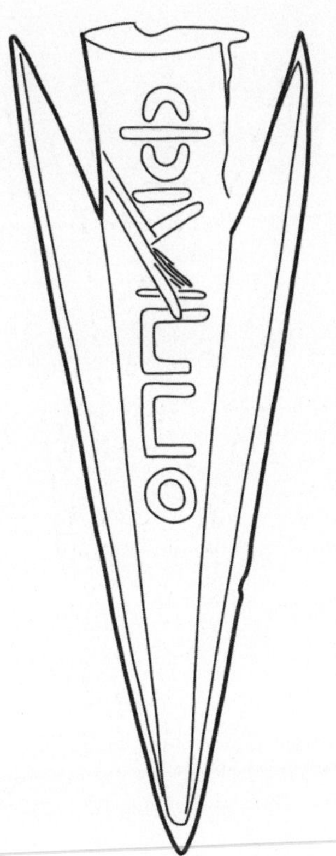

T0375865

Ancient Methone
2003–2013

UCLA COTSEN INSTITUTE OF ARCHAEOLOGY PRESS
Monumenta Archaeologica

Volume 48

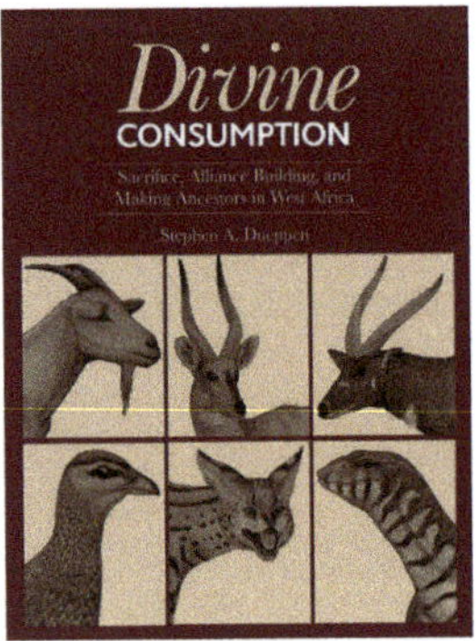

Divine Consumption: Sacrifice, Alliance Building, and Making Ancestors in West Africa

By Stephen A. Dueppen

Volume 47

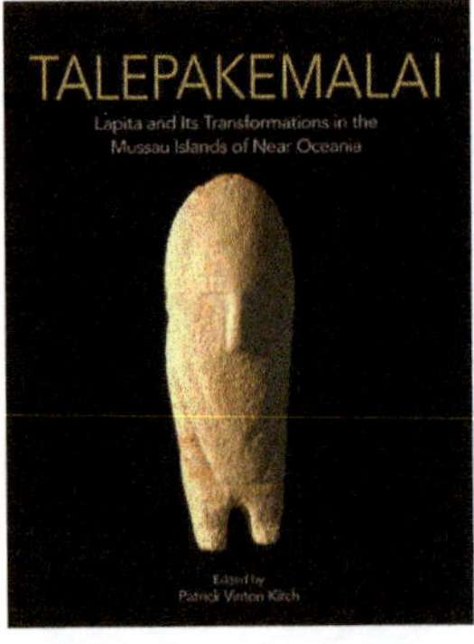

Talepakemalai: Lapita and Its Transformations in the Mussau Islands of Near Oceania

Edited by Patrick Vinton Kirch

Volume 46

Bikeri: Two Copper Age Villages on the Great Hungarian Plain

Edited by William A. Parkinson, Attila Gyucha, and Richard W. Yerkes

Volume 45

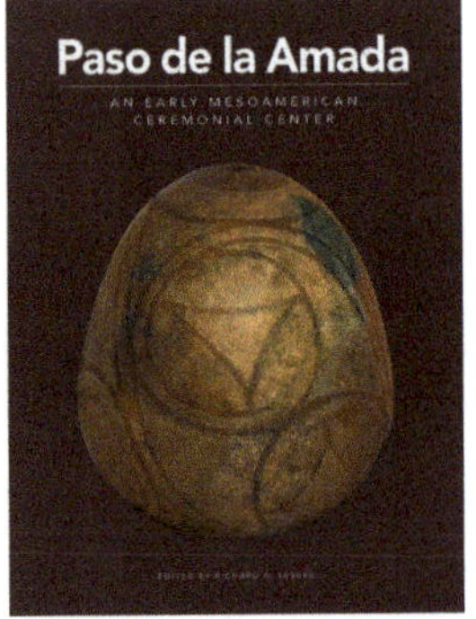

Paso de la Amada: An Early Mesoamerican Ceremonial Center

Edited by Richard G. Lesure

Volume 44

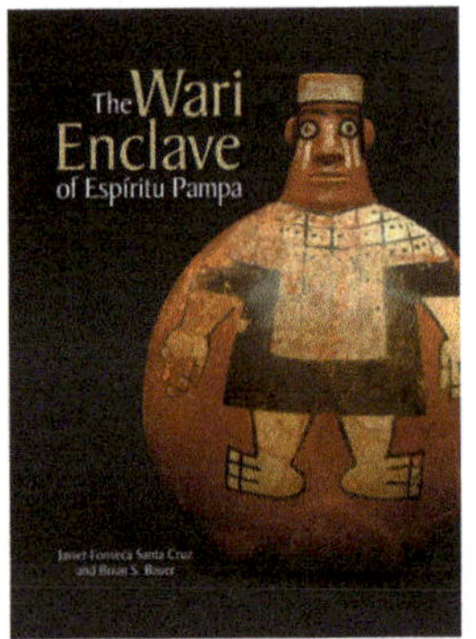

The Wari Enclave of Espíritu Pampa

By Javier Fonseca Santa Cruz and Brian S. Bauer

Volume 43

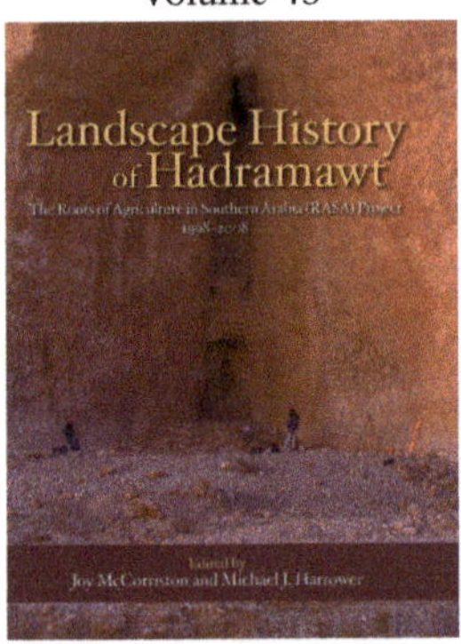

Landscape History of Hadramawt: The Roots of Agriculture in Southern Arabia (RASA) Project 1998–2008

Edited by Joy McCorriston and Michael J. Harrower

Volume 42

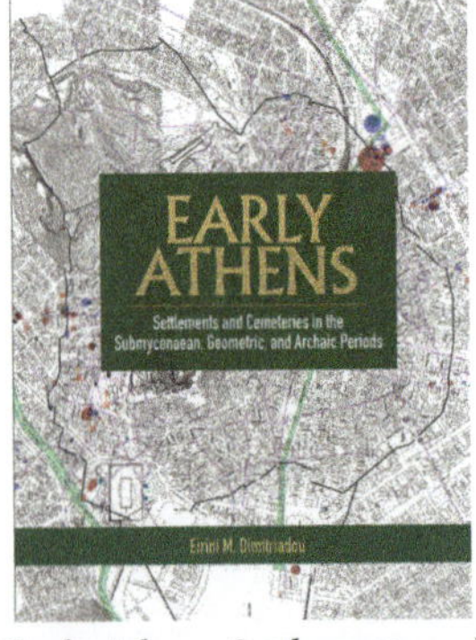

Early Athens: Settlements and Cemeteries in the Submycenaean, Geometric, and Archaic Periods

By Eirini M. Dimitriadou

Volume 41

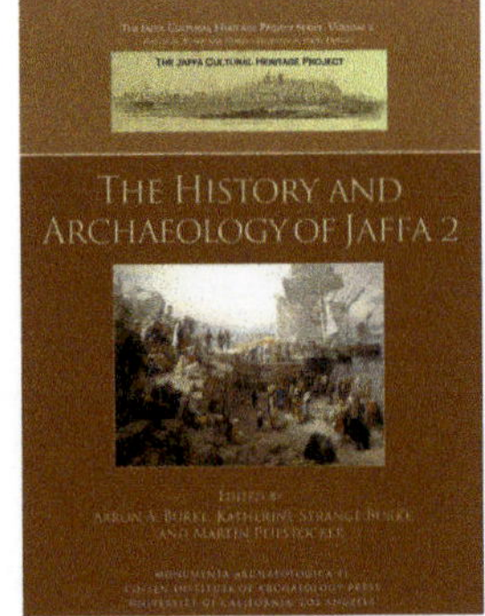

The History and Archaeology of Jaffa 2

Edited by Aaron A. Burke, Katherine Strange Burke, and Martin Peilstöcker

Volume 40

Tangatatau Rockshelter: The Evolution of an Eastern Polynesian Socio-Ecosystem

Edited by Patrick Vinton Kirch

See page 1445 for a complete list of volumes in the Cotsen Institute of Archaeology Monumenta Archaeologica series.

Ancient Methone
2003–2013

Excavations by Matthaios Bessios, Athena Athanassiadou, and Konstantinos Noulas

Volume 2

Edited by
Sarah P. Morris and John K. Papadopoulos

With contributions by (in alphabetical order)
Athena Athanassiadou, Matthaios Bessios, Angelos Boufalis, Brian Damiata, Elissavet Dotsika, Styliana Galiniki, Despina Ignatiadou, Petros Karalis, Alexandra Kasseri, Antonis Kotsonas, Alexandra Livarda, Antonio Longinelli, Ioannis Manos, Samantha L. Martin, Sarah P. Morris, Vanessa Muros, Marianna Nikolaidou, Konstantinos Noulas, Niki Oikonomaki, John K. Papadopoulos, Vaso Papathanasiou, Seth Pevnick, Llorenç Picornell-Gelabert, John Southon, Maria Tolia-Christakou, Sevi Triantaphyllou, Yannis Z. Tzifopoulos, Trevor Van Damme, Anastasia Vasileiadou, Samuel Verdan, Rena Veropoulidou, and Ioannis Vlastaridis

Monumenta Archaeologica 49

UCLA COTSEN INSTITUTE OF ARCHAEOLOGY PRESS

THE COTSEN INSTITUTE OF ARCHAEOLOGY PRESS is the publishing unit of the Cotsen Institute of Archaeology at UCLA, a premier research organization dedicated to the creation, dissemination, and conservation of archaeological knowledge and heritage. It is home to both the Interdepartmental Archaeology Graduate Program and the UCLA/Getty Program in the Conservation of Cultural Heritage. The Cotsen Institute provides a forum for innovative faculty research, graduate education, and public programs at UCLA in an effort to positively impact the academic, local and global communities. Established in 1973, the Cotsen Institute is at the forefront of archaeological research, education, conservation and publication, and is an active contributor to interdisciplinary research at UCLA.

THE COTSEN INSTITUTE OF ARCHAEOLOGY PRESS specializes in producing high-quality academic volumes in nine different series, including *Monumenta Archaeologica, Monographs, World Heritage and Monuments, Cotsen Advanced Seminars,* and *Ideas, Debates, and Perspectives*. Through a generous endowment by Lloyd E. Cotsen, longtime Institute volunteer and benefactor, the Press makes the fruits of archaeological research accessible to scholars, professionals, students, and the general public. Our archaeological publications receive critical acclaim in both academic communities and the public at large.

Edited by Jody Baboukis
Designed by Sally Boylan

The publication of this volume was made possible by a grant from the Institute for Aegean Prehistory and the Steinmetz Chair Endowment in Classical Archaeology and Material Culture at UCLA.

Library of Congress Cataloging-in-Publication Data

Names: Morris, Sarah P., 1954- editor. | Papadopoulos, John K., 1958- editor.
Title: Ancient Methone, 2003-2013 : excavations by Matthaios Bessios, Athena Athanassiadou, and Konstantinos Noulas / edited by Sarah P. Morris and John K. Papadopoulos.
Other titles: Excavations by Matthaios Bessios, Athena Athanassiadou, and Konstantinos Noulas
Description: [Los Angeles, California] : The Cotsen Institute of Archaeology Press, [2022] | Series: Monumenta archaeologica ; 49 |
Identifiers: LCCN 2022021422 | ISBN 9781950446285 (v. 1 ; hardback) | ISBN 9781950446285 (v. 2 ; hardback) | ISBN 9781950446339 (v. 1 ; ebook) | ISBN 9781950446339 (v. 2 ; ebook)
Classification: LCC DF901.M54 A53 2022 | DDC 938--dc23/eng/20220822
LC record available at https://lccn.loc.gov/2022021422

CONTENTS

Volume 1

VOLUME 2

PART III. METHONE IN THE ARCHAIC AND CLASSICAL PERIODS

ABBREVIATIONS

In addition to standard references (e.g., periodic table of elements), abbreviations of titles (Bibliography), and those defined in text (e.g., Chapter 6 appendix, Chapter 25 analysis)

A.D.	Anno Domini
ASL	above sea level
B.C.	Before Christ
BG	black-glaze
B.P.	before the present
cm	centimeters
D.	depth
DD	destruction deposit
Diam.	diameter
DRL	*Deckrandlampen* [covered-rim lamps]: Scheibler lamp type
DSL	(Scheibler lamp type)
EBA	Early Bronze Age
ed.	edited by, or edition
EG	Early Geometric
EIA	Early Iron Age
EPG	Early Protogeometric
ext.	exterior
Fig(s).	figures (in ms.)
FM	Furumark motif
FN	Final Neolithic
fr, frr	fragment(s)
FS	Furumark shape
g	gram
H.	height
HM	handmade

HPD	Highest Probability Density
HT	Howland Type (lamp)
int.	interior
kg	kilogram
km	kilometer
KSL	*Knickschulterlampen* [angled-shoulder lamps]: Scheibler lamp type
L.	length
LBA	Late Bronze Age
LG	Late Geometric
LH	Late Helladic
LN	Late Neolithic
LPG	Late Protogeometric
m	meters (all dimensions in meters, unless otherwise specified)
MBA	Middle Bronze Age
ME	μίκρο εύρημα (= SF: small find)
MG	Middle Geometric
MH	Middle Helladic
mm	millimeters
MN	Middle Neolithic
MPG	Middle Protogeometric
NH	neck-handled
N/R	not recoverable
P./p.	preserved
PG	Protogeometric
PSC	pendent semi-circle (skyphos/i)
pXRF	portable X-ray fluorescence [instrument]
SF	small find
SOS	Distinctive amphora decoration resembling the Greek letters ΣΟΣ
SPG	Subprotogeometric
RSL	*Rundschulterlampen* [rounded-shoulder lamps]: Scheibler lamp type
T	toichos (Wall)
Th.	thickness
W.	width
WM	wheelmade
Wt.	weight
XRF	X-ray fluorescence

LIST OF ILLUSTRATIONS

Volume 1

VOLUME 2

LIST OF TABLES

Volume 1

Volume 2

Part III

Methone in the Archaic and Classical Periods

18

BUILDING A ON THE EAST HILL OF ANCIENT METHONE

Samantha L. Martin

SETTING

The ancient settlement of Methone, as exposed to date, occupied two adjacent hills—referred to as the West and East Hills—of which the latter is lower in altitude. The East Hill originally formed a promontory that stretched northeast into the Thermaic Gulf.[1] However, this hill has witnessed extensive erosion by the sea over millennia, so much so that only its western edge has survived to the present day. It is in this general area, within a hollow between the two hills, that the ancient agora of Methone developed (Fig. 18.1). Building A, which is situated at the southern limit of the excavation area, was one of the first structures to emerge during investigations and it dominates the entire history of the site (Fig. 18.2).[2] It is crucial not only to our understanding of the topography of the ancient city, but also to the dating of civic structures in Greece in the 6th century B.C. and later.

Another principal building on the site, Building B, stands to the north of Building A and marks the northern limit of the excavations in this area. Furthermore, exposed remains of the agora indicate at least two other buildings, Δ and E, which stand immediately adjacent to Building A at the southwest and west, respectively. Only a small number of walls belonging to Buildings Δ and E have come to light; the rest of these structures remain beyond the limits of the area investigated.

Notably, a broad open area lies between Buildings A and B. The discovery of cobblestones in the general area suggests that the space likely served as a kind of paved central square or *plateia*.[3] Therefore, the relationship between this and the surrounding buildings is probably the closest thing we have to an urban unit at Methone thus far. While our understanding of the urban plan of the site is still relatively inchoate, we can begin to piece together the spatial order of the agora by considering how its buildings relate to one another as well as to the surrounding topography. For instance, as of yet we know relatively little about the ancient road system in and around Methone, but it is possible to surmise that at least one thoroughfare, and quite possibly more, connected with this open square. One likely scenario is the presence of a street running from the northwest of the agora, through the saddle between the East and the West Hills, and toward the area farther north that has been identified as the probable location of the harbor of the city (Fig. 3.13). Additionally, it is reasonable to presume that a road also linked the agora with regions farther southeast, although at this time we have no archaeological evidence to support such a hypothesis.

Although the site of ancient Methone was rediscovered in the 1970s, archaeological exploration of the area did not commence until the early 2000s. Between 2004 and 2007 the Greek Archaeological Service excavated Building A, and as a result of these investigations, directed by Manthos Bessios and supervised by Athena Athanassiadou, a general plan of Building A in its final

FIGURE 18.1. Aerial view of Building A and the agora and East Hill as exposed in 2014, from south, looking toward the harbor of Methone (see also Fig. 3.13). Photo H. Thomas

state can now be reconstructed with some accuracy (Fig. 18.3).[4] As we shall presently see, the story of this building is not clear-cut and many questions about its function and identity remain unanswered. Nonetheless, it must be emphasized that this structure, together with the other buildings in the agora, represents the earliest known monumental public architecture in Macedonia. Thus, without reservation, it can be argued that Building A provides crucial insight to studies of civic urbanism in the early Archaic period on the Greek mainland.

ARCHITECTURE

There are three principal construction phases for Building A, yet it is challenging to identify discrete building periods in the extant architectural fabric because several walls were refurbished, renovated, and possibly even rebuilt at various stages. Thus, it is possible to discern several subphases in the architecture, particularly within the second phase of construction. Despite the fact that Building A extends beyond the southern limit of the excavation area, we can state with some confidence that most corners of the building have been uncovered.

In its most basic sense, Building A is a rectangular limestone and mud-brick structure that runs east–west and is oriented north–south.[5] This structure, in its original design, consisted of a long narrow hall that was adjoined by two unequally sized rooms at the south. At some point Building A was

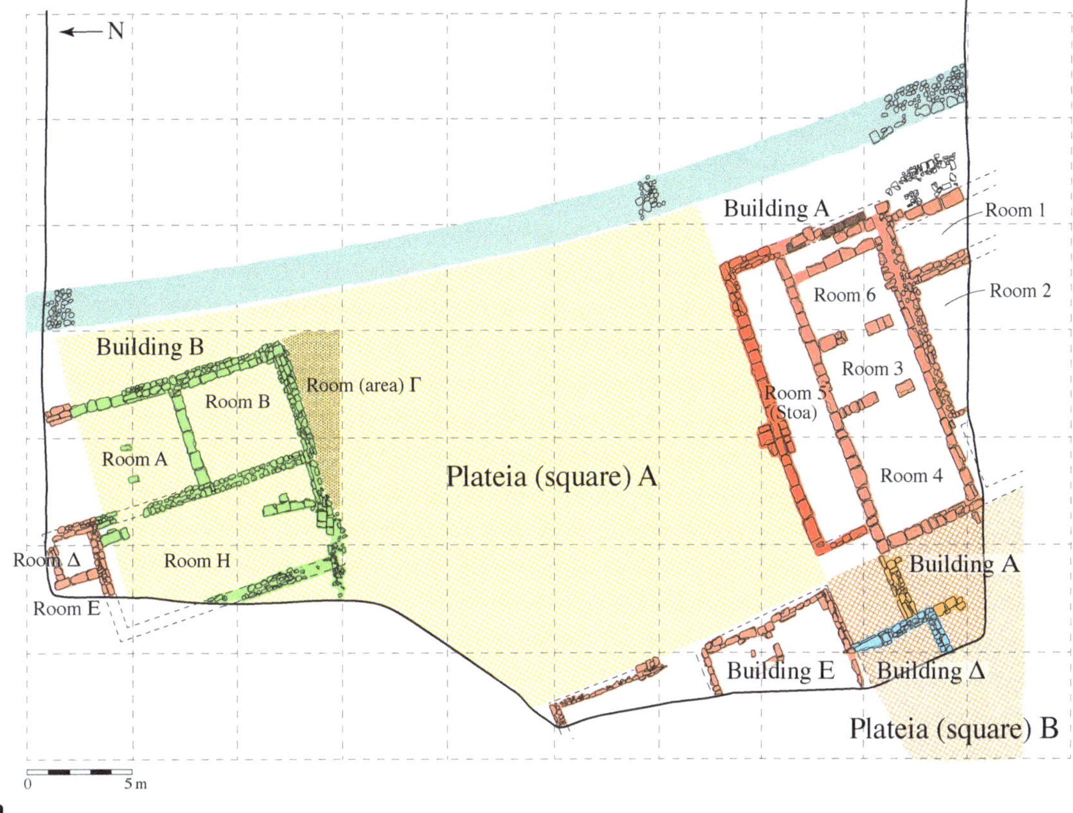

FIGURE 18.2. a) General plan of the agora of Methone. Drawing I. Moschou; b) Methone, East Hill, #274. Photogrammetric view of the Ephoreia excavations on the East Hill, generated by drone photography. Prepared by H. Thomas and M. Rocchio

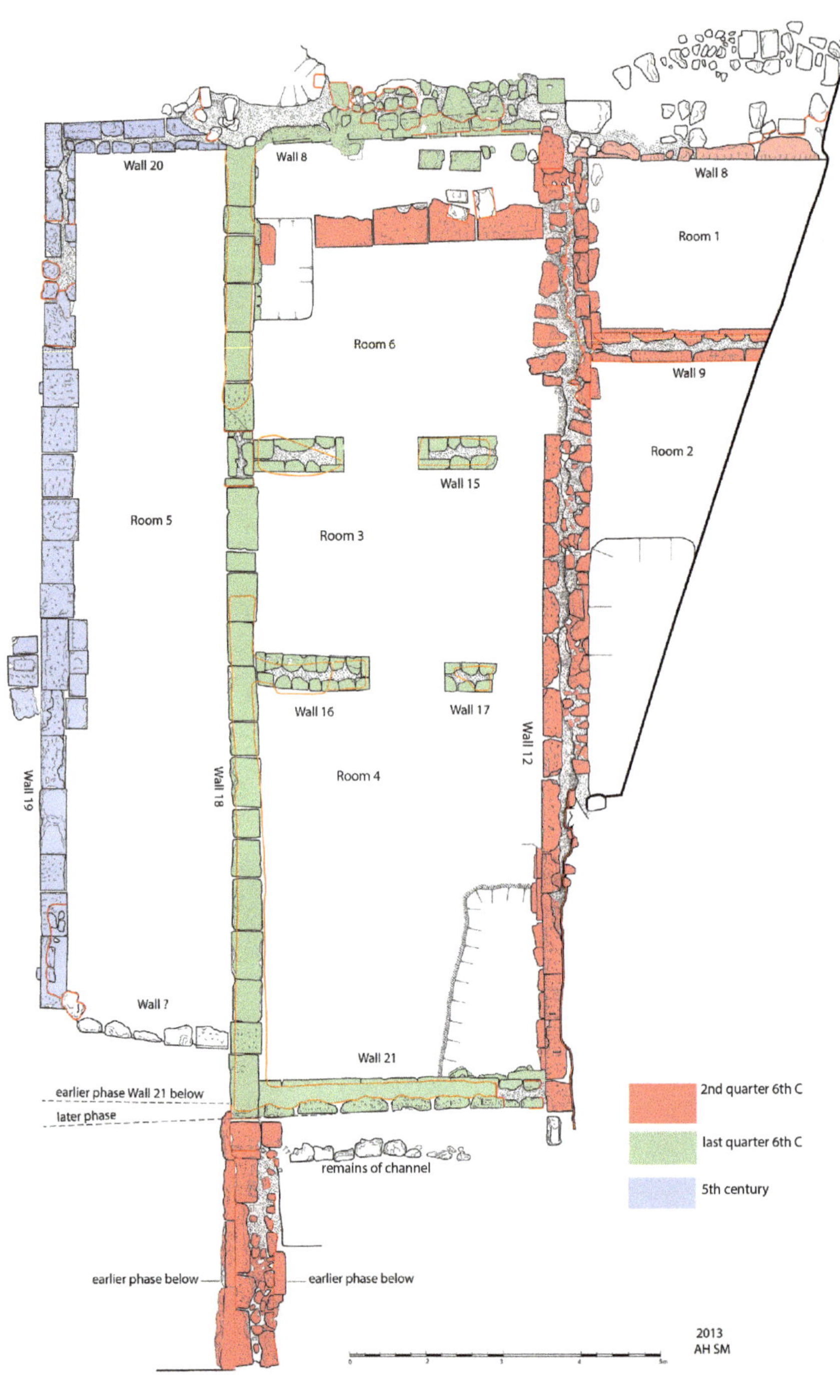

FIGURE 18.3. State plan of Building A, showing phases in color. Drawing A. Hooton and S. Martin

truncated at the west and the entire footprint of the central hall also shifted farther east by at least 1 m. These changes most likely spurred further modifications in the overall design of the building. A final period of expansion saw the addition of a long, slender porch to the northern façade of the building. Generally speaking, many of the walls of Building A are distinguished by an abundant use of ashlar masonry that is laid in orderly courses. For reasons of clarity, the architectural characteristics of the central space of the structure will be addressed here first, followed by the two southerly rooms, and then finally the porch.

The Central Hall of Building A

In the present state of the remains, the main hall of Building A is defined by Walls 8, 18, 21, and 12 (east, north, west, and south) and it measures 12.6 m x 4.6 m. Internally, this central space is divided into three unequally sized rooms by Walls 15, 16, and 17 (Fig. 18.4). Room 6, the terminal room at the east, is nearly square with dimensions of 4.7 m x 4.6 m. In the center lies Room 3 measuring 2.9 x 4.6 m, and at the west stands Room 4, the largest of the three internal spaces; this has dimensions of 6.1 x 4.6 m. Although none stand to their original height, the four main walls of this central hall are preserved in situ at their lower courses and they are supported by foundations that are composed of ashlar blocks of varying dimensions.

Figure 18.4. a) View of Building A from the west (2014); b) view of the 2014 cleaning operations to re-expose Building A, with workmen for scale. Photos J. Papadopoulos

At the east, the foundation of Wall 8 has been exposed to a height of 0.25 m; it consists of a series of highly worked orthogonal stones (Fig. 18.5). A single row of orthostates of different heights originally formed the lowest course of this wall: beginning at the northern end, there are three stones with a height of 0.20 m, followed by an area in the wall approximately 0.5 m wide that has disintegrated, and then, finally, another set of four orthostates measuring 0.4 m in height. Above the second and third orthostates of this latter section, two more stones from the second course have been preserved. The maximum preserved height of Wall 8 is 0.8 m, and it should be underscored that the excavators encountered substantial evidence that it was demolished from the west. In particular, a number of stones from the second course of this wall now lie due west in the floor of Room 6; at least five fallen stones were left in situ following investigations. In addition, a layer of mud brick, which contained broken tiles, both rough and highly worked, also came to light in this same area.

It deserves to be mentioned that Wall 8 is set against the western slope of the East Hill, a situation that not only corroborates the hypothesis that the wall was destroyed from the west, but also explains the large amount of rubble that has accumulated on top of it. For this reason, it is difficult to ascertain the original width of the wall; the current state of remains suggests a measurement in the region of 0.7–0.8 m. While the position of Wall 8 necessitated a design that was robust enough to resist the slope of the East Hill, it most likely was not a retaining wall. Rather, investigations farther east uncovered another wall, which does not belong to Building A, that served such a purpose. Wall 7 measures at least 1.7 m in width and extends a considerable distance north–south along the eastern limit of the excavation area (see Fig. 18.2).

Wall 18 extends east–west for 14.2 m at the northern side of Building A (Figs. 18.6–18.8). Generally speaking, it has a width of 0.5 m. Its foundations are in a good state of preservation and, therefore, they provide crucial insight into the original design and subsequent refurbishment of the building. From the outset, it is important to note that the foundations for this wall follow an irregular pattern that is difficult to gauge in its entirety. This is not only due to the fact that a ca. 2.0 m central portion of Wall 18 remains unexcavated, but also because the courses are stepped

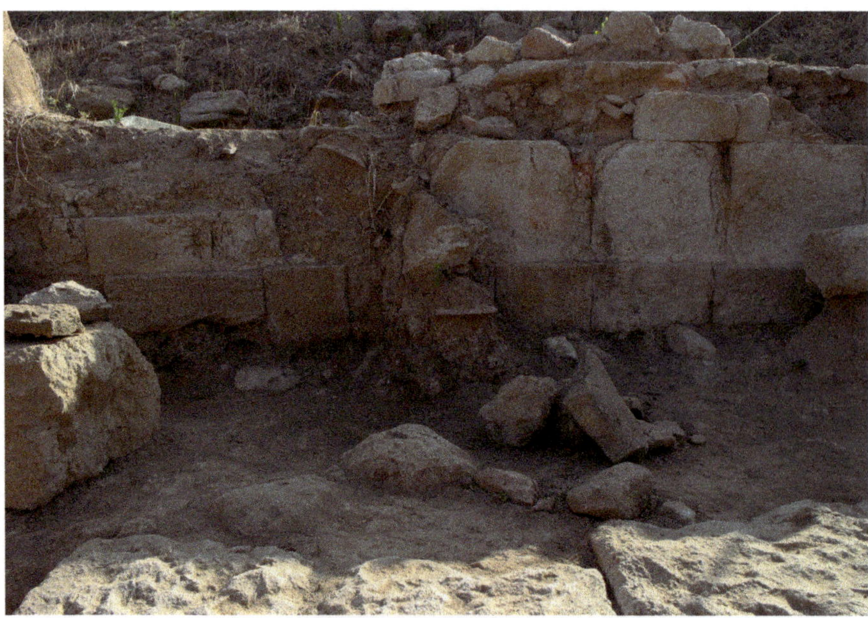

FIGURE 18.5. Wall 8, Room 6, view from west.
Photo S. Martin

FIGURE 18.6. Wall 18, east, view from northwest. Photo J. Papadopoulos

gradually downward toward the west using stones of various dimensions. Beginning in the east, the foundation is formed by a set of rectangular stones placed side by side measuring 0.20 m in height. Directly beneath the western corner of the second stone is packed a small, nearly square block measuring approximately 0.15 m in height. This first section of the foundation is then followed by a series of four orthogonal stones that have a height of 0.35 m; the top surfaces of these different-sized stones are flush and their joints are carefully aligned. However, somewhere between 5 m and 7 m from the eastern end of Wall 18, in the area concealed by the escarpment, this course discontinues and gives way to a pair of two highly worked orthogonal stones set side by side that are 0.35 m lower in elevation than the top of the foundation course at the east. These two stones have a height of 0.25 m; the first (at the east) is 0.30 m long and the second is 0.45 m. The remainder of this course of foundation includes two series of stones with a total height of 0.35 m. It is important to observe that there is also a second foundation course of Wall 18, but it only extends across the eastern half of the building. It commences beneath the second and third stones of the first course and continues until it reaches the escarpment. This course consists of a row of five stones with a height of only 0.15 m. In summary, the foundation of Wall 18 has two courses, the first (lower) of which has a maximum height of 0.35 m and is stepped near the midpoint of the wall. The second course is less than half the height of the first and only spans the eastern half of the wall.

At this point is must be noted that a single substantial stone with a height of 0.30 m and width of 0.52 m stands in the angle between the first and second foundation courses of Wall 18 (Fig. 18.9). This stone may be described as orthogonal but it is much more roughly worked than the stones belonging to Wall 18, and it has incurred damage to its lower western corner. As we shall see, this stone belongs not to Wall 18 but rather to an earlier course. In short, it is possible to state with some certainty that Wall 18 was built using a preexisting wall as a foundation. The particular characteristics and conditions of this precursor are discussed later in this section.

The lower courses of the superstructure of Wall 18, in particular the krepidoma and stylobate, are well preserved. The krepidoma spans the entire length of the wall, but at approximately 5.2 m from the eastern corner of the building it steps downward toward the west in order to correlate with the change in levels of the foundation. Accordingly, the destruction floor levels of Room 6

FIGURE 18.7. a) Wall 18, west, view from northwest. Photo S. Martin; b) view from east-northeast of Building A with Wall 18 at the center of the frame. Photo J. Papadopoulos

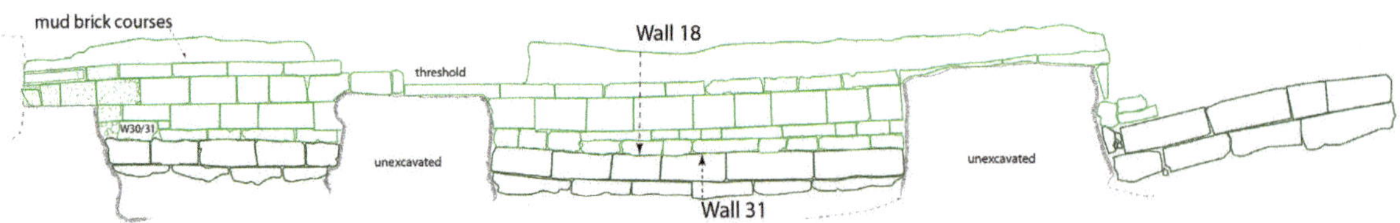

FIGURE 18.8. Wall 18 and Wall 31, elevation. Drawing S. Martin

FIGURE 18.9. Wall 30/31 cornerstone integrated into Wall 18.
Photo S. Martin

and Room 4 are also different as they correspond to the stepped elevation of the entire building. This eastern portion of the krepidoma consists of a single series of nine orthogonal stones measuring 0.45 m in height and reaching up to 0.8 m in length. These stones are set very carefully with tightly closed joints and their surfaces are finely dressed. Following this, there are two stones with a height of 0.30 m. The western stone is unusual insofar as its long side is positioned north–south, and therefore perpendicular to the other stones of the krepidoma. At present is it not possible to investigate the continuation of this course due to the presence of the escarpment. However, on the western side of this bank the krepidoma continues in a very similar series of nine highly worked orthogonal stones measuring 0.45 m in height.

Altogether, this substantial krepidoma of Wall 18 provides a solid platform for the stylobate, which is nearly intact, with the exception of a robbed stone just east of the doorway that leads into the main hall of the building. Nearly all of the stones comprising the stylobate are between 0.20 m and 0.25 m in height. Most are at least 0.6 m in length and several have drafted margins with stippling. A lifting boss can also be observed in the center of the south face of the easternmost stylobate block (Fig. 18.10). From the east there are a total of six stones comprising the stylobate; there was, as mentioned above, originally a seventh stone that was robbed at some point in antiquity. Therefore, there is at present a gap between the sixth stone of the stylobate course and the doorway of Wall 18. Notably, the surface of the doorway is ca. 0.25 m lower than the stylobate course to the east. The doorstep itself measures 1 m in length, 0.2 m in height, and 0.5 m in width and it bears some signs of use, but a form of wear and tear that is not typically associated with a threshold door (Fig. 18.11). For instance, along the top of the stone there is a raised section with a concave edge. Curiously, this detail continues across the two adjacent stones on the west (Fig. 18.12). In addition to this, there is a shallow depression in the surface of the stone with a ca. 0.15 m long groove leading to the eastern edge of the block. This kind of wear suggests an industrial process, perhaps casting, and thus it is entirely possible that this stone was introduced at a later period to replace the original doorway, which could have been composed of stone—perhaps marble—or

FIGURE 18.10. Lifting boss on stylobate block of Wall 18, southern elevation.
Photo S. Martin

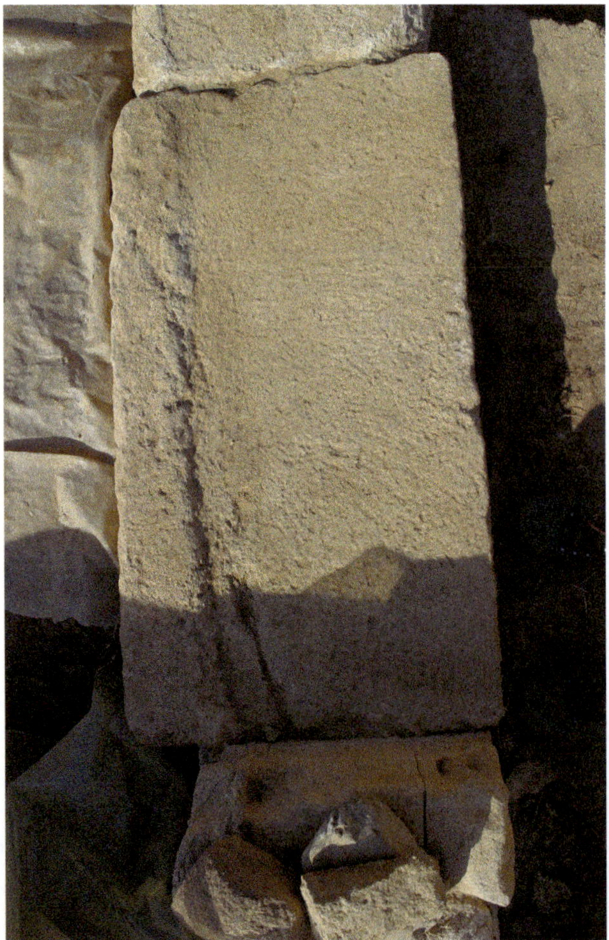

FIGURE 18.11. Doorstep (threshold block) of Wall 18, view from east.
Photo S. Martin

FIGURE 18.12. Doorstep and general threshold space of Wall 18, view from south. Photo S. Martin

FIGURE 18.13. a) Detail of Wall 18 with mud bricks in situ. Photo J. Papadopoulos; b) details of mud-brick superstructure (collapsed) from Wall 18 taken at the time of excavation. Photo KZ´ Ephoreia

wood. At present the precise history of this threshold remains an open and intriguing question. It is also important to point out that the corresponding stylobate block on the west is flush with the doorstep. This arrangement corroborates the argument that the building is stepped toward the west. The stylobate course on the western side of Wall 18 is composed of 13 blocks.

It is of especial note that considerable amounts of mud-brick superstructure from the walls of Building A survive. The entire length of Wall 18, with the exception of the areas on either side of the threshold, still retains mud-brick courses, and in some places these stand to a height of 0.4 m. To the north of Wall 18 the excavators encountered a layer of mud brick 1.3 m wide in total, which had collapsed from the wall. There were at least 14 rows in this layer, and the bricks had a width of 0.25 m (Fig. 18.13).[6]

Wall 21 stands perpendicular to Wall 18 at the western side of Building A (Fig. 18.14). In fact, the northernmost corner of the superstructure of Wall 21 keys into the krepidoma, stylobate, and mud-brick course of Wall 18. From this juncture, it extends 4.7 m in length to the south, where it abuts Walls 12 and 13. The full dimensions and composition of the lowest foundations of Wall 21 remain unknown, since the area to the immediate west of it has not been fully excavated. Nonetheless, it is possible to discern a line of foundations 3.5 m long at the bottom of the west face of the wall. Directly above this is another line of foundations 0.5 m tall. This course has a number of peculiar characteristics that deserve to be outlined in full. Put categorically, there are details in the construction of these foundations which suggest that Wall 21 not only was rebuilt at some stage, but also that it underwent a fundamental change in design.

FIGURE 18.14. Wall 21, exterior, western elevation (also visible in FIGURE 18.4a–b). Photo J. Papadopoulos

As mentioned above, the northern corner of the foundation of Wall 21 interlocks with Wall 18. A brief glance at the elevation reveals that the final stone of the krepidoma of Wall 18, which is 0.5 m in height and 0.2 m thick, abuts the first foundation stone of Wall 21 (Fig. 18.15). This is a very large ashlar block that measures 0.88 m in length. Following this there are three interlocked stones: the first is 1.15 m in length and 0.37 m in height; its top edge is flush with that of the preceding stone. However, this block rests upon another thin (0.13 m) but almost equally long stone; the third stone of this group is ca. 0.50 m long and 0.50 m tall, and interestingly, it has been cut in such a way that it has a ledge—an "L" in reverse—which protrudes ca. 0.10 m under the adjacent orthogonal block to its north. This third stone is also remarkable in that it has a margin of chisel marks approximately 0.15 m tall that runs across its bottom edge. Given the condition and configuration of this set of stones, it seems likely that at some point this section of Wall 21 had a doorway added, which was subsequently closed again. As such, the northernmost foundations of the wall were probably added during a period of extensive refurbishment. The southern half of the foundation course of Wall 21 has a completely different composition than the northern half. Immediately adjacent to the central block with the chisel marks there are two series of smaller orthogonal stones, which are also highly worked. The total length of this portion of the wall is 2.30 m. The top layer is comprised of seven stones with a height of 0.20 m. The lower layer has four stones and a height of 0.30 m.

Architecturally, the western, exterior face of Wall 21 is more straightforward than the foundations on which it stands. Like its foundation, this course also abuts Wall 18. The face of the wall is composed of six highly worked orthogonal stones that are fairly uniform in size: The stones are 0.4 m in height with the exception of the first stone at the north, which is 0.35 m. Most are between 0.20 and 0.25 m in width, and they range in length from 0.55 m to 0.85 m. One interesting further detail about this course is that the stones protrude in relation to the foundation. The north side of the wall projects 0.8 m, the center 0.13 m, and the south side 0.4 m.

Almost no mud brick survives from the top level of Wall 21; however, from the extant remains of the superstructure, it is clear that the internal face of the wall was constructed of mud brick (Fig. 18.16). Furthermore, during excavation, a substantial layer of mud bricks came to light farther west of Wall 21. The disposition of the deposited layer clearly indicated that it was a collapsed wall. Based on the dimensions of these bricks, as well as how far they fell from the wall, the original height of Wall 21 can be conjectured to reach approximately 3.0 m. Each row of mud brick had a

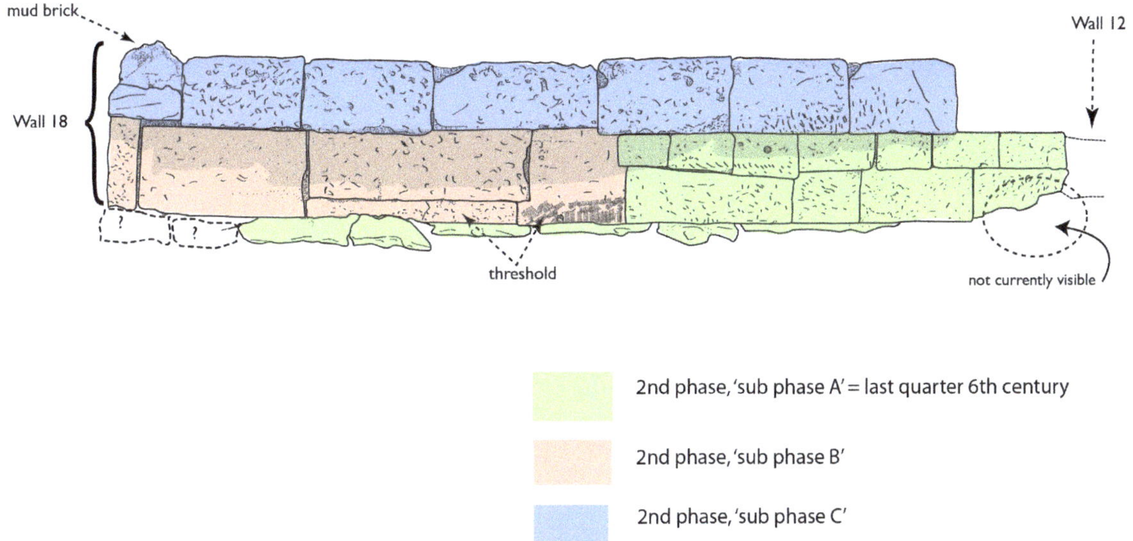

FIGURE 18.15. Wall 21, western elevation, drawn with phases indicated in color. Drawing S. Martin

FIGURE 18.16. Wall 21, eastern elevation, showing mud-brick interior. Photo J. Papadopoulos

height of 0.10 m; the bricks themselves measured 0.40 m in length and 0.35 m in width. In summary, the superstructure of Wall 21 originally stood to a height of 3 m. Its principal foundation course has a more or less continuous height of 0.50 m, but the composition of its stones suggests at least two construction phases.

Wall 12 comprises the southern side of the main hall of Building A and it measures approximately 14.5 m from east to west (Fig. 18.17). It is important to mention at this stage that the southwest corner of this wall abuts Wall 21 as well as Wall 13, of which only one block is presently visible; the remainder of Wall 13 runs beyond the excavation area and into the hillside (the solitary block is indicated on the plan, Fig. 18.3). Wall 12 is one of the most difficult walls in the building to read for a number of reasons: it was constructed in a variety of masonry styles, portions of it remain unexcavated, and its extant superstructure is in poor condition compared to Walls 18 and 21. There are two sections of the wall that have been fully exposed and remain visible from the foundation level to the superstructure: the northern elevation at the southwest (the rear corner of Room 4); and a ca. 3.80 m portion toward the center of the southern elevation.

FIGURE 18.17. Wall 12, general view from the west.
Photo J. Papadopoulos

The view toward Wall 12 from Room 4 is especially clear: the foundation consists of a layer of coarsely worked stones that range in height from 0.20 m to 0.33 m (Fig. 18.18). At approximately 2.0 m from the west this layer divides into two roughly equal layers. As a whole, this foundation level extends beyond the face of the superstructure by ca. 0.10 m. Above the foundation are three courses of superstructure, all of which are composed of highly worked orthostates whose joints are tightly closed. The lowest course is 0.17 m in height and has stones of varying length; the shortest is 0.20 m and the longest spans over 1.0 m. The second course has a height of 0.40 m, a width of 0.30 m, and was also constructed using stones with various lengths. It is worthwhile noting here that this particular section of Wall 12 has some of the largest stones found in Building A overall. At least two orthostates belonging to the second course exceed 1 m in length; one is nearly 1.45 m. Finally, there are two remaining orthostates from the third course of superstructure in this particular section of the wall, and these are distinguished by their scale and surface detail. At the far western corner sits an immense block measuring 0.95 m in length, ca. 0.33 m in width (the top surface is partially concealed by the escarpment), and 0.50 m in height. Adjacent to this stone at the east stands another orthostate with a length of 0.7 m and a width and height similar to its neighbor. Each of these stones has a clamp cutting in its top surface.

FIGURE 18.18. Wall 12, northern elevation as viewed from Room 4. Photo J. Papadopoulos

It is important to observe that the second course from the superstructure of Wall 12 is visible for nearly 9.5 m, measured from the southwest corner of Building A. Near the center of the wall, at approximately 4 m from its western end, another layer of superstructure is visible. This course reaches a maximum height of 0.60 m and is completely different from the two enormous orthostates that mark the western termination of the wall. Here, instead of carefully cut and dressed ashlar stones, we have a course of rubble masonry on the inside face of the wall and a polygonal-style construction on the exterior, southern face (Fig. 18.19). The rubble course is composed mostly of irregularly shaped stones and the polygonal masonry is minimally dressed; it has few matching joints. The full elevation of this section of the wall is clearly visible in the trench within Room 2. Beneath the polygonal masonry are two further courses of worked orthogonal stones, followed by a single foundation level.

In the northeastern corner of Room 2, the rubble masonry gives way to two rows of highly worked stones. This section of the superstructure runs to the termination point of Wall 12 at the east, where it abuts Wall 8 (Fig. 18.20). Overall, the wall in this section of the building is in very poor condition: only a single block, which measures 0.25 m in height, is preserved from the top row; then in the second row there are several more square stones, all of which have a height of 0.35 m. The foundation course at this end of Wall 12 has been exposed to a height of 0.05 m.

Earlier in this section it was noted that the central hall of Building A is divided internally into three rooms. In total there are two cross-walls and both of these are divided into two sections in order to provide interior passageways between the rooms. To clarify, while the eastern partition wall is composed of two discrete segments, both are referred to as Wall 15 in the archaeological record. However, the segments that constitute the western partition wall are referred to as Wall 16 (north) and Wall 17 (south), respectively. One peculiarity of both cross-walls is that they terminate about 0.7 m from the interior face of Wall 12. Based on the configuration of their remaining stylobate courses, it is likely that they originally continued farther south. However, at this time it is not possible to confirm whether they ever abutted or bonded with Wall 12.

FIGURE 18.19. Wall 12, southern elevation viewed from Room 2. Photo J. Papadopoulos

FIGURE 18.20. Eastern termination of Wall 12, where it meets Wall 8, view from west-southwest. Photo J. Papadopoulos

Wall 15 stands perpendicular to Wall 18 at a distance of 4.60 m from the eastern corner of the wall (Fig. 18.21). It is located just east of the doorway into the central hall at the north. The northern section of Wall 15 is 1.45 m in length and the southern is 1.25 m; both are 0.5 m wide. The passage between these two partitions measures 1.2 m. The stylobate and portions of the mud-brick superstructure survive in both sections of this wall. At the north the wall adjoins Wall 18 and its stylobate course is composed of eight blocks measuring 0.25 m in height. Several of the blocks are characterized by drafted margins. The mud brick is preserved to a height of 0.35 m and it is completely bound to the mud-brick course of Wall 18. In Room 3 to the west of Wall 15, the excavators encountered not only large quantities of smashed roof tiles, but also a good deal of pottery. In the southern section of Wall 15 there are seven stylobate blocks measuring 0.25 m in height, and here the mud brick survives to a height of 0.32 m.

Like its counterpart at the east, Wall 16 has survived in good condition (Figs. 18.21–18.22). It runs perpendicular to Wall 18 at a point 6.8 m from the western termination of the wall. Extending 1.8 m in length and 0.5 m in width, its stylobate course was constructed of 15 blocks averaging no more than 0.20 m in length. This course has not been excavated to its full height, however, and in several places it is possible to distinguish drafted margins and internal stippling on their exposed surfaces. In this wall the mud-brick course survives to a maximum height of 0.40 m and is also amalgamated with the superstructure of Wall 18. Out of all the internal cross-wall sections of Building A, Wall 17 is the least well preserved (Figs. 18.21 right foreground and 18.23). Almost none of its mud-brick superstructure remains, although the six stones comprising its stylobate are visible. This partition measures 0.75 m in length on its western elevation and 0.85 m on its eastern side. It is 0.48 m wide. Similar to Wall 15, the passageway between Wall 16 and Wall 17 is 1.20 m.

One very important detail in the archaeological record of Room 6 evinces a change in plan for the entire building. Beneath the floor of the room the excavations revealed a series of four very large, highly worked orthogonal stones (Fig. 18.24; the four blocks are also visible in the left

FIGURE 18.21. The western portion of the main hall of Building A, showing Wall 16 (left foreground), Wall 17 (right foreground), Wall 15 north (center left), and Wall 15 south (center right), view from west. Photo J. Papadopoulos

FIGURE 18.22. Eastern elevation of Wall 16, as preserved, view from east.
Photo S. Martin

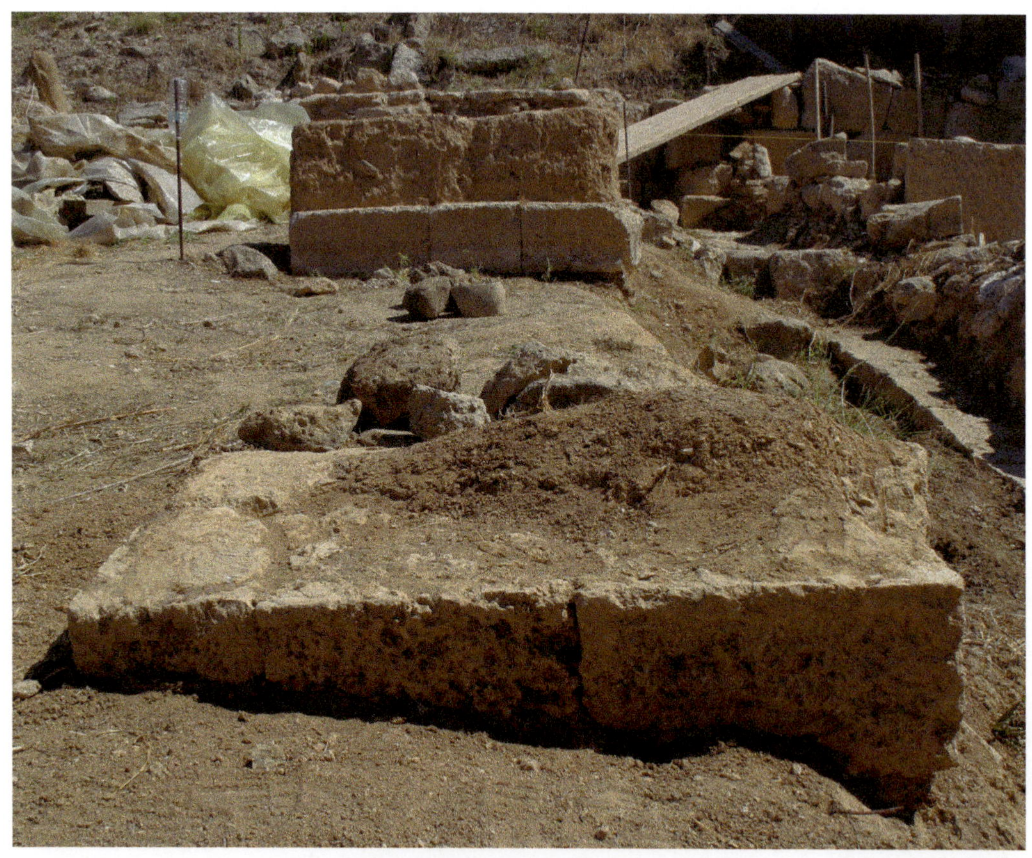

FIGURE 18.23. Detail of Wall 17, view from west.
Photo S. Martin

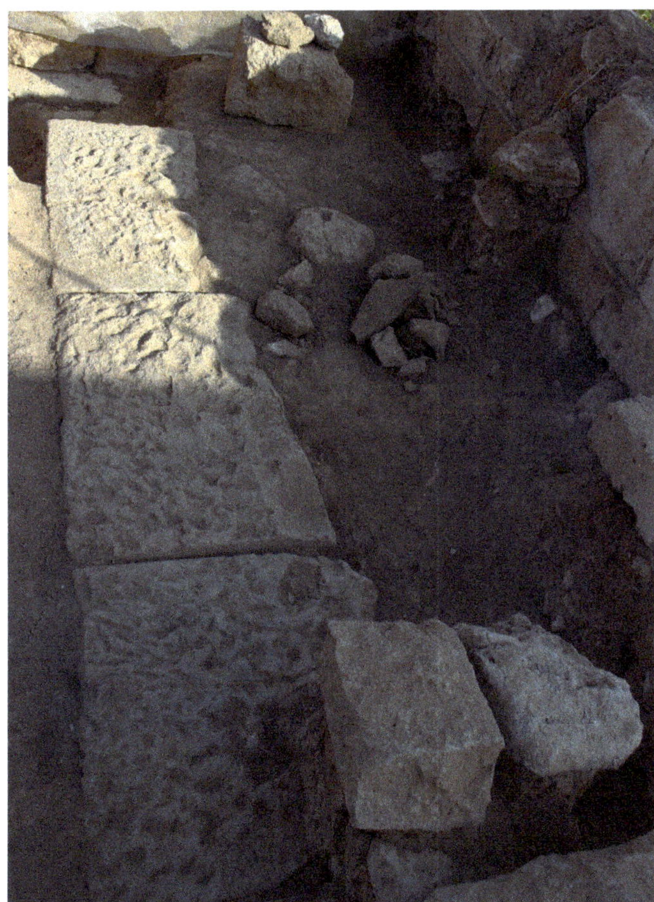

FIGURE 18.24. Detail of Wall 30, view from the south.
Photo S. Martin

portion of the frame of Fig. 18.20). Beginning from the south, the lengths for these stones are as follows: 1.10 m, 0.60 m, 0.88 m, and 0.95 m. Although they are closely aligned, there is a 0.05 m gap between each stone. The row runs parallel to Wall 8 at a distance approximately 1.0 m from its interior face. These blocks are highly damaged, especially at the east, and the northernmost stone is cracked down its middle, but overall they survive well enough intact to reveal the basic configuration of another wall: Wall 30. Crucially, while this wall does not explicitly link with Wall 12 at the south, it does clearly key into Wall 18 at the north (Fig. 18.9). Here it is necessary to recall the discussion of the foundations on the northeastern side of Wall 18, in particular the junction between the two courses and a stone measuring 0.30 m by 0.52 m. The conspicuousness of this stone was noted earlier: its highly porous and rough face stands in contrast to the more finely dressed blocks belonging to the foundation layers of Wall 18. It is now evident that this orthogonal block is either the northern terminal stone of Wall 30, or it is the eastern corner block of yet another wall, Wall 31, which extends for 18.20 m east–west beneath and, significantly, beyond the limit of Wall 18 (Figs. 18.3, 18.25). Directly beneath this stone runs a single course of superstructure that rests on one layer of foundation. This building method suggests that Wall 31 was stepped, thereby serving as a framework for the later construction of Wall 18.

Reading the elevation of Wall 31 presents difficulties not only because of the stepped construction but also because the entire wall bows near the western end of the building. To clarify, beginning in the eastern corner, Wall 31 slopes downward toward the west for ca. 12 m. At this point there is a clear bend in both the foundation and the superstructure of the wall. Thus, the final 4

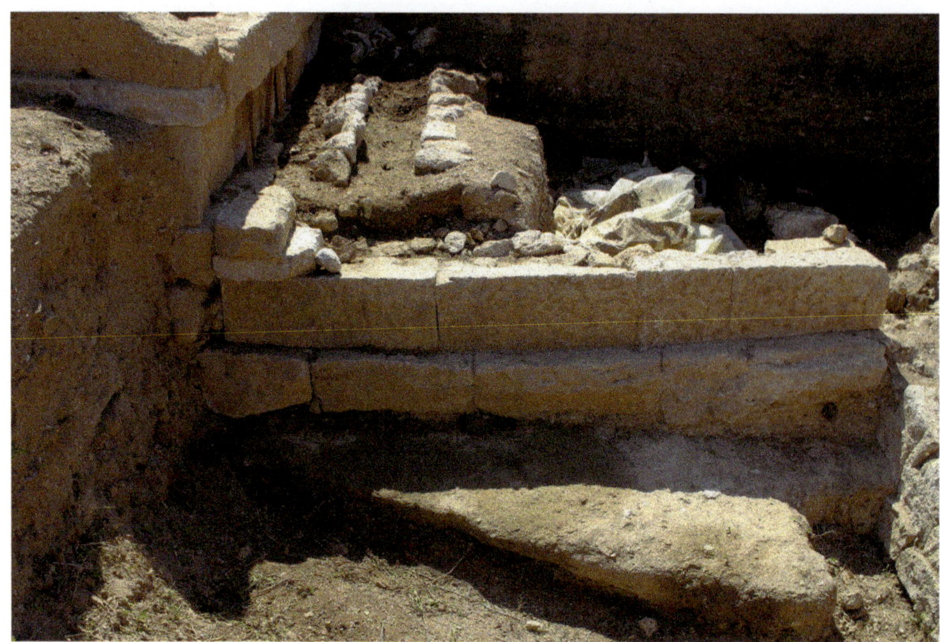

FIGURE 18.25. Wall 31, view from north.
Photo J. Papadopoulos

m of Wall 31 bends at the west slope in the opposite direction, from west to east. This situation is largely due to subsidence as the foundation of Wall 31 was not constructed on bedrock. In general, the foundation layer of this wall is composed of very large, roughly worked stones that protrude 0.15–0.25 m in relation to the superstructure. For the most part these blocks have lengths in excess of 0.7 m; many are nearly 1 m. At the west, the foundation terminates at the face of Wall 36, which belongs to another structure, Building Δ (Figs. 18.2, 18.25). The superstructure of Wall 31 was built of highly worked orthostates that stand at a fairly uniform height of 0.4 m. They vary in length from 0.25 m to well over 1 m. It also should be mentioned that Wall 18 slightly protrudes by 0.015 m over Wall 31. Considered together, Wall 30 and Wall 31 show without a doubt that the plan and scale of Building A were significantly altered over time. In its original state, the structure measured over l8 m in length, but at a later time the plan of the building shifted east by 1 m and its length was shortened to 14.2 m. At present, the precise reason for this transformation remains open to debate, but the possible causes will be considered later in the discussion of the chronology of Building A.

Room 1 and Room 2 at the South of Building A

Based on the extant architectural evidence, we may assume that there are two rooms of unequal size to the immediate south of the central hall of Building A. Although the presence of a precipitous and unstable escarpment precludes thorough investigations in the southwest area of the building, the presence of a single wall—Wall 9—running perpendicular to Wall 12 clearly indicates a division of space. Room 1, in the southeastern corner of the building, is 2.60 m in width (east–west) and at least 3.5 m in depth. Adjacent to this area at the west is Room 2, which is at least 7.0 m wide and 2.30 m deep. Wall 13, which is barely visible in the southwest corner of the Building A, marks the limit of Room 2. Gaining an accurate reading of the dimensions for either of these rooms is impossible because they both extend outside of the excavation area. At present it is not possible to ascertain whether the two southerly rooms were ever accessible from the central hall by a doorway.

It is necessary to point out here that while Wall 8 forms the southeastern boundary of Building A, it is not precisely contiguous with the section of Wall 8 in Room 6 to the immediate north; instead, it is positioned ca. 0.4 m farther west. At some point in the history of the building both these two sections were likely reconstructed to be the same wall. Only the western (interior) face of Wall 8 has been excavated (Fig. 18.26). Its foundation is partially revealed up to a maximum height of about 0.30 m, and the superstructure of the wall ranges from 1.1 to 1.50 m. It is, importantly, a polygonal structure. It is constructed of highly worked stones, several of which are nearly 1.0 m in width, and the joints are, for the most part, neatly matched. It is worthwhile mentioning here as well that in Room 1 the excavators encountered not only a layer of broken tile that covered a large portion of the space, but also two separate hearths or areas that contain evidence of firing.

Wall 9 runs parallel to Wall 8 and perpendicular to Wall 12 in a north–south direction (Fig. 18.27). In fact, it keys into the foundation course of Wall 12, but at present it is not possible to state with any certainty whether these two walls also met at an earlier phase; the floor of Room 2 has not been excavated beneath the destruction level of Building A. At present the maximum length of Wall 9 is 2.8 m; it continues into the escarpment at the southern limit of the excavation area. The total width of the wall is 0.47 m and at both the east and west of the wall the foundation has been revealed, which measures up to 0.20 m in height. It is constructed with highly worked ashlar stones. It deserves to be noted that the superstructure of this wall is of an exceptionally high quality and was clearly built with great care. It measures 0.5 m in height. On the eastern face there are two series of stones, each with a height of 0.25 m. These are constructed in an isodomic system. The western elevation consists of four very large orthostates, each measuring the full height of the wall (Fig. 18.28). The area in between the two faces of Wall 9 is filled with sand and small stones.

Overall, both Walls 8 and 9 are pivotal to our comprehension of the development of Building A, as well as the agora at Methone as a whole. As we shall see in the following section, they mark an early phase in the chronology of the building.

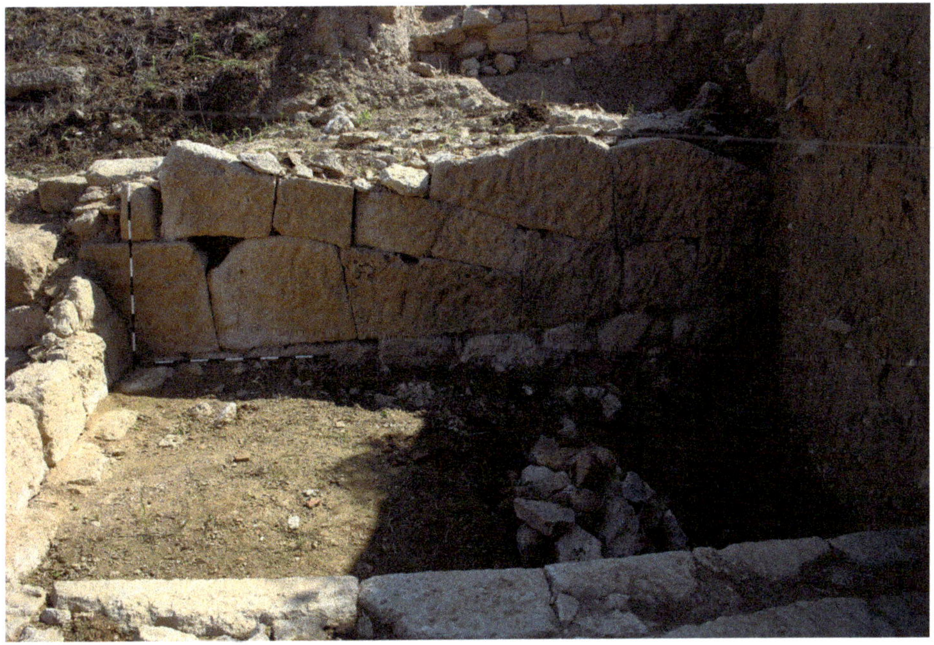

FIGURE 18.26. Wall 8, polygonal section in Room 1, view from west. Photo J. Papadopoulos

FIGURE 18.27. The western elevations of Walls 8 and 9, view from west-northwest. Photo J. Papadopoulos

FIGURE 18.28. a) The western elevation of Wall 9, with Wall 8 behind, view from west; b) eastern elevation of Wall 9, view from east. Photos S. Martin

The Porch of Building A

On the north side of Building A is preserved a porch ca. 2.50 m in depth that is defined by just two walls, 19 and 20. Wall 19 stands nearly parallel to Wall 18 and extends for 13.8 m east–west; the narrow interior space between these walls is referred to as Room 5 (Fig. 18.29). A number of details of Wall 19 make plain the particular conditions of the porch. One feature of this extension that deserves especial mention is its partially enclosed eastern corner. Beginning at the east there is a modest foundation course of small orthogonal stones measuring ca. 0.10 m in height that extends for 2.0 m. Notably, this first section of Wall 19 consists solely of a foundation and three very large orthostates; that is, there is no stylobate at the eastern front elevation of the porch, just the lower course of a solid wall (Fig. 18.30). At this time it is not possible to reconstruct the original wall height but it is reasonable to infer that the orthostates carried a mud-brick course similar to the other walls of the building.

Following the set of orthostates, the foundation steps down ca. 0.10 m and extends for 1.35 m. This short portion of Wall 19 appears to serve as a transition between the vertical wall course at the east and the non-load-bearing stylobate at the west. It is composed of a pair of smaller highly worked orthogonal blocks. The eastern block carries two very poorly preserved stones that are embedded into a compact mass of mud (Fig. 18.31). In contrast, the western block is devoid of any architectural remains on its top surface. Following this pair of blocks to the west, the foundation steps down yet again and then continues for about 4 m until it reaches the midpoint of the wall. The western end of Wall 19 has not been excavated below the level of the stylobate but it is unlikely to have foundations of any significance, the reason for this being that it was not load-bearing. Overall, like Walls 18 and 31, Wall 19 gradually steps downward toward the west.

In total, Wall 19 contains 14 stylobate blocks, and the width of the wall tapers from east to west. At the east it measures up to 0.58 m, whereas portions of the stylobate at the western end are as narrow as 0.40 m. A very large orthogonal stone measuring 1.10 x 0.43 m is situated toward the midpoint of the stylobate, and it is worthwhile pointing out that even though this stone does not

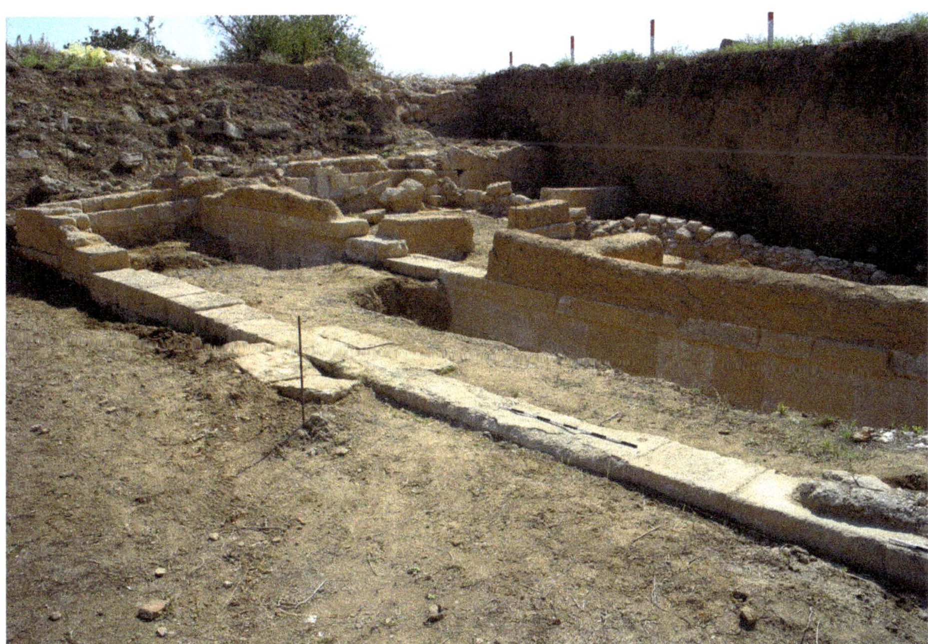

FIGURE 18.29. Walls 19 and 20, with Wall 18, general view from northwest. Photo J. Papadopoulos

FIGURE 18.30. Detail of the northeast corner of Wall 19, view from north. Photo S. Martin

FIGURE 18.31. Wall 19, northeast end, detail of transition between orthostate and stylobate, view from north. Photo S. Martin

mark the precise center point of the wall in numerical terms, it may be interpreted as a kind of threshold for the porch in general (Fig. 18.32). Certainly, it is distinguished by its size, but it also, importantly, demarcates a visible shift in the general shape of the stylobate blocks. To clarify, at the east of this large stone there are seven stylobate blocks, nearly all of which are almost square in dimension, whereas to the west there are six mostly rectangular stones. Two stones in the stylobate have preserved a lifting boss on their northern elevation. Even though it is probable that the stylobate carried some sort of colonnade—perhaps one composed of wooden columns—no setting marks have been observed.

FIGURE 18.32. Wall 19, threshold block and stylobate, view from north. Photo S. Martin

FIGURE 18.33. The western portion of Wall 19, view from north. Photo J. Papadopoulos

To the north and south of the 1.10 m stylobate block are preserved an additional seven highly worked orthogonal stones that align with Wall 19 (Fig. 18.33). For the most part these blocks are smaller in size than the stylobate blocks. It is likely that this group of stones belonged to Building A, but their original use remains an open question. During the excavation of Wall 19 a thin layer of hard sand was found across the stylobate and these surrounding blocks. This had clearly been deposited after the abandonment of the building.

The eastern side of the porch is closed by Wall 20, which is 2.45 m long and is contiguous with Wall 8 in Room 6 (Fig. 18.34). It is composed of a foundation course of small orthogonal stones, followed by two rows of highly worked rectangular orthostates. In the lower row there are eight blocks, some of which have drafted margins on the interior (western) elevation. The second row contains four much larger orthogonal stones, and this line of blocks is set back 0.2 m from the western face of Wall 20, thereby creating a kind of ledge. It is not clear whether this ledge was exposed or visible from Room 5 in antiquity.

Another peculiar characteristic of the porch of Building A is that it is not closed at the west by a wall. Rather, a single row of stones—four highly worked orthogonal stones and two orthogonal coarse stones—links the western corner of Wall 19 with the northern face of Wall 18 at a point approximately 1.10 m from its western corner (Figs. 18.3 and 18.35). It is likely that there were originally seven stones in total; this is justified by the fact that there is a space between the first stone at the north and the second stone. Significantly, these are neither foundation stones nor blocks belonging to a superstructure. The point to take from this is that these stones probably closed the

FIGURE 18.34. Wall 20, view from west.
Photo J. Papadopoulos

FIGURE 18.35. Line of orthogonal stones between Wall 18 and Wall 19 (at the left foreground), with drain west of Wall 21, view from north. Photo J. Papadopoulos

porch by acting as a kind of partition, a visual barrier that was not substantial enough to be identified as a wall. It is possible that the row may have served as a stylobate upon which columns could be placed. The area to the immediate west of this row has tentatively been identified as a small yard for Building A (Fig. 18.2). This raises questions about how the structure may have related to other buildings in the agora.

PHASES AND CHRONOLOGY

The masonry construction styles as well as the respective widths of the walls comprising Building A indicate three different major phases of construction. As mentioned in the opening discussion of the architecture, these phases, in particular the second phase, also show evidence of sub-phases as a result of rebuilding or remodeling. Generally speaking, phase one of Building A belongs to the first half—probably the second quarter—of the 6th century B.C., although there is no evidence available to date its construction precisely. Phase two dates from the last quarter of the 6th century, and the final period of construction, phase three, is from the 5th century B.C. (Fig. 18.3).

The first construction phase of Building A is represented by Walls 30, 31, 12, 9, and the polygonal portion of Wall 8 in Room 1. Wall 13 can be included in this list as well, although, as previously mentioned, only a fraction of this wall has come to light in the course of excavations. The walls comprising this earliest phase can reach to 0.80 m in width, as evinced by the western portion of Wall 31. These clearly abut an earlier structure in the agora, Building Δ, which is estimated to date to the end of the 7th century B.C. on the basis of the style of its walls and the stratigraphical relationship of the buildings.

The scale and craftsmanship of the walls belonging to this first phase arguably embody an ambition to construct public buildings of great significance at the earliest stages of development of the agora. Thus, it can be posited that Building A did not evolve into an important structure over time, and it was not overhauled or redesigned at a later stage. Rather, it was deliberately conceived and constructed as monumental architecture from the very beginning. Building in this manner set the precedent for ongoing urbanization at Methone. Generally speaking, with regard to symbolism, architecture is not as forthcoming as we would like it to be. Indeed, individual buildings rarely speak their meaning in a literal sense, especially in antiquity. However, these walls, in particular the polygonal and isodomic masonry construction methods of Wall 8 and Wall 9 (Figs. 18.26–18.28), respectively, do indeed signify change. They demonstrate that a community deliberately chose to erect public buildings that befit a burgeoning city.

Phase two of Building A can be described as an expansion of the first phase, but deciphering the particularities of the architectural construction is complicated because the structure at some point probably collapsed at its western end. The walls comprising this phase include 18, 21, interior Walls 15, 16 and 17, and the section of Wall 8 in Room 6. Wall 18 was constructed on top of Walls 30 and 31 and it directly follows the course of the latter. It is possible, but not certain, that Wall 18 originally extended farther west beyond its current length.

Notably, the second phase also has several sub-phases, many of which are illustrated in the western elevation of Wall 21 (Fig. 18.15). This particular wall appears to have three distinct building phases, the earliest of which belongs to the last quarter of the 6th century B.C. It is entirely likely that this wall once served as an interior, rather than terminal, wall for the structure. This is corroborated by the fact that the southern end of the wall is constructed of several orthostates that are much smaller in dimension than the blocks belonging to the northern end. Moreover, the configuration of the central portion of the lower course of the wall indicates that there was once a doorway, which was closed and then blocked in by new, larger orthostates. Thus, at some point toward the close of the 6th century, the central hall of Building A had two entranceways, one at the west and one in the north. A final sub-phase of Wall 21 is marked by the addition of another course, to which mud brick was also added.

A further detail in the archaeological evidence provides insight to the wider spatial context of Building A. To the immediate west of Wall 21 is a line of regular but uncut stones measuring in total ca. 3.0 m (Figs. 18.3, 18.4, 18.35). These are the remains of a gutter or drain that ran parallel to the building and which probably was used for the collection and removal of water. The drain does not continue beyond the northern limit of Wall 21 but it should be remembered that the area farther north has been identified as a yard for Building A. Both these details—the yard and the course of the drain—confirm that at some point Wall 21 demarcated the western limit of the building. They also imply the existence of some kind of alley or street bordering the building at the west.

The third and final construction phase of Building A is constituted by the porch at the north. There are only two walls comprising this addition—Wall 19 and Wall 20—and together they define a narrow space that is open at both its northern and western edges. The presence of this extension raises important questions about the identity and subsequent classification of Building A. These will be discussed in the final section of this study.

While the construction history of Building A is marked by successive changes in plan, deconstructions, and subsequent phases of rebuilding, its demise was straightforward and sudden: In 354 B.C., following a prolonged siege, Philip II laid waste to the city of Methone. Following this, the entire site was abandoned. A thick layer of destruction debris, including collapsed mud-brick walls, smashed tiles, and crushed cobblestones, was deposited at the site of Building A (see Chapter 29). This was eventually covered by a layer of collapsed or eroded deposits from the east that protected the remains of the agora.

USE AND IDENTIFICATION

Undoubtedly, the location, relative size, and construction technique of Building A indicate that this is a public structure of great significance. It is the natural assumption that the building served as either an administrative or a commercial center, perhaps both. In support of this we may refer to both tangible, material evidence that came to light during the excavation of the building, and wider considerations of the role of Methone as a coastal city on the Thermaic Gulf.

Methone was a prosperous city, especially during the Late Geometric and Archaic periods (Chapters 1, 2, 12, 14, 15, 21). In particular, excavations of the eastern edge of the agora have confirmed that the city was a significant place of production from at least the late Geometric period.[7] It is noteworthy that the excavators also came upon a considerable quantity of small finds within Building A itself. These provide some insight to the use of the structure. For instance, the preponderance of ceramic evidence clearly suggests that the building flourished as some sort of commercial depot for trade. Other finds, such as iron and bronze nails, loomweights, spindlewhorls, glass (Chapter 25), and fragments of metal tools and implements, point to industrial enterprise. This general picture of substantial activity and intensive use is further enhanced by other details in the archaeological record; for instance, the presence of pottery kilns and associated burning, as well as fragments of pottery.[8] Certainly, it is conceivable that Rooms 4, 3, and 6 of the central hall, and later Room 5 (the porch), served not only as workshops but also as commercial spaces; this is especially the case for Room 4 during the second phase of the building as it had an external doorway in its western wall. Rooms 1 and 2 were less accessible and thus were more likely used as storage facilities or workshops. In the period leading up to the destruction of the building, it is possible that the porch was utilized as a kind of lookout or shelter for the defenders of the city. Evidence for this is provided by debris from the floor area of Room 5. The material clearly indicates a form of burning, but, in this case, it resembles a handmade campfire rather than an established hearth.

While small finds provide discrete, particular glimpses into the life of Building A, other conditions and factors having to do with the wider topography allow us to think about the contributions this structure made to the urbanism of Methone. As mentioned at the start of this chapter, Building A faces north directly onto a *plateia*, and moreover, it is likely that a roadway led from this space in a northwesterly direction. While there could have been a harbor at the eastern edge of the East Hill, any evidence for this would have been destroyed long ago by coastal erosion. It is far more probable that the primary harbor of Methone was situated to the immediate north or northwest of the agora, just beyond the West and East Hills, in an area safely protected from the prevailing southern winds (Figs. 3.12–3.13). All of this means that Building A was strategically positioned and oriented to serve as a hub for goods moving between the agora and the harbor. To underscore this observation, we may adduce Methone's geostrategic importance to the general region. We know from ceramic evidence, together with that of other small finds presented in this volume, that the city played a pivotal role in trade throughout, as well as beyond, the Thermaic Gulf. It therefore required a form of architecture that not only could accommodate its manifold activities but could also reflect its economic and political status.

The overarching question regarding Building A concerns its identification. It is logical to surmise that the architectural characteristics of the porch—its permeable façade, long and narrow interior space, and position on the principal façade of the building—enable us to classify the structure as a stoa, at least in its final building phase. Yet this identification is more tenuous when we consider just the first two phases of the building. If it were evaluated strictly within the parameters of a formal building typology, then Building A, in its early form, would probably not meet the prerequisites for being labeled a stoa. However, this line of reasoning comes with a caveat: by requiring the building to demonstrate a set of predetermined formal characteristics, namely a colonnaded porch, in order to fit into a particular conceptual category, we are overlooking, indeed undermining, what Peter Carl describes as the "true depth of typicality" in architecture.[9] Thus, while it is customary to seek an identification for Building A according to its plan and construction details, it is equally important to take account of the structure as a setting for institutions and as a receptacle of typical situations; these latter attributes are generally omitted from formal building typologies. Moreover, it is worthwhile highlighting at this point that although typology is the dominant method of studying ancient architecture in the present day, this approach only came to the fore in post-Enlightenment discourse, in particular through Quatremère de Quincy's theory of type and Durand's codification of generic principles of design.[10] Although the Greeks certainly grouped buildings and developed a language to differentiate between them, we have no evidence to presume that this language was based on abstract forms and reified knowledge. Rather, it is much more likely that in antiquity buildings were referred to and described by a rich spectrum of situations and commonalities.

When we reflect more specifically on how Building A is positioned in the agora at Methone, and also review how it seemed to accommodate a range of activities, then it becomes reasonable to contend that the structure assumed the character of a stoa at even its earliest stages of existence. Regardless of geographical location or context—civic or sacred—stoas typically embody particular attributes and situations: they create a boundary or edge within a precinct or complex; their façades always maintain a spatial and visual reciprocity with an adjacent square or thoroughfare, sometimes both; and finally, one key commonality threading through all stoas is their calculated versatility. Even when a particular stoa tends to be associated with one activity above all others, more often than not it also maintains secondary uses, and importantly, these may change over time. Based on the available evidence, we can say that Building A conforms to all of these conditions.

NOTES

1 Unless otherwise noted, the photographs presented in this chapter are the work of Samantha L. Martin, Teresa Martin, and John Papadopoulos. The author wishes to thank Atteyeh Natanzi, who generously provided assistance with modern Greek translation.

2 Building A stands in Plot 274, one of the two main areas of archaeological investigation at ancient Methone (the other being West Hill, Plots 229, 245, Figs. 6.1, 19.1). It is important to note that while a majority of Building A has been revealed, it is a very real possibility that the structure continues farther south beneath the land that lies outside of the excavation area, as well as to a greater depth and age. Furthermore, in another excavation area, Plot 278, some 50 m southeast of Building A, architectural material has come to light and substantiates occupation from at least the Archaic period. Several large ashlar blocks, which together are referred to as Building Γ, most likely comprised a monumental structure (Bessios, Athanassiadou, and Noulas 2008, pp. 241, 245, fig. 9). The point is that any study of the agora of Methone as it is currently identified should not overlook the likelihood of a wider urban center, or indeed centers (Chapter 1).

3 It is referred to as Plateia A in the initial excavation report (cf. Chapters 1 and 29).

4 For the initial excavation report, see Bessios, Athanassiadou, and Noulas 2008, pp. 241–248; see also Bessios 2012b. It should be noted that the early exploration of the area in 2003 focused on the region immediately southeast of Building A. Note that in Chapter 29, Rooms 1–6 are labeled A–Z (Fig. 29.1).

5 The limestone was likely from Sfendami, which lies approximately 8 km southwest of the ancient site of Methone (Manthos Bessios, pers. comm.); cf. Koukouvou 2012, for poros quarries near Veroia.

6 Notebook photograph #274/077 (22/7/05).

7 Bessios, Athanassiadou, and Noulas 2008.

8 Two such installations were located north of Wall 18 in close proximity to its foundation course; these are described as pottery kilns in Chapter 19a.

9 Carl 2011, p. 39.

10 Quatremère de Quincy 1825; Durand 1802–1805.

19A

POTTERY WORKSHOPS OF ANCIENT METHONE

Matthaios Bessios

As noted in Chapter 1, the site of ancient Methone occupies a favorable coastal position, combined with immediate proximity to the main north–south road axis of antiquity.[1] This lent special geostrategic importance to the harbor of ancient Methone, particularly in terms of communication with central and west Macedonia, as well as with the Balkan hinterland.

We can easily understand, therefore, the prosperity of the settlement, especially during the Late Geometric and Archaic periods. An additional, special significance lies in the favorable circumstance of unearthing, for the first time in northern Pieria, well-preserved structural remains, including, most importantly, the administrative and commercial center—the ancient agora.

Specifically, in Plot 274 on the East Hill we located public buildings next to two squares (see Chapter 18). The finds indicate that intense workshop activity was taking place in the agora proper during the Archaic and Classical periods. Excavation in Buildings A and B also brought to light parts of two pottery kilns. Their investigation was not completed, because at that stage we were primarily interested in the horizontal exposure of the structures dating to the abandonment of the settlement, after its conquest by Philip II in 354 B.C. The pottery kilns in question were backfilled, to be further explored in the future.

Further excavations were carried out in Plots 245 and 229 on the West Hill, which is naturally defensible and thus must have functioned as the acropolis of the settlement (Fig. 19.1). Here we revealed pit graves of the Late Bronze Age (Chapter 6), along with deposits dating to the Early Iron Age and, mainly, to the Archaic period (Figs. 1.31–1.32, 6.2).

The focus of the excavations on the West Hill was on Sector B of Plot 229, where building remains of a distinctly industrial quarter came to light. So far, we have exposed parts of at least three buildings, with relatively thin walls (up to 0.40 m in thickness) made of local sandstone (Fig. 19.1a–c). Successive building phases span the second half of the 7th century B.C. to the second half of the 6th century B.C.

It must be noted that the richest phase is the one dating to the first half of the 6th century B.C., a phase that ended with visible evidence of burning in all the trenches that have been excavated so far. The destruction levels, apparently undisturbed, have already yielded a large number of finds, especially ceramics.

Despite the aforementioned good preservation of the architectural remains, which sometimes exceed one meter in height, the structures were simple and only scant fragments of roof tiles were found. Most of the roofs were, therefore, likely constructed of perishable materials.

While the possibility of a wartime event cannot be excluded as a cause of the conflagration, it is more likely that this resulted from the widespread use of fire in the context of workshop activities, coupled, of course, with the flammable nature of the building materials.

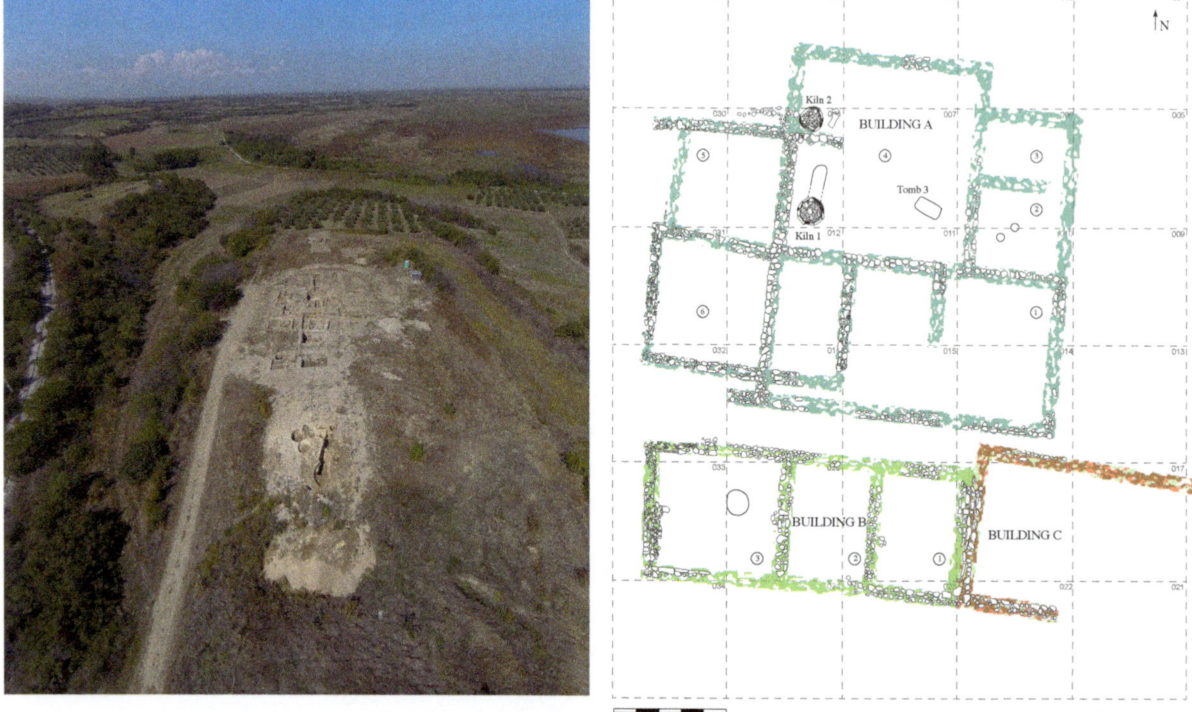

FIGURE 19.1. a) Aerial view from west of the West Hill at Methone as uncovered in 2014 (H. Thomas); b) 2014 aerial of the West Hill, from south (H. Thomas); c) plan of the buildings, kilns, and tombs excavated on the West Hill of Methone (Plot 229) up to the end of the 2011 season. Drone photography Hugh Thomas, drawing I. Moschou

We found evidence for a variety of industrial activities. Small pits containing molten copper were found on the floor of Room 2 in Building A, which can thus be interpreted as a metallurgical installation. This is also the case with Room 3 in Building A, the floor of which bore strong traces of fire and many pieces of molten copper. Fragments of stone molds, clay crucibles, and related materials were collected from this same room and from adjacent spaces.

In addition, most spaces in this quarter produced abundant waste from various stages of ivory-working (Fig. 1.37).

The excavations also brought to light two potting kilns, in Room 4 of Building A. This is quite a large space (7.80 x 8.00 m), which we may attribute to some outdoor or, more likely, a semi-roofed area—as would befit a pottery workshop (Figs. 19.2–19.3).

Immediately to the west of the two kilns, there was a thick gray layer that was plausibly associated with some workshop. This layer produced a large quantity of pottery, attributable to workshops of Corinth, Attica, the East Aegean, and so forth. There was also a considerable amount of grayware pottery, but no wasters or misfired pieces that would have allowed a secure connection with the products of this particular workshop.

Recent excavations have demonstrated beyond doubt that ancient Methone was, as anticipated, a major transit center. The principal novel contribution of our research is that we now have an industrial town which produced all kinds of commodities in various materials. Whereas these products obviously covered local demand, they were traded inland and overseas as well, along a wider chain of harbors in the Aegean and the Mediterranean in general.

FIGURE 19.2. West Hill (Plot 229), kiln 1.
Photo K. Noulas

FIGURE 19.3. West Hill (Plot 229), kiln 2.
Photo K. Noulas

19B

ARCHAIC POTTERY FROM THE ACROPOLIS (WEST HILL) OF ANCIENT METHONE

Matthaios Bessios and Konstantinos Noulas

The principal contribution of the investigations at Methone since 2003 lies in the documentation of an important industrial center of production on the site.[2] As a result, we know that Methone produced articles made of many different types of material: gold, silver, bronze, iron, ivory, animal bone, antler, and glass. These were usually luxury goods, the manufacture of which required specialized knowledge. Finds indicative of such extensive industrial activity include, for example, stone molds, clay crucibles for the pouring of metal (gold or bronze), ivory debitage, and a discoid ivory seal bearing the image of a centaur.[3]

Pottery workshops serve daily needs, of course, and their technology is relatively simple. Thus, they could not but be part of the diverse productive operations at Methone. Already since the Late Geometric period, the potteries of the town manufactured a great variety of ceramic wares, with clear influences from the Euboian sphere, the local Macedonian tradition, and Corinth, and very likely from the eastern Aegean as well.

We can, moreover, assume that the potters of Methone played a decisive role in the creation of the different ceramic categories in existence around the Thermaic Gulf. The presence of many production centers in this region—which operated in close mutual proximity and under common broader influences—makes it difficult to distinguish the individual contributions of each in the creation of specific vessel types. We must accept that the manufacture of items of all kinds at Methone did not serve only the local demand, or even that of the Macedonian hinterland, but that a portion of the products was also directed—by way of reciprocity or trade—to other centers in the Aegean and the wider Mediterranean. Future archaeological research will very likely attribute some finds from those centers to the Methonaian production.

In this chapter we will refer to the Archaic pottery from the West Hill of Methone, which is considered as the acropolis of the settlement because of its defensibility. Excavations in Plots 229 and 245 during the years 2001–2009 initially concentrated on the south part of the hill, where we expected to find remains of fortifications. Today we are certain that the course of the southern city wall ran here, of which, however, nothing has survived because of erosion and plundering. We nevertheless have so far located three tunnels that started immediately north of the wall and led outside of it (see Fig. 1.26). We must also see these as part of the Methonaian defensive strategy; likewise, the cutting of the hill—several meters deep—in front of the wall line sought to enhance the defensibility of the terrain.[4]

Although no architectural remains of habitation were found in the area immediately north of the wall—those having been lost to the aforementioned erosion—there survived parts of pithoi, and circular pits that were initially meant for storage and later used for refuse (Figs. 1.31–1.32).

FIGURE 19.4. Fragmentary locally made krater with Geometric ornament (ΜΕΘ 3559). Photo ΚΖ΄ Ephoreia

On the evidence of the collected pottery, most of these pits seem to have been filled in the second half of the 7th century B.C. There is Corinthian pottery, as well as vessels from the eastern Aegean, including Chian amphoras and Ionian cups. Grayware pottery is a distinctive group and includes both imports and, most likely, local products (Chapter 22). To the local workshops we must certainly attribute painted open shapes, the decoration of which preserves Geometric elements (e.g., Fig. 19.4).

By far the most important assemblage of Archaic pottery was excavated in Sector B of Plot 229, the central area of the acropolis plateau. Here were brought to light parts of at least three buildings of clear industrial character (Fig. 19.1c). These structures were densely arranged, their walls built of local sandstone of up to 0.40 m in width. Several construction phases have been detected; some of the older sections had been robbed, and later phases usually rested upon the earlier ones. More cursory extensions were also visible, on the upper level of the buildings. The surviving portions sometimes exceed one meter in height, and unbaked clay bricks are also attested. As noted above, two pottery kilns were uncovered in Building A, Room 4, which was most probably a semi-roofed area within a pottery workshop.

The initial phase of the buildings can likewise be dated to the second half of the 7th century B.C. Levels of the second half of the 6th century B.C. were preserved in fragmentary condition, because of the erosion on the hilltop. Classical remains have been almost completely lost, except for isolated surface finds, with most of the disturbance of these strata due to plowing. In Sector B, a pit in Square 13 constitutes the only secure indication for the use of the acropolis during the 4th century B.C.

Be that as it may, the richest horizon dates to the first half of the 6th century B.C, and is marked by strong traces of fire in all the trenches excavated so far. As was noted above, although an act of violence due to war cannot be ruled out as cause of the conflagration, it is more likely that this resulted from the widespread use of fire in the context of workshop activities within the buildings, coupled with the perishable nature of the building materials. The fortunate result, for our research purposes, is that the destruction layer came to light undisturbed and yielded a large number of movable finds, especially ceramics (Fig. 19.5).

FIGURE 19.5. Part of the destruction layer on the West Hill in Sector B, Plot 229. Photo K. Noulas

It must be noted that investigations have not uncovered all the spaces of Sector B, nor has the study of the respective finds yet been a priority among the Methone material.[5] Pottery conservation, especially of larger vessels, is time-consuming, and it has also been falling considerably behind. Nevertheless, the portion already restored allows a preliminary presentation of the corpus from the acropolis.

The first, obvious conclusion concerns as much the prosperity of the settlement as it does its multiple interactions with different trade hubs of the ancient world. This status is clear from the variety of transport amphoras, with numerous examples from Attica, Chios, Samos, Lesbos, and Miletos, as well as others from Corinth, and one that can be attributed to the Laconian workshop. In singling out diagnostic pieces from the above regions, we draw attention to an Attic amphora of the type *à la brosse* with interesting incised marks on both sides of the neck (see **21/9**, Fig. 21.7).[6] An almost complete example of a pointed-toe amphora from Chios demonstrates the shape development of this particular type, which took place from the last quarter of the 7th and the first half of the 6th centuries B.C.[7] The body and foot of this piece are already more slender, and the reduction of the neck diameter has resulted in a corresponding elongation of the handles (see **21/1**, Fig. 21.1). Following Pierre Dupont's classification, we could date this amphora to the transition from the second to the third quarter of the 6th century B.C.; however, it does not yet match the over-elongated examples—reaching 0.85–0.90 m. in height—of the late third quarter of the century, as known from other regions. The decoration is the standard red-on-white slip, consisting of bands around the lip, neck, and body, combined with curvilinear ornaments on the upper body and at the handle attachments.[8]

The Lesbian amphora ΜΕΘ 3543—its surface a distinctive gray and its handles cylindrical in section—belongs with examples of the type that are representative of the first half of the 6th century B.C. (see **21/6**, Fig. 21.5). The upper body bulges noticeably; the neck is wide at its base and is surmounted by a broad, emphatic lip.[9] Also of Lesbian origin is an amphora in orange-red fabric, similar to the previous one as regards the formation of the lip, foot, and handles.[10]

The Milesian products are easily recognizable by the high and rounded profile of the lip, the beveled base of the foot, and the single or multiple ridges around the neck.[11] Among the material from Plot 229, there is one unusual fragment with different types of handles, a feature that is described in the literature as being rare for Milesian amphoras;[12] it may have been the special trademark of a particular workshop. Both the complete and the more fragmentary Milesian amphoras from Methone (see **21/4** and **21/5**, Figs. 21.3–21.4) lack slip and decoration, in common with most vessels of this type that were meant for export from their place of production.[13] Chronologically, this piece belongs with examples which, toward the second quarter of the 6th century B.C, assume a curvilinear ("arched") body profile as a result of corresponding increases in height and diameter, and, before the mid-century, they also develop a distinctive fold at the base of the neck, which tapers toward the body.[14]

There are many fragments of Corinthian amphoras featuring the diagnostic broad horizontal rim (see **21/10** [ΜΕΘ 3544], Fig. 21.8). To a Lakonian workshop we can ascribe another, pointed amphora with wide ring foot and handles of rectangular section. The shape is broadly related to the SOS type, and the brown slip has been applied with a brush (see **21/11**, Fig. 21.9); this vessel, too, can be placed within the first half of the 6th century B.C.[15]

In addition, there are several other types of amphoras of unknown provenance, among which we must count the local production of Methone and the wider area of the Thermaic Gulf.[16] Some of these amphoras also bear incised marks and letters, the comprehensive study of which will hopefully assist in understanding interactions and exchanges among workshops. Especially noteworthy is the incised inscription ΤΕΛΙ on the neck of an amphora—most likely, the beginning of a name (see **21/12** [ΜΕΘ 3545], Fig. 21.10).

As for the finer pottery, the vast majority of banqueting ware was, as expected, Corinthian. There are large and smaller fragments of a significant number of column kraters that date to the Middle and Late Corinthian periods. One example bears on both sides animal images in panels (Fig. 19.6), possibly imitating works of the Potters' Quarter of Corinth.[17] On another column krater fragment, a point of interest is the yellow color of the robe of a figure riding a chariot.[18] To the smaller contemporary shapes belong kotylai and plates—among the plates a particularly fine example is ΜΕΘ 2695 (Fig. 19.7)[19]—together with small pyxides and flat-based aryballoi. Of the latter, one is decorated with warrior figures in a hoplite formation and scale pattern (Fig. 19.8).[20] An interesting work of Early Corinthian date is the alabastron with heraldic roosters (Fig. 19.9)—a popular decorative subject on Corinthian vases.[21]

The next major group can be attributed to east Aegean workshops. Representative examples include Ionian cups (**22/41–22/52**, Figs. 22.24–22.29), a "Samian" lekythos (**22/53**, Fig. 22.30),[22] fragments of Chian chalices (**22/38–22/39**, Fig. 22.22),[23] Chian amphoras (see above, and Chapter 21), as well as plates, and other vessel forms. A partially preserved high-footed plate, decorated with a bird on the interior (**22/40**, Fig. 22.23), likewise is East Greek, specifically from Miletos.[24]

Attic pottery also makes its appearance at this time, represented by fragments of kraters, cups (Fig. 19.10),[25] and plates, among other shapes (for a representative selection of Attic black- and red-figure pottery, see Chapter 23).

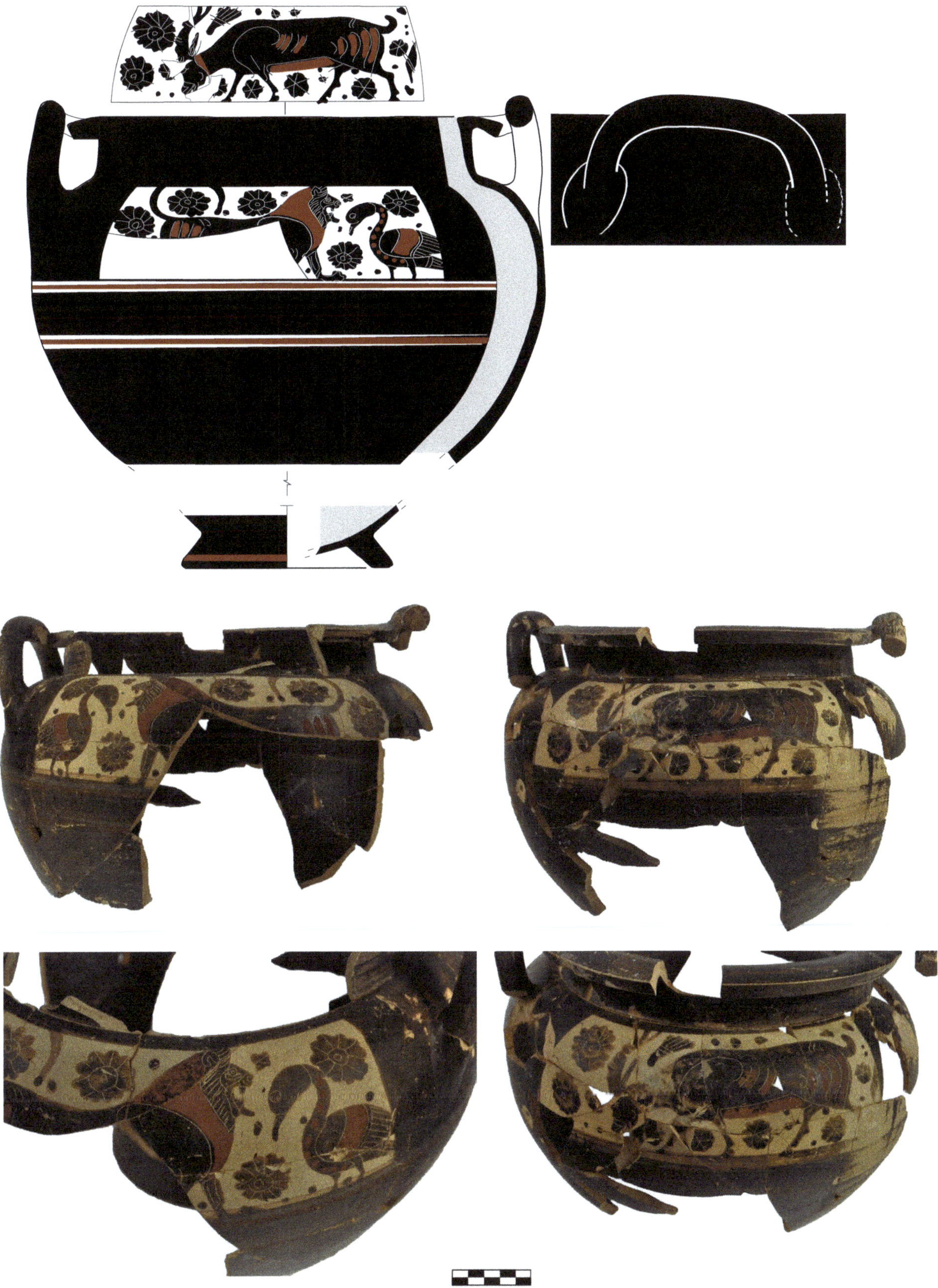

FIGURE 19.6. Drawing and four views of a Corinthian column krater (ΜΕΘ 2693). Drawing A. Hooton, photos I. Coyle

FIGURE 19.7. Corinthian plate (MEΘ 2695).
Drawing A. Hooton

It goes without saying that the largest portion of tableware was manufactured locally, by which—at this stage of research—we refer to the wider Thermaic Gulf area. There are oinochoai, eggshell-ware cups/kylikes, other types of cups, and skyphoi. A painted amphora measuring 0.25 m in height, with vertical handles on the shoulder, must be broadly attributed to a workshop in the Chalkidike (Fig. 19.11).[26]

Grayware pottery always constitutes a stable component of the total assemblage, represented by a variety of shapes such as amphoras, hydriai, oinochoai, skyphoi, cups, lekanides, dinoi, and other vessel forms. Among the large vessels there is also a stand and a kalathos. Notwithstanding the likely local production of this category, distinctive qualitative differences within the group suggest the possibility that different workshops operated at Methone, and that some of these vessels may have been imports (for the "Aiolian" grayware, see Chapter 22, **22/1–22/20**, Figs. 22.1–22.8).[27]

This brief presentation has highlighted the variety of Archaic pottery types from the acropolis at Methone. This material offers rich opportunities for research, on the level of specialized topics and case studies, as well as in works that address broader themes of trade, exchange, and interaction among different regions of the ancient world.

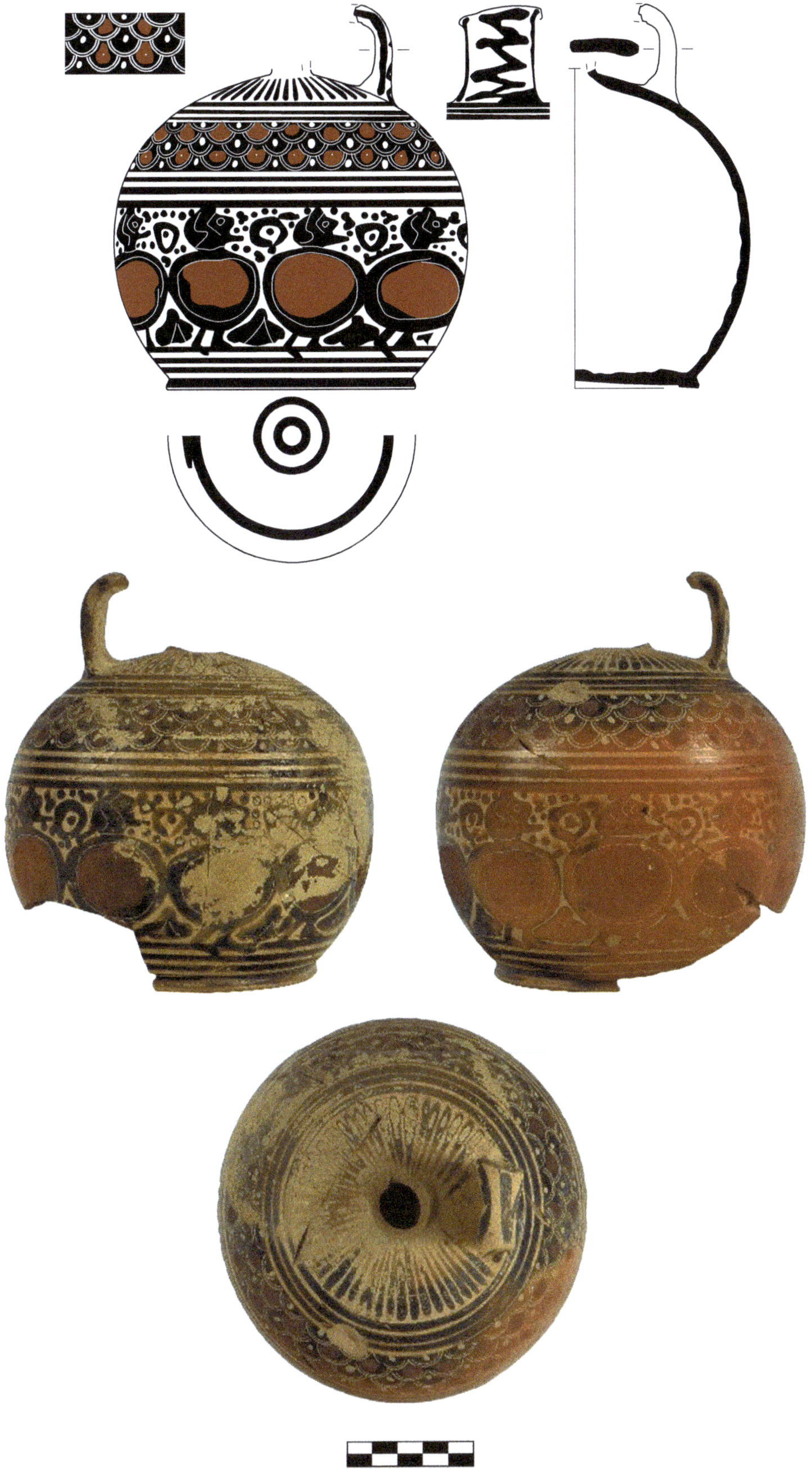

FIGURE 19.8. Drawing and three views of fragmentary Corinthian aryballos (ΜΕΘ 8361). Drawing A. Hooton, photos I. Coyle

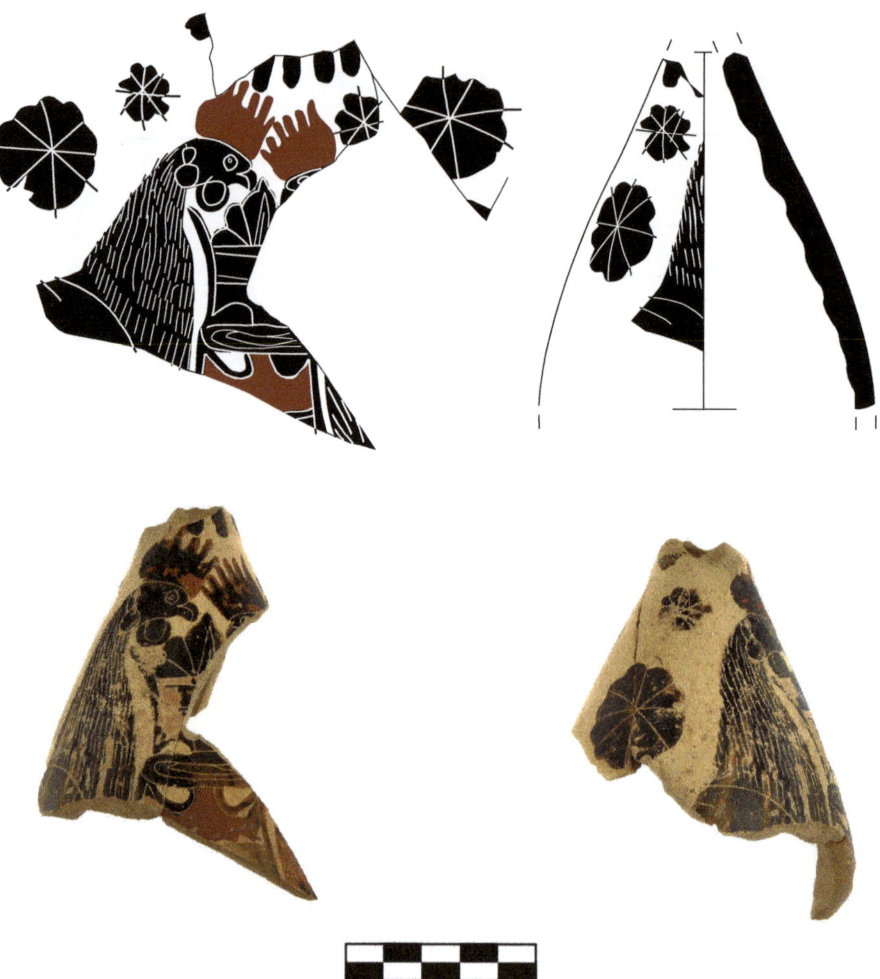

FIGURE 19.9. Fragmentary Corinthian alabastron (ΜΕΘ 3556).
Drawing A. Hooton, photos I. Coyle

FIGURE 19.10. Attic black-figure Siana cup by the Taras Painter (ΜΕΘ 5139).
Photo I. Coyle

FIGURE 19.11. Painted amphora from a workshop in the Chalkidike (ΜΕΘ 2707). Photo KZ′ Ephoreia

Completion of the study of the already excavated areas and the ongoing conservation of the ceramic material are the necessary preconditions for exploring the multifaceted contacts of Methone with other ancient emporia and sites across the Greek world and, more importantly, for confirming the activity of the local potteries.

NOTES

1 A Greek version of Chapter 19a appeared as Bessios 2013; Chapter 19b appeared in Greek as Bessios and Noulas 2012 (both translated here by Marianna Nikolaidou); both parts of this chapter have been amended and updated. For useful comparative material from other parts of the north Aegean, see Tiverios et al. 2012; Adam-Veleni, Kefalidou, and Tsiafaki 2013.

2 For the location of Methone, and its excavations beginning in 2003 with the limited resources of the Ephoreia, see Bessios 2003; for the harbor of Methone and for the excavations conducted between 2004 and 2009, see Bessios, Athanassiadou, and Noulas 2008; Bessios 2013. We know that in antiquity the sea reached deep into the land northwest of the city; for a general overview see Bessios 2017; see also Bessios, Athanassiadou, and Noulas 2021a, 2021b. In addition, the location of the settlement on the ancient north–south road axis secured favorable conditions for contacts, and possibilities of expansion into the hinterland of Macedonia and the Balkans in general. In ancient times, the route of the road from Pydna to Imathia passed through Methone. In antiquity, the stretch of the road from Pydna to Methone was coastal, as was also the portion from Methone to Aloros, which is mentioned as a coastal settlement; see Bessios and Krahtopoulou 2001, pp. 394–395. For the destruction of Methone in 354 B.C., see Chapters 1–2, and for "Macedonian Methone," founded at "Palaiokatachas" Methonis, see Bessios 2003, p. 444, n. 3; Bessios 2010, pp. 306–313; see also Bessios, Athanassiadou, and Noulas 2021a. The cemetery associated with Macedonian Methone was identified at the location "Melissia" Aiginiou (see Fig. 1.39); among the total of 94 excavated tombs, many were

richly furnished. With the exception of two graves that date to the Early Iron Age, the burials date to the 4th and 3rd centuries B.C.; see Bessios 2010, pp. 88–89, 314–319. For the jewelry, in particular, see Bessios and Tsigarida 2000; for the 4th- and 3rd-century B.C. pottery, see Kotitsa 2006. This cemetery was also attested by the existence of a burial tumulus—now leveled down—at the modern town of Aiginion. For the importance of Methone, especially in the Geometric and Archaic periods, see Bessios 2010, pp. 104–111.

3 Bessios 2010, p. 110; see also Fig. 1.14.

4 See Bessios, Athanassiadou, and Noulas 2008, 2021a; Bessios 2013.

5 Dr. Alexandra Kasseri has included part of the pottery, specifically the amphoras of the Archaic period, in her doctoral dissertation at Oxford (Kasseri 2015; for a summary, see Chapter 21; for the earlier, Geometric-period trade of amphoras, see Chapter 12). Further research will explore the commercial exchanges between Methone and other emporia and the conditions of Archaic trade. We are grateful to Dr. Kasseri for fruitful discussions and bibliographic suggestions on the topic of Archaic pottery.

6 ΜΕΘ 3202 (max. H: 0.625 m).

7 ΜΕΘ 2465 (max. H: 0.685 m).

8 For Chian amphoras, see Cook and Dupont 1998, pp. 146–151.

9 Max. H.: 0.610 m. This piece belongs to the so-called "gray series." The concave underfoot is an additional mark of early date. A representative example of this shape is illustrated in Cook and Dupont 1998, p. 175, fig. 23:4b.

10 ΜΕΘ 2462 (max. H: 0.600 m); see further, Cook and Dupont 1998, pp. 156–163; Birzescu 2005, pp. 46-49.

11 For Milesian amphoras, see Cook and Dupont 1998, pp. 170–177.

12 ΜΕΘ 3546. A characteristic example is illustrated in Cook and Dupont 1998, p. 172, fig. 23:8c.

13 ΜΕΘ 2675 (max H. 0.600 m); it bears incised marks on the shoulder and the outside of the handles (for which see Chapter 21). For decorated Milesian amphoras, see Bîrzescu 2009.

14 See discussion in Cook and Dupont 1998, pp. 170–177.

15 ΜΕΘ 2684 (max. P.H. 0.529 m). On the dating, compare the two examples of Lakonian amphoras in Pelagatti 1990, pp. 133, 135, figs. 47–48 (beginning of the 6th century B.C.) and p. 136, fig. 52 (second half of the 6th century B.C.), respectively. The shape of the Methone amphora is chronologically and stylistically intermediate between these two.

16 Characteristic examples include ΜΕΘ 2463 (Max. H. 0.632 m), ΜΕΘ 2464 (max. H. 0.640 m), ΜΕΘ 2708 (max. H. 0.538 m).

17 This is according to Professor Cornelius Neeft, who saw the piece. We are grateful to Professor Neeft for his thoughts on the Corinthian pottery from Methone.

18 For a comparable representation on a Middle Corinthian crater by the Detroit Painter, see Amyx 1988, p. 196, no. 5.

19 For further illustrations, see Fig. 1.35.

20 For an aryballos with comparable decoration by the Warrior Frieze Painter, see Amyx 1988, p. 154, no. 2.

21 Cf., for example, Amyx 1988, p. 83, no. 9.

22 For the shape, see *Kerameikos* IX, p. 84, pl. 18, fig. 2; for further discussion see Chapter 22.

23 For Chian pottery, see Lemos 1991.

24 For this category, compare an example from Miletos that was found in a stratum dating to the last quarter of the 7th century B.C., see von Graeve 1973–1974, p. 107, pl. 29, no. 116. General remarks on Milesian pottery and its decoration can be found in Voigtländer 1984.

25 In Chapter 23, Seth Pevnick classifies this (along with non-joining fragments ΜΕΘ 4644) as a Siana cup and attributes it to the Taras Painter (Fig. 23.2).

26 ΜΕΘ 2707. For the local painted pottery of Chalkidike, see Panti 2008, pp. 52–80, 192, and especially pp. 231–248; cf. Paspalas 1995.

27 For grayware pottery from the head of the Thermaic Gulf, see Panti 2008, pp. 81–86, 217, 250–255.

20

THE ROLE OF METHONE IN THE MACEDONIAN TIMBER TRADE

Angelos Boufalis

INTRODUCTION

Despite the fact that the Macedonian timber trade in the Classical period is well attested, little is actually known about it. This study aims at identifying the timberland(s) that served as the source(s) of Macedonian timber, as well as the port(s) that handled the exports. These are suggested to be, at least primarily, the Pieria mountains and the city of Methone respectively. To support this identification, geographical, botanical, and palynological data are considered along with literary and archaeological evidence.[1]

Macedonian timber resources, for both construction and shipbuilding, are well known from Theophrastos' *Historia Plantarum* (4.5.5, 5.2.1; cf. Plin. *HN* 16.197), where they are ranked as the finest in the regions around the Aegean and the Black Sea. The Macedonian timber trade is also well attested by a small number of testimonia, most of which concern the Athenian timber supply during the second half of the 5th and the first half of the 4th century B.C.[2] These historical sources have provided valuable information on aspects of Classical Greek political history and especially on the Macedonian kingdom in the period before Philip II; however, they provide no information on the timber trade itself, which would shed light on more specific matters, such as Macedonian political geography and administrative institutions.

A few indications regarding these matters are included in our evidence, enabling us to draw a few tentative, yet plausible, conclusions. The present study is intended to locate, on the one hand, the source(s) of Macedonian timber and pitch, and, on the other, the most likely place whence these products were exported. It has been argued before that these were, respectively, the Pieria mountains and the city of Methone.[3] The primary aim, then, is to explore the role of Pieria and more particularly that of Methone, and, to this end, botanical studies, pollen records, paleoenvironmental research, and the geography of the region are considered together, and in conjunction with the literary, epigraphic, and archaeological evidence.

The study is structured to follow this dual aim in an effort to investigate source(s) and export outlet(s) independently from each other. The chronological scope will be limited to the Classical period, as the bulk of the evidence dates from this period and the rapid expansion of the Macedonian kingdom from the mid-4th century B.C. onward created new conditions. Finally, the emphasis will be on shipbuilding timber and other naval supplies, namely oars and pitch, as these are the main concerns in the testimonia, and are also more indicative than the general timber trade, which would also involve entrepreneurs and enterprises on a smaller scale.[4]

THE SOURCE

Herodotos (8.136.1) mentions that Alexander I of Macedon, even though he was a vassal of the Persian king since his father had given earth and water to Darius I,[5] was a *proxenos* and benefactor of the Athenians. Charles Edson and Malcolm B. Wallace suggested that his benefaction, for which he was honored by the Athenians, was supplying the timber that made the construction of the Athenian fleet of 480 B.C. possible.[6] Russell Meiggs, however, has argued against a Macedonian provenance, suggesting alternatively south Italy as the most probable source.[7] He deemed it impossible that such an enterprise as the felling, processing, and transport of the great amount of timber needed for 200 triremes would not attract the attention of the Persians, who were stationed in Thrace as far as the Strymon River (Hdt. 5.11, 5.23). In contrast, Eugene Borza remarked that Macedonia proper at the time extended only to the west of the Axios River.[8] All mountainous regions of high altitudes, where trees that produce timber suitable for shipbuilding grow, as we will see below, extend from the south to the northwest of the plain of Emathia. According to Borza, the source of Macedonian timber was the Pieria mountains and Mt. Olympos, in the heart of the Macedonian kingdom, where any movements could go unnoticed by Persian officials in Thrace.

The land of Pieria is considered the first region to have been annexed to the newly founded Macedonian kingdom in the 7th century B.C.[9] The seat of the Macedonian kings itself, Aigai, identified with modern Vergina, was located in the northwestern foothills of the Pierian mountain range. The expansion of early Macedonia is not, as yet, fully understood; as tradition has it, it started from Mt. Vermion (Hdt. 8.138), then expanded to the plain of Emathia and into Pieria, then to the lower part of the valley of the Axios River, reaching farther to the east to Mygdonia, and also to Eordia to the west, as well as to

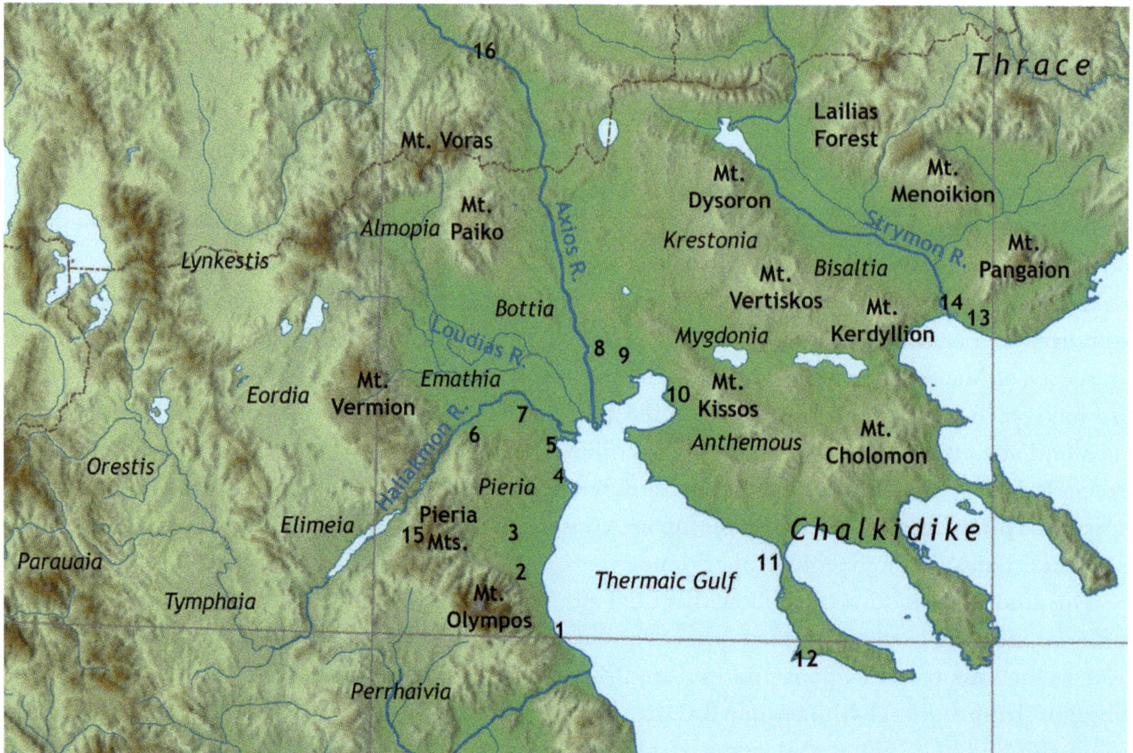

FIGURE 20.1. Physical map of northern Greece. The dashed line marks modern state borders; coastline as in modern time. 1. Herakleion, 2. Dion, 3. Katerini, 4. Pydna, 5. Methone, 6. Aigai, 7. Aloros, 8. Chalastra, 9. Sindos, 10. Therme, 11. Poteidaia, 12. Mende, 13. Eion, 14. Amphipolis, 15. Katafygi, 16. Demir Kapija. Map in the public domain (Wikimedia Commons), cropped and annotated by A. Boufalis

Almopia to the northwest, while also having subordinated Anthemous, Krestonia, and part of Bisaltia (Fig. 20.1). Furthermore, the people of Lynkestis, those of Elimeia, and other *ethne* of Upper Macedonia or farther west on the Pindos mountain range (probably of Orestis, Parauaia, and Tymphaia), possibly also of Thessalian Perrhaibia, were allied and/or subjected to the Macedonian king. Thucydides' (2.99) report of the above corresponds to the year 429 B.C., in the reign of Perdikkas II; the same territory, more or less, should also be true for the reign of Alexander I.[10]

There were many forested areas in the territory of the Macedonian kingdom; however, not every forest qualifies as timberland, especially for specialized uses such as shipbuilding. It is useful at this point to refer to the desirable properties and availability of shipbuilding timber, so as to consider how the forests of Macedonia conform to these prerequisites.

TREE SPECIES PRODUCING SHIPBUILDING TIMBER, OARS, AND PITCH ACCORDING TO THE LITERARY SOURCES

The superiority of the trireme as a warship resulted from its speed and maneuverability (Plut. *Cim.* 12.2). In order to acquire these capacities, its construction demanded the employment of light wood,[11] even though it would not have the durability or preservation properties in water that most hardwoods have. The timber from conifers would be ideal for this. In fact, fir (*elate*) and pine (*peuke*) are the most frequently recorded materials of a trireme in the ancient sources. Theophrastos, listing the woods employed in shipbuilding, records first fir (as does Plato) and then pine, if fir was not easily available, while in Crete and Syria, respectively, shipwrights substituted cypress and cedar for them. Conifers were used to make the hull of the ship, as they produce wood that combines light weight with good mechanical properties. Other woods employed came from alder, poplar, *pitys*, and possibly linden; for interior or structural parts of the ship that required hardness, mulberry, ash, elm, and plane were preferred; for the construction of the keel, which had to be extremely tough to stand hauling,[12] oak was most suitable, as it produces hard wood with a close grain, usually in combination with beech from which the χέλυσμα, false keel, was made.[13]

An inextricable part and probably the most vital component of a trireme, the oars were also made of conifers, and more particularly of fir.[14] Oars should be long but in one piece, straight, light, and not easily breakable. According to Theophrastos (*Hist. Pl.* 5.1.6–7), fir gives knot-free wood of straight grain,[15] in multiple distinct layers; removing the layers evenly along the oar shaft ensured that the grain of the wood was aligned to its axis, thereby making the oar strong for its weight.[16] Oars were made of a single trunk of a young fir tree and were purchased as such, perhaps only roughly worked.[17]

Among the non-timber supplies related to a trireme, pitch is also a tree product. The hull of the ship was coated with pitch, in order to become watertight;[18] even more so, the wood of resinous conifers (mostly pines), which was highly attractive to *teredon*, a saltwater mollusk responsible for rapid decay, had to be completely sealed in order to last.[19] Pitch is made from resin, either by boiling, or, particularly in Macedonia, through the process of pyrolysis, as described by Theophrastos (*Hist. Pl.* 9.3.1–3; see also Plin. *HN* 16.52, 16.58). The main source of pitch was apparently the resinous conifers, mostly pine, and to a lesser degree fir and *pitys*.[20]

THE FORESTS OF MACEDONIA

The natural habitat of the majority of the aforementioned trees is mountainous. Conifers in particular usually grow at high altitudes. An exception is the *pitys*. Nowadays the name denotes the *Pinus pinea* species (stone or umbrella pine), but such a correspondence is not necessarily correct for antiquity.[21]

For instance, the island of Chios was also known as *Pityoussa*, its forest comprising a large population of *Pinus brutia* (East Mediterranean pine), and the same was true for the island of Spetses, where *Pinus halepensis* (Aleppo pine) grew.[22] Theophrastos' account of the *pitys* does, in fact, hint at an identification with *P. halepensis*: in *Hist. Pl.* 3.9.5, the tree can regenerate after a fire, in contrast to *peuke* (pine), an ability characteristic of the Aleppo pine,[23] and in 5.7.3 it is employed as bentwood in triremes, a use dictated by its twisted trunk.[24] Overall, however, the name *pitys* probably referred to all lowland and coastal pine species, while *peuke* denoted the mountain pine in general.[25] This fits in with the reference to Cyprus (Theophr. *Hist. Pl.* 5.7.1), where the *pitys* is the coastal and *peuke* the mountain pine.[26]

It is obvious from the above that the higher the altitude, the better the timber.[27] Most secondary materials (namely plane, oak, linden, mulberry, manna-ash, and *pitys*) come from the Mediterranean vegetation zone extending up to 1000 m ASL. The rest (fir, pine, beech, and elm) belong to the beech-fir (*Fagetalia*) and oromediterranean pine zones, which extend between 500 and 1600 m ASL.[28] The terminology problem concerning the *pitys*, confronted above, could be applied to the names *peuke* (pine) and *elate* (fir) as well. The reason I call attention to this is the existence of the subalpine coniferous forest zone (1400–2000 m ASL) that can be found in most of the mountainous regions around Macedonia. In this zone, coniferous species other than those of the oromediterranean zone are found. Theophrastos does not distinguish between distinct species, and only seldom uses terms such as "resinous" (*Hist. Pl.* 5.4.2) or epithets such as "wild" (*Hist. Pl.* 3.3.1) and "cone-bearing" (*Hist. Pl.* 3.9.4). Taking into account the sum of characteristics he attributes to *peuke* (*Hist. Pl.* 3.9.4, 3.9.7, 5.1.5, 9.2.2), this may be identified with *Pinus nigra* (black pine): it gives light wood of average durability, it is highly resinous and subject to rapid decay, its resin has a strong smell, and it has no regenerating mechanisms following a forest fire. In the subalpine zone, however, there grows *Pinus sylvestris* (Scots pine), which differs significantly: its wood is relatively heavier and more durable, while still being soft, and of a lighter, though reddish, color, and its resin production is relatively low.[29] Unfortunately, Pliny's account (*HN* 16.43, 16.46) does not help; it seems that Pliny—who basically follows Theophrastos, although Latinizing the names—describes both species by the term *larix*, which should be equivalent to *peuke* or mountain pine. Similarly, there are two kinds of trees that could come under the term *elate*: *Abies borisii-regis* (Macedonian fir) and *Picea abies* (spruce), growing in the oromediterranean and the subalpine zone respectively. The two share similar characteristics, the hybrid Macedonian fir retaining the properties of both of its parental species, *Abies cephallonica* (Greek fir) and *Abies alba* (silver fir),[30] from which the spruce is differentiated mostly in appearance.

In addition to the above, the subalpine zone supports another significant tree species, albeit not very common in the region, *Betula pendula* (silver birch), which, besides timber of average quality, produces resin, being an addition to the resinous species mentioned by Theophrastos.

MACEDONIAN TIMBERLANDS

Extensive forests in Macedonia can be found on Mt. Olympos and the Pieria mountains in Pieria, Mt. Vermion in Emathia, Mts. Voras and Paiko in Almopia, Mts. Dysoron (modern Kroussia), Vertiskos, and Kerdyllion in Krestonia, Bisaltia, and northern Mygdonia, respectively, and Mts. Kissos (modern Chortiatis) and Cholomon in southern Mygdonia (Fig. 20.1). These shared in antiquity, as today, more or less similar vegetation: pines are dominant where higher altitudes are reached (i.e., except for Mts. Dysoron, Vertiskos, Kerdyllion, Kissos, and Cholomon),[31] with the addition of *Pinus peuce* (Macedonian pine) on Mt. Voras;[32] fir is present almost everywhere (not on Mt. Kissos and only in modern plantations on Mt. Cholomon), as are beech, poplar, elm, and oak; scarcer is birch, which, at least nowadays, grows in considerable numbers only on Mts. Voras and Paiko.[33]

In scouting for the source of Macedonian shipbuilding timber, we need to consider three parameters. First of all is the issue of transport, a major aspect of the timber trade. Although land transport from the felling location down the mountain was inevitable, proximity to some water feature—a river, a lake, or the sea—greatly facilitates the transport of timber. Water transport was generally preferable, land transport being relatively uneconomical and time-consuming.[34] Rivers in particular were of great importance, as they reached heavily forested hinterlands,[35] and proximity to a navigable river could automatically qualify a forested area as timberland (Dion. Hal. *Ant. Rom.* 1.37.4).[36] The Macedonian landscape (see Fig. 20.1), surrounding as it did a large gulf,[37] into which three major rivers empty themselves (Figs. I.1, I.3), presented no trouble in transporting timber. Mts. Voras and Paiko are edged by the Axios River to the east, while between them to the southwest is the inland drainage basin whence the upper Loudias (modern Moglenitsas) River issues. Mt. Vermion has several small rivers descending its northeastern slopes to join the Haliakmon River that passes along its southern limit, separating it from the Pieria mountains. These, extending in a slightly southwest-to-northeast direction, are edged all along their western side by the Haliakmon, while to the north and to the east their foothills reached the sea. Much closer to the sea was also the northeastern part of Mt. Olympos.

A second parameter is the existence of any direct or indirect evidence of forest exploitation in the ancient sources. The Pieria mountains, at least to my knowledge, provide the sole example for which we have attestations of the existence of a forest. Livy (44.43.1) mentions a "Pierian forest" between Pydna and Aigai, and Pliny the elder (*HN* 4.33) attributes the toponym *Pieria* to the forest ("*a nemore*"). Although neither indicates exploitation,[38] they reveal that the forest was a characteristic feature of the Pierian landscape, as can also be inferred from the phrase κλυτοδένδρου Πιερίης, "Pieria of renowned trees," in an epigram of Philip of Thessalonica (1st century A.D., *AP* 4.2.1). Positive evidence of exploitation of forest products may be the references to Pierian pitch by Herodotos (4.195.3) and Pliny (*HN* 14.128), also echoed by Kassianos Vassos (*Geoponika* 6.5.1).[39] One may wonder, however, whether the epithet "Pierian" reflects the origin of the product or was attached due to the pitch being traded at the ports of the Pierian coast, as was the case with "Sinopean ruddle," which originally came from Cappadocia (Theophr. *De Lap.* 52; Strabo 12.2.10). Pseudo-Aristotle (*Mir. ausc.* 842b) and Theopompos (cited in Plin. *HN* 16.59) merely refer to "Macedonian pitch."[40] An intriguing discovery at Krania, a coastal site identified as the port of ancient Herakleion (modern Platamon, Pieria), by the eastern foothills of lower Olympos, may have actually produced evidence for the Pierian origin of the pitch. The excavation of a pottery workshop, active between ca. 425 and 350 B.C., revealed dozens of empty Mendaian amphoras, some of them even branded as such by being stamped with ME on the handle, stored nearby.[41] These newly made Mendaian amphoras that were locally produced at Herakleion perhaps provide a background story for the nine Mendaian amphoras found in the 5th century B.C. shipwreck at Tektaş Burnu, which were filled with pine pitch produced, according to chemical analysis, most likely from *P. nigra* or *P. sylvestris*,[42] pine species absent from Mende's territory and characteristic of Mts. Olympos and Pieria (see below).

There is further evidence, albeit indirect, attesting to the production of pitch from mountain pines: analysis of the pine pitch found in the late 4th century B.C. shipwreck at Kyrenia (Cyprus) showed that it was produced through pyrolysis of wood,[43] as was the standard procedure in ancient Macedonia (Theophr. *Hist. Pl.* 9.3.1–3), and pitch produced through pyrolysis of pinewood has also been identified in Naukratis, where it had been used as lining inside East Greek clay vessels of the 6th century B.C.[44] Perhaps the exclusivity of Macedonia in this method of extracting pitch could be disputed; however, taking into account the strong trade ties between the Ionians and Macedonia in the Archaic period,[45] the Macedonian provenance of the Naukratis pitch is quite likely. Furthermore, in a trade agreement included in a treaty concluded between the Chalkidian confederacy and Amyntas III, specific reference is made to the import of pitch and timber from Macedonia.[46] The interest of the Chalkidians in acquiring pitch from Macedonia, even though the highly resinous *P. halepensis* grows extensively in Chalkidike, where it is still tapped today, implies that another species was targeted, either a mountain pine, most likely *P. nigra*, or *Betula pendula* (silver birch), which, however, may not have survived in sufficient numbers into the 1st millennium B.C.[47] The exact provenance of the pitch or timber is not specified in the treaty, and there is no indication that the Chalkidians would procure it themselves. For this reason it is highly unlikely that this agreement was attached to a deal concerning the ceding to, or claiming back from, the Chalkidians those borderlands, most likely Mygdonian, that Amyntas had entrusted to them when his kingdom was threatened by the Illyrians.[48] The aim of the Chalkidians was apparently to gain precedence over other buyers in the supply of the entire Macedonian pitch and timber production. The city-state of Mende was such a rival, as suggested above (p. 739), appearing in lines 18–23 of the same treaty among the independent states with which the two parties are not to enter an alliance independently of each other.

A final consideration should be the availability of shipbuilding timber, the wood used for oars above all. Oars were made of fir, which is common in most Macedonian timberlands. Still, I have made reference above to our shortcomings in identifying particular species by the nomenclature used in the ancient sources. Perhaps we should not trust even the most obvious cases, nor take Theophrastos' word at face value—after all, he also collected reports from lumberjacks and shipwrights,[49] and he himself points out this issue in regard to the Arkadians (*Hist. Pl.* 3.9.4, 3.9.8). Pliny, too, having already noted that even experts have trouble distinguishing between conifers (*HN* 16.45), notes the problem of the nomenclature of pines in some regions including Macedonia (*HN* 16.48).[50]

In *Hist. Pl.* 5.1.5–8 Theophrastos records the properties of the fir (*elate*) and the pine (*peuke*). All seem in place, except in 5.1.8, where he records that fir saplings grow at first in height, up to the point where they reach sunlight, and until then there is no lateral growth.[51] Yet stem elongation is a typical shade avoidance reaction, characteristic of shade-intolerant species, such as the pine,[52] while fir is a shade-tolerant species that has developed mechanisms, such as growth reduction and foliage morphology adjustment, in response to limited light conditions.[53] The distinction between shade-tolerant and intolerant species is, of course, not clear-cut, and depending on the exact circumstances of light availability, about which Theophrastos is not explicit enough, any tree can exhibit different growth patterns. In fact, in sunny places all trees invest in both woody and photosynthetic tissues, thus growing short, thick, with many branches, and not particularly straight (Theophr. *Hist. Pl.* 4.1.4). In full shade, however, the pine cannot survive for long, because, if light availability is not improved by increasing its height, its photosynthate production will be inadequate to meet the costs of maintaining the new tissues;[54] the fir, on the contrary, by reducing its growth rate can survive for decades until there is a gap in the canopy. Still, there is an exception: the fir could actually fit the description of Theophr. *Hist. Pl.* 5.1.8, even if in full shade, when growing in a thick, mixed stand, especially with beech. In that case, due to competition for a place in the canopy, both would exhibit strong apical dominance, thereby producing wood ideal for shipbuilding timber, masts, yardarms, and oars.[55] Such are the conditions in which fir grows on the Pieria mountains; however, the presence of *P. sylvestris*, which happens to be the most shade-intolerant species even among pines (Fig. 20.2), complicates the matter. If we refer back to the rest of Theophrastos' description, it suits *P. sylvestris* no less than it would a fir: it has soft and light wood, without (or rather low in) resin,[56] and of a whiter color than *peuke* (which would be *P. nigra*). It may also be identified with Pliny's (*HN* 16.43, 16.46, 16.187, 16.195) *larix*, which grows at the same places as and looks like fir, also being tall, with soft reddish wood. Moreover, several contradictions in Theophrastos' *Historia Plantarum* hinder full understanding of the distinction between *elate* and *peuke*: in 5.4.4 *peuke* is more inclined, due to the sweetness of its resin, to be rotted by *teredon* in the sea than *elate* is, while in 5.7.1 Theophrastos records that they build merchant ships of *peuke*, because it does not decay; in 1.7.2, 1.12.2, and 4.15.1 both *elate* and *peuke* are resinous, while in 5.1.5 *elate* is not; in 3.9.6 the foliage of *elate* is thick and dome-like, "similar indeed to a Boiotian hat,"[57] only fir resembles a cone, and the dome-like foliage is typical of a mature *P. sylvestris*.[58] Evidently, there is

FIGURE 20.2. A young *P. sylvestris* growing out of shade at Sarakatsana, Pieria Mts. Photo A. Boufalis (September 8, 2013)

confusion in Theophrastos' account, such that the information may be mistaken, the reports confused, or muddled by the existence of a local or regional name variant. I suggest, therefore, that the term *elate* in Theophrastos' account (*Hist. Pl.* 5.1.5–12) may correspond to *P. sylvestris*, not *Abies* sp.

The sole dominant stand of *P. sylvestris* in Macedonia is on the Pieria mountains (Fig. 20.3), where it grows surrounded by an extensive beech-fir and *P. nigra* forest in the middle part of the mountain range, above the modern villages of Rhetine (Ritini, literally "Resin"), Elatochori (literally "Fir-village"), and Katafygi, the people of the latter having exploited this particular species for its timber extensively in the past.[59] Intriguingly, this is one of just two dominant stands in Greece, the other being at the Lailias forest in the Strymon region,[60] where the interests of the timber-hungry Athenians were most bluntly expressed. The Athenians made multiple attempts during the 5th century B.C. to control this Thracian hinterland, where "ship-building timber [was] abundant along with many oars" (Hdt. 5.23.2).[61] The distinction Herodotos makes between shipbuilding timber and oars could by extension be a reference to distinct species preferred for each use, and it is significant that both *P. sylvestris* and *A. borisii-regis* grew there. If it is true that *P. sylvestris* is the species from which the masts, yardarms, and oars were preferably produced (Theophr. *Hist. Pl.* 3.7.1, 5.1.7),[62] then the Pieria mountains had a comparative advantage over the other timberlands around the Macedonian territory. The existence of *P. sylvestris* along with the large variety of forest tree species growing on the Pieria mountains (see Appendix 2) would have qualified the Pierian forest as a first-class shipbuilding timberland.

FIGURE 20.3. Mixed stand of young and mature *P. sylvestris* trees at Sarakatsana, Pieria Mts. Photo Y. Z. Tzifopoulos (September 8, 2013)

THE FOREST HISTORY OF MACEDONIA FROM POLLEN RECORDS

Unfortunately, pollen records, the only means to validate the above arguments, are not that helpful.[63] In particular, the pollen record from Pieria, which is of greater interest for this study, dates no earlier than 300 B.C., depriving us of the opportunity to glimpse any changes in forest vegetation before the Roman period. This period in Pieria is characterized by selective and intensive felling of fir,[64] which had probably been predominant earlier,[65] and the wiping out of the remnants of a presumably considerable population of birch.[66] Human activity is obvious in earlier periods as well, yet its effects seem to have been insignificant regarding forest vegetation.[67]

Conifers on the other mountains around the Macedonian kingdom exhibit signs of being affected by human activity by ca. 1000–900 B.C. This is most probably the result of a general decrease in forest vegetation caused by deforestation for the acquisition of agricultural land and pasture, as well as by the introduction of forest trees that bear fruit, namely chestnut and walnut.[68] Deforestation becomes more significant after ca. 700 B.C., when it is accompanied by increased percentages of poaceous and graminaceous plants indicating extensive grasslands. The fir seems to be more affected than the pine in the middle of the 1st millennium B.C. on Mts. Olympos, Voras, and Paiko, as well as in the forest of Lailias, where it was predominant earlier.[69] There is no reason not to assume that this was the case for the Pieria mountains as well.

Therefore, pollen records are in accordance with the literary sources, which unanimously rank the fir at the top of timber products, and this is further corroborated by the treaty between Amyntas III and the Chalkidians, where limitations are imposed on the exportation of fir, a measure clearly equating fir with naval material.[70] An obvious resolution would be to theorize that the fir offered Macedonian shipbuilding timber and oars, and the pine, perhaps along with the birch, Macedonian pitch. Still, the lack of information on the vegetal history of Pieria earlier than 300 B.C., and the difficulty in identifying specific forest products with specific tree species, hinder us from reaching any definitive conclusions.

THE COMMERCIAL OUTLET

The evidence on timber trade involves two main procedures, felling and exporting, both undertaken by the contractor.[71] This reduces the involvement of the state in the timber trade, and, as long as the *telos* (tax or duty) is paid, nothing seems to prevent the contractor from exporting the timber from a location of his choice, or from anywhere convenient. We have to assume, however, the necessity of a port, as a bulk commodity, such as timber, would be impossible to manage without a certain infrastructure. Gathering and towing timber along rivers and lakes does not have the technical limitations that sea travel has.

The most significant coastal cities around the Thermaic Gulf are known to have been Herakleion, Dion, Pydna, Methone, and Aloros on the western coast, in Pieria, and on the eastern coast, between Chalkidike and the Axios River, Therme, Sindos, and Chalastra. Although the case presented above strongly favors Mt. Olympos and the Pieria mountains as the source of Macedonian shipbuilding timber and pitch, the cities on the opposite coast need not be ignored. The mountains of Mygdonia may have been deprived of conifers, but according to Nicholas Hammond timber was floated down the Axios.[72]

The site of ancient Therme, identified with modern Cape Karabournaki south of Thessaloniki, is still today a coastal hill overviewing a harbor site.[73] The city is mostly known for giving its name to the Thermaic Gulf, and as the main camp site for Xerxes' army and naval station for his fleet in 480 B.C. (Hdt. 7.121–124, 127–128, 130, 179, 183). Obviously, it was the most important port in the area, which also explains the Athenian move to capture the city in 432 B.C. (Thuc. 1.61.2). The city was restored to Perdikkas in 429 B.C. (Thuc. 2.29.6) and it remained Macedonian as it was before.

The cities of Sindos and Chalastra have not been definitely identified, but they were most probably situated on the double trapeza of Anchialos and the trapeza Topsin, respectively, both coastal fortified hills between the outlets of the rivers Echedoros and Axios, as is also attested in Herodotos' account of the Persian camp on the Thermaic Gulf.[74] Chalastra is archaeologically rather unexplored,[75] but Sindos is well known to have been a vibrant trading center,[76] which presupposes that the city had a good port. The location of Chalastra, next to the mouth of the Axios, leaves no doubt that it also had a harbor.[77]

Herakleion is not a well-known city, but recent archaeological finds,[78] and its accession as a member to the Delian League,[79] show that at least its port was not unimportant.[80] Benjamin Meritt suggested Herakleion as a possible location for the Athenian shipbuilding operation in Macedonia in the late 5th century B.C. (as attested in *IG* I^3 117).[81] The city had immediate access to the forests of lower Olympos,[82] and, moreover, a fairly protected harbor from the south-southeast winds that affect the Pierian coast.[83] It could well have served, at least, as a local timber outlet.

A harbor site in a river mouth rather than a port should be placed at Dion,[84] which at the time lay no more than 1.2 km from the sea, and half of this distance was taken up by a marshland or a lagoon formed at the Baphyros River estuary.[85] Pausanias (9.30.8) reports that the river was navigable, suggesting that Dion was accessible by sea. This fits well with the importance of the city, which is recognized largely as a corollary of its religious character, but an economic function should not be dismissed. Several timber axes of Roman times that have been unearthed in Dion are intriguing finds indeed.[86]

Aloros is located in a most favorable location at the northernmost foothills of the Pieria mountains, not far from Aigai and close to the Haliakmon River.[87] Although the name of the city etymologically denotes close association with the sea,[88] and Pseudo-Skylax (66) includes the city in his *Periplous*, recent paleoenvironmental research has shown that the site should be already landlocked in the 5th century B.C., and the mouth of the Haliakmon was farther north.[89] However, the estuary of the river would still be in the territory of the city, and a harbor could nevertheless exist somewhere on the coast, although it is doubtful whether it could serve as a trading port. Still, a controversial reference by Strabo to Aloros as a flourishing city could perhaps support such a possibility.[90]

Pydna stood at the westernmost reaches of the Pierian coast and had a good port.[91] To judge by its confidence in revolting against the Macedonian king in 411/0 B.C. (Diod. Sic. 13.49.1–2), it must have been a prosperous city. In fact, the archaeological exploration of the area has found that the city grew during the 5th century B.C., becoming the largest urban settlement in Macedonia in the Classical period.[92] Pydna was definitely in a position to handle and control the Macedonian timber trade, as its proximity to the Pieria mountains and its extensive territory, presumably including them, made it possible.

The city of Methone occupied a cape to the north of Pydna, at the narrowest part of the Thermaic Gulf. The Methonaians controlled the best-protected harbor of the wider region on the north side of the cape, as the most habitual and high winds in the gulf during the navigation period (April to October)[93] blow from the southeast (Fig. 3.12), and probably there was also a harbor just south of the city, fairly protected from the winter north winds.[94] Methone was apparently a city with loose ties, politically or otherwise, with the Macedonian kingdom, and an Athenian ally in the Delian League by the late 430s B.C. The city has previously been associated with the Macedonian timber trade on account of a political development that highlights its importance to the Athenians in a period when they were in great need of shipbuilding timber.[95]

THE EVIDENCE FOR METHONE

In contrast to the perfectly good relations between the Athenians and Macedon throughout the reign of Alexander I, the case was different with his successor, Perdikkas II.[96] Although he had been "an ally and a friend at first," this had changed by 433/2 B.C., when the Athenians supported the coalition of his brother Philip and Derdas, king of Elimeia, against him (Thuc. 1.57.3). Thucydides fails, or finds it unnecessary, to inform us on the reasons for this development. It can hardly be unrelated to the foundation of Amphipolis in 437/6 B.C. that gave the Athenians access to the timberlands and mines of the Strymon region. Not only had the Macedonians had aspirations for this region since the time of Alexander I, but the Athenian presence there also entailed considerable damage to the economy and diplomatic arsenal of the Macedonian kingdom, as the Athenians would now be independent of Macedonian timber.[97] Perdikkas' change of stance was only natural, and the ensuing Athenian support to Philip must have been a response to that.

Perdikkas attempted to form a coalition of the Chalkidians of Chalkidike and the Bottiaians, with the support of the Spartans and the Corinthians, in order to oppose the Athenians.[98] His efforts may not have been in vain. In 432/1 B.C., while the army of the autonomous kingdom of Elimeia invaded from inland, the Athenians invaded Macedon from the sea, besieged Pydna, and captured Therme (Thuc. 1.59, 1.61.2), but soon, under the pressure of the Poteidaian revolt, they were forced to enter into an alliance with Perdikkas, which was breached, however, right afterward by both sides (Thuc. 1.61.3, 1.62.2). Later, in 429 B.C., the Odrysian king Sitalkes was prompted by the Athenians to invade Macedonia and install on the throne Amyntas, son of Perdikkas' brother Philip (Thuc. 2.95). The invasion ended without any serious engagement or development, after the intervention of Sitalkes' nephew, Seuthes, who was affiliated with Perdikkas' family by marriage (Thuc. 2.101.5). Perdikkas, now with some confidence, began harassing the Methonaians, while he also laid an embargo on their city. Interestingly, at this event the Athenians, instead of taking blunt action as usual, merely resorted to diplomacy.[99]

The inscription *IG* I³ 61, commonly known as the "Methone Decrees," is an epigraphic document of the 420s B.C. that displayed at least four successive decrees, of which only the first two are preserved (see Figs. 1.38, 2.1).[100] These enacted measures to help the city of Methone cope with its severe financial situation. With the first decree (lines 3–32), dated early in the decade,[101] the Athenians relieved the city of its financial obligations toward the League by exempting it from the main sum of the tribute, thenceforth being liable only for the *aparche* (1/60 of the total amount; see also *IG* I^3 282, lines 51–53), and providing for a favorable arrangement concerning previous debts. Moreover, ambassadors were to be sent to Perdikkas to advocate free shipping and trade in Macedonian territory, "as was the case before," and to reconcile the two sides, provided that Perdikkas would not have his army crossing the territory of the Methonaians against their will. With the second decree (lines 32–56), dated to 426/5 B.C., the Athenians made further accommodations for the Methonaians, allowing them to import grain from Byzantium, up to a certain amount (not preserved on the stone), completely tax-free. This decree also refers to the failure of at least two more embassies to Perdikkas, who seems to have been wasting time at Methone's expense.

The above measures of assistance were taken on the condition that the Methonaians would remain "useful (ἐπιτήδειοι) to the Athenians, as they are now and even more" (lines 11–12). How the Methonaians were useful to the Athenians is not stated. Meritt has proposed that an Athenian *archon* was present at Methone.[102] Such officers stationed at allied cities could be either military, in charge of a garrison (φρούραρχος), or administrative, in duty bound to oversee the payment of the tribute (ἐπίσκοπος).[103] Had an officer been installed at Methone, he would be administrative, as, according to the decrees, the Methonaians were expected to defend their own country, while the nearest garrison mentioned is that of Poteidaia (lines 27–28).[104] It follows that, although Methone's strategic position was undoubtedly of great importance to the Athenians, their interests there were probably not primarily military.

The foundation myth of the city, as recorded by Plutarch (*Quaest. Graec.* 293a–b), assigns Methone to the Eretrian colonies of the 8th century B.C. in the north Aegean. Eretrian settlers in Korkyra were ousted by Corinthian colonists and sailed back to Euboia. Yet their fellow citizens violently denied them repatriation, and thus they were forced to flee once again. They sailed to the north, where they occupied a local village. Although it is not stated in the myth, it is tenable that the Eretrian colonists sailed to familiar territories, maybe to a site where they had already established an *emporion*.[105] The term *polis* used for Methone in the myth could denote both a city and an *emporion*.[106] The archaeological finds are indicative: a late 8th to early 7th-century B.C. deposit excavated on the East Hill of the ancient city produced a pottery assemblage of both local Macedonian and foreign provenance, from all over the Aegean, and revealed a multicultural community of traders.[107] Such pluralism is characteristic of the Greek *emporion*.[108] By the Archaic period Methone must have been an independent city-state, as the archaeological finds show.[109] This does not mean that the commercial character of the city ceased. An *emporion* was not an autonomous political unit; rather it was a self-contained area primarily related to foreign trade, which could exist and function either as a discontiguous built area or a demarcated part within a settlement.[110] Situated on a cape, off which sea routes converge, Methone not only served as an outlet for the products from the hinterland, that is, northern Pieria, but also could receive and forward products coming down the Haliakmon and Loudias Rivers, which, flowing from upper (Elimeia and Almopia) through lower (Emathia and Bottiaia) Macedonia, reach the sea at a short distance.

Macedonia had many products and raw materials to offer. However, the plain to the north of Methone today was at the time largely still open sea,[111] while the narrow fertile plain between Pydna and the modern city of Katerini was a lagoon,[112] and the plain south of Katerini as far as Dion must have been much narrower. It is hard to imagine vast amounts of grain being exported from this part of Macedonia. As for mineral resources, and more particularly the gold and silver mines, they were mostly beyond the Axios and mainly in the valley of the Echedoros River (literally the "gift-bearing" river), in Chalkidike, and in the Thracian regions just east of Macedonia, where other colonies had been planted by the Eretrians.[113] What Pieria had in abundance was forest and animal products. The very presence of the Eretrians in Pieria is intriguing. The city of *ἐρέται*, "rowers," with its long nautical tradition, could hardly have had been unaware of, or indifferent to, Macedonia as a potential timber source.[114]

Once settled there, the Methonaians, quite unsurprisingly, used local timber to cover their needs. Somewhat unexpectedly, however, their reach exceeded Methone's immediate hinterland. The charcoal study from the aforementioned deposit has produced evidence for exploitation of mountain forest species already in the late 8th–early 7th century B.C. Charcoal analysis has identified, among other taxa, several pieces of *Pinus* type *sylvestris*, i.e., either *P. sylvestris* or *P. nigra*.[115] The city-state of Methone itself should not have such timber resources at hand.[116] Neighboring Aloros to the north and Pydna to the south,[117] both considerable cities, would have squeezed between them the territory of Methone, which probably occupied a rather narrow strip of hilly land extending to the west.[118] This is emphasized in the Methone Decrees by its apparent reliance on trade and its consequent need of grain. Even if it had some forest in its territory, the quality would be poor, as the Pieria mountains reach high altitudes farther to the west, probably in the territory of Aigai, and to the southwest, possibly in the territory of Pydna.[119] The literary and epigraphic sources are indisputable evidence: since the Macedonian king is involved in every single known timber transaction, the commodity must have been Macedonian.[120]

Borza convincingly remarked that there would be no reason for the Athenians to besiege Pydna in 432 B.C. if they already controlled Methone, and that the accession of the latter to the Delian League must have been a term in the peace treaty of 431 B.C.[121] with Perdikkas, to whom captured Therme would be restored in exchange (Thuc. 2.29.6). The objective of the Athenian campaign in 432 B.C., the departure of which preceded the Poteidaian revolt (Thuc. 1.59), was presumably to take hold of the ports that handled the Macedonian timber trade in Pieria and the metal trade in the regions west of the Axios (Thuc. 2.29.4). Their failure to capture Pydna and the urgency of the Poteidaian revolt forced them to compromise on a peace treaty favorable to Perdikkas, surrendering Therme, but formally admitting Methone, as an allied member in the Delian League.

The alliance of Methone with Athens was a reason for Perdikkas to feel uncomfortable; it was, undoubtedly, a constant threat having an Athenian ally between him and control over access to the Aegean.[122] Furthermore, if the Methonaians were liable for military service in the Macedonian army, as Greek residents in Macedonia were (Thuc. 4.124.1), joining the Delian League would entail serious military implications. However, the central issue in the Methone affair was the disruption of trade. From the Athenian perspective, if the ultimate purpose was keeping a base close to Aigai, it would be sufficient to sustain the city, as was indeed the case for the period covered by the Methone Decrees. Still, the Athenians insisted on free traffic and trade, while Perdikkas persisted in forbidding it. Methone's economy was obviously reliant on a Macedonian commodity, presumably timber, which the city would forward, process, or both. As an independent city-state, Methone would probably act as an agent on behalf of the Athenians in timber trade. Perhaps its "usefulness" was selling Macedonian timber to the Athenians at a low or even cost price. Perhaps the Methonaians had even been granted felling rights by Perdikkas. Such a role was played by the Athenian colony Amphipolis in the Strymon region, thus named likely from ἀμφιπολεύω (to serve, *LSJ*[9] s.v., cf. s.v. ἀμφίπολος), rather than its geographical location, "the Strymon flowing by the city on both sides (ἐπ' ἀμφότερα περιρρέοντος)" (Thuc. 4.102.3).[123]

Perdikkas' motives are difficult to discern. He was certainly suspicious toward the Athenians, and the hostility between them continued despite the peace of 431 B.C. Besides, since the Athenians were the chief customer for Macedonian timber and pitch, the convergence of trade on the port of Methone entailed considerably less revenue from Pydna, or any other Macedonian port involved in the timber trade. However, he certainly had sufficient reasons to impede the trade activities of Methone, even if that would cost him some timber deals in the immediate future.

Since there were at least two more decrees to cover the years 425/4–424/3 B.C., it follows that after losing Amphipolis in 424 B.C., an event that brought "great fear, because the city was especially useful to them (ὠφέλιμος) for shipping ship-building timber and bringing revenue" (Thuc. 4.108.1), the Athenians focused on Methone, and the fruit of their efforts was the treaty with Perdikkas in 423 B.C. (Thuc. 4.132.1). This must be the terminus post quem for *IG* I³ 89,[124] if not the treaty itself, by which Perdikkas is to sell oars exclusively to the Athenians.

CONCLUSIONS

The mountains surrounding the Macedonian kingdom were all heavily forested and easily accessible by water. Among them the Pieria mountains stand out. Their proximity to the sea, the convenience of being the backyard of Aigai, the location of two of the three major ports in the Thermaic Gulf (the other being Therme) at their foothills, the references to a Pierian forest and Pierian pitch in ancient sources, and the large variety of forest tree species, were all advantages that no other Macedonian timberland had. Moreover, if *P. sylvestris* was in fact the tree that oars were made of, the Pierian timberland would be unrivaled within Macedonia; and so would Macedonia, around the Aegean, at least, as long as the Athenians had no access to the Strymon region.[125]

Two neighboring Pierian cities—Pydna, the largest settlement in the Macedonian kingdom with a significant port, and Methone, an old Euboian colony with the best port in the Thermaic Gulf and, at least down to the 6th century B.C., a settlement specialized in manufacture and trade—are the best-qualified candidates for handling Macedonian timber exports. Their "Greekness," deduced from the label "πόλις Ἑλληνίς" ("Greek city") that Pseudo-Skylax (66) applied to both of them, may not be irrelevant, to the extent that it would reflect their trading activities.[126] It is more likely, however, that it echoes a short period of independence in the first half of the 4th century B.C., after the Athenian general Timotheos detached them from the Macedonian kingdom and brought them into the Athenian sphere of influence in 364/3 B.C. (Din. 1.14, 3.17; Dem. 4.4–5).[127] The end of Methone's membership in the Delian League came, presumably, either by revolt (see Thuc. 8.2.2) or by an agreement of mutual interest between the new king, Archelaos, who acceded to the throne of Macedon in 413 B.C., and the Athenians, who were anxious to rebuild their fleet in the winter of 412/1 B.C., following their devastating defeat in Sicily (Thuc. 8.4). This explains why the Athenians came to the assistance of Archelaos to subdue Pydna, when the city revolted in 411/0 B.C. (Diod. Sic. 13.49.1), as well as why Archelaos provided for the lodging and the timber and oar supply when the Athenians sent shipwrights to work locally in Macedonia in the years prior to honoring him as *proxenos* and benefactor in 407/6 B.C.[128] The friendship of Archelaos toward the Athenians is in itself evidence that they controlled no client states in or around Macedonia during his reign.

But where did the shipwrights work? Borza expected the shipyards to be located on the Pierian coast, at either Pydna or Methone, the cities closest to the Pieria mountains,[129] while Meritt suggested Herakleion,[130] which would also be a convenient place for the procurement of suitable timber (except of *P. sylvestris*, provided that the proposition presented above holds any truth), and William Greenwalt thought it more probable that such an enterprise would take place at the new capital, Pella, where Archelaos would be able to oversee the operation, and the location of the city would have facilitated both land and water transport of the timber from the surrounding mountains.[131] It is reasonable to assume that no city or port would have exclusive rights to the timber trade. Political circumstances would dictate trade partnerships that would still fit geographical considerations, that is, distance from, and accessibility to, felling locations, port capacity, and protection from weather, and, at the same time, would take advantage of local merchant communities, networked, experienced, and able to run the business.

The Athenians, who were eager to control all coastal cities in their attempt to win complete dominance over trade in the Aegean, targeted the Macedonian cities on the Thermaic Gulf as well (Thuc. 2.29.4). The Poteidaian revolt and the outbreak of the Peloponnesian War foiled their plans: Pydna and Therme remained within the Macedonian kingdom. However, they managed by a formal alliance to redouble their relations with Methone and consequently to gain a foothold in Macedonia. That meant only trouble for Perdikkas. He realized that the territorial integrity of his kingdom could not be ensured, unless he could eliminate Athenian influence in the city—something he apparently did not have the means or the resources to achieve. He had the power, however, to suspend trade, with the intention not so much to intimidate Methone into secession as to affect, even if indirectly, the Athenian interests furthered by the Methonaians, especially the Athenians' timber supply. Since Athenian relations with the Odrysians, who at the time controlled the Strymon region, were at their zenith,[132] the Athenians were not hard-pressed. But soon the loss of Amphipolis in 424 B.C. left them with no other choice than to come to terms with Perdikkas, whose interests in the meantime had also shifted toward friendship with the Athenians (Thuc. 4.128.5, 4.132.1). One part of the peace treaty of 423 B.C. was that Perdikkas would be selling oars exclusively to the Athenians (*IG* I^3 89); another stipulated that he would send aid for the recapture of Amphipolis—aid that never came (Thuc. 5.6.2, 5.83.4).

APPENDIX 1: THE ANCIENT LITERARY SOURCES NAMING TREE SPECIES THAT GAVE SHIPBUILDING TIMBER

Timber

Hom. *Il.* 13.389–391, 16.482–484

"ἤριπε δ᾽ ὡς ὅτε τις δρῦς ἤριπεν ἢ ἀχερωῒς
ἠὲ πίτυς βλωθρή, τήν τ᾽ οὔρεσι τέκτονες ἄνδρες
ἐξέταμον πελέκεσσι νεήκεσι νήϊον εἶναι"

"And he fell as when an oak falls, or a poplar,
or a tall pine, which on the mountains shipwrights
fell with whetted axes to be a ship's timber"

Hom. *Od.* 5.239

". . . κλήθρη τ᾽ αἴγειρός τ᾽, ἐλάτη τ᾽ ἦν οὐρανομήκης"

". . . alder and poplar and fir, which reaches to the skies"

Ar. *Eq.* 1310

". . . εἴπερ ἐκ πεύκης γε κἀγὼ καὶ ξύλων ἐπηγνύμην"

". . . as truly as I am made of pine and timbers"

Eur. *Alc.* 443–444

". . . λίμναν Ἀχεροντίαν πορεύ-
σας ἐλάτᾳ δικώπῳ"

". . . the lake of Acheron
he crossed on a two-oared fir"

Eur. *Andr.* 864

". . . πευκᾶεν σκάφος . . ."

". . . vessel of pine . . ."

Eur. *Hel.* 231–234

". . . [τίς]
ἔτεμε τὰν δακρυόεσσαν
Ἰλίῳ πεύκαν;
ἔνθεν ὀλόμενον σκάφος
συναρμόσας ὁ Πριαμίδας . . ."

". . . [who] felled the pine
that brought tears to Ilion?
From this the son of Priam
built his deadly ship . . ."

Eur. *IA* 172–178

"... Ἀχαιῶν τε πλάτας ναυσιπόρους ἡ-
μιθέων, οὓς ἐπὶ Τροίαν
ἐλάταις χιλιόναυσιν
[...]
στέλλειν ἐπὶ τὰν Ἑλέναν ..."

"... of Achaeans and the sea-going oars
of those godlike heroes, whom
on a thousand ships of fir against Troy...
they are sending for Helen ..."

Eur. *IA* 1319–1322

"μή μοι ναῶν χαλκεμβολάδων
πρύμνας ἅδ' Αὐλὶς δέξασθαι
τούσδ' εἰς ὅρμους ἐς Τροίαν
ὤφελεν ἐλάταν πομπαίαν ..."

"I wish that Aulis had never received
in these coves the sterns of the bronze-beaked ships
that were sailing to Troy in a fleet of fir..."

Eur. *Med.* 1–6

"Εἴθ' ὤφελ' Ἀργοῦς μὴ διαπτάσθαι σκάφος
Κόλχων ἐς αἶαν κυανέας Συμπληγάδας,
μηδ' ἐν νάπαισι Πηλίου πεσεῖν ποτε
τμηθεῖσα πεύκη, μηδ' ἐρετμῶσαι χέρας
ἀνδρῶν ἀριστέων οἳ τὸ πάγχρυσον δέρος
Πελίᾳ μετῆλθον"

"Would that Argo had never flown to the land
of the Colchians through the dark-blue Symplegades,
and that pines had neither been felled in the glens of Pelion
nor had furnished oars for the hands
of the excellent men who came for the Golden Fleece
at Pelias' command!"

Eur. *Phoen.* 208–209

"... Ἰόνιον κατὰ πόντον ἐλάτᾳ πλεύσασα περιρρύτῳ ..."

"... through the Ionian Sea
I sailed on a fir in the waves..."

Pl. *Laws* 705c

"ναυπηγησίμης ὕλης ὁ τόπος ἡμῖν τῆς χώρας πῶς ἔχει;—οὐκ ἔστιν οὔτε τις ἐλάτη λόγου ἀξία οὔτ' αὖ πεύκη, κυπάριττός τε οὐ πολλή· πίτυν τ' αὖ καὶ πλάτανον ὀλίγην ἂν εὕροι τις, οἷς δὴ πρὸς τὰ τῶν ἐντὸς τῶν πλοίων μέρη ἀναγκαῖον τοῖς ναυπηγοῖς χρῆσθαι ἑκάστοτε"

"What is the availability of ship-building timber in our country?—There is neither fir of any significance nor pine, and cypress not much: and one could find only a little *pitys* and plane, which are necessary for the shipwrights to use for the interiors of the ships"

Rhodes and Osborne 2003, no. 12, lines 10–11

"... ναυπηγισίμων δὲ πλὴν ἐλατίνων ..."

"... and of shipbuilding timbers except fir ..."

Theophr. *Hist. Pl.* 5.7.1–3

"Ἐλάτη μὲν οὖν καὶ πεύκη καὶ κέδρος ὡς ἁπλῶς εἰπεῖν ναυπηγήσιμα· τὰς μὲν γὰρ τριήρεις καὶ τὰ μακρὰ πλοῖα ἐλάτινα ποιοῦσι διὰ κουφότητα, τὰ δὲ στρογγύλα πεύκινα διὰ τὸ ἀσαπές· ἔνιοι δὲ καὶ τὰς τριήρεις διὰ τὸ μὴ εὐπορεῖν ἐλάτης. οἱ δὲ κατὰ Συρίαν καὶ Φοινίκην ἐκ κέδρου· σπανίζουσι γὰρ καὶ πεύκης. οἱ δ' ἐν Κύπρῳ πίτυος· ταύτην γὰρ ἡ νῆσος ἔχει καὶ δοκεῖ κρείττων εἶναι τῆς πεύκης. Καὶ τὰ μὲν ἄλλα ἐκ τούτων, τὴν δὲ τρόπιν τριήρεσι μὲν δρυίνην, ἵνα ἀντέχει πρὸς τὰς νεωλκίας, ταῖς δὲ ὁλκάσι πευκίνην· ὑποτιθέασι δ' ἔτι καὶ δρυίνην ἀπάν νεωλκῶσι, ταῖς δ' ἐλάττοσιν ὀξυίνην· καὶ ὅλως ἐκ τούτου τὸ χέλυσμα. [...] ἡ δὲ τορνεία τοῖς μὲν πλοίοις γίνεται συκαμίνου, μελίας, πτελέας, πλατάνου ... ταῖς δὲ τριήρεσιν ἔνιοι καὶ πιτυΐνας ποιοῦσι διὰ τὸ ἐλαφρόν. τὸ δὲ στερέωμα, πρὸς ᾧ τὸ χέλυσμα, καὶ τὰς ἐπωτίδας, μελίας καὶ συκαμίνου καὶ πτελέας"

"Now fir, pine, and cedar, generally speaking, are good for ship-building timber; for they make triremes and long-ships of fir because of its lightness, and round vessels of pine because of its resistance to rot; some make triremes also of pine because they are ill-provided with fir. The people of Syria and Phoenicia use cedar; for they lack pine as well. The people of Cyprus use the *pitys*; for this the island has and they deem it better than the pine. For the other parts they use the following: for the keel in triremes oak, in order to withstand the hauling up the ship-way, and in merchant vessels pine; and in addition they put underneath an oaken one when they are hauling, and in smaller vessels one of beech; and they make the false-keel of this entirely. [...] and bentwood in vessels is made of mulberry, ash, elm, plane ... in triremes, though, some make it of *pitys* as well because of its lightness. And the cutwater, to which the false-keel is attached, as well as the cat-heads, is made of ash, mulberry, and elm"

Theophr. *Hist. Pl.* 5.7.5

"ἐλάτη μὲν οὖν καὶ πεύκη, καθάπερ, εἴρηται, καὶ πρὸς ναυπηγίαν καὶ πρὸς οἰκοδομίαν καὶ ἔτι πρὸς ἄλλα τῶν ἔργων, εἰς πλείω δὲ ἡ ἐλάτη. πίτυϊ δὲ χρῶνται μὲν εἰς ἄμφω καὶ οὐχ ἧττον εἰς ναυπηγίαν, οὐ μὴν ἀλλὰ ταχὺ διασήπεται. δρῦς δὲ πρὸς οἰκοδομίαν καὶ πρὸς ναυπηγίαν ἔτι τε πρὸς τὰ κατὰ γῆς κατορυττόμενα. φίλυρα δὲ πρὸς τὰ σανιδώματα τῶν μακρῶν πλοίων ..."

"Now fir and pine, as has been said, are suitable both for ship-building and house building, and indeed for other works, though fir is useful for more purposes than pine. And the *pitys* is employed for both and no less in ship-building, although it rapidly rots. Oak is used for house building and ship-building, and indeed in mines. Lime for the decks of long-ships ..."

IG II^2 1492, lines 120–121

"... ἐδώκαμεν εἰς τὴν τ[ῶ]ν [ξύλω]ν κομιδ[ὴ]ν τῶν π[ε]υ[κῶν πα]ρὰ [βασιλ]έων [εἰ]ς τὰς ναῦς ..."

"... we paid to the ships for the transport of timber of the pines[133] given by the kings ..."

Lycoph. *Alex.* 32

"... *πεύκαισιν οὐλαμηφόροις* ..."

"... army-bearing pines ..."

Diod. Sic. 14.42.4

"... λαβὼν δ' ἐκ τῆς Ἰταλίας ἐξαγωγὴν ὕλης, τοὺς μὲν ἡμίσεις τῶν ὑλοτόμων εἰς τὸ κατὰ τὴν Αἴτνην ὄρος ἀπέστειλε, γέμον κατ' ἐκείνους τοὺς χρόνους πολυτελοῦς ἐλάτης τε καὶ πεύκης ..."

"[Dionysios of Syracuse] having obtained the right to export timber from Italy, half of the woodmen he sent to mount Aitna, which was full at that time of expensive fir and pine ..."

Diod. Sic. 17.89.4

"τῆς δὲ πλησίον ὀρεινῆς ἐχούσης πολλὴν μὲν ἐλάτην εὔτροφον, οὐκ ὀλίγην δὲ κέδρον καὶ πεύκην, ἔτι δὲ τῆς ἄλλης ὕλης ναυπηγησίμου πλῆθος ἄφθονον κατεσκεύασε ναῦς ἱκανάς"

"as the nearby mountainous country had a lot of thick firs, and no little cedar and pine, and indeed an ample quantity of other ship-building timber, he had good ships constructed"

Verg. *Aen.* 5.662–663

"... Furit immissis Volcanus habenis
transtra per et remos et pictas abiete puppis"

"Fire rages unbridled among
the thwarts and oars and sterns of painted fir"

Verg. *Aen.* 8.90–93

"Ergo iter inceptum celerant rumore secundo;
labitur uncta vadis abies; mirantur et undae,
miratur nemus insuetum fulgentia longe
scuta virum fluvio pictasque innare carinas"

"Thus their journey begins as they speed up making a rustle; the pitched fir glides on the water; and the waves marvel, the forest marvels unaccustomed to the sight of the shields of warriors gleaming from afar and the painted hulls floating on the river."

Verg. *Aen.* 10.206

"... Mincius infesta ducebat in aequora pinu."

"... the [river] Mincius led the hostile pines to the sea."

IG XII.5 739, lines 154–155

"δαμαζομένας δὲ θαλάσσας ὠκυπόροις ἐλάταις ..."

"the seas were tamed by far-going firs ..."

Plin. *HN* 16.39

"pinaster nihil est aliud quam pinus silvestris . . . easdem arbores alio nomine esse per oram Italiae quas tibulos vocant plerique arbitrantur, sed graciles succinctioresque et enodes liburnicarum ad usus"

"The *pinaster* is nothing else but a wild pine . . . many people believe this to be the same tree, under another name, as those that grow along the coasts of Italy, which are called *tibuli*, but these are slender and more compact, and being free from knots they are used in light galleys"

Plin. *HN* 16.42

". . . abieti expetitae navigiis . . ."

". . . the fir, which is in high demand for building ships . . ."

Plin. *HN* 16.219

"laricem in maritimis navibus . . ."

"larch used in seagoing vessels . . ."

Sil. *Pun.* 6.351–353

". . . iam nautica pubes
aut siluis stringunt remos, aut abiete secta
transtra nouant"

". . . then the young sailors shape oars from trees, and they cut new thwarts of fir"

Plut. *Quaest. Conv.* 676a

"[πίτυς] καὶ τὰ ἀδελφὰ δένδρα, πεῦκαι καὶ στρόβιλοι, τῶν τε ξύλων παρέχει τὰ πλωϊμότατα . . ."

"[*pitys*] and the related trees, namely pines and stone pines, provide the most floatable timber among all kinds of woods"

Orph. Argon. 259

"Ἀργῷ πεύκῃσιν τ' ἠδὲ δρυσὶν γομφωθεῖσα . . ."

"Argo made of pine and fastened with oak . . ."

Oars

Hom. *Il.* 7.5–6

". . . ἐϋξέστῃς ἐλάτῃσι πόντον ἐλαύνοντες"

". . . crossing the sea with polished oars of fir"

Hom. *Od.* 12.171–172

". . . οἱ δ' ἐπ' ἐρετμὰ
ἑζόμενοι λεύκαινον ὕδωρ ξεστῇς ἐλάτῃσιν"

"... and having sat at the oars
they were making the water white with their shaved firs"

Eur. *Hel.* 1461–1462

"... λάβετε δ' εἰλατίνας πλάτας,
ὦ ναῦται, ναῦται"

"... take up oars of fir,
oh sailors, sailors"

Eur. *IT* 407–409

"ἦ ῥοθίοις εἰλατίνας
δικρότοισι κώπας ἔπλευ-
σαν ἐπὶ πόντια κύματα ..."

"did they sail with double-beating
oars of fir dashing
over the waves of the sea ..."

Eur. *Hyps.*, fr. 752g (*TrGF* 5), line 14

"... εἰλατίνας ἀνάπαυμα πλάτα̣[ς]"

"... pause of the oars of fir"

Theophr. *Hist.Pl.* 5.1.6

"ἔστι δὲ καὶ πολύλοπον ἡ ἐλάτη, καθάπερ καὶ τὸ κρόμυον· ... δι' ὃ καὶ τὰς κώπας ξύοντες ἀφαιρεῖν πειρῶνται καθ'ἕνα καὶ ὁμαλῶς"

"moreover, the fir has many layers, like the onion; ... wherefore, when they are shaving the oars, they endeavor to take them off one by one and evenly"

Opp. *Hal.* 3.240

"... σπερχομένην τ' ἐλάταις ἄκατον ..."

"... a vessel hurried by firs ..."

Luc. 3.529–532

"Cornua Romanae classis validaeque triremes,
quasque quater surgens exstructi remigis ordo
commovet, et plures quae mergunt aequore pinus,
multiplices cinxere rates"

"The Romans put the fleet of powerful triremes in a horn formation, and those having four rows of oars they ordered to advance, and the more pines were being plunged into the sea, the more ships were surrounded"

Luc. 3.553–555

"Sed Graiis habiles pugnamque lacessere pinus ..."

"But the Greek galleys proved defter in the battle with pines ..."

Masts and Yardarms

Hom. *Od.* 2.424–426, 15.289–291

"ἱστὸν δ' εἰλάτινον κοίλης ἔντοσθε μεσόδμης
στῆσαν ἀείραντες . . ."

"A mast of fir they raised and set in the hollow socket on the beam . . ."

Theophr. *Hist. Pl.* 5.1.7

"ἔστι δὲ καὶ μακρότατον ἡ ἐλάτη καὶ ὀρθοφυέστατον. δι' ὃ καὶ τὰς κεραίας καὶ τοὺς ἱστοὺς ἐκ ταύτης ποιοῦσιν"

"fir is also of the longest and of the straightest growth; wherefore they make the yard-arms and the masts of this"

Plin. *HN* 16.195

"larici et magis abieti . . . , haec omnium arborum altissimae ac rectissimae. navium malis antemnisque propter levitatem praefertur abies"

"larch and great fir . . . , which is the tallest and straightest of all trees. Fir is preferred on account of its lightness for the masts and antennas of ships"

APPENDIX 2: THE FOREST VEGETATION OF NORTHERN PIERIA (BASED ON KLAPANES AND ABATZES 2011)

The Rhetine-Vrya Forest

This is the main forest complex in northern Pieria. It covers, for the most part, the higher altitudes of the northeastern slopes of the central Pieria mountains, peaking in these parts at 2,023 m ASL.[134] Two broad and deep ravines running roughly from west to east produce two pairs of slopes facing north and south, offering ample sunlight, wind protection, and increased humidity conditions, factors that favor forest vegetation. Slopes are generally steep, although they range between mild to very steep (mostly between 30 and 70%). Geologically, metamorphic rocks, and more particularly gneiss slate and micaceous schist, dominate, but sedimentary rocks, such as sandstones (flysch), limestone, and calcareous marls, are also present. The most common earth types are brown, brown podzolic, red (*terra rossa*), and illuvial deposits of clay. Climatic conditions are typically Mediterranean continental, with warm and humid summers, and moist and severely cold winters.

The fully wooded area within the limits of the forest reaches 89.34% of the total area, and within this a mixed forest of oak, chestnut, beech, fir, and pine predominates (58.16% of the fully wooded area). However, considerable dominant stands of oak (15.21%), beech (7.04%), and pine (19.59%) also exist. The main vegetation zones comprise broadleaf evergreens (*Quercus coccifera*) at lower altitudes, then broadleaf deciduous trees, mostly oak in the temperate zone (*Quercetum*) and mostly beech in the colder zone (*Fagetum*), and conifers at higher altitudes, represented by stands of fir and pine, the presence of the latter ranging from the beech-fir zone to the subalpine zone (*Picetum*). Within these formations the most common forest species are:

- broadleaves such as ash (*Fraxinus ornus* and *excelsior*) and lime (*Tilia parvifolia*), which give valuable wood and have suffered from felling to a destructive degree;
- poplar (*Populus tremula*), a hydrotropic species which spreads in gaps caused by human intervention;
- oak (*Quercus conferta, pubescens,* and *sessiliflora*), either in dominant stands or mixed with beech;
- beech (*Fagus sylvatica*), which exists mostly in mixed forest (mostly with fir and chestnut, but also hornbeam [*Carpinus betulus* and *orientalis*]), forming thick stands of premium quality timber;[135]
- chestnut (*Castanea vesca*), which exists usually mixed with beech, but also as individual trees or nesting in small groups;
- fir (*Abies hybridogenus/ borisii regis*), which is normally mixed with beech or pines and produces valuable timber;
- pine, which is found either in dominant stands or mixed with beech in lower altitudes and is represented by two distinct species: the black pine (*Pinus nigra*), a fast-growing species which produces good quality timber, and the Scots pine (*Pinus sylvestris*), a pioneer species which produces valuable timber; the latter crowns the forest complex and it is found in Pieria at the southernmost, warmest, and most arid limit of its distribution in Europe (Fig. 20.4).[136]

Apart from the above, wild pear and apple trees (*Pirus amygdaliformis* and *malus*), cornel (*Cornus mas*), hop hornbeam (*Ostrya carpinifolia*), elm (*Ulmus campestris*), willow (*Salix caprea*), and a few maple trees (*Acer pseudoplatanus* and *platanoides*) live scattered in the lower two vegetation zones (for a full account of the forest species on the Pieria mountains see Table 20.1, and for their distribution within the Rhetine-Vrya forest see Fig. 20.5; see also Fig. 20.6 for an overview of the vegetation in the entire prefecture, comprising the eastern Pieria mountains and northeastern Mt. Olympos).

Pollen records testify that this was the composition of the forest in antiquity as well. Regardless, due to long human activity and exploitation, and the fact that the forest has been under administration since the early 20th century, its natural state and the behavior of the trees under natural conditions are virtually unknown to us.

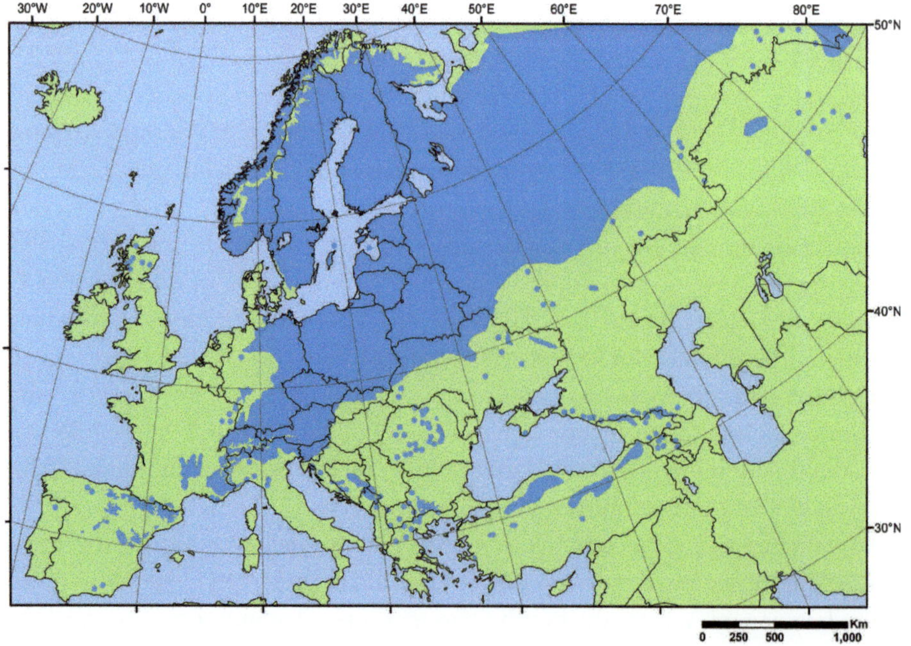

FIGURE 20.4. Distribution map of Scots pine (*Pinus sylvestris*) in Europe. © EUFORGEN 2009 (www.euforgen.org). Courtesy EUFORGEN 2009

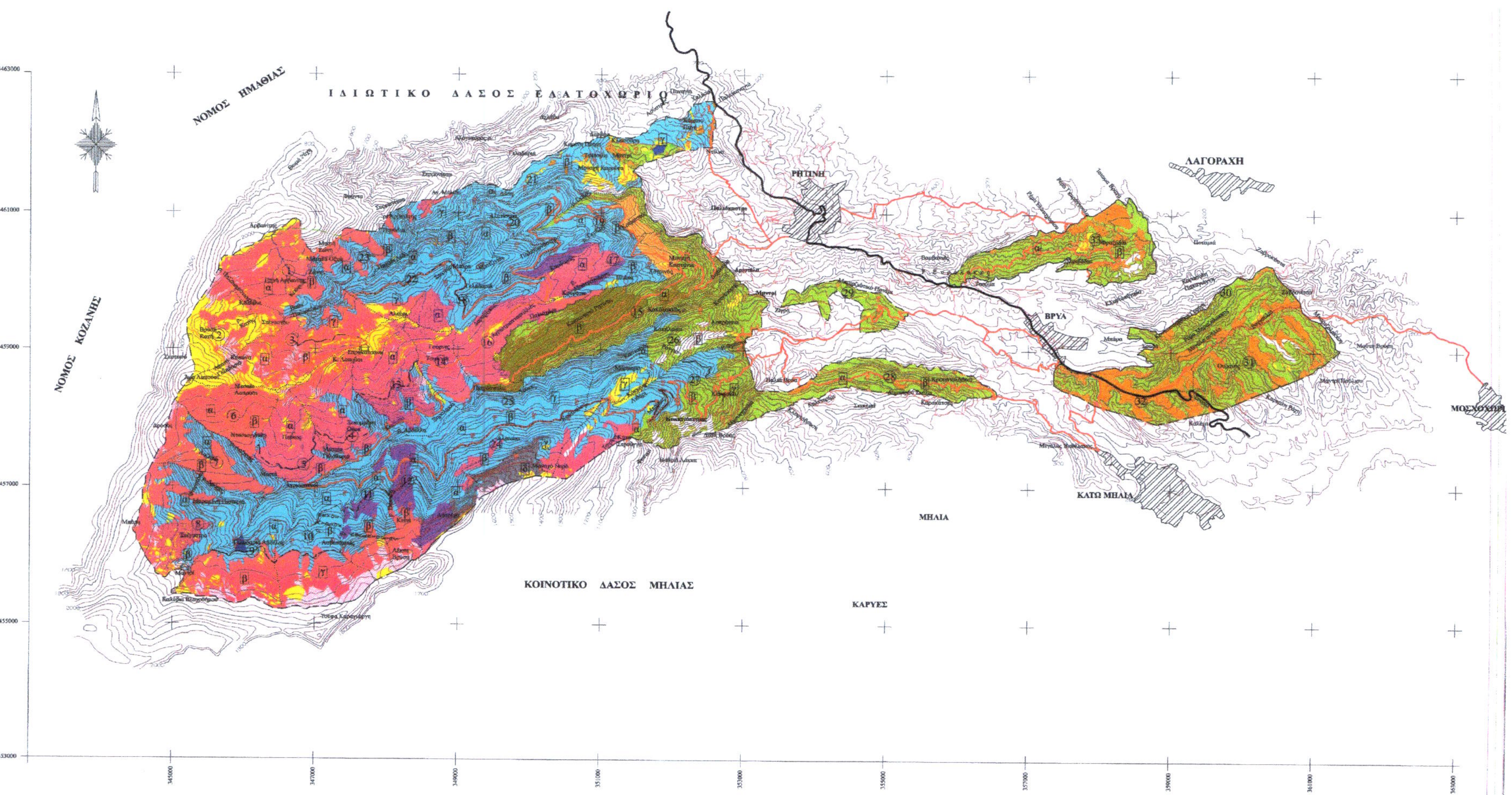

FIGURE 20.5. Map of forest coverage of the Rhetine-Vrya forest, Pieria Mts. Areas colored dark orange are agricultural land and yellow are arid/barren land; green stands for oak (*Quercus pubescens, conferta, sessiliflora*); light green for poplar (*Populus tremula*); dark green for chestnut (*Castanea sativa*); light orange for mixed beech-fir; light blue for beech (*Fagus sylvatica*); blue for fir (*Abies borisii regis*); gray for mixed black pine-fir; dark purple for mixed beech-black pine-fir; dotted purple for pine (reforested areas); light purple for black pine (*Pinus nigra*); and pink for scots pine (*Pinus sylvestris*) forest. Map by Klapanes and Abatzes 2011, © Pieria Prefecture Forestry Office. Courtesy Pieria Prefecture Forestry Office

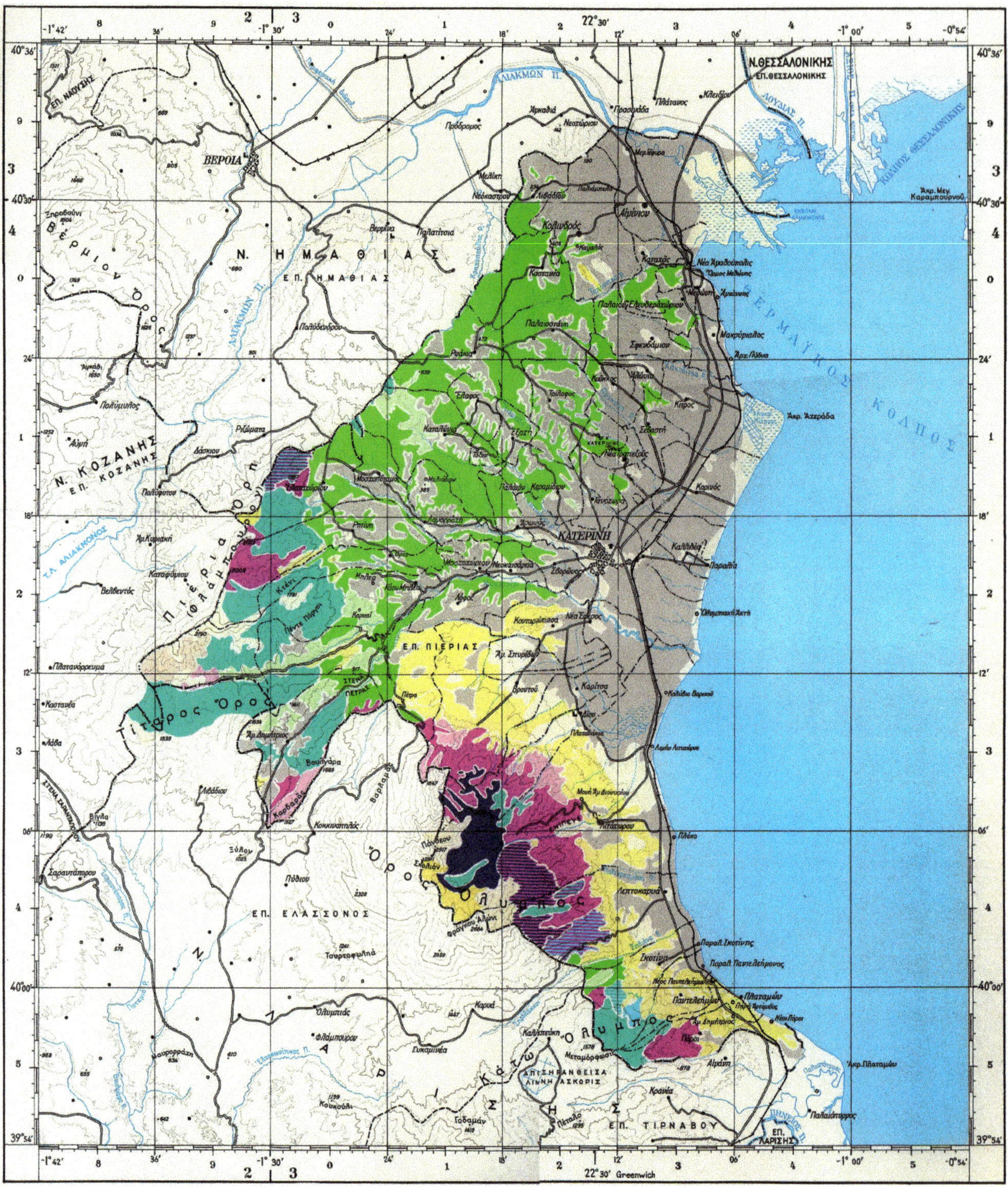

FIGURE 20.6. Map of forest coverage of Pieria Prefecture. Areas colored gray are agricultural land; yellow stands for scrublands of broadleaf evergreens forest (*Quercetalia ilicis*); green for oak and broadleaf deciduous forest (*Quercetalia pubescentis*); light blue for beech-fir forest (*Fagetalia*); purple for *Pinus nigra* forest; beige (at the westernmost end of the prefecture) for *Pinus sylvestris* forest; and dark blue for *Pinus leukodermis* or *heldreichii* forest. © Pieria Prefecture Forestry Office. Courtesy Pieria Prefecture Forestry Office

TABLE 20.1. The forest species on the Pieria Mts.

Vegetation zone	Vegetation complex	MASL	Scientific name	English name	Modern Greek name	Ancient Greek name	Wood	Wood properties	Special uses and products
subalpine (Vaccinio-picetalia)	Vaccinio-piceion	1400–1900	*Pinus sylvestris*	Scots pine	πεύκη (δασική), λιάχα	πεύκη (?)	soft	light, elastic, straight-grained	timber
subalpine (Vaccinio-picetalia)	Vaccinio-piceion	1400–1900	*Picea abies*	spruce	ερυθρελάτη	?	soft		timber
subalpine (Vaccinio-picetalia)	Vaccinio-piceion	1400–1900	*Betula pendula*	silver birch	συμήδα	?	soft	resinous	resin
oro-mediterranean / continental	Fagetum moesiacae	1200–1400	*Pinus nigra* (subsp. *pallasiana*)	black pine	μαύρη πεύκη, πεύκο, μαυρόπευκο	πεύκη	soft	resinous (ένδαδο)	timber, resin
oro-mediterranean / continental	Fagetum moesiacae	1000–1400	*Abies borisii regis / hybridogenus*	fir	ελάτη (υβριδογενής), έλατο	ἐλάτη	soft	light, elastic, straight-grained	timber
continental	Fagetum moesiacae	800–1200	*Fagus sylvatica*	beech	οξυά	ὀξυά	hard		spear shafts
continental	Fagetum moesiacae	500–1200	*Taxus baccata*	yew	ίταμος	ἴταμος, μίλος, (σ)μῖλαξ (?)	hard		
continental	Fagetum moesiacae	500–1200	*Ilex aquifolium*	holly	ελαιόπρινος, λιόπρινο, αρκουδοπούρναρο	κήλαστρον	hard		
supra-mediterranean / subcontinental	Quercion confertae	500–1200	*Castanea sativa / vesca*	chestnut	καστανιά (κοινή)	διοσβάλανος	hard	durable	fruit
supra-mediterranean	Quercion confertae	500–1200	*Carpinus betulus*	hornbeam	γαύρος, μαυρόγαυρο	?	hard		
supra-mediterranean	Ostryo-carpinion	500–1200	*Carpinus orientalis*	eastern hornbeam	γαύρος, ασπρόγαυρο	?	hard		
supra-mediterranean	Ostryo-carpinion	500–1200	*Ostrya carpinifolia*	hop hornbeam	οστρυά	ὀστρύα	hard		plane-foot (tool)
paramediterranean	Fagetum moesiacae	500–1200	*Sorbus aucuparia*	rowan, mountain-ash	σορβιά	?	hard		
paramediterranean		500–1200	*Juglans regia*	walnut	καρυδιά	καρύα	hard	heavy, open-grained, elastic	fruit
paramediterranean		500–1200	*Acer pseudoplatanus*	sycamore maple	σφένδαμος	σφένδαμνος	hard		
paramediterranean		500–1200	*Acer platanoides*	maple	σφένδαμος	σφένδαμνος	hard		
paramediterranean		500–1200	*Acer campestre*	field maple	σφενδάμι	ζυγία	hard		
paramediterranean	Quercion confertae	500–1200	*Corylus avellana*	hazel	φουντουκιά, λεπτοκαρυά	καρύα	no timber		fruit
paramediterranean		500–1200	*Cornus mas*	cornel	κρανιά (η άρρην)	κρανέα	hard		handles, spears, javelins, bows
paramediterranean		500–1200	*Pyrus amygdaliformis*	pear	αγριοαχλαδιά, αγριογκορτσιά	ἀχρίς/-άς	hard		
paramediterranean		500–1200	*Pirus malus*	apple	αγριομηλιά	μηλέα	hard	heavy	
hydrotropic		500–1200	*Ulmus campestris*	elm	φτελιά, καραγάτσι	πτελέα	hard	interlocking grain, extremely durable	keels and bows in triremes
hydrotropic		500–1200	*Alnus glutinosa*	black alder	(σ)κλήθρα	κλήθρα/-ον	soft	durable underwater	
hydrotropic	Quercion confertae	500–1200	*Fraxinus ornus*	manna ash	φράξος	μελία	hard		
hydrotropic		500–1200	*Fraxinus excelsior*	ash	μελιά, μέλιος	μελία	hard		spear shafts
hydrotropic	Quercion confertae	500–1200	*Tilia parvifolia*	lime tree, linden, basswood	φιλύρα, φιλουριά, τίλιο, φλαμουριά	φιλύρα	soft		boat oars (?)
hydrotropic		500–1200	*Populus tremula*	poplar	λεύκη, λεύκα, ασπρόλευκα	λεύκη, ἀχερωίς, αἴγειρος	soft	weak	furniture and utilities
hydrotropic		500–1200	*Platanus orientalis*	plane	πλάτανος, πλατάνι	πλάτανος	hard		
hydrotropic		500–1200	*Salix caprea*	willow	ιτιά (αίγειος), γιδοΐτιά	ἰτέα	soft		
para-/supra-mediterranean	Ostryo-carpinion	200–1200	*Quercus pubescens*	downy / pubescent oak	δρυς (η χνοώδης), μεράδι, βελανιδιά	φηγός (?)	hard		
para-/supra-mediterranean	Ostryo-carpinion	200–1200	*Quercus coccifera*	kermes oak	πρίνος, πουρνάρι	πρῖνος	hard		
para-/supra-mediterranean	Quercion confertae	200–1200	*Quercus conferta / frainetto*	Hungarian / Italian oak	δρυς (πλατύφυλλος), πλατίτσα	δρῦς (?)	hard		
para-/supra-mediterranean	Quercion confertae	200–1200	*Quercus sessiliflora*	sessile oak	δρυς (απόδισκος), δένδρο	δρῦς (?)	hard		
parameditterranean (Quercetalia pubescentis)	Quercion confertae	200–500	*Pistacia terebinthus*	terebinth	σχίνος, τερέβινθος, κοκορεβυθιά	τέρμινθος	no timber	resinous	resin
eumediterranean (Quercetalia ilicis)	Quercion ilicis	200–500	*Quercus ilex*	evergreen / holm oak	αριά, βελανιδιά	ἀρία	hard	tough	

NOTES

1 I would like to thank Nikos Paschaloudis, former director, and Theodosios Abatzis, active forester of the Pieria Prefecture Forestry Office, as well as George Koukouliatas, from the village of Rhetine (Ritini), and Antonis Chnoudas, from the village of Katachas, for willingly sharing their knowledge of Pieria's vegetation. Any errors in Table 20.1 are mine. I am also grateful to Dr. Maria Dinou for comments that proved most valuable, and to Professor Sarah Morris, Professor John K. Papadopoulos, Dr. Niki Oikonomaki, Dr. Antonis Kotsonas, and the anonymous reviewers, for their remarks and corrections on earlier versions of this paper.

2 The most straightforward of these are Xen. *Hell.* 6.1.11: "... Μακεδονίαν, ἔνθεν καὶ Ἀθηναῖοι τὰ ξύλα ἄγονται..." ("... Macedonia, whence the Athenians bring the timber ..."); and Dem. 17.28: "οὐ γὰρ δὴ ἔστι γ' εἰπεῖν ὡς Ἀθήνησι μὲν ἀφθόνων ὄντων τῶν ναυπηγησίμων ξύλων, τῶν μόγις καὶ πόρρωθεν εἰσκομιζομένων, ἐν δὲ τῇ Μακεδονίᾳ ἐπιλελοιπότων, τῇ καὶ τοῖς ἄλλοις τοῖς βουλομένοις εὐτελέστατα καθισταμένῃ" ("For it cannot be said that there is plenty of shipbuilding timber at Athens, where it is imported with great trouble from afar, but that it is scarce in Macedonia, where there is a cheap supply for whomever wants it"). See also Xen. *Hell.* 5.2.16: "ὅπου ξύλα μὲν ναυπηγήσιμα ἐν αὐτῇ τῇ χώρᾳ ἐστί, χρημάτων δὲ πρόσοδοι ἐκ πολλῶν μὲν λιμένων, ἐκ πολλῶν δ' ἐμπορίων, πολυανθρωπία γε μὴν διὰ τὴν πολυσιτίαν ὑπάρχει" ("... there is ship-building timber in this country, and revenues from many harbors and from many trading-posts, and of course there is a large population owing to the abundance of grain"), which refers to the expansion of Olynthos in 383 B.C., and thus it is unclear to which regions of Chalkidike or Macedonia the speaker alludes. On construction timber, see Dem. 19.265; *CID* 2.46, side B, col. III, lines 7–14; *IG* II^2 1672, lines 66–67, 433; *IG* XI.2.199, side A, line 57. The rest of the relevant ancient sources are examined below.

3 This is discussed in more detail below (p. 744 with n. 95).

4 See, for example, a lead letter found at Torone in Chalkidike (Henry 1991, 2001), documenting the correspondence between two traders regarding the supply of—probably—wood ([ξύ]λα, restored).

5 Hdt. 5.17–18; Edson 1970, pp. 25–26; Wallace 1970, p. 200, n. 13; see also Vasilev 2015, pp. 109–117. Perhaps with an interval concurrent with, and probably due to, the Ionian revolt as is inferred from Hdt. 6.44.1 (see Badian 1994, pp. 116–117). On the *Yaunā takabarā*, "Ionians with shield-like hats," who are listed in Old Persian inscriptions and appear in reliefs of the late 6th century B.C. among other people tributary to the Achaemenids, and who are identified with the Macedonians, see Rollinger 2006.

6 See further Badian 1994, pp. 122–126.

7 Meiggs 1982, pp. 123–124.

8 Borza 1987, p. 42; Borza 1990, p. 109.

9 That is according to Thuc. 2.99.3 (cf. Strabo 9.2.25, 10.3.17). On the chronology, which is far from clear, see Tzifopoulos 2012a, pp. 20–21, and more particularly his n. 32.

10 The Peisistratid Hippias, on his exile from Athens in 510 B.C., fled to Macedonia, where he was offered the city of Anthemous in northwest Chalkidike by king Amyntas I (Hdt. 5.94.1). During the reign of Alexander I, Macedonia begins past Mt. Dysoron, coming from the east, and the king also possesses a mine, most likely in the region of Mt. Pangaion (Hdt. 5.17.2). Mt. Dysoron may be identified with the Kroussia mountains (Krestonia) (see Xydopoulos 2016) or Mt. Menoikeion, east of the Strymon (Faraguna 1998, pp. 375–376; *BÉ* 2000, no. 436 [M. B. Hatzopoulos]). Either way, the mine referred to must have lain beyond the Strymon, and that is why, after having crushed the Thasian revolt (465 B.C.) and taken over their Thracian Peraia, Kimon on his return to Athens (463 B.C.) was prosecuted on the charge of not seizing the opportunity to advance on Macedonian territory (Plut. *Cim.* 14.2).

11 Most indicative among the trireme names preserved on inscriptions is Κουφοτάτη (*IG* II^3 1629, line 1), i.e., "lightest," which is curiously the only name pertaining to a ship's actual properties, and thus it is significant in its superlative. On the naval tactics demanding light crafts, see Casson 1991, pp. 77–78.

12 Theophr. *Hist. Pl.* 5.7.2. Triremes were hauled out of the water to be stored in ship sheds and presumably to be refurbished on a routine annual basis, as well as while the fleet encamped on shore or whenever—time allowing—maintenance was required (see for instance Hom. *Il.* 1.484–487, *Od.* 16.321–362; Thuc. 6.44.3, 7.12.3–5, 7.24.2, 8.55; Xen. *Hell.* 1.5.10). On the frequency of bringing triremes ashore, see Steinmayer and MacIntosh Turfa 1996, p. 109, and Steinmayer and MacIntosh Turfa 1997, who favor a rather improbable nightly (if possible) beaching; and Coates 1997; Coates 1999, pp. 113–114; Harrison 1999; Harrison 2003; Vortuba 2017, who argue against this practice.

13 See Appendix 1 (timber); see also Torr 1964, pp. 31–33; Meiggs 1982, pp. 119–120; Steffy 1994, pp. 256–259. Ancient warships have thus far escaped archaeology (the 3rd century B.C. Marsala shipwreck, previously identified as a Liburnian bireme [Frost 1973, 1974, 1975], is now considered a highly questionable case [Averdung and Pedersen 2012]), with a single exception: the prow timber parts preserved inside a bronze ram of the Hellenistic period found off Athlit, Israel, which, on the whole, verify the literary sources: planks, wales, and keel of pine, tenons and pegs of oak, ramming timber and stem of cedar, and elm for other parts (Steffy 1991, pp. 17, 36).

14 See Appendix 1 (oars); among the relevant sources, Lucan alone refers to oars as "pines."

15 Cf. Theophr. *Hist. Pl.* 5.2.2: "Ἰσχυρότατα δὲ τῶν ξύλων ἐστὶ τὰ ἄοζα καὶ λεῖα" ("The strongest among woods are those without knots and smooth").

16 For the same reasons, fir was preferred for the masts and yardarms; see Appendix 1 (masts and yardarms).

17 Hdt. 5.23.2: "...ἐν Θρηίκη, ἵνα ἴδη τε ναυπηγήσιμος ἐστὶ ἄφθονος καὶ πολλοὶ κωπέες καὶ μέταλλα ἀργύρεα" (". . . in Thrace, for there is abundant ship-building timber and many oars and silver mines"); *IG* I³ 182; Ar. *Lys.* 421–422; *IG* I³ 89; Andoc. 2.11; Verg. *Aen.* 10.207–208: "*It gravis Aulestes centenaque arbore fluctum | verberat adsurgens, spumant vada marmore verso*" ("Aulestes advances beating heavily the swelling waves with a hundred trees, leaving behind foam of water as white as marble," equating trees with oars); Sil. *Pun.* 6.352–353: "*aut silvis stringent remos*" ("from trees they shape oars"); Morrison, Coates, and Rankov 2000, pp. 188–189. See further Hom. *Od.* 6.268–269: "...ἔνθα δὲ νηῶν ὅπλα μελαινάων ἀλέγουσι, πείσματα καὶ σπεῖρα, καὶ ἀποξύνουσιν ἐρετμά" (". . . here they tend the outfit of their black ships, cables and sails, and shape the oar-blades"), and also note the κωποξύσται, "oar-scrapers," in late 2nd–early 1st century B.C. Kos (*IG* XII.4 293, line 17). The phrase "κωπέων πλατουμένων" (Ar. *Ach.* 552), oars being flattened, probably refers to the final shaping of oars taking place in the port as part of equipping a trireme (cf. Hsch. s.v. κώπης· τὸ ἄνω κώπαιον, τὸ δὲ κάτω πλάτην, "oar: the upper part oar, the lower blade").

18 Theophr. *Hist. Pl.* 5.4.5; Plin. *HN* 16.52, 16.56; cf. Genesis 6.14: "ποίησον οὖν σεαυτῷ κιβωτὸν ἐκ ξύλων τετραγώνων· νοσσιὰς ποιήσεις τὴν κιβωτὸν καὶ ἀσφαλτώσεις αὐτὴν ἔσωθεν καὶ ἔξωθεν τῇ ἀσφάλτῳ" ("then build for yourself an ark made of square timber; you will structure the ark as a nest and coat it on the inside and on the outside with bitumen"). The importance of pitch coating is emphasized in Plut. *Quaest. Conv.* 676a: ". . . πίττης τε καὶ ῥητίνης ἀλοιφήν, ἧς ἄνευ τῶν συμπαγέντων ὄφελος οὐδὲν ἐν τῇ θαλάττῃ" (". . . ointment of pitch and resin, without which anything fastened together by parts is no good at sea"). Accordingly, when the Peloponnesians sailed from Nisaia, the port town of Megara, in order to attack the unguarded Piraeus with 40 ships they hastily launched, and the Athenians were signaled in time to avert the surprise attack, the former aborted their mission, because they feared that the ships would not be watertight at all ("ἔστι γὰρ ὅτι καὶ αἱ νῆες αὐτοὺς διὰ χρόνου καθελκυσθεῖσαι καὶ οὐδὲν στέγουσαι ἐφόβουν"), obviously because in their haste they did not coat the hulls with pitch (Thuc. 2.93–94). The smell of pitch, which has a very strong odor, had actually become synonymous to war preparations in Athens (Ar. *Ach.* 190: "ὄζουσι πίττης καὶ παρασκευῆς νεῶν," "they smell of pitch and ship preparation"), and it is no surprise that pitch was considered part of the armament and was forbidden to export (Ar. *Ran.* 364–365: "... ἀσκώματα καὶ λίνα καὶ πίτταν διαπέμπων εἰς Ἐπίδαυρον, ἢ χρήματα ταῖς τῶν ἀντιπάλων ναυσὶν παρέχειν τινὰ πείθει," ". . . sending skins, linen, and pitch over to Epidaurus, or convincing anyone to provide equipment for the ships of the enemy"). Another relevant reference, showing the extent of

the practice, is the Homeric epithet "dark-colored" for ships, Hsch. s.v. μέλαιναι νῆες· αἱ βαθεῖαι, καὶ πισσόχριστοι ("smeared with pitch"). Archaeological evidence of this practice is also available; see, for example, Beck and Borromeo 1990; Connan and Nissenbaum 2003; Nieto 2008; Polzer 2009; Pomey 1998, pp. 148–149; Steffy 1985; Steffy 1991, p. 32).

19 Theophr. *Hist. Pl.* 5.4.5: "ἔστι δὲ ἡ τερηδὼν τῷ μὲν μεγέθει μικρόν, κεφαλὴν δ' ἔχει μεγάλην καὶ ὀδόντας· οἱ δὲ θρίπες ὅμοιοι τοῖς σκώληξιν, ὑφ' ὧν τιτραίνεται κατὰ μικρὸν τὰ ξύλα. καὶ ἔστι ταῦτα εὐΐατα· πιττοκοπηθέντα γὰρ ὅταν εἰς τὴν θάλατταν ἑλκυσθῇ στέγει· τὰ δὲ ὑπὸ τῶν τερηδόνων ἀνίατα" ("*teredon* is small in size, having a large head and teeth; wood-worms, by which the timber is afflicted to a lesser degree, are similar to earth-worms. And against these [ships] are easily curable; for if they are coated with pitch when launched at sea, they are protected; but they are incurable against *teredon*"); Plin. *HN* 16.219: "laricem in maritimis navibus obnoxiam teredini tradunt..." ("the larch used in seagoing vessels is said to be vulnerable to teredon"); see also Ar. *Eq.* 1308, where a young trireme protests against a new expedition, proclaiming her preference to grow old and rot by *teredon* in the port ("ὑπὸ τερηδόνων σαπεῖσ' ἐνταῦθα καταγηράσομαι"). On *teredon* (commonly known as "shipworm"), see Plin. *HN* 16.220; Turner 1966; Palma and Santhakumaran 2014, pp. 5, 15–22. On the effects of *teredon* infestation, see Steinmayer and MacIntosh Turfa 1996 (contested by Coates 1997).

20 Theophr. *Hist. Pl.* 1.12.2, 3.9.2–4, 4.16.1, 9.2.1–5; Plin. *HN* 16.38–49; Plut. *Quaest. Conv.* 676a: "[πίτυς] καὶ τὰ ἀδελφὰ δένδρα, πεῦκαι καὶ στρόβιλοι, τῶν τε ξύλων παρέχει τὰ πλωϊμότατα πίττης τε καὶ ῥητίνης ἀλοιφήν" ("[pitys] and the related trees, namely pines and stone pines, provide the most floatable timber among all kinds of wood as well as ointment of pitch and resin"); André 1964.

21 The existence of *Pinus pinea* in the Greek peninsula in antiquity is uncertain; see Konstantinidis 1995, who argues in favor, based on a false reading of Wright 1972 and a hasty identification of this species with the "cone-bearing" pine in Theophrastos. There is actually no evidence or mention of *P. pinea* antedating the Roman presence in Greece.

22 Strabo 13.1.18 (Chios); Pausanias 2.34.8 (Spetses). The Balearic Ibiza, too, was called *Pityoussa*, "full of pitys," again with *P. halepensis* (Plin. *HN* 3.76; Gómez Bellard 1995, p. 444).

23 Arianoutsou and Ne'eman 2000.

24 See Dafis 2010, p. 85.

25 Stephanou 1974, p. 22. Only Hom. *Il.* 13.390: "... πίτυς βλωθρή, τήν τ' οὔρεσι..." ("... tall pitys, which on the mountains...") indicates otherwise.

26 Today *P. brutia* is the most common pine species in Cyprus, extending up to 1600 m ASL, while *P. nigra* grows on the top of Mt. Troodos (Gumbricht, McCarthy, and Mahlander 1996, p. 274).

27 This is acknowledged by Theophrastos in *Hist. Pl.* 3.11.5.

28 Around the Aegean the strictly beech-fir zone (occasionally including *Castanea sp.*) extends from 800 to 1200 m ASL, and the oromediterranean pine zone (including also *Abies sp.*) from roughly 1200 to 1600 m ASL. Other species that grow among beech (such as hornbeam, maple, poplar, oak, elm, and plane) grow between 500 and 1200 m ASL. For a general account of vegetation zones in Greece, see Dafis 1972, pp. 75–87; Dafis 2010, pp. 55–57; for northern Greece in particular, see Gerasimidis and Athanasiadis 1995, pp. 110–111, and more specifically Gerasimidis 1985, pp. 14–17 (Lailias Forest); Athanasiadis and Gerasimidis 1986, pp. 218–220 (Mt. Voras); Athanasiadis and Gerasimidis 1987, p. 409 (Mt. Paiko); Gerasimidis 1985, pp. 29–33, and Gerasimidis et al. 2006, p. 232 (Pieria Mts.). On the Pieria mountains, see also Appendix 2 to this chapter.

29 Harris 1960, p. 121.

30 Meiggs (1982, p. 119) holds that the silver fir (*Abies alba*) produced the wood with the highest reputation in shipbuilding. Both the silver fir and the Greek fir are uncommon species in northern Greece.

31 Some pine forests existing there today are the result of modern reforestation; on the latter two mountains, see Gkaniatsas 1938 and Voliotis 1967, p. 63, respectively.

32 Gerasimidis, Athanasiadis, and Panajiotidis 2009, p. 316.

33 Gerasimidis and Athanasiadis 1995, p. 111. See also n. 47 below on birch growing in antiquity on the Pieria mountains and birch tar detected on Neolithic pottery in Pieria.

34 Plin. *Ep.* 10.41.2: "*Est in Nicomedensium finibus amplissimus lacus. Per hunc marmora fructus ligna materiae et sumptu modico et labore usque ad uiam nauibus, inde magno labore maiore impendio uehiculis ad mare deuehuntur*" ("At the borders of Nikomedia there is a large lake. This allows marble, fruits, firewood, and timber to be brought up to the roadway by boats on a moderate cost and with little effort, whereas it takes much labor and the cost is higher to take it from there to the sea on carriages"); Artem. 2.23: "διὰ θαλάσσης πλεῖν καὶ εὐπλοεῖν ἀγαθὸν μᾶλλον ἢ διὰ γῆς· βραδύτερα δὲ καὶ δυσχερέστερα καὶ μόλις ἐσόμενα τὰ ἀγαθὰ σημαίνει τὸ διὰ γῆς" ("sailing by sea and having a good voyage is better than by land; for transportation by land is slower and more troublesome and it means that the goods will be arriving hardly in time"); Meiggs 1982, pp. 245–246, 334–335, 377; Mulliez 1982, p. 118. The essential role of sea transport in timber trade is attested in [Xen.] *Ath.Pol.* 2.3 and 2.11–12: "εἰ γάρ τις πόλις πλουτεῖ ξύλοις ναυπηγησίμοις, ποῖ διαθήσεται, ἐὰν μὴ πείσῃ τὸν ἄρχοντα τῆς θαλάττης; [...] πρὸς δὲ τούτοις ἄλλοσε ἄγειν οὐκ ἐάσουσιν οἵτινες ἀντίπαλοι ἡμῖν εἰσιν ἢ οὐ χρήσονται τῇ θαλάττῃ" ("For if a city is rich in ship-building timber, where will it distribute it without the consent of the rulers of the sea? [...] and in addition, they will forbid export to wherever any of our enemies may be, or else they will be unable to use the sea").

35 Strabo 11.2.17: "ὕλην τε γὰρ καὶ φύει καὶ ποταμοῖς κατακομίζει" ("for it grows timber and brings it down by rivers as well"); Meiggs 1982, pp. 334–336; Borza 1987, pp. 37–38; cf. Pl. *Criti.* 118d–e: "τὰ δ' ἐκ τῶν ὀρῶν καταβαίνοντα ὑποδεχομένη ῥεύματα [...] τε ἐκ τῶν ὀρῶν ὕλην κατῆγον εἰς τὸ ἄστυ καὶ τἆλλα δὲ ὡραῖα πλοίοις κατεκομίζοντο" ("receiving the streams coming down from the mountains [...] and was bringing timber from the mountains down to the city and the other fineries on boats").

36 See also Harris 2013, p. 186.

37 Note that the sea reached farther inland at the time, even if in the form of a lagoon (Strabo 7.fr.20, 7.fr.23; *P.Köln* I 8; Ghilardi et al. 2008a; Ghilardi et al. 2008b; Fouache et al. 2008); see also [Skylax] 66, and Strabo 7.fr.20 and 7.fr.22 on the lower Loudias River being navigable.

38 A reference to a thick oak forest and implied exploitation, including transport and (trans)plantation, is found in Ap. Rhod. *Argon.* 1.28–31: "Φηγοὶ δ' ἀγριάδες, κείνης ἔτι σήματα μολπῆς, | ἀκτῆς Θρηικίης Ζώνης ἔπι τηλεθόωσαι | ἑξείης στιχόωσιν ἐπήτριμοι, ἃς ὅγ' ἐπιπρό θελγομένας φόρμιγγι κατήγαγε Πιερίηθεν" ("And wild oaks are still signs of that song on the Thracian coast of Zone, flourishing in orderly thick rows, those he [Orpheus] led forth charmed by the lyre down from Pieria"). However, the Pieria mentioned is not the Macedonian one, as further on (line 34) it is called "Bistonian" ("Πιερίῃ Βιστωνίδι"), but rather a Thracian region in the vicinity of Zone (in modern Rhodope Prefecture).

39 Although perhaps incidentally, the phrase πίειρα δρῦς, meaning "resinous wood," in Soph. *Trach.* 766, suggests that the toponym "Pieria" may allude to the productivity of the region in resin and pitch.

40 Ioanna Vassileiadou (2019, especially p. 112) assumes that Pieria was the main producer of pitch and thus accepts the term "Macedonian" as synonymous to "Pierian" pitch.

41 See Poulaki-Pantermali 2008a, pp. 127–129; and especially Bachlas and Syros 2018, pp. 279–282, and forthcoming, who identify it as a local workshop producing imitations of Mendaian amphoras. On the dominant mercantile presence of Mende in Herakleion, see also Bachlas 2018, where the author suggests that these amphoras were destined to contain wine of the Mendaian type produced by local country estates, in line with Papadopoulos and Paspalas' (1999, pp. 177–180) argument that several Chalkidian cities, apart from Mende, may have been involved in the production and export of "Mendaian" wine in matching containers.

42 Carlson 2003, pp. 587–589. On the possibility of extracting resin from pine species other than *P. nigra*, presumably *P. sylvestris*, in Macedonia in the Roman period, see Dimitrakoudi et al. 2011.

43 Beck and Borromeo 1990.

44 Stacey et al. 2010.

45 See Tiverios 1993; see further Chapters 12, 21, 22.

46 Rhodes and Osborne 2003, no. 12, line 9.

47 The presence of silver birch in Pieria has been confirmed by pollen records (Gerasimidis 1985, p. 116; Gerasimidis et al. 2006, p. 242). Organic residue analysis of pottery from the Neolithic sites of Makrygialos and Paliambela in northern Pieria has shown the wide use of birch-bark tar, which was most probably produced locally (Urem-Kotsou et al. 2002; Stern et al. 2006; Mitkidou et al. 2008). In only one case from Makrygialos was it found mixed with pine resin (Mitkidou et al. 2008, p. 493; Dimitrakoudi 2009, p. 257).

48 Probably in 393 B.C., see Diod. Sic. 14.92.3, 15.19.2. Whether there were one or two Illyrian invasions is debated (Lane Fox 2011a, pp. 221–225; Roisman 2010, pp. 159–160), although it seems obvious to me that both passages refer to the same invasion in 393/2 B.C., the second passage being an update on the matter of the lands given to the Olynthians, who in 383/2 B.C. were asked to return them and refused; that is, unless Diodoros has merged in his narrative the events of the Chalkidian expansion into Macedonia, known from Xen. *Hell.* 5.2.12–13, with the earlier Illyrian invasion. In any case, the treaty should be dated before 383 B.C. and probably even before the Illyrian invasion, right at the beginning of Amyntas' reign in 394/3 B.C. Furthermore, as far as I know, neither the fir nor any species of mountain pine grew in Mygdonia in antiquity (see above, p. 738).

49 See for instance *Hist. Pl.* 3.3.4, 3.3.8, 3.6.5, 3.9.2–3, 5.1.2, 5.4.4, 5.5.2.

50 *HN* 16.45: "*Omnia ea perpetuo virent nec facile discernuntur in fronde etiam a peritis; tanta natalium mixtura est*" ("all the aforementioned [species of conifers] are evergreen and not easily distinguished by the foliage from each other even by experts; that much interrelated they are"), and *HN* 16.48: "*nam in Macedonia et Arcadia circaque Elim permutant nomina, nec constat auctoribus quod cuique generi adtribuant*" ("Moreover, in Macedonia and Arcadia and around Elis names are swapped, so that authors are not in agreement as to which one to attribute to each species"); cf. Theophr. *Hist. Pl.* 3.9.2.

51 That is, nodes, branches, or increase in trunk diameter: "αὐξάνεται δὲ πρῶτον εἰς μῆκος, ἄχρι οὗ δὴ ἐφίκηται τοῦ ἡλίου· καὶ οὔτε ὄζος οὐδεὶς οὔτε παραβλάστησις οὔτε πάχος γίνεται· μετὰ δὲ ταῦτα εἰς βάθος καὶ πάχος· οὕτως αἱ τῶν ὄζων ἐκφύσεις καὶ παραβλαστήσεις."

52 Pacala et al. 1994, p. 2182; Messier et al. 1999, pp. 815–817; Gaudio et al. 2011, p. 191.

53 Messier et al. 1999, pp. 812, 816–818; Claveau et al. 2002, pp. 458, 461, 464; Robakowski et al. 2004, p. 225; Grassi and Giannini 2005, pp. 269, 273.

54 Messier et al. 1999, pp. 817, 819; also Theophr. *Hist. Pl.* 4.1.1.

55 Theophr. *Hist. Pl.* 4.1.2, 4.1.4; Dafis 2010, p. 120.

56 In *Hist. Pl.* 5.4.2 Theophrastos writes "resinous *peuke*," as if admitting there is also a non-resinous one; cf. Plin. *HN* 16.38: "*pinus fert minimum resinae, interdum et nucibus ipsis, de quibus dictum est, vixque ut adscribatur generi*" ("Pine yields the smallest amount of resin, sometimes also produced from its nuts themselves, about which we have spoken, and scarcely enough to justify its classification as a resinous tree," transl. H. Rackham, Cambridge, Mass., 1938). Neither is the fir totally deprived of resin.

57 On the form of the Boiotian helmet, see Waurick 1988, pp. 159–163.

58 Dafis 2010, p. 151. It is also characteristic of *P. pinea*, but see n. 21 above.

59 Gerasimidis, Panajiotidis, and Athanasiadis 2008, p. 641. Individual trees grow in most Macedonian mountains, but their number is insignificant (Pasayiannis 2000, p. 6; Chochliouros 2005, p. 211).

60 Gerasimidis 1985, pp. 31–33; Pasayiannis 2000, p. 6.

61 After having captured Eion, a fortified port town at the mouth of the Strymon River (by 474 B.C.; Hdt. 7.25.2, 7.107; Thuc. 1.98.1; Plut. *Cim.* 7.1–4), the Athenians launched in 465/4 B.C. an ambitious colonization campaign in the Thracian interior, which ended up a debacle (Hdt. 9.75; Thuc. 1.100.3, 4.102.3; Diod. Sic. 12.68.2; Paus. 1.29.4). In 437/6 B.C. a second attempt was made, which succeeded in founding Amphipolis (Thuc. 4.102.3; Diod. Sic. 12.32.3, 12.68.2). In 424 B.C. the Spartans captured the city, but it

was subsequently ceded to the Athenians by the peace treaty of 421 B.C. (Thuc. 5.18.5); notwithstanding, and despite multiple attempts to be brought back into Athenian control, the Amphipolitans remained independent thenceforth (Thuc. 5.21.1–2; Koukouli-Chrysanthaki 2011, p. 411).

62 The procurement of shipbuilding materials from *P. sylvestris* has been verified by merchantman shipwrecks of the Archaic and Classical periods (Bound 1991a, p. 43, and Bound 1991b, p. 34: hull planking; Nieto 2008, pp. 46, 57: hull planking [perhaps *P. nigra*]; van Duivenvoorde 2014, p. 22: frame). Alas, remains of masts are extremely rare, and those of yardarms and oars have never been found.

63 Note that pollen records have inherent limitations that make the acquisition of a full and accurate picture impossible; by recording percentages they only give a relative quantity of each species to the others, while the location from where the sample comes may or may not be fully representative, depending on altitude, orientation, predominant wind direction, and proximity to any geophysical features. Notwithstanding, large fluctuations in the values of different species types (but not specific species; see Panajiotidis, Gerasimidis, and Fotiadis 2009) can be discerned, even though their dating will be approximate.

64 From ca. 300–200 B.C. onward (and until ca. A.D. 200) forest vegetation is considerably reduced without corresponding increase in cultivation indicators (i.e., increased percentages of cereals, vines, etc.), thus indicating felling for timber production. A closer examination regarding forest species during this period reveals selective felling of conifers (Gerasimidis 1985, pp. 110, 116–117; Athanasiadis and Gerasimidis 1987, pp. 424–425, 434, 439; Gerasimidis 1995; Gerasimidis 2000, pp. 34–35; Gerasimidis, Athanasiadis, and Panajiotidis 2009, pp. 316–317), especially of the fir, which was severely damaged up to extinction (Gerasimidis 1995, p. 198).

65 Gerasimidis 1985, pp. 92, 115; Gerasimidis and Athanasiadis 1995, p. 114; Gerasimidis and Panajiotidis 2010, pp. 76–77.

66 Gerasimidis 1985, p. 93; Gerasimidis 1995, p. 196; Gerasimidis 2000, pp. 30–31.

67 Gerasimidis 1995, p. 195.

68 Athanasiadis and Gerasimidis 1986, pp. 239, 243; Athanasiadis and Gerasimidis 1987, pp. 419, 436; Athanasiadis 1988, p. 147; Gerasimidis 1995.

69 Athanasiadis 1975, pp. 120–122; Athanasiadis 1988, pp. 147, 151 (Mt. Olympos); Athanasiadis and Gerasimidis 1986, p. 243; Gerasimidis and Athanasiadis 1995, p. 114 (Mt. Voras); Athanasiadis and Gerasimidis 1987, pp. 421–422, 438–439; Gerasimidis 1995, p. 192; Gerasimidis and Athanasiadis 1995, p. 115 (Mt. Paiko); Gerasimidis 1985, p. 69; Gerasimidis 2000, pp. 34–35 (Lailias Forest).

70 Rhodes and Osborne 2003, no. 12, lines 9–13: "ἐ<ξ>αγωγὴ δ΄ ἔστω καὶ πίσσης καὶ ξύλων ọἰκοδομιστηρίωμ πάντων, ναυπηγισίμων δὲ πλὴν ἐλατίνων, ὅ τι ἂμ μὴ τὸ κοινὸν δέηται, τῶι δὲ κοινῶι καὶ τούτων εἶν ἐξαγωγήν . . ." ("There shall be export of pitch and timbers for building of all kinds but for shipbuilding except fir, whatever is not needed by the confederacy; but to the confederacy export of these will also be allowed . . ."); cf. the treaty between the Athenians and Perdikkas II (*IG* I^{3} 89, line 31), in which the Macedonian king takes an oath not to let anyone export oars, unless he is an Athenian ([- - - καὶ οὐδένα κο]πέας ἐχσάγεν ἐάσο ἐὰμ μὲ Ἀθε[ναίο- - -]).

71 Andoc. 2.11; Rhodes and Osborne 2003, no. 12, lines 9–14; Diod. Sic. 14.42.4.

72 Hammond 1972, p. 168; also Hammond and Griffith 1979, p. 52. This could be true for timber from the northern slopes of Mt. Voras, but only after the Demir Kapija defile had come under Macedonian control, possibly by the last decade of the 5th century B.C. (Borza 1990, p. 168). Noteworthy as possibly etymologically related to the name of the Axios River is a gloss in Hesychios, s.v. ἄξος· ὕλη, παρὰ Μακεδόσιν ("áxos: wood, among the Macedonians") (I owe this suggestion to Prof. S. Morris).

73 For an overview, see Flensted-Jensen 2004, pp. 818–819. Therme features as a coastal city in [Skylax] 66.

74 Hdt. 7.123.3; also 7.124.

75 Manakidou 2017, pp. 5–7.

76 Gimatzidis 2010; *Sindos* I–III.

77 The reference in Steph. Byz. s.v. Χαλάστρα: "... and there is a port (λιμήν) homonymous to the city" is doubtful as most manuscripts and other sources give λίμνη, "lake" (see Manakidou 2017, p. 31).

78 Poulaki-Pantermali 2003, pp. 337–338; Poulaki-Pantermali 2008a, pp. 127–129.

79 *IG* I³ 77, col. V, line 21 (422/1 B.C.); see also *IG* I³ 71, col. IV, line 108 (fully restored; 425/4 B.C.).

80 Herakleion served, even if only briefly, as a naval station for the Roman fleet in 198 B.C. (Livy 44.35.13–14).

81 Meritt 1936, p. 248, n. 8.

82 The forest vegetation of lower Olympos does not differ significantly from that of the Pieria mountains, with the exception of *P. sylvestris*, which is totally absent. Otherwise, the beech (*Fagus moesiaca*), the chestnut (*Castanea sativa*), the fir (*A. borisii-regis*), and the pine (*P. nigra*) form the main stands (Tsiaousi 1996).

83 Poulaki-Pantermali 2003, p. 336.

84 Hammond 1972, p. 125.

85 Strabo 7.fr.17; Livy 44.6.14–15; Bessios and Krahtopoulou 2001, p. 396.

86 Vassileiadou 2011, pp. 163–164, 246–248 (nos. 73–74, 76–77); also note the saws under nos. 80–82 (pp. 252–253).

87 On the identification of Aloros with modern Kypseli, see Hatzopoulos 1987, pp. 37–40; Apostolou 1988; Apostolou 1991.

88 By the prefix ἅλς, sea or salt, although a derivation from ἅλως, threshing floor, is also plausible (Suda, s.v. ἀλωρῆται). Either way, there is an economic aspect in the name suggesting control of sea traffic, salt harvesting, or agriculture.

89 Ghilardi 2007, pp. 358–360.

90 Strabo 7.fr.20: "ἔστι δ᾽ ἡ Ἄλωρος τὸ μυχαίτατον τοῦ Θερμαίου κόλπου· λέγεται δὲ Θεσσαλονίκεια διὰ τὴν ἐπιφάνειαν" ("Aloros is the most recessed part of the Thermaic Gulf; it is called Thessalonikeia because of its prominence"). The passage is problematic in that at the most recessed part of the Thermaic Gulf lay the city of Thessaloniki, already existing in Strabo's time. Hammond (1972, p. 133) attempts to resolve the problem by misreading Strabo 7.fr.22: "μετὰ τὸ Δῖον πόλιν ὁ Ἁλιάκμων ποταμὸς ἔστιν, ἐκβάλλων εἰς τὸν Θερμαῖον κόλπον· καὶ τὸ ἀπὸ τούτου (sc. Dion, rather than the Thermaic Gulf) ἡ πρὸς βορρᾶν τοῦ κόλπου παραλία Πιερία καλεῖται ἕως τοῦ Ἀξιοῦ ποταμοῦ ..." and suggesting that an inlet in the vicinity of Aloros would be regarded as the most recessed part of the Thermaic Gulf. I would rather side with Borza (1990, pp. 292–293), who comments on the untrustworthiness of Strabo regarding Macedonia.

91 The city features in all known *periploi* ([Skylax] 66; [Scymn.], line 626; Strabo 7.fr.20, 7.fr.22) and its port is directly referred to in Diod. Sic. 19.49.1. Apparently, its port served as a naval base for the Persians during the second Persian invasion (Diod. Sic. 11.12.3) and it seems that the city maintained a fleet at least in the 4th century B.C. (Diod. Sic. 19.69.3; see further Hauben 1978). Also, this is whence the exiled Athenian Themistokles sailed on his way to Persia in ca. 465 B.C. (Thuc. 1.137.1–2).

92 Bessios 1993, p. 1113.

93 Although James Beresford's (2013) thesis about wintertime seafaring merits serious consideration, transport of a bulk commodity, such as timber, would not be risked in harsh weather. One known voyage bound to bring timber from Macedonia back to Athens, that of Philondas (Dem. 49.28–29), took place in midsummer, sailing in April/May and returning in the following Attic year, i.e., after late July.

94 For a summary of predominant winds and their effects in the Thermaic Gulf, see Ghilardi 2006, pp. 26–28. For the second harbor site at Methone (Plot 278), see Chapter 1. See also Ghilardi 2006, pp. 84, 87–90, and Ghilardi et al. 2007 for possible additional harbor sites north of the city.

95 Meiggs 1982, p. 356; Borza 1987, pp. 38, 43, n. 47, and p. 49; Borza 1990, p. 75; Hammond 1998, p. 399; Millett 2010, p. 485; Tzifopoulos 2012a, pp. 20, 30.

96 The unstable relations between Athens and Perdikkas II (see Cole 1974; Psoma 2014, pp. 134–137) are uniquely commented on by Hermippos in his comedy *Phormophoroi* (426 B.C.). Listing the products imported to Athens, Hermippos mentions, among other commodities, that they receive from Perdikkas "cargoes of lies in many ships" (Athen. 27e), presumably referring to timber.

97 On the importance of the timber trade to the Macedonian economy, see Psoma 2015. See also Karathanasis 2019, who follows Theophrastos' text faithfully, assumes the identification of ἐλάτη with *Abies alba* (silver fir), and argues that the enmity of Perdikkas II toward the Athenians following the foundation of Amphipolis was not because it meant a heavy blow to the economy of his kingdom, but an anti-imperialistic response expressed by withholding timber sales of silver fir, of which he supposedly had a monopoly, and thus the Athenians sided with his brother Philip whose former dominion included the valley of Axios and Mt. Paiko, where the sole *A. alba* population grew in the 5th century B.C. Karathanasis fails to note, first, that the now extinct fir on Mt. Paiko is merely assumed to have been *A. alba* and not some other species (Cheddadi et al. 2014, pp. 114–115, especially p. 115), and, second, that it is at least equally probable that *A. alba* was also present along with *P. sylvestris* in the Strymon region, at the Lailias Forest (Mauri, de Rigo, and Caudullo 2016). He also downplays the extent and ignores the self-perpetuating necessity of the economic and political expansion that the Athenians aimed for. Even if the Athenians could cover or even exceed their need for *A. alba* (or *P. sylvestris*) from the Strymon region, they still would need to control Macedonian resources as well, if only to prevent them from being sold to others; the very concept of establishing a monopsony or a monopoly—terms misused by Karathanasis—is to overcome *all* competition (Robinson 1969). With regard to naval supplies especially, securing only the top-quality materials would just not be enough. Therefore, whether or not the Athenians were able to find an alternative source of *A. alba* (or *P. sylvestris*) by establishing themselves in the Strymon valley was irrelevant in terms of their imperialistic ambitions. Be that as it may, since the main concern seems to have been the oar supply, and oars were usually about 4–4.5 m long, harvested from young trees (see n. 17 above), the maximum height reached in maturity, in which in fact *A. alba* surpasses all other species, is also irrelevant; what matters is growth.

98 Thuc. 1.57–58; Diod. Sic. 12.34.2–4; West 1914.

99 Of course, the plague of 430 B.C. had reduced the Athenian force considerably, and in the following years the Athenians also had other urgent matters to attend to, such as the Mytilenian revolt in 427 B.C. Diplomacy may have been their last resort, rather than a choice of action.

100 See also Chapter 2, pp. 54–56.

101 In 430 B.C. according to Allen West (1925; see also Tzifopoulos 2012a, p. 22, n. 43 for further bibliography); in 427/6 B.C. according to Harold Mattingly (1961).

102 Meritt 1944, p. 217.

103 Nease 1949, pp. 107–109.

104 Poteidaia eventually yielded, its citizens were expelled, and Athenian colonists occupied the city in 429 B.C. (*IG* I^3 62, line 8; Thuc. 2.70; Meiggs and Lewis 1969, no. 66; Meritt 1980).

105 Bessios 2003, p. 448; Tiverios 2008, p. 19.

106 Hansen 1997, pp. 83–84, and 2006a, pp. 2–3.

107 Bessios, Tzifopoulos, and Kotsonas 2012; Chapters 9, 11, 12; see also Papadopoulos 2016.

108 Demetriou 2011, pp. 266–268.

109 Bessios 2003, p. 444; Bessios et al. 2004; Bessios, Athanassiadou, and Noulas 2008. On colonies as independent city-states, see Hansen 2006b, pp. 44–46; cf. Betcher 2012.

110 Hansen 1997, pp. 85–86, 97, 103, and 2006a, pp. 3–5, 23–25; Wilson 2005, pp. 110, 113.

111 Ghilardi et al. 2008a, 2008b; Fouache et al. 2008.

112 Krahtopoulou 2010, pp. 208–209.

113 Vavelidis 2004; Tiverios 2008, pp. 21, 32; Vavelidis and Andreou 2008, pp. 361–362.

114 Hammond 1998, p. 399; Tzifopoulos 2012a, p. 30.

115 See Chapter 10; L. Picornell-Gelabert, pers. comm.

116 A fragment attributed to Strabo (7.fr.20c Baladié = *P. Köln* I 8; Krebber 1972; Luppe 1994) cites Theopompos, who refers to a city called Methone as "ὑλήεσσα," "forested," in the context of naval preparations. Reinhold Merkelbach (1973) and Miltiadis Hatzopoulos, Denis Knoepfler, and Véra Marigo-Papadopoulos (1990, pp. 664–665) rejected its identification with Pierian Methone (although Strabo cites the fragment in a passage just prior to discussing Pella), suggesting identification with the Peloponnesian Methana and the Magnesian Methone respectively, but, more recently, Bruno Helly (2006) made a tenable case in favor of the Pierian Methone; see Chapters 2, 6.

117 [Skylax] 66; Strabo 7.fr.20, 7.fr.22.

118 The extent of its territory is unknown, and it is difficult to estimate its size. A rough estimation of a medium-sized *chora* (ca. 100 km^2) by Miltiadis Hatzopoulos and Paschalis Paschidis (2004, p. 804) is theoretically supported by Denise Demetriou (2011, pp. 262–265) and fits well on the map. The workshops of the 7th–6th centuries B.C. excavated on the West Hill (Bessios 2003, p. 449; Bessios et al. 2004, p. 369; Bessios, Athanassiadou, and Noulas 2008, p. 248) hint—if we accept them as operating through the Classical period—at a manufacturing economy, rather than subsistence, which would support a pessimistic view on the extent of Methone's territory.

119 Note that both *P. sylvestris* and *P. nigra* grow mainly on the west side of the Pieria mountains (Gerasimidis et al. 2006, p. 232; Gerasimidis and Panajiotidis 2010, p. 76).

120 *IG* I³ 89; *IG* I³ 117 = Meiggs and Lewis 1969, no. 91 = Walbank 1978, no. 90; Rhodes and Osborne 2003, no. 12, lines 9–14; Andoc. 2.11; Dem. 49.26, 29, 36–37; Theophr. *Char.* 23; Diod. Sic. 20.46.4; Plut. *Demetr.* 10.1; *IG* II² 1492, lines 120–121. According to Borza (1987, pp. 39–41, especially p. 39, n. 29), the fact that the king was making gifts of timber as an individual hints at forests owned by him personally, or rather ex officio. However, the exploitation was most probably leased out (Bissa 2009, pp. 112–115) or administered by royal agents (Hatzopoulos 1996, vol. 1, pp. 434–435; see also Roesch 1984 and Lane Fox 2011b, p. 263, for a possible identification of such a royal agent, perhaps from a family associated with timber trade). What is certain is the royal control exercised over timber exports.

121 Borza 1990, p. 148; against the date of 434 B.C. as suggested by Benjamin Meritt, Theodore Wade-Gery, and Malcolm McGregor (*ATL* 3, pp. 69, 134–135).

122 In 415 B.C. the Athenians shipped to Methone the Macedonian exiles who had taken refuge in Athens along with some of their own cavalry with orders to ravage Macedonian territory (Thuc. 6.7.3). The Athenian intervention in Macedonia continued in the 4th century B.C., again with Methone as a landing base (Diod. Sic. 16.2.6, 16.3.5–6), and resulted in the destruction of the city by Philip II (Diod. Sic. 16.34.4–5).

123 Thuc. 4.108.1; possibly also *IG* I³ 47, especially line 11.

124 On the debate over the date, see Borza 1987, p. 44, n. 49; Borza 1990, pp. 153–154, n. 56, and p. 295; also Mattingly 1996a, p. 155, n. 31.

125 Since the Strymon region had been annexed to the Macedonian kingdom by the time that *Historia Plantarum* was composed, Theophrastos' (*Hist. Pl.* 4.5.5, 5.2.1) ranking of Macedonia at the top of the Aegean timber-producing regions is not as specific as we would like it to be.

126 Yannis Tzifopoulos (2012a, p. 16) suggested that Pydna was another Greek colony, like Methone, that was later annexed by the Macedonian kingdom. In that case, a strong Greek element would be expected within the population of the city (Hansen 2004, pp. 150–151), as well as strong trade ties with south and east Greek cities.

127 Kahrstedt 1953; Kalléris 1954, p. 603; Flensted-Jensen and Hansen 1996, p. 151; Hatzopoulos 1996, vol. 1, p. 473; Mari 2007, pp. 32–33; Cohen 2013, pp. 362–363. Malcolm Errington (1990, p. 37) and Robin Lane Fox (2011b, pp. 266–267) objected to the date, favoring instead 360/59 B.C. Their independence

is further corroborated by a list of *thearodokoi* of ca. 360 B.C., where both cities appear as independent states along with Macedonia (*IG* IV² 94, fr. b, col. I, lines 7–9), as well as by numismatic evidence (Tselekas 1996, especially pp. 23–24; Psoma 2002).

128 *IG* I³ 117 = Meiggs and Lewis 1969, no. 91 = Walbank 1978, no. 90. That is, provided that the restoration of this fragmentary inscription is correct.

129 Borza 1990, p. 163, n. 9.

130 Meritt 1936, p. 248, n. 8.

131 Greenwalt 1999, pp. 175–176; see also King 2018, pp. 7–8. On Pella being reachable by sea and having a port, as is also attested by its inclusion in the *Periplous* of Pseudo-Skylax (66), see n. 37 above.

132 Thuc. 2.29, 2.67; Ar. *Ach.* 141–150; Pache 2001; Archibald 1998, pp. 118–120.

133 Meiggs (1982, p. 494, n. 87), although skeptical of the restoration on the whole, suggested alternatively that the kind of timber should be restored as π[ιτ]ύ[ων], which he justified as the wood was probably coming from Cyprus, where *pitys* was preferred over pine in shipbuilding (Theophr. *Hist. Pl.* 5.7.1).

134 The forest extends west of the ridge as well, in the area of Katafygi village, in Kozani Prefecture, where it occupies slopes of mostly north and northwest exposure. The bedrock and soil, and the composition of the forest, are the same; only the degree of degradation is much more severe (Boussios 2008; Gerasimidis, Panajiotidis, and Athanasiadis 2008).

135 This is a phenomenon characteristic of mixed stands, where the different species compete for a place in the canopy, unlike single-species stands, where, as trees compete on equal terms, balance becomes inevitable.

136 Critchfield and Little 1966, p. 13 and Map 32.

21

TRADE IN THE ARCHAIC NORTH AEGEAN: TRANSPORT AMPHORAS FROM THE WEST HILL OF METHONE

Alexandra Kasseri

Remains of three Archaic buildings were revealed after limited excavation on the central part of the West Hill at Methone (Figs. 1.33, 19.1).[1] The buildings are made up of several rooms, all of which contained clear stratigraphic evidence of fire; this destruction layer also extended across the entire trench. The fire, which occurred at some point during the 6th century B.C. and probably destroyed the buildings of the West Hill, sealed a layer of occupation, and together with it, a large amount of pottery.[2] Among this pottery, transport vessels, mainly amphoras, predominate and are the focus of this contribution. The assemblage is also made up of a considerable amount of fine imported decorated pottery; Early and Middle Corinthian products constitute the largest assemblage, but East Greek and Attic pottery is also present in significant quantities.[3] Although exact numbers are not yet known—as publications are ongoing—locally produced vases, transport vessels, and smaller pots represent a significant proportion of the overall pottery assemblage.

The function of these buildings is still uncertain. Nevertheless, important workshop-related remains have been discovered, including two kilns, a hearth with bronze slag, and potsherds with remnants of gold (for gold smelting), as well as jewelry molds and ivory debitage, all of which have been collected from several locations within the area of the Archaic buildings. It has, therefore, been suggested that the function of this area is related to various forms of industrial production and that it could be part of a workshop quarter. Evidence of workshop activity is also present in the Archaic levels excavated in the agora of Methone.[4]

The most distinctive aspect of this assemblage of transport vessels is the variety of types present, among both the imported and the locally manufactured amphoras. The imported transport vessels originate from several production centers in south and east Greece. Examples of transport vessels from Chios, Samos, Miletos, Lesbos, Athens, Corinth, and Lakonia are presented here. Alongside this rich assemblage of imported material, several locally manufactured transport containers, unclassified in the literature and distributed in several places in the north Aegean, have also been discovered. Some of these types will be briefly presented in this chapter as their study is still in progress.[5] The examples from each region are classified in different groups according to their fabric and/or their morphological characteristics. No petrographic analysis has been conducted yet on the Archaic amphoras from the West Hill, and, as such, fabric identification is based on macroscopic observations of both the clay and the morphological features of the vessels.[6]

CHIAN AMPHORAS AND RELATED SHAPES (21/1–21/3)

The most numerous amphora sherds in the West Hill assemblage originate from the island of Chios. From the pottery studied so far, at least 15 different vessels can be identified. Together with the published examples from the Hypogeion (fragments of six vessels),[7] Chian transport containers at Methone appear over a chronological period of one and a half centuries (from the late 8th until the middle of the 6th century B.C.).[8]

The identification and definition of Chian amphora fabrics have been the focus of several studies.[9] Workshops for the production of Chian amphoras have been located not only on the island but also in the Chian Peraia on the Anatolian mainland, in places such as Erythrai and Klazomenai.[10] The examples from the West Hill were classified under three fabric groups. The first consists of 45 examples made of a brownish clay with a gray core and contains many small and medium white inclusions, fewer small and medium dark inclusions, and abundant silver and gold mica (e.g., **21/1**). The second fabric is represented by 26 examples and is characterized by an orange clay with a gray or darker core and contains a slightly higher amount of mica compared to Group 1, many small and medium white inclusions, and fewer small and medium dark inclusions (e.g., **21/2**). The main representative of the third group is ΜΕΘ 4773, made in a brown fabric. It is significantly coarser when compared to Groups 1 and 2, and has a thick gray core. This last fabric group is represented by 12 examples.

A wide range of Chian transport vessels were found in the Methone West Hill assemblage, among which not only amphoras were identified, but also hydriai (e.g., **21/2**). The amphora **21/1** corresponds to the "standard Chian type" of the first half of the 6th century B.C.[11] This type is characterized by elongated morphological features when compared to the earlier type; these include a longer neck, a slender body, and a narrower foot. It is covered with a thin, whitish slip and painted with thin decorative bands. Examples of an earlier type, dated to the third quarter of the 7th century B.C., have also been found among the West Hill assemblage. This early type has a stouter neck and body and a wider foot compared to the "standard type," as well as differences in decoration; the vessel is covered with a thicker cream-colored slip and broader painted bands.[12] Some examples present characteristics of both types and have thus been dated to the transitional period between the two. Equally interesting is another example, which preserves decorative concentric circles over a cream slip (**21/3**). An identical example has been found in the Hypogeion at Methone (unpublished).[13] Examples of other closed vessels with similar decoration have also been found in the Methone West Hill assemblage (ΜΕΘ 4240 and ΜΕΘ 4355) and possibly belong to hydriai, as a similar and more complete example from the Hypogeion indicates.[14] Interestingly, the West Hill example was found together with Early Iron Age (EIA) local pottery of the middle/second half of the 7th century B.C. Concentric circles are not very common in the Chian repertoire, yet a vessel with similar decoration was identified by the author at Klazomenai.[15] Finally, another amphora type of Chian origin, the so-called Kolomak type, which is a smaller version, was also found in the Methone West Hill material (ΜΕΘ 4217, ΜΕΘ 4668).[16]

Chian transport vessels are largely thought to have carried wine;[17] however, a few scholars have argued that the Chian amphoras contained olive oil,[18] as well as other products.[19]

Twelve examples of Chian amphoras found on the West Hill at Methone carry incised marks, all made after firing. Some more elaborate examples appear to have been drawn with calipers.[20]

Chian amphoras were very common in the north Aegean from the 8th century, as attested by examples from the Hypogeion,[21] Sindos,[22] and Herakleion (Krania). Other early examples already known stem from Smyrna, Pithekoussai, Toscanos, and Carthage.[23] However, the bulk of Chian amphoras appeared toward the end of the 7th century and continue until the third quarter of the 5th century B.C. A few examples that date to the middle of the 7th century are known from the cemetery of Abdera.[24] Chian amphoras dating to the end of the 7th and the first half of the 6th century have been discovered at Krania and Kastro Neokaisareia in Pieria,[25] at Akanthos,[26] Poseidi, Dikaia, Thasos,[27] Fagris,[28] Oisyme,[29] Argilos,[30] Mende,[31] Sindos, Lebet (Polichni), Karabournaki,[32] Anchialos,[33] Archontiko,[34] Koufalia, Therme-Sedes, Toumba Thessalonikis,[35] Nea Kallikrateia,[36] Leivithra, on the north Aegean islands of Samothrace,[37] Lemnos (Hephaistia), and Mytilene,[38] and in western Anatolia at Troy, Daskyleion,[39] Eresos,[40] and Aiolian Kyme.[41]

SAMIAN AMPHORAS

At least 13 examples of Samian transport amphoras are preserved in the West Hill material and are divided into six different groups according to their fabric and morphological characteristics. Another 13 examples of Samian amphoras were identified from the Hypogeion of Methone.

A variety of Samian fabrics have been recognized within the West Hill material. This is not uncommon for Samian amphoras and has led to the conclusion that there must have been a number of production centers, many of which were scattered not only around the island, but also along the mainland and especially in the area of Miletos.[42] The clay is often light brownish red in color and has a dark core. The typical fabric usually contains dark brown inclusions, but the West Hill examples very often contain additional white inclusions, while the amount of mica varies significantly. The most characteristic feature of Samian transport amphoras is their well-levigated clay and excellent firing, which make the fabric resemble fine wares rather than transport vessels.

The majority of the examples from the West Hill are made of the typical well-burnished Samian fabric (ΜΕΘ 4772, ΜΕΘ 4737, ΜΕΘ 4852), similar to those found in the Hypogeion.[43] Nevertheless, some examples are made of a coarser fabric (ΜΕΘ 3549, ΜΕΘ 4635 a, b, ΜΕΘ 4721). One such example (ΜΕΘ 3549) contains very large fragments of crushed pottery or grog temper.[44] Dark inclusions are also frequent in the fabric of this example, but no mica is visible. Other examples contain large amounts of mica. The West Hill material includes examples of both Type I and Type II in Dupont's classification of the Samian amphoras.[45] The main difference between the types is the funnel (Type I) or straight (Type II) neck and the existence of a ring running around the transition of the neck to the shoulder (Type II).[46] Type I is dated to the end of the 7th century B.C. Type II must have been manufactured slightly later, after the beginning of the 6th century B.C., and according to an example from Gurna (Egypt) it lingers on until after the middle of the 6th century B.C.[47]

None of the examples from the material studied carry any graffiti.[48] In the north Aegean, Samian amphoras are popular, although not particularly so in the 6th century B.C. Early Samian amphoras of the 7th century B.C. have been found at Abdera,[49] Sindos,[50] Dikaia,[51] Zone,[52] Thasos,[53] Karabournaki,[54] Oisyme,[55] Poseidi,[56] Akanthos,[57] and Troy.[58]

MILESIAN AMPHORAS (21/4–21/5)

A wide range of transport amphoras originating from Miletos was identified in the West Hill assemblage. At least ten different vessels have been identified, while an additional inscribed example is known from the Hypogeion assemblage.[59] A typology of Milesian amphoras remains to be done, but based on the studies undertaken so far, the West Hill material was divided into three groups.[60]

Like Samian ones, Milesian amphoras come in a variety of fabrics. The typical Milesian amphora fabric has a beige/yellow-colored surface, which differs from the reddish surface of the Samian amphora. Milesian clay contains abundant silver and less gold mica, and quite a few small black inclusions. Occasionally, it contains small white inclusions, as well.

The standard type of Milesian transport amphora (Group 1), which reaches its final form in the first half of the 6th century B.C., is represented by several examples from the West Hill, **21/4** being one of them. The most distinctive morphological feature of the standard type is the high, thin rim, which flares outward. Below the rim there are always one or two ridges overhanging around the neck.[61] An example of a rim and neck of an amphora from Ephesos is very similar to **21/4** at Methone and is dated to the end of the 7th century B.C.[62] In Histria, an example identical to Methone **21/4** has been dated to the first half of the 6th century B.C.[63] The production of this type, therefore, spans the end of the 7th and first half of the 6th centuries B.C.

Many interesting examples of Milesian amphoras were found in the assemblage of the West Hill; among them is a very rare example (ΜΕΘ 4739) decorated with brown slip. Decorated Milesian transport containers are very rarely exported. In fact, they were once thought to have been produced and circulated exclusively within Miletos.[64] Another example of a Milesian amphora displays a handle peculiarity: it has one oval and one double-ribbed handle (ΜΕΘ 3546). This morphological feature is rare and only one other example has been recorded so far.[65] Such distinctive features reinforce the hypothesis that multiple workshops scattered around the area of Miletos and Caria, and down to south Ionia and Lycia, produced the same types of amphoras at the same time.[66] Conversely, such unusual characteristics could be specific markers to indicate different contents within the container.

The second group of Milesian amphoras from the West Hill consists of examples that do not resemble the standard Milesian type of the period (Group 1). **21/5**, which is the main representative of this group, is made of a fabric similar to the Group 1 amphoras (beige/buff in color with mica and black inclusions, while some white inclusions are present as well), but it is morphologically very different. It is a significantly smaller vessel and has a straight neck profile with a small straight rim. The handles also differ; they are flatter, thinner, and longer than **21/4**. Only two other examples like that of **21/5** are known, one from Salamis on Cyprus and another from Histria, and both have been dated to the first half of the 6th century B.C.[67]

A third group of Milesian amphoras with different fabric characteristics has also been identified in the Methone West Hill material.

Of the Milesian examples found at Methone, only three carry graffiti, in the form of either letters or other symbols.[68] The content of the Milesian amphoras is thought to have been olive oil.[69]

Milesian amphoras have a limited distribution in the north Aegean.[70] Examples from Krania[71] and Anchialos,[72] preserving traces of painted decoration and horizontal ridges on the neck, were dated to the Late Geometric II period and have been tentatively considered Milesian. The example from the Methone Hypogeion dates to the end of the 8th to the beginning of the 7th century B.C.[73] Furthermore, a table amphora originating from Miletos, discovered at Karabournaki in Thessaloniki, probably dates to the 7th century B.C.[74] The standard Milesian type, developed at the end of the 7th century and first half of the 6th century B.C., is found at Abdera,[75] on Thasos[76]—where some unpublished examples with painted decoration have also been discovered—at Karabournaki,[77] and at Oisyme.[78]

AMPHORAS FROM LESBOS (21/6–21/7)

There are 21 examples which, with relative certainty, can be attributed to workshops on the island of Lesbos. From these, at least nine different vessels can be identified. Another eight examples have been published by Antonis Kotsonas from the Hypogeion assemblage.[79]

Lesbian amphoras are traditionally divided into two series: gray and red. Mark Lawall was the first to argue that Lesbian transport vessels could be made from several other fabrics, with colors such as tan, brown, and white,[80] and an example made of brown clay could potentially be identified among the Methone material. Aside from the varying color, the Lesbian fabric is characterized by abundant mica, white inclusions, and grits. Examples of the gray or red series have been found in the Methone assemblage and have been classified into different groups (four groups corresponding to the gray series and two for the red series) according to the fabric and morphological characteristics of the amphoras identified.

The standard amphora type of the early 6th century B.C. is widely represented in the West Hill material (**21/6**). As Kotsonas has recently noted, the gray series of Lesbian amphoras can be made of either a dark gray fabric that tends to be handmade, or a light gray fabric that is usually wheelmade.[81] Examples of the group, typified by **21/6**, contain a lot of mica and many dark and white inclusions. This type has a thin protruding rim, a downward-slanting neck, and an emphatic bulbous belly with its diameter set high, while the body tapers toward a ring-shaped foot. The handles are circular in section and end in a so-called "rat tail," all typical characteristics of Lesbian amphoras.[82] Although a detailed analysis of these examples is beyond the scope of this chapter, it is important to note that there are examples that demonstrate continuity with imported Lesbian transport vessels from the late 8th until the middle of the 6th century B.C., well before the appearance of the standard type. In addition to their continuous presence, there is a noteworthy variety of Lesbian amphoras, which includes examples with pseudo-twisted handles, the distribution of which is limited.[83] It is tempting to think that a special type of Lesbian wine was carried in such a vessel. Examples of the standard type of the red series (dating to the first half of the 6th century B.C.) have been found at Methone (ΜΕΘ 4150, ΜΕΘ 4032, ΜΕΘ 4747, ΜΕΘ 4839), but another group of four examples, which seem to belong to the same type, have a coarser red fabric (ΜΕΘ 4595, ΜΕΘ 4600, ΜΕΘ 4668, and possibly ΜΕΘ 4813) with more white, and fewer red, inclusions.

Finally, **21/7** is an interesting example. It is made from a red-colored fabric with chunky white inclusions, smaller white and dark inclusions, and abundant mica. It is a tall vessel with a convex rim, a straight, cylindrical stout neck, and a pear-shaped body that tapers into a wide ring foot. Its profile does not match any of the classified Lesbian amphora types.[84] Nevertheless, this example preserves some features of the standard Lesbian amphora type, such as the circular-section handles, the pear-shaped body, and the ring-shaped foot; however, the short, squat, straight neck and the short handles are not typical of Lesbian amphora production of this period (beginning of the 6th century B.C.) and could more easily be associated with earlier examples of the Lesbian series that date to the beginning of the 7th century B.C.[85]

Similar amphoras seem to have been found at Akanthos and Oisyme and were named amphoras of "Lesbian type."[86] It is possible that these amphoras were manufactured in the north Aegean.[87] Bearing in mind that there is strong evidence of workshop activity at Methone,[88] including a misfired piece of a Late Geometric Euboianizing skyphos that suggests possible pottery production on site,[89] could Methone perhaps also be a possible place of production for this amphora type? Further evidence and a detailed study of the material will hopefully shed light on such a hypothesis.

Graffiti are often inscribed on Lesbian amphoras. An interesting assemblage comes from the Hypogeion of Methone, where a name in the genitive (ΑΝΤΙΚΥΔΕΟΣ) was incised after firing on the neck.[90] Interestingly, all "Lesbian type" amphoras from Akanthos have graffiti,[91] and the Methone example (**21/7**) is no exception, as it preserves a graffito below one handle (Fig. 21.6).

In the north Aegean, Lesbian transport amphoras are quite widely distributed.[92] Examples of the late 8th to early 7th century have been found in the Hypogeion at Methone.[93] Fragments of Lesbian amphoras dating to late 7th and first half of the 6th centuries B.C. have been recorded in sizable quantities at Karabournaki,[94] Nea Philadelphia, Sindos,[95] Archontiko, Therme, Chalastra, Gona, Toumba Thessalonikis, and Lebet (Polichni). Several sites in Chalkidike (Nea Kallikrateia,

Sane, Mende, Poseidi,[96] Aphytis,[97] and Akanthos),[98] many sites in eastern Macedonia and Thrace (Oisyme,[99] Argilos,[100] Neapolis, Thasos, Stryme,[101] Maroneia,[102] and Abdera[103]), and Hephaistia on Lemnos[104] also yielded Lesbian amphoras.

SOS AMPHORAS (ATTIC AND EUBOIAN) (21/8–21/9)

Examples of Attic amphoras that are attributed to either SOS or *à la brosse* types are particularly numerous among the West Hill pottery material. After Chian amphoras, they constitute the second largest group of such commodity containers. At least 19 different vessels were identified, four of which could be attributed to the *à la brosse* type and 11 to the SOS type. The remaining examples could not be securely attributed to a particular type. Seven inscribed examples of SOS amphoras were found in the Hypogeion of Methone,[105] and consequently SOS and *à la brosse* amphoras are present in Methone from the late 8th to the middle of the 6th century B.C.

The West Hill finds were divided into three fabric groups based on Kotsonas' classification of the Hypogeion material.[106] The classification was made on the basis of the frequency of mica, inclusions, and the color of the clay.

The SOS and *à la brosse* amphoras from the West Hill present a remarkable variety. However, due to the summary nature of this contribution and the incomplete state of the study, only two examples will be presented here. **21/8** is an example with a straight, cylindrical rim and a thick raised ring placed directly below it. The placement of the ring below the rim is typical of SOS amphoras dated before the beginning of the 6th century B.C., whereas the placement of the ring lower on the neck is an indication of a later date.[107] Chalkidian-Euboian SOS amphoras usually present a notch, instead of a groove, at this same spot.[108] Nevertheless, **21/8** presents an uncommon decoration that could possibly be Euboian: a circle with a cross in the middle and framed by two zigzag motifs covers the neck. This motif is known from examples in Eretria and Pithekoussai and dated to the Protocorinthian A period.[109] Together with **21/8**, a locally made Subgeometric skyphos and a fragment of an amphora from the Thermaic Gulf were found, and thus the date provided by the Eretrian example could apply to the Methone example as well, although the Methone piece could be slightly later. If the dating is correct, then this is one of the earliest fragments of the West Hill material.

21/9 is a complete example of the *à la brosse* type. It is characterized by a cup-shaped rim that flares outward and has no ring below it. These changes in the SOS rim profile take place toward the end of the 7th and the beginning of the 6th century B.C. Moreover, the handles arch and become smaller while the shoulder broadens and becomes very flat. The foot is tall and flares outward. **21/9** also displays the typical *à la brosse* decoration; the vessel is covered with red paint—usually worn off—while the neck, handles, and upper part of the shoulder are left plain and undecorated. This shoulder feature is what differentiates the *à la brosse* type from the SOS type with its decorated neck.

Finally, one other example from the West Hill assemblage deserves mention. It preserves part of the neck and shoulder of an amphora. The fragment is coated with a cream slip, and painted with orange zigzig lines. This is a rather odd decoration for an Attic workshop. Moreover, while Attic amphora fabrics include red and white inclusions of different sizes and frequencies, such inclusions are not present in the Chalkidian-Euboian amphoras. Instead their fabric is pink-to-red in color and devoid of inclusions. The clean fabric of the Methone example(s) contains very little mica and has very few small inclusions. For this reason, a Chalkidian-Euboian origin for this particular example is suggested. An example from the Hypogeion has also been identified as originating from Chalkis,[110] while a similar vessel was found in Mende.[111]

Five examples carry graffiti.[112] Three of these graffiti were scratched onto the vessels after firing and could be either elaborate commercial marks (Fig. 21.7), or parts of inscriptions. Two examples were incised before firing. SOS and *à la brosse* amphoras are found in quite a few settlements in the north Aegean,[113] such as Karabournaki,[114] Argilos, Poseidi,[115] Amphipolis, Oisyme,[116] Pitane,[117] Archontiko,[118] Anchialos,[119] Toumba Thessalonikis,[120] Mende,[121] Torone,[122] Abdera,[123] and on the island of Samothrace.[124]

CORINTHIAN AMPHORAS (21/10)

Twenty-three Corinthian amphora sherds were identified in the West Hill pottery assemblage, belonging to at least five different vessels. Among them there was a near-complete amphora (**21/10**) and the upper part of a hydria. One Corinthian amphora was published from the Hypogeion assemblage.[125]

The examples from the West Hill were divided into two different fabric groups. Both are equally coarse but the first has a more reddish fabric with red inclusions, while the second is made of a more yellowish fabric and contained more gray inclusions. All the examples belong to Corinthian amphora Type A. This type appears already in the 8th century B.C. It has a broad and trapezoidal projecting or outturned rim attached to a wide, cylindrical stout neck from where rounded handles arch down to the top of the shoulder. The large spherical body of Type A tapers to a cylindrical toe. This toe becomes narrower throughout the 7th century B.C. **21/10** has both the fabric and morphological characteristics of Type A, yet its dimensions are smaller and, therefore, it has been classified as a variant of the Corinthian Type A.[126]

Three of the Corinthian amphora examples carry graffiti, one having been made before firing. Corinthian amphoras are not widely distributed in the north Aegean.[127] Two examples found in Anchialos are dated to the middle of the 8th century B.C.[128] These pieces belong to the Geometric amphora tradition originally defined by Christopher Pfaff.[129] The example from the Hypogeion at Methone is dated to the same period. If this dating is correct, then these examples are among the earliest exports of Corinthian transport amphoras in the Mediterranean basin. Corinthian amphoras of the Archaic period in the north Aegean have been found in Karabournaki,[130] Oisyme,[131] Abdera,[132] Argilos, Poseidi, and Krania.[133]

LAKONIAN AMPHORA (21/11)

Among the West Hill pottery only one amphora from Lakonia was discovered. This Lakonian example has a buff purple fabric with many white inclusions and appears to match Alan Johnston's description of the Lakonian fabric from the Kommos examples.[134]

21/11 belongs to Paola Pelagatti's Lakonian amphoras Type 2 and Conrad Stibbe's Groups H and I. This type tends to have a paler red and less micaceous fabric than Pelagatti's Type 1.[135] The morphology is described as having a semicircular rim (the outer surface is concave), flat and horizontal on the top and, as a result, it projects outward quite a bit. This description perfectly matches the rim features of the Methone example. Usually Type 2 has a collar below the rim, which is angular and pointed,[136] but instead **21/11** has a ridge right in the middle of the neck. This type also has a squat neck with vertical strap handles that attach from the middle of the neck to the lower shoulder. The body is ovoid and rests on a wide ring foot, which is very similar to the SOS type, but is narrower than Type 1. Type 2 usually has its neck and shoulder unpainted, but some of the examples have a black painted neck, like one from Gravisca[137] and the example from Methone. Regarding the chronology, the "prototype," as Pelagatti calls it, is dated to the second quarter of the 6th century B.C.[138] This type, however, includes examples dated to the end of the 7th or the beginning of the 6th century B.C.[139] An earlier date is also indicated by the West Hill context, which suggests a date in the earlier part of the 6th century B.C., perhaps even slightly earlier if we take under consideration the morphological similarities of **21/11** to the Abdera examples, which are dated to the third quarter of the 7th century B.C.[140]

Lakonian transport amphoras have a limited distribution in the Aegean (21 examples),[141] and the same holds true for northern Greece.[142] So far, four examples are published from the cemetery in Abdera.[143] Fragments of Lakonian amphoras also come from the site of Karabournaki in Thessaloniki (unpublished) and from Akanthos, where only one out of the three examples can be dated to the 7th century B.C.[144]

LOCAL TRANSPORT AMPHORAS (21/12–21/13)

A final category of transport vessels from the West Hill assemblage includes those made from fabrics local to the north Aegean. Many of the forms identified remain unclassified but are dated to the first half of the 6th century B.C. (a more precise date will be provided after a closer examination of the fine pottery from relevant contexts) and thus constitute the earliest locally manufactured transport amphoras after the Thermaic Gulf type.[145] Their study has not as yet been completed, but a short summary is provided here.

Fragments of seven different groups/types of locally produced transport vessels have been identified up to now, two of which are presented here. **21/12** belongs to Group 2B. "Local Group 2" consists of 14 examples.[146] This group is divided into three subcategories, A, B, and C. Examples belonging to these subcategories share similarities in fabric composition but examples in Group 2A present different morphological characteristics compared to those of 2B and 2C.

21/12 is the most representative example of this group and one of the most interesting among the West Hill material. It is made of a yellow/beige-colored fabric with a sandy texture and contains a large amount of gold mica. The morphological features, however, are quite different from the ones identified for Group 2A. The key difference is that the handles of the Type 2B amphora are circular in section, whereas Type 2A has handles that are flat, straight, and cylindrical in section. In fact, the handles of **21/12** and the whole neck and rim profile look similar to **21/7**; the latter was initially classified as a Lesbian amphora of the red series but was later attributed to the "Lesbian type" category because of the absence of the "rat-tail" handles and other features typical of the Lesbian amphoras. **21/12** was found together with an example of the standard Milesian-type amphora and is therefore dated to the beginning of the 6th century B.C. Interestingly, **21/12** preserves an inscription made before firing on the neck, with the letters ΤΕΛΙ.

"Local Group 7" is another type of locally made amphora. **21/13** belongs to this type and is represented by six examples at Methone. They all share similar morphological and fabric characteristics. They are all made of a reddish brown fabric, which is very rich in gold mica, and contain dark and white inclusions (ΜΕΘ 3949 has the same composition but the fabric has a slightly rougher texture). Examples of this group display a convex and cylindrical rim section that has a notch on the upper part of the neck, and a long, straight cylindrical—and slightly funnel-shaped—type neck with long arching, circular-section handles, which preserve the potter's fingerprints on either side. A narrow groove is found at the juncture of shoulder and neck. The body is ovoid and tapers into a narrow ring foot.

Remarkably, all of the above examples preserve similar graffiti on the rim or neck, made either after or (in two cases) before firing (e.g., **21/13**). Examples of Group 7 amphoras have been examined by the author in Karabournaki, where a variant of this type was also unearthed. Two similar examples were also found in Poseidi in Archaic layers. It is therefore suggested that the type was produced somewhere in the north Aegean and circulated goods to north Aegean sites in the Archaic period.

DISCUSSION

It is hoped that the above synopsis has sufficiently illustrated the remarkable quantity and variety of the imported and local transport vessels found on the West Hill of Methone. Fine pottery also appears in significant quantities in the same assemblage, but the number of imported transport vessels demonstrates the direct or indirect commercial links that the settlement had with other regions in the Aegean and beyond. The commercial nature of Methone is further substantiated by the ceramic evidence from other excavated areas within the settlement, such as the Hypogeion, where imported transport vessels also suggest important commercial links with several regions.[147]

Following the study of the Archaic transport vessels from Methone, a number of questions have emerged primarily concerning the role of the site as a center of trade and production in the north Aegean. First of all, the new archaeological material enriches the known distribution of many types of commercial amphoras and offers an opportunity to reevaluate the commercial networks active in the Archaic period in which Methone clearly participated. At the same time, the results of this study contribute by identifying potential connections between Methone and other regions. Such considerations may clarify the possible reasons for such links and whether products from specific cities were favored more than others at the site. One can also consider the kind of commodities that were being traded, as well as what Methone was trading in exchange. These factors may help explain why and how Methone (or the north Aegean more generally) was incorporated into a well-developed and large-scale trading network from such an early period. Additional questions are related to the reasons why Methone was founded (Chapter 12), the nature of the settlement (Chapters 7–9), and the cultural identity of its residents. Finally, issues of possible leadership or control of Methone's trade may potentially be explored, as well as ideas about economic models and their applicability with Methone as a case study. Although it is impossible to discuss in detail all the issues raised from this study, some observations and general conclusions are presented below.

The first and most obvious conclusion we can draw from this short presentation of the West Hill material is that both long- and short-distance trade took place at Methone. Local trade conducted between settlements within the north Aegean was taking place in the Archaic period, as the new Archaic transport amphora types clearly attest (such as the local **21/12** and **21/13**). Furthermore, the pre-fired inscription of a name preserved on one of the locally manufactured vessels (**21/12**) not only demonstrates that these were vessels used to transport goods, but also suggests that they originated from different producers, who sometimes felt the need to brand their products with their maker's stamp. A signature mark incised or stamped before the firing of a vessel is more likely to indicate the producer or potter of the vessel and contents rather than the trader.

The commodities that these newly identified local types carried could have varied, as could the means of transportation. It is difficult to speculate on the type of commodities carried in these amphoras without the assistance of residue analyses, but if the Thermaic Gulf amphoras were for wine, as recent archaeobotanical evidence has shown,[148] then perhaps these new types may have replaced the earlier Thermaic Gulf amphoras. Their replacement could indicate the emergence of a new brand name or perhaps the product of another north Aegean settlement, which grew in prosperity and started exporting its surplus. The change may also result from the appearance of a different trend in pottery morphology and style. We should, however, note that on the West Hill, some 20 sherds of Thermaic Gulf amphoras were also found, which are not presented in this contribution; this fact indicates that the older and newer transport vessels overlapped for a period of time.[149] Also, at Karabournaki—a settlement with a harbor operating in a similar manner to Methone,[150] but on a smaller scale—a small example of a Methone "Local Type 7" was found. Whatever commodity these vessels were carrying, it must have been sought-after, if it was traded in vessels of different sizes.

Finally, it is important to emphasize that production and circulation of local products—so far primarily traced by the distribution of Thermaic Gulf amphoras—did not cease during the Archaic period and restart in the late 6th century B.C., as was previously thought. Such a conclusion seems improbable, as there are no obvious reasons for such an interruption to have taken place. In contrast, the newly identified Archaic containers from Methone indicate that the circulation of local products in the north Aegean continued throughout the Archaic period, with no sign of a hiatus, until mass-produced Mendaian, Thasian, and later Akanthian wine amphoras signal a shift in supply and dominate the market from the end of the 6th to the beginning of the 5th centuries B.C.[151] The production of a special vessel shape, regardless of the product it contained, in order to carry commodities, implies the existence of an enterprise built around the circulation of a certain product or products.

Local trade, however, is not only based on the circulation of local products. It is closely associated, instead, with the idea of a local redistributive exchange system. It is thus proposed that goods would flow in from different directions toward a central place or market. This central market place would then serve as a redistributive focal point from where goods would travel again to other settlements, primarily those inland. There is ample evidence to suggest that Methone served as such a place.

The number of imported transport vessels found at Methone provides strong evidence to support the existence of a large-scale, long-distance trade network between different regions during the Archaic period. In order for a site to conduct long-distance trade, certain prerequisites are essential. These include the establishment of a large urban center with specialized craft workshops. In addition to this, an efficient and cost-effective means of transportation was required; sea routes were traversed by merchant ships, while rivers or carts would have transported goods inland. In this way, packaging and transportation, which are major commercial concerns, are facilitated. The above requirements determined location and physical conditions, two of the most critical factors for the shaping of maritime routes and eventually the foundation of commercial towns.

Methone is ideally located for the implementation of such activities. Not only is it situated at the crossroads of major land routes leading to central and western Macedonia but, unlike other coastal settlements of the area, it is located next to one of the safest harbors of the Thermaic Gulf, a feature that gives it a unique advantage. In addition, several navigable rivers are located in close proximity to Methone, and would have offered easy access for the transport of goods to inland settlements and destinations. Finally, the location of Methone, on the doorstep of the Pierian mountains and the gold-rich Echedoros (Gallikos) river, was highly conducive to its transformation into such a large and successful commercial center in the area.

Given the advantageous location of Methone, and its constantly increasing quantity and variety of imports from a wide range of regions in the Mediterranean, one can securely identify it as a hub of commercial activity for central and western Macedonia. We can imagine voluminous heterogenous or homogenous cargoes of ships arriving at its harbor.[152] From Methone, another series of transportation and commercial transactions that involved retailers, middlemen, and navigable rivers would depart for inland settlements, such as Aiani in western Macedonia, which, despite having no direct access to the sea, appears to have been as cosmopolitan as the coastal settlements of the north Aegean.[153] For this reason, network theory, which acknowledges the importance of the good connection of a node to its local environment, enables us to explain how, from a particular trading transaction, a whole commercial network of transactions is built, and bearing in mind the numerous transactions taking place after goods arrived at Methone, this model seems applicable to north Aegean trade.[154] In conclusion, long-distance trade was clearly taking place and, alongside the interregional transactions, local redistribution allows us to identify Methone as a major redistribution or transshipment harbor of central Macedonia.

CATALOGUE

21/1. (ΜΕΘ 2465) Chian Amphora — Fig. 21.1

West Hill #229/020008 (8), destruction layer.

H. 0.685; Diam. (foot) 0.055; max. Diam. rim 0.127; Diam. (body) 0.334.

Reconstructed almost complete; small parts of rim and body missing.

Narrow ring-shaped base; tall body; rim convex and thin; long cylindrical handles.

Fabric Group 1: dark brown 5YR 5/4–6/4 (light reddish brown and reddish brown; core 5B/1 [gray]). Small to medium white inclusions, gray inclusions, and small black inclusions.

Entire vessel covered with chalky-white slip. Thin horizontal bands of red painted onto slip. One band covers the rim both inside and out; another band on the neck and three more on the body at the point of max. diameter. On the shoulder of the vessel on both sides an "S" or 8 pattern, also in red, placed horizontally. The upper and lower attachments of each handle are encircled by a band. Two more bands run along the upper surface of the handles. These bands extend onto the lower body of the vessel and terminate just below the next horizontal band, which runs around the vessel.

Graffito: X on the neck across band.

21/2. (ΜΕΘ 4648) Fragmentary Chian Hydria — Fig. 21.2

West Hill #229/007014, 019, 022–025, north of Wall 14.

P.H. 0.193; Th. (wall) 0.007; Diam. (rim) 0.255; Diam. (max, body) 0.394.

Incomplete, only upper part preserved (rim, neck, body), down to middle of the body, now restored in plaster.

Outturned rim, flat on top. Horizontal handles, thick and cylindrical in section.

Fabric Group 2: orange clay (7.5YR 6/6 reddish yellow) with large and plentiful white inclusions and fewer red inclusions; abundant mica.

Preserved vessel covered with creamy white slip and, on top of this, decoration in red paint. The central motif on the shoulder is not a figure-of-eight placed on its side, as on the amphora (**21/1**), but is a curved motif which covers the entire shoulder area on both sides. The rim is covered with orangey paint, but reserved on the flat rim top; the upper rim surface is instead decorated with sets of small vertical lines. Directly below the rim, three horizontal bands, below which is the central shoulder motif. The area below the shoulder is decorated with a set of four wavy lines. The handles are covered with red paint.

Graffito: X on the neck.

FIGURE 21.1. Chian amphora, **21/1** (MEΘ 2465).
Drawing I. Moschou and T. Ross, photos J. Vanderpool

21/3. (MEΘ 4650) Body Fr, Chian Amphora Fig. 21.2

West Hill #229/016007, 022, 023, Pit 7a.

P.H. (max) 0.065; Th. (wall) 0.009.

Single fr, broken on all sides, preserving small portion of the shoulder.

Preserved body slightly curved.

Fabric Group 1: brownish clay with gray core (5YR 5/4 reddish brown, in places with a brown core). Many small and medium white inclusions and fewer small and medium dark inclusions; abundant silver and gold mica.

Thick creamish slip. Painted decoration consists of two partially preserved sets of concentric mechanically drawn circles, each set consisting of five circles, in orange paint. Remains of a brown horizontal band below.

FIGURE 21.2. Chian hydria, **21/2** (MEΘ 4648), and shoulder fr of Chian amphora, **21/3** (MEΘ 4650). Drawings A. Hooton (**21/2**) and T. Ross (**21/3**), photos J. Vanderpool

21/4. (MEΘ 2675) Milesian Amphora Fig. 21.3

West Hill #229/019001, north section, depth: 0.50 m.

H. 0.600; Diam. (foot) 0.079; Diam. (rim) 0.142; max. Diam. (body) 0.425.

Almost complete, missing only a few small frr of the body.

Narrow, ring-shaped foot; rounded body; cylindrical, slightly flaring neck, which is distinguished from the shoulder by a neat groove. Tall convex rim, underlined by a thin ridge below. Vertical handles, flat and oval in section, slanting slightly inward toward the top, without forming a high arch.

Fabric orange, 5YR 6/6 (reddish yellow), with abundant silver and gold mica; frequent small black inclusions and a few small white inclusions.

Graffito: on both handles, inside one, and on the shoulder an "E" retrograde(?).

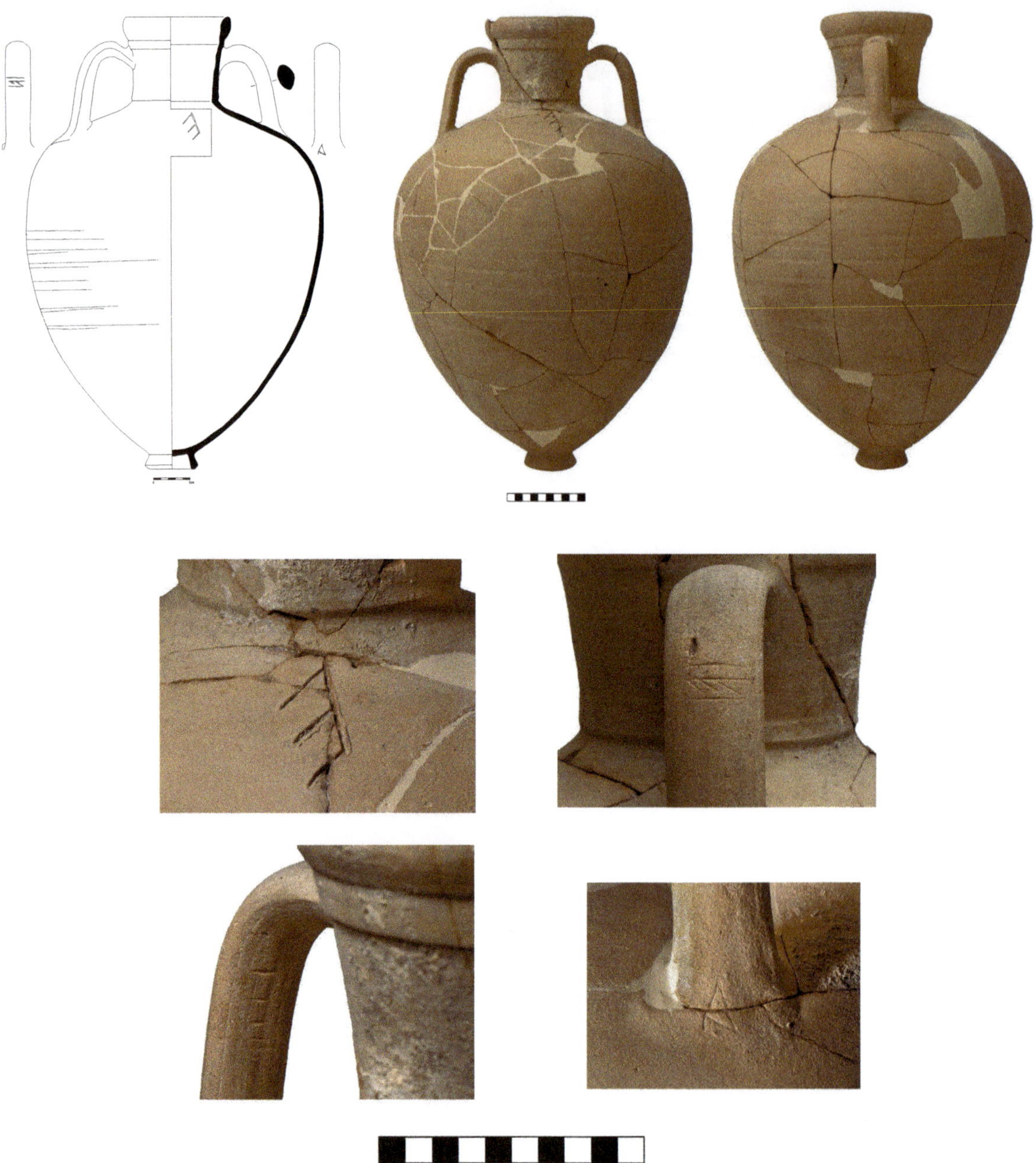

FIGURE 21.3. Milesian amphora, **21/4** (MEΘ 2675).
Drawing I. Moschou and T. Ross, photos J. Vanderpool

21/5. (MEΘ 3542) Fragmentary Milesian Amphora Fig. 21.4

West Hill #229/020 Sector B.

P.H. 0.480; Diam. (rim) 0.088.

Reconstructed from joining frr preserving upper body, neck, and rim of amphora. Evidence of having been fire-affected.

Body rounded; slightly swollen straight neck, with ridge at the transition to shoulder. Vertical rim. Handle long and arching, oval in section.

Fabric very light brown-beige, micaceous, but not as micaceous as **21/4**. Clay fired 7.5YR 7/3 (pink). Besides the white inclusions, there are also small to medium black inclusions that **21/4** does not have.

FIGURE 21.4. Milesian amphora, **21/5** (ΜΕΘ 3542).
Drawing I. Moschou and T. Ross, photos J. Vanderpool

FIGURE 21.5. Lesbian amphora, **21/6** (ΜΕΘ 3543).
Drawing I. Moschou and T. Ross, photos J. Vanderpool

21/6. (ΜΕΘ 3543) Lesbian Amphora Fig. 21.5

West Hill #229/019001 (1) North Section, A36.

H. 0.610; Diam. (base) 0.059; Diam. (rim) 0.127; Diam. (max, body) 0.420.

Reconstructed from frr, almost complete, except for one handle.

Very narrow ring-shaped foot; body with point of max. diameter set quite high. Thin rim, slightly outturned. Handles circular in section.

Fabric brownish, closer to the core orange reddish and gray core. Medium to large white inclusions and medium-size grits. Fabric fired 2.5Y 4/2 (dark grayish brown).

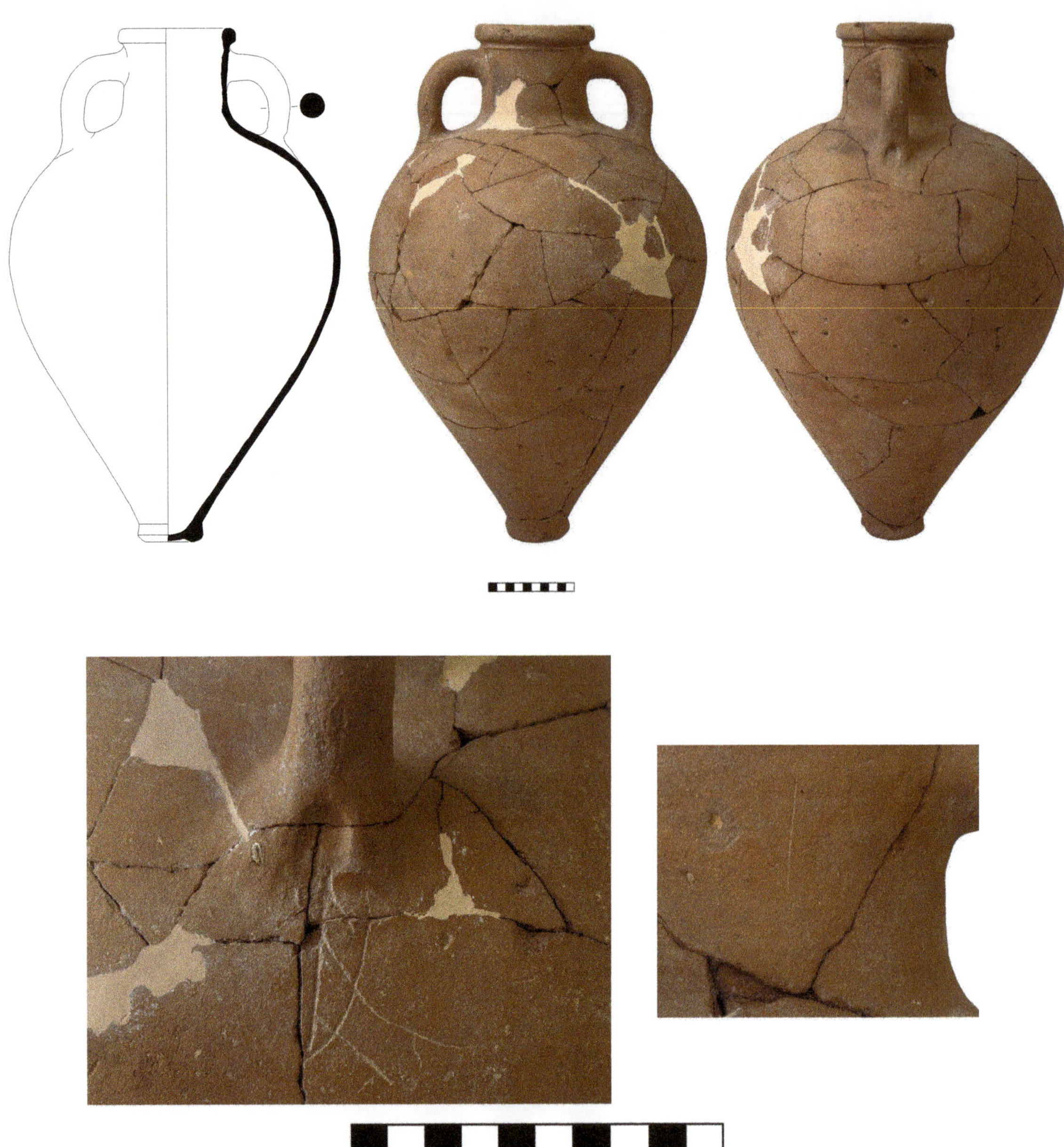

FIGURE 21.6. Lesbian amphora, **21/7** (MEΘ 2462). Drawing I. Moschou and T. Ross, photos J. Vanderpool

21/7. (MEΘ 2462) Lesbian Amphora — Fig. 21.6

West Hill #229/008002, west of Wall 4, depth 0.65 m.

H. 0.600; Diam. (base) 0.078; Diam. (max, body) 0.405.

Reconstructed from many frr almost complete, except for a few missing frr of the body, restored in plaster.

Narrow ring-shaped base; tall body; straight neck, with convex rim. Arching handles, circular in section; no "rat-tail."

Fabric orange, micaceous, and coarse, with many medium to large white inclusions and grit.

Graffito: under one of the handles, and a vertical incised line on the neck.

FIGURE 21.7. Euboian(?) SOS amphora, **21/8** (ΜΕΘ 4820), and SOS amphora *à la brosse*, **21/9** (ΜΕΘ 3202). Drawings I. Moschou and T. Ross, photos J. Vanderpool

21/8. (ΜΕΘ 4820) SOS Amphora (Euboian?) Fig. 21.7

West Hill #229/027004, southern part of the trench.

P.H. 0.090; Diam. (rim) 0.165; Th. 0.020.

Single fr preserving portion of rim and upper neck.

Vertical neck, flaring slightly upward; rounded rim, with small ridge immediately below.

Fabric clean reddish clay with some small black and some small white inclusions, fired 10YR 7/4.

Decoration in red paint, circle with cross framed by single vertical wavy lines on either side. Rim painted solid.

21/9. (MEΘ 3202) SOS Amphora (*à la brosse*) Fig. 21.7

West Hill 229/019001, north section together with A36.

H. 0.625; Diam. (base) 0.085; Diam. (rim) 0.179; Diam. (max, body) 0.400.

Reconstructed from frr almost complete, except for small missing parts of body.

Comparatively wide and thickish ring base, beveled; cylindrical neck with echinoid-shaped rim. Arching handles, circular in section.

Vessel covered with brownish slip, *à la brosse* technique; neck and handles reserved.

Graffito: one on each side of neck, as shown.

21/10. (MEΘ 3544) Corinthian Amphora Fig. 21.8

West Hill #229/013002, 0140003, black soil.

H. 0.452; Diam. (rim) 0.167; Diam. (max, body) 0.335.

Reconstructed from frr, missing parts of the lower body and one handle.

Rounded body, tapering toward base; cylindrical neck; thick, outturned horizontal rim, with trapezoidal profile. Thick handle, circular in section.

Fabric coarse, reddish yellow, with large inclusions (medium and large gray [quartz] and frequent while impurities). Surface color 10YR 8/3 (very pale brown).

21/11. (MEΘ 2684) Lakonian Amphora Fig. 21.9

West Hill #229/020002.

H. 0.529; Diam. (max, body) 0.367.

Reconstructed from frr almost complete, with only very small portions of the body not preserved.

Ring base, slightly protruding rim, with a rounded outer profile. Handles comparatively small, almost strap in section.

Fabric buff/pinkish, with white inclusions, fired 5YR 6/4 (light reddish brown).

Exterior covered with a brushed-on slip, except for the rim.

FIGURE 21.8. Corinthian amphora, **21/10** (MEΘ 3544).
Drawing I. Moschou and T. Ross, photos J. Vanderpool

FIGURE 21.9. Lakonian amphora, **21/11** (ΜΕΘ 2684).
Drawing I. Moschou and T. Ross, photos J. Vanderpool

21/12. (ΜΕΘ 3545) Local Amphora Fig. 21.10

West Hill #229/013002, 0.40 m south, 0.50 m west, A48, depth 0.42 m.

P.H. 0.380; Diam. (rim) 0.135; Diam. (max, body) 0.365.

Reconstructed from frr preserving only upper part of the vessel, including shoulder, neck, rim, and handles.

Vertical, cylindrical neck, convex protruding rim. Stout, arching handles, round in section.

Fabric yellow/ochre, very sandy, with abundant gold mica, fired 7.5YR 8/6 (reddish yellow).

Graffiti on neck on both sides, on one side: ΤΕΛΙ; on other side large, vertically oriented cross: +.

21/13. (ΜΕΘ 2464) Local Amphora Fig. 21.11

West Hill #229/020.

H. 0.640; Diam. (foot) 0.079; Diam. (rim) 0.142; Diam. (max, body) 0.425.

Reconstructed from frr almost complete, except for small parts of the body.

Narrow ring foot; tall body; vertical neck, sloping slightly in, surmounted by convex protruding rim as **21/12**. Ridge at the juncture of shoulder and neck, another at the height of the upper handle attachment. Arching handles, oval in section.

Fabric orange reddish, very micaceous (gold mica), with many small, medium, and large white inclusions, fired 2.5YR 5/8 (red). Remains of sediment. Unidentified Group 7.

Graffito, inscribed pre-firing, long diagonal stroke on neck.

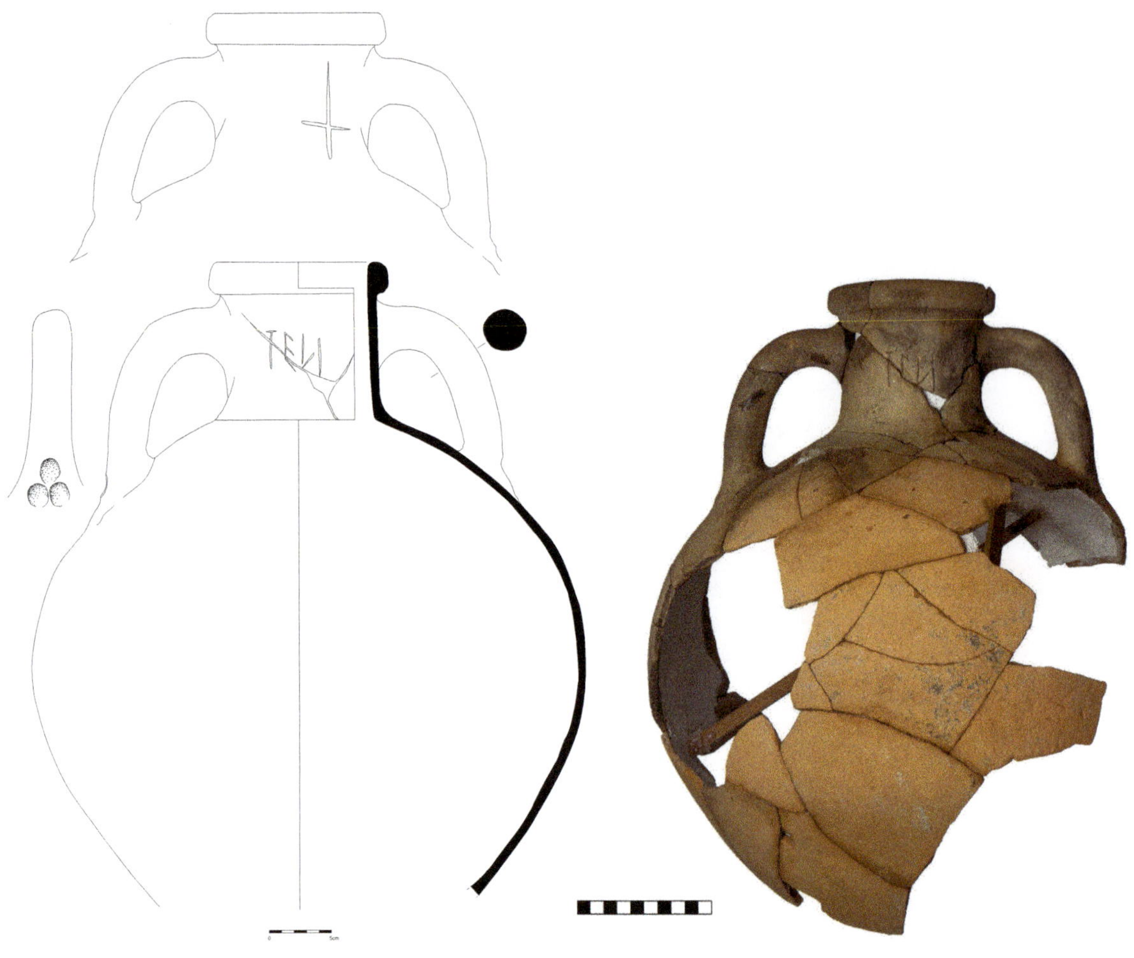

FIGURE 21.10. Local amphora, **21/12** (ΜΕΘ 3545).
Drawing I. Moschou and T. Ross, photos J. Vanderpool

FIGURE 21.11. Local amphora, **21/13** (ΜΕΘ 2464).
Drawing I. Moschou and T. Ross, photos J. Vanderpool

NOTES

1 The earliest evidence of habitation on the West Hill goes back to the Early Iron Age in the form of apsidal buildings, while during the Late Bronze Age (LBA) period, the hill was used as a cemetery for the settlement largely confined to the East Hill; see Bessios, Athanassiadou, and Noulas 2008, pp. 246–248; Chapters 1, 6.

2 For a summary, see Chapters 1 and 19.

3 Bessios and Noulas 2012; for an overview of some of the Corinthian, East Greek, and Attic fine pottery, see Chapters 1, 19, 22, and 23.

4 See Bessios, Athanassiadou, and Noulas 2008, and Chapters 1 and 18.

5 See also Kasseri 2015.

6 For fabric analyses of the amphoras from the Hypogeion, including petrographic studies, see Kiriatzi et al. 2012.

7 Kotsonas 2012, pp. 201–205: a total of 20 Chian amphoras are estimated to come from the Hypogeion deposit.

8 Chian amphoras continue to be imported to the area in later periods as well (see, for example, Filis 2019, pp. 244–245, fig. 1). Plenty of Chian amphoras have been found in the cemeteries of neighboring Pydna (Brachionidou 2019).

9 Lambrino 1938, pp. 100–113, 124–128; Ghali-Kahil 1960, p. 35; Zeest 1960, p. 16; Dupont 1982, pp. 194–198; Di Sandro 1986, p. 53; Jones 1986, p. 283; Slaska 1986, pp. 55–57; Oettli 1994, pp. 38–44; Sourisseau 1997, pp. 129–130, 133; Dupont 1998, p. 146; Monachov 1999, pp. 33–60; Aquilué Abadias et al. 2000, p. 330; de Domingo and Johnston 2003, p. 30; Monachov 2003a, pp. 10–24, 183–188; Seifert 2004, p. 22; Pelagatti 2006, pp. 64–65; Nedev and Gyuzelev 2011, pp. 63–64; for Mende, see Moschonissioti et al. 2005, pp. 249–267; for Methone, see Kiriatzi et al. 2012.

10 Boardman 1978, p. 288; Jones 1986, pp. 283–284. See also de Domingo and Johnston 2003, pp. 33–34. For chemical analysis see Seifert and Yalçin 1995, pp. 24–25; Seifert 1996, pp. 35–36; Seifert 2004, p. 49; Whitbread 1995, p. 143. See also Sezgin 2004, pp. 180–181, n. 18; Gassner 2011.

11 Dupont 1998, p. 148.

12 Dupont 1998, p. 146; Whitbread 1995, p. 135. For evidence of the earlier appearance of Chian amphoras, in the 8th century, see Cook 1958–1959, p. 14 (Smyrna); *Pithekoussai* I, p. 429, pl. 211, no. 397 (Pithekoussai); Docter 2000, p. 74 (Toscanos and Carthage); Kotsonas 2012, pp. 197–201 (Methone).

13 For further information on the amphoras from the Hypogeion, see Chapter 12.

14 The Hypogeion example is unpublished and has a slightly different decoration. It is decorated with concentric circles between sets of wavy lines, while the example from the West Hill is decorated with concentric circles between sets of straight lines.

15 The vessel was seen in the storerooms of archaeological material from Klazomenai in July 2013. Another Chian vessel (protocalyx) was found in Pitane, see A. Lemos 1991, p. 8, pl. 10, no. 100.

16 Kasseri 2015, p. 156, cat. no. 56, p. 415, from #229/01510, Pit 8. This type is dated to the end of the 7th and beginning of the 6th centuries B.C. The name comes from a site in Scythia (Krakhov, Ukraine) where it was first found. For further information about this type see Monachov 2000, pp. 172–173.

17 Johnston 1993, p. 375; Boardman 1999, p. 122; Panagou 2010, pp. 416–418; Dupont and Skarlatidou 2012.

18 Tiverios 1993b, pp. 1490, 1492; Hansson and Foley 2008, pp. 1169–1176; Chapter 12.

19 Lawall 2011a, p. 27; Kotsonas 2012, p. 203.

20 See ΜΕΘ 3730, ΜΕΘ 4021, ΜΕΘ 4248, ΜΕΘ 3738, ΜΕΘ 3847, ΜΕΘ 2465, ΜΕΘ 3715. See also Kotsonas 2012, p. 459, no. 131 for an identical graffito of overlapping circles drawn with calipers. For Chian graffiti see Csapo, Johnston, and Geagan 2000, p. 122, no. 53; Kenzelmann Pfyffer, Theurillat, and Verdan 2005, pp. 66–67, no. 26; *SEG* 55.980. BE 2005.385; Johnston 2004, p. 737.

21 Kotsonas 2012, pp. 201–205.
22 Gimatzidis 2010, p. 16; p. 288, n. 1789; p. 290, nos. 660, 662, pl. 89.
23 Cook 1958–1959, p. 14 (Smyrna); *Pithekoussai* I, p. 429, pl. 211, no. 397 (Pithekoussai), for examples that are probably Klazomenian; Docter 2000, p. 74, for early specimens in Toscanos and Carthage.
24 Skarlatidou 2010, pp. 130–131.
25 Jung and Gimatzidis 2008, p. 149, fig. 15b; Gimatzidis 2017, pp. 265–267.
26 Filis 2012a, pp. 266–267, fig. 1.
27 Bernard 1964, pp. 137–138, figs 10, 50, but much of the material is unpublished.
28 Nikolaidou-Patera 2007, p. 90, pl. 31, fig. 6b.
29 Koukouli-Chrysanthaki and Marangou-Lerat 2012, pp. 324–325, figs. 3, 4, 7.
30 Personal examination of the material.
31 Moschonissioti 2010, p. 215.
32 Tiverios 2009b, p. 392, fig. 10.
33 Tiverios 2010, p. 16.
34 Jung and Gimatzidis 2008, p. 149, fig. 15b.
35 Soueref 1992, fig. 108b.
36 Kefalidou 2012, pp. 94–95, fig. 5.
37 Karadima and Koutsoumanis 1992, p. 497.
38 Lungu 2010, pp. 50, 58.
39 Koçak Yaldır 2011, pp. 366–367.
40 Zachos 2012.
41 Frasca 1993, pp. 61–62, fig. 28.
42 This is why Samian and Milesian amphoras are often best studied together. Many recent sets of analyses have come to this conclusion and, more recently, on those from Eretria, see Johnston 1990, p. 47, n. 19; Dupont 1998, pp. 165, 176–177; Lawall 1995, pp. 186–191; Whitbread 1995, pp. 129–130; Dupont 2000, p. 59; de Domingo and Johnston 2003, p. 31; Gassner 2011, noting that there may have been production in Ephesos.
43 See, for example, Kotsonas 2012, pp. 457–458, no. 123.
44 Dupont (1998, p. 165) gives a similar description for Samian amphoras: "pieces of massive fabric."
45 Dupont (1998, p. 165) calls them a "closely related series of shapes that evolve side by side."
46 There have been some doubts as to Samian provenance of Type I. Type II most likely originates from Samos; see Dupont 2000, p. 59; Dupont 2007b, p. 43.
47 Dupont 1998, p. 165, n. 160.
48 See Kotsonas 2012, pp. 194–199 for inscribed examples from the Hypogeion.
49 Skarlatidou 2010, p. 165, n. 49; p. 193, n. 106, and personal examination of the material.
50 Gimatzidis 2010, p. 288, n. 1789; pp. 289–290, no. 576, pl. 72.
51 Karadima 2009, pp. 152, 162, fig. 17; Triantaphyllos and Tasaklaki 2012.
52 Karadima 2009, pp. 152, 162, fig. 18.
53 Empereur and Simosi 1989, p. 380.
54 Manakidou 2010, p. 463, n. 11.
55 Koukouli-Chrysanthaki and Marangou-Lerat 2012, pp. 326–327.
56 Moschonissioti 2012, p. 393, a general mention of Archaic East Greek pottery, but after personal examination of the material, Samian amphoras of both Types I and II were identified.
57 Filis 2012a, pp. 271–273; Filis 2013, pp. 70–71.
58 Lawall 2002, pp. 202–203, 223, no. 77.
59 Kotsonas 2012, pp. 199–201, Map 16; pp. 460–461, no. 126 (ΜΕΘ 2335).
60 Cf. Seifert 2004, pp. 36–49; Kerschner and Mommsen 2005; Mommsen, von Haugwitz, and Johrens 2010.

61 A single example with three ridges has been reported only at Miletos; see Naso 2005, p. 75, nos. 4 and 5. For a full description of the shape of the standard Milesian type see Dupont 1998, p. 174.
62 Kerschner and Mommsen 2005, pp. 119–120, figs. 1, 6.
63 Lambrino 1938, p. 175, fig. 127; for Histria, see further Dupont et al. 1999.
64 Dupont 1998, pp. 170–177; see also Seifert 2004, nos. 113–117 for decorated examples.
65 One example on the island of Kos (unpublished); see also Dupont 1998, p. 174.
66 Dupont 2000, pp. 57–58; Filis 2012a, p. 273.
67 Calvet and Yon 1977, pl. 11.120; Dupont 1998, p. 175, fig. 23.8 h, "funnel-shaped neck"; Dupont 2007a, p. 625.
68 For graffiti on Milesian amphoras, see Lawall 1995, pp. 191–193; Dupont 1998, p. 177; Dupont 1999, pp. 11, 15; Johnston 2004, pp. 742, 750–751; Dupont 2007a, p. 624.
69 Naso 2005; Bîrzescu 2009.
70 Kotsonas 2012, pp. 203–204, Map 17.
71 Filis 2012a, p. 273; Gimatzidis 2017, pp. 267, 270, figs. 9, 12a, 13–15.
72 Gimatzidis 2006.
73 Kotsonas 2012, pp. 199–201. The so-called "Methonaean" amphoras, originally believed to be locally produced (Kotsonas 2012, pp. 146–150), have eventually proven, through petrographic analysis, to come from Miletos, see Kiriatzi et al. 2012; Kotsonas et al. 2017, p. 9, n. 1.
74 Filis 2012a, p. 273, fig. 10.
75 Skarlatidou 2010, p. 89, no. K 193.
76 Grandjean 1992, nos. 29, 35, figs. 4, 5.
77 Tiverios 2009b, p. 392.
78 Koukouli-Chrysanthaki and Marangou-Lerat 2012, p. 326, fig. 8.
79 Kotsonas 2012, pp. 201–205. For Lesbian and Thasian amphoras, see Clinkenbeard 1982, 1986.
80 Lawall 2002, pp. 215–216; see also new examples from Spain in Aquilué Abadias et al. 2000, pp. 330–331, fig. 39.10–11.
81 Kotsonas 2012, p. 203. Examples of the wheelmade category have also been found on the West Hill.
82 Dupont 1998, pp. 156–157, fig. 23.4b.
83 The examples known are dated to the end of the 7th century B.C., see Csapo, Johnston, and Geagan 2000, p. 124, no. 67; p. 125, no. 74 (Kommos); and Skarlatidou 2010, p. 178, no. K63 (Abdera).
84 Dupont 1998, pp. 156–157; Bîrzescu 2005, pp. 45–75.
85 See, for instance, an example from the Hypogeion of Methone, Kotsonas 2012, p. 340, no. 4.
86 Dupont 2009, pp. 37–47, for detailed description of the type; for the Akanthos example see Filis 2013, p. 70, fig. 11:g.
87 Filis (2011) has proposed Oisyme.
88 See Chapter 19; see also Bessios, Athanassiadou, and Noulas 2008, p. 248.
89 See, for example, Bessios 2012a, p. 94, fig. 65.
90 Bessios, Tzifopoulos, and Kotsonas 2012, pp. 340–342, no. 4.
91 Filis 2011.
92 Kotsonas 2012, pp. 208–209, Map 18.
93 Kotsonas 2012, pp. 201–205. Examples are also known from other regions in the Mediterranean, including Lesbos, Smyrna, Kommos, and Tell Qudadi.
94 Tiverios 2009b, p. 392; Manakidou 2010, p. 463, n. 11. The majority of the samples are of the gray series.
95 Gimatzidis 2010, p. 16.
96 Both red and gray series examples of Lesbian transport amphoras were seen by the author.
97 All of the material above without references is unpublished.

98 For Akanthos, see Filis 2011.
99 Koukouli-Chrysanthaki and Marangou-Lerat 2012, pp. 323–324, fig. 3.
100 After personal examination of the material, two examples of the gray series and one of the red series can be confirmed.
101 Terzopoulou 1995, p. 658.
102 Karadima 2009, pp. 152, 162, fig. 19.
103 The example belongs to the second half of the 7th century B.C., see Skarlatidou 2010, p. 178, no. K63.
104 Beschi 2005, pp. 141–142, no. 197; Danile 2012, p. 87, fig. 14.
105 Kotsonas 2012, pp. 184–190.
106 Kotsonas 2012, pp. 184–186.
107 See *Agora* VIII, p. 42, nos. 25–28 for a comparative presentation of the late 8th- to late 7th-century examples.
108 Johnston and Jones 1978, pp. 111, 133, although it is noted that it is difficult to point to the origin of these details.
109 *Eretria* XX, p. 131, no. 354, pl. 72; Johnston and Jones 1978, pp. 136–137, fig. 8d; Andreiomenou 1983, pl. 53.28; Di Sandro 1986, pl. 1, sg. 2 (Attic?). The Eretrian piece is thought to be Euboian rather than Attic.
110 Kotsonas 2012, p. 191, which has clean clay and decoration peculiarities, such as triple concentric circles and triple triangles.
111 Vokotopoulou and Christidis 1995.
112 Graffiti on SOS and *à la brosse* amphoras are abundant, see Johnston and Jones 1978, pp. 128–132; Johnston 2004, pp. 738–740.
113 Kotsonas 2012, pp. 188–194, Map 14; Gimatzidis 2017, pp. 264–265.
114 Sizable quantities; an SOS amphora with the inscription ΚΑΛ(Λ)ΙΑΣ is dated to the beginning of the 6th century B.C., see Tiverios 2000, p. 519. See also Kotsonas 2012, p. 285, n. 1130 and an example in Panti 2008, p. 279, fig. 15.
115 At both Argilos and Poseidi, examples of SOS amphoras were seen by the author. The majority could be dated to the end of the 7th century B.C.; some are earlier.
116 Koukouli-Chrysanthaki and Marangou-Lerat 2012, p. 328, fig. 14.
117 Johnston and Jones 1978, pp. 112–113.
118 Chrysostomou 2011, p. 300.
119 Oettli 1994, pp. 22–23.
120 Chavela 2006, pp. 194–195.
121 Moschonissioti 2010, p. 215.
122 Paspalas 2001, pp. 320–321, no. 5.30.
123 Skarlatidou 2010, p. 136, n. 29.
124 Karadima and Koutsoumanis 1992, p. 497.
125 Kotsonas 2012, p. 186.
126 See Koehler 1992, table 1b; Cavalier 1985, fig. 2, no. 3 for parallels.
127 Kotsonas 2012, pp. 186–188, map 13.
128 Gimatzidis 2010, pp. 283–285, no. 617.
129 Pfaff 1988, pp. 29–31.
130 Manakidou 2010, p. 463, n. 11.
131 Koukouli-Chrysanthaki and Marangou-Lerat 2012, p. 329, fig. 15.
132 Skarlatidou 2010, p. 171.
133 At both Argilos and Poseidi, Archaic Corinthian transport amphoras of Type A were seen by the author. For Krania, see Gimatzidis 2017, pp. 263–264.

134 Johnston 1993, pp. 358–362.

135 Pelagatti 1992, pp. 134–135, fig. 49; Stibbe 2000, p. 71.

136 Not elongated and curving as in Group G, for which see Stibbe 2000, p. 71.

137 Boitani 1990, p. 56, no. 98, fig. 135.

138 Pelagatti 1992, pp. 134–135, fig. 49.

139 Stibbe 2000, p. 71.

140 Skarlatidou 2010, pp. 144, 146, nos. K98, K60, K269; p. 150, no. K83; the author identified six examples in total after personal examination.

141 For statistical data and distribution in the Mediterranean, see Coudin 2009, p. 15, table 1. The majority of Lakonian transport amphoras in the Aegean have been found at Kommos, see Johnston 1993, pp. 358–362.

142 For an overview of Lakonian pottery in the north Aegean, see Pipili 2012, pp. 197–208.

143 Skarlatidou 2010, pp. 144, 146, nos. K98, K260, K269; p. 150, no. K83.

144 Filis 2013, p. 71.

145 Fragments of Thermaic Gulf amphoras (Kotsonas 2012, pp. 121–122, 154–162, map 5, nos. 77–85, or Catling amphoras of Type II), which are generally dated between the early 8th and early 7th centuries B.C., but more likely continue in the 7th century (see Gimatzidis 2010, pp. 261–269; Kotsonas 2012, p. 158, n. 523, for a late example from Abdera), have also been found in the West Hill assemblage. For north Aegean amphoras of later date, see Filis 2019, pp. 248–249, fig. 5. See also Monachov 2003b for amphoras from unidentified centers of the north Aegean.

146 Classification has been made according to the study of the West Hill transport vessel material, examined for my doctoral thesis (Kasseri 2015).

147 Kotsonas 2012, pp. 184–213; Kotsonas, Chapter 12.

148 Valamoti 2003, p. 202; see also Kiriatzi et al. 2013; Kotsonas et al. 2017, p. 18, for residue analysis indicating plant resins and beeswax (if used as sealants, both could indicate wine).

149 Examples of the Thermaic Gulf amphoras have been found even in contexts of the beginning of the 6th century B.C., as noted by Kotsonas 2012, p. 158, n. 523 (a small amphora from Abdera in Skarlatidou 2010, p. 190, n. 100, no. K 117; 357); Filis 2019, pp. 248–249, fig. 5.

150 See below, discussion of the hypothesis about redistribution centers.

151 More categories of locally manufactured fine pottery, such as eggshell wares, were circulated but there are no transport amphoras known from this period.

152 For an argument concerning the relation between a heterogenous cargo and redistribution trade, see Nantet 2010, p. 107.

153 For an overview of Aiani, see Karamitrou-Mentesidi 2008.

154 For network theory, see Stein 2002; Stein 2005b, pp. 8–9, 29–30; Hodos 2006, pp. 6–9; Constantakopoulou 2007; Malkin, Constantakopoulou, and Panagopoulou 2009; Knappett 2011, pp. 28–30; Malkin 2011; Papadopoulos 2011, pp. 129–130; Sherratt 2011a; see also Sherratt 2011b, pp. 16–17; for the north Aegean, see Kotsonas 2012, pp. 233–234, 2015. There is a certain diversity in the way that network theory is conceived by the different researchers: compare, for example, Knappett 2011 and Malkin 2011.

22

THE EAST GREEK FINE POTTERY

John K. Papadopoulos

INTRODUCTION

Following the recently proposed classification of East Greek pottery by Michael Kerschner and Udo Schlotzhauer, I present a small selection of the East Greek pottery found at Methone between 2003 and 2011, beginning with presumed imports from the north, with the "Aiolian" graywares, and progressively moving south.[1] The new classification is based on a division by individual sites or regions of production, with subdivisions into chronological phases, in an open model that can be easily expanded to accommodate new finds or production centers. Moreover, this system incorporates all pottery—and eventually, I hope, other manufactured terracotta objects, including plastic vases, figurines, lamps, spindlewhorls, beads, or buttons[2]—figural or with ornamental decoration, as well as banded and undecorated pottery, into a uniform system.[3] Gone are all-encompassing terms, such as "Rhodian," once traditionally applied to pottery manufactured from Klazomenai to Miletos to various sites on the island of Rhodes,[4] although scholars had already clearly stated that Rhodes was far from the dominant purveyor of things "Rhodian," being rather the place where the so-called "Wild Goat Style" was first found.[5] In using South Ionia (abbreviated to "Si"), to illustrate their new classification, Kerschner and Schlotzhauer distinguish between SiG(eometric), SiA(rchaic), and SiC(lassical) and compare their scheme with Robert Cook's earlier classification of Early Orientalizing, followed by Early, Middle, and Late Wild Goat Style (with its various subphases), followed, in turn, by Fikellura.[6] The great advantage of this new classification system is that it is based on foundations well laid by Cook.

Despite the utility of this new classification system, the core of the problem has always been the all-encompassing term "East Greek," as it covers pottery of a vast region, akin to calling all the pottery from mainland Greece "Greek mainland pottery," rather than Attic, Corinthian, Lakonian, and so on. Furthermore, including some of the major islands of the east Aegean—especially Lesbos, Imbros, Tenedos, Chios, Samos, the Dodecanese, with Rhodes—as East Greek, is like adding Euboia, the Cyclades, and Crete to the same classification as "Greek mainland pottery." Although "East Greek" pottery remains a convenient term, the time is ripe to do away with it, as Kerschner and Schlotzhauer recommend, with new geographical and chronological coordinates.

A related issue, one that affects only a few of the fabrics discussed below—primarily the "Aiolian" graywares and, to a lesser extent, the Ionian cups (*Knickrandschalen*)—is that of local, north Aegean versions of East Greek wares. These are discussed in the relevant sections of this chapter, but I avoid altogether recent attempts to classify the local pottery of the north Aegean with terms such as "colonial," "semi-colonial," "indigenous," and "local," as these terms mean very little in the current state of our knowledge and they are, in and of themselves, highly problematic; terms such as "colonial" and "indigenous" as applied to pottery carry all sorts of assumptions.[7] Another issue is, with the "north Aegean" having now come into its own as a meaningful geographical term, where does East Greece start or stop? Put another way, is Troy, for instance, or Lesbos, for that matter, East Greek or north Aegean, or both?

The aim of this chapter is not to provide a definitive overview of the East Greek pottery from Methone (this would require an entire volume), but rather to present, by way of selected pieces, some of the main categories of the material as preserved.[8] As this chapter presents only the East Greek fine wares, it should be read in conjunction with Antonis Kotsonas's and Alexandra Kasseri's contributions (Chapters 12 and 21) on the commodity containers or amphoras, respectively from the Hypogeion and the West Hill, many of which derive from the same production centers as the fine ware pottery.

"AIOLIAN" GRAYWARE

Aiolis is the northernmost of the regions of East Greece. Long thought to have been "colonized" by immigrants from mainland Greece in the Early Iron Age, the historicity of the "Aiolian migration"—like the "Ionian migrations"—has recently been questioned.[9] Whatever the historicity of this migration, graywares were characteristic for the area, from the Troad in the north to Smyrna in the south, and especially on the large island of Lesbos (Mytilene), throughout prehistory and well into the Early Iron Age, Archaic, and later periods.[10] Cook believed that the Iron Age Greeks who settled this area "rather unusually" adopted the production of grayware.[11] As we shall see, I refer to this pottery as "Aiolian" because it may well have been made locally at Methone, not in Aiolis.

In reviewing where Aiolian grayware has been recorded, Cook noted that it has been found at various places on Lesbos, where, at several sites such as Antissa, it was virtually the only fine ware until the later 6th century B.C.[12] On mainland Aiolis, grayware, as Cook noted, is widespread, but perhaps not as dominant as on Lesbos.[13] It is reported in the Troad, while at Troy itself, as Carl Blegen and his collaborators noted, "About two-thirds of the pottery of Troy VIII consists of a monochrome Grayware, very similar to Lesbian bucchero."[14] Other sites noted by Cook include Pergamon (where grayware was still in use into the Hellenistic era), Myrina, Larisa (Buruncuk), and Phokaia; he also notes that grayware was plentiful at Smyrna before the 7th century B.C.[15] Of these sites, Pergamon has recently furnished important evidence of Aiolian grayware, providing several close parallels for the Methone material.[16] Moreover, Cook anticipated the existence of distinct local versions, if not schools, of Aiolian grayware, and it now seems that we can distinguish, on the basis of elemental analysis, at least a few production centers (see below) on the west coast of Asia Minor and elsewhere. At the time when Cook was working on *East Greek Pottery*, however, little was known archaeologically about Aiolian Kyme—a phenomenon replicated at various sites across mainland Aiolis—and the dearth of substantial stratified contexts of the Archaic period has limited our knowledge of the character and distribution of Aiolian graywares in their home region.

In discussing the technique of the Archaic graywares from Antissa on Lesbos, Winifred Lamb wrote: "The wares are usually light grey and sometimes reddish on the break, while the surface varies from silver-grey to gun-metal according to whether the surface has been polished, enhanced by a wash, or left rough."[17] Elsewhere she adds: "Mica is present in varying quantity."[18] Cook also describes the fabric and the fact that the surfaces were nicely finished, either polished/burnished, or covered with a wash. The burnished surface seen on all or most of the examples from Methone is noteworthy as it often resembles some of the finest examples of Middle Helladic Gray Minyan.[19]

Cook writes: "The clay is as a rule fairly fine and fired a lightish grey; often the exposed surface is polished or has a wash of finer clay. There is a full range of shapes, mostly of standard East Greek types, though they tend to be less precisely articulated than the painted wares. Decoration—on the comparatively few pieces that are decorated—is by incision or less often in relief and usually is sparse. For incision the staple is a wavy line or set of wavy lines."[20]

Nicholas Bayne goes further by pointing out the differences between the gray Aiolian wares of the prehistoric period and those of the first millennium B.C. Unlike the gray pottery of the Bronze Age, which could fire red or buff in addition to gray, the Early Iron Age and Archaic grayware is more consistently gray and is generally of a finer quality.[21] Bayne also noted that the fabric is well levigated, with intrusions never obtruding onto the surface, and that the pottery is better thrown than its prehistoric counterparts, with the result that vessel walls are thinner and made "with greater balance and precision than in the prehistoric period."[22] The color is usually a pale gray, which can be darker near the surface, and there is sometimes a reddish core, though more often than not the pots are fired evenly throughout and rather hard.[23]

Recent excavations beneath the acropolis of Eresos on Lesbos—the birthplace of Sappho—have brought to light an interesting, if only partial, assemblage of Aiolian grayware, in addition to three sherds of Aiolian Wild Goat style attributed to the London Dinos Painter or his/her workshop.[24] Published by Giorgios Zachos, the local grayware represents a wide variety of shapes, including various drinking vessels, amphoras, dinoi, lekanes, kraters, and strainers, as well as larger storage vessels and cooking wares.[25] Zachos notes that several of these shapes and their variants occur elsewhere on Lesbos, including Antissa, Methymna, and Pyrrha, while some, together with their incised decoration, trace their roots back to the local Bronze Age. He also notes that, despite the general uniformity of the series, differences in details show that the various cities of Lesbos followed their own separate paths.[26]

Beyond Lesbos and Aiolian Asia Minor, perhaps the most noteworthy locally produced grayware that has recently come to light is that from Lemnos, where a robust sequence of grayware has been mapped out by Laura Danile, from the very end of the Bronze Age and the beginning of the Early Iron Age through the 7th century B.C.[27] Although several sites on Lemnos have provided evidence of habitation in this period, including Myrina on the west coast and the sanctuary at Chloi on the north coast, only Hephaistia has yielded a broader, more comprehensive grayware sequence, the importance of which lies in the fact that grayware was the primary class of pottery used at the site from the Protogeometric period into the 7th century B.C.[28] Elemental analyses carried out on some of the grayware from Hephaistia have revealed a compatibility of the ware with the local clay sources of the island.[29] The range of shapes is impressive, but notably different from the assemblage of grayware at Methone, the primary vessel forms being the krater (of Danile's Type 1), the stemmed carinated kylix, the beaker, the kalathos, and the fenestrated stand.[30] In the later 8th and earlier 7th century B.C., the Lemnian grayware assemblage expands to include a new type of krater, as well as the carinated kantharos, the carinated kylix without handles, and the jug with cutaway neck.[31] By the 6th century B.C., the repertoire of Lemnian grayware shapes is replaced with something new, encompassing mesomphaloi phialai, small double-handled bowls, jugs, and trefoil oinochoai.[32] Not only is the range of shapes different from those of Methone (with the exception of the krater), most of the Lemnian profiles are different, as Danile notes, from those of Bayne's typology.[33] In her search for comparanda, Danile casts her net wide to include discussion of the Protogeometric and later black (and red) slip wares of Lefkandi, Skyros, and Thessaly, as well as those at Torone, together with related gray/black slip wares from Vergina and elsewhere in the north, including Anchialos-Sindos, Karabounaki, Toumba Thessalonikis, and Assiros, the sites of Mende-Poseidi, Sane, and Akanthos in Chalkidike, and related wares from various sites in northern Pieria, together with the north Aegean islands of Thasos, Samothrace, Lesbos, Chios, and Tenedos.[34] In the process, she also provides a useful overview of the graywares of Troy and that of the west coast of Asia Minor farther south.[35]

The "Aiolian" graywares form a significant component of most Archaic contexts at Methone, especially on the West Hill and its eastern slopes (Plots 229 and 245), but also in the area of the East Hill. All of the grayware presented in this chapter derives from various contexts on the West Hill, dating to the 7th and first half of the 6th centuries B.C. A few earlier pieces derive from the Hypogeion, the most noteworthy being the fragmentary karchesion, ΜΕΘ 2249 (figs. 1.12; 11.5 [**11/7**]) with the inscription ΦΙΛΙΟΝΟΣΕΜΙ (Φιλίōνος ἐμί) written retrograde, which is dated late 8th or early 7th century B.C.[36] The quantity of the material, coupled with the state of preservation of some of the pieces, is remarkable, indicating a substantial import—or local production—of this highly distinctive fabric. This is in many ways a surprise given the relative dearth of Aiolian exports elsewhere in the north Aegean. On this issue, Cook noted: "Very little Aeolian Grey ware was exported, and perhaps mainly from Lesbos. Some has been found on Chios and Samos, on Thasos, and at Al Mina and Naucratis. From other sites odd pieces have been reported, but identification is not always easy, since unpretentious Grey ware could be made locally, as for instance is claimed for Thasos and Histria."[37] In 1967, Aiolian grayware did not appear farther south than Chios, but John Boardman also noted that it was carried to Naukratis, Aziris, Al Mina, and the west.[38] Its popularity—and exportability to the coastal Levant, Egypt, and elsewhere—may have been due to the highly metallic look of the finished products, as if the vessels were made of silver. The well-thrown, often thin-walled, and highly burnished surfaces are features of the "Aiolian" graywares at Methone that highlight the metallic quality of this ceramic product. The makers of "Aiolian" grayware were consciously producing silver skeuomorphs in terracotta, often enhanced with incised decoration.

As for the place or places from where the "Aiolian" grayware at Methone derives, Lesbos looms large, not least because of the sheer quantity of Lesbian amphoras found at the site from the 8th century B.C. well into the Archaic period.[39] But I am not convinced that Lesbos was the sole purveyor of what we have come to regard as "Lesbian" amphoras (see Chapters 12 and 19).[40] In his discussion of Aiolian grayware found on Chios, Boardman noted that Phokaia may have been as important a center for its production as Lesbos.[41] This may well be true, but the other significant Aiolian center that has only recently come to light is Kyme.[42] Recent analytical work has not clinched with certainty the production center of Aiolian grayware, but Kerschner argues for Kyme and, perhaps on a smaller scale, Larisa as the production center(s) of fine Aiolian grayware.[43] Not only is Aiolian pottery now one group for which a good chemical profile exists (Aiolian subgroup "g"), it is, as a category, made up of a very wide variety of styles of decoration, "such as Wild Goat, black-figure and black-polychrome styles, including the so-called 'London Dinos group,' banded wares, meander-rim dishes and Grey ware pottery, to mention but a few."[44] What is also clear from elemental analysis is that several of the distinctively darker gray fine ware imports to Naukratis fall into the chemical group B-Troy.[45] Consequently, Trojan fine grayware was also exported, certainly to the Nile Delta.

As for the grayware at Methone, the closest parallels to date come from various sites on Lesbos, Kyme, as well as some from Assos, Larisa, and pre-Classical Pergamon. Yet close parallels from Aiolis for many of the forms found at Methone are lacking, perhaps the result of the dearth of systematic excavations of Archaic levels on both Lesbos and the Aiolian mainland.[46] This is especially the case for some of the most distinctive of the "Aiolian" graywares at Methone, such as the thin-walled skyphoi/bowls (nos. **22/10–12**), and the large shallow lekanai with the characteristic horizontal spur handles (nos. **22/14–15**), often with closer parallels from the Black Sea and Sicily than from the Aegean.[47]

In addition to the vessels and fragments of "Aiolian" graywares catalogued below, there are some fragments of a characteristic gray (reduced) fabric that appears to be locally made and highly micaceous. Unlike other categories of East Greek pottery (North Ionian bird kotylai and bowls, Milesian, Samian, Chian, etc.), only the graywares appear to have been singled out for local manufacture in the Archaic period at Methone. What I take to be clearly locally produced grayware is related to that produced in the kilns of Leukopetra in the Vermion Mountain range, and found in various places around the Thermaic Gulf, such as Karabournaki and Agia Paraskevi in Thessaloniki, in Chalkidike, and elsewhere in the north Aegean.[48] For the purposes of this report, my original intention was to include only examples of Aiolian graywares that I believed were imported. For to deal properly with all the locally produced graywares in the Thermaic Gulf would entail a more detailed and lengthy study of an entire category of pottery, which is beyond the scope of this volume. Although I originally thought that much of the "Aiolian" grayware at Methone presented in this chapter was imported from elsewhere, Camille Acosta has convinced me that this may not be the case, and that much of the grayware at the site, if not at all, was produced locally.

There is little doubt that the "Aiolian" graywares of Methone add a new dimension to the story of East Greek pottery and trade in the north Aegean. They also show how far we are, currently, from a synthetic overview of Aiolian graywares of the first millennium B.C.

As for their context and date, the "Aiolian" pottery from Methone, including that from Pit 8, was found together with Corinthian pottery dating to the end of the 7th century B.C. but also including material of the first half of the 6th century B.C. There is little, if any, grayware on the West Hill in a stratified deposit postdating the mid-6th century B.C. destruction by fire. In a similar vein, the Aiolian grayware recently published from Zone in Thrace—which includes, among other vessel forms, lebetes, oinochoai, and kyathia—is dated by Chrysafenia Pardalidou from the late 7th to the 6th century B.C.[49] Similarly, the imported Aiolian grayware from Abdera published by Eudokia Skarlatidou, primarily one-handled cups, olpai, and a phiale, is dated to the end of the 7th or the beginning of the 6th century B.C.[50] In contrast, the grayware from the cemetery at Thermi (Sedes), locally produced, dates mainly to the 6th century B.C.[51]

Closed Vessels

22/1. (ΜΕΘ 3552) Fragmentary Oinochoe Fig. 22.1

West Hill #229/013002 and 014003. Μαύρο χώμα ("black earth"). 2008.

Main body frr: p.H. 0.232; Diam. (base) 0.128; Diam. (neck, at its base) 0.090; non-joining frr of neck: p.H. 0.078. Original H. ca. 0.320.

Reconstructed from numerous frr preserving all of base and much of body, up to the neck, though with substantial missing parts of the lower body and rather less of the shoulder. A further group of three joining frr preserves about one-third of the neck, but nothing of the rim.

Tall ring foot, splaying out to resting surface, resulting in a broad resting surface; underside flat. Spherical body. Handle scar of lower handle attachment preserved on upper shoulder; enough survives of the opposite side of the vessel to suggest that this is a one-handled vessel. Juncture of shoulder and neck marked by a series of grooves, at least five and perhaps originally a few more. Vertical neck, flaring toward rim. Wheelmarks prominent on interior.

Fine gray fabric, dense, with few visible impurities and only a little fine silvery mica. Clay core and reserved surfaces fired close to gray 10YR 6/1 and 2.5Y 6/1.

Surface slipped/glazed, with a good black slip, flaked in places, with a slight sheen where best preserved. The contrast between the lustrous black exterior and the unslipped light gray interior is marked. In general, with this class of pottery, determining whether the surface is slipped or burnished may not be straightforward, but the slip on this vessel is clearer than on any other of this fabric.

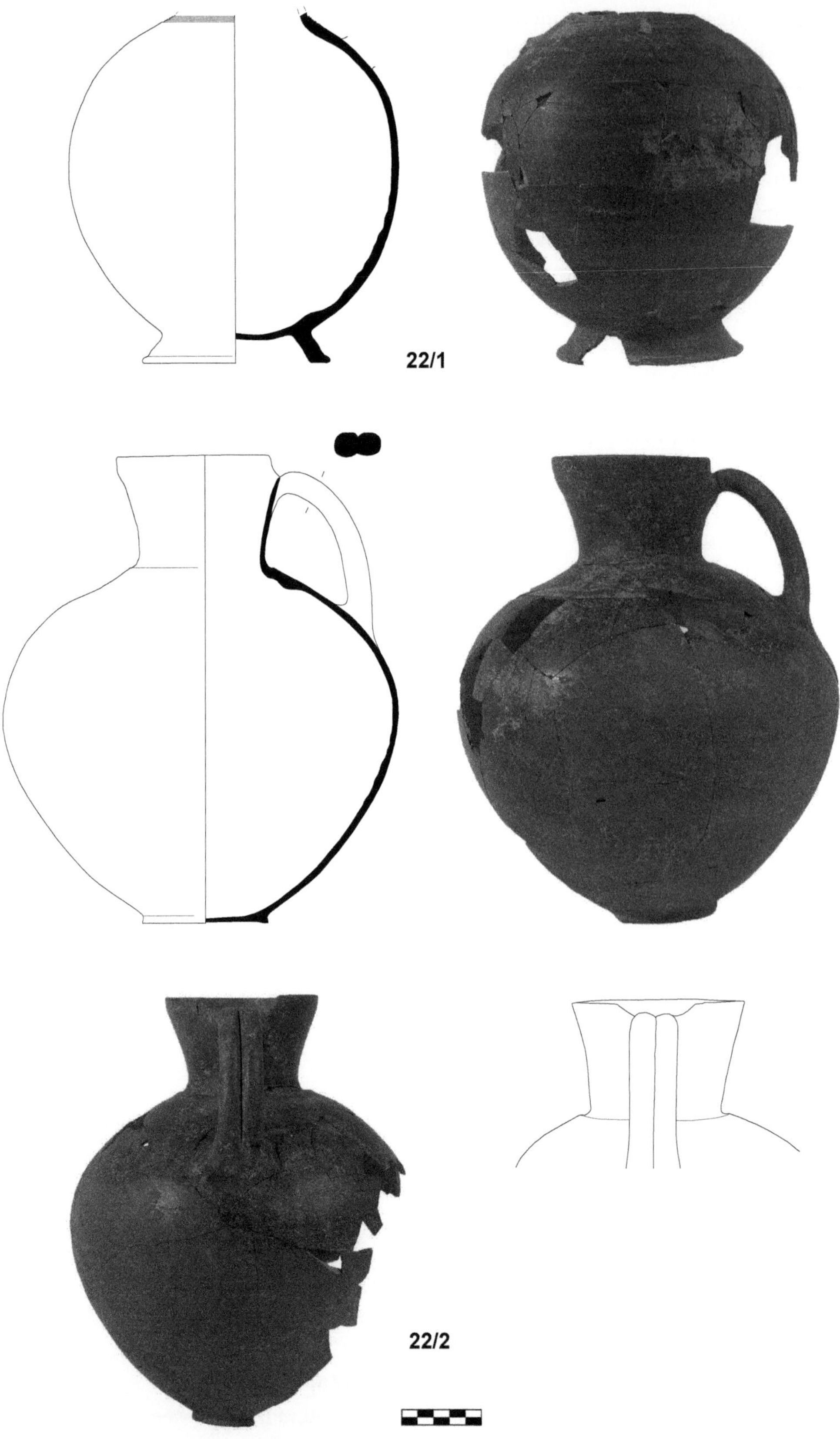

FIGURE 22.1. Two grayware jugs, **22/1** (ΜΕΘ 3552) and **22/2** (ΜΕΘ 5240). Drawings F. Skyvalida, photos I. Coyle

22/2. (MEΘ 5240) Fragmentary Oinochoe Fig. 22.1

Vessel reconstructed from numerous frr and contexts on the West Hill:

A 88: #229.020017 [6]. 3/8/2011.

A 98: #229.020019 [7]. 10/8/2011.

A 100: #229/020020 [7]. 11/8/2011.

H. 0.284; Diam. (rim) 0.107–0.109; Diam. (base) est. 0.080.

Reconstructed from numerous frr preserving small portion of base, over one-half of body and entire neck, rim, and handle of vessel.

Flat disk base, very thin-walled, articulated from body as shown; spherical body. Juncture of body and neck marked by a substantial thickening on interior and a slight ridge with corresponding shallow groove on exterior. Vertical lower neck flaring toward rim, which becomes vertical toward top, terminating in a plain rounded lip. Neck cutaway on one side of handle attachment. Double rolled or pulled handle, each element round in section, attached from upper shoulder directly to rim at cutaway.

Fabric as **22/1** (MEΘ 3552).

Surface as **22/1** (MEΘ 3552).

Cf. Gebauer 1992, p. 94, fig. 3, no. 10; note also p. 96, fig. 5, no. 17, for the double handle (see also p. 97, fig. 6, no. 22 for a triple handle on a jug); for similar double and triple handles from Troy, Level VIII, see *Troy* IV, pl. 291, nos. 5–6; for a double handle on a rather more slender grayware oinochoe, see Boardman 1967, pp. 135–136, no. 467; note also the Aiolian grayware double handle fr from Thasos, Ghali-Kahil 1960, p. 46, pl. 15, no. 26.

22/3. (MEΘ 5016) Rim, Upper Body, and Handle Frr, Trefoil Oinochoe Fig. 22.2

West Hill #229/015010 [10]. Pit 8. 2008.

P.H. 0.097; Diam. (lower neck) 0.061.

Eight joining frr preserving about one-half of neck and rather less of rim, most of handle, but only small portion of upper body.

Neck and upper body formed in one piece, with upper wall sloping in, lower neck vertical, flaring toward rim, which is formed into a trefoil. Lip toward handle beveled; more round toward front. Vertical strap handle, ovoid in section, attached from upper body directly to rim and rising slightly above level of rim. Preserved upper body and neck decorated with a series of grooves: at least two grooves at lower break; three on lower neck; two on upper neck.

Fabric contains noticeable white inclusions, occasional blowouts, and a little more mica than **22/1** (MEΘ 3552) and **22/2** (MEΘ 5240). Clay body and reserved surfaces fired dark gray 10YR 4/1 and 2.5Y 4/1.

Exterior body burnished rather than slipped.

Cf. Hertel 2007, p. 101, fig. 2 (right), nos. 1–2, 4 (Old Smyrna); Gebauer 1992, pp. 95–96, figs. 4–5, nos. 16–18 (Assos).

22/4. (MEΘ 5011) Rim Fr, Amphora (Rather than Oinochoe) Fig. 22.2

West Hill #229/015010 [10]. Pit 8. 2008.

P.H. 0.038; Diam. (rim) est. 0.135.

Three joining frr preserving about one-third of rim and upper neck.

Upper neck vertical, flaring to thickened rim, with an almost vertical outside edge and round on top. Handle scar of vertical handle, attached to uppermost neck. Shape more consistent with amphoras rather than oinochoai.

Fabric as **22/3** (MEΘ 5016).

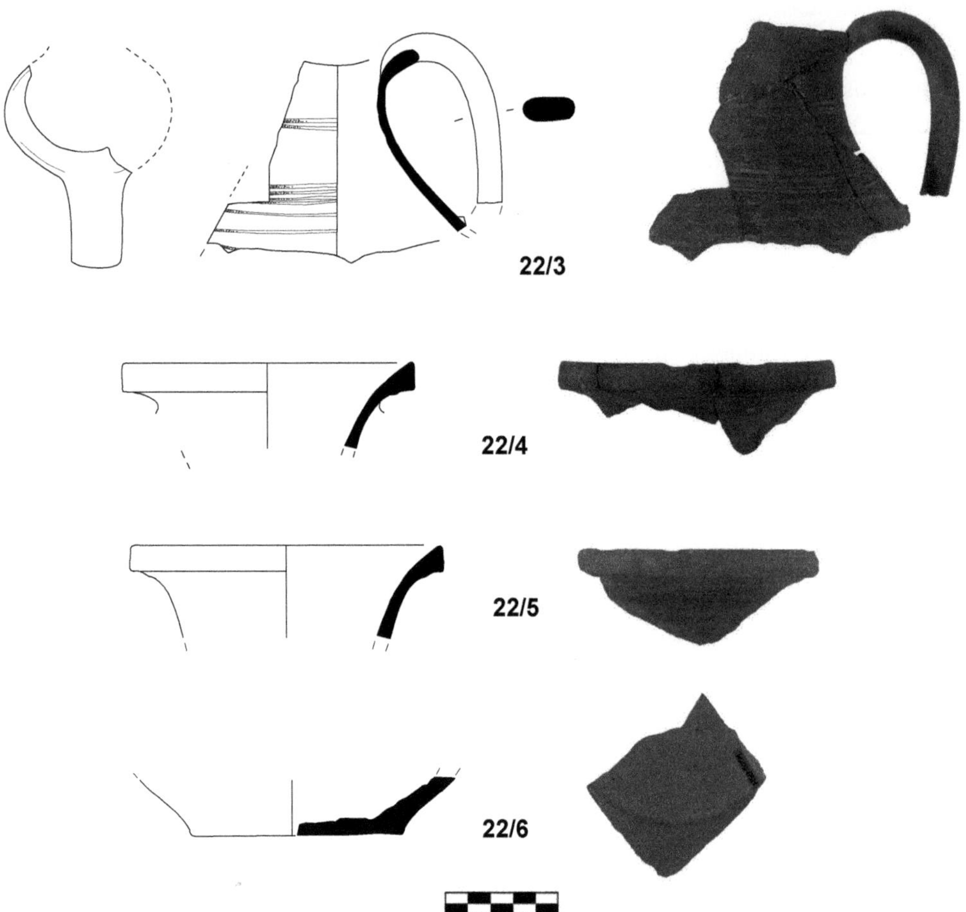

FIGURE 22.2. Selection of grayware fragments of closed vessels, **22/3** (MEΘ 5016), **22/4** (MEΘ 5011), **22/5** (MEΘ 5010), and **22/6** (MEΘ 5009). Drawings F. Skyvalida, photos I. Coyle

Exterior surfaces, especially on outer face of rim, burnished.

For the form of the rim, cf. İren 2008, p. 633, fig. 24, no. 7 (Kyme); Lagona and Frasca 2009, p. 302, fig. 12 (Kyme); for related amphora rims from Pergamon, cf. Hertel 2011, pp. 72–76, figs. 12–13, nos. 91–100.

22/5. (MEΘ 5010) Rim Fr, Amphora (Rather than Oinochoe) Fig. 22.2

West Hill #229/015010 [10]. Pit 8. 2008.

P.H. 0.040; Diam. (rim) est. 0.140.

Single fr preserving about one-third of rim and upper neck.

Shape as **22/4** (MEΘ 5011), but without a preserved handle attachment.

Fabric as **22/3** (MEΘ 5016) and **22/4** (MEΘ 5011).

Exterior surfaces as **22/4** (MEΘ 5011).

22/6. (MEΘ 5009) Base Fr, Medium-sized Closed Vessel Fig. 22.2

West Hill #229/015101 [10]. Pit 8. 2008.

P.H. 0.024; Diam. (base) est. 0.090.

Single fr preserving about one-quarter of base, but only a very small portion of lower body.

Flat disk base; lower wall rising steeply. Shape similar to **22/2** (MEΘ 5240). Wheelmarks prominent on interior (clearly a closed vessel).

Fabric as **22/3** (MEΘ 5016) and **22/4** (MEΘ 5011), with white and some darker (red) inclusions, but lighter colored, with clay body and reserved surfaces fired closer to gray 10YR 6/1 and 2.5Y 6/1.

Exterior surface burnished; underside and interior not burnished.

For the form of the base, cf. İren 2003, Beil. 5, no. 314.

22/7. (MEΘ 5014) Base Fr, Small to Medium-sized Closed Vessel Fig. 22.3

West Hill #229/015010 [10]. Pit 8. 2008.

P.H. 0.017; Diam. (base) est. 0.062.

Single fr preserving about one-third of base but only a very small portion of lower body. Rather worn.

Very low ring foot rather than flat disk base; lower wall rising steeply. Wheelmarks prominent on interior.

Fabric as **22/3** (MEΘ 5016) and **22/4** (MEΘ 5011), including color of fired clay.

Although surfaces are worn, the exterior is clearly burnished whereas the interior and underside are not.

22/8. (MEΘ 5013) Base Fr, Small to Medium-sized Closed Vessel Fig. 22.3

West Hill #229/015010 [10]. Pit 8. 2008.

P.H. 0.021; Diam. (base) 0.068.

Single fr preserving most of base but only a very small portion of lower body.

Ring foot of medium height, with a slight bulge (rather than nipple) at center of underside. Although worn, surfaces indicate a closed vessel.

Fabric as **22/3** (MEΘ 5016) and **22/4** (MEΘ 5011), but a little lighter, though not as pale as **22/6** (MEΘ 5009), with clay core and reserved surfaces fired closer to gray 10YR 5/1 and 2.5Y 5/1.

Although worn, the exterior is clearly burnished whereas the interior and underside are not.

For tall ring feet, see Frasca 1993, p. 53, fig. 3a–d (Kyme); cf. Gebauer 1993, p. 99, fig. 7, nos. 61–63 (all of which are stray finds from Assos and may be considerably later than Archaic in date).

FIGURE 22.3. Selected grayware base fragments, **22/7** (MEΘ 5014), **22/8** (MEΘ 5013), and **22/9** (MEΘ 5012). Drawings F. Skyvalida, photos I. Coyle

22/9. (ΜΕΘ 5012) Base Frr, Medium to Larger Closed Vessel Fig. 22.3

West Hill #229/015010 [10]. Pit 8. 2008.

P.H. 0.030; Diam. (base) est. 0.110–115.

Two joining frr preserving about one-third of base, but only a very small portion of lower wall.

Very low ring foot, as **22/7** (ΜΕΘ 5014); underside flat. Lower wall rising in a manner suggesting a spherical, and hence closed, body.

Fabric as **22/3** (ΜΕΘ 5016) and **22/4** (ΜΕΘ 5011); clay core and surfaces close to gray/dark gray 10YR 5/1–4/1 and 2.5Y 5/1–4/1.

Exterior surface burnished whereas the interior and underside are not.

For the form of the base, cf. İren 2008, p. 633, fig. 24, no. 7 (Kyme).

Open Vessels

22/10. (ΜΕΘ 5005) Fragmentary Skyphos/Bowl Fig. 22.4

West Hill #229/011003 [2]. Βόρεια τοίχου 1, στρώμα 2 (north of Wall 1, layer 2). 15/2/2008, 20/2/2008.

P.H. 0.086; Diam. (rim) est. 0.180.

Ten joining frr preserving just under one-half of rim and upper body, including one handle, but nothing of the base.

Lower wall curving up to vertical upper wall, which curves slightly in to rim; thin-walled. Tall rim, offset from body on interior and exterior, flaring slightly out and up to plain rounded lip. Horizontal handle, round in section, attached to uppermost wall near juncture with rim. Uppermost body decorated with two shallow grooves, the uppermost of which clearly extends below the handle, as it is visible within the handle arch (as does, probably, the lower one as well).

Fabric as **22/1** (ΜΕΘ 3552), with fewer visible impurities and only a little mica. Clay core and surfaces fired closest to gray 10YR 5/1 and 2.5Y 5/1.

Preserved interior and exterior very nicely burnished/polished, producing a surface not unlike the finest Minyan pottery.

Cf. Lungu 2009, p. 36, fig. 7a–b (Berezan); Bernard 1964, pp. 113–114, fig. 27, no. 96 (Thasos); Daragan 2009, p. 137, no. 1 (Black Sea).

22/11. (ΜΕΘ 5007) Rim and Upper Body Frr, Skyphos/Bowl Fig. 22.4

West Hill #229/015010 [10]. Pit 8. 2008.

P.H. 0.096; Diam. (rim) est. 0.240.

Two joining frr preserving about one-quarter of rim and upper body.

Shape as **22/10** (ΜΕΘ 5005), but larger; handle not preserved. Upper body decorated with two shallow grooves as **22/10** (ΜΕΘ 5005); very shallow groove at juncture of upper body and rim, which is not really visible on **22/10** (ΜΕΘ 5005).

Fabric as **22/10** (ΜΕΘ 5005), but a little darker, shading between gray/dark gray 10YR 5/1–4/1 and 2.5Y 5/1–4/1.

Burnishing on interior and exterior as **22/10** (ΜΕΘ 5005).

22/12. (ΜΕΘ 5008) Rim, Upper Body, and Handle Fr, Skyphos/Bowl Fig. 22.4

West Hill #229/015010 [10]. Pit 8. 2008.

P.H. 0.061; p.W. 0.083; Diam. (rim) est. 0.210.

Two joining frr preserving small portion of rim and upper body, including one handle.

Shape as **22/10** (ΜΕΘ 5005) and **22/11** (ΜΕΘ 5007), with handle circular in section. At least one and probably originally two shallow grooves on uppermost body, and a slight groove at juncture of body and rim. No real trace of the groove in the area below the handle arch.

Fabric as **22/3** (MEΘ 5016) and **22/4** (MEΘ 5011); color closer to **22/11** (MEΘ 5007). Burnishing as **22/10** (MEΘ 5005).

22/13. (MEΘ 5015) Base Fr, Probably Open Vessel (cf. Skyphos/Bowl) Fig. 22.4
West Hill #229/015010 [10]. Pit 8. 2008.
P.H. 0.024; Diam. (base) est. 0.065.
Single fr preserving about one-third of base, but very little of lower body.
Low ring foot; underside convex; preserved lower wall rising steeply. Surface treatment suggests open vessel.
Fabric as **22/3** (MEΘ 5016), but with some more substantial blowouts; color as **22/11** (MEΘ 5007).
Although worn, both the interior and exterior appear to have been burnished.

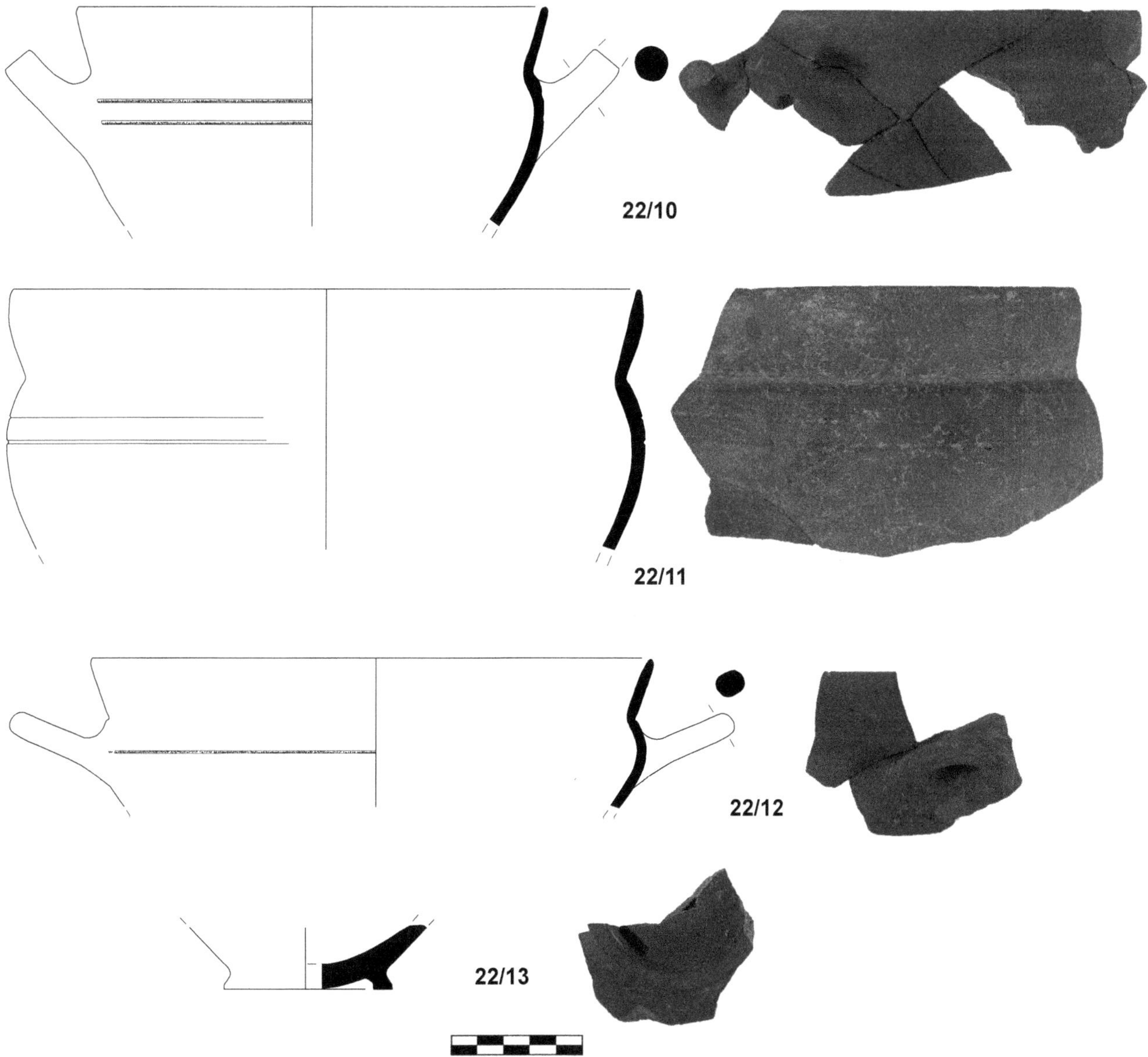

FIGURE 22.4. Selected grayware skyphoi/bowls, **22/10** (MEΘ 5005), **22/11** (MEΘ 5007), **22/12** (MEΘ 5008), and **22/13** (MEΘ 5015). Drawings F. Skyvalida, photos I. Coyle

22/14. (MEΘ 3554) Fragmentary Lekanis Fig. 22.5

West Hill #229/013002, #229/014003. 2008.

P.H. 0.075; Diam. (rim) 0.290.

Seventeen joining frr preserving three-quarters of rim and upper body, including one handle, but less of the lower body and nothing of the base. Several non-joining frr may be from this same vessel.

Broad and shallow basin, with flat floor; vertical, slightly incurved upper body and horizontal rim. Horizontal handles (only one preserved), thin and strap in section, with concave outer face, flanked on either side by pointed spur.

Fabric as **22/3** (MEΘ 5016) and **22/4** (MEΘ 5011), with some large blowouts; clay core and surfaces shading between gray/dark gray 10YR 5/1–4/1 and 2.5Y 5/1–4/1.

Interior and exterior surfaces burnished.

Among the closet parallels for **22/14** (MEΘ 3554) and **22/15** (MEΘ 5112) are lekanis rim frr from Megara Hyblaia (Sicily): Vallet and Villard 1964, p. 91, p. 80, nos. 1–2. For the form of the handle, see, among others, Lamb 1931–1932, p. 52, fig. 6a; Frasca 1993, p. 53, fig. 4a; for the form of the rim, cf. Lamb 1931–1932, p. 55, fig. 8, no. 33; Buchholz 1975, p. 97, fig. 28c–d; for the basic form, but significantly smaller, cf. Gebauer 1992, p. 99, fig. 8, no. 37; Utili 1999, p. 326, fig. 41, no. 742.

22/15. (MEΘ 5112) Rim, Body, and Handle Fr, Lekanis Fig. 22.6

West Hill #229/013002; #229/014003. 2008.

P.H. 0.059; Diam. (rim) est. 0.320.

Single fr preserving small portion of rim and upper body, including one complete handle.

Form of body, rim and handle as **22/14** (MEΘ 3554), but larger.

Fabric as **22/14** (MEΘ 3554), but with clay core fired light gray, close to light gray 10YR 7/1–6/1 and 2.5Y 7/1–6/1; surfaces closer to gray 10YR 5/1 and 2.5Y 5/1.

Interior and exterior surfaces burnished.

Cf. **22/14** (MEΘ 3554) and esp. the comparanda from Megara Hyblaia cited there.

22/16. (MEΘ 5121) Base Frr, Lekanis Fig. 22.6

West Hill #229/013002, #229/014003.

P.H. 0.022; Diam. (base) 0.125.

Three joining frr preserving much of base, but very little else; rather worn.

Ring foot of medium height, with comparatively flat underside; broad shallow floor.

Fabric as **22/15** (MEΘ 5112).

Although worn, it is reasonably clear that the exterior and interior of the vessel were burnished, whereas the underside was not.

Form of base goes with **22/14** (MEΘ 3554) and **22/15** (MEΘ 5112).

22/17. (MEΘ 5110) Rim and Upper Body Fr, Lekanis or "Fruit Stand" Fig. 22.7

P.H. 0.035; p.L. 0.065; Diam. (rim) est. 0.250.

Single fr preserving small portion of rim and upper wall.

Broad and shallow body with flat floor, smaller than **22/14** (MEΘ 3554). Shallow lower wall sharply carinated from short upper wall, the outer face of which is grooved (four grooves); horizontal rim, the flat top of which is also grooved (four grooves).

Fabric as **22/1** (MEΘ 3552), but very light colored, with clay core and surfaces fired close to light gray 10YR 7/1–7/2 and 2.5Y 7/1–7/2, in places shading to gray 10YR and 2.5Y 6/1.

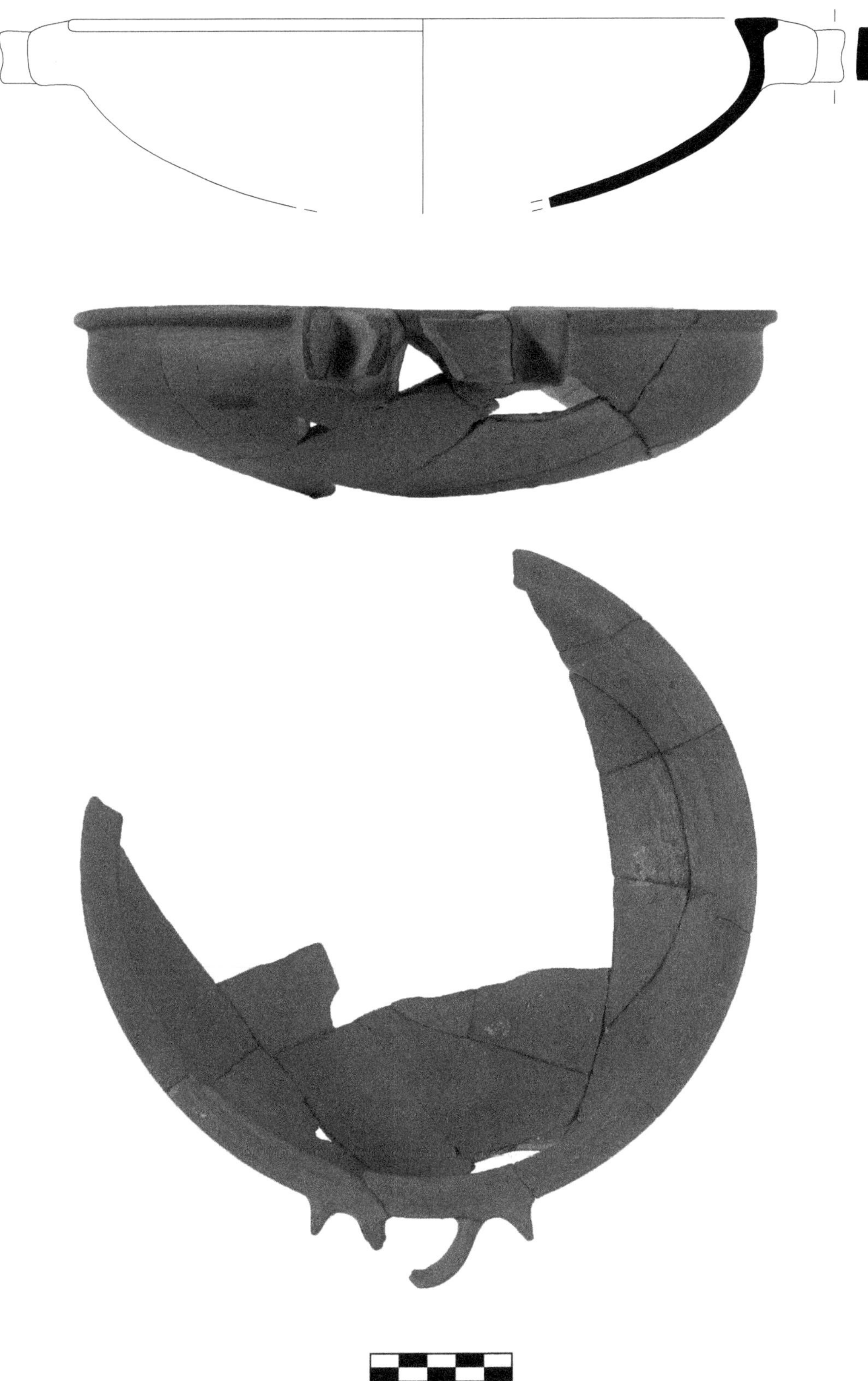

FIGURE 22.5. Grayware lekanis, **22/14** (ΜΕΘ 3554).
Drawing F. Skyvalida, photos I. Coyle

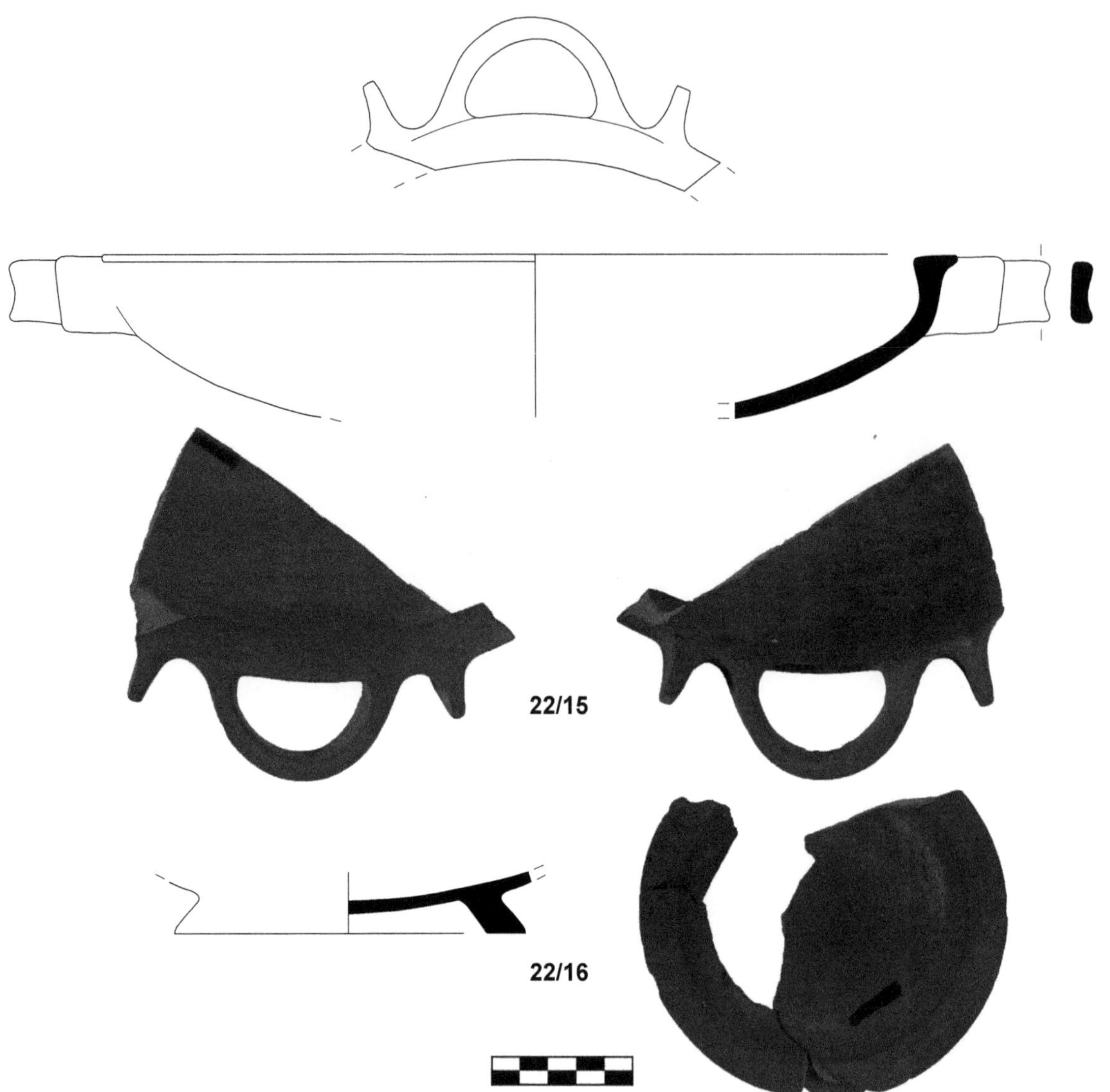

FIGURE 22.6. Grayware lekanides, **22/15** (ΜΕΘ 5112) and **22/16** (ΜΕΘ 5121). Drawings F. Skyvalida, photos I. Coyle

Exterior and interior surfaces burnished.

For the form of the rim, cf. Williams and Williams 1991, p. 185, fig. 4, nos. 2–4 (Mytilene); Lamb 1932, p. 6, fig. 2, no. 10 (Methymna); Buchholz 1975, p. 95, fig. 27, l–m (Methymna); Boehlau and Schefold 1942, p. 101, fig. 31b (Larisa); Gebauer 1992, p. 99, fig. 8, nos. 40–42; also p. 100, fig. 9, no. 46 (Assos); Hertel 2011, pp. 76–77, no. 103 (= p. 80, fig. 17, no. 2), labeled *Schüssel,* but with wavy-line decoration (Pergamon); Gantès 2000, p. 115, fig. 1, no. 13 (Marseille).

22/18. (ΜΕΘ 5111) Rim Fr, Lekanis or "Fruit Stand" Fig. 22.7

West Hill #229/013, 014.

P.H. 0.022; p.W. 0.047; Diam. (rim) est. ca. 0.230–0.240.

Single fr preserving very small portion of rim; worn.

Comparatively thick-walled, but broad and shallow body with flat floor. Rim thickened and tapering toward rounded lip; rim flat or obliquely-cut on top. Outer, thickened, face or rim decorated with incised wavy line below prominent groove.

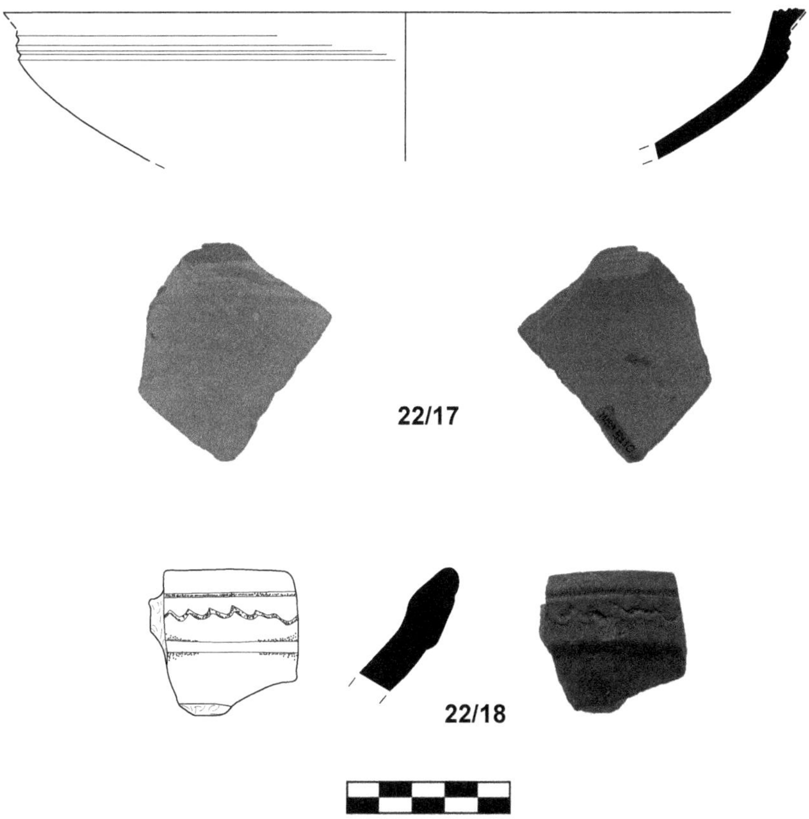

FIGURE 22.7. Grayware open vessels, **22/17** (ΜΕΘ 5110) and **22/18** (ΜΕΘ 5111). Drawings F. Skyvalida, photos I. Coyle and J. Vanderpool

Although thick-walled, the fabric is dense and relatively fine, with only occasional white and darker (red) inclusions, and very little mica. Clay core and interior surface fired close to gray 10YR and 2.5Y 6/1; exterior surface closer to gray 10YR and 2.5Y 5/1.

Interior and exterior surfaces burnished.

The form of the rim is closest to a large lekane from Kyme, see Frasca 1993, p. 54, fig. 5a. For the incised wavy-line decoration, but not for the form of the rim, see, among others, Lamb 1932, p. 4, fig. 1, nos. 1–3 (Methymna); p. 10, fig. 4, nos. 1–2 (from Pyrrha and Hanai Tepe); Lamb 1931–1932, pl. 22, no. 1 (Antissa); Buchholz 1975, p. 88, fig. 24a (Late Bronze Age Methymna); p. 95, fig. 27g, pl. 16j–k (Archaic Methymna); Hertel 2007, p. 107, fig. 8, no. 3 (Mytilene); p. 109, fig. 9, nos. 4–6 (Antissa); Hertel 2008a, pp. 168–169, figs. 49–50, nos. 106, 109, 114; Hertel 2008b, figs. 48a–b (Troy); Aslan 2009, p. 279, fig. 8 (bottom center); p. 280, fig. 10 (bottom center); p. 283, fig. 15 (Troy); Gebauer 1992, pp. 99–101, figs. 8–10, nos. 12–13, 18, and the body frr, nos. 58–59 (Assos); for similar wavy-line decoration on a broad variety of grayware shapes, see Utili 1999, pp. 315–316, figs. 30–31 (various examples); pp. 319–320 (various examples); pp. 326–327 (various examples), all from Assos; Frasca 1993, p. 53, fig. 2d–f (Kyme); Frasca 2000, p. 395, fig. 279 (Kyme, various examples); Ghali-Kahil 1960, p. 45, pl. 15, nos. 24–25 (Thasos); Bernard 1964, p. 111, fig. 24, nos. 75–76; p. 115, fig. 28, no. 98 (Thasos); Vallet and Villard 1964, p. 91, pl. 80, nos. 3, 5–6, 8 (Megara Hyblaia). For similar wavy-line decoration on the gray pottery from Lemnos, see Danile 2009, pp. 312–314, figs. 11, 13–14; Danile 2011, pl. 1, nos. 1–3; pls. 2–4; pl. 5, nos. 18, 20; Danile 2012, p. 81, fig. 2:a, c, d; p. 82, fig. 3:a, g. For the incised wavy-line grayware of Marseille, see Gantès 2000, esp. p. 115, fig. 1, nos. 6–9.

22/19. (MEΘ 5109) Rim and Upper Body Fr, Krater Fig. 22.8

West Hill #229/013, 014.

P.H. 0.071; p.W. 0.140; Diam. (rim) est. 0.380.

Single fr preserving small portion of rim and upper body; surfaces much worn.

Upper wall curving in to thickened triangular rim, flat on top and with rounded outside edge. Broad shallow groove at juncture of body and rim, another groove farther up on rim. Body thin-walled.

Fabric relatively dense and fine, with occasional white and some darker (red) inclusions, but highly micaceous. Clay core fired close to gray 10YR 6/1; reserved surfaces closer to grayish brown 10YR 5/2.

Interior and exterior surfaces burnished, but much worn.

For a related triangular krater rim from Pergamon, but with a ridge on the upper wall, see Hertel 2011, pp. 76–77, no. 101. Cf. Boehlau and Schefold 1942, p. 110, fig. 35, h and k; also Lamb 1932, p. 6, fig. 2, no. 1 (Methymna); İren 2008, p. 634, fig. 25, no. 18 (Kyme). For a krater from Krania in southern Pieria, ancient Herakleion, see Poulaki-Pantermali 2007, p. 643, fig. 19.

22/20. (MEΘ 5122) Fr, Grooved Handle Fig. 22.8

West Hill #229/016023. Pit 7.

P.H. 0.032; p.W. 0.043.

Single fr preserving greater portion of handle, but little of the corresponding body.

Small horizontal rolled handle, of a type normally associated with mortars, with ends articulated and central part grooved. Attachment to body at top and bottom flattened.

Fabric fine and dense, with only occasional small white and dark (red) inclusions and quite a bit of fine mica. Clay core and surfaces consistently fired close to gray 10YR 6/1 and 2.5Y 6/1.

Surfaces on interior and exterior burnished, though attachments to body immediately around handle less well finished.

For handle forms related to **22/20** (MEΘ 5122), but not exactly the same, see Boehlau and Schefold 1942, pl. 47, nos. 6, 9.

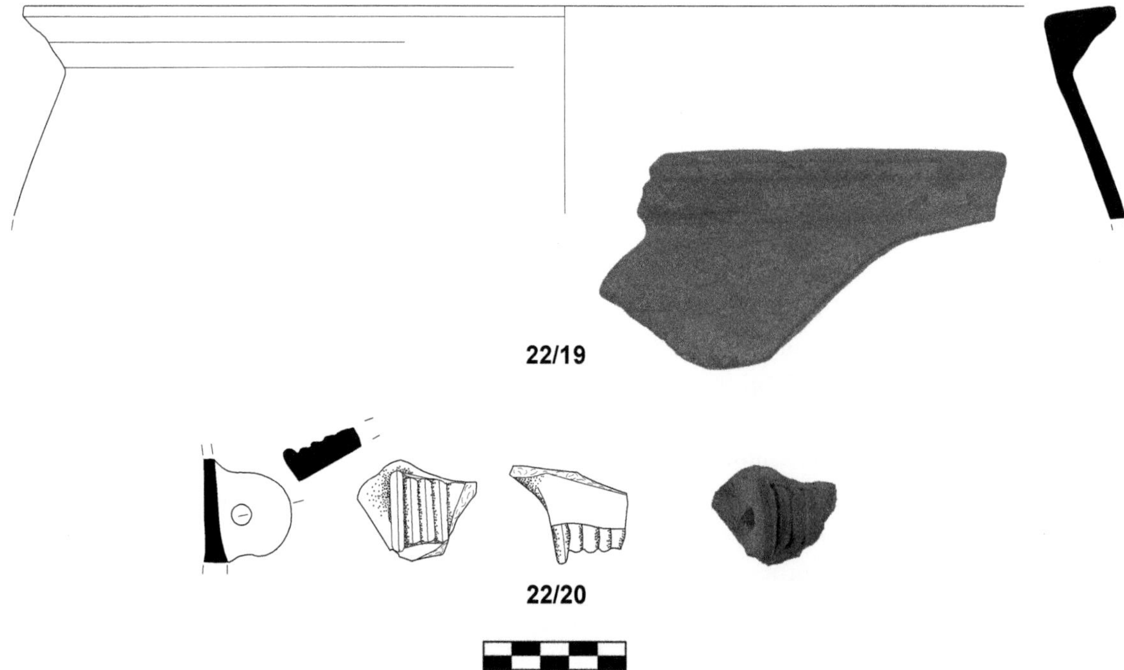

FIGURE 22.8. Grayware open vessels, **22/19** (MEΘ 5109) and **22/20** (MEΘ 5122). Drawings F. Skyvalida, photos I. Coyle

EAST GREEK BUCCHERO ("RHODIAN" BUCCHERO)

Although related to Aiolian grayware, what has come to be known as "Rhodian" bucchero is quite distinctive from the main series of Aiolian fine graywares, in both fabric and shape. While its provenance remains to be established, and despite the fact that the fabric was produced somewhere in southern East Greece, it seemed unnecessary to separate it from the Aiolian graywares and place it in a "miscellaneous" category. As for what is known of this type of ware, very little can be added to Cook's description in 1998:

> There is also what is called "Rhodian Bucchero"—"Rhodian" because of finds on Rhodes, then considered a major producer of East Greek pottery, and "Bucchero" since it has no Bronze Age pedigree to induce a change of name. It is a very minor product, technically similar to Aeolian Grey ware but, to judge by distribution, made in the southern part of the East Greek region. In older studies the two are sometimes conflated. As a rule, "Rhodian" Bucchero is, at least on its surface, considerably darker than Aeolian Grey ware. The principal shapes, modelled with some precision, are the aryballos, small and round, and the fusiform alabastron, often 20 cm long: the aryballoi may be vertically ribbed, the alabastra usually have lines incised sparsely round the body. There are also some larger bucchero pots, mainly oinochoai and plates or stemmed dishes, which are sometimes decorated in white and purple with lotus buds and other simple motives; shapes and ornaments recall the Middle II Wild Goat style. These two groups, the small plain pots and the larger decorated ones, may well come from different workshops. "Rhodian" Bucchero is found sporadically in the southern parts of the East Greek region and there was a little, although far-flung, export of the first group, alabastra in particular being relatively numerous in Sicily. Its floruit should be late seventh and early sixth century, contemporary roughly with Early and Middle Corinthian.[52]

At the cemetery of Sindos, there are several slightly later footed bucchero alabastra that are dated to the second half of the 6th century B.C.,[53] which represent a development from the solitary, earlier, alabastron from Methone presented here.

The context of **22/21** is the same as that of the "Aiolian" pottery presented above, with comparanda, including imports to other sites in the north Aegean, presented in the catalogue entry below.

22/21. (ΜΕΘ 5123) Fragmentary Base, Spindle Bottle (Alabastron) Fig. 22.9

West Hill #229/013, 014.

P.H. 0.065; Diam. (max) 0.041.

Reconstructed from frr preserving portion of base and lower body; much worn.

Tall, spindle-shaped closed vessel, with a tubular body tapering toward base. Three prominent but shallow grooves on lower wall.

Fabric thick-walled, but fine, with few visible impurities and only a little mica. Clay core fired close to reddish brown 5YR 5/3–5/4 and brown 7.5YR 5/3–5/4; surfaces on exterior closer to dark gray 5YR 4/1 and 7.5YR 4/1.

Exterior surfaces worn, but clearly burnished; interior surfaces very roughly finished.

The form of the base, together with the incised lines, is close to an example from Catania, see Pautasso 2009, pl. 1, no. 9; also cf. pl. 2, no. 42 (the site produced numerous alabastra, see pp. 25–30, figs. 1–3, pls. 1–2); Vallet and Villard 1964, pp. 90–91, pl. 79, no. 3; see also *Pithekoussai* I, p. 248, pls. 85 and CXXXIII, tomb 191, nos. 27–29. Among others, cf. Boehlau 1898, p. 46, no.

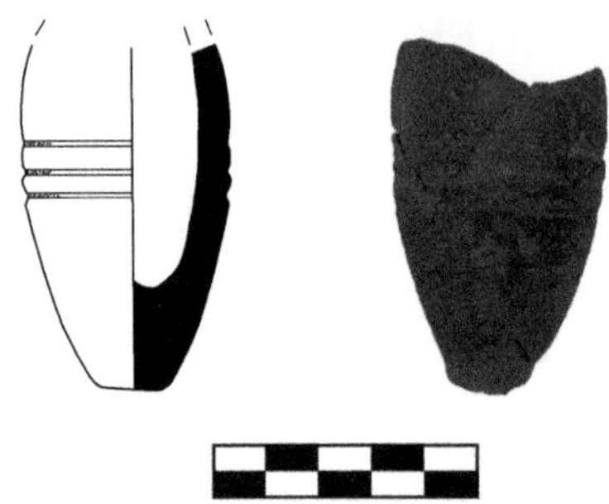

FIGURE 22.9. Bucchero alabastron, **22/21** (ΜΕΘ 5123). Drawing F. Skyvalida, photo I. Coyle

9.120; Boehlau and Habich 1996, p. 67, Grab 45, 37 (= *Samos* VI, p. 124, no. 270), with additional examples illustrated in *Samos* VI, p. 124, pl. 35, nos. 268–269 (judging by the curvature at the upper break, **22/21** [ΜΕΘ 5123] is substantially less tall than the examples from Samos); cf. also Orlandini 1978, pl. 55, fig. 23 (right). The bucchero alabastra from Kyrene offer close parallels for the Methone example, see Schaus 1985, pp. 73–74, fig. 9, pl. 27, nos. 447–454. For similar examples from the north Aegean, cf. Tsiafaki 2012, pp. 234–235, fig. 16 (Karabournaki); Chrysostomou and Chrysostomou 2012, p. 244, fig. 16.

NORTH IONIAN BIRD KOTYLAI AND BIRD BOWLS

BIRD KOTYLAI

All of the north Ionian bird kotylai, together with two examples of north Ionian bird oinochoai, were found in the Hypogeion on the East Hill (for context, see Fig. 22.10a and below). The two north Ionian bird oinochoai are presented above by Manthos Bessios (Chapter 9, nos. **9/93–9/94**; see also Fig. 22.10b below), so they are not catalogued here.[54] A select number of bird kotylai from the Hypogeion are presented here; numerous additional examples from the deposit are not included. A few fragments of these kotylai were also found in other contexts on the East Hill, such as ΜΕΘ 7528 (Fig. 22.10c).[55]

In discussing the "Bird-kotyle Workshop," Nicolas Coldstream stated:

> This workshop is named after its most striking ornament, and its commonest shape. The kotyle . . . first came to this area from Corinth at the end of MG. The first Corinthian model has a hemispherical profile, modified at the rim by a slight nick. Both features were copied in the earliest East Greek examples, and perpetuated in this workshop: the hemispherical form was preserved in the local LG style long after it has passed out of fashion at Corinth, and the nick was exaggerated so that the rim became inset. At the end of its long career, this kotyle was replaced not, as in Corinth, by the deeper variety, but by the shallow Subgeometric bird bowl.[56]

In his analysis, Coldstream listed 13 kotylai from various sites (Rhodes, the Purification Trench on Rheneia, Thera, Asine, Pithekoussai, and Al Mina), together with a krater from Myrina, an oinochoe from Delos, and a "lekythos-sprinkler" from Thera, which he collectively assigned to his first phase of the workshop. Coldstream's second phase comprised five kotylai from Rheneia, four jugs (one from Rheneia, the others in various museums said to come from Rhodes and Crete), and an oinochoe from Ialysos on Rhodes.[57]

In discussing the decoration, Coldstream noted that the workshop had evolved a simple metopal system that could be applied to almost any shape, though in its maturest form it appears most characteristically on the kotyle.[58] This metopal scheme consists of a main panel divided into four rectangular metopes, usually underlined by an ancillary zone, and the whole is surrounded by glaze. The four metope motifs in regular use are, in order of frequency: the lozenge, almost invariably cross-hatched, always on side panels, the tree ornament, the bird, and a pair of meander hooks. As Coldstream notes, the oldest kotyle with the full complement of four more or less equal metopes is probably the celebrated cup of Nestor, with its inscription, in the formula of a curse, from Pithekoussai on the island of Ischia (Fig. 22.11).[59] The ancillary zone below the primary metopal zone on Nestor's cup is a zigzag, which is also the most common ancillary zone on the Methone bird kotylai (see **22/23–22/33**); other ancillary motifs include double axes alternating with vertical lines (which occur on both of the Methone bird oinochoai, Fig. 22.10b, but not on the kotylai), and a horizontal row of cross-hatched lozenges (**22/22** [ΜΕΘ 1318]); the only other ancillary motif on the Methone kotylai is what appear to be plain horizontal bands (**22/34** [ΜΕΘ 3300]).[60] Coldstream followed Martin Robertson in assuming that the kotylai with three metopes belong to the most advanced stage—Coldstream's "second phase"—as their symmetrical scheme anticipates the decoration of the Subgeometric bird bowls (for which see below).[61] Indeed, Robertson's suggested stylistic sequence for the bird kotylai and bird bowls from Al Mina was fully corroborated by the stratigraphical sequence at Emporio on Chios and, most recently, from Yaşar Ersoy's excavations at Klazomenai.[62] Consequently, a Late Geometric date for the Methone kotylai is clear enough, while the stylistic similarity between some of the Methone bird kotylai (e.g., **22/22** [ΜΕΘ 1318] and **22/25** [ΜΕΘ 3302]) and the cup of Nestor, considered by Coldstream as among the earliest of the type, may suggest that some of the Methone examples are contemporary with the Pithekoussai kotyle.

As for the context of the north Ionian bird kotylai within the Hypogeion at Methone, this is best presented diagrammatically (Table 22.1). In the following table I have also included one of the better preserved kotylai that were not selected for the catalogue (ΜΕΘ 4396). The table was then converted into an illustration that shows better the joins between the various units (Fig. 22.10a). What is clear is that the fragments of several kotylai were encountered only in Phase I (**22/25**, **22/27**, **22/34**, and ΜΕΘ 4396); the joining fragments of several of the kotylai were found joining between phases I and II (**22/22**, **22/23**, **22/24**, **22/26**, **22/30**, **22/31**, **22/33**, and of these, two—**22/30**, **22/31**—only had one joining fragment in Phase II); the remainder were found with joins between Phases I and II and the mixed levels at the interface of Phases III and above. Not one fragment was found in the post–Phase III fill.

According to a recent study of the bird kotylai from Klaros by Onur Zunal, the onset of kotyle production begins at the end of the Middle Geometric, when the earliest kotylai are not decorated with birds, but with geometric meander motifs that originate from a Middle Geometric tradition.[63] Indeed, one of the early Klaros kotylai gives the impression of a five-metope zone. Zunal goes on to trace the development of kotylai from four metopal panels to three, which follows Robertson's and Coldstream's scheme.[64] Although the development from a four- to a three-metopal panel zone is clear, we are in need of a good stratigraphic sequence, preferably from multiple sites, to clinch the precise development of north Ionian bird kotylai.[65]

In dealing with the distribution of the bird kotylai, Coldstream noted that the influence of this workshop was felt all over the East Greek world, where the bird kotyle became the most universally popular drinking vessel of the Late Geometric period, citing numerous examples from Samos, Chios, Larisa, Smyrna, Ephesos, Miletos, Didyma, and Iasos.[66] Outside of the immediate area of East Greece, Coldstream documented the distribution of bird kotylai at Troy and Lesbos, in the northeast Aegean; to Rheneia, Thera, Naxos, Eretria, Chalkis, Aigina, and Asine, in the central and

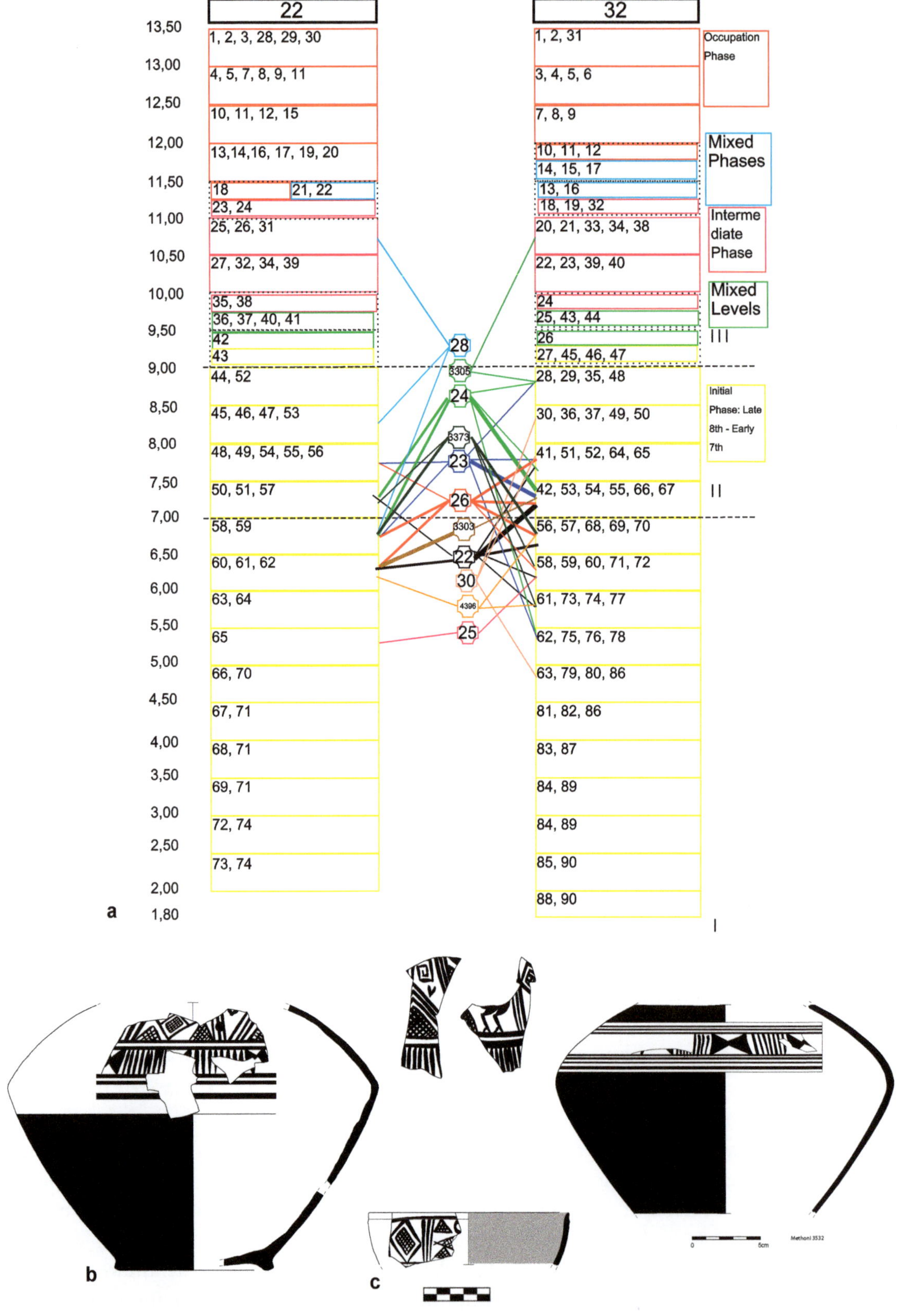

FIGURE 22.10. a) Distribution of north Ionian bird kotylai fragments across different levels of the Hypogeion; b) two north Ionian bird oinochoai from the Hypogeion (ΜΕΘ 4046 and ΜΕΘ 3532); c) North Ionian bird kotyle from the agora at Methone (ΜΕΘ 7528). Joins distribution prepared by A. DiBattista; drawings T. Ross

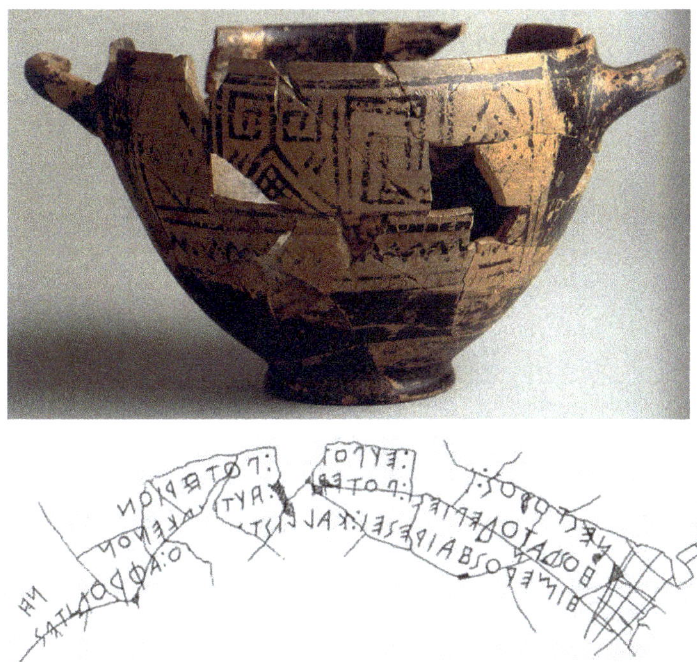

FIGURE 22.11. The cup of Nestor from Pithekoussai (after Papadopoulos 2016, p. 1245, fig. 5)

western Aegean; to Al Mina and Tarsus in the eastern Mediterranean; and to Pithekoussai, Megara Hyblaia, and Gela, in the western colonies.[67]

While the quantity of bird kotylai has been steadily growing in east Greece, various parts of the Aegean, and the Mediterranean beyond,[68] there has been a curious dearth of these shapes in the north Aegean. There is one published fragment from Torone in Chalkidike, and one or two fragments from Karabournaki that I know of.[69] The issue, in part, is that imports of the late 8th century B.C. and earlier tend to be rare in most parts of the north Aegean, the primary exceptions to date being Troy, Torone, and Methone. The sheer number of bird kotylai from this one context at Methone is a welcome addition, pointing to close contact between Methone and north Ionia precisely at the time when the site was being colonized by Eretrians, and at least half a century before the Klazomenian attempt to colonize Abdera in 654 B.C.[70] Here, it is interesting to note that although the Archaic cemetery of Abdera has yielded numerous examples of north Ionian bird bowls and related banded bowls, not one bird kotyle has been found at the site, at least from that area already excavated, precisely because the colonization of Abdera postdates bird kotylai.[71]

As for the provenance of the fabric, although noting the strong possibility of local imitations, Coldstream, in reviewing the available evidence in 1968, settled on a Rhodian origin, and argued specifically for Ialysos as the most probable center of production, with Kameiros as a second possibility. He also considered Ialysos and Kameiros as the likely production centers of the bird bowls, a conclusion questioned by John Hayes, who also suggested Samos and Kos as possibilities, adding, "a north Ionian origin for the present series is improbable."[72] The most recent evidence, however, does suggest north Ionia as the most likely place where the type originated and was largely produced.[73] Of the various north Ionian cities, I had originally considered Klazomenai as a likely producer, but the fabric of the bird kotylai, as well as that of the bird bowls from Methone, does not visually match that of Klazomenai, and the fabric is different from that normally found in the pottery from Smyrna, or at least that which I have seen.[74] The most recent results of elemental analysis, which remain to be confirmed, suggest that Teos may be a primary producer of north Ionian bird kotylai and bird bowls.[75]

TABLE 22.1. The Hypogeion contexts of the north Ionian bird kotylai (**22/22–22/34**, and MEΘ 4396)

Catalogue & MEΘ numbers	Context	Hypogeion Phase	Cold-stream Phase
22/22 (MEΘ 1318)	#274/022050, 022060, 022061, 032041, 032054, 032055, 032056, 032066, 032067, 032069, 032071, 032074	I, II	First
22/23 (MEΘ 1591)	#274/022055, 022058, 032041, 032048, 032053, 032054, 032055, 032062	I–II	First
22/24 (MEΘ 3239)	#274/022050, 022051, 022058, 022059, 022060, 032041, 032048, 032054, 032064, 032065	I–II	First
22/25 (MEΘ 3302)	#274/022065, 032060	I	First
22/26 (MEΘ 1592)	#274/022048, 022058, 022059, 022060, 022061, 032041, 032055, 032057, 032058, 032065, 032067, 032069	I–II	First
22/27 (MEΘ 3374)	#274/032062	I	First
22/28 (MEΘ 3198)	#274/022059, 022031, 022046	I, II & mixed levels	First
22/29 (MEΘ 3305)	#274/032038, 032048	II and in mixed levels	First
22/30 (MEΘ 3303)	#274/022060, 022061, 022062, 032054	I–II (only one fr Phase II)	First
22/31 (MEΘ 3373)	#274/022051, 022058, 022059, 032056, 032057, 032059, 032073	I–II (only one fr Phase II)	First
22/32 (MEΘ 2917)	#274/022043 (very last bucket)	Mixed levels	Unclear
22/33 (MEΘ 3306)	#274/032065, 032079, 032049	I–II	Second
22/34 (MEΘ 3300)	#274/022063	I	Second
MEΘ 4396	#274/022062, 032061, 032057	I	Unclear

The bird kotylai from the Hypogeion at Methone selected for presentation here provide only a sample of the available material at the site; there are many more examples, and, as with the Aiolian graywares, a closer study of this class of pottery is necessary. In order to assemble as representative a sample as possible, I have included examples of Coldstream's first and second phase of the bird kotylai, though it is clear that the majority can be assigned to Coldstream's first phase. Essentially, the examples of the first phase have four panels in the upper metopal zone (**22/22–22/31**, and probably **22/32**); those of the second phase have three (**22/33**, **22/34**). Of the former, kotylai with four panels that are more or less of equal width are rare; there are only two examples, **22/22** and **22/25**, and these two should be among the earliest thus far recorded from the site. The majority (**22/23**, **22/24**, **22/26–22/31**) are stylistically later, and one of the four panels is a narrow column of vertically arranged chevrons.

As for their fabric, the majority of the Methone bird kotylai belong to the primary series, which Coldstream originally thought was Rhodian, and is now almost certainly north Ionian. There are, however, exceptions, among which **22/34** is the most obvious. The fabric of this piece is very different from the main series, the decoration is also anomalous, and this kotyle was clearly made at some place other than that where the main series was produced. The only other piece of note is **22/32**; although its fabric and decoration fit within the normal range of the primary group, its clay shares some features that are more common with the pottery from Klazomenai, and I therefore wonder whether it was made there, or at some other north Ionian center.

The reserved surfaces of most, if not all, of the Methone bird kotylai are burnished, although in some the surfaces are worn.

Coldstream's first phase

22/22. (ΜΕΘ 1318) Fragmentary Bird Kotyle Fig. 22.12

East Hill, Hypogeion #274/022050 (2), 022060 (5), 022061 (6), 032041 (2), 032054 (1), 032055 (1), 032056 (3), 032066 (2), 032067 (1), 032069 (2), 032071 (2), 032074 (1).

H. 0.105; Diam. (base) 0.062; Diam. (rim) 0.147.

Reconstructed from many frr preserving most of vessel except for missing portion of body and rather less of the rim; both handles preserved. Surfaces worn.

Low ring base, with narrow resting surface; underside flat. Lower wall rising steeply to vertical, slightly incurved upper wall. Characteristic, very short rim, offset from the body by a slight nick; plain rounded lip. Small horizontal handles, circular in section.

Fabric fine and dense, with few visible impurities except for small white inclusions; little or no mica to speak of. Fabric more oxidized than normal; reserved surfaces fired close to light reddish brown 5YR 6/4.

Paint thickly applied and mostly well adhering, but worn in places, and variously fired from red to dark brown and black, mostly red on interior, variegated red/black on exterior. Base and lower wall painted solid. Standard metopal decoration, with four panels/metopes, on upper body. Sides of metopes framed by the usual three vertical lines; lower ancillary zone decorated with row of lined cross-hatched lozenges (six in all on both sides, with the two at the sides curtailed into triangles), framed by two bands above and two below; standard horizontal band at upper metope at juncture of body and rim. The metopal upper body thus framed has four decorated panels/metopes, each separated from the other by two vertical lines, decorated, from right to left, with: cross-hatched lozenge within a lozenge (or double-outlined lozenge); bird facing right, body cross-hatched, and with partial zigzag above left, in line with the head of the bird; tree, consisting of a cross-hatched triangle framed by a diagonal line on either side, with central vertical line extending upward from the apex of the triangle, and from which hang meanders, as shown; cross-hatched lozenge within a lozenge. Upper and outer faces of handles, rim top, and interior painted solid.

Clear evidence of use wear at the center of the floor.

22/23. (ΜΕΘ 1591) Fragmentary Bird Kotyle Fig. 22.13

Bessios, Tzifopoulos, and Kotsonas 2012, pp. 430–432, no. 92.

East Hill, Hypogeion #274/022055 (1), 022058 (2), 032041 (1), 032048 (1), 032053 (1), 032054 (6), 032055 (1), 032062 (1), 7.60/7.40 (2), 7.40/7.10 (4), 7.35/7.60 (1).

H. 0.090; Diam. (base) 0.054; Diam. (rim) 0.129.

Reconstructed from numerous frr preserving slightly more than one-half of vessel; complete profile preserved, including one complete handle, the other almost complete.

Ring foot, with flat underside; lower wall rising steeply, upper wall vertical, slightly incurved, with small offset (nick) 0.006–0.007 below lip; plain rounded lip. Two small horizontal handles, circular in section, rising fractionally above the level of the lip.

Thin-walled fabric, with few visible impurities; very occasional small white inclusions, and occasional blowout; no mica to speak of. Clay core mostly fired gray, close to gray 5YR 5/1; reserved surfaces evenly fired, closest to light brown 7.5YR 6/3–6/4; reserved underside a little lighter, closer to pink 7.5YR 7/3–7/4.

Paint in places evenly and quite thickly applied, especially on interior and around the handles on exterior, a little more dilute on lower wall, uniformly fired black. Base and lower wall painted solid,

FIGURE 22.12. North Ionian bird kotyle, **22/22** (ΜΕΘ 1318).
Drawing I. Moschou and T. Ross, photos I. Coyle

with paint extending onto small portions of resting surface, most of which is otherwise reserved. Outer faces of handles painted, inner faces reserved. Broad diagonal stripe of thick paint on either side of each handle, more or less creating a triangle that frames each handle. These broad stripes also define the reserved metopal decoration on the side of the upper body; the sides of the panels are further framed by three vertical lines, extending, as shown, from just below the rim to the area painted solid below, each vertical line tapering toward the bottom. Ancillary zone below each metopal panel decorated with thickish zigzag, with two horizontal bands below and two above, not one of the horizontal bands extending right across the metopal decoration. The upper metopal zone, thus defined, of four smaller panels/metopes, each separated by two vertical lines, decorated, left to right, with a cross-hatched lozenge within a lozenge; bird, facing right, outlined in black, with cross-hatched body and, on the side of the tail, an upright cross-hatched triangle below and a similar pendent cross-hatched triangle above; then panel with vertical row of chevrons (six in line); and, finally, another cross-hatched lozenge within a lozenge. (What little survives of the other side of the vessel is similarly decorated, with a cross-hatched lozenge within a lozenge, framed by vertical lines, and horizontal bands enclosing a zigzag.) Horizontal band above, right on the nick at juncture of the upper body and rim. Interior and most of the lip top painted solid.

Graffito, incised after firing, under the completely preserved handle: small circle (Diam. 0.006), incised with a pair of dividers with a pivot point at center. A similar graffito, only partially preserved, under the opposite handle and closer to one side rather than in the center. As the graffito is post-firing, it is unlikely to be a potter's mark.

Vessel mended in antiquity, with only a single preserved mending hole near the edge of the poorly preserved side of the vessel.

FIGURE 22.13. North Ionian bird kotyle, **22/23** (MEΘ 1591).
Drawing I. Moschou and T. Ross; photos KZ´ Ephoreia

22/24. (MEΘ 3239) Fragmentary Bird Kotyle Fig. 22.14

Bessios, Tzifopoulos, and Kotsonas 2012, pp. 434–435, no. 95.

East Hill, Hypogeion #274/022032, 022050 (1), 022051 (1), 022058 (14), 022059 (6), 032041 (1), 032048 (1), 032054 (1), 032064 (1), 032065 (1).

P.H. 0.079; Diam. (rim) 0.131.

Reconstructed from many joining frr preserving all of rim and upper body, including one complete and one partially preserved handle, but nothing of the lowermost body and base.

Shape as **22/23** (MEΘ 1591), with small nick at juncture of rim and upper body (0.006–0.009 below lip).

Fabric as **22/23**, but fired a little lighter. Clay core gray, closest to gray 5YR 5/1; reserved surfaces evenly fired close to reddish yellow 7.5YR 6/6.

Paint and decoration as **22/23**, and perhaps by the same painter/workshop, but with the following differences: paint on interior mostly fired red, with patches of grayish black. On one side of the vessel there are four (rather than three) vertical lines framing the metopal zone, and one of two smaller panels/metopes separated by three (rather than two) vertical lines. The primary difference is in the birds, here with body hatched rather than cross-hatched, birds facing left, not right, and with a small reserved ovule for the eye.

Graffito, as shown, incised after firing, under one of handles and closer to one side than center.

22/25. (MEΘ 3302) Rim and Body Frr, Bird Kotyle Fig. 22.15

East Hill, Hypogeion #273/022065 (1), 032060 (2).

P.H. (largest fr) 0.075; Diam. (rim) est. ca. 0.140.

Two groups of non-joining frr preserving small parts of rim and upper body from both sides of vessel, but nothing of base and handles.

Shape as **22/22** (MEΘ 1318).

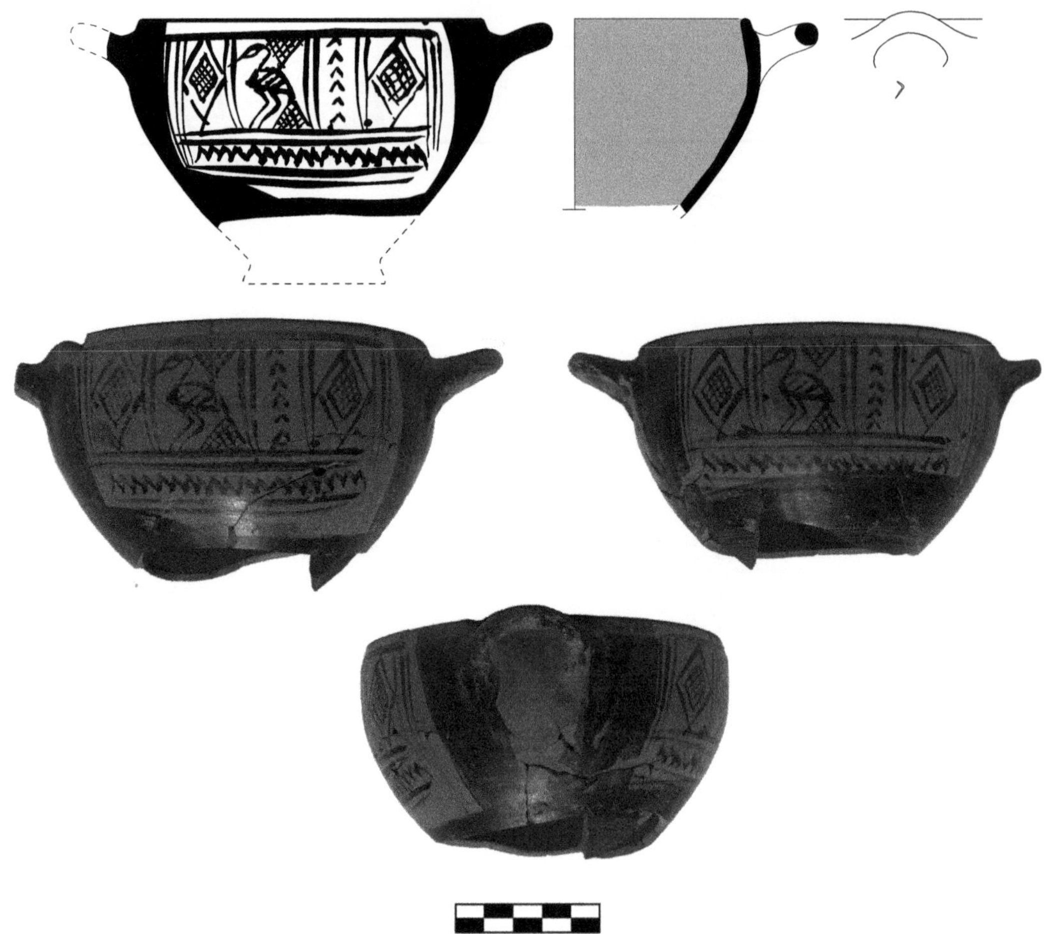

FIGURE 22.14. North Ionian bird kotyle, **22/24** (MEΘ 3239). Drawing T. Ross, photos I. Coyle

Fabric as **22/26** (MEΘ 1592) and **22/28** (MEΘ 3198), but with clay core and reserved surfaces more uniformly fired close to light reddish brown 5YR 6/4.

Paint as **22/26** (MEΘ 1592) and **22/28** (MEΘ 3198). Decoration closest to **22/22** (MEΘ 1318), but with careless ancillary zone, where the zigzag is in many places linked Xs, framed by one horizontal band below and two above. Panels in metopal zone each separated by two vertical lines and decorated, from right to left, with: cross-hatched lozenge within a lozenge; tree as on **22/22** (MEΘ 1318), and with reversed Ns on either side as filling motifs; bird facing right, body cross-hatched, with upright cross-hatched triangle below and pendent cross-hatched triangle above framing tail, and a reversed N above the body of the bird; cross-hatched lozenge within a lozenge. Interior and lip top painted solid.

22/26. (MEΘ 1592) Fragmentary Bird Kotyle Fig. 22.15

East Hill, Hypogeion #022048 (1), 0220058 (3), 022059 (1), 022060 (1), 022061 (1), 032041 (1), 032055 (1), 032057 (3), 032058 (1), 032065 (1), 032067 (1), 032069 (1).

H. 0.090; Diam. (base) 0.053; Diam. (rim) est. 0.150.

Reconstructed from many joining frr preserving entire base and lower body and just under one-half of upper body and rim, including one handle. At least one fr affected by fire directly joining with frr unburnt. At least one non-joining fr.

FIGURE 22.15. North Ionian bird kotylai, **22/25** (ΜΕΘ 3302) and **22/26** (ΜΕΘ 1592). Drawings I. Moschou and T. Ross, photos I. Coyle

Low ring base, with narrow resting surface and with small groove at center of resting surface; underside flat. Lower wall rising steeply to vertical, slightly incurved upper wall. Very short rim offset from body by slight nick; plain rounded lip. Small horizontal handle, circular in section.

Fabric fine and dense with few visible impurities except for small white inclusions; little or no mica to speak of. Clay core fired close to reddish gray 5YR 5/2 and weak red 2.5YR 5/2; reserved surfaces closer to light reddish brown 5YR 6/4.

Paint thickly applied and well adhering, uniformly fired black, thinning to dark brown in places on exterior where more dilute. Foot exterior and lower wall painted solid, so too the areas framing the handle. Ancillary zone decorated with zigzag, framed by two horizontal bands below and two above. Upper metopal zone framed by horizontal band at juncture of upper body and rim, the sides framed by three vertical lines. Metopal zone consists of four panels/metopes, each separated by two vertical lines and decorated, right to left, with: cross-hatched lozenge within a lozenge; vertical column of chevrons (six where complete); bird, only partially preserved, facing left, body hatched, with cross-hatched upright triangle below and pendent cross-hatched triangle above; cross-hatched lozenge within a lozenge. Interior and rim top painted solid.

Vessel mended in antiquity, with one preserved mending hole at midpoint near break on one side; another on the non-joining fr.

22/27. (ΜΕΘ 3374) Fragmentary Bird Kotyle Fig. 22.16

East Hill, Hypogeion #274/032062 (1), with additional sherds from various passes.

H. 0.099; Diam. (base) 0.056; Diam. (rim) est. 0.130–0.140.

Reconstructed from many frr preserving almost complete base and a little less than one-quarter of rim and upper body, including one handle.

Shape as **22/26** (MEΘ 1592), down to details.

Fabric as **22/26** (MEΘ 1592) and **22/28** (MEΘ 3198), but more oxidized. Clay core fired close to pinkish gray 5YR 6/2; reserved surfaces closer to reddish yellow 5YR 6/6.

Paint as **22/26** (MEΘ 1592) and **22/28** (MEΘ 3198), but fired red, shading to dark brown at limited points on exterior. Decoration as **22/26** (MEΘ 1592), except that bird faces right and its body is cross-hatched (it is possible that there were cross-hatched triangles as on **22/26** [MEΘ 1592] beyond the break).

22/28. (MEΘ 3198) Fragmentary Bird Kotyle Fig. 22.16

East Hill, Hypogeion #274/022059, 022031, 022046.

H. (to rim) 0.090; H. (to handle) 0.085; Diam. (base) 0.055; Diam. (rim) est. 0.120.

Three joining frr preserving all of base and about one-quarter to one-third of rim, including one handle, and corresponding body. At least one non-joining fr may belong to this vessel.

Low ring base, with narrow resting surface and small groove at center of resting surface; underside flat. Lower wall rising steeply to vertical, slightly incurved, upper wall. Short rim, offset from body by slight nick; plain rounded lip. Small horizontal handle, circular in section, rising very slightly above the level of the rim.

Fabric fine and dense with few visible impurities except for small white inclusions; little or no mica to speak of. Clay core fired gray, close to gray 5YR 5/1 and reddish gray 2.5YR 5/1; reserved surfaces lighter, closer to light reddish brown 5YR 6/4.

Paint thickly applied and well adhering, fired black, with a good sheen, especially on interior, thinning to dark brown in places on exterior where more dilute. Foot exterior and lower wall painted solid, as are areas framing handle (body immediately below handle reserved). Metopal zone similar to **22/26** (MEΘ 1592) and **22/27** (MEΘ 3374), but more carelessly executed. Sides of decorated upper body framed at sides by three vertical lines. Ancillary zone decorated with crude zigzag, becoming linked Xs at points; horizontal band defines upper zone at juncture of body and rim. The upper metopal zone is defined into four panels/metopes, but these are separated from each other sometimes with a single vertical line, sometimes with three vertical lines. The panels are decorated, from right to left, with: cross-hatched lozenge within a lozenge, but anchored to the horizontal line below by a short vertical stroke; vertical column of chevrons (nine in all); crudely drawn bird in silhouette, facing right, but with reserved inner head, and with a cross-hatched lozenge below and cross-hatched pendent triangle above, on either side of the tail; then anchored lozenge, precisely as on opposite side. Upper and outer faces of handle painted. Interior and rim top painted solid. The drawing overall is crude and hastily executed.

22/29. (MEΘ 3305) Rim and Handle Frr, Bird Kotyle Fig. 22.17

East Hill, Hypogeion #274/032038 (1).

P.H. 0.057; Diam. (rim) est. 0.150.

Four joining frr preserving portion of rim and upper body including one handle, but nothing of the base and lower body.

Shape as **22/28** (MEΘ 3198).

Fabric as **22/28** (MEΘ 3198) and **22/26** (MEΘ 1592).

Paint as **22/28** (MEΘ 3198) and **22/26** (MEΘ 1592). Decoration as **22/28** (MEΘ 3198), but with two vertical lines framing preserved left side. Decoration from left to right: cross-hatched lozenge within a lozenge; three vertical lines; bird facing left, body cross-hatched, with pendent cross-hatched triangles above and three N-motifs filling the open spaces.

FIGURE 22.16. North Ionian bird kotylai, **22/27** (MEΘ 3374) and **22/28** (MEΘ 3198). Drawings T. Ross, photos I. Coyle

22/30. (MEΘ 3303) Rim and Handle Frr, Bird Kotyle Fig. 22.17

East Hill #274/022060 (1), 022061 (3), 022062 (2), 032054 (1).

P.H. 0.062; Diam. (rim) est. 0.130.

Seven joining frr preserving small portion of rim and upper body, including one handle, but nothing of the lower body or base. At least one non-joining fr should be from this piece.

Shape as **22/28** (MEΘ 3198).

Fabric as **22/28** (MEΘ 3198), but reduced, with clay core and reserved surfaces fired close to gray 5YR 6/1.

Paint as **22/28** (MEΘ 3198), fired black, in places with minor streaks of dark reddish brown and gray. Decoration related to that of other bird kotylai, but different. Preserved side framed by at least two vertical lines; lower panel framed by zigzag, with two horizontal bands above but none below. Standard band framing upper panel at juncture with rim. The decorative panel thus defined, decoration from left to right consists of cross-hatched lozenge within a lozenge; two vertical lines; vertical cross-hatched lozenge chain; two vertical lines; then another motif at break, perhaps a meander extending from a vertical line, but this remains uncertain.

22/31. (MEΘ 3373) Rim, Body, and Handle Frr, Bird Kotyle Fig. 22.17

East Hill #274/022051 (9), 022058 (1), 022059 (1), 032056 (1), 032057 (1), 032059 (1), 032073 (2).

P.H. 0.079; Diam. (rim) est. 0.145.

Reconstructed from many frr preserving about one-half of rim and upper body, including one handle, but nothing of the base. At least one fire-affected fr joins frr that are not burned.

Shape as **22/28** (MEΘ 3198).

Fabric as **22/28** (MEΘ 3198), but with clay core closer to light reddish brown 2.5YR 6/4.

Paint as **22/28** (MEΘ 3198), but mostly fired brown to dark reddish brown. Decoration very similar to **22/22** (MEΘ 1318), but more crudely executed and with zigzag framing decorative panel, framed by two bands above, but none below. Decoration of the main zone is almost identical to **22/22** (MEΘ 1318), except that there is no bird; instead, the panel that would have held bird has a thick vertical zigzag. Also as many as four vertical lines framing the sides, many of which merge. Handle, rim top, and interior as **22/28** (MEΘ 3198).

Vessel mended in antiquity, with at least 12 mending holes preserved on the surviving frr.

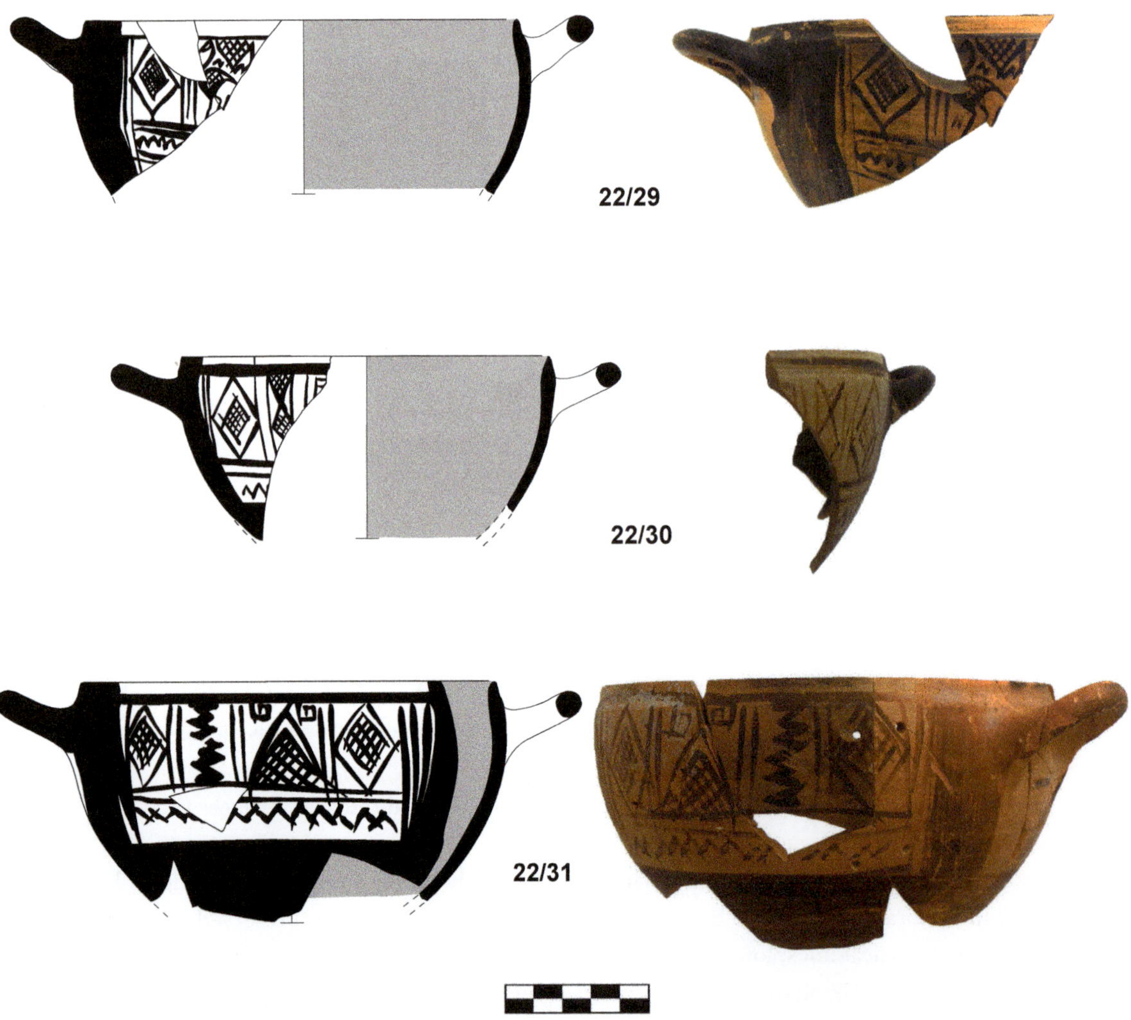

FIGURE 22.17. North Ionian bird kotylai, **22/29** (MEΘ 3305), **22/30** (MEΘ 3303), and **22/31** (MEΘ 3373). Drawings I. Moschou and T. Ross, photos I. Coyle

FIGURE 22.18. Fragmentary North Ionian bird kotyle, **22/32** (MEΘ 2917).
Photo I. Coyle

Too little survives of the following kotyle to determine, with certainty, whether it belongs to Coldstream's First Phase, but I am fairly sanguine that it most probably does.

22/32. (MEΘ 2917) Frr of Bird Kotyle Fig. 22.18

Bessios, Tzifopoulos, and Kotsonas 2012, pp. 433–434, no. 94.

East Hill, Hypogeion #274/022043 (11).

P.H. (largest fr) 0.062; Diam. (rim) est. 0.180.

Five frr in all, surviving as three non-joining groups of frr, preserving small portion of rim and upper body, including one complete handle.

Shape as **22/23** (MEΘ 1591) and **22/24** (MEΘ 3239), but clearly from a large kotyle, with offset (nick) about 0.008 below lip.

Fabric as **22/23** (MEΘ 1591), but with finest dusting of surface mica; clay core fired light gray, closest to reddish gray 10R 6/1; reserved surface fired closer to light reddish brown 2.5YR 6/4–7/4.

Paint as **22/23** (MEΘ 1591), but mostly fired reddish brown, in places approaching black and a mottled red to reddish brown, almost with a maroon tinge on interior. The little that survives of decoration resembles that of other bird kotylai, not least **22/22** and **22/23** (MEΘ 1318 and MEΘ 1591). There is a thickish zigzag framed by two horizontal bands above and two below; greater part of a cross-hatched lozenge within a lozenge survives, and on one fr there appears to be the lowest chevron of a vertical chevron column, to left of which there appears to be the lower legs of a bird, facing right.

Dipinto: small horizontal dash, painted before firing, below one of the handles.

Although fragmentary and difficult to establish with certainty whether the frr belong to Coldstream's first or second phase, it is likely that the kotyle originally had a four-panel metopal zone, and is, therefore, best assigned to the first phase.

Coldstream's second phase

22/33. (MEΘ 3306) Rim and Upper Body Frr, Bird Kotyle Fig. 22.19

East Hill, Hypogeion, side α: #274/032065 (2), 032079 (1); side β: 032049 (3).

P.H. (largest fr) 0.057; Diam. (rim) est. 0.140–0.150.

Three non-joining groups of frr preserving small portion of rim and upper body from both sides of the vessel, but nothing of base or handles. Traces of burning on one fr.

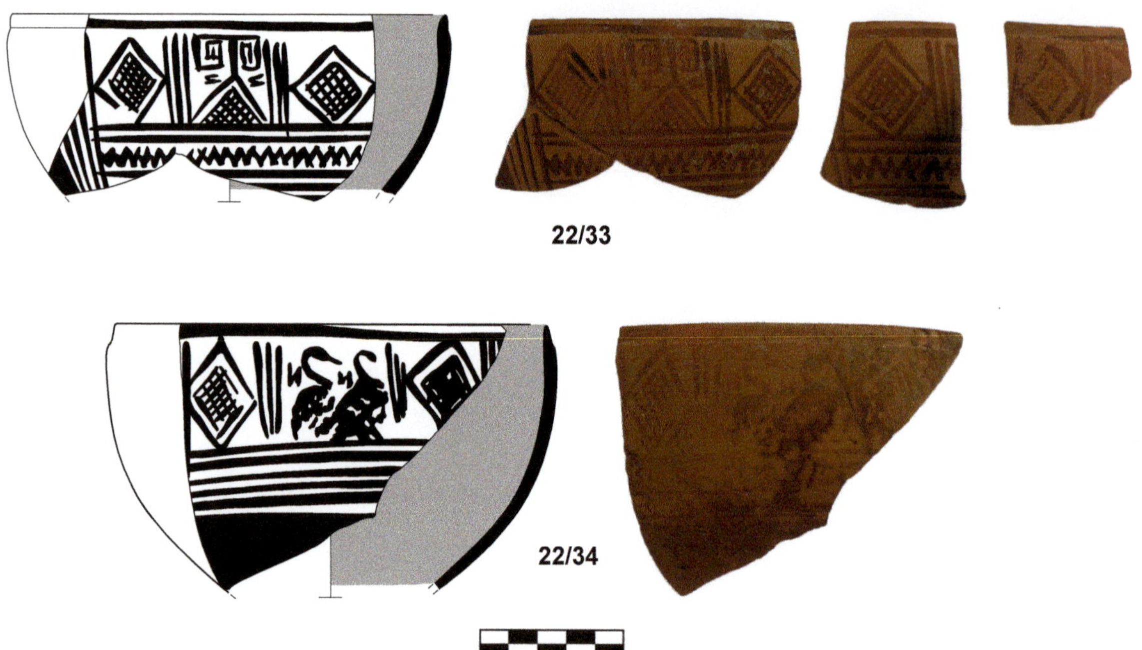

FIGURE 22.19. Fragmentary North Ionian bird kotylai, **22/33** (MEΘ 3306) and **22/34** (MEΘ 3300). Drawings T. Ross, photos I. Coyle

Shape as **22/28** (MEΘ 3198).

Fabric as **22/22** (MEΘ 1318).

Paint as **22/22** (MEΘ 1318), mostly fired red. Lower ancillary zone decorated with zigzag framed by two horizontal bands below and two above. Upper metopal zone made up of three panels/metopes, each separated by groups of three vertical lines (unlike the more common two on the earlier kotylai); four vertical lines frame entire zone on left side, and there is a horizontal band above at the juncture of upper body and articulated rim. The metopal zone thus defined was decorated, on either side, by a cross-hatched lozenge within a lozenge; the central motif is a tree, with a cross-hatched triangle base, a vertical line emanating from the apex of the triangle serving as the "trunk," and two heraldically arranged meanders suspended at the top of the trunk; two reversed Ns placed horizontally as filling motifs. Interior and rim top painted solid.

22/34. (MEΘ 3300) Rim and Upper Body Fr, Bird Kotyle Fig. 22.19

East Hill, Hypogeion #274/022063.

P.H. (largest fr) 0.087; Diam. (rim) est. 0.160.

Main group of joining frr preserving small portion of rim and upper body, but nothing of base or handles. Five or six additional small non-joining frr of body and rim are almost certainly from this kotyle. Surfaces much worn inside and out.

Standard shape, as **22/22** and others.

Fabric, although not unlike that of the main series, differs in the fact that it is very micaceous, with the occasional large white inclusion erupting onto the surface. Clay core fired close to reddish brown 2.5YR 5/4; reserved surfaces lighter, fired closer to light reddish brown 2.5YR 6/4.

Paint probably originally applied rather thickly, but much flaked, with central portion of decorated metope especially worn, which is an unusual feature of the bird kotylai from the Hypogeion. Upper part of preserved lower wall painted solid. The ancillary zone immediately above is very worn; there are at least three, and probably at least four, horizontal bands, and perhaps originally more (as indicated on the drawing); it is even possible that these enclosed a horizontal zigzag, but this is far from clear. Metopal zone consists of three panels/metopes, each separated by three vertical lines (there is only one surviving vertical line framing this zone on left side and portion of at least three on the right side). The metopal zone was decorated, on either side, by a cross-hatched lozenge within a lozenge; the central panel is decorated with a crudely drawn bird facing right, body evidently painted solid, but not even this is clear, with reversed Ns on either side serving as filling ornaments. What appears as a second bird may be more apparent than real, as the body here was especially encrusted, though there is a curved motif, very much resembling a bird's neck, to the right. Horizontal band above, at juncture of upper body and rim, at points extending to lip. Interior and rim top painted solid.

The combined features of the fabric and decoration of **22/34** suggest that it was made at some place other than that where the main series was produced.

For multiple birds on north Ionian bird kotyle from Klaros, see Zunal 2015, pp. 246–247, 343, fig. 3, with three birds in one panel, all painted solid.

Bird Bowls

Relatively few of the later Subgeometric and Archaic north Ionian bird bowls were found on the East and West Hills in comparison to the complete, semi-complete, and fragmentary examples of the Late Geometric bird kotylai from the Hypogeion, although larger quantities were more recently encountered in the 2014–2017 excavations on the summit of the West Hill. It is now more likely that there was continuous importation of north Ionian bird kotylai and bowls from the 8th through 6th centuries B.C. Only two fragments, both from the West Hill, are presented here (**22/35–22/36**, Fig. 22.20a–b); another fragment from the East Hill (ΜΕΘ 7529) was found in 2005 (Fig. 22.20c).[76]

In describing this characteristic shape, Cook begins:

> The Bird bowl—"bowl" is an unhappy but now hallowed description—is the most elegant product of East Greek Subgeometric, using traditional Geometric motives in an increasingly mannered and eventually careless way. It evolved from the Bird kotyle during the first quarter of the seventh century, simplifying the decoration and flattening the shape. A regular size is of 15 cm diameter at the rim.[77]

Cook goes on to describe the chronological development of the bird bowls and, following Coldstream, suggests absolute dates for the four successive phases: Group I: 700/690–675; Group II: 675–640; Group III: 650–615; Group IV: 615–600 or "after 615."[78] Of the two examples from Methone presented below, **22/36** (ΜΕΘ 5120) is too small to assign chronologically, but **22/35** (ΜΕΘ 5682) may be confidently assigned to Coldstream's Group II.

As for their fabric, the two pieces from Methone share a clay and finish similar to that of the main series of bird kotylai, and a north Ionian provenance seems clear enough (see above). This said, various workshops in East Greece and beyond have been claimed, from Rhodes to Chios, Samos to Miletos, and even Eretria.[79]

Bird bowls have a wide distribution throughout the eastern Aegean and have been found as far south as Crete;[80] in the north Aegean, bird bowls have been recorded at Karabournaki,[81] Abdera,[82] Thasos,[83] Torone,[84] Parthenonas (Mt. Itamos),[85] Aphytis,[86] Sane,[87] and Akanthos,[88] among other sites; they have been found in Sicily and southern Italy,[89] in the eastern Mediterranean,[90] in North Africa,[91] and in the Black Sea.[92]

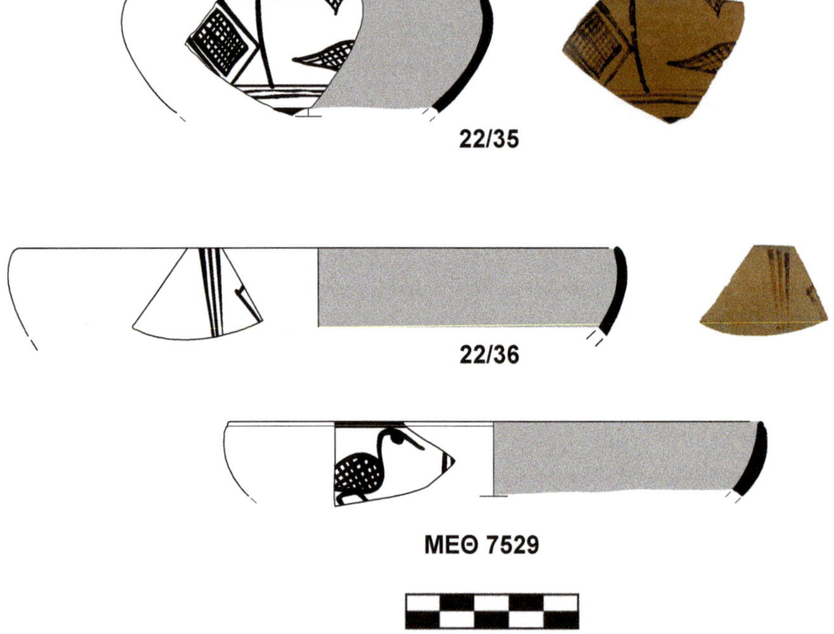

FIGURE 22.20. Fragments of North Ionian bird bowls, **22/35** (MEΘ 5682), **22/36** (MEΘ 5120), and MEΘ 7529. Drawings T. Ross and F. Skyvalida, photos I. Coyle

22/35. (MEΘ 5682) Rim Fr, Bird Bowl Fig. 22.20

West Hill #229/013004 [4].

P.H. 0.034; Diam. (rim) est. 0.100.

Single fr preserving small portion of rim and upper body.

Upper body curving up to vertical, slightly incurving rim, with plain round lip.

Fabric very fine and dense, with few visible impurities and no mica. Clay core and reserved surfaces closest to pink 7.5YR 7/3.

Reserved surface on exterior nicely burnished. Paint well applied and well adhering, fired black. Thick band or area painted solid at lower break; three thin bands above defining the decoration of the rim zone. The latter is decorated, to left, by a cross-hatched lozenge encased in a lozenge; vertical line to right extending from lip to the horizontal bands below. To right, portion of the body and tail of a bird, cross-hatched; small pendent cross-hatched triangle above. Thin band at lip, extending onto top of lip. Preserved interior painted solid.

Cf., among others, Kinch 1914, col. 133, fig. 44a–b; Yfantidis 1990, p. 185, no. 127 (labeled "Karisch?" and dated to 675–640 B.C).

22/36. (MEΘ 5120) Rim Fr, Bird Bowl Fig. 22.20

West Hill #229/011 (surface). 27/8/2007.

P.H. 0.023; p.W. 0.037; Diam. (rim) N/R.

Single fr preserving small portion of rim and upper body.

Upper body curving up to vertical rim, with plain rounded lip.

Fabric as **22/35** (MEΘ 5682), but with clay core and reserved surfaces closer to pink 7.5YR 7/4.

Reserved surface on exterior nicely burnished. Paint well applied and well adhering, fired black, reddish brown where more dilute. On exterior three vertical lines, each tapering toward bottom; to right painted motif, probably a lozenge. Interior and rim top painted solid.

CHIAN CHALICES

In comparison to other East Greek wares, fine decorated pottery of Chios was a rare import at Methone, particularly striking in light of the fact that Chian commodity amphoras were among the most common category of transport containers at Methone, especially on the West Hill.[93] The two small fragments presented below, both from the West Hill, represent the very few identified pieces of this category of the Archaic period thus far found at the site; nothing approaching a complete vessel has been found. This only holds true for the later Chian chalices of the later 7th and 6th century B.C. Earlier proto-chalices of the later 8th and earlier 7th century B.C. are known from the Hypogeion, and one of the inscribed examples of these earlier chalices is both catalogued and illustrated below (**22/37** [ΜΕΘ 3241 + 2308]).[94] It is, therefore, possible that there was a more continuous import of Chian fine wares at Methone, a pattern more in keeping with the occurrence of the Chian amphoras at the site, but clear evidence for this is not at present forthcoming. A few additional fragments of Chian chalices were found in the more recent excavations in 2014–2017 on the West Hill, but the quantity is not great.

As Cook noted, the Chian school is perhaps the best understood of the East Greek pottery production centers of its time, "its products in general easy to recognize by the whiteness of their slip (which becomes still whiter in the 6th century), the use of this slip under the dark paint that covers the surface inside open pots, and often the pinkish color of the clay. The dating too is assured roughly by the stratified deposits, properly published, of Emporio on Chios and Tocra in Libya, some contexts in Smyrna, and a very few graves."[95] In addition to the seminal publications of Chios and Tocra—supplemented by the publication of the Chian pottery from Kyrene[96]—the decorated styles of Chian pottery have received full and detailed analysis by Anna Lemos, who traces the distribution of the style throughout east Greece and Anatolia, mainland Greece and the Aegean islands, the north Aegean and Black Seas, Egypt and Cyrenaica, and the West, as well as the eastern Mediterranean.[97]

In discussing East Greek pottery in general, Boardman makes two important points that hold true of East Greek vase painting wherever it is produced. First of all, he states: "We are in an area of the Greek world where potters could be intermittently innovative but remained basically uninterested in developments elsewhere. The cities and islands, except for Rhodes, also remained relatively indifferent to reception of Corinthian or Attic decorated pottery."[98] The second point he makes is: "For reasons best known to themselves the East Greeks did not much use their pottery as a field for any notable range of narrative scenes such as we find in the rest of Greece . . . . Only Homer's island, Chios, seems an exception, but the evidence is meagre."[99]

The context of **22/38** (ΜΕΘ 5118) is 7th century B.C., that of **22/39** (ΜΕΘ 5119) is associated with the interior of Building Γ and is Archaic, but a date more precise than the 6th century B.C., and perhaps the first half or the middle of the century, is not possible. A late 8th century B.C. date for **22/37** is clear enough.[100]

Elsewhere in the north Aegean, Chian chalices are common. Perhaps the most spectacular single assemblage comprises the ten complete Chian chalices found in the Archaic tombs of the Agia Paraskevi cemetery in Thessaloniki.[101] Elsewhere in the north, Chian chalices, together with other Chian fine wares, have been found at Leivithra,[102] Karabournaki,[103] Souroti (Thessaloniki),[104] Oisyme,[105] Thasos,[106] Torone,[107] Parthenonas (Mt. Itamos),[108] Aphytis,[109] Zone in Thrace,[110] Mytilene and Eresos on Lesbos,[111] and elsewhere; the distribution of Chian pottery, particularly chalices, in the Black Sea is mapped out by Lemos (especially at Apollonia Pontica, Istros, and Berezan [Borysthenes]).[112] I do not include here the locally-produced pottery of the Chian workshop in Thrace, first isolated on Thasos, and found in Neapolis (Kavala), Oisyme, and Ainos (Enez).[113]

I begin with the proto-chalice, **22/37** (ΜΕΘ 3241 + 2308), as this is the earliest and belongs to a form not commonly found outside of its home region.[114] The shape and decoration of **22/37** is interesting as it is ancestral not only to the later Chian chalices, such as **22/38** and **22/39**, but also to the common Ionian banded cups (*Knickrandschalen*). This said, the fabric of the vessel is not exactly like that of the later Chian chalices, though it is in the broader range of Chian fabric of the period.[115] It goes without saying that the term "chalice" is conventional;[116] **22/37** could just as happily, perhaps even more so, be called a kylix or skyphos.

Late Geometric ΠΡΩΤΟ-ΚΑΛΥΚΑ (Proto-chalice)

22/37. (ΜΕΘ 3241 + 2308) Frr of Proto-chalice — Fig. 22.21

Bessios, Tzifopoulos, and Kotsonas 2012, pp. 436–437, no. 97.

East Hill, Hypogeion #274/022, 032067 (7). Larger fr: 032053 (10), 032055 (2), 7.60–7.40 m (5), 7.40–7.10 m (3), fill under Wall 14 (1); smaller fr: 032067 (7), 7.90–7.10 m.

P.H. (largest fr) 0.076; Diam. (rim) est. 0.160.

Two segments of the same vessel, each comprising many joining frr, but not joining among themselves, preserving portion of rim and upper body, including both handles, of large open vessel.

Upper body curving in to tall offset flaring rim, with plain rounded lip. Two thickish horizontal handles, round in section, attached to uppermost body.

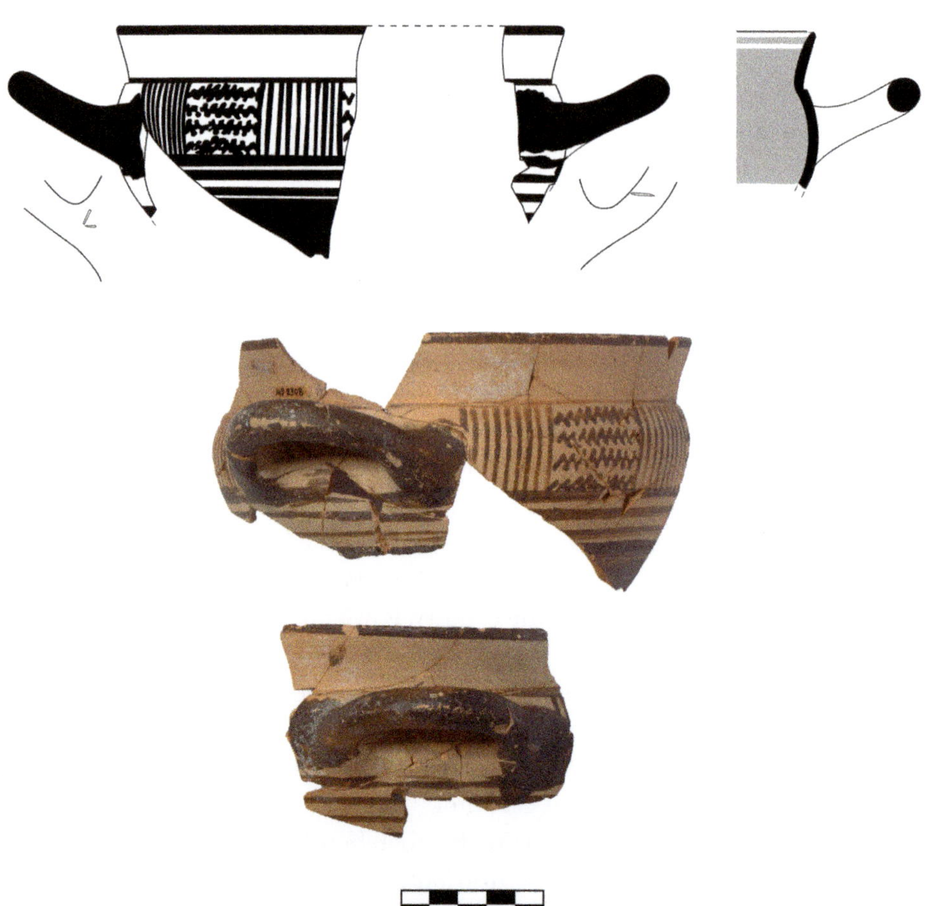

Figure 22.21. Early Chian chalice (πρωτο-κάλυκα) **22/37** (ΜΕΘ 3241 + 2308) from the Hypogeion. Drawing T. Ross, photo ΚΖ΄ Ephoreia

Fabric well levigated, with occasional small white inclusions, a few erupting onto the surface, and a few larger white inclusions, as well as rarer darker inclusions; fine dusting of surface mica. Clay core and reserved surfaces fired closer to light brown 7.5YR 6/4; reserved surfaces at points lighter, closer to pink 7.5YR 7/4 (the slightly darker 5YR reading in Bessios, Tzifopoulos, and Kotsonas 2012, pp. 436–437 was due to consolidant on the surface of the clay core). To my eye the fabric is closer to that of south Ionian kylikes (*Knickrandschalen*) than it is to the standard fabric of Archaic Chian chalices.

Paint evenly and generally quite thickly applied and well adhering. Paint fired dark reddish brown to dark brown, in places approaching black. Area painted solid at lower break, above which are three horizontal bands that extend below both handles. Outer, upper, and lower faces of handles painted; inner face reserved; paint on handle extending only slightly onto upper body. Handle zone decorated, as preserved, with one set of nine vertical lines framing the handle, then panel of four horizontally superimposed zigzags; another set of nine vertical lines, and another panel of at least three, and probably originally four, superimposed zigzags. Thin horizontal band of dilute paint at offset of upper body and lower rim; thicker horizontal band at upper rim, extending onto lip top. Preserved interior painted solid, except for two reserved bands at upper rim.

Graffiti: the small incised, post-firing, almost horizontal line on the lower handle attachment is clear enough; the more lightly incised vertical line at the handle base of the larger fr, which may or may not be accidental, is also clear. Multiple incisions on the interior are confined to one sherd only, and do not extend on to the joining frr, thus may not be graffiti.

Cf. Boardman 1967, p. 103, fig. 60, A–C; pp. 121–122, esp. nos. 235–237, 248; pls. 32–33 (various examples); Lemos 1991, pl. 1, esp. nos. 1–10.

Archaic Chalices

22/38. (ΜΕΘ 5118) Lower Rim and Upper Body Fr, Chian Chalice Fig. 22.22

West Hill #229/018007 [7]. 22–24/5/2008. Gray layer under the destruction deposit (γκρίζο χώμα κάτω από το στρώμα καύση [gray earth below the layer of burning).

P.H. 0.046; p.W. 0.038.

Single fr, broken on all sides, preserving small portion of upper body and lower rim.

Fairly squat, rounded body, as preserved, articulated from rim as shown. Lower rim tall and flaring toward lip, which is not preserved.

Characteristic Chian fabric, fine and dense, and very thin-walled, with minuscule specks of white and occasional darker inclusions, one or two blowouts, and little mica. Clay core fired close to light reddish brown 5YR 6/3, which describes well the characteristic maroon tinge of the fabric.

Thick, off-white slip, consistently applied on exterior and well adhering. Paint also well adhering, fired black, except where more dilute, where it is reddish brown. Thin horizontal band at juncture of body and rim. On body to left, portions of fine roughly parallel vertical lines. To right, at break, portion of unidentified motif. Preserved interior painted solid.

For the form of the body, and the decoration of the lower body inside and out, cf., among others, Akurgal 1950, pl. 16; Akurgal 1983, pl. 45a.

22/39. (ΜΕΘ 5119) Body Fr, Chian Chalice Fig. 22.22

West Hill #229/018003 [3]. 12–16/5/2008. East of Wall 14.

P.L. x p.W. 0.028 x 0.023.

Single fr, broken on all sides, preserving very small portion of body of open vessel.

Fr as preserved flaring; slightly thicker toward top, and from a larger and thicker-walled vessel than **22/38** (ΜΕΘ 5118).

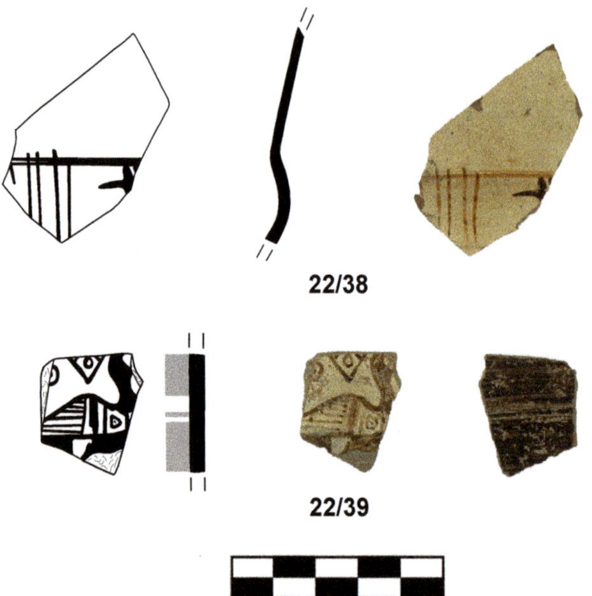

FIGURE 22.22. Fragments of Chian chalices from the West Hill, **22/38** (MEΘ 5118) and **22/39** (MEΘ 5119). Drawings F. Skyvalida, photos I. Coyle

Fabric as **22/38** (MEΘ 5118), but fired a little more gray, closer to pinkish gray 5YR 6/2 and gray 5YR 6/1, with occasional specks of mica.

Thick off-white slip, as **22/38** (MEΘ 5118). Paint fired black on interior, very dark brown approaching black on exterior. Partial bird on preserved exterior, with motifs floating above and to left, including lower portion of a lozenge, with a small circle within and dotted circle to left. Preserved interior painted solid and enlivened with horizontal bands in added white: thick band above thin band. It is also possible there was another thin band above, near upper break.

MILESIAN BOWL ("FRUIT STAND")

In comparison to the more common Aiolian graywares, the north Ionian bird kotylai and bowls, and the *Knickrandschalen*, the quantity of "Wild Goat Style" pottery at Methone from any of the East Greek production centers is not great. The solitary example presented below should be from Miletos, but on the basis of visual inspection only, not elemental analysis. In comparison, Milesian amphoras of the Archaic period are well represented among the finds from the West Hill, with at least ten examples known, and there is an earlier, late 8th or early 7th century B.C. Milesian amphora among the inscribed finds from the Hypogeion.[117]

This type of tall-footed bowl—although nothing of the foot of the example from Methone survives—is particularly well represented in Miletos and its surrounding area. One of the most important deposits of such bowls with stands comes from the sanctuary of Athena Assesia to the southeast of Miletos, which has yielded a good deal of south Ionian pottery.[118] Georg Kalaitzoglou has, to date, presented the fullest typology of this type of bowl, having distinguished, on the basis of the material from the Assesia sanctuary, several different types, with variants. He lists the bowl with stand among the south Ionian plates (*Teller*), labeling it Form A—the *Pokalfussteller*—which is divided into two types (1, with a plain rim; 2, with a flattened, horizontal rim).[119] The form of **22/40** (MEΘ 2704) accords well with Kalaitzoglou's Form

A, Type 1; the shallow form is close to Variant a, but the rim more closely resembles Variant d.[120] Among the many decorated examples from the sanctuary of Athena Assesia, the closest in terms of decoration is listed in the catalogue entry below (the distinctive rays can emanate from the rim into the center of the vessel, or vice versa); very similar birds with related subsidiary decoration are found on a variety of other vessel forms, not least Milesian kraters and jugs.[121]

As for its context, **22/40** was found in Building A, Room 2, on the West Hill, and should date before the Archaic destruction level of the middle of the 6th century B.C.; a date for **22/40** in the first half of the 6th century B.C. seems reasonable enough.

22/40. (ΜΕΘ 2704) Rim and Upper Body Fr, Bowl ("Fruit Stand") Fig. 22.23

West Hill #229/010005 [5]. Immediately north of Wall 1 (αμέσως βόρεια τοίχου 1). 25/2/2008.

Bessios and Noulas 2012, p. 405, fig. 14.

P.H. 0.039; p.L. x p.W. 0.112 x 0.103; Diam. (rim) est. 0.240.

Single fr preserving portion of rim and upper body, but nothing of the base.

Open bowl, flat toward center of floor, with upper body gently curving toward upturned rim, tapering slightly toward round lip.

Dense but grainy fabric, with several small to medium white inclusions, together with smaller dark inclusions but very little mica; some blowouts. Clay core with the characteristic maroonish tinge, close to reddish brown 2.5YR 5/3. Slipped and reserved surface on interior off-white, close to pinkish gray 5YR 7/2; reserved surface on exterior closer to light reddish brown 5YR 6/4.

Paint mostly dull, thickly applied and well adhering, fired dark brown approaching black; dark reddish brown at points on interior. Two preserved rings around center of floor, each separated/framed by two thin rings: the innermost, only partially preserved, seems to be decorated with a row of solid circles, but too little survives to be certain; the right circle has a smaller dot of added red at its center (indicated as gray on the drawing); outer ring decorated with solid squares alternating with reserved rectangles, each with small dot at center. Figured outer register decorated with bird protome in solid paint, except for eye and beak/mouth; added red circle on head and triangle on body (also indicated with gray on drawing). Dot rosette in field below beak of bird and slightly to the left, below which, and also to the left, is a dotted triangle. To upper left of bird's head a stylized half-tree, consisting of three curved arcs, the space between the outer two hatched, with a triangle at center; this motif extends from the rightmost of the six preserved rays. Two bands at rim. Horizontal band on rim exterior, with two horizontal bands immediately below and two more toward midpoint with base.

The combination of bird-head protomai, with ornamented pendent arcs and semicircles, and with similar filling ornaments, including the ring/dot rosette, is found on a number of vessels; cf. among others, Kalaitzoglou 2008, pl. 56, no. 336; Kinch 1914, pl. 4, 1a; pl. 17, no. 1; for a related bird-head protome on the shoulder of a jug, see Kinch 1914, col. 208, fig. 92 (Vroulia); Jacopi 1929, p. 84, fig. 74 (Ialysos); Jacopi 1931, p. 387, fig. 441 (Kameiros); Blinkenberg and Friis Johansen 1932, p. 56, pl. 75, esp. no. 1. For useful comparanda for Milesian filling ornaments, see Käufler 2004, pls. 62–72. For a related fruit stand from Tocra with a wild-goat protome (rather than a bird-head protome), see Boardman and Hayes 1966, pp. 48–49, fig. 24, pl. 33, no. 614.

22/40 (ΜΕΘ 2704) is bagged together with another Milesian fruit stand body fr, conceivably, but not certainly, from the same vessel, and shares the same inventory number (p.L. x p.W. 0.063 x 0.048).

FIGURE 22.23. Fragment of Milesian bowl ("fruit stand"), **22/40** (ΜΕΘ 2704). Drawing F. Skyvalida, photos J. Vanderpool

SOUTH IONIAN KYLIKES/CUPS (*KNICKRANDSCHALEN*)

Cook's short and to-the-point description of what he referred to as Ionian cups is worth quoting:

> Much more numerous are the plain cups, decorated only with simple horizontal bands, painted or reserved, and there are others that are completely covered with dark paint, except usually under the foot. Clay analysis has shown that Samos and Miletos were important producers in the later 7th and 6th centuries, but these so-called Ionian cups were probably made widely in southern workshops, not only of Ionia; and if South Ionian 3 turns out to be Aiolian, in Aiolis, too. North Ionia concentrated on the lipless Bird and Rosette bowls and their relatives. Ionian cups were exported to the East Mediterranean and Black Sea, where significant local manufacture has not yet been detected, and to the West, where it has and on a scale that is still often underestimated: cups were easy enough to shape and banded decoration still easier to apply nor does it necessarily need models. Here the old Panionist doctrine, rife a century ago, still lingers on. A large-scale investigation by clay analysis would be salutary.[122]

Boardman refers to Ionian cups collectively as representing "a *koine* with various centres of production, even outside Ionia and Rhodes (in mainland Greece and the west)."[123] Indeed, the fabric and gloss of several of the cups at Methone so resemble those of standard Attic that it is sometimes very difficult to distinguish between the two with certainty on the basis of visual inspection alone. Of the catalogued pieces, **22/41** (ΜΕΘ 3263) is the most similar to Athenian; its form is, in comparison to the other cups of this class, relatively shallow, with a lower lip, and its handles are thin, and more "pinched in" than their East Greek counterparts, a feature that was noted a long time ago by Brian Shefton.[124] Of the fragmentary examples selected for inclusion in this volume, **22/41** (ΜΕΘ 3263) was the primary example that the excavator considered Attic.

In a more recent analysis of the selected banded cups found at Methone, conducted with Trevor van Damme and Camille Acosta, we were happy to classify **22/41** (ΜΕΘ 3263) as Athenian. The fabric, glaze, and shape of **22/42** (ΜΕΘ 4407), particularly its shallow body, comparatively short rim, and overall elegant form, indicate that it is also an Athenian product. Of all the other cups, only **22/46** (ΜΕΘ 5698) may qualify as Attic. Although its rim is taller, its handles are characteristically thin, pinched in, and more horizontal, like those of **22/41** (ΜΕΘ 3263). Consequently, I begin the different sections on the cups from the East and West Hills with these three cups, **22/41** (ΜΕΘ 3263) and **22/42** (ΜΕΘ 4407) being almost certainly Attic, and **22/46** (ΜΕΘ 5698) probably Attic. I am sanguine that the other cups are all East Greek, but I am not absolutely certain about the small—almost miniature—**22/52** (ΜΕΘ 5689); its fabric is more micaceous with north Aegean overtones, and the vessel may be a local imitation of Ionian cups, perhaps from Methone, but not necessarily so.

It may seem odd to present Athenian cups in a chapter that deals with East Greek pottery, but the similarity between what I consider Athenian and Ionian is such that I think that, in many parts of the Mediterranean, Attic and East Greek versions of the shape have been confused. I am not the first to state this; as Brian Sparkes and Lucy Talcott have noted, the "origin of such cups . . . can only be recognized by a consideration of the glaze, shape, decoration and provenience; many cups with similar decoration have been called Ionian, and some certainly are so; a good number are Attic."[125] I consider it important to illustrate Athenian and East Greek examples side by side so that their similarities and differences may be more fully appreciated. Moreover, we should not lose sight of the fact that Athenians, too, were Ionians, and hence the terms "Ionian cups," as well as the more recent "Knickrandschalen" (for which see below), are both appropriate terms for these simply decorated and far-flung, in terms of distribution, drinking cups.

The most detailed study of the chronological development of "Ionian" cups is that of Udo Schlotzhauer, whose analysis focuses on the copious finds of such cups at Miletos.[126] Schlotzhauer recommends the abandonment of the term "Ionian" cups, and replacing it with "Knickrandschalen," a term that does not translate happily into English. A full analysis of the *Knickrandschalen* from the sanctuary of Athena Assesia near Miletos is presented by Kalaitzoglou and numerous examples from the Artemision at Ephesos are published by Kerschner.[127]

As a category, *Knickrandschalen* are fairly ubiquitous among the East Greek imports at Methone, consistently encountered throughout various contexts, particularly in the excavations of the West Hill, but also on the East Hill (the pieces selected below are presented according to where they were found on the site). This category of cup is characterized by a highly formal idiom of banded and glazed decoration. Despite this conservatism in design, there is an almost infinite variety of banded decoration among the fragmentary vessels selected for illustration. As a rule, the gloss of the Methone *Knickrandschalen* is normally fired black, often with a good metallic luster, but occasionally a piece is more oxidized, having fired red or reddish brown (e.g., **22/45** [ΜΕΘ 4409]). One of the most remarkable examples of this category of East Greek pottery, and among the largest, if not the largest, *Knickrandschale* known, is **22/47** (MEΘ 5691); its asymmetrical state is probably the result of its size. The multiple banding on its tall rim is characteristic of East Greek products.

Ionian cups are ubiquitous in the north Aegean, having been found at Sindos,[128] Archontiko (both Attic and east Ionian versions),[129] Karabournaki,[130] Nea Kallikrateia,[131] Amphipolis,[132] Oisyme,[133] Neapolis (Kavala),[134] Herakleitsa Cave,[135] Thasos,[136] Torone,[137] Parthenonas (Mt. Itamos),[138] Poseidi,[139] Akanthos,[140] Stageira,[141] and Troy,[142] among other sites.

Knickrandschalen from the East Hill

Attic

22/41. (MEΘ 3263) Fragmentary Cup Fig. 22.24

East Hill #274/067, 068. 8/10/2009.

H. 0073; Diam. (rim) 0.152; Diam. (base) 0.054.

Reconstructed from numerous frr encountered over a fairly large area, preserving most of cup, including complete profile and both handles.

Splaying conical foot; shallow, thin-walled body, with upper wall curving slightly in toward a relatively short flaring rim, offset from body on interior and exterior and tapering toward a rounded lip. Two thin horizontal handles, round in section, attached to upper body immediately below rim.

Fabric fine and dense, with a few small white and occasional darker inclusions and a few specks of mica. Clay core a little darker than canonical Attic, fired close to red 2.5YR 5/6; reserved surfaces a little paler, closer to light red 2.5YR 6/6.

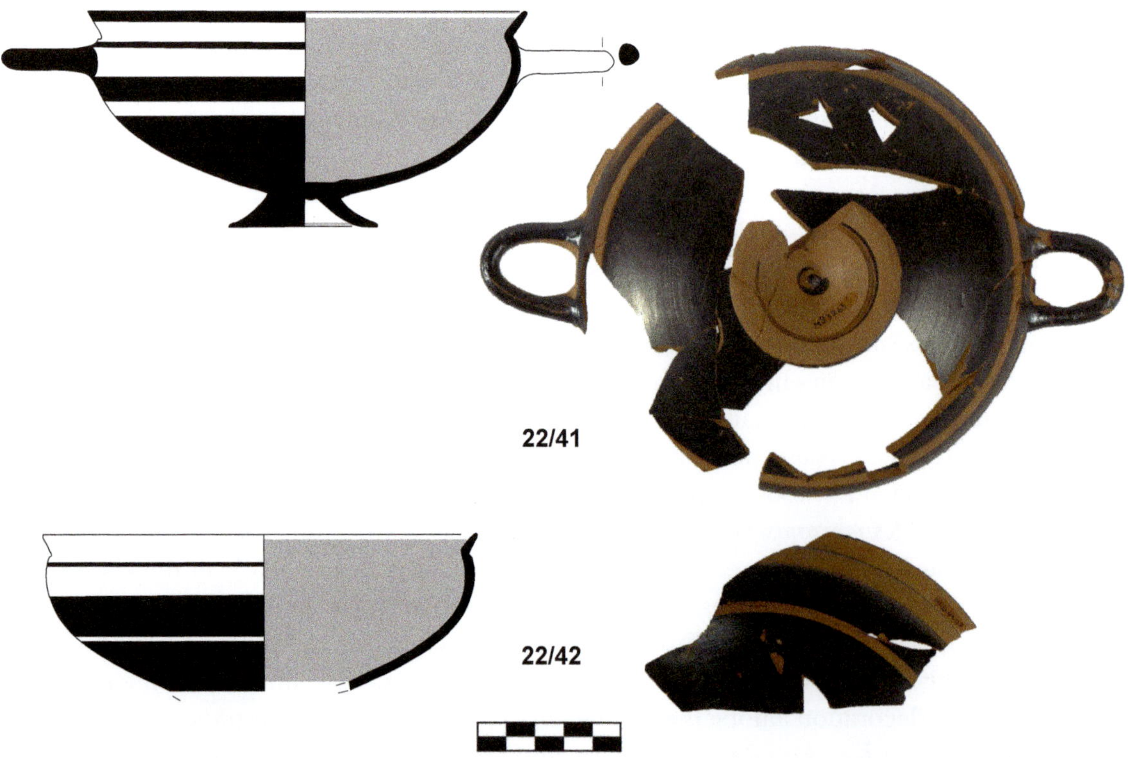

FIGURE 22.24. Athenian banded cups, Class of Athens 1104, **22/41** (MEΘ 3263) and **22/42** (MEΘ 4407). Drawings F. Skyvalida, photos I. Coyle

Good quality black gloss, with a good metallic luster, uniformly fired black. Ring around inner edge of resting surface on underside; partial ring around center of underside, with an irregular dot at center. Foot exterior and lower body painted solid. Thick band immediately below handles; thin band at juncture of body and rim; another thin band on rim, extending onto rim top. Lower, upper, and outer faces of handles, including the immediate area of their attachment to the body, painted; inner edges reserved. Interior painted solid, except for thin reserved band at lip.

22/42. (MEΘ 4407) Rim and Upper Body Frr, Cup Fig. 22.24

East Hill #274/036011 [4]. 6/6/2006.

P.H. 0.050; Diam. (rim) est. 0.140.

Reconstructed from nine joining frr preserving small portion of rim and upper body, plus two small non-joining frr.

Shape as **22/41** (MEΘ 3263).

Fabric similar to **22/41** (MEΘ 3263), but with a little more mica. Clay core and reserved surfaces similar to **22/41** (MEΘ 3263).

Paint as **22/41** (MEΘ 3263), but with an even greater metallic sheen; preserved decoration as **22/41** (MEΘ 3263). The gloss is particularly close to that of **22/44** (MEΘ 3265), which cannot be Attic.

East Greek

22/43. (MEΘ 3264) Fragmentary Cup Fig. 22.25

East Hill #274/067, 068. 8/10/2009.

P.H. 0.072; Diam. (rim) est. 0.160.

Main group reconstructed from 17 joining frr preserving portion of cup from rim to juncture with foot, itself not preserved. There is another group of three joining frr preserving portion of rim, plus 20 non-joining frr, most of which are from the same vessel, though several could be from another, similar, vessel. Foot and handles not preserved.

Shape as **22/41** (MEΘ 3263), but with taller rim, with offset from body less marked.

Fabric not canonically Attic, almost certainly East Greek. Clay with occasional white inclusions and a little more mica. Clay core fired close to red 2.5YR 5/6–4/6. Reserved surfaces closer to light red 2.5YR 6/6.

Paint similar to **22/41** (MEΘ 3263), mostly fired black, with a noticeable metallic sheen, thinning to reddish brown where more dilute. Lower preserved wall through upper wall painted solid; thin band at and just below upper rim, extending onto rim top. Interior banded: two thin partial rings around center of floor; thicker band near midpoint, with thinner band above, just below juncture with rim. Thick band on lower rim interior, then a thin reserved band and the gloss extending onto interior from the rim top.

22/44. (MEΘ 3265) Fragmentary Cup Fig. 22.25

East Hill #274/067, 068. 8/10/2009.

P.H. (main group of frr): 0.062; p.H. (base fr) 0.020; H. (restored) ca. 0.080; Diam. (base) 0.049; Diam. (rim) est. 0.120.

Main group reconstructed from 12 joining frr, preserving portion of rim and body; another group of five joining frr preserves more of the rim and upper wall, including one handle; another fr preserves almost complete base, and there are 14 additional frr, a few of which join among themselves.

Conical foot, with slightly convex outer profile, relatively broad resting surface, and small nipple at center of underside. Form similar to **22/41** (MEΘ 3263), but proportionately a little deeper; flaring rim sharply offset from body on interior and exterior. Horizontal handle, round in section, attached to uppermost body, immediately below rim.

Non-Attic fabric, fine and dense, with only very occasional white inclusions and only the finest dusting of fine silvery mica. Clay core relatively dark, fired close to red 2.5YR 5.6–6/6; reserved surfaces paler, closer to reddish yellow and light reddish brown 5YR 6/6–6/4.

Paint thickly applied and very well adhering, fired black, with a very noticeable metallic luster. Underside reserved. Exterior face of foot and lower body through the lower part of the upper body painted solid. Band on uppermost body immediately below rim; band on upper rim. Handle painted as **22/41** (ΜΕΘ 3263). Preserved interior painted solid, except for reserved band at rim.

22/45. (ΜΕΘ 4409) Fragmentary Cup Fig. 22.25

East Hill #274/067, 068. 19/9/2005.

P.H. (main group of frr) 0.059; p.H. (base) 0.018; H. (as restored) 0.077; Diam. (rim) est. ca. 0.130; Diam. (base) 0.050.

Main group of frr comprising ten joining frr preserving about one-quarter of rim and upper through lower body, including small portion of one handle. A separate, non-joining fr preserves the base. There are, in addition, five more non-joining frr, only one or two of which clearly belong to this vessel.

Shape as **22/44** (ΜΕΘ 3265), but with foot more splaying than conical, and with resting surface a little broader.

Fabric as **22/44** (ΜΕΘ 3265), but somewhat more oxidized. Clay core fired close to red and light red 2.5YR 5/6–6/6, with reserved surfaces closer to the latter.

Paint thickly applied and well adhering, uniformly fired red, close to red 2.5YR 5/6, with a good sheen. Decoration as **22/44** (ΜΕΘ 3265).

Cf. also Bessios, Tzifopoulos, and Kotsonas 2012, pp. 111, 507–508, no. 191 (ΜΕΘ 2022); Ionian kylix dated to the first half of the 6th century B.C.

Ionian Kylikes/Cups from the West Hill

The context of all the kylikes presented from the West Hill is the Archaic destruction level that is dated to the middle of the 6th century B.C.

Attic

22/46. (ΜΕΘ 5698) Fragmentary Cup Fig. 22.26

West Hill #229/013, 014. 2008.

P.H. 0.083; Diam. (base) 0.057; p.Diam. (body, max): 0.138.

Reconstructed from 14 frr preserving most of base and lower wall, about two-thirds of upper wall, but only small portions of lower rim; lip not preserved. One complete handle preserved, the other only partially.

Tall stemmed foot, splaying toward resting surface, with broad flat resting surface. Shallow lower wall, rising toward vertical upper wall. Rim offset from body and beginning to flare. Thin horizontal handles, circular in section, extending horizontally from uppermost body, just below juncture with rim.

Fabric as **22/47** (ΜΕΘ 5691), but with a very slight dusting of very fine mica. Clay body and reserved surfaces fired closest to light reddish brown 5YR 6/4.

Paint thickly applied and well adhering, fired black, with a good quality gloss, except on interior at center of floor, where the rings are in dilute paint. Foot and lower body painted solid; thin reserved band on lower wall; upper wall painted solid; handle zone reserved; thin band on uppermost body, immediately below offset with rim. Handles painted, except for inner faces. Preserved lower rim reserved. Interior painted solid, except for large reserved circle at center of floor decorated with three thin concentric rings, as shown, in dilute paint.

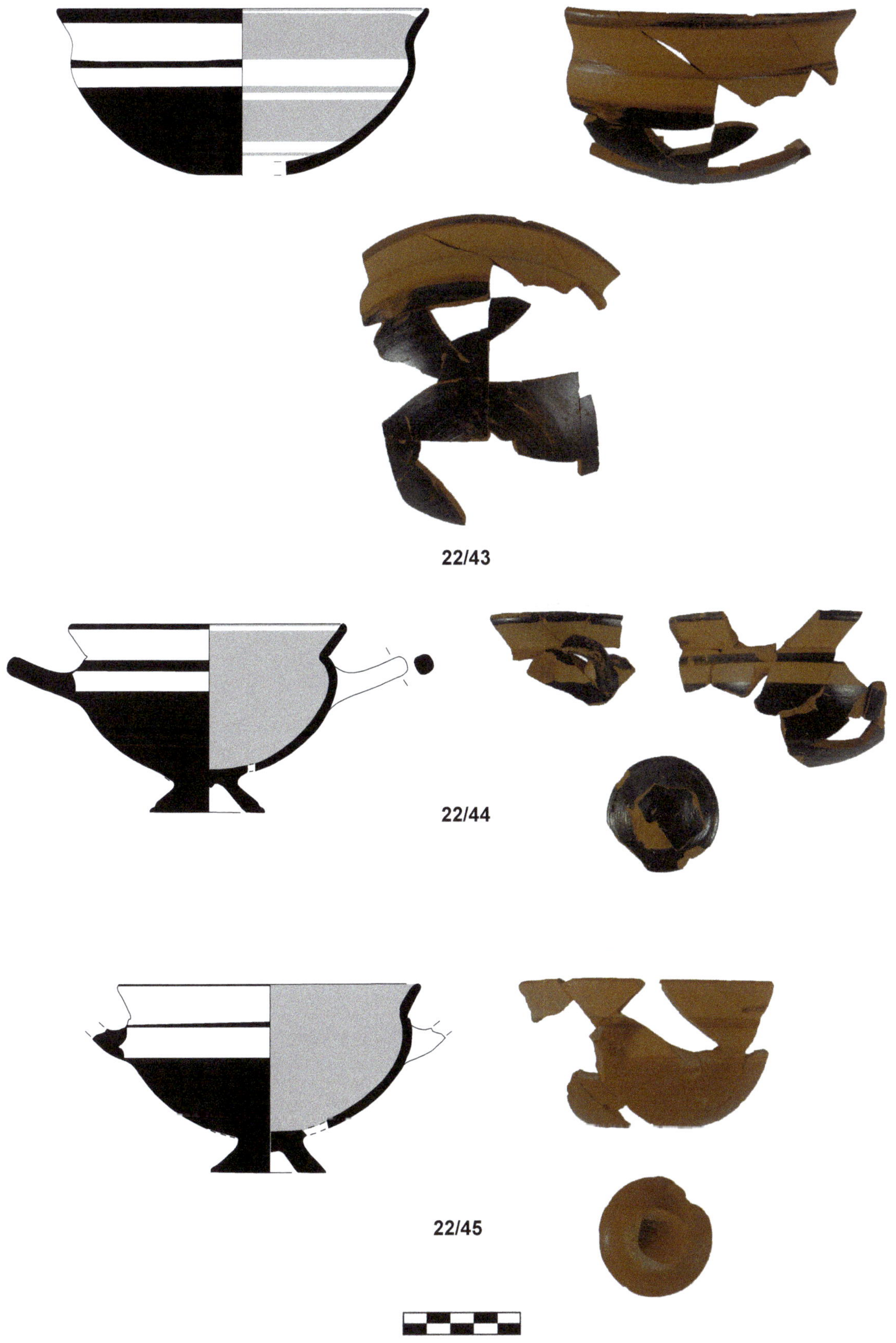

FIGURE 22.25. East Greek (South Ionian) kylikes/cups, **22/43** (ΜΕΘ 3264), **22/44** (ΜΕΘ 3265), and **22/45** (ΜΕΘ 4409). Drawings F. Skyvalida, photos I. Coyle

FIGURE 22.26. Athenian banded cup, Class of Athens 1104, **22/46** (MEΘ 5698).
Drawing T. Ross, photos I. Coyle

East Greek

22/47. (MEΘ 5691) Fragmentary Cup Fig. 22.27

West Hill #229/013, 014 Pass 6, 2. Frr originally found in 2008, some missing frr recovered in 2014 during the more recent excavations.

H. 0.190; Diam. (base) 0.135; Diam. (rim) 0.292.

Reconstructed from numerous joining frr preserving greater part of the vessel, except for portions of upper body and rim. A few floating non-joining frr survive from the missing areas. Parts of body restored in plaster.

Medium to tall splaying foot, with relatively broad, flat resting surface; underside flat. Broad curved body, with lower wall rising steeply and upper wall vertical, with uppermost wall curving slightly in to rim. Tall, flaring rim, offset from body, terminating in plain rounded lip. Two horizontal handles, circular in section, one completely preserved, the other only partially. Handles extend horizontally immediately below juncture of rim and upper body. This is among the largest of the *Knickrandschalen* known. Although generally thin-walled and well made, the vessel, especially the rim, is somewhat lopsided and not perfectly even.

Clay fine and dense, with few visible impurities, only a few very small white inclusions, and no mica to speak of. Clay body where visible fired closest to light brown 7.5YR 6/4 and light reddish brown 5YR 6/4. Reserved surfaces mainly closer to light reddish brown 5YR 6/4.

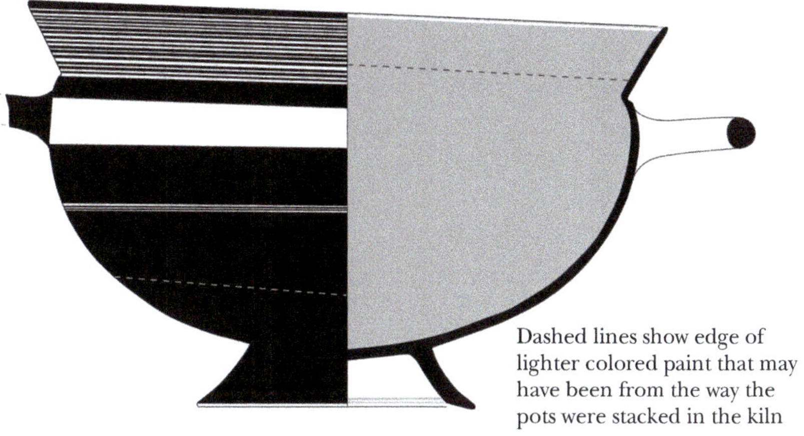

Dashed lines show edge of
lighter colored paint that may
have been from the way the
pots were stacked in the kiln

FIGURE 22.27. Large East Greek *Knickrandschale* **22/47** (ΜΕΘ 5691).
Drawing T. Ross, photos J. Vanderpool

Paint generally thickly applied and well adhering, mostly fired black on exterior, shading to red on one part of body; black on interior, but most of the surviving rim fired a chocolate brown. Underside reserved, except for very thin rings at juncture of resting surface and inner face of foot. Exterior of foot painted solid, except for lowest outside edge. Body exterior painted solid, except for two reserved bands: one thin below the handle zone, with two very thin bands in dilute paint; the other at the handle zone. Rim reserved, except for lip, which is painted; rim exterior decorated with numerous very thin bands in dilute paint (ca. 15). Handles painted solid, except for inner faces. Interior painted solid except for very thin reserved band on rim interior.

For similar multiple banding on interior (not exterior) of a much smaller Ionian cup, see Bakalakis 1938a, p. 113, fig. 5α, Type Δ.

22/48. (MEΘ 5683) Base and Body Frr, Cup Fig. 22.28

West Hill #229/013, 014 baulk, Pass 6, 2. Frr originally found in 2008, missing frr recovered in 2014.

P.H. 0.057; Diam. (base) 0.062; p.Diam. (max, at body near rim): 0.140.

Ten joining frr preserving all of base and much of lower body, but nothing of uppermost body, handles, and rim. Slight thickening at upper break indicates proximity of one handle. Two non-joining frr bagged with **22/48** (MEΘ 5683) are probably from a different vessel.

Medium to tall splaying foot, with comparatively broad and flat resting surface. Lower wall curving up to vertical upper wall.

Fabric with a fine dusting of mica. Clay body and reserved surfaces fired closest to pink 5YR 7/4.

Paint thickly applied and well adhering, mostly fired black, but variegated, with reddish brown and gray. Foot and body painted solid, except for outside edge of foot and at the upper break, which preserves the lower part of reserved band at handle zone. Decoration on interior as **22/46** (MEΘ 5698), but with reserved band around upper part of preserved interior at break and with somewhat thicker rings in reserved circle at center. Small blotch of paint between outer two rings.

22/49. (MEΘ 5684) Fragmentary Base and Lower Body, Cup Fig. 22.28

West Hill #229, 013, 014, Pass 6, 2. Frr originally found in 2008, some missing frr recovered in 2014.

P.H. 0.055; Diam. (base) 0.058; p.Diam. (body, max) 0.137.

Six joining frr preserving all of base and much of the lower wall, but nothing of the upper body, rim, or handles. Two non-joining frr bagged with **22/49** (MEΘ 5684) are from a separate vessel.

Shape as **22/48** (MEΘ 5683).

Fabric as **22/48** (MEΘ 5683), including mica, but with clay core fired closer to light reddish brown 5YR 6/4.

Paint as **22/46** (MEΘ 5698) and **22/48** (MEΘ 5683), fired black, in places beginning to shade to very dark brown. Decoration as **22/48** (MEΘ 5683), but with no preserved handle zone, and with central dot, rather than ring, on interior.

Cf. esp. **22/48** (MEΘ 5683).

22/50. (MEΘ 5701) Fragmentary Body and Rim, Cup Fig. 22.29

West Hill #229/013, 014. 2008.

P.H. 0.059; Diam. (rim) 0.145.

Reconstructed from 16 joining frr preserving most of upper body, both handles, and smaller portions of rim, but nothing of the base.

Shape as **22/46** (MEΘ 5698) and **22/48** (MEΘ 5683); base form unknown. Comparatively short flaring rim, with plain rounded lip. Handles as **22/46** (MEΘ 5698).

Fabric as **22/48** (MEΘ 5683).

FIGURE 22.28. East Greek (South Ionian) kylikes/cups, **22/48** (MEΘ 5683) and **22/49** (MEΘ 5684). Drawings A. Hooton and T. Ross, photos I. Coyle

Paint very similar to **22/48** (MEΘ 5683), but in places flaked. Exterior decoration closer to MEΘ 5698, but with thicker reserved band on lower body. Entire preserved interior painted solid, except for thin reserved band at rim. Center of floor not preserved, but from what survives it is clear that there is no substantial reserved circle as on **22/48** (MEΘ 5683) and **22/49** (MEΘ 5684), and the interior may be closer to **22/51** (MEΘ 5700).

22/51. (MEΘ 5700) Fragmentary Cup Fig. 22.29

West Hill #229/013, 014. 2008.

P.H. 0.062; Diam. (rim) est. 0.160–0.170.

Reconstructed from 12 joining frr preserving less than one-half of rim, and rather less of upper body, including most of one handle. Although the center of the floor is preserved on interior, with scar of the foot on exterior, it is impossible to determine precise form and height of the base.

Shape as **22/50** (MEΘ 5701).

Fabric as **22/49** (MEΘ 5684).

Paint as **22/49** (MEΘ 5684). Preserved body from articulation at base through handle zone painted solid. Handle zone reserved, with thin band just below juncture with base. Thin band on uppermost rim exterior. Handle painted, except for inner faces. On one side of preserved handle an irregular wavy line set diagonally, as shown. Preserved interior painted solid except for thin reserved band at lip. Enough survives of the center of floor to indicate that there was, in all probability, not even a very small reserved dot at center (cf. **22/50** [MEΘ 5701]).

22/52. (MEΘ 5689) Small Fragmentary Cup Fig. 22.29

West Hill #229/013, 014 Pass 6, 2. Frr originally found in 2008, some missing frr recovered in 2014.

H./p.H. 0.041; Diam. (base) 0.037; Diam. (rim) est. 0.075.

Four joining frr preserving all of base, about one-third of body, including most of both handles, but only small portion of rim. Due to wear, it is not certain whether the uppermost preserved edge is the actual rim or not.

Shape a miniature version of **22/47** (MEΘ 5691), **22/48** (MEΘ 5683), and **22/49** (MEΘ 5684).

Fabric as other cups, fine, with only a few very small white inclusions, rather more very small pinprick blowouts, and some mica. Clay core and reserved surfaces variously fired between light reddish brown 5YR 6/4–6/3 and pinkish gray 5YR 6/2–6/1.

Paint originally thickly applied, but substantially flaked, inside and out, fired black. Foot exterior and body below handle painted solid; handle zone reserved; likely thin band immediately below juncture with rim. No preserved paint on rim, but the little that survives of the rim is extremely worn. Handles painted, except for innermost edge at juncture with body. Preserved interior painted solid, except for likely reserved dot at center of floor, too worn to determine with certainty.

Cf., among others, Utili 1996b, pl. 15, no. 3 (where the foot is painted solid); Allamani-Souri 2012, p. 288, fig. 7 (left, from Souroti, Thessalonikis); Koukouli-Chrysanthaki and Marangou-Lerat 2012, p. 328, fig. 13:β (right) (Oisyme).

"SAMIAN" LEKYTHOS

In his study of banded and plain East Greek pottery, Cook described this distinctive type of lekythos: "There are also fancier flasks, often—without good reason—dubbed Samian, which have an angular shoulder and often noticeably concave belly: one version is illustrated (Figure 19.1c), another inverts the curve and is widest at the shoulder. These are attested at least for the sixth century."[143] The reason they were dubbed "Samian," I suspect, goes back to the fact that no fewer than six intact examples were discovered by Johannes Boehlau and Edward Habich in the Archaic cemetery of ancient Samos at Pythagoreion in 1894, deriving from six different tombs.[144] Today, this number pales before the quantities of the type found on the Italian peninsula and in Sicily.[145] The type is not uncommon in mainland and insular Greece, with ten such lekythoi found in the celebrated grave in the Kerameikos in Athens with the ivory couch dating to ca. 530 B.C., and

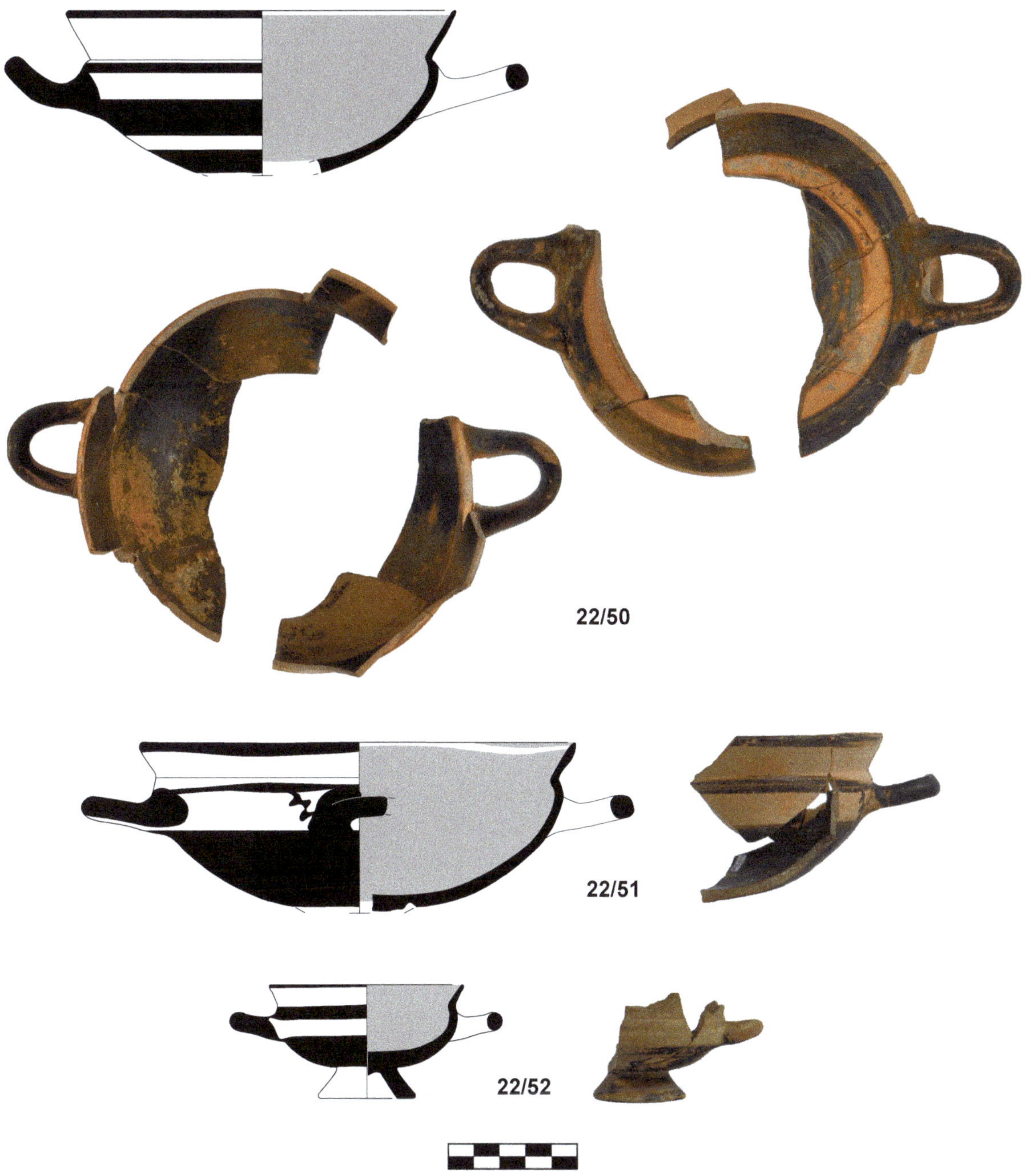

FIGURE 22.29. East Greek (South Ionian) kylikes/cups, **22/50** (ΜΕΘ 5701) and **22/51** (ΜΕΘ 5700), and East-Greek style cup, perhaps of north Aegean manufacture, **22/52** (ΜΕΘ 5689). Drawings A. Hooton and T. Ross, photos I. Coyle

several are particularly close to **22/53** (ΜΕΘ 2701) in terms of shape and size.[146] An almost intact example from Perachora has a considerably broader and more carinated shoulder, assigned to late in the first half of the 6th century B.C.[147] It has also been found in the Black Sea, at Berezan.[148] The place of manufacture of this distinctive type of lekythos remains to be determined. Its color and overall form seem to be reminiscent of Phoenician pottery.[149]

As for its context, **22/53** was found in Building A, Room 5 and should date to the middle or first half of the 6th century B.C.

FIGURE 22.30. "Samian" lekythos, **22/53** (ΜΕΘ 2701). Drawing F. Skyvalida, photo J. Vanderpool

22/53. (ΜΕΘ 2701 [A8]) Fragmentary "Samian" Lekythos Fig. 22.30

West Hill #229/012002 [2]. Immediately west of Wall 4 (αμέσως δυτικά τοίχου 4). 27/08/2007.

Bessios and Noulas 2012, p. 405, fig. 13.

P.H. 0.135; Diam. (base) 0.033–0.035; Diam. (lower body) max 0.064–0.065.

Complete except for upper neck, handle, and rim.

Thick-walled, heavy, and rather lopsided lekythos, with rounded ring base and with small nipple at center of underside. Sagging lower body, with point of max. Diam. set low, and vertical upper body. Sharply carinated shoulder, sloping into neck, becoming vertical. Lower handle attachment preserved at outer edge of shoulder; vertical handle, ovoid to plano-convex in section to judge from the break (flat section toward outside).

Red micaceous fabric, with few other visible impurities, but several blowouts. Clay core and surfaces fired close to red and light red 2.5YR 5/6–6/6.

Surfaces reserved; wheelmarks visible on sagging lower wall, but generally smoothed elsewhere.

Among the early examples of the type published by Boehlau, the closest in terms of shape and size is Boehlau 1898, pp. 45–46, pl. 7, no. 3 (H: 17. 8 cm) (= Boehlau and Habich 1996, p. 61, Grab 45.2); cf. also p. 38, pl. 7, no. 7 (H: 12 cm) (= Boehlau and Habich 1996, p. 35, Grab 19.1). The long and spindly body of **22/53**, together with the form of the base, resembles several of the lekythoi from the Elfenbein-Grab in the Kerameikos dated to ca. 530 B.C., see Knigge and Willemsen 1964, p. 44, pl. 39β; Scheibler 1973, p. 25, fig. 25; also one in Kassel, Kranz and Lullies 1975, pp. 16–17, pl. 53, no. 3, T. 446 (H: 0.153, which would be almost identical to the original height of **22/53**), and another from Talamone in Etruria (Museo Civico di Livorno, Cristofani 1978, p. 173, pl. 79, fig. 27).

NOTES

1 Kerschner and Schlotzhauer 2005, 2007. For discussion and assistance with various aspects connected to this chapter, I am especially grateful to Camille Acosta and Trevor Van Damme.

2 In other parts of the Greek world, pottery and other terracotta objects were being produced in the same workshops and often fired in the same kilns. For an overview of the early potters' deposits from the Athenian Agora, the original Kerameikos of Athens, see Papadopoulos 2003b.

3 Kerschner and Schlotzhauer 2005, pp. 1–4.

4 For the traditional use of the term "Rhodian" see, among others, Schiering 1957; Kardara 1963; Hayes in Boardman and Hayes 1966, 41; Hayes in Boardman and Hayes 1973, 16–17; Coldstream 1968, pp. 274–287.

5 E.g., Boardman 1998, p. 142; Cook and Dupont 1998, p. 32.

6 Cook and Dupont 1998; Kerschner and Schlotzhauer 2005, p. 8, compare the new system with the earlier classification of Cook; see further Schlotzhauer 2006, p. 141.

7 For such classifications, see Tiverios 2012b, 2013b.

8 A fuller study of the imported East Greek pottery from the 2014–2017 excavations at Methone by Camille Acosta and others is in progress.

9 For the settling of Aiolis, see, among others, Huxley 1966, pp. 36–39; Cook 1975, pp. 776–780; Coldstream 1977, pp. 262–264; Gschnitzer and Schwertheim 1996, cols. 337–339; for the historicity of the Aiolian migration, see Rose 2008; Parker 2008; for the historicity of the Ionian migration, see Papadopoulos 2005, pp. 580–588; Mac Sweeney 2017; for the Panionion and the Ionian migration, see Herda 2006.

10 See especially Lamb 1932; the fullest and most detailed survey of the graywares of northwest Anatolia, from the Middle Bronze Age through the Early Iron Age and into the Archaic period, is Bayne 2000 (based on the author's Oxford doctoral dissertation completed in 1963). For a useful overview of Aiolian grayware in the period of transition from the Bronze Age to the Early Iron Age, see Hertel 2007. For graywares on Lesbos see, most recently, Acheilara 2012, including closed shapes (e.g., amphoras: p. 59, figs. 4–5; "pithamphora": p. 63, fig. 11; amphoriskos: p. 64, fig. 16; trefoil oinochoe: p. 63, fig. 12; jug: p. 64, fig. 14), and open shapes (e.g., the karchesion: p. 61, figs. 6–7, two examples, the latter very similar in form to **11/7** [ΜΕΘ 2249, see Figs. 1.12 and 11.5 = Bessios, Tzifopoulos, and Kotsonas 2012, pp. 337–339, no. 1]; a variety of shallow lekanis-shaped vessels: p. 62, figs. 8–10; one-handled cup: p. 63, fig. 13; "kantharos": p. 64, fig. 15); Acheilara dates these vessels to the 7th and first half of the 6th centuries B.C.

11 Cook and Dupont 1998, p. 135. For the introduction of the "Wild Goat Style" in the Troad as a result of colonization in the Archaic period, see Aslan and Pernicka 2013.

12 Cook and Dupont 1998, p. 135; for Antissa, see Lamb 1930–1931, 1931–1932.

13 It should be noted, of course, that significant parts of the mainland opposite Lesbos were part of the Mytilenaian, or Tenedian, Peraia, for which see Cook 1973, pp. 189–198.

14 *Troy* IV, pp. 252–253; for more recent overviews of graywares at Troy, see Aslan 2009, 2011, esp. pp. 393–400, nos. 22–48; p. 415, fig. 25; pp. 418–419, figs. 27, 28 (top left and bottom right); and esp. Aslan 2019, p. 123, fig. 95; pp. 204–208; pp. 306–308, pls. 23–25, nos. 161–176; pp. 316–318, pls. 33–35, nos. 225–244; pp. 321–323, pls. 37–38, nos. 273–284; pp. 328–331, pls. 41–42, nos. 323–344; pp. 336–340, pls. 46–48, nos. 376–404.

15 In Cook and Dupont 1998, pp. 135–136.

16 Hertel 2011, esp. pp. 61–62, 64–68, 72–81 for Aiolian grayware; see also Hertel 2007.

17 Lamb 1931–1932, p. 51; cf. Lamb 1932, p. 3.

18 Lamb 1932, p. 3.

19 For the similarities and differences between Aiolian graywares and Gray Minyan of the Middle Helladic period, see *Troy* IV, pp. 252–253.

20 Cook and Dupont 1998, p. 136. For some wavy-line comparanda see **22/18** (ΜΕΘ 5111). For incised animals on two sherds of Archaic grayware from Mytilene, see Williams and Williams 1991, pl. VI.1; for relief, pl. VI.3.

21 Bayne 2000, p. 139. For the Late Bronze Age northwest Anatolian graywares, see Allen 1990.

22 Bayne 2000, p. 139.

23 Bayne 2000, p. 139.

24 For the Aiolian Wild Goat fragments, see Zachos 2012, p. 310, figs. 13, 14.

25 Zachos 2012, pp. 311–316, figs. 15–21.

26 Zachos 2012, p. 319.

27 Danile 2011, 2012, pp. 79–82.

28 Danile 2012, p. 80. Danile (2011, p. 171) notes that grayware accounts for 64% of the total pottery from the Early Iron Age levels at Hephaistia.

29 See Zacharias and Kaparou 2011.

30 Danile 2011; for a useful summary, see Danile 2012, pp. 79–82, figs. 2–3.

31 Danile 2012, p. 80.

32 Danile 2012, pp 84–85. Some of these vessel forms, though not all, are found elsewhere in the north Aegean, e.g., at Archontiko (Pella), for which see Chrysostomou and Chrysostomou 2012.

33 Danile 2012, p. 80; Bayne 2000.

34 Danile 2011, pp. 117–136, with full references; for Torone, see further Papadopoulos 2005, pp. 482–485; for northern Pieria, see Karliampas, Bessios, and Triantaphyllou 2004.

35 Danile 2011, pp. 136–146.

36 For related karchesia, see, among others, Acheilara 2012, p. 61, esp. fig. 7; Danile 2012, p. 86, fig. 12.

37 In Cook and Dupont 1998, p. 136. Cook adds that the grayware common in southern France was an indigenous product, neither imported nor related to Aiolian (cf. Villard 1970, pp. 116–117). For claims of locally made Aiolian on Thasos and at Histria, see Bernard 1964, pp. 109–114; Dupont 1983, p. 30. For a grayware jug with high handle from Apollonia Pontica, see Bozkova and Delev 2012, p. 73, fig. 6:c. For an Archaic workshop in Marseille producing "Greek" graywares, see Gantès 2000.

38 Boardman 1967, p. 135. For the Greek pottery from Naukratis see, most recently, Schlotzhauer and Villing 2006; Schlotzhauer 2012; Mommsen et al. 2012; for the findspots of Archaic Greek pottery from other sites in Egypt, see Weber 2012.

39 For the importance of Lesbos in the archaeology of the Aegean, see, among others, Spencer 1995a, 1995b.

40 At another north Aegean locale, amphoras referred to as "Mendaian" were, in fact, produced, with variations in fabric, at several production sites in Chalkidike: Papadopoulos and Paspalas 1999.

41 Boardman 1967, p. 135; it is worth adding that İren (2002) has argued that the workshop of the London Dinos Group was at Phokaia; for the importance of Phokaia and other Aiolian centers, see Langlotz 1975, esp. pp. 1–16. It is noteworthy that Phokaia was, much later on in the Roman period, an important production center of Phokaian red-slip ware, for which see Hayes 1980.

42 Especially useful is the "giornata di studio" organized by Giovanni Rizza at the University of Catania in 1990, see Rizza 1993; and esp. Frasca 1993, where, in addition to local gray and painted fine wares, imports from Corinth, Euboia, North Ionia (specifically Smyrna), Chios, Samos, and Athens are presented; see also Frasca 1998.

43 Kerschner 2006a; Mommsen and Kerschner 2006; Schlotzhauer and Villing 2006, p. 58.

44 Schlotzhauer and Villing 2006, p. 58.

45 Schlotzhauer and Villing 2006, p. 58, with figs. 11–13.

46 For Archaic grayware pottery from Mytilene, see, most recently, Acheilara 2012.

47 For much smaller lekanai, with the same types of handles from Assos, but with painted figural or patterned decoration, see Utili 1996a, pp. 59–70, pls. 18–19.

48 For the Leukopetra kilns, see Stefani 2013, esp. pp. 109–110, figs. 24–27 (Stefani 2012 for an overview of the region); for Agia Paraskevi, see Papakostas 2013, pp. 167–172, with figs. 1–8; the fullest study of this grayware ("τεφρόχρωμη κεραμική" in some Greek publications [Acheilara 2012, for

instance, refers to it as "γκριζόχρωμα"]) is that of Panti 2008, pp. 81–86, who not only provides a useful overview of shapes, especially from Akanthos, Karabournaki, and Sindos, but also traces the history of the study of this ware, going back to Heinrich Schliemann, and the various names applied to it, from "Lydian" pottery to "monochrome gray," and to "Minyan" and "gray Minyan." Panti also discusses the relationship of the north Aegean versions with the Aiolian, as well as with related gray-wares found elsewhere in the Mediterranean; see further Panti 2013; Saripanidi 2013.

49 Pardalidou 2012, p. 431, figs. 16, 17; *Αρχαία Ζώνη* I, pp. 654–663.

50 Skarlatidou 2010, pp. 305–307.

51 Skarlatidou et al. 2012, pp. 468–469, fig. 14; the range of shapes comprises the popular kantharoid bowl, the exaleiptron, and the krater, though there are also closed shapes, especially jugs of various forms; see further Allamani 2013, p. 184, fig. 1. For similar graywares locally produced in the kilns of Leukopetra, see Stefani 2013, pp. 109–110, figs. 24–27; cf. also the locally produced grayware from Agia Paraskevi in Thessaloniki (Papakostas 2013, esp. p. 168, fig. 2; p. 170, fig. 7) and from the Archaic-Classical cemetery of Sindos, Saripanidi 2013, esp. p. 220, fig. 1; with further notes and discussion by Saripanidi in *Sindos* II, pp. 182–192, 519–520, figs. 327–337, nos. 229–236.

52 Cook and Dupont 1998, pp. 136–137; in enumerating parallels for smaller aryballoi and the long alabastra, Cook lists, among others, Kinch 1914, pl. 31, no. 7; pl. 32, bb3; pl. 33, p4 (aryballoi); *Samos* VI, p. 35 (alabastra). For examples of East Greek bucchero from Francavilla Marittima in Calabria, see Tsiafaki 2008, pp. 40–44; Handberg 2010, pp. 325–327. For examples from Sicily, see esp. Vallet and Villard 1964, pp. 90–91, pl. 79, no. 3; Orlandini 1978, pl. 55, fig. 23 (right); Pautasso 2009, pl. 1, no. 9; also cf. pl. 2, no. 42. For the occurrence of the type in Black Sea, see, among others, Lungu 2009, p. 37, fig. 8 (Berezan [Borysthenes]).

53 *Sindos* II, pp. 35–37, 483, figs. 7–11, nos. 5–9. The other examples of bucchero from Sindos include two trefoil oinochoai and two mesomphalos phialai, see pp. 31–35, 482, figs. 1–6, nos. 1–4; for the pottery from the Sindos cemetery, see Saripanidi 2013, and in *Sindos* II.

54 Both of the Methone bird oinochoai are particularly close to Walter 1968, pl. 87, no. 490 (from Rhodes).

55 The piece was found in the agora of Methone (#274/068, northeast trench, Τομή ΒΑ τμήματος), consisting of three joining frr preserving a small portion of the rim and upper body, and measuring: p.H. 0.038; Diam. (rim) est. 0.150.

56 Coldstream 1968, p. 277, with pls. 61:c–d. The bird bowls are discussed in more detail below.

57 Coldstream 1968, p. 277.

58 Coldstream 1968, pp. 278–279.

59 Coldstream 1968, p. 278. For the cup of Nestor, see, most recently, Faraone 1996; Papadopoulos 2016, pp. 1244–1245, fig. 5; Węcowski 2017; Chapter 11.

60 For an alternative ancillary zone, including a row of short vertical bars, see von Miller 2015, pp. 184–196, 341, fig. 3 (from Panayırdağ, Ephesos); there is, occasionally, a double ancillary zone, such as the kotyle from Klaros that has a zigzag above a horizontal row of cross-hatched lozenges, for which see Zunal 2015, pp. 246–247, 343, fig. 3, no. 3.

61 Coldstream 1968, p. 278; Robertson 1940, pp. 14, 19, fig. 8:f–j.

62 Boardman 1967, pp. 132–134; Ersoy 2004, pp. 49–55.

63 Zunal 2015, p. 250.

64 Zunal 2015, p. 250–251.

65 Zunal 2015, p. 251, sums up the problem well: "However, it should be kept in mind that all of the above-mentioned kotyle types were in use contemporaneously, as can be understood by the different kotylai recovered in Teos from a cremation grave dated to the end of the eighth century B.C."

66 Coldstream 1968, p. 279, with n. 1 (and full references).

67 Coldstream 1968, p. 279, n. 2.

68 See, esp., Ersoy 2004, p. 50, fig. 6 (diagnostic pottery from a Late Geometric layer found under a 7th-century B.C. structure); with additional bird bowls and rosette bowls, pp. 51, 53, figs. 8, 12; see also Hürmüzlü 2004, pp. 83–84, figs. 12–13, with more bird bowls, e.g., p. 82, fig. 10; p. 85, fig. 16; and rosette bowls, p. 85, fig. 18.

69 For Torone, see Paspalas 2001, p. 313, fig. 51, pl. 51, no. 5.7; for Karabournaki, see Tsiafaki 2012, p. 231, fig. 8; I am grateful to Despoina Tsiafaki for letting me know of the material from Karabournaki (for further notes on East Greek pottery from Karabournaki, see Tsiafaki 2000).

70 See esp. Skarlatidou 2004, p. 249: "The ancient sources, most notably Herodotos, mention an unsuccessful attempt by the Clazomenians to establish a colony in 654 B.C. at the site that was to be Abdera, led by an oikistes called Timesios. They were repulsed by the local Thracian tribes and at the same site a century later (in 545 B.C.) a colony was founded by Teos. The chance discovery in 1982, and the subsequent excavation, of a cemetery dating to the second half of seventh and early sixth century B.C., clearly Greek in terms of its finds and its burial customs, leave no room for any doubt that it was connected with the Clazomenians' attempt to establish a colony at Abdera. For this reason, this discovery was unexpected." For the full publication of this important cemetery, see Skarlatidou 2010.

71 See Skarlatidou 2010, pp. 255–264.

72 Coldstream 1968, p. 298; Hayes, in Boardman and Hayes 1973, p. 20.

73 See Dupont 1983, pp. 40–41; Kerschner et al. 1993; Kerschner and Mommsen 1997; Kerschner 2000a, 2000b, esp. p. 489, fig. 343; Kerschner 2002a. In the 2008 edition of Greek Geometric Pottery, Coldstream (p. 479) stated: "but a laboratory analysis of its standard fabric (as opposed to local imitations) has made a persuasive case for transferring this workshop, and creation of its style, to a centre in North Ionia. Clazomenae is a likely candidate, in view of the survival there of several MG motifs in its earliest kotylai." Coldstream (2008, p. 479) also adds that bird kotylai were imitated by all the major East Greek regions, including Caria.

74 For Klazomenai, see Ersoy 1993, 2000, 2003, 2004, 2007, 2018; Özer 2004; Hürmüzlü 2004; Tzannes 2004; for the Early Iron Age pottery at Klazomenai, see Aytaçlar 2004; for Klazomenian wave-line pottery, see Uzun 2018. For the Geometric pottery from Smyrna see Özgünel 2003; for the non-figured wares of Old Smyrna, see esp. Paspalas 2006; for a recent overview of the archaeometric data on the East Greek pottery from Bayraklı (Old Smyrna), see Dupont 2018. I am grateful to Yaşar Ersoy for showing me the material from Klazomenai over the course of several days in 2011.

75 See esp. Kadıoğlu et al. 2015; see also Kerschner 2001, pp. 85–87; Kerschner 2002b; Schlotzhauer and Villing 2006, p. 56; Dupont and Thomas 2006; Kerschner 2006b; Posamentir 2006; Posamentir and Solovyov 2006.

76 The context (#274/088, Βόρειος μάρτυρας [north balk]. 9/5/2005) was uninformative as to date. Comprising a single fragment preserving a very small portion of the rim and upper body, the piece measures: P.H. 0.022; Diam. (rim) est. ca. 0.150.

77 Cook and Dupont 1998, p. 26; Cook and Dupont (1998, pp. 26–28) also discuss the related rosette bowls, for which see, most recently, Ersoy 2018, pp. 70–74, figs. 1–4, and the band, or banded, bowls: pp. 74–76, figs. 5–6.

78 Coldstream 1968, pp. 298–301; Cook and Dupont 1998, p. 26; the precise dates are based on bird bowls found in contexts with Protocorinthian and Corinthian pottery.

79 For discussion and references, see Paspalas 2001, p. 313, n. 21. For Rhodes, see Coldstream 1968, p. 279; for Chios, see Boardman 1967, pp. 132–134, esp. p. 134; for Samos, see Walter 1968, pp. 40–41, 58 (for bird kotylai, see pls. 42–44; for bird bowls, see pl. 85); for Miletos, see von Graeve 1973–1974, pp. 86, 95–97, pl. 23, nos. 47–58; for Eretria, see Descoeudres 1976, pp. 22–23, Beil. 10, no. FK 367/582.1; cf. p. 34, pl. 3, no. 49 (FK 1085).

80 For a good representation of Subgeometric and Archaic bird bowls from Assos, see Utili 1992, esp. pp. 57–58, figs. 1–2, pl. 13 (and for the closely related rosette bowls, cf. p. 60, fig. 4, pls. 14–15 [various examples]); Utili 1999, pp. 286–287, figs. 1–2, nos. 1–8 (bird bowls), nos. 15–20; fig. 3, nos. 22, 29 (rosette bowls); also p. 288, fig. 3, nos. 36–38 (meander bowls) and nos. 42–52 (banded bowls); for Smyrna, see Akurgal 1950, pl. 9a (bottom row); pl. 9b (center); pl. A, 1; Kerschner 1997, p. 110, pl. 1, nos. 1–2, 4; p. 122, pl. 4, no. 22; p. 126, pl. 5, no. 34; p. 130, pl. 6, nos. 42–43; p. 134, pl. 7, nos. 49–51; p. 138, pl. 8, no. 54; p. 146, pl. 10, nos. 73–78; p. 162, pl. 14, nos. 107–110; pp. 189–191, pls. 29–37 (Ephesos). For the bird bowls from Eresos on Lesbos, see Zachos 2012, p. 307, fig. 6; from the acropolis of Mytilene, see Schaus 1992, p. 358, pl. 80, no. 2; for those from Samos, see, among others, Walter 1968, pl. 85, nos. 476–482. For bird bowls from Rhodes, see, among others, Kinch 1914, col. 133, fig. 44a–b; pl. 23, nos. 1, 3; pl. 25, no. 11 (illustrated together with numerous rosette cups); pl. 36, nos. 2,34 and 2,41; pl. 42, no. 18,2 (Vroulia); Jacopi 1929, p. 48, fig. 37 (Ialysos); Jacopi 1931, p. 58, fig. 30; p. 274, fig. 301 (Kameiros); Jacopi 1932–1933, p. 64, fig. 64; p. 65, fig. 66 (top right); p. 67, fig. 70 (top left); p. 68, fig. 72; p. 102, fig. 114 (Kameiros). For Crete, see, among others, Stampolidis et al. 2019, p. 291, no. 131, from Knossos, dated to ca. 650 B.C.

81 Tsiafaki 2000, p. 422, fig. 307, top row; Tsiafaki 2012, pp. 230–231, figs. 8–10.

82 Skarlatidou 2004, p. 252, fig. 10, and cf. fig. 11, which is the same type of bowl but decorated only with banding; Skarlatidou 2010, p. 56, fig. 21; p. 88, fig. 89; p. 98, fig. 109; p. 118, fig. 153; pp. 255–257 (Type 1Aα); in addition to the bird bowls, Skarlatidou (2010, pp. 258–259, Type 1Aβ) illustrates numerous examples of plain banded bowls of the same shape; Skarlatidou 2012, p. 454, fig. 2 (top); p. 455, fig. 4 (two examples); p. 456, fig. 7 (bottom row, middle).

83 Ghali-Kahil 1960, pp. 17–18, pl. 1, nos. 1–8.

84 Paspalas 2001, pp. 313–314, fig. 51, pl. 51, nos. 5.8–5.12.

85 Vokotopoulou, Bessios, and Trakosopoulou 1990, pp. 428, 435, fig. 14; I have not seen this piece in person, but it could be from a bird kotyle rather than a bird bowl.

86 Misailidou-Despotidou 2009, p. 225, fig. 5.

87 Vokotopoulou 1993, pp. 195, 229–230, figs. 34–35, no. 25 (fragments of at least ten bird bowls).

88 *Akanthos* I, pl. 172, no. E14 (bottom right); see also Trakosopoulou-Salakidou 1996, pp. 305–306.

89 See, among others, Vallet and Villard 1964, p. 78, pls. 62–63; Orlandini 1978, pl. 53, fig. 4; Tsiafaki 2008, pp. 10–11, figs. 6–8; Handberg 2010, pp. 299–306.

90 See, among others, Courbin 1978, pl. 16, fig. 6 (Ras el Bassit); Calvet and Yon 1977, pl. IV, nos. 35–41 (together with rosette bowls); Calvet and Yon 1978, pl. 19 (Salamis on Cyprus); Gjerstad 1977, pl. X, nos. 3–7 (from Amathous and Salamis on Cyprus); Thalmann 1977, pl. I, nos. 5–14 (Amathous).

91 E.g., Schlotzhauer 2012, pl. 2, figs. e–f; pl. 3, figs. a–g (Naukratis); Boardman and Hayes 1966, pl. 38, no. 733 (together with many more rosette bowls); Boardman and Hayes 1973, pls. 12–13 (various examples, with bird bowls outnumbered by the rosette and meander bowls) (Tocra).

92 E.g., Posamentir 2006, p. 162, fig. 6 (Inv. B69-60, B70-56, B89-28); Posamentir and Solovyov 2007, p. 184, fig. 1a, nos. 1–3.

93 Kasseri (Chapter 21) notes that the most numerous amphora sherds in the West Hill assemblage originate from the island of Chios, with at least 15 different vessels identified. In addition, Kotsonas publishes another dozen or so pieces from the Hypogeion: in Bessios, Tzifopoulos, and Kotsonas 2012, pp. 201–205; pp. 368–369, no. 21; pp. 461–464, nos. 127–131; pp. 498–501, nos. 177–182, the earliest of which date to the later 8th or earlier 7th century B.C.

94 For the original publication of this piece, see Bessios, Tzifopoulos, and Kotsonas 2012, pp. 436–437, no. 97; for proto-chalices, see Boardman 1967, pp. 102–105, fig. 60; 119–122, fig. 74; Lemos 1991, pp. 7–13.

95 Cook and Dupont 1998, pp. 46–47; with reference to Boardman 1967; Boardman and Hayes 1966, pp. 57–63; Boardman and Hayes 1973, pp. 24–28; Cook 1965, pp. 138–141; see also Gjerstad 1977, pl. XVI, nos. 5–8.

96 Schaus 1985, pp. 77–85 for the Chian pottery, and esp. pp. 79–82, fig. 9, pls. 28–29, nos. 479–503 for the chalices.

97 Lemos 1991, pp. 191–208; see also Lemos 1986 for Archaic Chian pottery on Chios.

98 Boardman 1998, p. 150.

99 Boardman 1998, p. 150; for further discussion, see Lemos 2000.

100 For the chronology, see esp. Boardman 1967, pp. 102–105, with fig. 60, esp. A–C; Lemos 1991, pp. 8–13, pl. 1, esp. nos. 1–10.

101 Poulaki 2001, esp. pp. 55–133.

102 Poulaki-Pantermali 2008b, p. 32 (middle of the page).

103 Tsiafaki 2012, pp. 231–232, figs. 11–13.

104 Allamani-Souri 2012, p. 286, fig. 4 (middle).

105 Koukouli-Chrysanthaki and Marangou-Lerat 2012, p. 325, fig. 5.

106 Ghali-Kahil 1960, pp. 34–41, pls. 12–13.

107 Paspalas 2001, p. 315, fig. 52, pl. 52, nos. 20–21.

108 Vokotopoulou, Bessios, and Trakosopoulou 1990, pp. 428, 436, fig. 17. Although referred to as Chian, the authors note that it is not impossible that the fragments derive from a workshop on the Thasian Peraia.

109 Misailidou-Despotidou 2012a, p. 372, fig. 2:α; p. 375, fig. 8.

110 *Αρχαία Ζώνη* I, p. 665.

111 For Mytilene, see Schaus 1992, pp. 362–364, pl. 81, esp. nos. 20, 21 (in addition to these two chalices, there were several fragments of closed vessels, including an oinochoe, a kantharos rim, one or more fragments of Chian fruit stands, and several lid fragments); for Eresos, see Zachos 2012, pp. 306–307, figs. 1, 5.

112 Lemos 1991, p. 202.

113 Sometimes referred to as "ψευδοχιακών" or "ψευδοχιακοί" ("pseudo-Chian"), for which see Ghali-Kahil 1960, pp. 51–72, pls. 22–30; Boardman 1967, p. 157, n. 2; Salviat 1978; Giouri and Koukouli 1987, esp. p. 371; Lemos 1991, pp. 209–222; Lemos 1992; Coulié 1996; cf. Trakosopoulou-Salakidou 1996, p. 305.

114 As Lemos (1991, p. 8) notes, the earliest phase of the late 8th century B.C. is represented by a few fragments from Emporio, and some scraps reported from Old Smyrna, for which see Cook 1965, p. 140, fig. 19:a. The vessel was fully published by Kotsonas in Bessios, Tzifopoulos, and Kotsonas 2012, 436–437, no. 97.

115 For which see Boardman 1967, p. 102; Lemos 1991, pp. 1–3. Cook (1965, p. 140), in discussing differences in fabric of the Chian pottery from Old Smyrna, makes the point that "the difference is one of date rather than clay beds."

116 As Lemos (1991, p. 7) states, the term was first coined by Elinor Price and has since been followed, despite being inappropriate (see Price 1924, esp. pp. 205–222); on the celebrated Nikesermos "chalice" (Lemos 1991, p. 8, fig. 1), the term that the ancient potter used for the vessel was "kylix."

117 Bessios, Tzifopoulos, and Kotsonas 2012, pp. 460–461, no. 126; there is also at least one sherd disk from the Hypogeion that was formed from a fragment of a Milesian amphora, see Chapter 17 (**17/11**); for the Milesian amphoras from the West Hill, see Chapter 21.

118 For the location of the sanctuary of Athena Assesia, see Kalaitzoglou 2008, p. 9, fig. 1.

119 See esp. Kalaitzoglou 2008, p. 117, fig. 6, with full discussion on pp. 119–128.

120 Illustrated in Kalaitzoglou 2008, pls. 26–27.

121 Among many others, see, for example, Kalaitzoglou 2008, p. 118, no. 547 (krater); for Milesian jugs, cf. Käufler 2004, pl. 37 (various examples).

122 Cook and Dupont 1998, p. 129, with bibliography on p. 206; for recent publications of Ionian cups from their home region, see von Miller 2018 (for Ephesos, see further von Miller, Kerschner, and Betina 2019); see also Polat, Zunal, and Üney 2018, p. 204, fig. 2. For the occurrence of such types in

South Italy and Sicily, see Tsiafaki 2008, pp. 15–26, where a total of six groups are proposed just on the basis of the material from the extramural sanctuary of Sybaris at Francavilla Marittima; note also a series of related cups from Francavilla variously classified under the general heading of "Colonial Pottery," see van der Wielen-van Ommeren and Kleibrink 2008, esp. pp. 91–101 (some others presented in the same category, e.g., pp. 102–103, fig. 50a–b, no. C38, look Chian or Chian-inspired to me); for additional cups from Francavilla, see Handberg 2010, pp. 319–323. For a full list of *Knickrandschalen* found at sites in Calabria, particularly on the Ionian coast side, see Guzzo 1978, esp. pp. 123–128 ("Excursus II: Coppe cosi' dette ioniche"); see also Lo Porto 1978, pl. 64, fig. 7 (top right); pl. 66, fig. 14, top right; pl. 69, fig. 22 (bottom middle), all from Taranto; Cristofani (1978, pp. 195–204) lists some 260 *Knickrandschalen* from Etruria (with discussion on pp. 163–166; see also pls. 86–89); for such cups in Etruria, Pierro 1978, pls. 102–103, figs. 1–12; for Gravisca, see Boldrini 2000; for Campania, see, among others, Johannowsky 1978, pl. 72, figs. 3–4 (from Capua and Caudium); for the distribution of Ionian cups in southern Italy and Sicily more generally, see Van Compernolle 2000. For their occurrence in Spain, see Rouillard 1978, esp. pls. 120–123, 127, and Aquilué Abadias et al. 2000, esp. p. 298, fig. 14; p. 307, fig. 19; pp. 312–317, figs. 26–28, various examples (all from Emporion); for such cups in Carthage and Toscanos, see Docter 2000, pp. 79–83, figs. 14–16; for Languedoc, see Gailledrat 2000, esp. p. 154, fig. 3, nos. 1–2; p. 160, fig. 8, nos. 1–5. For East Greek imports in Sicily and the Sicilian production of East Greek types, see, among others, Vallet and Villard 1964, pp. 87–88, pls. 74–76; Kerschner and Mommsen 2009. For such cups in the eastern Mediterranean, see Calvet and Yon 1977, pls. VII–IX, nos. 65–98; Calvet and Yon 1978, pl. 22 (Salamis on Cyprus); Gjerstad 1977, pl. XIII, nos. 9–14; pl. XIV, nos. 1–10; pl. 15, nos. 1–8; pl. XVI, nos. 1–3 (from various sites on Cyprus); Karageorghis 1977, pl. II, nos. 24; pl. III, nos. 3–4 (Kition); Thalmann 1977, pl. III, nos. 8–15; pl. IV, nos. 1–13, 15 (Amathous). For North Africa, see Schlotzhauer and Villing 2006, 59–61, figs. 23–24, 27–29; Schlotzhauer 2012, pls. 9–15 (Naukratis); Schaus 1985, pp. 58–59, figs. 6–7, pl. 19, nos. 314–323. For the Black Sea, see, among others, Posamentir 2006, p. 162, fig. 7; Posamentir and Solovyov 2007, p. 205, fig. 9, nos. 1–3.

123 Boardman 1998, p. 149.

124 In *Perachora* II, pp. 377–378, Shefton notes the primary differences between Attic and East Greek banded cups: "Generally speaking Attic cups, as we might expect, show greater articulation than the East Greek ones; the lip is tooled off at the offset, the black band at the top of the handle zone usually emphasizes the division. On the other hand, Ionian cups tend to slur over these divisions, the black line often is a little way below the lip . . . . Also the underside of the foot of an Ionian cup of this type, resembling the Attic banded cups, is as a rule reserved throughout and has angular transitions . . . . The outlines of handles, as seen in plan, tend to be subtly different too; the Ionian cups favouring a more rounded shape." Shefton referred to these Athenian cups as "ST cups," so named after the sector in the Athenian Agora where a good example was found. In *Agora* XII, pp. 88–89, with n. 4, Sparkes and Talcott renamed these cups as "the Class of Athens 1104," noting that the relevant excavation sector was not ST, but ΣΤ´, the derivation being too recondite, the connection too slight.

125 *Agora* XII, p. 89 (Class of Athens 1104), with n. 6; see also Shefton in *Perachora* II, pp. 377–378. See further the comments of Thompson 1956, p. 59; Brann 1956, pp. 353, 370–371, pl. 60, nos. 78–79.

126 Schlotzhauer 2014; see also Schlotzhauer 2000. For *Knickrandschalen* in northwest Asia Minor, at the site of Assos, see Utili 1992, esp. pp. 62–63, figs. 7–8; İren 1993, p. 51, fig. 2; Utili 1999, pp. 289–291, figs. 4–6; only a few were encountered at Greek Emporio on Chios, see Boardman 1967, pp. 134–135, nos. 456–459; some from Thasos, see Ghali-Kahil 1960, pp. 28–30, pl. 8, nos. 5–15; and at Troy: *Troy* IV, p. 297, nos. 8–10.

127 Kalaitzoglou 2008, pp. 67–92; Kerschner 1997, p. 114, pl. 2, nos. 10–11; p. 118, pl. 3, nos. 12–13; p. 130, pl. 6, nos. 44–46; p. 138, pl. 8, no. 57; p. 150, pl. 11, nos. 79–86; p. 166, pl. 15, nos. 112–122; pp. 194–195, pls. 39–45; for an overview of the material from Ephesos, see Kerschner 2007.

128 *Sindos* II, pp. 37–39, 483, figs. 12–15, nos. 10–13.

129 Chrysostomou and Chrysostomou 2012, p. 240, figs. 2, 5.

130 Tsiafaki 2012, pp. 232–234, figs. 14–15.

131 Bilouka and Euthymoglou 2011, p. 414, fig. 7 (left).

132 Lazaridis 1964, pl. 23:α; cf. Lazaridis 1965, pl. 75:β.

133 Koukouli-Chrysanthaki and Marangou-Lerat 2012, p. 328, fig. 13:α, β.

134 Bakalakis 1938a, p. 110, fig. 3; pp. 112–113, figs. 5, 5α.

135 Bakalakis 1938b, p. 88, fig. 8 (bottom row, right).

136 Ghali-Kahil 1960, pp. 28–30, pl. 8, nos. 6–15.

137 Paspalas 2001, pp. 314–315, fig. 52, pl. 52, nos. 5.13–5.20.

138 Vokotopoulou, Bessios, and Trakosopoulou 1990, pp. 428, 436, fig. 18.

139 Vokotopoulou 1990, pp. 403, 410, fig. 16; Moschonissioti 2012, p. 389, fig. 9.

140 *Akanthos* I, pp. 225–228, fig. 12, pls. 173–174 (various examples).

141 Sismanidis 1996, p. 295, fig. 14.

142 See, for example, Aslan 2019, pp. 223, 348–350, pls. 53–54, nos. 459–473.

143 Cook and Dupont 1998, pp. 133–134, fig. 19.1c.

144 Boehlau and Habich 1996, pp. 30, 34–35, 61, 71, Graves 9.3, 16.4, 17.1, 19.1, 45.2, 46.1 (= Boehlau 1898, pp. 36–38, 45–47, pl. 7, nos. 3–4, 6–9). For further bibliography on the type, see Kranz and Lullies 1975, p. 16 (under pl. 53, 2); Yfantidis 1990, p. 167, no. 105.

145 This is not the place for a full account of the distribution of "Samian" lekythoi in the West, but among many others, cf. Haspels 1936, pp. 22–23, n. 3 (examples from Gela and Megara Hyblaia in Syracuse); Zancani Montuoro 1972 (Francavilla Marittima, also discussed in de la Genière 1984, pp. 93, 98, figs. 3, 8); Orlandini 1978, pl. 57, figs. 35 (grooved) and 36 (painted) (Gela); Lo Porto 1978, pl. 66, fig. 14, bottom left (Taranto); Cristofani 1978, pp. 171–173 (24 examples in all from Etruria, including Cerveteri, Tarquinia, Vulci, Grotte S. Stefano, Talamone, Populonia, Poggio Civitate, and Rome); also Pierro 1978, pl. 103, fig. 15 (Tarquinia).

146 Knigge and Willemsen 1964, p. 44, fig. 39β, illustrated four of the ten lekythoi; five are illustrated together with a few lydia in Scheibler 1973, p. 25, fig. 25. Additional examples from Greece are listed in Haspels 1936, p. 22, n. 3; Shefton 1962, p. 375, pl. 156, no. 4057; see also, among others from Greece: Kinch 1914, pl. 36, no. 2,27; pl. 38, nos. 6,5, 6,8; pl. 45, nos. 26,1–3 (Vroulia); Jacopi 1929, p. 64, fig. 54, nos. 11, 14; p. 83, fig. 73, two examples (Ialysos); Jacopi 1931, p. 55, fig. 26 (fourth row, third from left); pp. 282, 286, fig. 315, inscribed (after firing): Ἀμύρρητός ἠμι; p. 308, fig. 340 (two examples) (Kameiros); Pfuhl 1903, Beil. 22, no. 4, and cf. nos. 1, 3 (Thera). Among many others, cf. the marbled example from Sardis: Butler 1914, p. 435, fig. 8; see also Alexandrescu and Dimitriu 1968, p. 14, pl. 12, no. 1 (Bucharest).

147 Shefton 1962, p. 375, pl. 156, no. 4057.

148 Posamentir and Solovyov 2006, p. 126, fig. 35; Posamentir and Solovyov 2007, p. 203, fig. 7, nos. 7–8.

149 Culican 1975 identified them as Phoenician, calling them "Sidonian bottles," and see Fletcher 2011, pp. 29–30, fig. 8, center (who notes, p. 30: "the number of these bottles found in Phoenician contexts, their fabric and the development of the shape within the Phoenician repertoire make Culican's arguments convincing"); they are considered the ancestor of the Athenian lekythos shape.

23A

SELECTED ATTIC BLACK-FIGURE AND RED-FIGURE POTTERY FROM METHONE

Seth Pevnick

INTRODUCTION

The 2003–2011 excavations at Methone, Pieria have uncovered important and abundant pieces of Attic figured pottery. Mostly fragmentary, the Attic painted pottery found at Methone ranges from early black-figure through late red-figure, helping to confirm the existence of a long and continuous relationship between Athens and this very important northern center. In addition to contributing toward a fuller understanding of ancient Methone, this body of material contains a number of pieces that will be of interest to specialists in ancient painted pottery. Finally, because of its destruction by Philip II of Macedon in 354 B.C. and subsequent desertion, Methone provides us with a new fixed point in the chronology of late Attic red-figure, six years prior to the destruction of Olynthos (also sacked by Philip II, in 348 B.C.).

SELECT CATALOGUE

Although the body of material warrants a complete catalogue, I provide here only selected highlights, chosen to illustrate the range of pottery discovered at Methone thus far, in terms of date, shape, technique, and style. I have had to omit numerous important pieces, and I do not attempt here to quantify either the total amount of Attic painted pottery found at Methone, or the percentage of that total discussed here. This selection represents a tip of the proverbial iceberg, with plenty remaining in storage for future study, and still more in the ground, yet to be uncovered. The best-known piece from Methone, a fragmentary early red-figure cup discovered in 2004 and displayed for several years at Dion, is not included in this catalogue, but is given more comprehensive study and attribution by Maria Tolia-Christakou (see below, Chapter 23b).[1]

Contextually, the majority of the selected fragments of both Attic black- and red-figure were found in the excavations on the East Hill (**23/1**, **23/4**, **23/6–23/8**, **23/10–23/12**, **23/14–23/16**), in the area of the agora (Fig. 1.21; Chapter 29), and one was found in the area to the southeast of the East Hill (**23/3**, from Plot 278). In comparison, only three fragments were found on the West Hill (**23/2**, **23/5**, **23/9**), an area rich in Archaic finds (Chapters 19, 21–22), but destroyed by fire by the mid-6th century B.C., thus missing later Archaic and Classical layers (Chapter 1, Fig. 1.33).

For each entry I have provided dimensions and description (using BG for black gloss), with short commentary. For certain fragments, I have used Max. P. Dimension (Maximum Preserved Dimension) alongside or instead of P.H. or P.W. All dates mentioned in the commentary refer to years B.C.

ATTIC BLACK-FIGURE

23/1. (MEΘ 5159) Handle Plate Fr, Column Krater Fig. 23.1

East Hill #274/007005 [2]. Building B, Room B. 15.9.2003.

P.H.[= Th.] 0.023; p.L. 0.059; p.W. 0.062.

Single fr from handle plate of large column krater, with face of bearded man to left. Incised internal details include outer contour and pupil of eye, curved nose wing, and mouth, moustache (or cheekbone), and beard. Beard embellished with added red atop BG, with one stroke extending to edge of fr. BG streaky across outer edges and underside (with part of column running horizontally beneath, not continuing below into actual handle). Top side badly damaged, surface preserved only from left edge toward middle.

COMMENTARY

Column-krater handle plates decorated with vegetal ornament or a single animal (real or mythological) appear around 600 on vases from Corinth, where the shape is thought to have been invented (hence its ancient name, κρατὴρ κορίνθιος or κορινθιουργὴς, as noted by Sir John Beazley).[2] Soon thereafter, the shape appears in Athens, initially with the Komast Group, and then becoming most popular in the second quarter of the 6th century.[3] In this period, handle plates with male or female heads appear on both Corinthian and Athenian vases.[4] In addition, isolated male heads appear with some frequency on the necks of certain ovoid neck-amphoras of the same period.

Numerous parallels for the Methone piece can thus be found, on intact vases as well as fragments, and a date close to 560–550 seems likely. Attribution is more difficult, given the small extant painted area. The rounded nose and stray paint stroke extending beyond the beard are both unusual and difficult to parallel exactly; perhaps closest for their "cheerful quality" are the heads on either side of an ovoid neck-amphora in San Antonio (86.134.37) attributed to the Painter of Vatican 309, one of the "companions of Lydos." Also very similar is the male head on a column-krater handle plate "related to Lydos" now in Amsterdam, said to be from Italy.[5]

23/2. (MEΘ 4644, MEΘ 5139) Body and Rim Frr, Siana Cup (Overlap Type) Fig. 23.2

West Hill #229/014008 [8], Τομή B [Section 2], Building A; depth of 0.80 m. 27.6.2008 (MEΘ 4644); H229/016 NW. 19.8.2008 (MEΘ 5139).

Bessios and Noulas 2012, p. 405, fig. 15.

MEΘ 4644: p.H. 0.044; p.L. 0.101; Th. 0.003–004; Diam. (rim) est. 0.025.

MEΘ 5139, fr a: p.H. 0.029; p.L. 0.037; Th. 0.004; fr b: p.H. 0.047; p.L. 0.040; Th. 0.003–0.004.

FIGURE 23.1. Handle plate fragment, Attic black-figure column krater, **23/1** (MEΘ 5159). Photo I. Coyle

FIGURE 23.2. Body and rim fragments, Attic black-figure Siana cup, **23/2** (ΜΕΘ 4644, ΜΕΘ 5139). Photo I. Coyle, drawing A. Hooton

Three frr from rim and lower bowl of Siana cup (overlap type) with racing or parading horsemen (cavalcade). Interior BG, with reserved band just below lip, offset inside and out. Exterior with BG just over top of lip and thin BG band across lip-bowl junction, overlapping painted decoration (but not incision). Largest fr with horsemen to left, the first lost below seat, the second missing only his foot and the legs of his horse (which may once have been white); perhaps the muzzle of a third just preserved at right break. Smaller frr (non-joining) with horseman (front of face and torso, forearm and hand holding reins, upper thigh) on red or purple horse (head and neck) to left; and two rear horse legs to left, on BG ground line (above reserved line and glazed lower bowl), with likely tip of horsetail at left break. Horsemen with long hair, no indication of clothing; incision used primarily for overlap areas, not entire outline.

COMMENTARY

Siana cups, named for the cemetery on Rhodes where two examples now in London (B380, B381) were found, constitute the most significant type of Attic black-figure cup produced in the second quarter of the 6th century. Beazley devoted three chapters in *ABV* to the type, each now given its own volume by H. A. G. Brijder, who has also expanded the list of painters. Although we lack certain components of the cup which can be useful for attribution and dating, such as the foot and lower part of the bowl (including tondo), numerous details of the youths and horses suggest an attribution to the Taras Painter (called "the Shadow of the C Painter" by Beazley) in his early period (mid-560s and slightly earlier).[6] In particular, note the faces of the youths, which include several features characteristic of the Taras Painter: "strongly pronounced profiles with protruding noses, receding mouths, and prominent chins," and circular eyes "with a short horizontal stroke at the side." The single line for the mouth is an early characteristic, while the absence of anatomical details for riders is normal throughout the painter's career.[7]

An argument for a slightly later date could be made on the basis of the overall size of the cup, estimated at 25 cm, since this painter's cups diminish in size over the course of his career.[8] But this size is merely an estimate based on surviving fragments, and a diameter of 26 cm would be within his early size range.

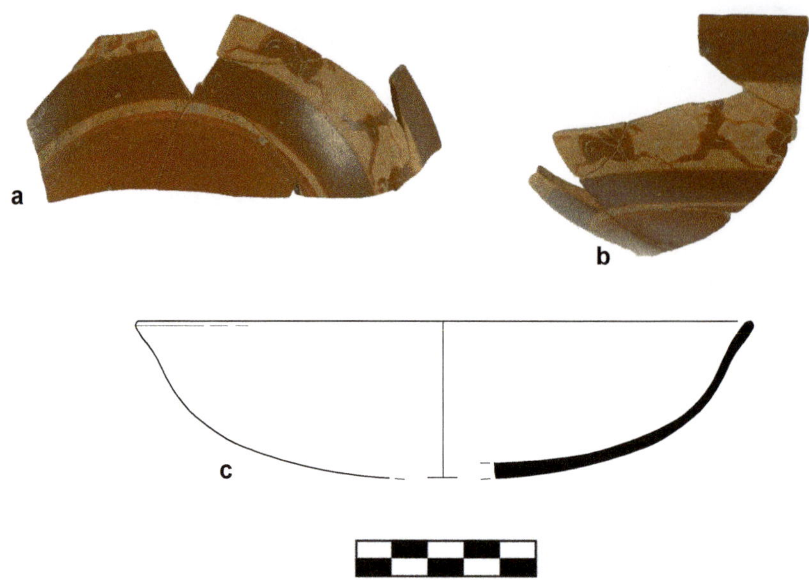

FIGURE 23.3. Fragmentary Attic black-figure Little Master band cup, **23/3** (ΜΕΘ 5160). Photos I. Coyle, drawing A. Hooton

23/3. (ΜΕΘ 5160) Body and Rim Fr, Little Master Band Cup Fig. 23.3

South side of East Hill #278/002, αγωγός ύδρευσης (water channel). 19.6.2006.

P.H. 0.045; p.L. 0.115; Th. 0.003–0.004.

Fr from bowl and rim of misfired Little Master band cup. Interior red (misfired BG). Exterior reddish brown (misfired BG) 0.015 below lip; reserved band with figures; BG band, reserved band, red (misfired BG) probably down to stem (now lost). BG red (2.5YR 4/8) and reddish brown (5YR 4/4) rather than black; alignment of darker color above reserved band, lighter color below and within bowl perhaps due to serendipitous stacking of cup in kiln atop vessel of same diameter as reserved band. Figure band: at left break, tendril (from palmette?), foot and lower leg of figure running right (toward horse); galloping horseman to right (lost above waist), nude male running right, looking back (top of head lost); palmette or lotus blossom lost at right break.

COMMENTARY

Little Master band cups develop just after Little Master lip cups, both flourishing in the third quarter of the 6th century. While lip cups often feature only one or two figures per side, band cups typically have three or more, as here.[9]

23/4. (ΜΕΘ 5158) Foot, Fillet, and Tondo Fr, Stemless Cup Fig. 23.4

East Hill #274/088, Χώρος Δ΄ (Building A, Room 4). [7]. 27.10.04.

P.H. (foot) 0.011; Diam. (foot) 0.075; p.H. (stem) 0.006; Diam. (stem) 0.046.

Torus foot with reserved outer face and resting surface, BG on slightly convex upper; hollow underneath, BG on conical underside, reserved under bowl. Added red fillet at base, BG bowl exterior and interior around tondo. Tondo with gorgoneion, set off with reserved outline; relief for eyes, eyebrows, ears (one mostly lost), mouth; incision for hair (alternating BG with added red on BG) and BG beard; mouth with red tongue, white teeth; BG dot centered in forehead.

FIGURE 23.4. Foot and tondo fragment, Attic black-figure stemless cup, **23/4** (ΜΕΘ 5158). Photos I. Coyle, drawing A. Hooton

COMMENTARY

Gorgoneia appear frequently across Greek art, but particularly within black-figure cup tondos and especially black-figure eye cups.[10] With its broad red fillet constituting the entire stem, this fragment likely derives from Beazley's Class of the Top-Band Stemlesses, a hybrid class of black-figure stemless (or very short-stemmed) band cups that often have eyes in the handle zone flanking additional figures, and gorgoneia in the tondos, ca. 530–520.[11]

23/5. (ΜΕΘ 5081) Body Frr, Kylix Fig. 23.5

West Hill #229/020001, Τομή (Sector) B, Building B. 19–20.8.08.

Max. P. Dimensions 0.152 x 0.200; Th 0.004.

Frr from kylix, comprising three contiguous groups, nearly joining. Interior BG, with reserved band (0.002) just below lip. Exterior with BG extending nearly all the way over offset lip section; below offset, reserved band with BG ground line supporting opposed ivy leaves, alternating black and red (both top/bottom and side/side), divided top and bottom by three dots (berries?); farther down, thick BG band atop thick reserved band with radiating tongues, alternating black and red, divided by BG, with triple BG bands above and below; BG below, presumably continuing to stem.

COMMENTARY

With varying patterned bands and no human or animal figures, these fragments call to mind the Cassel (or Kassel) Cups of the last decades of the 6th century (as named by Beazley).[12] But the BG bands below the lip and above and below the patterned bands do not accord with true Cassel Cup design. Moreover, the few instances of dots preserved between ivy leaves suggest an attribution to the Band-and-Ivy Group, which Brijder equates with the Taras Painter after his late period (i.e., 540s, probably first half).[13]

23/6. (ΜΕΘ 5051) Body Fr, Closed Pouring Vessel (Olpe?) Fig. 23.6

East Hill #274/074. 8.11.05.

P.H. 0.100; p.W. 0.055; Th. 0.002–0.007; Diam. (neck, interior) 0.060.

Single fr from body and neck of mid-sized closed vessel with lip offset outside, probably olpe. Interior BG at top (approx. 0.030 preserved beneath upper break) with thin purple band (0.025) just below break; unworked below. Exterior with BG (perhaps purple) dot on offset lip, perhaps from checkerboard pattern, above neck with decorative band (central BG band with ivy and berries springing from top and bottom, between BG bands [single above, double below]). Overlapping lowermost band, head of dancing maenad to left (ivy wreath: black, red, incised), holding krotala in raised right hand, skin white, drapery with incised and white ornament; below, head and upper body of satyr (beard, hair: black, red, incised) to right, perhaps holding maenad; background with grapevines.

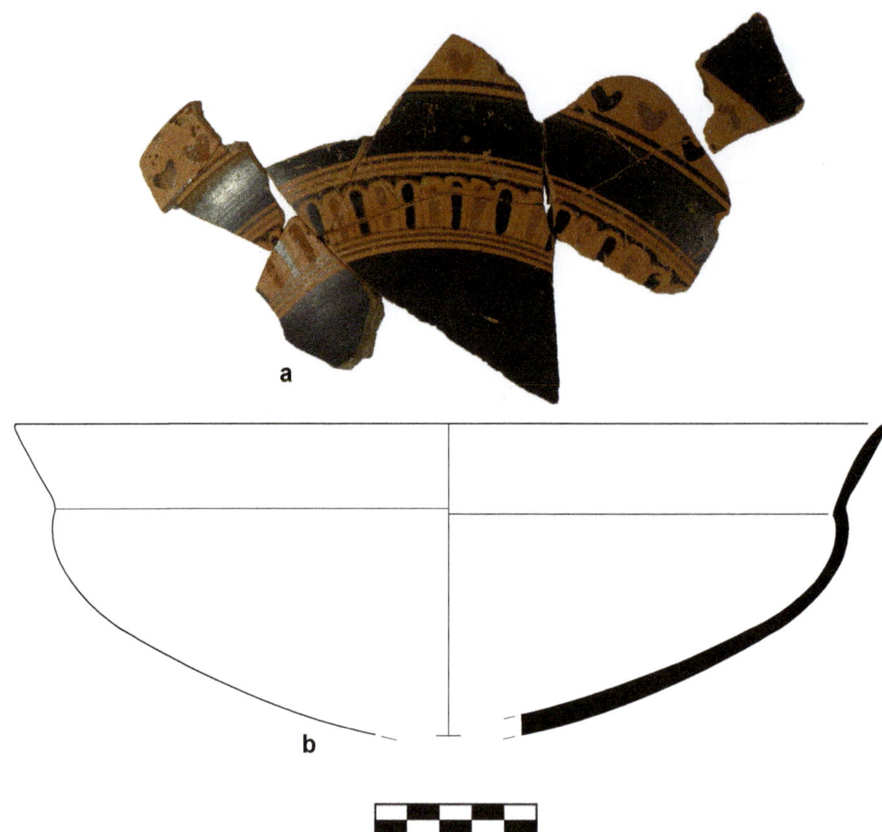

FIGURE 23.5. Fragmentary body, Attic black-figure kylix, **23/5** (MEΘ 5081).
Photo I. Coyle, drawing A. Hooton

FIGURE 23.6. Body fragment, Attic black-figure closed pouring vessel (olpe?), **23/6** (MEΘ 5051).
Photo J. Vanderpool

COMMENTARY

Both the shape and the general scheme of decoration follow those of the Daybreak Painter olpai, as described by C. H. Emilie Haspels: "The olpai are slender, pear-shaped, and long-necked . . . Above the picture there is usually an ivy pattern, and, on the front of the mouth, chequers."[14] The incision on the maenad and satyr, however, is perhaps not so detailed as in the finer olpai of the Daybreak Painter (e.g., the well-known olpe in Boston with Herakles in the pot of Helios),[15] and we may be safer in assigning this fragment to a painter of olpai within the Leagros Group, ca. 520–500.

23/7. (MEΘ 1988) Fragmentary Skyphos Fig. 23.7

East Hill #274/085, A87, ΒΔ τμήμα (NW sector). 4.11.05.

P.H. 0.099–0.105 [uneven base and rim]; Diam. (foot) 0.860–0.880; Th. 0.025–0.035.

Fragmentary skyphos with spreading ring foot, rising horizontal handle (only one preserved; round in section), and nearly vertical wall with slightly flaring lip. Resting surface, recessed bottom reserved, with BG band in between; BG band covering outer surface of foot from just above resting surface to upper surface, with reserved band at junction of base and bowl; above this, two BG bands (0.023, 0.003) supporting figured decoration: on either side, facing winged sphinxes between lotus buds. Incision delineating wings and lotuses; added white, now mostly lost, on faces. BG band (0.013) above figural zone, extending just over lip; reserved band (0.003) just inside lip, BG covering entire interior below (somewhat uneven, swirled).

COMMENTARY

Although somewhat sloppy in both potting and painting, this cup, with sphinxes as primary decoration, recalls several "Connected with the CHC Group."[16] Most of the sphinxes included there, however, lack incision. Within the CHC Group proper,[17] sphinxes tend to be subsidiary decoration, placed at the handles, often with palmettes, flanking a central scene. In any case, even a loose connection to the group suggests a date within the first quarter of the 5th century.

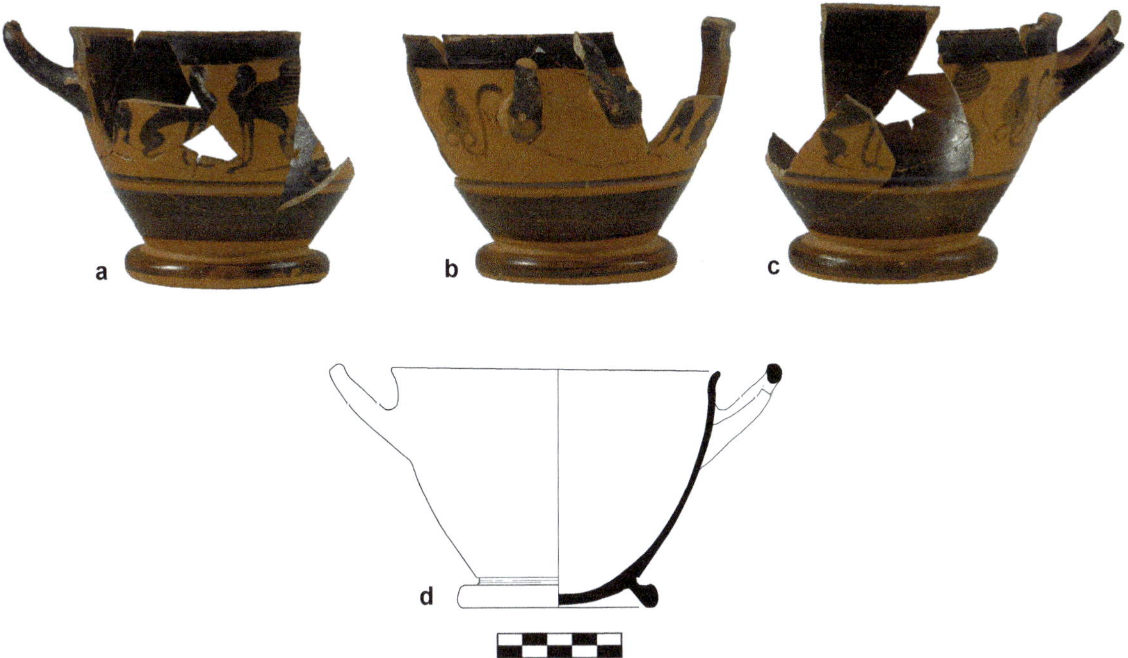

FIGURE 23.7. Fragmentary Attic black-figure skyphos, **23/7** (MEΘ 1988). Photos I. Coyle, drawing A. Hooton

ATTIC RED-FIGURE

23/8. (ΜΕΘ 4938) Body Fr, Krater Fig. 23.8

East Hill #274/089 (west of Building A). 11.7.06.

Max. p. Dimension 0.048; Th. 0.007.

Fr from massive krater (volute or calyx), broken just below slight groove setting off uppermost register below lip. Slight curvature, but nature of break (not in line with wheel marks) will not allow accurate measurement of diameter. Interior BG, exterior preserving small amount of painted decoration: head of Herakles to right, with lion skin covering forehead and chin up to break. Eye nearly frontal, with pupil and iris indicated, and very slight opening at outer edge. Mustache in dilute glaze, lion skin and facial features in relief contours. Two palm fronds at right also with relief contours, the lower disappearing behind nose of Herakles.

COMMENTARY

The presence of Herakles beside a palm tree suggests that this fragment derives from a representation of the hero in a sacred location—perhaps at Delphi in his struggle with Apollo over the tripod (as on the Pioneer Group amphora in Boston [Museum of Fine Arts, 63.1515]). The pupil-and-iris eye suggests a date fairly early within the development of red-figure, probably within the last quarter of the 6th century.[18]

23/9. (ΜΕΘ 4946) Base/Tondo Fr, Stemless Cup Fig. 23.8

West Hill #229/027. 29.5.09.

P.H. [= Th.] 0.008; p.L. 0.049; p.W. 0.018; Diam. (foot) est. 0.065.

Small fr from base/tondo of stemless cup. Base flat, reserved underneath, BG around lower edge, beneath reserved groove. Exterior of bowl largely lost, rising in three places, each preserving bits of coral-red gloss (also sometimes called "intentional red"). Interior with long-haired youth to left, implement in right hand behind; full relief contour, added red garland in hair. In field to right, four evenly spaced letters, perhaps from *kalos* name or potter/painter signature: *Σ Χ̣ Ο̣ Σ* [three-bar sigmas; the reading of the second and third letters is uncertain].

FIGURE 23.8. Body fragment, Attic red-figure krater, **23/8** (ΜΕΘ 4938); base/tondo fragment, Attic red-figure stemless cup, **23/9** (ΜΕΘ 4946); and body fragment, Attic red-figure uncertain vessel type, **23/10** (ΜΕΘ 4915). Photos I. Coyle, drawing A. Hooton

COMMENTARY

Despite the loss of most of the original cup, this small fragment deserves attention. The use of coral-red gloss on cup exteriors is rare, and although its use on a stemless cup might bring to mind well-known Sotadean vessels from the mid-5th century, the figural style here suggests an earlier date, ca. 500–480. The long hair and turned-back rear view, with rounded shoulder blade, call to mind the Pithos Painter, but the hand in particular is more finely drawn. Also, to my knowledge, no inscriptions appear on works attributed to the Pithos Painter. The inscription, if properly read as . . . *Σ Χ̣ Ο̣ Σ*, finds a parallel a bit earlier, on side B of a cup attributed to the Ambrosios Painter in Oxford (1911.616),[19] within the name ΚΡΑΛΑΙΣΚΟΣ; several scholars have seen this as a misspelled reference to Kallaischros, a relative of Kritias.[20]

23/10. (ΜΕΘ 4915) Upper Body Fr, Uncertain Vessel Type Fig. 23.8

East Hill, #274/089 (west of Building A). 3.10.07.

Max. p. Dimension 0.070; Th. 0.007.

Upper body fr from hydria, stamnos, neck amphora, or column krater. Interior partially glazed, exterior with BG tongues separated by relief lines above (just below neck, now lost), figural scene below: youth to right, wavy added red ivy garland in hair, dilute glaze for downy cheek, relief line for ear, eye, eyebrow, and chlamys draped over shoulders. Back of head not preserved, body (including arms and hands) lost below upper chest; missing arms and hands once held barbiton lyre to right, now with three preserved relief line strings. Behind lyre, right hand of another figure holds kylix (of Type C, with flaring lip offset by dilute glaze).

COMMENTARY

Probably from a komos scene, perhaps by the Pig Painter or another Earlier Mannerist (who far preferred column kraters to stamnoi), ca. 480–460. Cf., e.g., the komasts on column kraters in Paris (Musée Rodin 993 [note komast with lyre and kylix]) and Cleveland (Museum of Art 1924.197 [note man holding kylix]), or the pelike in Munich (Antikensammlungen 2346 [note added red garlands]).[21]

23/11. (ΜΕΘ 4914) Rim Fr, Calyx Krater Fig. 23.9

East Hill #274/089 (west of Building A). 28.9.07.

P.H. 0.048; Max. p. Dimension 0.165; Th. 0.005–0.020; Diam. (interior rim) est. 0.400; Diam. (exterior rim) est. 0.460.

Calyx-krater rim fr with torus lip. BG interior, with reserved line just below lip; BG exterior, now much worn, lost in places. Below lip, broad (0.0031) figured band, reserved above and below, with three sets of diagonally addorsed palmettes, linked by tendrils with relief contour.

COMMENTARY

Addorsed palmettes like these appear below the rims of calyx kraters for much of the 5th century. Among the earliest examples is a calyx krater attributed to the Kleophrades Painter now in Paris, although the Berlin Painter used similar ornamental bands to encircle the bodies of two Nolan amphoras perhaps slightly earlier (ca. 490–480).[22] The Aegisthus Painter, various Polygnotans, and others carry the motif into the middle of the century with more frequency, and a calyx krater in Richmond attributed to the Nikias Painter almost to the end (ca. 410).[23] Calyx kraters continue well into the 4th century, of course, but usually with laurel leaves below the rim.

FIGURE 23.9. Rim fragment, Attic red-figure calyx krater, **23/11** (MEΘ 4914). Photo I. Coyle, drawing A. Hooton

23/12. (MEΘ 4935) Spouted Head Fr, Askos Fig. 23.10

East Hill #274/075 (east of Building A). 9.6.06.

P.H, 0.036; p.L. 0.030; p.W. 0.045; Th. 0.003.

Head of zoomorphic askos/strainer, probably lion, with pierced hole (0.003) through mouth serving as spout. Interior unfinished, exterior with BG on ears, within mouth, underneath, on sides, and up above head, though not in a recognizable pattern. Eyes, muzzle (with whiskers?), nose, teeth, all molded in clay, unpainted. Area above head also decorated with five rows of piercings (perhaps imitating fur/mane), and above this a slight groove, perhaps offset for handle or larger spout to rise above, or—more likely—for central strainer section.

COMMENTARY

Probably part of a small group of strainers with lion's heads, this head would have joined to an askos on which the lion's body would appear in red-figure, perhaps together with other figures; above, a central disc with holes would serve as strainer. For a well-preserved example, with ring handle, see New York, Metropolitan Museum of Art 41.162.54.[24] The vessel probably dates to the late 5th or early 4th century.[25]

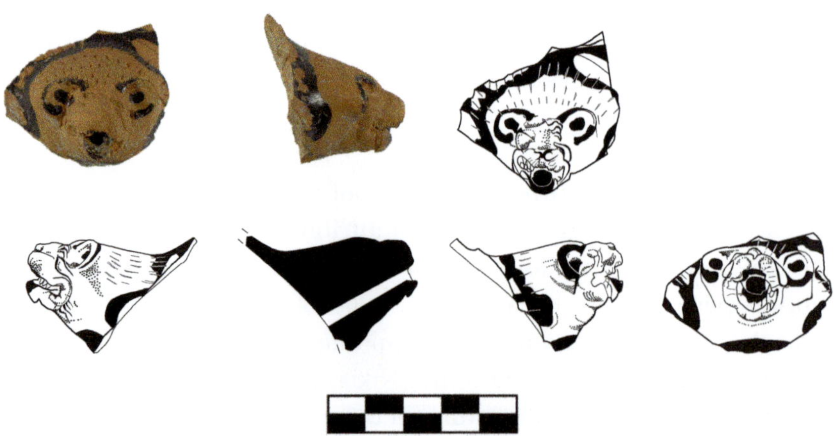

FIGURE 23.10. Spouted head fragment, Attic red-figure askos, **23/12** (MEΘ 4935). Photos I. Coyle, drawing A. Hooton

23/13. (ΜΕΘ 5154) Fragmentary Bell Krater Fig. 23.11

Handed over to the Ephoreia of Pieria (παράδοση) by A. Georgiadis, resident of Katachas (Καταχάς), from the acropolis (West Hill) of Methone, eastern flank. 20.8.99.

Diam. (exterior rim) est. 0.370; Diam. (exterior base) est. 0.150–0.160.

Fragmentary bell krater, comprised of three rim frr (α [H. 0.088; L. 0.275; W. 0.112; Th. 0.005–0.016]; β [H. 0.054; L. 0.242; W. 0.078; Th. 0.007–0.017]; γ [H. 0.039; W. 0.046; Th. up to 0.013]); two upper wall frr (δ [H. 0.045; W. 0.045; Th. 0.007]; ε [H. 0.032; W. 0.048; Th. 0.006–0.007]); one wall and handle fr (ζ [H. approx. 0.090; W. 0.118; Th. (wall) 0.005; Th. (handle) 0.020–0.040]); one body fr (η [H. approx. 0.190; W. approx. 0.270]); one base fr (θ [H. 0.044; L. 0.071; W. 0.039; Th. 0.008–0.010]); and two uncertain frr (ι [max. p. Dimension 0.053; Th. 0.006–0.009]; κ [max. p. Dimension 0.037; Th. 0.012]).

All frr with BG interior, badly misfired red (2.5YR 5/8) in many places. Rim/upper wall frr (α, β, γ) with reserved band just inside lip (0.002–0.004) and at top of bowl (0.003–0.006). Rim exterior with torus lip (BG above, *miltos* below?) above ornamental band (approx. 0.035) set off by very shallow groove above and below: laurel leaves to left (no berries); farther down, reserved band (approx. 0.005), overlapped by figured scene in places. Largest rim frr (α, β) each with part of ancient lead repairs (not joining) and figural decoration (described below), smallest (γ) with traces of laurel leaves and central rib. Reserved handle zone (approx. 0.010 wide) on rim fr β, almost certainly joining to handle fr ζ, although edges are too worn to be sure. Upper wall fr (δ) with part of laurel leaf and reserved band, above top and forehead of figure with hair and ivy crown (probably satyr), looking left; farther left, indeterminate reserved area (a hand?). Upper wall fr (ε) with right hand on branched staff. Wall and handle fr (ζ) with horizontal handle broken just beyond turn; BG exterior, reserved inside handle and on exterior wall facing handle, with dotted double kymation between relief lines around outer portion of handle root. Largest fr (η) preserves much of one side (probably A) of body, including portions of six figures (i–vi) above ornamental band (stopped double meander x 3 + dotted checkerboard). Starting at left, figures include male nude (i) standing to right, leaning slightly forward and down, both arms extended but missing buttocks and most of upper body; does not join to, but probably belongs with, head of bearded satyr to right, with ivy crown (plus added white) and two laurel branches, on rim fr β. Beside at right kneels a nude satyr (ii), wearing ivy garland and bearing offering dish; missing parts of head and hands. Farther right stands (iii), lost from the knees up, perhaps standing to right; perhaps belonging to head on fr δ and thyrsos on rim fr β. At center, male figure (iv), probably Dionysos, reclines on pedestaled platform, with dots across lower edge, indistinct pattern on upper. Figure wears drapery to waist with wave pattern at top, simpler decoration below; holding phiale in left hand, missing right arm, shoulder, and most of neck and head; wavy hair, back of neck suggests head turned left. Alongside sits female figure (v), perhaps Ariadne, to right, draped from waist down in bordered garment; above this, traces of white and yellow, perhaps from upper garment. Over left thigh and knee, ghost of left arm and hand, once in added white. At right break, nude male figure (vi) stands to left, right leg raised and passing behind figure v; between them, a branched staff (or tree) that may continue to become thyrsos on rim fr α; likewise, figure may join to head on fr α, and to hand on non-joining wall fr ε. Ivy-tipped thyrsos on rim fr β may belong to young satyr with head on non-joining wall fr δ. Base fr (θ) preserves small portion of foot with reserved concave underside (resting surface very worn, perhaps rounded and reserved). Uncertain frr (ι, κ) with little diagnostic value.

COMMENTARY

Bell kraters with Dionysian scenes are common in the 4th century, constituting many of the vases listed in Book XIX (Fourth-Century Pot-Painters) of *ARV*[2]. Often, as here, the rim bears laurel

FIGURE 23.11. Fragmentary Attic red-figure bell krater, **23/13** (ΜΕΘ 5154).
Photos I. Coyle

leaves, and the ornamental band below the figures a combination of meander and checkerboard. Somewhat unusual here is the reclining (rather than seated) Dionysos; especially unusual is his pedestaled platform. Also unusual is the kneeling satyr at left. Perhaps closest to our vase are those of "The Plainer Group," whose work Martin Robertson placed "mainly in the first quarter" of the 4th century.[26]

23/14. (ΜΕΘ 4944) Lid Fr, Lekanis Fig. 23.12

East Hill #274/085 (east of Building A). 1.11.05.

Max. p. Dimension: 0.152; p.H. 0.044; Th. (vertical outer edge): 0.0045; Th. 0.008–0.011; Diam. (exterior) est. 0.250.

Large lid fr from mid-sized lekanis. Underside BG, worn, scratched, and pitted in places; outer edge reserved, with double kymation; top with double kymation over double relief line just preserved around center (probably surrounding knob, now lost). Figural scene over main area: Eros (body white over reserved ground; wings reserved, with relief for long feathers below, dilute above) partially reclining on drapery, feet to left, head to right; before Eros, an object, perhaps a vessel, lost at left break; approaching from right break, a draped woman, bearing a tray; in the field before her, a reserved ring with double hash marks.

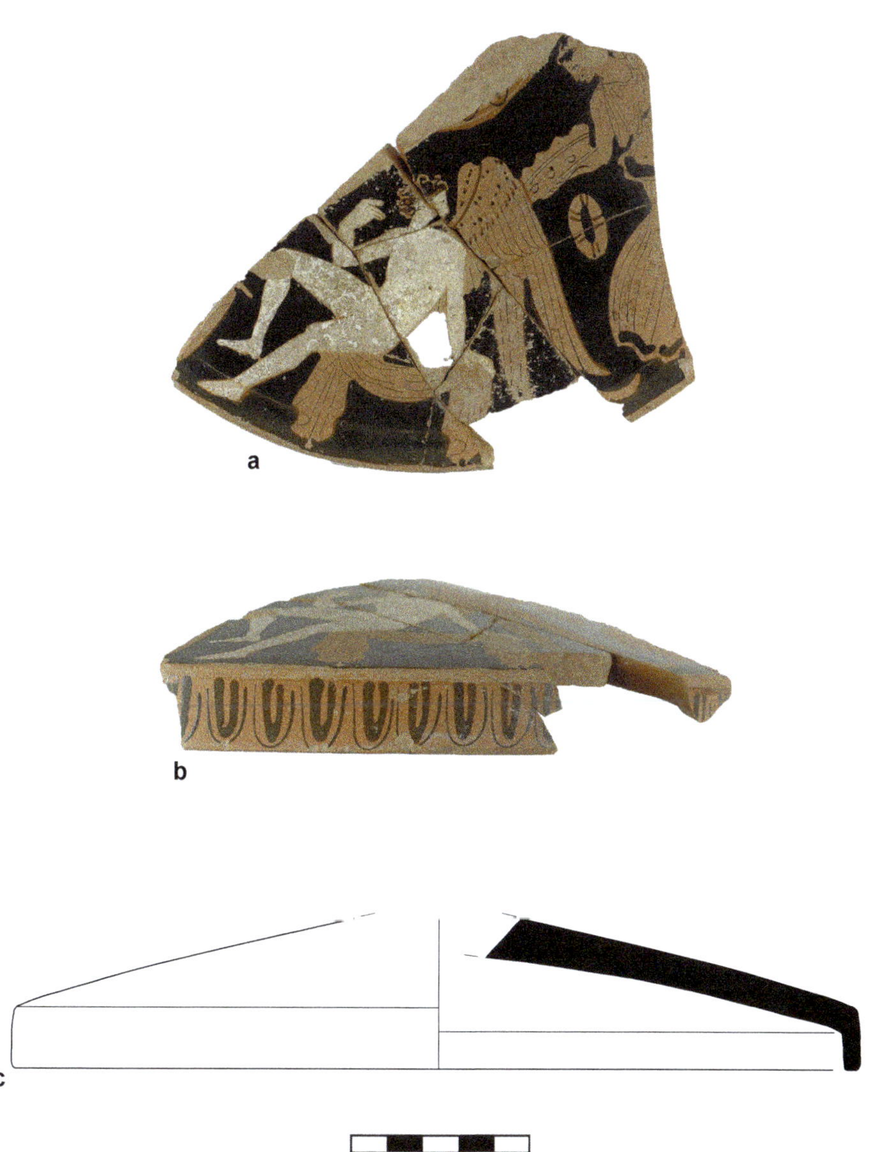

FIGURE 23.12. Lid fragment, Attic red-figure lekanis, **23/14** (ΜΕΘ 4944). Photos I. Coyle, drawing A. Hooton

COMMENTARY

Large lekanides are common in the 4th century, typically with an Eros, seated women, and a running maid (and sometimes also a seated youth). Here we have Eros and a running woman, but our Eros is unusual in sitting rather than running or fluttering. Perhaps the closest parallel is in London (British Museum F138 [1867,0508.1274]), listed by Beazley among "nuptial lekanides" of the Otchët Group.[27] Although the London lekanis was found in Apulia, many others in the Otchët Group come from northern Greece and the Black Sea region.[28] Probably dates 375–354.

23/15. (ΜΕΘ 5161) Fragmentary Pelike Fig. 23.13

Found across multiple units on the East Hill #274/059003, 059006, 059011 [2], 060001 [1], 068, 069, 078, 079. Between 2005 and 2009.

P.H. 0.270; Diam. (exterior rim) est. 0.190; Th. 0.002–0.010.

Fragmentary mid-sized pelike comprising two large rim frr, most of one handle, four body frr from side A, and one body, neck, and rim fr from side B. Rim frr preserving wide, flaring mouth and overhanging lip in two degrees; BG upper surface and underside, reserved outer edge, with double kymation band, dotted, below relief line. Vertical ribbed handle broken at lower join to body and at flat top, beginning tight turn back down to neck; BG on all preserved surfaces, save large palmette at base (12 leaves preserved). Four body frr (the largest measuring approx. 0.090 x 0.120) from side A, nearly joining, preserving figured scene atop ornamental band of double kymation, dotted, between relief lines (similar to that on lip). From left, scene includes four figures (i–iv): draped woman (i) moving left, probably looking right (head lost); nearly nude male (ii), with chlamys over left arm/shoulder (on non-joining fr, head lost) standing to right on right foot, left foot/knee raised, extending both hands to; reclining nude male (iii), seated to left atop drapery and looking right; and draped female (iv), leaning with right elbow on left shoulder of iii, looking left, stepping right. Single fr from side B preserves rim (matching description of rim frr above) and continuous profile of neck (including upper handle attachment) and portion of body; interior BG to neck, unworked below. Exterior with two fully draped youths facing one another beneath ornamental band of double kymation, dotted, between relief lines (similar to that on lip and below figures on side A). Left figure preserved from shoulder to knee, right from head to knee; both very cursorily drawn. Additional non-joining frr may also belong.

COMMENTARY

Among 4th-century pelikai, the grypomachies and griffin and Amazon heads that lend their names to Group G and the Amazon Painter are particularly abundant, but do not constitute particularly good parallels for our vase.[29] Instead, both the vase shape and the loose, sketchy contours of the figures suggest a connection to the mid-4th-century vases known as "Kerch-style" (after the city in the Crimea where many examples have been found). Although many such vases include polychromy and gilding, such embellishments are not found on all Kerch-style vases. Moreover, given the relatively poor condition of our vase, we should not be surprised if any such added colors once there will have been lost.[30] As preserved, the scene is not readily identifiable within the world of myth. Probably dates 375–354.

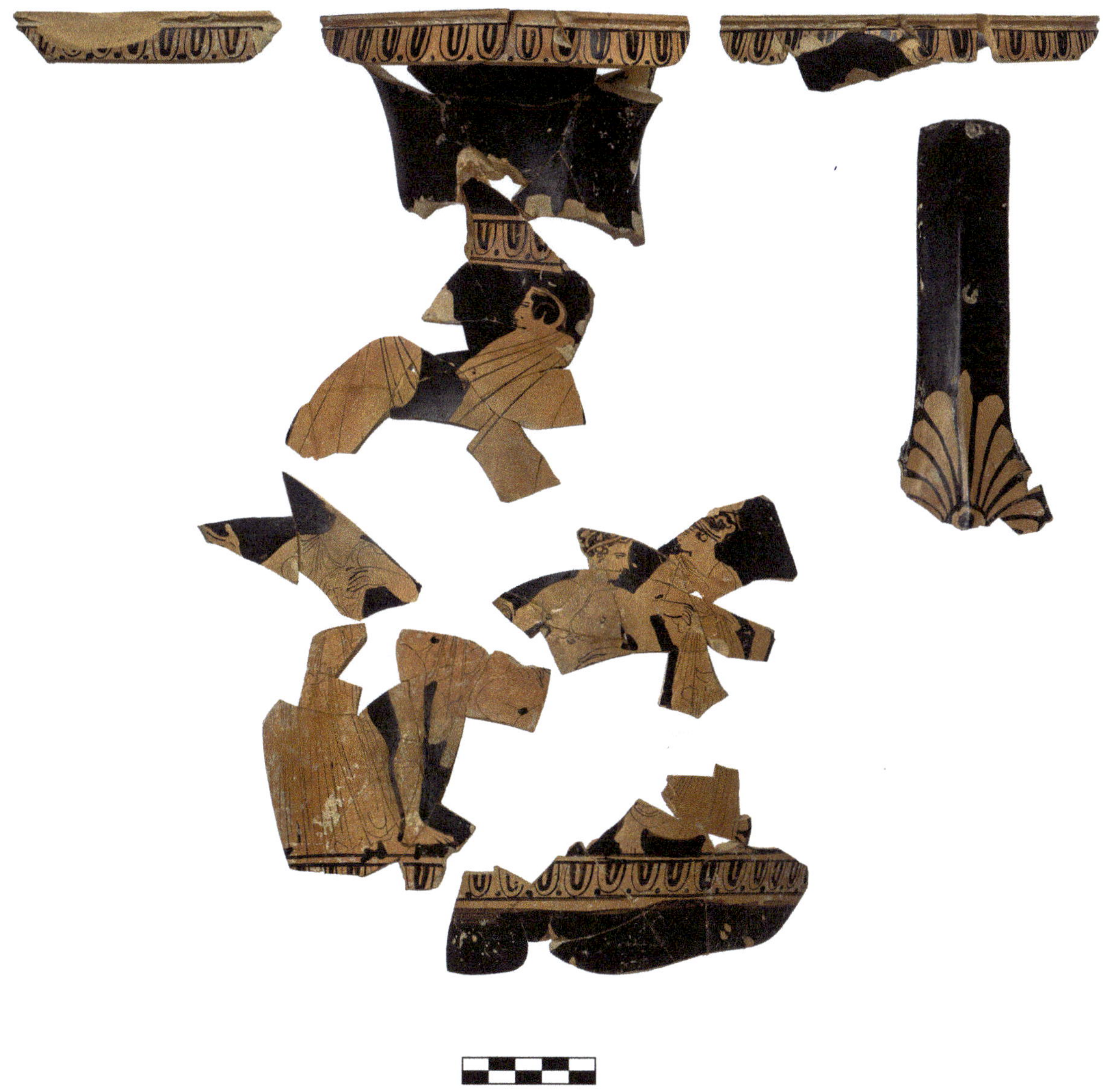

FIGURE 23.13. Fragmentary Attic red-figure pelike, **23/15** (ΜΕΘ 5161). Photos J. Vanderpool, drawings A. Hooton

23/16. (ΜΕΘ 1984) Miniature Squat Lekythos Fig. 23.14

East Hill #274/009003 [2], Building B, area of Rooms D, E. A52. 14.1.05.

P.H. 0.0585; Diam. (max) 0.041; Diam. (base): 0.035.

Nearly complete miniature squat lekythos. Spreading ring foot, flat resting surface, recessed bottom, reserved with two BG splotches (incidental?); outside of foot and most of body BG, worn and speckled. Irregular reserved space on front of vessel with schematic palmette, the central leaf rising above the rest and intersecting the reserved border above. Ribbon handle rising from shoulder, bending roughly 90° to join neck at break; neck joined to body with slight offset, broken below spout.

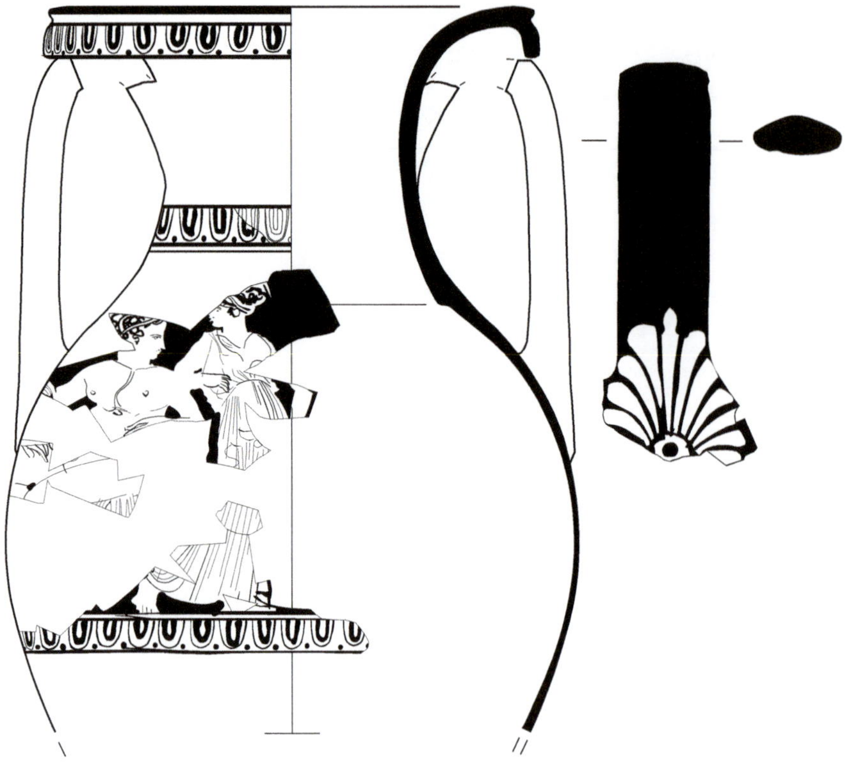

b

c

d

FIGURE 23.13. Fragmentary Attic red-figure pelike, **23/15** (ΜΕΘ 5161) *(continued)*.
Photos J. Vanderpool, drawings A. Hooton

FIGURE 23.14. Attic red-figure miniature squat lekythos, **23/16** (ΜΕΘ 1984). Photos I. Coyle, drawing A. Hooton

COMMENTARY

A common type produced in Athens and elsewhere during the first half of the 4th century, including in large numbers at Olynthos. David Moore Robinson notes that Olynthian palmette lekythoi with straight-sided lips may date from the first quarter of the century, while those with concave profile belong to the second quarter.[31] Since our vase lacks the mouth, such a distinction cannot be seen, and the palmette type, with long central leaf, does not provide additional chronological guidance. At Athens, where the type is extremely abundant, a similar dating scheme is in place, although the destruction of Methone provides a terminus ante quem for our piece, limiting the range to 400–354.[32]

23B

AN ATTIC RED-FIGURE CUP BY THE BONN PAINTER FROM METHONE

Maria Tolia-Christakou

During the excavations on the East Hill of ancient Methone in 2004, in the central room of Building A, fragments of a large Attic red-figure cup of the late 6th century B.C. were found, in the final phase of the stoa (**23/17** [MEΘ 1362]). The context of the vessel was the stoa Building A destroyed in Philip's sack of 354 B.C. (the destruction context and the building are described more fully in Chapters 1 and 18).[33]

23/17. (MEΘ 1362) Figs. 23.15–23.16
East Hill #274/ #274/087, Building A, Room 3 (Γ) destruction deposit.

The height of the vessel, including the handle, is 0.125 m, the diameter of the rim 0.317, the diameter of the base 0.125, while the diameter of the tondo is 0.150. The fabric is fine, with no visible inclusions (Munsell: 7.5YR 7/6) (Figs. 23.15–23.16).[34]

Just over half of the body is preserved with the base and one handle. The vessel was restored from many fragments; of what survives, two small rim fragments are missing, one with part of the shield held by one of the figures represented, the other undecorated. In addition, the cup has lost some small chips and flakes, especially at the edges of the joined fragments.

The vessel is an Attic Type B kylix (Fig. 23.15).[35] It stands on a low base with an articulated ring around its upper surface, a narrow and fairly high stem, and a shallow bowl. The rim is plain with a reserved line inside and outside rim. The side of the base, the resting surface, the interior of the stem, the inside of the upturned handle, and the panel between the handle roots are reserved. The underside of the base is glazed. A reserved line is also used for the tondo border and for the ground line on the exterior. The external contours and basic anatomical features of the human figures are executed in relief line; secondary anatomical details are drawn with diluted line; incision is used for the contours of the heads and the rim of the shields (which are compass-drawn). Added purple color is deployed for inscriptions, wreaths, flames on the altar, and blood. The preliminary sketch lines are abundant and fairly easy to discern, while in places there are also preserved traces of an applied red mineral color wash (*miltos*) which was applied to the vessel before firing.[36]

The exterior of the cup and the tondo are decorated with red-figure scenes (Fig. 23.16). Of the figural representation on the exterior, the left half of Side A and the right half of Side B are preserved, depicting a battle scene.

On the surviving half of Side A (Fig. 23.16), from the left, a young beardless male figure, wearing a wreath on his head, leaps to the right in a great stride, holding spear and shield. In front of him, to his right, appears an altar, on which a fire is burning. The altar rises from a two-stepped base and bears a crowning decorative element of a meander with volutes; the altar is inscribed ΚΑΛΕ (καλή) in dark paint, while two strokes of added purple depict blood from the sacrifice. From the right, two warriors are attacking the youth, of whom one, the bearded figure on the right, has already fallen to the ground, wounded in the chest and the right leg, as indicated by streaks of added purple that indicate the blood from his wounds. Behind these two figures there is yet another warrior, of whom only the left foot survives and part of the shield that he carries; he moves toward the warriors to the left.

There are four additional figures of warriors fighting in pairs on the preserved section of Side B (Fig. 23.16). On both sides of the cup, the warriors are shown nude, wearing only a helmet and, in some cases, greaves, while they carry a spear and a shield.

On two of the shields carried by the surviving warriors on Side B, the praise-name ΚΑΛΕ (καλή) is added in dark paint, while additional letters in added purple paint on the black gloss between the figures, somewhat difficult to make out, likewise represent the words ΚΑΛΟΣ or ΚΑΛΕ (καλή).[37]

The tondo shows a young horseman moving toward the left (Fig. 23.16e). The representation is missing the front part of the horse, including its head, most of the neck and chest, and the greater portion of the right, extended, leg. The young rider is barefoot and wears a wreath on his head, rendered in added purple; he wears a short chiton and on top of it a Thracian cloak, the so-called *zeira* (ζειρά), ornamented with geometric and circular motifs.[38] Behind him, near the periphery of the tondo, the dipinto ΚΑΛΟΣ is rendered in added purple, while below the hoofs of the horse can be discerned only the letters HO [ΠΑΙΣ?], written retrograde.

The vase is not signed, but on the basis of the style of painting, as well as details of its composition and iconography, it can be attributed to the Bonn Painter, one of the vase painters of the Athenian Kerameikos who worked at the end of the 6th century B.C.[39] To this artist, whose stylistic characteristics indicate that he trained near Oltos, have been assigned, so far until today, twelve other red-figure cups, all of substantial size.

The representations on the exterior of the cup show a battle, with no specific mythological content. Scenes of battle, similar in character, decorate four other cups by the painter, a fact that supports an equivalent interpretation for the scene on the cup from Methone.[40]

The depiction of the altar, around which the battle takes place on Side A of the vessel, is surely borrowed from the iconography of mythological battles. Examples of such battles derive for the most part from the Trojan cycle, and include representations of the duel between Hector and Achilles over the body of Troilos,[41] as well as scenes from the Ilioupersis with Priam as a suppliant at the altar of Zeus Herkeios.[42] The presence of the altar on the Methone cup functions to a certain degree as a sign that the battle that is in progress should not be mistaken for a real battle, but refers to the realm of myth. A similar iconographic allusion is to be understood in the nudity of the warriors, who are represented, in scenes of battle by this artist, as wearing at most a helmet and greaves, without the traditional hoplite outfit.[43]

The depiction of a young horseman in a Thracian cloak in the tondo of the kylix (Fig. 23.16e) represents a frequent choice of scene for artists of early and late Archaic red-figure. The subject is probably inspired by contemporary reality and perhaps reflects the custom of young Athenian horsemen adopting details of Thracian costume, in order to assume—as has been argued—by wearing such an outfit, the warrior capability, and the ferocity, of the Thracians in battle.[44]

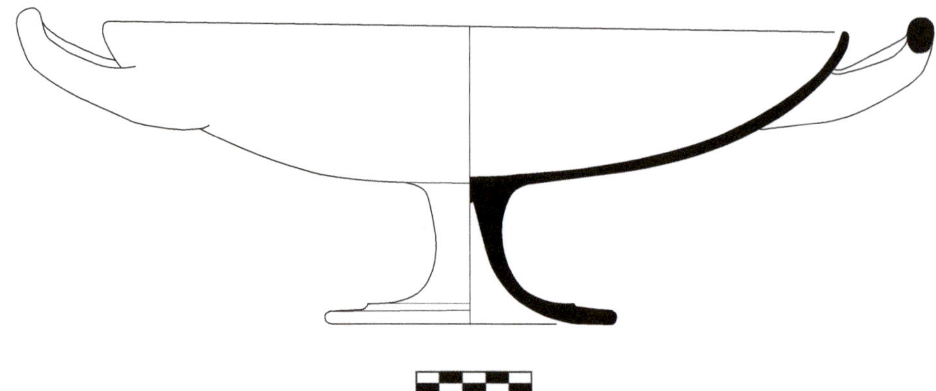

FIGURE 23.15. Attic red-figure cup, **23/17** (ΜΕΘ 1362).
Drawing A. Hooton

FIGURE 23.16. Attic red-figure cup, **23/17** (ΜΕΘ 1362).
Photos M. Tolia-Christakou

NOTES

1 See also Tolia-Christakou 2019. New excavations on the West Hill have now uncovered abundant Archaic and Classical remains in Pit 46, including Attic black- and red-figure pottery: see Van Damme 2020; Morris et al. 2020, figs. 58, 60–61.

2 Beazley 1941, p. 597.

3 *ABFV*, p. 187.

4 Bakir 1974, p. 66.

5 On the Painter of Vatican 309, see *ABV*, pp. 114, 120–122. On the San Antonio vase (BAPD 20272) and characterization of the painter's "cheerful quality," see entry by Kilinski in Shapiro et al. 1995, cat. 38 (p. 84). The Amsterdam fragment is Allard Pierson Museum 2098 (BAPD 13909, *CVA Netherlands 11 [Allard Pierson Museum 5]*, p. 48, Pl. 266.1), once in the Scheurleer collection (The Hague); BAPD follows *CVA The Hague 2* (III.H.d-e, p. 9, pl. 5.6 [inv. 2098]) in listing Rome as provenance, while the more recent *CVA* lists Taranto.

6 Brijder 1983, pp. 152, 167. Brijder (1983, p. 127) points out that sporting scenes appear in the oeuvre of the C Painter only in his late period (second half of the 560s), perhaps inspired by the Peisistratean reorganization of the Panathenaic Games in 566. On the Taras Painter more broadly, see Brijder 1983, pp. 151–165.

7 Brijder 1983, pp. 163–164 (quotation from p. 163). The same type of eye is also characteristic of this painter's horses (p. 164).

8 Brijder 1983, p. 155 and Table on p. 218.

9 On Little Master cups of all types, see Heesen 2011.

10 See Hedreen 2007, esp. pp. 221–227.

11 See *ABFV*, p. 109, and *Paralipomena*, pp. 100–102. Cf. New York, Metropolitan Museum of Art, 20.250 (BAPD 340246).

12 Beazley 1932, pp. 191–192.

13 Brijder 1983, pp. 151–152, 165–166, 168; see also Brijder 1993.

14 Haspels 1936, p. 59.

15 Museum of Fine Arts, Boston, 03.783: *ABV*, p. 378, no. 252; BAPD 302333; *ABFV*, fig. 232.

16 *ABV*, p. 623.

17 *ABV*, pp. 617–623.

18 It is worth noting, however, that some painters tend to portray Herakles with rounder eyes, even into the 5th century (e.g., the Berlin Painter, as seen by Kurtz 1983, p. 22). Museum of Fine Arts, Boston 63.1515: *ARV*², p. 1705 (then Basle market, "Somewhat recalls Euthymides"); *Paralipomena*, p. 324; BAPD 275680.

19 *ARV*², p. 173, no. 1; BAPD 201565.

20 Shapiro (1982, p. 72) points out that this Kritias would be "a descendant of Solon and grandfather of Kritias the Tyrant." See also *CVA Oxford, Ashmolean Museum 1*, pp. 2–3. The other instances of ". . . SCHOS" both appear on vases in Malibu: a fragmentary cup with erotic scene in the tondo, the youth labeled [M]OSCHOS (Tarquinia Painter, ca. 470 [BAPD 44984, J. Paul Getty Museum, 83.AE.321]); and a white-ground lekythos with the possible *kalos* name Μο[σχ]ος in an arming scene (Douris, early period, ca. 500 [BAPD 16229, J. Paul Getty Museum, 84.AE.770]). On coral-red gloss, see Cohen 2006, ch. 2; for coral-red phialai and stemless cups ca. 500–480, see Tsingarida 2014.

21 Paris: *ARV*², p. 564, no. 17, BAPD 206445; Cleveland: *ARV*², p. 564, no. 18, BAPD 206446; Munich: *ARV*², p. 565, no. 32 bis, BAPD 206462.

22 Kleophrades Painter: Paris, Musée du Louvre G162 (*ARV*², p. 186, no. 47, BAPD 201699); Berlin Painter: Naples, Museo Archeologico Nazionale 81550 [3137] (*ARV*², p. 201, no. 62, BAPD 201870), Paris, Musée du Louvre G201 (*ARV*², p. 201, 63, BAPD 201871).

23 E.g., Aegisthus Painter, New Haven, Yale University Art Gallery 1985.4.1 (BAPD 44751); Group of Polygnotos, New York, Metropolitan Museum of Art 56.171.48 (*ARV*[2], p. 1057, no. 104, BAPD 213734); Nikias Painter, Richmond, Virginia Museum of Fine Arts 81.70 (BAPD 10158).

24 On the type, which usually has a ring handle, see Schauenburg 1976. The New York askos is BAPD 13470.

25 But note that the British Museum allows for a broad range including a much earlier possible date for a similar vase (E764 [1890,0731.29], BAPD 2840, excavated at Marion-Arsinoe, Cyprus): between 470 and 400 (https://www.britishmuseum.org/collection/object/G_1890-0731-29, accessed Aug. 3, 2022).

26 Robertson 1992, p. 274. For the Plainer Group, see *ARV*[2], ch. 78, pp. 1418–1424.

27 *ARV*[2], p. 1498, no. 2; BAPD 230817.

28 On the Otchët Group, see *ARV*[2], pp. 1496–1499; Robertson 1992, pp. 274–275.

29 On Group G, see *ARV*[2], ch. 83 (pp. 1462–1471). On the Amazon Painter, see *ARV*[2], pp. 1478–1480.

30 On Kerch-style vases, with bibliography, see Lapatin 2006.

31 *Olynthus* XIII, pp. 146–150 (with plates 101-106).

32 For similar lekythoi at Athens, see Shear 1973, p. 131, incl. n. 27 and pl. 28, e–g; he counts 177 squat lekythoi and many more fragments from a single well excavated in 1971, "a great proportion of which are decorated with a single palmette in red figure." For dating, Shear cites examples from the Kerameikos, as well as Olynthos.

33 Bessios et al. 2004, p. 372; Bessios 2010, p. 103; Archibald 2011–2012, p. 99, fig. 158; Bessios 2012b, pp. 16, 20, fig. 17; BAPD 9038206. The findspot was Room 3 [Γ] in Stoa Building A (Fig. 1.21).

34 The kylix was on temporary exhibition in the Dion Museum for some years (until 2014). It is now stored in the new museum/*apotheke* in Makrygialos. The present contribution is a summary in English of a longer study on the kylix, its style, and iconography, now published (Tolia-Christakou 2019).

35 Cf. Bloesch 1940, pp. 56–57, pl. 14, 4.

36 For which see Richter 1923, pp. 53–59, 96–98; Noble 1988, pp. 125–127; Schreiber 1999, pp. 48–52; Cuomo di Caprio 2007, pp. 285–286, 309; Bentz, Geominy, and Müller 2010, pp. 28–29 (A. Boix).

37 For the female praise-adjective KALE (καλή), see Frontisi-Ducroux 1998; Hedreen 2016.

38 For the *zeira*, see Heuzey 1927, pp. 5–16; Best 1969, pp. 6–8; Cahn 1973, p. 13, with n. 2, with earlier bibliography; Lissarrague 1990, p. 211, with n. 62; Tsiafaki 1998, p. 32.

39 For the Bonn Painter, see *ARV*[2], pp. 351–352; *Paralipomena*, p. 363; Carpenter 1989, p. 221; *CVA* Basel 2 [Switzerland 6], pp. 31–34, pls. 14.1–2, 15.1–4, 35.1, 5; Tolia-Christakou 2019.

40 Cf. the kylix in Bologna, Museo Civico Archeologico, inv. NC 131 + 363 (*ARV*[2], p. 351, no. 5; Carpenter 1989, p. 221; *CVA* Bologna 1 [Italy 5], III I c, pl. 1, 1); the kylix in Kassel, Staatlichen Museen - Antikensammlung, inv. ALg 17 (*ARV*[2], p. 351, no. 6; *Paralipomena*, p. 363; Carpenter 1989, p. 221; Lullies 1968, p. 78–81, no. 34; Berger and Lullies 1979, pp. 97–100, no. 36); the kylix in the Vatican, Museo Gregoriano Etrusco Vaticano, inv. 505 (Side B) (*ARV*[2], p. 351, no. 4; Albizzati 1924–1938, pl. 70; *EAA* II [1959], p. 135, fig. 205 s.v.. Bonn, Pittore Falisco di [E. Paribeni]); the kylix once on the art market in London and New York (Sotheby's, London, 5/7/1982, p. 152, no. 390; Sotheby's, London, 10–11/7/1989, no. 201; Sotheby-Parke-Bernet, New York, 7/12/2005, p. 37, no. 35).

41 Kossatz-Deissmann 1981, pp. 87–90, no. 360; Aktseli 1996, pp. 44–45; Ekroth 2001, p. 119, nn. 16–17.

42 Wiencke 1954; Cassimatis 1988; Neils 1994, pp. 516–520; Papadakis 1994, pp. 148–154; Aktseli 1996, pp. 45–47; Mangold 2000, pp. 20–27; Hedreen 2001, pp. 64–80.

43 For the "heroic nude," see esp. Bonfante 1989; Himmelmann 1990, pp. 42–47; Hallett 2005, pp. 13, 18; Hurwit 2007, pp. 46–47, with n. 56, with additional bibliography.

44 Geddes 1987, p. 321.

24

TERRACOTTA LAMPS

John K. Papadopoulos

This chapter presents a representative sample of 16 Greek terracotta lamps from two parts of the site, the East Hill and the area to its south (Plots 274 and 278, see Fig. 1.1). The lamps were selected for their preservation, and for the range of fabrics and types. They are presented according to the area in which they were found, then by fabric and type.[1] Those lamps and lamp fragments that are clearly associated with the destruction deposit of 354 B.C. in the agora of Methone are published separately (in Chapter 29). The lamps presented here all date from the Archaic into the later Classical period.

EAST HILL: LAMPS FROM THE AREA OF THE AGORA

Attic Lamps

Type 16 B

This type of imported Attic lamp is fairly common at Methone, with at least four examples recorded, some of which are fairly well preserved (**24/1–24/3**, **24/15**). The prototype for this lamp is the earlier Corinthian version, which is fully discussed below (under **24/10–24/11**), corresponding to Type II at Corinth and Type 16 A in the classification of the Athenian Agora. Unlike the Corinthian prototype, which appears early in the 6th century B.C., the Athenian version is dated by Richard Howland, on the basis of the numerous examples from the Athenian Agora (13 catalogued plus another 59 inventoried), from the last quarter of the 6th century B.C. down to ca. 480 B.C.[2] What is especially important in terms of the chronology of this type from the Agora is that 19 inventoried examples, together with 25–30 uninventoried fragments, were found in the upper fill of the so-called "rectangular rock-cut shaft," dating to ca. 500–480 B.C., whereas there were no examples of Type 16 B found in the lower fill of the shaft, which was dated 575–535 B.C.[3] Agora Type 16 B is classified at the Kerameikos under the heading *Deckrandlampen* (DRL) by Ingeborg Scheibler, though she includes two examples that are of Howland's Type 17 A; following Howland, Scheibler dates the examples from the Kerameikos to the period 520–480 B.C.[4] Of the examples from Methone, the comparatively shorter rims of **24/3** and **24/15** are the earliest, with the broader rim of **24/1** the latest among the series.

Type 16 B is a close adaptation of its Corinthian prototype.[5] Howland's characterization of the type is worth quoting in part.

> There is a slightly concave bottom that rises into low curving sides topped by a flat or nearly flat overhanging rim. In the earlier examples the walls are low and rim narrow; in the later, the walls are somewhat higher and the rim much broader, covering a large proportion of the interior of the lamp so that it appears more like a flat top with a central aperture than a rim . . . . Type 16 B has no handle, following again the example set by Type 16 A. The nozzle is broad, coming to a narrow rounded termination, with a large oval wick-hole that may or may not intrude slightly onto the rim . . . . The Attic clay of these lamps is partially covered with a good black glaze that sometimes, owing to the conditions of firing, appears brown or red. The glaze is uniformly used throughout the interior, on the rim, and around the exterior of the nozzle in a neatly defined line. The remainder of the lamp, bottom and side walls, shows a diluted glaze wash, buff to orange to red in color. This was applied thickly or thinly to the entire exterior of the lamp before the black glaze was added on rim and nozzle . . . . An occasional lamp . . . may show an irregular circle on the rim where the glaze has fired orange or red; this blemish was caused by stacking in the kiln.[6]

In Chalkidike, there are no lamps of this type recorded at Torone, although one or two from Olynthos may be Type 16 Variants.

As for their context, **24/1** was found to the west of Building A on the East Hill, associated with material of the Archaic and early Classical period; **24/2** was found in the open area between Buildings A and B, associated with pottery primarily of the 6th century B.C., including Attic black-figure, but with at least one fragment of red-figure of the late Archaic or early Classical period; **24/3** was found outside of Building A, in the southeast quarter of the excavated area, beyond the retaining wall, in a mixed context including Archaic and late Classical pottery, near the preserved upper surface of the hill; **24/4** was found in a redeposited level overlying the destruction level of 354 B.C. and containing material from the Final Neolithic period through mid-4th century B.C.

24/1. (MEΘ 1140 [A132]) Fragmentary Lamp, Attic BG — Fig. 24.1

East Hill #274/079. 14/7/2006.

H. 0.026; Diam. (rim) 0.108.

Reconstructed from four joining frr preserving about two-thirds of lamp, but only small portion of nozzle. Slight discoloration around nozzle indicates use.

Flat base, slightly pushed up on underside; wall rising vertically; flanged rim, extending horizontally for short distance on exterior, with rim downward sloping on interior, terminating in sharply cut lip. Too little survives of nozzle to determine type.

Standard Athenian fabric. Clay body and reserved surfaces fired in the range of red 2.5YR 5/6–5/8.

Good quality black gloss, variously fired black and red, with a good luster. Exterior, including outer face of rim, reserved; underside nicely slipped/burnished. Rim top painted; center of floor painted, but wall on interior reserved. Surviving interior and exterior of nozzle painted.

Type as **24/2** (MEΘ 4430), but larger.

Cf., among others, *Agora* IV, pp. 31–33, pls. 4, 32, nos. 94–105; *Corinth* IV.2, p. 133, pl. 1, no. 52; Bovon 1966, p. 17, pls. A and 1, no. 12; Boardman 1967, pp. 233–234, fig. 154, no. 504 (dated late 6th–5th century B.C.).

24/2. (MEΘ 4430 [A134]) Fragmentary Lamp, Attic BG — Fig. 24.1

East Hill #274/036006 [4]. 25/5/2006.

H. 0.018; Diam. (rim) 0.092.

Single fr preserving about one-quarter of rim and rather more of base/floor. Non-joining fr of nozzle probably does not belong to this lamp.

Shape as **24/1** (MEΘ 1140), but smaller.

Standard Athenian fabric. Clay body and reserved surfaces fired closest to red 2.5YR 5/6.

Good quality black gloss, with good luster, uniformly fired black. Painted decoration as **24/1** (MEΘ 1140).

Type as **24/1** (MEΘ 1140) and cf. parallels cited there. Cf. also Bailey 1975, p. 32, pls. 6–7, no. Q 16.

24/3. (MEΘ 5349 [A242]) Rim, Body, and Nozzle Fr, Attic BG Lamp Fig. 24.1

East Hill #274/084008 [4]. 22/7/2003.

P.H. (close to original H.) 0.019; p.L. 0.068; Diam. (rim) est. 0.090.

Single fr preserving about one-quarter of rim and upper body, including small portion of nozzle. Clear traces of burning around nozzle indicate use.

Shape as **24/1** (MEΘ 1140), but with less broad flanged rim.

Standard Athenian fabric. Clay body and reserved surfaces fired closest to reddish yellow 5YR 6/6.

Good quality black gloss, mostly fired black, shading to very dark reddish brown at one point, with good sheen. Painted decoration, including nozzle, as **24/1** (MEΘ 1140), but with paint extending over outer edge of rim.

Cf., among others, *Agora* IV, p. 32, pl. 4, esp. nos. 94–95; *Isthmia* III, pp. 6–7, nos. 14–19; Bailey 1975, p. 33, pls. 6–7, no. Q 18.

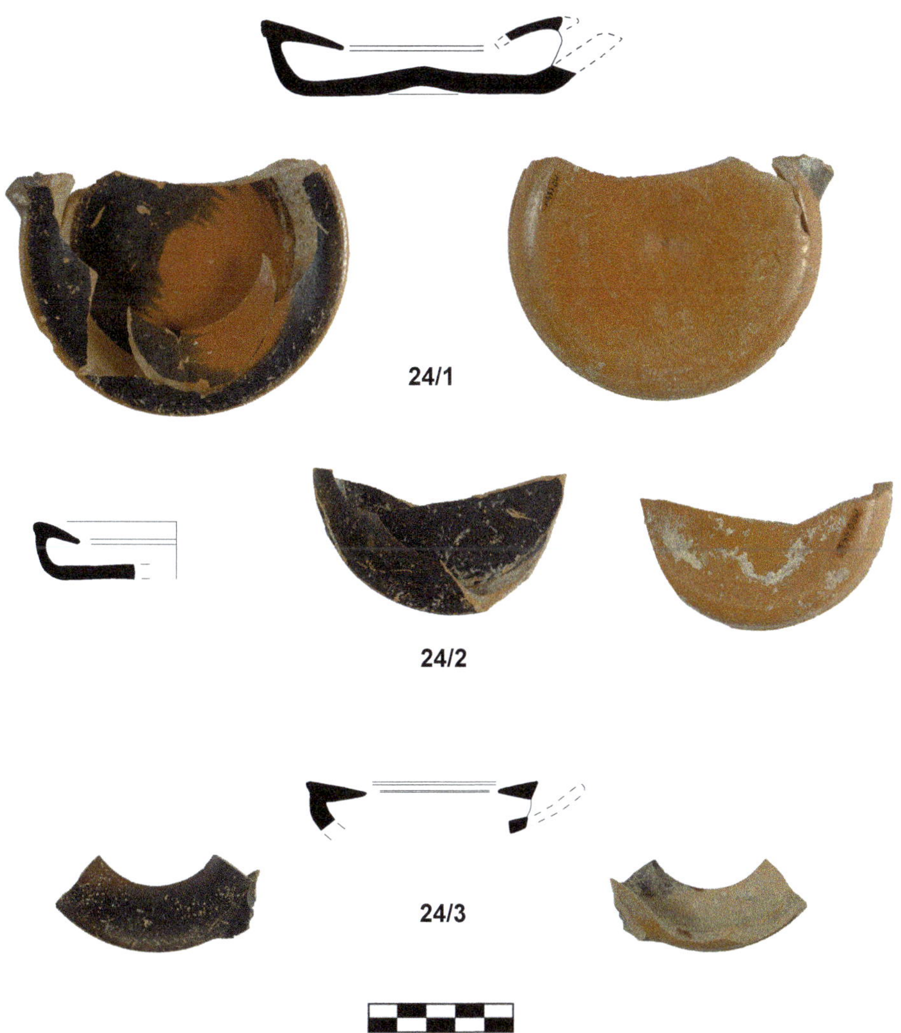

FIGURE 24.1. Attic black-gloss lamps, Type 16 B, from the area of the agora, **24/1** (MEΘ 1140), **24/2** (MEΘ 4430), and **24/3** (MEΘ 5349). Drawings F. Skyvalida, photos I. Coyle

Type 16 variants

The following fragmentary lamp is Attic and, on account of its profile, a variant of Type 16. Their chronological range is similar to that of Type 16 B: last quarter of the 6th century down to ca. 480 B.C., and although their rims are of Type 16 B, they have other features that set them apart.[7] These variances can be in the fact that they are glazed in a different manner from the normal Type 16 B lamps (e.g., **24/4**), or by the addition of a handle.

24/4. (ΜΕΘ 4431 [A42]) Lamp Fr, Attic BG Fig. 24.2

East Hill #274/067. Στρώμα διάβρωσης λιθόσωρος (layer of rubble collapse). 27/8/2004.

P.H. 0.022; p.L. 0.059; Diam. (rim) est. 0.090–0.100.

Single fr preserving about one-quarter of body and rim, but only outer edge of underside; nothing of the nozzle or handle preserved.

Base, body, and rim as **24/1** (ΜΕΘ 1140) and **24/2** (ΜΕΘ 4430), but with flanged rim flatter and less downturned, terminating in thicker beveled/cut rim.

Standard Athenian fabric, a little paler than **24/1** and **24/2** (ΜΕΘ 1140 and ΜΕΘ 4430), but well within the range of Attic. Clay body and reserved surfaces fired closest to reddish yellow 5YR 6/6.

Black gloss mostly dull, fired black, thinning to dark reddish brown where more dilute; lustrous only for thin band on flanged rim. Thin band around inner edge of flanged rim; inner edge of rim painted (rim underside reserved); remainder of preserved lower wall and floor reserved.

Shape as **24/1** (ΜΕΘ 1140) and **24/2** (ΜΕΘ 4430), but with different decoration.

Type 21 B

The following lamp (**24/5**) is a good example of Type 21 B in the Athenian Agora, which also corresponds to Corinth Type IV.[8] Dating between 480 and 415 B.C., Type 21 B is a long-lived variety that "has most of the usual characteristics associated with Type 21 A, with the addition of a well-defined flat raised base; this base is the distinguishing feature of Type 21 B; it is very rarely found in the long series of Type 21 lamps before 480 B.C."[9] All of the examples of Type 21 B in the Agora are made of Athenian clay and most are glazed inside and out, and at least two of the Athenian lamps have glazed undersides.[10] As Howland notes:

> Type 21 B is the commonest type of lamp during the second and third quarters of the 5th century. It was easy to make, convenient to use, and did not deviate from a standard form for two generations. It did not stop abruptly; the nozzles gradually became longer and wider. Examples with pronouncedly long and wide nozzles have been classified as Type 21 C, and belong to the last quarter of the 5th century B.C. and the early years of the 4th.[11]

The context of **24/5** is uninformative as to date.

24/5. (ΜΕΘ 5348 [A15]) Fragmentary Lamp, Attic BG Fig. 24.2

East Hill #274/066. Δοκιμαστική τομή. Στρώμα αμμώδις με μπάζωμα (trial trench; sandy layer with debris). 6/9/2004.

P.H./H. 0.024; Diam. (base) 0.061.

Two joining frr preserving half of base and rather less of rim and upper body.

Flat disk base, slightly pushed up on underside. Lower body curving sharply and turning in to rim, which is slightly downturned, terminating in sharp pointed lip. Traces of horizontal handle at one point.

Standard Athenian fabric. Clay body and reserved surfaces fired closest to reddish yellow 5YR 6/6.

Good quality black gloss, uniformly fired black, except for streak of red near rim top and on lower wall

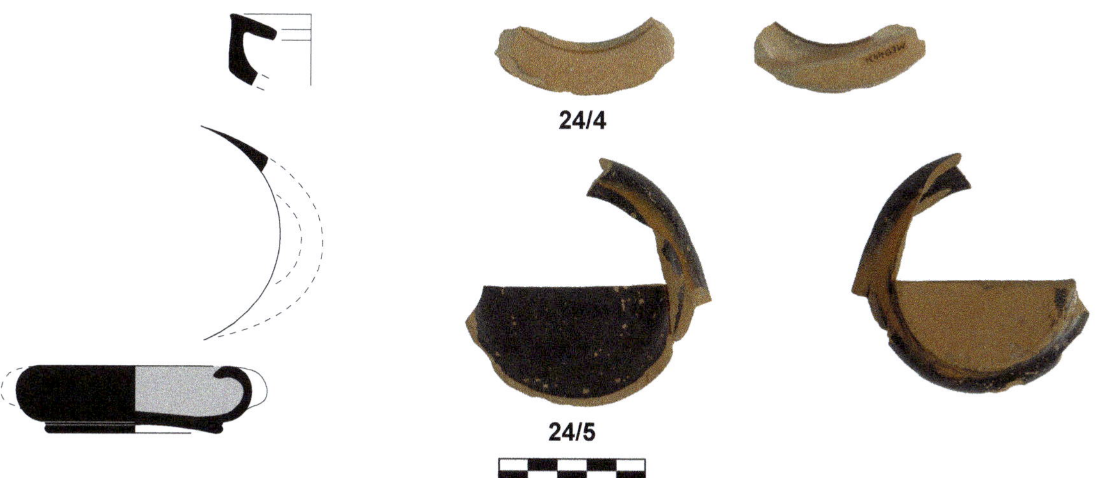

FIGURE 24.2. Attic black-gloss lamps from the area of the agora, **24/4** (ΜΕΘ 4431) (Attic Type 16 Variant) and **24/5** (ΜΕΘ 5348) (Attic Type 21 B). Drawings T. Ross and F. Skyvalida, photos I. Coyle

on exterior; good lustrous sheen. Painted solid inside and out, including surviving handle and edges and underside of rim. At least one small splash of paint on edge of underside.

Cf., among others, *Agora* IV, pp. 46–47, pls. 6, 34, esp. nos. 164–169; *Kerameikos* XI, pls. 14–15, esp. nos. 56–62; Drougou 1992, p. 33, fig. 1, pl. 4, nos. 13–14 (the former dating to the third quarter of the 5th century, the latter to the middle of the 4th century B.C.).

Type 25 A

The best preserved of the later lamps, **24/6**, is a good example of the Attic Type 25 A (Kerameikos *Rundschulterlampen*, RSL 4), which at Corinth is classified as Type VII, and as Type VII A at Isthmia.[12] Howland dates the type from the middle of the second quarter of the 4th century B.C. down into the first quarter of the 3rd century B.C., and he adds that the type is frequently found in the later deposits at Olynthos, so that it was established and exported well before 348 B.C.[13] The presence of the type at Methone now establishes that it was being exported well before 354 B.C. Additional examples of the type are also published from the Athenian Kerameikos (46 catalogued examples and 118 more inventoried), where some of the earliest examples may date as early as 400/380 B.C.[14] The type is common in the north Aegean: no fewer than 58 specimens were recorded from the excavations at Olynthos, the general type is well represented at Torone, with some 20 examples assigned to Type 25, and the later 4th-century B.C. examples of the type are fairly well represented at Pella.[15]

In dealing with the lamps of Types 25 A–D from the Athenian Agora collectively, Howland notes that this was the most common general type at the site.[16] The distinguishing features are a raised base—never a ring base—which is slightly concave; the sides are tall, with a pronounced curve, separated from the rim by a deep groove. Although the nozzle of **24/6** is not preserved, the nozzles are characteristically long, narrow, and flat on top.[17] Handle scars are preserved on **24/6**, but the handle itself does not survive. In dealing with the handles, Howland writes: "Lamps of Type 25 A may or may not have a thick horizontal strap handle. It is significant that more examples with handles are found in the earlier years of the type's floruit and more without handles in the later years."[18] Interestingly, all of the handles among the numerous Agora examples are broken, in precisely the same manner as the example from Methone, because "they are not really adequate to support the heavy bulk of the lamps caused by the enormous weight of the bases; it would seem that accidents occurred frequently, so that gradually the handles were omitted."[19] Lamps of this type are glazed inside and out, except for the underside.

This is a late type of lamp, perhaps contemporary with the destruction of Methone, but not from the actual destruction deposit.

FIGURE 24.3. Attic black-gloss lamp from the area of the agora, **24/6** (MEΘ 1981) (Attic Type 25 A). Drawing F. Skyvalida, photos I. Coyle

24/6. (MEΘ 1981) Fragmentary Lamp, Attic BG Fig. 24.3

East Hill #274/085017 [6]. 8/8/2003.

H. 0.036; Diam. (rim) 0.021 (inner), 0.038 (outer); Diam. (base) 0.042.

Single fr preserving most of lamp, except for nozzle and handle.

Disk base on raised foot; underside pushed up at center, resulting in prominent nipple on interior. Rounded body, curving in to rim, with sharply cut edge. Prominent groove around outer edge of flanged rim. Horizontal handle attested by both attachments on side opposite nozzle, itself not preserved.

Standard Athenian fabric. Clay body and reserved surfaces closest to light red 2.5YR 6/6.

Very good quality black gloss, fired uniformly black, with a good luster. Underside reserved; remainder of lamp painted solid inside and out, except for groove on rim.

Cf., among others, *Agora* IV, pp. 68–69, pls. 9, 38, nos. 269–272; Davidson and Burr Thompson 1943, pp. 48, 52–55, figs. 19, 22, various examples, esp. nos. 39, 51–52 (classified as Type VII [first group]); *Isthmia* III, p. 15, pls. 3, 16, no. 109 (= Caskey 1960, p. 173, pl. 56, no. 12, dated to around the middle of the 4th century B.C.; handle also missing); Bailey 1975, pp. 54–55, pls. 16–17, nos. Q 81–Q 83; Tidmarsh 2001, pp. 657–658, fig. 160, pl. 86, nos. 15/21–23; Drougou 1992, pp. 38–39, figs. 2–3, pls. 9–10, nos. 34–36, 42.

Other frr of Attic BG lamps not inventoried (all from East Hill #274/084008 4) Fig. 24.4

- Base fr, lamp of type as **24/1** (MEΘ 1140)
- Base fr, lamp of type as **24/1** (MEΘ 1140), but smaller than previous
- Two rim and upper body frr of same type as **24/1** (MEΘ 1140), but clearly from two different lamps
- Complete nozzle of another lamp type
- Small rim and body fr of yet another type of Athenian lamp

FIGURE 24.4. Additional fragments of Attic BG lamps from the area of the agora: a) top view; b) view of underside. Photos I. Coyle

NON-ATTIC BLACK GLOSS LAMPS (LOCAL?)

Type 19 A

Agora Type 19 A is classified by Howland in the following terms: "Lamps with sharp angle between body and rim; central tubes; imported fabric," and he dates the type to the "last quarter of the 6th century B.C. to ca. 480."[20] Five examples of the type are catalogued by Howland, and there are another 13 inventoried. At Corinth it is classified as Type III, but most of the specimens from Corinth and Isthmia lack the central tube.[21] It is noteworthy that the examples from Athens and Corinth are primarily imported, while the few examples from Isthmia can be either Attic (cf. Agora Type 19 B) or of local make, but of unusual fabric.[22] Howland describes the type in the following terms: Type 19 A

> consists of shallow saucer-like specimens, each of which has slightly convex bottom that curves up into low side walls; the rim is flat and slopes downward, overhanging the interior only. There is a wide central tube with a conical profile [not preserved on the example from Methone]; it seems probable that this central fixture is to facilitate holding the lamp while lighted . . . . The two nozzles, diametrically opposite, are unusual in that they tip upward . . . . The clay is thin and brittle, probably not Attic; it is light brown to buff in color, sometimes with small air bubbles and occasionally micaceous . . . . These lamps have appeared in other areas where they have been called variously South Russian, Rhodian, and Attic. The clay resembles that used for household pottery in the Lindos settlements . . . it is a thin brittle clay rather unlike the normal Attic product. The omission of glaze around the outside of the nozzle is not typical of Attic lamps of this period or any related period, and the tipped angle of the nozzle is at variance with Athenian traditions of lamp-making. One must look for a source elsewhere, but whether it is Rhodes or another eastern center cannot as yet be determined.[23]

Lamps of this general type are uncommon at Olynthos.[24] In discussing the examples from Olynthos, David Moore Robinson states that it "appears that the lamps of this Group are of local, Attic and some other foreign origin"; he goes on to cite the lamp from Lindos called "local" by Christian Blinkenberg, adding that Blinkenberg's ascription of an Ionian source should perhaps be carried over to those lamps from Olynthos that are neither Attic nor local.[25] What is clear is that the examples from Athens published by Howland of Type 19 A, together with **24/7** at Methone, are of a fabric that is not Attic or local Olynthian, and the possibility cannot be ruled out that it is

FIGURE 24.5. Non-Attic black-gloss lamp from the area of the agora, **24/7** (ΜΕΘ 5350) (Type 19 A). Drawing F. Skyvalida, photos I. Coyle

a local product of Methone, the Thermaic Gulf, or the north Aegean, especially in view of other early examples of lamps of other types in the same fabric from Methone (**24/8–24/9**). The context is topsoil and thus of no use chronologically.

24/7. (ΜΕΘ 5350 [A241]) Rim and Nozzle Fr, BG Lamp, Non-Attic — Fig. 24.5

East Hill #274/084002 [2]. 18/7/2003.

P.H. 0.011; Diam. (rim) est. 0.095.

Two joining frr preserving about one-third of rim and upper body and most of nozzle, but nothing of the base.

Shallow-walled lamp, with steeply rising upper wall, carinated from underside, most of which does not survive. Comparatively thin flanged rim, sloping downward, with plain rounded lip. Broad and shallow nozzle, showing signs of burning, indicating use.

Non-Athenian fabric, fine, dense, and thin-walled, with quite a dusting of fine silvery mica. Clay core and reserved surfaces fired close to reddish yellow 7.5YR 6/4.

Metallic gloss, with a slight sheen, fired a pale greenish/brownish color, approaching black. Preserved body reserved. Rim top painted solid, with paint extending slightly on to underside of rim for a short distance. Upper edges of nozzle also painted, though the remainder of the nozzle inside and out is reserved.

Cf. esp. *Agora* IV, pp. 39–40, pls. 5, 33, nos. 131–132; Blinkenberg 1931, cols. 615–616, pl. 122, no. 2557; see also, among others, Bailey 1975, pp. 33–34, pls. 3, 6–7, no. Q 20, which is compared to Howland Type 19, and stated to contain "much mica in very small particles."

Type 21 A

The following lamp (**24/8**) should be a non-Attic version of the type classified among the finds from the Athenian Agora as Type 21 A, which corresponds to Corinth Type IV.[26] Howland dates Type 21 A from the later years of the 6th century down to ca. 480 B.C., a chronology based partly on the fact that two examples served as ostraca (in 483 and in either 482 or 471 B.C.), as well as find contexts in the Agora.[27] The examples of the type catalogued by Howland (eight examples, plus five others inventoried) are all of Attic fabric, but in describing the type at Corinth, Oscar Broneer distinguishes three different clays used for lamps of this type: local Corinthian, Attic, and another, of the same color as Attic, but soft and mealy, with a glaze inferior to standard Attic, with a tendency to peel.[28]

As for the Athenian version, lamps with simple curved sides form a very large group, classified as Type 21 A–D, in vogue from the last years of the 6th down to the last years of the 5th century B.C.; Type 21 A has the typical curved rim and a plain base.[29] Type 21 A lamps have a single nozzle with an oval wick hole and they usually have a handle opposite the nozzle, horizontal and either flat or circular in section.[30] The versions of the type made in Athens are normally glazed inside and out, except for the base, which is always reserved and usually bears a thick coating of what Howland calls a dilute glaze wash; the glazed underside of **24/8** provides the only departure from the Athenian type (the reserved resting surface is on account of wear).[31] After the battles of Salamis and Plataia, the type changed into Type 21 B with the addition of a flat base (see **24/9** below).

The fabric of **24/8** is the same as that of **24/7** and **24/9**, and, as already noted, the entire group may be of local Methonaian or north Aegean manufacture. The context, although clearly associated with Classical pottery, is uninformative as to date.

24/8. (ΜΕΘ 1986 [A89]) Fragmentary BG Lamp, Non-Attic Fig. 24.6

East Hill #274/075. 10/11/2005.

H. 0.022; p.L. 0.072; Diam. (rim) 0.037; Diam. (base) 0.040.

Single fr preserving all of lamp except outer edge of nozzle and handle.

Possible, but very slight, traces of burning around edge of nozzle may indicate use, but as the nozzle end does not survive, this remains uncertain.

Plain flat disk base, very slightly pushed up on underside. Rounded body, with incurved rim; flat floor. Comparatively large nozzle, outer portion of which does not survive, on side opposite handle. Horizontal handle indicated by scars only.

Pale gray fabric, fine and dense, with few visible impurities, except for a dusting of fine silvery mica. Clay core and flaked surfaces fired closest to light gray 2.5Y 7/2 and 10YR 7/2.

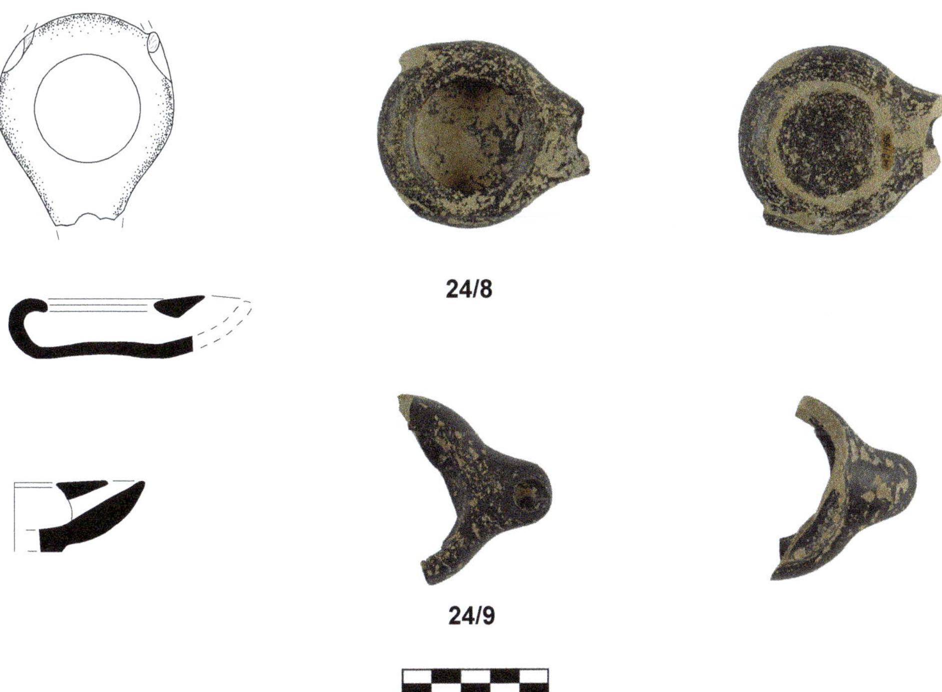

FIGURE 24.6. Non-Attic black-gloss lamps from the area of the agora, **24/8** (ΜΕΘ 1986) (cf. Attic Type 21 A) and **24/9** (ΜΕΘ 4433) (cf. Attic Type 21 B). Drawings F. Skyvalida, photos I. Coyle

Fairly good quality black gloss, much flaked/pocked, with a slight sheen, uniformly fired black. Entire preserved lamp inside and out painted solid, except for rough reserved ring on resting surface due to use. Gloss also on preserved interior of nozzle.

Cf., among others, *Agora* IV, pp. 44–46, pls. 6, 34, esp. nos. 157, 160; *Kerameikos* XI, p. 20, pl. 8, no. 22 (Scheibler conflates several different types under her *Knickschulterlampen* [KSL]); Bovon 1966, p. 18, pls. A, 1, no. 29, is especially close in profile; cf. also p. 19, no. 33 (not illustrated); *Isthmia*III, pp. 9–10, pls. 2, 15, nos. 36–37, 43. For the profile, cf. Bailey 1975, p. 35, pls. 8–9, no. Q 24.

Type 21 B

As was the case with **24/8**, so, too, with **24/9**, we are dealing with a non-Attic version of a lamp classified as Type 21 B in the Athenian Agora, which also corresponds to Corinth Type IV.[32] As noted above in the discussion associated with **24/5**, the type dates between 480 and 415 B.C., most of the Athenian examples are glazed inside and out, and at least two of the Athenian lamps have glazed undersides.[33] The context of **24/9** is the robbing of Wall 8 of Building A which contained numerous pieces of black- and red-figure and black-gloss pottery, the bulk dating to the 4th century B.C., and a date for the piece in the later 5th or earlier 4th century B.C. cannot be ruled out.

24/9. (ΜΕΘ 4433 [A124]) Lamp Fr, Non-Attic Fig. 24.6

East Hill #274/075. ΒΔ τμήμα-γκρίζο στρώμα (NW section, gray layer). 6/6/2006.

H. 0.027; p.L. 0.063; Diam. (rim) est. 0.040; Diam. (base) est. 0.050.

Single fr preserving entire nozzle about one-third of rim and upper body, but only small portion of base. Complete profile preserved.

Disk base on raised foot; rounded body curving in to rim, with sharply cut rim. Small but prominent nozzle. No clear traces of burning, but this may be obscured by the well-preserved glaze.

Fabric as **24/8** (ΜΕΘ 1986). Clay body fired closest to light gray 10YR 7/2; surfaces, where gloss has worn off, closer to very pale brown and pale brown 10YR 7/3–6/3.

Gloss as **24/8** (ΜΕΘ 1986), with similar flaking and pocking. Entire preserved lamp inside and out painted solid.

Agora IV, pp. 46–47, pls. 6, 34, nos. 164–170, esp. nos. 164–169; *Kerameikos* XI, pp. 20–21, pls. 8–9, various examples, esp. nos. 26–29; Blinkenberg 1931, cols. 615–616, pl. 122, nos. 2554, 2559; *Isthmia* III, pp. 9–10, pls. 2, 15, nos. 38, 42; Tidmarsh (2001, p. 655, fig. 159, nos. 15/3–15/4) classifies two examples from Torone as Type 21B, though they can equally be Type 21 A; cf. p. 656, fig. 159, nos. 15/9–15.10. For the articulated base and comparatively short nozzle, cf., among others, Bailey 1975, pp. 42–44, pls. 10–11, nos. Q 45–Q51 (compared to Howland Type 21 B); cf. also pp. 38–39, pls. 8–9, no. Q 36 (compared to Howland Type 22 C [with central tube]).

Corinthian Lamps

Corinthian Type II (= Type 16 A in the Athenian Agora)

The two Corinthian examples presented below are among the earliest lamps found to date at Methone. Both **24/10** and **24/11** can be assigned to Corinth Type II, with Corinthian imports found in Athens assigned to Type 16 A in the Athenian Agora classification.[34] In his introduction to Corinthian Type II lamps, Broneer wrote:

> In the course of the 6th century B.C., lampmaking in Greece progressed from a stage of experimentation, as shown in Type I, to assured craftsmanship, and by the end of the century several types evolved that held their shape for more than a century. The leading centers in this process were

> Corinth and Athens. In the beginning, Corinth held the lead and some early types apparently originated there, but the Corinthian clay was inferior in quality and the glaze tended to peel off. By the middle of the century the products of Athenian lampmakers had reached a stage of perfection that left their Corinthian competitors far behind. The Athenian lamps soon came to be preferred to the local products, which became progressively more imitative.[35]

This is precisely the pattern that we see at Methone.

Indeed, at least four Corinthian imports of this type of lamp are recorded from the Athenian Agora, where they are dated "as early as the early 6th century B.C. and well into the third quarter of the century," a dating that is based in part to the context of one of the examples from the Agora, in part on Corinthian comparanda, and in part on the fact that this type develops in Athens as Type 16 B in the third quarter of the 6th century B.C. (see **24/1–24/2**, above; **24/15** below).[36] Howland believed that these Corinthian lamps were exported in some quantity, in a period during which Corinthian wares still had a wide market. Type 16 A served as the Corinthian prototype and the models for the locally manufactured Athenian Type 16 B (see above). Later in the 6th century B.C., the Athenian version based on the Corinthian original was to be copied in Corinth, after trade conditions had been reversed and Athens had become the prime exporter.[37]

The defining characteristic of the type is the flat or slightly convex rim that overhangs the exterior, projecting slightly beyond the line of the wall, with the broad rim inclining inward and projecting over a great deal of the interior. As the type developed, the rim became wider so as to decrease the size of the central opening.[38] As Howland elaborates, there is no handle and the nozzle appears to be made separately, with a large hole that encroaches slightly on the wide rim (**24/11** preserves the articulation toward the nozzle), and Howland goes on to add:

> Glaze is conspicuously absent from the interior, but is used decoratively in dark brown concentric bands around the rim [a feature seen on both examples from Methone]. The end of the nozzle was dipped in glaze, so that color appears on its exterior and interior; this was done for a practical reason, to avoid absorption and discoloration from the burning wick that would otherwise create an untidy appearance on the pale porous clay.[39]

What is of particular interest is that, among the 15 lamps of this type found at Isthmia and catalogued, only two are Corinthian-made; the remainder are Athenian imports of Type 16 B.[40] The presence of at least two examples of this type at Methone not only confirms that the type was widely exported before the Attic versions of the type became well established (see discussion under **24/1–24/2**, **24/15**), but that they also made their way to the north Aegean, perhaps together with the fairly plentiful Corinthian pottery thus far found at the site (Chapter 19b). There is at least one Corinthian import of this type from Olynthos.[41] The context of **24/10** is uninformative as to date, that of **24/11** is Classical, but predating the destruction of Methone.

24/10. (ΜΕΘ 4434 [A233]) Fragmentary Lamp, Corinthian — Fig. 24.7

East Hill #274/085016 [5]. 6/8/2003.

H. 0.020; Diam. (rim) est. ca. 0.072–0.074.

Three joining frr preserving about one-quarter of rim and rather more of lower body and base.

Rounded body, with center of underside pushed up, creating a prominent omphalos rather than nipple on interior. Upper body marked off from lower body by carination. Prominent horizontal flanged rim, extending horizontally for a short distance on exterior and terminating in thin rounded lip on interior. Nothing preserved of nozzle or handle.

FIGURE 24.7. Corinthian Type II lamp from the area of the agora (= Type 16 A in the Athenian Agora), **24/10** (MEΘ 4434). Drawing F. Skyvalida, photos I. Coyle

Standard pale greenish gray Corinthian fabric, with clay body and reserved surfaces uniformly fired closest to pale yellow 2.5YR 7/3.

Pale gloss/paint, mostly flaked, originally fired black. Entire exterior and underside reserved. Flanged rim top decorated with rings: three encircling rim interior, then a thicker ring, and then either three thin rings or, more likely, another thicker ring; ring on outer edge of flanged rim, as well as another on inner edge. Thick ring encircling omphalos.

Cf. esp. *Corinth* IV.2, p. 134, pl. 1, no. 53 (for the decoration on the rim); p. 32, fig. 14, no. 12 (for the profile of the rim); Graham 1933, p. 268, pl. 197, no. 15; *Agora* IV, p. 31, pls. 4, 32, no. 92; *Isthmia* III, p. 7, pls. 1, 13, no. 13; cf. also Dunbabin 1962, p. 390, pl. 162, no. 4217.

24/11. (MEΘ 4432 [A137]) Fragmentary Lamp, Corinthian Fig. 24.8

East Hill #274/075. ΝΔ τμήμα-καστανό στρώμα (NW section—brown layer). 1/6/2006.

P.H. 0.025; p.L. 0.069; Diam. (rim) est. 0.090–0.100.

Three joining frr preserving portion of rim, body, base, and a tiny part of the nozzle; rather worn. Complete profile preserved.

Shape as **24/10** (MEΘ 4434), but with less sharp carination at juncture of upper and lower body. Articulation toward nozzle as shown.

Light-colored Corinthian fabric, but redder than **24/10** (MEΘ 4434), fired closer to very pale brown 10YR 7/4, shading to pink 7.5YR 7/4.

Glaze/paint better preserved and much better adhering than **24/10** (MEΘ 4434), mostly fired black, with a silvery metallic sheen at points; red where more dilute. Rim top as **24/10** (MEΘ 4434), decorated with rings; one broad ring near middle, with at least two, and probably originally more, encircling inner rim, the edge of which is not preserved. At least three bands toward outer edge, with another right at the outer edge. Broad ring around center of floor, encircling omphalos; remainder of interior reserved.

Type as **24/10** (MEΘ 4434). Cf. *Corinth* IV.2, p. 133, pl. 1, no. 47 (for the decoration on the rim); p. 32, fig. 14, no. 13 (for the profile of the rim).

LAMPS MADE OF SEMI-FINE LOCAL FABRIC

The context of **24/12** is interesting, as it is associated with Building Δ, which contained material of the Archaic and early Classical period; thus, a 6th-century B.C. date for the piece is likely. **24/13** was found in the open area—Plateia A—between Buildings A and B in a context that is clearly Archaic, and **24/14** was found west of Building A, which contained much Archaic material, though the latest pottery was of Classical date.

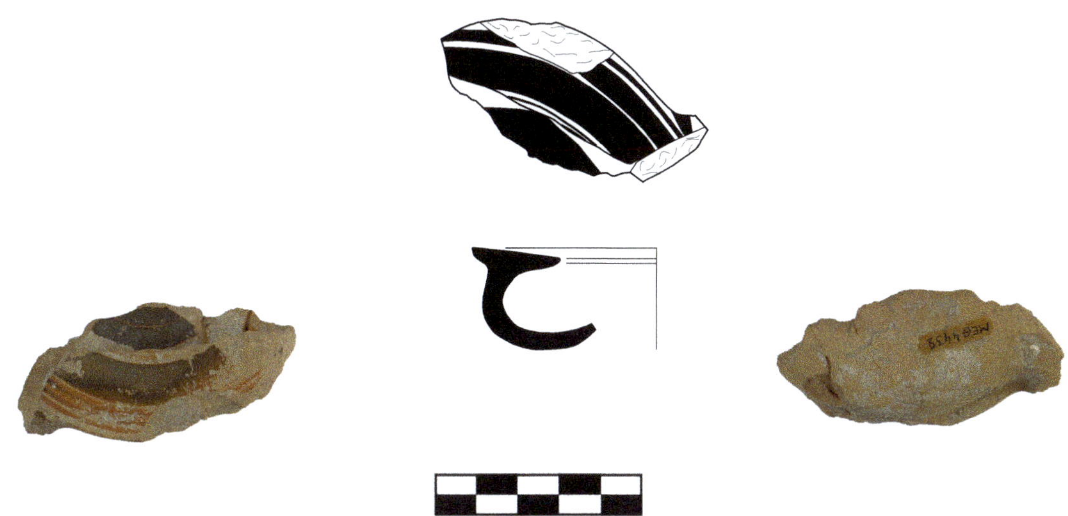

FIGURE 24.8. Corinthian Type II lamp from the area of the agora (= Type 16 A in the Athenian Agora), **24/11** (ΜΕΘ 4432). Drawing F. Skyvalida, photos I. Coyle

24/12. (ΜΕΘ 2179 [A186]) Semi-fine Undecorated Lamp Fig. 24.9

East Hill #274/090003 [2]. 29/10/2008.

H. 0.027; Diam. (base) 0.035; Diam. (rim) est. ca. 0.062.

Two joining frr preserving entire base and lower body, but only a small portion of the upper body and rim, and complete nozzle.

Heavy burning at and around nozzle indicates continual use.

Shape not unlike the Corinthian lamp **24/10** (ΜΕΘ 4434), but with considerably less broad rim. Flat disk base. Shallow lower wall, surmounted by vertical upper wall, the juncture of the two marked by a carination. Horizontal rim, extending on the side of the exterior; profile on interior very slightly incurved. Thin and rather elongated nozzle. Floor flat, except for small nipple at center. The body is wheelmade but crudely formed.

Semi-fine fabric, with small white inclusions and quite a bit of mica. Clay body and reserved exterior fired closest to light reddish brown and light brown 5YR 6/4 and 7.5YR 6/4.

Lamp undecorated.

Cf. Motsianos and Bintsi 2011, p. 67, no, 1.

24/13. (ΜΕΘ 3235 [A196]) Semi-fine Undecorated Lamp Fr Fig. 24.9

East Hill #274/067, 068. 2/10/2009.

H. 0.025; Diam. (rim) ca. 0.090.

Single fr preserving small portion of rim and body, including complete nozzle. Complete profile preserved except for center of underside.

Heavy burning at and around the nozzle indicates use.

Shape as **24/12** (ΜΕΘ 2179), but with broader horizontal rim, extending onto interior and exterior as shown. Nozzle rather broader and shorter than **24/12** (ΜΕΘ 2179). Although the center of the floor/underside is not preserved, it is possible that the center of the underside was pushed up, as on **24/10** (ΜΕΘ 4434), though this is not certain.

Fabric as **24/12** (ΜΕΘ 2179), perhaps a little more micaceous, but fired a darker reddish color, closest to reddish brown 2.5YR 5/4 and reddish brown 5YR 5/4, where not blackened.

Undecorated.

FIGURE 24.9. Lamps made of semi-fine local fabric from the area of the agora, **24/12** (MEΘ 2179) and **24/13** (MEΘ 3235). Drawings F. Skyvalida, drawings I. Coyle

24/14. (MEΘ 2059 [A143]) Semi-fine, Painted Lamp Frr Fig. 24.10

East Hill #274/089. 3/10/2007.

H. 0.026; Diam. (rim, outer edge) est. 0.110; Diam. (base) est. 0.090?

Two non-joining frr: one preserving portion of base, body, and rim (but not the inner edge); the other preserving portion of base, upper body, small portion of rim and entire nozzle. Complete profile preserved.

Burning at and around nozzle indicates use.

Flat disk base, slightly articulated from body as shown; curved body, with horizontal flanged rim, sharply offset from body; lip not preserved. Lamp clearly wheelmade.

Fabric as **24/12** (MEΘ 2179), with similar mica content and occasional blowouts. Clay body mostly fired light gray; reserved surfaces mostly light brown 7.5YR 6/4.

Although of similar fabric to **24/12** (MEΘ 2179) and **24/13** (MEΘ 3235), this is the only one of the three lamps that is painted. Paint dull, mostly fired red, shading to dark brown approaching black on interior; black around outer nozzle where blackened; red for the remainder of the nozzle. Exterior reserved; rim top decorated with broad band encircling inner rim, and at least one and perhaps originally more thin rings near midpoint; outer portion of rim top clearly reserved. Broad ring (or even area painted solid) around center of floor on interior. Interior of nozzle and its outer edges painted.

FIGURE 24.10. Lamp made of semi-fine local fabric from the area of the agora, **24/14** (ΜΕΘ 2059). Drawing F. Skyvalida, photos I. Coyle

LAMPS FROM THE AREA SOUTH OF THE EAST HILL

24/15 was found below the floor level of Building Γ in a context that predates the 354 B.C. destruction of Methone (see Chapter 1).

ATTIC LAMP

24/15. (ΜΕΘ 4998) Fragmentary BG Lamp, Attic Type 16 B Fig. 24.11

Area south of East Hill #278/002, 003. Επίχωση βόρεια του τοίχου 2 (fill north of Wall 2). 13/7/2006.

H. 0.018; Diam. (rim) 0.092.

Single fr preserving all of lamp except for nozzle.

Slight discoloration (black) at break on and near rim suggests proximity to nozzle.

Shape as **24/1** (ΜΕΘ 1140), but without the extension of the rim on the exterior. Rim downward sloping on interior, but less broad than **24/1** (ΜΕΘ 1140), terminating in a more rounded rather than sharply cut lip. It is clear that this lamp type does not have a handle.

Standard Athenian fabric. Clay core and reserved surfaces fired closest to light red 2.5YR 6/6 and reddish yellow 5YR 6/6.

Good quality black gloss, variously fired from red to black, with shades of reddish brown. Underside as **24/1** (ΜΕΘ 1140). Rim top painted solid; rim exterior reserved. Floor on interior painted solid; underside of rim and upper wall on interior reserved.

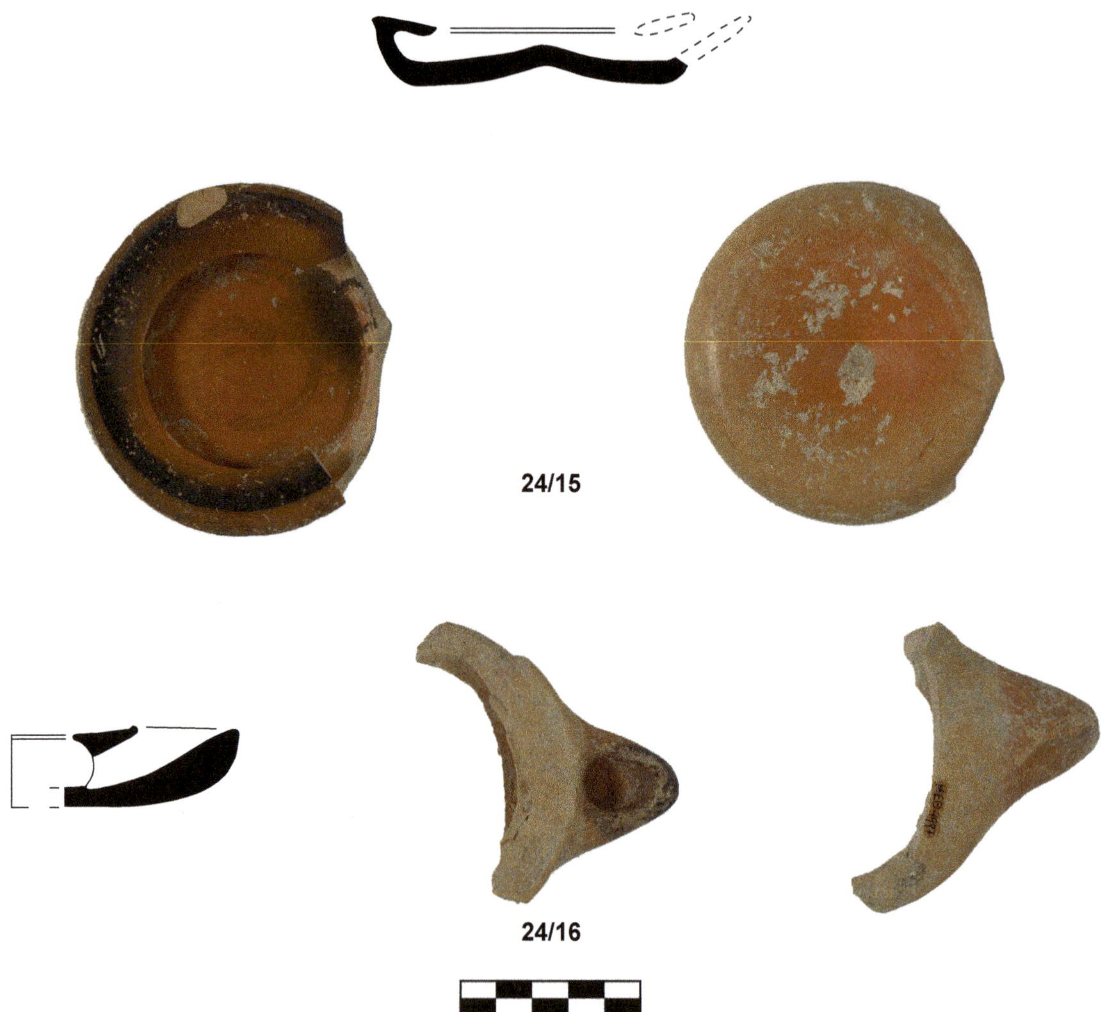

FIGURE 24.11. Lamps from the area south of the East Hill, **24/15** (MEΘ 4998) (Attic Type 16 B) and **24/16** (MEΘ 4997) (lamp made of semi-fine local fabric). Drawings F. Skyvalida, photos I. Coyle

LAMP MADE OF SEMI-FINE LOCAL FABRIC

The context of **24/16** was uninformative as to date.

24/16. (MEΘ 4997) Semi-fine Painted Lamp Rim, Body, and Nozzle Fr Fig. 24.11

Area south of East Hill #278/002. 19/6/2008.

H. 0.024; Diam. (rim) est. ca. 0.090.

Single fr preserving portion of rim and body, plus complete nozzle, but nothing of the center of the floor.

Blackening on nozzle top and inside indicates continuous use.

Type as MEΘ 2697 (unpublished, from the West Hill), but larger. Center of floor not preserved.

Fabric as **24/12** (MEΘ 2179) and MEΘ 2697. Clay core and reserved surfaces fired closest to light brown 7.5YR 6/4.

Gloss very dull, worn in parts, mostly fired red except at nozzle where blackened by use. Traces of ring along the top inner edge of the rim. Tip, exterior, and inside of nozzle painted. Traces of paint, very poorly preserved, on interior suggest that the interior of the floor was painted as MEΘ 2697.

NOTES

1 The lamps from the West Hill will be published by Konstantinos Noulas in a future study; they include a solitary non-Attic black-gloss lamp, ΜΕΘ 2697, the context of which is Archaic, found together with material dating to the end of the 7th century B.C., but also with material of the 6th century B.C.

2 *Agora* IV, p. 31.

3 Vanderpool 1946, pp. 332–333, pl. 68, nos. 330–337; *Agora* IV, p. 32, discussion under no. 96.

4 *Kerameikos* XI, pp. 16–17, pls. 6–7, nos. 10–16, where five examples of Type 16 B are catalogued (nos. 10–14), together with two examples of Type 17 A (nos. 15–16), in addition to which there are five other inventoried examples of the type from the Kerameikos excavations.

5 *Agora* IV, p. 31.

6 *Agora* IV pp. 31–32; Broneer (*Isthmia* III, p. 6), although agreeing with Howland's kiln-stacking hypothesis, believed that this may have been done on purpose to obtain differences in color.

7 *Agora* IV, pp. 33–35, pls. 4, 32, nos. 106–119.

8 *Agora* IV, pp. 46–47, pls. 6, 34, nos. 164–170; *Corinth* IV.2, pp. 39–42.

9 *Agora* IV, p. 46; seven examples of the type are catalogued by Howland, with another 41 inventoried but not catalogued.

10 *Agora* IV, pp. 46–47, nos. 167, 170.

11 *Agora* IV, p. 47.

12 *Agora* IV, pp. 67–69; *Kerameikos* XI, pp. 26–30; *Corinth* IV.2, pp. 45–46; *Isthmia* III, p. 15.

13 *Agora* IV, p. 67; he specifically cites Graham 1933, pp. 279–282, Group 8; additional lamps of this type from Olynthos were published in Robinson 1930, pp. 129–145 (various examples under Series 6 and 7); *Olynthus* XIV, pp. 385–391, where he distinguished an early (end of the 5th century B.C.) and a late form (first half of the 4th century B.C.).

14 *Kerameikos* XI, pp. 26–30, pls. 16–23, nos. 80–125 (RSL 4).

15 *Olynthus* XIV, p. 387; Tidmarsh 2001, pp. 650–651, 657–660, nos. 15/21–15/40 (Torone); Drougou 1992, pp. 38–39, figs. 2–3, pls. 9–10, nos. 34–36, 42, among others (Pella), with additional examples of Type 25 B.

16 *Agora* IV, p. 67; in addition to the 18 examples of the type catalogued by Howland from the Agora, there are an additional 67 others from the site inventoried.

17 *Agora* IV, p. 68.

18 *Agora* IV, p. 68.

19 *Agora* IV, p. 68.

20 *Agora* IV, p. 39.

21 *Corinth* IV.2, p. 32, fig. 14, profiles 14–16; pp. 38–39, 134, pl. 1, nos. 54–58; *Isthmia* III, pp. 8–9, pls. 1, 15, nos. 28–35. In his discussion of the type at Corinth, Broneer (*Corinth* IV.2, p. 38) notes that the lamps are made of three different fabrics: "The clay is of three kinds one of which is micaceous . . . . The lamps made of this clay have a dull brown or black glaze . . . . The second kind of clay, of which there are only three small fragments, is bluish gray, and the lamps of this kind have a lustrous black glaze. It is unsafe to draw conclusions from a few small fragments, but the glaze is so much like that of the Attic pottery, that even if the clay is of a different color it seems most likely that the lamps are of Attic workmanship . . . . The third kind is the local clay of Corinth, of which there is only one certain fragment of this type (no. 58)."

22 *Isthmia* III, p. 8.

23 *Agora* IV pp. 39–40, pls. 5, 33, nos. 131–135. The south Russian provenance was suggested by Waldhauer 1914, p. 21, pl. II, no. 24 (on the basis that it is not Attic and therefore probably local); the Rhodian provenance was suggested by Blinkenberg 1931, cols. 615–616, pl. 122, no. 2557; the Attic provenance was suggested by Furtwängler 1906, pp. 467–469, no. 10; pl. 9 (top right among the lamps).

24 Robinson 1930, pp. 129–132, 137, fig. 297, nos. 1, 4, 6–7 (several more of this type are listed by Robinson, but these are not the same as Type 19 A); Graham 1933, pp. 267–268, pl. 197, nos. 10, 12; *Olynthus* XIV, pp. 340–343, pl. 144, nos. 2–4.

25 *Olynthus* XIV, pp. 340–341. He adds (p. 341): "If, however, the similarities to those lamps from Lindos are as real as apparent, they may well have reached Olynthos with refugees from Persian aggression, or in trade, since there are many well attested contacts between the Thraceward region and Asia Minor."

26 For the Athenian version, see *Agora* IV, pp. 44–46, pls. 6, 34, nos. 156–163; for the type at Corinth, see *Corinth* IV.2, pp. 39–42; *Isthmia* III, pp. 9–12, where different types seem to be conflated.

27 *Agora* IV, p. 44.

28 *Corinth* IV.2, p. 41.

29 *Agora* IV, p. 45.

30 *Agora* IV, p. 45.

31 *Agora* IV p. 45.

32 *Agora* IV, pp. 46–47, pls. 6, 34, nos. 164–170; *Corinth* IV.2, pp. 39–42.

33 *Agora* IV, pp. 46–47, nos. 167, 170.

34 *Corinth* IV.2, pp. 32, 35–38, fig. 14 (profiles 11–13), pl. 1, nos. 44–53; *Isthmia* III, pp. 6–8, pls. 1, 14, nos. 13–27; *Agora* IV pp. 30–31, pls. 4, 32, nos. 92–93.

35 *Isthmia* III, p. 6.

36 *Agora* IV, p. 30, with reference to Campbell 1938, pp. 609–610, figs. 30–31, no. 235, the context of which at Corinth was 550–500 B.C.; two of the four examples from the Athenian Agora are inventoried and catalogued, and there are another two inventoried.

37 *Agora* IV, p. 31.

38 *Isthmia* III, p. 6.

39 *Agora* IV, p. 31.

40 *Isthmia* III, p. 6.

41 Graham 1933, p. 268, pl. 197, no. 15.

25

EARLY GLASS IN METHONE

Despina Ignatiadou

(With a contribution by Elissavet Dotsika, Petros Karalis, and Antonio Longinelli)

Excavations at Methone have revealed the presence of glass finds all over the site. The material derives from three primary contexts, in all three sectors: the agora, the Hypogeion, and the acropolis. Eye beads and plain glass beads were used in the city from the time of the colonial period in the 8th century B.C.[1] Later, in the 6th century B.C., poppy glass beads were manufactured from glass rods, also found in the agora. At the same time the first core-formed glass vessels made their appearance and their use continued until the destruction of the city.[2] The possibility that some of these were also locally made cannot be excluded, especially since evidence for the operation of workshops is ubiquitous in Methone. The presence of glass in Methone is in accordance with the strong presence of glass in Macedonia in general.[3]

TABLE 25.1. Glass finds in Methone according to area and type

		Vessels				**Beads**			**Rods**	**Gem**	**Unidentified**	**Workshop remains**	**Total**
	Core-formed vessels	Blown vessels	Modern vessel	Decorated poppy bead	Poppy beads	Decorated bead	Plain beads	Eye beads			Remains		
Agora	34	2	1	1	43	1	10	5	3+	1	4	—	105
Hypogeion	2	—	1	—	—	—	3	6	—	—	—	1	13
Acropolis	2	—	—	—	1	—	6	—	—	—	—	—	9

SOME GLASSWORKING TERMS[4]

Core-forming — The construction of a vessel around a core built at the end of a metal rod.

Mandril — Small metal rod around which beads and pendants are wound.

Marvering — The rolling of glass objects on a flat marble surface (*marver*), in order to smooth their surface or incorporate attached elements.

Mold-blown — Glass blown, by means of a blowpipe, into a mold of special shape.

Natural green color — The green/greenish color imparted to glass by the presence of iron oxide in its composition.

Dark color	A seemingly black color; in reality either very dark blue, green, or purple.
Opaque	Glass that is intentionally rendered impenetrable by light, by the addition of an opacifier.
Raw glass	Glass fused from raw materials but not yet made into an object.
Thread, trail	Filament of glass used in the decoration of glass objects.
Translucent	Glass that permits the passage of light.
Transparent	Glass that permits visibility.

THE HYPOGEION

Early glass finds, dating mainly from the Geometric period, were excavated in the Hypogeion (Chapter 8). They consist of six eye beads and three plain beads (**25/3–25/11**). Additionally, two fragments of core-formed vessels of the Classical period were also found (**25/1–25/2**) from the uppermost levels of the Hypogeion.

Core-formed Vessels (25/1–25/2)

Only two core-formed fragments were retrieved from the area of the Hypogeion excavation, from surface levels. They are both dated to the Classical period, but it is not possible to say whether they are 5th or 4th century B.C; that is, whether they are classified as Mediterranean Group I or II.[5]

Shape

Only one shape is represented: the alabastron, the most popular and widespread among the core-formed shapes.

Colors: body and added glass

25/1 (MEΘ 182) is a natural-green colored alabastron, decorated with white thread. This choice of body color is quite unusual. The other fragment, **25/2** (MEΘ 186), is the typical blue body decorated with yellow thread.

Decoration

25/1 (MEΘ 182) is decorated with a long zigzag (a design of the 5th century B.C.) or feather pattern (a design of the 4th century B.C.). **25/2** (MEΘ 186) is decorated with a festoon, a design shared by the 5th and 4th centuries B.C.

Context and dating

They were both found in the upper stratigraphy of the deposit (the Archaic fill C: 650–550 B.C.), but are probably later and intrusive, from the 4th century B.C.

Eye Beads (25/3–25/8)

Six eye beads have been found in the Hypogeion. They are all dated to the 9th–8th centuries B.C.

Type and decoration

The beads are all of the same type: triangular with three spiral eyes, **25/3**, **25/4**, **25/5**, **25/6**, **25/7**, **25/8** (MEΘ 179, MEΘ 341, MEΘ 1296, MEΘ 1297, MEΘ 1298, MEΘ 2836). The revolutions of the spirals vary between two and five.[6] Triangular beads with three spiral eyes are rare, unlike contemporary and similar triangular beads with stratified eyes. Isolated examples have been found in major excavations, for example, at Eretria (the sanctuary of Apollo Daphnephoros),[7] Lindos on Rhodes (the Acropolis),[8] and Emporio on Chios.[9] A considerable number was dedicated at the sanctuary of Athena Itonia in Philia.[10] In Macedonia, one example is known from an Archaic burial in Akanthos,[11] while 13 more are unfortunately unprovenanced.[12]

Colors

All the eye beads are made of dark glass with opaque white glass trails forming the spiral eyes. There is only one exception, a bead with two yellow and one white eye (**25/5** [ΜΕΘ 1296]); the eyes, too, differ in the number of revolutions. This particular bead displays an excellent state of preservation; the body glass is not at all corroded and has a shiny smooth surface that resembles a metallic surface, very similar to that of uncorroded iron. It is possible that the bead was originally intended to emulate an iron bead with inlaid eyes of gold and silver.

Context and dating

Five were found in the lower stratigraphy of the Hypogeion (fill A: 730–690 B.C.). The Hypogeion was dug around 700 B.C., but the materials used to fill it are earlier, mainly from the early phase of colonization, that is, 733–700/690 B.C., but with earlier isolated residual fragments, dating from the Late Neolithic into the Early Iron Age. The glass finds from fill A include: **25/4** (ΜΕΘ 341]), **25/5** (ΜΕΘ 1296), **25/6** (ΜΕΘ 1297), **25/7** (ΜΕΘ 1298), and **25/8** (ΜΕΘ 2836); only one fragment was from the upper fill C (650–550 B.C.): bead **25/3** (ΜΕΘ 179). All of these were, therefore, discarded already in the late 8th–early 7th century B.C., with the exception of one that was used or kept for 50–150 years or more.

Plain Beads (**25/9–25/11**)

Three plain beads were found in the Hypogeion. They are dated to the Geometric or Archaic period.

Type and decoration

Two beads are round, **25/9** (ΜΕΘ 340), **25/10** (ΜΕΘ 342) and one is ring-shaped **25/11** (ΜΕΘ 2835).

Colors

Two beads are transparent; one natural green, **25/9** (ΜΕΘ 340) and one turquoise, **25/10** (ΜΕΘ 342). One bead is blue, **25/11** (ΜΕΘ 2835).

Context and dating

25/9 and **25/11** (ΜΕΘ 340 and ΜΕΘ 2835) were found respectively in the lower or lower/middle stratigraphy (fill A: 720–690 B.C., or fill A or B: 720–690 or 690–650 B.C.); they were, therefore, discarded in the late 8th or 8th/7th century B.C. and are either Geometric or early Archaic. **25/10** (ΜΕΘ 342) was found in the middle/upper stratigraphy (fill B or C: 690–650 or 650–550 B.C.); it was, therefore, discarded in the 7th or 6th century B.C. and is probably Archaic.

Modern Glass (**25/12**)

A very small fragment of colorless glass, **25/12** (ΜΕΘ 8393), was retrieved from the surface layer. Its curvature and thin wall point to a vessel, but it is too small to be diagnostic. The total absence of color is probably an indication that it originates from a modern vessel made of decolorized glass.

Round Glass Fragment (**25/13**)

A small broken mass of glass with a round edge, **25/13** (MEΘ 8394), was retrieved from the surface layer. The round part of the find has been hot-formed. It is of translucent greenish glass used since pre-Roman times, and also until today in artistic glassworking. It is probable that it is a remnant of a workshop activity that involved the use of such glass either for beads or for vessels. Alternatively, it could be the lower part of a drop of molten glass, the result of a fluidity test carried out daily by Roman glassworkers; this may also explain the multiple cracks in the glass that resulted from non-controlled cooling.

THE AGORA

The excavation of the agora yielded most of the glass finds from Methone: 34 fragments (or groups of fragments) of core-formed vessels, fragments of two blown vessels, one fragment of a modern drinking glass, some 60 beads (including one decorated poppy bead, 43 poppy beads, one decorated bead, ten plain beads, five eye beads), at least three rods, and one gem.

Core-formed Vessels (**25/14–25/47**)

The core-formed fragments are particularly small, and therefore a typology of shapes cannot be established. They all seem to belong to core-formed vessels that are widespread in the eastern Mediterranean from the 7th century B.C. to the 1st century A.D. The core-formed fragments retrieved from the agora area are all dated to the Classical period, particularly the 5th or early 4th century B.C. They are all shapes of the Mediterranean Group I.[13] According to the established typology, this group includes four shapes: the alabastron, the amphoriskos, the aryballos, and the oinochoe, all tentatively recognized among the finds in the agora.

Shapes

The alabastron fragments derive from the necks and rims of vessels (**25/30** [MEΘ 906], **25/41** [MEΘ 2128], **25/45** [MEΘ 5565] and, possibly, **25/47** [MEΘ 5568]). The most informative is **25/30** (MEΘ 906), which is part of a blue neck with yellow thread on the rim. The piece shows extensive and unsuccessful tooling that resulted in a perforation on the neck; the product thus became unsuitable for use. Additionally, the yellow thread meant to accent the rim lip was not applied in sufficient length to cover the whole perimeter. The object was found east of Building A, in an area where other pieces of glass were rejected, along with pottery of the 6th and 5th centuries B.C. This particular find is perhaps an indication that core-forming was practiced in the agora; even if it was completed, a piece like this could hardly be offered for sale and it is more probable that it was discarded somewhere near the workshop. As alabastra can be identified with fair certainty, some body fragments from a cylindrical shape are perhaps of this shape: two decorated with zigzags (**25/21** [MEΘ 801], **25/23** [MEΘ 803]), three with festoons (**25/20** [MEΘ 800], **25/22** [MEΘ 802], **25/25** [MEΘ 805]), and one with horizontal revolutions (**25/26** [MEΘ 806]). Most of the remaining fragments can possibly be associated with the other forms which have a more or less rounded body shape, such as the oinochoe, the aryballos, and the amphoriskos (**25/14** [MEΘ 183], **25/15** [MEΘ 184], **25/31** [MEΘ 1074], **25/33** [MEΘ 1076], **25/34** [MEΘ 1077], **25/46** [MEΘ 5566]), and an inward-sloping mouth (**25/32** [MEΘ 1075]). Vessel **25/36** (MEΘ 1910] is an oinochoe beyond doubt; the surviving fragment is the central part of a trefoil mouth. **25/16** (MEΘ 185) is intensely curved and could be identified as an aryballos, albeit with reservations.

Colors: body and added

There is only one example of opaque white body glass, decorated with dark purple zigzags (**25/15** [ΜΕΘ 184]). This vessel is of excellent quality and is also very well preserved. Additionally, there is a natural-green colored fragment that could be part of a core-formed vessel, but its shape and decoration are difficult to identify (**25/17** [ΜΕΘ 191]). All the other vessels are of blue glass, ranging from light blue (**25/35** [ΜΕΘ 1905B], **25/36** [ΜΕΘ 1910]) to bright blue (**25/26** [ΜΕΘ 806]), and dark blue (the majority). The blue vessels are decorated with white, yellow, and light blue threads; only once does a turquoise thread appear (**25/45** [ΜΕΘ 5565]). The preference for light blue over turquoise thread must be noted as reflecting a particular (local?) artisan, a (local?) workshop, this particular period, or even a combination of the above.

Decoration

The majority of the decorated fragments show horizontal revolutions of white or colored threads (**25/14** [ΜΕΘ 183], **25/19** [ΜΕΘ 799], **25/24** [ΜΕΘ 804], **25/26** [ΜΕΘ 806], **25/27** [ΜΕΘ 807A], **25/37** [ΜΕΘ 1911], **25/38** [ΜΕΘ 1912], **25/40** [ΜΕΘ 1914], **25/47** [ΜΕΘ 5568]), zigzag (**25/17** [ΜΕΘ 191], **25/21** [ΜΕΘ 801], **25/23** [ΜΕΘ 803], **25/46** [ΜΕΘ 5566]), a combination of the above (**25/15** [ΜΕΘ 184], **25/16** [ΜΕΘ 185], **25/28** [ΜΕΘ 807B], **25/29** [ΜΕΘ 854], **25/31** [ΜΕΘ 1074], **25/33** [ΜΕΘ 1076], **25/34** [ΜΕΘ 1077]), or festoons (**25/20** [ΜΕΘ 800], **25/22** [ΜΕΘ 802], **25/25** [ΜΕΘ 805]). The zigzag pattern is either short or elongated, and the festoon is sometimes closer to a zigzag.

Context and dating

Almost all the fragments were found outside the two main buildings: to the north, east, and west of Building A, and to the east of Building B (Fig. 1.21, Fig. 25.1, Fig. 29.1–3). The excavated parts of the buildings are of the 6th century B.C. to 354 B.C.; most of the finds are therefore dated within this period.

Blown-glass Vessels

Shapes, colors, and dates

The few fragments of blown glass vessels found in the agora were either unearthed in the dump of excavated soil, or were surface finds from the balks. They can be attributed to two vessels of the Roman period. The shape of a transparent natural green (**25/49** [ΜΕΘ 190B]) cannot be identified. The other is a mold-blown prismatic bottle, of a transparent aqua color and good quality. Three pieces from the shoulder are preserved (**25/48** [ΜΕΘ 190A], **25/50** [ΜΕΘ 336], and **25/51** [ΜΕΘ 337]).

Modern Glass

A rim and body fragment from a decolorized glass vessel were surface finds in the agora. They probably belong to the upper part of a modern[14] drinking glass of the beaker type.

Poppy Beads

Terminology and symbolism

The term "poppy bead" is used here as a shorter version of the correct term "poppy-seedpod bead."[15] This type of bead emulates the seedpod of the opium poppy flower. The importance of the plant in antiquity cannot be overemphasized. The tall plant of the somniferous poppy, with red or white flowers, has been perhaps the most important medicinal plant since early prehistory. It has been used for the extraction of opium, appearing as drops along incisions made on the seedpod. Opium is mainly a sedative (it facilitates sleep, and hence the scientific name of the plant *papaver somniferum*) but also a strong painkiller, and a poison. Ancient authors elaborate on opium: it was usually swallowed or its fumes were inhaled, but also preparations were used as enemas, ointments, or eye drops. The poppy is local to central Anatolia and has been associated with Kybele; the goddess appears holding a poppy flower or pod in her hand while the rosette on top of the poppy seedpod decorates her headdress. The rosette became a most popular decorative element, appearing on pottery from the 6th millennium, and also on metal vessels of the Achaemenid International Style.[16]

History and distribution

Poppy beads were manufactured of crystal or gold since the Greek Bronze Age. They were intended to be used as necklace beads of different sizes, as pendants,[17] and also as heads of elaborate metal pins. Some of the most valuable rock-crystal examples of the 16th century B.C. were found at Mycenae as the heads of silver pins.[18] In the Archaic period those crystal-and-metal pins were reproduced entirely in gold and the poppy heads were rendered in embossed gold sheet with filigree and granulated decoration; the heads were usually topped by the multi-petaled rosette that appears also in nature.[19] The first glass poppy beads were made in the 9th/8th century B.C. of amber or dark glass.[20] Those early poppy beads have more ribs than the later examples, at least six. They are sometimes also decorated with transverse glass trails of a second color, wound spirally around the body of the bead. The beads were usually dedicated in sanctuaries, but could also be grave goods. Although they are a rare, luxury find, several isolated examples are known from all over Greece. In Macedonia, an 8th-century B.C. example, dark with reddish trail, was found in the sanctuary of Ammon-Zeus and the cave-sanctuary of Dionysos at ancient Aphytis (Chalkidike).[21] A dark bead with spiral yellow trail was found in a 7th-century B.C. grave in Therme (Sedes).[22] In the 6th century B.C. the spiral trail was replaced by a single ring around the middle of the bead, and later it disappeared completely. This horizontal decoration probably evoked the horizontal incision made on the natural seedpod to facilitate the extraction of liquid opium.

The plain poppy beads have five or six ribs and are made of transparent light blue-green glass. They appear in Macedonian burials in the Classical period, usually in the 5th century B.C., but rarely also before and after that. This fact indicates that they were valuable symbolic objects with a long life outside the grave. They were, therefore, sometimes two centuries old when they were deposited in the grave. A 6th- or 5th-century B.C. example, blue with five ribs, was unearthed in a grave in Aivasil, near the Langadas lake,[23] and a natural-green colored bead in a 6th/5th-century B.C. grave in Therme.[24] A necklace of 33 aqua beads (each with six ribs) was found in a 5th-century B.C. grave in Souroti, near Thessaloniki,[25] and contemporary isolated finds were also found in late 5th/early 4th-century B.C. burials in Therme (Sedes).[26] A seven-rib aqua example was found in a 350–300 B.C. burial in nearby Pydna;[27] seven more similar beads from the same site remain unpublished. A five-rib example, appearing white, was also found in an early Hellenistic context in the acropolis of Aigai.[28] Beyond Macedonia, in neighboring Thessaly, several beads were dedicated during the Late Geometric–Early Archaic period in the sanctuary of Athena Itonia in Philia.[29]

Types

In the agora of Methone one poppy bead was found decorated with a single revolution (**25/53** [ΜΕΘ 813]). It is larger than the undecorated poppy beads and, since the surviving half preserves four ribs, we can assume that the complete bead had eight ribs. It was made of aqua glass with a transverse opaque yellow revolution. Several similar beads were found in the Mieza cemetery, in a burial of the second quarter of the 5th century B.C. Five are aqua and one is blue, all with yellow trail.[30] They have more ribs than the Methone example, at least ten. The Methone bead was found with pottery of the late 6th–early 5th century B.C., and therefore the manufacture of these beads can be securely placed before that.

One small poppy bead is atypical because of its size, shape, and formation (**25/77** [MEΘ 1069]). It is smaller than the others, slightly biconical, and decorated with many closely packed ribs. Additionally, it has a very narrow perforation hole, only 1–3 mm wide, indicating that the bead was formed on a very thin mandril.

All the other 42 poppy beads share common characteristics. The only near-complete bead originally had, in all probability, seven ribs. The incomplete examples seem to have had originally between five and eight ribs. It is not certain whether the number of ribs indicates an evolution in style or different date. The diameter of the perforation varies between 4 and 9 mm; this is quite natural because the beads were formed around the tapering tip of the mandril, which was obviously 9 mm wide at its maximum.

Color

Most of the beads are of transparent aqua glass, in shades between the natural green color of glass and a light blue/bluish or turquoise color. One is amber-colored (**25/92** [MEΘ 4067]). One early find of the 6th–early 5th century B.C. is a blue fragmentary bead with irregular ribs that could number more than ten.

Context and dating

Poppy beads were isolated finds inside and outside both Buildings A and B. In Building A, beads were found in Rooms Δ and E (stoa), in strata dated to as early as the 6th century B.C. Most beads were found outside the building, mainly along the outer east and north wall, and also to the west where the earlier Buildings Δ and E were preserved at a lower level. In Building B, beads were found in Room A and outside the building, to the east. Several beads were found in the trench dug lengthwise to the east of both buildings. Most of the poppy beads were manufactured in the 6th/early 5th century B.C., but their use, of course, continued until the destruction of Methone in 354 B.C.

Glass Rods

Fragments of at least three glass rods were found in the agora (the five pieces of **25/112** could belong to one or more rods). They appear to be of the same fabric and color as most of the poppy beads, that is, of transparent aqua glass (Fig. 25.1). They are cylindrical but with oblique corrosion lines on their surface, indicating that they were drawn by twisting. The pulling and simultaneous twisting of hot glass is an ancient technique still used today to create rods, which are then used in a second stage for the fabrication and decoration of objects (Fig. 25.2).[31]

Context

A group of rod fragments (**25/112** [MEΘ 824]) and a tapering rod fragment of smaller diameter and slightly different color (**25/113** [MEΘ 825]) were found in Room Δ of Building A, in a trench dug deeper along the south interior wall. One more rod fragment (**25/114** [MEΘ 1909]) was found outside the building.

Dating

Black-figure pottery found together with the rods dates the stratum and shows that the rods were discarded in the 6th century B.C.

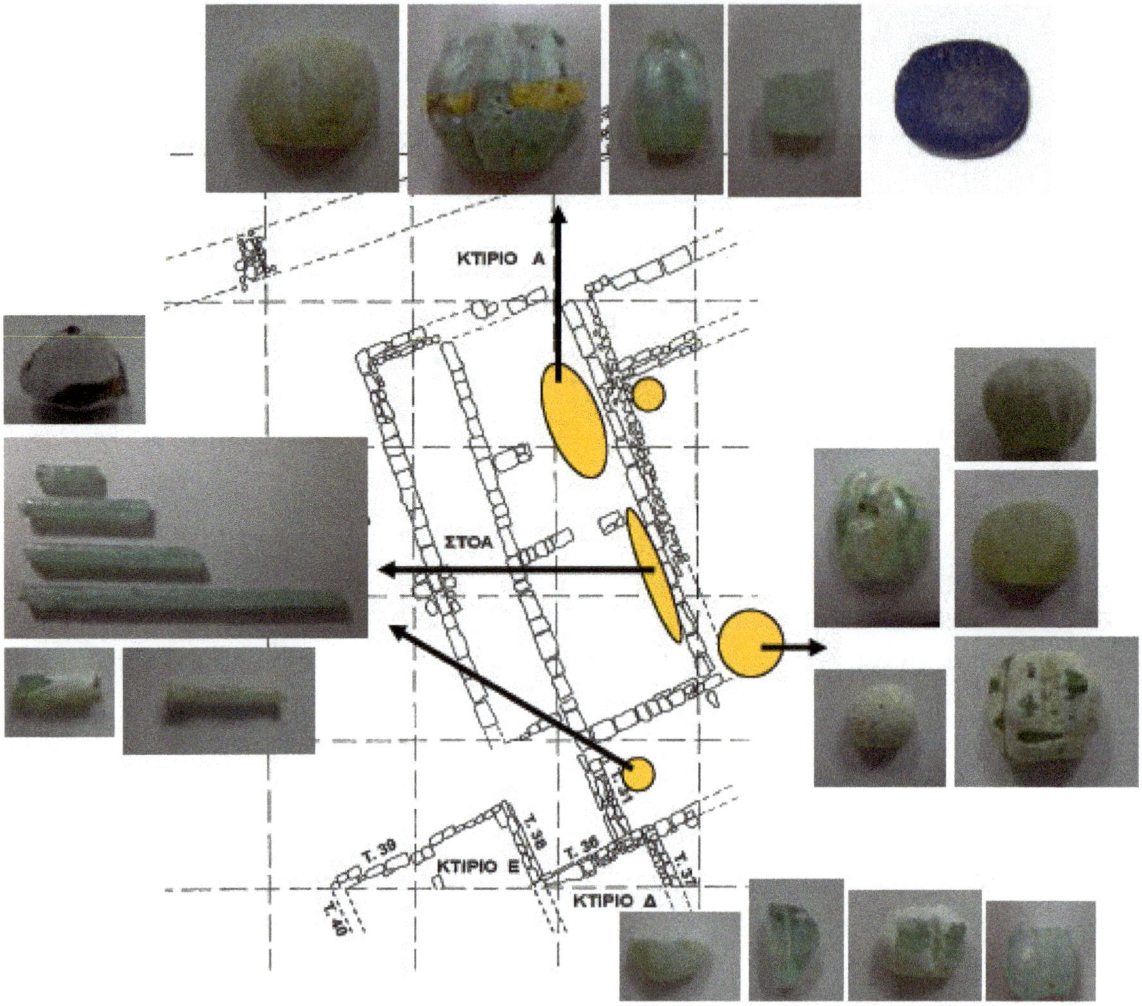

FIGURE 25.1. The agora area of Methone showing the findspots of aqua glass poppy beads and aqua glass rods. Prepared by D. Ignatiadou and A. Athanassiadou

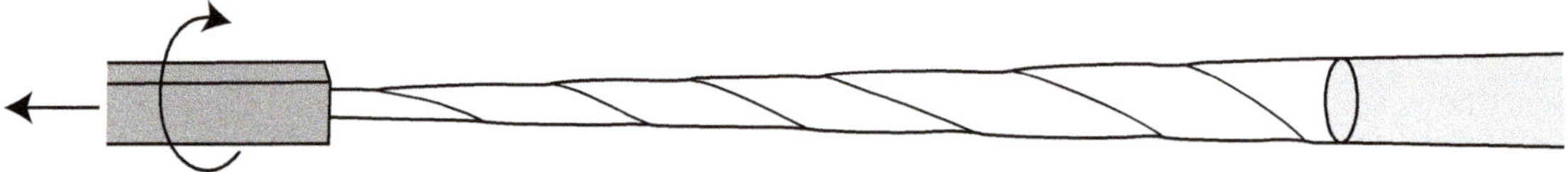

FIGURE 25.2. Pulling a mass of glass to make a twisted rod (after Spaer 2001, fig. 16). Drawing T. Ross

BEAD-MAKING AT METHONE

While most of the other types of beads from Methone survive intact, all of the aqua poppy beads from the agora were found broken.[32] The majority were either broken in antiquity, or present some kind of flaw; in both cases they were probably discarded as rejects. Some have disfiguring protrusions (**25/54** [ΜΕΘ 170], **25/55** [ΜΕΘ 171], **25/61** [ΜΕΘ 332], **25/63** [ΜΕΘ 334], **25/68** [ΜΕΘ 816], and **25/72** [ΜΕΘ 821]). One has a big pit which perhaps started as a bubble (**25/61** [ΜΕΘ 332]) and two more a transverse pit/dent, perhaps the result of awkward handling (**25/64** [ΜΕΘ 339], **25/65** [ΜΕΘ 808]). Others have irregular or flawed ribbing (**25/64** [ΜΕΘ

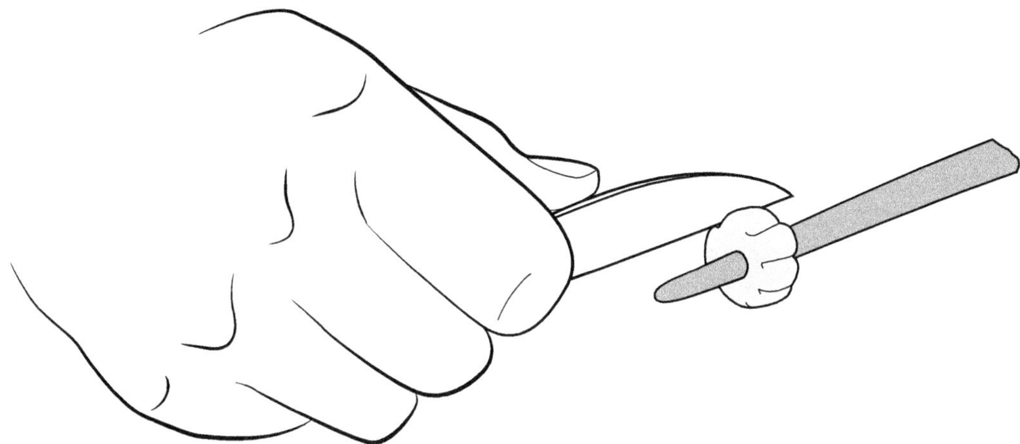

FIGURE 25.3. Making the ribs on a poppy bead (after Spaer 2001, fig. 24). Drawing T. Ross

339], **25/79** [MEΘ 1071]). An interesting find is that of a bead from which an oblique slice is missing (**25/70** [MEΘ 818]). The exposed surface has the same soft contour and corrosion as the rest of the surface; it therefore seems that the bead was exposed to heat after it was broken in antiquity and perhaps while still on the mandril.

The prevalence of the poppy beads among the finds, the fact that these were broken and discarded in antiquity, and the presence of rods for glassworking are strong indications that poppy beads were manufactured in the agora of Methone from as early as the 6th century B.C.

The technique used was winding around the mandril. From the diameter of the string-hole perforations on the surviving beads we can tell that the mandril was a maximum of 9 mm in width and narrower near the end. Several beads (**25/53** [MEΘ 813], **25/57** [MEΘ 173], **25/58** [MEΘ 174], **25/61** [MEΘ 332], **25/62** [MEΘ 333], **25/64** [MEΘ 339], **25/70** [MEΘ 818], **25/71** [MEΘ 820], **25/73** [MEΘ 1065], **25/74** [MEΘ 1066], **25/80** [MEΘ 1073], **25/81** [MEΘ 1898], **25/88** [MEΘ 1906], and **25/89** [MEΘ 1907])[33] preserve in the perforation the remains of the separating agent, used to facilitate the removal of the finished bead from the mandril; it is reddish brown (iron oxides?), sometimes with an off-white top layer. The raw glass was stored in the form of prefabricated glass rods like those found in the agora. The glassworker would heat-soften the tip of a rod and then wind the viscous glass in a few revolutions around the mandril. When pulling the glass away from the finished bead, the softened rod would diminish in diameter; the surviving tapering fragment (**25/113** [MEΘ 825]) is obviously testimony to this stage of the procedure. The ribs were created by pressing with a blade (Fig. 25.3).[34]

The source of heat can perhaps also be determined. It was certainly not a furnace of the open type, like the one used for traditional bead-making today, because that would presuppose the use of molten glass in crucibles. To use glass rods as raw glass today, one needs a steady flame that can be locally applied at the tip of the rod to be softened.[35] The technique is called "lamp-working" because it traditionally relied on the use of an oil lamp, the flame of which was directed by means of a blow tube or bellows to the desired spot. Contrary to the use of furnaces, lamp-working is an energy-saving technique that has been extensively used in the making of beads and other small objects. Its main advantage is that the glassworker has good visual control of the heat that is applied to the glass item from the side and from a short distance.[36] The study of ancient beads and pendants shows that lamp-working was practiced in antiquity, but this became possible only when the first closed oil lamps with wick spout appeared in the 6th century B.C.; the earlier open lamps could not provide the required concentrated heat. The necessary air flow that would direct and localize the flame with precision could be provided by any kind of tube with a nozzle, even a natural reed.[37] It is, therefore, perhaps not a coincidence that the earliest indications of bead-making in Methone are from the 6th century B.C. Since, however, lamp-working at this early period is considered a possibility but lacks strong evidence, it is also possible that bead-making was done with the help of a very simple furnace. Remains of a built curved truncated cone, with an opening at the top and a stoking hole near the bottom, and operated with bellows, were unearthed in Bronze Age Nuzi.[38] A similar construction is still used in traditional bead-making in Africa. Beads are made on the end of long metal rods that are repeatedly placed above the top opening to reheat the object. Since bead-making is based on the same principle as core-forming, it is now widely accepted that manufacture of both beads and core-formed vessels was done around the same type of furnace.[39]

Eye Beads

Five eye beads have been found in the agora. They were retrieved from different contexts and depths, and are dated from the Late Geometric period to the destruction of Methone in 354 B.C.

Types and decoration

The earliest type is the round bead with three stratified eyes. In a Late Geometric example, the (three) eyes are simple with two layers (**25/100** [ΜΕΘ 814]).[40] In an example of the Archaic period, the (six) eyes are more composite with six layers (**25/96** [ΜΕΘ 180]); three similar beads have been also found in Therme, in burials of the 6th and 5th centuries B.C.[41] In the Classical period the eyes are usually four with six layers (**25/97** [ΜΕΘ 809], **25/98** [ΜΕΘ 810]), or four pairs with four layers each (**25/99** [ΜΕΘ 811]). All the types are common,[42] except one rare bead with a combination of four eyes with eight yellow prunts (**25/97** [ΜΕΘ 809]).

Colors

Until the 5th century B.C. the beads have a dark body and decoration with opaque white, opaque yellow, and dark glass. From the 4th century B.C. there is one with opaque yellow and one with natural body, both decorated with opaque white and blue glass.

Context and dating

Four eye beads (**25/96** [ΜΕΘ 180], **25/97** [ΜΕΘ 809], **25/98** [ΜΕΘ 810], **25/99** [ΜΕΘ 811]) were found inside or near Building B; these are dated to the 5th/4th century B.C. One bead (**25/100** [ΜΕΘ 814]) was found outside Building A, in a mixed context, and is, stylistically, the earliest glass find in the agora, dating to the Late Geometric period.

Trail-decorated Bead

One dark green round bead is decorated with a yellow(?) trail (**25/101** [ΜΕΘ 1072]). It is very fragmentary and in a poor state of preservation.

Plain Beads

Ten plain beads have been found in the agora. They are dated to the Archaic period.

Type and decoration

The beads consist of three round (**25/102** [ΜΕΘ 175], **25/107** [ΜΕΘ 1064], **25/109** [ΜΕΘ

1915]), four round flattened (**25/103** [MEΘ 177], **25/104** [MEΘ 335], **25/108** [MEΘ 1900], and **25/110** [MEΘ 3191]), one ring-shaped (**25/105** [MEΘ 819]), one biconical (**25/106** [MEΘ 822]), and one too fragmentary to determine the form.

Colors
Five beads are aqua-colored (**25/102** [MEΘ 175], **25/103** [MEΘ 177], **25/104** [MEΘ 335], **25/105** [MEΘ 819], **25/108** [MEΘ 1900]), one is natural green (**25/110** [MEΘ 3191]), one is opaque light blue (**25/109** [MEΘ 1915]), two are amber (**25/106** [MEΘ 822], **25/111** [MEΘ 5573]), and one is impossible to tell.

Context and dating
Plain beads were found inside and outside of both Buildings A and B, in the same contexts as poppy beads, and are, therefore, dated to the Archaic period, though a few may be Classical.

GLASS GEM
The only glass gem found in Methone is a blue undecorated scaraboid (**25/115** [MEΘ 823]). It was found in the east room of Building A, under the fallen roof; it is, therefore, dated to the late 5th or the first half of the 4th century B.C., before the destruction of 354 B.C. Colorless glass scaraboid seals are known from 4th-century B.C. Macedonia, but this kind of undecorated blue scaraboid is rare. One blue seal of similar size has been found in a late 4th–early 3rd-century B.C. burial in Abdera.[43]

ACROPOLIS (WEST HILL)

Glass finds of the Archaic period from the West Hill were recovered mainly from Building B (Fig. 1.33) and consist of five plain beads (**25/124** [MEΘ 4265], **25/125** [MEΘ 4266], **25/126** [MEΘ 4267], **25/127** [MEΘ 8395], and **25/128** [MEΘ 8396]). One more plain bead (**25/123** [MEΘ 3044]) was found in Pit 3, in Sector Γ. Since the buildings were destroyed by fire sometime near the middle of the 6th century B.C., the stratified glass finds can be securely dated before this date. From Building A were retrieved the only poppy bead (**25/122** [MEΘ 3046]), an intact example, and two fragments of core-formed vessels of the Classical period (**25/120** [MEΘ 2986], **25/121** [MEΘ 4268]), all in the surface fill of the excavation.

CORE-FORMED VESSELS
The core-formed fragments retrieved from the acropolis excavation number only two. They are from surface levels and both dated to the 5th century B.C; they are, therefore, assigned to Mediterranean Group I.[44]

Shape
The fragments are so small that vessel shapes are difficult to identify. We can exclude the alabastron, which has an easily identifiable cylindrical shape; consequently, one or two of the remaining shapes are represented: the oinochoe or amphoriskos or aryballos.

Colors: body and added
Both vessels are blue and decorated with yellow and turquoise, but fragment **25/120** (MEΘ 2986) is a bright blue, while **25/121** [MEΘ 4268]) is a translucent light blue.

Decoration
Both vessels are decorated with yellow and turquoise in a combination of yellow horizontal revolutions, which develops below the midpoint into a mixed-color zigzag. But the decoration differs in width and spacing of the threads and zigzags, thus showing different manipulation, and perhaps also artisans.

Context
Both fragments were found in Building A, but in the surface fill.

POPPY BEAD
Only one poppy bead was found on the acropolis (**25/122** [MEΘ 3046]). It is complete but a stray find. The bead has five ribs and aqua color, similar to that of most of the poppy beads from the agora (for a general discussion of poppy beads, see the section on glass from the agora above).

Context
The bead was found near Building A, but is a stray find from surface fill.

PLAIN BEADS
Six plain beads have been found on the acropolis. They are dated to the Archaic period.

Type and decoration
The beads comprise one round flattened (**25/124** [MEΘ 4265]), one round conical (**25/123** [MEΘ 3044]), one conical (**25/125** [MEΘ 4266]), one disk-shaped (**25/126** [MEΘ 4267]), and two ring-shaped (**25/127** [MEΘ 8395], **25/128** [MEΘ 8396]).

Colors
Two beads are brown (**25/123** [MEΘ 3044], **25/127** [MEΘ 8395]), one is natural green (**25/124** [MEΘ 4265]), one is blue (**25/125** [MEΘ 4266]), and two are impossible to tell.

Context and dating
All the beads except one were found in Building B, which was destroyed in the middle of the 6th century; they are, therefore, dated to the 7th–earlier 6th century B.C.

CONCLUSIONS

Although very fragmentary, the glass finds from Methone testify to the use of glass from its historical beginnings to its final days. In the Geometric, Archaic, and Classical periods, triangular and, later, various eye and plain beads were a luxurious addition to personal adornment. In the Archaic period the city already had an established local production of aqua poppy beads, manufactured from prefabricated glass rods. Poppy beads were used singly, in rows around the neck, and also as pin heads, and were probably also exported to neighboring areas. A single and rare blue scaraboid gem had been worn as a pendant or had been set into a finger ring. Throughout the life of the city, rare commodities were kept in polychrome core-formed vessels. Their shapes we are now trying to deduce from the tiny fragments left behind after the larger ones had been—undoubtedly—collected to be recycled. In the centuries that followed the destruction of the city, only the occasional passersby would accidentally drop their precious glass vessels: their loss—our gain.

CATALOGUE OF THE GLASS OBJECTS

For the glass objects, all dimensions are given in mm.

THE HYPOGEION

Core-formed Glass Vessels

25/1. (MEΘ 182) Core-formed Glass Alabastron Fig. 25.4
East Hill #274/032005, 25.7.2003. Surface level.
11 x 21 mm.
Deteriorated surface with white iridescence.
Body fr. Natural green glass decorated with white feather pattern.
4th century B.C.

25/2. (MEΘ 186) Core-formed Glass Alabastron Fig. 25.4
East Hill #274/022002, 3.6.2003. Surface level.
8 x 16 mm. Deteriorated pitted surface, especially on the yellow thread.
Body fr. Blue glass decorated with yellow festoon in four revolutions.
5th or 4th century B.C.

Glass Eye Beads

25/3. (MEΘ 179) Glass Eye Bead Fig. 25.5
East Hill #274/032005, 25.7.2003. Post–Phase III.
L. 13; Diam. 23; Diam. (of perforation) 7; Diam. (of eyes) 12 mm.
Mended, small parts missing, brownish gray surface.
Triangular bead with three spiral eyes in five revolutions. Dark body, opaque white eyes.
9th–8th century B.C.

25/4. (MEΘ 341) Glass Eye Bead Fig. 25.5
East Hill #274. Phases I–III (late 8th–early 7th century B.C.).
L. 18, Diam. 21; Diam. (of perforation) 5; Diam. (of eyes) 11–15 mm.
Intact.
Triangular bead with three spiral eyes in five revolutions. Dark body, opaque white eyes.
9th–8th century B.C.

Figure 25.4. Core-formed glass vessels from the Hypogeion, **25/1** (MEΘ 182) and **25/2** (MEΘ 186). Photos I. Coyle

25/5. (MEΘ 1296) Glass Eye Bead Fig. 25.5
East Hill #022, north part zone, 10.11.2006. Phases I–III (late 8th–early 7th century B.C.).
L. 16–22 (with the projection); Diam. 25; Diam. (of perforation) 8; Diam. (of eyes) 13–15 mm.
Intact, protrusion near one end and dents near the other. Particularly well-preserved body, smooth and shiny.
Triangular bead with three spiral eyes: two yellow in four revolutions and one white in two revolutions. Dark grayish body, opaque yellow and opaque white eyes.
9th–8th century B.C.

25/6. (MEΘ 1297) Glass Eye Bead Fig. 25.5
East Hill #274/022059, 25.8.2006. Phases I–III (late 8th–early 7th century B.C.).
L. 17; Diam. (of perforation) 7; Diam. (of eyes) 15 mm.
In two joining frr preserving two eyes.
Triangular bead with three spiral eyes in five revolutions, closely packed and very regular. Dark body, opaque white eyes. White residue in the perforation.
9th–8th century B.C.

25/7. (MEΘ 1298) Glass Eye Bead Fig. 25.5
East Hill #274/032079, 4.10.2006. Phases I–III (late 8th–early 7th century B.C.).
L. 13; Diam. 23; Diam. (of perforation) 5; Diam. (of eyes) 11–12 mm.
Intact but corroded.
Triangular bead with three spiral eyes in three revolutions. Dark body, opaque white eyes. One end of perforation is very wide.
9th–8th century B.C.

25/8. (MEΘ 2836) Glass Eye Bead Fig. 25.5
East Hill #274/022045, 7.7.2004. Phases I–III (late 8th–early 7th century B.C.).
L. 13; Diam. 21; Diam. (of perforation) 4; Diam. (of eyes) 11–13 mm.
Intact but corroded.
Triangular bead with three spiral eyes: two in five revolutions and one in two revolutions. Dark gray body, opaque white eyes.
9th–8th century B.C.

Plain Glass Beads

25/9. (MEΘ 340) Glass Bead Fig. 25.6
East Hill #274/022045, 14.6.2004. Phases I–III (late 8th–early 7th century B.C.).
L. 11; P.W. 14, Diam. (of perforation) 3–5 mm.
One half preserved.
Round with conical perforation. Natural greenish glass.
Geometric or early Archaic period.

25/10. (MEΘ 342) Glass Bead Fig. 25.6
East Hill, field 274, #274/032040, 19.4.2004. Post–Phase III, fill B or C (early 7th–mid-6th).
L. 10; Diam. 14; Diam. (of perforation) 6 mm.
Almost complete, missing small part along its length. Small pits and one large.
Round. Transparent turquoise glass.
Archaic period.

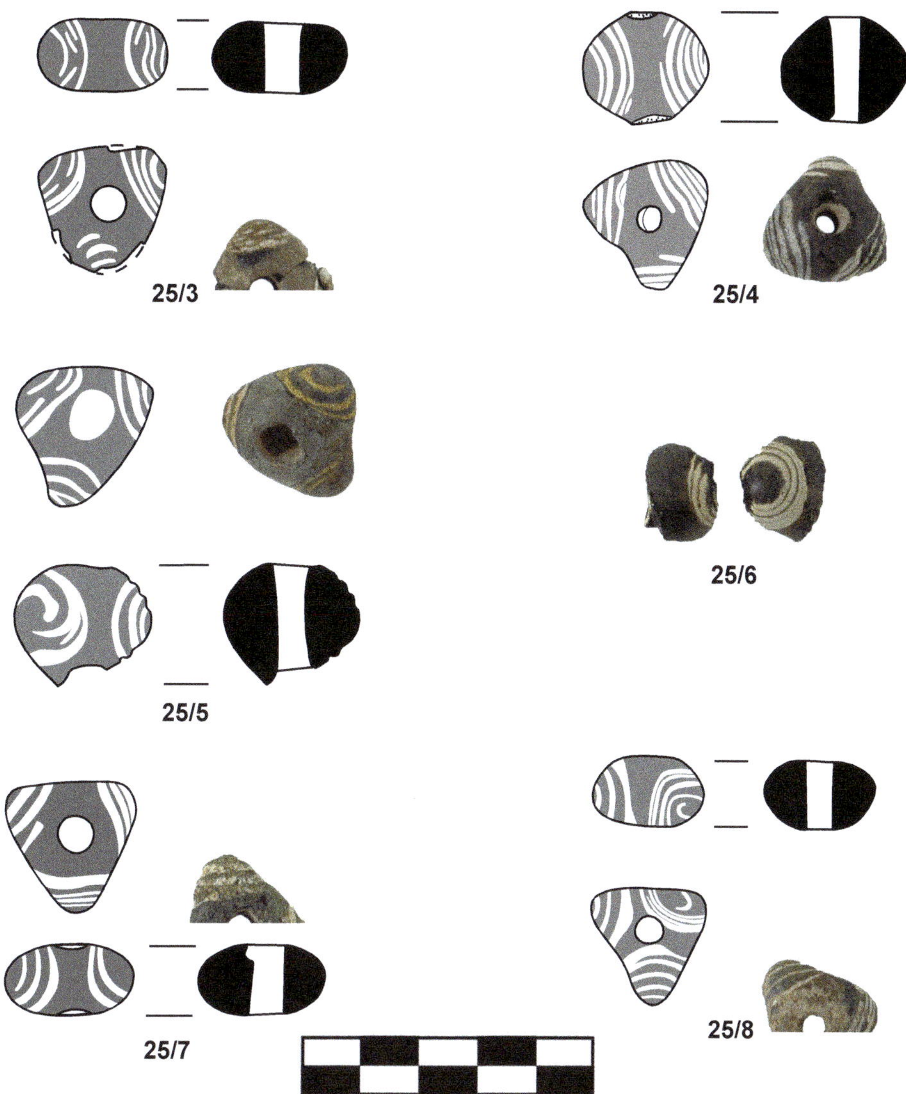

FIGURE 25.5. Glass eye beads from the Hypogeion, **25/3–25/8** (ΜΕΘ 179, ΜΕΘ 341, ΜΕΘ 1296, ΜΕΘ 1297, ΜΕΘ 1298, ΜΕΘ 2836). Drawings F. Skyvalida, photos I. Coyle

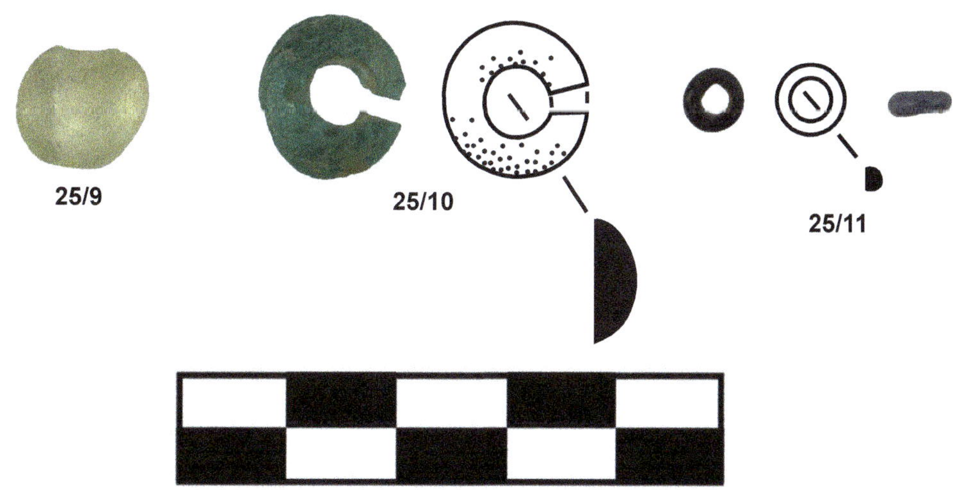

FIGURE 25.6. Plain glass beads from the Hypogeion, **25/9–25/11** (ΜΕΘ 340, ΜΕΘ 342, ΜΕΘ 2835). Drawings F. Skyvalida, photos I. Coyle

25/11. (MEΘ 2835) Glass Bead Fig. 25.6

East Hill #274/022043, 2.6.2004. Mixed levels above and at interface with Phase III (late 8th–mid-7th century B.C.

L. 2; Diam. 6; Diam. (of perforation) 3 mm.

Intact.

Ring shaped. Blue glass.

Geometric or Archaic period.

MODERN BLOWN-GLASS VESSEL

25/12. (MEΘ 8393) Fr Blown-glass Vessel Not illust.

East Hill #274/022030, east balk, surface layer. 17.3.2004.

20 x 23; Th. 2 mm.

Nearly flat body part. Transparent colorless glass.

Modern.

REMAINS OF GLASS OBJECT

25/13. (MEΘ 8394) Round Glass Fr Not illus.

East Hill #274/032086, east balk, surface layer. 22.11.2006.

L.7; Diam. 6 mm.

Broken end. Glass internally cracked.

Round edge of a broken mass of glass. Translucent greenish glass. Perhaps a workshop remnant or a fluidity-test drop.

Pre-Roman or Roman.

THE AGORA

CORE-FORMED GLASS VESSELS

25/14 (MEΘ 183) Fr Core-formed Glass Vessel Fig. 25.7

East Hill, #274/007017, pit, 26.9.2003. From a Classical stratum east of Building B.

H. 22; W. 19; Th. 2 mm.

Excellent quality, good condition; surface iridescence, remains of core inside.

Fr from middle body of an oinochoe, amphoriskos, or aryballos. Blue glass decorated with light blue zigzag in touch with one light yellow and one light blue revolution.

Perhaps from the same vessel as **25/24** (MEΘ 804).

5th century B.C.

25/15. (MEΘ 184) Fr Core-formed Glass Vessel Fig. 25.7

East Hill #274/007017, pit, 26.9.2003. From a Classical stratum east of Building B.

H. 14; W. 15; Th. 3 mm.

Excellent quality and condition, remains of core inside.

Fr from shoulder and upper body of an oinochoe or amphoriskos. White glass decorated with dark purple thread: one revolution on shoulder and four revolutions of zigzag on body. Unmarvered.

Late 6th or early 5th century B.C.

FIGURE 25.7. Core-formed glass vessels from the agora, **25/14–25/17** (MEΘ 183, MEΘ 184, MEΘ 185, MEΘ 191). Photos I. Coyle

25/16. (MEΘ 185) Fr Core-formed Glass Aryballos — Fig. 25.7

East Hill #274/087005, 6.11.2003. Building A (south of the stoa), Room B, possibly above floor, along with Corinthian and Ionian pottery.

H. 25; W. 22; Th. 3 mm.

Excellent quality and condition, remains of reddish core inside.

Fr from shoulder and upper body. Blue glass decorated with light blue and yellow thread: two and a half yellow revolutions on shoulder and three mixed-color revolutions of zigzag on body. Unmarvered.

5th century B.C.

25/17. (MEΘ 191) Core-formed Glass Vessel — Fig. 25.7

East Hill #274/007020, pit, 3.10.2003. From a Classical stratum east of Building B, along with iron slag.

L. 16; W. 10; Th. 1.5 mm.

White deteriorated surface. Mended.

Curved body fr of an oinochoe or amphoriskos(?). Natural green glass decorated with yellow thread; tips of two yellow zigzags are just preserved.

Classical period.

25/18. (MEΘ 338) Remnants of Core-formed Glass Vessel — Fig. 25.8

East Hill #274/067, trench north of Building A and Wall 19.

Dimensions not possible.

In small chunks/chips.

Blue body decorated with yellow thread.

Classical period.

25/19. (MEΘ 799) Fr Core-formed Glass Vessel Fig. 25.8

East Hill #274/007031. Building B, room A, 4.4.2005, below floor of last phase, along with pottery of the late 5th–early 4th century B.C., and workshop remains.

H. 23; W. 17; Th. 3 mm.

Good condition, surface iridescence, remains of core inside.

Fr from body. Blue glass decorated with light blue thread.

Classical period.

25/20. (MEΘ 800) Fr Core-formed Glass Alabastron Fig. 25.8

East Hill field 274, #274/007032, area between Walls 7 and 11, 19.4.2005. Classical stratum east of Building B, from its earlier phase.

H. 20; W. 15; Th. 3 mm.

Very deteriorated pitted surface with iridescence, remains of core inside.

Body fr. Blue glass decorated with yellow festoon in five revolutions.

Classical period.

25/21. (MEΘ 801) Fr Core-formed Glass Alabastron? Fig. 25.8

East Hill #274/074, SW part, 8.11.2005. Top of hill, east of Building A, east and outside of retaining Wall 7, surface.

H. 20; W. 16; Th. 3 mm.

Very deteriorated surface with iridescence, remains of core inside.

Body fr. Blue glass decorated with yellow and white zigzag in two or more revolutions.

Perhaps from same vessel as **25/23** (MEΘ 803).

5th century B.C.

25/22. (MEΘ 802) Fr Core-formed Glass Alabastron Fig. 25.8

East Hill #274/075, east part, 17.10.2005. Top of hill, east of Building A, above retaining Wall 7, along with prehistoric and Classical finds, and coin N 95.

H.16; W. 15; Th. 3 mm.

Surface with iridescence, remains of core inside.

Body fr. Blue glass decorated with short yellow festoon in five revolutions.

5th century B.C.

25/23. (MEΘ 803) Fr Core-formed Glass Alabastron Fig. 25.8

East Hill #274/078, west part, 31.5.2005. Destruction layer in Plateia A (northwest of the porch of Building A), along with bronze finds and coin N 81.

H. 12; W. 17; Th. 2 mm.

Very deteriorated surface with iridescence, remains of core inside.

Body fr. Blue glass decorated with long yellow curved zigzag in two revolutions.

Perhaps from a vessel similar to **25/21** (MEΘ 801).

5th century B.C.

25/24. (MEΘ 804) Fr Core-formed Glass Vessel Fig. 25.8

East Hill #274/078, stratum C, 16.8.2005. Building A, Room E, trench at foundation of Wall 18, along with pottery of 6th century B.C. and workshop finds.

H. 14; W. 16; Th. 3 mm.

Good condition, surface iridescence, remains of core inside.
Body fr. Blue glass decorated with one light blue and one light yellow revolution.
Perhaps from same vessel as **25/14** (ΜΕΘ 183).
6th/5th century B.C.

25/25. (ΜΕΘ 805) Fr Core-formed Glass Alabastron Fig. 25.8
East Hill #274/079, southeast part, 12.7.2005. Early phase, west of Building A, along with finds of 6th–4th century B.C., iron slag and coins N 86–N 88.
H. 16; W. 15; Th. 3 mm.
Good condition.
Body fr. Blue glass decorated with short yellow festoon in five revolutions.
5th century B.C.

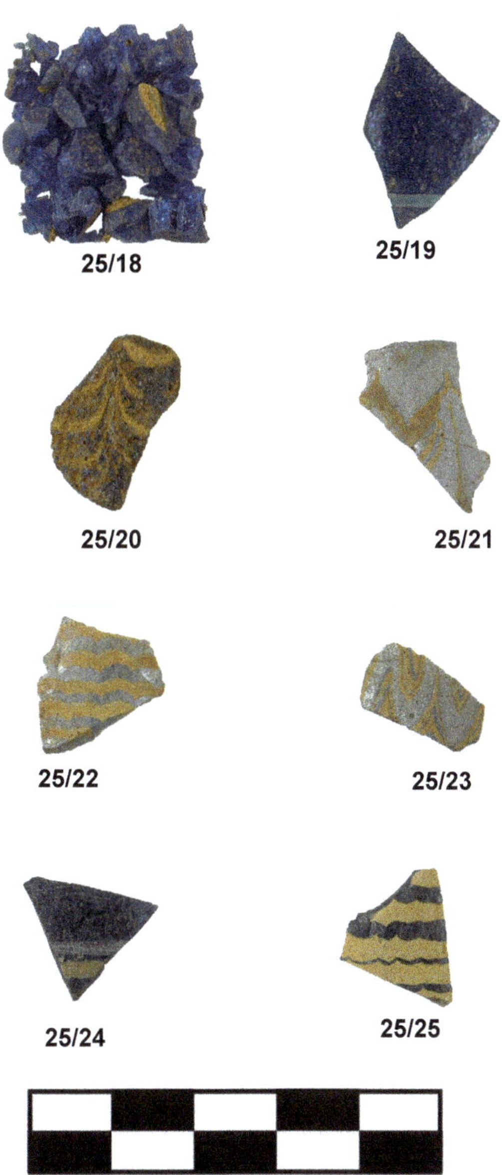

FIGURE 25.8. Core-formed glass vessels from the agora, **25/18–25/25** (ΜΕΘ 338, ΜΕΘ 799, ΜΕΘ 800, ΜΕΘ 801, ΜΕΘ 802, ΜΕΘ 803, ΜΕΘ 804, ΜΕΘ 805). Photos I. Coyle

25/26. (MEΘ 806) Fr Core-formed Glass Alabastron Fig. 25.9

East Hill #274/079, southeast part, 24.8.2005. Early phase, west of Building A, along with finds of 6th–4th century, and workshop finds.

H. 12; W. 10; Th. 4 mm.

Good condition.

Body fr. Bright blue glass decorated with white thread in four revolutions.

5th century B.C.

25/27. (MEΘ 807A) Fr Core-formed Glass Vessel Fig. 25.9

East Hill #274/079, southeast part, 24.8.2005. Early phase, west of Building A, along with finds of 6th–4th century, and workshop finds.

H. 15; W. 10; Th. 2 mm.

Good condition.

Body fr. Blue glass decorated with three mixed-color (white and yellow) revolutions.

5th century B.C.

25/28. (MEΘ 807B) Fr Core-formed Glass Vessel Fig. 25.9

East Hill #274/079, southeast part, 24.8.2005. Early phase, west of Building A, along with finds of 6th–4th century, and workshop finds.

H. 11; W. 8; Th. 2 mm.

Good condition.

Body fr. Blue glass decorated with yellow thread in two zigzags and one horizontal revolution.

5th century B.C.

25/29. (MEΘ 854) Frr (2) Core-formed Glass Vessel Fig. 25.9

East Hill #274/009010, area between 24 and 25, 17.5.2005. Building B, Room E (in use from 6th to 4th century B.C.), along with black- and red-figure pottery and workshop finds.

First fr: H. 10; W. 22; Th. 3 mm; second fr: H. 13; W. 10; Th. 2 mm.

Good condition, surface iridescence, remains of core inside.

Shoulder and body frr. Blue glass decorated with light blue and yellow thread. Shoulder fr with three light blue revolutions. Body fr with light blue and yellow zigzag in four revolutions, plus one yellow and one light blue horizontal revolution.

5th century B.C.

25/30. (MEΘ 906) Upper Part, Core-formed Glass Alabastron Fig. 25.9

East Hill #274/085, northwest part, 4.11.2005. Hard-packed soil, east of Building A, along with pottery of 6th–5th century B.C.

H. 20; W. 30; Th. of rim 4; est. Diam. (neck) 45 mm.

Deteriorated surface with iridescence in various directions. Pitting on yellow color.

Horizontal rim and cylindrical bulging neck of blue glass. Yellow thread around lip and one yellow revolution below.

Evidence for extensive tooling, irregular surface with depressions and one accidental perforation on neck.

5th century B.C.

25/31. (MEΘ 1074) Frr (2) Core-formed Glass Vessel Fig. 25.9

East Hill #274/016006, 10.5.2006. East of Building B, surface.

16 x 20 and 10 x 14 mm.

Shoulder and body frr. Blue glass decorated with yellow and light blue thread. Three yellow revolutions on shoulder and two–three zigzag revolutions (yellow and light blue) below.

5th century B.C.

25/32. (MEΘ 1075) Fr Core-formed Glass Vessel Fig. 25.9

East Hill #274/017016, 7.6.2006. Beyond and above east wall of Building B, along with red-figure pottery, slag, and coin N 125.

P.Diam. (rim) 21; P.H. 24 mm.

Good condition. Mended.

Mouth and neck fr of an oinochoe, amphoriskos, or aryballos. Blue glass decorated with yellow and light blue thread. Broad, inward-sloping mouth with yellow thread on lip. Neck with light blue thread.

5th century B.C.

FIGURE 25.9. Core-formed glass vessels from the agora, **25/26–25/32** (MEΘ 806, MEΘ 807A, MEΘ 807B, MEΘ 854, MEΘ 906, MEΘ 1074, MEΘ 1075). Photos I. Coyle

25/33. (ΜΕΘ 1076) Fr Core-formed Glass Vessel Fig. 25.10
East Hill #274/036006, 25.5.2006. Trench between Buildings A and B, along with Archaic and Classical pottery, gold earring, and workshop finds.
15 x 16 mm.
Good condition.
Upper body fr. Blue glass decorated with yellow and light blue thread in two mixed-color zigzags below one horizontal yellow revolution.
5th century B.C.

25/34. (ΜΕΘ 1077) Fr Core-formed Glass Vessel Fig. 25.10
East Hill, #274/085, central part, 25.5.2006. Found on hard-packed soil, east of Building A, along with pottery of 6th–5th century B.C.
11 x 12 mm.
Good condition.
Shoulder and upper body fr. Blue glass decorated with yellow thread in two zigzags below one horizontal revolution.
5th century B.C.

25/35. (ΜΕΘ 1905B) Fr Core-formed Glass Vessel Fig. 25.10
East Hill #274/089, north trench, 3.10.2007. Earlier buildings south of Building A, Wall 31, along with black- and red-figure pottery, parts of a musical instrument, bone object, and workshop finds.
10 x 4 mm.
Small piece of light blue glass.
6th century B.C.

25/36. (ΜΕΘ 1910) Fr Core-formed Glass Oinochoe Fig. 25.10
East Hill #274/027021, 12.9.2007. Surface stratum corresponding to interior of Building B.
P.H. 25; p.W. 15 mm.
Good condition, surface iridescence, several elongated bubbles.
Mouth, neck, and upper body fr, preserving central part of trefoil rim. Light blue glass decorated with yellow thread on lip and body.
5th century B.C.

25/37. (ΜΕΘ 1911) Frr Core-formed Glass Vessel Fig. 25.10
East Hill #274/079, south trench, 18.10.2007. West of Building A, below destruction deposit, along with black- and red-figure pottery, and workshop finds.
Max. 10 x 10 mm.
Good condition.
Four body frr. Blue glass decorated with white and yellow threads in horizontal revolutions.
5th century B.C.

25/38. (ΜΕΘ 1912) Fr Core-formed Glass Vessel Fig. 25.10
East Hill #274/089, central part, 21.6.2007. West of Building A, earlier than final phase, along with black- and red-figure pottery.
11 x 13 mm.
Deteriorated surface, large pit on yellow.
Body fr. Blue glass decorated with one yellow and one light blue thread in horizontal revolutions.
5th century B.C.

FIGURE 25.10. Core-formed glass vessels from the agora, **25/33–25/38** (MEΘ 1076, MEΘ 1077, MEΘ 1905B, MEΘ 1910, MEΘ 1911, MEΘ 1912). Photos I. Coyle and J. Vanderpool

25/39. (MEΘ 1913) Fr Core-formed Glass Vessel Fig. 25.11

East Hill #274/089, central part, 21.6.2007. West of Building A, earlier than final phase, along with black- and red-figure pottery.

8 x 15 mm.

Rim fr. Dark glass with red streaks edged with mixed yellow and decorated with light blue thread on lip. Surface irregular from tooling.

5th century B.C.

25/40. (MEΘ 1914) Fr Core-formed Glass Vessel Fig. 25.11

East Hill #274/089, central part, 21.6.2007. West of Building A, earlier than final phase, along with black- and red-figure pottery.

11 x 12 mm.

Body fr. Blue glass decorated with yellow thread in horizontal revolution.

5th century B.C.

25/41. (MEΘ 2128) Fr Core-formed Glass Alabastron Fig. 25.11

East Hill #274/090002, 30.9.2008. Plateia B, west of Building A, above destruction deposit, along with black- and red-figure pottery.

P.Diam. 27 (est.) 30; p.W. 14; p.H. 8 mm.

Good condition.

Mouth fr with horizontal added rim disk. Blue glass decorated with white thread on lip.

Late 5th–early 4th century B.C.

25/42. (MEΘ 5563) Fr Core-formed Glass Fig. 25.11

East Hill #274/086, north part, 6.9.2005. Building A, Room Z, under roof tiles.

P.L. 0.005.

Small blue chunk.

25/43. (MEΘ 5564) Frr Core-formed Glass Vessel Not illust.

East Hill #274/068, trial trench north, ditch, 4.11.2004. Plateia A, below level of destruction layer.

Minuscule chips of blue glass decorated with yellow thread, much deteriorated.

Classical period.

25/44. (MEΘ 5567) Fr Core-formed Glass Vessel Fig. 25.11

East Hill #274/089, central trench, 20.6.2007. West of Building A, below level of destruction deposit, along with black- and red-figure pottery.

13 x 10 mm.

Body fr. Transparent colorless glass.

Classical period?

25/45. (MEΘ 5565) Fr Core-formed Glass Alabastron? Fig. 25.11

East Hill #274/080005, 8.10.2009. Building E, below level of destruction deposit of the square, along with workshop finds.

L. 12 mm.

Rim fr. Blue glass decorated with white turquoise thread on lip.

Classical period.

25/46. (MEΘ 5566) Fr Core-formed Glass Vessel Fig. 25.11

East Hill #274/019001, 9.9.2008. Building B, Room H, under roof tiles, along with 4th-century B.C. pottery and coin N 207.

W. 10; H. 8 mm.

Body fr. Blue glass decorated with two yellow and one light blue zigzag.

5th century B.C.

25/47. (MEΘ 5568) Fr Core-formed Glass Vessel Fig. 25.11

East Hill #274/089, central part, 11.9.2007. West of Building A, below level of destruction deposit, near a 4th-century B.C. water channel?

L. 8 mm.

Small body fr with protrusion (lug?). Light blue glass decorated with yellow thread.

Classical period.

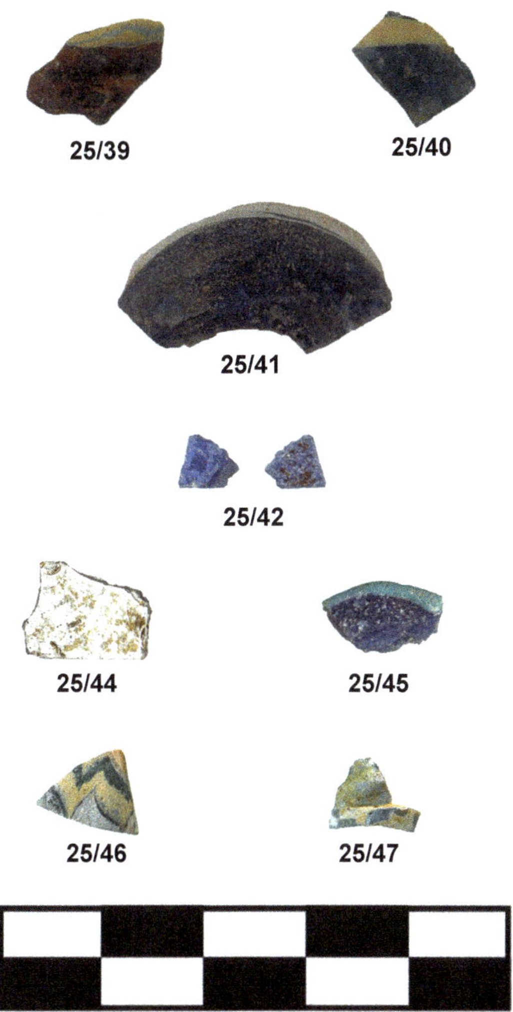

FIGURE 25.11. Core-formed glass vessels from the agora, **25/39–25/42**, **25/44–25/47** (ΜΕΘ 1913, ΜΕΘ 1914, ΜΕΘ 2128, ΜΕΘ 5563, ΜΕΘ 5567, ΜΕΘ 5565, ΜΕΘ 5566, ΜΕΘ 5568). Photos I. Coyle and J. Vanderpool

BLOWN-GLASS VESSELS

25/48. (ΜΕΘ 190A) Fr Mold-blown Glass Bottle — Fig. 25.12

East Hill #274/054001, east balk, surface, 13.6.2003, 17.6.2003.

L. 43; W. 23; Th. 4 mm.

Very good quality.

Convex shoulder from a prismatic bottle. Transparent, aqua glass. From same vessel as **25/50** (ΜΕΘ 336) and **25/51** (ΜΕΘ 337).

Roman period.

25/49. (ΜΕΘ 190B) Frr Blown-glass Vessel — Fig. 25.12

East Hill #274/044001, east balk, surface, 13.6.2003, 17.6.2003.

L. 24; W. 22; Th. 2 mm.

Very good quality. In two frr.

Convex body part. Transparent, natural green glass.

Roman period.

FIGURE 25.12. Blown-glass vessels from the agora, **25/48–25/51** (MEΘ 190A, MEΘ 190B, MEΘ 336, MEΘ 337). Photos I. Coyle

25/50. (MEΘ 336) Fr Mold-blown Glass Bottle Fig.25.12

East Hill, 30.9.2003, from the dump.

L. 45; W. 30; Th. 3 mm.

Very good quality. Round bubbles.

Convex shoulder part from a prismatic bottle. Transparent, aqua glass. From same vessel as **25/48** (MEΘ 190A) and **25/51** (MEΘ 337).

Roman period.

25/51. (MEΘ 337) Fr Mold-blown Glass Bottle Fig. 25.12

East Hill, 4.8.2004, from dump.

L. 37; W. 28; Th. 2 mm.

Very good quality.

Convex shoulder from a prismatic bottle. Transparent, aqua glass. From same vessel as **25/48** (MEΘ 190A) and **25/50** (MEΘ 336).

Roman period.

Modern Glass Vessel

25/52. (MEΘ 188) Colorless Glass Vessel Fig. 25.13

East Hill #274/012001. Top of hill, surface find, 26.5.2003.

H. 41; W. (rim) 15; Th. (rim) 4; Th. (lower body) 5; Diam. 55–60 mm.

Excellent quality, no corrosion, no bubbles.

Rim and body fr of a modern glass. Decolorized glass. It contains appr. 0.4 As. (XRF analysis conducted in the Archaeological Museum of Thessaloniki by the chemist Christos Katsifas).

20th century.

Decorated Glass Poppy Bead

25/53. (ΜΕΘ 813) Glass Poppy Bead Fig. 25.13

East Hill #274/074, extended trench north of Wall 18, second layer, 8.11.2005. East of retaining wall, along with pottery of various periods (including black-figure, black-glaze), unstratified.

L. 31; p.Diam. 32; Diam. (perforation) 12 mm.

One half preserved, ancient break. Surface pits. Yellow trail partly preserved. Reddish remains inside perforation.

Four preserved ribs. Aqua glass decorated with transverse opaque yellow trail in one revolution. An oblique short mark of blade used to create the ribs is left near one end.

Archaic or early Classical period.

Glass Poppy Beads

25/54. (ΜΕΘ 170) Glass Poppy Bead Fig. 25.13

East Hill #274/006, 007, collected from the dump, 22.10.2003. East of Building B.

L. 16; p.W. 15; Diam. (perforation) 4 mm.

One half preserved. Transparent but with bubbles and laminated surface.

Three preserved ribs and an end protrusion. Aqua glass.

Archaic or Classical period.

25/55. (ΜΕΘ 171) Glass Poppy Bead Fig. 25.13

East Hill #274/007016, pit, 25.9.2003. East of Building B, along with bronze pin and iron slag.

L. 16; p.W. 15; Diam. (perforation) 4 mm.

One half preserved. Bubbles and laminated surface.

Five preserved ribs, one very narrow, and an end protrusion. Aqua glass.

Archaic or Classical period.

Figure 25.13. Modern glass vessel, **25/52** (ΜΕΘ 188), decorated glass poppy bead, **25/53** (ΜΕΘ 813), and glass poppy beads, **25/54** (ΜΕΘ 170), **25/55** (ΜΕΘ 171), all from the agora. Drawing A. Hooton, photos I. Coyle

25/56. (MEΘ 172) Glass Poppy Bead Fig. 25.14
East Hill #274/006013, 10.9.2003. East of Building B, along with Archaic pottery.
L. 12; p.W. 15; Diam. (perforation) 8 mm.
One half preserved. Corroded off-white surface.
Three preserved ribs. Aqua glass.
Archaic or Classical period.

25/57. (MEΘ 173) Glass Poppy Bead Fig. 25.14
East Hill #274/007017, pit, 25.9.2003. East of Building B, early phase.
L. 19; p.W. 24; Diam. (perforation) 7 mm.
One half preserved. Very transparent but with bubbles and corroded surface. Reddish remains inside perforation.
Three preserved ribs. Aqua glass.
Archaic or Classical period.

25/58. (MEΘ 174) Glass Poppy Bead Fig. 25.14
East Hill #274/007016, pit, 25.9.2003. East of Building B, early phase.
L. 13; p.W. 19; Diam. (perforation) 7 mm.
One half preserved, ancient break. Corroded off-white surface. Reddish remains inside perforation.
Three preserved ribs. Aqua glass.
Archaic or Classical period.

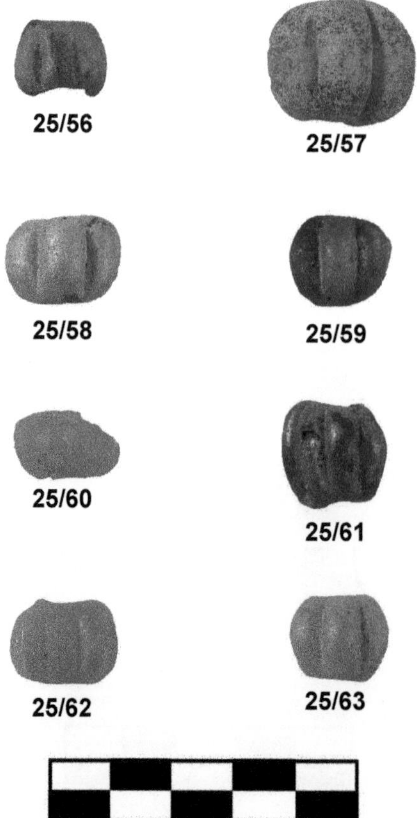

FIGURE 25.14. Glass poppy beads from the agora, **25/56–25/63** (MEΘ 172, MEΘ 173, MEΘ 174, MEΘ 176, MEΘ 178, MEΘ 332, MEΘ 333, MEΘ 334). Photos I. Coyle

25/59. (ΜΕΘ 176) Glass Poppy Bead Fig. 25.14

Stray find, possibly from the East Hill, 29.9.2003.

L. 14; p.W. 16; Diam. (perforation) 4 mm.

One half preserved. Iridescence and pits.

Three preserved ribs. Aqua to bluish glass.

Archaic or Classical period.

25/60. (ΜΕΘ 178) Glass Poppy Bead Fig. 25.14

East Hill #274/085022, 29.8.2003. Behind Building A, Room A, at face of polygonal wall.

L. 18; p.W. 10; Diam. (perforation) 4 mm.

Less than one-quarter preserved. Dull surface.

One preserved rib. Aqua glass.

Archaic or Classical period.

25/61. (ΜΕΘ 332) Glass Poppy Bead Fig. 25.14

East Hill #274/088, trial trench, southwest corner, 27.10.2004. Building A, Room Δ, below level of destruction deposit, along with 6th-century B.C. pottery.

L. 17; p.W. 17; Diam. (perforation) 7 mm.

One half preserved, ancient break. Bubbles and laminated surface. Large pit across one rib. Reddish remains inside perforation.

Five preserved ribs and an end protrusion. Aqua to greenish glass.

Archaic or early Classical period.

25/62. (ΜΕΘ 333) Glass Poppy Bead Fig. 25.14

East Hill #274/088, 27.10.2004. Building A, Room Δ, below the level of the destruction deposit, along with 6th–5th century B.C. pottery.

L. 13; p.W. 18; Diam. (perforation) 6 mm.

One half preserved. Dull surface and bubbles. Reddish remains inside perforation.

Five preserved ribs. Natural greenish glass.

Archaic or Classical period.

25/63. (ΜΕΘ 334) Glass Poppy Bead Fig. 25.14

East Hill #274/066, trial trench, 1.9.2004. Plateia A, north of Building A, destruction deposit, with black-figure and 4th-century B.C. pottery, and coin N 17.

L. 14; p.W. 16; Diam. (perforation) 7 mm.

One half is preserved, ancient break. Dull surface.

Three preserved ribs and an end protrusion. Aqua glass.

Archaic or Classical period.

25/64. (ΜΕΘ 339) Glass Poppy Bead Fig. 25.15

East Hill #274/088, trial trench, 26.10.2004. Building A, Room Δ, below level of destruction deposit, along with 6th–5th century B.C. pottery.

L. 15; p.W. 18; Diam. (perforation) 6 mm.

One half preserved, ancient break. Mended. Corroded off-white surface and large pit across one rib. Reddish remain inside perforations.

Three preserved ribs, one very wide. The ribs are not formed near the end where the surface is flat. Green glass.

Archaic or Classical period.

25/65. (MEΘ 808) Glass Poppy Bead Fig. 25.15

East Hill #274/017002, trench at the northeast part, 12.1.2005. Building B, Room A, erosion layer, along with coin N 56.

L. 14; p.W. 12; Diam. (perforation) 5 mm.

Less than one-quarter preserved; one longitudinal ancient break and one oblique modern break. Corroded off-white surface. Pit across one rib.

Two preserved ribs. Aqua glass.

Archaic or Classical period.

25/66. (MEΘ 812) Glass Poppy Bead Fig. 25.15

East Hill #274/068, trench at northeast part, 14.9.2005. North of Building A, under destruction deposit, with Archaic pottery and industrial workshop finds.

L. 14; p.W. 12; Diam. (perforation) 5 mm.

One-quarter preserved. Corroded off-white surface.

One and a half rib preserved. Aqua glass.

Archaic period.

25/67. (MEΘ 815) Glass Poppy Bead Fig. 25.15

East Hill #274/076, second layer, 10.8.2005. Building A, Room E, extended trench at foundation of Wall 18, along with handmade and 6th-century B.C. pottery and workshop finds.

L. 14; p.Diam. 17; Diam. (perforation) 7 mm.

One half preserved. Corroded off-white surface.

Four preserved ribs. Aqua glass.

Archaic or Classical period.

FIGURE 25.15. Glass poppy beads from the agora, **25/64–25/71** (MEΘ 339, MEΘ 808, MEΘ 812, MEΘ 815, MEΘ 816, MEΘ 817, MEΘ 818, MEΘ 820). Photos I. Coyle

25/68. (MEΘ 816) Glass Poppy Bead Fig. 25.15

East Hill #274/078, fourth layer, 16.8.2005. Building A, Room E, extended trench at the foundation of Wall 18, along with handmade and 6th-century B.C. pottery and workshop finds.

L. 20; p.W. 14; Diam. (perforation) 7 mm.

One-quarter preserved. Surface iridescence.

Two preserved ribs and an end protrusion. Aqua glass.

Archaic or Classical period.

25/69. (MEΘ 817) Fr Glass Poppy Bead Fig. 25.15

East Hill #274/078, fifth layer, 17.8.2005. Building A, Room E, extended trench below foundation of Wall 18, along with handmade and 6th-century B.C. pottery and workshop finds.

P.L. 11; p.W. 12; Diam. (perforation) 7 mm.

Small part with modern breaks.

Two partly preserved ribs. Aqua glass.

Archaic or early Classical period.

25/70. (MEΘ 818) Glass Poppy Bead Fig. 25.15

East Hill #274/079, southeast part, 24.8.2005. West of Building A, below destruction deposit, along with black-figure pottery, jewelry, bronze pin, and workshop finds.

L. 14; Diam. 20; Diam. (perforation) 7 mm.

Almost complete, missing an oblique part of one rib on one side, ancient break or heat-induced flattening. Reddish remains inside perforation.

Seven(?) ribs. Aqua glass.

6th century B.C.

25/71. (MEΘ 820) Glass Poppy Bead Fig. 25.15

East Hill #274/079, southeast part, 26.8.2005. West of Building A, below destruction deposit, along with bronze pin and workshop finds.

L. 13.5; p.W.10; Diam. (perforation) 7 mm.

One-quarter preserved. Reddish remains inside perforation.

Two preserved ribs. Aqua glass.

6th century B.C.

25/72. (MEΘ 821) Glass Poppy Bead Fig. 25.16

East Hill #274/085, east balk, upper layer, 1.9.2005.

L. 19; p.Diam. 21; Diam. (perforation) 5 mm.

One half preserved, ancient break. Surface iridescence.

Three preserved ribs and an end protrusion. Aqua to turquoise glass.

Archaic or Classical period.

25/73. (MEΘ 1065) Fr Glass Poppy Bead Fig. 25.16

East Hill #274/036008, 31.5.2006. Trench between Buildings A and B, along with Archaic and Classical pottery, and workshop finds.

P.L. 9; P.Diam. 14; Diam. (perforation) 6 mm.

Less than one-quarter preserved, ancient break. Corroded off-white surface. Reddish remains with off-white surface inside perforation.

Two preserved ribs. Aqua glass.

Archaic or Classical period.

25/74. (MEΘ 1066) Glass Poppy Bead Fig. 25.16

East Hill #274/036010, 5.6.2006. Trench between Buildings A and B, along with Archaic and Classical pottery, and workshop finds.

L. 16; p.Diam. 20; Diam. (perforation) 5–6 mm.

One half preserved. Corroded off-white surface. Reddish remains with off-white surface inside perforation.

Two preserved ribs. Aqua glass.

Archaic or Classical period.

25/75. (MEΘ 1067) Glass Poppy Bead Fig.25.16

East Hill #274/065, middle west part, 14.7.2006. East of Building A, along with coins N 162–N 167.

L. 20; p.Diam. 19; Diam. (perforation) 9 mm.

One half preserved. Corroded off-white surface.

Three preserved ribs. Aqua glass.

Archaic or Classical period.

25/76. (MEΘ 1068) Glass Poppy Bead Fig. 25.16

East Hill #274/075, northwest part, 9.6.2006. East of Building A.

L. 14; p.Diam. 17; Diam. (perforation) 6 mm.

One half is preserved, ancient break. Corroded off-white surface and pits in body.

Four preserved ribs. Aqua glass.

Archaic or Classical period.

FIGURE 25.16. Glass poppy beads from the agora, **25/72–25/77** (MEΘ 821, MEΘ 1065, MEΘ 1066, MEΘ 1067, MEΘ 1068, MEΘ 1069). Drawing A. Hooton, photos I. Coyle

25/77. (MEΘ 1069) Biconical Glass Poppy Bead Fig. 25.16

East Hill #274/077, fourth layer, 14.7.2006. Building A, Room E, Wall 31 (extended trench below foundation of Wall 18).

L. 7; Diam. 9; Diam. (perforation) 1.5–3 mm.

Complete. Corroded off-white surface. Longitudinal crack and a pit near one end of perforation.

Several ribs separated by irregular marks, showing that the blade used to create ribs was pressed on the surface from both ends. Aqua glass.

Archaic period.

25/78. (MEΘ 1070) Glass Poppy Bead Fig. 25.17

East Hill 25.5, central part, 2006#274/085. Trodden soil surface, east of Building A, along with pottery of 6th–5th century B.C.

L. 20; p.W. 14; Diam. (perforation) 7 mm.

One-quarter preserved, ancient break. Corroded off-white surface.

Three preserved ribs, separated by grooves that end at midpoint and start from alternating opposite sides. Blue glass, nearly opaque.

Archaic or early Classical period.

25/79. (MEΘ 1071) Glass Poppy Bead Fig. 25.17

East Hill #274/085, central part, 25.5.2006. Trodden soil surface, east of Building A, along with pottery of 6th–5th century B.C.

L. 14; p.Diam. 20; Diam. (perforation) 9 mm.

One half preserved. Dull surface. Pit near end of one rib.

Four preserved ribs, one wider than the others. Aqua glass.

Archaic or early Classical period.

FIGURE 25.17. Glass poppy beads from the agora, **25/78–25/85** (MEΘ 1070, MEΘ 1071, MEΘ 1073, MEΘ 1898, MEΘ 1899, MEΘ 1901, MEΘ 1902, MEΘ 1903). Photos I. Coyle

25/80. (MEΘ 1073) Glass Poppy Bead Fig. 25.17

East Hill #274/089, southwest trench, 7.7.2006. Above Building Δ, below level of destruction deposit, along with pottery of 6th–5th century B.C., and workshop finds.

P.Diam. 14; Diam. (perforation) 4 mm.

One-quarter preserved. Translucent, with bubbles. Reddish remains inside perforation.

Two preserved ribs. Aqua glass.

Archaic or early Classical period.

25/81. (MEΘ 1898) Glass Poppy Bead Fig. 25.17

East Hill #274/274/018001, 11.9.2007. Building B, Room A, erosion layer.

L. 18; W. 11; Diam. (perforation) 5 mm.

One-quarter preserved, ancient break. Bubbles, one transverse long. Corroded surface. Reddish remains inside perforation.

One preserved rib. Aqua glass.

Archaic or Classical period.

25/82. (MEΘ 1899) Glass Poppy Bead Fig. 25.17

East Hill #274/079, south trench, 18.10.2007. West of Building A, below destruction deposit, along with black-, red-figure, and Corinthian pottery, and workshop finds.

L. 18; W. 13; Diam. (perforation) 6 mm.

One-quarter preserved, ancient break. Dull surface.

Two preserved ribs. Aqua glass.

6th century B.C.

25/83. (MEΘ 1901) Glass Poppy Bead Fig. 25.17

East Hill #274/089, central trench, 21.6.2007. West of Building A, below level of destruction deposit, along with black- and red-figure pottery.

L. 16; p.Diam. 19; Diam. (perforation) 7 mm.

One half preserved, ancient break. Corroded and mended.

Four preserved ribs. Aqua glass.

Archaic or Classical period.

25/84. (MEΘ 1902) Glass Poppy Bead Fig. 25.17

East Hill #274/089, central trench, 11.9.2007. West of Building A, below level of destruction deposit, along with black- and red-figure pottery, bronze pins, and workshop finds.

L. 13; W. 8 mm.

One-eighth preserved. Surface iridescence.

One wide rib is preserved. Aqua glass.

Archaic or Classical period.

25/85. (MEΘ 1903) Glass Poppy Bead Fig. 25.17

East Hill #274/089, central trench, 11.9.2007. West of Building A, below level of destruction deposit, along with black- and red-figure pottery, bronze pins, and workshop finds.

L. 14; p.Diam. 18; Diam. (perforation) 7 mm.

One half preserved. Dull surface.

Four preserved ribs. Aqua glass.

From a 4th-century B.C. context.

Archaic or Classical period.

25/86. (MEΘ 1904) Glass Poppy Bead Fig. 25.18

East Hill #274/089, north trench, 28.9.2007. West of Building A, below level of destruction deposit, along with loomweights and workshop finds.

L. 16; p.Diam. 19; Diam. (perforation) 5 mm.

One half preserved. Dull surface, transparent with bubbles inside.

Three preserved ribs. Aqua glass.

Archaic or Classical period.

25/87. (MEΘ 1905A) Glass Poppy Bead Fig. 25.18

East Hill #274/089, north trench, 3.10.2007. Earlier buildings south of Building A, Wall 31, along with black- and red-figure pottery, parts of a musical instrument, bone object, and workshop finds.

L. 12; p.Diam. 15; Diam. (perforation) 6 mm.

Less than one-quarter preserved. Surface iridescence and erosion.

Three preserved ribs. Aqua glass.

6th century B.C.

25/88. (MEΘ 1906) Glass Poppy Bead Fig. 25.18

East Hill #274/089, north trench, 3.10.2007. Earlier buildings south of Building A, Wall 31, along with black- and red-figure pottery, parts of a musical instrument, bone object, and workshop finds.

P.L. 10; p.Diam. 20; Diam. (perforation) 6 mm.

One half preserved, ancient break. Dull surface. Reddish remains inside perforation.

Three preserved ribs. Aqua glass.

Archaic or Classical period.

25/89. (MEΘ 1907) Glass Poppy Bead Fig. 25.18

East Hill #274/089, central trench, 3.10.2007. West of Building A, below level of destruction deposit, along with black-figure pottery and workshop finds.

L. 16; p.Diam. 19; Diam. (perforation) 7 mm.

One half preserved. Dull surface with two dents and one pit on the break. Reddish remains inside perforation.

Two preserved ribs. Aqua glass.

Archaic period.

25/90. (MEΘ 1908) Glass Poppy Bead Fig. 25.18

East Hill #274/089, central trench, 8.10.2007. West of Building A, below level of destruction deposit, along with black-figure pottery and workshop finds.

L. 13; p.Diam. 16; Diam. (perforation) 8 mm.

One-quarter preserved. Dull surface.

Two preserved ribs, one wide. Aqua glass.

Archaic or Classical period, but from a 4th-century B.C. context.

25/91. (MEΘ 3192) Glass Poppy Bead Fig. 25.18

East Hill #274/080005, 8.10.2009. Building E, below destruction deposit of square, along with workshop finds.

L. 13; p.W. 17; Diam. (perforation) 5 mm.

One half preserved, ancient break. Off-white corroded surface with pits.

Three preserved ribs. Aqua glass.

Classical period.

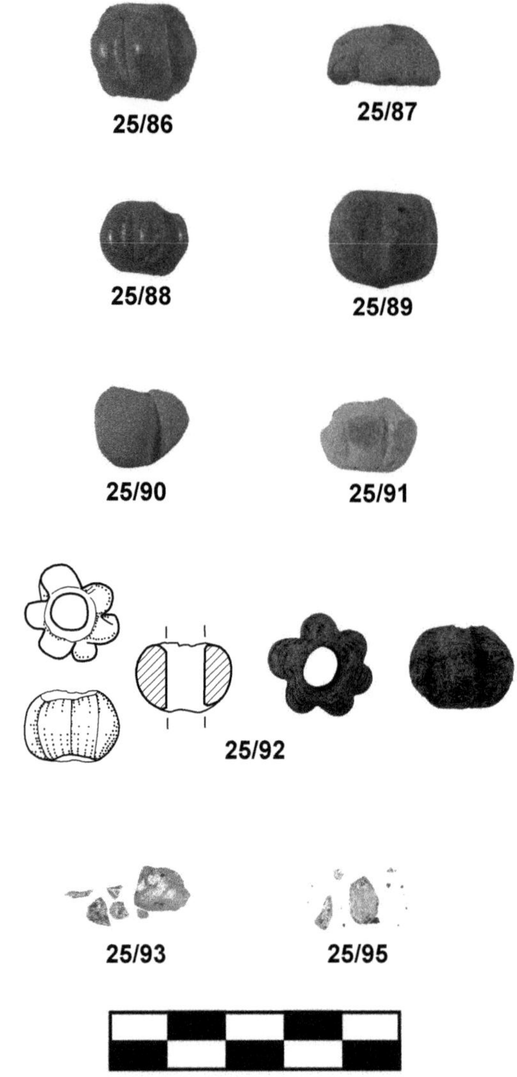

FIGURE 25.18. Glass poppy beads from the agora, **25/86–25/93** and **25/95** (ΜΕΘ 1904, ΜΕΘ 1905A, ΜΕΘ 1906, ΜΕΘ 1907, ΜΕΘ 1908, ΜΕΘ 3192, ΜΕΘ 4067, ΜΕΘ 5574, ΜΕΘ 5577). Drawing A. Hooton, photos I. Coyle and J. Vanderpool

25/92. (ΜΕΘ 4067) Glass Poppy Bead Fig. 25.18

East Hill from removal of topsoil at northwest part, 17.11.2004.

L. 13; Diam. 18; Diam. (perforation) 7 mm.

Complete. Off-white corroded surface with transverse corrosion lines.

Six ribs. Amber glass.

Unstratified find, possibly of Archaic or Classical period.

25/93. (ΜΕΘ 5574) Fr Glass Poppy Bead Fig. 25.18

East Hill #274/067, trial trench, east part, 6.9.2004. Building A, room E, possibly below destruction deposit.

P.L. 10; p.W. 8 mm.

Very transparent with bubbles.

Two preserved ribs. Aqua glass.

Archaic or Classical period.

25/94. (MEΘ 5576) Remnants of Glass Bead Not illust.

East Hill #274/077, trench north of Wall 18, fourth layer, 14.7.2006. Building A, Room E, Wall 31 (extended trench below foundation of 18).

Minuscule chips of aqua to bluish glass. Similar to **25/59** (MEΘ 176).

25/95. (MEΘ 5577) Small Remnants of Glass Poppy Bead Fig. 25.18

East Hill #274/066, east balk, 28.7.2006. North of Building A, above destruction deposit, along with bronze pin.

Chips of light blue glass. Aqua glass. Similar to **25/93** (MEΘ 5574).

Glass Eye Beads

25/96. (MEΘ 180) Glass Eye Bead Fig. 25.19

East Hill #274/007017, 29.9.2003. East of Building B, along with masses of clay and firing remains.

L. 14; p.W. 16; Diam. (perforation) 4 mm.

Intact, corroded surface with pits.

Round, flattened. Dark glass with six stratified eyes (three opaque white and three dark layers) in a three-plus-three arrangement.

Archaic period.

25/97. (MEΘ 809) Glass Eye Bead Fig. 25.20

East Hill #274/017006, 19.1.2005. Building B, Room A, below floor of final phase and of Wall 11, along with black-figure pottery and coin N 60.

L. 9; Diam. 14; Diam. (perforation) 6 mm.

Intact.

Round, flattened. Dark glass with four stratified eyes (three opaque white and three dark layers), separated by eight yellow prunts.

Classical period.

Figure 25.19. Glass eye bead from the agora, **25/96** (MEΘ 180) (five views).
Photos I. Coyle

25/98. (ΜΕΘ 810) Glass Eye Bead Fig. 25.20

East Hill #274/027011, 29.3.2005. Building B, Room Γ, erosion layer, along with coin N 65.

L. 16; p.W. 18; Diam. (perforation) 6 mm.

One-third preserved, with two eyes. Two large pits on broken side.

Round. Opaque yellow glass with (originally) four stratified eyes (three opaque white and three blue layers).

First half of the 4th century B.C.

25/99. (ΜΕΘ 811) Glass Eye Bead Fig. 25.20

East Hill #274/027013, east part, 6.4.2005. Building B, Room Γ, destruction deposit with extensive workshop finds, and a coin of Pydna.

L. 9; p.Diam. 13; Diam. (perforation) 5 mm.

Intact.

Round-cylindrical with deforming protrusions at both ends. Natural green glass with four pairs of stratified eyes (two opaque white and two blue layers).

First half of the 4th century B.C.

FIGURE 25.20. Glass eye beads from the agora, **25/97–25/99** (ΜΕΘ 809, ΜΕΘ 810, ΜΕΘ 811). Photos I. Coyle

25/100. (MEΘ 814) Glass Eye Bead Fig. 25.21

East Hill #274/075, east part, 30.9.2005. Above retaining Wall 7, erosion layer with Bronze Age to 4th century B.C. pottery.

L. 9; p.Diam. 13; Diam. (perforation) 5 mm.

One half preserved, with one complete and part of two more eyes. Corroded body and yellow layer but uncorroded dark layer.

Round. Dark glass with three stratified eyes (one yellow and one dark layer).

Late Geometric period.

Decorated Glass Bead

25/101. (MEΘ 1072) Glass Bead Fig. 25.21

East Hill #274/085, central part, 26.5.2006. Packed soil, east of Building A, along with pottery of 6th–5th century B.C.

P.L.17; p.Diam. 14; Diam. (perforation) 4 mm.

Two frr. Very corroded surface, most of yellow trail is missing. Residue inside perforation.

Round bead with transverse opaque yellow(?) trail in one revolution. Dark green glass that appears dark blue.

Archaic or early Classical period.

Plain Glass Beads

25/102. (MEΘ 175) Glass Bead Fig. 25.21

East Hill #274/006014, 10.9.2003. East of Building B.

L. 15. p.W. 18; est. Diam. (perforation) 4 mm.

One half preserved, mended. Laminated surface and pits.

Round. Aqua glass.

Archaic period.

Figure 25.21. Glass eye bead, **25/100** (MEΘ 814), decorated glass bead, **25/101** (MEΘ 1072), and plain glass beads, **25/102–25/104** (MEΘ 175, MEΘ 177, MEΘ 335), from the agora. Photos I. Coyle

25/103. (ΜΕΘ 177) Glass Bead Fig. 25.21

East Hill #274/006013, 10.9.2003. East of Building B.

L. 14; p.W. 16; Diam. (perforation) 4 mm.

One half preserved. Laminated surface and pits.

Round flattened. Aqua glass.

Archaic period.

25/104. (ΜΕΘ 335) Glass Bead Fig. 25.21

East Hill #274/088, 27.10.2004. Building A, Room Δ, below level of destruction deposit, along with 6th-century B.C. pottery.

L. 9; p.W. 12; Diam. (perforation) 5 mm.

One half preserved, ancient break. Corroded surface and pits.

Round flattened. Aqua glass.

Archaic period.

25/105. (ΜΕΘ 819) Glass Bead Fig. 25.22

East Hill #274/079, southwest part, 26.8.2005. West of Building A, below destruction deposit, along with 6th-century pottery, bronze pin, and workshop finds.

L. 4.5; Diam. 9; Diam. (perforation) 4 mm.

Intact.

Ring shaped. Aqua glass.

6th century B.C.

25/106. (ΜΕΘ 822) Glass Bead Fig. 25.22

East Hill #274/088, trench north of Wall 12, 29.8.2005. Building A, Room Δ, below level of destruction deposit, along with bronze pin, and 6th–5th century B.C. pottery.

L. 9; Diam. 13; Diam. (perforation) 1–3 mm.

Mended. Missing strip along edge and smaller missing parts along breaks. White corroded surface.

Biconical bead with one sloping and one nearly flat side. Amber glass. The sloping side has radial closely packed grooves and a depression; flat side is smooth with a circular mark around the perforation. Found together with glass rods **25/112** (ΜΕΘ 824) and **25/113** (ΜΕΘ 825).

6th century B.C.

25/107. (ΜΕΘ 1064) Glass Bead Fig. 25.22

East Hill#274/035, east face, 12.4.2006. Unstratified.

L. 11–13; Diam. 13; Diam. (perforation) 4–5 mm.

Intact, with off-white corroded surface.

Round; ring protrusion at one end, protrusion and a bump at the other. Impossible to see original color of glass.

6th century B.C.

25/108. (ΜΕΘ 1900) Glass Bead Fig. 25.22

East Hill #274/079, south trench, 18.10.2007. West of Building A, below the destruction deposit, along with black- and red-figure pottery, and workshop finds.

L. 7; p.Diam. 9; Diam. (perforation) 3 mm.

One half preserved. Corroded white surface.

Round flattened; protrusion at one end. Aqua glass.

6th century B.C.

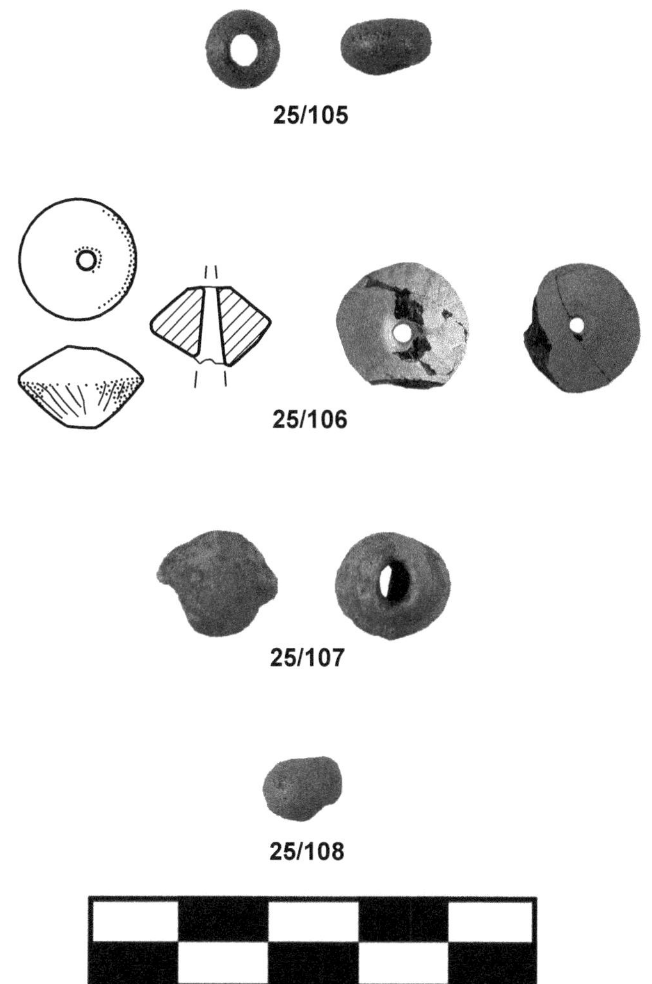

FIGURE 25.22. Plain glass beads from the agora, **25/105–25/108** (ΜΕΘ 819, ΜΕΘ 822, ΜΕΘ 1064, ΜΕΘ 1900). Drawing A. Hooton, photos I. Coyle

25/109. (ΜΕΘ 1915) Glass Bead Fig. 25.23

East Hill #274/036005, 23.5.2006. Trench between Buildings A and B, along with Archaic and Classical pottery, bronze pins, and workshop finds.

L. 5; Diam. 6; Diam. (perforation) 2 mm.

Corroded surface and big dent.

Round. Opaque light blue glass.

6th century B.C.

25/110. (ΜΕΘ 3191) Glass Bead Fig. 25.23

East Hill #274/067, 068, 29.9.2009. North of Building A, well below destruction deposit, along with Archaic and Classical pottery.

L. 6 (without the protrusions); Diam. 10; Diam. (perforation) 4 mm.

Corroded white surface.

Round flattened; pointed protrusions at both ends. Natural green glass.

Early Archaic period.

FIGURE 25.23. Plain glass beads from the agora, **25/109–25/111** (ΜΕΘ 1915, ΜΕΘ 3191, ΜΕΘ 5573). Photos I. Coyle and J. Vanderpool

25/111. (ΜΕΘ 5573) Fr Glass Bead Fig. 25.23

East Hill #274/088, trench north of Wall 12, 29.8.2005. Building A, Room Δ, below level of destruction deposit, along with bronze pin, and 6th–5th century B.C. pottery.

5 x 6 mm.

Amber glass.

Archaic period.

GLASS RODS

25/112. (ΜΕΘ 824) Glass Rod Fig. 25.24

East Hill #274/088, 29.8.2005. Building A, Room Δ, below level of destruction deposit, along with bronze pin, and 6th–5th century B.C. pottery.

L. (four largest frr) 103, 58, 41, 23; Diam. 5 mm.

Mended. Surface iridescence.

Five frr of slightly twisted cylindrical rod, originally from the same or different rods. Aqua glass. Found with glass rod **25/113** (ΜΕΘ 825) and amber-colored bead **25/106** (ΜΕΘ 822).

6th century B.C.

25/113. (ΜΕΘ 825) Glass Rod Fig. 25.24

East Hill #274/088, trench north of 12, 29.8.2005. Building A, Room Δ, below level of destruction layer, along with bronze pin, and 6th–5th century B.C. pottery.

L. 19; max Diam. 2 mm.

Dull surface.

Fr of twisted tapering cylindrical rod. Aqua glass. Found with glass rods **25/112** (ΜΕΘ 824) and amber-colored bead **25/106** (ΜΕΘ 822).

6th century B.C.

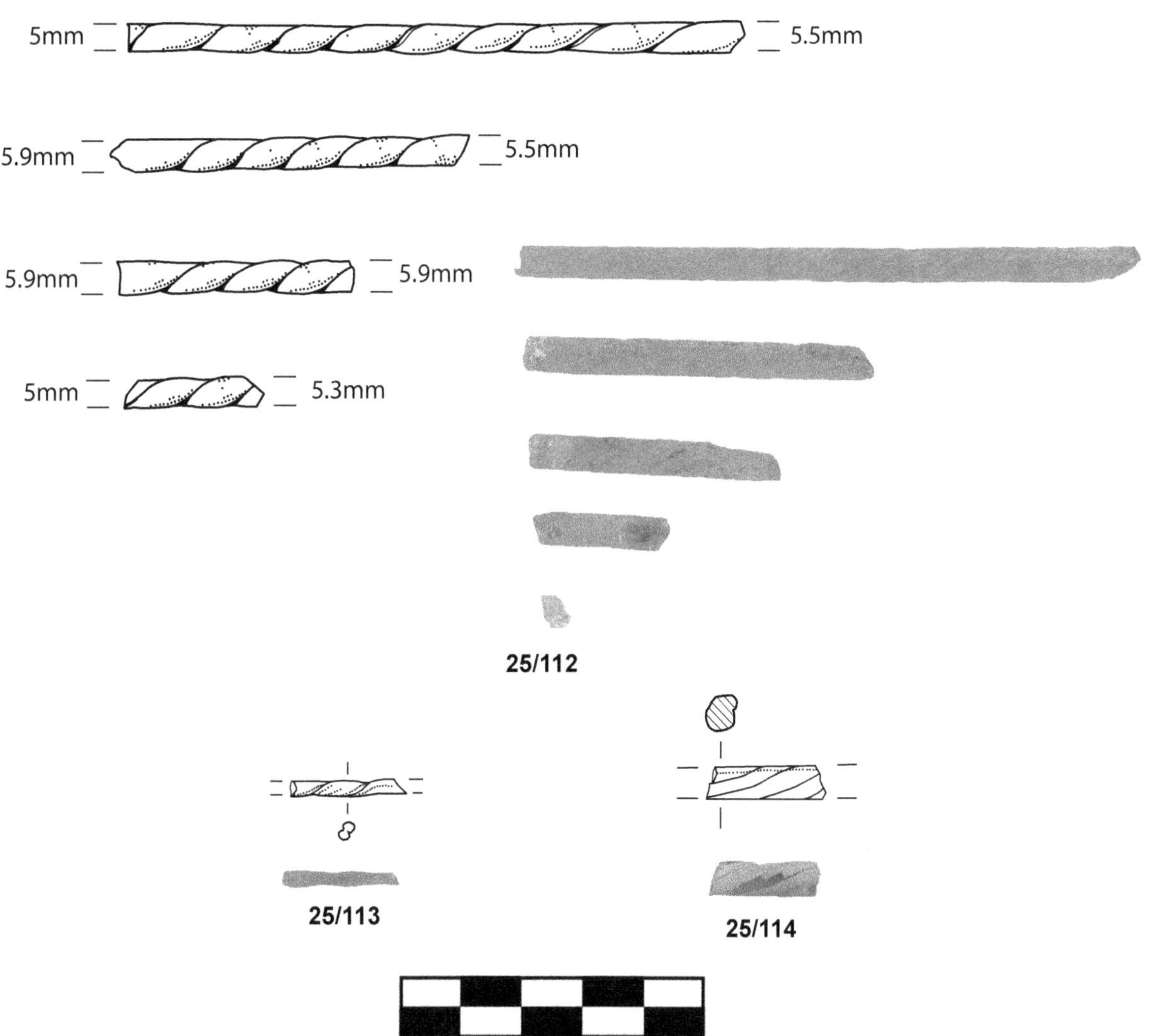

FIGURE 25.24. Glass rods, **25/112–25/114**: a–b) **25/112** (MEΘ 824); c) **25/113** (MEΘ 825); d) **25/114** (MEΘ 1909); e) **25/114** (top), **25/113** (bottom). Drawings A. Hooton, photos I. Coyle

25/114. (MEΘ 1909) Glass Rod Fig. 25.24

East Hill #274/089, central trench, 11.9.2007. West of Building A, below level of destruction deposit, along with black- and red-figure pottery, bronze pins, and workshop remains.

L. 18; Diam. 5 mm.

Surface iridescence.

Fr of slightly twisted cylindrical rod. Aqua glass.

6th century B.C.

GLASS GEM

25/115. (MEΘ 823) Glass Gem Fig. 25.25

East Hill #274/086, 6.9.2005. Building A, Room Z, final phase, along with iron pin and workshop finds.

17 x 14; Th. 6; min. Diam. (perforation) 1 mm.

Oval scaraboid gem, plano-convex with tapering vertical periphery and longitudinal perforation hole (wider on one end). Undecorated. Dark blue glass.

Before 354 B.C.

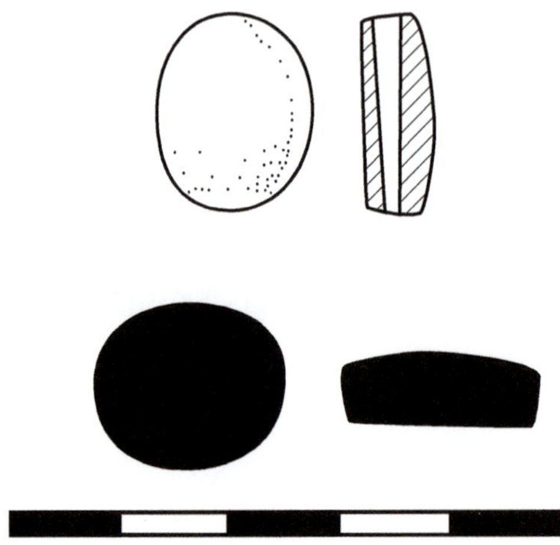

FIGURE 25.25. Glass gem from the agora, **25/115** (MEΘ 823). Drawing A. Hooton, photos I. Coyle

FIGURE 25.26. Remnants of glass object from the agora, **25/117** (MEΘ 5571). Photo J. Vanderpool

REMAINS OF GLASS OBJECTS

25/116. (MEΘ 5570) Remnants of Glass Poppy Bead or Rod — Not illust.

East Hill #274/078, west part, 31.5.2005. Plateia A, outside northwest corner of Building A, along with bronze pin, slag, and coin N 81.

Minuscule chips of aqua glass.

25/117. (MEΘ 5571) Remnants of Glass Vessel or Bead — Fig. 25.26

East Hill #274/079, southeast part, 29.8.2005. West of Building A, below destruction deposit, along with black- and red-figure pottery, and workshop finds.

Chunks of blue glass.

25/118. (MEΘ 5572) Glass Vessel or Bead (Powdered Remains) — Not illust.

East Hill #274/067, 068, 19.9.2005.

Powder of natural green glass.

25/119. (MEΘ 5575) Glass Bead (Remains)? — Not illust.

East Hill #274/089, southeast corner, 17.7.2006.

Powder of off-white glass.

THE ACROPOLIS (WEST HILL)

Core-formed Glass Vessels

25/120. (MEΘ 2986) Fr Core-formed Glass Vessel Fig. 25.27

West Hill #229/010001, 21.8.2007. Building A, east of Wall 2, surface fill.

H. 16; W. 16 mm.

Good condition, pit on the yellow thread.

Fr from shoulder and upper body of an oinochoe or amphoriskos or aryballos. Blue glass decorated with yellow thread in one wide and three narrow revolutions. Below them is the preserved tip of the turquoise zigzag edged with yellow.

5th century B.C.

25/121. (MEΘ 4268) Fr Core-formed Glass Vessel Fig. 25.27

West Hill #245/007001, 5.10.2004. Building A, surface fill.

H. 14; W. 33 mm.

Mended.

Two joining frr from shoulder and upper body of an oinochoe or amphoriskos or aryballos. Light blue translucent glass decorated with yellow thread in three wide revolutions. The thread continues as a yellow zigzag and then as a mixed-color (yellow and turquoise) zigzag in two revolutions.

5th century B.C.

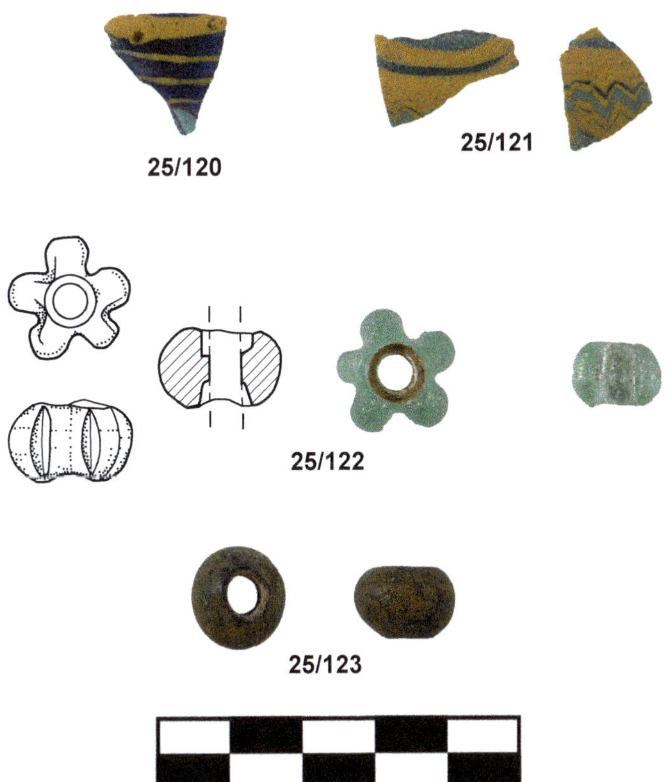

Figure 25.27. Core-formed glass vessels, **25/120** (MEΘ 2986), **25/121** (MEΘ 4268), glass poppy bead, **25/122** (MEΘ 3046), and plain glass bead, **25/123** (MEΘ 3044), from the acropolis (West Hill). Drawing A. Hooton, photos I. Coyle

Glass Poppy Bead

25/122. (MEΘ 3046) Glass Poppy Bead Fig. 25.27

West Hill #229/006, 9.6.2009. Near Building A, surface fill, stray find.
L. 11; Diam. 17; Diam. (perforation) 5–6 mm.
Complete. Small bubbles.
Five ribs. Aqua glass. Reddish remains with off-white surface inside perforation.
Archaic or Classical period.

Plain Glass Beads

25/123. (MEΘ 3044) Glass Bead Fig. 25.27

West Hill 13.4.2009, #229, Sector Γ, Pit 3.
L. 9; Diam. (perforation) 5 mm.
Intact.
Round conical. Brown glass.
Archaic period.

25/124. (MEΘ 4265) Glass Bead Fig. 25.28

West Hill #229/019031, 12.8.2011. Building B, Room 1.
L. 5; Diam. 10; Diam. (perforation) 4 mm.
Intact, with off-white corroded surface.
Round flattened. Natural green glass?
7th–early 6th century B.C.

25/125. (MEΘ 4266) Glass Bead Fig. 25.28

West Hill #229/019046, 31.8.2011. Building B, Room 1, northwest part.
L. 7; Diam. 10; Diam. (perforation) 4 mm.
Intact, with iridescence. Reddish remains with off-white surface inside perforation.
Conical. Blue glass.
7th–early 6th century B.C.

25/126. (MEΘ 4267) Glass Bead Fig. 25.28

West Hill #229/019050, 5.9.2011. Building B, Room 1, south part.
L. 3; Diam. 8; Diam. (perforation) 2 mm.
Intact, with off-white corroded surface.
Disk-shaped. Impossible to see original color of glass.
7th–early 6th century B.C.

25/127. (MEΘ 8395) Glass Bead Fig. 25.28

West Hill #229/020024, 17.8.2011. Building B, Room 2, northeast part.
L. 2; Diam. 5; Diam. (perforation) 2 mm.
Intact, local white surface corrosion.
Ring-shaped. Dark brown glass. Similar to **25/128** (MEΘ 8396).
7th–early 6th century B.C.

25/128. (MEΘ 8396) Glass Bead Fig. 25.28

West Hill #229/020014, 27.7.2011. Building B, Room 2, west part.
L. 2; Diam. 5; Diam. (perforation) 2 mm.

FIGURE 25.28. Plain glass beads from the acropolis, **25/124–25/128** (ΜΕΘ 4265, ΜΕΘ 4266, ΜΕΘ 4267, ΜΕΘ 8395, ΜΕΘ 8396). Photos I. Coyle and J. Vanderpool

Intact, with grayish corroded surface.
Ring-shaped. Impossible to see original color of glass. Similar to **25/127** (ΜΕΘ 8395).
7th–early 6th century B.C.

FAIENCE OBJECTS FROM METHONE

Two fragmentary faience objects were found in Methone. One is the curved fragment of a vessel **25/129** (ΜΕΘ 187); it was found in the Hypogeion and is of Archaic date. The other is a flat piece from an unidentifiable object **25/130** (ΜΕΘ 4978) and was found on the acropolis.[45]

25/129. (ΜΕΘ 187) Fr of Faience Vessel Fig. 25.29
East Hill, Hypogeion #274/022009, 11.6.2003. Post–Phase III.
L. x W. 14 x 18 mm.
Single fr broken on all sides.
Body fr of faience vessel. Turquoise glaze with yellow-glaze band or broader area. Off-white body.
Archaic period, 650–550 B.C.

25/130. (ΜΕΘ 4978) Faience Frr Fig. 25.29
West Hill #229, Trench Γ, pit 4, 21.8.2007.
L. x W. x Th. 46 x 18 x 8 mm.
Two joining frr preserving undetermined portion of unidentified object.
Flat as preserved. Turquoise glaze on off-white body.
Archaic.

FIGURE 25.29. Faience objects from Methone, **25/129** (MEΘ 187) (from the Hypogeion) and **25/130** (MEΘ 4978) (from the agora), and rock crystal, **25/131** (MEΘ 1078) (from the area of the agora). Photos I. Coyle

ROCK CRYSTAL FROM METHONE

Only one find of rock crystal was unearthed in Methone. It is unworked and was probably raw material to be fashioned into an object. The identification of the material, which contains approximately 90% SiO_2, was determined by XRF analysis conducted in the Archaeological Museum of Thessaloniki by the chemist Christos Katsifas.

25/131. (MEΘ 1078) Piece of Rock Crystal Fig. 25.29

East Hill, Agora #274/036007, trench between Buildings A and B, found together with Bronze Age, Archaic, and Classical pottery, and workshop finds.

L. x W. x Th. 20 x 20 x 16 mm.

Irregular shape, but with four adjacent flat surfaces.

Archaic or Classical period.

ANALYSES OF METHONE GLASS

Elissavet Dotsika, Petros Karalis, Antonio Longinelli, and Despina Ignatiadou

MATERIALS AND METHODS

In the present study eight glass samples, one natron salt sample, and a sand sample from the Pikrolimni area in central Macedonia[46] were chemically and isotopically analyzed. The artifacts analyzed originate from the Hypogeion and the agora (Table 25.2).

TABLE 25.2. Analyzed glass artifacts from Methone

Sample	Sector	Date	Artifact	Color
25/3 (ΜΕΘ 179)	Hypogeion	8th century B.C.	Triangular eye bead	Dark with opaque white spirals
25/6 (ΜΕΘ 1297)	Hypogeion	8th century B.C.	Triangular eye bead	Dark with opaque white spirals
25/18 (ΜΕΘ 338)	Agora	5th–4th century B.C.	Core-formed vessel	Blue
25/93 (ΜΕΘ 5574)	Agora	6th–4th century B.C.	Poppy bead	Aqua
25/94 (ΜΕΘ 5576)	Agora	6th–4th century B.C.	Poppy bead	Aqua
25/101 (ΜΕΘ 1072)	Agora	6th–5th century B.C.	Bead with trail	Dark green
25/106 (ΜΕΘ 822)	Agora	6th century B.C.	Biconical bead	Amber
25/112 (ΜΕΘ 824)	Agora	6th century B.C.	Glass rod	Aqua

The chemical compositions of the glass pieces were investigated using Electron Microprobe Analysis (EMPA) and X-Ray Fluorescence (XRF). The oxygen isotope ratios of the samples were measured with a FINNIGAN™ DELTA IV^{plus} Isotope Ratio Mass Spectrometer. The standard deviation of the measurements ranges on average 0.1% (2σ). The isotopic methods (^{18}O) have the potential to distinguish between different sources of the formers, fluxes, and stabilizers. The elemental and isotopic data are used for the identification of the fingerprint of raw materials and ancient glass, thus contributing to a better understanding of glass manufacture.[47]

RESULTS

The results of the chemical and isotopic analysis of the Methone glass artifacts are presented in Figure 25.30 (ternary plot of CaO vs Al_2O_3+TiO_2 vs K_2O+MgO) and Figure 25.31 (MgO vs K_2O, Na_2O vs SiO_2, CaO vs Al_2O_3, TiO_2 vs Al_2O_3, Na_2O vs $\Delta^{18}O$ and $\Delta^{18}O$). Major elemental data ranges: Na_2O (ranging from 17.5 to 20.5%), SiO_2 (ranging from 68 to 71%), MgO (ranging from 0.5 to 0.6%), K_2O (ranging from 0.1 to 0.5%), CaO (ranging from 5.7 to 9.8 %), Cl (ranging from 0.94 to 1.55%), SO_3 (ranging from 0.09 to 0.25%), Fe_2O_3 (ranging from 0.25 to 1.2%), and PO_4 (ranging from 0.04 to 0.09%). The isotopic data show $\Delta^{18}O$ values ranging from 12.2 to 17.7%. The oxygen isotopic ratio of the Pikrolimni natron and sand is 42% and 12.3% respectively.

DISCUSSION

Chemical Analysis: Hypogeion

Eye beads

Unfortunately, for samples **25/3** (ΜΕΘ 179) and **25/6** (ΜΕΘ 1297) there was not enough quantity of material for chemical analysis and only $\Delta^{18}O$ isotopic measurements were performed. They are both dark triangular beads with opaque white spirals but they show different oxygen values: 12.2% and 16%. The one with an oxygen value of 16%, **25/6** (ΜΕΘ 1297), shows an oxygen isotopic composition similar to the samples from the Archaic period (Fig. 25.32). This value suggests the use of Egyptian natron as raw material. The slightly enriched $\Delta^{18}O$ value in relation to the Pieria samples[48] can be explained by a greater addition of natron as flux to the glass batch. The other, **25/3** (ΜΕΘ 179), is a similar eye bead, with an oxygen value of 12.2%, showing a very different oxygen isotopic composition, indicating a different production procedure.

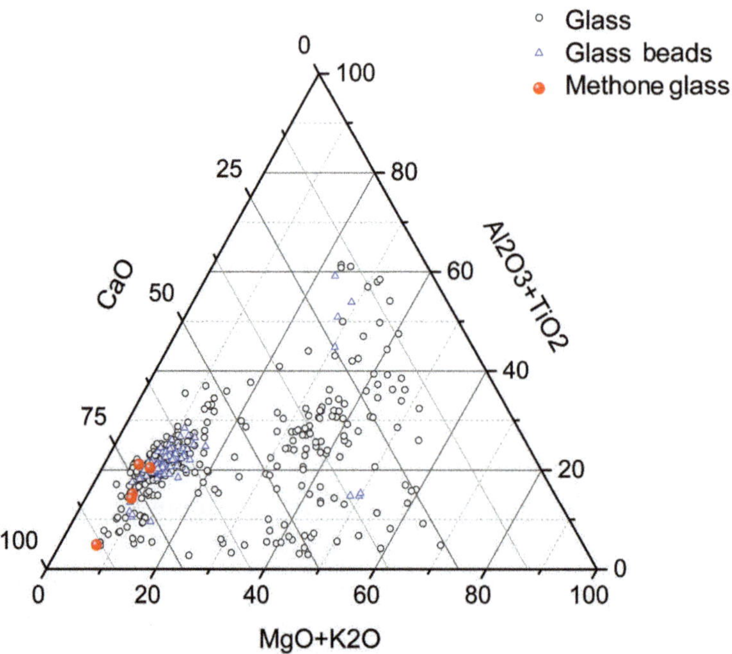

Figure 25.30. Ternary diagram of Methone glass compared with bibliographical data

Chemical Analysis: Agora

In Figure 25.31 we present the ternary plot of CaO vs. Al_2O_3+TiO_2 vs. K_2O+MgO of the Methone glass samples. In the same plot we quote the bibliographical data of Iron Age glass artifacts from Spina,[49] Bologna,[50] Mozia,[51] Aberdeenshire and Moray,[52] Cumae,[53] Pozzuoli and Chotin,[54] Sarno and Capua,[55] Adria,[56] Butrint,[57] and Pichvnari.[58] In general, the glass composition of the Methone samples is relatively homogenous and consistent with the bibliographical data.

The levels of K_2O and MgO (both less than 1.5%) of the Methone glass match those in the bibliographical data,[59] confirming that these glass objects were produced using the mineral natron (Fig. 25.31a). Furthermore, based on the analysis of soda, alumina, and lime contents, the glass samples were produced with natron and calcareous sand as the source of alkali flux and vitrifying component, respectively. This is also consistent with the detected levels of SiO_2 (Fig. 25.31b), Cl, SO_3, and PO_4, showing that Methone samples can be classified as soda-lime-silica natron-based glass.

Rod and poppy beads

One glass rod and two similar-colored poppy beads, all found in the agora, were analyzed. The rod sample was taken from the aqua glass rod **25/112** (ΜΕΘ 824) that we assume was raw glass used to fabricate the poppy beads. The two other bead samples were taken from the aqua poppy beads **25/93** (ΜΕΘ 5574) and **25/94** (ΜΕΘ 5576). In Figure 25.5c (CaO vs Al_2O_3) we demonstrate the relative homogeneity of the samples, which is also in agreement with the published data of contemporary glass artifacts found in the Mediterranean area from the 8th century B.C.[60] Furthermore, the higher soda content of **25/93** (ΜΕΘ 5574) and **25/94** (ΜΕΘ 5576) samples, in comparison to the glass rod **25/112** (ΜΕΘ 824), together with their higher isotopic signature, confirms that this glass [**25/112** (ΜΕΘ 824)] was the raw glass used to fabricate the poppy beads. The higher percentage of soda can be explained by a greater addition of natron from Wadi Natrun, or natron from Pikrolimni Lake, to the glass bath, causing enrichment of their isotopic values.

The Al_2O_3 and CaO diagram (Fig. 25.31c) also shows that the chemical data obtained for **25/93** (ΜΕΘ 5574), **25/94** (ΜΕΘ 5576), and **25/112** (ΜΕΘ 824) are also in agreement with those obtained for core-formed vessels of Mediterranean Group I (6th–5th century B.C.), originating from Spina in Italy,[61] and from Pichvnari in Georgia.[62] These data are also consistent with Roman "Levantine" glass,[63] suggesting that these three pieces from Methone were made with coastal sand from the Levant or from a similar source of sand. In conclusion, based on the soda, alumina, and lime levels, the same three samples were produced with natron and sand rich in silica, containing impurities of feldspar and carbonates,[64] as the source of alkali flux and vitrifying component respectively.

Core-formed vessel and biconical bead

One co0re-formed vessel found in the agora was analyzed. The sample was taken from the blue vessel with opaque yellow decoration **25/18** (ΜΕΘ 338), preserved in small fragments and probably dating from the 5th or 4th century B.C.

One sample was taken from the biconical bead **25/106** (ΜΕΘ 822). It is amber-colored but its surface has deteriorated to an opaque white, and it was found in the agora in a layer dating to the 6th century B.C. The content of K_2O and MgO of these samples (**25/18** [ΜΕΘ 338] and **25/106** [ΜΕΘ 822]), which is lower than 1.5%, together with the Na_2O compositions between 17.5 and 20.5 wt%, show that the analyzed glass artifacts were produced using mineral natron as the source of alkali flux. Additionally, the samples present the very low phosphorus oxide content

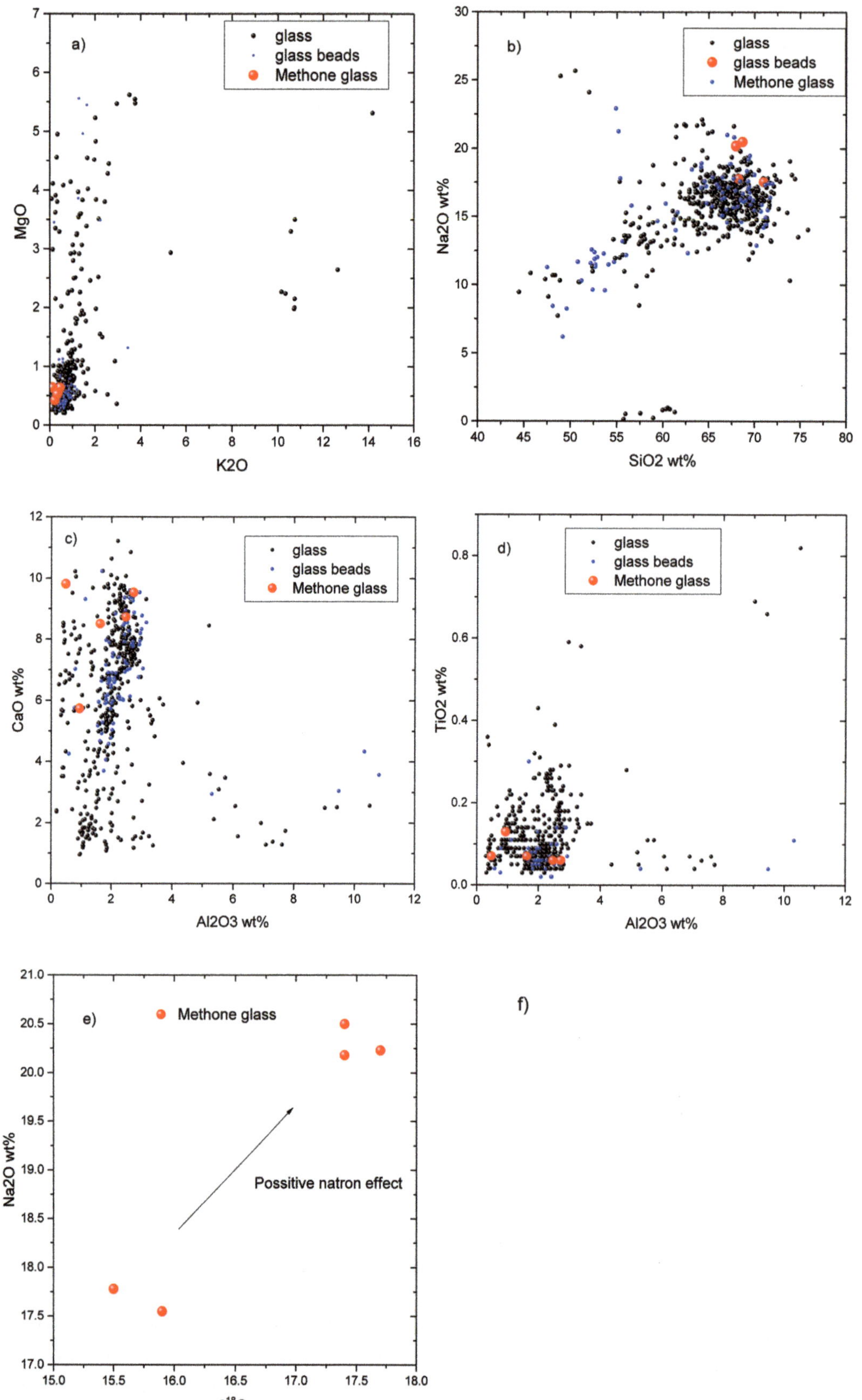

FIGURE 25.31. Methone samples against samples of contemporary glass (in general) and glass beads. K_2O versus MgO (a); Na_2O versus SiO_2 (b); Al_2O_3 vs CaO (c); Al_2O_3 versus TiO_2 (d); Na_2O versus ^{18}O (e) and $\delta^{18}O$ of samples

that is typical for glass artifacts produced with natron as fluxing agent. Furthermore, based on the low alumina levels, which range between 0.47% and 0.93%, these glass samples were produced with sand poor in feldspar as vitrifying component. The low content of Zn (<100ppm) and the high content of Sr (>300 ppm) of **25/106** (ΜΕΘ 822) suggest the use of Mediterranean coastal sand, which is rich in aragonite mineral. However, the other sample, **25/18** (ΜΕΘ 338), has different Sr (<250ppm) and Zr (>150ppm) contents, suggesting the use of inland sand containing carbonate. This is in agreement with the high content of TiO_2 (0.13%) (Fig. 25.31d), which implies the use of different sand, since titanium can be presented as accessory minerals.

The Colors of the Glass

Chemical differences are linked to the color of the samples. High levels of antimony were found in one aqua sample (> 1%, the rod, **25/112** [ΜΕΘ 824]). In contrast, the other two aqua samples, **25/93** (ΜΕΘ 5574) and **25/94** (ΜΕΘ 5576) contain lower levels of antimony (< 1%) and relatively high iron oxide contents (> 0.3%). Manganese and copper oxides were not detected in the samples, never exceeding 0.2%. Cobalt is present also in very low concentrations in two samples (**25/94** [ΜΕΘ 5576 poppy bead] and **25/18** [ΜΕΘ 338 core-formed vessel]) and none of the samples has CoO higher than 0.20%, the highest encountered in the blue sample (**25/18** [ΜΕΘ 338]). The sample **25/18** (ΜΕΘ 338) also has the higher SiO_2, TiO_2, Fe_2O_3 and CuO contents. As noted above, the major differences in the chemical composition of the samples are related to the level of antimony and iron oxide content. The aqua samples contain antimony oxide higher than 0.5% and the final colors of these samples are the result of the combination of antimony and iron oxide. It is probable that, during the raw glass production, antimony (probably in the form of an oxide) was added to a lime-rich glass batch.[65] Unfortunately, due to the small size of the samples, an X-Ray Diffraction analysis was not possible.

ISOTOPIC DATA

The Methone glass samples with oxygen ($\Delta^{18}O$) values between 15.5% and 17.7% show heterogeneous oxygen isotopic composition. Samples **25/18** (ΜΕΘ 338, core-formed vessel) and **25/112** (ΜΕΘ 824, rod) that have comparable isotopic values (15.5% and 15.9%) show different chemical compositions between them, except the Na_2O contents. The isotopic signature of these glass artifacts is in good agreement with the data glass from the bibliography, suggesting that both glasses were manufactured from similar raw material.[66]

The other samples with moderate isotopic enrichment (between 16 and 17.7%) also show variable chemical compositions, except the Na_2O and SiO_2 contents. These differences may be explained by the Positive Natron Effect (Fig. 25.31e), that is, the addition of further amounts of natron as flux to the glass batch, as suggested by their high percentages of soda. In fact, the samples with higher contents of Na_2O (**25/93** [ΜΕΘ 5574, poppy bead], **25/94** [ΜΕΘ 5576, poppy bead], and **25/106** [ΜΕΘ 822, biconical bead]) in respect to the other samples (**25/18** [ΜΕΘ 338, core-formed vessel] and **25/112** [ΜΕΘ 824, rod]) present the highest isotopic values (Fig. 25.31e). Moreover, isotopic values between 15 and 18% are very similar to the mean value of ancient glass reported in the literature. These values are very close to the value of "6th to 2nd B.C." glass reported by various scholars (Fig. 25.32).[67] These similarities may be explained by assuming that the Greek glass samples were produced with raw materials with equal or very similar oxygen isotopic composition with natron from Wadi Natrun and sand from the Levantine coast.

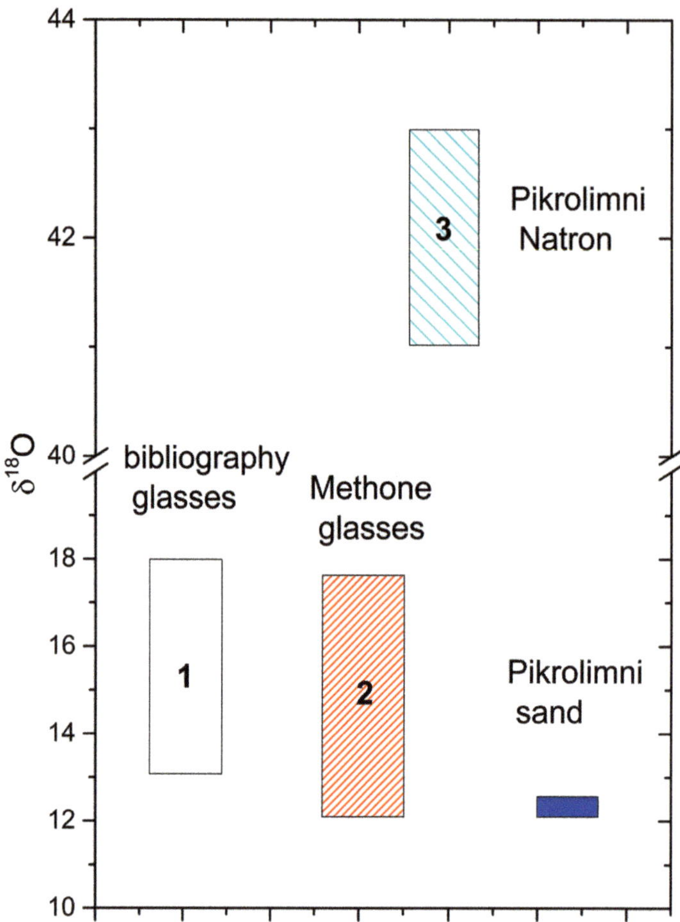

FIGURE 25.32. 1. 6th–2nd century B.C. glass in general (Brill et al., 1999); 2: 8th–4th century B.C. glass from Methone; 3: Pikrolimni natron

CONCLUSION

The possible origin of 8th- to 4th-century B.C. glass artifacts recovered at Methone was discussed on the basis of chemical and isotopic data. All glass samples could be classified as natron glass, made from a mixture of silica sand and natron.

The isotopic values show homogeneous $\Delta^{18}O$ values, ranging from 15.5% to 17.7% (VSMOW), except one sample (12.2%). These data are in good agreement with the signatures of glass artifacts from Pydna,[68] suggesting the use of identical raw materials. Samples **25/93** (MEΘ 5574, poppy bead), **25/94** (MEΘ 5576, poppy bead), and **25/106** (MEΘ 822, biconical bead) are slightly $\Delta^{18}O$ enriched. The range of $\Delta^{18}O$ values from 17.4 to 17.7%, measured on these glass objects, shows $\Delta^{18}O$ values slightly but systematically higher than in the other samples. Together with their higher percentage of soda, this can be explained by an increased addition of natron as a flux to the glass batch, showing that these three glasses may be produced by recycling glass in local secondary workshops.

The similarity of the elemental and isotopic composition of the Methone glass objects with the bibliographical data of Early Iron Age to Archaic period glass artifacts from the Mediterranean points to the potential provenance of the raw glass from the Syro-Palestinian coast. In conclusion, these glass samples from Methone can be seen as evidence for direct or indirect commercial exchange between the Near East and Greece.

NOTES

1 Glass beads have a very long history, and have also influenced the manufacture and decoration of glass vessels. On beads in general see Beck 1928; Kunter 1995; Spaer 2001.

2 On core-formed vessels in general see Grose 1989, and from Greece see Weinberg 1992; esp. McClellan 1992.

3 For an overview see Ignatiadou 2010; Ignatiadou and Athanassiadou 2012 [2017]. Furthermore, some glass finds are among other surface finds collected from the area in the past by Stamatis Tsakos and donated to the Archaeological Museum of Thessaloniki (cf. Chapter 27). These consist of four fragments of core-formed vessels, two poppy beads, part of a bracelet, and one suspension handle of a blown-glass vessel.

4 For further terminology see Ignatiadou and Antonaras 2008.

5 Grose 1989, pp. 130–131.

6 On the technique, see Spaer 2001, p. 52.

7 *Eretria* XXII, pp. 135–136, nos. 443 and 444, pl. 106.

8 Blinkenberg 1931, no. 151, with more parallels.

9 Boardman 1967, no. 552, fig. 162, pl. 95.

10 Kilian-Dirlmeier 2002, pp. 77–86, nos. 1309, 1321, 1322, 1333:d, 1336:a, 1337:e, 1338, 1339:e, 1341:a, 1342:k, 1343:a, 1347:a–b, 1348:a–b, 1349:k, 1350:b, c, 1351:h–k, 1352:Ae–f, 1352:Bb–c.

11 Trakosopoulou 2002, pp. 80–81, fig. 2.

12 Ignatiadou 2010, nos. 386–387 (A. Dimoula).

13 Grose 1989, p. 130.

14 This identification is based on macroscopic examination in combination with XRF analysis that showed it contains approximately 0.4% arsenic. The analysis was conducted in the Archaeological Museum of Thessaloniki by the chemist Christos Katsifas.

15 Beads of this type are usually called melon (or ribbed) beads, because they were considered a survival of the Egyptian Bronze Age melon beads. Those are, however, more elongated and have closer ribbing: Beck 1928, pp. 24–25.

16 Merrillees 1962; Kritikos and Papadaki 1963; Mitsopoulou-Leon 2001; Ignatiadou 2006, 2012a, 2012b.

17 E.g., a gold pendant from Argos, see Despoini 1996, no. 111.

18 Dimakopoulou 1990, no. 223 (K. Dimakopoulou).

19 For the rosette as part of the poppy seedpod, see Ignatiadou 2006. For the connection of the long petals to the poppy rosette, see Ignatiadou 2004, 2012b.

20 Containing a high amount of colorant and appearing nearly black.

21 Ignatiadou 2010, no. 443 (D. Ignatiadou).

22 Ignatiadou and Chatzinikolaou 2002, pp. 63–65, fig. 15, chart B1a; also Ignatiadou 2010, no. 307 (E. Skarlatidou).

23 Gardner and Casson 1918–1919, p. 22, fig. 16.

24 Ignatiadou 2010, no. 308 (E. Skarlatidou).

25 Ignatiadou 2010, no. 321 (K. Chavela and D. Ignatiadou).

26 Ignatiadou and Chatzinikolaou 2002, chart A5. See the same publication for references to more finds from southern Greece, but note that the earlier erroneous term "melon bead" was used. See also Skarlatidou 2007, p. 68.

27 Ignatiadou 2010, no. 87 (D. Ignatiadou). Also Ignatiadou 1993, 207–208, fig.1.

28 Ignatiadou 2010, no. 64 (P. Faklaris and V. Stamatopoulou).

29 Kilian-Dirlmeier 2002, pp. 77–86, nos. 1250:b, 1251:b, 1280:a, 1281:a, 1293:g, 1299:a, 1301:c, 1332:a, 1333:c, 1343:b, 1344:k, 1346:b–c.

30 P 1673, grave 93, see Rhomiopoulou and Touratsoglou 2002, p. 95, pl. 13, with bibliography, and also chart 1.

31 E.g., Spaer 2001, fig. 16c.

32 The two intact examples are unstratified finds, one amber-colored from the agora (**25/92** [MEΘ 4067] and one aqua but from the acropolis (**25/122** [MEΘ 3046]).

33 Also the decorated bead **25/101** (MEΘ 1072) from the agora, and the aqua poppy bead **25/122** MEΘ 3046), and the conical blue bead **25/125** (MEΘ 4266) from the acropolis.

34 Cf. Gam 1993, fig. 2.

35 Chunks of preheated raw glass could also be used in the same manner as glass rods.

36 In present-day bead-making, the source of flame is a gas burner, enhanced with air supply.

37 We owe these remarks, and the path-breaking specialized research on this subject, to Rosemarie Lierke; see Lierke 1992.

38 For Nuzi glass, see Starr 1937, pp. 53–54; Vandiver 1983.

39 Giberson 1996.

40 Similar beads were dedicated during the Late Geometric–Early Archaic period at the sanctuary of Athena Itonia in Philia, Thessaly; see Kilian-Dirlmeier 2002, pp. 77–86, nos. 1306, 1316, 1324:e, 1325:a, 1326:g, 1327:a, 1329:a, 1331:a, 1334:o, 1350:a, 1352:Ac.

41 Ignatiadou and Chatzinikolaou 2002, chart B5, p. 69.

42 Ignatiadou and Chatzinikolaou 2002, chart B.

43 Ignatiadou 2010, no. 494 (K. Kallintzi, K. Hatziprokopiou, and M. Chrysafi).

44 Grose 1989.

45 There is, in addition, one faience fragment with yellow and green glaze among other surface finds collected from the area of ancient Methone by Stamatis Tsakos and now in the Archaeological Museum of Thessaloniki.

46 See Dotsika et al. 2009, 2012.

47 Blomme et al. 2017.

48 Blomme et al. 2017.

49 Arletti et al. 2010; Arletti et al. 2011.

50 Arletti et al. 2010; Conte et al. 2016a.

51 Arletti et al. 2010; Arletti, Ferrari, and Vezzalini 2012.

52 Bertini et al. 2011.

53 Conte et al. 2016a, 2016b.

54 Conte et al. 2016a.

55 Conte et al. 2016b.

56 Panighello et al. 2012.

57 Schibille 2011.

58 Shortland and Schroeder 2009.

59 See Arletti et al. 2010, 2011; Arletti, Ferrari, and Vezzalini 2012; Bertini et al. 2011; Conte et al. 2016a, 2016b; Panighello et al. 2012; Schibile 2011; Shortland and Schroeder 2009.

60 Cf. Arletti et al. 2010, 2011; Arletti, Ferrari, and Vezzalini 2012; Bertini et al. 2011; Conte et al. 2016a, 2016b; Panighello et al. 2012; Schibile 2011; Shortland and Schroeder 2009.

61 Arletti et al. 2010.

62 Shortland and Schroeder 2009.

63 Freestone, Ponting, and Hughes 2002.

64 Sayre and Smith 1961, 1967.

65 Shortland 2002; Arletti et al. 2006a, 2006b.

66 Silvestri et al. 2010.

67 Brill et al. 1999; Silvestri et al. 2017.

68 Blomme et al. 2017.

26

METAL OBJECTS IN ARCHAIC AND CLASSICAL METHONE: ACROPOLIS AND ITS EAST SLOPE, THE AGORA, AND THE SOUTH HARBOR AREA

John K. Papadopoulos

Unlike Chapter 15, which presented a more representative selection of the metal objects from the Hypogeion, the current chapter aims to provide a summary overview of the metal objects from Archaic and Classical Methone. The material derives from four different areas of the site, covered in other sections of this volume (Chapters 1, 6, 18, 19, and 29). It begins with the metal objects from the West Hill, the acropolis of Methone, followed by those from the acropolis east slope and the small quantity of material from the more circumscribed excavations in the area of the so-called south harbor of Methone, before dealing with the more copious deposits from the agora of the settlement on the East Hill.

Given the agricultural use of the West Hill over much of the 20th century, most of the Classical layers were destroyed in this part of the site. Consequently, the material largely derives from Archaic levels, when much of the area was given over to industrial activities, including metallurgical, ceramic, ivory, and bone-working, as well as the working of glass. Some of the material, however, is clearly later, deriving either from surface deposits or from limited contexts associated with the destruction of the city by Philip II in 354 B.C. Much of the material in the agora and the south harbor area also derives from the 354 B.C. destruction of Methone and thus complements the pottery from this context presented in Chapter 29. Additional metal objects were encountered in two other contexts in the area, those from the pre-destruction collapse deposits from the higher slopes of the East Hill that subsided onto the destroyed agora at some undetermined later time, and from smaller, isolated pre-existing deposits.

The material is presented first according to the area and context from which it derives, and then by type of object, following as far as possible the categories as presented in Chapter 15. Certain types of objects, especially items of personal ornament mostly of bronze, but also categories of iron tools and weapons, together with common lead implements such as mending clamps and fishnet weights, received discussion, with comparanda, in Chapter 15. In such cases, I refer back to that discussion, offering supplementary material, especially in terms of chronology, where it is needed.

THE METAL OBJECTS FROM THE WEST HILL (ACROPOLIS) OF METHONE

As noted above, the metal objects from the West Hill mostly derive from the Archaic industrial deposits, when much of the area was given over to the various craft industries, including the working of metal, ivory and bone, glass, and the manufacture of pottery. Most of the buildings uncovered in the central portion of the excavations on the West Hill were associated with these activities, including Buildings A, B, and Γ (see Figs. 1.33, 19.1a–b). Two pottery kilns were clearly associated with Building A (Figs. 19.2–19.3). A third pottery kiln was excavated in the area just south of Buildings B and Γ, together with evidence of an ironsmithing operation, in the more recent excavations of 2014–2017.[1] From the earlier excavations at the site up to and including 2011, there were essentially two types of Archaic deposits on the West Hill.[2] The first was a mid-6th-century B.C. destruction deposit by fire that covered much of the excavated area of the West Hill. Unlike the 354 B.C. destruction deposits of Methone, which were associated with large quantities of weaponry,[3] this Archaic destruction was not clearly associated with a historical episode of violence, and may well have been the result of an industrial or domestic accident (see Fig. 19.5). Additional metal objects were found in preexisting deposits, including a number of refuse fills that are mainly of the 7th century B.C. Prominent among these preexisting deposits were a number of refuse pits, several of which yielded many of the Archaic amphoras published in Chapter 21.[4] In addition to the amphoras, this deposit brought to light some of the most magnificent examples of Archaic Corinthian, Attic, Chalkidian, East Greek, and other imported pottery.[5]

The Archaic buildings on the West Hill, together with their associated industrial deposits, overlay earlier remains. The most prominent of these were the Bronze Age tombs located primarily in the area to the south of the cluster of Buildings A–Γ, although a few tombs, including Tomb 229/3, were uncovered in the area below these buildings (Fig. 1.33). The Bronze Age tombs on the West Hill (Plot 229) extended into Plot 245 on the upper east slopes of the West Hill. These tombs, which were mainly of Late Bronze Age date with quantities of Mycenaean pottery, included a few earlier tombs (late Early Bronze Age or Middle Bronze Age date) and are fully presented in Chapter 6. The phases between the Bronze Age tombs and the Archaic industrial deposits were not extensively exposed in the initial excavations. Although Early Iron Age postholes and a few refuse pits associated with buildings of the period were uncovered in certain parts of the West Hill (e.g., Fig. 1.32), these were limited.[6] It was only in the later excavations of 2014–2017 that a fuller stratified sequence was uncovered, including deposits predating the Eretrian colonization of Methone in the late 8th century B.C.[7] A few of the metal finds were encountered in topsoil and some of these, not least the lead "branch" for the casting of sling bullets (**26/40**), are associated with the 354 B.C. siege of Methone by Philip II.

The context of each of the metal objects presented below is provided in the catalogue entry, with further commentary, as needed, in the introductory sections that precede these entries, and there is a summary as well in Table 26.1. The material is exclusively of bronze, iron, and lead. The only gold objects were encountered in the Late Bronze Age tombs (there were no silver objects). The catalogue begins with the jewelry and other items of personal ornament: pendants, fibulae, dress pins, beads, rings (not all the latter are necessarily jewelry). Although not formally an item of jewelry, the cheese grater (**26/13**)—τυρόκνηστις—presented below under "implements," is certainly a personal item, not least for any self-respecting hero.

TABLE 26.1. Summary listing the context and type of the metal objects from the West Hill at Methone. The "date" column lists the contextual date of each piece

ΜΕΘ	Metal	Context	Object	Date
26/1 (ΜΕΘ 5272)	Bronze	#229/008012	Pendant ("jug stopper")	Archaic
26/2 (ΜΕΘ 5283)	Bronze	#229/016022	Pendant	Archaic
26/3 (ΜΕΘ 5281)	Bronze	#229/007014	Arched fibula	Archaic
26/4 (ΜΕΘ 5285)	Bronze	#229/010001	"Phrygian" fibula	Archaic
26/5 (ΜΕΘ 5278)	Bronze	#229/027	Fibula a navicella	Context unclear
26/6 (ΜΕΘ 5277)	Bronze	#229/016023	Fibula a navicella	Archaic
26/7 (ΜΕΘ 5282)	Bronze	#229/015008	*Rollenkopfnadel*	Archaic
26/8 (ΜΕΘ 5280)	Bronze	#229/018007	*Rollenkopfnadel*	Archaic
26/9 (ΜΕΘ 5296)	Bronze	#229/018009	Fragmentary double pin	Archaic
26/10 (ΜΕΘ 5298)	Bronze	#229/033006	Small bead	Archaic
26/11 (ΜΕΘ 5302)	Bronze	#229/016023	Ring	Archaic
26/12 (ΜΕΘ 5295)	Bronze	#229/019011	Small ring	Surface find
26/13 (ΜΕΘ 5279)	Bronze	#229/011010	Cheese grater	Archaic
26/14 (ΜΕΘ 5288)	Bronze	#229/014001	Needle(?)	Uncertain
26/15 (ΜΕΘ 5286)	Bronze	#229/	Nail	354 B.C. destruction
26/16 (ΜΕΘ 5299)	Bronze	#229/008012	Thin rod	Archaic
26/17 (ΜΕΘ 5300)	Bronze	#229/014002	Rod (leaded?)	Archaic
26/18 (ΜΕΘ 5294)	Bronze	#229/007025	Twisted wire	Archaic
26/19 (ΜΕΘ 5297)	Bronze	#229/023001	Small strip	Undetermined
26/20 (ΜΕΘ 5287)	Bronze	#229/012011	Thin rectangular strip	Archaic
26/21 (ΜΕΘ 5305)	Bronze	#229/020008	Large sheet	Archaic
26/22 (ΜΕΘ 5273)	Bronze	#229/022001	Arrowhead	Surface find
26/23 (ΜΕΘ 5276)	Bronze	#229/019013	Arrowhead	Archaic
26/24 (ΜΕΘ 5274)	Bronze	#229/008002	Arrowhead	Uncertain
26/25 (ΜΕΘ 5275)	Bronze	#229 context unclear	Arrowhead	Uncertain
26/26 (ΜΕΘ 5284)	Bronze	#229/010014	Cone	Probably Archaic
26/27 (ΜΕΘ 4973)	Iron	#229/020010	Knife	Archaic
26/28 (ΜΕΘ 4970)	Iron	#229/008009	Axe/adze/hoe	Archaic
26/29 (ΜΕΘ 4968)	Iron	#229/010017	Pointed chisel	Archaic
26/30 (ΜΕΘ 4969)	Iron	#229/006016	Chisel fragment	Archaic
Cf. 26/30 (ΜΕΘ 4976)	Iron	#229/013001	Cf. chisels	Backfill (uncertain)
Cf. 26/30 (ΜΕΘ 4977)	Iron	#229/2007	Cf. chisels	Surface
26/31 (ΜΕΘ 4971)	Iron	#229/012 or 011	Nail	Surface (uncertain)
26/32 (ΜΕΘ 4972)	Iron	#229/016003	Axe pendant	Archaic
26/33 (ΜΕΘ 4975)	Iron	#229/	Obelos	Probably Archaic
26/34 (ΜΕΘ 4963)	Lead	#229/020010	Fishnet weight	Archaic
26/35 (ΜΕΘ 4966)	Lead	#229/ unstratified	Uncertain, clamp/plug	Archaic
26/36 (ΜΕΘ 4961)	Lead	#229/018004	Rod	Archaic
26/37 (ΜΕΘ 4960)	Lead	#229/011004	Disk	Archaic
26/38 (ΜΕΘ 4965)	Lead	#229/ unstratified	Disk	Archaic
26/39 (ΜΕΘ 5292)	Lead	#229/019003	Unidentified object	Archaic
26/40 (ΜΕΘ 4964)	Lead	#229/023001	Sling bullet "branch"	Topsoil (354 B.C.)

Objects of Bronze

Jewelry and other items of personal ornament

Pendants

The first of the pendants, **26/1**, is a classic example of what has been variously termed in the modern literature a "jug stopper," or even a "bottle stopper" (*Kannenverschluß* in German). Ironically, the earliest published examples, including one from a tomb in situ at Donja Dolina in Bosnia published in 1904, evidently attached to a belt, were clearly pendants.[8] As Michael Vickers noted, in "1932 E. J. Forsdyke thought of the objects as pendants, but with the flat studs at the lower ends pieced through a strap, and Theodore Makridis had the same idea."[9] The idea was that, although pendants, they were associated with a horse harness. The term "*Kannenverschluß*" we owe to Ulf Jantzen, who, in 1953, suggested that they were "jug stoppers," arguing that the disks or knobs were wrapped in resin-soaked cord in order to seal or stop the pouring hole of a jug.[10] Despite Vickers' noble attempt to end the notion that these objects were ever jug stoppers, the term is still in use. Even in Imma Kilian-Dirlmeier's comprehensive study of pendants in Greece from the Mycenaean to the Late Geometric period, they appear as *"Kannenverschluß"-Anhänger* ("jug stopper" pendants).[11] Such terms, when established, die hard.

As for its context, **26/1** was found in the fiery mid-6th-century B.C. destruction level on the West Hill. Although the possibility that the pendant is an earlier residual piece cannot be dismissed, a contextual date in the 7th or earlier 6th century is most likely, if not assured. That such objects were made at ancient Methone is established by a terracotta lost-wax mold from the Hypogeion for precisely this type of pendant that dates to the late 8th or early 7th century B.C. (Fig. 14.3). As Samuel Verdan notes in Chapter 14, it is generally believed that the more "naturalistic" figures at the top of these pendants are earlier than the more "schematic."[12] In terms of discerned types, **26/1** is closest to Kilian-Dirlmeier's Type B (*"Kannenverschluß"-Anhänger mit schematisiertem Hockendem auf Basis*).[13] The fact that the two examples from Methone are so well dated provides further confirmation that the type is well established by the Late Geometric and early Archaic period. This is of some importance, since the type evidently persisted well into the 5th century B.C.[14]

The fragmentary **26/2** preserves only the upper part of the pendant and its incomplete state impedes a more detailed identification. As preserved, there is a simple eyelet at the top for suspension and a beaded stem, with a lower continuum that does not survive. The context is Archaic, but a more precise date in the course of the 7th and 6th centuries B.C. is not possible. Although the upper finial of **26/2** resembles some examples of the so-called "Gestielte Glockenanhänger"—or stemmed bell pendant[15]—the fragment as preserved resembles more closely some examples of Kilian-Dirlmeier's "Geschlossene Bommeln mit einfacher Öse und unterem Fortsatz,"[16] as well as a few of the so-called "*Stabbommeln*," although the latter normally have several of the larger beads along the stem.[17]

26/1. (ΜΕΘ 5272) Bronze Pendant — Fig. 26.1

West Hill #229/008012 [12].

L. 0.087; Diam. (head) 0.013–0.014; Diam. (max) 0.015; Wt. 25.6 g.

Intact (preserved in one piece), cracked and corroded in places, but condition otherwise good.

Pendant, with lower portion consisting of four symmetrical rows of connected disks, six in each row, all four suspended from a central stem, circular in section, with a disk finial below. Upper part consists of a schematic "crouching monkey" or "thinker" or "drinker," as shown, with knees bent and arms raised to the head, which is roughly triangular-shaped, but with rounded corners.

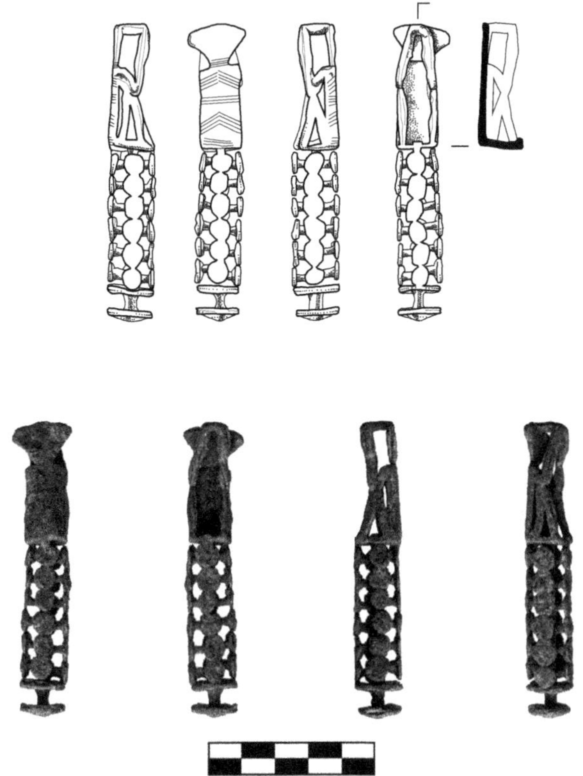

FIGURE 26.1. West Hill bronze pendant, **26/1** (MEΘ 5272). Drawing A. Hooton, photos J. Vanderpool

The back is decorated, as shown, with three sets of incised parallel horizontal bands, one in the middle, one at the juncture of shoulder and head, another at the bottom, defining two panels, each decorated with a set of parallel incised herringbone pattern. Suspension from the opening formed by the head and raised arms.

Cf. various examples in Bouzek 1974b, p. 78, fig. 23; and especially Kilian-Dirlmeier 1979, pp. 197–199, pls. 64–67, nos. 1198–1229, including a good parallel from Donja Dolina, p. 267, pl. 108, no. 12; Kilian 1975a, pl. 87, esp. nos. 30–31; Maier 1956, p. 65, fig. 1, no. 4.

Context mid-6th century B.C. destruction level.

26/2. (MEΘ 5283) Bronze Pendant Fig. 26.2

West Hill #229/016022 [22].

P.L./L. 0.046; W. (max) 0.009–0.010; Wt. 4.8 g.

Single fr preserving upper part of presumed pendant. Lower shaft too worn to determine whether broken or intact.

Top formed into an open loop or eyelet to allow suspension; below this loop four small beads, with a larger and more biconical bead at point of max. Diam. The shaft that forms the lower component, which tapers slightly toward the bottom, is also beaded; at least seven smaller beads are clearly visible.

Context suggests an Archaic date.

Related to **15/1** (MEΘ 1473), but a variant of the same type; cf. also **26/41** (MEΘ 5038) from the east slope of the West Hill and discussion related to it. Among others, cf. esp. Kilian-Dirlmeier 1979, pp. 59–60, nos. 354–367, esp. nos. 365, 363, 375–376; Kilian 1975a, pl. 80, nos. 27, 31–35, 39; Kilian-Dirlmeier 2002, pl. 60, esp. no. 927.

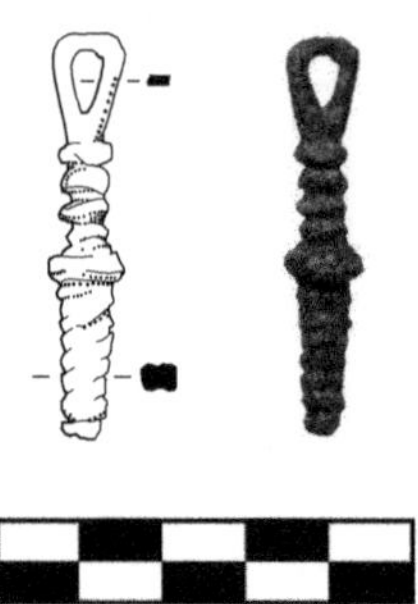

FIGURE 26.2. West Hill bronze pendant, **26/2** (ΜΕΘ 5283). Drawing A. Hooton, photos J. Vanderpool

Fibulae

Although the quantity and range of fibulae from the summit of the West Hill are not great, the fact that two of the handful of examples found there were of the Italian boat type (a navicella) is noteworthy, together with an arched fibula and a "Phrygian" fibula. The contexts of **26/3**, **26/4**, and **26/6** are Archaic; **26/5** was found on the surface, but is also clearly of Archaic date.

Arched fibula

The solitary example of an arched fibula from the West Hill, **26/3** is essentially a better-preserved example of two similar fibulae from the Hypogeion, **15/8** (ΜΕΘ 1393) and **15/9** (ΜΕΘ 1394), especially the former. The type corresponds to Blinkenberg Type II and to Sapouna-Sakellarakis Type II.[18] The arch of **26/3** is clearly symmetrical, but judging from the position of the broken catchplate, it may have had a fairly large and more triangular catchplate. This type of fibula in fully discussed in Chapter 15.

26/3. (ΜΕΘ 5281) Arched Fibula — Fig. 26.3
West Hill #229/007014 [14].
L. 0.040; H. 0.027; Wt. 2.3 g.
Almost complete, except for the lower portion of the catchplate and the tip of the pin.
Small arched fibula, with shaft circular in section. Catchplate, as preserved, hammered flat and spreading; judging from what survives, it would have been comparatively large. Spring one turn.
Context Archaic.
Cf., among others, **26/44** (ΜΕΘ 5039); cf. also Raubitschek 1999, p. 157, pl. 65, no. M5 (in *Isthmia* VIII, pl. 65, no. M5, 8th century B.C. = *Isthmia* VII, p. 52, pl. 35, no. 198); Kilian-Dirlmeier 2002, pl. 15, nos. 251–260.

"Phrygian" fibula

The fibula **26/4** is especially close to **15/14** from Phase I of the Hypogeion. The basic type corresponds to Blinkenberg's Type XII 12 and XII 13 (= Muscarella Type XII, 12, 13), and finds especially close parallels among some of the Aegean islands and a few from Gordion. The type is more fully discussed in Chapter 15 and among the many more examples of the type from the agora of Methone below.

26/4. (ΜΕΘ 5285) "Phrygian" Fibula — Fig. 26.3
West Hill #229/010011 [11].
P.L./L. 0.026; H. 0.022; Wt. 3.5 g.
Single fr, corroded, preserving most of arch and catchplate, but nothing of the spring or pin.

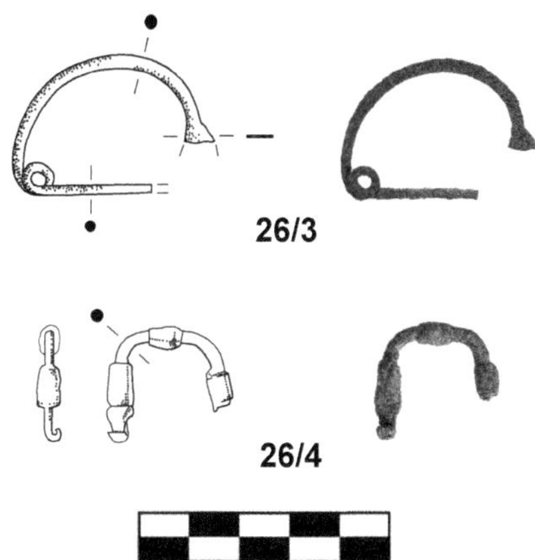

FIGURE 26.3. West Hill bronze fibulae, arched fibula **26/3** (MEΘ 5281), "Phrygian" fibula **26/4** (MEΘ 5285). Drawings A. Hooton and F. Skyvalida, photos I. Coyle and J. Vanderpool

Fibula more Π-shaped than arched, with three prominent beads, one on the horizontal arm, one on each of the vertical arms; beads undecorated. Catchplate hammered flat and curved up.

Context Archaic.

Cf. esp. **15/14** (MEΘ 1392), and discussion and comparanda there cited. Cf., among others, Sapouna-Sakellarakis 1978, p. 127, pl. 52, nos. 1657 (Samothrace) and 1659 (Chios); pl. 53, nos. 1661 (Chios), 1676–1677 (Ialysos); for related examples primarily, but not exclusively, from Gordion, see Caner 1983, pp. 86–87, pl. 37, Variante C 1,1, esp. nos. 479–482.

Fibula a navicella

The two boat fibulae presented below, **26/5** and **26/6**, are close to **15/16** from the Hypogeion. As discussed at greater length in Chapter 15, the fibula a navicella is a classic Italian type, found in over 50 variants.[19] The earliest examples on the Italian Peninsula are assigned to the 8th century B.C., with most dating to the 7th and 6th centuries B.C., and only a few lasting into the earliest 5th century. The basic type corresponds to Blinkenberg's Type XI 6–7, and with Type XId of Sapouna-Sakellarakis, who illustrates examples from Lindos and Exochi on Rhodes, as well as from Samos, Emporio, and Aigina.[20]

26/5. (MEΘ 5278) Bronze Fibula a Navicella — Fig. 26.4

West Hill #229/027. Surface find.

P.L. 0.030; W. (max) 0.017; Wt. 4.1 g.

Single fr, corroded, preserving most of bow, but nothing of the spring, catchplate, or pin.

Solid bow/arch, concave on interior as shown, imitating a schematic form of a boat; one small knob on either side at point of max. W. Four light incised parallel lines at either end, one near spring, the other near the catchplate.

Context gives no clue as to date of this piece, though the type is best accommodated in the Archaic period on the basis of Italian comparanda, and the date of **26/6** (MEΘ 5277) is clearly Archaic, and the date of **15/16** (MEΘ 1510) is probably 7th century B.C.

Cf. **15/16** (MEΘ 1510) and **26/6** (MEΘ 5277).

26/6. (MEΘ 5277) Fibula a Navicella — Fig. 26.4

West Hill #229/016023 [23].

P.L. (= L. of bow or arch) 0.036; W. (max.) 0.019; Wt. 6.5 g.

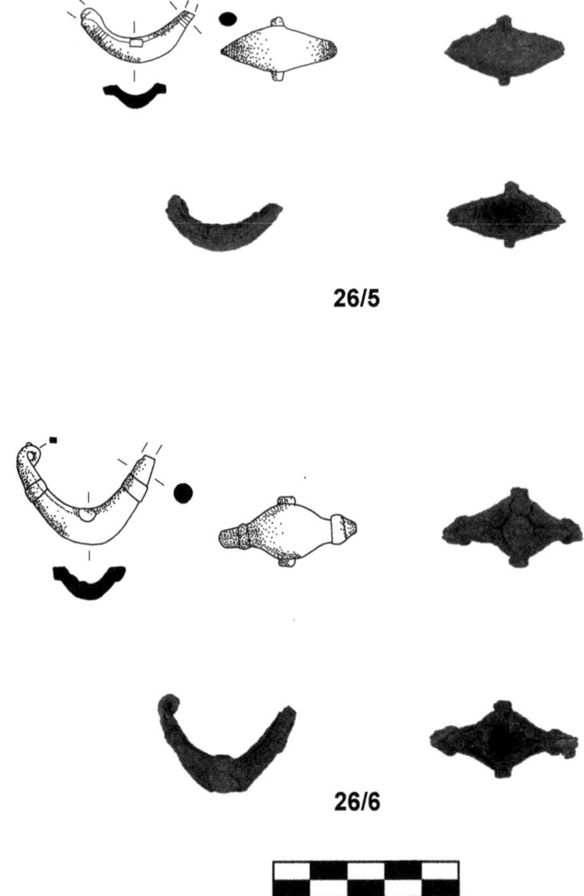

FIGURE 26.4. West Hill bronze fibulae a navicella, **26/5** (MEΘ 5278), **26/6** (MEΘ 5277). Drawings F. Skyvalida, photos I. Coyle

Two joining frr, corroded and cracked, preserving all of bow/arch and portion of fibula spring. Catchplate and pin not preserved.

Solid bow/arch, concave on interior as **26/5** (MEΘ 5278), in imitation of a boat; small knob on either side at point of max. W. Thin and narrow applied sheet of bronze on either side near the terminals (instead of incised parallel lines as on **26/5** [MEΘ 5278]). Spring at least two turns.

Context Archaic.

Cf. **15/16** (MEΘ 1510) and **26/5** (MEΘ 5278).

Dress pins

There are only two different type of dress pin from the early excavations on the West Hill: the Rollenkopfnadel, of which there are two examples, **26/7** and **26/8**, and a fragmentary double pin, **26/9**.

Rollenkopfnadeln

Although the ubiquitous dress pin with rolled head enjoys a venerable history from the Chalcolithic into the Classical period and beyond, the context of both **26/7** and **26/8** is Archaic. This type of dress pin is fully discussed in Chapter 15, with comparanda, including Bronze Age examples (cf. also **6/16**, from a Bronze Age tomb), assembled under **15/18–15/20**.

26/7. (MEΘ 5282) *Rollenkopfnadel* Fig. 26.5

West Hill #229/015008 [8].

P.L. 0.067; Diam. (head) 0.008; Wt. 2.9 g.

Three joining frr preserving entire head and portion of shaft of pin; pin tip not preserved.

Standard *Rollenkopfnadel*, with shaft circular in section, tapering slightly toward point, which is not preserved. Head hammered flat and rolled.

Although *Rollenkopfnadeln* are found from the Chalcolithic, and continue well into the Classical period and beyond, the context of this piece is Archaic.

Context Archaic.

Cf. **15/18** (MEΘ 1418), **15/19** (MEΘ 1403), and **15/20** (MEΘ 1434). Also Casson 1919–1921, pp. 15–16, fig. 11 (middle left).

26/8. (MEΘ 5280) Small *Rollenkopfnadel* Fig. 26.5

West Hill #229/018007 [7].

L. (as bent) 0.055; L. (original) 0.062; Wt. 2.0 g.

Complete, but bent.

Small pin, with shaft circular in section tapering to well-preserved point. Head hammered flat, rectangular in section, and rolled.

Context Archaic.

Cf. **26/7** (MEΘ 5282).

Additional *Rollenkopfnadel* from the West Hill

(ME 230) West Hill #229/015010 [10] Pit 8 (context Archaic). Three joining frr.

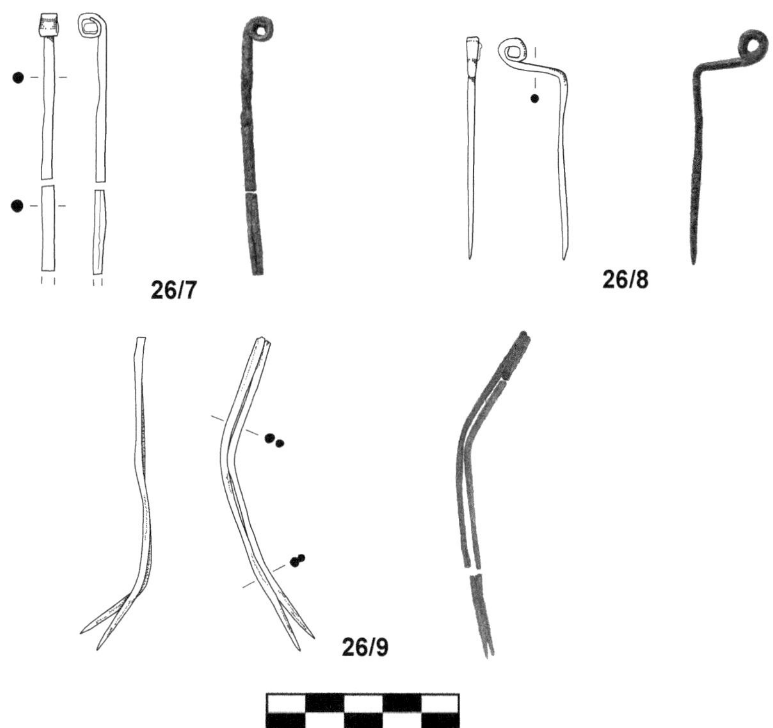

FIGURE 26.5. West Hill bronze dress pins, *Rollenkopfnadeln*, **26/7** (MEΘ 5282), **26/8** (MEΘ 5280), fragmentary double pin **26/9** (MEΘ 5296). Drawings A. Hooton and T. Ross, photos I. Coyle and J. Vanderpool

Fragmentary double pin

Given its fragmentary state, especially the missing head and the tips of both terminals, little can be said of **26/9**. That the fragment, as preserved, is from a double pin and not some other type of object is clear enough, as is its mid-6th-century B.C. date. This type of pin will be discussed in more detail below (under **26/77** and **26/78**). Given the manner in which the two shafts are preserved, **26/9** is probably of the type represented by **26/77** (ΜΕΘ 1611).

26/9. (ΜΕΘ 5296) Fragmentary Bronze Double Pin — Fig. 26.5

West Hill #229/018009 [9], mid-6th-century destruction level.

P.L. 0.080; Wt. 1.7 g.

Three joining frr preserving much of the pin shafts, but little of the head and nothing of the tips. Corroded.

Thin continuous bronze wire, round in section, formed into a double pin, as shown.

Mid-6th century B.C. or earlier.

Cf. **26/77** (ΜΕΘ 1611) and **26/78** (ΜΕΘ 1613).

Bead

Despite its small size and unprepossessing form, **26/10** is a full-fledged bead, with a diameter of 0.007–0.008 and a height of 0.004 m, rectangular to plano-convex in section. Although such small beads are more common in glass or faience, bronze examples are known, and a few of these are cited in the catalogue entry below.[21]

26/10. (ΜΕΘ 5298) Small Bronze Bead — Fig. 26.6

West Hill #229/033006 [6].

Diam. 0.007–0.008; H. 0.004; Wt. 0.6 g.

Intact, but heavily corroded.

Small round bronze bead, rectangular to plano-convex in section.

Context Archaic.

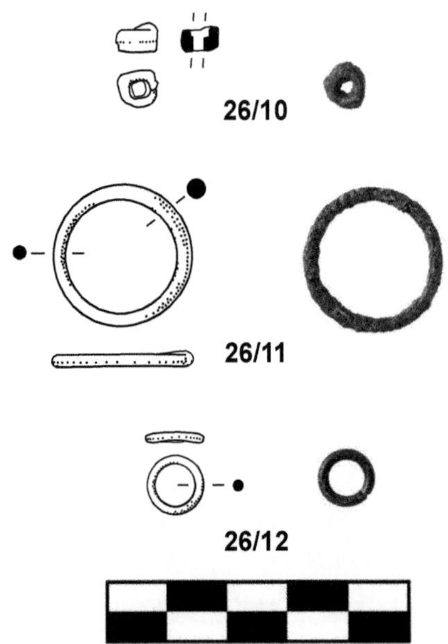

FIGURE 26.6. West Hill bronze bead, **26/10** (ΜΕΘ 5298), bronze rings/*krikoi*, **26/11** (ΜΕΘ 5302), **26/12** (ΜΕΘ 5295). Drawings A. Hooton, photos J. Vanderpool

Cf., among others, Kilian 1975a, p. 201, pl. 75, esp. no. 21, from Pherai, which is only fractionally larger than **26/10**; Felsch 2007, pp. 333–334, pl. 45, esp. nos. 1452–1453, 1466, 1469–1471. Note also Kilian-Dirlmeier 2002, p. 159, pl. 164, nos. 2651–2659, where they are classified as "*Blechringchen*," i.e., small to minuscule rings made of sheet metal. Cf. the similarly small bronze rings with faience/ glass inserts, **26/87** (ΜΕΘ 1650 α).

Rings/*krikoi*

Finger or signet rings, known as δακτύλιος in Greek, which are items of jewelry, are fully discussed in Chapter 15, as are κρίκοι, or rings of various shapes and sizes that are not clearly items of personal ornament, and which functioned in a variety of ways (Greek literature from as early as Homer was full of references to κρίκοι and their various functions). Of the two selected examples from the West Hill, the context of **26/11** is Archaic, whereas **26/12** was a surface find that cannot be dated precisely. **26/11**, evidently cast in one piece, with the band round in section, is certainly in the size range to be worn as a finger ring. In contrast, **26/12**, which is clearly open-ended without overlaps, is too small to have been worn on the finger, although it may have been associated with some other item of jewelry.

26/11. (ΜΕΘ 5302) Bronze Ring — Fig. 26.6
West Hill #229/016023 [23].
Diam. 0.023; H. 0.002; Wt. 1.5 g.
Complete, corroded.
Ring band round in section, probably cast in one piece. Probably a finger ring.
Context Archaic.

26/12. (ΜΕΘ 5295) Small Ring — Fig. 26.6
West Hill #229/019011 [11]. Surface find.
Diam. 0.009–0.010; H. 0.002; Wt. 0.4 g.
Intact.
Small bronze ring, round in section and clearly open-ended, though with no overlaps.
Not clearly an item of jewelry, though it may have been suspended from another item of jewelry, such as a necklace.

Implements and other bronzes

Cheese grater

The poorly preserved fragments of **26/13** derive from a cheese grater—τυρόκνηστις—of Archaic date. Greek literature is replete with references to such graters, and it was passages in Aristophanes that prompted Paul Jacobsthal to publish the first list of some 60 graters in 1932.[22] In a similar vein, Athenaios has Anaxippos enumerate various kitchen utensils: "Bring a soup ladle, a dozen skewers, a meat hook, mortar, small cheese scraper, skillet, three bowls, a skinning knife, four cleavers . . . ."[23] But the earliest and most critical passage is in Homer's *Iliad* (11, 680–683), the action taking place in the camp of the Greeks, specifically in Nestor's hut:

Into the cup [of Nestor] Hekamede, beautiful as a goddess,
Poured Pramnian wine, grated goat cheese into it
With a brazen grater, and sprinkled white barley on top.
She motioned them to drink . . .[24]

In addition to the literary evidence, a number of Boiotian terracotta figurines depict the use of graters.[25] Since Jacobsthal's 1932 paper, the number of cheese graters has expanded greatly. The earliest examples include three from Lefkandi, two dating to SPG II (875–850 B.C.), the third to SPG IIIa (850–800 B.C.).[26] There is also a Geometric example in bronze from Eretria, classified as a strainer (*passoire?*), that could be a grater.[27] Archaic and later examples were sometimes dedicated at Greek sanctuaries, such as at Pherai, Philia, and Kalapodi in Thessaly and central Greece,[28] Olympia and Perachora,[29] and various Aegean islands, including Samos, Lindos, Paros, and Aigina.[30] Early Italian examples have been assembled by David Ridgway, those from dated contexts all 7th century, and mostly 675–650 B.C., a date that agrees nicely with **26/13.**[31] Archaic graters from Morgantina and elsewhere on Sicily are noted by Claire Lyons, and at Selinunte graters were represented from the earliest (Archaic) levels into the 4th and 3rd centuries B.C.[32] Similar graters from Olynthos establish their continued use into the Classical period and beyond.[33] Several fragments of Classical or Hellenistic date from Stymphalos are referred to as "screens," although the possibility of their serving as cheese graters is noted.[34]

26/13. (ΜΕΘ 5279) Cheese Grater Frr — Fig. 26.7
West Hill #229/011010 [9].
Dimensions of largest fr: 0.039 x 0.019; Wt. (all frr) 3.4 g.
Five frr in all (four illustrated); although preserved in small broken frr, what survives is in relatively good condition.
Thin sheet bronze perforated in such a way as to serve as a grater. The preserved edge of the largest fr is clearly curved, as opposed to straight.
Context Archaic.

Needle(?)

Little can be said of **26/14.** I present it as a possible needle on account of the clear concave articulation at the broken end opposite the tapering point that may form the eye of a needle. Found on the surface of the West Hill, the piece cannot be dated, but its bronze composition, as determined by pXRF, is the same as that of the other ancient bronzes. Although fragmentary, its size suggests that, if a needle, it is a large one.[35] Discussion, with comparanda, for the two basic types of needles from the Hypogeion at Methone is provided in Chapter 15, under **15/45** and **15/46.**

26/14. (ΜΕΘ 5288) Bronze Needle? — Fig. 26.7
West Hill #299/014001 [1]. Surface find.
P.L. (as bent) 0.054; Wt. 4.2 g.
Single fr, bent out of shape, with both ends broken.
Shaft circular in section, tapering clearly toward one side to point, the tip itself not preserved. Opposite end preserves a clear concave articulation, which looks intentional, but perhaps broken in this way. If intentional, the object is a needle.
Context uncertain.
Cf., among others, esp. Kilian-Dirlmeier 2002, pl. 169, notably larger examples like nos. 2843–2844.

Nail

Found at the opening of one of the Methonaian defensive tunnels dug to provide active defense against Philip II and to bring in supplies, the context is clearly mid-4th century B.C. Bronze nails of various forms and sizes of Archaic and Classical date are known from both Greek sanctuaries and tombs.[36] Classical and Hellenistic examples from the Athena Itonia sanctuary near Philia in

Thessaly are especially close to **26/15**.[37] A good series of bronze nails and the larger nails referred to as spikes from Isthmia, mostly of Classical and Hellenistic date, are presented by Isabelle Raubitschek.[38] In discussing these, Raubitschek notes that bronze nails were manufactured from cast bronze rods that were cut to the desired length with the head formed from that part of the rod which projected beyond the anvil.[39] Similar bronze nails, tacks, and spikes have been found at many other sites in Greece.[40]

26/15. (ΜΕΘ 5286) Nail Fig. 26.7

West Hill #229. Sector A, defensive tunnel, south opening/entrance.

L. 0.045; Diam. (head) 0.009; Wt. 4.9 g.

Intact, condition quite good.

Small but sturdy bronze nail, with plain round/disk head, and shaft mostly square/rhomboidal in section, tapering toward point.

Context mid-4th century B.C. destruction of Methone.

Cf., among others, Kilian-Dirlmeier 2002, pp. 124–125, pl. 115, nos. 1901–1905; *Isthmia* VII, pp. 134–135, 140, pl. 77, nos. 499–503 (for Classical and Hellenistic bronze nails); also pl. 78, nos. 507–508 (for the larger Classical and Hellenistic bronze spikes); *Selinus* V, p. 149, pl. 47, no. 921 (dated to the second half of the 5th century B.C.).

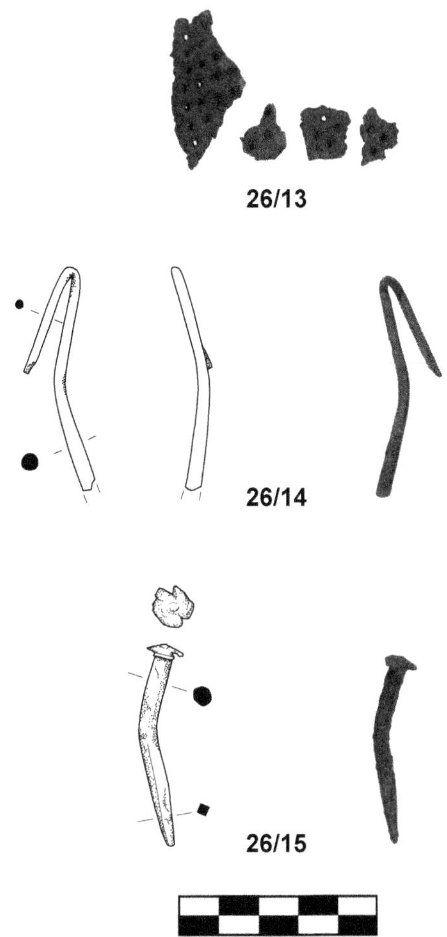

FIGURE 26.7. Various bronze implements from the West Hill: cheese grater **26/13** (ΜΕΘ 5279), needle(?) **26/14** (ΜΕΘ 5288), nail **26/15** (ΜΕΘ 5286). Drawings T. Ross, photos I. Coyle

Bronze rods, strips, and wire

Three of the pieces presented below are Archaic in date (**26/16–26/18**) and one is of uncertain date as it was found in topsoil (**26/19**). **26/16** is a thin bronze rod, square in section. The shaft of the rather heavier leaded bronze rod **26/17** is rhomboid in section, thicker in the middle, and bent. **26/18** is a length of twisted bronze wire, not unlike **15/61**. In contrast, **26/19** is a thin strip of bronze. Comparanda to similar pieces from the Hypogeion are given in the entries below, except for **26/17**, which finds no clear parallels.

26/16. (MEΘ 5299) Thin Bronze Rod Fig. 26.8
West Hill #229/008012.
P.L. (as bent) 0.072; L. (measured with string) 0.113; Wt. 5.7 g.
Bent out of shape; unclear whether either end is original or broken.
Thin rod, roughly square in section. As preserved, one end appears intact, the other probably broken.
Context Archaic.
This is a thinner version of the bronze rod **15/64** (MEΘ 4121) from the Hypogeion.

26/17. (MEΘ 5300) Leaded Bronze Rod Fig. 26.8
West Hill #229/014002 [2].
P.L. (as bent) 0.066; Wt. 13.3 g.
Complete, except for terminals.
Shaft rhomboid in section, thicker in the middle, tapering noticeably toward point (not preserved); bent at opposite end, and evidently hammered flat (probably broken at this point).
High lead content (determined by pXRF).
Context Archaic.

26/18. (MEΘ 5294) Twisted Bronze Wire Fig. 26.8
West Hill #229/007025 [25], Pit 16.
P.L. 0.059; p.W. (of object, as preserved) 0.023; Wt. 5.0 g.
Single fr preserving unknown portion of original object. Condition quite good.
Two strands of thin bronze wire, both square to rectangular in section, twisted together, as shown. The resultant form resembles, but is not, a double pin (like **26/9** [MEΘ 5296]).
Context Archaic.
Cf. **15/61** (MEΘ 4135) and comparanda cited there.

26/19. (MEΘ 5297) Small Strip of Bronze Fig. 26.8
West Hill #229/023001. Topsoil.
L. (as bent) 0.037; W. (max.) 0.006; Wt. 0.9 g.
Evidently intact, but misshaped. Condition poor (reinforced with Japanese tissue).
Thin strip of bronze, bent over at one end; opposite end thinner, evidently hammered flat.
Context undetermined (topsoil).
Cf. **15/68** (MEΘ 1517).

Bronze sheet

The two pieces of bronze sheet from the West Hill both derive from Archaic contexts, **26/20** specifically from the mid-6th century B.C. destruction deposit. Neither piece preserves perforations, unlike **15/70** and **15/71**, which would qualify them as elements of binding sheaths. Similar bronze sheet, perforated and unperforated, is discussed, and comparisons cited, above in Chapter 15 (see **15/70–15/74**).

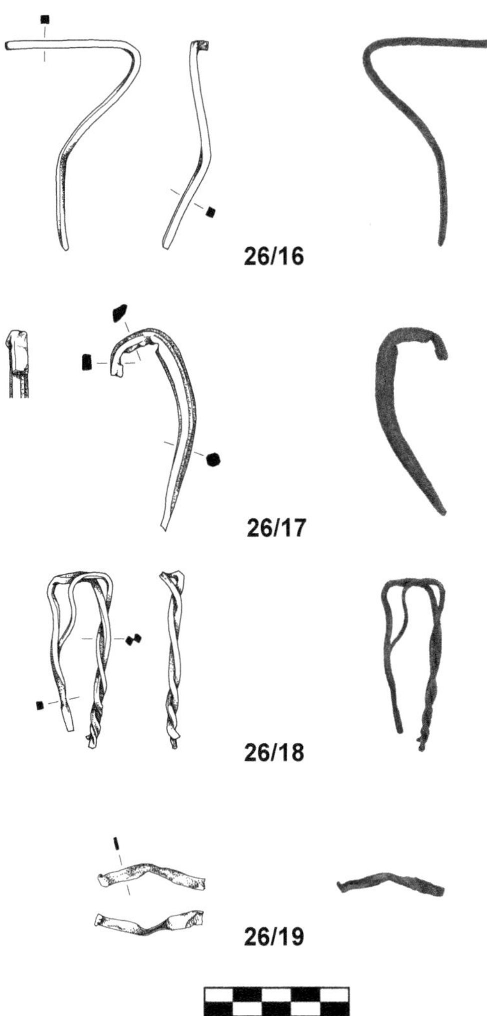

FIGURE 26.8. West Hill bronze rods, strips, and wire, **26/16** (ΜΕΘ 5299), **26/17** (ΜΕΘ 5300), **26/18** (ΜΕΘ 5294), **26/19** (ΜΕΘ 5297). Drawings T. Ross, photos I. Coyle

26/20. (ΜΕΘ 5287) Thin Strip/Sheet — Fig. 26.9

West Hill #229/012011 [11]. Mid-6th century B.C. destruction level.

P.L./L. 0.039; W. 0.013; Wt. 3.6 g.

Single fr preserving what may be a complete strip or small sheet of bronze. The two long edges are original, as is one of the shorter edges; other short edge is less certain. What appear as small dots on the surface of both sides are corrosion, not decoration.

Thin rectangular sheet or strip of bronze, tapering very slightly toward one end.

Mid-6th century B.C. or earlier.

26/21. (ΜΕΘ 5305) Large Fr Sheet Bronze — Fig. 26.9

West Hill #229/020008 [8].

P.H. 0.067; W. 0.045; Wt. 11.5 g.

Single fr, cracked (reinforced with Japanese tissue). Broken at both shorter ends; longer edges are original.

Thin sheet, roughly rectangular, as preserved, hammered flat.

Context Archaic.

Weapons

Arrowheads

Although I have catalogued only four arrowheads from the summit of the West Hill for this volume, their variety, especially in terms of size, is interesting. As for their date, as tempting as it is to see them as the weaponry of Philip's siege of 354 B.C., whether Macedonian or Methonaian, at least one, **26/23**, is clearly earlier, as it was found in the mid-6th-century B.C. destruction deposit. Two of the arrowheads (**26/22** and **26/24**) were found on the surface or in topsoil, and the context of **26/25** was not informative as to date.

All of the arrowheads presented below are socketed and accord with Snodgrass Type 3 arrowheads. The largest of the West Hill arrowheads, and probably one of the largest of the bronze arrowheads at Methone, **26/22**, best accords with Anthony Snodgrass's Type 3A3, although the solitary example illustrated by Snodgrass has a longer socket, and **26/22** with its form, including "blood channels," is more complex.[41] For Type 3A3, Snodgrass states: "This comparatively unusual variant was considered by Weber to be a Greek type," and he concludes by noting: "It was probably an archaic type which was later replaced by the more efficient three-edged heads."[42] He notes its rarity farther east, occurring only in Cyprus and Egypt, although it was known at northern sites from the Russian steppe to Bavaria. In Greece, Snodgrass cites examples from Olympia, Marathon, and Perachora, and in Sicily.[43]

The earliest of the four arrowheads from the West Hill, **26/23**, is a barbed three-edged socketed arrowhead of Snodgrass's Type 3B4. This type is known from as early as the 7th century, extending into the late 4th century B.C.; an example from Gordion may be as late as Hellenistic.[44] Its context at Methone may suggest that it is among the earliest examples of this type in Greece. The smaller **26/24** and **26/25** are closely related to **26/23**, and they are both good examples of Snodgrass's Type 3B5, which are also barbed, three-edged socketed arrowheads, but differ from Type 3B4 in that the socket lacks a shaft, what Snodgrass refers to as a "barbed interior socket."[45] In dealing broadly with Types 3B4 and 3B5, Snodgrass writes: "Perachora, Delos, Olympia, and Cyrene provide some likely archaic examples; Marathon and Aegina may testify to its use in the Persian Wars; at Vouni in Cyprus examples date from about 500–450, while the Olynthos finds show that it was used (perhaps exclusively) by the Macedonian royal archers in the mid-fourth century."[46]

26/22. (MEΘ 5273) Bronze Arrowhead — Fig. 26.10

West Hill #229/022001 [1]. Surface find (topsoil).

L. 0.053; W. (max): 0.018; Diam. (socket): 0.009; Wt: 11.4 g.

Complete, except for tiny chips; condition otherwise quite good.

Thin blade with central thickening running the length of the arrowhead, with a small groove ("blood channel") on one side. Two small barbs on either side. Small round tang, not very deep, rather than a socket, which must surely be broken as there is no other means of attachment. The tang extends to form the conical thickening at the juncture with the blade.

This is one of the largest arrowheads from Methone.

Type should be of Archaic date.

26/23. (MEΘ 5276) Bronze Arrowhead — Fig. 26.10

West Hill #229/019013 [13].

L. 0.031; W. (max.) 0.011; Diam. (socket) 0007–0.008; Wt. 3.5 g.

Intact, slightly chipped here and there.

Triangular three-barbed arrowhead, with prominent round socket extending well below the blade/head (the socket of **26/24** [MEΘ 5274]) does not extend this far).

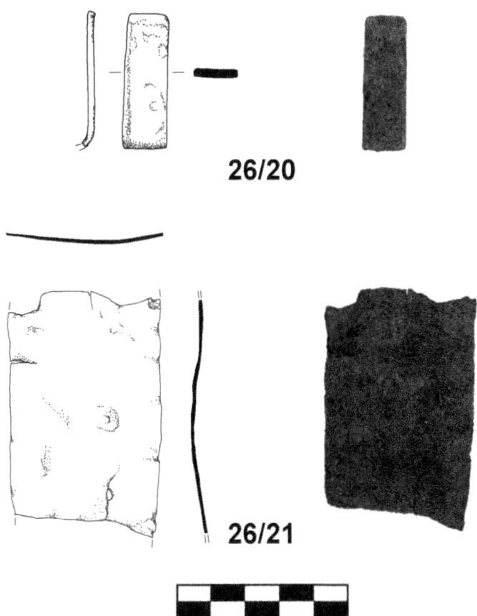

FIGURE 26.9. West Hill bronze sheet, **26/20** (MEΘ 5287), **26/21** (MEΘ 5305). Drawings T. Ross, photos I. Coyle

Cf. **26/24** (MEΘ 5274); and, among many others, Boardman 1967, pp. 226–227, fig. 148, no. 406.
Context mid-6th-century B.C. destruction level.

26/24. (MEΘ 5274) Bronze Arrowhead Fig. 26.10
#229/008002 [2]. Topsoil.
L. 0.017; W. 0.008–0.009; Diam. (socket) 0.006; Wt. 1.6 g.
Intact, but slightly damaged out of shape.
Small triangular three-barbed arrowhead, with small round socket.
Context uncertain.
Cf. **26/25** (MEΘ 5275); also Boardman 1967, pp; 226–227, fig. 148, no. 405; *Torone* I, p. 729, fig. 171, no. 18.16; Kilian-Dirlmeier 2002, pl. 110, no. 1779 (Classical).

26/25. (MEΘ 5275) Bronze Arrowhead Fig. 26.10
West Hill #229/Sector A.
L. 0.020; W. (max.) 0.007; Diam. (socket) 0.005; Wt. 1.8 g.
Complete, except for chipping and flaking.
Small three-barbed arrowhead, triangular in shape, with small round socket.
Cf. **26/24** (MEΘ 5274).
Context undetermined.

Cone

I do not know what function these small cones served. They are made of a thin sheet of bronze hammered flat and formed into a cone, resembling in shape a dunce's cap. Similar small cones are common all over the site, from the agora area on the East Hill (e.g., **26/122** [MEΘ 1784], **26/123** [MEΘ 295], **26/124** [MEΘ 296], **26/125** [MEΘ 299], **26/126** [MEΘ 2138]), and even on the surface of the site as found by the 2014 pedestrian surface survey.[47] In the area of the agora, similar cones are found both in the destruction deposits of 354 B.C. and in pre-destruction layers, and a related object from the Hypogeion, **15/55** (MEΘ 1504), was noted as a possible, but uncertain, arrowhead. The fact that they are found from as early as the Late Geometric or early

Archaic period into the mid-4th century B.C. is certainly interesting, and in light of the quantity of real arrowheads from the site in bronze and iron, their interpretation as arrowheads seems most unlikely. Although not unlike bronze spindle hooks, such as **26/121** (MEΘ 1781), and of a similar size, they are clearly finished products as is, not hooks.[48]

26/26. (MEΘ 5284) Small Bronze Cone Fig. 26.10
West Hill #229/010014 [14].
L. 0.021–0.022; Diam. 0.007; Wt. 0.5 g.
Complete.
Thin sheet bronze hammered flat and formed into a cone, resembling a dunce's cap.
Probably Archaic.
Cf. Morris et al. 2020, p. 675, fig. 16:b.

Objects of Iron

The quantity of iron objects from the early excavations on the West Hill was not great and consists largely of implements, including a knife (**26/27**), an axe/adze or possible hoe (**26/28**), several chisels (**26/29**, **26/30**), and a large nail (**26/31**). Two other objects are more interesting: one is an axe-shaped pendant of iron, **26/32**, which is of unique form (although bronze axe pendants are common in Greece and the Mediterranean, iron ones are few and far between); the other is a fragmentary iron obelos, **26/33**.

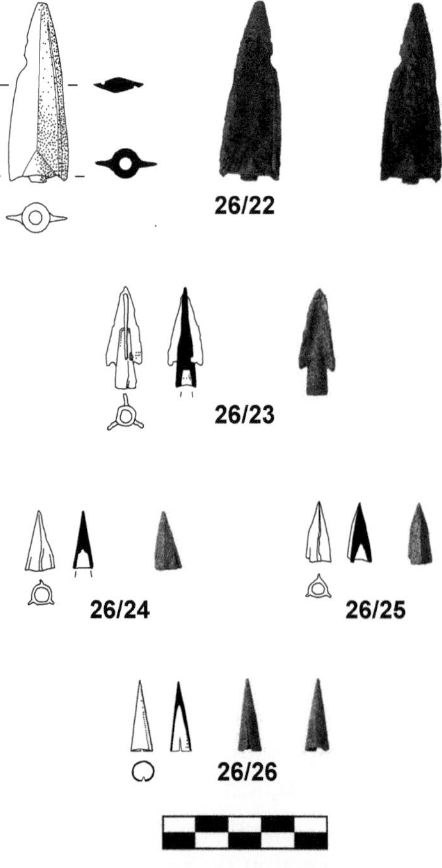

Figure 26.10. West Hill bronze arrowheads, **26/22** (MEΘ 5273), **26/23** (MEΘ 5276), **26/24** (MEΘ 5274), **26/25** (MEΘ 5275), and bronze cone, **26/26** (MEΘ 5284). Drawings A. Hooton and S. Skyvalida, photos J. Vanderpool and I. Coyle

Implements

Knife

The one knife from the West Hill presented below has a context indicating an Archaic date. Iron knives are fully discussed with comparanda in Chapter 15, under **15/79–15/88**. Individual comparanda more specifically for **26/27** are presented in the catalogue entry below.

26/27. (ΜΕΘ 4973 [ΜΕ 656]) Iron Knife Fig. 26.11

West Hill #229/020010 [10].

L. 0.133; W. (max) 0.024; Wt. 23.3 g.

Four main frr preserving greater part of knife, except for very tip of point. Additional chips of corrosion.

Pointed knife, with cutting edge along the concave side. Haft slightly less pointed than tip and more consistently thicker in section.

Context Archaic.

Cf., among others, *Vergina* I, p. 267, fig. 104, Ζπ1α and Κιβ; Kilian-Dirlmeier 2002, p. 71, pl. 68, no. 1063; p. 72, pl. 70, nos. 1095–1096 (dated "Spätgeometrische bis hocharchaische Zeit"); p. 149, pls. 155–156, nos. 2439, 2443 (undated context); Kilian 1975a, pl. 93, no. 10; Vokotopoulou 1986, figs. 91:δ, 91:ι, 91:ιδ.

Axe/Adze/Hoe

Axes, together with adzes and possible hammers, are discussed above in Chapter 15 (see **15/89–15/92**). Among the latter, **26/28** most closely resembles **15/92**, which I have classified as a possible hammer. The primary difference between the two is that **26/28** tapers toward a sharp edge on one side, making it a likely axe or adze. The possibility that it functioned as an agricultural implement for digging—a hoe?—is also possible. According to Nicholas Blackwell, differentiating between tools and weapons in the Early Iron Age can be difficult and determining a single function for an

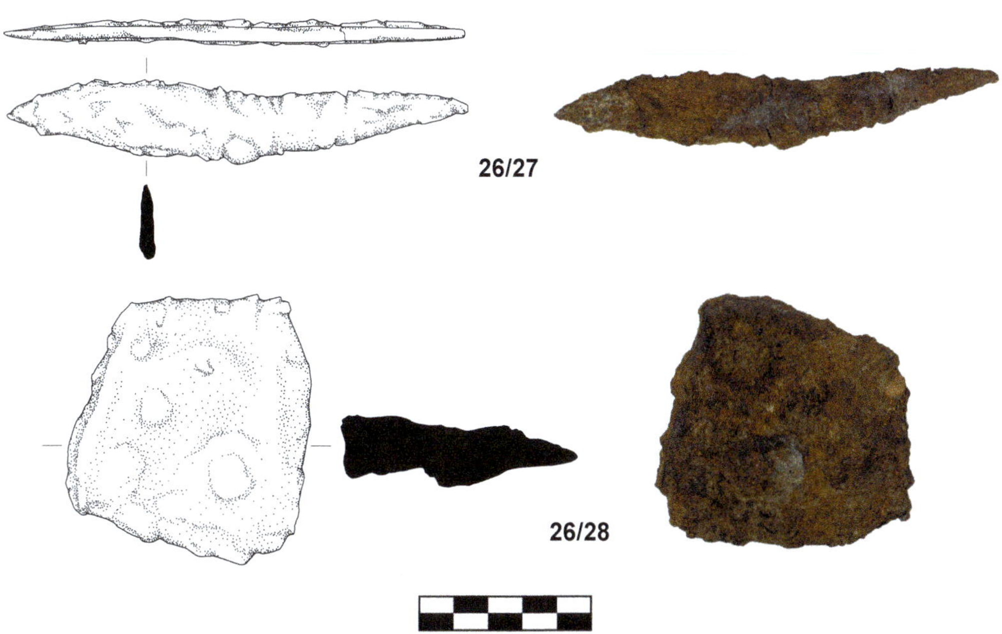

FIGURE 26.11. West Hill iron knife, **26/27** (ΜΕΘ 4973), iron axe/adze/hoe, **26/28** (ΜΕΘ 4970). Drawings T. Ross, photos I. Coyle

implement can sometimes be challenging.[49] A classic case in point is the Late Geometric II tomb 678 at Pithekoussai, thought to contain nine iron tools of a carpenter, all of which were found next to, and above, the lower part of the legs of the deceased.[50] The "tools" included an "ascia di ferro a cannone," which could be interpreted as an axe or scraper, three pointed chisels ("scalpelli"), two of which (nos. 678-7 and 678-8) resemble iron sauroters or spear butts (cf. **26/190**), which if found in another context could be classified as weapons; an "asta di ferro" or iron rod with a small hook at one end, the function of which is unclear; two awls ("punteruoli"), which would have been equally useful to a carpenter, metalworker, or leatherworker; and two all-purpose knives (a "coltello" and a "lama").

26/28. (MEΘ 4970 [ME 542]) Iron Axe/Adze/Hoe Fig. 26.11
West Hill #229/008009 [9].
P.L. x p.W. x Th. 0.078 x 0.070 x 0.024; Wt. 213.4 g.
Single piece preserving undetermined portion of implement, plus chips and flakes of corrosion.
Large and heavy piece of iron, thicker at upper preserved edge as shown, tapering toward opposite end to a sharp edge.
Context Archaic.
Cf. **15/92** (MEΘ 1553).

Chisels

Of the two examples presented below, the better preserved **26/29** is clearly a pointed chisel, as opposed to the more common flat chisels that were in use in the Bronze Age. Iron chisels are discussed in more detail in Chapter 15, where Early Iron Age, Archaic, and Classical comparanda are assembled (see **15/93–15/97**). As I noted in Chapter 15, citing Raubitschek, the pointed iron chisel was in use in Greece from the Early Geometric period, continuing through the 7th century B.C., into the late Archaic, Classical, and later periods.[51]

26/29. (MEΘ 4968 [ME 677]) Pointed Chisel Fig. 26.12
West Hill #229/010017 [17].
L. 0.126; Diam. (max) 0.017; Wt. 112.4 g.
One main piece, plus flaked chips of corrosion, probably preserving most of the original object.
Thick spike, evidently circular in section at the end opposite the point, but becoming square toward the point, where it tapers toward a point.
Context Archaic.

26/30. (MEΘ 4969 [ME 610]) Fragmentary Chisel Fig. 26.12
West Hill #229/006016 [16].
P.L. 0.066; W. (shaft) 0.021 x 0.017; Wt. 43.4 g.
Single fr preserving top flat edge, but undetermined portion of shaft.
Shaft thick, square to rectangular in section, tapering toward a sharp edge.
Context Archaic.

Additional possible chisels

Both of the following pieces are fragmentary and corroded. Although both probably derive from chisels, the possibility that they were bolts/projectiles cannot be categorically dismissed, especially since one was found on the surface, the other, although probably from a deeper deposit—Archaic or earlier—in backfill.

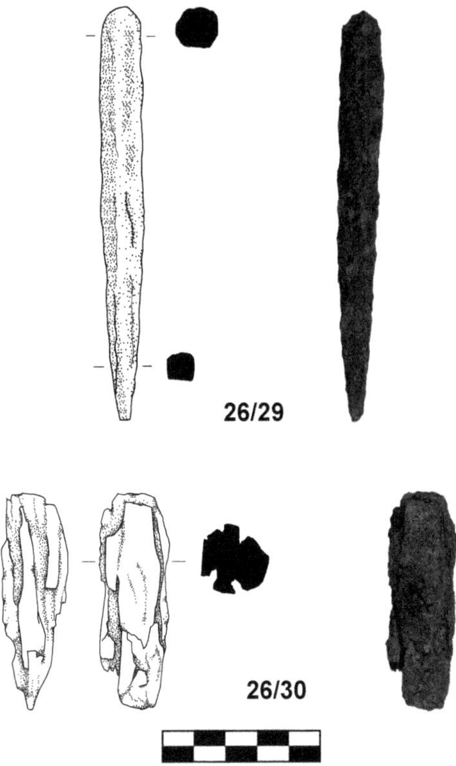

FIGURE 26.12. West Hill iron chisels, **26/29** (MEΘ 4968), **26/30** (MEΘ 4969). Drawings T. Ross and F. Skyvalida, photos I. Coyle

- MEΘ 4977. West Hill #229.2007. From backfill, no clear context. P.L. 0.050; Th. 0.013 x 0.011; Wt. 13.8 g.
- MEΘ 4976. West Hill #229/013001 [1]. Surface. P.L. 0.045; Th. 0.08; Wt. 4.8 g.

Large iron nail

As it is essentially a surface find, the date of **26/31** is undetermined. Nails, especially those of bronze, have been discussed in greater detail above, under **26/15**, and below, **26/133–26/146**. In dealing with different sized iron nails, Raubitschek distinguishes between nails, which have lengths of more than 0.035 and less than 0.100 m, and spikes, which have a length of more than 0.101 m.[52] With a preserved length of 0.065, **26/31** is a clearly a nail, albeit a large one. Raubitschek notes that iron spikes were used where stronger attachments were needed, and she goes on to make an interesting point: "Since wooden parts had to be protected from the weather, lead sheathing was often required, and great quantities of lead sheets have in fact been found in the excavations."[53] At nearby Sindos, Aikaterini Despoini distinguishes three types of iron nails from tombs: Type I (550 to mid-5th century B.C.) have shafts that are square in section, with one terminal bent back to serve as the head; Type II (mid-6th–mid-5th century B.C.) have a disk head, and are square in section; Type III (mostly 560–500 B.C., one dating to the mid-5th century B.C.) nails are primarily associated with stone-lined tombs, with one end triangular in shape, and the extending shaft that tapers to a point usually circular in section.[54] It is worth noting that the iron nails of Classical and Hellenistic date from the sanctuary of Athena Itonia near Philia resemble **26/31** in that those with bent-back heads are square or rectangular in section.[55] Although most of the head of **26/31** is on one side of the shaft, the slight overhang on the other side of the head may have resulted when it was hammered into place.

26/31. (MEΘ 4971 [ME 444]) Large Iron Nail Fig. 26.13

West Hill #229/012 or 011. Surface.

P.H. 0.065; L. x W. (head) 0.018 x 0.015; Wt. 17.7 g.

Single fr preserving greater part of nail except for the lower tip.

Shaft square/rectangular in section, tapering toward point, itself not preserved. Head roughly oval-shaped and extending largely to one side of shaft as if intentionally bent.

Context undetermined.

Axe Pendant(?)

Were **26/32** made of bronze, I would have no qualms in categorizing it as an axe pendant; with a second suspension hole, one could classify it as an attachment. But as an iron pendant with a single suspension hole it is something of a curiosity. The form is very clearly a trunnion axe, one of the most basic types of Early Iron Age and Archaic axes, usually, but not exclusively, made of iron. I have already discussed this basic type of iron axe from the Kerameikos, in several tombs at Lefkandi, in Troy (level VIIb1), Karphi, and elsewhere, in Chapter 15.[56] But the latter are all real axes, not miniatures with a single suspension hole. The *locus classicus* for axe pendants from the Mycenaean through the Late Geometric period is Kilian-Dirlmeier's *Prähistorische Bronzefunde* volume, where she distinguishes several different types, none of which is close to **26/32**.[57] I know of no parallel for **26/32**,[58] but the ubiquity of the trunnion axe form with projections in the Greek world of the period, together with a miniature axe pendant made of iron, need come as no surprise.

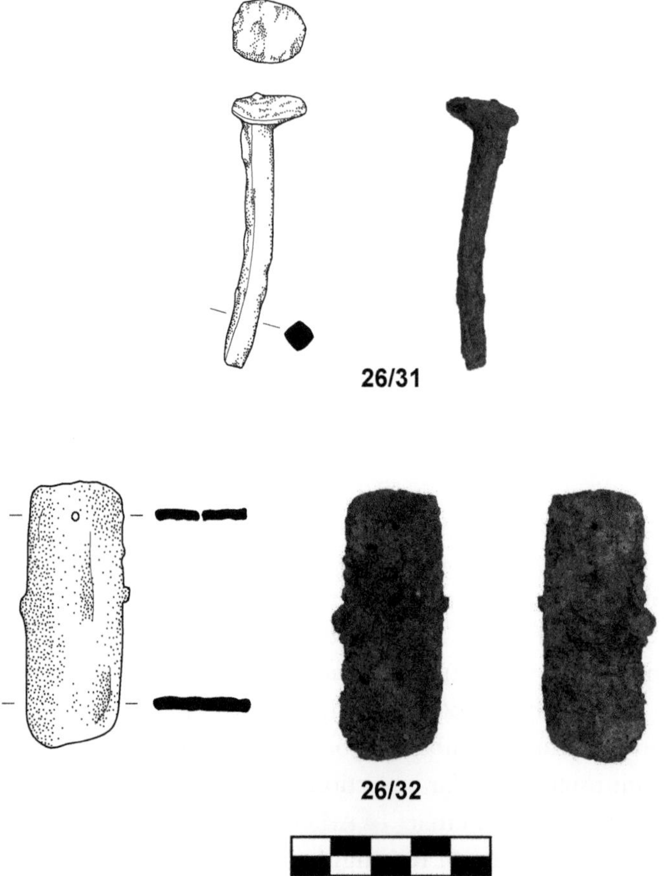

FIGURE 26.13. West Hill large iron nail, **26/31** (MEΘ 4971), and iron axe pendant, **26/32** (MEΘ 4972). Drawings T. Ross and F. Skyvalida, photos I. Coyle

26/32. (ΜΕΘ 4972 [ΜΕ 67]) Iron Axe Pendant Fig. 26.13
West Hill #229/016003 [3].
L. x W. x Th. 0.064 x 0.030 x 0.004; Wt. 11.7 g.
Largely intact, though shorter edges may be chipped.
Roughly rectangular sheet of iron, with corners more rounded than squared; one short projection on each of the long sides. Small hole at top, as shown. The form is that of a miniature Early Iron Age trunnion axe with short projections, in this case serving as a pendant.
Context Archaic.

Fragmentary iron obelos

When first confronted with **26/33**, in its uncleaned state prior to conservation, I thought this may have been a much-damaged spearhead, but it is no spearhead, nor is it a product of overzealous conservation.[59] The long shaft is rectangular in section and there is no socket. The context of **26/33** is probably Archaic. The preserved length is 0.230, and the original length would have been greater than 0.300 m, perhaps even considerably longer. In dealing with the iron spits from Fortetsa, which include the earliest iron obelos I am aware of (Early Protogeometric), James King Brock writes: "These are large rods of square section . . . . None is completely preserved but the length is 30 cm. or more. The fact that most occur in bundles tends to confirm their identification as spits."[60] Unfortunately, none of the spits and related objects from the Fortetsa tombs near Knossos were illustrated by Brock, and several were missing. Obeloi, together with what Brock termed pikes, were very common elsewhere at Knossos, including the North Cemetery, where over 20 examples were traced in one tomb alone (tomb 285.f48/50) by Anthony Snodgrass, who lamented their fragmentary state.[61] Despite their sad state, some of the Knossian obeloi were over 1 m in length, and many were found associated with firedogs.[62] In determining the date of the obeloi from Knossos, including those from Fortetsa, it was clear that obeloi were not uncommon at the site from Protogeometric times on, but their most intensive period of deposition was in the later 8th and 7th centuries B.C.[63] Related obeloi from tombs in Argos were of Late Geometric date,[64] and the Sindos cemetery yielded numerous obeloi mostly of the 6th century B.C. (see below). There are also a number of obeloi from the sanctuary of Zeus at Nemea that date to the 5th century B.C., and fragmentary examples from Stymphalos are mostly of the 4th century B.C., although some may date to the 5th century.[65]

Snodgrass's chronology, in which the greatest number of obeloi date to the 8th and 7th century, was confirmed and supplemented by what must be the largest published selection of iron obeloi or spits in Greece, at least 130, from the sanctuary of Zeus at Olympia.[66] A variety of grip ends were distinguished on the Olympia spits, with the four basic types including: a) round or oval grips/terminals (only seven, which appear to be the earliest, later 8th/7th century continuing into the last quarter of the 6th century B.C.); b) half-moon or crescent-shaped grips (48 examples, beginning in the second quarter of the 6th century and continuing into the third quarter of the 5th century B.C.; c) lozenge- or lancet-shaped (17 examples, which are not as well dated, but appear to date from the 7th to the early 5th century B.C.); and d) triangular grips (only five, also poorly dated, although one is clearly from an early 5th-century B.C. context).

In the central and northern Aegean, some of the best-illustrated examples of obeloi were encountered in the Protogeometric to Archaic deposits at the sanctuary of Athena Itonia near Philia in Thessaly, where some 17 "eiserne Bratspieße (Obeloi)" were published in exemplary detail.[67] The majority of the Philia obeloi have a flattened circular or oval disk at one end that served as the grip, with a smaller rectangular projection at the midpoint of the shaft. Only one of the Philia obeloi has a circular projection hammered flat at its midpoint.[68] The Methone obelos most closely resembles the latter of the Philia obeloi, but its circular projection/grip does not appear to be at the midpoint of the shaft, but closer toward one end (the top as illustrated). In this respect, it also resembles one of the 5th century B.C. Nemea obeloi that has not a circular, but more of a crescent half-moon projection close to one of its terminals (like the obeloi of type b at Olympia), together with a smaller rectangular projection near its midpoint.

Closer to home, the cemetery at Sindos has brought to light no shortage of obeloi, many of them found in bundles (δέσμη ὀβελῶν), often in association with firedogs (κρατευτὲς).[69] Virtually all of the Sindos obeloi come from tombs dated to the 6th century B.C. The earliest, from tomb 28, is assigned to ca. 560 B.C.; the latest, from tomb 30, 480–470 B.C.; the remainder falling between the mid-6th century and ca. 500 B.C.; the associated firedogs are of similar date. Several of the Sindos obeloi have their terminals or grips hammered flat, with a short, pointed projection extending from it, which is not as long as that on **26/33**, and some have a crescent-shaped projection near the terminal not unlike the Nemea and Olympia obeloi already noted.[70] None of the Sindos obeloi have the smaller rectangular projection near the midpoint found on most of the Philia examples.

It is important, by way of conclusion, to heed Snodgrass's comment on the function of obeloi: "Our finds do not do much to reinforce the belief that obeloi had significance as a primitive currency at Knossos in the period of the cemetery."[71] That they may have served in certain contexts as stores of value is certainly possible,[72] but their clear association in so many tombs with firedogs indicates that they served a very different purpose altogether: to skewer and cook meat.

26/33. (ΜΕΘ 4975 [ΜΕ 11) Iron Obelos Fig. 26.14

West Hill #229. Τομή Β (Sector B).

P.L. 0.230; W. (max) 0.027; Wt. 68.8 g.

One main piece, plus numerous chips and flakes due to corrosion, preserving substantial portion of object, except for both terminations.

Lower long portion of surviving shaft rectangular in section, splaying out very slightly toward the bottom as preserved. Central portion ovoid, with a shorter, as preserved, continuing shaft, evidently also rectangular in section, but much corroded. The latter does not clearly taper to a point and the broken top edge suggests an object other than a spearhead.

Context probably Archaic.

Objects of Lead

There was a somewhat broader array of lead objects from the West Hill in comparison to those from the Hypogeion presented in Chapter 15. Most are implements, like the common fishnet weights (**26/34**) and a possible clamp/plug (**26/35**); other objects include a rod or possible ingot (**36/36**), two small disks of undetermined function (**26/37**, **26/38**), and an uncertain object labeled here a "domed attachment(?)" (**26/39**). The only weapon was a characteristic "branch" for the casting of lead sling bullets (**26/40**).

Implements

Fishnet weight

Three identical fishnet weights were found in the Hypogeion (**15/104–15/106**), which are fully discussed with comparanda cited in Chapter 15.

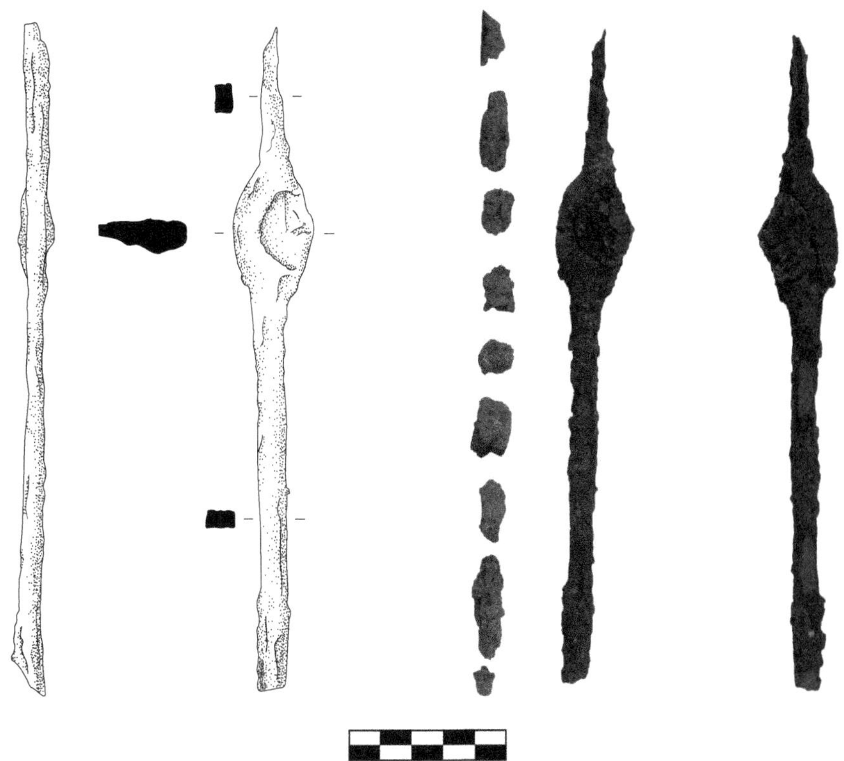

FIGURE 26.14. West Hill fragmentary iron obelos, **26/33** (ΜΕΘ 4975). Drawing F. Skyvalida, photos I. Coyle

26/34. (ΜΕΘ 4963) Fishnet Weight Fig. 26.15
West Hill #229/020010 [10].
L. 0.060; Wt. 15.7 g.
Probably complete; slightly cracked on one side.
Standard fishnet weight, made of thin lead strip, roughly hammered flat and folded over to grip one of the primary cords of the net.
Context Archaic.
Cf. **15/104–15/106**.

Undetermined, conceivably a mending clamp/plug

Preserved in three joining fragments, **26/35** essentially remains an undetermined object. I have listed it here conceivably as a mending plug rather than a conventional clamp on the basis of a lead clamp/plug on an Early Iron Age krater from Torone.[73] The Torone clamp was partially preserved in two joining fragments, comprising a large flattened disk of lead employed not only to hold together the broken fragments of the pot but also to seal a hole created at the base of the krater by the breaking of its foot. With a max length x width of 0.062 x 0.055 m, the Torone example is of comparable size to **26/35**, although not of similar form. Lead clamps/plugs similar to the Torone example are known from Olynthos and Torone of Classical date that may have served a similar function, as well as in a much earlier Bronze Age example from Poliochni on Lemnos.[74] Given its form, and especially its weight, **26/35** seems a most unlikely clamp/plug for pottery, although it may have been used for other materials, not least stone. A number of related objects, some with drilled holes, from Isthmia of Archaic to Classical date are presented as lead filling for statuette bases.[75]

26/35. (MEΘ 4966) Undetermined; Possible Mending Plug Fig. 26.15

West Hill #229/ Sector Γ (3).

P.H. 0.038; p.L. 0.078; Wt. 344.4 g.

Three main joining frr preserving undetermined portion of object.

Object clamp-like on account of its form: flat on one side (bottom, as shown) and on adjacent perpendicular side; prominent mushroom-shaped projection on top, as shown. The form is such that it should be intentional, as opposed to misshapen.

Context Archaic.

Lead rod

26/36 is a strip-like rod, rectangular in section, with a nicely cut terminal at one end; it is unclear whether the opposite end is intact or damaged, and the rod, as preserved, is slightly twisted. The rod was probably cast in an open form, and then cut and hammered to shape. Its context is Archaic. Related rods or bars of Archaic and Classical date from Isthmia—over 70 in all—are referred to as ingots, and **26/36** resembles some of these, although it does not seem to have a clearly defined head, and there are certainly no incised letters as on some of the Isthmia ingots.[76] In discussing the latter, Raubitschek casts her net wide to include discussion of Minoan and Mycenaean predecessors, and established weights of Archaic and Classical date. Although the length of **26/36** is similar to some of the Isthmian ingots, its weight does not really accord with any of them. As a rod, **26/36** may well have served as a convenient way of storing lead for later use, and as such its function as an ingot is possible, if not likely.

FIGURE 26.15. West Hill lead fishnet weight, **26/34** (MEΘ 4963) and uncertain lead object, possible mending clamp/plug, **26/35** (MEΘ 4966). Drawing F. Skyvalida, photos I. Coyle

26/36. (MEΘ 4961) Lead Rod (Ingot?) Fig. 26.16

West Hill #229/018004 [4].

P.L. 0.094; Wt. 23.9 g.

Single fr preserving undetermined portion of rod, including one clear terminal; perhaps intact?

Strip-like rod, rectangular in section, with nicely cut terminal/edge at one end. Rod slightly twisted, as shown.

Context Archaic.

Cf., among others, *Isthmia* VII, pl. 90, nos. 593, 597.

Disks

Of Archaic date are two small, crudely shaped lead disks, for want of a better word, **26/37** and **26/38**. Both are evidently complete, although **26/37** may be slightly damaged on one side. A number of "disks" from Isthmia are listed under the heading of lead pieces unidentified as to use, but not catalogued or listed, which are slightly larger than the two Methone examples presented here (diameter/length ranging between 0.043 and 0.060).[77]

26/37. (MEΘ 4960) Lead Disk Fig. 26.16

West Hill #229/022004 [11].

Diam./L. 0.024; Th. (max.) 0.003; Wt. 11.1 g.

Evidently complete; perhaps broken or damaged on one side, but uncertain.

Thin lead disk, shaped as shown.

Context Archaic.

26/38. (MEΘ 4965) Lead Disk Fig. 26.16

West Hill #229/ Sector B, level 3.

Diam./L. 0.034–0.035; Th. (max.) 0.008; Wt. 36.9 g.

Evidently complete.

Somewhat thicker disk than **26/37** (MEΘ 4960), slightly articulated on one side, as shown, as if preserving an edge.

Context Archaic.

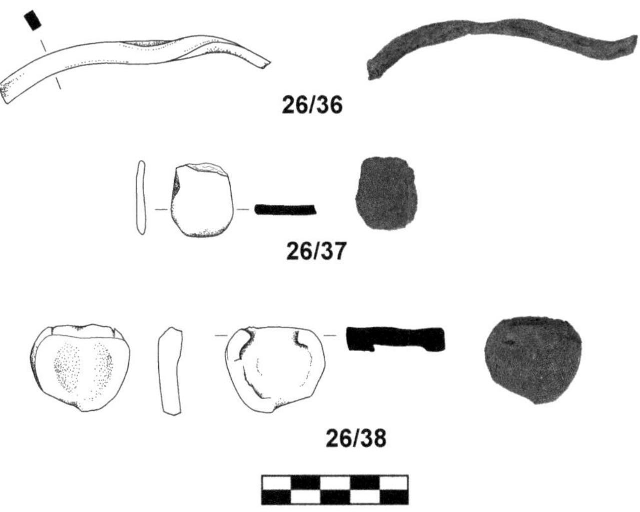

FIGURE 26.16. West Hill lead rod, **26/36** (MEΘ 4961), lead disks, **26/37** (MEΘ 4960) and **26/38** (MEΘ 4965). Drawings T. Ross, photos I. Coyle

Unidentified domed object

The function of **26/39** is far from certain, but it was found in the mid-6th-century B.C. destruction deposit on the West Hill and is clearly of Archaic date. In the catalogue entry below, I note that it resembles the pommel of a sword, but it is clearly not from a sword. Its shape and size are very close to a lead object interpreted as a lead door pivot socket and thus an architectural fixture from Isthmia of uncertain date.[78] The latter, however, is concave on the interior to serve as the pivot for a door, lacking the more carefully made almost cylindrical lower element below the dome of **26/39**. Consequently, **29/39** remains a problem—but well-dated—piece in need of interpretation.

26/39. (5292) Domed Attachment(?) Fig. 26.17

West Hill #229/019013 [13]. Mid-6th-century B.C. destruction level.

P.H. 0.025; H. (dome, without the attachment below) 0.023; Diam. 0.047; Wt. 266.6 g.

Single piece preserving entire dome and portion of the attachment on flat underside.

Nicely formed lead dome, with circular and evidently flat disk-shaped attachment below. In shape the piece, as preserved, resembles the pommel of a sword, but is clearly not from a sword. Original object unclear.

Context mid-6th century B.C. or earlier.

Weapons

"Branch" for casting lead sling bullets

The lead sling bullets from Methone are thoroughly presented and discussed in Chapter 28. Found in topsoil, well away from the fortifications of the West Hill defined by the underground tunnels dug by the Methonaians, **26/40** provides an evocative glimpse of the final desperate days of the settlement at Methone during Philip's siege of 354 B.C. The well-preserved cluster of lead sling bullets, **28/62**, has four surviving bullets, all inscribed ΕΥΓΕΝΕΟΣ.

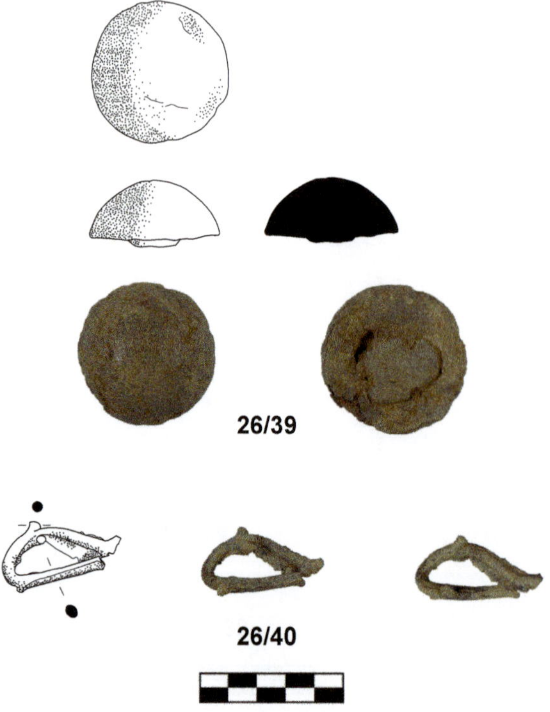

FIGURE 26.17. West Hill unidentified domed object, **26/39** (ΜΕΘ 5292), and lead "branch" for the casting of lead sling bullets, **26/40** (ΜΕΘ 4964). Drawings F. Skyvalida, photos I. Coyle

26/40. (ΜΕΘ 4964) "Branch" for Casting Sling Bullets Fig. 26.17

West Hill #229/023001 [1]. Topsoil.

P.L. (max.) 0.043; Wt. 14.4 g.

Single fr, bent over as shown, preserving undetermined portion of branch.

Cast rod, mostly circular in section, with casting seam running its length. At least four clearly preserved small branches supporting individual sling bullets, and perhaps originally more.

Although the context is uncertain, **26/40** can only be associated with the siege and destruction of Methone in 354 B.C.

THE METAL OBJECTS FROM THE ACROPOLIS (WEST HILL) EAST SLOPE

The metal objects from the east slope of the West Hill or acropolis of Methone come from the excavations in Plot 245 (Chapter 1). The material is in many ways a continuation of that on the summit of the West Hill and only a short distance to the east. But unlike the summit of the West Hill, the nature of the deposits was rather different, with no clear evidence of substantial workshop activity of the Archaic period. As outlined in Chapter 1, it was in Plot 245 that one of the first of the tunnels excavated by the Methonaians during the siege of the city in 354 B.C. was brought to light, indicating the line of the fortification wall of Methone otherwise destroyed (Fig. 1.26). Apart from residual material, the earliest remains in situ were the Late Bronze Age tombs presented in Chapter 6 (see especially Fig. 6.2). As is outlined in Chapter 1, in the ensuing Early Iron Age, especially in the Protogeometric and Subprotogeometic periods, there is a clear increase in the size of the fortified settlement, and it is during this period that the West Hill was included as part of the settlement. It was especially in Plot 245 on the upper part of the fortified settlement of the hill that a fortification trench had been cut in the course of the Early Iron Age (Fig. 1.31). Adjacent to it was an apsidal building, as indicated by the arrangement of its postholes. In the same area were a number of Early Iron Age refuse pits. The pits were critical for providing various finds ranging in date from the Early Iron Age into the earlier Archaic period. By the 4th century B.C., it was into these preexisting deposits that the Methonaian fortification tunnel was dug, together with other isolated pockets of the Classical period. The result was the palimpsest as indicated on Figure 6.2.

As with the material from the summit of the West Hill presented above, the context of the metal objects from Plot 245 is provided in the catalogue entries below, and is further discussed in the various introductory sections as needed. I also present a summary listing in Table 26.2. The date provided for individual finds is the date suggested by the context of the piece.

Objects of Bronze

Jewelry

Pendants

The first pendant, represented by **26/41**, is of a type largely confined to northern Greece and the Balkans. It corresponds to Kilian-Dirlmeier's "Geschlossene Bommeln mit erweiterter Öse, Stiel und unterem Fortsatz," more specifically to the variant with a biconical bead ("Doppelkonisch").[79] Of the 14 examples assembled by Kilian-Dirlmeier, all have a north Aegean provenance: Agios Panteleimon (Pateli, in the Florina district) (4), Pherai in Thessaly (3), Vergina (2), Philia (1); two others are said to be from "Chalkidike," and another two from "northern Greece."[80] A pendant that is very close to **26/41** comes from Donja Dolina, and the Glasinac region of Bosnia-Herzegovina has produced a number of related pendants, including two from Osovo where the triangular element is actually at the bottom, with pendent rings, and the top is a ring from which the pendant itself was suspended;

TABLE 26.2. Summary listing of the context and type of the metal objects from the eastern slopes of the acropolis (West Hill) in Plot 245. The "date" column lists the contextual date of each piece

MEΘ	Metal	Context	Object	Date
26/41 (MEΘ 5038)	Bronze	#245/007007	Pendant	Probably EIA/Archaic
26/42 (MEΘ 5040)	Bronze	#245/013019	Triangular sheet (pendant?)	EIA/Archaic
26/43 (MEΘ 5034)	Bronze	#245/002003	Spectacle fibula fr	Probably EIA/Archaic
26/44 (MEΘ 5039)	Bronze	#245/007013	Small arched fibula	EIA/Archaic
26/45 (MEΘ 5031)	Bronze	#245/005011	"Phrygian" fibula	EIA/Archaic
26/46 (MEΘ 5036)	Bronze	#245/005/	"Phrygian" fibula	Classical
26/47 (MEΘ 5032)	Bronze	#245/017021	Tutulus/small boss	EIA/Archaic
26/48 (MEΘ 5035)	Bronze	#245/002018	Cheese grater	EIA/Archaic
26/49 (MEΘ 5033)	Bronze	#245/001014	Tack	EIA/Archaic
26/50 (MEΘ 5037)	Bronze	#245/005/	Nail	Classical
26/51 (MEΘ 5043)	Iron	#245/002020	Large nail	EIA/Archaic
26/52 (MEΘ 5044)	Lead	#245/002019	Large mending clamp	EIA/Archaic
26/53 (MEΘ 5046)	Lead	#245/001018	Disk-shaped mending plug?	Context unclear
26/54 (MEΘ 5045)	Lead	#245/002014	Small bead, button, weight	EIA/Archaic

and five such pendants, replete with dangling rings, hanging pendent from a considerably larger rectangular element, were found at Arareva Gromila.[81]

I am not certain that **26/42** is a pendant, but I cannot see what else it may be. Although reconstructed from three joining fragments, the object is complete, and the folded-over top, not unlike the heads of rolled-head pins, must be intentional. The only parallels I can cite for **26/42** are Minoan bronze pendants, some Early Minoan, others Late Minoan II–III, most of which are of similar dimensions to **26/42**, though a few are smaller.[82] The early context for **26/42** may suggest that the type survives into the Early Iron Age.

26/41. (MEΘ 5038 [ME 22]) Fragmentary Pendant — Fig. 26.18

Acropolis east slope #245/007007 [4]. 8/10/2004.

P.L. 0.054; Wt. 8.0 g.

Two frr, probably joining, but heavily corroded especially at their juncture, preserving most of pendant, except for the bottom, which is clearly broken.

Central portion of lower shaft circular in section, beaded as shown, with larger biconical bead near center, with two beads above and two below, spaced apart. The shafts of the triangular head or top are also round in section, with bead "ears" at either end. On the basis of comparanda, the lower terminal of **26/41** would not have extended much farther.

Context probably Early Iron Age/Archaic.

Cf., among others, Kilian-Dirlmeier 1979, pl. 24, esp. nos. 431, 437–438; also pl. 108, no. 5 (from Donja Dolina); Makridis 1937, pl. III:1; Bräuning and Kilian-Dirlmeier 2013, p. 203, fig. 104, no. 27 (Vergina Grave LXIV E:27); p. 273, fig. 217, AE 345 (far right).

26/42. (MEΘ 5040 [ME 154]) Triangular-shaped Pendant(?) — Fig. 26.18

Acropolis east slope #245/013019 [8]. Pit 26.

L./H. 0.041; W. (max) 0.027; W. (head): 0.009–0.010; Wt. 9.1 g.

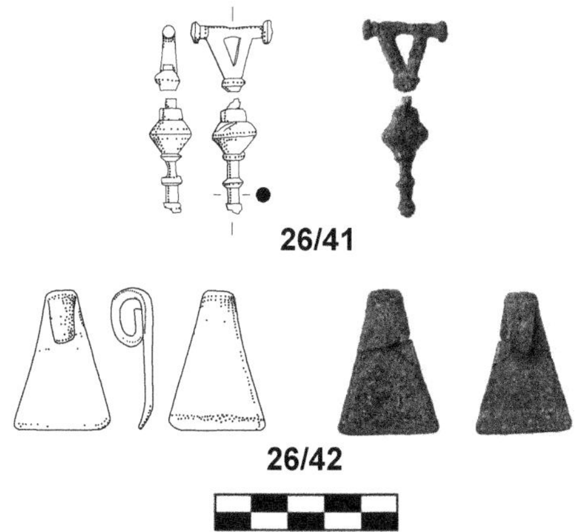

FIGURE 26.18. Acropolis east slope bronze pendants, **26/41** (MEΘ 5038), and **26/42** (MEΘ 5040). Drawings A. Hooton, photos J. Vanderpool

Three joining frr preserving complete pendant.

Thickish sheet of bronze, hammered flat, and worked into a triangle, with a thinner projecting tongue at top, folded over as shown.

Context Early Iron Age/Archaic.

Fibulae

Spectacle fibula

Although badly corroded, **26/43** is clearly a spectacle fibula made of bronze wire coiled to form a spiral. Only the outer ring is clearly visible, with the remainder of the spiral fused together,[83] but also the end near the center that is curled up to form part of the catchplate. Corresponding to Blinkenberg Type XIV and Sapouna-Sakellarakis Type X, spectacle fibulae are fully discussed, with comparanda, in Chapter 15 (under **15/2–15/5**).[84]

26/43. (MEΘ 5034 [ME 6]) Fragmentary Spectacle Fibula Fig. 26.19

Acropolis east slope #245/002003 [3].

Diam. 0.026–0.027; Wt. 7.2 g.

Two joining frr, very heavily corroded, with most of bronze wire fused together and only really visible in the broken section, preserving about one-half of fibula, and what may be portion of catchplate.

Bronze wire, circular in section, coiled to form a spiral. End, near center, curled up to form likely catchplate.

Context probably Early Iron Age/Archaic.

For the catchplate, see esp. Kilian-Dirlmeier 2002, pl. 40, no. 580.

Arched fibula

26/44 is a small arched or bow fibula, with a small, flattened, and roughly triangular catchplate. It corresponds generally to Blinkenberg's Type II "fibules à arc symétrique" (under the general heading of "types submycéniens"), and to Type IIa of Sapouna-Sakellarakis.[85] The type begins with Submycenaean examples from Lefkandi and Salamis, and Subminoan examples from Gortyn and Karphi, and continues into the Geometric and Archaic periods.[86] Although the arch resembles the Aegean twisted bows normally classified as Submycenaean, this is not a true twisted bow, but rather one decorated with lightly incised spiral grooving.[87] Most of the Aegean examples differ from **26/44** in that their catchplates are normally smaller and much less triangular, although a few pieces get close to the general form of **26/44**.[88] The distinctively triangular catchplate of **26/44**, especially bearing in mind that the lower portion of the catchplate is missing, more closely resembles the size and general form of a northern fibula type, classified by Rastko Vasić as "zweischleifige Bogenfibeln mit dreieckigem Fuss," which comes in variants with plain, twisted, and other types of bows, dating from the late 8th and early 7th, well into the 6th century B.C.[89] The similarity between these fibulae and **26/44** is noteworthy, but the Methone fibula lacks the second loop on the side of the catchplate. Some fibulae in Bulgaria without the second loop are close, as is a small silver fibula from Thessaly.[90] It is almost as if **26/44** is a fusion between a standard Aegean and a standard central Balkan fibula.

26/44. (ΜΕΘ 5039 [ΜΕ 240]) Small Arched Fibula Fig. 26.19

Acropolis east slope #245/007013 [8]. Pit 79.

L. 0.025; H. 0.016; Wt. 1.2 g.

Four joining frr preserving complete fibula, but with pin broken and lower part of the catchplate missing.

Small bow fibula, with small, flattened, roughly triangular catchplate. Spring two turns; pin shaft circular in section, tapering toward point. Although corroded and not clearly visible, the arch appears to be decorated with a lightly incised spiral grooving rather than twisting.

Context Early Iron Age/Archaic.

"Phrygian" fibulae

I have provided an introduction to the so-called "Phrygian" fibulae in Chapter 15, with discussion and comparanda under **15/13–15/15**, and additional notes and examples in my discussion (below) of the more numerous fibulae of the type in the agora of Methone (**26/57–26/67**). Of the two fibulae presented below, **26/45** is earlier, and it accords primarily with examples of Blinkenberg's and Muscarella's Type XII 12 and XII 13.[91] It is particularly close to **15/14**, except that the beads on **26/45** are filleted rather than plain. Especially close to **26/45** is an Archaic fibula from Lindos published by Blinkenberg, several others from Chios, and at least five examples from the Athena Itonia sanctuary near Philia in Thessaly, cited in the catalogue entry below. It is worth noting that related fibulae in Anatolia with three beads on the arch tend to have more complex springs and catchplates, and the closest parallels come from the Aegean.[92]

In contrast, **26/46** is of Classical date. It has four small beads more or less equally spaced on its arch and a volute-shaped catchplate with the bottom curved up to accommodate the pin. The "spring" has two elements that hold the pin in place, usually with a smaller pin or rivet; although the pin does not survive, it was clearly made separately from the rest of the fibula. I know of no related fibula from Anatolia, either in Blinkenberg's and Muscarella's typology of "Phrygian" fibulae, or in Ertuğrul Caner's corpus, although the latter dealt with fibulae to the end of the 6th century B.C. The closest parallels for **26/46** come from the nearby tombs of Sindos and were perhaps even made at Methone; they are noted in the catalogue entry, together with the contextual date for each of the tombs in which they were found. A number of similar fibulae from Classical levels at the Athena Itonia sanctuary in Thessaly are also cited in the entry below.

26/45. (ΜΕΘ 5031 [ΜΕ 322]) "Phrygian" Fibula Fig. 26.19

Acropolis east slope #245/005011 [5]. Τομή Β΄, Τάφρος 2 (Sector 2, Ditch 2).

L. 0.035; H. 0.024; Wt. 5.5 g.

Single fr preserving complete fibula except for pin.

Arched fibula, with three relatively low filleted beads. Extension for catchplate hammered flat, with end folded up to accommodate pin; spring at least two and probably originally three turns.

Context Early Iron Age/Archaic.

Cf. esp. **15/14** and comparanda cited there. Cf., among others, Blinkenberg 1926, p. 221, fig. 250, Type XII 13k (= Blinkenberg 1931, col. 88, pl. 8, no. 111), though the catchplate of **26/45** is simpler; Sapouna-Sakellarakis 1978, pl. 53, nos. 1665, 1668 (Emporio, Harbor Sanctuary = Boardman 1967, pp. 209–210, fig. 138, esp. nos. 212–221, Type H); Kilian-Dirlmeier 2002, p. 96, pl. 93, nos. 1465–1469.

26/46. (ΜΕΘ 5036 [ΜΕ 230]) "Phrygian" Fibula Fig. 26.19

Acropolis east slope #245/005. Τάφρος ιστορικών χρόνων (Classical ditch).

L. 0.029; H. 0.022; Wt. 7.5 g.

Single fr preserving all of fibula except pin.

Small fibula of "Phrygian" type, with four small beads more or less equally spaced apart on arch, which is circular in section, each comprising a large bead framed on either side for the two central beads by smaller beads. The beads at the catchplate and spring framed by smaller beads only on the side of the arch. Volute-shaped catchplate, with bottom curved up to accommodate pin. Two-part spring, holding the pin, itself not preserved, which was made separately.

Context Classical.

As noted above, the closest published parallels for **26/46** come from the cemetery at Sindos, see esp. *Sindos* III, pp. 189–190, 455, figs. 167–171, no. 349 (470–460 B.C.), no. 350 (mid-5th century B.C.), no. 351 (perhaps the closest to **26/46**: 460–450 B.C.), no. 352 (with three rather than four beads: 450–440 B.C.), and no. 353 (made of "wire beads": second quarter of the 5th century B.C.). For the related fibulae from Philia, see Kilian-Dirlmeier 2002, pp. 119–120, pls. 112–113, nos. 1828–1829, 1832–1834; cf. also nos. 1847–1849, 1854–1859, where the central bead in each set is further decorated with a band of raised dots.

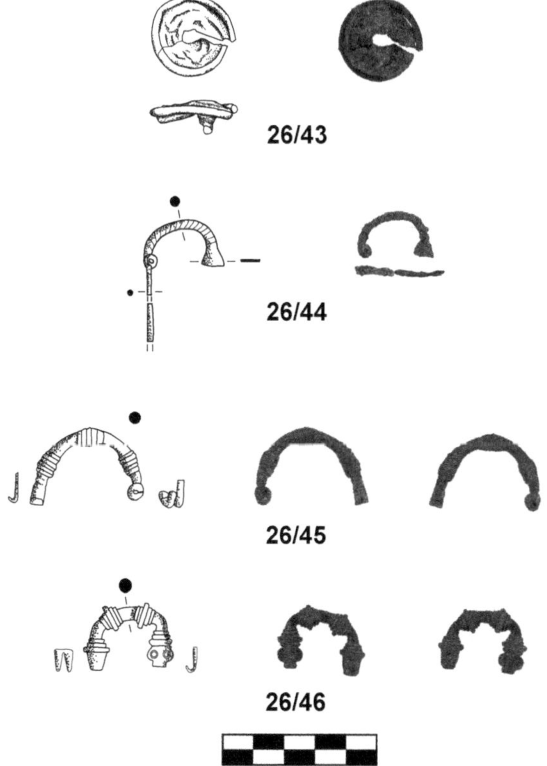

FIGURE 26.19. Acropolis east slope bronze fibulae: fragmentary spectacle fibula, **26/43** (ΜΕΘ 5034), arched fibula, **26/44** (ΜΕΘ 5039), "Phrygian" fibulae, **26/45** (ΜΕΘ 5031), **26/46** (ΜΕΘ 5036). Drawings T. Ross and F. Skyvalida, photos I. Coyle

Tutulus/small boss

A full discussion of the eight tutuli from the Hypogeion is provided in Chapter 15, under **15/36–15/43**. **26/47** is a good example of a tutulus or small boss with no clear method of attachment, such as a loop/eyelet on the underside or a piercing at the top of the dome. A few Archaic parallels are given in the entry below. A variety of uses for such objects is discussed by David Robinson on the basis of numerous examples from Olynthos.[93] The remnants of the compound on the underside of **26/47** were shown by pXRF to be corroded lead with a little tin; a related lead/tin solder was found on the underside of two of the three Archaic examples of such bosses from Francavilla Marittima in southern Italy.[94]

26/47. (ΜΕΘ 5032 [ΜΕ 315]) Tutulus/Small Boss Fig. 26.20
Acropolis east slope #245/017021 [20].
Diam. 0.015; H. 0.007; Wt. 1.8 g.
Complete, but cracked and much worn.
Circular omphaloid tutulus or small boss, convex on exterior, concave on interior.
Noticeable incrustation on the underside composed of corroded lead with a little tin.
Context Early Iron Age/Archaic.
Cf. **15/43**; Boardman 1967, pp. 227, 229, fig. 149, nos. 429–430; Felsch 2007, pp. 383–384, pl. 63, no. 2257; Kilian-Dirlmeier 2002, pl. 170, nos. 2884–2885; Papadopoulos 2003a, pp. 87–88, fig. 110, nos. 246–248.

Fragmentary cheese grater

Despite its poor state of preservation, the fragments of **26/48** are clearly of a cheese grater, of the general type of **26/13**, from the summit of the West Hill, fully discussed with comparanda above.

26/48. (ΜΕΘ 5035 [ΜΕ 43]) Cheese Grater Frr Fig. 26.20
Acropolis east slope #245/002018 [5]. Pit 5.
P.L. x p.W. (largest fr) 0.029 x 0.024; Wt. 2.8 g.
One main fr, folded over, plus several smaller pieces, including minuscule chips, preserving portion of grater, corroded.
Very thin sheet bronze, pricked through with numerous small holes to serve as grater.
Context Early Iron Age/Archaic.
Cf. **26/13** and the parallels cited there.

Nails/tacks

The following two objects are presented chronologically. The context of the small tack, **26/49**, is Early Iron Age, and as such, it is a good complement in bronze of the closely related and roughly contemporary iron tack from the Hypogeion, discussed in Chapter 15 under **15/100**. A variety of bronze nails and tacks of Archaic and later date are discussed above under **26/15**.[95] The fragmentary bronze nail, **26/50**, which derives from a Classical deposit, is of the same basic type, but with a slightly larger head, as **26/15**; it differs from the latter in that the shaft of **26/50** is circular in section, whereas that of **26/15** is square or rhomboidal.

26/49. (ΜΕΘ 5033 [ΜΕ 83]) Tack Fig. 26.20
Acropolis east slope #245/001014 [5]. Pit 5.
H. 0.022; L. x W. (rectangular head) 0.019 x 0.012; Diam. (upper flattened part of circular head) 0.008; Wt. 1.5 g.

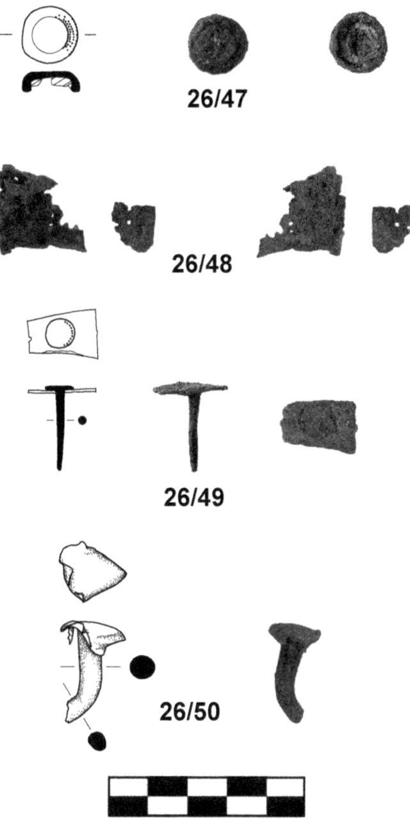

FIGURE 26.20. Acropolis east slope bronzes: tutulus/small boss, **26/47** (ΜΕΘ 5032); cheese grater, **26/48** (ΜΕΘ 5035); nails/tacks, **26/49** (ΜΕΘ 5033), **26/50** (ΜΕΘ 5037). Drawings A. Hooton and T. Ross, photo I. Coyle and J. Vanderpool

Complete.

Small tack, with circular head encased in a larger, roughly rectangular head; lower shaft circular in section.

Context Early Iron Age/Archaic.

Cf. **15/100** for discussion of bronze and iron tacks and nails.

26/50. (ΜΕΘ 5037 [ME 134]) Fragmentary Nail Fig. 26.20

Acropolis east slope #245/005. Από τα χώματα της τομής τάφρος ιστορικών χρόνων (from fill in ditch of Classical period).

P.L. 0.025; L. x W. (head, as bent) 0.016 x 0.012; Wt. 6.1 g.

Single fr preserving entire head and upper part of shaft, but not the lower shaft.

Shaft circular in section, tapering toward point, itself not preserved. Originally circular head, bent out of shape as shown.

Context Classical.

Same basic type as the nail, **26/15**.

IRON OBJECT[96]

Large nail

Although fragmentary, **26/51** is clearly a large nail, with a preserved length, as broken and bent, of 0.140 m. Such large nails, often referred to spikes, are especially common in the Classical period, and they can have a bent-back head, or a distinct round head as **26/51**.[97] Archaic or earlier examples this large are rare, and **26/51** is a welcome addition to large iron nails of the period.

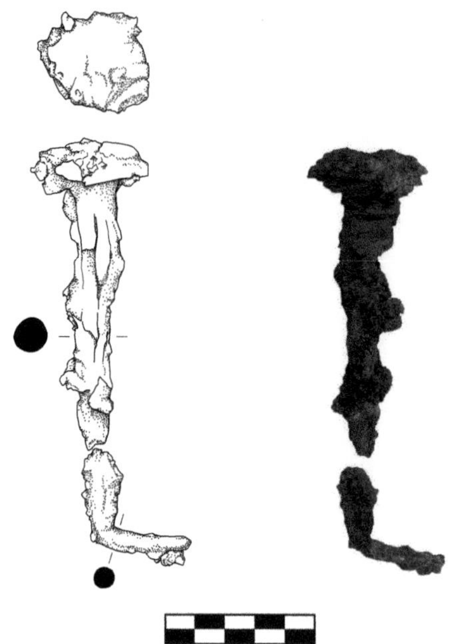

FIGURE 26.21. Acropolis east slope large iron nail, **26/51** (MEΘ 5043). Drawing T. Ross, photo I. Coyle

26/51. (MEΘ 5043 [ME 55]) Fragmentary Nail Fig. 26.21

Acropolis east slope #245/002020 [5]. Pit 5.

P.L. (as bent) 0.140; Diam. (head) 0.041; Wt. 64.9 g.

Two joining frr preserving the greater part of a large nail. Bent and very heavily corroded.

Shaft section difficult to determine on account of corrosion, but probably originally square or rectangular; comparatively large circular head.

Context Early Iron Age/Archaic.

OBJECTS OF LEAD[98]

Implements

Mending clamp and mending plug

Despite its broken state, **26/52** is among the largest of the lead mending clamps at Methone. It is of the same general type as **15/107**, which is fully discussed in Chapter 15. In many ways **26/53** is both a more interesting and a more enigmatic object. Described in the entry below, it is unclear whether it is fragmentary or complete or near complete. In form it resembles, but is slightly smaller than, a lead clamp/plug on an Early Iron Age krater from Torone, referred to under **26/35** from the summit of the West Hill (see discussion and comparanda under **26/35**).[99]

26/52. (MEΘ 5044 [ME 49]) Large Mending Clamp Fig. 26.22

Acropolis east slope #245/002019 [5]. Pit 5.

P.L./L. 0.105; W. (max, at horizontal flattened struts) 0.020; Diam. (connecting strut) 0.011; Wt. 96.0 g.

Two joining frr, plus smaller chips, preserving substantial part of clamp, missing portion of one of the horizontal struts and with only one of the vertical connecting struts.

Preserved vertical strut circular in section. The better preserved of the horizontal struts plano-convex in section; what survives of the other horizontal strut is more or less flat.

Context Early Iron Age/Archaic.

Cf. **15/107** and parallels cited there.

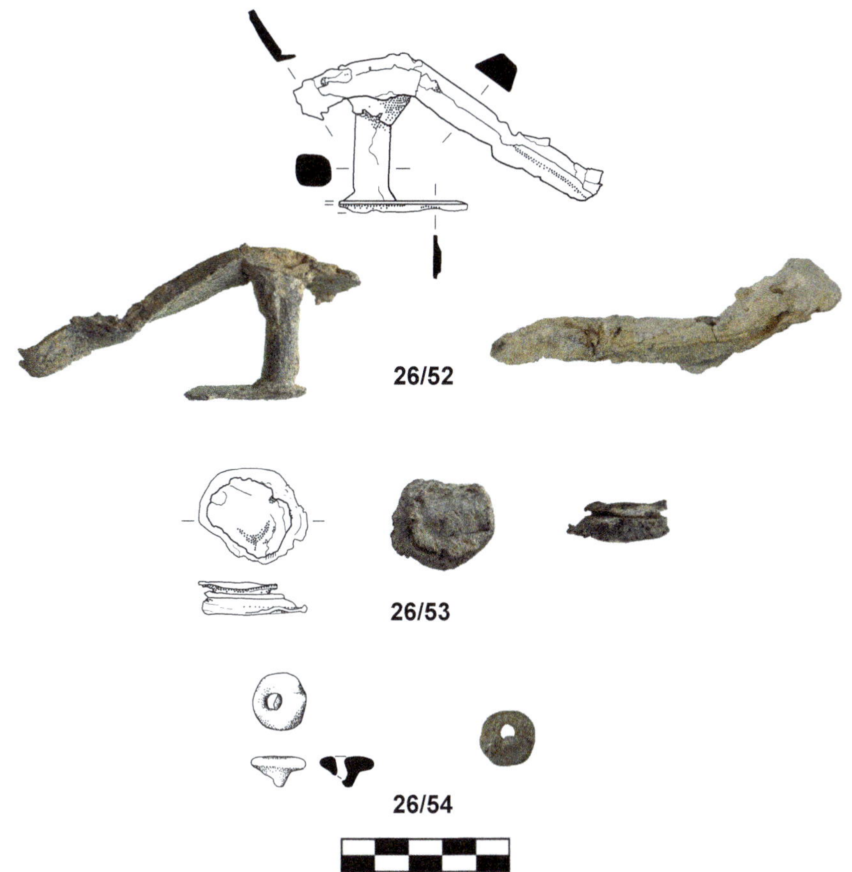

FIGURE 26.22. Acropolis east slope lead objects: large mending clamp, **26/52** (MEΘ 5044); mending plug/clamp, **26/53** (MEΘ 5046); small bead, button, or weight, **26/54** (MEΘ 5045). Drawings A. Hooton and T. Ross, photos I. Coyle and J. Vanderpool

26/53. (MEΘ 5046 [ME 107]) Disk, Possible Mending Plug(?) Fig. 26.22

Acropolis east slope #245/001018 [1]. Τομή Δ (Sector 4).

L. 0.031; W. 0.026; Th. 0.009; Wt. 38.3 g.

Unclear whether complete or broken.

Two rough disks, one smaller than the other, separated by shallow groove; the larger disk is flatter than the smaller one.

Context unclear.

Cf. **26/35**, and esp. Papadopoulos 2005, pp. 151, 563, fig. 135, pl. 330:a, b, T79-1.

Small bead, button, or weight

26/54 has no convincing parallel that I could find. Its form, as preserved, is intentional and thus it clearly served a function. It may have served as a small bead, button, or even a weight.

26/54. (MEΘ 5045 [ME 37]) Small Bead, Button, or Weight Fig. 26.22

Acropolis east slope #245/002014 [5]. Pit 5.

Diam. 0.017; H. 0.008; Diam. (hole) 0.004; Wt. 7.6 g.

Single piece preserving undetermined part of object, perhaps near-complete.

Small circular disk with small hole slightly off-center; flat on one side, with a small shaft-like extension on the other. The small visible grooves are probably accidental(?).

Context Early Iron Age/Archaic.

METAL OBJECTS FROM THE AGORA OF METHONE

The results of the excavations of the agora of ancient Methone are summarized in Chapter 1, and the early stoa building (Building A) is more fully discussed in Chapter 18. Thanks to excellent contextual control during excavation, the context date of each piece is, whenever possible, provided below in Table 26.3. The complex stratigraphy essentially consists of three different deposit types. The most important is the destruction deposit of 354 B.C. itself, a well-preserved and clear level, with numerous finds (pottery presented in Chapter 29, lead sling bullets in Chapter 28). Providing as it does a useful terminus ante quem for all the material contained within, this deposit gives us a useful fixed point in the chronology of the mid-4th century B.C., not only for the north Aegean. Then there was the collapsed fill above the destruction deposit. This layer, at points several meters in depth, collapsed from the higher part of the East Hill, in the area of the Hypogeion, immediately to the east of the agora. The collapse of a portion of the hill, which happened at some undetermined time after the destruction of Methone in 354 B.C., exposed some of the earliest remains at the site, including, only a few centimeters below the summit of the hill, the series of prehistoric defensive trenches on the top of the East Hill (see Chapters 1 and 4). It was from this collapsed fill that much of the Bronze and Early Iron Age material presented in Chapters 4, 5, and 7 derives. Essentially redeposited, this fill contained material from the later stages of the Neolithic period through the mid-4th century B.C. and thus provides no clear contextual dates. The third type of deposit was encountered in isolated patches below the level of the destruction deposit. Wherever encountered, these areas were only partially explored, and they varied in date from Early Iron Age to Archaic.

As with the presentation of the metal objects from the Hypogeion, I begin with the bronzes, before presenting the objects of iron and lead. The copious number of metal objects from the area of agora precludes a full presentation of the material, and in the selection of the material for this chapter my aim was to provide as representative a sample as possible of the range of material present at this part of the site, which was, before it ever became the agora of Archaic and Classical Methone, the primary area of settlement beginning in the Neolithic period.

TABLE 26.3. Summary listing of the context and type of the metal objects from the area of the agora of Methone (Plot 274). The "date" column lists the contextual date of each piece (this table was prepared with the collaboration of Athena Athanassiadou) (DD = destruction deposit)

MEΘ	Metal	Context	Object	Date
26/55 (MEΘ 4196)	Bronze	Pre-destruction deposit	Violin-bow fibula	EIA/Archaic
26/56 (MEΘ 1605)	Bronze	Destruction deposit	Fibula pin & spring	Mid-4th c. or earlier
26/57 (MEΘ 1636)	Bronze	Destruction deposit	"Phrygian" fibula	Mid-4th c. or earlier
26/58 (MEΘ 1629)	Bronze	Context unclear	"Phrygian" fibula	Context unclear
26/59 (MEΘ 1634)	Bronze	Context unclear	"Phrygian" fibula	Context unclear
26/60 (MEΘ 1627)	Bronze	Destruction deposit	"Phrygian" fibula	Mid-4th c. or earlier
26/61 (MEΘ 1631)	Bronze	Pre-destruction deposit	"Phrygian" fibula	Archaic or Classical
26/62 (MEΘ 1637)	Bronze	Destruction deposit	"Phrygian" fibula	Mid-4th c. or earlier
26/63 (MEΘ 1630)	Bronze	Context unclear	"Phrygian" fibula	Context unclear
26/64 (MEΘ 1628)	Bronze	Destruction deposit	"Phrygian" fibula	Mid-4th c. or earlier
26/65 (MEΘ 1632)	Bronze	Collapsed fill above DD	"Phrygian" fibula	Prehistoric–4th c. B.C.
26/66 (MEΘ 1635)	Bronze	Destruction deposit	"Phrygian" fibula	Mid-4th c. or earlier

ΜΕΘ	Metal	Context	Object	Date
26/67 (ΜΕΘ 2130)	Bronze	Water channel associated with DD	"Phrygian" fibula	Mid-4th c. or earlier
26/68 (ΜΕΘ 1621)	Bronze	Pre-destruction deposit	*Rollenkopfnadel*	EIA–Archaic
26/69 (ΜΕΘ 1609)	Bronze	Pre-destruction deposit	Possible *Rollenkopfnadel*	EIA–Archaic
26/70 (ΜΕΘ 1608)	Bronze	Destruction deposit	Small knot-headed pin	Mid-4th c. or earlier
26/71 (ΜΕΘ 2133α)	Bronze	Destruction deposit	Small knot-headed pin	Mid-4th c. or earlier
26/72 (ΜΕΘ 1603)	Bronze	Context unclear	Ribbed-head pin	Context unclear
26/73 (ΜΕΘ 1610)	Bronze	Context unclear	Ribbed-head pin	Context unclear
26/74 (ΜΕΘ 1614)	Bronze	Collapsed fill above DD	Pin with beaded head	Prehistoric–4th-c. B.C.
26/75 (ΜΕΘ 1787)	Bronze	Context unclear	Pin with flattened head (spatula, stylus?)	Context unclear
26/76 (ΜΕΘ 1604)	Bronze	Destruction deposit	Poppy/pomegranate head pin	Mid-4th c. or earlier
26/77 (ΜΕΘ 1611)	Bronze	Destruction deposit	Double pin	Mid-4th c. or earlier
26/78 (ΜΕΘ 1613)	Bronze	Pre-destruction deposit	Double pin	Archaic/earlier Classical
26/79 (ΜΕΘ 1622)	Bronze	Context unclear	Pin finial	Context unclear
26/80 (ΜΕΘ 1654)	Bronze	Destruction deposit	Finial (for pin?)	Mid-4th c. or earlier
26/81 (ΜΕΘ 2132)	Bronze	Destruction deposit	Pin shaft	Mid-4th c. or earlier
26/82 (ΜΕΘ 2143)	Bronze	Destruction deposit	Pin or needle shaft	Mid-4th c. or earlier
26/83 (ΜΕΘ 1655)	Bronze	Collapsed fill above DD	Elongated biconical bead	Prehistoric–4th-c. B.C.
26/84 (ΜΕΘ 1653)	Bronze	Collapsed fill above DD	Small biconical bead	Prehistoric–4th-c. B.C.
26/85 (ΜΕΘ 1651)	Bronze	Backfill	Biconical bead with rims	Context unclear
26/86 (ΜΕΘ 1649)	Bronze	Context unclear	Biconical bead with rims	Context unclear
26/87 (ΜΕΘ 1650 α,β,γ)	Bronze	Pre-destruction deposit	Three small beads, faience inlays	EIA–early Classical
26/88 (ΜΕΘ 1665)	Bronze	Pre-destruction deposit	Finger ring	EIA–Archaic
26/89 (ΜΕΘ 1640)	Bronze	Collapsed fill above DD	Finger ring	Prehistoric–4th-c. B.C.
26/90 (ΜΕΘ 1639)	Bronze	Pre-destruction deposit	Finger ring with bezel	Archaic–Classical
26/91 (ΜΕΘ 1642)	Bronze	Context unclear	Finger ring with bezel	Context unclear
26/92 (ΜΕΘ 1641)	Bronze	Context unclear	Finger ring with bezel	Context unclear
26/93 (ΜΕΘ 1797)	Bronze	Pre-destruction deposit	Earring/hairring	EIA–Archaic
26/94 (ΜΕΘ 1798)	Bronze	Context unclear	Earring/hairring	Context unclear

TABLE 26.3. *(Continued)*

ΜΕΘ	Metal	Context	Object	Date
26/95 (ΜΕΘ 1796)	Bronze	Scarp cleaning	Earring/hairring	Context unclear
26/96 (ΜΕΘ 1794)	Bronze	Pre-destruction deposit	Ring (κρίκος)	EIA–Archaic
26/97 (ΜΕΘ 2135)	Bronze	Destruction deposit	Ring (κρίκος)	Mid-4th c. or earlier
26/98 (ΜΕΘ 2136)	Bronze	Context unclear	Ring (κρίκος)	Context unclear
26/99 (ΜΕΘ 1669)	Bronze	Pre-destruction deposit	Small ring (κρίκος)	EIA–Archaic
26/100 (ΜΕΘ 1645)	Bronze	Pre-destruction deposit?	Bracelet	Archaic–Classical?
26/101 (ΜΕΘ 1647)	Bronze	Destruction deposit	Bracelet	Mid-4th c. or earlier
26/102 (ΜΕΘ 1646)	Bronze	Context unclear	Bracelet	Context unclear
26/103 (ΜΕΘ 3095)	Bronze	Destruction deposit	Bracelet	Mid-4th c. or earlier
26/104 (ΜΕΘ 1690)	Bronze	Scarp cleaning	Tutulus	Context unclear
26/105 (ΜΕΘ 1691)	Bronze	Destruction deposit	Tutulus	Mid-4th c. or earlier
26/106 (ΜΕΘ 1673)	Bronze	Context unclear	Tutulus (omphaloid disk)	Context unclear
26/107 (ΜΕΘ 4143)	Bronze	Backfill	Aulos terminal	Context unclear
26/108 (ΜΕΘ 1795)	Bronze	Collapsed fill above DD	Unidentified (musical instrument?)	Prehistoric–4th-c. B.C.
26/109 (ΜΕΘ 1780)	Bronze	Destruction deposit	Tripod stand, with feline leg	Mid-4th c. or earlier
26/110 (ΜΕΘ 4142)	Bronze	Destruction deposit	Small phiale	Mid-4th c. or earlier
26/111 (ΜΕΘ 4187)	Bronze	Context unclear	Roundel attachment for vessel	Context unclear
26/112 (ΜΕΘ 4188)	Bronze	Destruction deposit	Cheese grater	Mid-4th c. or earlier
26/113 (ΜΕΘ 1671)	Bronze	Context unclear	"Ear spoon"	Context unclear
26/114 (ΜΕΘ 1670)	Bronze	Collapsed fill above DD	Spoon-shaped implement	Prehistoric–4th-c. B.C.
26/115 (ΜΕΘ 1672)	Bronze	Pre-destruction deposit	Spatulate implement/instrument	EIA–Archaic
26/116 (ΜΕΘ 2134)	Bronze	Destruction deposit	Needle	Mid-4th c. or earlier
26/117 (ΜΕΘ 1658)	Bronze	Context unclear	Needle	Context unclear
26/118 (ΜΕΘ 1659)	Bronze	Destruction deposit	Needle	Mid-4th c. or earlier
26/119 (ΜΕΘ 2133β)	Bronze	Destruction deposit	Small needle	Mid-4th c. or earlier
26/120 (ΜΕΘ 4197)	Bronze	Context unclear	Small needle	Context unclear
26/121 (ΜΕΘ 1781)	Bronze	Context uninformative	Spindle hook	Context uninformative
26/122 (ΜΕΘ 1784)	Bronze	Pre-destruction deposit	Cone	Archaic–Classical
26/123 (ΜΕΘ 295)	Bronze	Destruction deposit	Cone	Mid-4th c. or earlier
26/124 (ΜΕΘ 296)	Bronze	Collapsed fill above DD	Cone	Prehistoric–4th-c. B.C.
26/125 (ΜΕΘ 299)	Bronze	Destruction deposit	Cone	Mid-4th c. or earlier
26/126 (ΜΕ 2138)	Bronze	Destruction deposit	Cone	Mid-4th c. or earlier
26/127 (ΜΕΘ 1681)	Bronze	Destruction deposit	Fishhook	Mid-4th c. or earlier
26/128 (ΜΕΘ 1683)	Bronze	Context unclear	Fishhook	Context unclear

ΜΕΘ	Metal	Context	Object	Date
26/129 (ΜΕΘ 1686)	Bronze	Collapsed fill above DD	Fishhook	Prehistoric–4th-c. B.C.
26/130 (ΜΕΘ 1685)	Bronze	Context unclear	Fishhook	Context unclear
26/131 (ΜΕΘ 1688)	Bronze	Context unclear	Fishhook	Context unclear
26/132 (ΜΕΘ 4310)	Bronze	Context unclear	Knife?	Context unclear
26/133 (ΜΕΘ 3097)	Bronze	Context unclear	Nail	Context unclear
26/134 (ΜΕΘ 4194)	Bronze	Collapsed fill above DD	Nail	Prehistoric–4th-c. B.C.
26/135 (ΜΕΘ 4195)	Bronze	Collapsed fill above DD	Nail	Prehistoric–4th-c. B.C.
26/136 (ΜΕΘ 4193)	Bronze	Collapsed fill above DD	Nail	Prehistoric–4th-c. B.C.
26/137 (ΜΕΘ 4192)	Bronze	Context unclear	Nail	Context unclear
26/138 (ΜΕΘ 4293)	Bronze	Context unclear	Nail	Context unclear
26/139 (ΜΕΘ 4292)	Bronze	Destruction deposit	Nail	Mid-4th c. or earlier
26/140 (ΜΕΘ 4145)	Bronze	Destruction deposit	Large nail head	Mid-4th c. or earlier
26/141 (ΜΕΘ 1695)	Bronze	Destruction deposit	Nail	Mid-4th c. or earlier
26/142 (ΜΕΘ 2141)	Bronze	Destruction deposit	Nail	Mid-4th c. or earlier
26/143 (ΜΕΘ 2142)	Bronze	Destruction deposit	Nail head	Mid-4th c. or earlier
26/144 (ΜΕΘ 4305)	Bronze	Destruction deposit	Nail	Mid-4th c. or earlier
26/145 (ΜΕΘ 1693)	Bronze	Context unclear	Tack	Context unclear
26/146 (ΜΕΘ 1692)	Bronze	Scarp cleaning	Tack	Context unclear
26/147 (ΜΕΘ 2129)	Bronze	Destruction deposit	Staple	Mid-4th c. or earlier
26/148 (ΜΕΘ 4190)	Bronze	Destruction deposit	Staple	Mid-4th c. or earlier
26/149 (ΜΕΘ 1633)	Bronze	Context unclear	Staple	Context unclear
26/150 (ΜΕΘ 1778)	Bronze	Context unclear	Bindings/sheaths	Context unclear
26/151 (ΜΕΘ 1779)	Bronze	Destruction deposit	Bindings/sheaths	Mid-4th c. or earlier
26/152 (ΜΕΘ 4146)	Bronze	Destruction deposit	Bindings/sheaths	Mid-4th c. or earlier
26/153 (ΜΕΘ 4304)	Bronze	Destruction deposit	Binding plate	Mid-4th c. or earlier
26/154 (ΜΕΘ 4291)	Bronze	Surface find	Binding plate	Surface find
26/155 (ΜΕΘ 4311)	Bronze	Pre-destruction deposit	Binding plate	EIA–early Classical
26/156 (ΜΕΘ 4227)	Bronze	Collapsed fill above DD	Binding plate	Prehistoric-4th-c. B.C.
26/157 (ΜΕΘ 1775α)	Bronze	Destruction deposit	Binding plate/attachment	Mid-4th c. or earlier
26/158 (ΜΕΘ 1775β)	Bronze	Destruction deposit	Binding plate/attachment	Mid-4th c. or earlier
26/159 (ΜΕΘ 4231)	Bronze	Destruction deposit	Perforated disk	Mid-4th c. or earlier
26/160 (ΜΕΘ 1777)	Bronze	Collapsed fill above DD	Disk	Prehistoric–4th-c. B.C.
26/161 (ΜΕΘ 1776)	Bronze	Context unclear	Disk	Context unclear
26/162 (ΜΕΘ 4233)	Bronze	Context unclear	Small rectangular sheet	Context unclear

TABLE 26.3. *(Continued)*

MEΘ	Metal	Context	Object	Date
26/163 (MEΘ 4235)	Bronze	Destruction deposit	Rectangular sheet	Mid-4th c. or earlier
26/164 (MEΘ 4228)	Bronze	Collapsed fill above DD	Triangular sheet	Prehistoric–4th-c. B.C.
26/165 (MEΘ 4308)	Bronze	Backfill	Small rectangular strip	Uncertain
26/166 (MEΘ 4229)	Bronze	Destruction deposit	Thin narrow strip	Mid-4th c. or earlier
26/167 (MEΘ 1648)	Bronze	Pre-destruction deposit	Rod	EIA–Archaic
26/168 (MEΘ 4230)	Bronze	Destruction deposit	Large rod	Mid-4th c. or earlier
26/169 (MEΘ 4309)	Bronze	Collapsed fill above DD	Perforated rod shaft	Prehistoric–4th-c. B.C.
26/170 (MEΘ 4232)	Bronze	Destruction deposit	Hinged plate & pin	Mid-4th c. or earlier
26/171 (MEΘ 4234)	Bronze	Context unclear	Fragmentary hinged object	Context unclear
26/172 (MEΘ 2140)	Bronze	Building Δ	Wedge-shaped object	Mid-4th c. or earlier
26/173 (MEΘ 4191)	Bronze	Context unclear	Attachment, decorative rivet	Context unclear
26/174 (MEΘ 5303)	Bronze	Destruction deposit or just above	Tube	Mid-4th c. or earlier
26/175 (MEΘ 1675)	Bronze	Context unclear	Arrowhead	Context unclear
26/176 (MEΘ 294)	Bronze	Destruction deposit	Arrowhead	Mid-4th c. or earlier
26/177 (MEΘ 1791)	Bronze	Destruction deposit	Arrowhead	Mid-4th c. or earlier
26/178 (MEΘ 1679)	Bronze	Pre-destruction deposit	Arrowhead	Archaic to Classical
26/179 (MEΘ 1676)	Bronze	Context unclear	Arrowhead	Context unclear
26/180 (MEΘ 1678)	Bronze	Building B fill, above DD	Arrowhead	Classical or earlier
26/181 (MEΘ 1677)	Bronze	Building B fill, above DD	Arrowhead	Classical or earlier
26/182 (MEΘ 1674)	Bronze	Destruction deposit	Arrowhead	Mid-4th c. or earlier
26/183 (MEΘ 1730)	Iron	Scarp cleaning	Arrowhead	Context unclear
26/184 (MEΘ 1731)	Iron	Surface find	Arrowhead	Surface find
26/185 (MEΘ 1734)	Iron	Above destruction deposit	Arrowhead	Context unclear
26/186 (MEΘ 1723)	Iron	Context unclear	Arrowhead	Context unclear
26/187 (MEΘ 1728)	Iron	Destruction deposit	Arrowhead	Mid-4th c. or earlier
26/188 (MEΘ 1746)	Iron	Cleaning of Wall 7	Spearhead	Context unclear
26/189 (MEΘ 1752)	Iron	Destruction deposit	Spearhead	Mid-4th c. or earlier
26/190 (MEΘ 1766)	Iron	Context unclear	Small sauroter	Context unclear
26/191 (MEΘ 1747)	Iron	Pre-destruction deposit	Sword fr	EIA–Archaic
26/192 (MEΘ 1753)	Iron	Destruction deposit	Sword	Mid-4th c. or earlier
26/193 (MEΘ 1751)	Iron	Destruction deposit	Fragmentary knife	Mid-4th c. or earlier
26/194 (MEΘ 1737)	Iron	Context unclear	Scythe or large sickle	Context unclear
26/195 (MEΘ 1755)	Iron	Above destruction deposit	Tongs/poker	Pre-destruction deposit
26/196 (MEΘ 1774)	Iron	Destruction deposit	Large scraper	Mid-4th c. or earlier
26/197 (MEΘ 5291)	Iron	Context unclear	Ring	Context unclear

ΜΕΘ	Metal	Context	Object	Date
26/198 (ΜΕΘ 1754)	Iron	Context unclear	Two interconnected rings	Context unclear
26/199 (ΜΕΘ 4260)	Iron	Destruction deposit	Nail	Mid-4th c. or earlier
26/200 (ΜΕΘ 5333)	Iron	Destruction deposit	Nail	Mid-4th c. or earlier
26/201 (ΜΕΘ 5345)	Iron	Immediately below DD	Nail	Early 4th c. or earlier
26/202 (ΜΕΘ 4345)	Iron	Immediately below DD	Nail	Early 4th c. or earlier
26/203 (ΜΕΘ 1769)	Iron	Destruction deposit	Tube	Mid-4th c. or earlier
26/204 (ΜΕΘ 1771)	Iron	Destruction deposit	Attachment(?)	Mid-4th c. or earlier
26/205 (ΜΕΘ 4368)	Lead	Collapsed fill above DD	Mending clamp	Prehistoric–4th-c. B.C.
26/206 (ΜΕΘ 4367)	Lead	Destruction deposit	Fragmentary mending clamp	Mid-4th c. or earlier
26/207 (ΜΕΘ 4372)	Lead	Context unclear	Mending clamp	Context unclear
26/208 (ΜΕΘ 2146)	Lead	Pre-destruction deposit	Mending clamp	EIA–Archaic
26/209 (ΜΕΘ 1712)	Lead	Context unclear	Mending clamp	Context unclear
26/210 (ΜΕΘ 4371)	Lead	Context unclear	Mending clamp	Context unclear
26/211 (ΜΕΘ 4366)	Lead	Context unclear	Circular clamp & plug	Context unclear
26/212 (ΜΕΘ 2182)	Lead	Destruction deposit	Weight	Mid-4th c. or earlier
26/213 (ΜΕΘ 1710)	Lead	Destruction deposit	Weight	Mid-4th c. or earlier
26/214 (ΜΕΘ 1526)	Lead	Surface find	Weight?	Uncertain
26/215 (ΜΕΘ 2149)	Lead	Destruction deposit	Unidentified suspended object	Mid-4th c. or earlier
26/216 (ΜΕΘ 1713)	Lead	Surface find	Wheel	Uncertain
26/217 (ΜΕΘ 4378)	Lead	Destruction deposit	Thin sheet (*pinakion*)	Mid-4th c. or earlier
26/218 (ΜΕΘ 4365)	Lead	Pre-destruction deposit	Rectangular sheet	Late EIA–Archaic
26/219 (ΜΕΘ 4374)	Lead	Destruction deposit	Thin sheet, perforated	Mid-4th c. or earlier
26/220 (ΜΕΘ 4375)	Lead	Destruction deposit	Thick elliptical sheet	Mid-4th c. or earlier
26/221 (ΜΕΘ 4376)	Lead	Context unclear	Thinner elliptical sheet	Context unclear
26/222 (ΜΕΘ 2147)	Lead	Destruction deposit	Sheet	Mid-4th c. or earlier
26/223 (ΜΕΘ 4364)	Lead	Pre-destruction deposit	Rod (ingot?)	Late EIA–Archaic
26/224 (ΜΕΘ 2148)	Lead	Destruction deposit	Fragmentary rod (ingot?)	Mid-4th c. or earlier
26/225 (ΜΕΘ 4363)	Lead	Pre-destruction deposit	Pierced strip	Late EIA–Archaic
26/226 (ΜΕΘ 4373)	Lead	Context unclear	Globular piece of lead (ingot?)	Context unclear
26/227 (ΜΕΘ 4377)	Lead	Context unclear	Lead filling	Context unclear
26/228 (ΜΕΘ 1711)	Lead	Destruction deposit	Amorphous strip	Mid-4th c. or earlier
26/229 (ΜΕΘ 4370)	Lead	Context unclear	Amorphous piece	Context unclear
26/230 (ΜΕΘ 3100)	Lead	Immediately below DD	Amorphous piece	Archaic–Classical

Objects of Bronze

Jewelry and other items of personal ornament

Fibulae

Violin-bow fibula

The solitary example of a violin-bow fibula from the agora, **26/55**, is closely related to **15/6** from the Hypogeion. Designated "en archet" by Blinkenberg, this fibula type enjoys a Mycenaean pedigree, continuing through the Early Iron Age into the Archaic period.[100] Sapouna-Sakellarakis follows Blinkenberg in classifying this as Type I, and distinguishes at least eight varieties.[101] For further discussion and comparanda, see Chapter 15 under **15/6.**

26/55. (MEΘ 4196 [ME 3801]) Violin-bow Fibula Fig. 26.23

Agora #274/089. Τομή στη βόρεια πλευρά (trench on the north side).

P.L. (main joining frr) 0.032–0.033; W. (max) 0.010; Wt. 2.0 g.

Four main frr, two of which join, preserving portion of arch and spring.

Arch/bow hammered flat and lozenge-shaped in plan, tapering toward both ends, only the end on side of spring preserved. Spring has at least three turns.

Context Early Iron Age/Archaic.

Cf. **15/6**, and discussion and comparanda provided there.

Pin and spring of large fibula

Although only partially preserved, without any of the arch surviving, **26/56** is of interest for its size, as it does not correspond to the smaller, more normal fibulae found at Methone. Although its type is unknown, it may derive from a violin-bow fibula, any of the larger bow fibulae ("Bogenfibeln"), or even one of the larger mainland Greek fibulae.

26/56. (MEΘ 1605 [ME 1375]) Fibula Pin and Spring Fig. 26.23

Agora #274/076. Στρώμα καστανέρυθρο (red-brown layer) [3].

P.L. 0.072; Diam. (spring) 0.008; Diam. (shaft) 0.002–0.003; Wt. 3.2 g.

Single fr preserving most of pin and spring of fibula, except for pin point; nothing of bow/arch survives.

Large fibula of unknown type. Pin shaft square/rectangular in section, tapering toward point, the tip of which is not preserved. Spring end slightly hammered flat; at least two turns.

Context destruction deposit, mid-4th century B.C. or earlier.

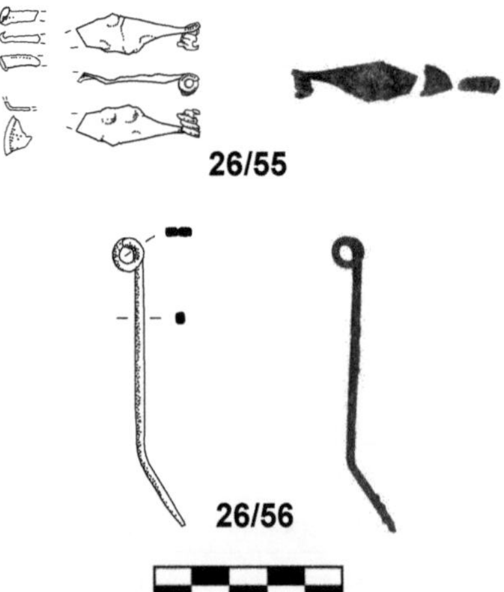

Figure 26.23. Agora bronze fibulae, violin-bow fibula, **26/55** (MEΘ 4196), and pin and spring of large fibula, **26/56** (MEΘ 1605). Drawings A. Hooton and F. Skyvalida, photos I. Coyle and J. Vanderpool

"Phrygian" fibulae

I provided a brief introduction to "Phrygian"—or "Asia Minor/Anatolian"—fibulae in Chapter 15 under **15/13–15/15**, with supplementary comments above under **26/45**. I refer to them as "Phrygian"—in quotation marks—because, with the possible exception of **15/13**, they were made in the Aegean. Most of the Hypogeion examples were earlier, late 8th or 7th century B.C., whereas most of the examples presented below are later, many of them from the mid-4th century B.C. destruction deposit. I present them below, trying to follow, as far as is possible, the typology established by Blinkenberg and further elaborated by Muscarella (Type XII). Most typologies of "Phrygian" fibulae focus on Archaic examples, whereas those of Classical date are somewhat less known. Wherever possible, I provide comparanda for each fibula in the catalogue entry.

Although broadly related to Blinkenberg's and Muscarella's Type XII, most of the Methone fibulae differ from the main series of Phrygian fibulae from Gordion and Anatolia, and correspond to Blinkenberg's and Muscarella's Type XII, 15–17, about which the latter writes: "These types should be discussed separately from the other types in the group XII category. None of the examples known to me come from Gordion or Anatolia; all were found in Greece or Macedonia. Their mouldings and catches are not like those on group XII fibulae and none are demonstrably earlier than the 6th century B.C. In fact, they, like XII, 13q-s and XII, 14q, are Greek fibulae derived from types XII, 13 and 14 prototypes."[102]

The first two, **26/57** and **26/58**, correspond generally to Type XII, 2. In describing the type, Muscarella writes: "The arc is semi-circular and plain, except for milling on some examples. The arc is round in section and the end mouldings consist of various types of tori, abaci, and discs in combination. The spring-plate is usually shield-shaped but sometimes cylindrical." The arch of **26/57** is decorated by milling, whereas that of **26/58** is plain, although there is a very slight swelling at the top. The arch of the former connects directly with both the catchplate and the springplate; the latter has decorated beads at either end. The horns on the catchplate of **26/58** are found on a fibula in northern Greece, now in Oxford, mentioned in the catalogue entry below. The catchplates and springplates of both fibulae are different from the main series of Phrygian fibulae from Anatolia, and both are better classified under the general heading of Type XII, 15–17 of Greek manufacture.

The next six fibulae (**26/59–26/64**) correspond broadly to Blinkenberg's and Muscarella's Type XII, 12 and XII, 13, especially the latter. One example of this type was also encountered in the Hypogeion, with full discussion in Chapter 15, under **15/14**, and another on the summit of the West Hill (**26/4**). Most should be equated with what Muscarella classifies as Type XII, 16A, which correspond to Blinkenberg's Type XII, 16a and b from Dodona and Eretria.[103] About this type, Muscarella writes: "The arc has three to five mouldings and the pin turns on a pivot set into a disc or palmette. There is no group XII catch."[104] He goes on to cite parallels from Olynthos and other sites in the north Aegean, adding: "The Olynthus destruction of 348 B.C. established a 4th-century date for this type."[105] The final three fibulae I distinguish from the previous six, on account of five beads or moldings on their arch, but it is clear from Muscarella's typology that these also belong with his Type XII, 16A. Well-dated examples of such fibulae from the tombs at Sindos date to the 6th century B.C.[106] A number of the "Phrygian" fibulae preserve traces of iron corrosion indicating that the pin, or the small rivet keeping it in place, was made of iron.

26/57. (ΜΕΘ 1636 [ΜΕ 1375]) "Phrygian" Fibula — Fig. 26.24

Agora #274/069.

L. 0.023; H. 0.017; Wt. 2.8 g.

Two frr preserving virtually complete fibula: one of arch with catchplate, the other the pin.

Milled or ribbed arch, resembling continuous spiral, circular in section. Catchplate circular in plan and plano-convex, almost cone-shaped in profile, with catch hammered flat and bent up to accommodate pin. The spring consists of two parallel circle disks resembling a yo-yo that hold the pin in place. Pin thin, circular in section, tapering to a sharp point.

Context destruction deposit, mid-4th century B.C. or earlier.

Cf. Sapouna-Sakellarakis 1978, pl. 50, nos. 1595–1600 (Type XII, 2), which are earlier than **26/57**; Boardman 1967, pp. 209, 211, fig. 138, nos. 228–230 (Type K, compared with Blinkenberg Type XII, 1).

26/58. (ΜΕΘ 1629 [ΜΕ 2255]) "Phrygian" Fibula Fig. 26.24

Agora #274/075. Ανατολικό τμήμα (east section).

L. 0.037; H. 0.026; Wt. 7.0 g.

Intact. Condition good.

Arch circular in section, swollen very slightly at the top, with bead on either side near spring and catchplate, each bead set off by fillet on either side. Spring double disk, yo-yo-shaped, as **26/57**, but with two small "ears" or "horns" at the top, as shown, to which the pin is attached. Circular catchplate, also with two small "ears/horns," with lower portion hammered flat and bent up to accommodate the pin. Pin circular in section tapering toward point.

Context unclear.

For the horned catchplate, cf. two fibulae in Oxford from northern Greece noted by Muscarella 1967, p. 34, n. 53. Cf. also the plain arch of Sapouna-Sakellarakis 1978, pl. 50, no. 1597 (Type XII, 2); Caner 1983, pl. 38, nos. 489–491, plain arch with very slight swelling at top (his Type D I; his Type D II has a more noticeable swelling at midpoint); cf. also Boardman 1967, pp. 209, 211, fig. 138, no. 227 (also Type K). Cf. also Kilian-Dirlmeier 2002, pl. 93, no. 1464.

26/59. (ΜΕΘ 1634 [ΜΕ 3714]) "Phrygian" FIibula Fig. 26.24

Agora #274/017019 [2]. Βόρειας μάρτυρας (north balk).

L. 0.025; H. 0.016; Wt. 1.6 g.

Single piece preserving entire arch, catchplate and most of springplate, but nothing of the pin itself.

Arch circular in section and decorated with three beads, each of the three sets with a larger central bead flanked by a fillet or smaller bead on either side. Circular two-part yo-yo springplate, with traces of iron corrosion suggesting that the pin, or the smaller rivet holding it in place, was of iron. Simple catchplate as shown, hammered flat and curved up to accommodate pin.

Context unclear.

Cf. Blinkenberg 1926, p. 227, fig. 260, XII 16a; Sapouna-Sakellarakis 1978, pl. 53, nos. 1670–1673 (from Emporio, Chios).

26/60. (ΜΕΘ 1627 [ΜΕ 960]) "Phrygian" Fibula Fig. 26.24

Agora #274/077.

L. 0.025; H. 0.020; Wt. 5.1 g.

Single piece preserving complete arch and springplate, but nothing of catchplate and pin.

Arch circular in section, decorated with three substantial beads, each ribbed or filleted (five ribs). Circular, two-part disk springplate as **26/59** (ΜΕΘ 1634).

Context destruction deposit, mid-4th century B.C. or earlier.

Cf., among others, the general form of Sapouna-Sakellarakis 1978, pl. 53, no. 1662 (Phana, Chios); Kilian-Dirlmeier 2002, pl. 93, no. 1468; Mazarakis Ainian 2019, p. 114, fig. 190.

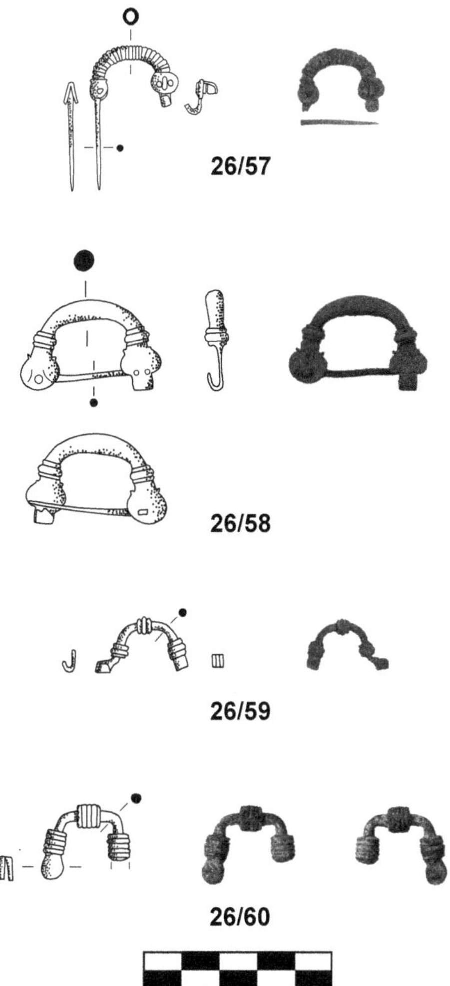

FIGURE 26.24. Agora bronze "Phrygian" fibulae, **26/57** (ΜΕΘ 1636), **26/58** (ΜΕΘ 1629), **26/59** (ΜΕΘ 1634), **26/60** (ΜΕΘ 1627). Drawings F. Skyvalida, photos I. Coyle and J. Vanderpool

26/61. (ΜΕΘ 1631 [ΜΕ 2077]) "Phrygian" Fibula Fig. 26.25

Agora #274/079. ΝΑ Τμήμα (SE section).

L. 0.022; H. 0.018; Wt. 3.6 g.

Single piece preserving arch, catchplate, and springplate, but nothing of the pin.

Arch circular in section with three symmetrically placed ribbed or filleted beads (mostly four ribs). Volute-shaped catchplate, which lacks the plano-convex bulge on one side. Hammered flat, with lower part curved up to accommodate pin. Standard two-part disk springplate as **26/59** (ΜΕΘ 1634).

Context pre-destruction deposit, Archaic or Classical.

Cf., among others, Kilian 1975a, pl. 50, nos. 1732–1736.

26/62. (ΜΕΘ 1637 [ΜΕ 3974]) "Phrygian" Fibula Fig. 26.25

Agora #274/069. Δάπεδο (floor).

L. 0.036; H. 0.020; Wt. 3.4 g.

Single piece preserving arch, catchplate, and springplate, but nothing of the pin.

Type as **26/59** (ΜΕΘ 1634) and **26/60** (ΜΕΘ 1627), with volute catchplate. Traces of iron corrosion suggest that the pin or the small rivet attaching it to springplate was of iron.

Context destruction deposit, mid-4th century B.C. or earlier.

Cf. **26/61** (ΜΕΘ 1631); Kilian-Dirlmeier 2002, pl. 93, nos. 1468–1469; pl. 112, no. 1827; Rhomiopoulou and Touratsoglou 2002, pp. 79–80, M 1063α (Mieza, last quarter 5th century B.C.), also p. 120, M 1046 (mid-5th century B.C.); *Sindos* III, pp. 190, 455, fig. 170, no. 352 (dated 450–440 B.C.).

26/63. (ΜΕΘ 1630 [ΜΕ 2378]) "Phrygian" Fibula Fig. 26.25

Agora #274/075. Μέσο νότιου τμήματος (middle of south part).

L. 0.019; H. 0.012; Wt. 0.8 g.

Single piece preserving arch, catchplate, and springplate, but nothing of the pin.

Type as **26/59** (ΜΕΘ 1634) and **26/62** (ΜΕΘ 1637), but smaller and with three single beads, the bead on side of springplate separated by fillets. Volute catchplate, with lower part hammered flat and curved up to accommodate pin. Standard two-part disk springplate, with traces of iron corrosion.

Context unclear.

Cf. Blinkenberg 1926, p. 227, fig. 260, XII 16a; Kilian-Dirlmeier 2002, pl. 93, no. 1474; *Sindos* III, pp. 187, 454, fig. 163, no. 344 (dated 460–450 B.C.).

26/64. (ΜΕΘ 1628 [ΜΕ 1679]) "Phrygian" Fibula Fig. 26.25

Agora #274/008008 [3].

L. 0.026; H. 0.019; Wt. 2.2 g.

Single piece preserving arch, catchplate, and springplate, but nothing of the pin.

Type as **26/60** (ΜΕΘ 1627) and **26/62** (ΜΕΘ 1637), but with each set of beads consisting of a broader central bead flanked by fillets. Traces of iron corrosion associated with springplate.

Context destruction deposit, mid-4th century B.C. or earlier.

Cf. esp. Kilian 1975a, pl. 50, no. 1732; Kilian-Dirlmeier 2002, pl. 94, nos. 1478–1479; Rhomiopoulou and Touratsoglou 2002, p. 103, M 1092 (5th–early 4th century B.C.), p. 105, M 1097 (5th century B.C.); also the silver fibulae, *Sindos* III, pp. 188, 455, fig. 166, no. 347 (dated second quarter of the 5th century B.C.).

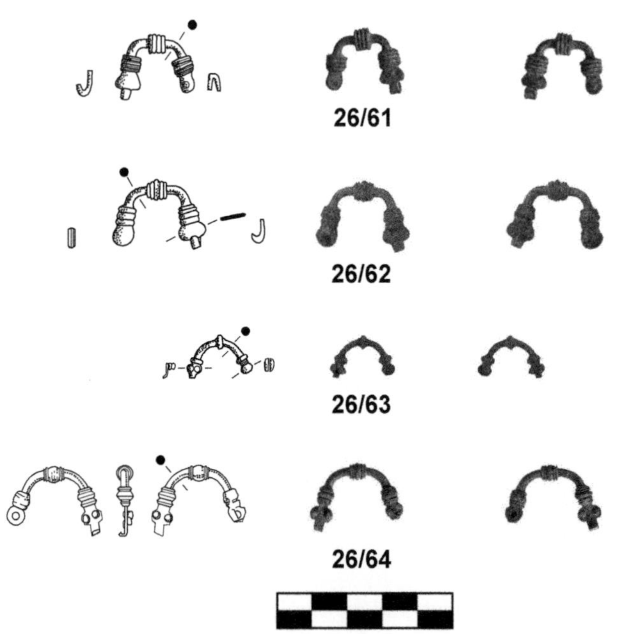

FIGURE 26.25. Agora bronze "Phrygian" fibulae, **26/61** (ΜΕΘ 1631), **26/62** (ΜΕΘ 1637), **26/63** (ΜΕΘ 1630), **26/64** (ΜΕΘ 1628). Drawings A. Hooton and F. Skyvalida, photos I. Coyle and J. Vanderpool

26/65. (ΜΕΘ 1632 [ΜΕ 2535]) "Phrygian" Fibula Fig. 26.26

Agora #274/016005 [1].

P.L. 0.023; p.H. 0.017; Wt. 3.0 g.

Single piece preserving arch, springplate, and most of the catchplate, but nothing of the pin.

Arch, circular in section, with five beads or moldings, all rosette-shaped. Volute-shaped catchplate, as shown, the lower end hammered flat; circular, double-disk, yo-yo shaped springplate. Traces of iron corrosion indicate that the pin, or what held it in place, was of iron.

Context collapsed fill above destruction deposit, prehistoric to mid-4th century B.C.

Cf. **26/66** (ΜΕΘ 1635); and cf., among others, Kilian 1975a, pl. 50, nos. 1747, and 1745; Kilian-Dirlmeier 2002, pl. 94, nos. 1505–1506 (for the general form); Rhomiopoulou and Touratsoglou 2002, p. 66, α.α (bottom, from Mieza), also p. 106, M 1098 (5th–early 4th century B.C.), p. 109, M 1101 (5th century B.C.). Note also the four silver fibulae associated with the chain, *Sindos* III, pp. 185, 431, fig. 70, no. 337 (dated 450–440 B.C.); also the silver fibulae pp. 183–184, 452, figs. 153–154, nos. 328–330 (all of the latter dated to the end of the 6th century B.C.); Benac and Čović 1957, pl. XLIX, nos. 6–9.

26/66. (ΜΕΘ 1635 [ΜΕ 3960]) "Phrygian" Fibula Fig. 26.26

Agora #274/069. Δάπεδο (floor).

P.L. 0.024; p.H. 0.016; Wt. 3.0 g.

Condition as **26/65** (ΜΕΘ 1632), but with most of the catchplate preserved.

Form as **26/65** (ΜΕΘ 1632), with beginning of curved-up portion of catchplate to accommodate pin.

Context destruction deposit, mid-4th century B.C. or earlier.

Cf. **26/65** (ΜΕΘ 1632); Kilian-Dirlmeier 2002, pl. 94, nos. 1481, 1497–1498, 1505–1506; Rhomiopoulou and Touratsoglou 2002, p. 66, α.α (Mieza, 5th–4th century B.C.).

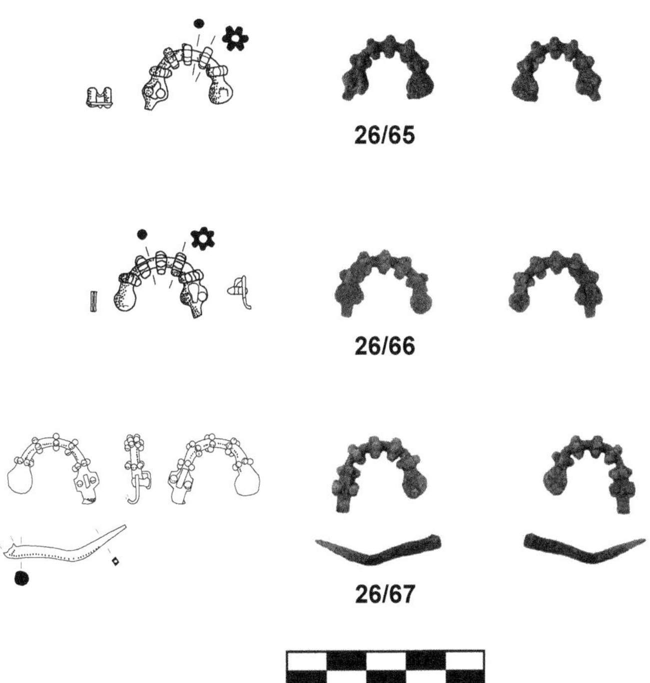

FIGURE 26.26. Agora bronze "Phrygian" fibulae, **26/65** (ΜΕΘ 1632), **26/66** (ΜΕΘ 1635), **26/67** (ΜΕΘ 2130). Drawings A. Hooton and F. Skyvalida, photos I. Coyle and J. Vanderpool

26/67. (ΜΕΘ 2130 [ΜΕ 4080]) "Phrygian" Fibula Fig. 26.26

Agora #274/059010 [3]. Αυλάκι (small channel).

L. 0.023–0.024; H. 0.017; L. (pin) 0.031; Wt. (both frr) 4.3 g.

Two non-joining frr, one preserving arch, catchplate, and springplate, the other preserving greater part of pin. It seems clear that, although found together, the pin and the fibula arch are not from the same object.

Form as **26/65** (ΜΕΘ 1632).

Context water channel associated with the destruction deposit, mid-4th century B.C. or earlier.

Cf. **26/65** (ΜΕΘ 1632) and **26/66** (ΜΕΘ 1635); Rhomiopoulou and Touratsoglou 2002, p. 79, M 1062 (Mieza, first half 4th century B.C.), also p. 89, M 1077 (end of the 5th century B.C.), p. 96, M1080, M 1081 (silver, 5th century B.C.); Benac and Čović 1957, pl. XLIX, nos. 8–9.

Additional "Phrygian" fibulae not catalogued:

ΜΕΘ 1638 (ΜΕ 3909). Agora #274/079. Τομή στη νότια πλευρά. P.L. 0.035; Wt. 4.6 g.

ΜΕΘ 1626 (ΜΕ 422). Agora #274/007008 [3]. P.L. 0.025; Wt. 2.4 g.

ΜΕΘ 4307 (ΜΕ 3558). Agora #274/008012 [6]. Collapsed fill above destruction deposit. Not unlike the springplate for **26/58**. P.L. 0.018; Diam. (max) 0.012; Wt. 5.6 g.

Dress pins

Rollenkopfnadeln

The one clear example of a dress pin with rolled-head ("Rollenkopfnadel" or "Rollennadel"), **26/68**, was found in a pre-destruction context that can be dated Early Iron Age or Archaic. This distinctive pin type, one of the oldest in the Aegean, is discussed more fully, with comparanda, in Chapter 15 (under **15/18–15/20**), with additional examples from the summit of the West Hill (**26/7**, **26/8**). Closely related is a more damaged pin that is probably of this type, **26/69**. As noted in the catalogue entry below, it is unlikely to be a pin with a ring head ("*Ringkopfnadel*"). Like **26/68**, **26/69** can also be dated to the Early Iron Age or Archaic period.

26/68. (ΜΕΘ 1621 [ΜΕ 2743]) *Rollenkopfnadel* Fig. 26.27

Agora #274/036011 [4].

P.L. 0.061; Diam. (head) 0.009–0.010; Th. (shaft, max) 0.003; Wt. 2.3 g.

Single fr preserving head and much of upper shaft of pin; shaft worn.

Portion of shaft is circular in section, but in parts appears to be square, but difficult to tell due to wear. Top hammered flat and rolled to form the distinctive head.

Cf., among others, Mazarakis Ainian 2019, p. 116, fig. 199.

Context pre-destruction deposit, Early Iron Age or Archaic.

26/69. (ΜΕΘ 1609 [ΜΕ 2103]) *Rollenkopfnadel*(?) Fig. 26.27

Agora #274/079. ΝΑ Τμήμα (SE section).

L. (as bent) 0.084; L. (head) 0.010; Diam. (shaft) 0.002; Wt. 1.3 g.

Single fr preserving complete pin; shaft in relatively good condition; head very poorly preserved and appears broken at one point.

Comparatively thin shaft of medium length, circular in section, tapering toward a point. Shaft continues onto head, but its original form is difficult to determine; as preserved, it appears to be looped or rolled over, but it is possible that it originally may have had two loops, as **26/70** (ΜΕΘ 1608). Although broken, it is unlikely to be a pin with a ring head ("*Ringkopfnadel*"), such as Kilian-Dirlmeier 1984a, pp. 284–285, pl. 113, nos. 4904–4913.

Context pre-destruction deposit, Early Iron Age or Archaic.

Possible additional rolled-head pins:

ΜΕΘ 1620 (ΜΕ 2639). Agora #274/036016 [4]. Fr preserving head and two additional frr of shaft, highly corroded. P.L. (all frr) 0.066; Wt. 5.8 g.

ΜΕ 4218. Agora #274/080005 [3]. Head of comparatively small *Rollenkopfnadel.* P.L. 0.010; L. (head) 0.005; Wt. 0.3 g.

Knot-head pins ("*Schlaufennadeln*" or "*Schleifennadeln*")

The "knot-headed" or "looped-headed" pin is a relatively long-lived type that comes in a variety of sizes ranging from small to medium, but is rarely large.[107] Jacobsthal grouped together a number of such pins from Perachora, Corinth, Olympia, Prosymna, Psychro Cave, Praisos, Palaikastro, and Lasithi, and noted that, although they first appear in the Early Bronze Age in Europe, the Near East, and Egypt, the context of those found in Greece cannot be earlier than the 8th or 7th century B.C.[108] Both **26/70** and **26/71** are very small, with a preserved length of 0.041, and unlikely in their original state to have been much larger; an example from Mantineia has a total length of 0.073.[109] The type corresponds to the "Schlaufennadeln" (Jacobsthal prefers "Schleifennadeln"), which begin in the late 7th or early 6th century, and although numerous pins of the type from Crete (Paliakastro, Praisos, the Diktaian Cave) are difficult to date, seven examples of the type from Tegea are assigned

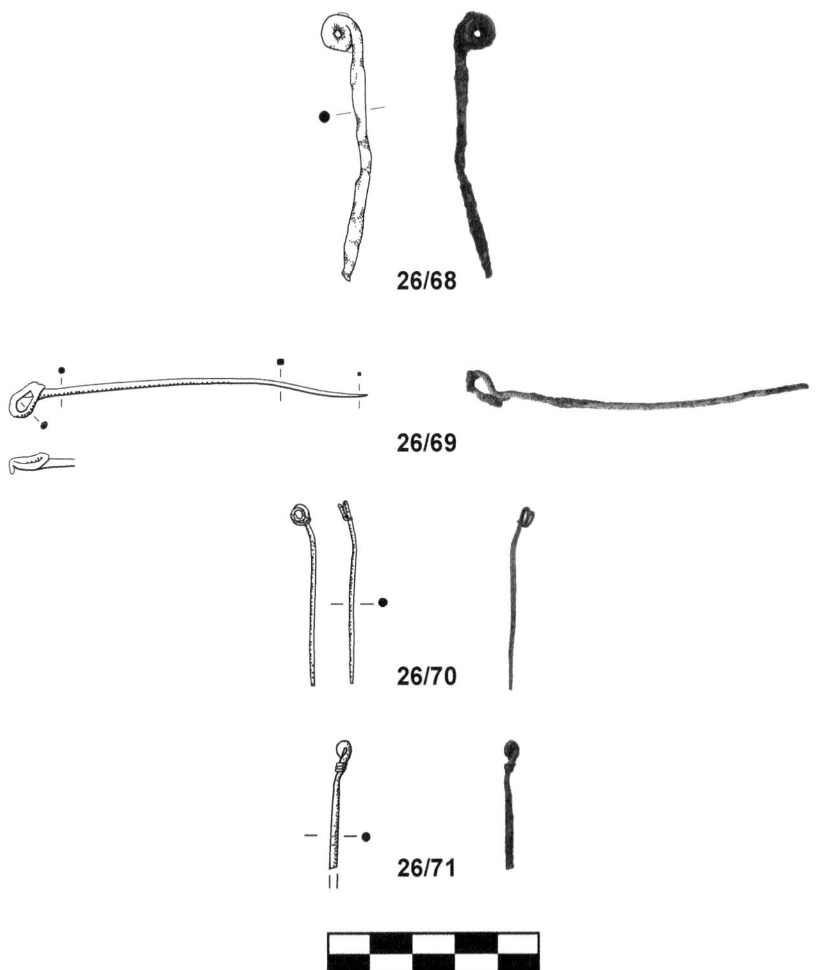

FIGURE 26.27. Agora bronze dress pins, *Rollenkopfnadeln*, **26/68** (ΜΕΘ 1621) and **26/69** (ΜΕΘ 1609), knot-headed pins, **26/70** (ΜΕΘ 1608) and **26/71** (ΜΕΘ 2133α). Drawings A. Hooton, T. Ross, and F. Skyvalida, photos I. Coyle and J. Vanderpool

by Mary Voyatzis to the 8th–7th centuries B.C., while an example from Deposit F at the Demeter sanctuary at Knossos is of Hellenistic date.[110] A fragmentary example of this type was found at Corinth next to a late antique grave in a context of the 6th century A.D. that shows that the type continued well into the Late Roman period.[111] A related pin type at Sindos, in silver and bronze, has a figure-of-eight knot at the head.[112] The appearance of **26/70** and **26/71** in the destruction deposits of the mid-4th century B.C. at Methone helps to secure the chronological range of the type.

26/70. (ΜΕΘ 1608 [ΜΕ 1818]) Knot-headed Pin Fig. 26.27
Agora #274/078. Ανατολικός.μάρτυρας (east balk).
P.L. 0.041; Diam. (head) 0.004; Diam./Th. (shaft) 0.002; Wt. 0.4 g.
Single fr preserving all of pin except, perhaps, for the tip of the point.
Very small pin, with shaft circular in section, tapering toward point. Top of shaft partially hammered flat and coiled to form head, which itself tapers to a point and has two turns, with the terminal looped around upper shaft.
Context destruction deposit, mid-4th century B.C. or earlier.
Cf., among others, Kilian-Dirlmeier 1984a, pls. 112–113, nos. 4884, 4886, 4888–4892, 4895–4896 (from Tegea, the Argive Heraion, Mantineia, and Olympia); *OlForsch* XIII, pl. 36, nos. 296, 299–300; cf. also p. 116, fig. 200 (Kythnos).

26/71. (ΜΕΘ 2133α [ΜΕ 4094α]) Knot-headed Pin Fig. 26.27
Agora #274/059010 [3]. Αυλάκι (small channel).
P.L. 0.029; Diam. (head) 0.003–0.004; Diam. (shaft, max) 0.002; Wt. 0.3 g.
Single fr preserving all of head and upper portion of shaft.
Shaft circular in section. End of pin head partially hammered flat, coiled to form head, with the terminal, consisting of thin bronze wire, continuing from head and coiled over uppermost shaft.
Context destruction deposit, mid-4th century B.C. or earlier.
Cf. esp. Kilian-Dirlmeier 1984a, pl. 112, no. 4893, also nos. 4880–4881 (from Corinth, Perachora, and Tegea).

Ribbed-head pins with small finial

Both **26/72** and **26/73** are poorly preserved, but their main elements are clear: the circular pin shaft is surmounted by a ribbed head, rather than one that is more clearly beaded (**26/73** is ribbed, though it is possible that **26/72** has one or two beads below the finial, unclear due to corrosion). At the top of the heads of both pins there is a small finial. That on **26/72** is damaged and corroded, but on **26/73** it seems that the finial had a minuscule eyelet. Some related pins from Thessaly have heads that are more clearly profiled with beads and ribs, and surmounted by small finials with an eyelet. These are generally compared by Kilian-Dirlmeier with the "*Mehrkopfnadeln,*" or multi-headed pins, discussed below under **26/74**, the small eyelet, according to Kilian-Dirlmeier, permitting pairs of such pins to be worn together connected with a chain, as was popular in late Archaic times.[113] As for the date of **26/72–26/73**, it is unfortunate that the context of both was uninformative. Although a late Archaic date is possible, it is far from assured, and I would not be surprised if both of the Methone pins of this type are of Classical date (two unpublished examples of this pin type from Liatovouni are early Classical, dating to 480-460 B.C.).

It is also worth noting a few related pins from farther north. Although not unlike some of the central Balkan "club-headed" pins (cf. **15/22**, "Keulenkopfnadeln, Variant mit verziertem Kopf"), **26/72** and **26/73** are different in that their heads are ribbed, not decorated with incised diagonal, zigzag, dogtooth, or other motifs, and they have a small terminal at the top (with or without eyelet), unlike the *Keulenkopfnadeln*.[114] Another central Balkan type may also be compared, the so-called "Kolbenkopfnadel" or "piston-head" pin, but this is rather rare, and different in that their heads are more beaded rather than ribbed and lack the small finial on top.[115]

26/72. (ΜΕΘ 1603 [ΜΕ 1311]) Ribbed-head Pin — Fig. 26.28

Agora #274/067. Στρώμα αμμώδης (sandy layer).

P.L. 0.050; L. (head) 0.015; Diam. (shaft) 0.002; Wt. 1.4 g.

Single fr preserving entire head and upper portion of pin shaft.

Shaft circular in section, surmounted by decorated head, also circular in section, but thicker, ribbed as shown. Small, but worn, pointed finial at top.

Context unclear.

Cf. **26/73** (ΜΕΘ 1610).

26/73. (ΜΕΘ 1610 [ΜΕ 1981]) Ribbed-head Pin — Fig. 26.28

Agora #274/084. ΝΑ τμήμα (SE section).

P.L. 0.030; L (head) 0.018; Diam. (head) 0.005; Diam. (shaft) 0.002–0.003; Wt. 2.1 g.

Single fr preserving head, but only small portion of upper shaft of pin.

Form as **26/72** (ΜΕΘ 1603). Small finial on top worn.

Context unclear.

Cf. **26/72** (ΜΕΘ 1603).

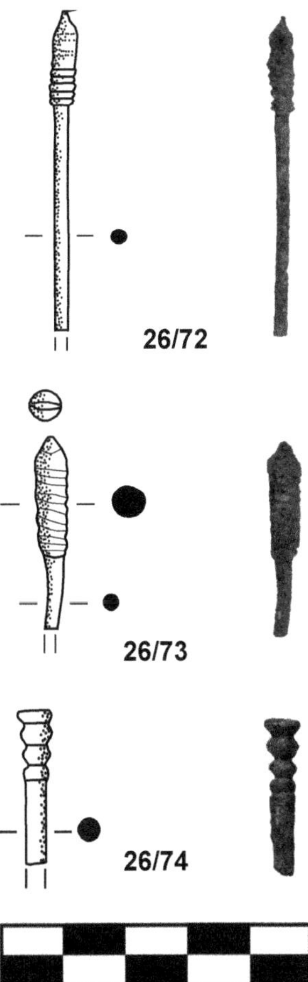

FIGURE 26.28. Agora bronze pins, ribbed-head pins, **26/72** (ΜΕΘ 1603) and **26/73** (ΜΕΘ 1610), pin with beaded head, **26/74** (ΜΕΘ 1614). Drawings F. Skyvalida, photos I. Coyle and J. Vanderpool

Additional pin heads as **26/72** and **26/73**:

MEΘ 1618 (ME 2756). Agora #274/017016 [5]. P.L. 0.022; L. (head) 0.016; Diam. (head, max) 0.006; Wt. 1.2 g.

MEΘ 3092 (ME 4251). Agora #274/066. Περιοχή Ν του Τ.19. Upper shaft and pin head. P.L. 0.035; L. (head) 0.012; Th. (shaft) 0.002; Wt. 0.8 g.

Pin with beaded head

The head of **26/74** has a beaded head consisting of four beads, with a flat plain circular top, with three beads below, the latter more or less biconical, the lowermost the smallest. The upper shaft is circular in section. Found in the collapsed fill above the destruction deposit, the piece could date from the prehistoric period into the 4th century B.C. Although not unlike **15/25**, **26/74** is more clearly beaded, rather than of the pin type that is sometimes referred to as "vase-headed" or "poppy-headed" or with "pomegranate" head (see discussion under **15/25**). **26/74** closely resembles some of the so-called "*Mehrkopfnadeln*" or "multi-headed" pins that are common in central and southern Greece, some of which have four beads like **26/74** (see catalogue entry for references). Although many of the "*Mehrkopfnadeln*" have a large protruding disk on the uppermost part of the head, quite a few have a smaller head like **26/74**.[116] Most of the central and southern Greek comparanda are Late Geometric or earlier Archaic.

26/74. (MEΘ 1614 [ME 2480]) Pin with Beaded Head — Fig. 26.28

Agora #274/016001 [1].

P.L. 0.024–0.025; Diam. (max) 0.006; Wt. 1.6 g.

Single fr preserving all of head but only small portion of upper shaft.

Upper shaft circular in section, surmounted by a decorated head consisting of four beads, as shown, three lowermost biconical, the uppermost flat on top.

Context collapsed fill above destruction deposit, prehistoric to mid-4th century B.C.

Cf. **15/25** (MEΘ 4137). Among the numerous so-called "*Mehrkopfnadeln*" amassed by Kilian-Dirlmeier (1984), those headed like **26/74** with four beads, the uppermost small and flat on top, include pl. 65, nos. 2017–2020 (from the Argive Heraion, Olympia, and the sanctuary of Artemis Orthia at Sparta).

Pin with flattened head, variant of *Blattkopfnadel* (spatula/stylus)?

The following piece is presented as a possible pin. **26/75** is of the same type as **15/23**, which I have also classified in Chapter 15 as a possible dress pin, noting its resemblance to a spatula and also discussing the possibility of it being a stylus. Deriving from Phase I of the Hypogeion, **15/23** can be confidently assigned to the Late Geometric or early Archaic period. It is, therefore, all the more unfortunate that the context of **26/75** was uninformative as to date. The type is fully discussed in Chapter 15 under **15/23**, with comparanda. The only substantive difference between **26/75** and **15/23** is that the former has a shaft square/rectangular in section, the latter one that is circular.

26/75. (MEΘ 1787 [ME 1787]) Pin with Flattened Head — Fig. 26.29

Agora #274/017006 [4].

L. 0.103; W. (head) 0.006; Wt. 4.2 g.

Intact. Condition quite good.

Longish shaft, mostly square/rectangular in section, tapering toward a well-preserved point. Shaft hammered flat at the top to produce the distinctive head.

Context unclear.

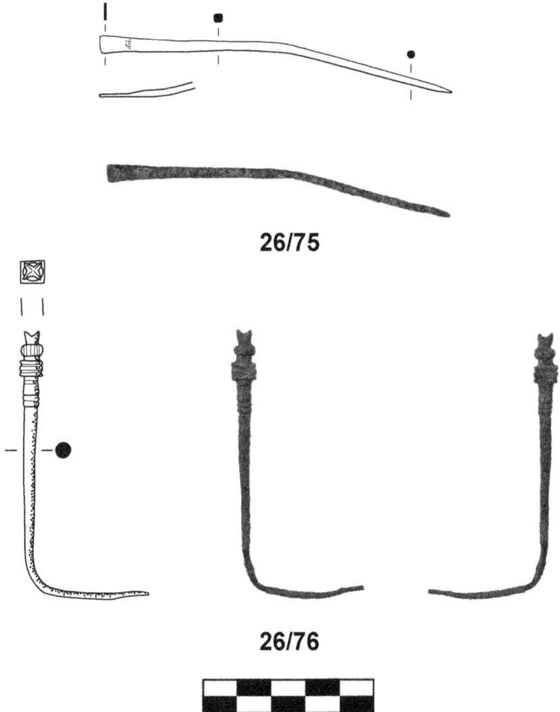

FIGURE 26.29. Agora bronze pins, pin with flattened head, **26/75** (MEΘ 1787), poppy- or pomegranate-headed pin, **26/76** (MEΘ 1604). Drawings A. Hooton and F. Skyvalida, photos I. Coyle and J. Vanderpool

Cf. **15/23**.

Inventoried fragments related to **26/75** (MEΘ 1787):
MEΘ 1790 (ME 3605). Agora #274/089. P.L. 0.050; W. (head) 0.004; Wt. 2.8 g.
MEΘ 1789 (ME 2557). Agora #274/065. P.L. 0.066–0.067; W. (head) 0.005; Wt. 3.7 g.
MEΘ 1788 (ME 2227). Agora #274/075. P.L. 0.040; W. (head) 0.003; Wt. 1.3 g.

Poppy- or pomegranate-headed pin

Encountered in the heart of the destruction deposit, **26/75** is one of the best preserved of the Methone dress pins, and a mid- or slightly earlier 4th-century B.C. date cannot be doubted. In discussing Greek pins with heads in the form of flowers or fruit, Jacobsthal noted: "I have compared their heads with buds and fruits, pears, and melons, leaving it open whether these comparisons were just a means of describing forms, or whether it is to be understood that the artists and the wearers of the pins saw them as fruits."[117] Jacobsthal refers to certain pins from Ephesos and Perachora of the Orientalizing period as pomegranate-headed, whereas a not dissimilar pin from Ephesos is described as "an ordinary globe head but enriched with 'a flower of six raised petals with a cup-like centre (pomegranate?).'"[118] In a similar vein, Kilian-Dirlmeier admits that, for these floral elements: "unverbindliche Bezeichnungen wie 'Blute, Knospe, Kapsel' eher angemessen sind; 'Granatapfel' kann allenfalls als konventioneller Terminus verstanden werden."[119] Whatever we call **26/76** is moot, but that it is a flower- or fruit-headed pin is clear enough.

For Jacobsthal, the examples known to him prior to 1956 were largely those from Ephesos and Perachora of Orientalizing date. In a fuller catalogue, Kilian-Dirlmeier brings together many more examples of these and related types under the heading "archaische Nadeln, Typengruppe F," including pins from Argos and the Argive Heraion, Corinth, Lousoi, Mantineia, Olympia, Perachora, Sparta, and others said to be from "Arkadia" and the "Argolis," variously dated to the 6th,

5th, and 4th centuries B.C.[120] I would not call all of the pins classified under this heading flower- or fruit-headed, and **26/76** differs from many in the small cube below the actual fruit or flower. I cite some of the closer comparanda in the catalogue entry below, but none is identical to **26/76.**

26/76. (MEΘ 1604 [ME 981]) Poppy/Pomegranate-headed Pin Fig. 26.29

Agora #274/076. Στρώμα καταστροφής (destruction level).

P.L. (as bent) 0.076; p.L (when straight) 0.104; L. (decorated head) 0.023; Diam. (shaft, max) 0.004; Wt. 6.4 g.

Single fr preserving virtually complete pin, except for very tip of point. Condition good.

Shaft of medium length, circular in section, tapering toward point, itself not preserved. Head decorated with three elements, from bottom to top: uppermost shaft immediately below head, articulated with two small beads, framing a small undecorated portion of shaft, and then two more beads or incised lines. This is surmounted by a small cube that is ribbed, defining three beads; the sides of the central bead are further enhanced with faint vertical incised lines. This, in turn, is surmounted by the poppy or pomegranate finial, as shown, with the circular element decorated with vertical incised lines/strokes, and a four-petaled top.

Context destruction deposit, mid-4th century B.C. or earlier.

Cf., among others, Jacobsthal 1956, pp. 36, 38, 187, figs. 141, 145–147, 161. Kilian-Dirlmeier 1984a, pls. 111–112, esp. nos. 4763–4845 (which includes several variants).

Double pins

There are two fairly well-preserved double pins from the agora of Methone, together with a few others listed below. **26/77** was found in the destruction deposit, and is thus mid-4th century B.C. or perhaps a little earlier, but unlikely to be much earlier. **26/78** was found in a pre-destruction deposit context in association with material of the Archaic and earlier Classical period. In dealing generally with what he termed double-shanked pins, John Alexander noted that they were made by folding the wire back on itself to provide two shanks.[121] Such pins were earlier studied by Ferdinand Maier and Jacobsthal, both of whom agreed that the type was of Bosnian origin, which was subsequently imported into Greece, and, on the basis of the Greek evidence, mostly of 8th–7th century B.C. date.[122] In her 1984 study of pins from the Early Bronze Age to the Archaic period in Greece, Kilian-Dirlmeier distinguished three types of double pins: the Trebenište type, which was the most common in Greece in the Archaic period; the Glasinac type, and the Kozani type, of which there was only one example in Kilian-Dirlmeier's catalogue.[123] The number of Kozani-type double pins in Greece has now increased exponentially, thanks to the excavations at Mieza and elsewhere.[124]

The characteristic form of **26/77** corresponds to Alexander's Type II and Vasić's Type IV, which Maier, Jacobsthal, and Kilian-Dirlmeier refer to as the Trebenište type, even though the general form was not very common there.[125] This type of double pin was the most common in Greece. As for their chronology, the majority of the examples amassed by Kilian-Dirlmeier are Archaic, beginning in the 7th century, continuing through the 6th and into the 5th.[126] The examples from Glasinac, which are quite numerous (see catalogue entry), are assigned to period IVc (625–500 B.C.),[127] but on the basis of the Greek evidence, Alexander notes: "they are dated to the late 7th–4th centuries with most coming from the end of the period."[128] An iron pin of this type from Vitsa Zagoriou in Epirus is dated to 490–475 B.C.[129] Closer to home, the cemetery at Sindos has produced no shortage of such pins, made of silver, bronze, and iron; referred to as περόνες με τρίλοβη κεφαλή ("pins with three-lobed heads"), the earliest date to the very end of the 6th or beginning of the 5th century, the latest to the very end of the 5th century B.C.[130] On the basis of the numerous examples of the type from the central Balkans, which he classifies as Type IV, Rastko Vasić provides the most up-to-date distribution of the type in Greece, the central Balkans, and central Italy, and dates Type IV between the 6th and 2nd centuries B.C.[131] Given its context, a 4th-century B.C. date for **26/77** is assured.

Although the form of **26/78** is not unlike **26/77**, it differs in that the head consists of a single loop that projects above the "shoulders" of the pin. This is a fairly rare type, especially in Greece. Among the examples presented by Kilian-Dirlmeier, the closest is the so-called Glasinac type, but these differ from **26/78** in that the central loop is flanked by two smaller loops at the juncture to the shoulder.[132] Farther north, Alexander's Type III double pins are related, but they differ in having their shoulders curving out before rejoining the two shanks of the pin, their distinctive shape inspiring Alexander to refer to them as "trefoil."[133] The closest parallels for **26/78** are a series of bronze and iron double pins of Vasić's Type IIa (simply referred to as "Variante mit rundem Kopf").[134] Vasić traces the distribution of the type in northern Greece, North Macedonia, Albania, Kosovo, and Bosnia, and in dealing with their chronology, notes that the earliest examples date from the end of the 7th or the beginning of the 6th century B.C., and that they continue into the 5th century B.C.[135] Seven pins of this type of silver, bronze, and iron were recently published from the cemetery at Sindos, just to the north of Methone, the earliest from a tomb dated 530–520 B.C., the latest from a tomb dating to ca. 450 B.C.[136] As such, the context of **26/78** nicely confirms both Vasić's chronology and that from Sindos published by Aikaterini Despoini. A few of the closest bronze parallels from the central Balkans, together with the examples from Sindos of various metals, are given in the catalogue entry below.

26/77. (ΜΕΘ 1611 [ΜΕ 1869]) Double Pin — Fig. 26.30

Agora #274/085, 086.

P.L. 0.094; L. (head) 0.022; Diam. (shaft, max) 0.002; Wt. 6.2 g.

Single piece preserving virtually complete pin, except for tips of both shafts.

Pin formed of continuous bronze wire, circular in section and tapering toward both points, themselves not preserved. Head formed into triple loop, as shown, also referred to as a double-end loop in Alexander 1964.

Context destruction deposit, mid-4th century B.C. or earlier.

Cf., among others, Jacobsthal 1956, pp. 135–139, figs. 393, 399; Kilian-Dirlmeier 1984a, pls. 113–114, nos. 4925–4942 (mostly from Olympia, but with one example each from Nemea and Phigaleia, and two silver examples said to be from "Patras"); *OlForsch* XIII, pp. 97–102, pl. 37, nos. 309–318; Rhomiopoulou and Touratsoglou 2002, p. 77, M 2056 (2nd quarter of the 5th century B.C.) p. 85, M 1069 (5th century B.C.), both examples from Mieza; Benac and Čović 1957, pl. VIII, nos. 3, 13; pl. IX, nos. 3–4; pl. XLVI, no. 7; pl. XLVII, nos. 13–14, 19; pl. XLVIII, no. 5 (with added spirals); pl. LXIX, nos. 12–13; Vokotopoulou 1986, fig. 115:θ, ι; Klebinder-Gauss 2007, pp. 75–76, 241, pl. 21, no. 299 (with further references).

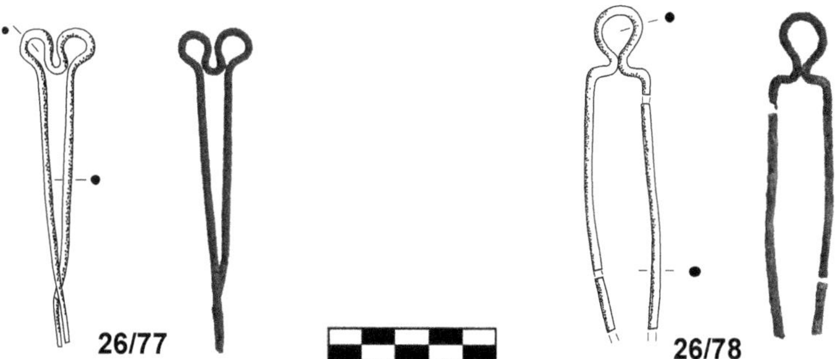

FIGURE 26.30. Agora bronze double pins, **26/77** (ΜΕΘ 1611) and **26/78** (ΜΕΘ 1613). Drawings F. Skyvalida, photos I. Coyle

26/78. (MEΘ 1613 [ME 2099]) Double Pin Fig. 26.30

Agora #274/088. Building A, Room 4. Τομή βόρεια του T12 (trench north of Wall 12).

P.L. (min) 0.093; L. (head) 0.020; Diam. (shaft, max) 0.003; Wt. 5.8 g.

Nine main frr, joining, plus chips, preserving greater part of pin, except for tips of both points.

Type not unlike **26/77** (MEΘ 1611), formed of continuous bronze wire, circular in section, but with head consisting of a single loop, as shown, projecting above the "shoulders" of the pin.

Context pre-destruction deposit, Archaic or earlier Classical.

Cf., among others, Jacobsthal 1956, pp. 135–139, fig. 402 (and one example on fig. 403, upper right); Vasić 2003, p. 116, pl. 43, nos. 836, 837, 844, 846, 848 (from Belaćevac, Marvinci, Trebenište, Valandovo, and Visoji); *Sindos* III, pp. 449–450, figs. 145–149, nos. 317–322.

Additional double pins:

MEΘ 1619 (ME 2633). Agora #274/036005 [3]. P.L. (min) 0.088+; Diam. (shaft) 0.002; Wt. 5.5 g. Type related to **26/78** (MEΘ 1613).

MEΘ 1601 (ME 458). Agora #274/007016 [3]. Λάκκος (pit). P.L. 0.030; Wt. 0.8 g. Likely double pin of uncertain type, consisting of two pin shafts crossing one another.

Bronze finials for pins

The two following heads may well be from different types of pin. **26/79** is hollow underneath to accommodate the insertion of a pin shaft made separately, which would have been circular in section, with a small side opening to keep the inserted pin shaft in place. Such bronze finials often served as the heads for iron pin shafts, as indicated by a few such bimetallic pins from the cemetery at Sindos.[137] The Sindos pins differ from **26/79** in that the stem into which the pin shaft was inserted is slightly longer, and both have a smaller circular finial on the top.[138] Related bronze pins of the Archaic period are discussed by Kilian-Dirlmeier under her broad heading of "archaische Nadeln, Typengruppe F."[139] In dealing with related pins from Trebenište, Vasić writes: "Das Herstellungszentrum dieser Nadeln ist wahrscheinlich in der Umgebung von Thessaloniki zu suchen."[140] Given the plentiful evidence for metalworking at Methone, the site may have been a production center for this and other types of pin. The context of **26/79** is uncertain, but the related pins from Sindos and Trebenište already cited date to the later 6th and 5th centuries B.C., and such a date, or one perhaps a little later, for **26/79** is likely. The form of the head of **26/80** is closely related to **26/79**, but differs in that it is not hollow underneath, and appears to be connected directly to its shaft. With its minuscule finial on top, it resembles more closely the examples from Sindos and Trebenište already cited, as well as another pin from Sindos and several from the Athena Itonia sanctuary near Philia in Thessaly cited in the entry below. According to its context, in the destruction deposit of 354 B.C., its date cannot be much earlier than the mid-4th century B.C.

26/79. (MEΘ 1622 [ME 2530]) Finial for Pin Fig. 26.31

Agora #274/065. Βόρειο τμήμα (north section).

H. 0.011; Diam. 0.010; Wt. 2.3 g.

Head evidently intact. Nothing of pin shaft survives.

Circular, roughly conical finial, surmounting a narrow shaft, with articulated ring below, as shown. Underside of finial hollow to permit insertion of the pin shaft, which would have been circular in section, with a small side opening to accommodate the insertion of the pin shaft and to keep it in place.

Context uncertain.

Cf., among others, *Sindos* III, pp. 155, 438, 593, fig. 90, pl. 269, no. 250; Vasić 2003, p. 105, pl. 39, nos. 762–763.

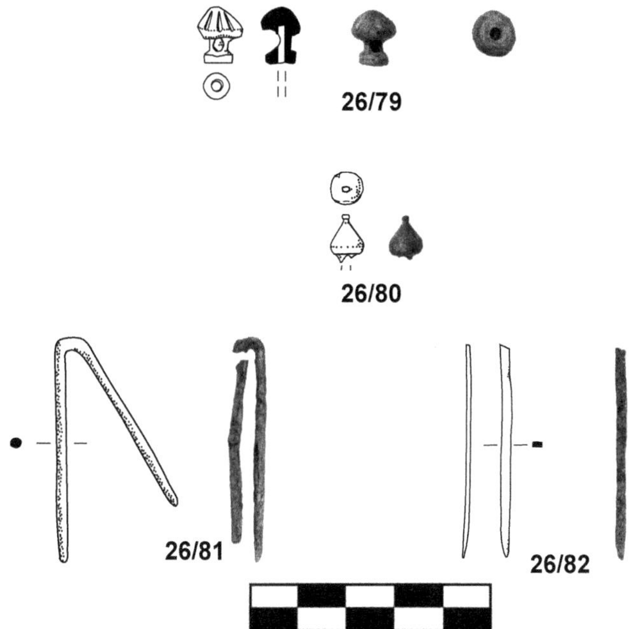

FIGURE 26.31. Agora bronze finials for pins, **26/79** (MEΘ 1622) and **26/80** (MEΘ 1654), shafts of bronze pins (or needles), **26/81** (MEΘ 2132) and **26/82** (MEΘ 2143). Drawings A. Hooton, T. Ross, and F. Skyvalida, photos I. Coyle and J. Vanderpool

26/80. (MEΘ 1654 [ME 2861]) Finial for Pin Fig. 26.31

Agora #274/089. NA τμήμα (SE section).

P.H. (= H. of head) 0.009; Diam. 0.007; Wt. 1.2 g.

Single fr preserving complete head, but virtually nothing of the shaft of the pin, except for remnants indicating that there was a shaft of bronze. Condition good.

Small globular bead-shaped head, with minuscule circular finial on top.

Context destruction deposit, mid-4th century B.C. or earlier.

Cf. parallels cited for **26/79**, and see further *Sindos* III, pp. 155, 438, fig. 91, no. 251; Kilian-Dirlmeier 2002, pl. 95, esp. nos. 1527–1529. A particularly well-preserved bronze pin head with an iron shaft of this type was found in the more recent excavations (2014–2017) on the West Hill at Methone, in Hypogeion 2 (MEΘ 7682).

Shafts of bronze dress pins

A number of inventoried and uninventoried shafts of bronze dress pins were found in the agora of Methone. I catalogue here only two, **26/81**, with a shaft circular in section, and **26/82**, with a rectangular shaft, both from the destruction deposit, and several others are listed. I am fairly certain that **26/81** is from a dress pin, although probably not from a double pin, whereas **26/82** may well be from a needle.

26/81. (MEΘ 2132 [ME 1367]) Fragmentary Pin Shaft Fig. 26.31

Agora #274/018006 [2].

P.L. (as bent) 0.045; Diam. (shaft) 0.002–0.003; Wt. 1.9 g.

Three frr, all originally joining (now broken), preserving substantial portion of dress pin.

Shaft mostly circular in section, tapering toward point, which is not preserved.

Context destruction deposit, mid-4th century B.C. or earlier.

26/82. (MEΘ 2143 [ME 4039]) Fragmentary Pin/Needle Shaft Fig. 26.31

Agora #274/028003 [1]. Δάπεδο (floor).

P.L. 0.043; W. 0.002–0.003; Th. 0.001; Wt. 0.5 g.

Single fr preserving portion of shaft and point.

Thin and narrow shaft, rectangular in section hammered flat, tapering toward point.

Context destruction deposit, mid-4th century B.C. or earlier.

Inventoried fragments of pin shafts not catalogued:

MEΘ 1624 (ME 2872). Agora #274/089. Two frr. P.L. 0.037; Wt. 0.9 g.

MEΘ 1600 (ME 57). Agora #274/004012 [5]. P.L. 0.084; Wt. 4.5 g.

MEΘ 1612 (ME 1876). Agora #274/085, 086. Two frr. P.L. 0.040; Wt. 0.7 g.

MEΘ 1623 (ME 2814). Agora #274/065. ΝΔ Τμήμα (SW section). P.L. 0.039; Wt. 0.5 g.

MEΘ 1615 (ME 2508). Agora #274/016002 [1]. P.L. 0.031; Wt. 0.6 g.

MEΘ 1617 (ME 2526). Agora #274.016004 [1]. Two joining frr. P.L. 0.034; Wt. 0.5 g.

MEΘ 1602 (ME 567). Agora #274/087006 [5]. Two joining frr. P.L. 0.032; Wt. 0.6 g.

MEΘ 1606 (ME 2316). Agora #274/066. ΝΑ Τμήμα (SE section). Four joining frr. P.L. 0.051; Wt. 1.1 g.

MEΘ 1616 (ME 2517). Agora #274/016003 [1]. P.L. 0.048; Wt. 1.3 g.

MEΘ 1607 (ME 2320). Agora #274/066. ΝΔ Τμήμα (NW section). P.L. 0.032–0.033; Wt. 0.9 g.

Beads

Although small in number, there was a noteworthy range of early bronze beads. Of the five examples presented below, **26/83** and **26/84** were both found in the collapsed fill above the destruction deposit, and although they can date from anywhere between the prehistoric period and the mid-4th century B.C., both are classic examples of beads of the Early Iron Age and Archaic periods. The context of **26/85** and **26/86** was unclear, but both are also standard in the Early Iron Age to Archaic periods, especially in Macedonia.[141] The three minuscule beads that constitute **26/87**, two of bronze with faience inlays, and one of faience, were found in a pre-destruction deposit in association with material from the Early Iron Age through early Classical period.

It is clear that beads like **26/83–26/86** were manufactured at Methone on the evidence of terracotta lost-wax molds, like the one found in the Hypogeion of late 8th- or early 7th-century B.C. date (Fig. 14.4, and see also discussion in Chapter 15 under **15/28**). Examples from Macedonia, Thessaly (where such beads are particularly common),[142] and central and southern Greece are cited in the catalogue entries below.

26/83. (MEΘ 1655 [ME 3949]) Elongated Biconical Bead Fig. 26.32

Agora #274/018005 [1].

L./p.L. 0.024; Diam. (max) 0.013; Wt. 6.5 g.

Single piece preserving most of bead, except for chipped terminals. Surfaces worn and flaking.

Plain, elongated biconical bead, cast.

Context collapsed fill above destruction deposit, prehistoric to mid-4th century B.C.

Cf., among others, Bräuning and Kilian-Dirlmeier 2013, p. 277, fig. 224, no. 17 (top row); p. 248, fig. 178, no. 231; p. 280, fig. 228, 26α-ζ; 282, fig, 231, no. 32β (various examples, Vergina); Bouzek 1974b, p. 90, fig. 27, no. 11 (Ephesos); p. 99, fig. 30, nos. 5–7, 9 (Olynthos); p. 102, fig. 31, nos. 1–2 (Amphipolis); Vickers 1977, p. 28, fig. III, nos. 10–12 (Poteidaia); Kilian 1975a, pl. 75, nos. 36–49 (Pherai); Kilian-Dirlmeier 2002, pl. 10, nos. 192–193 (Protogeometric-Archaic from Philia); Felsch 2007, pl. 46, no. 1513 (Kalapodi); Klebinder-Gauss 2007, pp. 111, 265, pl. 55, no. 771 (Ephesos); DeCou 1905, pl. CXII, no. 1547 (Argive Heraion); Voyatzis 1990, p. 279, pl. 133, no. L26 (Lousoi); *Selinus* V, p. 68, pl. 18, esp. no. 318.

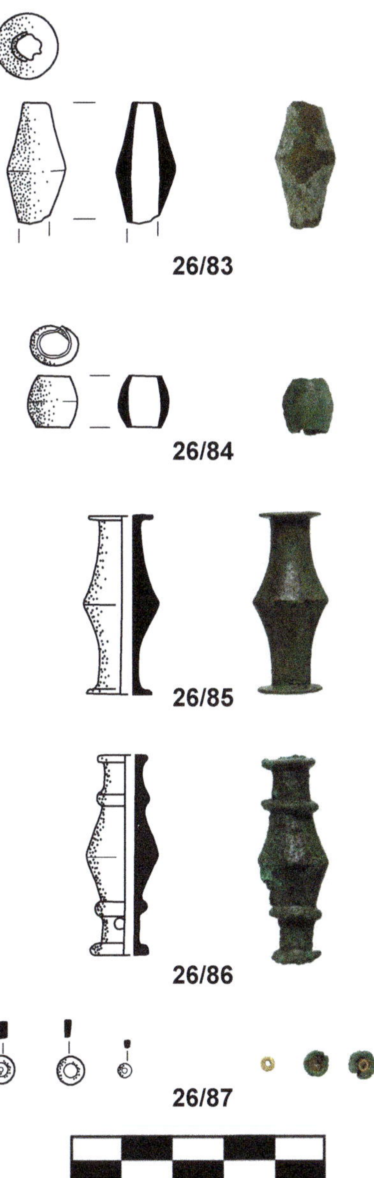

FIGURE 26.32. Agora bronze beads, **26/83** (ΜΕΘ 1655), **26/84** (ΜΕΘ 1653), **26/85** (ΜΕΘ 1651), **26/86** (ΜΕΘ 1649), **26/87** (ΜΕΘ 1650α, β, γ). Drawings F. Skyvalida, photos I. Coyle and J. Vanderpool

26/84. (ΜΕΘ 1653 [ΜΕ 2477]) Small Biconical Bead Fig. 26.32

Agora #274/065. Βόρειο τμήμα (north sector).

L. 0.010; Diam. (max) 0.010; Wt. 1.5 g.

Intact, but slightly pushed in at one point.

Small biconical bead, almost approaching globular in places. Relatively thin bronze sheet, with seam clearly preserved (clearly not cast in one piece).

Context collapsed fill above destruction deposit, prehistoric to mid-4th century B.C.

Cf., among others, Bouzek 1974b, p. 90, fig. 27, no. 10 (Ephesos); p. 99, fig. 30, no. 14 (Olympia); Vickers 1977, p. 28, fig. III, nos. 14–15 (Poteidaia); Kilian 1975a, pl. 75, nos. 26, 35; pl. 95, no. 10 (Valanida); Felsch 2007, pl. 45, nos. 1431, 1433, 1481–1482 (Kalapodi); Voyatzis 1990, p. 336, pl. 123, no. B170 (Tegea); Klebinder-Gauss 2007, pp. 111, 265, pl. 55, no. 772 (Ephesos).

26/85. (ΜΕΘ 1651 [ΜΕ 2567]) Biconical Bead, Articulated Terminals Fig. 26.32

Agora #274. Backfill.

L. 0.034; Diam. (max) 0.015; Diam. (terminals) 0.013; Wt. 9.9 g.

Intact. Condition good.

Large biconical bead, with concave sides, thickest in section at the center, and with relatively broad, flat/horizontal terminals.

Recovered from the backfill, context unclear.

Cf., among others, Casson 1919–1921, p. 15, pl. 1 (middle) (Tsaoutsitsa); Bräuning and Kilian-Dirlmeier 2013, p. 190, fig. 87, no. 4; p. 200, fig. 100, no. 10; p. 275, fig. 222, no. 7 (Vergina); *Olympia* IV, pl. 24, no. 444; DeCou 1905, pl. CXII, nos. 1548, 1549 (Argive Heraion); Voyatzis 1990, p. 337, pl. 132, nos. B182, B183 (Tegea); Blinkenberg 1931, col. 95, pl. 10, no. 171 (Lindos); Bouzek 1974b, p. 90, fig. 27, no. 9 (Ephesos); pl. 2 (second from left) (Tsaoutsitsa); Vickers 1977, p. 28, fig. III, nos. 21–26; pl. A, nos. 6–7 (Poteidaia); Kilian 1975a, pl. 76, nos. 22–33, esp. nos. 26–27, 30, 32–33; Kilian-Dirlmeier 2002, pl. 97, nos. 1573, 1578–1579 (Philia); Felsch 2007, pl. 46, no. 1515 (Kalapodi); Klebinder-Gauss 2007, pp. 109–111, 264, pl. 54, nos. 761–765, esp. no. 763 (Ephesos); also Makridis 1937, pl. III:γ, δ, ε; Maier 1956, p. 65, fig. 1, no. 3 (middle).

26/86. (ΜΕΘ 1649 [ΜΕ 1805]) Biconical Bead, Articulated Terminals Fig. 26.32

Agora #274/007032 [11]. Περιοχή ανάμεσα T.7 and T.11 (area between Walls 7 and 11).

L. 0.040; Diam. (max) 0.015; Diam. (terminals) 0.011; Wt. 11.7 g.

Intact, a little bronze disease.

Type as **26/85** (ΜΕΘ 1651), but slightly larger, and with a raised fillet on either side of the carination. Small hole at one end.

Context unclear.

Cf., among others, Casson 1919–1921, p. 15, pl. 1 (bottom) (Tsaoutsitsa); Vickers 1977, p. 28, fig. III, nos. 27–29; pl. A, no. 8 (Poteidaia); Kilian 1975a, pl. 76, nos. 35–39, also no. 40 (with perforations) (Pherai); pl. 95, no. 2 (Valanida); Kilian-Dirlmeier 2002, pl. 97, no. 1582 (Philia); Klebinder-Gauss 2007, pp. 109–111, 264, pl. 54, no. 766 (Ephesos); note also the example from Aineia, Vokotopoulou 1990, p. 98, fig. 50, no. 7613; p. 102, fig. 52, no. 7627; p. 106, fig. 56, nos. 8095–8097; pl. 61:γ (left); pl. 63:δ (lower center and right); pl. 65:ε (center and right); Makridis 1937, pl. III:α, β; Maier 1956, p. 65, fig. 1, no. 3 (top).

The three following beads—two of bronze with faience inlays, and one of faience—were all found together in #274/079, ΝΑ τμήμα (SE section). Context is pre-destruction deposit, Early Iron Age to Archaic or early Classical.

26/87. (ΜΕΘ 1650α [ΜΕ 2080]) Small Bronze Bead Fig. 26.32

H: 0.003–0.004; Diam. 0.006; Wt. 0.2 g.

Intact.

Small open-ended ring bead made from a thin strip of bronze, rectangular in section. Smaller faience bead, as ΜΕΘ 1650γ, inlay.

Cf. Kilian-Dirlmeier 2002, p. 159, pl. 164, nos. 2651–2659 (Philia); Felsch 2007, pl. 45, nos. 1466–1471, 1503–1504 (Kalapodi); Klebinder-Gauss 2007, pp. 112, 265, pl. 55, no. 778 (Ephesos); for related small glass/faience beads of similar form, see, among others, Kilian 1975a, pl. 78, nos. 1–2 (Pherai).

(ΜΕΘ 1650β) Small Bronze Bead Fig. 26.32

H. 0.003–0.004; Diam. 0.005; Wt. 0.2 g.

Intact.

As ΜΕΘ 1650α, but fractionally smaller; also with traces of faience inlay.

(ΜΕΘ 1650γ) Minuscule Faience Bead Fig. 26.32

H. 0.001; Diam. 0.003; Wt. < 0.1 g.

Intact.

Minuscule ring bead of white faience.

Cf. Kilian 1975a, pl. 78, nos. 1–2 (Pherai).

Rings

Plain finger rings

Finger rings, especially those that are plain and of Early Iron Age or Archaic date, are fully discussed in Chapter 15 (under **15/30–15/32**).[143] Of interest is that **26/88** comes from a pre-destruction context of Early Iron Age or earlier Archaic date, and the date of **26/89**, although from the collapsed fill overlying the destruction deposit, which cannot be dated with certainty as the material recovered from it could be of prehistoric to mid-4th century B.C., may well be broadly contemporary with **26/88.** In his discussion of the bronze finger rings from Lefkandi, Hector Catling noted that, in addition to the rings with shield-shaped bezels, there were two other common varieties. One was the closed ring, fairly solid and usually plano-convex in section. **26/88** is a good example of this type. The other common variety at Lefkandi was the open ring with overlapping terminals, normally made of a flat, hammered strip of bronze, coiled into a ring. **26/89** is most probably of this variety, although its fragmentary state makes certainty difficult.[144] The simple form of such rings is conservative, lasting into Archaic, Classical, Hellenistic, and Roman versions.[145]

26/88. (ΜΕΘ 1665 [ΜΕ 4912]) Finger Ring Fig. 26.33

Agora #274/067.

Diam. 0.020; H./Th. 0.003; Wt. 2.7 g.

Intact.

Plain band, cast in one piece, mostly circular in section, in places approaching plano-convex.

Context pre-destruction deposit, Early Iron Age to Archaic.

26/89. (ΜΕΘ 1640 [ΜΕ 1327]) Finger Ring Fig. 26.33

Agora #274/067. Στρώμα διάβρωσης (erosion layer: collapsed fill).

Diam. (as preserved) 0.026; H./Th. (band) 0.002; Wt. 1.6 g.

Two joining frr preserving complete or almost complete ring (it is unclear whether ring was open-ended or missing a small portion, probably the former).

Plain ring, with band mostly circular in section.

Context collapsed fill above destruction deposit, prehistoric to mid-4th century B.C.

Additional inventoried ring not catalogued:

ΜΕΘ 1664 (ΜΕ 1381). Agora #274/066. Two joining frr. Diam. 0.020; H./Th. 0.002; Wt. 0.4 g.

Finger rings with bezels

Three well- or moderately well-preserved finger rings with bezels were recovered from the agora, one from a pre-destruction deposit context (**26/90**), the other two from uncertain contexts (**26/91–26/92**). In the post–Bronze Age period, finger rings with bezels begin in the very earliest stages of the Early Iron Age with the characteristic rings with shield-shaped bezels, essentially continuing a tradition well established in the Mycenaean era.[146] The examples presented below are all later, and related rings with bezels, decorated and plain, are commonly found in Greek sanctuaries of Archaic, Classical, and later date.[147] Two bronze rings with bezels from Isthmia date to the

Classical period, and a silver example is Archaic.[148] The sanctuary at Kalapodi has yielded a bronze and an iron ring with bezels labeled as "archaische und klassische Plattenringe," both assigned to the 5th century B.C.[149] Four bronze finger rings with bezels from the sanctuary of Athena Itonia near Philia are broadly dated to the Classical period, and compared to the typology established by John Boardman.[150] The date of these examples is in keeping with the Archaic–Classical date for **26/90**. An array of similar rings from the sanctuary of Demeter at Knossos are mostly dated to the 4th century, and some to the 3rd century B.C.[151] Similarly, numerous rings with bezels from Olympia date from the 5th–4th centuries B.C.,[152] and among the 52 finger rings from Stymphalos, 40 have bezels, mostly dating to the 4th century B.C.;[153] many of the Olympia and Stymphalos rings, together with those from Knossos, are contemporary, stylistically, with **26/91–26/92**. The numerous rings from Olynthos, including those with bezels, are all dated before the destruction of the city in 348 B.C.[154]

In terms of its overall form, **26/90** is a classic example of Boardman's Archaic Type N ring and is in keeping with his chronology: "Type N, with the long, flat, leaf-shaped bezel and stirrup hoop, is important since from it stems the whole series of Classical finger rings. It is mainly Late Archaic."[155] **26/91** and **26/92** are of similar form to one another, although the bezel of **26/91** is fractionally more oval than leaf-shaped. Both rings best correspond in form to Boardman's Classical Type II, about which he notes: "Type II has the slim hoop shaped more to the finger and the thin bezel too is often bent out in sympathy with the line of the hoop. The bezel is still leaf-shaped but some swell, and one or two are slim ovals. This is current from the middle to the end of the fifth century."[156] Some of Boardman's other Classical types, particularly those with a more oval bezel like Types VI–VIII, are not unlike.[157]

In terms of bezel designs, only **26/91** has anything that is at all clear; although begging for decoration, none is clearly visible on **26/90**, despite the slight depressions seen especially under raking light, and there is nothing clearly visible on **26/92**. As noted in the entry below, the incised decoration on the bezel of **26/91** clearly shows a bird, perhaps a dove(?), in flight, with a smaller, unidentified ovoid motif below in what almost appears to be an exergue. Although birds, whether flying or standing, are common on Classical finger rings, I know of no identical parallel for **26/91**.[158]

26/90. (ΜΕΘ 1639 [ΜΕ 1861]) Finger Ring with Bezel Fig. 26.33
Agora #274/009010 [4]. Building B, Room 4. Ανάμεσα σε Τ.24 and Τ.25 (between Walls 24 and 25).
H./Diam. 0.020; L. x W. x Th. (bezel) 0.019 x 0.020 x 0.010; Wt. 1.5 g.
Four joining frr preserving complete ring, including bezel.
Closed finger ring with band circular in section; bezel elliptical in plan, and flat. Bezel cries out for decoration, but none is clearly visible, despite the fact that in raking light there are slight depressions in the bronze indicating the possibility of decoration, indicated on drawing.
Context pre-destruction deposit, Archaic to Classical.

26/91. (ΜΕΘ 1642 [ΜΕ 2164]) Finger Ring with Bezel Fig. 26.33
Agora #274/085. Ανατολικός μάρτυρας (east balk).
H. 0.021; Diam. 0.020; L. x W. (bezel) 0.015 x 0.010; Wt. 3.4 g.
Intact. Well preserved.
Closed, cast finger ring, with band mostly circular in section, although faceted near the juncture with bezel. Nicely cast elliptical bezel, cast together with the hoop, with incised decoration clearly depicting a flying bird (dove?), with smaller unidentified ovoid motif in what appears to be an exergue.
Context unclear.

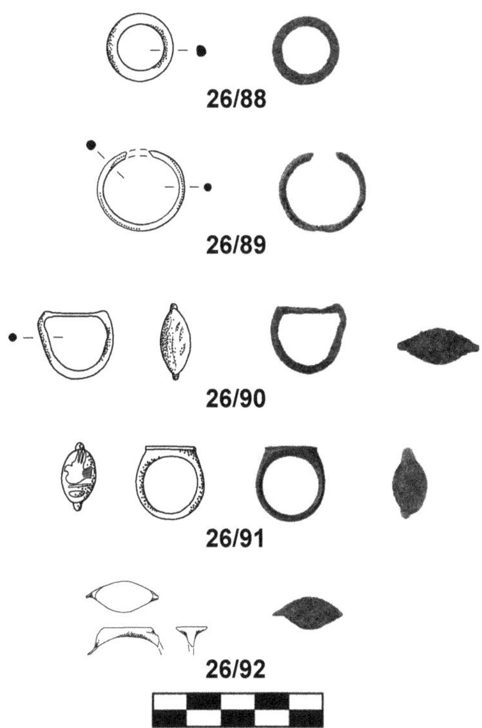

FIGURE 26.33. Agora bronze finger rings: plain finger rings, **26/88** (ΜΕΘ 1665) and **26/89** (ΜΕΘ 1640), finger rings with bezels, **26/90** (ΜΕΘ 1639), **26/91** (ΜΕΘ 1642), **26/92** (ΜΕΘ 1641). Drawings A. Hooton, T. Ross, and F. Skyvalida, photos I. Coyle and J. Vanderpool

26/92. (ΜΕΘ 1641 [ΜΕ 2617]) Finger Ring with Bezel Fig. 26.33
Agora #274/075. ΝΔ τμήμα, ξήλωμα Τ.8 (SW section, collapse of Wall 8).
P.H. 0.008; L. x W. (bezel) 0.018 x 0.009; Wt. 1.5 g.
Single fr preserving complete bezel, but virtually nothing of the ring.
Type as **26/91** (ΜΕΘ 1642), but with no clearly visible decoration on bezel.
Context unclear.

Earrings/hairrings

Without the panacea of examples found in situ in tombs worn by the deceased, distinguishing between an earring or hairring, and sometimes a finger ring, is not straightforward. In dealing with what he labeled as "δακτύλιοι μὴ ἐφαπτομένων περάτων"—which are of different types from the Methone examples presented below—Andronikos notes that they are usually found at the cranium of the deceased and served as hair ties ("σφηκωτῆρες"), whereas some were found associated with the hands of the deceased and thus worn as finger rings.[159] In a similar vein, Raubitschek, in dealing with related objects, writes: "Earrings, beads, and pendants are here discussed as a group since it is often impossible to determine to which category an object belongs . . . . This caveat also applies to simple metal circuits that may have been either finger rings or earrings or, if very delicate, hair spirals."[160] In her publication of the jewelry from Olympia, Hanna Philipp often classified very similar rings as earrings or as finger rings.[161] Of the three examples from Methone presented below, **26/93** should be an earring; **26/94** could be either an earring or a hair tie, whereas **26/95** is perhaps best classified as a hair tie. The only one with a firm context is **26/93**, which was encountered in a pre-destruction deposit of Early Iron Age to Archaic date; the contexts of **26/94–26/95** are unclear. Given their different forms and chronologies, I have preferred to cite parallels for each piece in the entries below.

26/93. (MEΘ 1797 [ME 923]) Earring/Hairring Fig. 26.34

Agora #274/086.

Diam. 0.018; Th. 0.002; Wt. 1.5 g.

Single fr preserving perhaps complete earring/hairring, though one of the terminals may be broken

Small earring/hairring made of bronze wire, circular in section, tapering toward a point at one end. The terminals overlap for about one-quarter of ring.

Context pre-destruction deposit, Early Iron Age to Archaic.

Cf., among others, *Isthmia* VII, pp. 66, 69, pl. 40, nos. 254–258 (three of Archaic date, the remaining two of uncertain date); Felsch 2007, p. 351, pl. 47, nos. 1893, 1895 (Kalapodi, classified under earrings, "Ohrringe archaischer Typen"); *OlForsch* XIII, p. 141, pl. 42, nos. 511–513 (classified under finger rings, "submykenische, geometrische, früharchaische Fingerringe"); for Archaic examples from colonial southern Italy, see Papadopoulos 2003a, pp. 75–76, fig. 98, esp. nos. 203, 207; esp. close are a number of bronze earrings from Lofkënd, see Papadopoulos and Kurti 2014, pp. 362–263, fig. 10.30, nos. 10/80–10/81 (with further references to examples in Greece, Macedonia, and southern Italy). Related earrings from Ephesos are thicker on one side, tapering sharply toward a point on the other, see Klebinder-Gauss 2007, pp. 83–85, pls. 37–39, nos. 447–606, esp. the undecorated nos. 447–543.

26/94. (MEΘ 1798 [ME 2192]) Earring/Hairring Fig. 26.34

Agora #274/085. Ανατολικός μάρτυρας (east balk).

L./Diam. (as preserved) 0.020; Th. (max) 0.003; L. (decorated head) 0.012; Wt. 3.2 g.

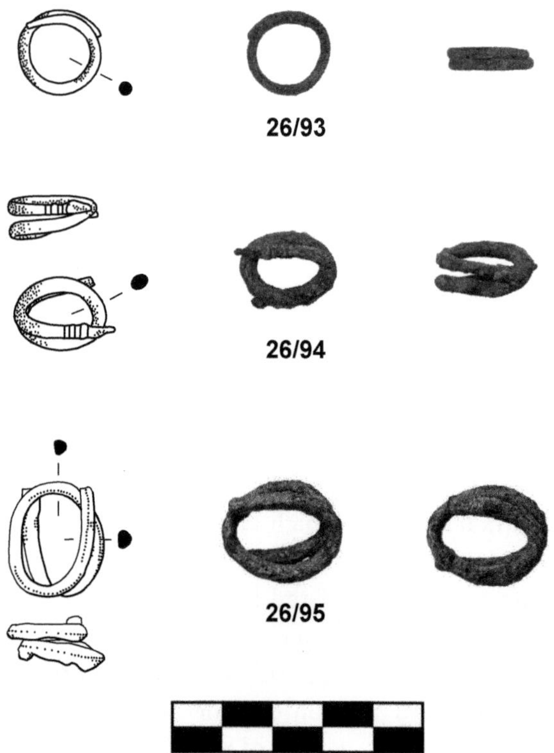

FIGURE 26.34. Agora bronze earrings/hairrings, **26/93** (MEΘ 1797), **26/94** (MEΘ 1798), **26/95** (MEΘ 1796). Drawings A. Hooton and F. Skyvalida, photos I. Coyle and J. Vanderpool

Intact, but corroded.

Thickish bronze wire, circular in section looped over to form an earring or hairring. Decorated terminals leaf- or palmette-shaped, with ribbed element before juncture to the rest of the shaft.

Context unclear.

Cf., among others, Coldstream 1973, pp. 154–155, fig. 38, no. 192 (Knossos, Demeter sanctuary, classified as earring); Felsch 2007, pp. 350–351, pl. 47, nos. 1888–1891 (Kalapodi, Archaic, 5th century B.C., classified under earrings); *OlForsch* XIII, p. 116, pl. 41, no. 399 (classified as earring of Geometric to early Archaic date); p. 131, pl. 41, nos. 469–470 (classified as finger ring of Archaic–Classical date); Klebinder-Gauss 2007, pp. 85, 256, pl. 40, no. 609 (classified as earring).

26/95. (ΜΕΘ 1796 [ΜΕ 1400]) Earring/Hairring Fig. 26.34

Agora #274/076. Από τον καθαρισμό της βόρειας παρείας (from cleaning north scarp of trench).

L./Diam. 0.025; Th. 0.005; Wt. 5.3 g.

Intact, but heavily corroded.

Earring or hair tie made of thick bronze wire, circular in section, looped (two turns) to form ring. Shaft tapering toward a blunt point at one end; thickened at the other.

Context scarp cleaning, context unclear.

Cf., among others, *Nichoria* III, pp. 300, 306, figs. 5-12, 5-13, nos. 18–19 (spiral rings); Kilian 1975a, pl. 70, no. 26 (Pherai, classified as a finger ring); Klebinder-Gauss 2007, pp. 85–87, p. 258, pl. 41, no. 638 (Ephesos, classified as earring); Papadopoulos 2003a, p. 76, fig. 98:c–d, no. 204 (Francavilla Marittima).

Krikoi

I have already discussed, in Chapter 15 (under **15/33–15/34**), κρίκοι (*krikoi*)—sometimes κίρκος—in Greek, as opposed to δακτύλιος (used specifically for finger ring or signet), to refer to rings of various shapes and sizes that are not clearly items of personal ornament, and which functioned in a variety of ways. Of the rings presented below, **26/96** (ΜΕΘ 1794) is in many ways the most interesting. Despite its fragmentary state, the piece was encountered in a pre-destruction deposit in a context that is Early Iron Age or earlier Archaic. As noted in Chapter 15, various items of jewelry, such as rings, bracelets, and anklets, functioned as fungible items, more or less as money, in an era before coinage. In the context of Early Iron Age Greece, Phanouria Dakoronia has argued that bronze rings (*krikoi*) served as recognized values or weights in a premonetary system in the Geometric period, and she pointed specifically to rings with spurs, like **26/96.**[162] More complete rings with spurs elsewhere in Greece can have three, four, or even five spurs, and in one case from Pherai, perhaps only two.[163] A few comparanda from other sites are provided in the entries below.

Similarly early is **26/99** (ΜΕΘ 1669), the smallest of the rings presented here. Although the possibility that it once served as a bead cannot be dismissed, it is fractionally larger and thinner than most minuscule disk beads of the period. I know of no good parallel for it of such a date. **26/97** (ΜΕΘ 2135) was found in the destruction deposit and must date to the earlier or mid-4th century B.C.; with a cast band square in section, its shape and size preclude a finger ring or some other item of personal ornament. In contrast, **26/98** (ΜΕΘ 2136) may well have served as a finger ring, although if so, for a child, adolescent, or petite adult; the possibility that it served as an earring or hair tie cannot be excluded. Parallels for **26/97** and **26/98** are given in the catalogue below.

26/96. (MEΘ 1794 [ME 3826]) Fragmentary Ring (*Krikos*) Fig. 26.35

Agora #274/089. Τομή στη βόρεια πλευρά (north side of trench).

Diam. 0.033–0.036; Th. (shaft/band) 0.005; Wt. 4.4 g.

Single fr preserving about one-half of ring; corroded.

Ring formed of thick bronze wire/band, circular in section. At least two small preserved spurs, 0.027 apart.

Context pre-destruction deposit, Early Iron Age or Archaic.

See, generally, Dakoronia 1989; cf., among others, Kilian 1975a, pl. 73, nos. 28–37; pl. 74, nos. 1–18; Vokotopoulou 1990, pl. 61:δ (two examples, center right, with three spurs); pl. 63:ε (two examples, lower right, with three spurs); Kilian-Dirlmeier 2002, pl. 58, nos. 883–896 (from Philia, most with four or five spurs, dated "spätgeometrische bis hocharchaische Zeit"); Felsch 2007, pl. 44, nos. 1358–1360 (with three and four spurs).

26/97. (MEΘ 2135 [ME 4109]) Fragmentary Ring (*Krikos*) Fig. 26.35

Agora #274/089. Κάτω απ'το στρώμα κεραμιδιών (below layer of roof tiles).

Diam. 0.016; Th. 0.002–0.003; Wt. 1.1 g.

Two joining frr preserving a little more than three-quarters of ring; terminals not preserved.

Band square in section. Unclear whether cast in one piece and broken, or with open-ended terminals as **26/98** (MEΘ 2136), probably the former.

Context destruction deposit, mid-4th century B.C. or earlier.

Cf., among others, Kilian 1975a, pl. 73, esp. nos. 1–15 (Pherai); Kilian-Dirlmeier 2002, pls. 168–169, nos. 2817, 2826, 2829, 2832, 2835, 2838–2841 (Philia); Felsch 2007, pl. 41, nos. 1124–1125; pl. 42, no. 1186 (Kalapodi).

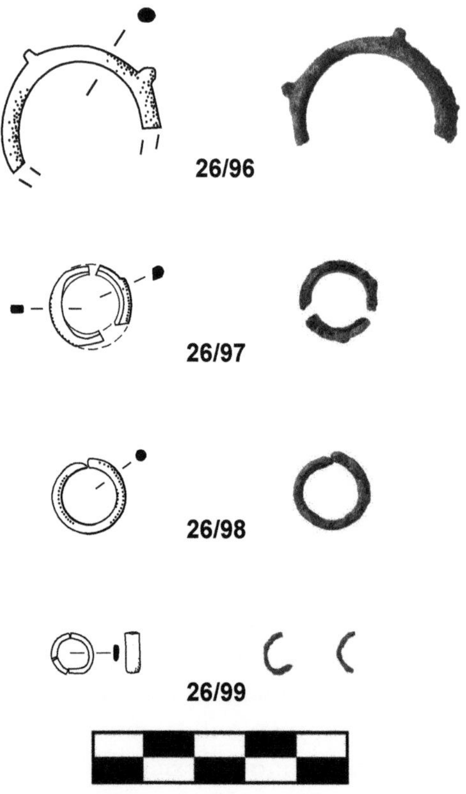

FIGURE 26.35. Agora bronze rings (*krikoi*), **26/96** (MEΘ 1794), **26/97** (MEΘ 2135), **26/98** (MEΘ 2136), **26/99** (MEΘ 1669). Drawings A. Hooton, T. Ross, and F. Skyvalida, photos I. Coyle and J. Vanderpool

26/98. (ΜΕΘ 2136 [ΜΕ 4119]) Ring (*Krikos*) Fig. 26.35

Agora #274/090003 [2].

Diam. 0.015; Th. 0.002–0.003; Wt. 0.7 g.

Intact.

Open-ended ring, tapering toward a point at one end, more blunt at the other, circular in section.

Context unclear.

Cf., among others, Kilian-Dirlmeier 2002, pl. 58, nos. 897–898; pl. 107, no. 1749; pl. 165, nos. 2684–2685, 2688–2690, 2705–2706, 2710; pl. 166, nos. 2711, 2717, 2725; pl. 167, no. 2782 (Philia); Felsch 2007, pl. 40, no. 940; pl. 44, no. 1254 (Kalapodi).

26/99. (ΜΕΘ 1669 [ΜΕ 3802]) Small Ring (*Krikos*) Fig. 26.35

Agora #274/089. Τομή στη βόρεια πλευρά (trench on north side).

Diam. 0.009; H. 0.003–0.004; Wt. 0.2 g.

Three joining frr preserving complete ring.

Small circular ring, with outer face slightly concave.

Context pre-destruction deposit, Early Iron Age to Archaic.

Additional inventoried *krikoi* not catalogued:

ΜΕΘ 1666 (ΜΕ 2048). Agora #274/076. Diam. 0.009; H./Th. 0.002; Wt. 0.4 g.

ΜΕΘ 1667 (ΜΕ 3737). Agora #274/017022 [4]. Βόρειος μάρτυρας (north balk). Diam. 0.020; Th. 0.002; Wt. 0.6 g.

ΜΕΘ 1668 (ΜΕ 3913). Agora #274/079. Τομή στη νότια πλευρα(trench on south side). Diam. 0.008; H./Th. 0.001; Wt. < 0.1 g.

Bracelets

There are four fairly well-preserved examples catalogued below, together with an additional example listed. **26/101** and **26/103** were found in the destruction deposit and are thus mid-4th century B.C. or a little earlier; **26/100** appears to be from a pre-destruction deposit context, in association with material of Archaic and Classical date, whereas the context of **26/102** is unclear. In terms of nomenclature, such items of personal ornament are normally referred to as "bracelet" when the diameter is less than 0.080 and as "armlet" or "anklet" when the diameter is 0.080 m and above.[164] Bracelets, together with armlets/anklets, are comparatively rare in the later Bronze and Early Iron Age.[165] Throughout the earlier stages of the Early Iron Age, there are essentially two types of bracelets; one made of a bronze strip, hammered, with overlapping terminals, and most often plano-convex in section rather than oval or perfectly flat; the other is cast, often with incised decoration.[166] Examples of both types, together with bracelets of various other types, from Olympia, the Enodia sanctuary at Pherai and the Athena Itonia sanctuary near Philia in Thessaly, and at Kalapodi, to mention just a few sites, continue into the Archaic and Classical periods.[167] Parallels for the individual bracelets are provided below in the catalogue entries.

26/100. (ΜΕΘ 1645 [ΜΕ 1848]) Fragmentary Bracelet Fig. 26.36

Agora #274/009009 [3]. Building B. Περιοχή ανάμεσα Τ.24 and Τ.25 (area between Walls 24 and 25).

P.L. 0.044; L. (terminal) 0.011; Th. (band) 0.003–0.004; Wt. 3.2 g.

Single fr preserving about one-half of bracelet.

Cast and perhaps slightly hammered. Band circular in section. Molded triangular head resembling snake head.

Context pre-destruction deposit? Archaic or Classical period.

Cf. *OlForsch* XIII, pp. 222–230, pl. 52, nos. 823–824, 826–827, 832, 835; pls. 53–55, various examples (all Archaic–Classical); Kilian-Dirlmeier 2002, p. 100, pl. 96, no. 1546; cf. also the pin with a snake-head finial, pl. 96, no. 154 (Philia, Archaic); Rhomiopoulou and Touratsoglou 2002, p. 105, M 1094, M 1095 (Mieza, silver, dated 470–440 B.C.); Felsch 2007, p. 299, pls. 8 and 36, no. 617 (Kalapodi, 5th century B.C.); Vokotopoulou 1990, pp. 107–108, fig. 57, pl. 66:γ (two silver bracelets from Aineia, ca. 600 B.C.); Klebinder-Gauss 2007, pp. 80–81, 248, pl. 35, no. 434 (Ephesos, Archaic).

26/101. (ΜΕΘ 1647 [ΜΕ 3847]) Bracelet Fig. 26.36

Agora #274/018003 [2]. Δάπεδο (floor).

L. 0.053; L. (terminals) 0.018; Th. (band) 0.004–0.005; Wt. 12.2 g.

Intact, except for minor chipping around one terminal.

Cast in one piece. Thick band, circular in section, diagonally grooved (resembling twisting). Molded decorated terminals, as shown, resembling snake heads.

Context destruction deposit, mid-4th century B.C. or earlier.

Cf. Kilian 1975a, pl. 65, no. 9 (Pherai); Kilian-Dirlmeier 2002, pp. 54–55, pl. 57, nos. 870–871 (Philia, referred to as "Armringe" of "spätgeometrische bis hocharchaische Zeit"); Rhomiopoulou and Touratsoglou 2002, p. 70, M 1037 (Mieza, 4th century B.C.); Felsch 2007, pl. 34, nos. 552–553, 555, 560 (Kalapodi, "tordierte Armreife").

26/102. (ΜΕΘ 1646 [ΜΕ 2356]) Fragmentary Bracelet Fig. 26.36

Agora #274/075. ΝΔ τμήμα (SW section).

P.L. 0.063; Th. (band) 0.005–0.006; Wt. 8.0 g.

Single fr preserving over one-half of bracelet; heavily corroded.

Thick band, square to rhomboid in section, rather than circular. Broken at one end; the other end thickened into a terminal, as shown, with no clear decoration.

Context unclear.

Cf. Vickers 1977, p. 29, fig. IV, nos. 1–5, 8–10 (Poteidaia); *OlForsch* XIII, p. 198, pl. 45, no. 725 (under "protogeometrische Armreifen"); Kilian-Dirlmeier 2002, p. 100, pl. 96, no. 1547; Papadopoulos 2003a, pp. 77–78, fig. 90:e–f, g–h, nos. 211–212 (Archaic from Francavilla Marittima); Felsch 2007, pp. 292, 297, pl. 33, nos. 532, 534; pl. 36, nos. 593–595 (Kalapodi).

26/103. (ΜΕΘ 3095 [ΜΕ 4226]) Possible Bracelet? Fig. 26.36

Agora #274/066. Βόρειο Τμήμα (north section).

P.L. 0.076; Th. (band) 0.002–0.003; Wt. 4.1 g.

One end intact, the other broken.

Probably bracelet rather than length of bronze wire. Band more oval than circular in section. Preserved terminal nicely rounded, with slight traces of fillet near the edge (more visible on the photo).

Context destruction deposit, mid-4th century B.C. or earlier.

Cf., among others, Felsch 2007, p. 292, pl. 33, no. 533 (Kalapodi).

Additional fragmentary bracelet:

ΜΕΘ 1643 (ΜΕ 1310). Agora #274/067. P.L. 0.068; Th. (band, max) 0.004; Wt. 7.2 g.

Tutuli, buttons, or bosses

One of the tutuli presented below, **26/105**, was encountered in the destruction deposit of 354 B.C.; the context of the other two was unclear. Tutuli are more fully discussed above in Chapter 15 (under **15/36–15/43**), with supplementary notes on the example from the acropolis east slope

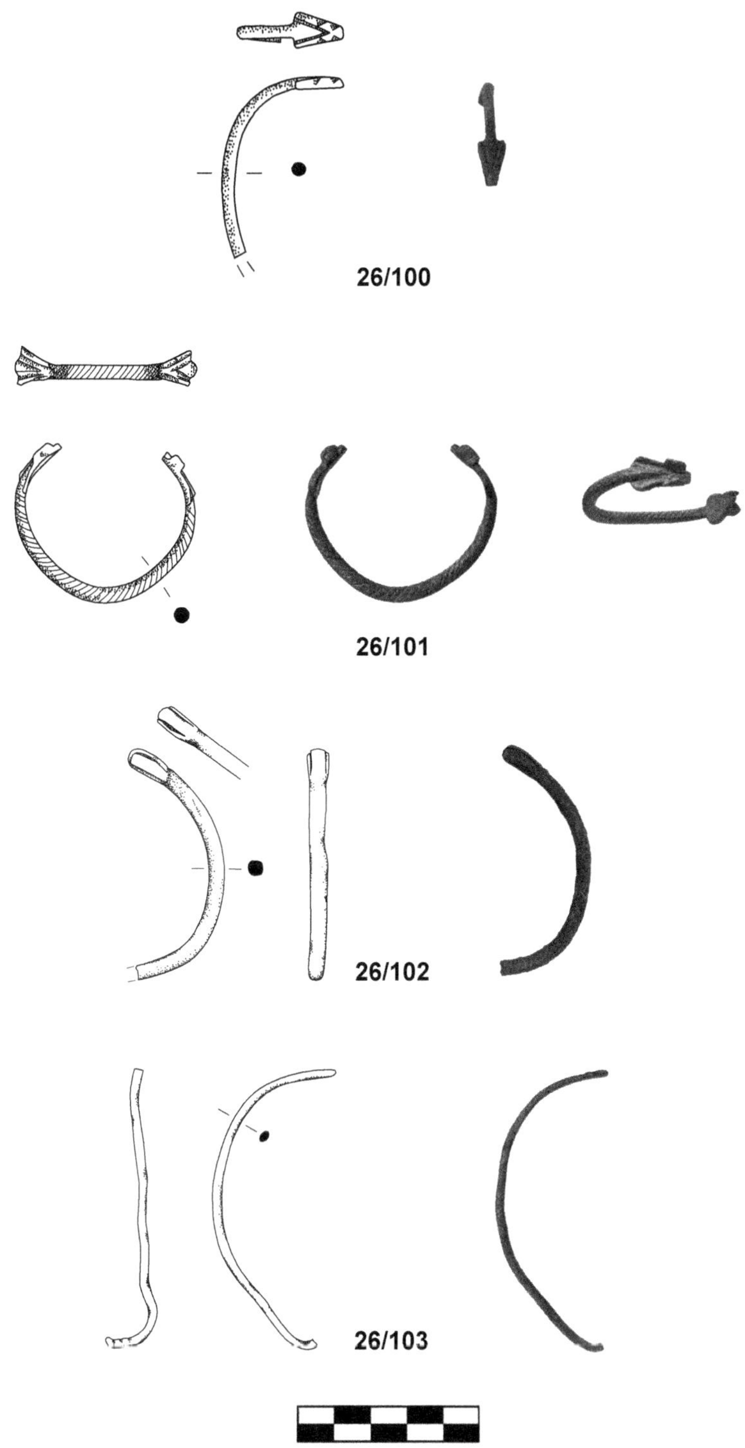

FIGURE 26.36. Agora bronze bracelets, **26/100** (MEΘ 1645), **26/101** (MEΘ 1647), **26/102** (MEΘ 1646), **26/103** (MEΘ 3095). Drawings T. Ross and F. Skyvalida, photos I. Coyle and J. Vanderpool

(**26/47**). Both **26/104** and **26/105** are small domes, with no clear method of attachment; the closest parallels come from Francavilla Marittima in Archaic southern Italy (see catalogue entry below). **26/106** is the largest of the three, but only fractionally, with its edge articulated to form a rim of sorts. A variety of uses for such tutuli or small bosses is discussed by Robinson for the numerous examples from Olynthos.[168]

26/104. (MEΘ 1690 [ME 934]) Tutulus, Button, or Boss Fig. 26.37

Agora #274/. Scarp cleaning.

H. 0.003; Diam. 0.010; Wt. 0.4 g.

Intact.

Thin small dome. Method of attachment unclear.

Context unclear.

Cf., among others, Zancani Montuoro 1983–1984, p. 72 (referred to as "bottoni tondi di bronzo," as opposed to "bottonicini"); Papadopoulos 2003a, pp. 87–88, fig. 100, esp. nos. 246, 248; cf. Boardman 1967, pp. 227, 229, no. 430; Coldstream 1973, pp. 148–150, fig. 35, esp. no. 145.

26/105. (MEΘ 1691 [ME 965]) Tutulus, Button, or Boss Fig. 26.37

Agora #274/077.

H. 0.003; Diam. 0.008; Wt. 0.2 g.

Intact.

As **26/104** (MEΘ 1690) but slightly smaller.

Context destruction deposit, mid-4th century B.C. or earlier.

Cf. **26/104** (MEΘ 1690) and parallels cited there.

26/106. (MEΘ 1673 [ME 1811]) Tutulus, Omphaloid Disk Fig. 26.37

Agora #274. Περιοχή κτιρίου Α (area of Building A).

H. 0.003; Diam. (max) 0.013; Th. 0.001; Wt. 0.3 g.

Intact.

Small disk, dome shaped, with edge articulated to form a rim.

Context unclear.

Cf., among others, Papadopoulos 2003a, p. 88, fig. 111, esp. no. 249.

Additional tutulus, button, or boss:

MEΘ 1625 (ME 3848). Agora #274/018003 [2]. Εστία (hearth). Found together with a fr of a pin shaft (and inventoried under the same number). H. 0.005; Diam. 0.010; Wt. 0.6 g.

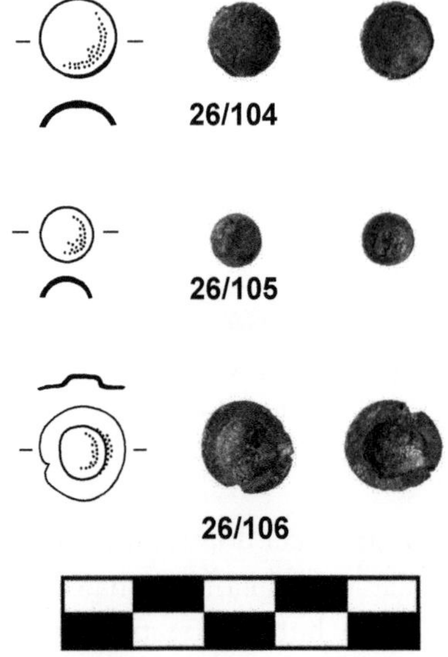

FIGURE 26.37. Agora bronze tutuli, **26/104** (MEΘ 1690), **26/105** (MEΘ 1691), **26/106** (MEΘ 1673). Drawings A. Hooton, photos J. Vanderpool

Musical instrument

Bronze terminal for wind instrument

It is unfortunate that the solitary musical instrument of metal from Methone derives from a context that is undetermined, the object having been found in the backfill of the excavations in the agora of Methone. All that can be said about it is that it dates before 354 B.C., although comparanda from various parts of Greece will assist in establishing the chronological range of this type of instrument. With a diameter, as preserved, of 0.037 m, **26/107** is fully described in the catalogue entry below. I have written more fully about this class of object in a recent paper focusing on identical objects from Epirote tombs, where **26/107** was briefly noted.[169] In that paper I referred to the wind instrument as an "aulos," largely on the basis of a much better-preserved example from Dourouti in Epirus, replete with a bone cylinder forming the main body, onto which a bronze terminal resembling **26/107** was attached, with a diameter of 0.040, and described as a "καλοδιατηρημένη καμπάνα (κώδων) αυλού που διατηρεί τμήμα του οστέινου κέρατος."[170] Although auloi do not normally have such domed bronze terminals, they are often equipped with bronze rings at their ends, such as the example from the Kabeireion on Lemnos.[171]

More numerous terminals similar to **26/107** are quite common in the Greek world, even though they have been rarely identified as components of musical instruments. The largest number of such terminals were found in tombs at the Molossian site of Liatovouni in Epirus.[172] There are at least five examples, each appearing individually in a tomb, and as a group they have a height of 0.008–0.015 (usually closer to 0.015) and a diameter of 0.030–0.040 m. All are from tombs that date to the Archaic or earlier Classical period.[173] Three virtually identical bronzes were found in tombs at the other Molossian cemetery extensively excavated and fully published, at Vitsa Zagoriou, all dating to the 5th century B.C., referred to by Vokotopoulou as "χάλκινα ομφαλωτά κομβία," and thought to be associated with boots or sandals.[174] Elsewhere in northern Greece, two further examples illustrated by Georgia Karamitrou-Mentessidi from Aiani in western Macedonia were interpreted as bronze nozzles of aryballoi, the bodies of which were thought to be made of an organic material otherwise not preserved,[175] and another, also identified as the mouth of a bronze aryballos, from Sindos.[176]

Similar bronze terminals are equally common, perhaps even more so, in southern Greece, especially in the Corinthia, although examples are known from other Peloponnesian sites, including Olympia.[177] Several of the small bronzes from the temenos of Hera Limenia at Perachora are virtually identical to the Methone, Liatovouni, and Vitsa pieces discussed above, and three of the Perachora examples are especially close.[178] One of the Perachora pieces is referred to as the mouth of a round aryballos, and two are thought to be the mouthpieces of lekythoi, a shape that is stressed as uncommon in bronze.[179] In terms of size, the Perachora "lekythos mouths" are the same as those from Methone and Epirus: the diameters range between 3.3 and 4.3 cm, and although there is nothing to clinch their absolute chronology, they are considered to be 6th century B.C. Elsewhere in the Corinthia, such bronzes are well represented at the sanctuary of Poseidon at Isthmia. In her study of the metal objects from the site, Raubitschek writes: "Eleven identifiable tops of lekythoi were found, six of which . . . are almost identical in size and shape.[180] They were all found in the pronaos of the Archaic temple with other small and valuable objects.[181] Farther afield, there is an identical bronze, with a diameter of 0.038, from tomb 93 at Pithekoussai, thought to be a bronze mouthpiece of a leather aryballos, dating to the 5th century B.C.[182] Elsewhere in the Greek world, musical instruments are not uncommon dedications at Greek sanctuaries, especially in colonial Italy and Sicily.[183]

The few examples presented here are not meant to be exhaustive, and there may very well be many more. They are presented here in the hope that more examples may be noted and published, especially ones from well-preserved contexts that could provide additional evidence of the type of instrument from which such pieces derive.[184]

26/107. (MEΘ 4143 [ME 4147]) Terminal of Wind Instrument Fig. 26.38

Agora #274. Backfill.

Diam. (as preserved) 0.037; Wt. 5.8 g.

Single fr, crumpled and chipped, preserving almost complete terminal for wind instrument, except for the cylindrical stem used for attachment to the main cylinder of the musical instrument, made of organic material.

Sheet bronze of medium thickness, formed into a disk, with lower edges folded up. The main body would originally have been dome-shaped. Central hole at top (as shown), much chipped, would have originally had a short upturned cylinder, for insertion into the main stem of the musical instrument.

Context unclear.

Related?

The following piece was, and still is, an enigma, for which I have no convincing parallel. Its shape and size, however, resemble **26/107**, although **26/108** is significantly heavier. It is not a convincing neck and rim of a closed bronze vessel, unless the rest of its body, of which nothing survives, is open latticework, which may result in a thymiaterion of sorts, for which I also know of no convincing parallel. It is presented here as another problem piece, in proximity to both the terminal of what I am sure is a musical instrument, and also close to the few fragmentary bronze vessels from the site. Found in the collapsed fill above the destruction deposit, its context is unhelpful in terms of its date.

26/108. (MEΘ 1795 [ME 2791]) Undetermined; Instrument Terminal? Fig. 26.38

Agora #274/027016 [1].

Diam. 0.033–0.034; L./H. 0.022; Wt. 15.1 g.

Single fr preserving undetermined portion of object. The narrow cylindrical end seems broken, but perhaps not all around. Outer edge of cone heavily chipped.

Circular cone, with slightly concave underside as shown, outer edge heavily chipped, although it may have originally been articulated all around as shown. This conical, funnel-like element is elaborated with petal-like depressions and holes (i.e., some of these are pierced through, others are not); this decoration, for want of a better word, was intentionally cast. The broader conical element is surmounted by a narrow cylinder, as shown.

Context collapsed fill above destruction deposit, prehistoric to mid-4th century B.C.

Bronze vessels

There were no demonstrable vessels, or fragments of vessels, from the Hypogeion fill, and none from the other areas of the site investigated thus far. The three pieces presented here were the only diagnostic fragments of bronze vessels from the agora of Methone, a small and eclectic number. Two were found in the destruction deposit, **26/109** and **26/110**, whereas the context of the third, **26/111**, was unclear as to date.

Tripod stand

Figured tripod feet, whether anthropomorphic, combination anthropomorphic and zoomorphic, or zoomorphic—most commonly felines and bulls—are common dedications in Greek and South Italian sanctuaries.[185] In mainland Greece and the Aegean tripodiskoi with zoomorphic feet are well represented in various sanctuaries, including the Athenian Acropolis, Dodona, Perachora, Olympia, the Argive Heraion, Sparta, Delphi, Samos, and Lindos.[186] A well-preserved

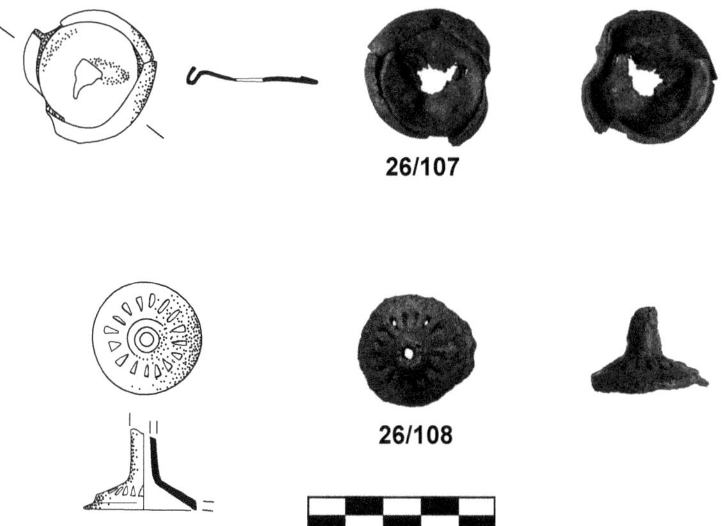

FIGURE 26.38. Agora bronze musical instrument, bronze terminal for wind instrument, **26/107** (ΜΕΘ 4143), and related, **26/108** (ΜΕΘ 1795). Drawings F. Skyvalida, photos J. Vanderpool

example close to **26/109** was found at Rhitsona in Boiotia,[187] as were at least three fragmentary tripodiskoi at Kalapodi.[188] In southern Italy, the type is well represented at the Timpone della Motta at Francavilla Marittima, the sanctuary of Hera Lakinia at Capo Colonna, at Rosarno Medma, and the cemetery at Lokroi Epizephyrioi, to mention only a few sites in Calabria, as well as in Apulia.[189] A number of well-illustrated examples from the cemetery at Trebenište are published by Bogdan Filow.[190] Much closer to Methone are the tripod-footed lekanai and exaleiptra from Sindos in Macedonia, of late Archaic date.[191]

26/109. (ΜΕΘ 1780 [ΜΕ 1520]) Fragmentary Tripod Stand — Fig. 26.39

Agora #274/088. Στρώμα καταστροφής, χώρος Δ′ (ανατολικός μάρτυρας). Destruction level, Room 4 (Stoa Building A), east balk.

H. 0.040; p.W. 0.035; Wt. 30.3 g.

Feline leg complete and well preserved; ring above clearly broken at one end, less so on the opposite end. Some corrosion at upper left.

Upper horizontal part that forms the ring supported by the one preserved feline leg, slightly curved in profile. Substantial groove on outer face at juncture of ring and leg stand. Feline leg, with four-toed paws.

Context destruction deposit, mid-4th century B.C. or earlier.

Small phiale

It is a shame that **26/110** is so fragmentary and poorly preserved; without its base, it is uncertain whether its bottom was round, flat, or mesomphalic. The tear in the bronze at the lower break gives the impression of a mesomphalos phiale, but nothing of its base is actually preserved. Similar phialai, ranging in size from miniature to large (5–25 cm in diameter), are ubiquitous at most sanctuary sites of the Archaic period, and, as such, an example like **26/110** of the first half of the 4th century B.C. establishes the continuity of the type well into the Classical period. In his publication of the bronzes from the temenos of Hera Limenia at Perachora, Thomas Dunbabin listed Greek comparanda known at the time from the Argive Heraion, Arkadian

Orchomenos, Sparta, Olympia, Corinth, the Athenian Acropolis, Boiotian Orchomenos, Delphi, Dodona, Ephesos, Lindos, and "most other temple sites."[192] Dunbabin placed the earliest datable Greek phialai to the 7th century B.C. and noted: "Earlier examples in Greece and Etruria are certainly Phoenician imports. The phiale mesomphalos came to Greece, and, in the first place, it appears, to Corinth, probably from Syria or Phoenicia."[193] Dunbabin's suggestion that the Asiatic phiale first appeared in Greece at Corinth is generally accepted by Raubitschek, but with a more prominent role assumed by Perachora and Isthmia.[194] Similar phialai are also very common in southern Italy.[195] The numerous examples in Cyprus, both bronze and silver, decorated and plain, are assembled and discussed by Hartmut Matthäus and others.[196]

26/110. (ΜΕΘ 4142 [ΜΕ 4037]) Small Phiale Fragment Fig. 26.39

Agora #274/028002 [1]. Δάπεδο (floor).

P.H. 0.013; Diam. (rim) est. ca. 0.065.

Single fr preserving small portion of rim and upper body. Bronze torn near lower break.

Small and shallow open bowl, with upper wall rising gently toward plain rim, flat (cut) on top.

Context destruction deposit, mid-4th century B.C. or earlier.

Decorative roundel/reel

26/111 is an example of a decorated roundel or reel, sometimes referred to as spools, usually associated with a handle or else as a rim attachment for bronze vessels. A very wide variety of handles and their attachments are a common feature among the bronze finds from various contexts throughout Greece and Italy.[197] A few close Greek, Balkan, and south Italian comparanda for **26/111** may be cited from Olympia, the Argive Heraion, Perachora, Isthmia, Lindos, Kalapodi, Philia, Trebenište, Francavilla Marittima, Krotone, Foce del Sele, and Metapontion, among many other sites.[198] The cemetery at Sindos has yielded no shortage of complete or near-complete bronze vessels, some of which are equipped with decorated roundels/reels associated with both handles, but also placed adjacent to the rim.[199]

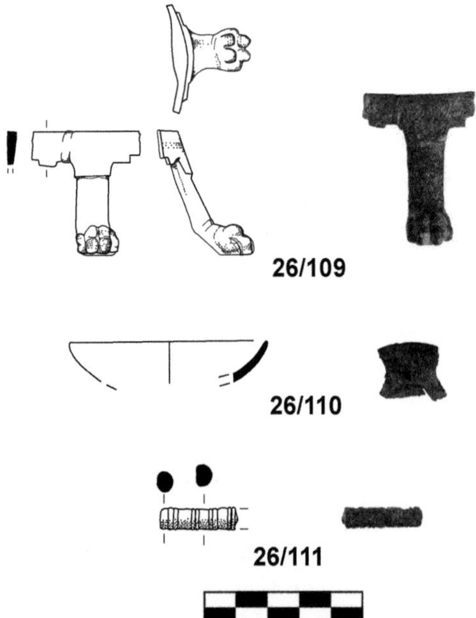

FIGURE 26.39. Agora fragmentary bronze vessels: tripod stand with feline leg, **26/109** (ΜΕΘ 1780); rim fragment of small phiale, **26/110** (ΜΕΘ 4142); decorative roundel for vessel, **26/111** (ΜΕΘ 4187). Drawings A. Hooton and F. Skyvalida, photos I. Coyle and J. Vanderpool

26/111. (ΜΕΘ 4187 [ME 1985]) Decorative Roundel/Reel Fig. 26.39

Agora #274/084. NA Τμήμα (SE section).

L. 0.026; Diam. (max) 0.007; Wt. 4.5 g.

The roundel itself is intact, but at one end there are traces of the stem to which it was attached to a handle.

Roundel/reel plano-convex in section (i.e., flattened on one side for attachment), with a version of the common bead-and-reel decoration, though the beads in between are not very prominent.

Context unclear.

Various implements/tools

Cheese grater

Cheese graters have been fully discussed, with comparanda, under **26/13** from the summit of the West Hill, with an additional fragmentary example, **26/48**, from the acropolis east slope. Both **26/13** and **26/48** are early: the former is Archaic, the latter Early Iron Age or Archaic. Although the majority of published cheese graters cited above date to the Early Iron Age or Archaic period, the importance of **26/112** lies in the fact that it was recovered from the destruction deposit and must date to the first half of the 4th century B.C., thus establishing that cheese graters continue well into the later Classical period.

26/112. (ΜΕΘ 4188 [ME 1399]) Cheese Grater Fig. 26.40

Agora #274/088. Ανατολικός μάρτυρας, στρώμα καστανέρυθρο 3 (east balk, red-brown layer 3).

P.L. (largest fr) 0.041; p.W. 0.031; Wt. 1.6 g.

Three main joining frr plus smaller chips, preserving relatively small portion of grater.

Thin sheet bronze, with holes all created from one side, with the grating surface on the opposite side. Also preserved is portion of the straight unperforated side that frames the grating surface, but not the edge itself. The holes are all punched, not drilled, and are square, rectangular, or rhomboidal.

Context destruction deposit, mid-4th century B.C. or earlier.

Additional fragments of cheese graters from the agora of Methone:

ME 3616. Agora #274/089. P.L. x p.W. 0.014 x 0.011; Wt. 0.4 g.

ME 2306. Agora #274/075. Ανατολικό τμήμα (east section). One main fr plus chips. P.L. x p.W. 0.013 x 0.013; Wt. 0.5 g.

Ear spoons

There are two examples of such objects from the agora of Methone, **26/113** and **26/114**, the former from an unclear context, the latter from the collapsed fill above the destruction deposit; in terms of their date, all that can be said is that they are 354 B.C. or earlier.

The term "ear spoon"—"ὠτογλυφίδα" (plural ὠτογλυφίδες) in Modern Greek, "Ohrlöffel" in German—that has entered the archaeological literature was inspired by a fragment of the comic poet Plato, a contemporary of Aristophanes, which refers to an ὠτογλυφὶς as a medical implement.[200] In dealing with a fairly large number from Corinth, of Roman and Byzantine date, Gladys Davidson refers to them as "ear and unguent spoons."[201] A useful discussion of the term, together with other related terms for medical implements—such as μήλη and μηλωτρίς—is provided by Despoini in her presentation of two ear spoons from Sindos closely related to **26/113** (one of the Sindos examples was found in tomb 106, dating to the last quarter of the 6th century B.C., the other a chance find in the area of the cemetery without a clear context).[202] Despoini further notes that "ear spoons" were used from the Bronze Age into Roman times, and lists comparanda, many very close to **26/113** and

26/114, from Thebes, Vitsa Zagoriou in Epirus (first quarter 5th century B.C.), Olynthos (348 B.C. or earlier), the Athena Itonia sanctuary near Philia (some Classical, others Roman-Byzantine), Corinth (of bronze and bone, mostly Roman, some Byzantine), and Thessaloniki (Roman).[203] Additional examples from Delos (Greek period), Olympia (Roman period), Novaesium (Neuss) in Germany, and Hungary (8th century A.D.) are given by Davidson.[204] To these, two examples may be added from the Minoan peak sanctuary at Agios Georgios sto Vouno on Kythera.[205] For an Archaic ear spoon from the Artemision at Ephesos, Gudrun Klebinder-Gauss compares examples from Boğazköy (dating to the 2nd millennium B.C.) and Gordion (620–600 B.C.), on the basis of which she not only dates the Ephesos *Ohrlöffel* to the 7th century B.C., but suggests that it is perhaps an import from Phrygia; an undated "cure-oreilles" from Dodona is also published by Constantin Carapanos.[206]

In the catalogue entries I cite a few close comparanda for **26/113** and **26/114**. Many of the published examples similar to **26/113** are as early as Archaic, whereas many of the comparanda for **26/114** are Roman or Byzantine, although at least one example from Pherai should be Archaic (as already noted, the date of **26/114** lies anywhere between the prehistoric period and the mid-4th century B.C.). It is interesting to add that for the examples from Philia already noted, Kilian-Dirlmeier distinguishes between "Ohrsonde" ("ear probes"), which resemble **26/114**, and "Ohrlöffel" ("ear spoons"), like **26/113**, most of which are of Roman or Byzantine date, although two are of Classical date.[207]

26/113. (ΜΕΘ 1671 [ΜΕ 2844]) Ear Spoon Fig. 26.40

Agora #274/065. ΝΔ τμήμα (SW section).

P.H. 0.037; p.L. (decorated terminal) 0.018; L. x p.W. (spoon) 0.005 x 0.004; Wt. 1.3 g.

Single fr preserving uncertain portion of implement, and although side opposite the spoon is clearly broken, the piece, on the basis of comparanda, is unlikely to be significantly larger.

Miniature spoon, essentially composed of thin bronze sheet hammered into shape. Opposite end molded (cast) and beaded, as shown, with five preserved beads, with fillets in between.

Context unclear.

Cf., among others, Klebinder-Gauss 2007, pp. 169–170, pl. 86, no. 888 (7th century B.C.); *Sindos* III, pp. 276–277, 467, 632, fig. 226, pl. 574, nos. 553–554 (last quarter of the 6th century B.C); Vokotopoulou 1986, pl. 37:α, fig. 114:λ (Vitsa, first quarter 5th century B.C.).

26/114. (ΜΕΘ 1670 [ΜΕ 2946]) Ear Spoon Fig. 26.40

Agora #274/016002 [1].

P.L. 0.098; L. x W. (spoon) 0.007–0.005; Th. (shaft, max) 0.003; Wt. 4.2 g.

Single fr preserving most of implement, except for the terminal on the side opposite the spoon.

Comparatively long shaft, circular in section, broken at one end and formed into a small spoon at the other. It remains uncertain whether or not the terminal opposite the spoon was decorated.

Context collapsed fill above destruction deposit, prehistoric to mid-4th century B.C.

Cf., among many others, Kilian 1975a, p. 212, pl. 88, no. 16 (Pherai, under "Toilettenzubehör"); *Corinth* XII, pl. 82, esp. nos. 1319–1323; Kilian-Dirlmeier 2002, pl. 117, nos. 1938–1940; *Selinus* V, p. 134, pl. 42, no. 750 (dated end of the 4th into the beginning of the 3rd century B.C.).

Spatulate implement/instrument

In her discussion of various implements and instruments, Davidson distinguishes between "true spatulae," which are rare, and "spatulate instruments." About the latter she writes: "These instruments are distinguished from the spoons by the fact that the working end is flat, not concave. They were probably used for mixing unguents or similar materials."[208] In discussing the

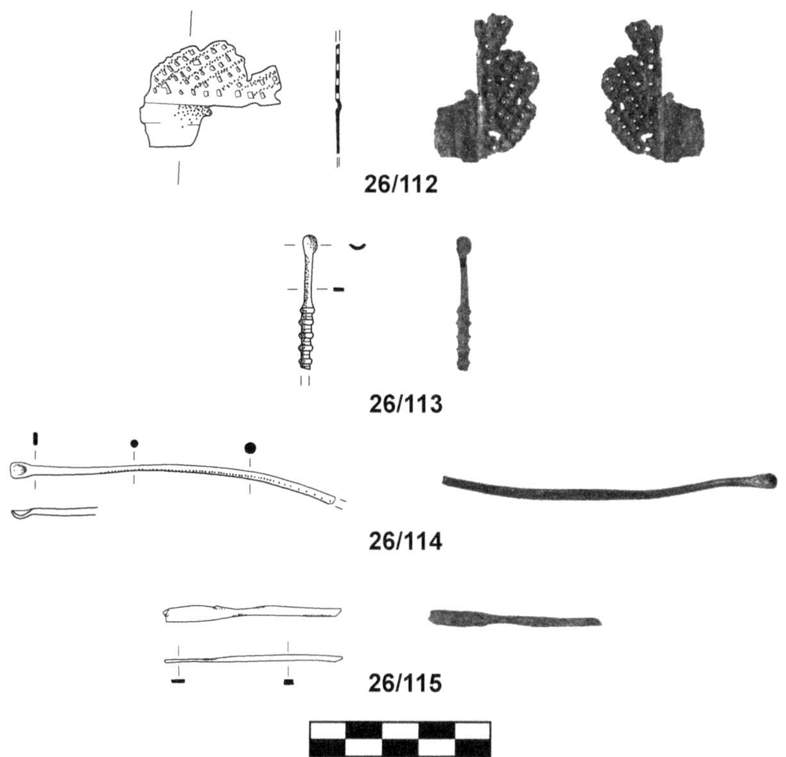

FIGURE 26.40. Agora, various bronze implements: cheese grater, **26/112** (ΜΕΘ 4188); ear spoons, **26/113** (ΜΕΘ 1671), **26/114** (ΜΕΘ 1670); spatulate implement/instrument **26/115** (ΜΕΘ 1672). Drawings A. Hooton, T. Ross, and F. Skyvalida, photos I. Coyle and J. Vanderpool

related "spatulae" of bone, she compares them to a common medical instrument called a "spatula probe."[209] All of the Corinth examples presented by Davidson are Roman and mostly of bone, although at least one (no. 1341) is bronze; also of Roman or Byzantine date is a "Spatelsonde" from Philia.[210] In its basic form, **26/115** is similar to **15/65**, from Phase I of the Hypogeion, and therefore of late 8th or earlier 7th century B.C. date; both have shafts that are rectangular in section. The importance of **26/115** and **15/65** is their context, which suggests an Early Iron Age or Archaic date, and thus establishes that this type of object is of earlier date. That such spatulate objects were used for mixing and applying unguents, ointments, cosmetics, and the like is indicated by similarly shaped bone pins from the Late Bronze Age tombs at Methone.[211]

26/115. (ΜΕΘ 1672 [ME 2294]) Spatulate Implement Fig. 26.40

Agora #274/068. Τομή ΒΔ τμήματος (NW section of trench).

P.L. 0.051; p.L. x W. (head) 0.018 x 0.005; Wt. 1.2 g.

Single fr preserving portion of implement, including most of the spatulate head, except for the very edge, but unknown portion of the shaft.

Small spatulate implement, made of thin bronze strip, hammered flat, with shaft rectangular in section.

Context pre-destruction deposit, Early Iron Age to Archaic.

Related:

ΜΕΘ 4306 (ME 2604). Agora #274/065. Single fr preserving portion of head and shaft, bent out of shape. P.L. 0.042; W. (head) 0.005; Th. (shaft) 0.003 x 0.003; Wt. 2.7 g.

ME 2163. Agora #274/085. Ανατολικός μάρτυρας (east balk). P.L. (as bent) 0.021; Wt. 0.7 g.

Needles

The needles from the Hypogeion, late 8th to 7th century B.C., are presented above in Chapter 15 (under **15/45–15/48**). There are relatively more needles from the agora than from other areas of the site. Essentially, the two basic types of needles encountered in the Hypogeion were also encountered in the agora: the first is the classic needle with an eyelet, which comes in a variety of sizes (long: **26/116** and **26/117**, and short: **26/118**); the second type, including **26/119** and **26/120**, accords with **15/47** from the Hypogeion. Of the two examples of this type from the agora, **26/119** is the more characteristic: the needle is short and sturdy, its head triangular in profile and articulated from the shaft by an inset to accommodate the thread, which could have been quite thick. One side of the needle is flat, the other has a groove running down the central portion of the needle, terminating well before the point. **26/120** is related, but less sturdy, and with its head only slightly wider than the shaft, hammered flat, thus allowing the thread to be tied around it in the same manner as the fishhooks (for which see below, **26/127–26/131**).

As for the longer versions of the needles with eyelets (**26/116** and **26/117**), they are sometimes classified as dress pins, such as the distinctive examples with eyelets of Bronze Age date from Greece and the central Balkans.[212] Later examples are normally referred to as sewing needles ("Nähnadeln").[213] In discussing the more numerous needles from Corinth, where there is no evidence for the existence of needles before the 1st century A.D., Davidson makes the point that household sewing in the modern sense was almost nonexistent.[214] Be that as it may, bronze needles of Classical date, mostly of the 4th century B.C., are known from Olynthos, Knossos, and probably also Delos, although the latter are more difficult to date.[215] Against such a backdrop, the Methone examples are important; needles of both types and of various sizes were common from the Late Geometric period, if not earlier, to the time of the destruction of the city in 354 B.C., and need not have been used primarily or exclusively for the sewing of cloth, but for other materials and purposes as well. That some of the bone pins in the Bronze Age tombs of Methone were used for the application of ointments or unguents, rather than as dress or hair pins, is clear from their context (see Chapter 6), and many of the Methone needles, especially the sturdier ones of Geometric to Classical date, would have been well suited for sewing leather, while the longer needles may well have been used for finishing, or even repairing, textiles. As noted in Chapter 15, the needles of Methone should be seen against the backdrop of both industrial and domestic activity at the site, which include textile production (note the spindlewhorls and loomweights from the Hypogeion in Chapter 16), and the working of animal products, not least leather. Moreover, they help to bridge the chronological gap between the "Nähnadeln" of the Bronze Age and the needles of Classical, Hellenistic, Roman, and Byzantine date, suggesting that needles enjoyed a long history from the Bronze Age into modern times.[216]

26/116. (ΜΕΘ 2134 [ΜΕ 4056]) Needle Fig. 26.41

Agora #274/009012. Δάπεδο (floor).

L. (as bent) 0.077; W. (max, at head) 0.002–0.003; Wt. 0.9 g.

Intact.

Thin shaft, circular in section, tapering to a sharp point. Small oval eyelet at head.

Context destruction deposit, mid-4th century B.C. or earlier.

26/117. (ΜΕΘ 1658 [ΜΕ 2370]) Fragmentary Needle Fig. 26.41

Agora #274/075. Μέσο νότιου τμήματος (middle of south side).

P.L. 0.069; Th. (max) 0.001–0.002; Wt. 0.8 g.

Single fr preserving greater part of needle, except for uppermost portion of eyelet and point.

Comparatively long, thin needle, circular in section, tapering toward point, itself not preserved. Small eyelet, as **26/116** (ΜΕΘ 2134) broken.

Context uncertain.

26/118. (ΜΕΘ 1659 [ΜΕ 1903]) Small Needle Fig. 26.41

Agora #274/078. Δυτικό τμήμα (west section).

L. 0.027; W. (head) 0.004; Th. (max) 0.001; Wt. 0.1 g.

Single fr preserving almost complete needle; small portion of eyelet broken.

Small needle, with short shaft, circular in section, tapering to sharp point. Head hammered flat, with a comparatively broad eyelet.

Context destruction deposit, mid-4th century B.C. or earlier.

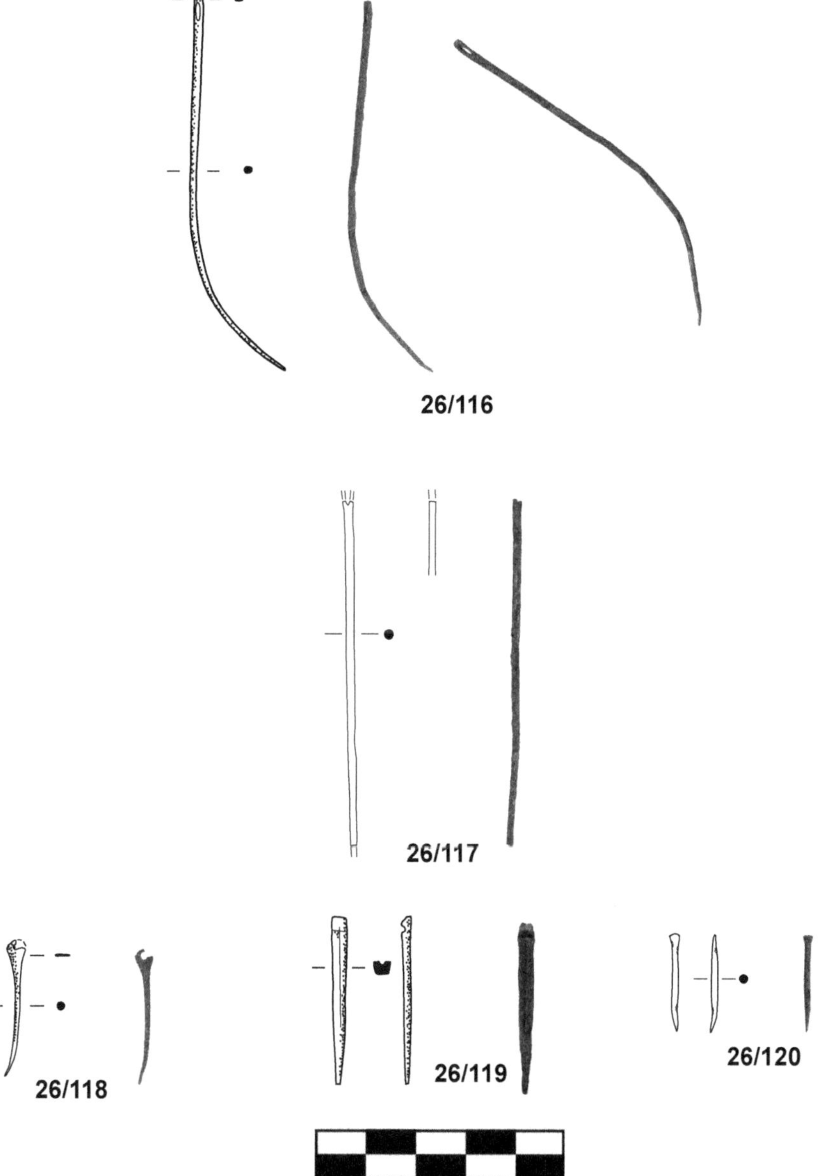

FIGURE 26.41. Agora bronze needles, **26/116** (ΜΕΘ 2134), **26/117** (ΜΕΘ 1658), **26/118** (ΜΕΘ 1659), **26/119** (ΜΕΘ 2133β), **26/120** (ΜΕΘ 4197). Drawings T. Ross and F. Skyvalida, photos I. Coyle and J. Vanderpool

26/119. (ΜΕΘ 2133β [ΜΕ 4094 β]) Small Needle Fig. 26.41

Agora #274/059010 [3]. Αυλάκι (small channel).

L. 0.034; W. (max, at top) 0.003–0.004; Th. (max) 0.002–0.003; Wt. 1.1 g.

Intact.

Small, but comparatively broad needle, with head triangular in profile, articulated from shaft by inset to accommodate the thread. One side of needle is flat, the other has a groove running down the central portion of needle, terminating well before the point. The lower shaft tapers to a sharp point.

Context destruction deposit, mid-4th century B.C. or earlier.

26/120. (ΜΕΘ 4197 [ΜΕ 2256]) Small Needle Fig. 26.41

Agora #274/075. Ανατολικό τμήμα (east section).

L./p.L. 0.020; W. (head) 0.002; Th. (shaft, max) 0.001–0.002; Wt. 0.1 g.

Complete, though uppermost part of head may be broken and could have extended slightly more.

Small needle, with shaft circular in section, tapering to point; head at opposite end hammered flat and thus slightly wider in order to accommodate the thread (as is also the case for fishhooks, see below).

Context unclear.

Additional inventoried fragments of needles not catalogued:

ΜΕΘ 1660 (ΜΕ 2156). Agora #274/085. Ανατολικός μάρτυρας (east balk). P.L. 0.053; Th. (shaft) 0.002; Wt. 0.6 g.

ΜΕΘ 1661 (ΜΕ 2189). Agora #274/085. Ανατολικός μάρτυρας (east balk). Two joining frr. P.L. 0.067; Th. (shaft) 0.002; Wt. 0.9 g.

ΜΕΘ 1656 (ΜΕ 312). Agora #274/085012. Two joining frr. P.L. 0.048; Wt. 0.7 g.

ΜΕΘ 1662 (ΜΕ 2917). Agora #274/066. Ανατολικός μάρτυρας (east balk). Two joining frr. P.L. 0.050; Wt. 0.6 g.

ΜΕΘ 1663 (ΜΕ 3921). Agora #274/079. Τομή στη νότια πλευρά (south wall of trench). Four joining frr. P.L. 0.075; Wt. 0.8 g.

ΜΕΘ 1657 (ΜΕ 1582). Agora #274. ΝΔ γωνία κτιρίου χώρον Δ΄ (SW corner of building, Room 4). P.L. 0.025; Wt. 0.1 g.

ΜΕΘ 1793 (ΜΕ 1996). Agora #274/077. Ανατολικός μάρτυρας (east balk). P.L. 0.033; Wt. 0.6 g.

Spindle hook

In discussing the spindle hooks of Corinth, Davidson states: "The bronze spindle hooks, of which great numbers have been found, are all quite alike: a strip of metal, folded into conical shape, forms a hook at one end, while the other end is left open to form a socket for the wooden spindle. A fragment of wood still remains in one hook . . . . While all the Corinthian spindle hooks were found in contexts of Byzantine or later times, such hooks are known to have been in use in the classical period as well."[217] As for the date of **26/121**, its context was uninformative, and all that can be said with certainty is that it can be dated to 354 B.C. or earlier. A Classical date for **26/121** fits well, as 4th-century B.C. examples are known from Olynthos,[218] a solitary spindle hook from tomb 258 at Metapontion is dated to 320–275 B.C., and one from the agora of Selinunte is similarly dated to the 4th/3rd century B.C.[219] Spindle hooks from most other sites—including the Diktaian Cave, Lindos, Olympia, Delos, Isthmia, Corinth, Philia, Kalapodi, Oropos, and Kythera, to mention only a few—are either undated precisely by context, or else of Roman, Byzantine, or later date.[220] Although later (Roman and Byzantine) material was found in the Diktaian Cave and at Lindos, the quantity was certainly not great, and it remains possible that some of the spindle hooks from these sites may be of late Archaic or earlier Classical date.

26/121. (ΜΕΘ 1781 [ΜΕ 2256]) Spindle Hook Fig. 26.42

Agora #274/066. Ανατολικός μάρτυρας (east balk).

L. 0.036–0.037; Diam. (max) 0.005; Wt. 1.0 g.

Intact.

Proportionately long and narrow cone, with upper shaft circular in section, bent over to form a hook. Opposite end open to accommodate the spindle.

Context uninformative.

Small cones

As noted above (under **15/55** and **26/26**), I do not know how these small cones were used, and I know of no clear published parallel. The only thing that comes close are some cones presented as spindle hooks, but where the hook broke away, leaving only the cone, or some intact cones that were classified as possible spindle hooks in the absence of comparanda.[221] There is, however, nothing broken about the Methone examples; they are intentionally made as is.

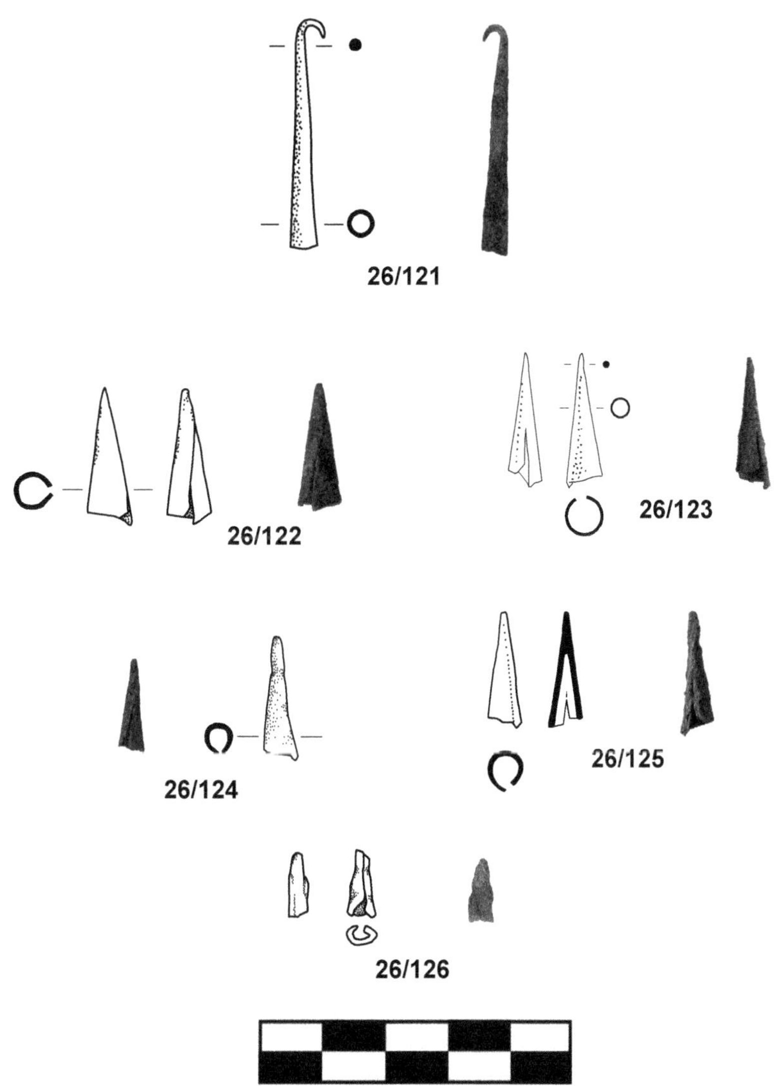

FIGURE 26.42. Agora bronze spindle hook, **26/121** (ΜΕΘ 1781); bronze cones, **26/122** (ΜΕΘ 1784); **26/123** (ΜΕΘ 295); **26/124** (ΜΕΘ 296); **26/125** (ΜΕΘ 299); **26/126** (ΜΕΘ 2138). Drawings A. Hooton, T. Ross, and F. Skyvalida, photos I. Coyle and J. Vanderpool

Six small cones are catalogued below, and as many again are listed. Most were found in the destruction deposit of 354 B.C. (**26/123**, **26/125**, **26/126**, together with the majority of those inventoried but not catalogued, including ΜΕΘ 297 and ΜΕΘ 298). At least one, however, is clearly earlier, **26/122**, found in a pre-destruction deposit in association with material of Archaic to Classical date; and **26/124** may also predate the destruction deposit, although how much earlier remains unclear. It was the quantity of these small cones in the destruction deposit that first gave rise to the idea that they may have been hastily made projectiles in times of distress.

26/122. (ΜΕΘ 1784 [ΜΕ 2145]) Small Cone Fig. 26.42

Agora #274/086. Stoa Building A. Μέσο δυτικό τμήματος, βόρεια του Τ.12 (middle of west section, north of Wall 12).

L. 0.021; Diam. (max) 0.007–0.008; Wt. 0.9 g.

Intact.

Small cone, made of thin sheet bronze, formed into a small cone.

Context pre-destruction deposit, Archaic to Classical.

26/123. (ΜΕΘ 295 [ΜΕ 920]) Small Cone Fig. 26.42

Agora #274/085. Στρώμα καστανέρυθρο [3]. Red-brown layer [3].

L. 0.021; Diam. 0.006; Wt. 0.4 g.

Intact, but chipped.

Form as **26/122.**

Context destruction deposit, mid-4th century B.C. or earlier.

26/124. (ΜΕΘ 296 [ΜΕ 922]) Small Cone Fig. 26.42

Agora #274/086. Στρώμα διάβρωσης (erosion layer: collapsed fill).

L. 0.015; Diam. 0.004–0.005; Wt. 0.2 g.

Intact.

Form as **26/122** and **26/123.**

Context collapsed fill above destruction deposit, prehistoric to mid-4th century B.C.

26/125. (ΜΕΘ 299 [ΜΕ 1547]) Small Cone Fig. 26.42

Agora #274/086. ΣΤρώμα καΣΤανέρυΘρο [3]. Red-brown layer [3].

L. 0.020; Diam. 0.006; Wt. 0.4 g.

Intact.

Form as **26/122.**

Context destruction deposit, mid-4th century B.C. or earlier.

26/126. (ΜΕΘ 2138 [ΜΕ 4097]) Small Cone Fig. 26.42

Agora #274/59009 [2]. Δάπεδο (floor).

P.L. 0.011; Diam. 0.004–0.005; Wt. 0.1 g.

Almost complete except for tip of point. Bent slightly out of shape.

Form **26/122**, but smaller. Cf. also **15/55.**

Context destruction deposit, mid-4th century B.C. or earlier.

Additional small cones:

ΜΕΘ 297 (ΜΕ 924). Agora #274/086. Στρώμα καστανέρυθρο [3]. Red-brown layer [3]. L. 0.017–0.018; Diam. 0.005–0.006; Wt. 0.3 g.

ΜΕΘ 298 (ΜΕ 1546). Agora #274/086. Στρώμα καστανέρυθρο [3]. Red-brown layer [3]. P.L. 0.017; Wt. 0.3 g.

Two small cones ΜΕΘ 1782α, β (ΜΕ 523). Agora #274/086017 [3]. ΜΕΘ 1782α: L. 0.018; Diam. (max) 0.007; Wt. 0.9 g. ΜΕΘ 1782β: L. 0.023; Diam. (max) 0.009–0.010; Wt. 1.0 g.

ΜΕΘ 1783 (ΜΕ 2064). Agora #274/078. P.L. 0.016; Diam. (as flattened) 0.007; Wt. 0.5 g.

ΜΕΘ 1785 (ΜΕ 2150). Agora #274/086. L. 0.019; Diam. (max) 0.008; Wt. 0.9 g.

Related:

ΜΕΘ 1786 (ΜΕ 2785). Agora #274/075. P.L. 0.013; Diam. (max, as preserved) 0.005; Wt. 0. 3 g.

Fishhooks

That bronze fishhooks were cast at Methone in the Archaic period in the industrial area on the West Hill is established by the mold found there, which, in addition to other items, including jewelry, had two channels for casting fishhooks (Fig. 1.36a–c, ΜΕΘ 2977). The Methone fishhooks are all of the same basic type, with a tanged or barbed point, a shaft circular in section, and a small head hammered flat to permit the line to be tied at its base for purchase. Throughout antiquity, this was one of the primary types of fishhooks, and virtually the only type from the Geometric period to the 4th century B.C., as shown by examples from various sanctuary sites, including Chios, Perachora, Isthmia and Corinth, Nemea, Petalidi in Messenia, Philia, Olympia, and Kythera,[222] as well as from domestic and other non-votive contexts at Olynthos, Delos, Torone, Selinunte, and Metapontion.[223]

The history of bronze fishhooks in the Aegean spirals back to the Early Bronze Age, and fishhooks fashioned from natural materials—such as animal bone or antler—go back to the Neolithic and Mesolithic.[224] For the later Bronze Age, Spyridon Iakovidis lists examples from the Diktaian Cave, Gournia, and Palaikastro on Crete, Ialysos on Rhodes, Thebes, and Teichos Dymaion, as well as at Enkomi on Cyprus.[225] In presenting the two fishhooks from Perati, Iakovidis notes that they are rare in Crete and on the mainland in comparison to the more numerous lead fishnet weights. For the historic period this is echoed by Davidson, who notes: "it is likely that nets were used extensively and fishhooks very little."[226] Fishhooks of the same form continued through late antiquity and post-antiquity into the modern era.

26/127. (ΜΕΘ 1681 [ΜΕ 2007]) Fishhook Fig. 26.43

Agora #274/077. Ανατολικός μάρτυρας είσοδος κτίριο Ζ. East balk, entrance to Building Z.

L./p.L. 0.028–0.029; Wt. 0.9 g.

Complete, except perhaps for very tip of head.

Cast fishhook with tanged point. Shaft circular in section. Head hammered flat to permit line to be tied at its base.

Context destruction deposit, mid-4th century B.C. or earlier.

26/128. (ΜΕΘ 1683 [ΜΕ 2013]) Fishhook Fig. 26.43

Agora #274/077. Area west of Wall 15.

L. 0.020; Wt. 0.4 g.

Intact.

Form as **26/127**, but smaller.

Context unclear.

26/129. (ΜΕΘ 1686 [ΜΕ 2013]) Fishhook Fig. 26.43

Agora #274/036002 [1].

L. 0.013; Wt. 0.1 g.

Form as **26/127** and **26/128**, but even smaller.
Context collapsed fill above destruction deposit, prehistoric to mid-4th century B.C.

26/130. (ΜΕΘ 1685 [ΜΕ 2544]) Fishhook Fig. 26.43
Agora #274/016006 [1].
L. 0.020; Wt. 0.2 g.
Complete, except for tang; head well preserved.
Form as **26/127**.
Context unclear.

26/131. (ΜΕΘ 1688 [ΜΕ 2787]) Fishhook Fig. 26.43
Agora #274/075. ΒΔ τμήμα καστανό στρώμα. NW section, brown layer.
P.L. 0.016; Wt. 0.2 g.
Almost complete, except for tang; head worn.
Form as **26/127** but smaller.
Context unclear.

Additional inventoried fishhooks not catalogued:
ΜΕΘ 1680 (ΜΕ 1329). Agora #274.087, 077. Building A. Χώρος Γ΄. Δάπεδο. Room 3, floor. P.L. 0.010; Wt. < 0.1 g.
ΜΕΘ 1682 (ΜΕ 2010). Agora #274/077. East balk, area west of Wall 15. P.L. 0.025; Wt. 0.3 g.
ΜΕΘ 1684 (ΜΕ 2210). Agora #274/085. Ανατολικός μάρτυρας (east balk). P.L. 0.020–0.021; Wt. 0.3 g.
ΜΕΘ 1687 (ΜΕ 2942). Agora #274/036002 [1]. P.L./L. 0.028; Wt. 0.4 g.
ΜΕΘ 1689 (ΜΕ 2899). Agora #274/077. Τομή βόρεια του Τ.18, δ΄ στρώμα (trench north of Wall 18, 4th level). Fragmentary. P.L. (largest fr) 0.016; Wt. < 0.1 g.
ΜΕΘ 1792 (ΜΕ 2819). Agora #274/065. P.L. 0.028; Wt. 0.7 g.

Bronze knife?

Although marked with a query, **26/132** should be a bronze knife. While bronze knives are standard in the Bronze Age tombs of Methone, they are rare in the Early Iron Age and later periods, when iron knives were common, although there were some.[227] The only other bronze knife from Methone presented in this volume is **15/54**, from the Phase II fill of the Hypogeion (Late Geometric or early Archaic); the context of **26/132** is uncertain as to date. The shape of **26/132** is unlike that of **15/54**, its cutting edge being on the concave side, whereas on **15/54** the cutting edge is on the convex side. As with **15/54**, so too with **26/132**, bronze knives should be seen as all-purpose implements rather than primarily as weapons, and against the backdrop of the industrial and domestic activity at Methone.

26/132. (ΜΕΘ 4310 [ΜΕ 2391]) Bronze Knife Fig. 26.43
Agora #274/075. Μέσο νότιου τμήματος (middle of south side).
P.L. 0.057; W. (max) 0.017; Wt. 5.4 g.
Single fr preserving uncertain portion of object. It is unclear whether the broader short end is broken or not.
Blade-shaped; wider at one short end, tapering toward the other. One of long edges is clearly thicker than the other, thus suggesting a knife, with cutting edge on the slightly concave side (bottom as shown).
Context uncertain.
Cf. **15/54**.

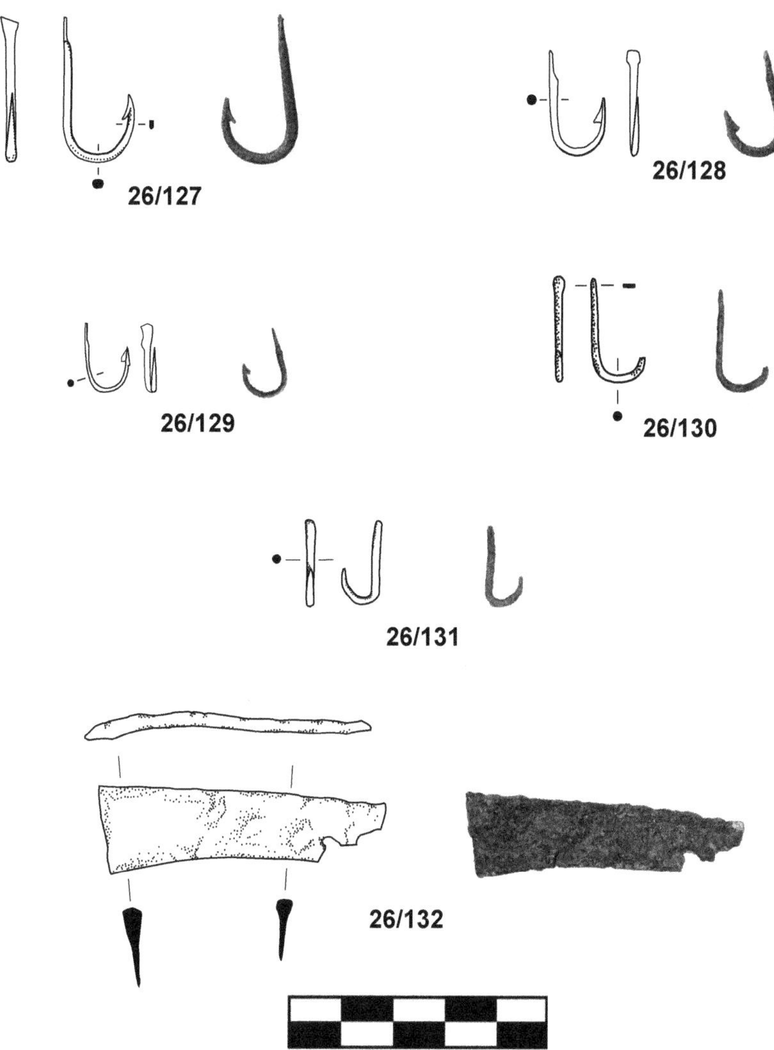

FIGURE 26.43. Agora bronze fishhooks, **26/127** (ΜΕΘ 1681), **26/128** (ΜΕΘ 1683), **26/129** (ΜΕΘ 1686), **26/130** (ΜΕΘ 1685), **26/131** (ΜΕΘ 1688); bronze knife, **26/132** (ΜΕΘ 4310). Drawings A. Hooton, T. Ross, and F. Skyvalida, photos, I. Coyle and J. Vanderpool

Nails

I have already provided a fuller discussion of bronze nails, together with comparanda from various Greek contexts, in Chapter 15 (under **15/57–15/58**), as well as from other parts of the site (see discussion associated with **26/15** and **26/50**), so further comment here is unnecessary. The importance of the agora bronze nails from Methone lies in the fact that many of them were encountered in the destruction deposit of 354 B.C. (**26/134**, **26/139–26/144**, inclusive), and as such extend the chronological range of such nails to the mid-4th century B.C.[228] Two additional nails from the area of the agora (**26/135**, **26/136**) were found in the collapsed fill above the destruction deposit, whereas the contexts of the remainder were unclear (**26/133**, **26/137–26/138**). In the catalogue entries below I cite parallels for individual nails from other parts of the site. It is worth noting that many of the Methone bronze nails find close parallels to Archaic examples from Ephesos and Lindos,[229] as well as among the nails of unclear date from Kythera.[230] Nails from the cemetery at Sindos, whether of bronze or iron, with circular disk heads are classified as Type II, whereas those with the head bent toward one side are Type I.[231]

26/133. (MEΘ 3097 [ME 4191]) Nail Fig. 26.44

Agora #274/080001 [1].

L. (as bent) 0.051; Diam. (head) 0.014; Th. (shaft) 0.005 x 0.005; Wt. 11.0 g.

Intact, but bent, with shaft and head defining something of an S-curve.

Shaft square in section, tapering toward well-preserved point. Circular, disk-shaped head, only very slightly domed.

Context unclear.

Cf. **26/15** and **15/57**.

26/134. (MEΘ 4194 [ME 1778]) Nail Fig. 26.44

Agora #274/017011 [1].

L. (as bent) 0.118; Diam. (head) 0.014; Th. (shaft) 0.005 x 0.005; Wt. 11.6 g.

Intact.

Long shaft, almost circular in section near juncture with head, square for the remainder of its length, tapering toward a point. Head as **26/133** (MEΘ 3097).

Context collapsed fill above destruction deposit, prehistoric to mid-4th century B.C.

26/135. (MEΘ 4195 [ME 426]) Nail Fig. 26.44

Agora #274/086008 [1].

L. 0.079; Diam. (head) 0.015; Diam. (shaft, at top) 0.006; Wt. 10.4 g.

Intact.

Nail as **26/134** (MEΘ 4194), with head circular in section toward the top, square for the remainder of its length.

Context collapsed fill above destruction deposit, prehistoric to mid-4th century B.C.

26/136. (MEΘ 4193 [ME 2485]) Nail Fig. 26.44

Agora #274/016002 [1].

P.L. (as bent) 0.067; Diam. (head) 0.016; Diam. (shaft) 0.005; Wt. 11.8 g.

Single fr preserving almost complete nail, except for tip of point.

As **26/133** (MEΘ 3097) and **26/134** (MEΘ 4194), but with shaft mostly circular in section, and with slight faceting throughout (rather than square/rectangular).

Context collapsed fill above destruction deposit, prehistoric to mid-4th century B.C.

26/137. (MEΘ 4192 [ME 1828]) Fragmentary Nail Fig. 26.44

Agora #274/009004 [2].

P.L. 0.042; Diam. (head) 0.016; Diam. (shaft) 0.006–0.007; Wt. 10.7 g.

Fr preserving most of nail, except for lower part of shaft.

As **26/136** (MEΘ 4193), with shaft circular in section.

Context unclear.

26/138. (MEΘ 4293 [ME 1828]) Nail Fragment Fig. 26.44

Agora #274/075. ΝΔ Τμήμα—ξύλωμα Τ.8 (SW section, dismantling of Wall 8).

P.L. 0.034; Diam. (head) 0.017; Diam. (shaft) 0.006; Wt. 10.7 g.

Single fr preserving complete head and upper part of shaft.

Form as **26/133** (MEΘ 3097), but with shaft circular in section.

Context unclear.

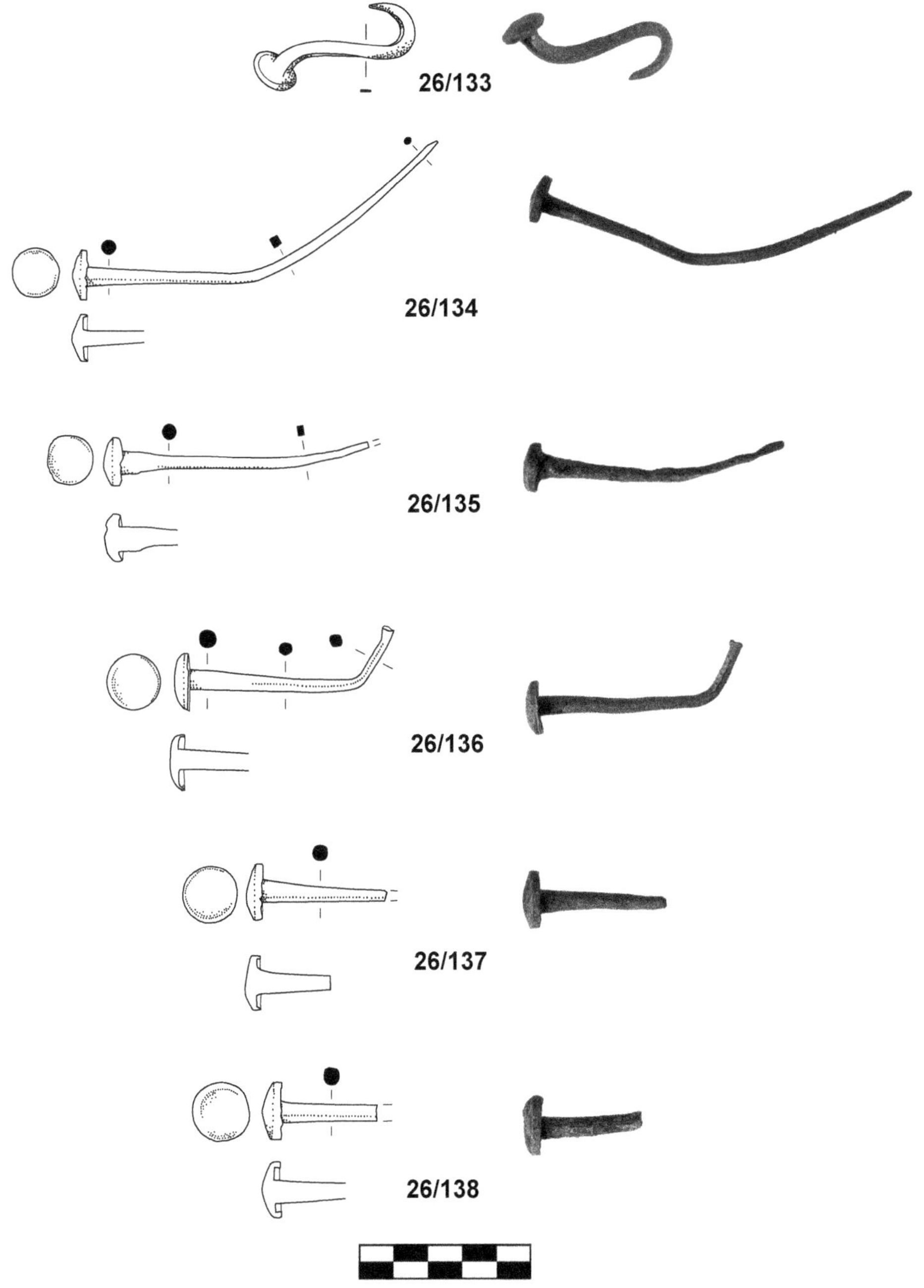

FIGURE 26.44. Agora bronze nails, **26/133** (ΜΕΘ 3097), **26/134** (ΜΕΘ 4194), **26/135** (ΜΕΘ 4195), **26/136** (ΜΕΘ 4193), **26/137** (ΜΕΘ 4192), **26/138** (ΜΕΘ 4293). Drawings A. Hooton and F. Skyvalida, photos I. Coyle and J. Vanderpool

26/139. (ΜΕΘ 4292 [ΜΕ 1844]) Nail Fragment Fig. 26.45

Agora #274/009008 [3]. Building B. Περιοχή ανάμεσα Τ.22 και Τ.23 (area between Walls 22 and 23).

P.L. 0.061; p.L./p.Diam. (head) 0.017; Diam. (shaft) 0.006; Wt. 14.8 g.

Single fr preserving portion of head and upper shaft of nail. Head, as preserved, roughly triangular, but this is the result of breakage.

Shaft circular to rhomboidal in section (i.e., only slightly faceted); head originally as **26/133** (ΜΕΘ 3097).

Context destruction deposit, mid-4th century B.C. or earlier.

26/140. (ΜΕΘ 4145 [ΜΕ 3992]) Fragmentary Head, Nail Fig. 26.45

Agora #274/019006 [2]. Δάπεδο (floor).

P.L. 0.021; Diam. (head) 0.023; Diam. (shaft) 0.012; Wt. 14.6 g.

Single fr preserving all of head, but only the uppermost portion of shaft; head chipped and bent.

Rounded head, with edges comparatively thin. Thick and solid shaft, circular in section.

Context destruction deposit, mid-4th century B.C. or earlier.

Cf. **15/57**, also **26/50**.

26/141. (ΜΕΘ 1695 [ΜΕ 1916]) Nail Fig. 26.45

Agora #274/079. Ανατολικό τμήμα (east section).

P.L. 0.038; Diam. (head) 0.008–0.009; L. x W. (shaft) 0.003–0.004; Wt. 2.7 g.

Single fr preserving almost complete nail, except for tip of point.

Shaft square/rectangular in section. Solid, domed head.

Context destruction deposit, mid-4th century B.C. or earlier.

26/142. (ΜΕΘ 2141 [ΜΕ 3988]) Nail Fig. 26.45

Agora #274/018006 [2]. Δάπεδο (floor).

L. 0.069; Diam. (head, max) 0.012; Diam. (shaft, max) 0.007; Wt. 13.1 g.

Intact.

Head more triangular in plan than circular, flat on top and extending largely to one side of shaft as if intentionally bent. Thick shaft, circular in section toward top, with slight articulation below head as shown, but appears to be more faceted farther down its length. Point flattened, tapering to blunt point.

Context destruction deposit, mid-4th century B.C. or earlier.

26/143. (ΜΕΘ 2142 [ΜΕ 4025]) Nail Head Fig. 26.45

Agora #274/028001 [1]. Δάπεδο (floor).

P.L. 0.008; Diam. (head) 0.009; Diam. (shaft) 0.007; Wt. 1.9 g.

Single fr preserving entire head, but little of shaft.

Form as **26/142** (ΜΕΘ 2141), but with head more circular, and only extending slightly to one side; upper preserved shaft circular in section.

Context destruction deposit, mid-4th century B.C. or earlier.

26/144. (ΜΕΘ 4305 [ΜΕ 2142]) Fragmentary Nail Fig. 26.45

Agora #274/086. Stoa Building A. Ανατολ. παρεία/στρ. καταστροφής, χώρου Ζ (east side, destruction level, Room 5).

P.L. 0.023; Diam. (head, as preserved) 0.006; Diam. (shaft) 0.004–0.005; Wt. 1.7 g.

Fr preserving head and upper shaft.

Shaft circular in section, with small, roughly circular head, barely larger than the shaft, extending slightly to one side.

Context destruction deposit, mid-4th century B.C. or earlier.

Cf. **15/58**.

Additional nail:

ΜΕΘ 2139 (ΜΕ 4133). Agora #274/090003 [2]. Likely point, flattened, as **26/142** (ΜΕΘ 2141).

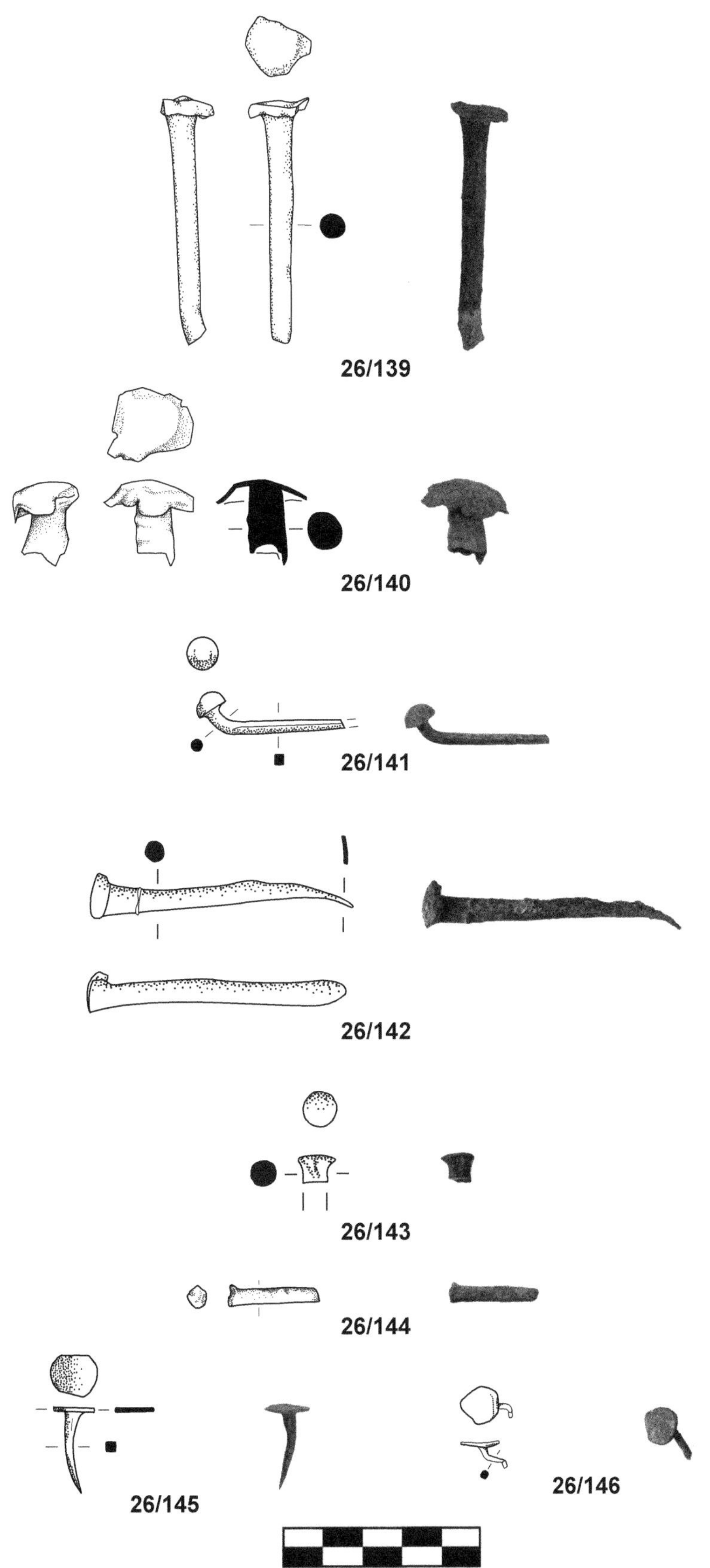

FIGURE 26.45. Agora bronze nails and tacks, **26/139** (MEΘ 4292), **26/140** (MEΘ 4145), **26/141** (MEΘ 1695), **26/142** (MEΘ 2141), **26/143** (MEΘ 2142), **26/144** (MEΘ 4305); and tacks, **26/145** (MEΘ 1693), **26/146** (MEΘ 1692). Drawings A. Hooton, T. Ross, and F. Skyvalida, photos I. Coyle and J. Vanderpool

Tacks

I have briefly discussed tacks above (under **26/49**), and also in Chapter 15 (under **15/100**, an iron tack). Although the contexts of both **26/145** and **26/146** provide little information as to their dates, similar tacks are known from Olynthos, and Manthos Bessios (pers. comm.) notes that such tacks were often found with klinai in the 4th-century B.C. tombs in the area of Pydna, usually to keep in place a leather backing or some other organic material.[232]

26/145. (ΜΕΘ 1693 [ΜΕ 2375]) Tack Fig. 26.45

Agora #274/086. Μέσο νότιου τμήματος (middle of south section).

L. 0.022; Diam. (head) 0.012; Th. (shaft) 0.003–0.004; Wt. 1.4 g.

Intact.

Small tack, with shaft thicker toward head, tapering to sharp point, square in section. Flat, and comparatively broad, disk head.

Context unclear.

26/146. (ΜΕΘ 1692 [ΜΕ 1783]) Leaded Bronze Tack Fig. 26.45

Agora #274/027.

L. (as bent) 0.016; Diam. (head) 0.010; Th. (shaft, max) 0.002–0.003; Wt. 1.0 g.

Almost complete, except for point of shaft.

Form as **26/145** (ΜΕΘ 1693), but slightly smaller.

Context unclear.

Other inventoried tacks, not catalogued:

ΜΕΘ 1696 (ΜΕ 2125). Agora #274/086. Βόρειο τμήμα (north section). P.L. 0.021; Diam. (head) 0.012; Wt. 1.1 g.

ΜΕΘ 1694 (ΜΕ 1911). Agora #274/079. Ανατολικό τμήμα (east section). P.L. 0.004; Diam. (head) 0.009; Wt. 0.5 g.

ΜΕΘ 1697 (ΜΕ 3717). Agora #274/017020 [5]. Βόρειας μάρτυρας (north balk). P.L. 0.011–0.012; Diam. (head) 0.007; Wt. 0.4 g.

T-shaped staples

There are three examples of T-shaped staples from the agora at Methone, two from the destruction deposit (**26/147**, **26/148**), and one with an unclear context (**26/149**). In discussing the bronze "T-förmige Bronzeklammern" from the sanctuary of Athena Itonia near Philia, Kilian-Dirlmeier notes two varieties, one with a long, pointed, T-shaped shank that is often folded over, and another with a short-riveted shank.[233] The Methone examples all conform to the first of these varieties. The Philia staples are all of Classical date. Similar bronzes in both varieties and of similar date are known at Olynthos, dating mainly to the 4th century B.C.,[234] and they are also found in domestic contexts at Tarsus dating to the Classical and Hellenistic periods.[235] In discussing the Philia examples, Kilian-Dirlmeier notes that they were also found in sanctuary contexts at Mazi, Isthmia, and at Kourion on Cyprus.[236] Contextually, however, there are no clear indications for the function of these bronzes, and Kilian-Dirlmeier goes on to note that the numerous examples of them at Thermopylai suggests their use in the production of weapons, perhaps for connecting the leather cover and wooden core of shields.[237] That they are somehow connected with wood, and also perhaps leather, is reasonable enough, but their shape is such to have facilitated the connection of elements of various wooden—or other organic—implements, not just weapons.

26/147. (ΜΕΘ 2129 [ΜΕ 4030]) T-shaped Staple Fig. 26.46

Agora #274/028002 [1]. Δάπεδο (floor).

L. 0.046; H. 0.016; Wt. 2.3 g.

Intact.

Essentially cast in one piece, with a horizontal element and a vertical element, which is bent, defining the characteristic T-shape. Shaft square to rectangular in section throughout, tapering toward three sharp points.

Context destruction deposit, mid-4th century B.C. or earlier.

26/148. (ΜΕΘ 4190 [ΜΕ 1833]) T-shaped Staple Fig. 26.46

Agora #274/009005 [3]. Building B. Περιοχή ανάμεσα Τ.26 and Τ.25 (area between Walls 25 and 26).

L. 0.035; H. 0.039; Wt. 2.0 g.

Evidently complete, although it is possible that one of the terminals may be broken.

Form as **26/147** (ΜΕΘ 2129), but a little smaller.

Context destruction deposit, mid-4th century B.C. or earlier.

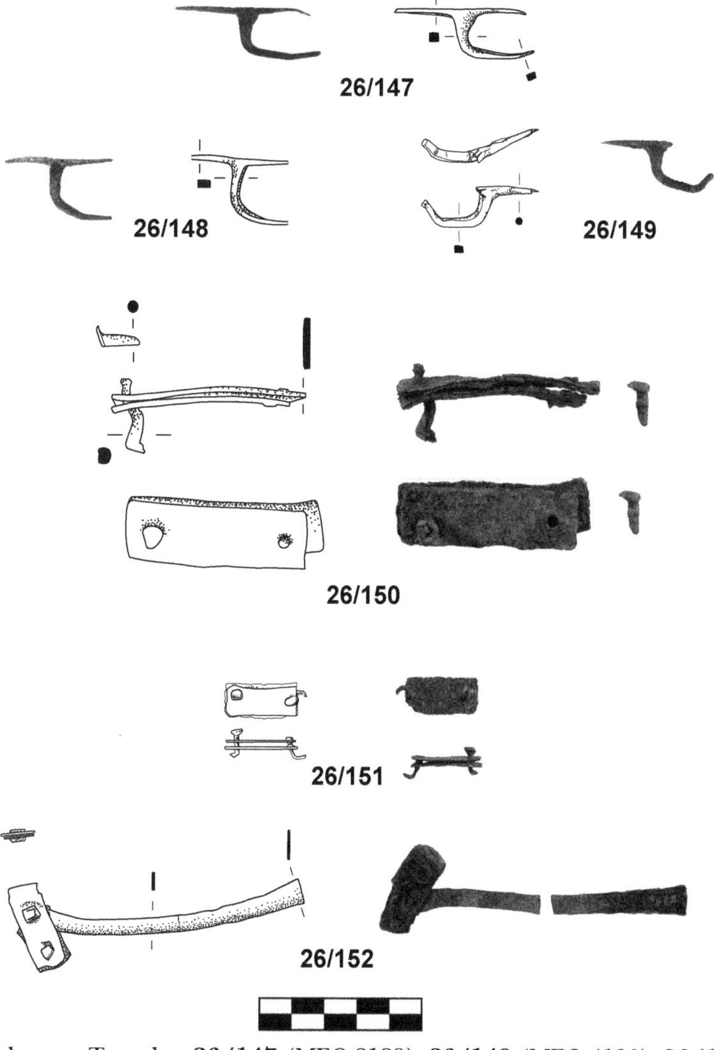

FIGURE 26.46. Agora bronze T-staples, **26/147** (ΜΕΘ 2129), **26/148** (ΜΕΘ 4190), **26/149** (ΜΕΘ 1633); bronze bindings/sheaths, **26/150** (ΜΕΘ 1778), **26/151** (ΜΕΘ 1779), **26/152** (ΜΕΘ 4146). Drawings A. Hooton, T. Ross, and F. Skyvalida, photos I. Coyle and J. Vanderpool

26/149. (MEΘ 1633 [ME 2804]) T-shaped Staple Fig. 26.46

Agora #274/065. ΝΔ τμήμα (SW section).

P.L. 0.036; H./p.H. 0.015; Wt. 1.8 g.

Single fr preserving almost complete staple, except for one of the horizontal terminals of the T; the terminal of the vertical, bent-back element is damaged.

Form as **26/147** (MEΘ 2129), size as **26/148** (MEΘ 4190).

Context uncertain.

Bronze bindings/sheaths

This distinctive group of metal reinforcements, which vary in shape and size, appear to have been used primarily as sheathings for wood, whether ornamental or non-decorative. **26/150** and **26/151** are closely related, with **26/150** twice as large as **26/151**. The date of the former is uncertain, but **26/151** was found in the destruction deposit and should date to the first half of the 4th century B.C. Since the organic material rarely, if ever, survives, determining the function of such bindings is difficult. It is important, however, to note that such reinforcements may well have been for bronze objects. In discussing the bronze belts from Archaic Emporio on Chios, Boardman illustrates a number of hinge plates or hinge reinforcements that are not unlike **26/150** and **26/151**, and at Isthmia a related reinforcement was a fixture of a bronze vessel believed to be a jug.[238] Related bronze reinforcements similar to **26/150** and **26/151** of Archaic date are known from the Athenian Acropolis and the sanctuary of Apollo at Bassai.[239] There are a number of closely related bronze reinforcements from Olynthos that date to the earlier 4th-century B.C.,[240] and a few, perhaps, from the Argive Heraion.[241] Some of the closest parallels to **26/150** and **26/151** come from the Archaic extramural sanctuary of Sybaris at Francavilla Marittima in northern Calabria.[242] Several related iron objects at Isthmia dating to the Archaic and Classical periods are presented as clamps.[243]

As for the roughly T-shaped, as preserved, binding reinforcement **26/152**, the basic idea is the same as for **26/150** and **26/151**, but its fragmentary state impedes any clear identification of function; it may have served as a reinforcement for a bronze vessel? Its date, however, is clear, first half of the 4th century B.C.

26/150. (MEΘ 1778 [ME 1860]) Bindings/Sheaths Fig. 26.46

Agora #274/009010 [4].

L. 0.062; W. 0.020; Wt. 17.0 g.

Four joining frr preserving more or less complete binding or metal reinforcement; the loose rivet (p.L. 0.013; Diam. [head] 0.007–0.008), fits in the empty hole at one end.

Binding consists of two rectangular sheets of bronze hammered flat, both perforated at one end with a single hole, and held together by a single rivet at either end (L. of the better-preserved rivet 0.025).

Context uncertain.

26/151. (MEΘ 1779 [ME 1891]) Bindings/Sheaths Fig. 26.46

Agora #274/079. Ανατολικό τμήμα (east section).

L. 0.023 (L., including bent tack, 0.026); W. 0.012; Wt. 1.2 g.

Intact, except for one of the rivets, which is slightly broken.

Two thin rectangular sheets of bronze, hammered flat, as **26/150** (MEΘ 1778), but smaller, held together by two rivets (p.L. x Diam. of better-preserved rivet 0.009 x 0.003).

Context destruction deposit, mid-4th century B.C. or earlier.

26/152. (ΜΕΘ 4146 [ΜΕ 4006]) Bindings/Sheaths Fig. 26.46

Agora #274/028001 [1]. Building B. Πάνω στον Τ.22 (above Wall 22).

P.L. 0.090; L. x W. (binding sheaths): 0.029 x 0.012; W. (long strip) 0.010; Wt. 7.8 g.

Two joining frr preserving undetermined portion of binding; second rivet on binding sheaths at one end indicates that there would have been another strip of bronze. The opposite end is preserved in such a way that it seems unbroken, but this is far from certain.

The long strip is hammered flat, rectangular in section, wider toward one end (that opposite the bindings/sheaths). Attached at one end are two smaller strips of bronze, held in place, as preserved, by two rivets, one holding the preserved longer strip. The strips holding together the longer strip are the same in form as **26/154** (ΜΕΘ 4291), and of similar dimensions.

Context destruction deposit, mid-4th century B.C. or earlier.

Binding plates

The first four binding plates, **26/153–26/156**, are individual elements from bindings/sheaths like **26/150–26/152** and require little further comment, except for their date. Although **26/153** was encountered in the destruction deposit and is therefore from the first half of the 4th century B.C., **26/155** is from a pre-destruction deposit associated with material from the Early Iron Age to the early Classical period. **26/156** may also be early, although it may also be associated with the destruction deposit; **26/154** is a surface find. As suggested under **15/70** and **15/71**, some of these could well have served as patches for repairing bronze vessels.

The two remaining pieces are rather different, both on account of their shape—**26/157** is lozenge-shaped and **26/158** circular—and the fact that the former has a more substantial square hole in the center. Both were found in the destruction deposit. A number of triangular and lozenge-shaped attachments are noted among the binding plates from Archaic Francavilla Marittima, as well as a few oval-shaped and related attachments.[244]

26/153. (ΜΕΘ 4304 [ΜΕ 1791]) Binding Plate Fig. 26.47

Agora #274/017013 [2].

L. 0.044; W. 0.014; Th. 0.001; Wt. 2.7 g.

Two joining frr preserving complete binding sheet; slightly torn in places.

Small sheet bronze, hammered flat, roughly rectangular in shape, with long edges bent over for attachment. Two small holes, one at center near both of the short edges (Diam. [hole] 0.002).

Context destruction deposit, mid-4th century B.C. or earlier.

26/154. (ΜΕΘ 4291 [ΜΕ 2491]) Binding Plate Fig. 26.47

Agora #274/016. Επιφανειακό στρώμα (surface layer).

L. 0.035; W. 0.013–0.014; Th. 0.002; Wt. 2.2 g.

Complete, slightly bent.

Small, rectangular sheet of bronze, hammered flat. Comparatively large hole at either end.

Surface find.

26/155. (ΜΕΘ 4311 [ΜΕ 3882]) Binding Plate Fig. 26.47

Agora #274/079. Τομή στη νότια πλευρά (trench on the south side).

L. 0.039; W. (max) 0.014; Th. 0.001–0.002; Wt. 2.1 g.

Intact. Slightly bent in places.

As **26/153** (ΜΕΘ 4304) and **26/154** (ΜΕΘ 4291) but with concave long sides, and thus resembling a schematic double axe of sorts (cf. **15/52** [ΜΕΘ 1508]).

Context pre-destruction deposit, Early Iron Age to early Classical.

26/156. (ΜΕΘ 4227 [ΜΕ 1323]) Binding Plate Fig. 26.47

Agora #274/066. Στρώμα διάβρωσης (collapsed fill).

P.L. 0.031; W. 0.015; Th. 0.002–0.003; Wt. 9.3 g.

Single fr preserving greater portion of sheet; one short end intact, the other broken.

Thickish (cast rather than hammered) rectangular sheet of bronze, with squared edges, and portion of hole (Diam. 0.004) at the broken short end.

Context collapsed fill above destruction deposit, prehistoric to mid-4th century B.C.

26/157. (ΜΕΘ 1775α [ΜΕ 374]) Binding Plate/Attachment Fig. 26.47

Agora #274/085022 [8]. Κάτω από στρώμα καύσης (below burnt layer).

L. 0.039; W. 0.024; Th. 0.001; Wt. 1.7 g.

Two joining frr preserving complete lozenge.

Lozenge-shaped sheet of bronze, hammered flat, with large square hole at center. Found together with **26/158**.

Context destruction deposit, mid-4th century B.C. or earlier.

26/158. (ΜΕΘ 1775β [ΜΕ 374]) Binding Plate/Attachment Fig. 26.47

Agora #274/085022 [8]. Κάτω από στρώμα καύσης (below burnt layer).

P.L. (largest fr) 0.028; p.W. 0.021; Th. < 0.001; Wt. 1.4 g.

Three joining frr preserving slightly less than half of perforated disk.

Circular, disk-shaped binding/attachment, hammered flat, with small hole near edge.

Context destruction deposit, mid-4th century B.C. or earlier.

Disks

I begin with **26/159**, encountered in the destruction deposit, because it is similar to the form of **26/158** and its central perforation is not unlike that on **26/157**. Whether the piece is classified under this heading or the previous one is moot. It is also closely related to **15/49** from the Hypogeion, for which I noted that it may have served as a disk element for a bronze dress pin.[245] Such a possibility cannot be ruled out for **26/159**, but also cannot be verified. In discussing a similar pierced bronze disk from the Harbor Sanctuary at Emporio on Chios, Boardman compared it to a disk from Lindos associated with a fibula.[246] In presenting a pierced disk of Classical date from Isthmia, Raubitschek classified it as a boss, which she considered to be a bronze furniture fixture or an appliqué for boxes or other articles of furniture.[247] A pierced disk very similar to **26/159** from Philia was considered to be part of "Ringgriffe" by Kilian-Dirlmeier; it consisted of a hinged ring connected to a pierced disk, and was thought to have been used for a variety of functions at various times.[248] Related perforated disks are also known in various parts of the Balkans, not least Albania.[249] A common form of pierced disks in the Greek world are the so-called omega-shaped staples, loops, or hasps ("omegaförmige Bügel"), which, although of similar size, are invariably equipped with two perforations to accommodate the omega-shaped loop, and are often slightly domed; they are common in various contexts from the Geometric period, through the Archaic and Classical, into Roman times.[250]

As for the unperforated **26/160** and **26/161**, they are more closely related to the sheet bronze presented under the following heading. A few of the disks from the Argive Heraion and Isthmia are unperforated.[251]

26/159. (ΜΕΘ 4231 [ΜΕ 3734]) Perforated Disk Fig. 26.48

Agora #274/017021 [2]. Δάπεδο (βόρειος μάρτυρας). Floor (north balk)

Diam. 0.024; Th. 0.002–0.003; Wt. 3.8 g.

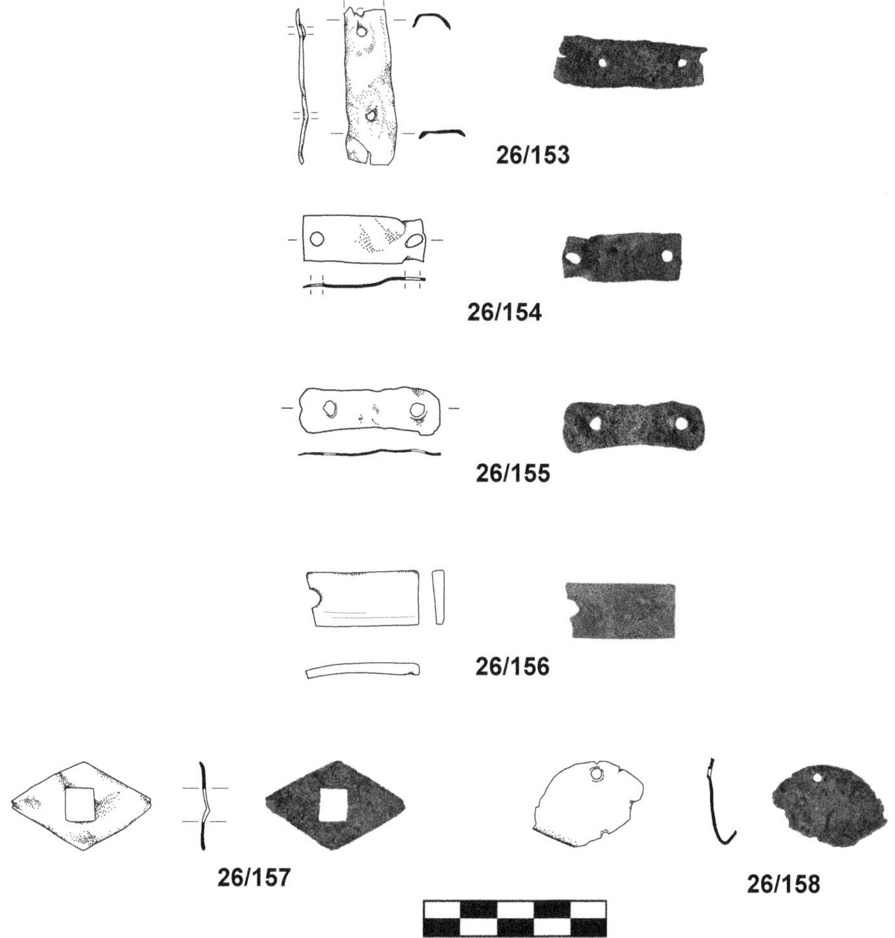

FIGURE 26.47. Agora bronze binding plates, **26/153** (ΜΕΘ 4304), **26/154** (ΜΕΘ 4291), **26/155** (ΜΕΘ 4311), **26/156** (ΜΕΘ 4227), **26/157** (ΜΕΘ 1775α), **26/158** (ΜΕΘ 1775β). Drawings A. Hooton and T. Ross, photos I. Coyle and J. Vanderpool

Intact.

Cast round disk, with edges nicely rounded and small square perforation at center.

Context destruction deposit, mid-4th century B.C. or earlier.

26/160. (ΜΕΘ 1777 [ΜΕ 2563]) Disk Fig. 26.48

Agora #274/036001 [1].

Diam. 0.018; Th. 0.001; Wt. 1.1 g.

Intact.

Small round disk, made of thin hammered sheet bronze, slightly concave on one side.

Context collapsed fill above destruction deposit, prehistoric to mid-4th century B.C.

26/161. (ΜΕΘ 1776 [ΜΕ 2301]) Disk Fig. 26.48

Agora #274/075. Ανατολικό τμήμα (east section).

Diam. 0.018; Th. 0.001; Wt. 1.1 g.

Almost complete, but slightly frayed at one point.

Form as **26/160** (ΜΕΘ 1777).

Context unclear.

Sheet bronze (including strips)

A number of thin bronze sheets from the Hypogeion, perforated and unperforated, have been discussed (under **15/70–15/74**), as well as similar objects from the summit of the West Hill (under **26/20–26/21**). The sheet bronze, including thinner strips, from the agora of Methone comprises a variety of shapes. **26/162** and **26/163** are roughly rectangular; the context of the former is uncertain, but the latter was found in the destruction deposit and can thus be assigned to the earlier 4th century B.C. As preserved, **26/164** is triangular, and rather thicker than the other bronzes of this category; encountered in the collapsed fill above destruction deposit, it may well be earlier, but its date can be anywhere from the prehistoric period to mid-4th century B.C. **26/165** and **26/166** are thin and narrow strips of bronze; the context of the former is uncertain, the latter was found in the destruction deposit.

26/162. (ΜΕΘ 4233 [ΜΕ 1967]) Small Rectangular Sheet Fig. 26.48

Agora #274/088, 089.

L./p.L. 0.025; W. 0.015; Th. < 0.011; Wt. 1.4 g.

Probably complete, but one of the shorter edges may be broken(?).

Small rectangular sheet, hammered flat. Corners on one short side nicely rounded; corners on opposite side sharper.

Context uncertain.

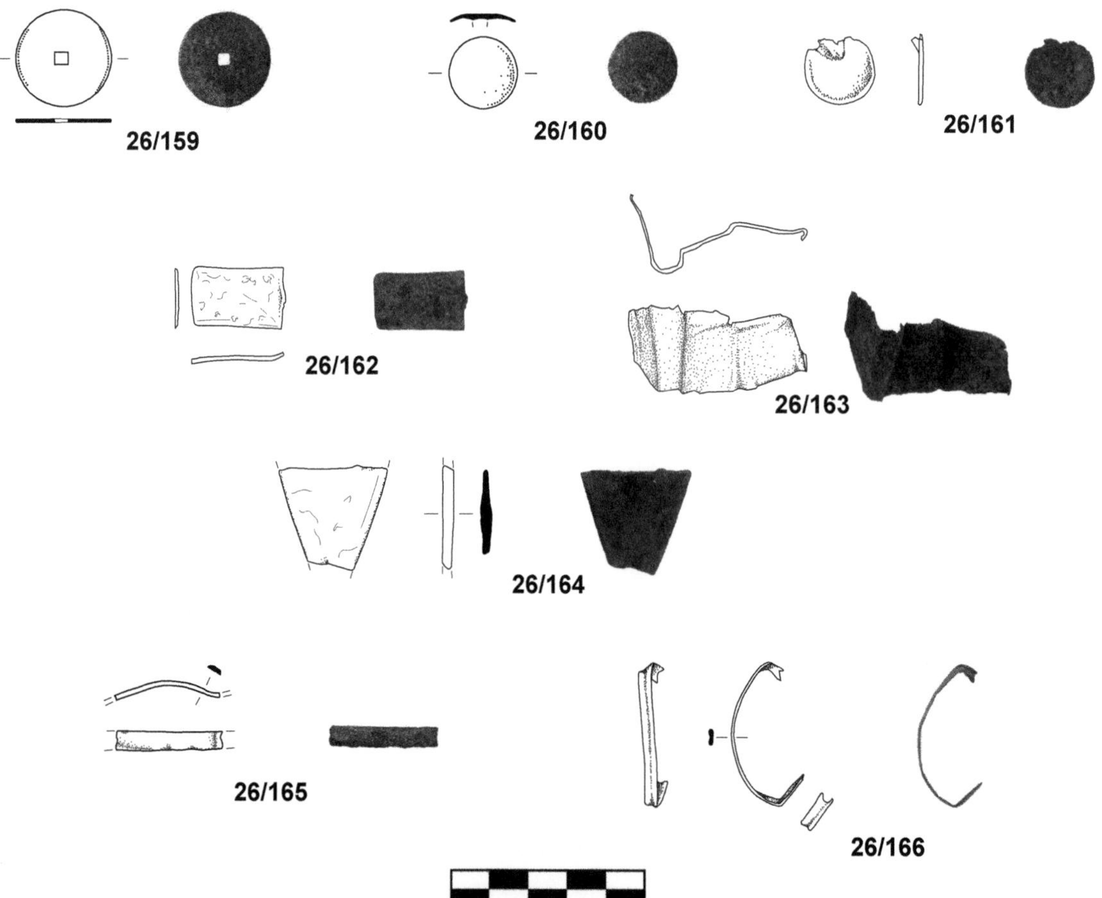

FIGURE 26.48. Agora bronze disks, **26/159** (ΜΕΘ 4231), **26/160** (ΜΕΘ 1777), **26/161** (ΜΕΘ 1776); bronze sheet (including strips), **26/162** (ΜΕΘ 4233), **26/163** (ΜΕΘ 4235), **26/164** (ΜΕΘ 4228), **26/165** (ΜΕΘ 4308), **26/166** (ΜΕΘ 4229). Drawings A. Hooton and T. Ross, photos I. Coyle and J. Vanderpool

26/163. (ΜΕΘ 4235 [ΜΕ 3886]) Rectangular Sheet Fig. 26.48

Agora #274/027023 [3].

L. (as bent) 0.045; W. 0.021; Th. < 0.001; Wt. 3.1 g.

Intact, but bent, chipped around the edges and slightly torn in places.

Rectangular sheet, hammered flat. One short side slightly wider than the other.

Context destruction deposit, mid-4th century B.C. or earlier.

26/164. (ΜΕΘ 4228 [ΜΕ 1857]) Triangular Sheet Fig. 26.48

Agora #274/017014 [1].

P.L. 0.027; p.W. 0.028; Th. 0.003; Wt. 8.8 g.

Single fr, broken at top and bottom.

Roughly triangular and thicker sheet as preserved, with surviving edges rounded. Possible, but unclear, lower edge of perforation at bottom, as shown.

Context collapsed fill above destruction deposit, prehistoric to mid-4th century B.C.

26/165. (ΜΕΘ 4308 [ΜΕ 254]) Small Rectangular Strip Fig. 26.48

Agora #274/084004 [3]. Δυτικά Τ.7 (στα μπάζα). West of Wall 7 (in backfill).

L. x W. 0.028 x 0.005; Wt. 1.2 g.

Possibly intact, but unclear whether one or both short ends are original or broken.

Thin and narrow rectangular strip of bronze, slightly plano-convex in section.

Context uncertain.

26/166. (ΜΕΘ 4229 [ΜΕ 1910]) Thin Narrow Strip Fig. 26.48

Agora #274/079. Ανατολικό τμήμα (east section).

P.L. 0.036; W. 0.004; Th. 0.001; Wt. 0.6 g.

Single fr preserving undetermined but significant portion of strip.

Thin and narrow strip, bent as shown. Terminals do not appear to be preserved, but both surviving ends seem to be perforated, unless this is simply the way piece has broken.

Context destruction deposit, mid-4th century B.C. or earlier.

Additional small sheets of bronze:

ΜΕ 3769. Agora #274/018001 [1]. L./p.L. x W. 0.034 x 0.013; Th. 0.001–0.002; Wt. 2.5 g.

ΜΕ 2122. Agora #274/086. Building A. Από το ξύλωμα του Τ.12 (from dismantling of Wall 12). P.L./L. 0.049; W. 0.017; Th. 0.001; Wt. 1.4 g.

Rods and related

The three objects presented below are an eclectic series of bronze rods. When first encountered, **26/167** was thought to be a possible bronze bracelet, but this seems unlikely given that there is no curvature whatsoever. A very similar rod from the agora of Methone listed below also lacks curvature. **26/167** is of interest as its context is Early Iron Age to Archaic. Similar rods elsewhere with a clearly molded rectangular head are perforated for attachment, which is not the case here.[252] The rather amorphous and damaged form of **26/168**, from the destruction deposit, does not suggest a clear function. Although only partially preserved, the form of **26/169** is of interest both for its heptagonal to octagonal section, and the fact that it is perforated at both preserved ends, which are clearly broken, but splaying outward. The piece was recovered from the collapsed fill above the destruction deposit; its fragmentary nature impedes a clear identification of the original object, and I know of no parallel for **26/169**.

26/167. (ΜΕΘ 1648 [ΜΕ 3825]) Rod Fig. 26.49

Agora #274/089. Τομή στη βόρεια πλευρά (north part of trench).

P.L. 0.081; L. x W. x Th. (rectangular terminal) 0.006 x 0.005 x 0.004; Wt. 8.0 g.

Two joining frr preserving substantial portion of implement; side opposite rectangular terminal obscured by bronze disease, but clearly broken.

Thickish cast shaft, circular to elliptical in section. One end terminating in a well-molded rectangular head; opposite end slightly thickened as preserved, but broken.

Context pre-destruction deposit, Early Iron Age to Archaic.

Related to **26/167**:

ΜΕΘ 1644 (ΜΕ 935). Agora #274/087 [3]. P.L. 0.067; L. x W. x Th. (rectangular head) 0.006 x 0.005 x 0.004; Wt. 6.1 g.

26/168. (ΜΕΘ 4230 [ΜΕ 3867]) Large Rod Fig. 26.49

Agora #274/018003 [2]. Περιοχή ανάμεσα σε α σειρά λίθων και T.22. Area between first row of stones and Wall 22.

P.L. 0.144; Th. (shaft, max) 0.008; Wt. 19.7 g.

Single fr preserving large portion of shaft, but no clear terminal. Bronze split at thickest point.

Long and thickish shaft, mostly square to rhomboidal in section, tapering toward point at one end, which may have been flattened, whether intentionally or accidentally, with an articulation resembling a perforation probably the result of damage. Opposite end thicker, but not well defined.

Context destruction deposit, mid-4th century B.C. or earlier.

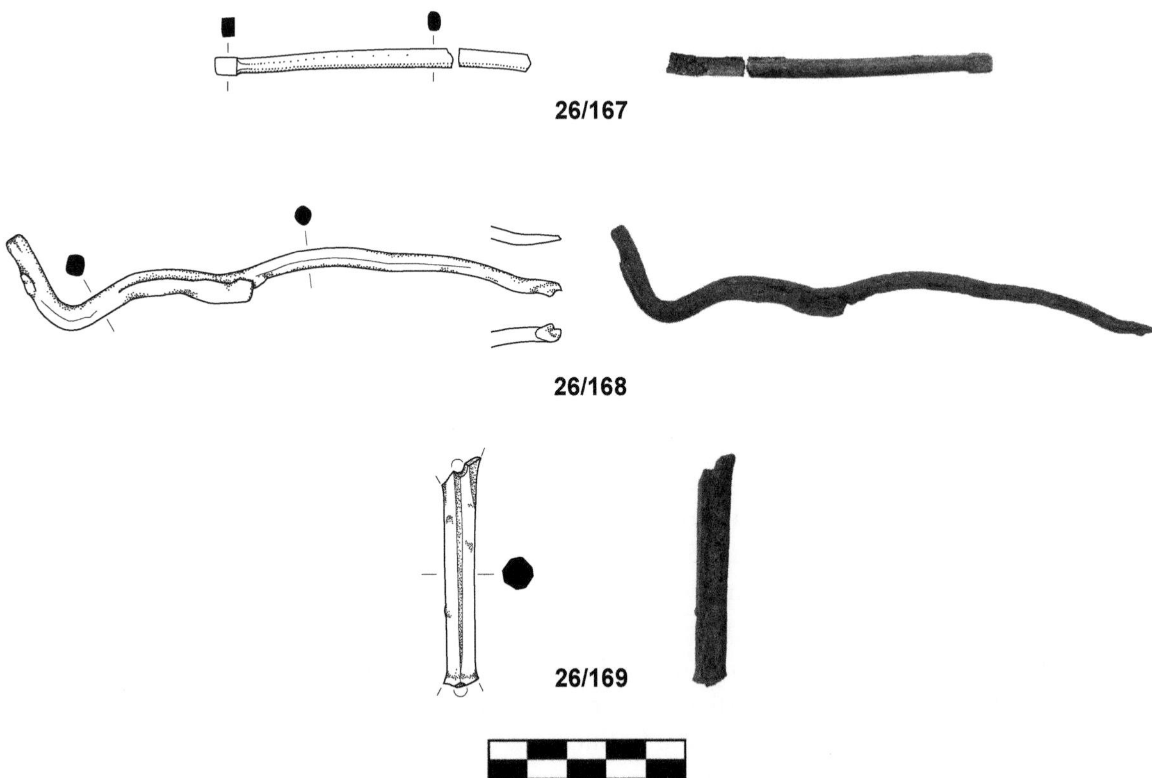

FIGURE 26.49. Agora bronze rods and related, **26/167** (ΜΕΘ 1648), **26/168** (ΜΕΘ 4230), **26/169** (ΜΕΘ 4309). Drawings A. Hooton and T. Ross, photos I. Coyle and J. Vanderpool

26/169. (MEΘ 4309 [ME 2518]) Fragmentary Perforated Rod Fig. 26.49

Agora #274/016003 [1].

P.L. 0.058; L. x W. (shaft) 0.009 x 0.009; Wt. 22.0 g.

Single fr preserving undetermined portion of object.

Thick faceted shaft, heptagonal to octagonal in section, and splaying out at both preserved ends, both of which are perforated, but broken, with the holes only partially preserved.

Context collapsed fill above destruction deposit, prehistoric to mid-4th century B.C.

Varia

Hinged objects

Hinges of various shapes and sizes are known in a variety of contexts in the Greek world, but few, if any, are shaped quite like **26/170** and **26/171**. The former is late Classical; the context of the latter gives no firm clue as to its date. Various bronze and iron hinges are known from Dodona, Bassai, Isthmia, Olynthos, and Philia in Greece, as well as in southern Italy.[253] Larger hooked and hinged elements are known from bronze belts,[254] helmets,[255] and an object from Isthmia interpreted as a "drain cover" is not unlike **26/170**.[256] The form and size of **26/170** suggests that it may have been a hinge or latch associated with a small case or diptych. In many ways, **26/171** is larger, heavier, and more complex than **26/170**, all the more a shame that the piece is so fragmentary; I know of no convincing parallels.

26/170. (MEΘ 4232 [ME 949]) Hinged Plate with Pin Fig. 26.50

Agora #274/087. Στρώμα καταστροφής [5] (destruction layer [5]).

Rectangular hinged plate: L. x W. 0.024 x 0.019; Th. 0.001; pin: L. 0.027; Wt. (both pieces) 2.6 g.

Pin intact; hinged plate preserved in three joining frr complete, except for folded-over edge, which is partially preserved.

Thin rectangular plate, made of sheet bronze, hammered flat, with small hole at center of long side opposite the pin. Side accommodating the pin hinged and folded over to hold pin. Pin shaft ovoid in section, with rounded, slightly thickened terminals to prevent pin from slipping out of its mount.

Context destruction deposit, mid-4th century B.C. or earlier.

26/171. (MEΘ 4234 [ME 2337]) Fragmentary Hinged Object Fig. 26.50

Agora #274/085. ΒΔ τμήμα (NW section).

Main fr: p.L x p.W. 0.031 x 0.026; Th. 0.010; pin: p.L. 0.037; Wt. (total, both pieces) 20.6 g.

Two non-joining pieces, both fragmentary. One fr preserves thick articulated bronze plate with groove; two joining frr preserve portion of pin.

Main fr thick and multifaceted; articulated as shown. One side preserves broad groove, thought to accommodate pin. There is also a corresponding but partial groove on the opposite side, large enough for the lower portion of the pin to fit. Pin thicker at preserved top, tapering to a well-preserved point, circular in section.

Context unclear.

Wedge-shaped object

It is likely that **26/172** is complete or near complete; only the bottom edge may be broken, but this remains uncertain, and even if it was, it is unlikely to have been originally much larger. One can imagine the wedge shape serving any number of functions in keeping wooden elements in place. Furthermore, the small rounded globe or ball seems to facilitate either purchase or the securement of a line around it, in the same manner that a line would be tied around the head of the fishhooks presented above. If the latter is entertained, the object could be a weight of sorts, but lead, which is plentiful at Methone, would have served such a purpose more efficiently. If the purpose of the small globe was to accommodate the fastening of string, then the possibility of a pendant cannot be ruled out, but the lack of a suspension hole seems odd; the only small pendant that is close to **26/172** is one of similar size from the Enodia sanctuary at Pherai, which has a rectangular projection with no suspension hole.[257]

26/172. (MEΘ 2140 [ME 4136]) Wedge-shaped Object — Fig. 26.50

Agora #274/090004 [3].

P.L. 0.030; W. (max) 0.011; Wt. 4.0 g.

Single fr, conceivably intact; bottom edge as shown seems to be broken but difficult to tell due to corrosion.

Roughly triangular body in plan, broader at bottom, but with a small rounded globe/ball at top (Diam. 0.005–0.006).

Context Building Δ, mid-4th century B.C. or earlier.

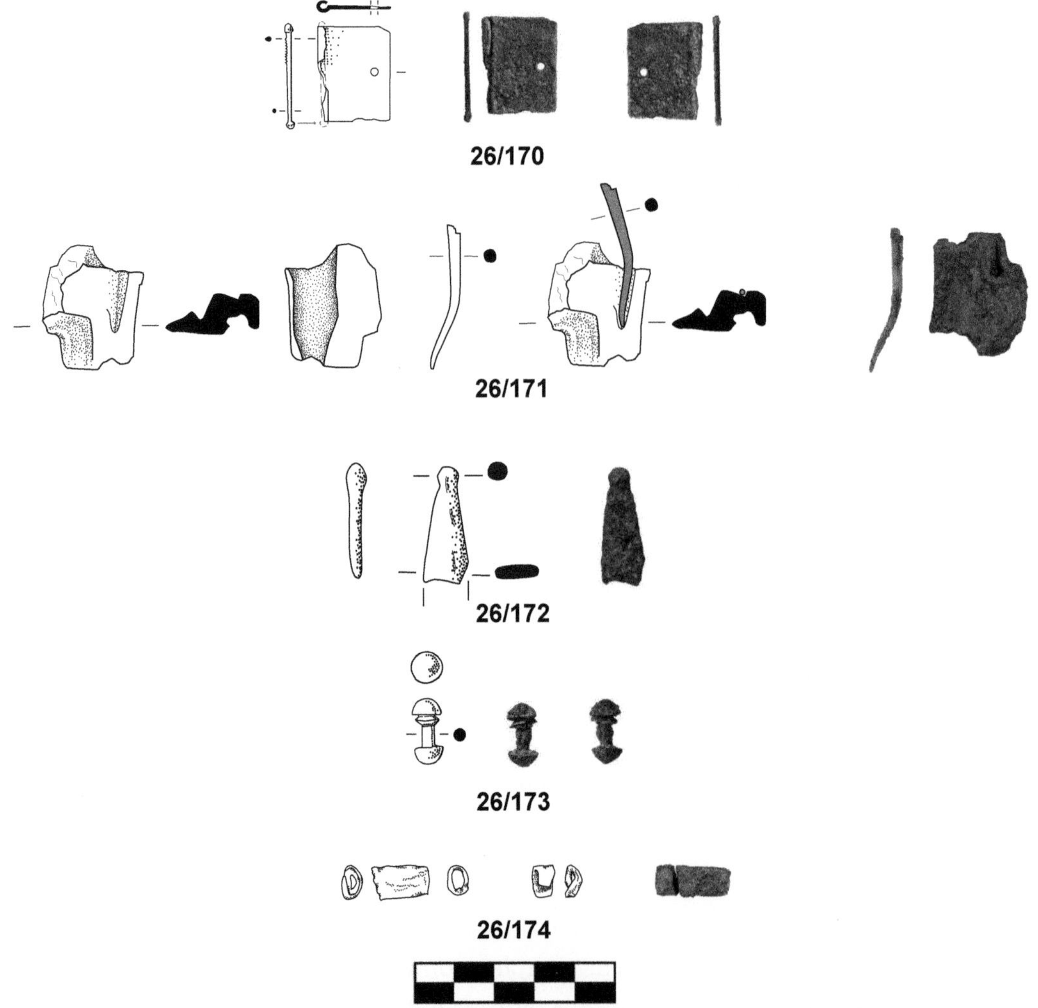

FIGURE 26.50. Agora bronze varia: hinged objects, **26/170** (MEΘ 4232), **26/171** (MEΘ 4234); wedge-shaped object, **26/172** (MEΘ 2140); attachment (decorative rivet), **26/173** (MEΘ 4191); folded sheet/small tube, **26/174** (MEΘ 5303). Drawings A. Hooton, T. Ross, and F. Skyvalida, photos I. Coyle and J. Vanderpool

Attachment (decorative rivet?)

26/173 is best described as an "attachment," for want of a better term. Although it is very closely related to the finials of the so-called *T-Nadeln* dress pins of Kilian-Dirlmeier's Type XVIIIC, there is no perforation in the central shaft of **26/173** to accommodate the pin, which is an almost invariable feature of such pins, and the small ring on the side of one of the finials is also unusual.[258] Although I do not rule out the possibility that **26/173** is from a *T-Nadel*, the possibility that it served some other function is worth consideration, which is why I have placed the piece here. The form of **26/173** is not unlike two bone/ivory "ἐξαρτήματα" ("components" or "accessories") from Sindos.[259] In discussing the latter, Despoini notes the similarity of the form to Bronze Age parallels from Zygouries, Mycenae, and Eleusis, whereas similar examples from Archaic and later sanctuaries are either described in general terms, or characterized as buttons; other examples from Mycenae and Cyprus discussed by Despoini were thought to be associated with shields or swords by their excavators.[260] These parallels, although referring to bone or ivory pieces of related form, illustrate that such objects may well have served a variety of purposes.

26/173. (ΜΕΘ 4191 [ΜΕ 2194]) Attachment Fig. 26.50

Agora #274/085. Ανατολικός μάρτυρας (east balk).

L. 0.016; Diam. (max) 0.008; Diam. (connecting shaft) 0.003; Wt. 1.3 g.

Intact, but corroded.

Two conical finials, connected by shaft, circular in section. Below one of the finials what appears to be a ring.

Context unclear.

Folded sheet/small tube

I have vacillated between presenting **26/174** as a bead or small thin folded sheet of bronze, and even including it at all. It is presented here instead in the hope that, isolated, it may find parallels from elsewhere.

26/174. (ΜΕΘ 5303 [ΜΕ 926]) Fragmentary Tubular Object Fig. 26.50

Agora #274/086.

P.L./L. 0.019; Diam. 0.008; Wt. 1.0 g.

Two joining frr preserving uncertain portion of object.

As preserved, small tube, evidently formed of sheet bronze rolled over.

Context destruction deposit or immediately above, mid-4th century B.C. or earlier.

Weapons

Arrowheads

The only weapons in bronze from the agora of Methone are arrowheads. Other weapons, of which there was no shortage, are of iron (see below), or else the numerous lead sling bullets (Chapter 28). The bronze arrowheads presented below essentially follow the order of Snodgrass's typology. The first, **26/175**, despite its damaged state, is a good example of Snodgrass's Type 3A1, the plain two-edged type, which makes its earliest appearance in Greece in the 8th century B.C.[261] He goes on to note that during and after the Persian Wars, two-edged arrowheads were largely ousted by the various three-edged forms, "no doubt because of their liability to bend on impact."[262] Unfortunately, the context of **26/175** was such that it could not provide a clear date for the piece.

I have classified **26/176** and **26/177** as examples of Snodgrass's Type 3B1, which, as Snodgrass notes, is not always easily distinguished from the shaftless Type 3B3, even though the socket of

26/177 does not project for any great length.[263] This type is found as early as Type 3A1, and they are often found in the same contexts as the latter. Both examples from Methone were found in the destruction deposit; both may be confidently assigned to the first half of the 4th century B.C., and are likely to have been used in the siege of 354 B.C. Although almost twice the size of **26/176** and **26/177**, **26/178** is of the same type, differing only in being equipped with a spur, and is thus an example of Type 3B2.[264] This may well be the earliest of the bronze arrowheads from the agora at Methone, as it was found in a pre-destruction context in association with material of the Archaic and earlier Classical period. It is important to note that a stone mold for producing this type of arrowhead was found at Samos.[265] Similarly, **26/179** and **26/180** are examples of three-edged arrowheads, but without a projecting socket, corresponding to Snodgrass's Type 3B3, and about which Snodgrass noted that there is little to add to Types 3B1 and 2, except that it is a later development of the three-edged form with projecting socket. Its development largely complete by the 5th century B.C., this form was almost universal at Thermopylai, the Athenian Acropolis North Slope, and Olynthos, "and became the commonest single variety of arrowhead in Greece."[266] The context of **26/179** is uncertain, whereas **26/180** was found in the fill of Building B, immediately above the destruction deposit, and is therefore Classical or a little earlier.

The last two bronze arrowheads, **26/181** and **26/182**, are essentially like Types 3B1 and 3B3, but differ only in that their edges are barbed. They are good examples of Snodgrass's Types 3B4 and 3B5, but distinguishing between the former, with a projecting socket, and the latter, with "interior socket," is not always straightforward.[267] This appears to be a very popular type among Greek mercenaries in the later Classical and Hellenistic periods; in Greece the barbed triangular type was common perhaps from Archaic times (the context of **26/181** is the same as **26/180**, Classical or a little earlier, and **26/182** was encountered in the destruction deposit of 354 B.C.).[268] As already noted, Snodgrass believes that the Olynthos finds show that they were used (perhaps exclusively) by the Macedonian royal archers in the mid-4th century.[269] The variety of arrowheads in the agora of Methone, especially those from the destruction deposit, amplified by the iron arrowheads presented below (**26/183–26/187**), provide something of an evocative glimpse of the final days of the settlement at Methone and its siege conditions.

26/175. (ΜΕΘ 1675 [ΜΕ 2204]) Arrowhead — Fig. 26.51

Agora #274/085. Ανατολικός μάρτυρας (east balk).

P.L. 0.022; W. 0.009; Diam. (socket/tang) 0.005; Wt. 1.6 g.

Almost complete, but chipped and rather worn, perhaps the result of use/impact?

Relatively broad, leaf-shaped blade, with prominent central rib, terminating, as preserved, in an almost rounded point. Very small circular socket, rather than long tang.

Context unclear.

26/176. (ΜΕΘ 294 [ΜΕ 987]) Arrowhead — Fig. 26.51

Agora #274/067. Δοκιμαστική τομή—ανατολικά. Στρώμα καταστροφής (trial trench, east; destruction level).

L. 0.019; W. 0.007; Diam. (socket) 0.006; Wt. 1.4 g.

Complete, but one or two of the lower edges may be chipped.

Triangular, three-edged blade/head. Small circular socket. Small hole, 0.006 from socket edge, to aid attachment.

Context destruction deposit, mid-4th century B.C. or earlier.

Cf., among others, *Selinus* V, p. 26, pl. 2, nos. 33–34, 38, variously dated from the second half of the 5th century to the end of the 4th century B.C.

26/177. (MEΘ 1791 [ME 1372]) Arrowhead Fig. 26.51

Agora #274/066. Στρώμα καταστροφής, ερυθρό με πλιθιά (destruction level, red with mud bricks).

L. 0.018; W. 0.007; Diam. (socket) 0.006; Wt. 1.4 g.

Intact, but chipped.

As **26/176** (MEΘ 294), with very small hole 0.008 from the point to aid attachment. Small socket, slightly flattened on one side.

Context destruction deposit, mid-4th century B.C. or earlier.

Cf., among others, *Selinus* V, p. 29, pl. 3, esp. no. 76 (assigned to the 6th century B.C.).

26/178. (MEΘ 1679 [ME 3933]) Arrowhead Fig. 26.51

Agora #274/079. Τομή στη νότια πλευρά (south side of trench).

L. 0.036; W. 0.009; Diam. (socket) 0.006–0.007; Wt. 3.1 g.

Intact, but chipped.

Three-edged triangular blade, with prominent spur (chipped) projecting from juncture of blade and socket. Type as **26/176** (MEΘ 294), but larger (twice the length), and with a much longer socket.

Context, pre-destruction deposit, Archaic to Classical.

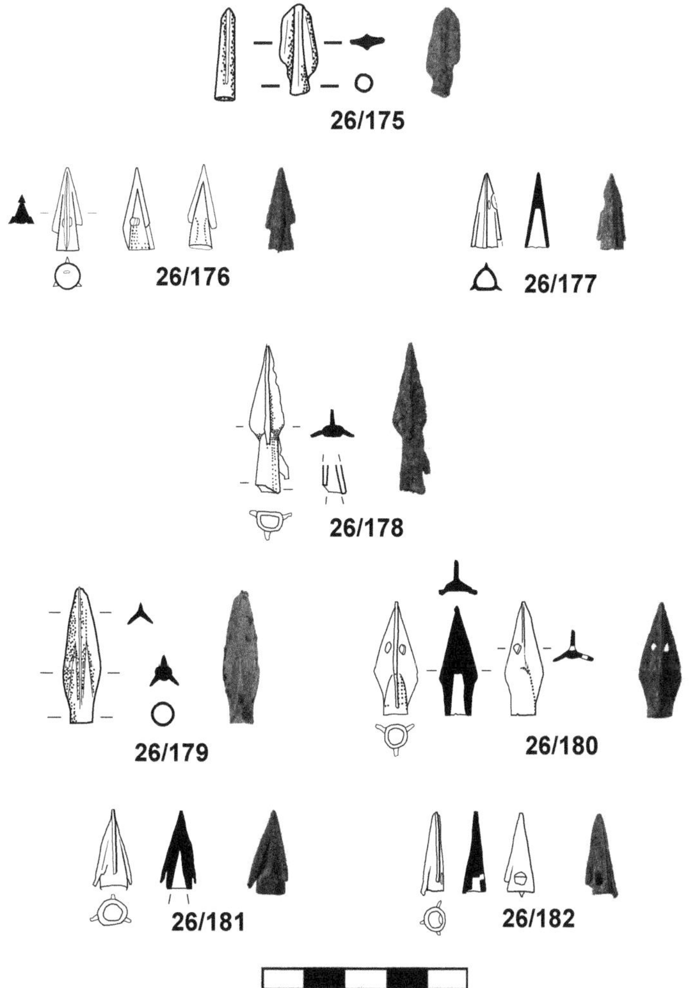

FIGURE 26.51. Agora bronze arrowheads, **26/175** (MEΘ 1675), **26/176** (MEΘ 294), **26/177** (MEΘ 1791), **26/178** (MEΘ 1679), **26/179** (MEΘ 1676), **26/180** (MEΘ 1678), **26/181** (MEΘ 1677), **26/182** (MEΘ 1674). Drawings A. Hooton and F. Skyvalida, photos I. Coyle and J. Vanderpool

26/179. (MEΘ 1676 [ME 2676]) Arrowhead Fig. 26.51

Agora #274/085. NW corner.

P.L. 0.033; W. 0.011; Diam. (socket) 0.007; Wt. 3.5 g.

Almost complete, except for very tip of point. Originally heavily encrusted, with an atypical lighter green patina.

Triangular three-edged blade, rather substantial, but with very short socket, approaching an interior socket; type as **26/180** (MEΘ 1678).

Context unclear.

26/180. MEΘ 1678 [ME 3557]) Arrowhead Fig. 26.51

Agora #274/008012 [6].

L. 0.027–0.028; W. 0.010; Diam. (socket) 0.007; Wt. 2.2 g.

Intact.

Type as **26/179** (MEΘ 1676), but a little smaller. Two of the three leaves of the blade each have a small hole that appears to be intentional.

Context Building B fill, above destruction deposit, Classical or earlier.

26/181. (MEΘ 1677 [ME 3556]) Arrowhead Fig. 26.51

Agora #274/008012 [6].

L. 0.019; W. 0.009–0.010; Diam. (socket) 0.007; Wt. 2.3 g.

Intact, but chipped.

Triangular three-edged blade, but with barbs. Circular socket, barely extending below the barbs; cf. **26/182** (MEΘ 1674).

Context Building B fill, above destruction deposit, Classical or earlier.

26/182. (MEΘ 1674 [ME 1909]) Arrowhead Fig. 26.51

Agora #274/079. Ανατολικό τμήμα (east portion).

L. 0.020; Diam. (socket) 0.006; Wt. 1.5 g.

Complete, except for two of the three barbs.

Type as **26/181** (MEΘ 1677), with interior socket, well below the level of the best-preserved barb.

Context destruction deposit, mid-4th century B.C. or earlier.

Objects of Iron

The iron objects from the agora of Methone complement those from the Hypogeion, but provide various classes of weaponry not found in the earlier context, as well as a rich and varied collection of tools and implements. In this section, I begin with the weapons, specifically the iron arrowheads, as they complement well the bronze examples from the agora presented above (**26/175–26/182**). Other iron weapons include spearheads, sauroters, and swords. The tools/implements include nails, rings, and a knife, together with a large scraper, a fragment of a pair of tongs (or a poker), and a few other items (only a representative sample of the iron objects from the agora is presented here).

Weapons

Arrowheads

All of the iron arrowheads are of the same type, Snodgrass's Type 4, which comes in two main varieties: a) straight sides; b) curved sides; although the type has been plausibly associated with Cyprus, the evidence is far from conclusive.[270] All of the Methone examples are straight-sided and all are, thus far, of iron. The form is narrow, in terms of both the blade (or head) and the tang, and they are invariably square in section (blade and tang), although the lowermost tang on some examples can be more rounded. They are large in comparison to the bronze arrowheads, all of which are under 0.040, and often considerably smaller, whereas the iron examples of Type 4 can reach 0.085 m. Their size and form gives them the appearance of a bolt. The quantity of the type at a site in the north Aegean is noteworthy. They are found in both pre-destruction and destruction deposit contexts, and thus can be securely dated from the Archaic period, if not earlier, through 354 B.C.

In discussing the origin of the type, especially the straight-sided Type A, Snodgrass notes Anatolian Bronze Age prototypes in both bronze and bone from Alishar Hüyük and other sites in Anatolia, continuing into the Phrygian period.[271] As for the type in Greece, Snodgrass writes:

> Its occurrences in Greece are limited, and not entirely attributable to the Persian invasions, when there may have been Cypriote archers present. By the 8th century it had already reached Crete in its iron form, no doubt as a direct import. It appears on the Acropolis slopes at Athens and at Dodona in bronze, at Marathon in both bronze and iron, and at Olynthus in iron, dating from the Macedonian siege of 348 B.C. Possibly the type could penetrate bronze armour: the famous Crowe corselet from Olympia is pierced by two small, square holes such as a solid-headed arrow might make.[272]

The earliest example of the type may now be from the Early Iron Age tomb 13 in the Athenian Agora, which is Early Geometric I.[273] The type is also common at the sanctuary at Kalapodi,[274] and there is at least one example from Vitsa in Epirus, and another from the cemetery at Sindos.[275] A number of iron arrowheads of this type from Torone were found on Hill 2 (Thucydides' [4.110.2] ἀνωτάτω φυλακτήριον), and are dated to the middle of the 4th century B.C., the fateful date when Torone, together with Mekyberna (the port of Olynthos), fell to Philip, according to Diodoros of Sicily (16.53.2) by means of "treasonable surrender."[276] Northern examples aside, this is a very popular arrowhead in central and southern Greece. In discussing over 90 examples of this type of arrowhead, Christopher Hagerman, who refers to them as "bodkin arrowheads" (not the happiest term), notes comparanda from Olympia, Pylos, and elsewhere.[277]

Given the ubiquity of the type at Methone in 354 and at Olynthos in 348 B.C., not to mention Torone, it is tempting to link them to either the Macedonian or the local archers: was this the βέλος that Aster of Methone fired at the Macedonians that took out the right eye of Philip II?[278] Or were these large arrowheads/bolts used by the Macedonians? Or by both sides? That the type is largely confined to the area of the agora of Methone does not clinch the matter, and it is probably best to regard this type of arrowhead as a popular one in the later Classical period. The fact that Type 4 arrowheads are attested in Archaic Methone suggests that the type enjoyed, as noted above, a long history at the site.

26/183. (ΜΕΘ 1730 [ΜΕ 2466]) Arrowhead Fig. 26.52

Agora #274/052. Ανατολική παρειά (east section).

P.L. 0.082; p.L. (blade) 0.042; Wt. 12.9 g.

Single fr preserving greater part of arrowhead. Tang bent.

Large and sturdy blade, without barbs, square in section, tapering toward point, the tip of which is not preserved. Tang considerably narrower than blade/head, rectangular in section for the upper and much of the tang, more rounded in section toward the tang point.

Context unclear.

26/184. (ΜΕΘ 1731 [ΜΕ 3582]) Arrowhead Fig. 26.52

Agora #274. Επιφανειακό στρώμα (surface layer).

P.L./L. 0.079; L./p.L. (blade); 0.034; Wt. 9.0 g.

Single fr preserving most of arrowhead, except for the very tip of the point.

Form as **26/183** (ΜΕΘ 1730). Most of the tang square, except for the tip of the point where it is a little more rounded.

Surface find.

26/185. (ΜΕΘ 1734 [ΜΕ 3953]) Arrowhead Fig. 26.52

Agora #274/069.

P.L. 0.075; p.L. (blade) 0.048; Wt. 6.5 g.

Single fr preserving all or most of blade/head, but undetermined portion of tang.

Type as **26/183** (ΜΕΘ 1730), but with proportionately longer blade. Upper tang square/ovoid in section, lowermost tang more rounded, suggesting that it may be almost complete.

Context unclear.

26/186. (ΜΕΘ 1723 [ΜΕ 2263]) Arrowhead Fig. 26.52

Agora #274/075. Ανατολικό τμήμα (east section).

P.L. 0.061; L. (blade) 0.048; Wt. 7.9 g.

Single fr preserving all of blade, but undetermined portion of tang.

Type as **26/183** (ΜΕΘ 1730); uppermost tang rectangular in section.

Context unclear.

26/187. (ΜΕΘ 1728 [ΜΕ 1897]) Arrowhead Fig. 26.52

Agora #274/079. Ανατολικό τμήμα (east section).

P.L. 0.063; L./p.L. (blade) 0.047; Wt. 11.5 g.

Single fr preserving all of blade, except for tip of point, but undetermined portion of tang.

Type as **26/183** (ΜΕΘ 1730).

Context destruction deposit, mid-4th century B.C. or earlier.

Additional arrowheads of the same type:

ΜΕΘ 1720. Agora #274/076. Βόρειος μάρτυρας, χώρος Ε΄, στρώμα καστανό. North balk, Room 5, brown layer. P.L. 0.069; p.L. (blade) 0.034; Wt. 7.5 g.

ΜΕΘ 1721. Agora #274/077. Χώρος Ε΄, στρώμα καταστροφής (Room 5, destruction deposit). P.L. 0.060; p.L. (blade) 0.037; Wt. 9.8 g.

ΜΕΘ 1722. Agora #274/007. Backfill. P.L. 0.034; p.L. (blade); Wt. 7.2 g.

ΜΕΘ 1724. Agora #274/075. Ανατολικό τμήμα (east section). P.L. 0.056; p.L. (blade) 0.045; Wt. 6.5 g.

ΜΕΘ 1725. Agora #274/075. Μέσο νότιο τμήματος (middle of south section). P.L. 0.053; p.L. (blade) 0.036; Wt. 9.9 g.

ΜΕΘ 1726. Agora #274/078. P.L. 0.051; p.L. (blade) 0.041; Wt. 9.5 g.

ΜΕΘ 1727. Agora #274/079. Ανατολικό τμήμα (east section). P.L. 0.040; p.L. (blade) 0.033; Wt. 6.7 g.

ΜΕΘ 1729. Agora #274/089. Ανατολικό τμήμα (east section). P.L. 0.045; p.L. (blade) 0.039; Wt. 9.6 g.

ΜΕΘ 1732. Agora #274/017019 [2]. Βόρειος μάρτυρας (north balk). P.L. 0.046; p.L. (blade) 0.033; Wt. 7.2 g.

ΜΕΘ 1733. Agora #274/027023 [3]. P.L. 0.069; p.L. (blade) 0.043; Wt. 13.1 g.

ΜΕΘ 1735. Agora #274/089. ΒΔ τμήμα (NW section). P.L. 0.057; p.L. (blade) 0.052; Wt. 11.6 g.

ΜΕΘ 1736. Agora #274/089. Τομή στο κέντρο του τετραγώνου (trench in center of square, pre-destruction deposit, Archaic to Classical). P.L. 0.064; p.L. (blade) 0.052; Wt. 13.0 g.

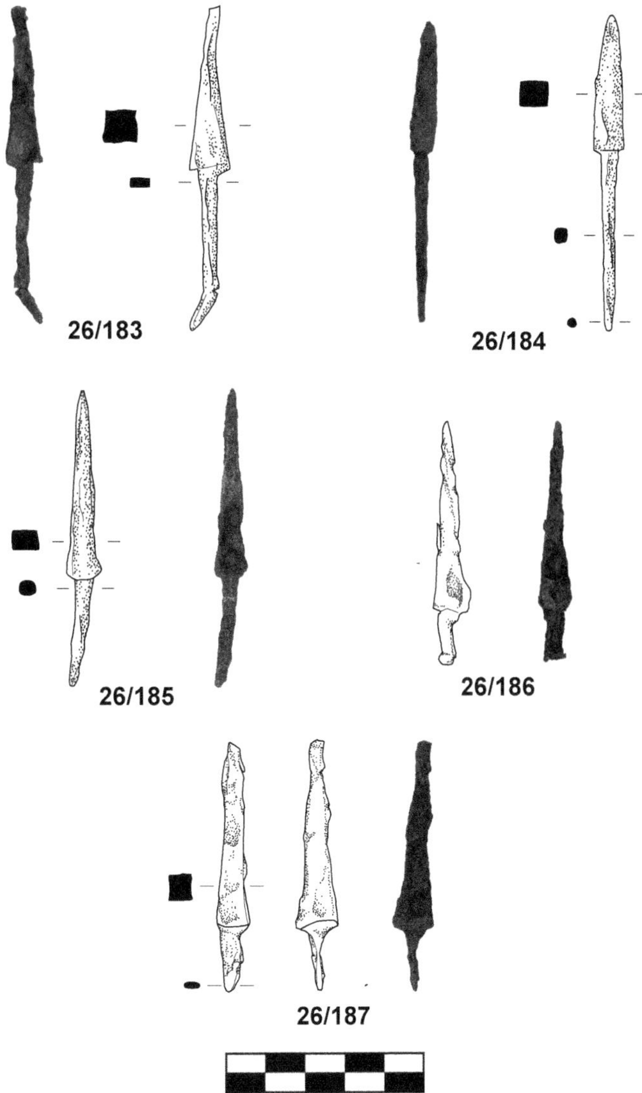

FIGURE 26.52. Agora iron arrowheads, **26/183** (MEΘ 1730), **26/184** (MEΘ 1731), **26/185** (MEΘ 1734), **26/186** (MEΘ 1723), **26/187** (MEΘ 1728). Drawings T. Ross and F. Skyvalida, photos I. Coyle

Spears (spearheads and sauroters)

The one diagnostic spear, albeit poorly preserved, from the Hypogeion is of Snodgrass's Type M, and is fully discussed, with comparanda, in Chapter 15 (under **15/75**). Of the two spearheads presented below, the poorly preserved **26/189** is probably of this type.[279] The flat blade of **26/188** is certainly reminiscent of Snodgrass's Type M spears, although, from what survives, it appears to be proportionately broader and larger, and, as such, it may be an example of Vokotopoulou's Type Ω spears from Vitsa Zagoriou.[280] The context of **26/188** was unclear as to date, but **26/189** was found in the destruction deposit.

I have catalogued only one sauroter—spear butt, spear end, "Lanzenschuh" in German—from the agora at Methone, but I have listed several others. Although the context of **26/190** is unclear, several of those listed were from the destruction deposit and can be assigned to the first half of the 4th century B.C., and were no doubt in use in the siege of 354 B.C. Referred to as σαυρωτήρ or οὐρίαχος in Greek, and once thought to be a rarity before the 6th century, there are, as Snodgrass notes, several examples that are earlier, including one from Kallithea that is Mycenaean, another from Ialysos of Late Protogeometric date, and a third from Corinth that should be 7th century.[281] To these, an 8th–7th century sauroter from Vitsa can be added.[282] The form and size of **26/190** is fairly standard for the more simple sauroters throughout the Greek world.[283] More complex Archaic and Classical examples of bronze sauroters are known from, among other sites, Olympia, Philia, Kalapodi, Selinunte, Krotone, and Francavilla Marittima,[284] and it is worth adding that simpler sauroters are not uncommon in pre-Greek cemeteries in south Italy and Sicily.[285]

Spearheads

26/188. (ΜΕΘ 1746) Spearhead Fig. 26.53

Agora #274/ Καθαρισμός Τ.7 (cleaning of Wall 7).

P.L. 0.122; W. (blade) 0.042; W. (socket) 0.008–0.009; Wt. 53.2 g.

Primary fr, plus chips of corrosion, preserving most of blade, except for tip, but only uppermost part of the transition to the socket.

Broad, flat, leaf-shaped blade, without a central spine. The socket itself does not survive, only the square/rectangular-in-section transition from blade to socket.

Context unclear.

26/189. (ΜΕΘ 1752 [ΜΕ 3731]) Spearhead Fig. 26.53

Agora #274/017021 [2]. Βόρειος μάρτυρας (north balk).

P.L. (main fr) 0.098; p.W. (blade) 0.019; Wt. 30.3 g.

Two main frr, plus numerous smaller frr and chips, preserving portion of spearhead, much damaged and corroded, with most of the edges of the blade not preserved.

Although poorly preserved, the form of the blade would have originally been close to **26/188** (ΜΕΘ 1746), but perhaps not as broad. Comparatively narrow round socket.

Context destruction deposit, mid-4th century B.C. or earlier.

Additional spearhead:

ΜΕΘ 1749 (ΜΕ 3760). Agora #274.018001 [1]. Socket primarily preserved, with little of the blade. P.L. (main fr) 0.094; Wt. 28.1 g.

Sauroters

26/190. (ΜΕΘ 1766 [ΜΕ 2467]) Small Sauroter Fig. 26.53

Agora #274/025. Ανατολική παρειά (east side of trench).

L./p.L. 0.055; Diam. (socket) 0.014; Wt. 9.4 g.

Single fr preserving virtually complete object.

Made from iron sheet, hammered flat, and rolled into a cone, but with thick bottom tip, square in section.

Context unclear.

Additional sauroters:

ΜΕΘ 1738 (ΜΕ 563). Agora #274/087055 [3]. As **26/190** (ΜΕΘ 1766) but slightly larger. L. 0.064; Diam. (socket) 0.017; Wt. 16.5 g.

ΜΕΘ 1757 (ΜΕ 1528). Agora #274/077. Building A. Χώρος Ε΄, δυτικά στρώμα καταστροφής (Room 5, west destruction deposit). P.L. 0.056; Diam. (socket) 0.015; Wt. 15.4 g.

ΜΕΘ 3099 (ΜΕ 4262). Agora #274/070002 [1]. Possible sauroter, with small hole to accommodate nail. P.L. 0.078; Diam. (max) 0.016; Wt. 17.7 g.

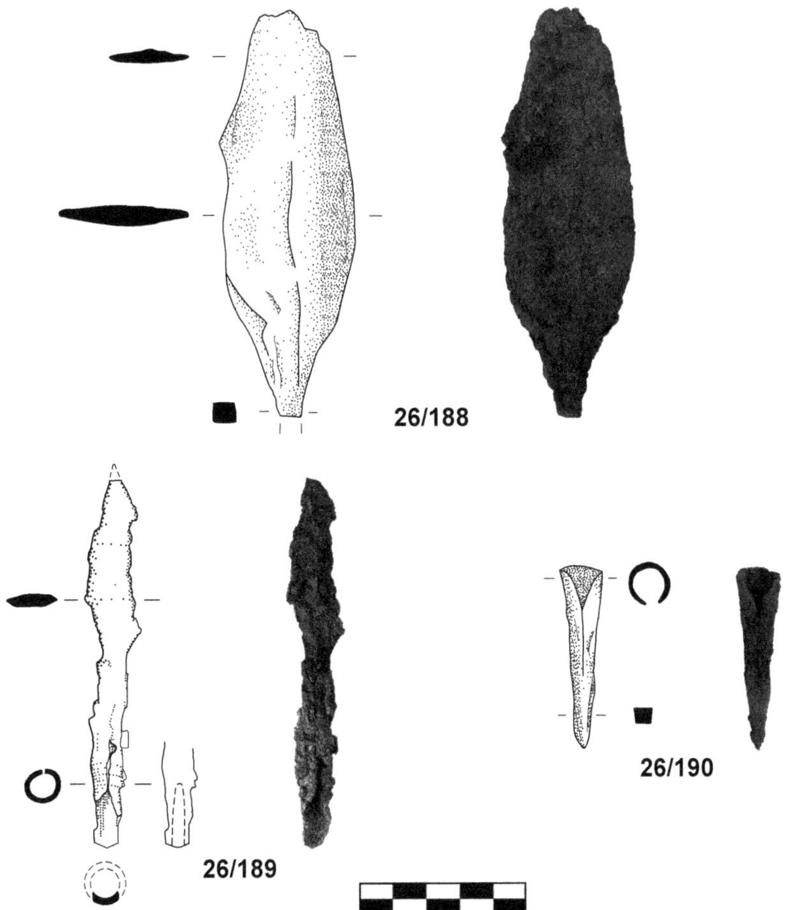

FIGURE 26.53. Agora iron spearheads, **26/188** (MEΘ 1746), **26/189** (MEΘ 1752); sauroter, **26/190** (MEΘ 1766). Drawings A. Hooton and F. Skyvalida, photos I. Coyle and J. Vanderpool

Swords

There are two iron swords from the agora that preserve enough details to warrant comment, **26/191** and **26/192**. The former is from an Early Iron Age to Archaic context, the latter was found in the destruction deposit of 354 B.C. It is important to note that there were no swords in bronze or iron in the Hypogeion. The earliest sword, **26/191**, is a good example of Snodgrass's Type II, which is a single-edged "hacking" sword; in describing the type, Snodgrass notes that it is not clear that these are in fact weapons of war, as opposed to large knives.[286] Indeed, a few of the iron knives from the Hypogeion are closely related in form, but are smaller (cf., esp. **15/86**). Whether it is a sword, dagger, or large knife (used, for instance, as a cleaver of sorts) may be moot, but the size of **26/191** would suggest its potential use as a weapon (its original length, if complete, would be at least in the vicinity of 0.50 m, and Late Geometric examples of the type from Vitsa Zagoriou in Epirus have a preserved length of 0.735, longer than many full-fledged swords).[287] Although such blades could well have been used for butchery, they could just as easily be used as weapons; thus Ioulia Vokotopoulou's cogent description of them as μαχαιροειδή ξίφη (knife-like swords).[288] The examples listed by Snodgrass—from Fortetsa, Halos, Arkades (Afrati), Tsaoutsitsa, and Olympia—are Late Geometric or Orientalizing, dates that accord nicely with **26/191**. The examples from Vitsa already noted are as early as the later 8th century B.C., but the earliest examples may now be several swords of this type from the Athena Itonia sanctuary near Philia, which are classified by Kilian Dirlmeier as Early to Middle Geometric, as well as a Middle Geometric example from the North Cemetery at Knossos.[289]

Dating as it does to the destruction deposit, **26/192** is chronologically much later than the period covered by Snodgrass. Unfortunately, too little survives of its hilt and shoulders to assist in determining the type more specifically. Long straight-sided blades of similar form and size are common in Greece from the 6th century B.C. into the Hellenistic period.[290] Straight-sided and related swords, often with elaborate hilts and shoulders or handguards, are standard among the graves at nearby Sindos in the late Archaic and Classical periods.[291]

26/191. (ΜΕΘ 1747 [ΜΕ 2671]) Sword Fragment Fig. 26.54

Agora #274/036007 [4].

P.L. 0.144; W. (max) 0.045; Wt. 89.9 g.

Two joining frr, plus three smaller frr, preserving portion of sword, including the tip.

Large, thick blade tapering to a well-preserved point. Cutting edge, if there was one, on the convex side, which is slightly thinner in section than the opposite straight edge.

Context pre-destruction deposit, Early Iron Age to Archaic.

26/192. (ΜΕΘ 1753 [ΜΕ 3856]) Fragmentary Sword Fig. 26.54

Agora #274/018003 [2]. Περιοχή ανάμεσα α σειρά λίθων και Τ.22 (area between 1st series of stones and Wall 22).

P.L. (main frr) 0.330+; W. (max) 0.027; Wt. 119.1 g.

Six main frr, several of which join, plus numerous frr and chips, preserving substantial portion of the sword, primarily the blade; tip not preserved.

Long, straight-sided blade, with similar edges on both sides. One fr may preserve portion of the haft/hilt (on the left side of the drawing, as shown), but this is not certain.

Context destruction deposit, mid-4th century B.C. or earlier.

Additional possible sword:

ΜΕΘ 1742 (ΜΕ 2196). Agora #274/085. Ανατολικός μάρτυρας (east balk: context unclear). Type as **26/192** (ΜΕΘ 1753)? P.L. 0.111; p.W. (max) 0.011; Wt. 16.2 g.

Knife

I catalogue below only one fragmentary iron knife from the agora, **26/193**, encountered in the destruction deposit. Iron knives from the Hypogeion and the summit of the West Hill are fully discussed in Chapter 15 (under **15/79–15/88**) and above (under **26/27**). A few parallels for **26/193** from Vergina, Sindos, Pherai, Philia, and Sindos are provided in the entry below.

26/193. (ΜΕΘ 1751 [ΜΕ 1899]) Fragmentary Knife Fig. 26.55

Agora #274/089. Ανατολικό τμήμα (east section).

P.L. 0.072; W. 0.021; Wt. 13.8 g.

Primary fr, plus smaller fr preserving much of knife, except the point.

Relatively straight blade, tapering toward point, which is not preserved. Opposite edge straight and should represent the haft. Cutting edge on the slightly convex side.

Context destruction deposit, mid-4th century B.C. or earlier.

Cf., among others, *Vergina* I, p. 267, fig. 104, ΚΙβ; Kilian 1975a, pl. 93, esp. nos. 4–6; Kilian-Dirlmeier 2002, pl. 70, esp. nos. 1102–1104; pl. 100, nos. 1652, 1654; pl. 108, no. 1758; pls. 154–155, nos. 2418, 2430–2432; *Sindos* III, p. 460, fig. 194, no. 433; p. 461, fig. 196, no. 435.

Additional knife:

ΜΕΘ 1750 (ΜΕ 1744). Agora #274/007029 [10]. Two frr. P.L. (main, larger fr) 0.085; Wt. 46.6 g.

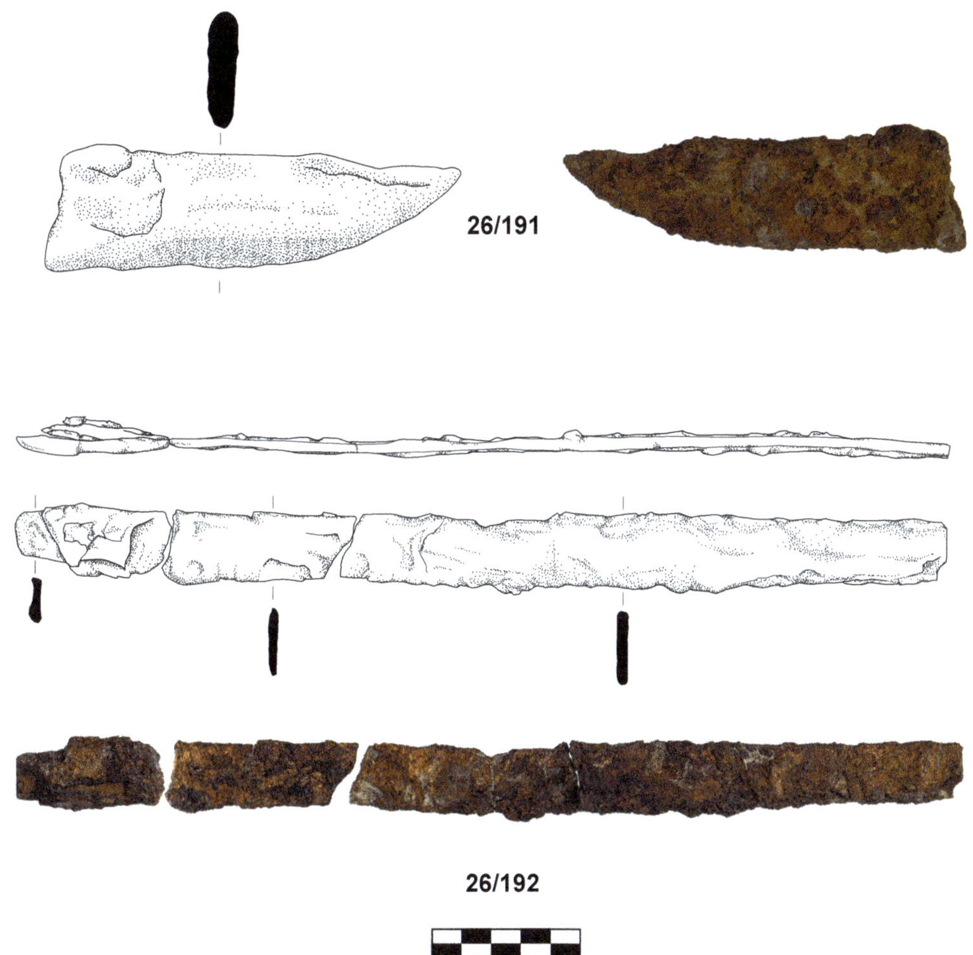

FIGURE 26.54. Agora iron swords, **26/191** (ΜΕΘ 1747), **26/192** (ΜΕΘ 1753). Drawings T. Ross and F. Skyvalida, photos I. Coyle and J. Vanderpool

Large sickle/scythe/pruning knife/hook

Although smaller sickles—or what are often referred to as sickle-shaped knives—are commonly found in Greek sanctuaries (whether of bronze or iron),[292] in funerary contexts,[293] and in domestic contexts,[294] a large sickle with such a prominent curved point as **26/194**, its size approaching a scythe, is rare indeed, and it is unfortunate that its context provides no clear idea of its date (except that 354 B.C. provides a terminus ante quem). Occasionally, some of the larger sickles or sickle-shaped knives approach the form of **26/194**,[295] but none that I know of is so substantial. Among the closest comparanda are several sickle-shaped iron objects from Isthmia referred to as "pruning hooks," all of which are of Classical or early Hellenistic date; two additional Hellenistic "sickles" from Nemea may also be cited.[296] In discussing these, Raubitschek makes reference to the "science of pruning grape vines" in Hesiod (*Works and Days* 570).[297] The preserved length of **26/194** is 0.110 m (its original size is unknown, but it may have been considerably larger); the lengths of the Isthmia examples vary between 0.084 and 0.230 m. Most modern pruning hooks, whether serrated or plain—oftentimes clippers are preferred to hooks—are small, and never as broad or substantial as **26/194**. There is a good example of an iron pruning knife ("falcetto") from the Pantanello Sanctuary in Metapontion, that is somewhat smaller than **26/194**, but of related form. Whether **26/194** is referred to as a sickle, scythe, or pruning hook or knife, it is surely an agricultural tool.

26/194. (MEΘ 1737 [ME 1899]) Large Sickle/Scythe Fr Fig. 26.55

Agora #274/007017 [3].

P.L. 0.110; W. (max, near tip) 0.060; Wt. 101.5 g.

Main fr, plus numerous flakes and chips, preserving portion of large sickle or scythe, including most of the point.

Large sickle or scythe with prominent curved point, which is complete or almost complete; opposite end broken; fairly even in section. Cutting edge on the concave side.

Context unclear.

Tongs/poker fragment

What survives of **26/195** is almost identical to the preserved terminal of the somewhat better-preserved set of tongs (or poker) from Phase I of the Hypogeion (**15/98**), which is fully discussed, with comparanda, such as they are, in Chapter 15. The only difference between **15/98** and **26/195** is that the shaft of the latter is somewhat thinner, and more rectangular, as opposed to the thicker and squarer shaft of **15/98**. What is of special interest is the fact that there are several examples of this type of industrial object at Methone. **15/98** dates to the later 8th–early 7th century, whereas **26/195** was encountered immediately above the destruction deposit of 354 B.C., in the collapsed fill from the higher sector of the East Hill. All that can be said about its date is that it is pre-destruction deposit, but how much earlier is impossible to tell.

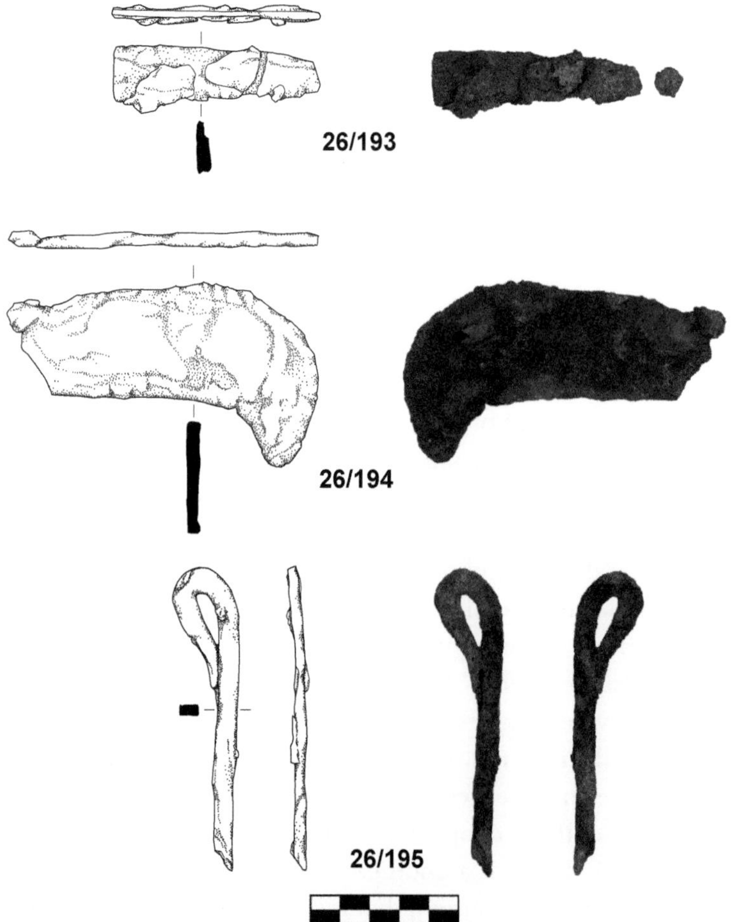

FIGURE 26.55. Agora iron tools/implements: knife, **26/193** (MEΘ 1751); large sickle/scythe, or pruning hook, **26/194** (MEΘ 1737); tongs/poker fragment, **26/195** (MEΘ 1755). Drawings T. Ross, photos I. Coyle

26/195. (ΜΕΘ 1755 [ME 977]) Tongs/Poker Fr Fig. 26.55

Agora #274/067. Στρώμα καστανό (brown layer).

P.L. 0.103; W. (head, max) 0.020; W. x Th. (shaft) 0.008 x 0.004; Wt. 19.9 g.

Single fr preserving handle and portion of shaft.

Rectangular shaft or strip of iron, with preserved terminal hammered and looped over to form handle.

Context pre-destruction deposit.

Large scraper

In many ways, **26/196** is among the most interesting of the iron objects at Methone. Despite its heavily corroded state, the scraper is essentially like a very large iron spearhead, but with a flat triangular blade, sharp along its broadest edge, and a comparatively broad socket to accommodate the wooden handle shaft. Precisely the same object, replete with a sturdy wooden shaft, was used to scrape back the scarps of the trenches at Pylos, in the excavations directed by Jack Davis and Sharon Stocker (Fig. 26.56d). This type of object, hand-held, without the use of feet, would have been ideal to straighten the sides of a large pit or underground installation, such as the Hypogeion on the East Hill, and especially the narrower Hypogeion 2 uncovered on the West Hill in the 2014–2017 excavations at Methone.[298] Such a tool would not have been useful, however, for the actual digging of the Hypogeion from above, since, unlike a spade, one cannot use the feet to push the tool down into the earth or bedrock.

Given the importance of timber at Methone, not least for shipbuilding and especially the oars of the Athenian triremes (see Chapter 20), an alternative use for **26/196** may have been for working wood. Such a tool would be ideal for scraping off the bark and any small adjoining branches of logs, as well as for the first rough shaping of the logs into beams or planks. The possibility that this was one of the κωποξύσται—"oar-scrapers"—mentioned in the Classical sources, is very likely.[299] The fact that there may have been at least three other iron objects of the same or similar form from Methone, listed below, suggests that this was a fairly common tool at the site, and should be seen together with other metal tools used for working timber, such as the axes, adzes, chisels, and other implements presented in Chapter 15 (under **15/89–15/92**) and above (under **26/28**). As already noted, Blackwell makes the point that determining a single function for an implement can sometimes be challenging.[300] I know of no comparanda from ancient contexts, although there is a smaller triangular scraper (L. 0.185; W. 0.053) from Torone of post-Byzantine date.[301] Not unlike the Methone object is a tool of Geometric date from Kavousi but with a broad bent tip, actually called a "scraper" by the excavators, and thought to have been used possibly for scraping hides or wood; another example from Kavousi published a few years earlier was originally referred to as a "chisel with a bent tip."[302] The latter are not unlike, but not the same as, a more common axe, typified by examples from Crete and Pithekoussai of Late Geometric date.[303] The heads of the Pithekoussai axes are square, but the two larger examples are socketed, though it is difficult to determine from the illustrations how sharp the edges were. From the foregoing discussion, it is clear that I cannot offer any compelling comparanda for **26/196.** Dating as it does to the destruction horizon of 354 B.C., **26/196** is a welcome addition to the tools of Classical antiquity.

26/196. (ΜΕΘ 1774 [ME 3891]) Large Scraper Fig. 26.56

Agora #274/027023 [3]. Δάπεδο (floor).

L./p.L. 0.227–0.235; W. (blade, max) 0.116; Diam. (socket) 0.030; Wt. (total, all frr) 820 g; Wt. (not including flakes and chips) 608.4 g.

Several primary frr, plus numerous flakes and chips, preserving greater part of scraper; corroded.

Roughly triangular blade, with sharp edge along its widest point. Comparatively broad socket to accommodate a sturdy wooden shaft.

Context destruction deposit, mid-4th century B.C. or earlier.

Fragments of additional scrapers:
ΜΕΘ 1741
ΜΕΘ 1774
ΜΕΘ 1767

Rings *(krikoi)* and related

Although resembling a finger ring, **26/197** is probably misformed into its current shape, and is too large to serve as a finger ring. Consequently, it is more likely a *krikos* serving a wide variety of purposes (see especially discussion in Chapter 15, under **15/33–15/34**, and above, under **26/11–26/12**, **26/96–26/99** [bronze]). Heavily corroded, **26/198** resembles two interconnected rings rather than part of a linked chain, such as the bronze **15/51**. In its current form it could have served any number of functions, like most *krikoi*.

26/197. (ΜΕΘ 5291 [ΜΕ 2303]) Ring Fig. 26.57

Agora #274/075. Ανατολικό τμήμα (east section).

L. (as bent) 0.035; Wt. 4.4 g.

Two joining frr preserving complete ring; evidently bent.

Thick rod/wire of iron, circular in section, formed into a ring, ovoid as preserved, and flattened on top.

Context unclear.

26/198. (ΜΕΘ 1754 [ΜΕ 2352]) Two Interconnected Rings Fig. 26.57

Agora #274/085. ΒΔ τμήμα/στρώμα λίθων (NW section/layer of stones).

L. 0.063; H./W. 0.032; Wt. 31.0 g.

Main fr, plus smaller flakes, preserving most of object (assuming there were only two rings).

Figure-of-eight double rings, unclear whether square/rectangular or circular in section due to corrosion, but most probably square.

Context unclear.

Nails

Four selected nails are presented below from the agora; two were encountered in the destruction deposit (**26/199**, **26/200**) and two immediately below; the latter are hence earlier 4th century B.C. or earlier (**26/201**, **26/202**). The iron nails from the agora at Methone should be seen in the context of the bronze nails from the same area of the site, many of which were encountered in the destruction deposit (**26/133–26/144**). Additional bronze nails and tacks from the Hypogeion (Late Geometric and earlier Archaic) and other parts of the site (down to 354 B.C.) are more fully discussed in Chapter 15 and above (under **15/57**, **26/49**, **26/145–26/146**), as are iron nails and tacks (under **15/100**, **26/31**, **26/51**, **26/233**).

There are two types of iron nails from the agora, one with the head bent back toward one side (or folded head: **26/199–26/201**) and one with a broad and flat elliptical or circular head (**26/202**). Among the nails listed but not catalogued below, there were also some with a plain circular head. The definitive history of the nail in the Greek world has yet to be written, but typologies based on nails from specific sites have been provided from the Korykian Cave, Isthmia, Corinth, Kommos, Knossos, Olynthos, Torone,[304] and more recently at Stymphalos and Sindos.[305] There are, moreover, numerous iron nails, especially those with the head bent back, from the "royal"

FIGURE 26.56. a)–c) Agora large iron scraper, **26/196** (ΜΕΘ 1774); d) the author holding a modern tool of similar form and size, from the excavations at Pylos. a)–c) Drawing F. Skyvalida, photos I. Coyle; d) Photo Sarah Morris, courtesy of Jack Davis and Sharon Stocker, 2019

tombs at nearby Vergina, particularly in Tomb II, although these have not been systematically studied.[306] Perhaps the fullest treatment of nails is the study of those from Stymphalos by Monica Munaretto and Gerald Schaus, who distinguish six types: I, with large heads; II, medium heads; III, small heads; IV, tacks; V, folded heads; and VI, bolts; indeed, the same types of iron nails continue into the Hellenistic and later periods.[307] I have eschewed following these typologies, except in a very general way, as none covers the full range of nails and tacks at Methone.

26/199. (ΜΕΘ 4260 [ΜΕ 4125]) Nail Fig. 26.57

Agora #274/029001 [1].

L. (as bent) 0.086–0.087; L. x W. (head) 0.020 x 0.013; L. x W. (shaft) 0.007–0.008 x 0.007 x 0.008; Wt. 14.9 g.

Intact, but bent as shown; corroded.

Shaft square in section, tapering toward point, which is bent. Head roughly triangular in shape and extending only onto one side of the shaft.

Context destruction deposit, mid-4th century B.C. or earlier.

26/200. (ΜΕΘ 5333 [ΜΕ 4084]) Nail Fig. 26.57

Agora #274/059010 [3].

P.L. 0.087; L. x W. (head) 0.020 x 0.019; Th. (L. x W., shaft) 0.009 x 0.009; Wt. 25.7 g.

Single fr preserving most of nail, except for lower point. Corroded, but condition quite good.

Shaft square in section, beginning to taper toward point, which is not preserved. Head flattened and extending only onto one side.

Context destruction deposit, mid-4th century B.C. or earlier.

26/201. (ΜΕΘ 5345 [ΜΕ 4247]) Nail Fig. 26.57

Agora #274/066. Περιοχή βόρεια του Τ.19 (area north of Wall 19).

P.L. 0.065; L. x W. (head) 0.012 x 0.008; Th. (shaft, max) 0.006 x 0.007; Wt. 8.9 g.

Single fr preserving most of nail, except for lower point. Corroded.

Type as **26/200** (ΜΕΘ 5333), but smaller, with shaft rectangular in section, in places more ovoid. Head flattened, and extending onto one side as shown.

Immediately below destruction deposit, early 4th century B.C. or earlier.

26/202. (ΜΕΘ 4345 [ΜΕ 4252]) Fragmentary Nail Fig. 26.57

Agora #274/066. Περιοχή βόρεια του Τ.19 (area north of Wall 19).

P.L. 0.049; Diam. (head, max) 0.032; Wt. 15.7 g.

Single fr preserving nail head and portion of upper shaft. Corroded.

Shaft circular or square in section (difficult to tell due to corrosion). Comparatively large and rather thin elliptical to circular head, bent as shown.

Immediately below destruction deposit, early 4th century B.C. or earlier.

Additional iron nails:

ΜΕ 4101. Agora #274/019002 [1]. Type as **26/199–26/201**. L. 0.090; L. x W. (head) 0.015 x 0.11; Th. (shaft) 0.006 x 0.006; Wt. 14.6 g.

ΜΕ 4106. Agora #274/019002 [1]. Κάτω απ'το στρώμα κεραμιδιών (below layer of tiles). Type with circular head. P.L. (main fr) 0.052; Diam./L. (head, max) 0.016; Wt. 8.1 g.

ΜΕ 4202. Agora #274/066. Βόρειο τμήμα (north section). Head much worn, probably circular. L. (as bent) 0.092; p.Diam. (head) 0.013–0.015; Th. (shaft) 0.006 x 0.005; Wt. 12.2 g.

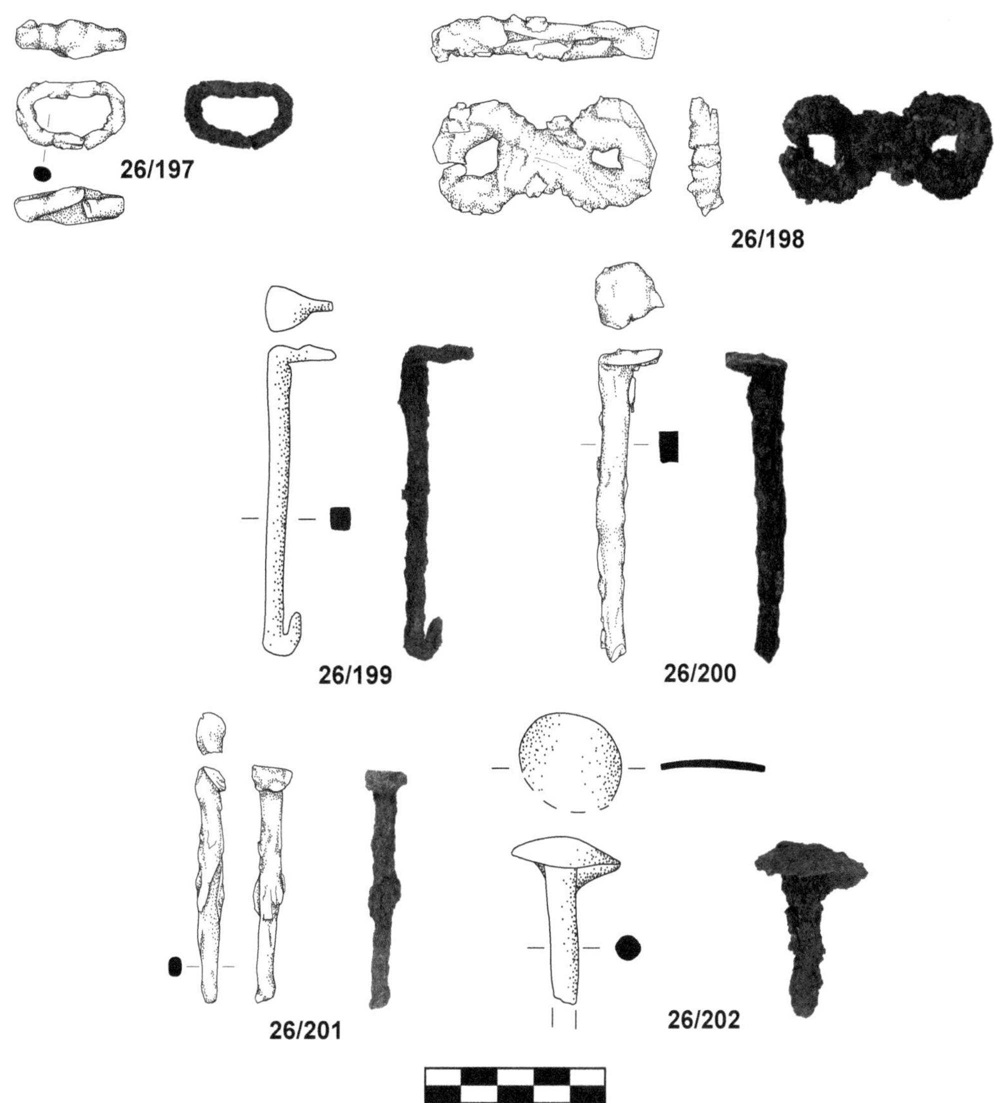

FIGURE 26.57. Agora iron rings (*krikoi*) and related, **26/197** (ΜΕΘ 5291), **26/198** (ΜΕΘ 1754); iron nails, **26/199** (ΜΕΘ 4260), **26/200** (ΜΕΘ 5333), **26/201** (ΜΕΘ 5345), **26/202** (ΜΕΘ 4345). Drawings T. Ross and F. Skyvalida, photos I. Coyle and J. Vanderpool

Cylinder/tube segment

The solitary tubular segment, **26/203**, was found in the destruction deposit. The slight articulations near the center on either side are almost certainly the result of corrosion rather than an intentional feature. Although **26/203** resembles the tubular iron beads that are not uncommon in tombs in Early Iron Age Albania, it is twice the size of the Albanian beads, and of a type that is rare in Greece.[308] The piece, which seems to be complete as is, is best seen as something more functional rather than an item of personal ornament.

26/203. (ΜΕΘ 1769 [ΜΕ 3730]) Cylinder Segment Fig. 26.58

Agora #274/027020 [2]. Βόρειος μάρτυρας, γκρίζο στρώμα (north balk, gray layer).

L./H. 0.025; Diam. 0.030; Wt. 12.4 g.

Single fr preserving segment of cylinder/tube; evidently complete, but corroded.

Flat sheet of iron formed into a tube.

Context destruction deposit, mid-4th century B.C. or earlier.

Attachment(?)

26/204 preserves an unknown portion of an incomplete object of unclear function. That it served as an attachment is also moot; this was suggested by a possible, but unclear, rivet-like connection on one side, but which does not extend through the piece. Although vaguely reminiscent of some of the architectural fixtures, such as those from Isthmia, nothing comes close in shape or purpose.[309] **26/204** is thus presented as a problem piece in need of an interpretation.

26/204. (ΜΕΘ 1771 [ΜΕ 3962]) Attachment(?) Fig. 26.58

Agora #274/027020 [2]. Βόρειος μάρτυρας, γκρίζο στρώμα (north balk, gray layer).

P.L/H. 0.068; W. (max) 0.032; W. (min) 0.018; Wt. 36.6 g.

Two joining frr preserving undetermined portion of object; corroded.

Circular end (at top, as shown), with volute-like extensions on either side, seems to be original; this stands above a thin flat strut that splays out toward the opposite end. Possible, but unclear, rivet-like connection/strut toward bottom, but only on one side.

Context destruction deposit, mid-4th century B.C. or earlier.

Objects of Lead

In comparison to other areas of the site, the excavations in the area of the agora of Methone brought to light a good number of lead objects, many of them from the destruction deposit of 354 B.C. In comparison to the material from the Hypogeion—a few lead fishnet weights and a fragmentary lead clamp—the agora of Methone presents a significant increase in the number of lead objects. There is, moreover, a broader range of such objects in the Classical period than in earlier times, including mending clamps, weights (both a square weight or balance and suspension weights), a lead wheel or wheel pendant, lead sheet, including one with a fragmentary inscription, rods and strips of lead, together with a rounded or globular lump, some of which may have served as ingots, as well as amorphous lumps of lead ready to be worked.

FIGURE 26.58. Agora iron cylinder/tube segment, **26/203** (ΜΕΘ 1769); iron attachment(?), **26/204** (ΜΕΘ 1771). Drawings T. Ross, photos I. Coyle

Mending clamps

The seven lead clamps presented below are mostly of the standard type, with horizontal struts usually plano-convex in section, less commonly rectangular, and their vertical struts circular in section. A full discussion is provided in Chapter 15 for the solitary lead clamp from the Hypogeion (under **15/107**), with supplementary notes above (under **26/52**), including comparanda for prehistoric, Early Iron Age to Classical clamps (see especially Chapter 15). The standard clamps are presented below according to size, beginning with the largest (**26/205**, L. 0.090) to the smallest (**26/209**, L. 0.027), except for **26/210**, which is much damaged. In addition to the standard clamps, **26/211** is a circular mending clamp that also served as a plug; it is similar to two others, **26/35** from the summit of the West Hill, and **26/53** from the east slopes of the West Hill, as well as a very similar Early Iron Age example from Torone.[310] Contextually, the earliest of the agora lead clamps is **26/208**, which is Early Iron Age to Archaic; the latest is **26/206** from the destruction deposit; the contexts of the majority were unclear (**26/207**, **26/209–26/211**), and one was found in the collapsed fill above the destruction deposit (**26/205**), which yielded material from the prehistoric period to the 4th century B.C.

26/205. (ΜΕΘ 4368 [ΜΕ 1336]) Mending Clamp Fig. 26.59

Agora #274/066. Στρώμα διάβρωσης (collapsed fill).

L. 0.090; H. 0.025; Wt. 61.5 g.

Intact.

Large clamp, with horizontal struts plano-convex in section; vertical struts circular in section.

Context collapsed fill above destruction deposit, prehistoric to mid-4th century B.C.

26/206. (ΜΕΘ 4367 [ΜΕ 3918]) Mending Clamp Fig. 26.59

Agora #274/018004 [2]. Δάπεδο (floor).

P.L. (as bent) 0.064; Wt. 50.7 g.

Single fr preserving all or most of horizontal strut, much of one vertical strut, but only the stump of the second.

Large clamp, with horizontal strut plano-convex in section; vertical strut circular in section. The stump of the second strut, unlike the first, is not at the edge of the clamp.

Context destruction deposit, mid-4th century B.C. or earlier.

26/207. (ΜΕΘ 4372 [ΜΕ 404]) Mending Clamp Fig. 26.59

Agora #274/007004 [1].

L. 0.037; H. 0.017; Wt. 11.3 g.

More or less intact.

Smaller clamp, with horizontal struts plano-convex in section; vertical struts circular.

Context unclear.

26/208. (ΜΕΘ 2146 [ΜΕ 4154]) Mending Clamp Fig. 26.59

Agora #274/068. Βόρειος μάρτυρας (north balk).

L. 0.028; W. 0.023; Wt. 13.1 g.

Single fr preserving complete clamp, except for edges of one horizontal strut, which are slightly chipped.

Small clamp, with horizontal struts more rectangular than plano-convex in section; vertical struts circular.

Context pre-destruction deposit, Early Iron Age to Archaic.

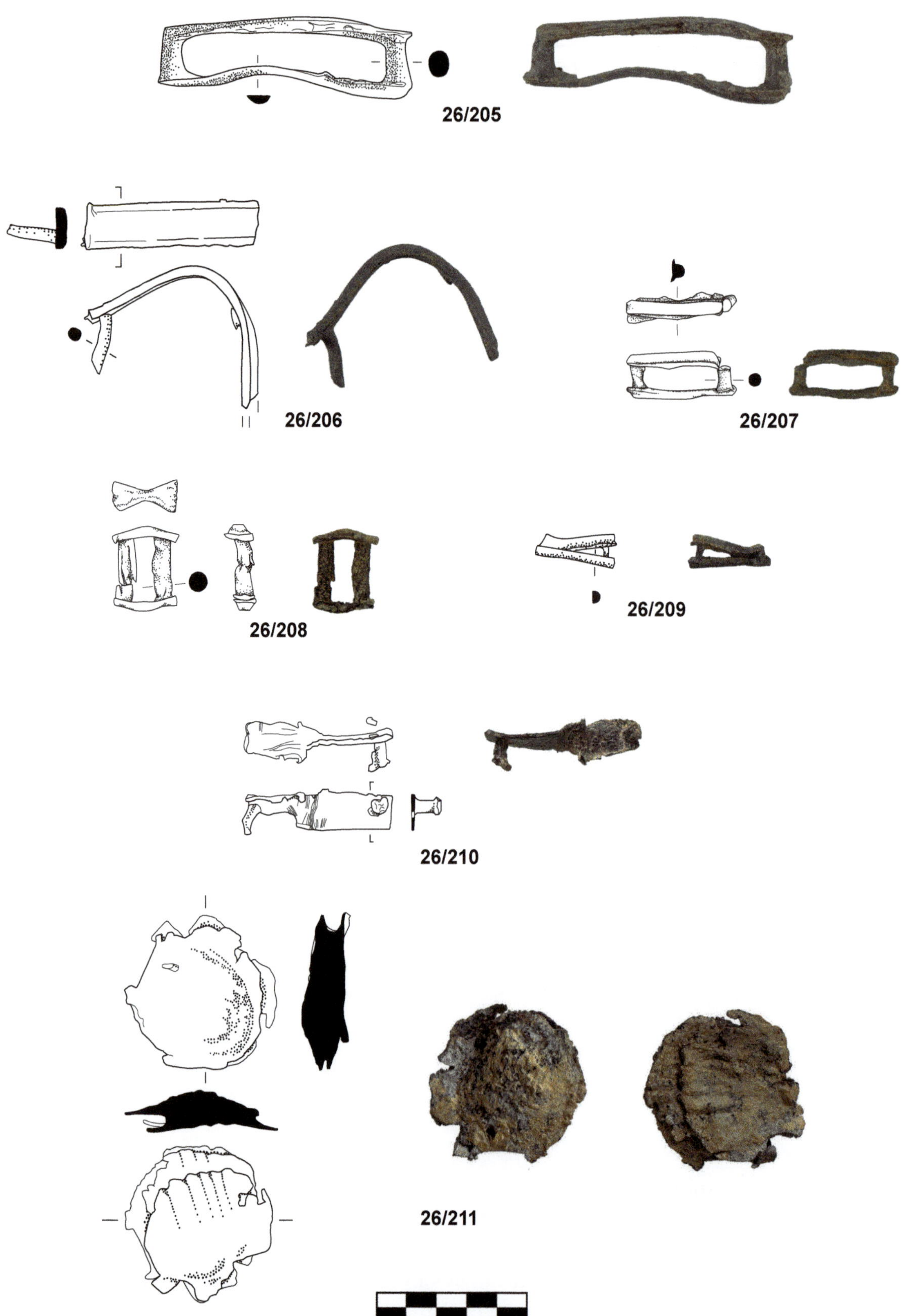

FIGURE 26.59. Agora lead mending clamps, **26/205** (ΜΕΘ 4368), **26/206** (ΜΕΘ 4367), **26/207** (ΜΕΘ 4372), **26/208** (ΜΕΘ 2146), **26/209** (ΜΕΘ 1712), **26/210** (ΜΕΘ 4371), **26/211** (ΜΕΘ 4366). Drawings A. Hooton, T. Ross, and F. Skyvalida, photos I. Coyle and J. Vanderpool

26/209. (ΜΕΘ 1712 [ΜΕ 2851]) Mending Clamp Fig. 26.59
Agora #274/065. ΝΔ τμήμα (SW section).
L. 0.027; H. 0.011; L. x W. (horizontal struts) 0.024 x 0.007, 0.027 x 0.005; Wt. 5.5 g.
Complete, but pushed down onto itself on one side.
Small clamp, with horizontal struts plano-convex in section; well-preserved strut circular in section, the other completely pushed down.
Context unclear.

26/210. (ΜΕΘ 4371 [ΜΕ 447]) Fragmentary Mending Clamp Fig. 26.59
Agora #274/056006 [3].
L. 0.052; p.H. 0.013; L. x W. (horizontal strut) 0.052 x 0.012; Wt. 12.1 g.
Single fr preserving one horizontal strut and portions of two vertical struts; bent and chipped in parts.
Larger but damaged clamp, with horizontal strut rectangular as preserved; one vertical strut more or less circular in section, the other elliptical.
Context unclear.

26/211. (ΜΕΘ 4366 [ΜΕ 1866]) Mending Clamp & Plug Fig. 26.59
Agora #274/009011 [3]. Περιοχή ανάμεσα Τ.22 και Τ.25 (area between Walls 22 and 25).
P.L./Diam. 0.054; p.H. 0.016; Wt. 146/6 g.
Single piece preserving substantial portion of clamp.
Two roughly circular plates, one thinner than the other, connected only on one side, serving as both clamp and plug.
Context unclear.

Weights

The most characteristic example of a lead weight or balance from Methone is **26/212**, encountered in the destruction deposit of 354 B.C. Intact, and more or less square (0.028 x 0.026, with a thickness of 0.005 m), the piece weighs 32.8 g. Two similar nearly square lead weights are known from Sardis, but they are larger and significantly heavier (one measures 0.046 x 0.048, with a weight of 253.20 g; the other 0.047 x 0.048, with a weight of 182.15 g).[311] Both are considered Lydian, and one is dated to the 6th century B.C.[312] The surfaces of both the Sardis examples are not carefully smoothed, and one seems to have a slight inset, not unlike **26/212**. Three similar lead weights from Corinth, all three inscribed, are of similar date to **26/212**, two dating to the 5th or 4th century B.C., and one to the 4th or 3rd century B.C.; they are also larger than the example from Methone (no. 1580: W. 0.084, Wt. 825 g; no. 1581: W. 0.093; Wt. 1,195 g; no. 1582, W. 0.052, Wt. 137.45 g), with slight insets on one side of all three.[313] In terms of established weights, it is difficult to discern what standard **26/212** conforms to. For example, dividing the Solonian mina (436.60 g) by 32.8 g gives 13.31; doing the same with the μνᾶ ἀγοραῖα (654.9 g) and the μνᾶ ἐμπορική (602.6 g) gives 19.96 and 18.37 respectively, with **26/212** representing about 1/20 of the μνᾶ ἀγοραῖα.[314] Two related lead weights of the Classical period from Torone (one L. x W. 0.048 x 0.039, Wt. 216.9 g; the other 0.053 x 0.041, Wt. 205.95 g), both inscribed with the letter H, are discussed in the context of the Euboian standard.[315] Similar weights of Hellenistic and Roman date may be noted from the Athenian Agora, and Olynthos has yielded various weights.[316] It is worth mentioning that at some sites, lead disks of various sizes, both perforated and unperforated, have been considered as weights.[317]

Both **26/213** and **26/214** are suspension weights. The former was also encountered in the destruction deposit; the latter was found in a surface level and, as such, its date is uncertain. I can certainly imagine **26/213** used as a sinker for fishing,[318] but such weights could have served any number of functions, such as the suspected lead loomweights from Corinth, Isthmia, and Olynthos.[319] Elsewhere, such lead weights have been found with stamped impressions.[320] Although it lacks a suspension eyelet or perforation, **26/214** should be a suspension weight, the upper stem slightly wider to accommodate the tying of thread; its bottom is flat. I can also imagine this as a weight used for fishing, but again, any number of functions may be noted. Several similar bronze, lead, or stone weights from Corinth can be cited as comparanda, but all are either Late Roman or Byzantine.[321] Among alternative functions that have been suggested for suspended lead objects, loomweights, pendants, and sinkers have been noted, but another interpretation of interest is a conical lead weight with suspension loop at the top, encountered in the foundation trench of the later Classical/early Hellenistic fortification wall at Torone, thought to be a plumb bob used in construction work.[322] Its shape is rather different, however, from **26/213** and **26/214**.

26/212. (ΜΕΘ 2182 [ΜΕ 257]) Weight or Balance — Fig. 26.60

Agora #274/018006 [2]. Δάπεδο (floor).

L. x W. x Th. 0.028 x 0.026 x 0.005; Wt. 32.8 g.

Intact; well preserved.

Roughly square block of lead, flat on one side, but with a slight inset, as shown, on other side. No visible inscriptions.

Context destruction deposit, mid-4th century B.C. or earlier.

26/213. (ΜΕΘ 1710 [ΜΕ 950]) Suspension Weight — Fig. 26.60

Agora #274/087. Στρώμα καταστροφής (destruction layer).

H. 0.036; L. x W. (bottom) 0.014 x 0.009; L. x W. (top) 0.009 x 0.006; Wt. 27.3 g.

Intact.

Small, roughly pyramidal weight, nearly rectangular at top and bottom, with small elliptical hole.

Context destruction deposit, mid-4th century B.C. or earlier.

26/214. (ΜΕΘ 1526 [ΜΕ 786]) Suspension Weight — Fig. 26.60

Agora #274. Επιφανειακό στρώμα (surface layer).

H. 0.018; Diam. (max) 0.014; Wt. 17.4 g.

Single fr preserving complete or near-complete object (uncertain is original length of stem); pitted at points.

Small globe, flattened at the bottom, with a small cylinder of lead extending from center of top. Form of suspension uncertain, but slight thickening at top of stem would have facilitated the tying of thread.

Surface find, context uncertain.

Related

There are no cogent parallels for **26/215**, which is placed here because, whatever its original function, it was meant to be suspended. I do not think it is a weight, but it may have served as a pendant of sorts, even though lead pendants are not common. Among the standard pendants in the Greek world, the only ones that are in any way related are the so-called "Vögel auf Scheibe"—or "bird-on-disk"—pendants, which are invariably of bronze, and without the bird, only the suspension rod, tied back on itself to form a loop.[323] The only thing that can be said about **26/215** with any certainty is its date, as it was found in the destruction deposit of 354 B.C.

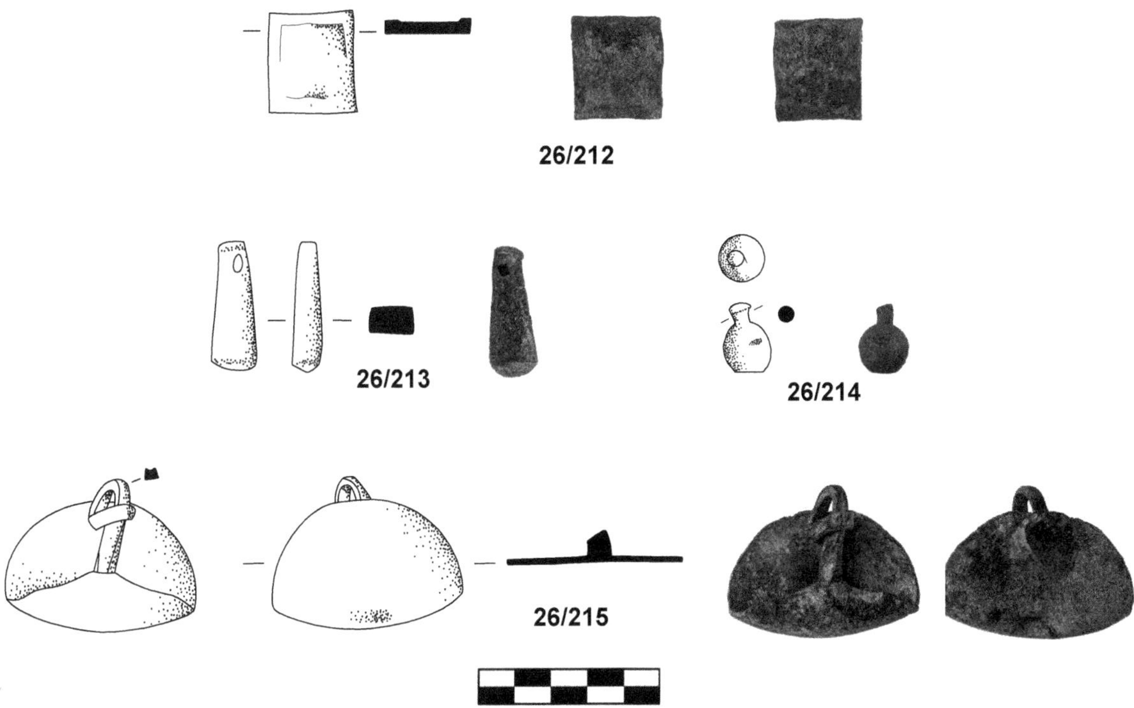

FIGURE 26.60. Agora lead weights, **26/212** (MEΘ 2182), **26/213** (MEΘ 1710), **26/214** (MEΘ 1526); related, **26/215** (MEΘ 2149). Drawings F. Skyvalida, photos I. Coyle and J. Vanderpool

26/215. (MEΘ 2149 [ME 4018]) Unidentified Suspended Object Fig. 26.60

Agora #274/028001 [1].

Diam. (disk, original Diam.) 0.056; Th. (disk) 0.002; L. (rod and tie) 0.026; Wt. 47.9 g.

Evidently intact, but bent onto itself (as if intentionally "killed").

Thin, circular disk, bent over onto itself, with a rod attached at upper edge on one side of disk. Rod square/rectangular in section, rising well above level of the disk and tied back on itself, in a loop, as shown.

Context destruction deposit, mid-4th century B.C. or earlier.

Wheel or wheel pendant

The solitary lead wheel from the agora at Methone, **26/216**, was a surface find, and its date is thus uncertain. It is not unlike a four-spoked lead wheel, of the same size, from the Archaic sanctuary on the Timpone della Motta at Francavilla Marittima, the extramural sanctuary of Sybaris.[324] Such small lead wheels are uncommon in comparison to the more numerous bronze wheels, often thought to have once been attached to votive model chariots or carts, like the many published examples from Olympia, as well as some from Delphi, and elsewhere.[325] Related wagons, both life-size and model votives, are a common feature of Bronze and Early Iron Age Italy.[326] The recent publication of the cemetery at Sindos near Methone has brought to light no shortage of model two- and four-wheeled bronze and iron carts in tombs.[327] The possibility that some of these may have been toys cannot be dismissed. Alternatively, such small wheels may have served as pendants or other items of jewelry.[328] There are also a number of bronze wheels from various sanctuaries in the Greek world that are inscribed, sometimes with a dedication to a particular deity, sometimes with the name of the dedicant, that may have been offerings in themselves, and not part of a votive wagon or pendant.[329]

26/216. (MEΘ 1713 [ME 1878]) Wheel Fig. 26.61

Agora #274/. Surface find.

L. (as preserved = original Diam.) 0.034; Diam. (central hole) 0.005–0.006; Wt. 3.5 g.

Intact, but misformed, bent back onto itself.

Four-spoked wheel, made of thin sheet lead, with elliptical hole at center. There is only one outer circle of the wheel (no second circle).

Surface find, context uncertain.

Lead sheet

The epigraphic habit at Methone was not limited to post-firing inscriptions on pottery or pre-firing potters' marks and other notations on vases (Chapter 11). Although never common, inscriptions on metal at Methone were not unknown, and **26/217**, found in the destruction deposit of 354 B.C., is one of the rare inscriptions on lead from the site. It is a small and thin rectangular lead sheet that resembles some of the *pinakia* from the Athenian Agora, although with a length of 0.047, it is smaller than those.[330] As is outlined in *Agora* XXVIII, the "pinakia that are used in various dikastic procedures are of three sorts: (1) the πινάκιον τιμητικόν on which dikasts would mark an assessment; (2) the tablets on which parties to an action would write down notes, memoranda, and challenges; (3) the tablets of bronze (later, boxwood) that served as dikasts' identification tags."[331] Poorly preserved in the upper left corner of the plaque, the few surviving letters are barely visible, and they are presented in the catalogue entry below in a preliminary reading by Yannis Tzifopoulos. The nature of the letters, the fact that the sheet appears to have been folded, and that the opposite side of the *pinakion* may have been smoothed, with earlier letters possibly

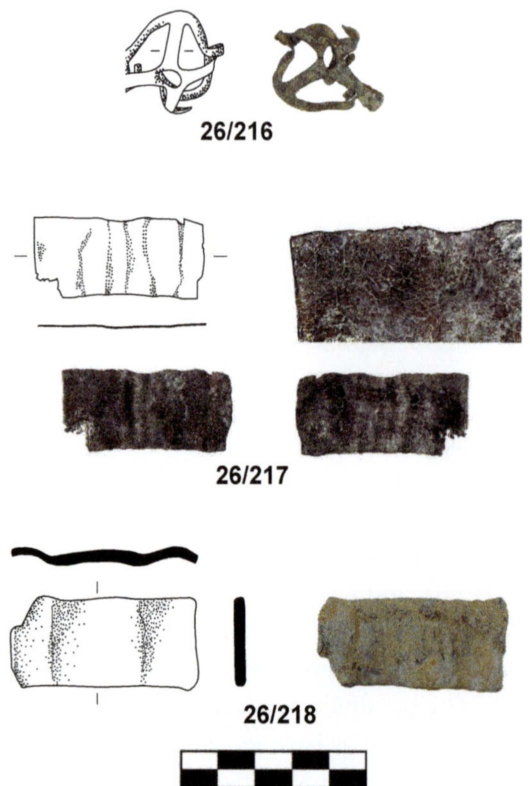

FIGURE 26.61. Agora lead wheel, **26/216** (MEΘ 1713); lead sheet, **26/217** (MEΘ 4378, including detail), **26/218** (MEΘ 4365). Drawings A. Hooton and F. Skyvalida, photos I. Coyle and J. Vanderpool

erased, is more in keeping with Greek private letters written on lead sheets, although **26/217** is smaller than most of the known letters.[332] A fuller assessment of the inscription will be presented by Tzifopoulos.

Although of similar dimensions, **26/218** is not only thicker and heavier than **26/217**, it is also earlier, found in a pre-destruction context in association with material of the later Early Iron and Archaic date. There are no visible traces of letters. Even less can be said of the fragmentary **26/219**, except that it is perforated and was also encountered in the destruction deposit. **26/220** and **26/221** are smaller, and both are roughly elliptical; they recall the small lead disks from Isthmia that Raubitschek refers to as lead weights, though most of those are more rounded.[333] A further fragment of a lead sheet, **26/222**, was found, bent out of shape, in the destruction deposit of 354 B.C.

26/217. (MEΘ 4378 [ME 1878]) Sheet (*Pinakion*) Fig. 26.61

Agora #274/059003 [2].

L. 0.047; W./H. 0.022; Th. 0.001; Wt. 5.0 g.

Single fr preserving almost complete sheet, except for lower left corner, as shown (on side with inscription), and minor tears along edge.

Thin rectangular sheet of lead, now flat, but evidently once folded over. On one side incised, but very faint letters, beginning at upper left corner and oriented left to right. The letters are difficult to make out, but on a preliminary reading, Yannis Tzifopoulos reads: Line 1: I I Λ A; Line 2: NA or NΛ (perhaps). On the opposite side the surface displays tool marks running horizontally, suggesting that the surface may have been smoothed, with earlier letters possibly erased.

Context destruction deposit, mid-4th century B.C. or earlier.

26/218. (MEΘ 4365 [ME 1762]) Sheet Fig. 26.61

Agora #274/007031 [10].

P.L. x W./H. 0.052 x 0.025; Wt. 27.5 g.

Single fr preserving undetermined portion of sheet, and probably most of it; creased as points, as if it was once folded.

Roughly rectangular sheet of lead, but thicker than **26/217** (MEΘ 4378).

Context pre-destruction deposit, Early Iron Age to Archaic.

26/219. (MEΘ 4374 [ME 2577]) Fragmentary Sheet, Perforated Fig. 26.62

Agora #274/059003 [2].

P.L. 0.053; Wt. 9.1 g.

Single fr preserving undetermined portion of sheet, but with one edge clearly preserved (along left edge of drawing, as shown).

Thin lead sheet, perhaps originally rectangular. At least one pierced hole, with two others, either intentional or accidental, at break. Perhaps more holes originally?

Context destruction deposit, mid-4th century B.C. or earlier.

26/220. (MEΘ 4375 [ME 1755]) Elliptical Sheet Fig. 26.62

Agora #274/007030 [10].

L. x W. 0.038 x 0.025; Th. 0.004; Wt. 30.0 g.

Intact.

Thick, roughly elliptical sheet, pointed at one end, more rounded on the other.

Context destruction deposit, mid-4th century B.C. or earlier.

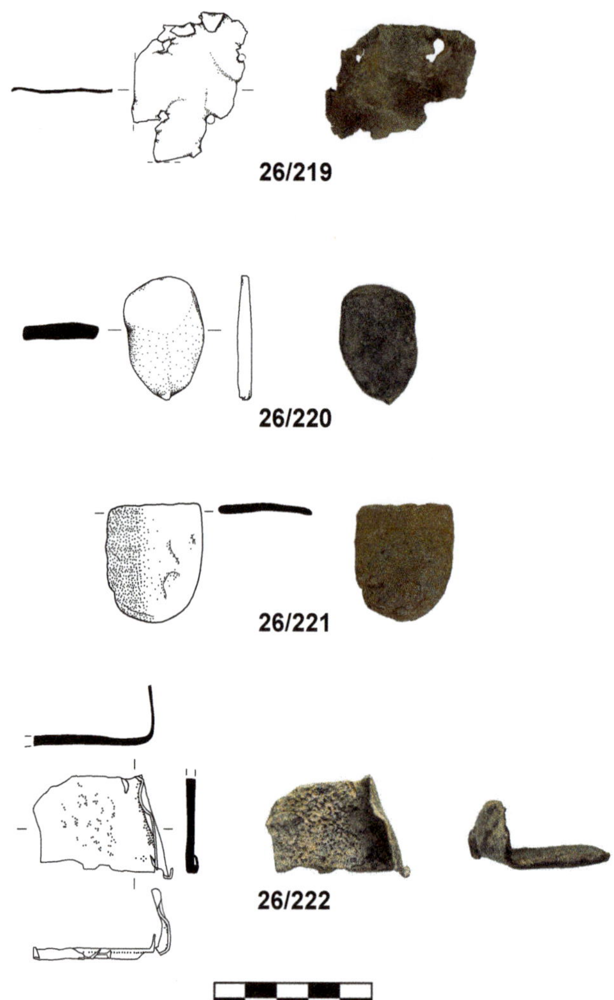

FIGURE 26.62. Agora lead sheet (continued), **26/219** (ΜΕΘ 4374), **26/220** (ΜΕΘ 4375), **26/221** (ΜΕΘ 4376), **26/222** (ΜΕΘ 2147). Drawings A. Hooton, T. Ross, and F. Skyvalida, photos I. Coyle and J. Vanderpool

26/221. (ΜΕΘ 4376 [ΜΕ 1347]) Elliptical Sheet Fig. 26.62

Agora #274/066. Στρώμα καστανό [2] (brown layer [2]).

L. x W. 0.037 x 0.032; Wt. 22.3 g.

Intact.

Roughly elliptical, almost semicircular sheet, rounded at one end, straight at the other; thinner in section to **26/220** (ΜΕΘ 4375).

Context unclear.

26/222. (ΜΕΘ 2147 [ΜΕ 3994]) Fragmentary Sheet Fig. 26.62

Agora #274/018006 [2]. Δάπεδο (floor).

P.L. (as bent) 0.045; W. (max) 0.033; Th. ranging from 0.002–0.005; Wt. 41.6 g.

Single fr preserving undetermined portion of lead sheet, and conceivably much of it; bent over, as shown, and frayed around the edges.

Mostly thin sheet, but noticeably thicker in parts, with clear edge along one side (along the top edge on the first of the two photographs).

Context destruction deposit, mid-4th century B.C. or earlier.

Rods (ingots?) and strip of lead

There are two rods of lead, **26/223** and **26/224**, and one strip, **23/225**; of these, **26/223** and **26/225** were found in pre-destruction contexts in association with material of the late Early Iron Age and Archaic period, whereas **26/224** was encountered in the destruction deposit of 354 B.C. The two lead rods or bars are related to the more than 70 lead "ingots" from the sanctuary of Poseidon at Isthmia, dating to the Archaic and Classical periods, dates that accord nicely with both **26/223** and **26/224**.[334] Some of the Isthmia bars were marked either with cast letters, or incised, or bore graffiti, or both incised letters and graffiti, but many had no markings.[335] Related bars, some with markings, are known from the sanctuary of Zeus at Nemea, as well as from Classical Olynthos.[336] Similar rods or bars from Olympia and the Aphaia sanctuary on Aigina have been interpreted as architects' and workmen's "pencils" ("Bleistifte"), and their contexts, together with that of the examples from Isthmia, suggest that they may well have been used as markers during construction.[337] Although attempts have been made to calculate standardized weights for these "ingots," the paucity of examples from Methone, coupled with their fragmentary state, does not allow any conclusive statements.[338]

The perforated strip of lead, **26/225**, is of interest for its form, which is described in the entry below. How it functioned is unclear, nor is it known whether there were perforations on the side opposite the well-preserved terminal.

26/223. (ΜΕΘ 4364 [ΜΕ 3908]) Rod — Fig. 26.63

Agora #274/079. Τομή στη νότια πλευρά (trench on south side).

P.L./L. (as bent) 0.074; Diam. (shaft, max) 0.006; Wt. 18.6 g.

Single fr preserving undetermined portion of rod, though both ends, as preserved, may be original terminals.

Rod composed of shaft, circular in section, with one end evidently hammered flat and tapering to a point; opposite end very slightly concave.

Context pre-destruction deposit, late Early Iron Age to Archaic.

26/224. (ΜΕΘ 2148 [ΜΕ 3995]) Fragmentary Rod — Fig. 26.63

Agora #274/018006 [2]. Δάπεδο (floor).

P.L. 0.047–0.048; W. (max) 0.010; W. (central portion of rod) 0.006; Wt. 6.6 g.

Single fr preserving portion of rod.

Central portion of rod rectangular/rhomboidal in section, flattened at both ends, as shown. It is unclear whether the piece originally extended on either side.

Context destruction deposit, mid-4th century B.C. or earlier.

26/225. (ΜΕΘ 4363 [ΜΕ 3805]) Perforated Strip — Fig. 26.63

Agora #274/089. Τομή στη βόρεια πλευρά (trench on north side).

L./p.L. (as bent) 0.055; W. 0.013; Th. 0.002; Wt. 18.4 g.

Single fr preserving undetermined portion of strip, perhaps near complete; one short end probably broken, the other bent and damaged. Slightly torn in places.

Relatively thin and narrow strip of lead, with a small ridge running down the center on one side; the other side is plain and flat. Two small holes near one end, next to one another on one side of the small ridge. Long edges nicely beveled.

Context pre-destruction deposit, late Early Iron Age to Archaic.

Globular piece of lead (ingot?)

I have placed the globular piece of lead, **26/226**, here because such domed but flattened pieces of lead—essentially plano-convex in shape—may also have served as ingots of sorts. Indeed, the round, plano-convex or "bun"-shaped ingots from the Cape Gelidonya and Uluburun shipwrecks certainly allow the possibility that **26/226** was an ingot.[339] Its context did not provide any clear information as to its date.

26/226. (ΜΕΘ 4373 [ΜΕ 2222]) Globular Piece of Lead Fig. 26.63

Agora #274/085. Ανατολικός μάρτυρας (east balk).

Diam. 0.036; H. 0.023; Wt. 73.4 g.

Intact.

Small globular piece of lead, flattened on one side, rounded or domed on the other. Slight and partial groove on one side as shown.

Context unclear.

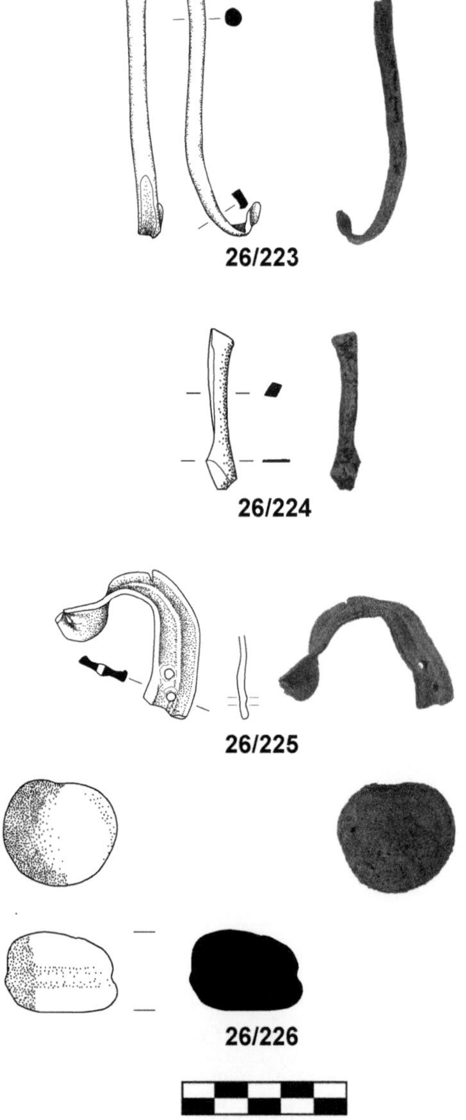

FIGURE 26.63. Agora rods and strips of lead, **26/223** (ΜΕΘ 4364), **26/224** (ΜΕΘ 2148), **26/225** (ΜΕΘ 4363); globular piece of lead (ingot?), **26/226** (ΜΕΘ 4373). Drawings T. Ross and F. Skyvalida, photos I. Coyle

Lead filling

One of the most common uses of lead was as a filling for all sorts of fixtures and implements, from handle and base fillers of bronze vessels, to fillers of statues, or mounts for statue bases, in which case they were often set into a stone.[340] The form of **26/227** suggests that it was a fairly substantial filling, the domed and rounded bottom inserted, probably into stone, and hence its rough finish, and the carefully smoothed opposite side, the top, with prominent groove would, if more complete, provide a better idea of what it was originally associated with. A number of cup-shaped pieces of lead from Isthmia were interpreted as the linings of pivot holes to receive metal rods on which the door swung, and these match pieces actually in situ in ancient houses elsewhere, but **26/227** is too large to serve such a purpose.[341] It is clearly associated with something more substantial than a door pivot or setting.

26/227. (ΜΕΘ 4377 [ΜΕ 360]) Lead Filling Fig. 26.64

Agora #274/085018 [7].

P.L. 0.082; p.H. 0.032; Wt. 307.7 g.

Single fr preserving undetermined portion of large object.

There is a rounded or domed side, which was left rough (what I take to be the bottom), whereas the opposite side (or top) was nicely finished, with a substantial groove parallel to the edge.

Context unclear.

Amorphous lead

The first two pieces, **26/228** and **26/229**, are standard amorphous pieces of lead encountered occasionally at the site, that were evidently molten lead, spilled, whether intentionally or accidentally, and solidified, usually flat on one side, irregular on the other. Given the relatively low melting point of lead (327.5° C), such amorphous pieces would have been convenient sources of lead, particularly in periods of stress. **26/228** was encountered in the destruction deposit of 354 B.C., whereas the context of **26/229** was unclear.

When first encountered in its uncleaned state, **26/230** resembled an attachment of sorts, not unlike the bronze bindings/sheaths, especially **26/150** and **26/151**. Despite its roughly rectangular shape, the piece, once cleaned, was rather amorphous, perhaps representing a lead object melted out of its original form. The small finger-like extensions of lead resembled those, slightly larger, on **26/229**, and the rough surface on one side is very similar to the rougher surfaces of **26/228** and **26/229**.

26/228. (ΜΕΘ 1711 [ΜΕ 1545]) Amorphous Strip of Lead Fig. 26.64

Agora #274/076. Χώρος Ζ, στρώμα καταστροφής (Room 6, destruction level).

L. 0.305; W. (max) 0.042; H. 0.017; Wt. 521.5 g.

Single piece preserving long strip of spilled and cooled lead.

Irregular on one side, more or less flat on the other.

Context destruction deposit, mid-4th century B.C. or earlier.

26/229. (ΜΕΘ 4370 [ΜΕ 2762]) Amorphous Piece of Lead Fig. 26.65

Agora #274/075. ΝΔ τμήμα. Ξήλωμα Τ.8 (SW section, collapse and removal of Wall 8).

P.L. (max) 0.070; Wt. 87.7 g.

Single piece; unclear whether or not broken.

Amorphous and quite irregular lump of spilled and hardened lead, extending in various directions.

Context unclear.

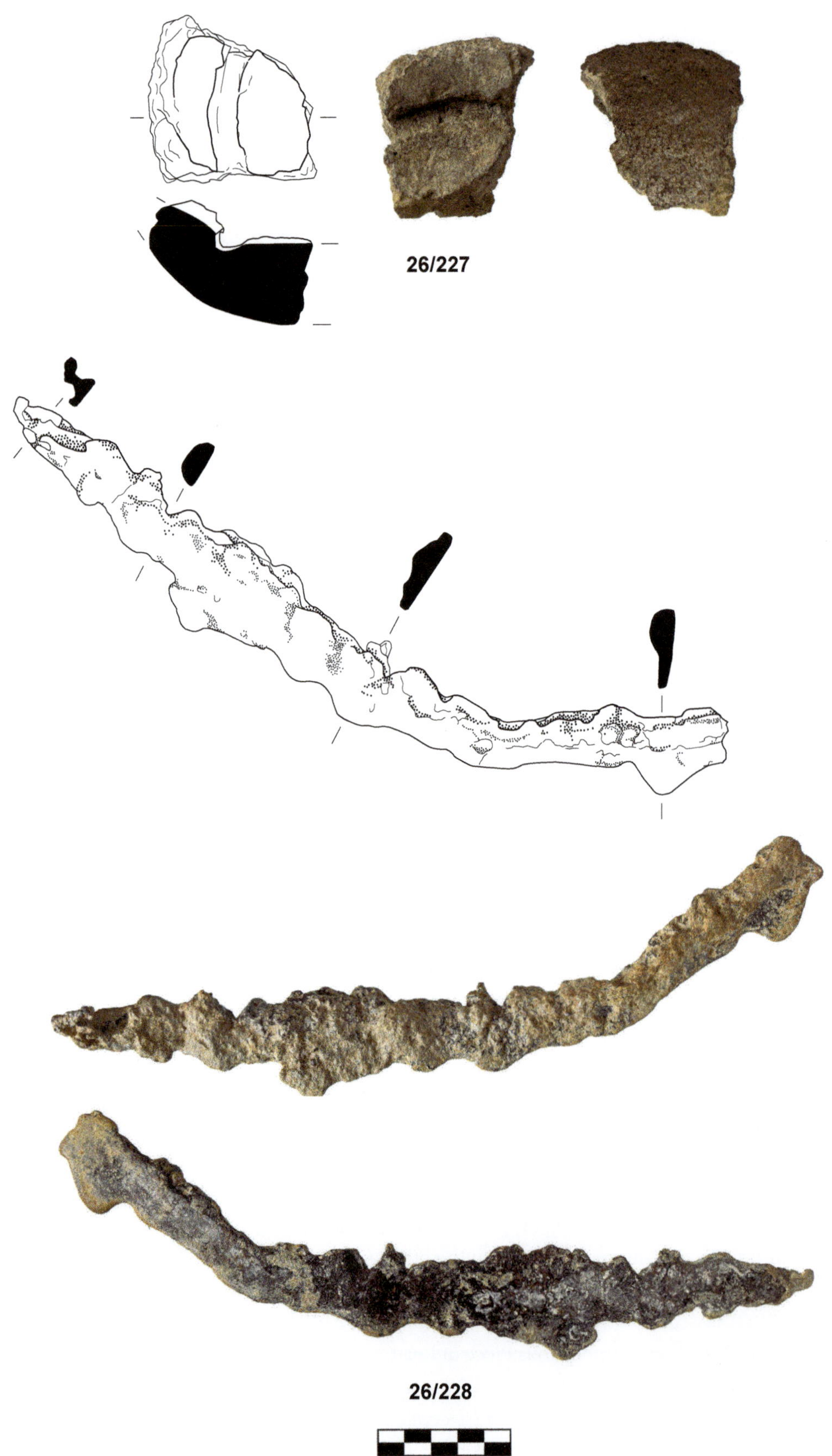

FIGURE 26.64. Agora lead filling, **26/227** (ΜΕΘ 4377); amorphous lead, **26/228** (ΜΕΘ 1711). Drawings A. Hooton, photos J. Vanderpool

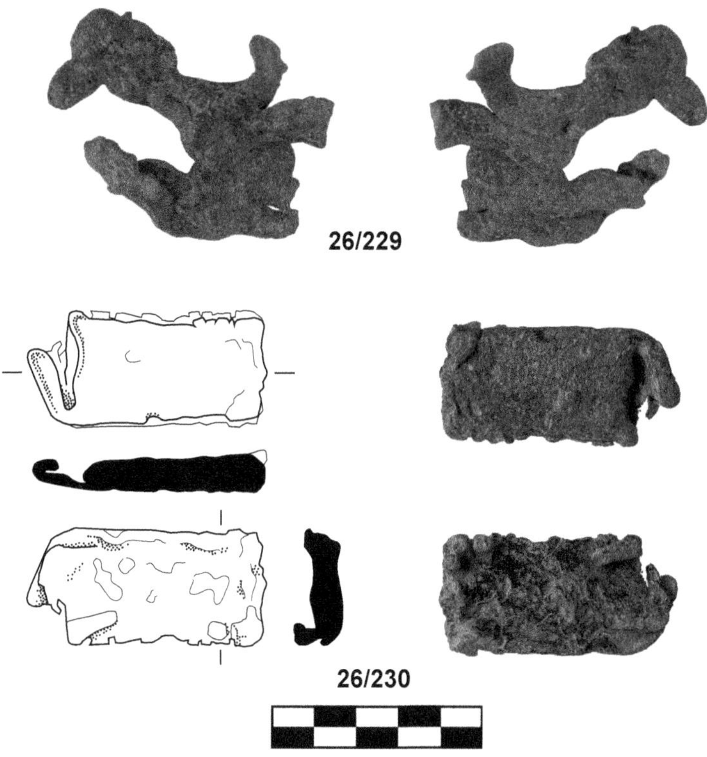

FIGURE 26.65. Agora amorphous lead (continued), **26/229** (ΜΕΘ 4370), **26/230** (ΜΕΘ 3100). Drawing A. Hooton, photos I. Coyle and J. Vanderpool

26/230. (ΜΕΘ 3100 [ΜΕ 4245]) Amorphous Piece of Lead Fig. 26.65

Agora #274/066. Χώρος βόρεια του Τ.19 (area north of Wall 19).

P.L. x W. 0.058 x 0.028; Wt. 81.3 g.

Single piece, which may be complete or almost complete as preserved.

Roughly rectangular piece, smoother on one side, rough on the other. A finger-like extension, plano-convex in section to one side, as shown, with thinner sheet of lead immediately below. Similar finger-like extension on opposite side, bent back. Small circular "boss" of sorts on lower left corner, probably accidental.

Context immediately below destruction deposit, Archaic to Classical period.

METAL FINDS FROM THE SOUTH HARBOR AREA (PLOT 278)

Only limited excavations were conducted in Plot 278, located on the eastern slope of the East Hill (Chapter 1). These excavations showed that, at least from the Archaic period, the settlement had extended to this area as well. For this to have occurred, a coastal zone had already existed or had been created here that prevented waves from eroding the hill. As is noted in Chapter 1, there is a strong possibility that there was a secondary harbor here, but this was always exposed to the severe southern winds that often batter the coast of Pieria. It was in Plot 278 that a small portion of another monumental building (Building Γ) was investigated, and it is even possible that there was another small square or open area here. Only a small portion of this area was investigated (for the location of Plot 278 see Fig. 1.1), and the excavations conducted in the area only yielded a small number of finds. The number of metal objects was paltry, and the three selected pieces include the most representative and diagnostic.

TABLE 26.4. Summary listing of the context and type of the metal objects from the area of the south harbor (Plot 278). The "date" column lists the contextual date of each piece

MEΘ	Metal	Context	Object	Context date
26/231 (MEΘ 2771)	Bronze	#278/002, 003 unstratified	Fishhook	Unclear
26/232 (MEΘ 2773)	Bronze	#278/005 unstratified	Triangular object	Backfill
26/233 (MEΘ 5017)	Iron	#245/004	Nail	Backfill

OBJECTS OF BRONZE

There are only two bronze objects from Plot 278, a fishhook and a small triangular object of uncertain function. Fishhooks have been fully discussed above, with comparanda (under **26/127–26/131**) and require no further comment. The small, roughly triangular object as preserved, **26/232**, which may have been originally lozenge-shaped, seemed rather heavy for its size and it may have been leaded; it also had a small, semicircular notch along one side. Whether intact or fragmentary, a clear function did not suggest itself. Although resembling **26/42**, **26/232** is a solid piece of metal, not a bronze sheet rolled up at one end, and it is a thicker version of **26/164**.

26/231. (MEΘ 2771) Bronze Fishhook Fig. 26.66

South harbor area #278/002, 003. Επίχωση βόρεια του τοίχου 2 (fill north of Wall 2).

L. 0.026; W. 0.015; Wt. 0.8 g.

Intact; heavily corroded.

Small shaft of bronze, circular in section and tapering toward a point formed into a barb. Opposite end hammered flat, and thus slightly wider than shaft to accommodate string.

Cf. *Isthmia* VII, pp. 121, 127, 129, pl. 71, nos. 453 (19 fishhooks), and 454.

26/232. (MEΘ 2773) Bronze Triangular Object Fig. 26.66

South harbor area #278/005. Backfill.

P.L./p.H. 0.030; W. 0.022; Th. 0.006; Wt. 15.4 g.

Bottom edge as shown evidently broken; condition otherwise good.

Thick and comparatively heavy (perhaps leaded?) bronze, triangular-shaped as preserved, with a consistent thickness and a small semicircular notch at the middle of the bottom. If broken, the original object may have been lozenge-shaped.

OBJECT OF IRON

The following object was originally found, in its unconserved state, together with another object and inventoried as one.[342] Following conservation, it was clear that the two were from separate objects. Only the main fragment preserving what is clearly an iron nail is presented below. Iron nails are fully discussed above, with references (under **26/31**, **26/51**, **26/199–26/202**), as are bronze nails (under **15/57–15/58**, **26/15**, **26/49–26/50**, **26/133–26/146**), and need no additional comment here.

26/233. (MEΘ 5017) Iron Nail Fig. 26.66

South harbor area #278/004. Backfill.

P.L. 0.068; Diam. (head) 0.053; Wt. 57.9 g.

One main fr preserving most of head and upper part of shaft of nail, with several smaller frr or crumbs; heavily corroded.

Large circular disk head. Comparatively thin upper shaft, square/rectangular in section, but in parts approaching triangular due to corrosion.

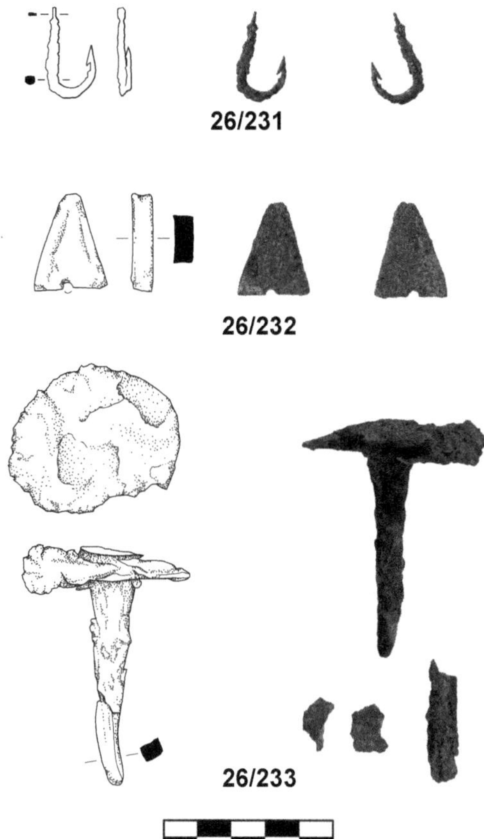

FIGURE 26.66. South harbor area, bronze fishhook, **26/231** (ΜΕΘ 2771); bronze triangular object, **26/232** (ΜΕΘ 2773); iron nail, **26/233** (ΜΕΘ 5017). Drawings A. Hooton and T. Ross, photos I. Coyle and J. Vanderpool

NOTES

1 Morris et al. 2020, pp. 701–703, figs. 52–53.

2 I am grateful to my colleagues Manthos Bessios and Konstantinos Noulas, excavators of the West Hill, for going over this material with me in detail.

3 Including the large number of lead sling bullets published in Chapter 28, and some of the weapons presented in this chapter.

4 For the earlier amphoras from the Hypogeion, see Chapter 12.

5 See Chapter 19, Figs. 19.6–19.9 (for Corinthian imported pottery), Fig. 19.10 (for Attic), and Fig. 19.11 (for Chalkidic). For the East Greek pottery from this deposit, see Chapter 22.

6 See, for example, the fragmentary Early Iron Age vessel illustrated in Fig. 19.4.

7 See Morris et al. 2020.

8 Truhelka 1904, p. 125, pl. 72, no. 12.

9 Vickers 1977, p. 17; see further Forsdyke 1931, pp. 82–83, and pl. XXXIII; Makridis 1937, col. 517 (pendants for a horse harness). Robinson (*Olynthus* X, pp. 521–522, pl. CLXVII, no. 2624) suggested, but quickly dismissed, the possibility that they were used to tighten lyre strings; he also suggested that they may have been associated with weaving.

10 Jantzen 1953. The notion remained unchallenged, especially among German scholars, well into the early 1970s. For actual jug stoppers in the Bronze Age, made of clay, see Van Damme 2019.

11 Kilian-Dirlmeier 1979, pp. 194–208.

12 Their chronological development was first suggested by Vickers (1977, pp. 19–21, with fig. 1); cf. Kilian-Dirlemeier (1979, pp. 206–208) on the chronology of these pendants.

13 Kilian-Dirlmeier 1979, pp. 197–199, pls. 64–67, nos. 1198–1229. For Type B, Kilian-Dirlmeier states: "Charakteristisches Merkmal der 'Kannenverschluß'-Anhänger von Typus B bildet die formelhaft schematisierte Figur des Hockenden. Der Körper ist zu einem blechartig dünnen Rechteck mit kaum einschwingenden Langsseiten reduziert, auf dem mit der Spitze nach unten ein ebenso flaches Dreieck als Kopf aufsitzt." In terms of Vickers' (1979, p. 20, fig. 1) more circumscribed development, **26/1** accords best with his nos. 3 and 4.

14 See discussion in Vickers 1977, pp. 30–31; for a fuller chronological discussion, see Kilian-Dirlmeier 1979, pp. 206–208.

15 For which, see generally Kilian-Dirlmeier 1979, pp. 45–48, pls. 18–19, nos. 277–294; see also the stemmed bell pendant from Pherai, Kilian 1975a, pl. 78, no. 72.

16 Kilian-Dirlmeier 1979, pp. 59–60, nos. 354–367, esp. nos. 365, 363, 375–376.

17 Kilian-Dirlmeier 1979, pp. 74–75, pl. 25, nos. 478–487.

18 Blinkenberg 1926, esp. pp. 58–60; Sapouna-Sakellarakis 1978, pp. 41–54; see also von Eles Masi 1986, pp. 14–40, pls. 3–15.

19 One of the fullest corpora of this type of fibula, with 51 variants, is presented by von Eles Masi 1986, pp. 85–143, pls. 49–111.

20 Blinkenberg 1926, pp. 200–201; Sapouna-Sakellarakis 1978, pp. 118–120, pl. 49.

21 For small glass and faience beads of a form related to **26/10**, see, among others, Kilian 1975a, pl. 78, esp. nos. 1–5; Kilian-Dirlmeier 2002, pl. 72, nos. 1165–1183; pl. 73, nos. 1224–1232, and various examples on pls. 74–85.

22 Jacobsthal 1932, with reference to Aristophanes, *Wasps*, 938, 963; *Birds*, 1579; *Lysistrata*, 231. Some of the well-known Archaic examples include Jacopi 1929, p. 192, fig. 186, no. 5 (inv. 10642); *Perachora* I, p. 182, pl. 81, no. 11; see also Blinkenberg 1931, col. 215, pl. 29, no. 693.

23 *Deipnosophistai* 4, 169b–c (trans. C.B. Gulick, Loeb ed.).

24 Trans. Stanley Lombardo (with my own amendment).

25 See, esp., Burrows and Ure 1907–1908, pp. 296–297, figs. 20–21, pl. VII:B.

26 From Toumba T 79B, and T Pyres 13 and 14, see *Lefkandi* III, pl. 78, B2; pl. 146:d (tomb 79B); pl. 48, no. 8 (T Pyre 13); pl. 87, no. 18; pl. 146:c (T Pyre 14). For the grater from tomb 79B, see, further, Popham and Lemos 1995, p. 154, fig. 6; for T Pyres 13 and 14, see Popham, Touloupa, and Sackett 1982a, p. 229, pl. 26, no. 8; pl. 33:g; Popham, Calligas, and Sackett 1988–1989, p. 118, fig. 2.

27 *Eretria* XXII, vol. 2, pp. 24, 156, pl. 103, 402.

28 Kilian 1975a, p. 215, pl. 94, no. 33 (*Käsereibe*); Kilian-Dirlmeier 2002, p. 16, pl. 11, no. 213 (*Käsereibe*); Felsch 2007, p. 386, pl. 65, nos. 2294 (iron "*Reibe*"), 2295–2296 (bronze "*Reibenfrgt*").

29 See *Olympia* IV, p. 197, no. 1272; *Perachora* I, p. 182, pl. 81, no. 11.

30 For the Heraion on Samos, see Gehrig 1964, pp. 9–10, nos. 50–54; pp. 97–98; Brize 1989–1990, p. 323, fig. 3; for Lindos, see Blinkenberg 1931, col. 215, pl. 29, no. 693; for the Delion on Paros, see Rubensohn 1962, pp. 70–71, pls. 12, 18, no. 32; for Aphaia on Aigina, see Maass and Kilian-Dirlmeier 1998, p. 99, fig. 18, nos. 140–141.

31 Ridgway 1997, esp. pp. 331–335.

32 Lyons 1996, p. 110, with n. 19; *Selinus* V, pp. 115–119, pls. 67–69, nos. 588–626.

33 *Olynthus* X, pp. 191–194, pls. XLVIII–XLIX, for both cheese graters (nos. 600–608) and strainers (nos. 609–612), the latter of bronze and lead. It is worth noting here that a well-preserved grater from tomb 210 (a multiple burial) at Metapontion is dated 480–440 B.C., see Prohászka 1998, p. 819, H9 (for the grater); Carter and Hall 1998, p. 352 (for the tomb itself).

34 Schaus 2014b, p. 173, fig. 7.12, nos. 140–144. For a distinction between "cheese grater" and "sieve," see *Perachora* I, p. 182. For a well-preserved strainer/sieve resembling a modern colander from the sanctuary of Aphrodite on Mt. Aphrodision in Arkadia, see Kardara 1988, pl. 115, referred to as an οὐλοχόϊον, literally the vessel in which the sacred barley was kept, see LSJ s.v. οὐλοχοεῖον or οὐλοχόϊον.

35 The clear taper toward one end would preclude the possibility of a netting needle, such as Blinkenberg 1931, cols. 146–147, pl. 15, no. 406.

36 Cf., among others, Blinkenberg 1931, cols. 202–203, pl. 26, nos. 626–629, with reference to examples from Olympia, the Argive Heraion, Aigina, Lokroi Epizephyrioi, Dodona, Priene, and tombs in Syracuse.

37 Kilian-Dirlmeier 2002, pp. 124–125, pl. 115, nos. 1901–1905 (bronze), nos. 1906–1914 (iron nails); additional iron nails are presented on pls. 158–159; for smaller bronze nails and tacks from the sanctuary that cannot be dated precisely, see pl. 170, nos. 2871–2873, 2875.

38 *Isthmia* VII, pp. 134–135, pls. 77–78, nos. 499–503, 507–508.

39 *Isthmia* VII, p. 134, n. 24, with reference to Rostoker and Gebhard 1980, pp. 359–360.

40 See, among others, *Olynthus* X, pp. 309–323, pls. XCI–XCIV, nos. 1352–1485 (for bronze nails and tacks, the larger bronze nails referred to as spikes); pp. 323–328, pl. XCV, nos. 1486–1540 (for the larger iron spikes); *Corinth* XII, pp. 140–143, pl. 72; *Corinth* XV.1, p. 119, pl. 48, nos. 43–47; *Olympia* IV, pp. 190–191, figs. 1210–1213; *Perachora* I, p. 181, pl. 82, esp. nos. 5, 6 (the latter a tack), and nos. 1–4, 7–9 for the larger nails; Schaus 2014b, pp. 174–175, fig. 7.13, nos. 155–165 (bronze nails and tacks from Stymphalos).

41 Snodgrass 1964, pp. 151–152, fig. 10.

42 Snodgrass 1964, pp. 151, 253, where he cites Weber 1944 in *OlForsch* I, p. 162.

43 Snodgrass 1964, pp. 151, 253, with n. 42.

44 Snodgrass 1964, pp. 153, 253, with n. 45, with additional references to its distribution.

45 Snodgrass 1964, pp. 152–153, with fig. 10.

46 Snodgrass 1964, pp. 153, 253–254, with n. 47. For examples of various Type 3 arrowheads, together with other types, at Lindos, see Blinkenberg 1931, cols. 194–195, pl. 23, esp. nos. 601 and 608.

47 Morris et al. 2020, p. 675, fig. 16:b.

48 The bronze spindle hooks ("*Spindelhaken*") from the sanctuary of Athena Itonia near Philia in Thessaly are either intact with the small hook preserved, or with their apex clearly bent to form a hook, which is broken. The one example that is longer and thinner than the rest and preserves no hook is different in shape and proportions from **26/26**; see Kilian-Dirlmeier 2002, pp. 164–165, pl. 169, nos. 2849–2852.

49 Blackwell 2020, p. 533, caption for fig. 3.6.2. For the bronze axes and adzes of the Bronze Age in Israel, see Miron 1992.

50 For Pithekoussai tomb 678, see *Pithekoussai* I, pp. 657–660, esp. pls. 15 (lower right), 190, nos. 678-5–678-13.

51 *Isthmia* VII, p. 120. Of the pointed chisels from Isthmia, those that can be dated are Archaic, see *Isthmia* VII, pp. 125–127, fig. 25, esp. nos. 441–442.

52 *Isthmia* VII, pp. 178–180.

53 *Isthmia* VII, pp. 134–135, with n. 26; for the iron spikes from Isthmia, see p. 140, pl. 78, nos. 504–506, all of which are of Classical date. Among the iron spikes from Isthmia, **26/31** is closest in form to pl. 78, nos. 504–505.

54 *Sindos* III, pp. 267–272, 466, figs. 220–222, nos. 525–548.

55 Kilian-Dirlmeier 2002, pp. 124–125, pl. 115, nos. 1906–1910; two types of *Nägel* are distinguished from the Athena Itonia sanctuary, those with bent-back heads (nos. 1906–1910) and those with rolled-over or looped heads (nos. 1911–1914).

56 See discussion, with full references, in Chapter 15, under **15/89–15/91**, esp. n. 253. Additional examples from the Aegean, Italy, and Spain are assembled in Bouzek 1997, pp. 105–106, fig. 100.

57 Kilian-Dirlmeier 1979, pp. 243–258, pls. 90–99, nos. 1562–1755. Her basic types of *Beil-Anhänger* include an essentially Italian type (nos. 1562–1563, *Beile mit Tierprotomen*), of which there are only two examples in Greece, one in the Benaki Museum of unknown findspot and another from Dodona; good examples of this type are found at Francavilla Marittima, the extramural sanctuary of Sybaris, see Papadopoulos 2003a, pp. 68–69, fig. 88, nos. 175–176, with further references. Kilian-Dirlmeier's other types include the triple-axe pendants (nos. 1564–1570, *Drillingsbeil-Anhänger*), five from Vergina (see *Vergina* I, pp. 248–251, fig. 87 (referred to as Τρίδυμοι διπλοῖ πελέκεις), and two from North Macedonia (from Kumanovo and Beranci). There are also double-axe pendants with eyelet or looped suspensions (nos. 1571–1579, *Doppelbeile mit Aufhängöse*), straight double-axe pendants with handle with one or two suspension holes (nos. 1580–1596, *geradseitige Doppelbeile mit flacher Klinge*), some of which have no obvious means of suspension (e.g., nos. 1587–1592, 1594), a similar but much more common double-axe pendant with a thickened center from which the pendant is suspended (nos. 1597–1683, *geradseitige Doppelbeile mit verdickter Klingenmitte*), the small flat double-axe pendants with perforated blades (nos. 1684–1690, *flache Doppelbeile mit Klingenausschnitten*), and the larger and closely related type without the perforated blades (nos. 1691–1755, *Doppelbeile ohne Klingenausschnitten*); the double axes of the last two types are in the form of Boiotian or Dipylon shields; many of the standard bronze axe pendants are found in the sanctuary at Olympia, see *OlForsch* XIII, pls. 80–81, nos. 1322–1351; for many of these types, see Bouzek 1974b, p. 154, fig. 48; for related double axes from the sanctuary of Artemis at Ephesos, see Klebinder-Gauss 2003; 2007, pl. 57, nos. 791–792; for that from the tombs at Aineia, see Vokotopoulou 1990, p. 98, fig. 50, no. 7616, pl. 61:γ (lower right).

58 The only piece that I am aware of that comes even remotely close is a small bronze of unknown function from the Athena Itonia sanctuary near Philia, which is classified as a possible votive axe (*Votivbeil?*) in Kilian-Dirlmeier 2002, p. 171, pl. 175, no. 3006. It is, however, very different from **26/32** in that both of the "blades" of the putative axe taper in toward the center.

59 I am grateful to Ciarán Lavelle, one of our conservators in 2012 who specialized in iron, for working on this and several other problematic iron pieces from various parts of the site.

60 Brock 1957, p. 202, and cf. the related pikes; the earliest obelos is no. 114 from Tomb VI, see pp. 11–15, which was unfortunately missing. The so-called pikes were shown by Karageorghis (1974, pp. 171–172) to be the same as the spits and thus increased their number; see discussion in *Agora* XXXVI, pp. 959–960; for related "obeloi" from Kavousi, see Boardman 1971. For bronze and iron obeloi from various sites on Cyprus, see Haarer 2000, esp. p. 12 (table); the earliest of the Early Iron Age obeloi, dating to ca. 1050 B.C., come from Kition, Lapithos, and Palaepaphos.

61 Snodgrass 1996, pp. 590–591; on p. 590 Snodgrass writes, "Desperately fragmentary, corroded to the point where reconstruction is usually impossible and even recognition often difficult, they defy any kind of accurate quantification."

62 Snodgrass 1996, pp. 591–592.

63 Snodgrass 1996, p. 591, a chronology further supported by the finds from Kavousi published in Boardman 1971.

64 Courbin 1957, p. 369, fig. 53; Courbin 1974, pp. 13, 32, 41, 136.

65 Miller 1983, p. 79, pl. 23:f, IL 421; Miller 1984, p. 181, pl. 37:d, IL 470, IL 471. For the Stymphalos obeloi, see Schaus 2014b, pp. 175–177, 460, fig. 7.14, nos. 171–178.

66 *OlForsch* XXXII, pp. 66–87; the selection of published examples is only a portion of the iron spits found at the site.

67 Kilian-Dirlmeier 2002, p. 9, pls. 4–6, nos. 15–31.

68 Kilian-Dirlmeier 2002, pl. 4, nos. 15–20, for the standard obelos type with one terminal hammered flat and a smaller rectangular projection at the midpoint of the shaft; for the obelos with a circular projection at its midpoint, see pl. 5, no. 21.

69 For obeloi, see *Sindos* III, pp. 242–247, nos. 462–473; pp. 464–465, figs. 216–218; pp. 621–622, figs. 488–501; for firedogs, see pp. 248–251, nos. 474–480; p. 621, fig. 492; pp. 622–623, figs. 502–510. For a general overview see Haarer 2000.

70 *Sindos* III, p. 464, fig. 216, no. 464 (for the circular projections with a short pointed extension); p. 465, fig. 217, no. 465 (for the crescent-shaped projection near one terminal).

71 Snodgrass 1996, p. 591.

72 One of the most cogent discussions of the value of spits, particularly in the context of Greek sanctuary sites and ritual, including reference to Bernhard Laum's seminal study *Heiliges Geld* (see Laum 1924), is in *Perachora* I, pp. 187–190, pl. 86, nos. 9–13; see further Papadopoulos 2012.

73 Papadopoulos 2005, pp. 151, 563, fig. 135, pl. 330:a, b, T79-1.

74 *Olynthus* X, p. 334, pl. 100, no. 1592; the only other instance of a clamp at Torone, similar to that on the Early Iron Age krater T79-1, was encountered in an earlier Classical deposit, inv. 82.623 (unpublished). For a much earlier clamp/plug from Lemnos, see Bernabò-Brea 1976, p. 292, pl. 234:s.

75 *Isthmia* VII, pp. 159–161, pls. 91–92, nos. 606–609.

76 *Isthmia* VII, pp. 155–159, 182–183, pls. 89–90, nos. 584–605, with full discussion and comparanda.

77 *Isthmia* VII, p. 184, three examples, all from Rachi.

78 *Isthmia* VII, p. 138, pl. 75, no. 487; a similar but less well preserved lead piece (IM 456) is presented and illustrated with Isthmia no. 487.

79 Kilian-Dirlmeier 1979, pp. 66–68, pl. 24, nos. 426–439; cf. also p. 73, pl. 25, nos. 478–479 (one of unknown provenance, the other from Korçë in Albania).

80 Kilian-Dirlmeier 1979, pp. 66–67. For Vergina, cf. Bräuning and Kilian-Dirlmeier 2013, p. 203, fig. 104, no. 27; p. 273, fig. 217, AE 345 (far right). For Pherai, see further Kilian 1975a, pl. 80, esp. nos. 17–18. There is also a variant from Pherai that has a similar triangular upper element, set on top of a ring rather than a beaded shaft; see Kilian 1975a, pl. 74, nos. 31–32; pl. 75, nos. 1–2. Note also a related type with a larger single bead: Kilian-Dirlmeier 2002, p. 60, nos. 929–930.

81 For the pendant from Donja Dolina, see Kilian-Dirlmeier 1979, p. 267, pl. 108, no. 5; for the related pendants from Osovo, Tumulus II, see Benac and Čović 1957, pl. XXVII, which are somehow associated with no. 3; for the complete arrangement with five related pendants from Arareva Gromila, see pl. XL, no. 4.

82 Boardman 1961, pp. 45–46, fig. 20, pl. XV, nos. 210–216, esp. nos. 213, 215, 216, with full discussion and references.

83 A similar pattern of corrosion can be seen on a spectacle fibula from Tumulus X at Mladj, see Benac and Čović 1956, pl. XXIX, no. 1; see also Vasić 1999, pl. 15, no. 201.

84 Blinkenberg 1926, pp. 253–262, Type XIV "agrafes en spirales"; Sapouna-Sakellarakis 1978, pp. 110–116, classified as "Fibeln nördlicher Form oder nördlicher Herkunft (Typ X)." The most detailed study of their origin remains Alexander 1965, esp. pp. 7–8.

85 Blinkenberg 1926, pp. 58–72; Sapouna-Sakellarakis 1978, pp. 42–45, pls. 3–4, nos. 51–89.

86 See Sapouna-Sakellarakis 1978, pp. 44–45.

87 Arched fibulae with twisted bows: Sapouna-Sakellarakis 1978, pp. 49–51, pls. 6–7, nos. 194–215.

88 The closest, without the incised decoration, are two fibulae from Gortyn, Sapouna-Sakellarakis 1978, p. 42, pl. 3, nos. 51A, 51B.

89 Vasić 1999, pp. 48–54, pls. 25–27, nos. 286–318 (with plain bow), nos. 319–330 (with twisted bow), and nos. 331–334 (for further variants).

90 Gergova 1987, pp. 22–23, pls. 1–2, no. 18, which is about the same size as **26/44**, and nos. 14–15, which are larger (classified as "Bogenfibeln mit dreieckiger Fussplatte"); Kilian 1975a, p. 23, pl. 1, no. 21, which is made of silver.

91 Blinkenberg 1926, pp. 218–222; Muscarella 1967, pp. 21–24.

92 These generally fall under "phrygische bzw. anatolische Fibeln Variante G and H," in Caner 1983, pls. 44–49, various examples.

93 *Olynthus* X, p. 260.

94 See Papadopoulos 2003a, p. 207. I am grateful to Vanessa Muros for her pXRF work on the Methone metal objects.

95 See especially n. 37 above.

96 The quantity of iron objects from the acropolis east slope of Methone was not great. In addition to the large iron nail, **26/51**, which was the most diagnostic of all iron objects, there was a possible iron staple, misformed (ΜΕΘ 5042), and a possible iron projectile (ΜΕΘ 5041).

97 See, for example, *Olynthus* X, pp. 323–328, pl. XCV, nos. 1486–1540; *Isthmia* VII, pp. 134–135, 140, pl. 78, nos. 504–506; among the latter, the largest measures 0.230 in length, the smallest 0122.

98 As with the iron finds, the quantity of lead objects from the east slopes of the West Hill was low. The three pieces presented here are the most diagnostic, representative, and interesting of the pieces encountered (lead sling bullets from this area are presented in Chapter 28).

99 Papadopoulos 2005, pp. 151, 563, fig. 135, pl. 330:a, b, T79-1; the Torone clamp/plug measures 0.062 x 0.055 m (L. x W.).

100 See esp. discussion in Blinkenberg 1926, pp. 41–58; Sapouna-Sakellarakis 1978, pp. 34–35. **26/55** is closest to Blinkenberg's (1926, pp. 50–51) Type I 7, described thus: "l'arc a été élargi et aplati par le martelage; pas de décoration."

101 Sapouna-Sakellarakis 1978, pp. 34–41.

102 Muscarella 1967, p. 26, with reference to Jacobsthal 1956, p. 205, n. 2. He also refers to two fibulae in the Ashmolean Museum, Oxford, that were found in "Thrace" by Stanley Casson (no. 1921-1250), each with a horned catch (like our **26/58**).

103 Muscarella 1967, p. 27 (under Type XII, 16); Blinkenberg 1926, p. 227, fig. 260.

104 Muscarella 1967, p. 27.

105 Muscarella 1967, pp. 27, 34, n. 56, with reference to *Olynthus* X, p. 107, pl. XXI, nos. 368–373; pl. XXIII, nos. 364–367, 375–376; they are dated 432–348 B.C., but according to Muscarella (1967, p. 34, nos. 54, 56) may be closer to the later date. See further, Casson 1921, p. 210, pl. VII, fig. 2 (from Kalindoia); Keramopoullos 1932, col. 75, fig. 39, no. 10.

106 For examples with five beads, see *Sindos* III, pp. 183–184, 452, figs. 153–154, nos. 328–330 (all of which are silver fibulae).

107 The type is referred to as "knot-headed pin" by Sylvia Benton, 1939–1940, p. 55.

108 Jacobsthal 1956, pp. 133–134, figs. 390, 391, 391a.

109 Kilian-Dirlmeier 1984a, p. 282, pl. 112, no. 4887.

110 Voyatzis 1990, p. 372, pl. 162, nos. B242a, B242b (seven examples from Tegea); for Knossos, see Coldstream 1973, pp. 147–148, fig. 35, no. 126; Kilian-Dirlmeier 1984a, p. 283; see further Benton 1939–1940, p. 55, pl. 29, no. 34, citing Early Bronze Age examples from Bohemia, and later examples from Greece; Boardman 1961, pp. 32–34, fig. 13, pl. XIII, no. 144.

111 Wiseman 1967, p. 428, no. 24, pl. 91:l; the pin head was found in dark fill of the 6th century A.D. next to Grave 26; for the Hellenistic example from Knossos, see Coldstream 1973, pp. 147–148, fig. 35, no. 126; see further Kilian-Dirlmeier 1984a, p. 283.

112 *Sindos* III, pp. 163–164, 443, figs. 278 (second quarter 5th century B.C.), 281 (not precisely datable), 283 (ca. 500 B.C.).

113 Kilian-Dirlmeier 2002, p. 98, pl. 95, nos. 1516–1523 (from the Athena Itonia sanctuary near Philia); she also cites a related silver pin from Pherai, see Kilian 1975a, p. 191, pl. 64, no. 44.

114 For "Keulenkopfnadeln," see Vasić 2003, pp. 82–86, pls. 31–34, nos. 536–630.

115 For "Kolbenkopfnadeln" and related pins, see Vasić 2003, pp. 81–82, pl. 31, esp. nos. 532–533.

116 Kilian-Dirlmeier 1984a, pp. 163–203, pls. 65–83, nos. 2017–3330, where an almost bewildering number of variants of "*Mehrkopfnadeln*" is presented.

117 Jacobsthal 1956, p. 36; also discussed at length in Appendix I, headed "A Chapter on Fruits," on lifelike representations of poppies, apples, and pomegranates, together with pomegranate vases, pendants, and finials (pp. 185–200).

118 Jacobsthal 1956, pp. 38, 187, figs. 145–147, 161 (pomegranate-headed); p. 36, fig. 141, for the ordinary globe enriched with a flower (with reference to Marshall).

119 Kilian-Dirlmeier 1984a, p. 273.

120 Kilian-Dirlmeier 1984a, pp. 273–281, pls. 111–112, nos. 4738–4859.

121 Alexander 1964, pp. 170–174.

122 Maier 1956, pp. 68–69, fig. 2; see also the examples illustrated on p. 65, fig. 1; Jacobsthal 1956, p. 135.

123 Kilian-Dirlmeier 1984a, pp. 286–289, pls. 113–144, nos. 4925–4942 (Trebenište type); nos. 4943–4948 (Glasinac type); and no. 4949 (Kozani type).

124 Rhomiopoulou and Touratsoglou 2002, p. 48, M 1050 (three examples, 5th–4th century B.C.); p. 66, α.α. (one pin, last quarter of the 5th century B.C.); p. 73, α.α. (one pin, late 6th–5th century B.C.); there are also two examples from the Iron Age cemetery at Arnissa, see Chrysostomou 2016, p. 11, fig. 4 (top right); for an example of the type from Ephesos, see Klebinder-Gauss 2007, pp. 76, 241, pl. 21, no. 300.

125 Alexander 1964, pp. 171–172, fig. 7 (type II); see also p. 173, fig. 8, nos. 11, 16; Kilian-Dirlmeier 1984a, pp. 386–387 (where Trebenište and Glasinac were wrongly placed); Vasić 2003, pp. 123–128, pls. 45–47, nos. 902–958; see also Vasić's earlier study (1982).

126 Kilian-Dirlmeier 1984a, pp. 288–289.

127 Benac and Čović 1957, typological foldout.

128 Alexander 1964, p. 172.

129 Vokotopoulou 1986, p. 29, T67, no. 7.

130 *Sindos* III, pp. 172–175, 447–449, figs. 129–144, nos. 300–316.

131 Vasić 2003, pl. 69 for the distribution of the type, pp. 125–128 for their chronology.

132 For the Glasinac type, see Kilian-Dirlmeier 1984a, p. 287, pl. 114, nos. 4943–4948.

133 Alexander 1964, pp. 171–172, fig. 7, Type III (which corresponds to Vasić's Variante III a, see Vasić 2003, pp. 118–120, pl. 44, esp. nos. 857–873).

134 Vasić 2003, p. 116, pl. 43, nos. 836–849.

135 Vasić 2003, p. 116 for discussion of the chronology, pl. 67 for the distribution of the type.

136 *Sindos* III, pp. 175–176, 449–450, figs. 145–149, nos. 317–322 (referred to as "περόνες με μονόλοβη κεφαλή").

137 *Sindos* III, pp. 155, 438, 593, fig. 90, pl. 269, no. 250 (two iron pin shafts with bronze heads); both of the Sindos pins were found in fill 1.80 m southeast of tomb 14, in a context that should be of 5th-century B.C. date.

138 Despoini in *Sindos* III, p. 155, compares the two Sindos pins to two from Trebenište, which Vasić 2003, p. 105, pl. 39, nos. 762–763, referred to as "Haubenkopfnadeln."

139 Kilian-Dirlmeier 1984a, pp. 273–281, especially some of those under Type FIIIc, see pp. 278–279, nos. 4845–4848 (from the Argive Heraion, Mantineia, Lousoi, and Sparta).

140 Vasić 2003, p. 106.

141 See, among others, Bouzek 1974b, pp. 105–117, figs. 32–33; Bouzek 1987, pp. 91–100, esp. for the distribution of the type; Vickers 1977, pl. III.

142 For Thessaly see, among others, Kilian 1975a, pl. 76, esp. nos. 15, 20–25 (Pherai); pl. 95, nos. 4–6 (Valanida); Kilian-Dirlmeier 2002, p. 102, pl. 97, esp. nos. 1573–1575, and the larger nos. 1578–1979, which are of similar form (Philia).

143 For a good introduction, see Higgins 1980, p. 89, and see further discussion and comparanda in Chapter 15.

144 For Catling's discussion of the Lefkandi bronze finger rings, see *Lefkandi* I, p. 247. For further discussion, see, among others, Lemos 2002, pp. 115–117. Such rings could be worn by women and men, see *Lefkandi* I, p. 248; *Kerameikos* I, p. 85; Styrenius 1967, pp. 48–70, 109. For central and southern Greece, I have enumerated the five main varieties of Early Iron Age finger rings in Chapter 15; see further Higgins 1980, pp. 88–93, 210–212; Desborough 1972, p. 304; *Kerameikos* XVIII, pp. 206–216.

145 The following examples from Isthmia serve to illustrate the chronological range of such rings, *Isthmia* VII, p. 63, pl. 38, nos. 233–239.

146 In dealing with this type of ring, Snodgrass (1971a, p. 320) noted that "this basic shape of ring, with a roughly elliptical bezel set at right-angles to the hoop, had been the standard type of the Aegean Bronze Age, and was again to become common in the Geometric period." Similarly, Desborough (1972, p. 304) noted that "the ring with oval or rather angled bezel reflects the Mycenaean tradition." For further discussion, see Higgins 1980, pp. 88–93, 210–212; *Kerameikos* XVIII, pp. 206–216; *Agora* XXXVI, pp. 924–925 (for bronze examples), and pp. 946–947 for a Submycenaean example made of bone (T63-17).

147 For 6th-century B.C. rings with bezels, see Higgins 1980, p. 131; for 5th-century examples from Corinth, see *Corinth* XV.1, p. 126, pl. 49, no. 60.

148 *Isthmia* VII, p. 63, pl. 38, nos. 230, 231 (bronze); p. 64, pl. 39, no. 246 (for the Archaic silver ring), and cf. p. 64, fig. 9, no. 244 (for another silver ring with bezel of Classical date).

149 Felsch 2007, p. 329, pl. 44, nos. 1361, 1362.

150 Kilian-Dirlmeier 2002, p. 121, pl. 113, nos. 1871–1874; Boardman 1970, pp. 212–213, fig. 217.

151 Coldstream 1973, pp. 140–142, fig. 32, nos. 71–80.

152 *OlForsch* XIII, pp. 157–166, pls. 8–9, 42–43, nos. 578–613.

153 Young 2014, pp. 113–119, esp. nos. 97–135; of these, only nos. 97–118 are bronze, of which one is late 6th–early 5th centuries B.C. (no. 97); one or two are 5th century B.C. (nos. 98, 102?); a few are 3rd or 2nd century B.C. (nos. 113, 118), whereas the remainder are 4th century B.C. (99–101, 103–112, 114–116).

154 *Olynthus* X, pp. 132–158, pl. XXVI–XXVII, no. 447.

155 Boardman 1970, pp. 156–157, fig. 198, Type N; the Classical successor of the Archaic Type N ring is Type I, see Boardman 1970, pp. 212–213, fig. 217, Type I, about which Boardman notes (p. 212), "the Archaic form remains the only usual shape to the middle of the 5th century. There are some very flimsy rings of this form which may be later."

156 Boardman 1970, pp. 212–214, fig. 217, Classical Type II.

157 Boardman 1970, pp. 213–214. Of these, Type VI persists from about 400 B.C. through the 4th century B.C., Type VII is 4th century, while Type VIII is most popular during the middle and late 4th century B.C.

158 For birds on Classical finger rings, see, among others, Boardman 1970, p. 231, figs. 248, 249; pls. 468–469, 488–490, 492, 494–495, 518–519, 549, 554–557, 700. For a standing pigeon on a carnelian ring stone, see pl. 625.

159 *Vergina* I, p. 240, with fig. 80.

160 *Isthmia* VII, p. 64.

161 *OlForsch* XIII, pp. 112–137 for earrings (nos. 394–399 Geometric to early Archaic; nos. 400–486 Archaic to Classical; no. 487 Hellenistic; nos. 488–507 Roman); pp. 138–190 for finger rings (nos. 508–565 Submycenaean through early Archaic; 566–575 "archaisch-etruskische Fingerringe"; nos. 576–617 5th–4th centuries B.C.; nos. 618–638 Hellenistic to Roman periods; nos. 639–680 Roman; nos. 681–694 classified as "Fingerringe: Einzelstücke").

162 Dakoronia 1989.

163 Dakoronia 1989; Kilian 1975a, pl. 73, nos. 28–37 (the ring with perhaps only two spurs is no. 30, although there are slight bulges that may indicate an additional spur or spurs); pl. 74, nos. 1–18 (all from Pherai); additional comparanda are given in the catalogue entry for **26/96**.

164 Catling 1964, pp. 230–232. Two bronze bracelets encountered in situ in an Early to Middle Protogeometric tomb in the Athenian Agora, worn by a child, measure 0.056–0.057 m, see *Agora* XXXVI, p. 927.

165 See esp. *Lefkandi* I, p. 247; Snodgrass 1971a, p. 270; *Agora* XXXVI, pp. 927–928; cf. Higgins 1980, p. 89; Catling 1964, pp. 230–232 for the Late Bronze Age.

166 The two types are discussed in Lemos 2002, pp. 114–115. Both cast and hammered bracelets are well represented in the collection of the University of Mainz; see *CVA*, Mainz 1 [Germany 15], pp. 14–15, figs. 6–8 (cast, with incised decoration); figs. 9, 10 (hammered).

167 *Olympia* IV, pp. 56–58, pl. 23, nos. 380–398; *OlForsch* XIII, pp. 195–259, pls. 12–17, 45–58, nos. 721–983 (PG: nos. 721–730; Geometric–Archaic: nos. 731–797; Archaic–early Classical: nos. 823–937; Late Roman: nos. 938–983); Kilian 1975a, various examples of both forms, pls. 66–68 (Pherai); Kilian-Dirlmeier 2002, pp. 53–56, pls. 55–57, nos. 844–882 (Armbänder and Armringe) (Philia); Felsch 2007, pp. 143–158, 292–299, pls. 33–36, nos. 529–617 (Kalapodi). For bracelets made of various metals in the 7th century, see Hampe 1936, pp. 5, 7–8; Wolters 1892, pl. 11:3–5.

168 *Olynthus* X, esp. pp. 260–269, pls. LXX–LXXI, nos. 1037–1107.

169 Papadopoulos 2017b.

170 Andreou 2000, p. 33. Rescue excavations were conducted at the site until 1981, and from 1995 as a systematic excavation by I. Andreou. By 2000, some 150 tombs were cleared, mostly dating from the 7th–4th centuries B.C. The Dourouti instrument was encountered in Tomb XVI; see I. Andreou 1977, p. 150, pl. 93δ; I. Andreou 2000, p. 33, fig. 5. The Dourouti instrument is also illustrated in Papadopoulos 2017b, p. 272, fig. 6.

171 See Beschi 2001, p. 176, fig. 1:d, pl. 18, no. 3. Bronze rings are also known on the auloi from Meroë (present-day Sudan), see Bodley 1946, pl. IV, no. 9.

172 Douzougli and Papadopoulos 2010, pp. 60–61; all five Liatovouni examples are illustrated in Papadopoulos 2017b, p. 269, fig. 3.

173 They are as follows: T65-2 (8331), T71-5 (8474), T73-7 (8433), T85-4 (8434), T90-11 (8330); for a summary overview of the Liatovouni cemetery, see Douzougli and Papadopoulos 2010. Although most of the tombs are later Archaic to earlier Classical, the latest example may be that from Tomb 90, which should be third quarter of the 5th century B.C.

174 Vokotopoulou 1986, p. 318, fig. 115:κδ; they were found in Tombs 66, 72, and 77; two of the Vitsa examples are illustrated in Papadopoulos 2017b, p. 270, fig. 4.

175 Karamitrou-Mentessidi 2008, p. 139, fig. 237. It is not absolutely clear from the publication whether this is one piece or two; the label of the Greek text refers to the two illustrations as if they were different views of the same piece; the English edition, however, clearly refers to "nozzles of aryballoi" in the plural.

176 *Sindos* II, pp. 314–315, 471, 550, figs. 86 and 544–545, no. 438 (from tomb 76, 420–410 B.C.), with further references.

177 Raubitschek, in *Isthmia* VII, p. 26, mentions two unpublished examples from Olympia, inv. B 7995 and Br 4608.

178 *Perachora* I, p. 158, pl. 61, nos. 2–4. Of these, which I have not seen in person, I am certain that nos. 3 and 4 are similar to the Methone and Epirus examples discussed above, but I am less certain about no. 2.

179 *Perachora* I, p. 158. The cited parallel (Payne 1931, p. 211), is simply a common Corinthian aryballos in clay, with the statement that "there were occasionally metal versions of the shape." One of the Perachora examples is also illustrated in Papadopoulos 2017b, fig. 8.

180 *Isthmia* VII, pp. 26–27, pl. 21, nos. 104–113 (the six that were virtually identical were nos. 104–109, plus also no. 106A). The Isthmia terminals are also illustrated in Papadopoulos 2017b, p. 273, fig. 9.

181 Raubitschek (*Isthmia* VII, p. 26) writes: "The mouth, shaped like a funnel, is composed of a sheet that is bent back at the lip with a considerable overhang." She also cites a fragmentary example that is perhaps from such a bronze from the Korykian Cave north of Delphi, for which see Rolley 1984, pp. 273–274, fig. 22, no. 51, simply referred to as an "objet bombé" (with a diameter of 5.5 cm, the piece from the Korykian Cave is slightly larger than the examples from Methone and Epirus noted above).

182 *Pithekoussai* I, p. 115, pls. 30 and CVI, 93-3 (inv. 166441), described as an "imboccatura di bronzo di aryballos di cuoio."

183 Such as the so-called chalkophones and their related tubes, as well as the "dischi compositi," from Archaic Francavilla Marittima; see discussion, with references, in Papadopoulos 2003a, pp. 110–117.

184 For the literary sources for ancient Greek music, see West 1992.

185 For the various types of figured tripod feet, see Papadopoulos 2003a, pp. 22–27, figs. 24–30. For a magnificent combined anthropomorphic/zoomorphic tripod leg, in this case a gorgon, see Rolley 1982, pl. XLV, 204–205. For related anthropomorphic/zoomorphic examples in Greece, see *Olympia* IV, p. 137, pl. I.1, no. 857; Evangelidis 1956, pl. 59:γ; Vokotopoulou 1973, pl. 26; Dakaris 1998, pl. 33, no. 2. See also Stoop 1970–1971, p. 40, fig. 1 (from Francavilla Marittima).

186 De Ridder 1896, pp. 25–37, Keramopoullos and Pelekidis 1915, p. 26, figs. 20–22; Carapanos 1878, pl. XXIII, no. 2 (and 2 *bis* inscribed), also pl. XLI, nos. 1–5, 8–10; Evangelidis 1955, pl. 58:β; *Perachora* I, pls. 70–71 (various examples); *Olympia* IV, p. 136, pl. LI, no. 853; *OlForsch* XX, pls. 63–67 (numerous examples), also pl. 110:6a–b, 7; DeCou 1905, esp. pp. 295–296, pls. CXXIV–CXXV, nos. 2227–2230, also nos. 2231–2234; Dawkins 1929a, pl. LXXXIII:c, e–f; *FdD* V.1, esp. p. 71, figs. 229–234; for the examples from Samos that may have supported larger tripod cauldrons with griffin protomai, see Jantzen 1955, pl. 63, nos. 1–3; Blinkenberg 1931, col. 223, pl. 31, nos. 745–746.

187 Burrows and Ure 1907–1908, p. 286, fig. 16, center, no. 242.

188 Felsch 2007, p. 379, pl. 61, nos. 2195–2197 (under the heading "Dreifussuntersätze von Becken [Podanipteres], Exaleiptra, Räuchergefässen oder Oinochoen[?])." Cf. also the somewhat larger "Löwentatze" from the Athena Itonia sanctuary near Philia, Kilian-Dirlmeier 2002, p. 94, pl. 93, no. 1455.

189 For Francavilla, see Stoop 1980, pp. 171, 184, figs. 21–22; Papadopoulos 2003a, p. 26, figs. 28–29, nos. 22, 23; for Hera Lakinia, see Spadea 1994, pl. IV:e, and esp. Spadea 1996, pp. 111–112, nos. 17–20; also Orsi 1911, p. 92, fig. 65. For Rosarno Medma, see Orsi 1913, pp. 138, 140, fig. 185 (left); for Lokroi, see Orsi 1913, p. 28, fig. 34 (bottom row), also p. 26, fig. 30; Orsi 1917, p. 125, fig. 30 (bottom left). Note also the stand from the cemetery at Melfi, published in Adamesteanu 1965–1966, pl. LVIII:b; also that from Ugento published in Lo Porto 1970–1971, pl. XLVIII:a. For tripodiskoi from Apulia, see esp. Tarditi 1996, pp. 23–33, nos. 27–41; pp. 117–118, nos. 263–266; pp. 128–130, figs. 6–11 (*podanipter*).

190 Filow 1927, pp. 68–80, figs. 72–90 (also figs. 94–95), nos. 81–89.

191 Vokotopoulou et al. 1985, p. 93, no. 139 (lekane, inv. 8548, tomb 20, ca. 510–500 B.C.), and the tripod stand for the exaleiptron, pp. 110–111, no. 162 (tomb 59, ca. 530–520 B.C.); *Sindos* II, pp. 307–310, 469, 548, figs. 80–81, 531–534, nos. 432 and 433 (bronze lekanai, the former dating 545–535 B.C., the latter to the end of the 6th century B.C.); also the bronze exaleiptra, pp. 311–313, 470, 549, figs. 82–83, 535–540, nos. 434–435 (from tomb 25, 545–535 B.C.; tomb 59, 530–520 B.C.; tomb 67, 510–500 B.C.). For the relationship of these tombs to one another, see *Sindos* I, foldout plan A, and plans I–II.

192 *Perachora* I, p. 150, with nn. 5–14. See further DeCou 1905, various examples, pp. 279–284, pls. CXIII–CXV, including numerous plain phialai, such as nos. 1908, 1914, 1916, 1921, 1980; at nearby Prosymna, Carl Blegen (1937, fig. 462) came across a similar phiale, probably an intrusion in one of the Bronze Age tombs; for miniature phialai from the Argive Heraion, see also Caskey and Amandry 1952, p. 180, pl. 46, nos. 78–79. See also *Corinth* VII.1, p. 28; *Corinth* XII, pp. 68–70, fig. 1, no. 517 (with further references to the earlier literature); *Corinth* XV.1, p. 115, pl. 47, no. 2; Lamb 1926–1927, p. 105 (Sparta); *Olympia* IV, pl. LII, no. 879; de Ridder 1896, p. 74, no. 222 (Athenian Acropolis, inscribed ἀ[θη]ν[αίᾳ]); de Ridder 1895, p. 210 (Boiotian Orchomenos); Maass and Kilian-Dirlmeier 1998, pp. 92, 95, fig. 16, no. 120 (Aigina); *FdD* V.1, p. 90, figs. 304–305, with reference to "un assez grand nombre de phiales à ombilic φιάλαι ὀμφαλωταί, μεσόμφαλοι; Carapanos 1878, pl. XXIII, no. 6 (Dodona); Hogarth 1908, pl. 15, no. 13 (Ephesos); Blinkenberg 1931, pl. 31, no. 749. To Dunbabin's list add, among many others, Kilian 1975a, pl. 88, esp. no. 24 (Pherai); Furtwängler 1981, pl. 31, nos. 3–4 (Samos, Heraion); Kardara 1988, pl. 34:γ–δ, and esp. pl. 116:δ (sanctuary of Aphrodite Erykine, Arkadia); Kilian-Dirlmeier 2002, pp. 92–94, pl. 92, esp. nos. 1443, 1447, 1448–1449 (Philia, Archaic); pp. 156–157, pl. 163, esp. nos. 2602–2603, 2606, 2609 (Philia, uncertain date); Felsch 2007, p. 375, pl. 60, nos. 2149–2152 (Kalapodi).

193 *Perachora* I, p. 151; see further *Corinth* XII, pp. 68–70, discussion under no. 517. For possible Phoenician complexities at Corinth, see Morris and Papadopoulos 1998.

194 *Isthmia* VII, pp. 21–23, pls. 17–18; most of the Isthmia phialai are Archaic, although at least one is Classical.

195 About ten examples were published by Stoop (1980, pp. 177, 188–189, figs. 38, 39:a, c, 40, 43:d) from the Timpone della Motta at Francavilla Marittima, and there are numerous other examples in the storerooms; an additional 68 phialai, both complete and fragmentary, from Francavilla were published in Papadopoulos 2003a, pp. 38–53, figs. 55–69. Similar phialai are particularly well represented at the sanctuary of Hera Lakinia at Capo Colonna south of Krotone; see Spadea 1994, pl. IV:b ("patera mesonfalica"); Spadea 1996, pp. 115–117, nos. 46–54. Phialai are also common in south Italian tombs, see discussion in Tagliente 1983, p. 24 (with illustrated examples on pl. XV, nos. 200742, 200745), with references to similar phialai in tombs at Armento and Roccanova. At least 121 mesomphalos phialai were recorded by Orsi from Rosarno (Medma), both plain and decorated, see Orsi 1913, pp. 138–140, fig. 186.

196 Matthäus 1985, pp. 139–145; see also the discussion in Howes Smith 1981, 1984.

197 In Greece, bronze handles and their attachments are particularly well represented at Olympia, fully presented in *OlForsch* XX; see also, among other sites, *FdD* V.1, pp. 74–76, figs. 250–258; Blinkenberg 1931, pl. 30 (various examples); *Perachora* I, esp. pls. 65–66 (various examples, esp. pl. 65, nos. 3, 6, 8; pl. 66, nos. 19–24); *Isthmia* VII, pls. 15–16.

198 *OlForsch* XX, pl. 23:8b–e (Le 174, Le 172, Le 170, Le 175), also pl. 23:2 (Le 162), 7a–7b (Le 168, Le 169), and various examples on pl. 24; DeCou 1905, pp. 292–293, pl. CXXII, no. 2187 (Argive Heraion); *Perachora* I, pl. 66, no. 21; *Isthmia* VII, pp. 18–19, pl. 15, nos. 63–68; Blinkenberg 1931, col. 219, pl. 30, no. 714 (Lindos, with numerous further references to examples in the earlier literature); Felsch 2007, pp. 377–378, pl. 61, nos. 2180, 2181 (Kalapodi); Kilian-Dirlmeier 2002, p. 92, pl. 92, no. 1433 (Philia); Filow 1927, p. 31, fig. 28, nos. 5, 7, 8, 10 (Trebenište); Papadopoulos 2003a, p. 33, fig. 43, esp. nos. 48–50; also Stoop 1980, p. 183, fig. 18:b (Francavilla); Spadea 1996, p. 115, nos. 39–41 (Hera Lakinia near Krotone); Zancani Montuoro 1965–1966, pl. XLIII:c (center top, from Foce del Sele); *Metaponto* I, pp. 45–46. For later examples from Stymphalos, see Schaus 2014b, p. 156, fig. 7.5, nos. 39–43.

199 *Sindos* II, pp. 285–286, 455–457, 540–541, figs. 50–52, 486–488, 491, nos. 404–406, all from bronze lebetes (from tomb 115, ca. 520 B.C.; tomb 20, end of the 6th century B.C.; tomb 52, ca. 500 B.C.).

200 *Comicorum Atticorum Fragmenta* I, fr. 148, 1 (Kock); Vol. II, fr. 3, 1 (Meineke); Edmonds 1957, p. 534, no. 148. For surgical/medical implements, see Milne 1907, pp. 63–68. For medical instruments in antiquity, including ear spoons, see further Béal 1983, p. 24; Riha 1986, pp. 56–63; Bliquez 1994, pp. 48–49; Uzel 1999, pp. 212–213.

201 *Corinth* XII, pp. 181, 184, pl. 82, nos. 1318–1327. Davidson also distinguishes a number of related small bone spoons that she classifies as "cosmetic or unguent spoons," see pp. 181, 184, pl. 82, nos. 1328–1333.

202 *Sindos* III, pp. 276–277, 467, 632, fig. 226, pl. 574, nos. 553–554.

203 For the Bronze Age, see Iakovidis 1969–1970, vol. 2, p. 376; Branigan 1974, pp. 34, 174, nos. 1278–1280; Papaefthymiou-Papanthimou 1979, pp. 251–252; Keramopoullos 1917, p. 198, fig. 42, 3, no. 4 (Thebes). For later periods, see, among others, Vokotopoulou 1986, pl. 37:α, fig. 114:λ (Vitsa); *Olynthus* X, pp. 354–355, pl. CXIII, nos. 1705–1712; Kilian-Dirlmeier 2002, pp. 121–122, pl. 113, nos. 1875, 1876 (Classical); pp. 129–130, pl. 117, nos. 1938–1940, 1942–1943 (Roman-Byzantine); *Corinth* XII, pp. 181, 184, pl. 82, nos. 1318–1327. For the example from Thessaloniki, see Trakosopoulou-Salakidou 1986, p. 123, inv. 11557. Despoini (*Sindos* III, p. 276) also refers to additional examples from southern Italy. See also, among others, Babelon and Blanchet 1895, p. 609, no. 1616.

204 *Corinth* XII, p. 181, nos. 75–76. See further, *Olympia* IV, pp. 181, 209, nos. 1109–1118; *Délos* XVIII, pp. 223–224.

205 Brokallis 2013, pp. 364, 377, 398, 407, pl. 2, figs. 7–8, nos. X194, X195.

206 Klebinder-Gauss 2007, pp. 169–170, pl. 86, no. 888; for Dodona, see Carapanos 1878, p. 95, pl. LI, no. 12.

207 Kilian-Dirlmeier 2002, pp. 121–122, pl. 113 (Classical period, referred to as "Ohrlöffelchen"); pp. 129–130, pl. 117, nos. 1938–1940 ("Ohrsonde") and nos. 1942–1943 ("Ohrlöffel").

208 *Corinth* XII, pp. 182, 184–185, pls. 82–83, nos. 1336–1347, esp. nos. 1336–1342.

209 *Corinth* XII, p. 181. For the "spatula probe," see Milne 1907, pp. 58–61, pl. XIII, 3.

210 Kilian-Dirlmeier 2002, p. 129, pl. 117, no. 1932.

211 Cf., among others, **6/10α–γ** (Fig. 6.8e–h), **6/31** (Fig. 6.18), and **6/48** (Fig. 6.33h–i).

212 Kilian-Dirlmeier 1984a, p. 59, pl. 5, nos. 145A–145E (from Tiryns and Midea, though they differ slightly from **26/116** and **26/117** in that their eyelets tend to be slightly lower down on the shaft). Cf. also the "Nähnadeln" of the central Balkans, such as Vasić 2003, pp. 130–133, pl. 48, nos. 963–1000.

213 Kilian-Dirlmeier 2002, p. 164, pl. 169, nos. 2843–2848 (all of uncertain date).

214 *Corinth* XII, pp. 173–174, 176–177, pls. 78–79, nos. 1234–1262 (made of bronze and bone).

215 *Olynthus* X, pp. 362–363, nos. 1750–1754; Coldstream 1973, pp. 151–152, fig. 36, pls. 91–92, nos. 164–178; *Délos* XVIII, p. 266, figs. 296–297 (various examples). Hogarth (1899–1900, p. 111) mentions over 50 pins with eyelets from the Diktaian Cave, and although not precisely dated by context, many of these may be earlier than the Classical period.

216 For the difficulty of dating needles without context, see Brokallis 2013, p. 371. For needles from Crete, which are rarely found on Minoan sites, see Boardman 1961, p. 35, fig. 15, pl. XIII, nos. 151–155 (Diktaian Cave). For numerous bone needles of Bronze Age date from Tiryns, see *Tiryns* XVI, pp. 190–198, pls. 72–73.

217 *Corinth* XII, p. 173; for the spindle hooks themselves, see p. 176, pl. 78, nos. 1223–1228. For a spindle hook of late Hellenistic or Roman date, see, among others, the example from Megalo Gardiki in Epirus, Soueref 2016, p. 73, no. 39 (referred to as a "hook" ["άγκιστρο"]).

218 *Olynthus* X, pp. 376–377, pl. CXIX, nos. 1884–1892.

219 Prohászka 1998, p. 819, H10; for the date of the tomb, see Carter and Hall 1998, p. 328, tomb 258; *Selinus* V, p. 125, pl. 35, no. 676.

220 Hogarth 1899–1900, 111–112, fig. 46, right (three illustrated examples out of five mentioned); Blinkenberg 1931, col. 136, pl. 13, no. 343, with reference to *Olympia* IV, p. 61, pl. 23, no. 422; cf. also *Délos* XVIII, pp. 164–166, pls. LVII, LVIII, nos. 447–484; *Isthmia* VII, pp. 111, 116, pl. 63, nos. 401–404 (three

of bronze, one iron); *Corinth* XII, pp. 173, 176, pl. 78, nos. 1223–1228; Kilian-Dirlmeier 2002, pp. 164–165, pl. 169, nos. 2849–2852 (Philia, with references to further examples of Roman, Byzantine, and later date); Felsch 2007, p. 386, pl. 65, no. 2292 (Kalapodi, "späte Störung; Byz?"); Petrakos 1968, p. 127, pl. 52:β, no. 45 (Oropos); Brokallis 2013, pp. 370–371, 400, 410, pl. 4, fig. 32, no. X 223 (Kythera). For other late examples, see, among others, Kallipolitis 1961, pl. 74α (Korkyra); Aupert 1980, p. 706, fig. 14, top (Philippi); Russel 1982, p. 137, fig. 4.32 (Anemurium); Gill 1986, pp. 253–254, pl. 352, no. 404 (Saraçhane, Istanbul); Boardman 1989, p. 131, fig. 53, F62, F63 (Byzantine Chios).

221 See, for example, *Isthmia* VII, pl. 63, no. 404 (IM 3282); Kilian-Dirlmeier 2002, pl. 169, no. 2852; *Corinth* XII, pl. 78, no. 1226 (left).

222 Lamb 1934–1935, p. 151, pl. 32, nos. 7–8 (Kato Phana, Chios); Boardman 1967, p. 226, fig. 147, pl. 93, nos. 395–396 (Emporio, Chios); *Perachora* I, p. 182, pl. 80, no. 6; *Isthmia* VII, pp. 121, 127–129, pl. 71, nos. 453 (19 bronze fishhooks, Archaic to Classical), no. 454 (Classical); *Corinth* XII, pp. 190, 193, pl. 88, nos. 1447–1448 (date uncertain, and not demonstrably from a votive context); Versakis 1916, pp. 98–99, fig. 40 (Petalidi); Kilian-Dirlmeier 2002, p. 165, pl. 169 (Philia, "Angelhaken"); *OlForsch* XXXII, pp. 57–62, pl. 16, nos. 172–212; Brokallis 2013, pp. 365, 377, 398, 408, pl. 2, fig. 12, no. X198.

223 *Olynthus* X, pp. 365–374, pls. CXVII–CXIX, nos. 1788–1882; *Délos* XVIII, pp. 201–202, nos. 551–553; *Torone* I, pp. 730–731, fig. 171, nos. 18.20–18.23; *Selinus* V, pp. 127–128, pls. 38, 72, nos. 689–701, variously dated from the first half of the 6th into the 4th century B.C.; Prohászka 1998, p. 819, H11 (Metapontion).

224 For fishing in the Aegean Mesolithic and Neolithic, see, among others, Powell 2003; Theodoropoulou and Stratouli 2009; Theodoropoulou 2011; Mylona 2014. For the earlier stages of the Bronze Age, see, among others, Buchholz, Jöhrens, and Maull 1973, pp. 170–173, pl. 55; Tsountas 1899a, col. 104, pl. 10, nos. 38–39 (Syros); Goldman 1931, p. 218, fig. 286 (Eutresis); Caskey and Caskey 1960, p. 156, pl. 53, VIII.60 (Eutresis); Lamb 1936, p. 176, pl. XLVII (Thermi); Milojčić 1961, p. 54, nos. 16–20; pl. 50, nos. 8–10, 15–16 (Samos); Bernabò-Brea 1964, pp. 353, 354, 375, 456, 665, pl. 175, no. 2; pl. 177, nos. 16–19 (Poliochni); Powell 1992, 1996, pp. 122–166.

225 Iakovidis 1969–1970, pp. 354–355, fig. 156. For the Bronze Age, Iakovidis distinguished two main types of fishhooks, one smaller with a notched head, with either one or two small notches, that permitted the line to be fastened easily around the head, and a larger fishhook, made of thicker bronze but without a preserved "eye" or top. For a variant with a looped-over head from Teichos Dymaion, see Mastrokostas 1966, p. 162, fig. 191 (right); cf. also Powell 1996, p. 152, no. 43, from Petromagoula, Volos, and various examples on fig. 90. Bronze fishhooks with "eyes," like modern needles, are rare in the Bronze Age, though see an example from Mycenae, made of silver from Grave Circle B: Powell 1996, p. 150, no. 35.

226 *Corinth* XII, p. 190; Iakovidis 1969–1970, pp. 354–355.

227 See, for example, Koukouli-Chrysanthaki 1992, pp. 404–408, fig. 90 (Thasos); Morricone 1978, p. 210, fig. 433 (Kos); Bianco Peroni 1976, pl. 39, nos. 346, 354 (bronze knives from 8th–7th century B.C. Italy). For Geometric or later bronze knives at Kalapodi, see Felsch 2007, pp. 384–385, pl. 64, nos. 2271–2274.

228 For various bronze nails from Olynthos, dated 348 B.C. or earlier, see *Olynthus* X, pp. 309–323.

229 See Klebinder-Gauss 2007, pp. 191–192, pls. 99–102, nos. 979–1000; Blinkenberg 1931, pl. 26, nos. 626–628.

230 Brokallis 2013, pp. 374–375, made of bronze, iron, and lead, and of various shapes and sizes, including tacks.

231 *Sindos* III, p. 466, figs. 220, 221. There are no clear examples at Methone of the Sindos Type III nails.

232 For bronze nails and tacks, see *Olynthus* X, pp. 309–323, pl. XCI–XCIV, nos. 1352–1485.

233 Kilian-Dirlmeier 2002, pp. 117–118, pl. 111; the first variety includes nos. 1800–1810, the second nos. 1811–1821.

234 *Olynthus* X, pp. 329–330, pl. XCVI, nos. 1544–1552 (first variety, shaped like a small letter *h*), and p. 330, pl. XCVI, nos. 1553–1555 (second variety). Some of the first variety were associated with hearths in houses at the site, see *Olynthus* X, p. 329, n. 257, with reference to *Olynthus* VIII, pp. 122–123.

235 *Tarsus* I, p. 392, fig. 266, nos. 83–85.

236 Kilian-Dirlmeier 2002, p. 117; see further *Isthmia* VII, pp. 152–153, pl. 88, nos. 578–583 for the various T- and h-shaped staples.

237 Kilian-Dirlmeier 2002, p. 117, with n. 496.

238 Boardman 1967, pp. 214–221, esp. pp. 220–221, fig. 143, nos. 329, 330; *Isthmia* VII, p. 27, pl. 22, no. 115 ("bronze reinforcement plaque for a vase").

239 Keramopoullos and Pelekidis 1915, p. 27, fig. 25:β; Kourouniotis 1910, col. 328, fig. 53 (left), the latter referred to as "χαλκαῖ ἐπενδύσεις σκευῶν."

240 *Olynthus* X, pp. 301–306, pls. LXXXVII–LXXXIX, nos. 1309–1336; cf. also some of the rivets that are closely related to those on **26/150** and **26/151**, *Olynthus* X, pp. 309–310, pl. LXXXIX, nos. 1354–1359.

241 DeCou 1905, pl. CIV, esp. 1803–1804 (referred to as "plates of bronze").

242 Papadopoulos 2003a, pp. 129–130, fig. 161, nos. 450–454.

243 *Isthmia* VII, p. 101, n. 28, pp. 106–108, figs. 18–20, pl. 58, nos. 351–362; p. 171, pl. 95, appendix II; cf. also an example from Crete published in Boardman 1971, pl. Δ′ (center left, from Early Iron Age Kavousi).

244 Papadopoulos 2003a, pp. 127–129, figs. 158–160 (with discussion and references to related pieces).

245 Cf., for example, Kilian-Dirlmeier 1984a, pl. 44, nos. 1282–1302.

246 Boardman 1967, pp. 227, 229, fig. 149, no. 424, with comparison to Blinkenberg 1931, pl. 9, no. 132.

247 *Isthmia* VII, pp. 146, 149, pl. 85, no. 550.

248 Kilian-Dirlmeier 2002, pp. 157–158, pl. 163, esp. no. 2626, about which she writes: "Ringgriffe, bestehend aus einer Zwinge mit beweglich eingehängtem Ring und einer runden Beschlagscheibe, sind zu allen Zeiten in unterschiedlichsten Funktionen verwendet worden." She goes on to cite parallels from Olynthos and elsewhere.

249 See, for example, Papadopoulos and Kurti 2014, pp. 355–356, fig. 10.25, esp. no. 10/62 (with references).

250 The earliest example, in iron, is from the Early Geometric "warrior grave" in the Athenian Agora, tomb 13, see *Agora* XXXVI, pp. 114–118, figs. 2.62–2.64, T13-17; also pp. 968–969 (the disk of the Agora example does not survive). The type in bronze is especially common in Archaic and Classical sanctuaries throughout the Greek world, including the Athenian Acropolis, Lindos, Olympia, the Argive Heraion, Dodona, and Philia, to mention only a few sites; see Keramopoullos and Pelekidis 1915, p. 27, fig. 25:λ; Blinkenberg 1931, col. 204, pl. 26, nos. 636, 638, 639; *Olympia* IV, p. 95, no. 663; DeCou 1905, pp. 267–269, pls. CXIX–CI, nos. 1600–1718 (mostly perforated, plain and ornamented); Caskey and Amandry 1952, pl. 46, no. 110; Carapanos 1878, pl. LIII:21; Kilian-Dirlmeier 2002, pp. 109–111, pls. 106–107, nos. 1694–1744. The type is also very popular in Archaic and later sites in southern Italy; see Papadopoulos 2003a, pp. 132–133, fig. 167, with full discussion and comparanda. Examples from the sanctuary of Poseidon at Isthmia are of Classical or uncertain date, see *Isthmia* VII, pp. 150–152, fig. 33, pl. 87, nos. 567–574. Classical and Roman examples are known from Olynthos and Sardis, among other sites, see *Olynthus* X, p. 84, pl. XVII, nos. 288, 289 (under earrings); p. 221, pls. LVII, LIX, nos. 767–769 (under bronze handles); p. 246, pl. LXV, nos. 977, 981 (bronze cotter pins); *Sardis* 8, pp. 77, 94–95, 140, nos. 142, 534, 923, 938, pls. 26, 36, 53 (Sardis). For discussion of the large group of related staples from Salamis on Cyprus, associated with a chariot or cart, see Karageorghis 1973, pp. 18–19, pls. XLII, CCLIV, nos. 111, 112 (two bronze examples); pp.

43–45, pls. LXXV, CCLII, nos. 416/4, 8, 12, 14, 26, 30A, 33, 35 (iron examples), with further discussion in *Agora* XXXVI, pp. 968–969.

251 DeCou 1905, pls. C–CI, nos. 1706, 1708 (among others); *Isthmia* VII, p. 149, pl. 85, no. 549.

252 See, for example, Boardman 1967, p. 228, fig. 150, no. 417.

253 See, among others, Evangelidis 1952, p. 297, fig. 27, no. 1; Kourouniotis 1910, col. 328, fig. 53 (right), referred to as a binding plate; *Isthmia* VII, p. 136, pl. 74, no. 479 (referred to as a "keyplate"); pp. 133–134, 136 ("hinges," mostly iron); cf. also some of the 4th-century B.C. hinges in *Olynthus* X, pp. 299–301, pl. LXXXVI, nos. 1301–1307. For southern Italy, see Stoop 1987, pp. 29, 31, fig. 37; Papadopoulos 2003a, pp. 130–131, fig. 162, no. 455; see also the Hellenistic "elemente di cassetta," de Juliis, Alessio, and di Puolo 1989, pp. 365–366, no. 336.

254 For bronze belts, see, among others, Boardman 1967, pp. 214–221 (Chios); Klebinder-Gauss 2007, pp. 102–103, pls. 51–53, 108, nos. 738–756, and cf. also the so-called "Hakenenden," pp. 101–102, pls. 44, 45, 51, 108, nos. 710, 711, 732–737 (Ephesos).

255 Kilian-Dirlmeier 2002, pp. 115–116, pl. 110, nos. 1782–1793, esp. nos. 1782–1785 ("Ausstattung von Helmen"), with full discussion and comparanda.

256 *Isthmia* VII, pp. 135–136, 144, pl. 81, no. 524 (IM 3241). It is only slightly larger than **26/170**.

257 Kilian 1975a, p. 206, pl. 80, no. 1 (inv. M 1599). I see no compelling parallels in Kilian-Dirlmeier 1979. A small silver bead/pendant in *Sindos* III, pp. 136–137, 432, 588, fig. 227, pl. 246, no. 227 (from tomb 68, 470–460 B.C.), is vaguely reminiscent of **26/172**, though different, and is equipped with a suspension hole.

258 For the T-Nadeln, which are especially common at the Argive Heraion, Tiryns, Argos, Corinth, and Tegea, see Kilian-Dirlmeier 1984a, pp. 149–150, pls. 61–62, nos. 1865–1905; Voyatzis 1990, p. 341, pl. 155, no. B225.

259 *Sindos* III, pp. 280–281, 468, figs. 228, 229, nos. 559, 560 (both from tombs dating to the end of the 6th century B.C.). Both of the Sindos tombs were disturbed; thus, the position of the two pieces in situ could not be determined.

260 *Sindos* III, p. 280, with full discussion and references. Among others, Blinkenberg 1931, cols. 124–125, pl. 12, nos. 305–308, refers to examples from Lindos as "bâtonnets en os."

261 Snodgrass 1964, pp. 151–152, fig. 10, Type 3A1 (plain); the earliest example presented by Snodgrass is from Asine (see Frödin and Persson 1938, p. 333, fig. 225, no. 2); he goes on to cite (p. 252, n. 40) probable Archaic comparanda from Smyrna, Daphnae, Naukratis, Lindos, Chios, and Sparta, noting that some of the Olympia examples have a terminus ante quem of 460 B.C.

262 Snodgrass 1964, p. 151. Such a date is corroborated by recently published examples from Selinunte; the closest to **26/175** are dated to the Archaic period; see, among others, *Selinus* V, p. 25, pl. 2, nos. 17, 25.

263 Snodgrass 1964, pp. 151–152, fig. 10, Type 3B1 (projecting socket).

264 Snodgrass 1964, pp. 151–152, fig. 10, Type 3B2 (with spur).

265 Reinholdt 1992, p. 228, fig. 15a, Samos B 46, and cf. some of the arrowheads on fig. 15b from Samos, Delphi, Troy, and Olympia.

266 Snodgrass 1964, pp. 152–153, fig. 10, Type 3B3 (interior socket), with references on p. 253, n. 44. There are two bronze arrowheads of this type in *Sindos* III, pp. 315, 492, figs. 302α, 303, nos. 659 (tomb 84, 360–350 B.C., a date that accords nicely with the destruction of Methone) and 660 (chance find near kiln 4).

267 Snodgrass 1964, pp. 152–153, fig. 10, Types 3B4 and 3B5.

268 Snodgrass 1964, pp. 153, 253–254; Snodgrass cites examples thought to be associated with Greek mercenaries from Carchemish (7th century B.C.), Al Mina (late 4th century B.C.), Athlit, and Gordion (the latter Hellenistic). Likely Archaic examples from Greece and in Greek colonies are noted from Perachora, Delos, Olympia, and Kyrene.

269 Snodgrass 1964, p. 153.

270 Snodgrass 1964, p. 154, Type 4; Snodgrass 1996, p. 585, Type C (Knossos, probably Late Geometric); see, most recently, *Agora* XXXVI, pp. 959–962, which questions the Cypriot origins of this type of arrowhead in Greece.

271 Snodgrass 1964, pp. 154, 254, with references.

272 Snodgrass 1964, pp. 154, 254, with reference to the type in Olynthos, for which see *Olynthus* X, pp. 392–397, pls. CXXIII–CXXIV, nos. 1972–2026 (where it is classified as Type E); for the Crowe corselet at Olympia, see *Olympia* IV, pl. 59.

273 *Agora* XXXVI, pp. 114–118, 959–962, figs. 62–64, T13-18, and cf. T13-14.

274 Schmitt 2007, pls. 94–96, nos. 368–390.

275 Vokotopoulou 1986, fig. 107:ζ; *Sindos* III, pp. 315, 492, fig. 304, no. 661 (chance find).

276 *Torone* I, pp. 727–728, fig. 171, no. 18.14; for Philip II at Torone, see *Torone* I, p. 50; for the ἀνωτάτω φυλακτήριον, see p. 221.

277 Hagerman 2014, pp. 87–89, figs. 5.2–5.3, nos. 100–191.

278 See Chapter 28, with n. 181; see also Chapter 1.

279 Snodgrass 1964, pp. 125, 127–128, fig. 8:b.

280 Vokotopoulou 1986, pp. 300–301, fig. 106, where seven examples of the type are illustrated; cf. also Kilian 1975a, pl. 93, no. 22 (Pherai).

281 Snodgrass 1964, pp. 132–133; for Corinth, see further *Corinth* XV.1, p. 120, pl. 48, no. 32.

282 Vokotopoulou 1986, p. 304, fig. 104:ζ.

283 Apart from the examples already noted in Snodgrass 1964 (pp. 132–134, 174), cf., among many others, *Olympia* IV, pl. LXIV (various types); Weber 1944, pp. 154–157, pls. 63–64 (bronze), and pp. 157–158, pls. 65–66 (iron examples from Olympia); Kilian 1975a, p. 216, pl. 92, no. 6 (Pherai); Kilian-Dirlmeier 2002, pp. 142–143, pls. 147–148, nos. 2248–2261 (Philia); *Torone* I, pp. 726–727, fig. 171, nos. 18.12, 18.13; Schmitt 2007, pp. 543–544, pls. 91–92, nos. 318–349 (Kalapodi). For examples of the Classical period, see *Olynthus* X, pp. 416–418, pls. CXXVIII–CXXIX (bronze and iron), note esp. the type B sauroters, such as no. 2174.

284 *Olympia* IV, p. 177, pl. LXIV, no. 1064; Kilian-Dirlmeier 2002, p. 114, pl. 110, nos. 1771–1776; Schmitt 2007, pl. 92, nos. 340–342; Gàbrici 1927, cols. 365–367, figs. 157:f, i; pl. 158:b; Mazza 1992, p. 32; Ardovino 1980, pl. XVII:2; Papadopoulos 2003a, p. 65, fig. 82:a–b, no. 169. Note also the copper and iron sauroter associated with a statue at Isthmia, see *Isthmia* VII, pp. 11–12, pl. 9, no. 43 (with further discussion).

285 See, among others, Orsi 1926, col. 130, fig. 125 (right), with further discussion in col. 173 (Calabria); Orsi 1913, p. 142, fig. 188 (second from left, from Rosarno Medma); Orsi 1914, col. 901, fig. 141 (right, from Kaulonia); Bedello and Fabbricotti 1975, p. 72, no. 4; p. 89, fig. 16, no. 7; cf. p. 128, no. 7 (bottom, from Veii); Marzoli 1989, pl. 33, no. 5 (Quattro Fontanili); as well as from Scicli in Sicily, see Di Stefano and Giardino 1990–1991, p. 507, fig. 13, no. 37.

286 Snodgrass 1964, pp. 100–101, fig. 6:g; Wace and Thompson 1912, pp. 26–27, fig. 15, nos. 6, 7 (esp. no. 6, Halos, pyre XV, dated to the 8th century B.C.).

287 Vokotopoulou 1986, p. 200, fig. 88:β, γ, T157-8 (last quarter of the 8th century B.C.). In terms of size, an example in *Sindos* III, pp. 235, 460, fig. 190, no. 429 (from tomb 28, ca. 560 B.C.), which is intact, including haft, has a length of 0.317, and is described, rightly in my view, as a knife. Many of the knives of Late Geometric and earlier Archaic date from Philia have related tips, but are also smaller, see Kilian-Dirlmeier 2002, pp. 71–72, pls. 68–71, various examples.

288 Vokotopoulou 1986, figs. 88–89 (various examples).

289 Kilian-Dirlmeier 2002, p. 8, pl. 2, nos. 3–8 (classified as "Hiebmesser," slashing knives); Snodgrass 1996, p. 578, 125.f1a.

290 See esp. Kilian-Dirlmeier 1993, pp. 118–126, pls. 55–57, nos. 404–442; the possibility cannot be ruled out that **26/192** is a late iron example of a Naue II sword (or related type), see Kilian-Dirlmeier 1993, pp. 113–118, pls. 48–54, nos. 352–400; Vokotopoulou 1986, esp. figs. 86–87, swords from tombs 76 (5th century B.C.), 119 and 166 (both 4th century B.C.); note also the late Archaic to Classical swords from Philia, Kilian-Dirlmeier 2002, pp. 107–108, pls. 102–104, nos. 1664–1683, as well as some of the swords, daggers, and related blades from Philia from contexts that cannot be dated precisely, pp. 133–135, pls. 119–120, nos. 1985–2008 ("Schwerter," "Dolche," "Fragmente von Schwertklingen oder Lanzenspitzen," and "Hiebmesser"); Schmitt 2007, pls. 102–105 (various examples, Kalapodi).

291 *Sindos* III, pp. 291–304, 474–485, figs. 251–272, nos. 595–622 (with references).

292 See esp. Kron 1998; to which add: Kilian 1975a, pl. 93, nos. 1–2 (Pherai); Kilian-Dirlmeier 2002, pp. 113–114, pls. 108–109, nos. 1761–1770 (Philia).

293 See, among others, *Vergina* I, p. 267, fig. 104, Zπ1α; Vokotopoulou 1986, fig. 91:α–ΣΤ (Vitsa); Snodgrass 1996, pp. 586–587, Types C and D (Knossos, North Cemetery); *Sindos* III, pp. 462–464, figs. 208–215, nos. 450–461.

294 Such as the so-called "pruning hooks" from the Rachi settlement at Isthmia, see *Isthmia* VII, pp. 121, 127, pls. 69–70, nos. 446–449 (mostly of Classical date, one early Hellenistic).

295 See, for example, Vokotopoulou 1986, fig. 91:α. Two examples that may be larger are *Selinus* V, p. 126, pl. 36, nos. 677 and 678, esp. 677, which is dated 550/540–530 B.C.

296 In *Isthmia* VII, pp. 121, 127, pls. 69–70, nos. 445–449, Raubitschek (esp. p. 121, with n. 12) refers to pruning hooks in Asia (citing McClellan 1975, p. 324, no. 231, pls. 17, 32); she also refers to *Perachora* I, pp. 189–190, pl. 86. For the two iron sickles from Nemea see Miller 1976, p. 191, pl. 37d.

297 *Isthmia* VII, p. 121, n. 12. Note also the "vinedresser" (ἀμπελουργός) in Philostratus *Heroicus*, *passim*. The *Heroicus* presents a conversation between a devout farmer, "vinedresser," and a skeptical Phoenician, at the site of the hero-shrine of Protesilaos at or near Elaious, on the Gallipoli peninsula opposite Troy, about the powers and worship of the Homeric heroes. See, esp., the new edition of the *Heroicus* edited and translated by J. Rusten and J. King, *Philostratus, Heroicus, Gymnasticus, Discourses 1 and 2*, Cambridge, Mass. 2014 in the Loeb Classical Library.

298 For Hypogeion 2, see Morris et al. 2020, pp. 702–712, figs. 54–56.

299 For "oar-scrapers" see Chapter 20, n. 17.

300 Blackwell 2020, p. 533, caption for fig. 3.6.2.

301 *Torone* I, p. 760, fig. 174, pl. 98, no. 18.107, of the 17th century A.D., perhaps used in leatherworking.

302 Gesell, Coulson, and Day 1991, p. 153, pl. 58:g; see also Gesell, Day, and Coulson 1988, p. 286.

303 See, among others, Gesell, Coulson, and Day 1991, p. 153, pl. 58:e; *Pithekoussai* I, p. 517, pl. 154, no. 515–119 (inv. 168039); p. 555, pls. 165 and CLXXIV, no. 557-7 (inv. 168226); p. 659, pl. 190, no. 678-5 (inv. 168662), all Late Geometric II.

304 For a useful summary and discussion of these, see Munaretto and Schaus 2014, p. 185. See further Rolley 1984, p. 277, figs. 32–33, no 64 (Korykian Cave); *Isthmia* VII, pp. 134–135, 175–181; *Corinth* XII, pp. 140–143, nos. 1014–1055 (various types in bronze and iron); Shaw and Shaw 2000, pp. 373–386, 412–413 (Kommos, with references); Branigan 1992, p. 367 (Knossos); *Olynthus* X, pp. 309–329, pls. XCI–XCVI; *Torone* I, pp. 740–744, fig. 172, pl. 97, nos. 18.44–18.60.

305 Munaretto and Schaus 2014, pp. 184–192; *Sindos* III, p. 466, figs. 220–222 (type I–III).

306 For timber, hammers, and nails in the royal tombs of Vergina, see Andronikos 1984, pp. 71, 74, 217.

307 Munaretto and Schaus 2014, pp. 186–192; for Hellenistic and later examples, see, among others, Soueref 2016, p. 58, no. 13.

308 Papadopoulos and Kurti 2014, pp. 367–370, fig. 10.39, nos. 10/89–10/101; with references to parallels from other Albanian sites, including, among others, Katundas, Shtoj, and Luaras.

309 *Isthmia* VII, pp. 131–144.

310 Papadopoulos 2005, pp. 151, 563, fig. 135, pl. 330:a, b, T79-1.

311 *Sardis* 8, p. 87, pl. 30, nos. 480–481.

312 *Sardis* 8, p. 87, no. 480.

313 *Corinth* XII, pp. 204, 208, pl. 94, nos. 1580–1582.

314 For the weights, see *Corinth* XII, pp. 203–204 (with references).

315 *Torone* I, pp. 758–759, fig. 174, nos. 18.102, 18.103.

316 *Agora* X, p. 32, pl. 10, nos. LW 74, 76, 79; for the lead and bronze weights of Olynthos, see *Olynthus* X, pp. 447–471, pls. CXXXVIII–CLII; for the form of **26/212**, see, among others, no. 2383.

317 See, among others, *Isthmia* VII, pp. 112, 116–117, pl. 64, nos. 406–412, though some of these may have served other functions; Raubitschek notes that at least one of the perforated disks may have been a pendant. For solid, unperforated, flat disks, see also *Olynthus* X, pp. 467–468, pl. CXLVIII, nos. 2451–2455.

318 For two suspected lead sinkers of rather different form, see *Sardis* 8, p. 87, pl. 30, nos. 485 (Hellenistic-Roman?), 486 (Late Byzantine). One is conical with a round perforation through the center, the other domed, with a similar perforation.

319 There is only one lead suspension weight (thought to be a loomweight) from Corinth, dating to the Hellenistic or Roman period, *Corinth* XII, pp. 163, 172, pl. 77, no. 1212; see also the bell-shaped suspension weight of bronze, its interior filled with lead, in *Corinth* XII, p. 213, pl. 96, no. 1640; for lead loomweights dating to the 4th century B.C., see esp. *Olynthus* X, pp. 471–474, pls. CLIII–CLV, nos. 2479–2501; *Isthmia* VII, pp. 111–112, 116, pl. 63, nos. 405, 405a (both 3rd century B.C.).

320 See *Délos* XVIII, pp. 155–156, for discussion and references.

321 *Corinth* XII, p. 213, pl. 96, nos. 1642 (bronze), 1644 (lead, with a tiny projection for suspension), and 1645 (stone).

322 *Torone* I, p. 758, fig. 174, no. 18.104, with references to Orlandos 1968, pp. 68–69, fig. 62.

323 Kilian-Dirlmeier 1979, pp. 154–158, pls. 49–51, nos. 887–937.

324 Papadopoulos 2003a, p. 142, fig. 176, no. 558 (Diam. 0.033 is virtually identical to the Diam. of **26/216** (0.034); for related bronze wheels from Francavilla, see Stoop 1987, p. 22, fig. 6; also Stoop 1980, pp. 177, 187, fig. 36. For an almost identical wheel, but in bronze, from Sala Consilina, see Kilian 1970, pl. 72, I, no. 3:f; and others from Olympia, see *OlForsch* XIII, pp. 346, 348, pl. 76, no. 1239; *OlForsch* XII, pl. 119, nos. 939–941.

325 For Olympia, see Heilmeyer 1981, 1994; for Delphi, *FdD* V.1, pp. 118–119, figs. 433–437. See also Alexandri 1973, p. 104, nos. 7–8, pl. 56:α–β; Kardara 1988, pl. 113:γ; Bammer 1990, p. 30, fig. 14; Klebinder-Gauss 2007, pp. 175–176, pl. 88, no. 900, with further references; Filow 1927, p. 31, fig. 28, no. 4.

326 Woytowitsch 1978.

327 *Sindos* III, pp. 213–213, 611–616, nos. 416–428, figs. 428–450, nos. 416–428, with full discussion and references. The Sindos carts date from the 6th into the 5th centuries B.C.

328 The fullest discussion of wheel pendants ("Radanhänger") is Kilian-Dirlmeier 1979, pp. 16–29, pls. 4–10, nos. 54–152. See also Amandry 1953, pl. XXVII, no. 184a; *OlForsch* XIII, pp. 345–348, pl. 76, nos. 1233–1244; Kilian 1975a, pl. 79 (various examples from Pherai); Voyatzis 1990, p. 334, pl. 117, nos. B151–B152; Mazarakis Ainian 2019, p. 119, fig. 212 (Kythnos); cf. also the various types of wheel ornaments, such as Bouzek 1974b, pp. 135, 139, figs. 43–44. Also, further discussion in *Perachora* I, p. 183, pl. 83, no. 19; *Vergina* I, p. 255 (with fig. 90); for the wheel pendants of Ithaka, see Robertson 1948, pl. 49, nos. E185, E186. At Francavilla Marittima in northern Calabria, wheel pendants were common both as dedications in the sanctuary (see Stoop 1987, pp. 22, 24,

fig. 6 [FM 65555]) and as offerings in graves, often worn by the deceased, see Zancani Montuoro 1977–1979, p. 14, fig. 4, no. 5; p. 22, fig. 8, no. 4, pl. XLIII:c (left); Zancani Montuoro 1980–1982, p. 15, fig. 3, pl. III:b, no. 6; p. 103, fig. 37, no. 12; Zancani Montuoro 1983–1984, p. 20, fig. 2, pl. V, no. 8; p. 36, fig. 8, no. 7; pl. XXVII:b, no. 8; pl. XLI, no. 12; pl. LXIII:a, no. 11; see also de la Genière 1968, p. 118; Kilian 1970, pl. 72, I, no. 3:f.

329 The fullest list of these is assembled in Dunst 1972, pp. 139–140, in the context of presenting a new example from Samos; a few of these are conveniently illustrated in Jeffery and Johnston 1990, pl. 15, no. 17; pl. 67, no. 13. Among many others see, for example, *Isthmia* VII, p. 11, pl. 8, no. 41 (inscribed with a dedication to Poseidon); another inscribed wheel, said to come from Galaxidi near Delphi, Caskey 1936, pp. 310–311, fig. 5, appears to be a dedication to Apollo; Kontis 1949–1951, p. 347, fig. 1. An inscribed bronze wheel from the Athenian Acropolis has the name of the dedicant: Πίθηκος ἀνέθηκεν, see Bather 1892–1893, p. 127, pl. VI, no. 42; for uninscribed bronze wheels or wheel pendants from the Athenian Acropolis, see Keramopoullos and Pelekidis 1915, p. 28, fig. 26:γ; note also the bronze wheel in Lilibaki-Akamati and Akamatis 2012, p. 22, fig. 5, second from the left. Note also the example from Rhamnous published in Petrakos 1987, p. 285, fig. 13.

330 *Agora* XXVIII, pp. 59–64; the complete *pinakia* associated with the kleroteria were usually double the length of **26/217** (Agora P 8 measures 0.080, and Agora P 9 0.139 m in length). The term *pinakion* in Greek is generic, akin to "plaque" or "tablet."

331 *Agora* XXVIII, p. 10, n. 2. See further, Dow 1963; Kroll 1967, 1972.

332 Such as the lead letter from Torone (H. 0.052; W. [top] 0.127; W. [bottom]; Th. 0.001 m), for which see Henry 1991, 2001, with references to other examples, as well as to *defixiones*.

333 *Isthmia* VII, pp. 116–177, pl. 64, esp. nos. 407–412.

334 *Isthmia* VII, pp. 155–159, pls. 89–90, nos. 584–605 (with full discussion).

335 *Isthmia* VII, p. 156.

336 See Miller 1979, p. 81, pl. 25:a, inv. IL 242 (Nemea); *Olynthus* X, pp. 477–481, pls. CLV, CLVII, esp. nos. 2525–2527, see also nos. 2514–2520.

337 See *OlForsch* XVIII, p. 164, pl. 60; Furtwängler 1906, p. 424, pl. 119, nos. 74–78. See further Bankel 1984. Raubitschek (*Isthmia* VII, p. 157, n. 14) notes that Manolis Korres found many such lead pieces behind the Parthenon metopes (pers. comm.). For Roman lead marking pens from Ostia, see Drescher 1989, pp. 59–60, figs. 1, 4–5.

338 For standardized weights, see *Isthmia* VII, p. 156.

339 Bass 1967, pp. 62–69, 74; Bass 1986, pp. 270–272, 275–276, pl. 17, fig. 1 (top right).

340 For lead fillers for bronze vessels, see Papadopoulos 2003a, pp. 26–27, fig. 30 (a magnificent cast bronze tripod foot in the form of a cow's or bull's hoof, largely filled with lead); also p. 142, fig. 177, nos. 559, 560 (Francavilla Marittima); cf. Furtwängler 1981, pl. 31, no. 2 (Samos); *Perachora* I, pp. 160–161, pl. 64:2, 5, 6 lead fillers for ring feet; Kakavoyiannis 1984, p. 131, fig. 4:a. For bronze statues or statuettes, see the bronze panther in *Isthmia* VII, p. 23, pl. 19, no. 89; with further discussion of the technique in Rostoker and Gebhard 1980, pp. 353–354, 362, pl. 106:b; also the lead-filled bronze lion from Dodona, Dakaris 1974, pp. 48–50, figs. 38, 39 (the lead filling is noted on p. 50); and, more generally, *Isthmia* VII, pp. 157, 159–161, pls. 92–93, nos. 606–616.

341 *Isthmia* VII, pp. 133–134, 138, pl. 75, nos. 486, 487. For such lead pivots in situ see, among others, *Délos* XVIII, pl. LXXVII, no. 635; *Délos* VIII, pp. 265–266, 272, 275–276, 280, 284–285, figs. 128–130, 136, 152, 157; see also Leinas 1973, p. 327, fig. 33; *Olynthus* VIII, pp. 249–256; *Olynthus* X, pp. 295–296, pl. LXXXV, nos. 1286–1287. Note also the lead door socket in situ on a threshold block in the Classical structure 3 at Torone, see *Torone* I, pp. 142–170, pl. 25:g.

342 The surviving fragments of the other object are illustrated together with **26/233** in the photograph (Fig. 26.66).

27

JEWELRY MOLDS FROM METHONE IN THE ARCHAEOLOGICAL MUSEUM OF THESSALONIKI (STAMATIOS TSAKOS COLLECTION)

Styliana Galiniki

The use of molds for the manufacture of various items of clay, metal, or glass cullet (recycled glass) is found all over the ancient world, at different historical periods.[1] Molds were mostly made of stone or clay; when durable, they could be reused for the production of multiple identical objects. Because their basic technological features remained unchanged through time, the dating of the molds relies primarily on the patterns that were carved on them.[2] What should be stressed is that each mold is a distinct object, with its own particular characteristics.

The molds with inventory numbers ΤΣ 1080, ΤΣ 1081 and ΤΣ 1082 in the Stamatios Tsakos Collection in the Archaeological Museum of Thessaloniki (AMTh/ΑΜΘ) are on display in the permanent exhibition "Macedonia from the 7th Century B.C. until Late Antiquity."[3] According to the collector, they were chance finds from the area of Methone, Pieria. All three molds bear various carved patterns for jewelry. The differences in the shape, size, and raw material of the molds, in conjunction with the diverse types of the carved designs and the presence or absence of pouring funnels, are related to the manner of use of the molds and to the potential application of distinct technologies in each case.

As became apparent in the course of this project, the study of mold technology and manufacture can be particularly complex and complicated. The present publication posed a challenge to investigate further issues that had arisen during the original publication of these artifacts. During this new study various hypotheses were confirmed or refuted, and emphasis was placed on details that had previously escaped due attention; at the same time, new questions emerged and new fields of inquiry opened up.

STONE MOLD FOR THE MANUFACTURE OF A SPECTACLE FIBULA (ΤΣ 1080, FIGS. 27.1–27.24)

The mold with inventory number ΤΣ 1080 (8.9 x 8 x 3.2 cm) (Fig. 27.1) is rectangular in shape and in section.[4] It is made of polished dark-brown stone with a gray-green patina, which has been identified by stereoscopic observation as micrite fossiliferous limestone that occurs in the Peloponnese.[5] This is a dense rock which, however, can be easily etched and is resistant to temperatures of up to 900º C. The surface bears patches of accretion, shallow abrasions, and discolorations—probably the result of wear during casting[6]—while the upper horizontal surface has been chipped off, and thus only about one-half of this surface survives.[7]

FIGURE 27.1. Stone mold ΤΣ 1080, made of micrite fossiliferous limestone.
Photo J. Vanderpool

The mold bears a carved figure-of-eight pattern and a pouring funnel on the one ("main") horizontal surface, while the other ("secondary") horizontal surface bears only a funnel in a corresponding position. The figure-of-eight—or so-called spectacle—motif is found mainly on fibulae of ivory and bone, and more rarely among metal fibulae. Spectacle fibulae have been found at various sites of island and mainland Greece, and in the wider Mediterranean basin.[8] They date from the late 8th to the 6th century B.C., with most examples belonging to the 7th and 6th centuries. Sometimes the back surface preserves the fastening pin.

Spectacle fibulae of ivory or bone have been found in sanctuary deposits (Sparta, Perachora, Vryokastro on Kythnos, Paros, Thasos, Sybaris, Lokroi Epizephyrioi, Olympia, Chios),[9] while they are rarer in graves, including the cemeteries of Thera, Aineia, and Oropos.[10] A silver-plated bone specimen was found in a pyre at the Telesterion in Eleusis;[11] bone examples from the sanctuary of Artemis Orthia in Sparta had amber inlays in the centers of the disks.[12]

Metal fibulae of this type are rarer. Most are made of bronze and have been found in sanctuaries, for example, at Sparta, Despotiko, and Vryokastro,[13] as well as in tombs at Knossos,[14] in Serbia, and in Bulgaria.[15] The earlier spectacle fibulae from Vitsa are made of iron and come from graves dating to the 9th and 8th centuries B.C.,[16] while an iron example from a grave in southern Italy,[17] and another from Kalapodi, date to the 6th century B.C.[18] A lead specimen has been found at Tegea.[19] Three figure-of-eight-shaped gold sheets with embossed decoration, now in Berlin, were intended for the plating of spectacle fibulae made of bone, or for other objects.[20] A spectacle fibula of silver and part of a second one have been found at Vryokastro;[21] another such ornament was placed on a grave at Tarra, on Crete.[22]

The pattern of a spectacle fibula is also carved on the mold ΤΣ 1081 of the Tsakos Collection (see below), as well as on a stone mold fragment from Kalapodi.[23] A mold from Vergina likewise bears a figure-of-eight design, combined with the motif of the sacral knot, for the manufacture of a pendant.[24] A disk-shaped design on a fragment of a stone mold from Karabournaki, dating to the second half of the 5th century,[25] was possibly also intended for a spectacle fibula.

With regard to the decorative motif of the concentric dotted circlets, variations are seen on several spectacle fibulae, as well as on diverse objects of ivory, bone, and metal, since the Late Bronze Age. Most comparanda date to the 7th–6th century,[26] although the motif occurs sporadically into Roman times.[27] On our mold the circles adjoin or intertwine, as if attempting to render a braid pattern.[28]

On the basis of the comparanda noted above, a date for the mold ΤΣ 1080 in the 7th–6th centuries B.C. is most likely.

Technical Features of the Mold: Observations and Questions

One of the main initial questions was whether the mold ΤΣ 1080 was composed of two joined blocks, as is hinted by the perimeter groove on the vertical sides A, B, C, and D (Fig. 27.2), or preserves one component of a two-part (bivalve) or multi-part mold—in which case the perimeter groove is simply superficial. This question was already answered in the original publication: the mold belongs to the closed type, which consists of two halves fitted together.[29] Having established this, the following discussion addresses both old pending issues and new questions that arose in the context of the present restudy.

The blocks (upper: max. Th. 1.6; lower: max. Th. 1.3 cm), are still attached together; the mold has not been opened since it was last used by an ancient craftsman. On the main horizontal surface—that is, the outside of the upper half (Figs. 27.3–27.4)—the figure-of-eight pattern is placed symmetrically on the diagonal axis, and ends in a pouring funnel (L. 1.9; max. W. 0.8; min. W. 0.3 cm) that is carved perpendicular to the corner of sides A and B, its mouth slightly flaring and bent over that corner. The figure-of-eight design consists of two large disks (the second one barely preserved, because of the mold's fracture) and, between them, a pair of adjoining smaller circles placed at 1 cm distance from each other. The whole measures 1 mm in disk depth and 4.2 cm of maximum width at the central area where the two small disks adjoin, with an estimated length of 8 cm—assuming that the large disks were of equal size. The intact large disk (Diam. 3.5 cm) is divided by an incised concentric circle (Diam. 1.9 cm) into two registers, of which the outer one is embellished with a row of incised and dotted concentric circlets arranged in pairs, some of them adjoining and others intersecting. The same decoration is repeated on the preserved part of the other large disk. The center of the intact disk is defined by a depression (Diam. 0.6 cm; measurable depth 0.2 cm), the shape of which (conical or hemispherical) is obscured by accretions. Likewise, the smaller disks (Diam. 1.6 cm) are defined by a conical or hemispherical central depression that is covered by encrustation (Diam. 0.6 cm; measurable depth 0.3 cm).

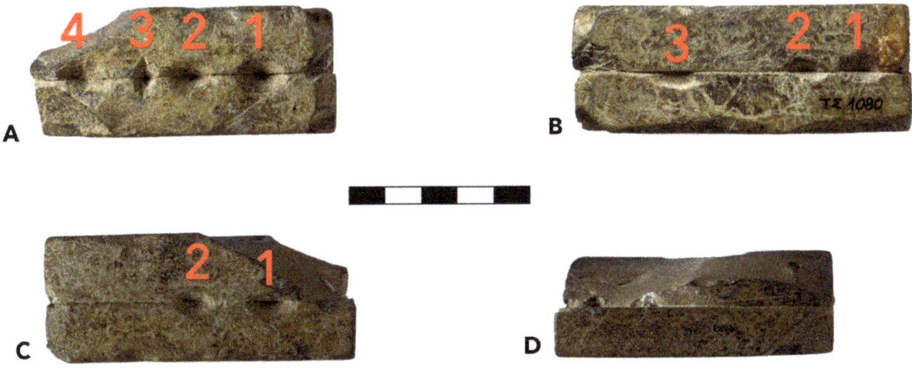

Figure 27.2. ΤΣ 1080 showing the perimeter groove on all four vertical sides (A, B, C, D as shown on Fig. 27.1). Photo J. Vanderpool

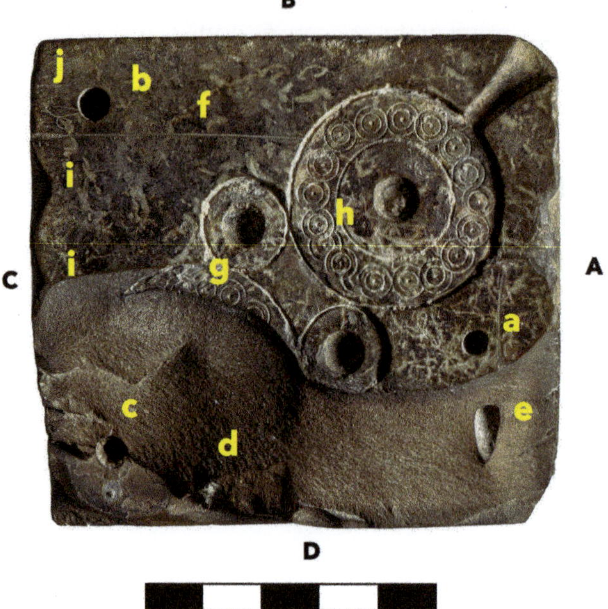

FIGURE 27.3. Primary surface of ΤΣ 1080 showing various points of interest noted in the text. Photo J. Vanderpool

FIGURE 27.4. ΤΣ 1080. Drawing T. Ross

In addition, two fully pierced vertical perforations (Diam. 0.4 cm) are positioned on the primary surface of the upper block (see Fig. 27.3, at points *a* and *b*); in their interior, at respective depths of 0.7 and 0.5 cm, they bear metal rivets that end at the secondary surface. Two more perforations exist in the fractured area but do not exit through the secondary surface. Of these, perforation *c* (Diam. 0.4 cm; D. 0.5 cm), at the corner, does not have a rivet, while perforation *d* (0.35 x 0.5 cm), farther to the right, is covered with metal—probably a rivet. We assume that perforations *c* and *d* also did not exit through the main surface, because, in that case, they would have adjoined the large preserved disk and thus damaged it. These are, therefore, internal perforations, which were opened symmetrically on the surfaces that would be in contact when the two halves of the mold were joined in another position (see the section below on "adjoined surfaces," especially position 2).

In the fractured area, near perforation *a* and at a level at least 0.5 cm lower than the figure-of-eight motif, there is a tear-shaped cavity, *e* (L. 0.9 cm; max. W. 0.3 cm), possibly a part of another carved design that may have existed on the primary surface.

From approximately the middle of the large preserved disk begins a longitudinal incision, *f* (L. 4.7 cm) that runs parallel to the edge of side surface B and ends (slightly wider) perpendicular to the edge of side surface C (Fig. 27.3); this is likely a vent. Vents in the shape of multiple incised, oblique lines are reported for earlier molds from Sicily[30] and Bulgaria,[31] as well as for later molds.[32]

Part of the lower interior surface of the block is visible in the area of the fracture and at the corner of sides C and D. The interior shows a dark discoloration, probably the result of burning on contact with the molten metal,[33] and also a grayish stain. There are additional spots of friction wear, and a series of scratches *g* (Figs. 27.3–27.5) that have damaged the decorative zone of circlets on the preserved part of the second large disk. It is not clear whether these scratches are traces of the tools used to carve the mold, or were made after the circlets were drawn—the latter explanation being more likely. By contrast, it seems that faint wavy marks at *h* (Figs. 27.3–27.5) on the intact large disk were left by the carving tools.

The secondary surface of the mold, that is, the horizontal exterior of the lower half (Fig. 27.6, see also Fig. 27.4), is flat, with a funnel (L. 2 cm; max. W. 0.7 cm, min. W. 0.35 cm) placed on the diagonal axis and in a position corresponding to the funnel on the main surface; namely, perpendicular to the corner of sides A and B. The mouth of the funnel flares slightly and bends over the corner of sides A and B; that is, it faces the mouth of the funnel on the main surface. In addition to the funnel, other features visible on the secondary surface include the ends of the rivets of perforations at points *a* and *b*, a semicircular incision around rivet *a*, and many other incised lines or scratches running in various directions. Several of these lines are located at approximately the center of the surface and are almost straight and parallel (Fig. 27.7), while others are diagonal (Fig. 27.8). Some of the straight lines are located near the corner of sides B and C (Fig. 27.9). Two additional parallel incisions, running diagonally, are visible on the vertical surface B of both halves (Fig. 27.10). These lines look like scratches left by a wire that had been tied around the block or had bound the two blocks together.[34] Their possible correlation with the aforementioned scratches (*g*) on the main surface will be discussed below.

Three of the vertical surfaces (A, B, C) of the joined halves bear depressions that are symmetrical as to their size and position on both, whereas no such depression exists on surface D. Side A bears four depressions (*A1* [L. 1.3; W. 0.8; D. 0.6 cm], *A2* [1.1 x 0.7 x 0.5 cm], *A3* [0.4 x 0.5 x 0.3 cm], and *A4* [1.2 x 0.7 x 0.3 cm]); side B has two (*B2* [0.8 x 0.3 x 0.2 cm], *B3* [1.2 x 0.5 x 0.2 cm]), and a third one (*B1* [0.8 x 0.2 x 0.1 cm]) only on the lower half; side C has two depressions (*C1* [1 x 0.5 x 0.2 cm], *C2* [1.2 x 0.4 x 0.3 cm]) (see Fig. 27.2). Although these depressions look like funnels, their inner profile is not at all clear, nor do they exhibit in any way the careful shaping of the funnels on the main and secondary surfaces. Two additional, rhomboid depressions (*i*) on side C (Fig. 27.11, see also Fig. 27.3) are positioned symmetrically at the edges of the main and the

FIGURE 27.5. Details of the primary surface of TΣ 1080.
Photos J. Vanderpool

secondary surface. Similar formations are visible on the edges of side A, but it is not clear whether those were made on purpose or caused randomly by wear.

Finally, there are some noteworthy incised marks, which—unlike the many other use- and wear-related scratches over almost the entire surface of the mold—seem to have been purposeful and point to "recognition marks," such as have been identified on the Vergina mold,[35] and on another from Samos:[36] that is, symbols of the identity of the workshop or even signs meant to distinguish each half, or the mold itself, from others. Inscriptions on the mold from Kalapodi, as well as on Roman examples from Pantikapaion and Chersonessos, have been interpreted as indicative of the craftsman's identity.[37] A similar purpose was perhaps served by a shallow, rather cursory figure-of-eight-shaped incision (*j*) (see Fig. 27.3) on the main surface, near the corner of sides B and C

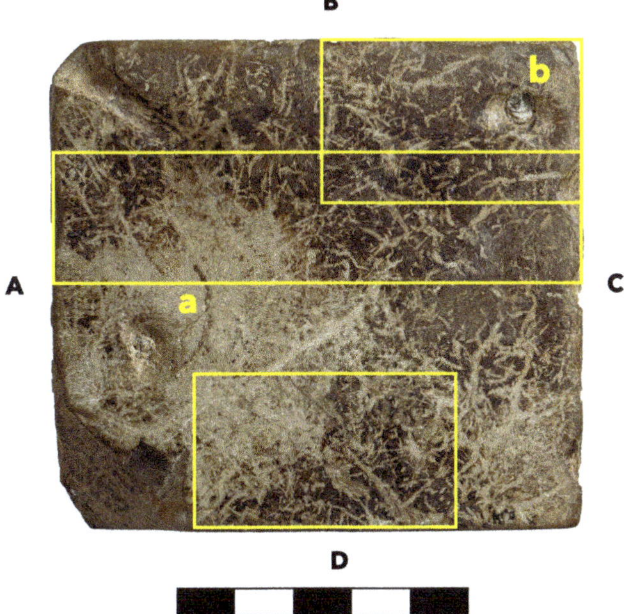

FIGURE 27.6. The secondary surface of the mold ΤΣ 1080.
Photo J. Vanderpool

FIGURE 27.7. Detail of the top right corner of the secondary surface of ΤΣ 1080 (as shown on FIGURE 27.6). Photo J. Vanderpool

(above the endpoint of the vent and beside perforation *b*), as well as by a mark in the form of the letter "A" on side A of the lower block (Fig. 27.12). It is not clear, however, whether some other incisions, around that mark and between the mouths of the funnels on the main and secondary surfaces, were intentional or random.

On side A of the upper block, there are some faint incisions of relatively consistent size and interval, running perpendicularly to a shallow horizontal line in a manner reminiscent of an inscription (Fig. 27.13); the obscurity of the lines does not permit any safe conclusion, however. Particularly unclear is also another incision, within the plain interior register of the large disk of the figure-of-eight pattern (Fig. 27.14).

FIGURE 27.8. Detail of the upper central portion of ΤΣ 1080 (cf. Fig. 27.6). Photo J. Vanderpool

FIGURE 27.9. Detail of the lower central portion of ΤΣ 1080 (cf. Fig. 27.6). Photo J. Vanderpool

FIGURE 27.10. Two parallel incisions, running diagonally, visible on the vertical surface B of both halves of ΤΣ 1080. Photo J. Vanderpool

FIGURE 27.11. Detail of vertical face C of ΤΣ 1080.
Photo J. Vanderpool

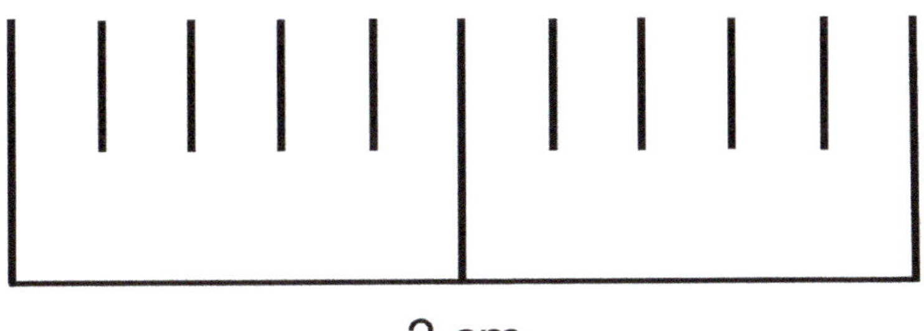

FIGURE 27.12. Detail of mark in the form of the letter "A" on side A of the lower block of ΤΣ 1080.
Photo J. Vanderpool

FIGURE 27.13. Closer details of side A of ΤΣ 1080 showing possible, but uncertain, inscriptions above the letter "A." Photos J. Vanderpool

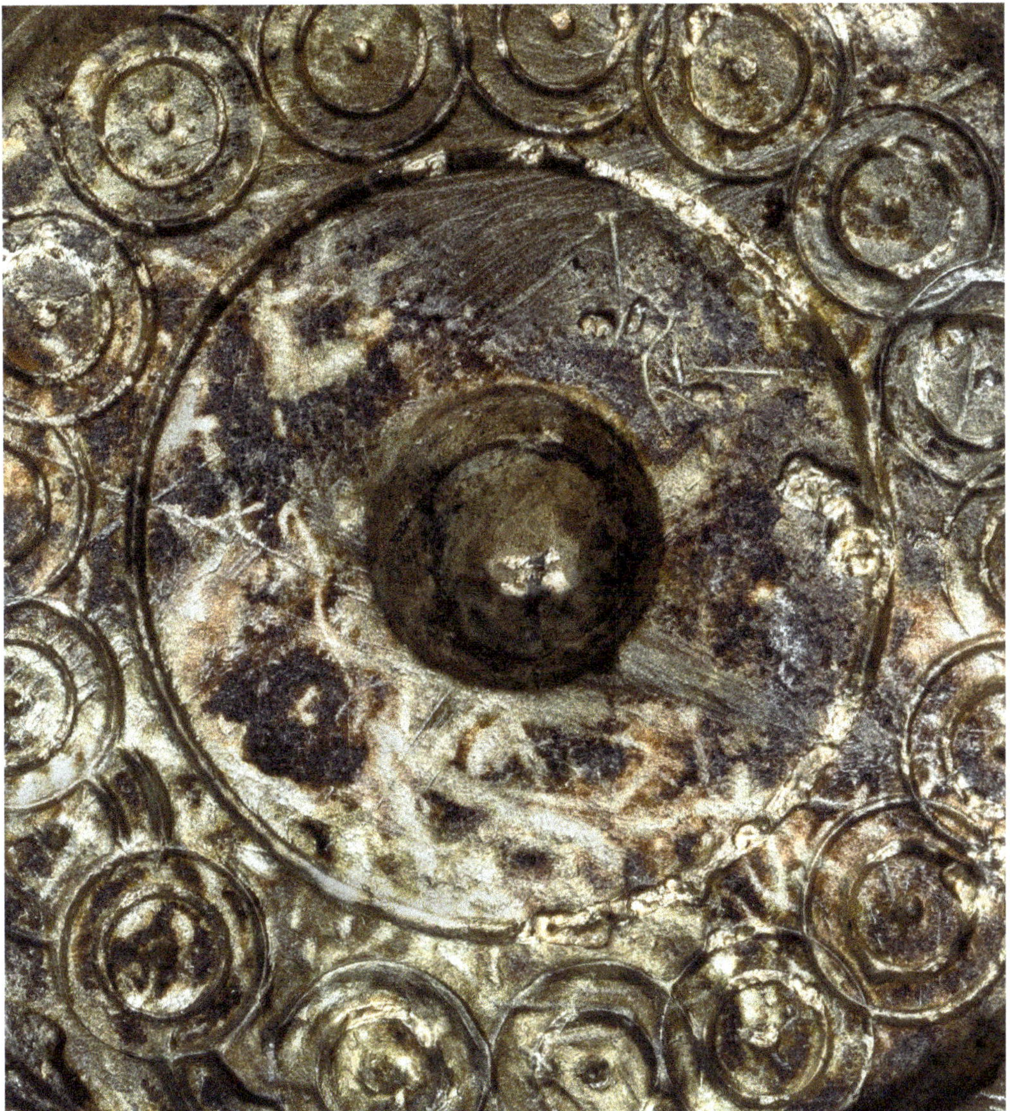

FIGURE 27.14. Detail of the carved decoration on the primary surface of TΣ 1080. Photo J. Vanderpool

Adjoined Surfaces: Investigating How the Mold Was Used

In order to produce a figure-of-eight-shaped foil of only 0.1 cm in thickness (Fig. 27.15)—likely a plating for a fibula of ivory or bone—and given that such ornaments are decorated on one side only, there had to be fitted onto the primary surface one additional flat stone block, with a funnel in a corresponding position; in other words, a slab with the features of the secondary surface of the mold.[38] Consequently, it would suffice to use the two blocks in a reversed position (what can be referred to as "position 1"), so that the main surface would be covered by the secondary one. In such a hypothetical rearrangement, the funnels of the two blocks match precisely. The rhomboid depressions (*i*) would have been used as guides for the proper fitting of the two blocks in this position.[39] The same depressions (*i*) could have been used as sockets for the binding material that held the blocks together in "position 2."

I consider here two possible explanations for the recovery of the mold with the two halves fitted in "position 2," that is, facing each other and with their respective active surfaces placed on the outside:[40]

1. It is accidental: for example, the blocks were so positioned during storage and could not be separated afterward. If this was the case, we must consider two other possibilities:
   a) the adjoined surfaces are undecorated or at least they show traces of carving attempts.
   b) the adjoined surfaces do bear carved designs, but the blocks operate as two independent, open-type molds for producing ornaments by casting the metal slowly and directly into the carved patterns, without a funnel. Consequently, two different methods of casting—open-type (without a cover) and closed-type—would have been used for the manufacture of the artifacts; such a combination is known from both ancient and more recent molds.[41]

2. There are carved patterns on the adjoined surfaces, and the mold functioned as a closed-type in both positions 1 and 2. Casting in position 2 would be possible only if all or some of the depressions on the vertical side surfaces are in fact funnels. According to this scenario, the mold has four active surfaces (two on each half), and is, therefore, bivalve and double. The recovery of the mold with the two halves in position 2 shows that it has not been opened since it was last used, and there is possibly metal still preserved between the two blocks.

The investigation precluded any potentially destructive attempt to open the mold, opting instead for non-invasive methods of analysis. The most important result of the initial X-ray testing (Fig. 27.16) was the discovery of perforation *k* between the funnels of the main and secondary surfaces, which confirmed the existence of two attached blocks.[42] Moreover, the analysis verified the existence of rivets within perforations *a*, *b*, and *c*, and the diameter of these perforations was shown to be larger than that of their respective rivets. Finally, lines could be seen radiating from rivet *a*, which were most likely caused by the cracking of the mold and do not constitute intentional incisions.

For the purposes of the present study, the mold was examined anew by detailed stereoscopic and portable-microscope observation as well as by computer tomography,[43] with additional pXRF testing for the detection of metal.

FIGURE 27.15. Modern figure-of-eight-shaped fibula made from rubber copy of ΤΣ 1080. Photo J. Vanderpool

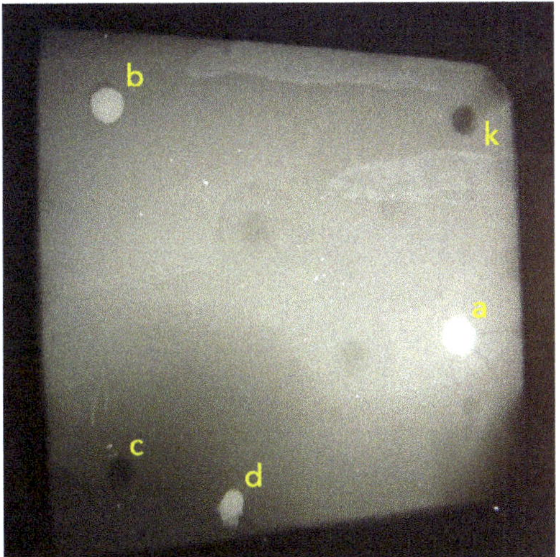

FIGURE 27.16. Initial X-ray testing of ΤΣ 1080 in 2005. X-ray image I. G. Artopoulos

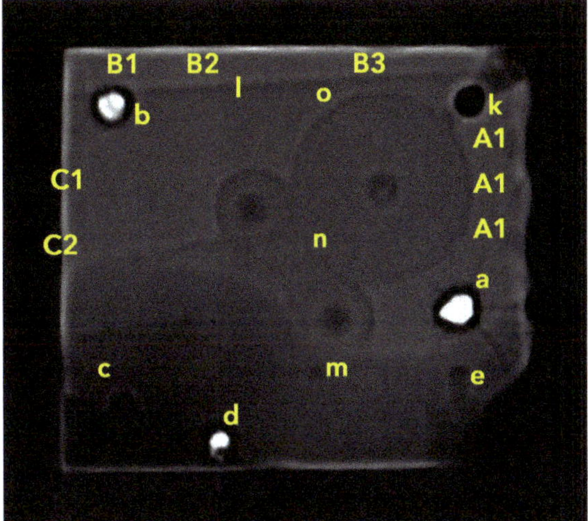

FIGURE 27.17. Top-view scan of ΤΣ 1080 in 2019. Tomography Euromedica General Clinic of Thessaloniki

The method of computed tomography was chosen in order to look for additional traces of treatment on the adjoined surfaces of the blocks, in position 2. The tomography produced a horizontal scan of the main surface of the mold, zooming in on the figure-of-eight pattern, as well as vertical sections of the entire mold at 1 mm intervals. It should be noted that the oblique positioning of the mold on the CT scanner affected the direction of the sections. Additional disadvantages included the overexposure of the artifact to light (it was not possible to conduct advance testing) and the low resolution of the photographs taken; the overmagnification of the light spectrum of the rivets also had a negative influence on the final result.

The CT detection of carved patterns on the interior of the mold relies on color differences, which correspond to areas or materials of different density and, accordingly, ability to absorb radiation. More specifically, the following was established:

1. Possible carved patterns

- In the top-view scan (Fig. 27.17) of the mold one can discern (in addition to the figure-of-eight pattern on the main surface) a dark-colored area (*l*) with a slanting edge toward side B and between perforations *b* (exterior) and *k* (interior, near the funnel). Perhaps the slanting edge corresponds to a carved channel; alternatively, the whole dark-colored, approximately rectangular area may represent a carved pattern of analogous shape—although no corresponding cavity is visible on the side scans.
- A circular dark-colored area in position *m* (see Figs. 27.17 and 27.18) seems to be a carved depression that is symmetrically placed on the two blocks. In contrast, a dark-colored depression between perforation *c* and side C likely represents a small cavity in the fractured area.
- Of the visible depressions on the vertical surfaces (see the section above on the technical features of the mold), A3 seems to meet one of the lines radiating from rivet *a* (see Fig. 27.17).
- In the top-view scan (Fig. 27.17) one can barely see four light-colored, straight, and parallel lines (*n*) that run horizontally, at approximately the center of the main surface and across its entire width, and are parallel to the oblique edge of the aforementioned dark-colored area *l*. These lines start from depression C2 and continue up to depression A3. Perpendicular to them, two other straight and parallel lines (*o*) run between depressions B2 and B3 on side surface B, reaching approximately up to the outer decorated register of the preserved large disk of the figure-of-eight

motif. Moreover, a light-colored stain in the center of the large disk points to the possible presence of metal underneath the accretions, as is also indicated by stereoscopic observation; alternatively, the stain may have resulted from the carving of a pattern on the adjoining surfaces of the two halves of the mold. In a vertical section scan (Fig. 27.19), we see, on the contact surfaces, black cavities (indicated by arrows on the image) running from side surface A toward the interior of the mold, which probably correspond to the interior terminations of the depressions on side A. Another black area on the upper block likely corresponds to the figure-of-eight pattern and is a result of the oblique positioning of the mold on the CT scanner.

- Other indications of carved patterns exist on the main surface, under the tear-shaped depression (*e*) and toward the corner of side surfaces A and D (Figs. 27.17 and 27.19).

2. Perforations and rivets

- The interior perforation *k* opens into both blocks and deviates slightly from its vertical axis, which means that either it was not pierced in precise symmetry between the two mold halves, or that the halves did not fit exactly together when placed in position 2.
- In the CT scan, as also in the earlier X-ray, the perforations appear wider than their respective rivets (see perforations *a* and *b* on Fig. 27.17). In addition, radiating lines are visible around rivet *a*, which in section appears to penetrate both blocks (Fig. 27.17) and to deviate slightly from its vertical axis on the lower one. This deviation, as well as the uneven surface along the height of the rivet, may be due to the repeated melting and reheating of the rivet during successive castings. I conclude that perforations *a* and *b* functioned to join the blocks together in both positions 1 and 2, while perforation *d*—which also has a rivet—was used to attach the two halves in position 2. Perforations *c* and *k* apparently served the same purpose for the attachment of rivets; even if we suppose that a rivet existed but has not been preserved in perforation *c*, the question remains why perforation *k* lacks a rivet (see Fig. 27.20).

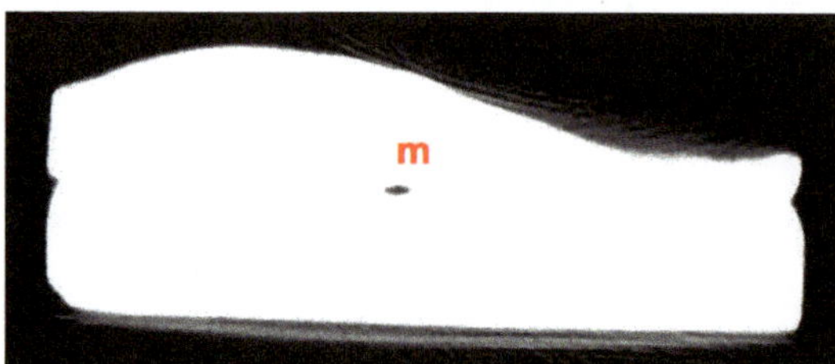

FIGURE 27.18. Scan of vertical face C showing the small depression *m*. Tomography Euromedica General Clinic of Thessaloniki

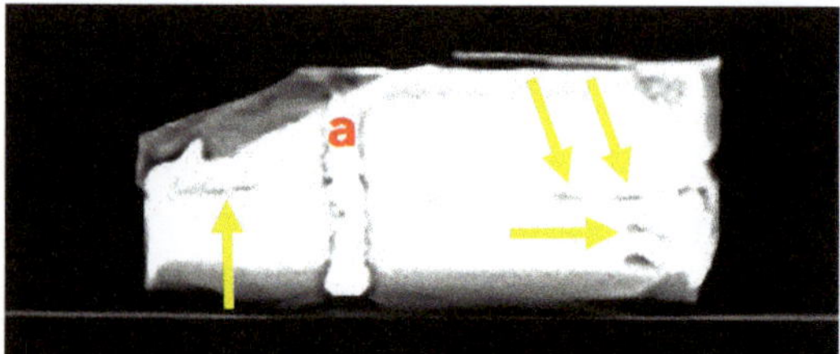

FIGURE 27.19. Vertical scan of ΤΣ 1080. Tomography Euromedica General Clinic of Thessaloniki

FIGURE 27.20. Vertical scan of ΤΣ 1080 showing perforation *k*. Tomography Euromedica General Clinic of Thessaloniki

Remains of Metal

No metal could be traced by pXRF testing at random points of the carved pattern on the main surface, because this particular device cannot target individual points. The same testing method was also applied to the visible areas of the rivets, which were found to consist not of lead (as had been originally assumed),[44] but of exceptionally pure tin.

The following were stereoscopically observed on the main surface:[45]

- traces of metal that are estimated to be silver oxides, inside the circlets of the decorative register of the large disk and in the depression at the center of the disk (Fig. 27.21)
- traces of unidentified metal, on the perimeter of the tear-shaped depression (Fig. 27.22)
- grains with metallic glitter, at various points of the figure-of-eight pattern[46]
- grains of unidentified metal, in the depressions/funnels *A2* (Fig. 27.23) and *A3*

Figure 27.21. Detail of the circlets of the decorative register of the large disk and in the depression at the center of the disk of ΤΣ 1080 showing traces of metal estimated to be silver oxides. Photo J. Vanderpool

Figure 27.22. Detail showing traces of unidentified metal, on the perimeter of the tear-shaped depression on ΤΣ 1080. Photo Jeff Vanderpool

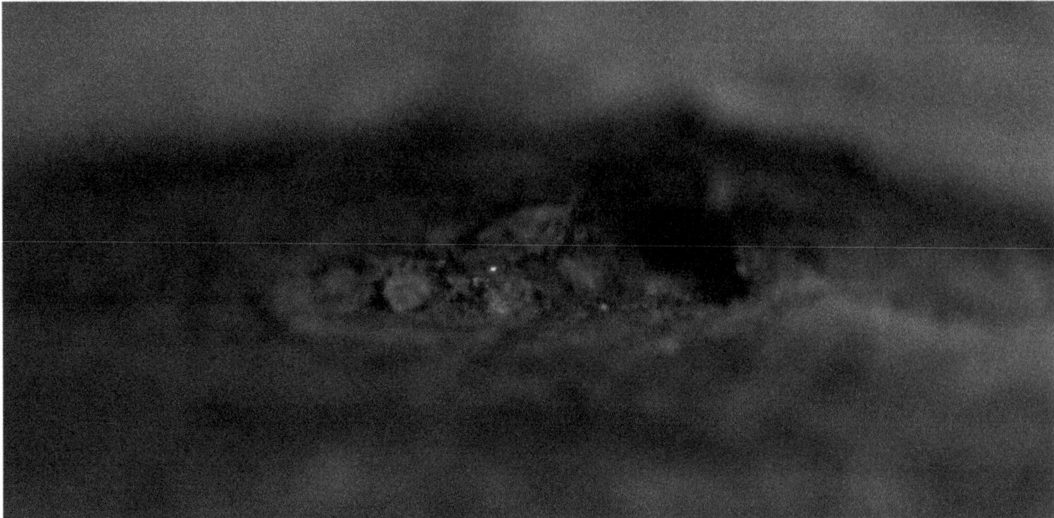

FIGURE 27.23. Detail of ΤΣ 1080 showing grains of unidentified metal, in the depressions/funnel A2. Photo Styliana Galiniki

STAGES IN THE USE OF THE MOLD: CONCLUSIONS AND PENDING QUESTIONS

The few new results from the non-invasive methods of analysis do not help clarify the ways in which the mold was used. In all likelihood, the mold was of the bivalve type with two or more active surfaces. Understanding the methods of its use relies on the interpretation of the depressions on the vertical sides: are they funnels or not?

If the depressions are not funnels but belong instead to existing carved patterns on the adjoined surfaces, then the mold could function in a combination of casting methods—open- and closed-type—according to one of the hypotheses proposed above. For the production of a figure-of-eight (spectacle) ornament, the two blocks should be brought to position 1 (Fig. 27.24 left), with the two halves of the pouring funnel (one on each block) touching each other and the diagonal axis of the mold placed vertically, so that the figure-of-eight pattern would be in an upright position. The release of gases would be achieved by means of an air channel, when the mold was placed in an upright position after casting. As modern applications show, the following is recommended for the successful release of the gases during casting: a) a narrow and slightly slanted air channel, so that the liquid metal does not spill over through it, and b) tilting the mold during casting and positioning it upright afterward.[47] The attachment of the two halves of the mold in position 1, in which the surfaces that are now touching would have been placed on the outside, would have been guided by the rhomboid depressions *i* as well as by the rivets of perforations *a* and *b*.

It is possible, of course, that the carving of the now adjoined surfaces had been merely attempted but not completed; this means that the mold would be of the bivalve type, with only the main and the secondary surfaces active, and the manufacture of the ornament would follow the process described above—with the two halves joined in position 1 (Fig. 27.24, left). If this was the case, some of the depressions on the vertical side surfaces A, B, and C, which are symmetrically placed on the two blocks, may have served for the fastening of a wire that bound the blocks together. We might then surmise that the two sets of parallel lines, *n* and *o*, which are discernible in the top-view CT scan (see above, Fig. 27.17), are the effects of fastening wire which could not be removed for some reason—for example, hot temperature or even incorrect attachment of the blocks in this position. According to one interpretation,[48] the depressions on the vertical surfaces, between the two blocks, were caused by the tools of the ancient craftsman, in an attempt to separate the two halves of the mold.

FIGURE 27.24. Two alternative methods of the use of the mold ΤΣ 1080.
Photo Styliana Galiniki

If, however, some of the aforementioned depressions were in fact funnels, such as *A2* and *A3*, which have a minimal opening and preserve grains of unidentified metal around their openings, then the mold was both bivalve and double, and casting took place in successive stages by reversing the blocks: in position 1 for the spectacle fibula, in position 2 for the production of objects the patterns of which were possibly carved on one or both of the adjoined surfaces—depending on whether these objects would be cast in the round or with only one decorated surface. The small passage opening of the depressions/funnels *A2* and *A3* may be related to the casting material, or to the size and type of the carved patterns. The narrow passage certainly necessitated a slow casting flow, which was dictated either by the kind of metal poured or by the types of items to be cast from the carved patterns. In the case of patterns with many decorative details, the controlled flow would secure the pouring of metal into those; at the same time, it would avert the possible destruction of the mold by abrupt contact with a large quantity and high temperature of molten metal, or of the cast object because of accidentally trapped gases. The latter, as well as the excess metal, may have been released through channels that exited into some of the depressions on side surfaces B and C.[49] These depressions would thus have served as channels when the mold was used in position 2, whereas the air duct *f* operated in position 1. Another possible function of these depressions is as sockets for shafts, which would serve to open attachment or suspension holes on the produced artifacts.[50] Finally, they could have a matching—and yet reverse—function to that of the rhomboid cavities *i*; in such a scenario, depressions B1–B2 and C1–C2 would be guides for locking the valves in position 2.

As regards the carved pattern(s) on one or both adjoined surfaces, the CT scan offered inconclusive indications (see Fig. 27.17). Does the dark-colored area with the slanting edge (*l*) correspond to a carving? Do the sets of parallel lines *n* and *o* indicate decorative channels? Finally, is there metal preserved between the connected blocks—perhaps in the shape of a flat sheet with one edge oblique and various decorative details? Be that as it may, why does this dark-colored area include perforations *b* and *k*?

It is conceivable, of course, that after several uses the mold operated only in position 2; in other words, that its use in position 1 had been abandoned. This seems to be suggested by the existence of the parallel incisions *g* on the figure-of-eight pattern (see Fig. 27.5, left), which are possibly the continuation of those incisions on the secondary surface (for which see Figs. 27.7–27.9) that have been interpreted as traces of binding material. If the two blocks had indeed been held together with wire which left, during a casting, its imprint not only on the secondary surface but also on the main one—where it damaged the figure-of-eight pattern—then this would have meant the end of the use of the mold in position 1.

It is also possible to consider the hypothesis that had been proposed in the original publication, namely, that the mold ΤΣ 1080 may be the preserved part of a tri- or multi-part object. If so, then the two blocks would not be reversed; instead, a third slab-like part would be placed on top of the figure-of-eight pattern (Fig. 27.24, right). In such a case, the funnel on the secondary surface would simply have resulted from an incomplete attempt to carve that side of the block. This hypothetical third cover would have both sides flat, so that both a mono-facial fibula could be produced and the connecting wire could pass around the exterior of the cover—the remains of the wire are now visible on the secondary surface of the preserved block. Lastly, one may also think of a fourth part, bearing a carved pattern and attached onto the so-called secondary surface. Thus, there would be essentially two bivalve molds joined together, so that casting occurred simultaneously on both.

The detection of high-purity tin is puzzling and unexpected, because it is a rare find in the 7th–6th centuries. Given that the origin and circulation of tin in the Mediterranean remain constant topics of archaeological enquiry,[51] the use of this metal—indeed in an almost unalloyed form—for the manufacture of a secondary element such as rivets poses new questions concerning, for example, the value of the metal, its circulation and use, and its role in the metallurgical technology of the period. It also raises questions concerning the exchange networks in which the metalsmiths at Methone were involved.[52] Could it be that the use of tin was dictated by the value or the intended use of the produced artifacts?

MULTIFACETED STONE MOLD FOR THE MANUFACTURE OF PENDANTS AND OTHER ORNAMENTS (ΤΣ 1081, FIGS. 27.25–27.33)

The mold with inventory number ΤΣ 1081 (measuring 5.3 x 4.9 x 3.4 cm) (Figs. 27.25–27.26) is pyramidal in shape, made of creamy white-colored limestone. The surface shows abrasions and chipped-off spots. The mold has seven faces, of which those with carved designs include the almost square horizontal surface, the two rectangular lateral surfaces, and the one vertical triangular surface, with an additional attempted carving on the other vertical triangular surface. The exterior of the mold has dark-colored areas, possibly the result of contact with molten metal during casting. Each of the remaining two elongated, wedge-shaped surfaces—between the horizontal surface and the rectangular sides—carries the opening of a funnel, for casting patterns on the base and on one of the lateral surfaces.

Horizontal Surface

The almost square horizontal surface (4.9 x 4.6 cm) (Fig. 27.27) bears three carved motifs, all very shallow (about 1 mm in depth) and decorated in a cursory and asymmetric fashion. The surface is divided in the middle by an elongated groove (likely a funnel), measuring 0.4 cm at its mouth, that starts from edge B and is directed toward the design that is located along edge D. The surface of the groove/funnel bears longitudinal lesions.

- In approximately the center of the surface and along edge D, there is a figure-of-eight carved motif (L. 2.9; W. 1.4 cm) for an ornament, most likely a spectacle fibula (see Fig. 27.28, lower

FIGURE 27.25. Pyramidal stone mold ΤΣ 1081.
Photo J. Vanderpool

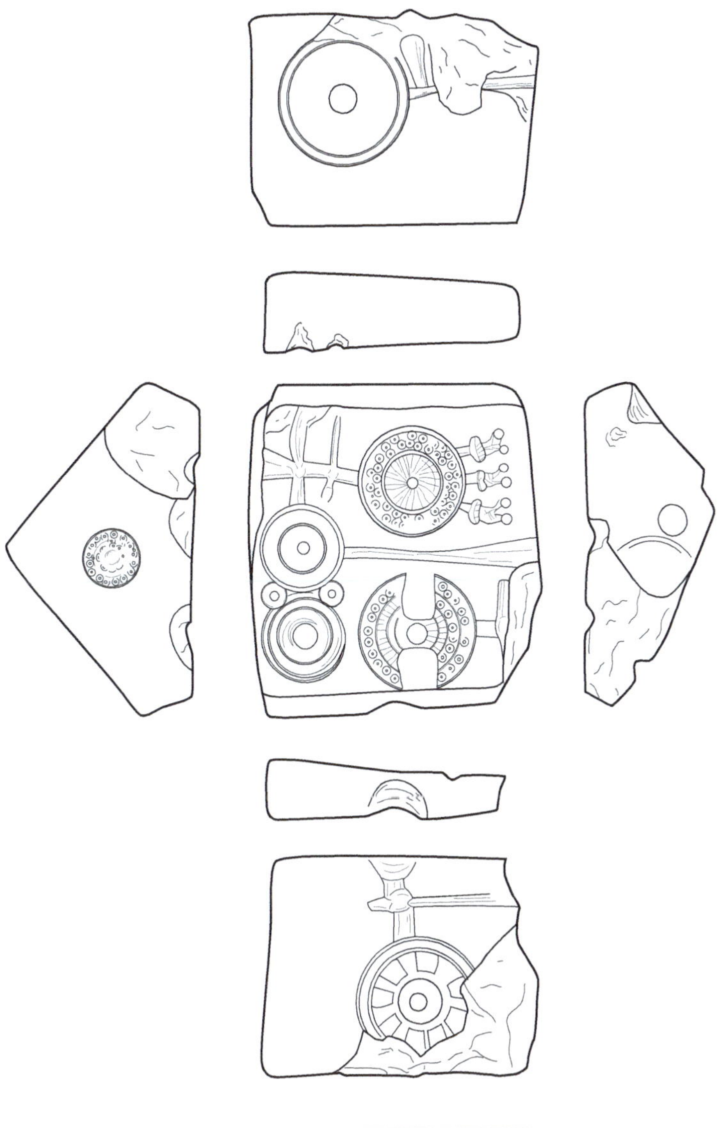

FIGURE 27.26. ΤΣ 1081.
Drawing T. Ross

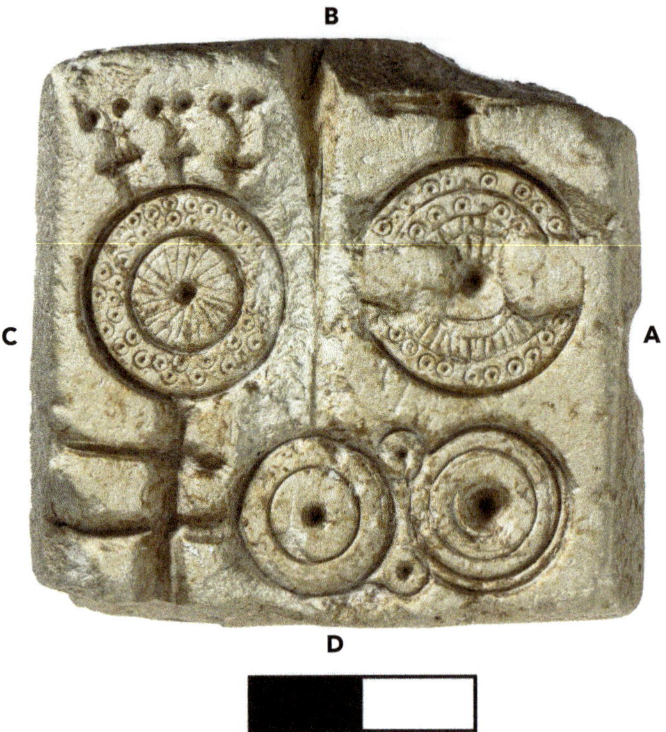

FIGURE 27.27. One of the primary carved horizontal surfaces of ΤΣ 1081, which is almost square. Photo J. Vanderpool

right).[53] Both of the large disks have the same diameter (1.4 cm) and bear an incised interior circle, but they are otherwise asymmetric in their decoration: one (on the left) has a solitary interior concentric circle and a small circular depression at the center (0.1 cm in depth), whereas the other (on the right) features a second incised circle around a relatively deep (0.2 cm) central depression, and an additional incised line around its circumference, which apparently was intended to enlarge the diameter of the disk. Of the large disks, the right one preserves traces of unsuccessful carving attempts. The two small disks at the center of the pattern are not decorated, but they also have a central depression like the large ones. Two grooves end at the circumference of the left large disk: the long groove/funnel mentioned above, and another that starts from edge C and intersects with a funnel running from edge D to the carved disk pattern along edge C (see below). This funnel seems to intersect with another groove in the lightly chipped-off edge of the mold. In the cavity of the funnel, a shiny metallic grain was detected stereoscopically.

- In the area between edges A and B, there is a carved motif in the shape of a double axe inscribed in a circle (Diam. 2 cm). This pattern was likely designed for a pendant, as is indicated by the preserved part of a groove that runs perpendicular to the axis of the pouring funnel, in which a rod was inserted for the creation of a suspension hole (see Fig. 27.29, lower right). The shape of the pattern recalls the motif of the figure-of-eight (Boiotian/Dipylon) shield. It is similar to the double axe on the mold from Vergina[54]—both belong to Jan Bouzek's type 3 of small double axes[55]—and has further parallels among Geometric finds (mainly of bronze) from sanctuaries, including Sparta,[56] Kalapodi,[57] Olympia,[58] and Pherai,[59] as well as with the double axe ("figure-of-eight shield") on a gold plaque-shaped component of a diadem from a 5th century B.C. pyre at Eleusis.[60] Double axes of lead have been found at Sparta,[61] while another lead example of a different type comes from a 7th–6th century assemblage at Isthmia.[62] Pendants in

FIGURE 27.28. Some of the modern jewelry made on the basis of the stone mold ΤΣ 1081. Photo J. Vanderpool

FIGURE 27.29. Additional modern jewelry made on the basis of ΤΣ 1081. Photo J. Vanderpool

the shape of a double axe, in a variety of materials, types, and sizes, have been found at many sites in Macedonia, such as the cemeteries of Aineia, Sindos, and Nea Philadelphia,[63] the dates of which range from the 9th/8th to the 5th centuries B.C. In no other example, however, does the suspension stem extend perpendicularly to the blades of the axe.[64] All comparanda bear a suspension hole that is perforated at the convergence point of the blades or starts from it.[65] The decoration lacks symmetry. One blade is divided into four ornamental registers: the two outer ones feature randomly placed and occasionally adjoining circlets with a central dot, while the other two are filled with poorly executed, parallel vertical incisions. The other blade is divided into three registers, of which the outer one bears the same ornament of randomly placed, dotted circlets, the middle one is filled with cursory incised lines, and the inner one is left blank. Visible remains of an arc on the straight (inner) section of one blade (the lower one in Fig. 27.27) indicate that the perimeter of the axe motif was drawn with a compass. At the convergence point of the blades there is a depression of 0.2 cm in depth.

- Along edge C, there is a carved pattern in the shape of a disk (Diam. 1.8 cm), which was probably meant for a pendant or earring (Fig. 27.29, lower left). Three stems with bifurcated, dotted ends radiate from the circumference of the disk. On the opposite side of the circumference (near the corner of edges C and D), a funnel groove extends perpendicular to the disk and intersects with the groove of a socket for a suspension stem, and with the funnel that ends at the motif of the spectacle fibula (see above).
- The disk (Diam. 1.7 cm), its center marked by a small round depression, is divided into two registers by an incised concentric circle. The inner register is decorated with radiating, slightly oblique lines in a whorl-like motif that runs counter to the direction of the three pendent stems; the outer register has pairs of dotted circlets, some of them adjoined and others not. The decorative motif of the dotted circlets—common on various objects of metal, ivory, or bone[66]—shows the same cursory execution as on the other patterns of the mold; the type has parallels among the earliest, late 8th-century lead votives at the sanctuary of Artemis Orthia in Sparta.[67] The whorl motif occurs on metal jewelry of the Archaic period.[68]

Lateral Surfaces

The two rectangular lateral surfaces bear discoid patterns, carved near their common edge (Fig. 27.30). On surface A, a groove that is probably a funnel starts from one of the short edges and ends at a flat circular pattern, the circumference of which is defined by a deeply carved ring and its center by a deep depression (almost 1 cm in depth). An additional groove of unknown function is visible on the same surface, but at some distance from the disk.

Surface B bears the carved pattern of a disk, with rectangular spokes arranged wheel-like around a central circular perforation, 1 cm deep. The circumference of both the disk and the perforation are defined by relief rings. The pattern ends in a funnel, the opening of which is located on the elongated side between surface B and the horizontal square surface (Fig. 27.31). The funnel intersects with a groove, probably the socket of a shaft for the formation of a suspension hole.

Molds with discoid, ring-shaped patterns such as the one on surface A have been found at various sites,[69] as have other artifacts of the same form. It is also possible that the same carved pattern could produce a solid, disk-shaped object featuring a pronounced outer ring and a central perforation or protuberance—probably the decorative finial on the head of a pin, such as those on Archaic examples from Lousoi and Olympia.[70] The item that came from the pattern of surface B was most likely a wheel-shaped earring or pendant, such as are known from the Peloponnese, Thessaly, and other regions.[71] This ornament could be either solid or perforated (Fig. 27.29, top), as indicated by examples from Pherai.[72]

FIGURE 27.30. Two rectangular lateral surfaces of ΤΣ 1081 bearing discoid patterns. Photo J. Vanderpool

FIGURE 27.31. Lateral view of ΤΣ 1081. Photo J. Vanderpool

The form of the cast objects may have ultimately depended on the type of covers that were used for the mold surfaces during casting. In the case of flat covers, the resulting objects would be perforated; by contrast, if the covers themselves carried carved patterns corresponding to the circumference of the ornament, then the products could be solid and thicker. Each cover may even have been pierced through by a vertical shaft, which penetrated the central holes of the carved patterns in order to create a perforation at the center of the ornament, and at the same time secured the attachment of the covers on the surfaces of the mold during casting. We cannot, of course, rule out that the cast items were decorative appendages of other ornaments, as is indeed suggested by the presence, on both types, of a deep central perforation with suspected remains of metal in the interior. Specifically, the wheel with fused vertical stem at its center could be attached to a bird-shaped metal ornament that featured a central supportive shaft and a wheel-shaped base; such objects from Pherai have been interpreted as pendants, while others from Argos and Lakonia have been seen as decorative belt attachments.[73] In such a case, of course, the groove that runs perpendicular to the pouring funnel on the surface of the mold could not have served as the socket of a shaft for the creation of a suspension hole (as proposed above), but would have functioned in some other way.

Vertical Triangular Surfaces

One vertical surface (Fig. 27.32) carries the carved pattern of a disk with a hemispherical depression at its center, divided by a concentric circle into a ring of adjoining dotted circlets around the circumference and a rosette of eight more such circlets surrounding the central cavity. Any further decoration inside the cavity has been obscured by surface wear. The design was probably intended for a decorative element such as the head of a pin (Fig. 27.28, lower left).[74] In the absence of a funnel, metal would have been poured directly into the pattern to cast the ornament. After casting, a core of other material might have been used in order to keep the underside of the artifact convex.

The other vertical triangular surface is broken off at one of its lower corners. Two incised concentric circles (Fig. 27.33) and a small depression are visible in the preserved area; they probably indicate an attempt to draw a motif—a practice known from other molds as well.[75]

The technical features of the mold are summed up as follows:

1. Although the stone is especially soft, the decoration of the carved patterns is careless.
2. Before casting, each surface required the attachment of a cover.
3. The shape of the mold would have rendered simultaneous casting on all surfaces rather difficult.
4. The mold probably operated as both closed and open, depending on the surface in use each time. The presence of pouring funnels on three surfaces indicates the use of the mold in the closed mode, with attached covers that could be flat or bear carvings corresponding to the respective patterns on the surfaces. As there are no rivet holes on the main surface, the cover would probably be fastened by means of a twine or wire; in contrast, the deep perforations in the center of the patterns on the side surfaces could, as was mentioned above, have received rivets for the attachment of a cover. The lack of a funnel on the vertical triangular surface means that in this case the mold functioned in the open mode.
5. In the case of two carved motifs, namely, the disk with three fused stems and the disk in the form of a wheel, the grooves intersecting with the funnels were potential sockets for the insertion of a shaft, which was intended to produce suspension holes in the cast ornaments.

Figure 27.32. View and detail of one of the vertical triangular surfaces of ΤΣ 1081. Photos J. Vanderpool

6. The horizontal, square surface is covered completely by the three patterns that are carved on it. Two of these are joined by a network of grooves, all of which could operate as funnels that facilitated the flow of liquid matter between the patterns. It would actually suffice to pour the metal into one funnel only, albeit at the risk of it over-flowing the mold through the other outlets.
7. Grains and accretions of metallic glitter are visible at several spots on the various motifs, and inside the central perforations of the motifs on the side surfaces.
8. Localized traces of engraving tools are visible.

The nature of the casting material remains an open question, but a clue may be offered by the pattern of the disk pendant on the horizontal surface. This motif seems to have parallels among the earliest lead votive offerings at the sanctuary of Artemis Orthia in Sparta, which date to the end of the 8th century B.C.[76] On the basis of the objects themselves, which were intended as offerings to the goddess and not as actual items of adornment—although they do resemble real ornaments—Alan Wace made a series of suggestions regarding the type of molds that had been used to produce such items. Since the backs of all the votives were flat, he assumed that they were cast in simple one-part molds, which were covered with some other flat object so that they could be used in the closed mode. He also thought that the carved patterns on the molds were shallow and connected to each other by funnels, because on some of the finished products the metal rods corresponding to the funnels had been left uncut. In his view, the presence of a "rim" around the finished forms indicates that the motifs had been carved very close to the edges of the mold. He thus concluded that the molds could have been used to manufacture additional ornaments of other metals.

Many of the features discussed by Wace find parallels on our mold ΤΣ 1081. The cast metal was quite likely lead, to judge from the quality of the stone of the mold.[77] Nevertheless, experimental methods have shown that even molds made of stones vulnerable to heat could, under certain conditions, be used for the casting of metals that melt at high temperatures.[78]

FIGURE 27.33. The other vertical triangular surface of ΤΣ 1081.
Photo J. Vanderpool

STONE MOLD FOR THE MANUFACTURE OF PINS (ΤΣ 1082, FIGS. 27.34–27.38)

ΤΣ 1082 (measuring 4.9 x 5.2 x 2 cm) (Figs. 27.34–27.35) is the preserved half of a bivalve, closed-type mold. Its material was initially thought to be clay, upon which a pattern motif had been created by pressing the desired objects to be copied.[79] According to the recent reassessment, however, the mold was made of stone, specifically micrite fossiliferous red limestone which had probably been mined in the Peloponnese.[80]

The main surface bears two funnels corresponding to two carved patterns in parallel arrangement: the upper-part halves of two pins, of the same form but of different sizes. Each pin pattern consists of a longitudinal groove, topped by the halves of two disk-shaped elements on either side of a hemispherical depression, and crowned by the half-portion of another, large disk. The type of pin, with a disk-shaped head and decorative smaller disks flanking a spherical bead, probably dates to the Archaic period (Fig. 27.36).[81]

The parts of the pins that correspond to the funnels may well have been hammered into an elongated needle shape.[82] It is equally possible, however, that the groove part of each pin would have received a cast rod, which would create an open perforation into the lowest disk for the subsequent insertion of a needle made of other material.[83] The now-missing second part of the mold could either bear the corresponding halves of the carved motifs, or be flat; in the latter case, the pins produced would have been formed by casting both of their halves on the one carved block and then welding them together.

The secondary surface (Fig. 27.37) carries two parallel semi-cylindrical grooves that are crossed in two places by short, slightly oblique bars. Their use is not clear: either they had to do with the attachment of another block onto the main surface, or they were intended for the manufacture of wire rods with horizontal crossbars, possibly a type of pin similar to an isolated example from Kalapodi.[84] The latter function would have required a third block or a cover of sorts, although the absence of funnels would have made it difficult to conduct the casting solely through the ends of each groove. The notches at the edges of the mold surface could have been guiding marks for fastening a cover onto

FIGURE 27.34. View of the primary surface of the stone mold ΤΣ 1082, made of micrite fossiliferous red limestone probably mined in the Peloponnese. Photo J. Vanderpool

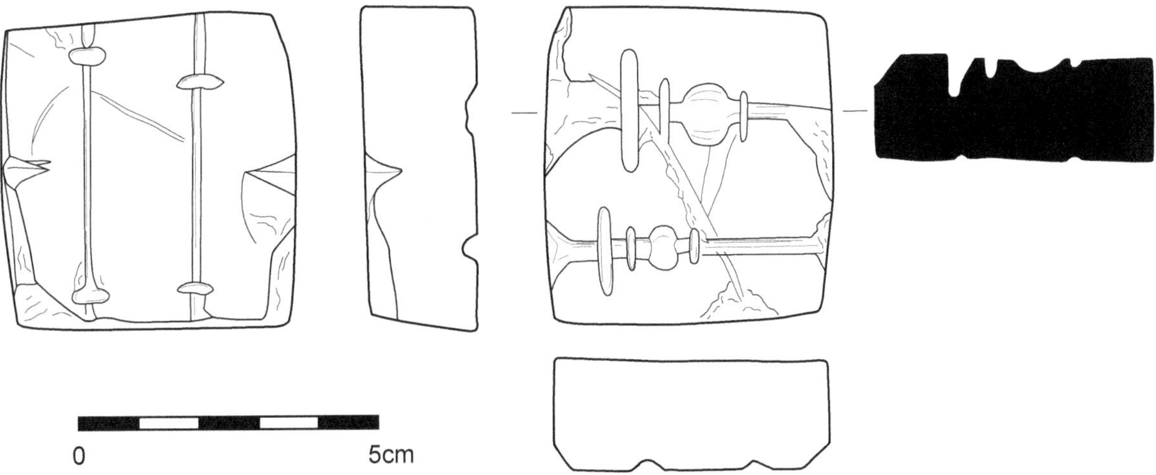

FIGURE 27.35. Mold ΤΣ 1082.
Drawing T. Ross

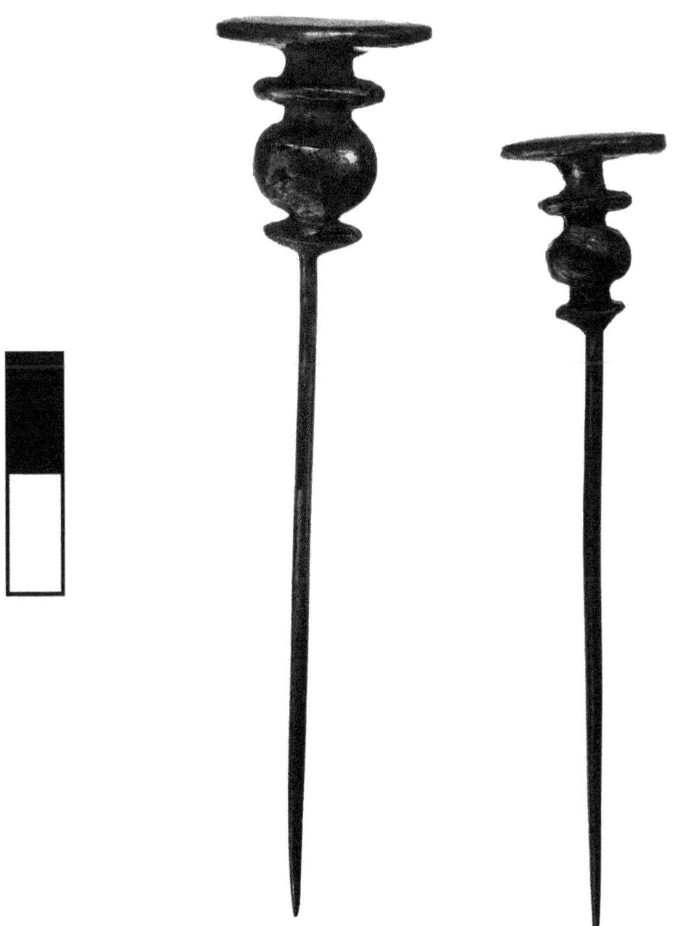

FIGURE 27.36. Modern pins made on the basis of the mold ΤΣ 1082.
Photo J. Vanderpool

FIGURE 27.37. The secondary surface of ΤΣ 1082.
Photo J. Vanderpool

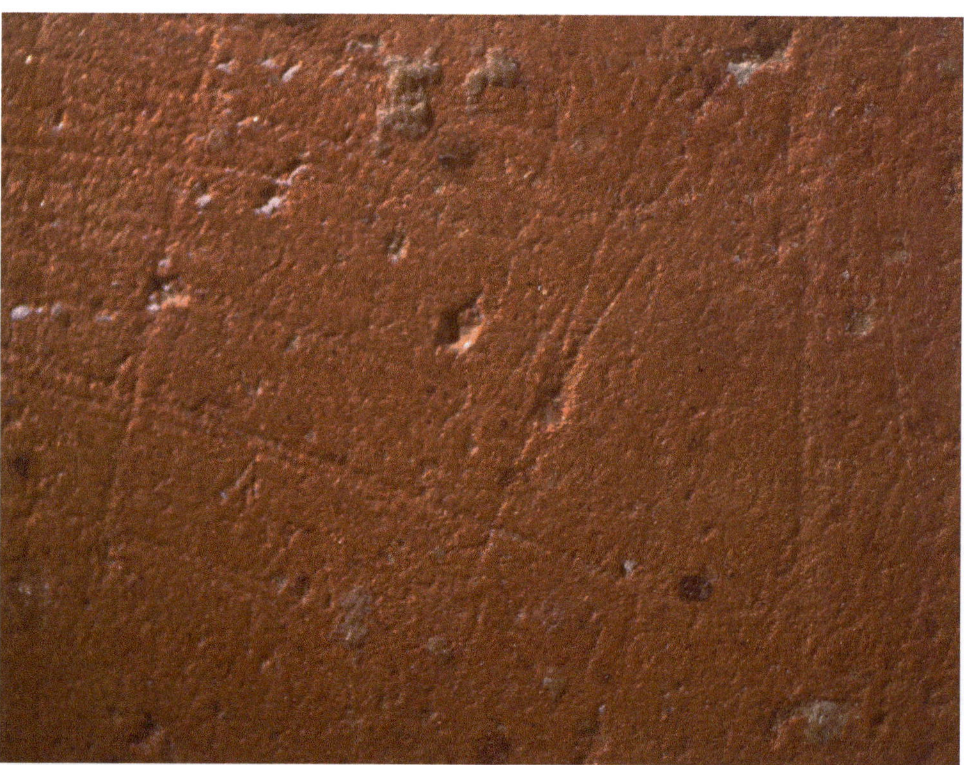

FIGURE 27.38. Detail of assorted localized incisions, probably traces of binding material that joined the existing block with another. Photo Thessaloniki Museum

the main surface in order to produce the pins, or for attaching a similar cover onto the secondary surface.[85] Assorted localized incisions can be interpreted as traces of binding material that joined the existing block with another (Fig. 27.38). Dark-colored wear on the interior of the pin patterns, around the funnel openings, and at various spots on the surface was probably caused by contact of the stone with the molten metal. There are also unconfirmed indications of remnants of metal.

EPILOGUE

The molds in the Stamatios Tsakos Collection are not the only ones from ancient Methone; excavations at the site by the Ephoreia of Antiquities of Pieria and, since 2014, as a collaboration between the Ephoreia and the American School of Classical Studies at Athens, have brought to light many additional ornament molds of stone or clay (Figs. 1.15–16, 1.36, 14.3–14.4),[86] some from the Hypogeion, others from the excavations on the West Hill, together with large quantities of pottery and industrial debitage from the working of metals, ivory/bone, glass, and other materials.

On the evidence of typology, the origin of the raw materials, and comparanda for the carved patterns, it is likely that the molds in the Tsakos Collection had been imported to Methone from southern Greece, or else they had been brought by artisans who settled in this region of Macedonia or happened to be there temporarily. In either case, archaeometric identification of the stone, and of the surviving traces of metal, will produce more information about the circulation of molds in antiquity.

NOTES

1 The molds presented in this chapter were first published, in a more circumscribed manner and with fewer illustrations, in Galiniki 2006. Unless otherwise noted, all measurements are in cm. The present study would not have been possible without the trust and full encouragement of John Papadopoulos. Thanks are also due to the support team of this publication: Dr. Marianna Nikolaidou (translation), Jeffrey Vanderpool (photographs), Vanessa Muros and Gazmend Elezi (pXRF testing), and Tina Ross (drawings). Additional examination of the mold ΤΣ 1080 by computer tomography was possible thanks to the interest and help of Agni Apostolidou and the generosity of orthopedic surgeon Vassilis Lykomitros, to both of whom I express my sincere gratitude. The input and unfailing support of Annareta Touloumtzidou were crucial in encouraging me to examine multiple parameters of research. For discussion and their apt remarks, I am grateful to Nikos Kantiranis, Christos Katsifas, Yiannis Nazlis, and Vasso Michalopoulou. I am further indebted to the late Evangelia Stefani, then director of the Archaeological Museum of Thessaloniki (AMTh/AMΘ), and to my colleagues Evangelia Tsangaraki, Dimitris Karolidis, Sofia Athanassiadou, Kalliope Chatzinikolaou, Eleonora Melliou, and Angeliki Moneda, for their contributions at different stages of the project.

2 At times, products from the same mold can be found in archaeological strata of different date (see Cavanagh and Laxton 1984, p. 33).

3 On display in the Archaeological Museum of Thessaloniki, together with the molds, are modern copies of ornaments cast from them, which were reproduced by the gold- and silversmith Nikos Xanthopoulos (illustrated in Figs. 27.28-29, 27.36) on the occasion of the reopening of the museum galleries in 2006. To produce the casts, the goldsmith made rubber molds by copying the ancient prototypes through optical observation and measurements. Consequently, the modern ornaments are not exact copies of the ones that would have been produced from the ancient molds, but imitations of the closest possible degree. The molds ΤΣ 1081 and ΤΣ 1082 were also included in the temporary exhibition "Copying (in) the Past: Imitation and Inspiration Stories," Archaeological Museum of Thessaloniki, November 24, 2018–end of 2019; see Stefani and Koukouvou 2019, pp. 60–61, nos. 50, 51.

4 The copyright on the ancient objects depicted in figures 27.1–27.38 belongs to the Ministry of Culture and Sports–Archaeological Museum of Thessaloniki.

5 The identification was made by Nikos Kantiranis, Professor of Geology at the Aristotle University of Thessaloniki, who also pointed to the possible place of origin. Prehistoric quarries for the extraction of micrite fossiliferous limestone have been located at Tiryns; see Kokkorou-Alevra et al. 2014, p. 163, nos. 589, 590.

6 Similar wear has been observed on a mold from Aigina (Reinholdt 1992, pp. 216–217, h.1).

7 According to Professor Kantiranis, this is a recent fracture, because there are no accretions deposited around it.

8 For example, Boardman and Hayes 1966, p. 163, nos. 72, 73, 77, pl. 104; *OlForsch* XIII, pp. 143, 298, 303, no. 1099, pl. 21; *Olynthus* X, pp. 99–101, pl. XX. For examples from Methone, see Chapter 15, 15/2–15/5 (Fig. 15.2), and Chapter 26, 26/43 (Fig. 26.19).

9 Blinkenberg 1926, pp. 263–272; Boardman 1967, pp. 206, 211, nos. 231–239, pl. 86; Dawkins 1929b, pp. 224–225, pls. CXXXII–CXXXIII; Dawkins 1929a, pl. LXXXII (s); *Perachora* II, pp. 433–437, pls. 183–185; Kourayos and Burns 2004, p. 150, fig. 20; *OlForsch* XIII, pp. 298, 303, pl. 21, no. 1099; Stampolidis 2003, pp. 544–546, nos. 1074 (M. Sgourou), 1075–1076 (Y. Kourayos and S. Detoratou), 1078 (M. Eustathiou), 1081 (M. T. Granese), and 1082 (M. M. Macri [variant of the type]); Varvarinou 2017, pp. 168–169, figs. 2–8.

10 Stampolidis 2003, p. 545, no. 1079 (M. Eustathiou); Vokotopoulou 1990, p. 109, pl. 66, ε–στ; Vlachou 2007, pp. 216, 223.

11 Kokkou-Vyridi 1999, p. 244, no. B250, pl. 60.

12 Droop 1926, p. 199, pl. LXXXII (s); Ignatiadou and Chatzipanagiotou 2018, p. 276, fig. 13; see also Boardman 1967, p. 211, no. 238, pl. 86 (with depressions in the centers of the disks for inlays of other material).

13 Blinkenberg 1926, p. 271; Stampolidis 2003, p. 566, no. 1136 (Y. Kourayos, S. Detoratou, and B. Burns); Touloumtzidou 2017, pp. 204–205, fig. 41.

14 Stampolidis et al. 2018, p. 301, no. 141 (M. Roussaki).

15 Vasić 1977, p. 21, pl. 24 (13) and 26 (20, 21); Gergova 1987, p. 54, no. 233, pl. 19.

16 Vokotopoulou 1986, vol. 1, p. 71, pl. 99a, fig. 108γ (750–720 B. C.); p. 137, pl. 216β, fig. 108 δ–ε (end of 9th century); p. 141, pl. 223 γ–δ, fig. 108 α–β (end of 9th century); p. 310. See also volume 2 of same publication, fig. 108α–ε.

17 Felsch 2007, pp. 139–140, no. 517, pl. 32; Stampolidis 2003, p. 551, no. 1088 (T. Calo).

18 Felsch 2007, pp. 139–140, no. 517, pl. 32.

19 Dugas 1921, p. 428, no. 370, fig. 42.

20 Blinkenberg 1926, pp. 267, 268, 272. For another example see Deppert-Lippitz 1985, p. 87, fig. 42.

21 Koukoulidou 2017, p. 202, fig. 108.

22 Weinberg 1960, p. 101, no.10, pl. 32, c.

23 Felsch 2007, pp. 139–140, no. 518, pl. 32.

24 Michailidou and Tzachili 1986, p. 370.

25 Tiverios, Manakidou, and Tsiafaki 1997, pp. 330–331, fig. 8.

26 See, for example, Dawkins 1929b, p. 238, pl. CLXIV; Kilian 1975a, p. 117, pl. 48 (1357, 1366); *OlForsch* XIII, p. 144, no. 528, pl. 42; Stampolidis 2003, p. 543, nos. 1071 (S. Lupino), 1072 (M. Cavalier–M.C. Martinelli), p. 550, no. 1087; Varvarinou 2017, pp. 166–170, fig. 2, 6, 12; Voyatzis 2014, pp. 210–215, no. LdN 27, pl. 14.

27 Stampolidis et al. 2018, p. 313, no. 178 (M. Roussaki), relief dotted circlets on the lead model of a table from Knossos, 1st century A.D. Boardman (1967, p. 211) considers the dotted-circlet decoration of fibulae a sign of Near Eastern influence.

28 On an ivory spectacle fibula from Sybaris (end of 8th–beginning of 7th century), adjoining or intersecting circlets indicate unsuccessful attempts to repeat a braid pattern that has been partly achieved in the decoration; Stampolidis 2003, p. 546, no. 1081 (M. T. Granese).

29 For the methods of use of open- and close-type molds, see Hodges 1964, pp. 70, 71; Golani 2019, pp. 45, 51–53.

30 Vassallo 2004, pp. 24–26, fig. 3 (8, 10).

31 Marazov et al. 1997, pp. nos. 131, 163.

32 Evans and Wixom 1997, p. 305, no. 207 (P. Dandridge and O. Z. Pevny). Vents are not necessary when the mold is made of porous material or when the halves do not fit perfectly; see Hodges 1964, p. 71.

33 Such traces of thermal shock indicate that the casting material was metal and not wax or plaster, as has been occasionally mentioned in the literature; see commentary and references in Tsakos 2016, pp. 700–701. On the question whether a wax template was shaped in the molds, even in ones made of stone, see Higgins 1980, pp. 16, 17; also Despoini 1996, p. 21, with references; Golani 2019, pp. 55, 56, with references.

34 Traces of a binding material are preserved on an Iron Age mold from Kastanas (Hochstetter 1987, p. 41, pl. 5 [3]), and a mold preserving the binding wire was found at Gournia (Konstantinidi-Syvridi and Kontaki 2009, p. 316, who also mention the use of wire on molds from Sparta and Knossos).

35 Michailidou and Tzachili 1986, pp. 368, 373.

36 Tsakos 2016, pp. 698–699, fig. 1. A mark similar to the one on the Samos mold exists on a Late Bronze Age bronze ingot from Haifa and has been interpreted as a Cypro-Minoan (Maddin, Wheeler, and Muhly 1977, p. 44, fig. 23) or pseudo–Cypro-Minoan (see Ferrara 2012, p. 234, footnote 52) sign.

37 Felsch 2007, pp. 139–140, no. 518, pl. 32; Treister and Zolotarev 1993; Treister 2007, p. 570, fig. 3,2, where the inscription is accompanied by a sketch of the craftsman's face.

38 We should not exclude the possibility that this cover block also bore the figure-of-eight motif, carved relatively deeply in case it was desirable to produce a thicker ornament.

39 On depressions or incisions that serve as "guides" for the attachment of the blocks, see Stampolidis 2003, p. 470, no. 840 (F. Spatafora); Michailidou and Tzachili 1986, p. 372; Vassallo 2004, pp. 21–23, nos. 1, 3, figs. 1, 2.

40 By the term "active" I mean that the surface played a role in the process of casting the metal to produce the object, irrespective of whether or not this surface bore a carved pattern.

41 For ancient molds, see Papaefthymiou-Papanthimou 1973, pp. 393–395; also Michailidou and Tzachili 1986, p. 368. According to Golani, "open casting molds are seldom used in jewelry production" (Golani 2019, p. 45, with references). For more recent molds combining both types—open and closed—for jewelry production, see Farooq Swati and Khan 2001, pp. 190–193, fig. 1–6, where the rear surfaces of bivalve molds bear carved patterns but no funnels, and were used as separate one-part molds—although it is not clarified whether metal had been cast directly into the patterns. One surface (p. 193, fig. 6) bears incised designs which, according to the authors, had been used in preliminary stages of decoration. This assemblage of medieval (A.D. 1000–1500) molds from Pakistan also includes three-part specimens (pp. 194–195, figs. 12–15), with the middle block bearing carved designs on both surfaces, which correspond to the designs on the interior surfaces of the two other parts. In this way, the first and second blocks constitute a bivalve mold, likewise the second and third ones. Casting could be carried out simultaneously, by attaching all three parts together. The exterior surfaces (of the first and third blocks) bore guiding patterns for secondary decorative work. The presence of incised designs on the narrow sides of some molds (p. 196, figs. 16–17) has been interpreted as indication for the hammering of metal sheets upon these surfaces; the sheets would have been preheated, so that the soft stone of the molds could stand the impact of such an application. This method could be considered as another technique of using an open mold. For a secondary use of the single part of a bi-valve mold for stamping gold leaf into shallow matrices, see Dimakopoulou 1974, pp. 166–167.

42 The X-ray was performed in 2005 at the General Hospital of Thessaloniki "Agios Dimitrios" by Dr. I. G. Artopoulos.

43 The computer tomography was conducted in 2019 at the Euromedica General Clinic of Thessaloniki, by courtesy of physician Dr. Vassilis Lykomitros and the Head Administrator of the clinic, Aikaterini Kechayia.

44 See Galiniki 2006, p. 348.

45 Stereoscopic observation for the tracing of metal remains was conducted by Professor N. Kantiranis of the Geology Department at the Aristotle University of Thessaloniki.

46 These grains were identified stereoscopically by Ch. Katsifas and A. Touloumtzidou.

47 Untracht 1986, pp. 395, 401.

48 As proposed by V. Michalopoulou, antiquities conservator.

49 On a mold from Aptera on Crete (Stampolidis et al. 2018, p. 76, nos. 46–47 [L. Flevari]), the funnel is thought to have served also as a drainage duct for the excess metal and, we may suggest, for the air, too. On a much later example, a 12th–13th century A.D. mold from Kiev (Kyiv), triangular depressions on the lower part of the carved pattern and opposite the funnel have been likewise interpreted as channels, through which the metal could escape from the center of the deeply carved and concave pattern, with the casting method of "quick flow" or "slush casting"; Evans and Wixom 1997, p. 316, no. 216 (P. Dandridge and O. Z. Pevny).

50 Tsountas 1897, cols. 100–101; Michailidou and Tzachili 1986, pp. 367–368. See also Hochstetter 1987, p. 42, pl. 5 (3), where it is suggested that, instead of the two channels having received shafts, they may have alternatively functioned as funnels in a subsequent casting.

51 Tin has been described as "the mystery metal of the ancient Near East" (Maddin, Wheeler, and Muhly 1977).

52 See, for example, Asimenos in Touloumtzidou 2011, p. 84, on the use of a tin-bronze for the production of metal vessels in Macedonia since the Archaic period. On the tin-plating of vessels from Pieria dating to the late 5th and 4th centuries, see Kotitsa 2012a, pp. 114–118. See also Treister 1996, pp. 28–29, 152–164, especially p. 156, on the rarity of tin among the alloys dating to the second half of the 8th century B.C.

53 For parallels compare the mold ΤΣ 1080, above.

54 Michailidou and Tzachili 1986, p. 370.

55 Bouzek 1974b, p. 148, fig. 48: 3.

56 Droop 1926, p. 199, pl. LXXXV, β–λ; closest in shape are nos. β and γ, which date to the Geometric period.

57 Felsch 2007, pl. 22, nos. 194, 195.

58 Kilian-Dirlmeier 1981, pp. 371–372, pl. 80, nos. 1322–1332.

59 Kilian 1975a, p. 175, pl. 75 (8–20).

60 Kokkou-Vyridi 1999, p. 258, no. Γ72, pl. 58, no. Γ72. Around the perimeter of the axe runs a row of small concentric circles in pairs, which at points form a braid motif.

61 Wace 1929, p. 254, 264, pls. CLXXIX, no. 18, CLXXX, no. 34.

62 Voyatzis 2014, pp. 211, 215, no. LdN 30, fig. 12, pl. 14. To different types belong also the double-axe pendants from Kalapodi (Felsch 2007, nos. 186, 187, 188) and those from Lousoi (Reichel and Wilhelm 1901, p. 49, figs. 67–68).

63 Vokotopoulou 1990, p. 97, pl. 60γ, no. 9 (inv. ΜΘ 7616); Misailidou-Despotidou 2012b, pp. 473–477, the closest parallel, albeit of larger size, being no. 8, which dates to the 7th century B.C.

64 The only exceptions are the axe-shaped ends of the fastening wire on arch fibulae of type B II 2 from Bulgaria (Gergova 1987, pls. 15 (nos. 190–195]), 16 (nos. 197–199, 201, 202, 210), 17 (nos. 212, 216–220).

65 A double axe with perforated suspension holes at the edges of the blades, as well as at the center, has been reported from an Early Iron Age grave at Spilaio Grevenon (Rhomiopoulou 1971, p. 40, fig. 4).

66 For references, compare the mold ΤΣ 1080, above.

67 Wace 1929, pp. 250–253, pl. CLXXIX, nos. 6–17, 19–21.

68 Voyatzis 2014, p. 215, no. LdN 20, fig. 12, pl. 14, on a 7th-century round sheet of lead—probably a shield from a pendant in the shape of a warrior—from Tegea, with parallels from the sanctuary of Artemis Orthia (Wace 1929, p. 254); Kilian 1975a, p. 9, pl. 64, no. 28, on the head of an Archaic pin from Pherai; Kilian-Dirlmeier 1984a, pl. 106, no. 4472, on the head of a pin from Sparta.

69 Dimakopoulou 1974, pp. 166–167; Treister 2007, p. 570, pl. 72, no. 3.

70 Mitsopoulou-Leon 2012, pp. 80, 150, no. 120, pl. 16; *OlForsch* XIII, p. 57, no. 98, pl. 29.

71 Wace 1929, pp. 254, 258, 265, pls. CLXXX, nos. 10–13, CLXXXVI, nos. 10–14, with references to gold and bronze parallels from other regions. Comparable ornaments of lead come from Perachora (*Perachora* I, p. 186, pl. 85, no. 19 [this one bifaced]) and Pherai (Kilian 1975a, p. 176, pl. 79, no. 14, and pl. 79, no. 31). Wheel-shaped pendants of Bronze Age date are widespread in central Europe, Italy, and Greece (see De Angelis and Gori 2017; also Bouzek 1974b, pp. 137–138).

72 Kilian 1975a, p. 176, pl. 79, no. 14, and pl. 79, no. 31.

73 Kilian 1975a, pp. 182–183, pl. 84, nos. 18–20, 22–23; see also Bouzek 1974b, pp. 20–21, fig. 3, nos. 6, 7 (type E, parallels from Serbia and Pherai); pp. 135, 140–141, fig. 43, no. 8 (another variation). For examples from Argos see Ström 1995, pp. 64–65, no. NM 16971, fig. 28.

74 Kilian-Dirlmeier 1984a, pl. 106, no. 4468) (Archaic pin from Lousoi), also pl. 5, no. 126 (decoration on the upper part of a Mycenaean pin head from Myrsinochori); see further pl. 87, no. 3579 (Archaic pin from the Argive Heraion), and pl. 83, nos. 3331–3344 (examples from various sites in the Peloponnese); see also Mitsopoulou-Leon 2012, pl. 24, no. 285.

75 See, for example, the mold from Vergina, Michailidou and Tzachili 1986, p. 371, fig. 5; compare also a 3rd–2nd century B.C. mold for the manufacture of lead objects from Aptera, Crete, Stampolidis et al. 2018, p. 76, nos. 46–47.

76 Wace 1929, pp. 250–253, pl. CLXXIX, nos. 6–17, 19–21. The wheel-shaped, lead comparanda from the same site date to the 7th century B.C. (Wace 1929, pp. 254, 258, 265, pls. CLXXX, nos. 10–13, CLXXXVI, nos. 10–14).

77 Lead melts at a lower temperature than other metals—327º C versus 1063º C and 1000º C, the respective melting points of gold and bronze. Alloys melt at lower temperatures (see Hodges 1964, p. 97).

78 See Craddock, Freestone, and Dawe 1997, for experimental proof that open molds of limestone were used for the direct casting of simple-shaped, undecorated objects. Tylecote (1973) also demonstrated that coating a sandstone mold with soot helped increase its resistance to the increased temperature of the molten metal.

79 See Galiniki 2006, pp. 352–353.

80 See Kokkorou-Alevra et al. 2014, p. 163, no. 590 on an ancient quarry for micrite fossiliferous, reddish brown limestone at Tiryns.

81 For close parallels, in many different variations, see *Perachora* I, p. 172, pl. 74, nos. 12, 15, 17–20; Kilian-Dirlmeier 1984a, pl. 85, nos. 3422–3425, 3429; Felsch 2007, pl. 27, no. 380; pl. 28, no. 410.

82 Reinholdt 1992, p. 222.

83 See, for example, Misailidou-Despotidou 2011, p. 70.

84 Felsch 2007, pp. 83, 84, 85, no. 198, pl. 22.

85 For references, compare ΤΣ 1080 above.

86 Bessios 2003; Bessios et al. 2004; cf. Chapters 1, 14; see also Morris et al. 2020, fig. 56:f–g.

28

THE LEAD SLING BULLETS FROM METHONE: WARFARE (UN)INSCRIBED

Angelos Boufalis, Niki Oikonomaki, and Yannis Z. Tzifopoulos

INTRODUCTION

The present study publishes a total of 108 plain and inscribed sling bullets (counting the cluster of four bullets **28/62** individually), which were found during the excavations conducted by the Pieria Ephoreia of Antiquities (former KZ′/27th Ephoreia of Prehistoric and Classical Antiquities) at the site of ancient Methone in the period 2003–2008. The bullets are associated with the siege of the city by the Macedonian king Philip II in 354 B.C. and are related to other identical or similar sling bullets found throughout Macedonia, Chalkidike, and Thrace. This material is accompanied by a full archaeological, historical, and epigraphic commentary, as well as an exhaustive overview of what is known to date about slings, slinging, and slingers, and a critical review of earlier research on sling bullets. From this study several challenging, if problematic, topics emerge, such as the meaning, function, and purpose of the inscriptions and devices on sling bullets, which inevitably touch upon scholarly debates on warfare and literacy in antiquity. Here it is argued that the inscriptions and devices are most probably related to the production of the bullets rather than to their use.

Of the 108 bullets, 68 have inscriptions in relief and 40 are plain (including one with an incised mark). Most bullets come from stratified contexts dated to the later part of the first half of the 4th century B.C. and were found mainly in the agora (East Hill) and along the city walls of the West Hill.[1] Their provenance presents clear evidence as to the narrative of their deposition there: the siege and subsequent capture of the city by Philip II in 355/4–354/3 B.C.[2] Moreover, the inscribed bullets bear standardized inscriptions, most of which are already known from other sites, that is, other cities or forts besieged by the Macedonians under Philip II, and therefore strongly suggest that they are part of a larger group of lead sling bullets associated with the military operations of the army of Philip II along the Macedonian coast, in the Chalkidike Peninsula, and across Thrace during the 350s and 340s B.C.[3]

The quantity of bullets that was found—especially taking into account not only those that escaped collection by archaeologists, but also all those that were reclaimed after battle in order to be recycled or reused[4]—should be considered as non-representative of the total amount that was shot.[5] As one can judge from archaeological reports, such finds are common throughout Macedonia and are found, in fact, in great numbers; however, the publication rate does not keep up with the numbers coming to light in excavations. Thus far, about 500 bullets found at Olynthos and its port town Mekyberna form the largest and first systematically published group in northern Greece,[6] followed by a few much smaller groups from Pella,[7] Torone,[8] and Amphipolis.[9]

However few, their number is still revealing of the extent to which slingers were employed in war operations and indicative of their involvement in sieges, as is attested in literary sources. In any battle, slingers seem to have had a prominent role in the tactics advanced by both sides.[10] Lead sling bullets, however, are carriers of far more information than what can be inferred from their number and findspot. Their material and casting technique may be important to the discussion of political geography and metallurgy in antiquity, while inscriptions and devices that are often found on bullets may provide evidence for military campaigns, army organization and logistics, state armories, and weapon production and distribution, as well as prosopography.

The aim of this chapter is to present a thorough examination of the sling bullets from Methone and their archaeological and historical context. Thus, by way of introduction to the catalogue, the historical circumstances that led to the siege of Methone, and the archaeological contexts wherein the bullets were found are explored. The catalogue itself also comprises a short section on typology so as to set out some general facts and common characteristics, and a full commentary on the inscriptions and devices, which appear on the bullets under study. But first, a short history of the weapon, its use, and its users is necessary.

ON SLINGS, SLINGING, AND SLINGERS

The sling is an easily made, yet efficient, weapon that has been in use in the Aegean since at least the Neolithic period.[11] Although its use as a combat (as well as hunting) weapon in earlier prehistoric times has been contested[12] (depending on the presumed socioeconomic frame of those communities in question), the sling, as civilization progressed, soon found its way into domination disputes. Thus, the sling is employed by defenders, along with the bow, in a siege scene depicted on the celebrated silver rhyton found at Mycenae (Appendix II.1); later it appears on two vases of the Geometric period, where slingers are attacking the advancing enemy apparently before the hoplites clash with each other (Appendix II.2–3);[13] in Homer's *Iliad* the sling is employed in pitched battle by the invading army, in order to throw the Trojans into disarray;[14] and Archilochos (mid-7th century B.C.) refers to bows and slings only to praise swords and spears,[15] even though on a late 7th-century B.C. vase, a hoplite has divested himself of his arms and operates as a slinger against the approaching enemy, taking cover behind a fellow hoplite (Appendix II.4). Although still not common, illustrations of slingers increase considerably by the 6th century B.C. (see Appendix II), and from the 5th century B.C. onward slingers (and slings) are mentioned far more often in literary sources, usually together with bows in war contexts.[16]

The Greek word for sling, σφενδόνη, literally means a strap of cloth, and as such it is attested in the *Iliad* (13.716: ἐϋστρεφεῖ οἶος ἀώτῳ), where a strap of twisted wool is employed in one instance as a weapon, and in another as gauze to treat a wound (*Il.* 13.599–600).[17] This must be the simplest form of the sling: a strap of cloth, wider in the middle,[18] folded once breadthwise around the object that would serve as the missile. A weapon, however, which took so much training to master,[19] would hardly maintain its primal form, while techniques and ammunition evolved. Although no actual ancient Greek sling survives, nor is iconography of much help, as the portrayal of slings is rarely detailed enough to determine the structure of the sling,[20] literary sources offer a fairly good picture. There were two types:[21] one braided from end to end and forming an ellipsoid slot in the middle; and one made of three distinct parts: a rectangular leather pouch with two straps or cords fastened on either end.[22] The straps or cords were called κῶλα, which is technically translated as "parts," and the pouch in the middle μέσον.[23] The κῶλα were made of wool, leather, flax, horsehair, tendons or sinews, or *melancranis* (sedge).[24]

Of the two κῶλα, one is the retention cord, which ends in a loop to accommodate the slinger's middle finger, thereby securing the sling to the slinger's arm, and the other is the release cord, which ends in a knot that was held between index and thumb and was released to launch the missile. The sling functioned as an extension of the arm; a simple back-and-forth movement or a more dexterous swing of an arm throwing a stone was the pattern on which the slinging technique was based and from which it evolved. Additionally, the sling offered the possibility of swinging in a full circle that the human arm cannot achieve, and this became the typical way of slinging as it allowed the development of momentum,[25] thus multiplying the velocity and thereby the power and range of the shot.[26] Although styles vary,[27] the common method of slinging is to raise the sling above the head, rotating it a few times, and then release the missile at the moment when the sling forms a 90° angle to the prospective target, or, in other words, when the missile is on the tangent to its orbit aligned to the prospective target. This technique takes full advantage of the acceleration achieved by swinging, and it goes without saying that a longer sling would achieve a longer range than a shorter one—no doubt the reason why Balearic slingers carried three slings of different lengths.[28]

Obviously, swinging demanded space, as well as time to develop momentum. As both were rather limited in the course of battle, simpler techniques developed, involving fewer swings and whip-like moves.[29] The latter technique is probably the one most often illustrated in Greek iconography (see Appendix II), where the slinger is depicted with his arms raised, holding the sling taut above his head; he would then swing it over and around, and, using his back and shoulder muscles, he would toss it forward. For the loss of momentum and, therefore, of velocity and range, accuracy and speed of reflexes would compensate.[30]

Although the accuracy of slingers is explicitly noted in several instances in the sources,[31] it is noteworthy that, when their tactical importance in battle is commented upon, it is always when slingers are deployed and expected to act en masse;[32] there are no references to snipers or anything like that in the ancient sources. During a siege the slingers of the attacking party would carry out a variety of tactical aims, from bringing havoc to the besieged to providing cover fire for light-armed troops as they advanced to scale the walls, while the besieged would use the firepower of slingers to repulse any such attempt.[33] Accordingly, in open battle slingers were always appointed as a unit to harass and prevent the enemy infantry from relocating or advancing, and they almost always did so from a safe distance.[34] On the whole, it is to be deduced that a slinger's most important capability was to outrange the enemy.

The fact that the sling, before the invention of the hand-held ballista, was the projectile weapon with the longest range in antiquity is certainly attested in many instances.[35] There is, however, no evidence and no consensus among scholars as to the actual range:[36] classicists deduce from the ancient sources a range as high as 350–500 m, while ethnographic and experimental research usually produces results below 100 m. A range of 70–150 m seems more reasonable in order to reconcile different materials, techniques, and a slinger's gender and age. Yet a shot reaching as far as 200 m should be considered normally achievable by skilled slingers and a range of ca. 300 m under specific circumstances (depending on sling length, technique, and shape and material of ammunition) could still be possible.[37]

The commonest ammunition was, of course, stones, preferably natural rounded pebbles, as angular rocks do not perform well in flight, but also manually rounded stones. Stones are the most commonly mentioned sling ammunition in literary sources,[38] and the only type visible in iconography, either already in the pouch of the sling or stocked in the slinger's pouch.[39] Other materials, namely clay and lead,[40] were also used: the former in regions scarce in suitable natural stones, and the latter by well-organized armies that had the motivation and the resources to provide for the supply. Clay sling bullets were also used for special purposes such as starting fires with incandescent bullets.[41]

Lead sling bullets[42] first appear in literary sources at the end of the 5th century B.C., and more specifically in Xen. *Anab.* 3.3.17 (written sometime in the first half of the 4th century B.C., but referring to the year 401 B.C.). How much earlier lead bullets were invented is unknown. In comparison to the standard stone ammunition (λίθοι χειροπληθεῖς) which weighed about a *mna* (ca. 435 g),[43] lead bullets are rather light. This led Tracey Rihll to argue that lead bullets were designed and used primarily as catapult ammunition, which was developed in the same period,[44] although she does not exclude the possibility that they were thrown with a hand sling as well.[45] Indeed, the stone or clay bullets of the Neolithic period, had a weight equivalent to the lead bullets of the Classical and Hellenistic period (ca. 30 g);[46] however, leaden examples that securely predate the 4th century B.C. are lacking. At Enkomi on Cyprus, Porphyrios Dikaios found, among a few clay sling bullets and many pebbles that have been interpreted as such, one lead bullet in an apparently securely stratified context of Late Cypriot IIIA (12th century B.C.),[47] and five in Late Cypriot IIIB (early 11th century B.C.) contexts.[48] Furthermore, on Crete, Arthur Evans reported two bullets from a Late Minoan III (13th–12th century B.C.) stratum at Knossos with no evidence of later intrusion, which differ in weight and caliber from one inscribed ΚΝΩ found in the area of the Greco-Roman city.[49] Paul Åström and Ino Nicolaou published a few lead sling bullets from Hala Sultan Tekke found in supposedly undisturbed Late Cypriot IIIA contexts;[50] but one bullet which was found in an otherwise securely dated Late Cypriot IIIA1 context is inscribed in Greek,[51] and thus casts doubt on the Late Bronze Age dating of the other bullets as well. All these cases should be treated with extreme caution.

A cluster of lead sling bullets was found in a metallurgical workshop at Gravisca, Etruria, which seems to have been active during the 6th and in the early 5th century B.C.;[52] but in the area there are also metallurgical waste pits of the 4th–3rd century B.C., which is a more acceptable date for the bullets.[53] The bullets allegedly from Marathon and associated with the famous battle of 490 B.C. (according to the antique dealers) are identified as plain bullets of unknown provenance and chronology, bearing forged inscriptions (incised, as opposed to molded which is typical).[54] David Robinson speculated that some bullets inscribed Ἀθηναίων from Mekyberna, the port town of Olynthos, may date from the Athenian occupation of the port in the 420s B.C. or its recapture by the Olynthians in 421 B.C. (Thuc. 5.39.1; Diod. 12.77.5);[55] such a dating, however, is hardly compatible with their Ionic script, although not impossible. Two bullets inscribed ΜΕΡ|ΝΑ from Pydna and Poteidaia were mistakenly dated to the 5th century B.C. (see the commentary on *Μερ|να(–)? vel Να|μερ(–)* below). A bullet inscribed ΚΛΕΟΜΑΧ(ΟΥ) found at the excavation of a chamber tomb of the late 5th–early 4th century B.C. at Brasda, north of Skopje,[56] was actually found in the fill, which is dated to ca. 400–350 B.C.[57] As for the bullets of Tissaphernes,[58] they may be contemporary to Xenophon's account, only if the named individual is in fact the satrap of Lydia (413–395 B.C.), a precondition not supported by the use of lunate sigma, which, although it appears already in the late Archaic period, becomes common only in the early 3rd century B.C.[59] The fact that Xenophon (*Anab.* 3.3.16–17) picked out the Rhodians as being familiar with this particular ammunition material is perhaps indicative, as it may imply that the use of lead sling bullets was not widespread at the time. This is odd, as lead was an inexpensive material,[60] widely used in various applications, and well known for providing maximum weight for any given size, while being easily cast. What is certain is that by the mid-4th century B.C. lead bullets had entered the arsenal of—at least—state armies.

A variety of reasons made slingers an essential part of any properly organized army: the relative ease of manufacturing a sling, the low cost of the materials for both sling and ammunition (stone, clay, lead), which, moreover, were easily recycled and replenished even in battle,[61] the lethal nature of the weapon, even as a blunt projectile,[62] and, most importantly, the range of the sling. Almost all accounts enumerating military forces list slingers along with archers and javelin throwers,[63] and perhaps their presence is to be assumed in other instances, as their existence may have been covered under the umbrella term "light-armed" (ψιλοί),[64] or even "naked" (γυμνῆται).[65] Still, in literary sources, as well as in vase iconography, there is a disparity in the frequency with which they appear in comparison to hoplites and other military classes. Although depictions of slingers are not unusual (see Appendix II), they are not nearly as numerous as those of horsemen, hoplites, Amazons, etc. This is due to the status of slingers in an army that was a reflection of contemporary society. In Greek city-states, the honored guardians of the homeland had to be the citizens; and even among the citizens, prowess in battle was measured in metal. Until the rowing masses were upgraded to "saviors of the city" in the context of the Athenian empire, the only σωσίπολις was the one who had the means to arm himself.[66] In Greek tradition, dominated by Homer's glorified aristocratic duels, a poor citizen with no means to arm himself for close combat was technically excluded from any honorable martial practice. Slingers, as well as archers, received little, if any, recognition for their achievements in battle, and their weapon, as much as all other long-range projectiles (spears excluded), was considered a dishonorable one, befitting only those of servile status.[67] Interestingly, however, warriors also using the sling are attested. Apart from the Trojan hero Agenor in the *Iliad* (13.598–600),[68] there are telling depictions of warriors with slings in vase iconography: a hoplite who has divested himself of his arms and armor, which are set in front of him, except his greaves (Appendix II.4); a light-armed warrior wearing a helmet (Appendix II.10); Iolaos in full hoplite gear readying his sling against the Stymphalian birds (Appendix II.15); a warrior with helmet and greaves, but wearing light armor instead of a cuirass (Appendix II.14); a slinger with a linen(?) chiton and a helmet (Appendix II.19); but more significantly, Herakles himself is often depicted using a sling (Appendix II.7–9, 11, 15).[69] All these instances, dating to the Archaic period and to the mid-5th century B.C. at the latest, reveal that, although it was not promoted, the use of the sling was acceptable to an extent even by hoplites.[70] The inferiority of projectile weapons was clearly one in concept and the depreciation of the light-armed military classes by the aristocracy was essentially politically motivated.[71]

THE HISTORICAL CONTEXT

It is intriguing to find that the Methonaians, albeit coincidentally, had a special relationship with slinging long before the Macedonian king Philip II besieged the city. According to the city's own foundation myth, as Plutarch relates, the Eretrians who colonized Methone were first settled on Korkyra from where they were ousted by Corinthian colonists and sailed home, where their compatriots "forbade their landing by slinging" (ἀποβαίνειν ἐκώλυον σφενδονῶντες). Unable to prevail through either violence or words, they sailed north, where they occupied a Thracian village. The new settlement was named Methone, and they were nicknamed by their neighbors "those who were repulsed by slings" (ἀποσφενδόνητοι).[72] There is no reason to doubt the validity of this foundation story, even though Plutarch, or his source,[73] may have been inaccurate in interpreting the term ἀποσφενδόνητοι, which could simply mean "slung out."[74] Whether or not the story holds any truth, it seems to foreshadow the expulsion of the Methonaians after they yielded their city to Philip II.[75]

After the death of Perdikkas III, the new king Philip II continued his predecessors' military reforms of the Macedonian kingdom,[76] while maintaining his antagonism with the Athenians, especially over Amphipolis. In 356/5 B.C. (see below), the Athenians sent a force of 3,000 hoplites along with a considerable naval force to help the pretender Argaios ascend to the throne (Diod. 16.2.6). The whole operation ended in a disaster for the Athenians, as Philip met them in battle and destroyed their force (Diod. 16.3.5–6; cf. Dem. 23.121), and an even greater one for the Methonaians, whose city was soon besieged, with the Athenians being either unable or unwilling to help.[77]

According to Diodoros' account (16.31.6, 16.34.4), the siege of Methone took place soon after the unsuccessful coup of Argaios, in 354 B.C.[78] An honorary decree, however, for a certain Sochares from Apollonia, who offered some services (not preserved on the stone) to Methone[79] in December 355 B.C.,[80] implies that the city was already under siege by this date. Perhaps Diodoros' chronology (written in the 1st century B.C.) admits revision, dating Argaios' coup in 356/5 B.C., rather than 354 B.C., so as to allow that Methone was besieged and fell in 355/4–354/3 B.C.[81]

THE ARCHAEOLOGICAL CONTEXT

The archaeological context cannot offer such a precise dating, but the dated material from the destruction layer excavated in the agora of Methone, within or around which most of the bullets were found, can certainly support one. This dates to the end of the first half of the 4th century B.C.[82] and contains enough evidence for the identification of the destruction event with the aftermath of the surrender of Methone, which the Macedonians razed to the ground (Diod. 16.31.6, 16.34.5; Dem. 9.26).

Diodoros' narrative (16.34.5: καὶ μέχρι μέν τινος οἱ Μεθωναῖοι διεκαρτέρουν, ἔπειτα κατισχυόμενοι συνηναγκάσθησαν παραδοῦναι τὴν πόλιν τῷ βασιλεῖ) suggests that the Methonaians held firm to their city until they surrendered, but archaeological finds attest to the contrary. Apart from those bullets found along the fortification walls, a considerable number was found inside the buildings of the agora, the city center. This recalls the distribution pattern noticed at Olynthos, where urban combat has been documented,[83] and Polyainos' account, which suggests that Methone may actually have been captured.[84]

East Hill (Plot 274)

Plot 274 is situated on the western slope of the middle part of the East Hill, where the agora of the city has been discovered. Four buildings (A, B, Δ, and E), by all evidence not of domestic character, have been partially excavated around an open space (Fig. 1.21) with a paved road leading presumably to and from the port lying to the north.[85] A number of sling bullets, as well as a few bronze arrowheads, were found in relation to the destruction layer inside the buildings around this open space.[86]

Apart from a few bullets that were found in topsoil (**28/2** [ΜΕΘ 285], **28/73** [ΜΕΘ 1699], **28/75** [ΜΕΘ 1704]), the rest were found in the fill deposits of the rooms and in most cases in close relation to the destruction layer. Three bullets were found on the floor below the destruction layer (**28/45** [ΜΕΘ 1702], **28/47** [ΜΕΘ 2144], **28/74** [ΜΕΘ 1703]), 14 within the destruction layer (**28/1** [ΜΕΘ 281], **28/3** [ΜΕΘ 287], **28/4** [ΜΕΘ 291], **28/37** [ΜΕΘ 283], **28/38** [ΜΕΘ 286], **28/39** [ΜΕΘ 288], **28/44** [ΜΕΘ 1701], **28/58** [ΜΕΘ 292], **28/59** [ΜΕΘ 1708], **28/63** [ΜΕΘ 289], **28/64** [ΜΕΘ 290], **28/66** [ΜΕΘ 282], **28/67** [ΜΕΘ 280], **28/68** [ΜΕΘ 284]), and five in the fill above the destruction layer (**28/6** [ΜΕΘ 1705], **28/8** [ΜΕΘ 1709], **28/43** [ΜΕΘ 1700], **28/46** [ΜΕΘ 1706], **28/72** [ΜΕΘ 1698]); additionally, one was found in a drainage channel (**28/48** [ΜΕΘ 2145]) and one in the fill of a cut in a 4th-century B.C. stratum (**28/7** [ΜΕΘ 1707]). The assemblage is mixed as regards the inscriptions, except on the floor level, where two out of three bear the name Μικίνας, but their number is too small to draw any conclusions.

East Hill (Plot 278)

At the neck of the East Hill, 30 m south of Plot 274, lies Plot 278, where a narrow trench was opened, partially revealing Building Γ. This building has a strong southern wall, 1 m thick, running parallel to a ditch along its southern, external side. Inside the space north of this wall, which seems to have been an interior space, although there were no roof tiles in the deposit or on the floor level, a total of 46 sling bullets was found (**28/9** [ΜΕΘ 2854], **28/10** [ΜΕΘ 2862], **28/11** [ΜΕΘ 2863], **28/12** [ΜΕΘ 2864], **28/13** [ΜΕΘ 2865], **28/14** [ΜΕΘ 2866], **28/15** [ΜΕΘ 2867], **28/16** [ΜΕΘ 2868], **28/17** [ΜΕΘ 2869], **28/18** [ΜΕΘ 2870], **28/19** [ΜΕΘ 2871], **28/20** [ΜΕΘ 2872], **28/21** [ΜΕΘ 2873], **28/22** [ΜΕΘ 2875], **28/23** [ΜΕΘ 2878], **28/24** [ΜΕΘ 2879], **28/49** [ΜΕΘ 2853], **28/50** [ΜΕΘ 2856], **28/51** [ΜΕΘ 2857], **28/52** [ΜΕΘ 2858], **28/53** [ΜΕΘ 2859], **28/54** [ΜΕΘ 2860], **28/55** [ΜΕΘ 2861], **28/60** [ΜΕΘ 2847], **28/65** [ΜΕΘ 2891], **28/76** [ΜΕΘ 2846], **28/77** [ΜΕΘ 2848], **28/78** [ΜΕΘ 2849], **28/79** [ΜΕΘ 2850], **28/80** [ΜΕΘ 2851], **28/81** [ΜΕΘ 2852], **28/82** [ΜΕΘ 2855], **28/83** [ΜΕΘ 2874], **28/84** [ΜΕΘ 2876], **28/85** [ΜΕΘ 2877], **28/86** [ΜΕΘ 2880], **28/87** [ΜΕΘ 2881], **28/88** [ΜΕΘ 2882], **28/89** [ΜΕΘ 2883], **28/90**[ΜΕΘ 2884], **28/91** [ΜΕΘ 2885], **28/92** [ΜΕΘ 2886], **28/93** [ΜΕΘ 2887], **28/94** [ΜΕΘ 2888], **28/95** [ΜΕΘ 2889], **28/96** [ΜΕΘ 2890]), along with a few coins and many iron objects.[87] The substantial south wall, the ditch in front of and parallel to it, and the location of the building in close proximity to the supposed course of the south city wall fit well with a military use of it as a guardhouse, even if this was temporary.[88] Still, the number of bullets found is not extraordinary, and the assemblage of different inscriptions may indicate that the concentration was probably by chance: a walled, but not roofed, space by the city wall could presumably have received a considerable number of missed shots. Another sling bullet was collected from the excavation debris of the trench (**28/25** [ΜΕΘ 2892]).

West Hill (Plot 229)

The course of the south city wall is far better defined on the West Hill. The neck of the hill had been dug up to strengthen the defense of this part of the fortification, which seems to have been one of the weak points. Part of this fortification trench was found filled with an artificial deposit containing extremely few pottery sherds, but a significant number of sling bullets.[89] In the same area, to the south of the fortification trench, excavations in 2014 partially revealed an earthen ramp rising toward the north.[90] Both earthworks were obviously made by the besieging army in order to scale the city wall.[91] The course of the wall can be determined by the south slope of the West Hill in conjunction with the location of several tunnels found along its course to the north, with a north–south orientation.[92] These were narrow descending rock-cut stairways leading, presumably, underneath the wall, and having some defensive function on the other side—possibly leading to sally ports.[93] Sling bullets were a common find in the fill, especially in close proximity to the course of the wall (**28/31** [ΜΕΘ 2898], **28/33** [ΜΕΘ 2907], **28/34** [ΜΕΘ 2909], **28/35** [ΜΕΘ 2910], **28/36** [ΜΕΘ 2911], **28/56** [ΜΕΘ 2901], **28/57** [ΜΕΘ 2912], **28/61** [ΜΕΘ 2900], **28/97** [ΜΕΘ 2899], **28/98** [ΜΕΘ 2902], **28/101** [ΜΕΘ 2906], **28/102** [ΜΕΘ 2908]). Notably absent here are the Εὐγένεος bullets, which, at any rate, are very few at the site, but the rest of the inscribed names are all represented.

West Hill (Plot 245)

The course of the south city wall was also traced in Plot 245, which, according to the excavators, is evident mainly from a steep cut in the hill, namely the fortification trench (as above), and by surface finds,[94] namely a few sling bullets found in topsoil (**28/71** [MEΘ 654]) and in the upper layers of the deposits (**28/5** [MEΘ 655], **28/26** [MEΘ 2893], **28/42** [MEΘ 656]).

Another tunnel was found here, and was partially excavated (Figs. 1.26, 6.2). Apparently, the entrance was situated inside or underneath a roofed structure, as indicated by a thick layer of roof tiles and mud bricks, as well as a few cornerstone blocks that were found inside the tunnel.[95] Apart from three bullets found in topsoil (**28/27** [MEΘ 2894], **28/28** [MEΘ 2895], **28/30** [MEΘ 2897]), another six were found inside the tunnel: one on the lower steps in an intentional (human-made) fill covering the staircase (**28/41** [MEΘ 653]), two in the natural fill above (**28/29** [MEΘ 2896], **28/70** [MEΘ 652]), two in a layer of fallen roof tiles within the natural fill (**28/62** [MEΘ 651], **28/69** [MEΘ 650]), and one in the fill above the layer of fallen roof tiles (**28/40** [MEΘ 649]).

It is interesting that, excluding the finds in Plot 278, the greater number of bullets was found in the agora, rather than along the walls. This may be due to the extent of the excavated area in each part of the site, or to the morphology of the terrain, the hilltops being liable to erosion and the fold between the two hills being liable to sedimentation, thus concentrating more material. However, the presence of bullets in interior spaces in the agora and, moreover, within the destruction layer leaves no doubt that the fighting took place not only outside and on the city walls. Urban combat following the breach of the city walls by the besiegers is well documented, as is the capture and occupation of the agora in order to secure control of a city.[96] Athena Athanassiadou points out that the pottery assemblage of the destruction layer in the agora is dominated by cooking pots and tableware, which must be seen in relation to the hearths that were found in every interior space of Building A, and she goes on to conclude that "the concentration of lead sling bullets in the eastern part of the stoa porch [of Building A], as well as in Building Γ, which was found to the south, leaves no doubt about the occupation of public buildings, either by besieged Methonaians or by troops of the army of Philip II."[97] Only a small part of the site of ancient Methone has been explored by excavation, and, therefore, it is impossible to say at this point whether combat took place in residential areas, as is argued for Olynthos.[98] As for using missile weapons in interior spaces, as Lee argues,[99] the evidence so far is also inconclusive. Most of the bullets in the interior spaces of the buildings around the agora were found within the layer of fallen roof tiles, and the rest below as often as above it (see above, Plot 274). Nicholas Cahill notes that in Olynthian houses, bullets were often found "on floor levels rather than in debris above the floor, as they presumably would have been if they had fallen onto the roofs of the houses," and thus he suggests that these bullets were shot at Olynthian defenders positioned on roofs.[100] Roofs, however, do not usually fall flat, and objects can slip through damaged roofs, while shooting through window and door openings is another possibility. Arrowheads, too, according to the excavation notebooks, were found in interior spaces at Methone (mostly in Plot 274, squares 26, 75, and 85), but there is no consistency in their stratigraphic relation to the destruction layer, other than a close association with it. One interesting observation from the excavation notebooks is that, except in square 79 of Plot 274, the findspots of sling bullets do not coincide with those of arrowheads.

The presence of bullets inside tunnels is more easily explained. The presence of collapsed structural debris inside the tunnels from the fortifications that once rose above suggests that bullets fell along with the superstructure. The layer of roof tiles found on the floor of the tunnels must surely be associated with the fortification walls, where roofing would serve both to protect the mud-brick superstructure from weather[101] and to provide shelter for the defenders on the *parodos* (wall walk).[102] If we accept Polyainos' (4.2.5) testimony that the Macedonians managed to scale and take the walls, consequently bringing the battle on top of them or on the inside, then the presence of bullets even north of the course of the city wall is not surprising. What is strange is that the cluster of bullets (**28/62** [ΜΕΘ 651]), which one would expect to find in an interior space serving as an arsenal or guardhouse or the like, was found within the fallen roof-tile layer inside a tunnel (Plot 245). There is no explanation for this, other than that bullets were perhaps cast on the walls, or inside a room of a tower, although it is not impossible that the cluster ended up there by chance.

TYPOLOGY AND GENERAL CHARACTERISTICS

All known bullets coming from Greek antiquity are of similar size[103] and form, that is, a rounded, elongated body of ellipsoid, or close to round, midsection with more or less pointed ends.[104] Variations may include sharper edges, a more slender body, flattened sides, and so on. This form was already conceived and, judging from the effort invested in the manufacture of stone bullets, favored in the Neolithic Age, and was applied in the manufacturing of both stone and clay bullets all across the Mediterranean.[105] The persistence of the form is not surprising, as this is the most aerodynamic shape one could achieve. In fact, modern-era ballistics rediscovered the form in the 19th century after centuries of using round missiles, and fully adopted it for ammunition of all types of firearms.[106]

Many studies have attempted a typology of sling bullets, but none is comprehensive enough to comprise all types, while at the same time taking into account the chronological sequence of variations, which may indicate evolution of forms; some scholars tend to focus on minor variations in seeking to attribute groups of similar bullets to mold sets, overlooking general typological characteristics.[107] Moreover, most studies examine bullets of the Roman era, when a number of variants had developed or had been invented.[108] The sling bullets examined here are all of the same period and conform to two particular types that seem to have been standard in the Classical and Hellenistic period. The two types are distinguished by (i) the difference in ratio between width and thickness,[109] (ii) the sharpness of the edges (perhaps a corollary of [i]), and (iii) the sharpness of the ends.[110]

- Type A (almond-shaped) has an ellipsoid midsection with acute, pointed ends (at least the bullet point), and sharp edges.
- Type B (olive-shaped) has a round or near round midsection, rather rounded ends, and the edges are far from sharp.

Further characteristics differentiating the two types are due to the meticulous production that is consistently noted in Type A, and rarely, if ever, in Type B. Type A has distinct edges, smooth sides (even appearing polished), carefully placed and executed inscriptions, rarely visible traces of casting defects, and no deformities due to mold shift.[111] Overall, bullets of this type are noticeably more refined than those of Type B. Evidence of the relatively careless production of Type B bullets (especially the ΜΕΡΝΑ ones) is the flattening (after deflashing) of the edges by hammering,[112] as opposed to cutting and filing that has produced the fine edges of the Type A examples. It must be noted that the same case could be made to distinguish the

Μικίνα from the MEPNA bullets, both identified as Type B, just by focusing more closely on their differences. Still, as the same disparity has been noted at Olynthos between Chalkidian sling bullets and the rest,[113] the above typology is probably a useful tool. Nonetheless, such variations may be irrelevant to typology and perhaps are simply due to the mold specifications of each particular issue of sling bullets; therefore, they may not pertain to distinct types or subtypes, so that in a comprehensive typology of sling bullets, both these types could be merged into one.

It is indeed questionable whether an artisan commissioned to manufacture a mold for sling bullets would also receive exact specifications of the end result, that is, precise dimensions and appearance. The fact that the finer shape of Type A bullets is always accompanied by fine finishing attests to the overall care taken in production, and rougher bullets, such as those inscribed MEPNA, were presumably not ordered to be made more roughly, but are simply the products of a rough mold, the cavities of which would have been carved out without respect to a specific depth or the smoothness of the surface. A number of surviving molds exhibit such discrepancies in quality of manufacture that would, by extension, result in the same discrepancy in the quality of the bullets produced. The published sling bullet molds of the type that produced treelike clusters, such as **28/62** (ΜΕΘ 651), are the following:[114]

- clay mold with seven (preserved) cavities, uninscribed, found at Olynthos, ante 348 B.C.;[115]
- clay mold with at least six (five preserved) cavities, uninscribed, found on Delos, 2nd century B.C.;[116]
- bronze mold with six cavities, inscribed ΤΙΜΩΝΟΣ, in the Paul Kanellopoulos Collection in Athens.[117]

There also exist molds with serial, instead of branching, channeling:

- casting channel connecting the cavities laterally:[118]
  - clay mold with two series of cavities (of which three are preserved), uninscribed, adapted from a Corinthian-type roof tile and found at Pella, Hellenistic period;[119]
  - clay mold with a series of six (preserved) cavities, uninscribed, adapted from a Corinthian-type roof tile and found at Pella, Hellenistic period;[120]
  - limestone mold (both halves) with eight cavities arranged in series of two, three uninscribed and the rest inscribed with single letters (Μ, Δ, Α, Χ, Χ), found at Aptera, Crete, Hellenistic period;[121]
  - clay mold with three preserved cavities, uninscribed, found at Phanagoria, Roman(?) period, now in the Hermitage, St. Petersburg;[122]
- casting channel connecting the cavities serially:
  - limestone mold with nine cavities (preserved), uninscribed, the latter four unfinished as to the funnel and channel, and a fragment of the same, or of the other half of the mold with only an incision of the outline of one cavity at the bullet point, found at Aptera, Hellenistic period;[123]
  - limestone mold with three cavities (preserved), uninscribed, found at Aptera, Hellenistic period;[124]
- type uncertain:
  - red brick mold with two cavities, inscribed ΧΑΛΚΙ, found at Mekyberna, 348 B.C.;[125]
  - clay mold with three cavities (preserved), inscribed EVLG, found at Saint-Martin Rivoli, Paris, late 1st century B.C.–early 1st century A.D.[126]

It is likely that Εὐγένεος bullets were cast in a finely manufactured, perhaps bronze, mold, while the MEPNA, Μικίνα, and Κλεοβούλō ones could have been cast in cavities carved into a clay or stone mold. Therefore, the above two forms (Type A and B) may not pertain to typology, but to the degree of care in the preparation of the molds.[127]

The manufacturing process of sling bullets is illustrated by **28/62** (ΜΕΘ 651). This belongs to a series of similar clusters in the form of a lead "tree," with a main stem branching out in regular intervals to pairs of shorter stems ending in bullets. Comparable finds come from different geographical areas and periods:

- cluster of five bullets out of nine (four are missing) found in a metallurgical context at Gravisca (port of Tarquinia), Etruria, late Archaic(?) period;[128]
- cluster of seven bullets (inscribed ΔΙΟΝΥ|ΣΙΟ), in the Feuardent Collection, National Museum of Copenhagen;[129]
- six fragments of cast stems with no bullets attached, of which three complete with stalks for nine bullets in total, found at Miletos, 350–300 B.C.;[130]
- ten bullets (inscribed ΛΙΠΟΔΩΡΟΣ) attached together along their edges and some with the rear part of their connecting stalk found at Kazaphani (Keryneia), Cyprus, late 4th century B.C.;[131]
- three clusters of nine bullets each (inscribed ΔΙΟΝΥ [sc. verso not illustrated, probably –|ΣΙΟ]) found in the Piraeus, 3rd(?) century B.C., in the National Archaeological Museum at Athens;[132]
- cluster of ten bullets, twisted and with extensive casting flashes, found together with two pairs of bullets joined together at the stem and other bullets joined together by casting flashes, and along with scrap lead and many other lead objects, in an interior space at Populonia, Etruria, 2nd(?) century B.C.;[133]
- cluster of six bullets (inscribed ΑΓΡΟΙΤΑ) found at Eretria, 198 B.C.;[134]
- a single bullet still attached to the casting stem and preserving a lead sheet in between, in a private collection in Blagoevgrad, southwest Bulgaria, 181 B.C.[135]
- two fragments of cast stems with no bullets attached, of which one almost complete with stalks for nine bullets in total, found at Vigla, Cyprus, undated;[136]

Most clusters are twisted and present excess overflowed material forming sheets (flashing) between the bullets. This is caused by leakage of the material between the two halves of a mold. Proper design of the mold can reduce or eliminate flash; nevertheless, old or worn mold cavities that no longer fit tightly together are still prone to flashing. The rest of the bullets of the same issue as **28/62** (ΜΕΘ 651) (Εὐγένεος) are of a fine finish, which is probably due to post-casting treatment (deflashing).[137] As for the twisted appearance, Cédric Brélaz and Pierre Ducrey suggest that this may be caused by the force used to detach the bullets, which is further indicated by some marks on the three free bullets found alongside the cluster they publish, possibly made by the tool used to break them loose.[138] One of the bullets from Methone has such marks (**28/75** [ΜΕΘ 1704]); most bullets, however, do not, and were evidently easily detached by cutting them at the connecting stalk with the casting stem, leaving a blunt end with an even cut surface.

A recurring feature is the presence of one or more holes in the body of the bullet. While some holes of extremely small or large size, irregular opening, and most often near the stem end of the bullet, are obviously casting defects (blowholes), others certainly look drilled.[139] All holes on MEPNA bullets (**28/5** [ΜΕΘ 655], **28/10** [ΜΕΘ 2862], **28/15** [ΜΕΘ 2867], **28/17** [ΜΕΘ 2869], **28/18** [ΜΕΘ 2870], **28/24** [ΜΕΘ 2879], **28/28** [ΜΕΘ 2895], **28/29** [ΜΕΘ 2896], **28/31**

[ΜΕΘ 2898], **28/34** [ΜΕΘ 2909]) as well as on uninscribed bullets (**28/84** [ΜΕΘ 2876], **28/104** [ΜΕΘ 2914]) are blowholes. On Μικίνα bullets, with the exception of **28/56** (ΜΕΘ 2901), which has a small hole paired with tiny ones of irregular opening (porosities) on the other side, holes are round, of one size, and usually at the same spot, that is mostly above (**28/37** [ΜΕΘ 283], **28/38** [ΜΕΘ 286], **28/40** [ΜΕΘ 649], **28/54** [ΜΕΘ 2860]) or below the device (**28/41** [ΜΕΘ 653], **28/46** [ΜΕΘ 1706], **28/47** [ΜΕΘ 2144], **28/55** [ΜΕΘ 2861])—once above the inscription (**28/51** [ΜΕΘ 2857]), and near the bullet point—once in the middle (**28/46** [ΜΕΘ 1706]). This is the case with holes on Κλεοβούλō bullets as well: all are of similar size and opening shape, and found above or below the inscription near the stem end (**28/58** [ΜΕΘ 292], **28/60** [ΜΕΘ 2847], **28/61** [ΜΕΘ 2900]). Although holes on ΜΕΡΝΑ bullets are just another casting defect among the many this group exhibits, those on Μικίνα and Κλεοβούλō bullets are intentional. While a few suggestions have been made, from carrying messages to delivering poison,[140] their purpose has yet to be determined.

Another recurring feature is having either one of the ends obliquely cut.[141] Except for some cases where the traces of impact, such as uneven surface (**28/24** [ΜΕΘ 2879], **28/67** [ΜΕΘ 280], **28/70** [ΜΕΘ 652]) or an adjacent bulge formed by material that was pushed aside (**28/27** [ΜΕΘ 2894]), are apparent, in most cases the cut surface is clean, occasionally only with shearing traces (**28/4** [ΜΕΘ 291], **28/20** [ΜΕΘ 2872], **28/23** [ΜΕΘ 2878], **28/44** [ΜΕΘ 1701], **28/48** [ΜΕΘ 2145], **28/59** [ΜΕΘ 1708]). What is more, in one case (**28/66** [ΜΕΘ 282]) an alphabetic(?) mark has been incised on the cut surface,[142] eliminating (since it was found within the destruction layer) the possibility that the cut was caused by impact damage. The purpose of this feature remains unknown. Perhaps it was a way to form a sharper end, or it may have been the result of a central decision to economize material by reclaiming part of the lead from each bullet, in order to make more bullets, while their body would still maintain an aerodynamic shape. It may be significant that the bullets among the uninscribed ones presenting this feature are the thicker ones in the catalogue (**28/66** [ΜΕΘ 282], **28/73** [ΜΕΘ 1699], **28/76** [ΜΕΘ 2846], **28/82** [ΜΕΘ 2855], **28/83** [ΜΕΘ 2874], **28/94** [ΜΕΘ 2888], **28/96** [ΜΕΘ 2890]).

COMMENTARY ON THE INSCRIPTIONS

Inscribed sling bullets are not a rare find; it seems, however, that they constitute the minority in every group of sling bullets known from publications in northern Greece. Hence it is striking that, in the material from Methone, the ratio of inscribed to uninscribed bullets is reversed: counting the cluster of bullets individually, 68 out of 108 bullets are inscribed (73.44%), that is, a ratio of 1.7:1, while only one-fifth of the bullets found at Olynthos and only one-seventh of those found at Argilos is inscribed.[143] There is no apparent reason for this and it may well be without significance.

Not unexpectedly, the inscribed sling bullets have drawn much attention. And yet, being short and simple, the inscriptions remain puzzling as to their meaning and purpose. After reviewing the relevant bibliography, the categories and suggested interpretations of the (Greek and Latin) inscriptions found on sling bullets can be summarized as follows:[144]

1) personal name
   a) in the genitive
      i) the ruler as the army leader or the issuing authority,[145] occasionally abbreviated
      ii) the division commander;[146] occasionally substituted by legion number in the Roman era[147]

b) in the nominative[148]

i) the manufacturer (followed by ἐπο(ί)ησε/*fecit*)[149]

ii) a distinguished slinger[150]

2) ethnic

b) a city-state or confederacy as the issuing authority, usually abbreviated (to be read in the genitive case)[151]

3) other words (verbs, adjectives, adverbs, etc.) and phrases

a) taunt (by means of sarcasm or direct insult)[152]

b) exhortation

i) to the slinger(?)[153]

ii) to the bullet (possibly, depending on the reading)[154]

c) exclamation

i) of pain (a single example; false reading)[155]

d) invocation

i) to victory[156]

ii) to a deity[157]

4) single or couple of letters, occasionally ligatures

a) abbreviation of 1a–b and 2a, as above[158]

b) other abbreviation (patronym, perhaps ethnic)[159]

c) numeral[160]

Some issues of sling bullets feature, either on their own or in addition to inscriptions, pictorial devices. These may depict:[161]

a) animals (e.g., wasp, scorpion, snake, eagle)

b) weapons (e.g., spearhead, bow and arrow, trident, club)

c) other (e.g., thunderbolt, bucranium, star, phallus[162])

Suggested references/symbolisms and functions include:

- symbols "representative of the act of striking" or denoting the result of being hit by a bullet[163]
    - as a taunt
    - as a lucky charm or curse
    - as a simile/reference to the ensuing injury
    - as a reference to the launching machine[164]
- royal, military or ethnic/city-state insignia
    - issuing authority[165]
    - group identity (on levels of military division, state, kingdom)[166]
    - "look who hit you" (seen after being hit) or "look who's coming for you" (seen on the ground)[167]
    - insignia of military divisions or particular commanders[168]
- divine insignia
    - invocation to a deity[169]

Much effort has been invested in trying to determine the meaning, purpose, and function of the inscriptions and devices on sling bullets. Early attempts followed the attested categories and ascribed a different meaning to each one of them, without much consideration or discussion of the purpose or function of these legends.[170] More recent attempts regarded these legends as a uniform phenomenon and made generalized claims about the purpose and function of the legends in the context of war. The entire discussion has revolved around two main inquiries: (i) the identity and/or capacity of the named individuals, and (ii) the intended audience.

Every inscription has an intended reader. It is, however, impossible to judge who the intended reader might have been, unless the purpose of the inscription is already known. Inscriptions of Type 3a–b above are the only ones among the numerous inscribed sling bullets with a clear purpose. Verbal abuse is a customary component of every dispute, and it serves both to elevate the offender and to belittle the opponent. This, however, may not always reach both sides and, as Steven Tuck aptly put it, "the true audience is the slinger himself. These inscriptions would serve to develop confidence and to boost the morale of the attacking forces."[171] Amanda Kelly reinforces this argument by considering modern comparanda, instances from 20th-century wars between enemies of different language, and observing that these messages were never intended to be read or understood by the target, and if they did anyway, that "would certainly constitute a bonus."[172] As regards the devices, however, she argues that images on bullets, such as scorpions and thunderbolts, had "evidently malign symbolism" even for the illiterate, as "the malign aspect inherent in the choice of these symbols is purposeful in terms of the aggressive intention that they advertise to the enemy," and that "through their reliance on visual metaphor slingshots dispense with the need for mass literacy and a common tongue."[173] Kelly draws heavily on the work of John Ma, who considers the symbolical and ideological functions of inscriptions and emblems in the construction and forging of group identities within the army,[174] and deems it clear enough that, intentionally or not, they would have had a psychological effect on the other side as well, as they would violate the borders and intrude the realm of the enemy, causing not only physical damage, but also terror.[175]

Indeed, missiles, such as javelins, arrows, and sling bullets, belong to a category quite distinct from close combat weapons. To begin with, they are projected at the enemy's side and thus, they enter the opponent's realm; they are also expendable and, therefore, they were most likely mass-produced by a central authority and not privately supplied by their users;[176] finally, their users were recruited from the lower socioeconomic stratum among the free men, who were fighting as slingers because they could not afford any arms or armor.[177] Consequently, it is not far-fetched to assume that lead sling bullets were products issued by a central authority, and they would be recognized by the recipient side as such. In this regard, they were an ideal medium to convey propaganda or threats, although a written message is only one form of achieving this—others being the devices on the bullets, oral taunts, and feint shots.[178]

Missiles as message carriers in ancient literary sources are not rare. Projectiles have been used in antiquity to communicate with parties outside a besieged city, although this communication is usually between allies or the means of betrayal.[179] Exchange of menacing or insulting messages between the opposed parties is also attested and, interestingly enough, Methone features again in a relevant anecdotal incident. During the siege of the city in 355/4 B.C., Philip was inspecting the "machines" (see Appendix I), when an arrow hit him across the eye. The arrow is said to have been shot by Aster, whom some versions of the story introduce as a master archer, who had inscribed on it: "Aster sends to Philip a lethal arrow" (Ἀστὴρ Φιλίππῳ θανάσιμον πέμπει βέλος). As the story goes, Philip replied with another arrow carrying the inscription "If Philip catches Aster, he will hang him" (Ἀστέρα Φίλιππος, ἢν λάβῃ, κρεμήσεται).[180] Plutarch's call on citizens to play fair in lawsuits and "not to engrave on and poison like missiles the arguments of the case with blasphemies, calumnies, and threats making them irreparable, great, and public"[181] is perhaps the most illustrative reference to this long-standing practice that is well known up to the modern period.[182]

However, actual evidence of this practice is rather scarce. Among the hundreds of sling bullets, no more than 30 examples of insults and exhortations are known and, moreover, nearly half of them are of uncertain reading and some are even suspected to be forgeries.[183] These admittedly impressive, yet isolated, examples have attracted the most attention, and one wonders how much they have influenced the interpretation of the practice of inscribed lead sling bullets.

The "epigraphic habit" on sling bullets has not been systematically studied. Apart from publications of new material, most studies present an aggregate collection of published inscriptions. Moreover, they tend to focus on the highlights, such as insults and royal names, and disregard both the date of each particular bullet, and consequently any chronological variation that could attest to the evolution of the practice. Actually, the bulk of the inscriptions comprise (non-royal) personal names, as well as inscriptions (e.g., fabricants' signatures) and devices (see n. 187) that do not conform to preconceived ideas of group identity and malign symbolism. Therefore, attempts to reach an overall interpretation of the practice are bound to be misguided.

All published inscribed sling bullets securely dated to the 4th century B.C., that is, found at excavations of securely dated contexts, are limited to categories 1a–b (personal names), 2a (ethnics), 4a–b (1–2 letter abbreviations), and possibly 3b.i (exhortations to the slinger), in this order of frequency.[184] Of these, only two isolated examples possibly correspond to Type 3b.i and only a few belong to Type 4a–b; those of Type 1a–b and Type 2a constitute the vast majority. Devices, up to the late 4th century B.C., appear far less frequently than inscriptions; apart from the bullets of Μικίνα, which are securely dated by their archaeological context in Methone, only a few issues carrying devices can be dated to the 4th century B.C.[185] The majority of inscribed bullets, even in the following centuries and up to the Roman era, have alphabetic inscription(s) without a device, and it is noteworthy that there is no bullet securely dated to the 4th century B.C. that carries only a device.

Thus, as far as securely dated published material allows us to conclude, in the 4th century B.C. the inscribed sling bullets bear no insults, no sarcastic expressions, no exclamations or exhortations—in short, no text addressing the enemy or the bullet. The two *kalos* inscriptions, although, like other praise inscriptions, they possibly refer to certain Chalkidians,[186] may equally well be irrelevant to the particular events of 349/8 B.C., or may not even belong to Type 3b.i at all (see n. 153). Furthermore, devices are uncommon and, at least in the 4th century B.C., seem to be randomly selected and adopted; that is, unless the pitchfork/torch(?) is some unknown weapon or harmful implement (see the commentary on *Μικίνα* below). Even in later periods, besides the weapons and the symbols possibly metaphorically associated with stinging or striking, there are other devices, apart from the pitchfork/torch(?), with no such—at least apparent—connotations: a bucranium, a star, an anchor, a shield.[187] Therefore, it is rather difficult to sustain the argument that the devices on sling bullets carry a malign message and supposedly substitute for the inscription for the sake of the illiterate among slingers or recipients.

The lack of securely dated Type 3a inscriptions in the 4th century B.C. casts further doubt on the theory of psychological warfare via inscribed sling bullets. The letter forms suggest that this was not the case until Late Hellenistic or Roman times, when the earliest Type 3a inscriptions appeared, and even these constituted only a very small discrete group in their time and, therefore, should be regarded as a deviation from the rule. As the literary sources indicate, the exchange of insults inscribed on missiles must have been sporadic and rather individualized until that period. In the act of delivering an insult, the launcher is the active party and the act of composing the insult is normally performed by him—this is clearly the case in all known literary references (see nn. 180–181), as well as in modern comparanda. The issue of ready-made insults on missiles demands as a prerequisite either a decision made by an issuing authority or an initiative taken by someone involved in any stage of production. Both could be true, but, in any case, the purpose and function of such an inscription should not be confused with, or considered identical to, the purpose and function of the vast majority of the inscriptions on sling bullets, which comprises personal names and ethnics.

Personal names have been variously interpreted, but mostly as names of the military officers under whose command the slingers participated in a battle (Type 1a.ii). This interpretation has become a fact beyond dispute through uncritical repetition, but actual proof of its validity is lacking. The evidence is at best circumstantial and based on the identification of named individuals on sling bullets with individuals vaguely known from the ancient literary sources.[188] The assumption that personal names refer to military commanders has given rise to further inferences about the function of the inscriptions, which are thus considered almost inescapably within the context of ongoing military campaigns.[189] Ma is careful to make the distinction clear between the purpose of the inscriptions and devices and the effect they could have had on both sides. He underlines that inscriptions and emblems on weapons could have functioned as assertions of legitimation of authority, advertisements of military power, and proclamations of collective intention for violence toward the other side, while the presence of the name, ethnic, or emblem of one's own group on weapons could have evoked for individuals an *esprit de corps*, contributing to the construction of group identity and the cohesion of the group.[190] Even so, he nevertheless maintains that inscriptions and devices reflect the organization and logistics of military supply.[191]

However tenable and tempting, claims about the psychological impact of the inscriptions and devices on either side cannot be verified, nor should it be taken for granted that, in the course of a siege, slingers could afford the time to have a look at their ammunition or that soldiers and citizens alike in the besieged city would care to examine them.[192] Furthermore, although the military and political structural organization in Macedonia of the Classical period, or in city-states other than Athens, is basically unknown, one must perforce wonder why the Macedonian king would allow his inferior noblemen to advertise themselves militarily next to him; or for that matter why a city-state would allow generals to advertise themselves politically as individuals; and also what the chances were that each side was familiar with the names of the commanders of the other and was also intimidated by them individually.

Inscriptions of Type 1a–b are found in the following combinations:

- single name (occasionally with a device)
- name + patronym
- name + ethnic
- name + name
- name + single letter or ligature (occasionally with a device)

With the exception of a few cases, in which a ruler is identified with more or less certainty, all other names are open to interpretation.[193] As the inscriptions are not extensive enough to offer any other indications, the grammatical case of the name has been used to discern between different intended meanings: names in the genitive, which implies an omitted noun (e.g., the bullet or the army), have been considered as denoting the military commander in charge of a particular division of slingers, and names in the nominative, which implies an omitted verb (e.g., "made" or "shot"), as denoting the fabricant or the slinger himself. Yet the inscriptions ΜΙΚΙΝΑΣ and ΜΙΚΙΝΑ (see the commentary on *Μικίνα* below) show that the distinction between the nominative and the genitive probably has no merit.[194]

Thus far, attempts to decipher the inscriptions on sling bullets have concentrated on this specific group of inscribed objects and the similarities and differences within it. But in order to understand their structure and meaning, and ultimately their purpose and function, examination of the phenomenon in the wider "epigraphic habit" of the time is required, beyond the confines of this specific material and its particular context of use.

As Tracey Rihll aptly remarked, "the natural desire of scholars to associate a name on a *glans* with a known individual favours commander of the unit. But other inscribed everyday objects record information about (i) production, (ii) contents (e.g., weight or other measure), (iii) distribution, or (iv) ownership (Harris 1993), and we should assume one or other of these for *glandes*."[195] Similarly, Tuck considered the possibility that "the names could have served a more mundane purpose of distinguishing the bullets of certain units and insuring that particular units were issued bullets of the correct weight, a critical factor for range and accuracy."[196] The fact that sling bullets are categorized by modern scholars as *instrumenta domestica* may be a matter of methodological convenience,[197] but their affinity with other inscribed *instrumenta* of this category is far from accidental, an affinity that may indeed potentially provide answers about ancient administration and economy.[198]

The content and structure of the inscriptions on sling bullets (basically, an ethnic or a name in the genitive, occasionally in the nominative, and occasionally paired with a device) find exact or nearly exact parallels with those on coinage, amphora stamps, and tile stamps.[199]

Inscriptions on coins are common and correspond to the issuing authority (ethnic or head of the state), which appears unfailingly in the genitive, although it is usually abbreviated. Despite the fact that these would also function as advertisement of authority within the state and as advertisement of sovereignty abroad, their initial and primary purpose was to indicate provenance and certify the weight of the bullion and perhaps also denote the metrical system employed.[200] By the early Hellenistic period, administrative data, known as "control" or "mint marks," were being recorded in the form of devices, monograms, and names in the nominative, which appear in addition to the main image and inscription. These have been variously interpreted as indicating mint magistrates/officials or even sponsors (by monogram or abbreviated name), emission (by device, chosen by the magistrate), date of issue (by monogram), and perhaps provenance of the bullion that would indicate the quality of the metal (by monogram).[201] The reason for their existence is probably the result of new regulations imposed on minting coins and they are only supplements to the main legend, that is, the issuing authority.

Amphora stamps were not uncommon prior to the 4th century B.C., but they acquired extended texts which began to be applied in a systematic way in Thasos in the early 4th century B.C. as a means of state control over production.[202] Information encoded in Thasian amphora stamps most often included the name of an official denoting the date and the name of the fabricant, and, from the late 4th century B.C. onward, devices appeared which could correspond to either of the names, but more often corresponded to the fabricant.[203] These elements, along with other information, appear in various combinations.[204] In Rhodian amphora stamps the device (a rose) is the emblem of the city-state, and they use the genitive for both the official and the fabricant, while names on the Thasian stamps appear mostly in the nominative.[205]

Tile stamps carry devices and rarely inscriptions until the late 4th–early 3rd century B.C., but, when these coexist, it is evident that the device is the trademark of the fabricant, as must have been the case in the earlier periods.[206] By the 3rd–2nd century B.C. texts on tile stamps found at Sparta and Elateia in Phokis become longer, including at least the following information: chronological formula (ἐπὶ + name of magistrate), ownership or building allocated for (e.g., δημόσιος or τειχέων), and name of contractor.[207] In other regions, texts tend to become shorter;

roof tiles of the 2nd century B.C. in Macedonia feature inscriptions like ΠΥΔΝΗΣ, ΠΕΛΛΗΣ, and ΒΑΣΙΛΙΚΟΣ with no other information, while in the early 3rd century B.C. the indication ΒΑΣΙΛΙΚΟΣ appears in abbreviated form as a ligature Β͡Α accompanying personal names in the genitive (contractor or fabricant).[208] This development perhaps indicates that from the late 4th to the 2nd century B.C. state and city authorities took over production from individuals (contractors) in certain parts of ancient Greece.

Obviously, similarities among coinage, amphora stamps, tile stamps, and inscriptions on sling bullets are not limited to the structure and contents of the text. The development of the practice is attested in the same period and the combinations of information recorded seem to evolve concurrently for all these groups. Devices supplement the inscriptions from the late 4th century B.C. and become more common in the 3rd and 2nd centuries B.C. Also, they accompany or substitute for the name of the official or the fabricant and they are not necessarily associated with the use of the object. In fact, amphora stamps often depict weapons, showing that these devices are simply insignia, with no connotations or further relation to the purpose of the containers on which they feature, or their contents. Single letters and monograms also appear on amphora stamps in the mid-4th to the beginning of the 3rd century B.C., as they do on sling bullets (see nn. 271–272), and they are probably employed instead of devices.[209] Claims about the assumption of production by the state or vice versa cannot be made as regards production of sling bullets, since the available evidence is insufficient,[210] but in terms of frequency of such finds (ethnic or ruler's name) their percentage is roughly the same as for tile stamps. Finally, it must be emphasized that not all coins carry mint marks, nor were all amphoras and tiles stamped, just as in the case of sling bullets.

Yet the most crucial similarity is that all these inscribed groups are mass-produced and issued or approved by the state, which may appoint a state official or commission their production to a contractor. As tile stamps indicate, and building inscriptions attest, such contracts were comprehensively laid out, strictly regulated, and meticulously audited by the state.[211] Thus, indication of the producer (official or contractor) and perhaps additional information concerning the production of a batch of sling bullets would be a tenable interpretation. If the personal names are those of military commanders of particular divisions, then the inscription of state ethnics and ruler's names on other bullets seems rather odd and redundant. Peter Weiss has suggested the possibility that these were (freelance) mercenary commanders, issuing and providing their own ammunition.[212] But if so, then the bullets found in Olynthos inscribed with the city-state ethnic Ὀλυ(νθίων) on one side and, abbreviated or not, a personal name on the other become incomprehensible.[213] If, however, the personal names are those of state officials (not excluding the possibility that military commanders acted as such), the attestation of both the state (indicated by ethnic or ruler's name) and its representative makes sense. Likewise, if the personal names are those of fabricants, as opposed to state foundries (indicated by ethnic or ruler's name), their coexistence is again completely understandable. Even the possibility that these were names of sponsors who financed and undertook the production of a batch of sling bullets alongside batches financed by the state would be tenable.[214]

It is, therefore, more likely that the named individuals appear on sling bullets in a capacity that does not render them mutually exclusive with the state or the ruler in terms of authority. Thus, the most probable interpretations of the Type 1a–b inscriptions on sling bullets are:

- name of official/magistrate/sponsor (+ trademark/name of fabricant)
- name of fabricant (+ trademark of fabricant)

The occasional presence of the ethnic supplementing the name (examples of uncertain date) does not seem to fit in with any of the above interpretations,[215] but these should not be regarded as definitive, nor as limiting the variations in structure and content of the inscription, which both gradually evolved during the Hellenistic period. As for bullets that carry two personal names, they parallel, perhaps, the New Style Athenian owls of the late period, where a pair of officials were regularly recorded on the coins,[216] as well as tile stamps, on which the presence of two names has been convincingly explained as two contractors who had entered a partnership.[217] Finally, according to this interpretation, the monograms and the devices are simply trademarks, bureaucratic imprints or personal devices, equivalent to those on coins, amphora stamps, and tile stamps, and not symbols related to the purpose of the carrier object.[218] After all, this is exactly the case with the devices on shields, on which a bird, a *triskelion,* a thunderbolt, a gorgon, a hare, and even pottery could be depicted.[219]

There is, moreover, a particular group of mass-produced inscribed objects that proves the above argument. The excavation of a Ptolemaic military camp in Attica produced several nails bearing inscriptions of the same type discussed here: a few of them bear the inscription Βα(σιλέως) Πτο(λεμαίου) along with a trident,[220] one the inscription Δη(μητρίου) along with a shield,[221] and another a name or ethnic ΦΡΑΣΙΤΩΝ followed by a number(?) Γ (or Λ).[222] Whatever their purpose, these nails were neither an offensive weapon nor the main part of whatever they were fixed on. What is even more important is that these inscriptions were molded on the inside of the nailhead and, thus, absolutely invisible when the carrier object was actually in use (nailed into place). One wonders where the inscriptions and devices on sling bullets would be, had the bullets been of another shape.

Perhaps it is time to set aside the entire discussion of military propaganda and psychological warfare and accept the idea that both the inscriptions and the devices have a purpose distinct from that of the object that carries them. Although the Greeks waged wars quite frequently, most of the time they had peace, a period ideal to prepare for war. It is more plausible to suggest that the intended audience was neither the users nor the recipients of these missiles, but the state officials in charge of the state armories. This does not reject definitively the possibility of any emotional effects caused by inscriptions and devices during wartime, but, if they did occur, these should be regarded as a side effect rather than the primary purpose of the inscriptions and devices on sling bullets.

THE INSCRIPTIONS ON THE SLING BULLETS FROM METHONE

ΜΕΡ|ΝΑ(–)? VEL ΝΑ|ΜΕΡ(–) (**28/1–28/36** = 36 bullets)

Bullets of the same issue are the following:

- two bullets found at Olynthos, 348 B.C.[223]
- one bullet found at Pydna, undated (found along with a sherd of the 5th century B.C. in the fill of Trench A1, not necessarily a closed context)[224]
- one bullet in the Kanellopoulos Collection in Athens, undated[225]
- one bullet in a private collection in Osuna, Spain; probably from the market,[226] 1st(?) century B.C.[227]
- one bullet from Greece with no other indication, now in the Zagreb Archaeological Museum, undated[228]

- one bullet purchased in Athens, now in the Museum of Art and Archaeology, University of Missouri-Columbia, 4th century B.C.[229]
- five (?) bullets found at Poteidaia, mid-4th century B.C. (one in a structure between Buildings A and B, active throughout the 5th and abandoned sometime in the 4th century B.C.)[230]
- two bullets found at Torone, ante 349 B.C.[231]
- three bullets found at Amphipolis, mid-4th century B.C.[232]
- one bullet bought in Trieste in 1876, now in Civici Musei di Storia e d'Arte di Trieste, mid-4th century B.C.[233]
- unspecified number of bullets found at the acropolis of Carevi Kuli, Strumica, commonly identified with ancient Astraion, 4th century B.C.[234]
- two bullets auctioned in London and six auctioned by Gorny & Mosch in Munich[235]
- five bullets in the Gorny & Mosch Gallery in Munich[236]
- one bullet in the British Museum[237]

Claude Brixhe and Anna Panayotou dated the MEPNA bullets possibly to the end of the 5th century B.C., based on the report by Aikaterini Despoini on the sling bullet from Pydna that was found along with a sherd of the 5th century B.C. in the fill of Trench A1; this, however, was just one of the finds in a fill that, as Despoini notes, comprised pottery of the Classical and Hellenistic periods in general.[238] The bullets in a private collection in Osuna,[239] Spain, and in the Zagreb Archaeological Museum,[240] erroneously considered as probably Latin, cannot be dated to the 1st century B.C. The bullets from Amphipolis and Pydna set the terminus ante quem in 357 B.C.

This particular inscription has spurred many attempts to read it but to no avail. As a number of different readings are equally possible, a definitive text is impossible. Robinson considered the possibility of a thus far unattested personal name Μέρνας, before he suggested that the inscription is an abbreviation of Μ(ηκύβ)ερνα,[241] the harbor town of Olynthos, or more probably Μ(ηκυβ)ερνα(ίων), as an ethnic should be expected. Although abbreviations of ethnic names on sling bullets are common, this one would be unique and of a type so far unattested in Greek antiquity; abbreviations by contraction where letters are dropped from the middle of a word do not occur until the Roman period.[242] A similar case from Antikythera is the presumed abbreviation παρὰ Φ(αλασ)α<ρ>νίων, a heavily restored and, thus, highly problematic reading.[243] Nevertheless, the abbreviation of an ethnic Μερνα(ίων), from an unknown city called Merna, remains a possibility.[244] Robinson's first thought, that it is the genitive of the personal name Μέρνας, found support from Brixhe and Panayotou, who pointed out the plausibility of the dialectic ending of the genitive in –α for names of the first declension in Macedonia.[245] The letter sequence –ερν–, however, is quite unusual in Greek, and the only comparable proper names are the personal name Βέρνας (Ουέρνας, with initial *digamma*),[246] a Roman name, and place names of probably prehellenic origin or not at all Greek.[247]

On all bullets from Methone, the inscription runs dextrograde, and the letters MEP are written starting from the stem end running toward the bullet point, while the letters NA start from the bullet point running toward the stem end. This layout is similar on all published bullets: the inscription, as a rule, starts from the stem and runs toward the end of the bullet, and it ends again before the stem, even if the text runs sinistrograde or changes to sinistrograde script on the reverse.[248] However, as examples like **28/65** (ΜΕΘ 2891) illustrate,[249] engravers did not pay too much attention to such trivialities and, therefore, this is not a rule by which to determine the beginning of the inscription. Consequently, it is impossible to decide between the readings MEP|NA and NA|MEP. Thus, the editors of the bullets from Torone preferred the reading of the abbreviated personal name Ναμέρ(τας) or Ναμερ(τίδας), or even Ναμέρ(τιος)[250] as possible and "less strained" readings than Robinson's abbreviation of Μ(ηκύβ)ερνα.[251] They reached this conclusion on the basis of two bullets inscribed with only the letters NA on one side (nos. 18.4 and 18.5), which they considered a shorter abbreviation of the same name, and thus they regarded the syllable Να– as the beginning of the intended name, a conclusion accepted by Alexandru Avram.[252] A similar unpublished sling bullet from Pydna (Πυ 12577),[253] however, has a significantly more refined appearance than all the MEPNA bullets, and it is doubtful whether they are of the same issue (see above, "Typology") and, therefore, whether the same inscription was intended.

John Ma[254] accepted the reading Να|μερ(τ–), a personal name deriving from the adjective ναμερτής/–τές (the negative prefix νη– and ἁμαρτάνω, LSJ, s.v.), which means not to make a mistake and is often used with the meaning of hitting the mark;[255] but he doubted the possibility of reading either ναμερ(τές), an adjective referring to the bullet itself, or ναμερ(τέως), an adverb referring to the act of slinging, although admittedly both are epigraphically and contextually satisfactory readings. The adjective ναμερτής/–ές is not attested as qualifying a missile, but it is often found in literature accompanying nouns such as λόγος, ἔπος, and βουλή,[256] that is, forms of speech, which is often metaphorically associated with βέλος, as in ἔπεα πτερόεντα (Hom. *Od.* 2.269) alongside ἰὰ πτερόεντα (Hom. *Il.* 20.68). Other adjectives synonymous or antonymous to ναμερτής/–ές, such as ἀψευδής (unmistaken) or ἅλιος/–ον (fruitless, idle), are attested qualifying both speech and missiles.[257] It may not, therefore, be far-fetched to see ναμερτής/–ές as qualifying missiles as well. This would be the earliest example of a Type 3b.ii inscription on a sling bullet, but a problematic one: the reason for abbreviating a metaphor is rather obscure, and moreover it is doubtful whether its meaning would be immediately perceived.[258]

The form and overall appearance of the bullets and the distribution of the inscription in northern Greece (see below, p. 1165) indicate that these bullets are Macedonian. If so, reading an ethnic Μερνα(ίων) is rather improbable, but a personal name Μέρνας or Ναμερ(–) is not, as such a name may identify the official overseeing their production, or the manufacturer that produced them, or a Macedonian military officer in charge of a military division stationed in Pieria.

MIKINA (**28/37–28/57** = 21 bullets)

Bullets of the same issue are the following:

- one bullet found at the palatial building at Bylazora, early 3rd century B.C.[259]
- one bullet in a private collection in Osuna, Spain, undated[260]
- seven bullets auctioned by Hirsch Nachfolger in Munich[261]
- one bullet of unknown provenance auctioned in London, ca. 300 B.C.[262]
- six bullets found at Argilos, 357/6 B.C.[263]

Μικίνας/-ης (from the adjective μικ(κ)ός, Doric and Boiotian form of (σ)μικρός;[264] LSJ, s.v.) is a fairly common name in central Greece from the 5th century B.C. onward,[265] also appearing in Rhodes (Diod. 17.113.1). It is also attested as Μικκίνας,[266] and it is equivalent to the far more common Μικ(κ)ίων.

Two different issues(?) are known with this name: (i) the name in the nominative running dextrograde on both sides of the bullet, and (ii) the name in the genitive running, with (published) exceptions **28/41** (ΜΕΘ 653) and B-349.6 from Argilos, sinistrograde on one side, and a device on the other. All the bullets of Μικίνα from Methone belong to the latter type.[267]

Alexandru Avram, Costel Chiriac, and Ionel Matei propose two different persons with the same name,[268] and date the bullets with the name in the nominative to 349 B.C., based on the published example from Torone, and those in the genitive to the end of the 4th century B.C., based on the similarity of the device to that on the bullets of Thearos and Euboulidas, which have been associated with the siege of Kameiros in 305 B.C.,[269] and with that of Tharypos from Vigla, Cyprus, dated to 306 or 294 B.C.[270] The bullets from Methone, however, render both the dating and, probably, the assumption of two Μικίνας erroneous.

On the reverse of the bullets, the depiction shows a four-pronged implement with a short handle and a cross-guard from which the prongs extend curving downward toward their end. This particular, as yet unidentified, object is also depicted on bullets inscribed with the names Θέαρος,[271] Εὐβουλίδας,[272] and Θάρυψ.[273] With the exception of the latter, which differs only by having one more prong, on the bullets of Thearos and Euboulidas the object has shorter prongs and an apparently cylindrical handle, or rather socket, as it looks like a pitchfork. This identification was already made by Karl Zangemeister, who pointed out that the pitchfork was already known as a device on the coinage of Metapontion.[274] The pitchfork is also certainly depicted on sling bullets,[275] as well as on amphora stamps.[276] In these cases, however, it differs in form from the device on the Methone bullets, having shorter straight prongs and a long handle/socket. In a series of ineffective attempts to identify the object, Amedeo Maiuri suggested that it could be a *penteakontion*,[277] an otherwise unknown object; M. García Garrido and Luis Lalana identified it with a rudder,[278] which, however, has a far different form; and Marie-Christine Hellmann suggested it could also be a monogram,[279] which is impossible.

Peter Weiss and Niels Draskowski, in spite of all the above attempts for a plausible identification, conclude that the object remains unidentified.[280] After considering the obvious possibilities, that of a rake or a pitchfork,[281] they re-examine the pitchfork featuring on the silver stater of Metapontion, issued in the period ca. 330–290 B.C., which has a long handle and five bent prongs, and to these depictions they add those on some rare bronze coinage of neighboring Lucanian Herakleia, where the device marked particular issues supplementing the ear of wheat, the main city emblem. In addition, they point out that the monogramme X͡A, which could equally be read as A͡X, resembles that of the Achaean League, and, as it happens, Metapontion was an Achaean colony.[282] They also entertain the identification with a trident, but reject it because of the curving prongs, as well as with the κρεάγρα and the like (λύκος, ἅρπαξ, ἁρπάγη), which do have five curved prongs, but are of a significantly different form, and also with the πεμπώβολον,[283] which, however, still remains unidentified archaeologically and its exact form is unknown.[284]

Given the affinity between the inscriptions and devices on bullets and those on amphora stamps (see above, "Commentary on the Inscriptions"), this is the most likely domain to look for parallels. Among the devices featured on amphora stamps, there are several objects similar to the one on the sling bullets, and these are identified by the editors as rakes or pitchforks,[285] but in one or two cases could possibly be a torch.[286] Depictions of torches with linear flames stemming apart from each other are rare, but they do exist.[287] This may just be a convention in depicting flames, while the curving end is characteristic of almost all depictions of fire. What is more, a torch (of the usual form) features as a device on uninscribed bullets found at Amphipolis.[288] At present, identification of the device as a torch is not definite, but it is possible.

ΚΛΕΟΒΟΥΛŌ (**28/58–28/61** = 4 bullets)

Bullets of the same(?) issue are the following:

- fifteen bullets found at Olynthos, 348 B.C.[289]
- unspecified number of bullets found at Stageira, mid-4th century B.C.[290]
- unspecified number of bullets found along the north wall (the least defensible part of the fortification) at Apollonia, Mygdonia, mid-4th century B.C.[291]
- one bullet found at Torone, 349 B.C.[292]

- one(?) bullet found at Amphipolis, 357 B.C.[293]
- one bullet found at Carevi Kuli, Strumica, 4th century B.C.[294]
- six bullets found at Kozi Gramadi, 340s B.C.[295]
- one bullet in the Gorny & Mosch Gallery in Munich[296]
- one bullet found (allegedly) at Kolopenishteto, Sotyria, Sliven, 340s B.C.[297]

Κλεόβουλος is a common name throughout Greece from the 6th century B.C. onward, and in Macedonia from the 4th century B.C. onward.[298]

Robinson assumes that he was a high-ranking officer of Philip II,[299] next to Ἱππόνικος,[300] whose name frequently appears on bullets found at the same places as those of Κλεοβούλō.[301] Rihll, on the basis of the deviation of mean weight within the group (by 10.4% of the mean weight), which is equivalent to the bullets of the Chalkidians and far from the consistency in weight of those inscribed Φιλίππου and Ἱππονίκου, attributes these bullets to the Olynthian side.[302] But their presence at Methone indicates otherwise.

Apart from a few cases, where the editor gives the text in non-diplomatic transcription or the reading of the final upsilon cannot be confirmed by the photographs, there is one that, technically, constitutes a different inscription. This is the variation ΚΛΕΟΒ|ΟΥΛΟΥ, which not only has the letter B inscribed on the side where the inscription begins, but also has an Y at the ending of the genitive, probably the reason why B was transferred to the other side, in order to produce a symmetrical inscription with five letters on each side. The difference may seem insignificant, but it may have chronological implications, as it is rather unlikely that the same person would at the same time use on the same mold both graphemes (O and OY) for the genitive ending of second declension names.[303] They may correspond to two different issues, that is, molds. Notwithstanding, since the sling bullets in the area of Amphipolis were most probably deposited there during the siege of the city by Philip II in 357 B.C., the two variations are most likely contemporary.[304] This would make the Κλεοβούλου issue one of the earliest examples of the grapheme OY for the second declension genitive ending in Macedonia.

ΕΥΓΕΝΕΟΣ (**28/62–28/65** = 7 bullets, of which 4 are in a cluster, **28/62** [ΜΕΘ 651])
Since by far the most usual inscription on sling bullets is a personal name in the genitive, it seems inevitable to read the uncontracted genitive Εὐγένεος of the name Εὐγένης/-ους, which is epigraphically attested in Thespiai in the 5th century B.C.,[305] and in Attica,[306] Skione,[307] Karystos,[308] and Kolophon[309] in the 4th century B.C.[310]

Another, far less probable, but not impossible reading is εὖγε | νέος or νέος | εὖγε, addressed either as an exhortation to the slinger (inscription Type 3b.i) or as sarcasm addressed to the enemy (inscription Type 3a).[311] The adverb εὖγε is normally followed by a name in the vocative, but the use of the nominative in exclamations is not unattested.[312] The adjective νέος could also be read as the personal name Νέος,[313] even though it would be too individualized to be meaningful in this context; but cf. Ἀρχίης | ὡραῖος and Ὀρ - - δας | καλός.[314]

Similarly, the reading αἰσχρὸ(ν) δῶρο(ν), suggested by Robinson for the inscription ΑΙΣΧΡΟΔΩΡΟ on a bullet from Olynthos,[315] was rejected by William Kendrick Pritchett, who pointed out the unusual omission of the final nû on both words and proposed, alternatively, the genitive of a fabricated mock name Αἰσχρόδωρος (otherwise unattested),[316] a proposal in line with the idea that inscriptions were addressed to the receivers of the bullets. But names with the stem αἰσχρ- are quite common, e.g., Αἶσχρος or Αἴσχρων,[317] and Αἰσχρόδωρος need not be a fabricated name purposefully invented for the occasion.[318] Other inscriptions with ambiguous readings, either as insults or as names, are tackled by Ma, who maintains that most texts are actually personal names.[319]

CONCLUDING REMARKS

The dating of the sling bullets from Methone is unproblematic. The archaeological context, whenever there is one, is in full accordance with the historical sources, and with the findspots of identical bullets at the sites of other cities and forts besieged by the army of Philip II during the 350s and 340s B.C. The siege of Methone in 355/4 B.C., however, is only a terminus ante quem. There is no evidence to exclude the possibility that sling bullets were produced in advance and kept in store for years. This is definitely the case with the bullets of Κλεοβούλō, for example, which are used throughout the 350s and 340s B.C. Still, a starting date of production earlier than 359 B.C., the year of Philip's II accession to the throne of Macedon, would rely entirely on historical inferences. The manufacture date of the Methone material can be dated to the period ca. 359–357 B.C. for the bullets of MEPNA and Κλεοβούλō,[320] and ca. 359–355 B.C. for the bullets of Μικίνα and Εὐγένεος. These dates accord as well with the letter forms (especially A, E, M, N, O, Σ, Y), which are rather characteristic of the mid-4th century B.C. and a little earlier, while the grapheme –ō, instead of –ου, for the genitive ending of the second declension is also typical of the period.

The bullets inscribed MEPNA and Μικίνα form the majority of the inscribed bullets found in Methone. This indicates that those few examples that have been found elsewhere—at least as far as published material is concerned—were most probably first used in Pieria, during the sieges of Pydna and Methone, and later either they were reused, or the surplus that remained in stock was used in the sieges of Torone (349 B.C.), Olynthos (348 B.C.), and the military campaign of Philip II in Thrace (340s B.C.). One of the earliest uses of the Κλεοβούλō bullets took place also in Pieria, but this particular issue seems to have been a long-lived one that was produced by more than one mold. As for the bullets of Εὐγένεος, they could belong to a single issue in anticipation of the siege of Methone, but their fine quality indicates that, at least, the mold had already been manufactured in prior years.

A question that has been discussed in some of the publications of new sling bullets from excavations is whether certain groups of bullets can be ascribed to the besiegers or to the besieged. Such attempts have mostly relied on the inscriptions, but other methods have considered the physical characteristics of the bullets, assuming a standardization of lead bullet production with discernible differentiation in shape, form, and weight. Robinson noticed that "the slingstones of the Chalkidians (nos. 2260–2264) in general weigh about one-third less [than those inscribed ΦΙΛΙΠΠΟΥ]," and assumed different weight classes between the Macedonian and the Chalkidian bullets.[321] Aris Tsaravopoulos used the ratio of width to thickness in order to distinguish between different types and to ascribe the bullets to each of the opposing parties in conjunction with their findspot.[322] In the material from Methone, weight does not seem to play a role. The MEPNA bullets weigh between 23.5 and 28.5 g with a mean weight of 25.6 g, the Μικίνα ones between 21 and 29 g with a mean weight of 27.4 g, and the Κλεοβούλō ones between 28.7 and 29 g with a mean weight of 28.9 g, while the Εὐγένεος bullets weigh between 23.5 and 27 g with a mean weight of 25.8 g, roughly the same as those of MEPNA. Shape and form, on the contrary, are distinguishing criteria, which, however, can be safely employed to distinguish between issues but not necessarily armies (see above, "Typology"). Uninscribed bullets are generally larger and heavier, although not considerably (see also n. 103): their length ranges between 0.029 and 0.0332 m, their width between 0.0141 and 0.018 (plus one deformed example at 0.0204) m, their thickness between 0.0132 and 0.0162 m, and their weight between 28.7 and 34.5 g with a mean weight of 31.5 g. There is, however, no apparent correlation between form and dimensions or weight that would divide them into distinct groups.

Another criterion, when trying to ascribe certain groups of bullets to one or the other side, is findspot, by making a distinction between bullets found inside and those found outside city walls.[323] As shown in the case of Methone, there is no horizontal or vertical distribution pattern, and this must be due, at least partially, to the reuse of ammunition and urban warfare. The distribution of inscribed sling bullets on a regional level is more indicative. The fact that bullets of MEPNA, Μικίνα, and Κλεοβούλō have been found in cities besieged by Philip II throughout Macedonia, Chalkidike, and Thrace indicates that these are most probably issues of the Macedonian army, as reclamation and reuse seem quite inadequate to explain their discovery in so many of those sites.[324]

Irrespective of shape, weight, and the fact that the sling bullets of Εὐγένεος have been, thus far, only recorded from Methone, the cluster (**28/62** [ΜΕΘ 651]) affirms that they are Methonaian. However, whether or not Εὐγένης is a Methonaian cannot be determined with certainty. This uncertainty about the identity of named individuals, and the capacity in which they feature on sling bullets, despite many attempts and some highly indicative names, persists throughout the corpus of inscribed sling bullets, and has a bearing on the discussion about the meaning, purpose, and function of the inscriptions and the devices on sling bullets.

Inferences have mostly revolved around the idea of psychological warfare, supposing that inscriptions helped boost the moral of the slingers and shatter that of their enemy. But, as usual, the truth is probably more mundane. At least in the Classical period, evidence of non-official function of these inscriptions is scarce, and thus it is more probable that they parallel those (equally puzzling) inscriptions on coins, amphora stamps, and tile stamps, on which the standard information recorded seems to have been the issuing authority and the manufacturer or a city official along with trademarks and state insignia. Even in the case of the—admittedly more eloquent—amphora and tile stamps, this matter is not yet resolved. Most probably, however, these notations had a bureaucratic function and were related to production regulations,[325] rather than trade. In this regard, inscriptions on sling bullets may be seen as evidence for military organization, army supply and logistics, and actual proof of state armories, which is corroborated by epigraphic sources (see n. 176), while inferences about the psychological aspects of warfare should be reserved when trying to explain the overall practice.

While the focus has inevitably been on the inscribed sling bullets, a major part of the material is uninscribed, and has thus been ignored in the discussion that has revolved mostly around the dating of particular military events, siege tactics, and ancient prosopography. Equally full and thorough publication of the uninscribed material has much to offer toward building a pool of data that will eventually allow a better understanding of the manufacture as well as a better-defined typology of sling bullets. The uninscribed material is also a reminder that a good part of ancient history is undocumented.

Either by conquest or by surrender, Methone fell. The victorious army, on orders of Philip II, razed the city to the ground. Perhaps the fact that most bullets (except those in Plot 278) were found within or above the destruction layer indicates that in the meantime the soldiers collected all visible missiles from the ground for recasting or reuse. Or perhaps excavations at Methone have not yet been extensive enough for the material to be representative. Only further excavations at the site will tell.

CATALOGUE

ΜΕΡ|ΝΑ( )? *VEL* ΝΑ|ΜΕΡ( )

28/1. (ΜΕΘ 281) Fig. 28.1

East Hill #274/067, eastern part, trial trench, destruction layer.

L. 0.0305; W. 0.015; Th. 0.0125; Wt. 25.0 g.

Olive-shaped (Type B); flattened lower edge. Treated.

Molded inscription in relief on both sides, running dextrograde. Letter H. 0.006–0.008; letter W. 0.0045–0.0075.

Μερ|ν̣α( )? *vel* Να|μερ( ).

28/2. (ΜΕΘ 285) Fig. 28.1

East Hill #274, surface find.

L. 0.028; W. 0.014; Th. 0.0128; Wt. 25.3 g.

Olive-shaped (Type B); flattened upper edge. Treated; impact damage on the side near the bullet point.

Molded inscription in relief on both sides, running dextrograde. Letter H. 0.0055–0.0078; letter W. 0.0042–0.0082.

Μερ|ν̣α( )? *vel* Ν̣α|μερ( ).

The right vertical stroke of N.

28/3. (ΜΕΘ 287) Fig. 28.1

East Hill #274/066, Building A, Room E, destruction layer.

L. 0.029; W. 0.0148; Th. 0.0132; Wt. 25.2 g.

Olive-shaped (Type B); flattened lower edge. Not treated; oxidized, covered by white patina.

Molded inscription in relief on both sides, running dextrograde; N is worn flat. Letter H. 0.0055–0.0071; letter W. 0.004–0.0083.

Μερ|να( )? *vel* Να|μερ( ).

28/4. (ΜΕΘ 291) Fig. 28.1

East Hill #274/076, balk B, destruction layer.

L. 0.029; W. 0.016; Th. 0.0145; Wt. 28.7 g.

Olive-shaped (Type B). Not treated; oxidized, covered by thin layer of white patina; one end obliquely cut off, severely hit twice on the side (ΜΕΡ).

Molded inscription in relief on both sides, running dextrograde. Letter H. 0.0066–0.0078; letter W. 0.006–0.008.

Με[ρ]|να( )? *vel* Να|με[ρ]( ).

28/5. (ΜΕΘ 655) Fig. 28.1

West Hill #245/005003, defensive trench 2, pass 2.

L. 0.030; W. 0.015; Th. 0.0125; Wt. 25.0 g.

Olive-shaped (Type B); flattened lower edge, casting flash of upper edge folded above letter P; porosities on letter M (casting defect). Not treated; oxidized, covered by white patina; minor hit below letter A.

Molded inscription in relief on both sides, running dextrograde. Letter H. 0.005–0.007; letter W. 0.004–0.007.

Μερ|να( )? *vel* Να|μερ( ).

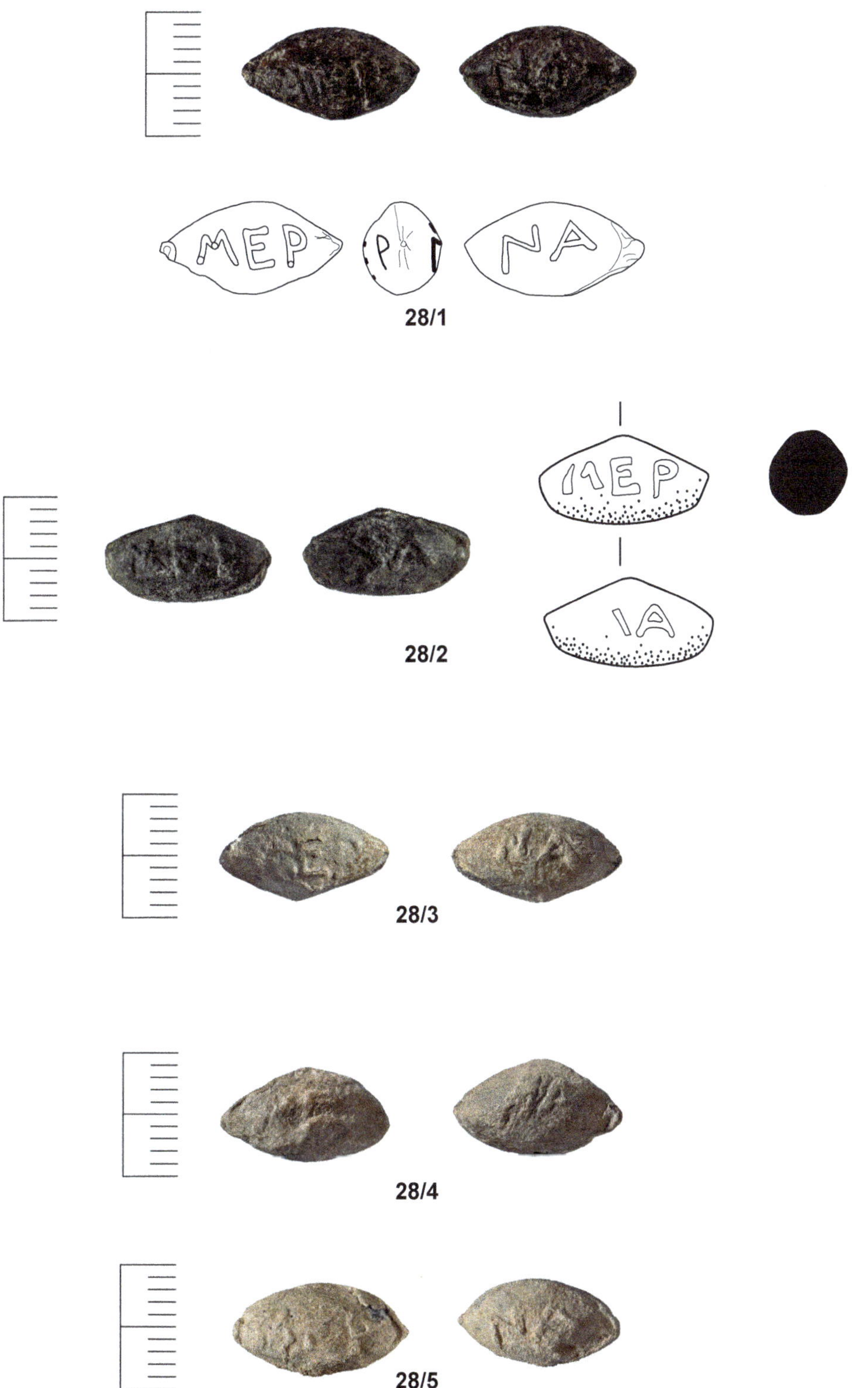

FIGURE 28.1. Inscribed lead sling bullets: ΜΕΡ|ΝΑ( )? *VEL* ΝΑ|ΜΕΡ( ). **28/1** (ΜΕΘ 281), **28/2** (ΜΕΘ 285), **28/3** (ΜΕΘ 287), **28/4** (ΜΕΘ 291), **28/5** (ΜΕΘ 655). Photos J. Vanderpool, drawings A. Boufalis and F. Skyvalida

28/6. (ΜΕΘ 1705) Fig. 28.2

East Hill #274/065, southern part.

L. 0.031; W. 0.015; Th. 0.013; Wt. 25.7 g.

Olive-shaped (Type B). Not treated; oxidized, covered by white patina; hit below letter N.

Molded inscription in relief on both sides, running dextrograde. Letter H. 0.0055–0.0078; letter W. 0.0037–0.0078.

Μερ|να( )? *vel* Να|μερ( ).

28/7. (ΜΕΘ 1707) Fig. 28.2

East Hill #274/075, southwestern part, fill of trench for dismantlement of Wall 8a.

L. 0.0277; W. 0.0145; Th. 0.012; Wt. 24.5 g.

Olive-shaped (Type B); hole of irregular opening above letter M. Not treated; oxidized, covered by white patina; severely hit on the side (MEP), minor hit on lower edge.

Molded inscription in relief on both sides, running dextrograde. Letter H. as preserved 0.007–0.0084, letter W. 0.0073–0.0088.

Με̣[ρ]|να( )? *vel* Να|με̣[ρ]( ).

The middle part of the vertical and the middle horizontal stroke of E.

28/8. (ΜΕΘ 1709) Fig. 28.2

East Hill #274/018001, pass 1.

L. 0.026; W. 0.014; Th. 0.013; Wt. 23.9 g.

Olive-shaped (Type B); flattened lower edge. Not treated; minor hit on the side, an incised curved line extends to both sides crossing the bullet point.

Molded inscription in relief on both sides, running dextrograde. Letter H. 0.005–0.007; letter W. 0.005–0.008.

Μερ|να( )? *vel* Να|μερ( ).

28/9. (ΜΕΘ 2854) Fig. 28.2

East Hill #278/002003, fill north of Wall 2.

P.L. 0.028; W. 0.0162; Th. 0.0126; Wt. 26.6 g.

Olive-shaped (Type B); deformed due to mold shift. Not treated; oxidized; the bullet point damaged, two deep nicks on the side (MEP).

Molded inscription in relief on both sides, running dextrograde. Letter H. 0.006–0.008; letter W. 0.004–0.008.

Μερ|να( )? *vel* Να|μερ( ).

28/10. (ΜΕΘ 2862) Fig. 28.2

East Hill #278/002003, fill north of Wall 2.

P.L. 0.0254; W. 0.0147; Th. 0.0128; Wt. 24.1 g.

Olive-shaped (Type B); two small holes of irregular opening (casting defects), one on either side. Not treated; oxidized, covered by thin layer of white patina, sediments on both sides; the bullet point missing due to severe impact damage.

Molded inscription in relief on both sides, running dextrograde. Letter H. 0.0057–0.0078; letter W. 0.0041–0.008.

Μερ|να( )? *vel* Να|μερ( ).

28/11. (ΜΕΘ 2863) Fig. 28.2

East Hill #278/002003, fill north of Wall 2.

L. 0.0315; p.W. 0.0145; p.Th. 0.0129; Wt. 28.1 g.

Olive-shaped (Type B). Not treated; one side almost completely damaged, hit on the lower edge.

Molded inscription in relief on both sides, running dextrograde. Letter H. 0.0055–0.0072; letter W. 0.004–0.0077.

Μερ|[να]( )? *vel* [Να]|μερ( ).

The possibility that the side where the letters NA are restored was uninscribed cannot be excluded.

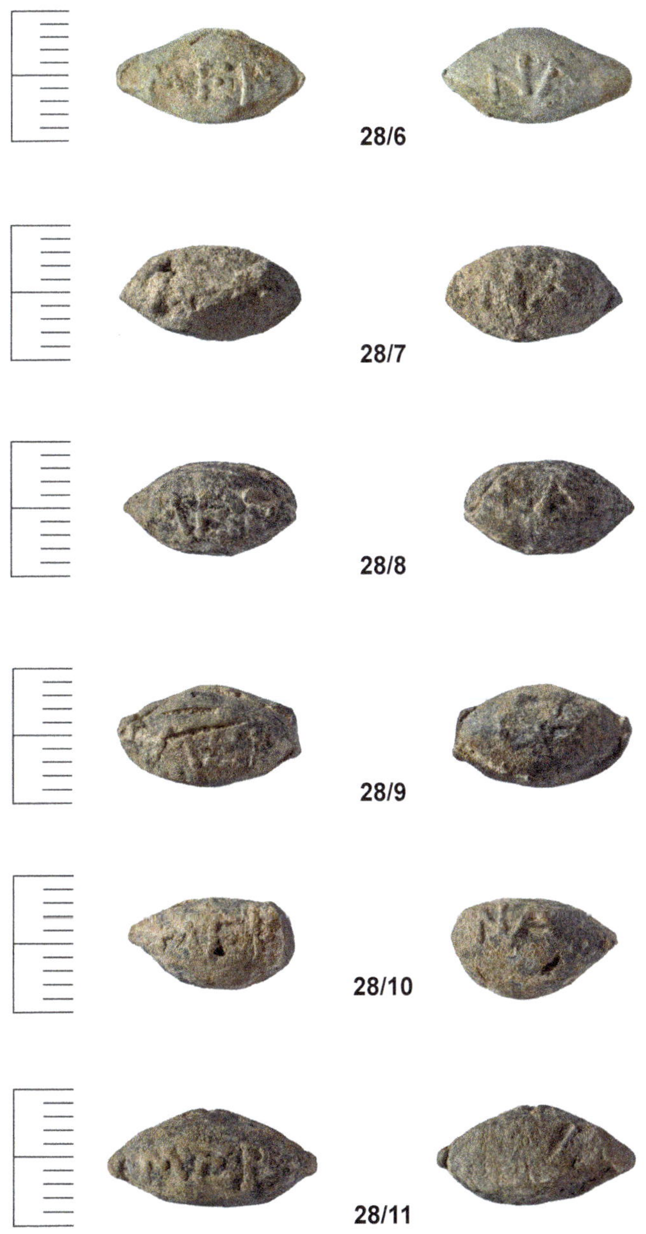

FIGURE 28.2. Inscribed lead sling bullets: ΜΕΡ|ΝΑ( )? *VEL* ΝΑ|ΜΕΡ( ). **28/6** (ΜΕΘ 1705), **28/7** (ΜΕΘ 1707), **28/8** (ΜΕΘ 1709), **28/9** (ΜΕΘ 2854), **28/10** (ΜΕΘ 2862), **28/11** (ΜΕΘ 2863). Photos J. Vanderpool

28/12. (ΜΕΘ 2864) Fig. 28.3

East Hill #278/002003, fill north of Wall 2.

P.L. 0.0276; W. 0.0145; Th. 0.0127; Wt. 25.9 g.

Olive-shaped (Type B). Not treated; sediments on letter E; the stem end obliquely cut off by severe impact, hit at the bullet point, hit on the upper edge.

Molded inscription in relief on both sides, running dextrograde. Letter H. 0.006–0.0067; letter W. 0.004–0.007.

Μερ|να( )? *vel* Να|μερ( ).

28/13. (ΜΕΘ 2865) Fig. 28.3

East Hill #278/002003, fill north of Wall 2.

L. 0.0286; W. 0.0158; Th. 0.0133; Wt. 25.7 g.

Olive-shaped (Type B). Not treated; heavily oxidized on one side (NA); severe impact damage on the upper edge.

Molded inscription in relief on both sides, running dextrograde. Letter H. 0.0056–0.008; letter W. 0.0045–0.008.

Μερ|να( )? *vel* Να|μερ( ).

28/14. (ΜΕΘ 2866) Fig. 28.3

East Hill #278/002003, fill north of Wall 2.

P.L. 0.0281; W. 0.0146; Th. 0.0138; Wt. 25.6 g.

Olive-shaped (Type B); casting flashes folded on both sides. Not treated; the bullet point obliquely cut off due to impact.

Molded inscription in relief on both sides, running dextrograde. Letter H. 0.0055–0.0066; letter W. 0.0038–0.0078.

Μερ̣|να( )? *vel* Να|μερ̣( ).

The upper part of P.

28/15. (ΜΕΘ 2867) Fig. 28.3

East Hill #278/002003, fill north of Wall 2.

L. 0.0293; W. 0.0156; Th. 0.0134; Wt. 26.0 g.

Olive-shaped (Type B); two shallow cavities on one side above letter M, a wide and deep one on the other side next to the stem end (casting defects). Not treated; minor hit (recent) on one side (MEP).

Molded inscription in relief on both sides, running dextrograde. Letter H. 0.0063–0.0075; letter W. 0.0038–0.0078.

Μερ|να( )? *vel* Να|μερ( ).

28/16. (ΜΕΘ 2868) Fig. 28.3

East Hill #278/002003, fill north of Wall 2.

L. 0.0272; W. 0.0154; Th. 0.0109; Wt. 23.6 g.

Olive-shaped (Type B); deformed due to mold shift. Not treated; sediments; severe impact damage on the lower edge deforming the body of the bullet, hit on the edge next to letter A, minor hit on letter E.

Molded inscription in relief on both sides, running dextrograde. Letter H. 0.005–0.006; letter W. 0.0033–0.0076.

Μερ|να( )? *vel* Να|μερ( ).

FIGURE 28.3. Inscribed lead sling bullets: ΜΕΡ|ΝΑ( )? *VEL* ΝΑ|ΜΕΡ( ). **28/12** (ΜΕΘ 2864), **28/13** (ΜΕΘ 2865), **28/14** (ΜΕΘ 2866), **28/15** (ΜΕΘ 2867), **28/16** (ΜΕΘ 2868). Photos J. Vanderpool

28/17. (ΜΕΘ 2869) Fig. 28.4

East Hill, Plot 278, #002003, fill north of Wall 2.

L. 0.0304; W. 0.0155; Th. 0.0131; Wt. 26.3 g.

Olive-shaped (Type B); flattened upper edge; two holes of irregular opening above letter A (casting defects). Not treated; oxidized.

Molded inscription in relief on both sides, running dextrograde. Letter H. 0.0055–0.0075; letter W. 0.004–0.0076.

Μερ|να( )[?] *vel* Να|μερ( ).

28/18. (ΜΕΘ 2870) Fig. 28.4

East Hill #278/002003, fill north of Wall 2.

L. 0.029; W. 0.015; Th. 0.013; Wt. 26.4 g.

Olive-shaped (Type B); small cavity below letter M, tiny holes around letter A (casting defects). Not treated; two recent hits on the side (NA).

Molded inscription in relief on both sides, running dextrograde. Letter H. 0.0056–0.0074; letter W. 0.0045–0.008.

Μερ|να( )[?] *vel* Να|μερ( ).

28/19. (ΜΕΘ 2871) Fig. 28.4

East Hill #278/002003, fill north of Wall 2.

P.L. 0.027; W. 0.0145; Th. 0.013; Wt. 26.6 g.

Olive-shaped (Type B). Not treated; severely hit at the stem end and on the upper edge, both being obliquely cut off, severe impact damage below letter N, minor nick on letter N, minor hit below and to the right of letter A, deep nick at the bullet point above letter P.

Molded inscription in relief on both sides, running dextrograde. Letter H. 0.005–0.007; letter W. 0.0042–0.0052.

Μ̣ερ|να( )[?] *vel* Να|μ̣ερ( ).

The lower part of the right exterior slanting stroke of M.

28/20. (ΜΕΘ 2872) Fig. 28.4

East Hill #278/002003, fill north of Wall 2.

L. 0.028; W. 0.015; Th. 0.0133; Wt. 25.5 g.

Olive-shaped (Type B); casting flash folded below letter P. Not treated; obliquely cut off above letters ME.

Molded inscription in relief on both sides, running dextrograde. Letter H. 0.0054–0.0075; letter W. 0.0035–0.007.

Μερ|να( )[?] *vel* Να|μερ( ).

28/21. (ΜΕΘ 2873) Fig. 28.4

East Hill #278/002003, fill north of Wall 2.

L. 0.0284; W. 0.0142; Th. 0.013; Wt. 26.0 g.

Olive-shaped (Type B). Not treated; oxidized; sediments; flattened lower edge, obliquely cut off above letter N.

Molded inscription in relief on both sides, running dextrograde. Letter H. 0.0053–0.0074; letter W. 0.0042–0.008.

Μερ|να( )[?] *vel* Να|μερ( ).

FIGURE 28.4. Inscribed lead sling bullets: ΜΕΡ|ΝΑ( )? *VEL* ΝΑ|ΜΕΡ( ). **28/17** (ΜΕΘ 2869), **28/18** (ΜΕΘ 2870), **28/19** (ΜΕΘ 2871), **28/20** (ΜΕΘ 2872), **28/21** (ΜΕΘ 2873). Photos J. Vanderpool

28/22. (ΜΕΘ 2875) Fig. 28.5

East Hill, Plot 278, #002003, fill north of Wall 2.

L. 0.027; W. 0.0155; Th. 0.0125; Wt. 25.7 g.

Olive-shaped (Type B); deformed due to mold shift. Not treated; hit at the stem end, hit on the edge near the bullet point.

Molded inscription in relief on both sides, running dextrograde; letters are worn flat. Letter H. 0.0055–0.007; letter W. 0.0043–0.007.

Μερ|να( )? *vel* Να|μερ( ).

28/23. (ΜΕΘ 2878) Fig. 28.5

East Hill #278/002003, fill north of Wall 2.

P.L. 0.0292; W. 0.0162; Th. 0.0126; Wt. 25.6 g.

Olive-shaped (Type B); deformed due to mold shift. Not treated; the bullet point obliquely cut off, the stem end hit and deformed, minor nick on one side (MEP), minor hit on the upper edge.

Molded inscription in relief on both sides, running dextrograde. Letter H. 0.0054–0.008; letter W. 0.0043–0.0082.

Μερ|να( )? *vel* Να|μερ( ).

28/24. (ΜΕΘ 2879) Fig. 28.5

East Hill #278/002003, fill north of Wall 2.

P.L. 0.0263; W. 0.016; Th. 0.0153; Wt. 26.4 g.

Olive-shaped (Type B); small hole of irregular opening below M (casting defect). Not treated; part of the bullet broken off.

Molded inscription in relief on both sides, running dextrograde. Letter H. 0.0063–0.0081; letter W. 0.0047–0.0072.

Μερ|να( )? *vel* Να|μερ( ).

The vertical stroke of P.

28/25. (ΜΕΘ 2892) Fig. 28.5

East Hill #278/004, from the excavation debris.

L. 0.028; W. 0.0155; Th. 0.013; Wt. 26.5 g.

Olive-shaped (Type B). Not treated; oxidized, covered by thin layer of white patina; hit on the edge above the stem end, minor hit on letter N, a nick on either edge toward the bullet point, a nick below letter M.

Molded inscription in relief on both sides, running dextrograde. Letter H. 0.0057–0.0077; letter W. 0.004–0.0073.

Μερ|να( )? *vel* Να|μερ( ).

28/26. (ΜΕΘ 2893) Fig. 28.5

West Hill #245/005, western part, defensive trench 2, cleaning of the sides of the excavation trench.

L. 0.029; W. 0.0145; Th. 0.013; Wt. 23.5 g.

Olive-shaped (Type B); a large cavity by the stem end, causing discontinuity to the surface on the other side. Not treated; oxidized, covered by thin layer of white patina, minor hit (recent) on letter E, minor linear hit above letter P.

Molded inscription in relief on both sides, running dextrograde. Letter H. 0.0055–0.007; letter W. 0.004–0.008.

Μερ|να( )? *vel* Να|μερ( ).

FIGURE 28.5. Inscribed lead sling bullets: ΜΕΡ|ΝΑ( )? *VEL* ΝΑ|ΜΕΡ( ). **28/22** (ΜΕΘ 2875), **28/23** (ΜΕΘ 2878), **28/24** (ΜΕΘ 2879), **28/25** (ΜΕΘ 2892), **28/26** (ΜΕΘ 2893). Photos J. Vanderpool

28/27. (MEΘ 2894) Fig. 28.6

West Hill #245/007010, pass 5, topsoil.

P.L. 0.027; W. 0.015; Th. 0.0124; Wt. 23.8 g.

Olive-shaped (Type B). Not treated; severe impact damage at the stem end.

Molded inscription in relief on both sides, running dextrograde; MEP is placed unusually low on the surface. Letter H. 0.006–0.008; letter W. 0.004–0.007.

Μερ|να( )? *vel* Να|μερ( ).

28/28. (MEΘ 2895) Fig. 28.6

West Hill, surface find, 5 m north of #245/013, collected by Th. Avramides.

L. 0.030; W. 0.015; Th. 0.0133; Wt. 26.3 g.

Olive-shaped (Type B); deformed due to mold shift; small hole of irregular opening by the stem end (casting defect). Not treated.

Molded inscription in relief on both sides, running dextrograde. Letter H. 0.0055–0.008; letter W. 0.0045–0.007.

Μερ|να( )? *vel* Να|μερ( ).

28/29. (MEΘ 2896) Fig. 28.6

West Hill #245/001016, Sector Γ, pass 2.

L. 0.029; W. 0.016; Th. 0.0135; Wt. 28.4 g.

Olive-shaped (Type B); porosities above letter M (casting defect). Not treated; covered by thin layer of white patina; minor hit above letter E.

Molded inscription in relief on both sides, running dextrograde. Letter H. 0.0055–0.0078; letter W. 0.004–0.0075.

Μερ|να( )? *vel* Να|μερ( ).

28/30. (MEΘ 2897) Fig. 28.6

West Hill #245/#001025, Sector E, pass 1, topsoil.

L. 0.029; p.W. 0.015; Th. 0.0123; Wt. 25.4 g.

Olive-shaped (Type B); deformed due to mold shift. Not treated; oxidized, covered by white patina; upper edge severely damaged.

Molded inscription in relief on both sides, running dextrograde. Letter H. 0.005–0.008; letter W. 0.0045–0.007.

Μερ|να( )? *vel* Να|μερ( ).

28/31. (MEΘ 2898) Fig. 28.6

West Hill #229, Sector A, northern side.

L. 0.029; W. 0.015; Th. 0.013; Wt. 24.3 g.

Olive-shaped (Type B). Not treated; oxidized, covered by white patina; hit on the upper edge, lower edge damaged around the opening of a small oblong hole (casting defect), minor nick below letter A.

Molded inscription in relief on both sides, running dextrograde. Letter H. 0.006–0.007; letter W. 0.004–0.008.

Μερ|να( )? *vel* Να|μερ( ).

FIGURE 28.6. Inscribed lead sling bullets: ΜΕΡ|ΝΑ( )? *VEL* ΝΑ|ΜΕΡ( ). **28/27** (ΜΕΘ 2894), **28/28** (ΜΕΘ 2895), **28/29** (ΜΕΘ 2896), **28/30** (ΜΕΘ 2897), **28/31** (ΜΕΘ 2898). Photos J. Vanderpool

28/32. (ΜΕΘ 2903) Fig. 28.7

West Hill #229, Sector A, collected from the excavation debris.

L. 0.028; W. 0.0155; Th. 0.013; Wt. 25.6 g.

Olive-shaped (Type B); deformed due to mold shift; casting flash folded below letter A. Not treated; oxidized, covered by patches of white patina; hit above letter M.

Molded inscription in relief on both sides, running dextrograde. Letter H. 0.005–0.0073; letter W. 0.004–0.007.

Μερ|να( )? *vel* Να|μερ( ).

28/33. (ΜΕΘ 2907) Fig. 28.7

West Hill #229, Sector A, fill south of tunnel entrance.

L. 0.030; W. 0.014; Th. 0.0134; Wt. 26.5 g.

Olive-shaped (Type B); flattened edges. Not treated; oxidized, covered by patches of white patina.

Molded inscription in relief on both sides, running dextrograde. Letter H. 0.006–0.007; letter W. 0.0045–0.008.

Μερ|να( )? *vel* Να|μερ( ).

28/34. (ΜΕΘ 2909) Fig. 28.7

West Hill #229, Sector A, fill south of tunnel entrance.

L. 0.031; W. 0.015; Th. 0.0133; Wt. 27.0 g.

Olive-shaped (Type B); a cavity by the stem end and a small shallow hole at the lower edge (casting defects). Treated.

Molded inscription in relief on both sides, running dextrograde. Letter H. 0.0055–0.0075; letter W. 0.0035–0.0073.

Μερ|να( )? *vel* Να|μερ( ).

28/35. (ΜΕΘ 2910) Fig. 28.7

West Hill #229, Sector A, fill south of tunnel entrance.

L. 0.030; W. 0.016; Th. 0.013; Wt. 25.9 g.

Olive-shaped (Type B). Not treated; oxidized, covered by patches of white patina; minor nick on one side (NA).

Molded inscription in relief on both sides, running dextrograde. Letter H. 0.006–0.008; letter W. 0.004–0.008.

Μερ|να( )? *vel* Να|μερ( ).

28/36. (ΜΕΘ 2911) Fig. 28.7

West Hill #229, Sector A, fill south of tunnel entrance.

L. 0.027; W. 0.0155; Th. 0.013; Wt. 26.6 g.

Olive-shaped (Type B); flattened upper edge. Not treated; significantly oxidized, covered by patches of yellowish patina.

Molded inscription in relief on both sides, running dextrograde. Letter H. 0.006–0.007; letter W. 0.005–0.008.

Μερ̣|να( )? *vel* Να|μερ̣( ).

The bottom part of the vertical stroke of P.

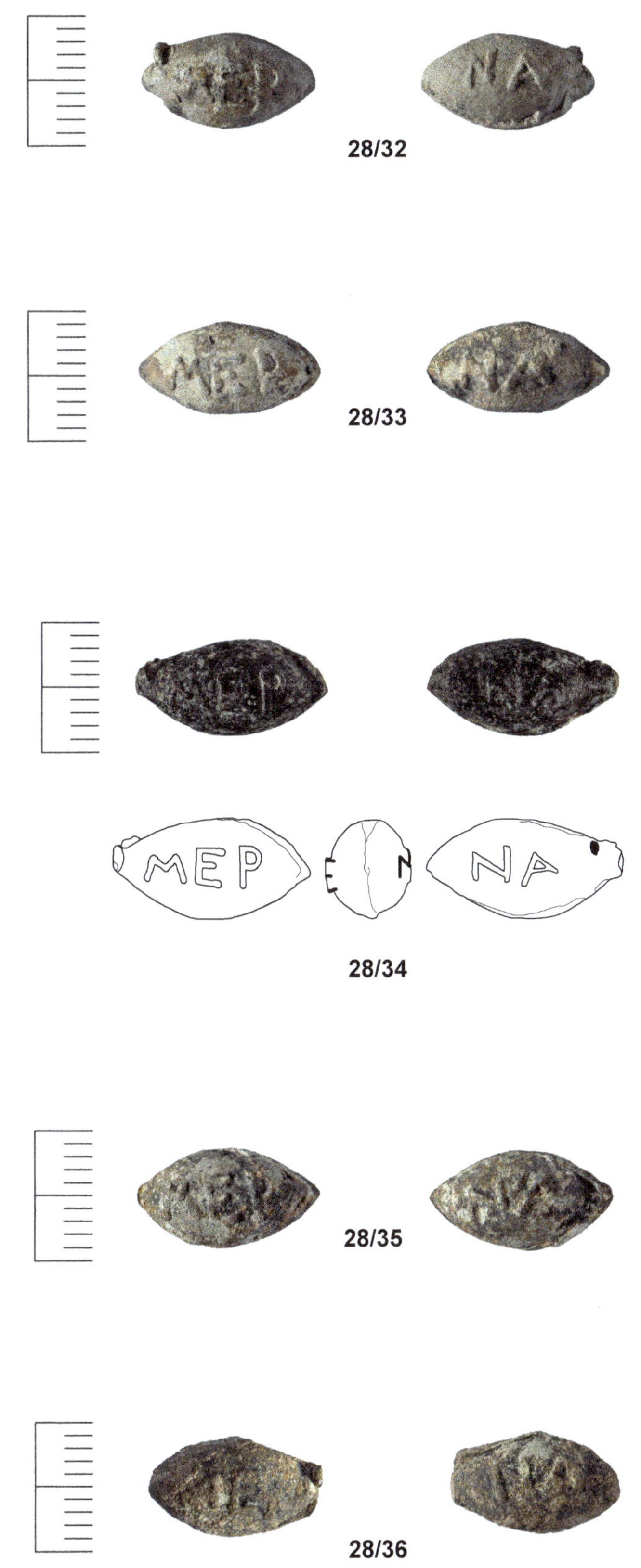

FIGURE 28.7. Inscribed lead sling bullets: ΜΕΡ|ΝΑ( )? *VEL* ΝΑ|ΜΕΡ( ). **28/32** (ΜΕΘ 2903), **28/33** (ΜΕΘ 2907), **28/34** (ΜΕΘ 2909), **28/35** (ΜΕΘ 2910), **28/36** (ΜΕΘ 2911). Photos J. Vanderpool, drawing A. Boufalis

MIKINA

28/37. (ΜΕΘ 283) Fig. 28.8

East Hill #274/067, northen part, trial trench, destruction layer.

L. 0.029; W. 0.016; p.Th. 0.013; Wt. 27.7 g.

Olive-shaped (Type B); small round hole above the device, apparently drilled. Not treated; the stem end cut off (probably by the manufacturer's detachment tool), two severe hits on the device.

Molded inscription in relief on one side, running retrograde; device in relief on the other side. Letter H. 0.003–0.005; letter W. 0.003–0.0055; device: p.L. 0.0172; p.W. 0.0093.

Μικίνα ← | pitchfork/torch(?).

Half a letter space between M and I.

28/38. (ΜΕΘ 286) Fig. 28.8

East Hill #274/087, destruction layer.

P.L. 0.027; W. 0.016; Th. 0.013; Wt. 28.5 g.

Olive-shaped (Type B); one hole above letter K and one above the device. Treated; the bullet point hit and deformed, three parallel nicks above the letters; two small shallow cavities with white fill probably caused by corrosion.

Molded inscription in relief on one side, running retrograde; device in relief on the other side. Letter H. 0.0035–0.0055; letter W. 0.0035–0.0047; device: L. 0.0172; W. 0.0093.

Μικίνα ← | pitchfork/torch(?).

28/39. (ΜΕΘ 288) Fig. 28.8

East Hill #274/066, Building A, Room E, destruction layer.

P.L. 0.028; W. 0.016; Th. 0.013; Wt. 27.1 g.

Olive-shaped (Type B); deformed due to mold shift. Not treated; severely hit above letter K, hit at the bullet point.

Molded inscription in relief on one side, running retrograde; worn surface; device in relief on the other side. Letter H. 0.004–0.005; letter W. 0.003–0.0045; device: L. 0.0153; W. 0.0077.

Μ̣ικίν̣α ← | pitchfork/torch(?).

The right half of M; the left vertical stroke and the upper corner of N.

28/40. (ΜΕΘ 649) Fig. 28.8

West Hill #245/001013, pass 5, Pit 5 (tunnel).

P.L. 0.026; W. 0.016; Th. 0.013; Wt. 27.2 g.

Olive-shaped (Type B); wide and deep hole near the bullet point. Not treated; oxidized, covered by bluish patina; part of the bullet broken off, hit on letters MI, minor hit below the device.

Molded inscription in relief on one side, running retrograde; device in relief on the other side. Letter H. 0.0035–0.005; letter W. 0.003–0.004; device: p.L. 0.016; W. 0.0095.

[Μι]κίνα ← | pitchfork/torch(?).

28/41. (ΜΕΘ 653) Fig. 28.8

West Hill #245/002026, pass 5, Pit 5 (tunnel).

L. 0.030; W. 0.016; Th. 0.0133; Wt. 28.2 g.

Olive-shaped (Type B); wide and deep hole below the device near the stem end. Not treated; considerably damaged around the stem end, minor hit at the bullet point, hit on the edge.

Molded inscription in relief on one side, running dextrograde; device in relief on the other side. Letter H. 0.003–0.004; letter W. 0.0028–0.0042; device: L. 0.021; W. 0.011.

Μικίνα | pitchfork/torch(?).

FIGURE 28.8. Inscribed lead sling bullets: MIKINA. **28/37** (ΜΕΘ 283), **28/38** (ΜΕΘ 286), **28/39** (ΜΕΘ 288), **28/40** (ΜΕΘ 649), **28/41** (ΜΕΘ 653). Photos J. Vanderpool

28/42. (ΜΕΘ 656) Fig. 28.9

West Hill #245/005005, defensive trench 2, pass 2.

L. 0.028; W. 0.016; Th. 0.0135; Wt. 29.0 g.

Olive-shaped (Type B); surface depression below letter K. Treated; small shallow cavities caused by corrosion(?).

Molded inscription in relief on one side, running retrograde; device in relief on the other side. Letter H. 0.0033–0.005; letter W. 0.0035–0.0052; device: L. 0.0184; W. 0.0078.

Μικίνα ← | pitchfork/torch(?).

28/43. (ΜΕΘ 1700) Fig. 28.9

East Hill #274/087033, pass 2.

P.L. 0.027; W. 0.016; Th. 0.0135; Wt. 26.4 g.

Olive-shaped (Type B). Not treated; oxidized, covered by greenish patina; damaged near the stem end, the bullet point hit and obliquely cut off, nick on the device.

Molded inscription in relief on one side, running retrograde; device in relief on the other side. Letter H. 0.0036–0.0045; letter W. 0.0027–0.0032; device: p.L. 0.0165; W. 0.0076.

[Μ]ικίνα ← | pitchfork/torch(?).

28/44. (ΜΕΘ 1701) Fig. 28.9

East Hill #274/068, western part.

P.L. 0.027; W. 0.016; Th. 0.0135; Wt. 28.5 g.

Olive-shaped (Type B). Not treated; one end obliquely cut off, worn surface, minor nick on letter A.

Molded inscription in relief on one side, running retrograde; device in relief on the other side. Letter H. 0.0035–0.0045; letter W. 0.003–0.005; device: p.L. 0.0186; W. 0.0104.

Μικίνα ← | pitchfork/torch(?).

28/45. (ΜΕΘ 1702) Fig. 28.9

East Hill #274/079, eastern part.

L. 0.0275; W. 0.0155; Th. 0.0125; Wt. 27.2 g.

Olive-shaped (Type B). Not treated; small surface depression below the device.

Molded inscription in relief on one side, running retrograde; device in relief on the other side. Letter H. 0.003–0.005; letter W. 0.003–0.004; device: L. 0.0209; W. 0.0098.

Μικίνα ← | pitchfork/torch(?).

28/46. (ΜΕΘ 1706) Fig. 28.10

East Hill #274/065, southern part.

L. 0.028; W. 0.0155; Th. 0.0135; Wt. 27.0 g.

Olive-shaped (Type B); hole below the device. Not treated; oxidized, covered by white patina; minor hit below letters MI.

Molded inscription in relief on one side, running retrograde; device in relief on the other side. Letter H. 0.0035–0.005; letter W. 0.003–0.0045; device: L. 0.0213; W. 0.0098.

Μικίνα ← | pitchfork/torch(?).

28/47. (ΜΕΘ 2144) Fig. 28.10

East Hill #274/019001, pass 1, below the layer of fallen roof tiles.

P.L. 0.026; W. 0.016; Th. 0.0135; Wt. 26.9 g.

Olive-shaped (Type B); hole near the bullet point. Not treated; the stem end broken off, hit on the device.

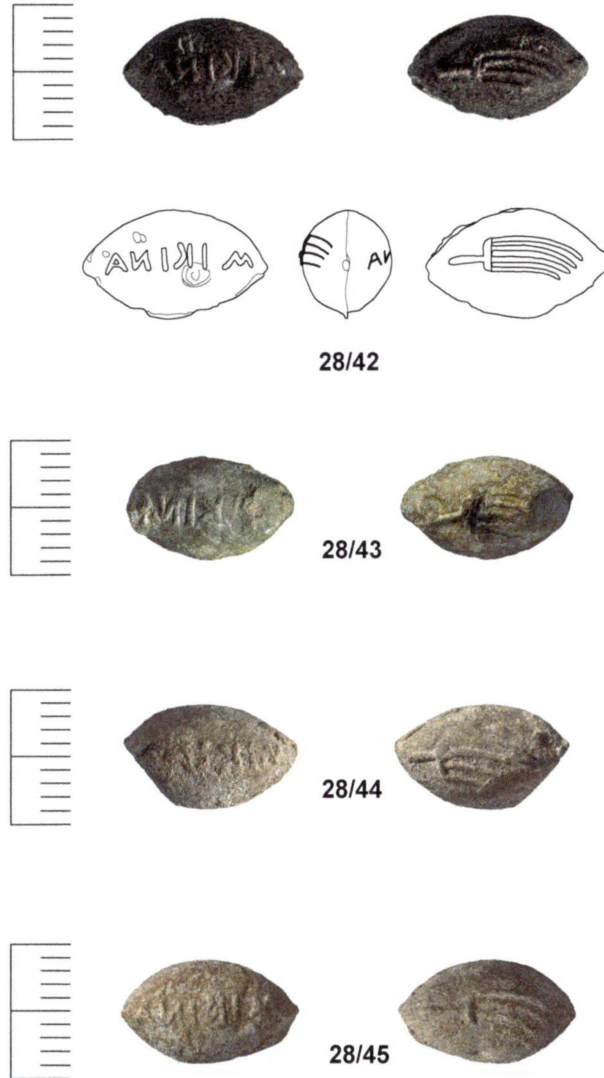

FIGURE 28.9. Inscribed lead sling bullets: MIKINA. **28/42** (MEΘ 656), **28/43** (MEΘ 1700), **28/44** (MEΘ 1701), **28/45** (MEΘ 1702). Photos J. Vanderpool, drawing A. Boufalis

Molded inscription in relief on one side, running retrograde; device in relief on the other side. Letter H. 0.0025–0.004; letter W. 0.003–0.006; device: p.L. 0.0132; p.W. 0.071.

Μικίν[α] ← | pitchfork/torch(?).

28/48. (MEΘ 2145) Fig. 28.10

East Hill #274/059010, pass 3, drainage channel.

P.L. 0.0285; W. 0.0165; Th. 0.0133; Wt. 28.2 g.

Olive-shaped (Type B). Not treated; one end obliquely cut off, severe impact damage on the device.

Molded inscription in relief on one side, running retrograde; device in relief on the other side. Letter H. 0.0035–0.0045; letter W. 0.003–0.006; device: p.L. 0.0165; p.W. 0.0083.

Μικίνα̣ ← | pitchfork/torch(?)

Part of the left slanting stroke of A.

28/49. (ΜΕΘ 2853) Fig. 28.10

East Hill #278/002003, fill north of Wall 2.

P.L. 0.0255; W. 0.0162; Th. 0.0142; Wt. 28.3 g.

Olive-shaped (Type B); casting flash folded below letter M. Not treated; sediments; severe impact damage at one end, which is broken off, severely hit on the lower edge.

Molded inscription in relief on one side, running retrograde; device in relief on the other side. Letter H. 0.0035–0.0044; letter W. 0.003–0.005; device: L. 0.018; W. 0.009.

Μικίνα ← | pitchfork/torch(?).

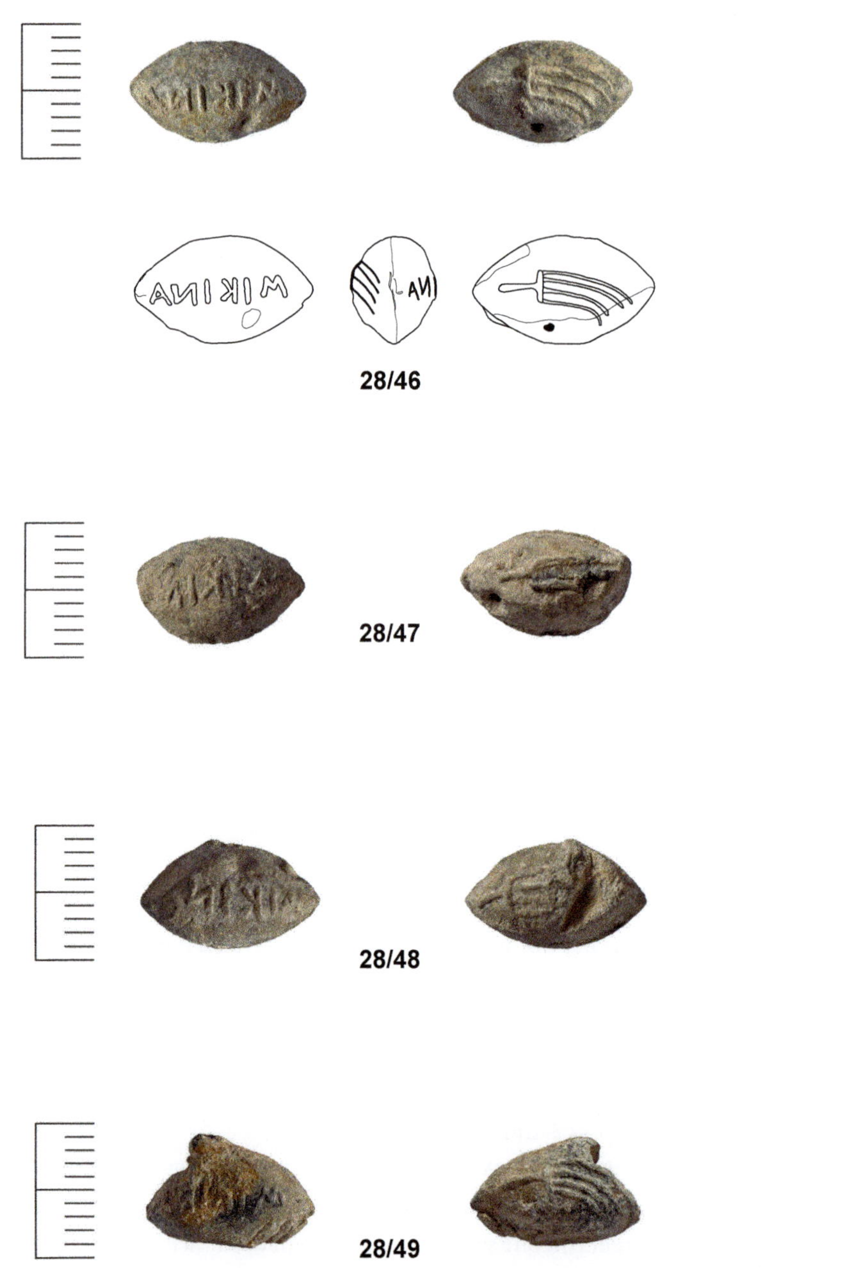

FIGURE 28.10. Inscribed lead sling bullets: MIKINA. **28/46** (ΜΕΘ 1706), **28/47** (ΜΕΘ 2144), **28/48** (ΜΕΘ 2145), **28/49** (ΜΕΘ 2853). Photos J. Vanderpool, drawing A. Boufalis

28/50. (ΜΕΘ 2856) Fig. 28.11

East Hill #278/002003, fill north of Wall 2.

L. 0.0267; W. 0.0167; Th. 0.0132; Wt. 28.0 g.

Olive-shaped (Type B). Not treated; few sediments; surface damage below the inscription, small surface depression below the device.

Molded inscription in relief on one side, running retrograde; device in relief on the other side. Letter H. 0.0032–0.004; letter W. 0.003–0.005; device: L. 0.0195; W. 0.008.

Μικίνα ← | pitchfork/torch(?).

28/51. (ΜΕΘ 2857) Fig. 28.11

East Hill #278/002003, fill north of Wall 2.

L. 0.0285; W. 0.0166; Th. 0.0133; Wt. 29.1 g.

Olive-shaped (Type B); hole above letter K. Not treated; sediments; hit above letter I, hit on the device, damaged on the lower edge.

Molded inscription in relief on one side, running retrograde; device in relief on the other side. Letter H. 0.003–0.005; letter W. 0.0035–0.0045; device: L. 0.018; W. 0.008.

Μικίνα ← | pitchfork/torch(?).

28/52. (ΜΕΘ 2858) Fig. 28.11

East Hill #278/002003, fill north of Wall 2.

L. 0.0273; W. 0.0156; Th. 0.0138; Wt. 21.1 g.

Olive-shaped (Type B). Not treated; sediments; large cavity on the side of the device, hit on the upper edge, minor hit on the inscription.

Molded inscription in relief on one side, running retrograde; device in relief on the other side. Letter H. 0.004–0.0055; letter W. 0.003–0.005; device: p.L. 0.011; W. 0.009.

Μικ[ίν]α ← | pitchfork/torch(?).

Half a letter space between M and I.

28/53. (ΜΕΘ 2859) Fig. 28.11

East Hill #278/002003, fill north of Wall 2.

L. 0.028; W. 0.0155; Th. 0.013; Wt. 27.0 g.

Olive-shaped (Type B). Not treated; sediments on the device; nick on the inscription.

Molded inscription in relief on one side, running retrograde; device in relief on the other side. Letter H. 0.003–0.004; letter W. 0.0035–0.005; device: L. 0.018; W. 0.006.

Μι[κ]ίνα ← | pitchfork/torch(?).

28/54. (ΜΕΘ 2860) Fig. 28.12

East Hill #278/002003, fill north of Wall 2.

L. 0.0268; W. 0.0155; Th. 0.0132; Wt. 27.0 g.

Olive-shaped (Type B); hole near the bullet point. Not treated; oxidized, covered by thin layer of white patina; hit on the upper edge near the stem end, minor nick on the side.

Molded inscription in relief on one side, running retrograde; device in relief on the other side. Letter H. 0.0038–0.0053; letter W. 0.003–0.0045; device: L. 0.021; W. 0.0096.

Μικίνα ← | pitchfork/torch(?).

Half a letter space between M and I.

FIGURE 28.11. Inscribed lead sling bullets: MIKINA. **28/50** (ΜΕΘ 2856), **28/51** (ΜΕΘ 2857), **8/52** (ΜΕΘ 2858), **28/53** (ΜΕΘ 2859). Photos J. Vanderpool

28/55. (ΜΕΘ 2861) Fig. 28.12

East Hill #278/002003, fill north of Wall 2.

L. 0.028; W. 0.0155; Th. 0.0135; Wt. 28.2 g.

Olive-shaped (Type B); hole near the bullet point; part of casting flash remains. Not treated; oxidized.

Molded inscription in relief on one side, running retrograde; device in relief on the other side. Letter H. 0.0037–0.0064; letter W. 0.0032–0.0045; device: L. 0.020; W. 0.0105.

Μικίνα ← | pitchfork/torch(?).

28/56. (ΜΕΘ 2901) Fig. 28.12

West Hill #229, northern side, Sector A, south of tunnel entrance.

L. 0.027; W. 0.0155; Th. 0.0134; Wt. 28.4 g.

Olive-shaped (Type B); very small hole below the device, and porosities on the other side; casting flash folded below letter M. Not treated; oxidized, covered by thin layer of white patina.

Molded inscription in relief on one side, running retrograde; device in relief on the other side. Letter H. 0.003–0.0045; letter W. 0.003–0.0045; device: L. 0.020; W. 0.0088.

Μικίνα ← | pitchfork/torch(?).

28/57. (ΜΕΘ 2912) Fig. 28.12

West Hill #229, northern side, Sector A, fill south of tunnel entrance.

P.L. 0.026; W. 0.0142; Th. 0.015; Wt. 28.3 g.

Olive-shaped (Type B). Not treated; oxidized, covered by white patina; hit at the bullet point, above the inscription, and on the lower edge.

Molded inscription in relief on one side, running retrograde; device in relief on the other side. Letter H. 0.0033–0.0039; letter W. 0.0023–0.0031; device: p.L. 0.0162; W. 0.009.

Μ̣ικίνα ← | pitchfork/torch(?).

The right half of M. Half a letter space between M and I.

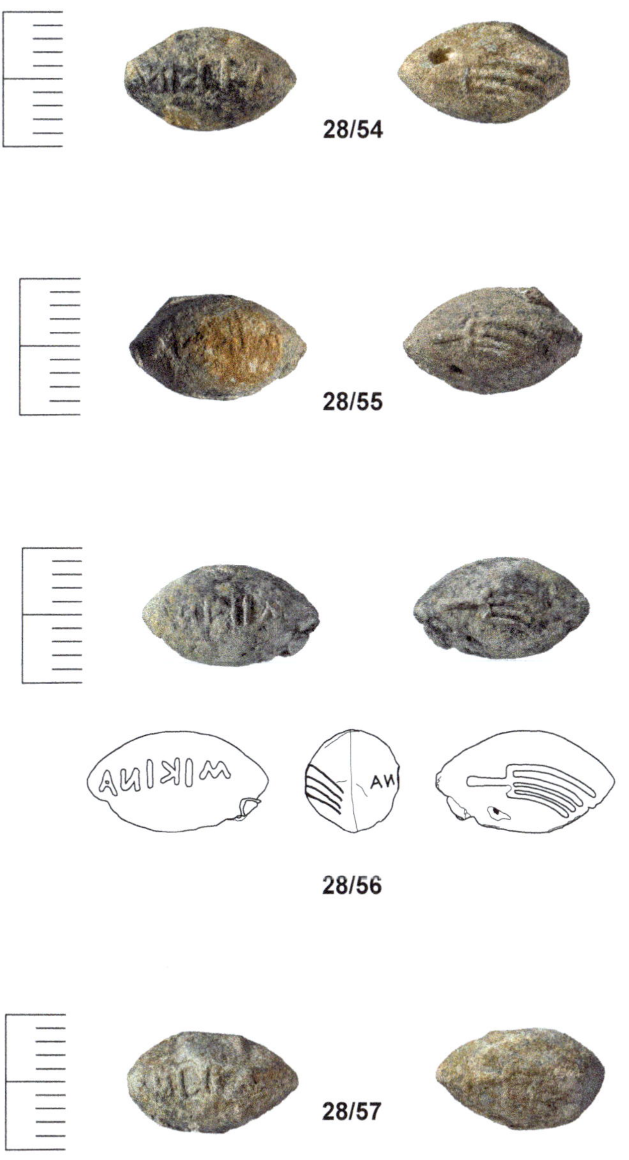

FIGURE 28.12. Inscribed lead sling bullets: MIKINA. **28/54** (ΜΕΘ 2860), **28/55** (ΜΕΘ 2861), **28/56** (ΜΕΘ 2901), **28/57** (ΜΕΘ 2912). Photos J. Vanderpool, drawing A. Boufalis

ΚΛΕΟΒΟΥΛŌ

28/58. (ΜΕΘ 292) Fig. 28.13

East Hill #274/076, Building A, Room E, northern balk, destruction layer.

L. 0.028; W. 0.0165; Th. 0.013; Wt. 29.0 g.

Olive-shaped (Type B); two oblong holes below the inscription on either side of the edge near the stem end. Treated; severely hit above letters ΚΛ, worn surface at the central part of the same side and minor nicks around.

Molded inscription in relief on both sides, running dextrograde. Letter H. 0.0027–0.0043; letter W. 0.0022–0.0027.

[Κλ]εο|βούλō.

A thin retrograde F-shape in very low relief is discerned above Y, but whether or not it was intentionally carved on the mold is unclear.

28/59. (ΜΕΘ 1708) Fig. 28.13

East Hill #274/017021, northern balk, pass 2.

P.L. 0.026; W. 0.016; Th. 0.014; Wt. 28.3 g.

Olive-shaped (Type B). Not treated; oxidized, covered by white patina; one end obliquely cut off, the other blunted, a wavy incised line below letters ΥΛ.

Molded inscription in relief on both sides, running dextrograde. On side A only O is partially in relief; the strokes of the other letters look as if they are carved. Letter H. 0.0026–0.0048; letter W. 0.0026–0.0034.

Κλεο|βο̣ύλ[ō].

The upper right part of O.

28/60. (ΜΕΘ 2847) Fig. 28.13

East Hill #278/002-003, deposit north of Wall 2.

L. 0.028; W. 0.016; Th. 0.013; Wt. 28.7 g.

Olive-shaped (Type B); deep oblong hole above the inscription near the stem end; casting flash folded above letter B. Not treated; oxidized, covered by white patina; minor hit at one end, a few minor hits, worn surface on both sides.

Molded inscription in relief on both sides, running dextrograde. Letter H. 0.002–0.004; letter W. 0.002–0.004.

Κ[λ]εο|βού[λ]ō.

28/61. (ΜΕΘ 2900) Fig. 28.13

West Hill #229, Sector Γ, cleaning east of the trench after the removal of the topsoil.

L. 0.0275; W. 0.016; Th. 0.0135; Wt. 28.9 g.

Olive-shaped (Type B); wide and deep hole near the stem end next to a surface depression (an attempt to open another hole?). Treated; a nick next to letter O, hit on letters ΒΟΥ, minor hit below letters ΥΛ.

Molded inscription in relief on both sides, running dextrograde. Letter H. 0.0026–0.0035; letter W. 0.0026–0.0034.

Κλεο|β̣[ο]ύ̣λō.

The upper left part of B; the upper part of Y.

FIGURE 28.13. Inscribed lead sling bullets: ΚΛΕΟΒΟΥΛΟ̄. **28/58** (ΜΕΘ 292), **28/59** (ΜΕΘ 1708), **28/60** (ΜΕΘ 2847), **28/61** (ΜΕΘ 2900). Photos J. Vanderpool, drawings A. Boufalis

ΕΥΓΕΝΕΟΣ

28/62. (ΜΕΘ 651) Fig. 28.14

West Hill #245/001014, pass 5, Pit 5 (tunnel), layer of fallen roof tiles.

L. of cluster 0.063; W. of cluster 0.036; Th. of cluster 0.029; total Wt. 117.0 g; dimensions of individual bullets as follows: L. (a) 0.028; (b) 0.028; (c) 0.0285; (d) 0.0285; W. (a) 0.016; (b) 0.015; (c) 0.0165; (d) 0.0165; Th. (a) 0.012; (b) 0.0115; (c) 0.0125; (d) 0.012.

Four bullets, almond-shaped (Type A), stemming from a central stem in pairs; overflow material forms a sheet between the bullets (a) + (c) and sharp flashes along the edges of all four. Treated; the stem possibly extended at the upper part bearing more bullets—no funnel is preserved at its end; toward the lower end the stem is twisted to the right; bullet (d) is covered by reddish corrosion (as of iron, probably from another object) at its point.

Molded inscription in relief on both sides of all four bullets, running dextrograde. Letter H. (a) 0.0025–0.0038; (b) 0.0025–0.0033; (c) 0.003–0.0038; (d) 0.0025–0.0038; letter W. (a) 0.0022–0.0035; (b) 0.002–0.0034; (c) 0.0018–0.0042; (d) 0.0022–0.0037.

a) Εὐγέ|νεος.

b) Εὐγέ|νεος.

c) Εὐγέ|νεος.

Half a letter space between E and O.

d) Εὐγέ|νεος.

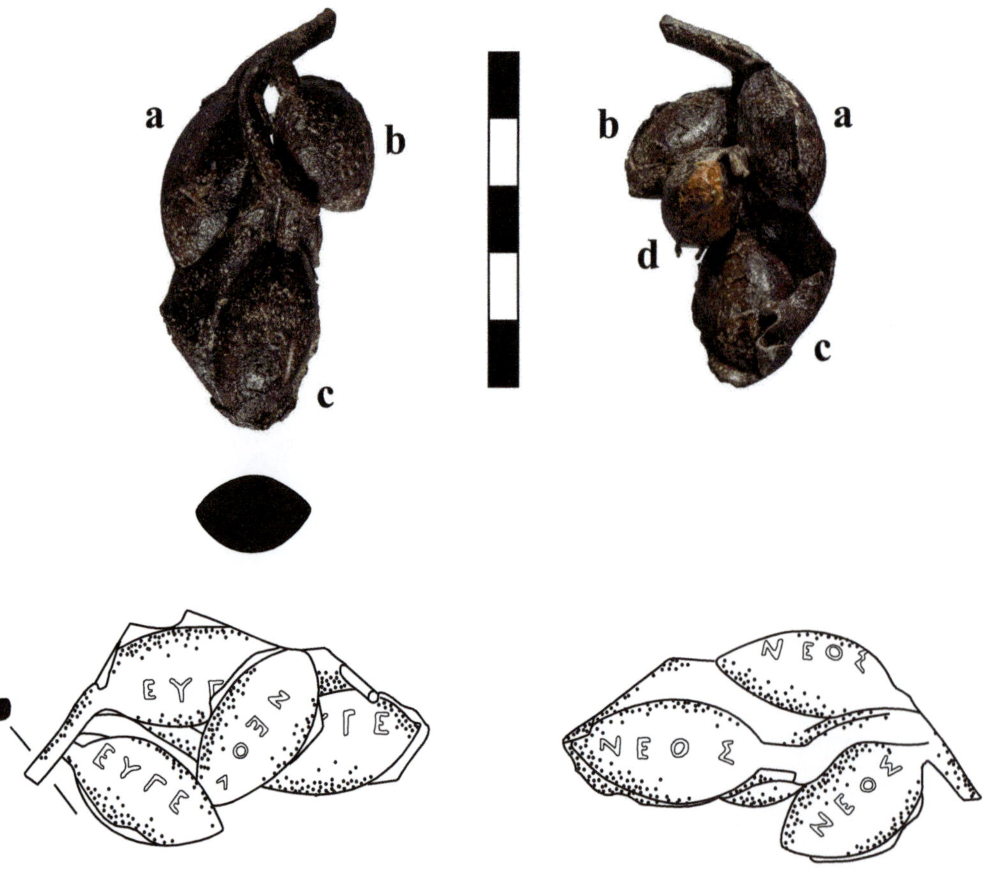

FIGURE 28.14. Cluster of inscribed lead sling bullets: ΕΥΓΕΝΕΟΣ. **28/62** (ΜΕΘ 651). Photos J. Vanderpool, drawing F. Skyvalida

28/63. (ΜΕΘ 289) Fig. 28.15

East Hill #274/066, Building A, Room E, destruction layer.

L. 0.0275; W. 0.0155; Th. 0.011; Wt. 23.4 g.

Almond-shaped (Type A). Treated; small surface depression centrally on letters EO, minor nick near the stem end next to letter E.

Molded inscription in relief on both sides, running dextrograde. Letter H. 0.0022–0.004; letter W. 0.002–0.0025.

Εὐγέ|νεος.

28/64. (ΜΕΘ 290) Fig. 28.15

East Hill #274/066, Building A, Room E, destruction layer.

L. 0.028; W. 0.0163; Th. 0.012; Wt. 26.6 g.

Almond-shaped (Type A). Not treated; oxidized, covered by white patina; minor damage (recent) above letters EO.

Molded inscription in relief on both sides, running dextrograde. Letter H. 0.0022–0.004; letter W. 0.002–0.003.

Εὐγέ|νεος.

28/65. (ΜΕΘ 2891) Fig. 28.15

East Hill #278/002003, fill north of Wall 2.

L. 0.0285; W. 0.016; Th. 0.0125; Wt. 27.3 g.

Almond-shaped (Type A). Treated.

Molded inscription in relief on both sides, running dextrograde. Letter H. 0.0023–0.0042; letter W. 0.0022–0.0043.

Εὐγέ|νεος.

ORIGINALLY UNINSCRIBED WITH GRAFFITO

28/66. (ΜΕΘ 282) Fig. 28.16

East Hill #274/067, northern part, trial trench, destruction layer.

P.L. 0.0286; p.W. 0.016; Th. 0.0162; Wt. 30.6 g.

Olive-shaped (Type B). Not treated; oxidized, covered by thin layer of white patina; one end obliquely cut off, minor hit on the edge, minor nick and a round swelling of the material on one side, partially worn surface near the preserved end.

Incised alphabetic(?) mark, facing dextrograde, on the flat surface where the bullet is cut; the incision is shallow, executed with a very fine point. Letter H. 0.0058; letter W. 0.0044.

Γ.

UNINSCRIBED

28/67. (ΜΕΘ 280) Fig. 28.17

East Hill #274/067, eastern part, trial trench, destruction layer.

L. 0.0315; W. 0.018; Th. 0.015; Wt. 34.1 g.

Olive-shaped (Type B); one edge rather sharp; similar form to **28/93** (ΜΕΘ 2887). Not treated; oxidized, covered by thin layer of white patina; severely hit and broken off near one end.

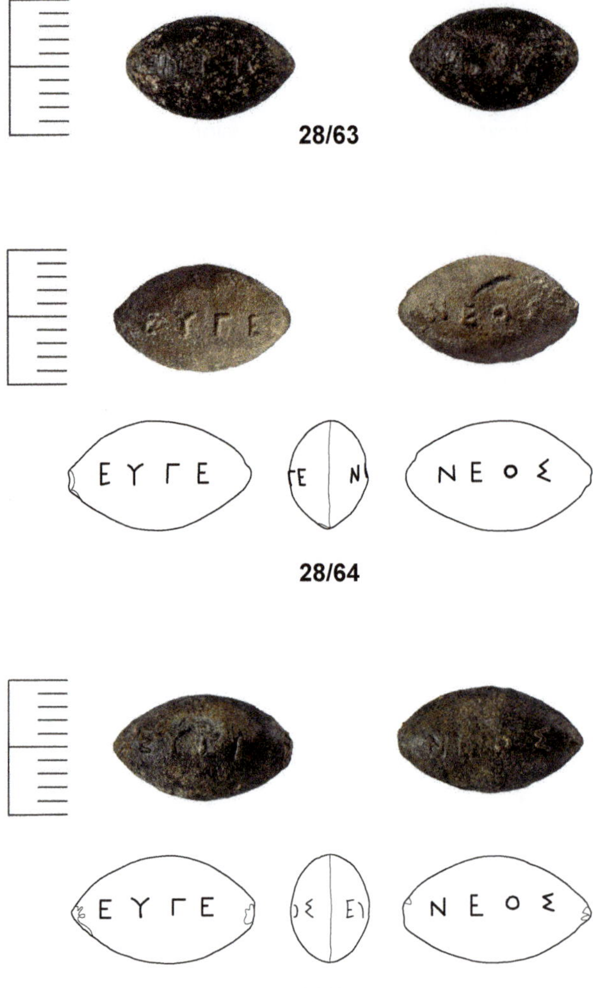

FIGURE 28.15. Inscribed lead sling bullets: ΕΥΓΕΝΕΟΣ. **28/63** (ΜΕΘ 289), **28/64** (ΜΕΘ 290), **28/65** (ΜΕΘ 2891). Photos J. Vanderpool, drawings A. Boufalis

FIGURE 28.16. Originally uninscribed lead sling bullet with graffito: **28/66** (ΜΕΘ 282). Photos J. Vanderpool

28/68. (MEΘ 284) Fig. 28.17
East Hill #274/067, northern part, trial trench, destruction layer.
L. 0.030; W. 0.0165; Th. 0.0135; Wt. 31.1 g.
Olive-shaped (Type B). Not treated; oxidized, covered by thin layer of white patina; minor hit near the bullet point.

28/69. (MEΘ 650) Fig. 28.17
West Hill #245/001014, pass 5, Pit 5 (tunnel), layer of fallen roof tiles.
L. 0.0325; W. 0.016; Th. 0.0135; Wt. 31.9 g.
Olive-shaped (Type B); flattened edges. Not treated; oxidized, covered by white patina.

28/70. (MEΘ 652) Fig. 28.17
West Hill #245/002020, pass 5, Pit 5 (tunnel).
P.L. 0.031; p.W. 0.0165; Th. 0.0145; Wt. 31.0 g.
Olive-shaped (Type B). Not treated; heavily oxidized, covered by white patina; broken off at the bullet point and at the edge.

28/71. (MEΘ 654) Fig. 28.17
West Hill #245/005001, pass 1, topsoil.
L. 0.0305; W. 0.014; Th. 0.0135; Wt. 28.8 g.
Olive-shaped (Type B); smoothed edges. Not treated; oxidized, covered by thin layer of white patina; minor hits on the sides.

28/72. (MEΘ 1698) Fig. 28.17
East Hill #274/084004, pass 3.
L. 0.030; W. 0.0155; Th. 0.0135; Wt. 28.9 g.
Olive-shaped (Type B). Not treated; oxidized, covered by white patina; hit on the edge near the bullet point.

28/73. (MEΘ 1699) Fig. 28.18
East Hill #274/086003, pass 1.
L. 0.031; W. 0.015; Th. 0.016; Wt. 31.3 g.
Olive-shaped (Type B); casting flashes not cared for. Not treated; about 1/3 is obliquely cut off, minor hit at the stem end.

28/74. (MEΘ 1703) Fig. 28.18
East Hill #274/079, eastern part.
L. 0.033; W. 0.0204; Th. 0.014; Wt. 34.0 g.
Olive-shaped (Type B); deformed due to mold shift. Not treated; severe impact damage on the edge and on one side, minor hit (possibly recent) on the other.

28/75. (MEΘ 1704) Fig. 28.18
East Hill #274/016, topsoil.
L. 0.032; p.W. 0.016; Th. 0.014; Wt. 33.6 g.
Olive-shaped (Type B). Not treated; two impressed oblique linear marks on either side by the stem end, hit on the edge.

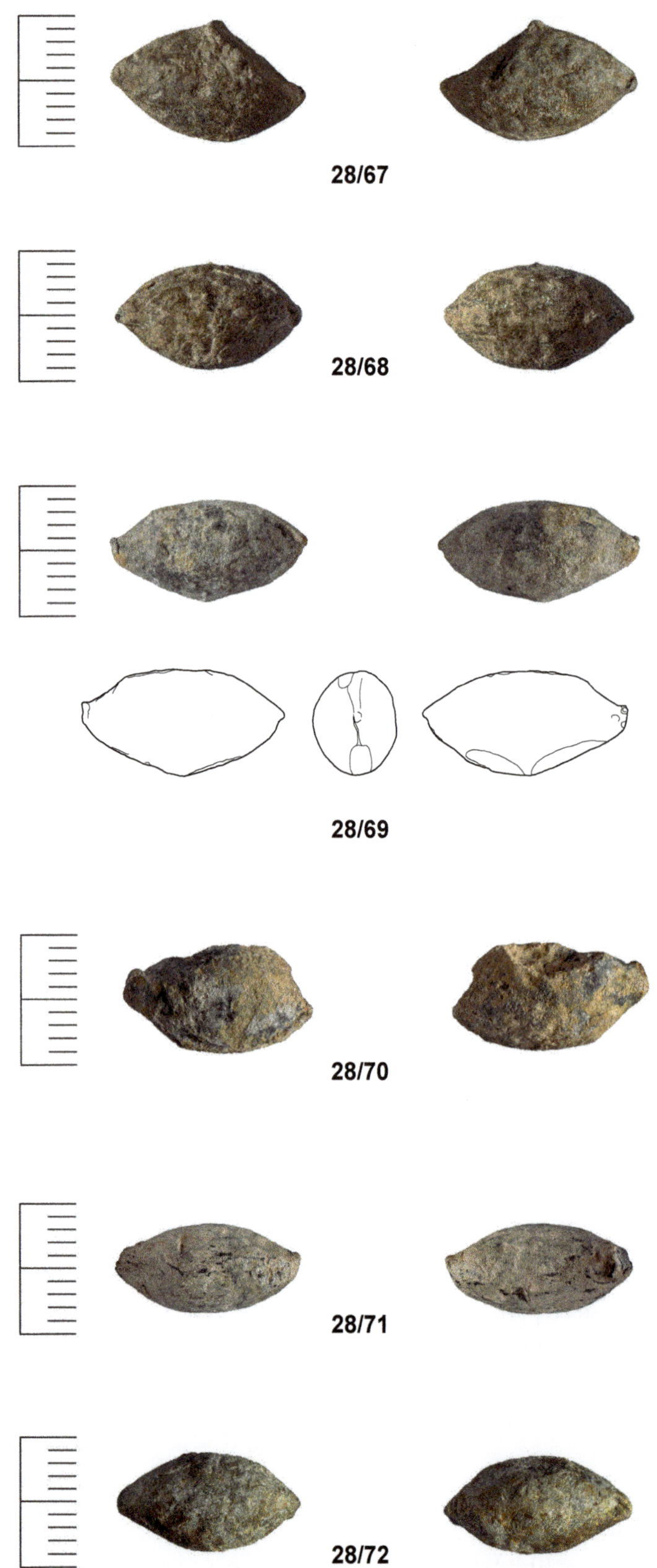

FIGURE 28.17. Uninscribed lead sling bullets: **28/67** (ΜΕΘ 280), **28/68** (ΜΕΘ 284), **28/69** (ΜΕΘ 650), **28/70** (ΜΕΘ 652), **28/71** (ΜΕΘ 654), **28/72** (ΜΕΘ 1698). Photos J. Vanderpool, drawing A. Boufalis

28/76. (ΜΕΘ 2846) Fig. 28.18
East Hill #278/002-003, deposit north of Wall 2.
P.L. 0.029; p.W. 0.0175; Th. 0.015; Wt. 33.8 g.
Olive-shaped (Type B). Not treated; oxidized, covered by white patina; one end obliquely cut off.

28/77. (ΜΕΘ 2848) Fig. 28.18
East Hill #278/002-003, deposit north of Wall 2.
P.L 0.0295; W 0.0155; Th 0.0135; Wt. 32.1 g.
Olive-shaped (Type B). Not treated; oxidized, covered by white patina; hit at one end.

28/78. (ΜΕΘ 2849) Fig. 28.18
East Hill #278/002-003, deposit north of Wall 2.
L. 0.031; W. 0.015; Th. 0.014; Wt. 30.7 g.
Olive-shaped (Type B); flattened edge. Not treated; sediments; heavily oxidized at the central part of one side.

28/79. (ΜΕΘ 2850) Fig. 28.18
East Hill #278/002-003, deposit north of Wall 2.
L. 0.030; W. 0.016; Th. 0.0145; Wt. 32.0 g.
Olive-shaped (Type B); folded casting flashes on one side. Not treated; one end hit, surface damage on the side.

28/80. (ΜΕΘ 2851) Fig. 28.19
East Hill #278/002-003, deposit north of Wall 2.
L. 0.031; W. 0.0155; Th. 0.014; Wt. 34.3 g.
Olive-shaped (Type B). Not treated; sediments.

28/81. (ΜΕΘ 2852) Fig. 28.19
East Hill #278/002-003, deposit north of Wall 2.
L. 0.030; W. 0.0155; Th. 0.014; Wt. 29.9 g.
Olive-shaped (Type B). Not treated; severely hit near one end, several hits all over.

28/82. (ΜΕΘ 2855) Fig. 28.19
East Hill #278/002-003, deposit north of Wall 2.
L. 0.029; W. 0.0165; Th. 0.0145; Wt. 31.2 g.
Olive-shaped (Type B). Not treated; oxidized, covered by thin layer of white patina; obliquely cut off near the bullet point.

28/83. (ΜΕΘ 2874) Fig. 28.19
East Hill #278/002-003, deposit north of Wall 2.
P.L. 0.0265; W. 0.017; Th. 0.015; Wt. 31.4 g.
Olive-shaped (Type B). Not treated; oxidized, covered by thin layer of white patina; traces of iron oxide on one side; one end obliquely cut off.

28/84. (ΜΕΘ 2876) Fig. 28.19
East Hill #278/002-003, deposit north of Wall 2.
L. 0.0295; W. 0.017; Th. 0.014; Wt. 32.3 g.
Olive-shaped (Type B); very small, shallow hole near the stem end (casting defect); protruding casting flashes on one side. Not treated; oxidized, covered by white patina; minor hit on the side.

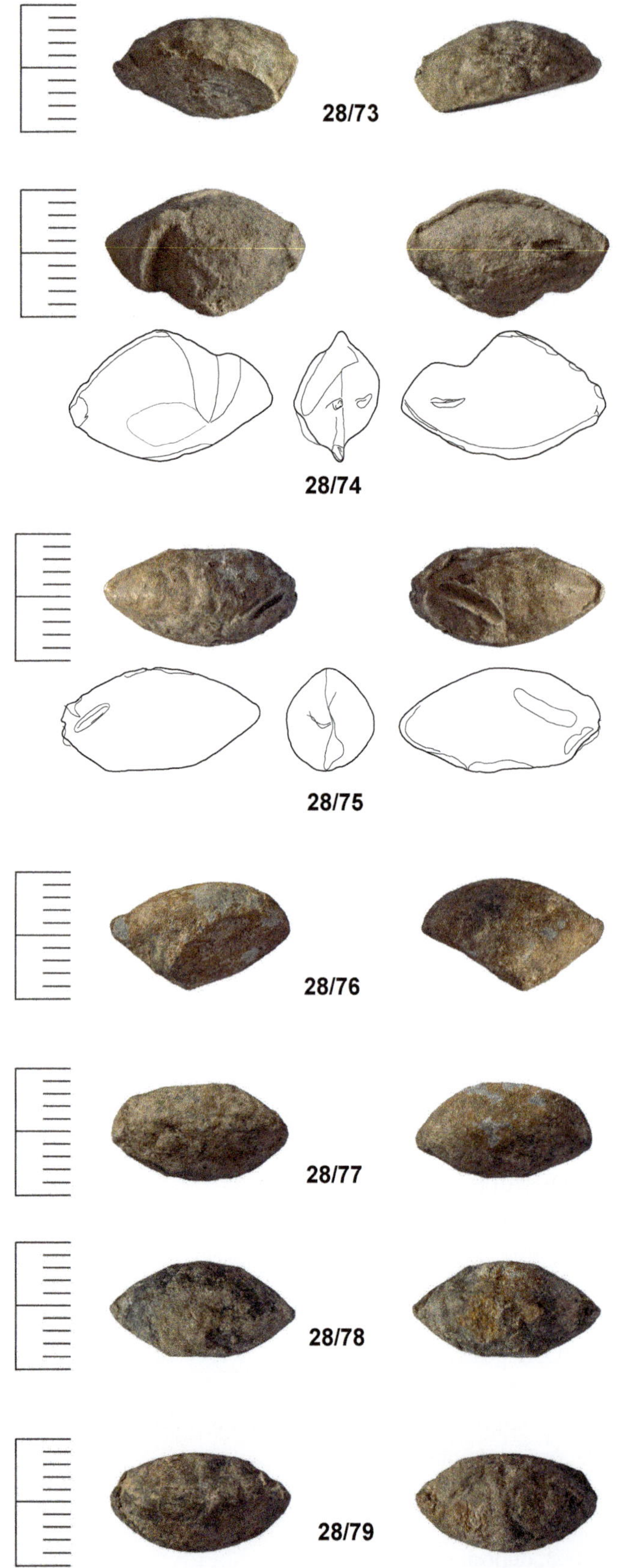

FIGURE 28.18. Uninscribed lead sling bullets: **28/73** (ΜΕΘ 1699), **28/74** (ΜΕΘ 1703), **28/75** (ΜΕΘ 1704), **28/76** (ΜΕΘ 2846), **28/77** (ΜΕΘ 2848), **28/78** (ΜΕΘ 2849), **28/79** (ΜΕΘ 2850). Photos J. Vanderpool, drawings A. Boufalis

FIGURE 28.19. Uninscribed lead sling bullets: **28/80** (ΜΕΘ 2851), **28/81** (ΜΕΘ 2852), **28/82** (ΜΕΘ 2855), **28/83** (ΜΕΘ 2874), **28/84** (ΜΕΘ 2876), **28/85** (ΜΕΘ 2877), **28/86** (ΜΕΘ 2880). Photos J. Vanderpool

28/85. (MEΘ 2877) Fig. 28.19
East Hill #278/002-003, deposit north of Wall 2.
L. 0.0315; W. 0.0155; Th. 0.013; Wt. 29.5 g.
Olive-shaped (Type B). Not treated; oxidized, covered by white patina; minor hit near the bullet point.

28/86. (MEΘ 2880) Fig. 28.19
East Hill #278/002-003, deposit north of Wall 2.
L. 0.031; W. 0.0165; p.Th. 0.013; Wt. 30.8 g.
Olive-shaped (Type B); protruding edges on one side. Not treated; oxidized, covered by white patina; one side severely hit in the middle, hit on the edge.

28/87. (MEΘ 2881) Fig. 28.20
East Hill #278/002-003, deposit north of Wall 2.
L. 0.030; W. 0.0165; Th. 0.0145; Wt. 31.6 g.
Olive-shaped (Type B); casting flashes not fully taken care of. Not treated; oxidized, covered by white patina; minor hits on the side and near one end.

28/88. (MEΘ 2882) Fig. 28.20
East Hill #278/002-003, deposit north of Wall 2.
L. 0.030; W. 0.016; Th. 0.014; Wt. 32.5 g.
Olive-shaped (Type B). Not treated; oxidized, covered by thin layer of white patina; minor nick on one side.

28/89. (MEΘ 2883) Fig. 28.20
East Hill #278/002-003, deposit north of Wall 2.
L. 0.032; W. 0.014; Th. 0.0135; Wt. 30.0 g.
Olive-shaped (Type B). Not treated; oxidized, covered by white patina; minor hits on the sides.

28/90. (MEΘ 2884) Fig. 28.20
East Hill #278/002-003, deposit north of Wall 2.
L. 0.031; W. 0.016; Th. 0.014; Wt. 30.9 g.
Olive-shaped (Type B); casting flashes not fully taken care of. Not treated; oxidized, covered by white patina; hit on the edge.

28/91. (MEΘ 2885) Fig. 28.20
East Hill #278/002-003, deposit north of Wall 2.
L. 0.029; W. 0.016; Th. 0.013; Wt. 29.6 g.
Olive-shaped (Type B); casting flashes not fully planished. Not treated; surface damage on one side near the bullet point, large surface depression of considerable depth (impact damage?) on the other side.

28/92. (MEΘ 2886) Fig. 28.20
East Hill #278/002-003, deposit north of Wall 2.
L. 0.031; W. 0.016; Th. 0.0145; Wt. 34.5 g.
Olive-shaped (Type B). Not treated; hit on the edge.

FIGURE 28.20. Uninscribed lead sling bullets: **28/87** (ΜΕΘ 2881), **28/88** (ΜΕΘ 2882), **28/89** (ΜΕΘ 2883), **28/90** (ΜΕΘ 2884), **28/91** (ΜΕΘ 2885), **28/92** (ΜΕΘ 2886), **28/93** (ΜΕΘ 2887). Photos J. Vanderpool

28/93. (ΜΕΘ 2887) Fig. 28.20

East Hill #278/002-003, deposit north of Wall 2.

L. 0.030; W. 0.018; Th. 0.013; Wt. 32.0 g.

Olive-shaped (Type B); one edge rather sharp; similar form to **28/67** (ΜΕΘ 280). Not treated; minor nick on one side.

28.94. (ΜΕΘ 2888) Fig. 28.21

East Hill #278/002-003, deposit north of Wall 2.

P.L. 0.030; W. 0.016; Th. 0.015; Wt. 32.5 g.

Olive-shaped (Type B). Not treated; oxidized, covered by patches of white patina; one end obliquely cut off.

28/95. (ΜΕΘ 2889) Fig. 28.21

East Hill #278/002-003, deposit north of Wall 2.

L. 0.0315; W. 0.016; Th. 0.0135; Wt. 32.4 g.

Olive-shaped (Type B). Not treated.

28/96. (ΜΕΘ 2890) Fig. 28.21

East Hill #278/002-003, deposit north of Wall 2.

P.L. 0.0305; W. 0.018; Th. 0.015; Wt. 34.4 g.

Olive-shaped (Type B). Not treated; one side corroded; one end obliquely cut off.

28/97. (ΜΕΘ 2899) Fig. 28.21

West Hill #229, Sector A, north end, at 0.25 m depth, red soil.

L. 0.031; W. 0.0165; p.Th. 0.0135; Wt. 27.3 g.

Olive-shaped (Type B); cavity on one side. Not treated; oxidized, covered by white patina; both sides heavily corroded.

28/98. (ΜΕΘ 2902) Fig. 28.21

West Hill #229, Sector A, north end, south of tunnel entrance, red soil.

L. 0.032; W. 0.017; Th. 0.014; Wt. 31.5 g.

Olive-shaped (Type B). Not treated; minor hits all over.

28/99. (ΜΕΘ 2904) Fig. 28.21

West Hill #229, Sector A, collected from the excavation debris.

L. 0.0315; W. 0.017; Th. 0.0145; Wt. 33.9 g.

Olive-shaped (Type B). Not treated; oxidized, partially covered by thin layer of white patina; hit on the edge, a nick on the side.

28/100. (ΜΕΘ 2905) Fig. 28.22

West Hill #229, Sector A, collected from the excavation debris.

L. 0.0295; W. 0.015; Th. 0.0135; Wt. 28.7 g.

Olive-shaped (Type B). Not treated; oxidized, fully covered by white patina; breakage on one side.

28/101. (ΜΕΘ 2906) Fig. 28.22

West Hill #229, Sector A, south of tunnel entrance.

L. 0.031; W. 0.016; Th. 0.0145; Wt. 31.0 g.

Olive-shaped (Type B). Not treated; oxidized, covered by white patina; one side severely corroded, minor breakages by corrosion on the other.

FIGURE 28.21. Uninscribed lead sling bullets: **28/94** (ΜΕΘ 2888), **28/95** (ΜΕΘ 2889), **28/96** (ΜΕΘ 2890), **28/97** (ΜΕΘ 2899), **28/98** (ΜΕΘ 2902), **28/99** (ΜΕΘ 2904). Photos J. Vanderpool, drawing A. Boufalis

28/102. (MEΘ 2908) Fig. 28.22

West Hill #229, Sector A, south of tunnel entrance.

L. 0.030; W. 0.016; Th. 0.0145; Wt. 30.6 g.

Olive-shaped (Type B). Not treated; oxidized, covered by white patina; severely hit on the edge.

28/103. (MEΘ 2913) Fig. 28.22

West Hill #229, Sector A, collected from the excavation debris.

L. 0.031; W. 0.016; Th. 0.0145; Wt. 32.2 g.

Olive-shaped (Type B). Not treated; oxidized, covered by patches of white patina; hit on the edge.

28/104. (MEΘ 2914) Fig. 28.22

West Hill #229, Sector A, collected from the excavation debris.

P.L. 0.0255; W. 0.017; Th. 0.0145; Wt. 30.8 g.

Olive-shaped (Type B); a hole with irregular opening on one side (casting defect). Not treated; oxidized, fully covered by white patina; one end completely scraped off; hit on the edge.

28/105. (MEΘ 2915) Fig. 28.22

West Hill #229, Sector A, collected from the excavation debris.

L. 0.0305; W. 0.015; Th. 0.014; Wt. 31.1 g.

Olive-shaped (Type B); flattened edges. Not treated; oxidized, covered by white patina; minor hit on the side, breakages by corrosion on the other.

APPENDIX I

AN INSCRIBED BRONZE CATAPULT BOLT FROM METHONE

This solitary inscribed catapult bolt is essentially a large bronze three-finned arrowhead.[326] The piece can be described as follows:

28/106. (MEΘ 293) Fig. 28.23

East Hill #274/088, Building A, room Δ, southwest corner, 3rd brownish red stratum, 3/11/2004. Now in the Archaeological Museum of Thessaloniki.

L. 0.068 (0.070 incl. the longest fin); W. (between the two shorter fins) 0.024; Diam. of socket (exterior) 0.013, (interior) 0.012.

Bronze arrowhead, three-finned. The fins are triangular, with sharp edges, running along a conical hollow shaft (socket, αὐλός), and ending in an undercut barb. Two of the fins are of about the same length as the shaft, while the third (the one opposite the inscription) is a bit longer; short casting at one side of the shaft. Treated; short linear scratches on the shaft.

Molded inscription in relief, running retrograde, on the shaft at the interspace between two of the fins (the two shorter ones). Letter H. 0.0045–0.009; letter W. max. 0.007.

Φιλίππō. ←

Identical Finds

- five arrowheads found at Olynthos, 348 B.C.[327]
- one arrowhead reportedly found near Olynthos, undated[328]

FIGURE 28.22. Uninscribed lead sling bullets: **28/100** (ΜΕΘ 2905), **28/101** (ΜΕΘ 2906), **28/102** (ΜΕΘ 2908), **28/103** (ΜΕΘ 2913), **28/104** (ΜΕΘ 2914), **28/105** (ΜΕΘ 2915). Photos J. Vanderpool

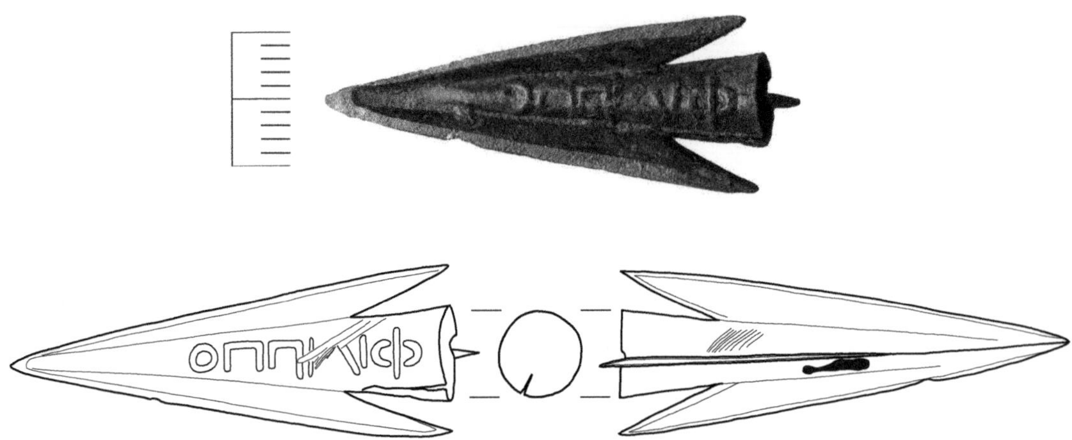

FIGURE 28.23. Inscribed bronze catapult bolt **28/106** (ΜΕΘ 293). Photo O. Kourakis, drawing A. Boufalis

The dating of these arrowheads to 348 B.C., based on the examples from Olynthos, can now be pushed back to 354 B.C. on account of the presence of **28/106** (ΜΕΘ 293) at Methone.

The dimensions and weight are unusual for arrowheads. This led Anthony Snodgrass to suggest that this particular type of arrowhead was actually fitted on catapult bolts shot from a *gastraphetes*.[329] Eric Marsden took this idea further by considering the possibility that these specific missile heads were used with small types of the non-torsion catapult.[330] It is noteworthy, even if coincidental, that all known (that is, published) examples come from Olynthos and Methone, both cities reported as the place where Philip II lost his eye while inspecting the (presumably launching) siege engines (see n. 180). The findspot of the arrowhead, in an interior space of Building A in the agora of Methone, is perhaps unexpected, but it does not preclude that it is a catapult bolt head.

The named individual of the inscription has been identified by Robinson as the Macedonian king Philip II,[331] and there is not much room for doubt. Robinson also associated the arrowheads with sling bullets from Olynthos with the inscription Φιλίππου (see below), and suggested that there was a personal troop of royal archers and slingers. He also suggested that, as all such arrowheads were found in the same area, along the west part of the city on the North Hill of Olynthos, the king's regiment was attacking on that side. This, however, is not corroborated by the findspots of Philip's sling bullets that were found all around the city.[332] Both the identification of the Philip on the sling bullets with Philip II, and the question as to whether names are to be identified as the slingers' commanding officers, remain debatable issues.[333]

SLING BULLETS INSCRIBED ΦΙΛΙ|ΠΠΟΥ:

- fourteen bullets found at Olynthos[334]
- three bullets in the Froehner Collection, housed in the Cabinet des Médailles de la Bibliothéque Nationale in Paris[335]
- unspecified number of bullets found at Stageira[336]
- two bullets from the Haskovo area (Bulgaria), now in the Regional Museum of History in Haskovo[337]
- one bullet found at Aiani[338]
- three bullets found at Argilos, 357/6 B.C.[339]

Eugene Borza noted that the findspots of these arrowheads were "on the west slope of Olynthus' North Hill outside the walls, as well as inside an Olynthian house,"[340] and he challenged the above interpretation by wondering whether the arrowheads should be ascribed to the Chalkidian side, and whether the inscription may feature a local Olynthian dative, meaning "for Philip."[341] The idea was rejected by John Lee on probability grounds: it is unlikely that the Olynthians would invest in quality missiles bearing their opponent's name.[342] In addition, at least according to Lee's plan of the site of Olynthos (see n. 332), all of these arrowheads were found inside houses at the western part of the North Hill, and not on the slope outside the walls. Furthermore, the letter Ω was already widely used for the long /o/ sound in the mid-4th century B.C. and the absence of iôta adscript would be rather unusual. Thus, there is no supporting evidence for Borza's suggestion, and the second declension genitive ending in –ō remains the only possible reading.

APPENDIX II

ILLUSTRATIONS OF SLINGERS: A NON-EXHAUSTIVE CATALOGUE[343]

1. Slingers and archers before hoplites sallying out from a besieged city. Silver conical rhyton, 16th century B.C., Shaft Grave IV, Mycenae.[344]
2. Slinger and spearmen standing by. Amphora(?) fragments ("vaso chiuso"), 7th century B.C. (Rizza) / Protogeometric period, ante 850 B.C. (Biondi), Prinias, Crete.[345]
3. Slingers before hoplites, against hoplites and horsemen; arrows indicate they are also being hit by projectiles. Black-figure amphora, Geometric period, Paros.[346]
4. Slinger operating behind a hoplite; the armor and arms in front of the slinger indicate he is also a hoplite. Corinthian alabastron, 625–600 B.C., Delos.[347]
5. Pygmies hunting cranes with clubs; the one at the far left uses a sling and carries a pouch. Attic black-figure aryballos (Nearchos Aryballos), ca. 570 B.C., Attica.[348]
6. Pygmies mounted on wild goats hunting cranes with slings, while others on foot are armed with clubs (frieze on the foot of the vase). Black-figure volute krater (François vase), ca. 570–560 B.C., Chiusi, now in Florence, Museo Archeologico Etrusco.[349]
7. Herakles hunting the Stymphalian birds with a sling. Attic black-figure amphora, ca. 575–525 B.C., Vulci, Etruria, now in the British Museum, no. 1843/1103.40.[350]
8. Herakles hunting the Stymphalian birds with a sling. Attic black-figure amphora, ca. 575–525 B.C., Musée de Boulogne-sur-Mer, no. 420.[351]
9. Herakles hunting the Stymphalian birds with a sling. Attic black-figure amphora fragment, ca. 575–525 B.C., Munich, Staatliche Antikensammlungen, no. 8701.[352]
10. Slinger operating behind a hoplite; the slinger has light armor, helmet, and sword on. Relief pithos, 6th century B.C., Sparta.[353]
11. Herakles slinging against an Amazon armed as a hoplite. Attic black-figure pelike, ca. 525 B.C., Cerveteri, now in Leipzig, Antikenmuseum der Universität, no. T3329.[354]
12. Slinger (barbarian) with pouch facing an advancing hoplite; on the other side, similar scene with an archer. Attic black-figure stemless band cup, ca. 520 B.C., Vulci, Etruria, now in Munich, Staatliche Antikensammlung, no. 2104.[355]
13. Slinger wearing a pilos, crouching. Attic red-figure cup, ca. 525–475 B.C., Leipzig, Antikenmuseum der Universität, no. T519.[356]

14. Slinger wearing light armor and a helmet and carrying a pouch. Attic black-figure (interior) and red-figure (exterior) cup, ca. 525–475 B.C., British Museum, no. 1896/6-21.3.[357]
15. Herakles and Iolaos (on either side) hunting the Stymphalian birds with slings: Herakles covers himself with a pelt hanging from his left hand; Iolaos with hoplite gear (cuirass, helmet, sword, shield, two spears) covers himself with a himation hanging from his left hand. Attic black-figure amphora, ca. 500–490 B.C., Vulci, Etruria, now in Paris, Musée du Louvre, no. F387.[358]
16. Slinger, wearing light armor, with pouch and a couple of spears beside him; arrows hit the ground before him. Attic red-figure cup, ca. 490 B.C., Kurashiki, Ninagawa Museum, no. 34.[359]
17. Kephalos slinging(?) at Eos.[360] Attic red-figure column krater, ca. 500–450 B.C., Bologna, Museo Civico.[361]
18. Slinger wearing a pilos and covering himself with an aegis; advancing hoplite on the other side. Red-figure amphora, ca. 475–450 B.C., Nola, Italy, once in Rouen, Bellon, no. 609 (now lost).[362]
19. Slinger, wearing a chiton and a helmet, with a pair of spears beside him; on the other side a hoplite ready to strike with his spear. Attic red-figure amphora, ca. 460–450 B.C., British Museum, no. 1772/0320.266.[363]
20. Slinger wearing a pilos. Boiotian black-figure cup, 5th century B.C., Athens, National Museum, no. 484.[364]
21. Amazon slinger, wearing a nebris, with a bow by her feet and a couple of spears beside her. Attic white-ground lekythos, ca. 440 B.C., now in New York, The Metropolitan Museum of Art, no. 10.201.11.[365]
22. Slinger. Coin (stater) of Aspendos, Pamphylia, verso, late 5th–early 4th century B.C.[366]
23. Slinger carrying a pouch and/or sword, with a couple of spears beside him. Coins (silver didrachms) of the Ainianes, Thessaly, verso, 168–146 B.C.[367]

POSSIBLE DEPICTIONS

24. Athletes; one of them in a pose of a slinger and with a black line extending from hand to hand. Attic red-figure mastoid vase, ca. 525–475 B.C., Paris, Musée du Louvre, no. CP10783.[368]
25. Warrior (cuirass, helmet, spear) holding a sling(?). Clay relief plaque, 500–450 B.C., Apollonia Pontica, now in Paris, Musée du Louvre, no. CA1748.[369]
26. Warrior, naked with a helmet on, standing like a slinger at ease. Bronze statuette, 3rd–2nd century B.C., Pompeii, Campania.[370]

A NOTE ON GEAR

Although most slingers on vase iconography do not wear armor, there are several who do show some armor. Apart from Herakles with his casual hide (nos. 7–9, 11; cf. no. 15), and Iolaos (no. 15) and the warrior in no. 4, who are otherwise hoplites, there are a few who wear a helmet (nos. 10, 14, 19; cf. no. 26) and a few who wear light armor (nos. 10, 14, 16).[371] In nos. 10 and 14 this armor seems to be made of hide or pelt; in no. 16 it looks like fleece. From literary sources we know of another type of armor possibly worn by slingers, linen armor,[372] which is probably worn by the warrior in no. 25.[373]

APPENDIX III

FURTHER NOTES ON LEAD SLING BULLETS IN LITERATURE

1. The Heat: Incandescent Sling Bullets

A phenomenon that is pointed out in Arist. *Cael.* 289a, 19–25 (Bekker): ἡ δὲ θερμότης ἀπ' αὐτῶν καὶ τὸ φῶς γίνεται παρεκτριβομένου τοῦ ἀέρος ὑπὸ τῆς ἐκείνων φορᾶς [. . .]· οἷον καὶ ἐπὶ τῶν φερομένων βελῶν· ταῦτα γὰρ αὐτὰ ἐκπυροῦται οὕτως ὥστε τήκεσθαι τὰς μολυβδίδας (sling bullets burning and melting in flight because of friction), is echoed in Latin poetry:

- Lucr. 6.176–178: *ut omnia motu | percalefacta vides ardescere, plumbea vero | glans etiam longo cursu volvenda liquescit.*[374]
- Lucr. 6.305–307: *non alia longe ratione ac plumbea saepe | fervida fit glans in cursu; cum multa rigoris | corpora dimittens ignem concepit in auris.*[375]
- Verg. *Aen.* 9.586–589: *stridentem fundam positis Mezentius hastis | ipse ter adducta circum caput egit habena | et media adversi liquefacto tempora plumbo | diffidit ac multa porrectum extendit harena.*[376]
- Sen. *QNat.* 2.57.2: *sic liquescit excussa glans funda et attritu aeris velut igne destillat.*[377]
- Luc. *Pharsalia* 7.513: *inde sagittae, | inde faces et saxa volant, spatioque solutae | aeris et calido liquefactae pondere glandes.*[378]
- Ov. *Met.* 2.726–729: *obstipuit forma Iove natus* (sc. Mercury) *et aethere pendens | non secus exarsit quam cum Baleriaca plumbum | funda iacit; volat illud et incandescit eundo, | et quos non habuit sub nubibus invenit ignis.*[379]
- Ov. *Met.* 14.824–826: *corpus mortale per auras | dilapsum tenues, ceu lata plumbea funda | missa solet medio glans intabescere caelo.*[380]
- Stat. *Theb.* 10.531–536: *at Tyrii, quae sola salus, caput omne coronant | murorum, nigrasque sudes et lucida ferro | spicula et arsuras caeli per inania glandes | saxaque in adversos ipsis avolsa rotabant | moenibus: exundant saevo fastigia nimbo | armataeque vomunt stridentia tela fenestrae.*[381]

The same remark is also made in Onasander's *Strategikos* (19.3): ἡ δὲ τῆς σφενδόνης ἄμυνα χαλεπωτάτη τῶν ἐν τοῖς ψιλοῖς ἐστιν· ὅ τε γὰρ μόλιβδος ὁμόχρους ὢν τῷ ἀέρι λανθάνει φερόμενος, ὥστ' ἀπροοράτως ἀφυλάκτοις τοῖς τῶν πολεμίων ἐμπίπτειν σώμασιν, αὐτῆς τε τῆς ἐμπτώσεως σφοδρᾶς οὔσης καὶ ὑπὸ τοῦ ῥοίζου τριβόμενον τῷ ἀέρι τὸ βέλος ἐκπυρωθὲν ὡς βαθυτάτω δύεται τῆς σαρκός, ὥστε μηδ' ὁρᾶσθαι, ταχὺ δὲ καὶ τὸν ὄγκον ἐπιμύειν.[382] No such observation has been made by experimenting with lead bullets and it remains unconfirmed whether or not air flight could cause so much friction as to heat the lead to its melting point. Perhaps this notion was originally formed because of bullets that had been heated in advance.[383] See for example Caes. *BGall.* 5.43.1–2: *Septimo oppugnationis die maximo coorto vento ferventes fusili ex argilla glandes fundis et fervefacta iacula in casas, quae more Gallico stramentis erant tectae, iacere coeperunt. Hae celeriter ignem comprehenderunt et venti magnitudine in omnem locum castrorum distulerunt.*[384]

2. Stealth: Invisibility of Incoming Sling Bullets

Another characteristic of sling bullets that made them fairly frightening in battle was being invisible in flight. Onasander (as above) attributes this to the color of the lead, which merges with the color of the sky.

This characteristic has also been poetically exploited in Latin poetry:

- Val. Flacc. 6.192–194: *Dipsanta Caresus | Strymonaque obscura spargentem vulnera funda | deicit.*[385]
- Sil. 1.314–318: *hic crebram fundit Baliari verbere glandem | terque levi ducta circum caput altus habena | permissum ventis abscondit in aere telum, | hic valido librat stridentia saxa lacerto, | huic impulsa levi torquetur lancea nodo.*[386]

3. It's Raining Bullets: Slinging as a Meteorological Phenomenon

A few hundred slingers, or archers, shooting at the same time, certainly made an impression in battle. Not unexpectedly, sling bullets are often compared to hail and rain in literary sources.[387] Similes of rain almost always correspond to a massive pouring of bullets, usually compared to a storm.

- Hom. *Il.* 12.278–289: ὣς τώ γε προβοῶντε μάχην ὄτρυνον Ἀχαιῶν. | τῶν δ', ὥς τε νιφάδες χιόνος πίπτωσι θαμειαὶ | ἤματι χειμερίῳ, ὅτε τ' ὤρετο μητίετα Ζεὺς | νιφέμεν ἀνθρώποισι πιφαυσκόμενος τὰ ἃ κῆλα· | κοιμήσας δ' ἀνέμους χέει ἔμπεδον, ὄφρα καλύψῃ | ὑψηλῶν ὀρέων κορυφὰς καὶ πρώονας ἄκρους | καὶ πεδία λωτοῦντα καὶ ἀνδρῶν πίονα ἔργα, | καί τ' ἐφ' ἁλὸς πολιῆς κέχυται λιμέσιν τε καὶ ἀκταῖς, | κῦμα δέ μιν προσπλάζον ἐρύκεται· ἄλλά τε πάντα | εἴλυται καθύπερθ', ὅτ' ἐπιβρίσῃ Διὸς ὄμβρος· | ὣς τῶν ἀμφοτέρωσε λίθοι πωτῶντο θαμειαί, | αἱ μὲν ἄρ' ἐς Τρῶας, αἱ δ' ἐκ Τρώων ἐς Ἀχαιούς, | βαλλομένων· τὸ δὲ τεῖχος ὕπερ πᾶν δοῦπος ὀρώρει.[388]
- Livy 36.18.5: *Macedones pro vallo locati primo facile sustinebant Romanos, temptantes ab omni parte aditus, multum adiuvantibus, qui ex loco superiore fundis velut nimbum glandes et sagittas simul ac iacula ingerebant.*[389]
- Livy 37.41.9–10: . . . *et ex omnibus simul partibus tela ingerere; haec velut procella partim vulneribus missilium undique coniectorum partim clamoribus dissonis ita consternavit equos, ut repente velut effrenati passim incerto cursu ferrentur.*[390]
- Stat. *Theb.* 8.416–418: *stridentia funda | saxa pluunt, volucres imitantur fulgura glandes | et formidandae non una morte sagittae.*[391]
- Stat. *Theb.* 10.541–543: *non ora virum, non pectora flectit | imber atrox, rectosque tenent in moenia voltus | immemores leti et tantum sua tela videntes.*[392]
- *Historia Alexandri Magni* (Recensio β) 2.16: οἱ μὲν λίθους ἔβαλλον, οἱ δὲ τόξα ἔπεμπον ὡς ὄμβρον ἀπὸ οὐρανοῦ φερόμενον, <οἱ δὲ ζιβύνας ἔβαλλον,> ἕτεροι δὲ βολίδας ἐσφενδόνιζον, ὥστε ἐπικαλύπτειν τὸ τῆς ἡμέρας φέγγος . . . γνοφερὸς δὲ ἦν ὁ ἀὴρ καὶ αἱματώδης.[393]
- Sid. Apoll. *Carm.* XXIII.342–347: *non sic fulminis impetus trisulci, | non pulsa Scythico sagitta nervo, | non sulcus rapide cadentis astri, | non fundis Balearibus rotate | umquam sic liquidos poli meatus | rupit plumbea glandium procella.*[394]

Interestingly, the name of a launching machine, possibly also using sling bullets as missiles (see n. 45, and cf. n. 164), was καταπέλτης,[395] similar to the adjective καταπαλτός/-ή, -όν.[396]

Less often, but more aptly, bullets are compared to hail.

- Ar. *Nub.* 1124–1127: (Chorus of Clouds speaking) ἡνίκ' ἂν γὰρ αἵ τ' ἐλαῖαι βλαστάνωσ' αἵ τ' ἄμπελοι, | ἀποκεκόψονται· τοιαύταις σφενδόναις παιήσομεν. | ἢν δὲ πλινθεύοντ' ἴδωμεν, ὕσομεν καὶ τοῦ τέγους | τὸν κέραμον αὐτοῦ χαλάζαις στρογγύλαις συντρίψομεν.[397]
- Pacuvius *Paulus* fr. 3: *nivit sagittis, plumbo et saxis grandinat.*[398]

- Ov. *Met.* 9.216–225: *Dicentem genibusque manus adhibere parantem | corripit Alcides et terque quaterque rotatum | mittit in Euboicas tormento fortius undas. | Ille per aerias pendens indurvit auras, | utque ferunt imbres gelidis concrescere ventis, | inde nives fieri, nivibus quoque molle rotatis | adstringi et spissa glomerari grandine corpus: | sic illum validis iactum per inane lacertis | exsanguemque metu nec quicquam umoris habentem | in rigidos versum silices prior edidit aetas.*[399]
- Livy 28.37.7: … *tanta vis lapidum creberrimae grandinis modo in propinquantem iam terrae classem effusa est.*[400]

Although probably unrelated,[401] it is noteworthy that Zeus is the god who sends rain and hail to the earth,[402] and Zeus' thunderbolt is one of the most common devices on sling bullets.[403]

NOTES

1 See pp. 1146–1149, "Archaeological Context," and Chapter 29. The authors wish to thank Manthos Bessios, Athena Athanassiadou, and Konstantinos Noulas for the permit to study the material and for facilitating the actual study, Iordanis Poimenidis for constructing a sling for us and instructing us in its use, Vanessa Muros for treating unconserved bullets and performing the XRF analysis, photographers Jeff Vanderpool (photographs of all bullets) and Orestis Kourakis (photograph of ΜΕΘ 293), Fani Skyvalida for the drawings of ΜΕΘ 651 and ΜΕΘ 285, and the editors of this volume, Sarah Morris and John Papadopoulos, for their meticulous editing, as well as the anonymous reviewers for their emendations. Unless otherwise noted, all dimensions are expressed in meters (m); the weight (Wt.) is as preserved.

2 For which, see pp. 1144–1145, "Historical Context."

3 The reader may refer to the comparanda for each inscription in the "Commentary on the Inscriptions." For an overview of such finds in Thrace in relation to the Thracian campaigns of Philip II, see Nankov 2015, pp. 2–5.

4 The practice of reusing missiles is attested for arrows in Xenophon (*Anab.* 3.4.17) and Alkidamas (fr. 2, 31–34), as well as for javelins in Polybios (6.22), Livy (10.29.6), and Sallust (*Jug.* 58); thus, it is reasonable to assume it applied to sling bullets as well (Kelly 2012, p. 275). Fougères (1896b, p. 1611) also considers it probable that ammunition was reclaimed from the battlefield after the battle. See also Romero 2021, p. 212, for the discovery of a total of 1,189 sling bullets, which he presumes to have been collected and stocked by the Macedonians following the conquest of Argilos in a room interpreted as an armory.

5 To this argument may be added the case of natural stones and pebbles, which were widely used as sling bullets and presumably have escaped identification as such during excavation, assuming of course that they were in fact present.

6 *Olynthus* X, pp. 418–443. This is the largest as long as Romero 2015 remains unpublished; for a summary see Romero 2021.

7 Papakonstantinou-Diamantourou 1997.

8 Cambitoglou et al. 2001, pp. 723–726.

9 Kosmidou and Malamidou 2006, pp. 135–136.

10 See pp. 1142–1145, "On Slings, Slinging, and Slingers."

11 Voutiropoulos 1996; Adamidou 2008. For a full list of sling bullets from prehistoric sites around the Aegean, see Pritchett 1991b, pp. 39–43.

12 Voutiropoulos 1996, p. 68; Adamidou 2008, p. 59.

13 On the position of the slingers ideally in front of the phalanx, see Onasander 17.

14 Hom. *Il.* 13.712–722: οὐδ᾽ ἄρ᾽ Ὀϊλιάδῃ μεγαλήτορι Λοκροὶ ἕποντο· | οὐ γάρ σφι σταδίῃ ὑσμίνῃ μίμνε φίλον κῆρ· | οὐ γὰρ ἔχον κόρυθας χαλκήρεας ἱπποδασείας, | οὐδ᾽ ἔχον ἀσπίδας εὐκύκλους καὶ μείλινα δοῦρα, | ἀλλ᾽ ἄρα τόξοισιν καὶ ἐϋστρεφεῖ οἷος ἀώτῳ | Ἴλιον εἰς ἅμ᾽ ἕποντο πεποιθότες, οἷσιν ἔπειτα | ταρφέα βάλλοντες Τρώων ῥήγνυντο φάλαγγας· | δή ῥα τόθ᾽ οἳ μὲν πρόσθε σὺν ἔντεσι δαιδαλέοισι | μάρναντο Τρωσίν τε καὶ Ἕκτορι χαλκοκορυστῇ, | οἳ δ᾽ ὄπιθεν βάλλοντες ἐλάνθανον· οὐδέ τι χάρμης | Τρῶες μιμνήσκοντο· συνεκλόνεον γὰρ ὀϊστοί.

15 Archil. fr. 3, 1–5 (West) (text in n. 67).

16 In addition to the sources mentioned elsewhere in the text, see also Aesch. *Ag.* 1010; Pl. *Lach.* 193b; Verg. *Aen.* 9.586–589 (text in Appendix III.1); Luc. *VH* 16.

17 The latter of the Homeric references is perhaps less clear: Menelaus strikes Helenos' arm with his spear, and then "great-hearted Agenor pulled it out from the arm, and that he bound up with a band of well-twisted plucked wool, which his retainer was carrying for the herder of people" (*Il.* 13. 598–600: τὸ μὲν ἐκ χειρὸς ἔρυσεν μεγάθυμος Ἀγήνωρ, | αὐτὴν δὲ ξυνέδησεν ἐϋστρεφεῖ οἰὸς ἀώτῳ | σφενδόνῃ, ἣν ἄρα

οἱ θεράπων ἔχε ποιμένι λαῶν). Richard Janko (1994, p. 119) identifies in this instance the epic hapax σφενδόνη as the projectile weapon, although the term is absent from 13.716 (ἀλλ' ἄρα τόξοισιν καὶ ἐϋστρεφεῖ οἷος ἀώτῳ), pointing out other instances where a retainer carries a warrior's weapon (*Il.* 12.372: τοῖς δ' ἅμα Πανδίων Τεύκρου φέρε καμπύλα τόξα, and 13.709–711: ἀλλ' ἦτοι Τελαμωνιάδῃ πολλοί τε καὶ ἐσθλοὶ | λαοὶ ἕπονθ' ἕταροι, οἵ οἱ σάκος ἐξεδέχοντο | ὁππότε μιν κάματός τε καὶ ἱδρὼς γούναθ' ἵκοιτο).

18 Eust. *Comm. on Dionys. Per.* 7: Σφενδόνῃ δὲ τὴν οἰκουμένην εἰκάζει ὁ Διονύσιος ἢ τῷ λιθοβόλῳ ὀργάνῳ ἢ καὶ αὐτῇ τῇ σφενδόνῃ τοῦ δακτυλίου. Εἰ δέ τις ὀκνεῖ τοῦτο παραδέχεσθαι, ἀφαιρείσθω καὶ τῆς τοῦ δακτυλίου σφενδόνης καὶ τὸ ὄνομα. Ἔοικε γὰρ καὶ αὐτὴ τοιαύτη πάλαι ποτὲ οὖσα κατὰ τὸ ἀρχαῖον ἐφ' ἑκάτερα μὲν εὐρύνεσθαι, ἐπὶ θάτερα δὲ καθ' ὁμοιότητα τῆς ὁμωνύμου πετροβόλου σφενδόνης συνάγεσθαι εἰς ὀξύτερον. Οἱ δὲ παλαιοί [i.e., scholiasts] φασι καὶ κόσμον τινὰ γυναικεῖον σφενδόνην καλεῖσθαι, ὅμοιον τῇ τηλεβόλῳ σφενδόνῃ ὄντα, πλατὺν μὲν καὶ αὐτὸν τὰ μέσα καὶ πρὸς τῷ μετώπῳ πίπτοντα, ἐκ λεπτοτέρων δὲ καὶ ὀξυτέρων τῶν ἄκρων ὀπίσω δεσμούμενον. Ἦν δὲ, φασί, καὶ ὀπισθοσφενδόνη παρὰ τοῖς κωμικοῖς ἐκ τοῦ ἐναντίου τῇ τοιαύτῃ σφενδόνῃ, διὰ τὸ γελοιότερον περιτιθεμένη τῇ κεφαλῇ, καὶ ὀπίσω μὲν ἔχουσα τὰ πλατύτερα, τὰ δὲ ὀξύτερα καὶ τὸν δεσμὸν περὶ τὸ ἔμπροσθεν. See also Curt. 5.6.18 (on the customs of the Mardians, an Iranian tribe or ethnic group in the Elburz, a mountain range south of the Caspian Sea): *Ne feminis quidem pro naturae habitu molliora ingenia sunt: comae prominent hirtae, vestis super genua est, funda vinciunt frontem: hoc et ornamentum capitis et telum est.*

19 This is mostly emphasized in the case of the famed Balearic slingers, who trained from early childhood (see Diod. 5.18.4; Strabo 3.5.1; Lycoph. *Alex.* 637–641), and is also mentioned in regard to the Achaeans in Livy 38.29.3–4.

20 For the very few Roman detailed depictions, see Völling 1990, pp. 27–30.

21 See also Garlan 1970, pp. 625–630, for a possible depiction of a staff sling in the Archaic period, a type that is otherwise only known from the Roman era onward.

22 Livy 38.29.5–6: *et est non simplicis habenae, ut Baliarica aliarumque gentium funda, sed triplex scutale, crebris suturis duratum, ne fluxa habena volutetur in iactu glans, sed librata cum sederit, velut nervo missa excutiatur* (about the slingers from Aegium, Patrae and Dymae, ". . . the sling is not composed of a single strap, like those of the Baleares and other peoples, but the bullet-carrier is triple, strengthened with numerous seams, so that the missile may not fly out at random, from the pliancy of the strap at the moment of discharge, but, seated firmly while being whirled, may be shot out as if from a bowstring," transl. E. T. Saege, T. E. Page, E. Capps, and W. H. D. Rouse, London and Cambridge, Mass., 1936); cf. Lycoph. *Alex.* 636: τριπλαῖς δικώλοις σφενδόναις ὡπλισμένοι, along with *Scholia* in *Lycoph. Alex.* 636: τριπλαῖς· ἐκ γ΄ σχοινίων πεπλεγμένας ss³s⁴ ἔχοντες τὰς σφενδόνας ss³A N t.

23 Polyb. 27.11.5: δυεῖν κώλων ἀνίσων ὑπαρχόντων τῆς σφενδόνης, εἰς τὸ μέσον ἐνηγκυλίζετο τῶν κώλων εὐλύτως; Suda, s.v. κῶλα: τὰ τῆς σφενδόνης ἑκάτερα μέρη; *Scholia in Lycoph. Alex.* 636: . . . κῶλα δὲ λέγεται τὰ ἑκατέρωθεν τῆς σφενδόνης σπαρτία. ss³ δικώλοις· διπλαῖς πεφυκυίαις, μέσον ὅπου καὶ αἱ πέτραι τίθενται.

24 Hom. *Il.* 13.599–600 and 13.716, along with *Scholia in Hom. Il.* 13.599 (Erbse, vol. 3, p. 514): οἰὸς ἀώτῳ: ἐξ ἐρίων γὰρ πάλαι συνέπλεκον τὰ κῶλα τῆς σφενδόνης, οὐχ ὡς νῦν νεύροις, ἵνα διατείνοντο ἐν τῇ ἀπορρίψει. [. . .] b (BCE³E⁴) T νῦν δὲ τὸ τοῦ ἐρίου λεπτότερον καὶ καθαρώτερον, ὅθεν καὶ αἱ σφενδόναι ἐπλέκοντο. b (BCE³E⁴); Xen. *Anab.* 3.4.17: ηὑρίσκετο δὲ καὶ νεῦρα πολλὰ ἐν ταῖς κώμαις καὶ μόλυβδος, ὥστε χρῆσθαι εἰς τὰς σφενδόνας, along with 3.3.18: . . . σφενδόνας . . . πλέκειν . . . (see also Ma [2010a, p. 428, no. 2], who refutes Rihll's [2009, pp. 164–165] arguments against the use of sinews as structural part for slings); Strabo 3.5.1: (on the Baleares) σφενδόνας δὲ περὶ τῇ κεφαλῇ τρεῖς μελαγκρανίνας ἢ τριχίνας ἢ νευρίνας (μελαγκρανίς is identified with *Schoenus nigricans*, see Philet. 25.1; Fougères 1896a, p. 1363, n. 20); Veg. *Mil.* 3.14: *fundis lino vel saetis factis—has enim dicunt esse meliores*; *Anth. Pal.* 7.172, lines 3–4: ῥίνου (leather) χερμαστῆρος (sling) ἐΰστροφα κῶλα τιταίνων Ἀλκιμένης, πτανῶν εἶργον ἄπωθε νέφος. See also Ar. *Ach.* 178–185: ἐγὼ μὲν δεῦρό σοι σπονδὰς φέρων | ἔσπευδον· οἱ δ' ὤσφροντο πρεσβῦταί τινες | Ἀχαρνικοί, στιπτοὶ γέροντες πρίνινοι | ἀτεράμονες Μαραθωνομάχαι σφενδάμνινοι. | ἔπειτ'

ἀνέκραγον πάντες, ὦ μιαρώτατε | σπονδὰς φέρεις τῶν ἀμπέλων τετμημένων; | κἀς τοὺς τρίβωνας ξυνελέγοντο τῶν λίθων· | ἐγὼ δ' ἔφευγον· οἱ δ' ἐδίωκον κἀβόων, along with *Scholia in Ar. Ach.* 181b: (i) σφενδάμνινοι: ἰσχυροί· τοιοῦτον γὰρ τὸ τῆς σφενδάμνου ξύλον. ἀντὶ τοῦ σφενδονῆται. REΓLh vet (ii) ἄλλως: τὸ "σφενδάμνινοι" ταὐτόν ἐστι τῷ "πρίνινοι". σφένδαμνος γὰρ εἶδος ἰσχυροῦ ξύλου. ἔστι δὲ καὶ εἶδος καννάβεως ἡ σφένδαμνος· ἡ γὰρ σφενδόνη ἀπὸ καννάβεως γίνεται. EΓ = Suda, s.v. σφενδάμνινοι (κάνναβις is hemp, otherwise known as being widely used for making ropes); it cannot be verified whether this particular name was also applied to a species of hemp, or the scholiast is employing a false etymology; however, cf. Verg. *Georg.* 1.309: *stuppea torquentem Balearis verbera fundae* ("swinging the hempen cords of the Balearic sling"). Fougères (1896a, p. 1363, n. 21) also notes a possible case of cords made of metal chains. For some ethnographical comparanda, see Skov 2011, p. 114.

25 Pollux 1.175: ἐρεῖς δὲ τὰς σφενδόνας πληρώσασθαι, τὰς σφενδόνας στρέψαι, τὰς σφενδόνας ἐναγκυλίσασθαι.

26 [Arist.] *Mech.* 852a–b: διὰ τί πορρωτέρω τὰ βέλη φέρεται ἀπὸ τῆς σφενδόνης ἢ ἀπὸ τῆς χειρός; καίτοι κρατεῖ γε ὁ βάλλων τῇ χειρὶ μᾶλλον ἢ ἀπαρτήσας τὸ βάρος. καὶ ἔτι οὕτω μὲν δύο βάρη κινεῖ, τό τε τῆς σφενδόνης καὶ τὸ βέλος, ἐκείνως δὲ τὸ βέλος μόνον. πότερον ὅτι ἐν μὲν τῇ σφενδόνῃ κινούμενον τὸ βέλος ῥίπτει ὁ βάλλων (περιαγαγὼν γὰρ κύκλῳ πολλάκις ἀφίησιν), ἐκ δὲ τῆς χειρὸς ἀπὸ τῆς ἠρεμίας ἡ ἀρχή· πάντα δὲ εὐκινητότερα κινούμενα ἢ ἠρεμοῦντα. ἢ διά τε τοῦτο, καὶ διότι ἐν μὲν τῷ σφενδονᾶν ἡ μὲν χεὶρ γίνεται κέντρον, ἡ δὲ σφενδόνη ἡ ἐκ τοῦ κέντρου· ὅσῳ ἂν ᾖ μείζων ἡ ἀπὸ τοῦ κέντρου, κινεῖται θᾶττον. ἡ δὲ ἀπὸ τῆς χειρὸς βολὴ πρὸς τὴν σφενδόνην βραχεῖα ἐστίν.

27 See Diessl 1979, pp. 7–8; Skobelev 2009.

28 Lycoph. *Alex.* 633–636: οἱ δ' ἀμφικλύστους χοιράδας Γυμνησίας | σισυρνοδῦται καρκίνοι πεπλωκότες | ἄχλαινον ἀμπρεύσουσι νήλιποι βίον, | τριπλαῖς δικώλοις σφενδόναις ὡπλισμένοι, along with *Scholia* in *Lycoph. Alex.* 636: τριπλαῖς· γ΄ γὰρ σφενδόνας εἶχον s^3 μίαν περὶ τὴν κεφαλὴν καὶ μίαν περὶ τὸν ὦμον καὶ ἄλλην περὶ τὴν γαστέρα ss^3 A N t; Diod. Sic. 5.18.3: ὁπλισμὸς δ' ἐστὶν αὐτοῖς τρεῖς σφενδόναι, καὶ τούτων μίαν μὲν περὶ τὴν κεφαλὴν ἔχουσιν, ἄλλην δὲ περὶ τὴν γαστέρα, τρίτην δ' ἐν ταῖς χερσί; Strabo 3.5.1: σφενδόνας δὲ περὶ τῇ κεφαλῇ τρεῖς . . . τὴν μὲν μακρόκωλον πρὸς τὰς μακροβολίας, τὴν δὲ βραχύκωλον πρὸς τὰς ἐν βραχεῖ βολάς, τὴν δὲ μέσην πρὸς τὰς μέσας.

29 See, for instance, Onasander 17: (the slingers positioned in the middle of the phalanx) οὐδὲ μὴν οἱ σφενδονῆται κυκλόσε τὸν δῖνον ἀποτελεῖν τῆς σφενδόνης παρὰ πλευρὰν ἑστώτων φιλίων ὁπλιτῶν καὶ πρὸς τὸν ῥόμβον ἀντιπταιόντων; Veg. *Mil.* 2.23.9: *Adsuescendum est etiam, ut semel tantum funda circa caput rotetur, cum ex ea emittitur saxum* (advice to the slingers to swing once instead of three times); Richardson 1998a, p. 45.

30 Richardson (1998a, p. 45) is probably wrong to assume that the main difference in this technique was in the starting point and direction of swinging; slinging trials have convinced us that the raised-arms technique aimed to shorten the swings to only a half-swing, and since it is impossible for a person of average height to use a long sling in this way, this means that range was not intended.

31 The accuracy of a (trained) slinger is evident from the use of the sling for hunting birds; see Martha 1889, p. 400, no. 10, and p. 399, fig. 272: wall-painting in a tomb in Tarquinia, ca. 510 B.C.; Brélaz 2007, p. 76; cf. Ar. *Av.* 1186–1188 (army of birds hunting winged Iris); one could add to these the proverbial saying "to kill two birds with one stone." On the accuracy of Achaean slingers, see Livy 38.29.5 and 38.29.7; and Suda, s.v. Ἀχαΐα καὶ ἐπὶ τῶν εὐστόχως βαλλόντων, παρ' ὅσον πάντων ἐπιτηδειότατόν ἐστι τὸ τοιοῦτον βέλος πρὸς πολιορκίαν, τὸ τῶν ἐξ Ἀχαΐας σφενδονητῶν βέλος (the term βέλος here stands for any missile; LSJ, s.v. βέλος); the ethnic Ἀχαιός along with the personal name Δαμοκλῆς on a sling bullet (Weiss and Draskowski 2010, pp. 132–133) could, perhaps, be a reference to Damokles' expertise (for interpretations of names in the nominative, see pp. 1152–1159, "Commentary on the Inscriptions").

32 See esp. Archil. fr. 3, 1–2 (West): θαμειαὶ | σφενδόναι; also, Philo *On Sieges* 101/D66 (Whitehead 2016): βάλλοντες καὶ οἱ λιθοβόλοι καὶ οἱ τοξόται καὶ οἱ σφενδονῆται ὡς πλεῖστοι καὶ ἄριστοι. See further Appendix III.3.

33 Diod. 5.18.3, 13.54.7, and 20.54.4–5; Livy 38.29.8; App. *Mith.* 32.33; Veg. *Mil.* 1.16; Tac. *Ann.* 13.39; *Historia Alexandri Magni*, lines 2221–2228; Sall. *Jug.* 57 and 94; see also Gracia Alonso 2000, pp. 138–148; and Echols 1950, p. 229; Pritchett 1991b, pp. 57–58; Paunov and Dimitrov 2000, p. 46.

34 Xen. *Cyr.* 3.3.60; Onasander 17–20; Sall. *Jug.* 57 and 94; Brélaz and Ducrey 2003, pp. 111–112. Before the development of the phalanx, in open terrain battles, slingers would also operate behind the cover of hoplites, as in Appendix II.4 and 10, and Hom. *Il.* 13.721: οἳ δ᾽ ὄπιθεν βάλλοντες ἐλάνθανον; cf. Tyrtaeus fr. 11 (West), 35–38, who advises the light-armed soldiers to throw stones and javelins while protected behind the shields of the heavily armed (ὑμεῖς δ', ὦ γυμνῆτες, ὑπ' ἀσπίδος ἄλλοθεν ἄλλος | πτώσσοντες μεγάλοις βάλλετε χερμαδίοις | δούρασί τε ξεστοῖσιν ἀκοντίζοντες ἐς αὐτούς, | τοῖσι πανόπλοισιν πλησίον ἱστάμενοι).

35 Thuc. 2.81.8: ἄπωθεν δὲ σφενδονώντων καὶ ἐς ἀπορίαν καθιστάντων· οὐ γὰρ ἦν ἄνευ ὅπλων κινηθῆναι. δοκοῦσι δὲ οἱ Ἀκαρνᾶνες κράτιστοι εἶναι τοῦτο ποιεῖν; Eur. *Phoen.* 1141–1143: καὶ πρῶτα μὲν τόξοισι καὶ μεσαγκύλοις ἐμαρνάμεσθα σφενδόναις θ᾽ ἑκηβόλοις πέτρων τ᾽ ἀραγμοῖς; Xen. *Anab.* 3.4.16: μακρότερον οἵ τε Ῥόδιοι τῶν Περσῶν ἐσφενδόνων καὶ† τῶν τοξοτῶν; Strabo 8.3.33: ἀπαντησάντων δὲ τῶν Ἐπειῶν μεθ᾽ ὅπλων, ἐπειδὴ ἀντίπαλοι ἦσαν αἱ δυνάμεις, εἰς μονομαχίαν προελθεῖν κατὰ ἔθος τι παλαιὸν τῶν Ἑλλήνων Πυραίχμην Αἰτωλὸν Δέγμενόν τ᾽ Ἐπειόν, τὸν μὲν Δέγμενον μετὰ τόξου ψιλόν, ὡς περιεσόμενον ῥᾳδίως ὁπλίτου διὰ τῆς ἑκηβολίας, τὸν δὲ μετὰ σφενδόνης καὶ πήρας λίθων, ἐπειδὴ κατέμαθε τὸν δόλον· τυχεῖν δὲ νεωστὶ ὑπὸ τῶν Αἰτωλῶν εὑρημένον τὸ τῆς σφενδόνης εἶδος· μακροβολωτέρας δ᾽ οὔσης τῆς σφενδόνης πεσεῖν τὸν Δέγμενον, καὶ κατασχεῖν τοὺς Αἰτωλοὺς τὴν γῆν ἐκβαλόντας τοὺς Ἐπειούς; Arr. *Tact.* 15: ὠφέλιμοι δ᾽ ἐν μάχῃ τοξόται τε καὶ ἀκοντισταὶ καὶ σφενδονῆται καὶ πάντες ὅσοι ἑκηβόλοις ὅπλοις διαχρῶνται πολλαχῇ· καὶ γὰρ ὅπλα συντρῖψαι τῶν πολεμίων ἱκανοί, μάλιστα δὲ οἱ τοῖς λίθοις ἀκροβολιζόμενοι, καὶ τραύματα ἐκ μακροῦ ἐμβαλεῖν, εἰ δὲ βιαιοτέρα πληγὴ γένοιτο, καὶ κατακτανεῖν. χρήσιμοι δ᾽ ἐκκαλέσασθαι ἐκ χωρίου ὀχυροῦ πολεμίους τῷ διὰ μακροῦ τὰ βέλη ἀφιέντες ἐλπίδα παρέχειν ὅτι ἐπιόντας οὐκ ἂν δέξαιντο. χρήσιμοι δὲ καὶ φάλαγγα τεταγμένην διαλῦσαι καὶ ἵππον ἐπιφερομένην ἀναστεῖλαι καὶ χωρία ὑπερδέξια καταλαβέσθαι τῷ τε ταχεῖς εἶναι διὰ κουφότητα καὶ τῷ, εἰ καταλάβοιεν, τῇ συνεχείᾳ τοῦ ἀκροβολισμοῦ μηδένα πελάσαι αὐτοῖς ἄνευ πολλῶν τραυμάτων. χρήσιμοι δὲ καὶ ἀποκρούσασθαι ἀπὸ χωρίου τοὺς κατειληφότας, οὐχ ὑπομένοντας τὰ τραύματα, ἐπιτήδειοι δὲ καὶ τὰ ὕποπτα χωρία διερευνήσασθαι, ὠφέλιμοι δὲ καὶ ἐς ἐνέδραν ἐγκαθέζεσθαι, ἑνί τε λόγῳ καὶ προαγωνίσασθαι τῶν πεζῶν ἀγαθοὶ καὶ συναγωνίσασθαι ὠφέλιμοι καὶ ἐπιμαχόμενοι ἱκανοὶ τελέαν τὴν ἧσσαν τοῖς πρὸς τῶν πεζῶν τραπεῖσι βαρβάροις καταστῆσαι; Cassius Dio 49.26.2: οἱ γὰρ σφενδονῆται πολλοί τε ὄντες καὶ μακροτέραν τῶν τόξων ἱέντες πάντα καὶ τὸν κατάφρακτον ἰσχυρῶς ἐλυμαίνοντο.

36 Skov 2011, p. 115: "there has been wild disagreement among researchers and enthusiasts alike. Those expressing high-end estimates tend to cite historical evidence, ethnographic evidence and personal experience, while low-end estimates are usually the result of controlled experimentation."

37 On range, see Fougères 1896a, p. 1366; Korfmann 1973, p. 37; Foster 1978, p. 13; Richardson 1998a, p. 46; Brown Vega and Craig 2009 (with a review of earlier results and estimates). On the ballistics of slinging, see Baatz 1990; Skov 2011, p. 115–121; and also Diessl 1979, pp. 11–19; Richardson 1998a, 1998b; Dohrenwend 2002; Borrini, Marchiaro, and Mannucci 2012, pp. 34–38.

38 E.g., Xen. *Anab.* 3.3.16–17: χειροπληθέσι τοῖς λίθοις σφενδονᾶν; Dion. Hal. *Ant. Rom.* 9.63.4: οὔτε βελῶν ὑπὸ τοξοτῶν οὔτε χερμάδων ἀπὸ σφενδόνης.

39 This was a small leather bag (the nomenclature varies among πήρα, ἄγγος, διφθέρα, and κώρυκος) which held the ammunition of slingers and stone-throwers. It is occasionally illustrated (Appendix II.6, 12, 14, and 16; Garlan 1970, pp. 625–630: staff slinger(?) with pouch; Fougères 1896a, p. 1365 and fig. 3328), and also attested in literary sources: Xen. *Anab.* 5.2.12: ὁ δὲ τοῖς πελτασταῖς πᾶσι παρήγγειλε διηγκυλωμένους ἰέναι, ὡς, ὁπόταν σημήνῃ, ἀκοντίζειν, καὶ τοὺς τοξότας ἐπιβεβλῆσθαι ἐπὶ ταῖς νευραῖς, ὡς, ὁπόταν σημήνῃ, τοξεύειν δεῆσον, καὶ τοὺς γυμνῆτας λίθων ἔχειν μεστὰς τὰς διφθέρας· καὶ τοὺς ἐπιτηδείους ἔπεμψε τούτων ἐπιμεληθῆναι; Diod. 3.49.4: ὁ δ᾽ ὁπλισμὸς αὐτῶν (sc. τῶν Λιβύων) ἐστιν οἰκεῖος

τῆς τε χώρας καὶ τῶν ἐπιτηδευμάτων· κοῦφοι γὰρ ὄντες τοῖς σώμασι καὶ χώραν οἰκοῦντες κατὰ τὸ πλεῖστον πεδιάδα, πρὸς τοὺς κινδύνους ὁρμῶσι λόγχας ἔχοντες τρεῖς καὶ λίθους ἐν ἄγγεσι σκυτίνοις; Strabo 8.3.33: τὸν δὲ μετὰ σφενδόνης καὶ πήρας λίθων; Menander *Colax* 29 (Austin, *CGFP* 163): [ὁ διμοιρίτης] φέρων αὐτός ποτε | [ ]ον, πήραν, κράνος | [ ]ον, διβολίαν, κώιδιον | [δυστ]υχὴς ὄνος φέρει | [ἐξ]αίφνης Βίας.

40 The reportedly "bronze" bullet from Korkyra (BM 1868/0110.61.a; *IG* IX.1 836; its material described as *Erz*, i.e., ore, by Vischer 1878a, no. 4) is actually lead (Zangemeister 1885, p. 13; Fougères 1896b, p. 1609, n. 12).

41 Caes. *BGall.* 5.43.1 (text in Appendix III.1).

42 The term used in antiquity for a lead sling bullet was μολυβδίς (Xen. *Anab.* 3.3.17; Pl. *Rep.* 519b; Arist. *Cael.* 289a; *IG* II^2 1488; Polyb. 27.11.6–7; Plut. *Ant.* 41.5; Plut. *Non posse* 1107c), which also describes large lead weights (Luc. *Anach.* 27. 8–10). The same is the case with the term μολύβδαινα/-αίνη (App. *Mith.* 33; App. *BCiv.* 5.4.36; Anonymus Lexicographus, *Συναγωγὴ λέξεων χρησίμων* (Versio antiqua), s.v. *μολύβδαινα· μολυβδίδα*, also in Photios, *Lexicon*, s.v.; Lexica Segueriana, s.v.; and Suda, s.v.; see also App. *Mith.* 34: ἐπυργομάχουν πρὸς ἀλλήλους, ἑκατέρωθεν πυκνὰ καὶ θαμινὰ πάντα ἀφιέντες, ἕως ὁ Σύλλας ἐκ καταπελτῶν, ἀνὰ εἴκοσιν ὁμοῦ μολυβδαίνας βαρυτάτας ἀφιέντων), which first appears in the Roman period and also describes many other lead objects (e.g., fishing sinker, metal weight for training, loomweight; see LSJ, s.v.). The term βολίς is also used to denote missiles hurled with slings (Curt. 2.16: ἕτεροι δὲ βολίδας ἐσφενδόνιζον = Id. (Recensio byzantina poetica (cod. Marcianus 408)) line 3622: κατεσφενδόνιζον βολίδας), but it is most likely a generic term, not necessarily corresponding to sling bullets (*Scholia in Hom. Il.* 24.80a (Erbse, vol. 5, p. 535): ex. ἡ δὲ μολυβδαίνῃ ἰκέλη: τῷ μολίβδῳ, ὃ πρὸς τῇ ὁρμιᾷ καὶ τῷ ἀγκίστρῳ ἐστὶ πρὸς τὸ θᾶττον καθικνεῖσθαι τοῦ βυθοῦ. (BC E3E4)T οἱ δὲ τὴν βολίδα. ἢ „μόλιβον" δέ φησιν (sc. Λ 237) ἢ μόλυβδον. T). See also App. *Mith.* 31 (cf. 35): δύο δ' ἐκ τοῦ Πειραιῶς Ἀττικοὶ θεράποντες . . . πεσσοῖς ἐκ μολύβδου πεποιημένοις ἐγγράφοντες αἰεὶ τὸ γιγνόμενον ἐς τοὺς Ῥωμαίους ἠφίεσαν ἀπὸ σφενδόνης; since elsewhere in the same narrative the missiles are called μολύβδαιναι, here πεσσός (from πίπτω, drop) is probably used for a makeshift lead object, perhaps a thick sheet of lead inscribed, folded, and thrown with a sling just to convey a message over the wall to the enemy's camp. The Latin term *glans*, i.e., acorn, recalls a particular form that was given to bullets in the Roman era.

43 Diod. 19.109.1–2: τοὺς σφενδονήτας τοὺς ἐκ τῶν Βαλιαρίδων νήσων, [. . .]· οἱ γὰρ ἄνδρες οὗτοι μναιαίους λίθους βάλλειν; cf. Xen. *Anab.* 3.3.16–17: χειροπληθέσι τοῖς λίθοις σφενδονᾶν.

44 Diod. 14.42.1: καὶ γὰρ τὸ καταπελτικὸν εὑρέθη κατὰ τοῦτον τὸν καιρὸν ἐν Συρακούσαις (referring to the year 399 B.C.).

45 Rihll 2009, pp. 160–163, with additional arguments on pp. 163–167. *Contra*: Ma 2010a; Campbell 2011, pp. 692–698. The lead bullets used with a catapult in App. *Mith.* 7.34 are referred to as "heaviest" (μολυβδαίνας βαρυτάτας) and presumably belong to a different type, if they are identical to regular sling bullets at all. Richardson (1998a, pp. 46–47, based on Salazar 1998, p. 178: "variety of missiles . . . that they would have sufficient impact to penetrate skin and connective tissue, with effects similar to long-range gunshot wounds," who in turn draws on Paul. Aeg. 6.88.9), made an admittedly interesting suggestion that they may have been designed to be used as grapeshot, which would produce a "shotgun effect."

46 Voutiropoulos 1996, p. 65.

47 Dikaios 1969, p. 279, inv. no. 626: ellipsoid, L. 0.038 m.

48 Dikaios 1969, p. 139, inv. no. 1225; p. 141 and p. 296, inv. no. 1296; p. 296, inv. nos. 1141 and 1200.

49 Evans 1928, pp. 344–345. On the fluctuation of weight and dimensions that proves nothing about the dating, see the section on "Typology."

50 Åström and Nicolaou 1980.

51 Åström and Nicolaou 1980, no. 4: Λιπ(όδωρος).

52 Colivicchi 2004, no. 204; Fiorini and Torelli 2007, pp. 88–89.

53 Fiorini and Torelli 2007, p. 91.

54 Zangemeister 1885, pp. 88–142; Fougères 1896b, p. 1609; Foss 1975, p. 27.

55 *Olynthus* X, pp. 423–424.

56 Mikulčić and Sokolovska 1991, p. 79 (*SEG* 46.803 and 47.895).

57 Paunov and Dimitrov 2000, p. 52.

58 Foss 1975; Weiss and Draskowski 2010, nos. 1–2.

59 For a graffito using the lunate sigma in the late 6th–early 5th century B.C., see Johnston 2010; see further Gorissen 1978; and below, n. 185. If the identification is correct, these bullets are the second earliest epigraphic attestation of the lunate sigma, and the earliest sling bullets, perhaps along with the bullets of Δρόμας the Ainian, which may be connected with the mercenary troops employed by Cyrus the Younger against Tissaphernes; see Weiss 1997, no. I.2 and p. 151.

60 On the price of lead in antiquity, see Treister 1996, pp. 250–251: about 2.5 drachmas per talent in the Classical period; Papadimitriou 2008, pp. 111–114: very low, and could be even lower if produced by the state.

61 On reusing missiles, see n. 4. On casting bullets during a siege, see Caes. *BAfr.* 20: *officinas ferrarias instruere, sagittas telaque ut fierent complura curare, glandis fundere, sudis comparare*... (Caesar established foundries within his camp to cast lead bullets and other missiles); and Bosman 1995, who identified bullets made on the spot in the last phases of a siege by their distribution on the battlefield and their shape, which betrayed that they were being cast in depressions made in soil by a stick (Type II) or finger (Type I).

62 Diod. 19.109.1–2; Arr. *Tact.* 15.1–2; Veg. *Mil.* 1.16. On bullets penetrating the human body, see n. 140. Ferdinard Moog (2002) makes a negative assessment of the effectiveness of sling bullets in causing fatal wounds, based on the absence of relevant evidence in paleopathology and on the few and sporadic references to such injuries in ancient medical authors, and overemphasizes inscriptions addressed to the enemy (see Type 3a, pp. 1153–1155) and devices depicting stinging animals, completely neglecting to refer to the majority of inscriptions and devices that do not support his argument. First, only a comparative list of injuries made by different types of weaponry would be a suitable basis for such a conclusion; second, all references in ancient sources establish that sling bullets mostly caused damage to the soft tissues, thus any ex silentio paleopathological argument pointing out the lack of bone traumas by bullets is nugatory; and third, see the "Commentary on the Inscriptions" about the meaning and function of inscriptions and devices.

63 See, for instance, Hdt. 7.158.4; Thuc. 4.100.1, 6.22, 6.25, 6.43, and 7.31.5; Pl. *Crit.* 119b; Pl. *Laws* 8.834a; Arr. *Tact.* 15.1–2; Aristid. *Orat.* 26 (Jebb p. 346); Livy 42.58.9–10.

64 Thuc. 4.32.4: κατὰ νώτου τε αἰεὶ ἔμελλον αὐτοῖς, ᾗ χωρήσειαν, οἱ πολέμιοι ἔσεσθαι ψιλοὶ καὶ οἱ ἀπορώτατοι, τοξεύμασι καὶ ἀκοντίοις καὶ λίθοις καὶ σφενδόναις ἐκ πολλοῦ ἔχοντες ἀλκήν, οἷς μηδὲ ἐπελθεῖν οἷόν τε ἦν; Thuc. 6.69.2: καὶ πρῶτον μὲν αὐτῶν ἑκατέρων οἵ τε λιθοβόλοι καὶ σφενδονῆται καὶ τοξόται προυμάχοντο καὶ τροπὰς οἵας εἰκὸς ψιλοὺς ἀλλήλων ἐποίουν; Xen. *Hell.* 2.4.33: ἐκεῖ δὲ ἔτυχον ἐξοπλιζόμενοι οἵ τε πελτασταὶ πάντες καὶ οἱ ὁπλῖται τῶν ἐκ Πειραιῶς. καὶ οἱ μὲν ψιλοὶ εὐθὺς ἐκδραμόντες ἠκόντιζον, ἔβαλλον, ἐτόξευον, ἐσφενδόνων; Diod. 15.85.4: τῷ δὲ πλήθει καὶ τῇ παρασκευῇ τῶν ψιλῶν καὶ τῇ στρατηγικῇ συντάξει πολὺ τῶν ἐναντίων ἐλείποντο. αὐτοὶ μὲν οὖν ὀλίγους εἶχον ἀκοντιστάς, οἱ δὲ Θηβαῖοι τριπλασίους σφενδονήτας καὶ ἀκοντιστὰς τοὺς ἐκ τῶν περὶ τὴν Θετταλίαν τόπων ἀπεσταλμένους; Onasander 17.1 and 19.3: ἡ δὲ τῆς σφενδόνης ἄμυνα χαλεπωτάτη τῶν ἐν τοῖς ψιλοῖς ἐστίν; Arr. *Tact.* 3.2–3: τὸ δὲ ψιλὸν ἐναντιώτατα ἔχει τῷ ὁπλιτικῷ πάντα, ὅτιπερ ἄνευ θώρακος καὶ ἀσπίδος καὶ κνημῖδος καὶ κράνους ἐκηβόλοις ἐστὶν ὅπλοις διαχρώμενον, τοξεύμασιν ἢ ἀκοντίοις ἢ σφενδόναις ἢ λίθοις ἐκ χειρός (= Ael. *Tact.* 2.8); Ael. *Tact.* 4.3: καί, ἐάν τε διά τινας χρείας ὥστε ἐπὶ τριάκοντα δύο ἄνδρας γενέσθαι, ἢ συναιρῆται καὶ ἐπ' ὀκτὼ ἄνδρας βαθύνηται, οὐδὲν ἐμπόδιον γενήσεται τοῖς ὄπισθεν τασσομένοις ψιλοῖς· ἄν τε γὰρ ἀκοντίζωσιν ἢ σφενδόναις

χρῶνται ἢ τοξεύμασιν, εὐκόπως ὑπερθήσουσι ταῖς βολαῖς τὸ τῆς φάλαγγος βάθος; Dion. Hal. *Ant. Rom.* 8.65.2: ἐπεὶ δ' ἀγχοῦ ἐγένοντο ἀλλήλων ἔθεον ἀλαλάξαντες ὁμόσε, πρῶτον μὲν οἱ ψιλοὶ σαυνίων τε βολαῖς καὶ τοξεύμασι καὶ λίθοις ἀπὸ σφενδόνης μαχόμενοι, καὶ πολλὰ τραύματα ἔδοσαν ἀλλήλοις; Asclepiodotus *Tact.* 2.1: οὐδὲν γὰρ ἔμποδον ἔσται τοῖς ὄπισθεν μαχομένοις ψιλοῖς ἀκοντίζουσιν ἢ σφενδονῶσιν ἢ καὶ τοξεύουσιν; Hsch., s.v. ψιλούς· γυμνούς. σφενδονιστάς. τοξότας; Suda, s.v. ὁπλῖται· . . . μὲν γὰρ λέγονται οἱ βαρυτάτῃ κεχρημένοι καθοπλίσει . . . ψιλοὶ δὲ, οἳ κουφοτάτῃ· κέχρηνται γὰρ τόξῳ καὶ ἀκοντίοις καὶ λίθοις ἐκ σφενδόνης ἢ ἐκ χειρός. See also *SEG* 3.354; *SEG* 23.271, lines 25–26; *IG* VII 2714.

65 Thuc. 4.32.4: οἱ πολέμιοι ἔσεσθαι ψιλοὶ καὶ οἱ ἀπορώτατοι, τοξεύμασι καὶ ἀκοντίοις καὶ λίθοις καὶ σφενδόναις ἐκ πολλοῦ ἔχοντες ἀλκήν; Hsch., s.v. γυμνῆτες· οἱ μὴ ἔχοντες ὅπλα· οἱ δὲ τοὺς σφενδονητάς· οἱ δὲ τοὺς γυμνοὺς μαχομένους; Eur. *Phoen.* 1145–1147: ὦ τέκνα Δαναῶν, πρὶν κατεξάνθαι βολαῖς, | τί μέλλετ' ἄρδην πάντες ἐμπίπτειν πύλαις, | γυμνῆτες ἱππῆς ἁρμάτων τ' ἐπιστάται, along with *Scholia in Eur. Phoen.* 1147 (Dindorf 1863): γυμνῆτες, ἱππεῖς· φροντισταί. ἐπιστάται. Μ. ὄνομα στρατιωτῶν οὐ πανοπλίᾳ χρωμένων, ἀλλὰ τῇ σφενδόνῃ, πεζοί, οἱ σφενδονῆται, ἢ οἱ τοξόται. B.C.M.T.I.

66 Ar. *Arch.* 162–163: ὁ θρανίτης λεὼς | ὁ σωσίπολις; the term is also attested as a name of an old trireme in 377/6 B.C. (*IG* II² 1604, line 70; also *IG* II² 1607, line 47: 373/2 B.C.; *IG* II² 1611, line 95: 357/6 B.C.; *IG* II² 1612, line 17: 356/5 B.C.). On the naval successes gaining acknowledgment for the nautical mob, see Pl. *Laws* 707a–c; Arist. *Pol.* 1304a; Pritchard 2018. On Athenian oarsmen aiming to leech on the Athenian empire in order to preserve themselves, see Thuc. 6.24.3 and 8.76.4; and also Galpin 1984, pp. 107–108.

67 Xen. *Cyr.* 7.4.14–15: ἦγε δὲ καὶ Λυδῶν οὓς μὲν ἑώρα καλλωπιζομένους καὶ ὅπλοις καὶ ἵπποις καὶ ἅρμασι καὶ πάντα πειρωμένους ποιεῖν ὅ τι ᾤοντο αὐτῷ χαριεῖσθαι, τούτους μὲν σὺν τοῖς ὅπλοις· οὓς δὲ ἑώρα ἀχαρίτως ἑπομένους, τοὺς μὲν ἵππους αὐτῶν παρέδωκε Πέρσαις τοῖς πρώτοις συστρατευομένοις, τὰ δὲ ὅπλα κατέκαυσε· σφενδόνας δὲ καὶ τούτους ἠνάγκασεν ἔχοντας ἕπεσθαι. καὶ πάντας δὲ τοὺς ἀόπλους τῶν ὑποχειρίων γενομένων σφενδονᾶν ἠνάγκαζε μελετᾶν, νομίζων τοῦτο τὸ ὅπλον δουλικώτατον εἶναι· σὺν μὲν γὰρ ἄλλῃ δυνάμει μάλα ἔστιν ἔνθα ἰσχυρῶς ὠφελοῦσι σφενδονῆται παρόντες, αὐτοὶ δὲ καθ' αὑτοὺς οὐδ' ἂν οἱ πάντες σφενδονῆται μείνειαν πάνυ ὀλίγους ὁμόσε ἰόντας σὺν ὅπλοις ἀγχεμάχοις. On contrasting close combat weapons with projectiles, see Archil. fr. 3, 1–5 (West): οὔτοι πόλλ' ἐπὶ τόξα τανύσσεται, οὐδὲ θαμειαὶ | σφενδόναι, εὖτ' ἂν δὴ μῶλον Ἄρης συνάγῃ | ἐν πεδίωι· ξιφέων δὲ πολύστονον ἔσσεται ἔργον· | ταύτης γὰρ κεῖνοι δάμονές εἰσι μάχης | δεσπόται Εὐβοίης δουρικλυτοί; Eust. *Il.* 10.256 (van der Valk, vol. 3, p. 62): ὁ γὰρ Διομήδης ἴσως ἀπαξιοῖ τὸ ἐκηβόλον ὅπλον οἷα σταδαῖος ὁπλίτης καὶ ἀγχέμαχος, and Eust. *Il.* 3.82 (van der Valk, vol. 1, p. 611): ἔστι δ' ἐν τούτοις συναγαγεῖν ἐκ τοῦ «ἐπετοξάζοντο Ἀχαιοὶ καὶ ἰοῖσι λάεσσί τε ἔβαλλον», ὅτι καὶ τοξόταις πολλοῖς ἐχρῶντο καὶ σφενδονήταις, εἰ καὶ ὁ ποιητὴς οὐδεμίαν που ἐν αὐτοῖς ἀνδραγαθίαν ἐπισημαίνεται, ὅς γε καὶ τοξοτῶν ἀριστέων ὀλιγίστων τινῶν μέμνηται; Eunapius, *Vitae Sophistarum* 10.5.6: ὥσπερ οἱ τῶν βασιλέων ἔννομον καὶ ὀρθὴν μάχην νενικημένοι καὶ ἐν τοῖς ἀπόροις εἰς τὸ ἔσχατον συνελθόντες, ἐπὶ ψιλοὺς καὶ σφενδονήτας καὶ γυμνήτας καὶ τὸ εὐτελὲς ἐπικουρικὸν καταφεύγουσιν, οὐ ταῦτα τιμῶντες ἐξ ἀρχῆς, ὅμως δὲ δι' ἀνάγκην ταῦτα τιμῶντες. See also Brélaz and Ducrey 2007, pp. 342–347, for a general account. Regarding bows, see also Eur. *Her.* 159–161: ὃς οὔποτ' ἀσπίδ' ἔσχε πρὸς λαιᾶι χερὶ | οὐδ' ἦλθε λόγχης ἐγγὺς ἀλλὰ τόξ' ἔχων, | κάκιστον ὅπλον, τῆι φυγῆι πρόχειρος ἦν; Nilus Ancyranus, *Scr. Eccl. Epistulae* 3.198, line 5: αἰσχροβόλα τόξα.

68 See further Janko 1994, p. 119.

69 Four of these instances (Appendix II.7–9, and 15) concern bird-hunting (the Stymphalian birds), and in only one (Appendix II.11) is Herakles using a sling in battle, in a rather awkwardly composed scene, where the figure of Herakles seems copied from some other scene (perhaps Stymphalian bird hunting) or some model; however, as he is far more often depicted with a bow, another undervalued projectile weapon, the argument stands.

70 For archaeological finds confirming the use of projectiles even by heavy-armed aristocrats in the Geometric and Archaic period, see Wheeler 1987, pp. 164–173. Cf. Pl. *Laws* 794c: πρὸς δὲ τὰ μαθήματα

τρέπεσθαι χρεὼν ἑκατέρους, τοὺς μὲν ἄρρενας ἐφ' ἵππων διδασκάλους καὶ τόξων καὶ ἀκοντίων καὶ σφενδονήσεως, ἐὰν δέ πῃ συγχωρῶσιν, μέχρι γε μαθήσεως καὶ τὰ θήλεα, where the training of all children in both horse riding and the use of projectile weapons is somewhat unexpected, but it was, apparently, a regular training curriculum, as also attested by the ephebes law from Amphipolis (Lazaridou 2015), lines 56–58: παιδευ|έσθωσαν δὲ πρῶτον μὲν ἐπὶ τοῖς ἵπποις, ἔπειτα τοξεύειν καὶ ἀκον|τίζειν καὶ σφενδονᾶν καὶ λιθάζειν.

71 Dion. Hal. *Ant. Rom.* 7.59.5–6: πέμπτη δ' ἐκαλεῖτο συμμορία τῶν ὀλίγου πάνυ τετιμημένων ἀργυρίου, ὅπλα δ' ἦν αὐτῶν σαυνία καὶ σφενδόναι· οὗτοι τάξιν οὐκ εἶχον ἐν φάλαγγι, ἀλλὰ ψιλοὶ καὶ κοῦφοι συνεστρατεύοντο τοῖς ὁπλίταις εἰς τριάκοντα λόχους διῃρημένοι. οἱ δ' ἀπορώτατοι τῶν πολιτῶν οὐκ ἐλάττους τῶν ἄλλων ἁπάντων ὄντες ἔσχατοι τὴν ψῆφον ἀνελάμβανον, ἕνα μόνον ἔχοντες λόχον· οὗτοι στρατειῶν τ' ἦσαν ἐλεύθεροι τῶν ἐκ καταλόγου καὶ εἰσφορῶν τῶν κατὰ τιμήματα γινομένων ἀτελεῖς καὶ δι' ἄμφω ταῦτ' ἐν ταῖς ψηφοφορίαις ἀτιμότατοι, and 7.59.9: ἵνα μήθ' οἱ πένητες τῶν πλουσίων μειονεκτῶσι μήθ' οἱ ψιλοὶ τῶν ὁπλιτῶν ἀτιμοτέραν χώραν ἔχωσι. See also van Wees 1995; and Brélaz and Ducrey 2003, pp. 112–113, who point out that archers, javelin throwers, and slingers in the Athenian army were often foreign auxiliaries (p. 112), and that distinction was made garment-wise from the hoplites (p. 113), adding that they could also be poor Athenians (Pipili 2000, p. 164: *psiloi* wearing the pilos, a mark of their low class; see also Blatter 1964, who distinguishes between hoplites and *psiloi* by their headgear; see further the slingers wearing the pilos in Appendix II.13, 18, 20).

72 Plut. *Quaest. Graec.* 293a–b: 'τίνες οἱ ἀποσφενδόνητοι;' Κέρκυραν τὴν νῆσον Ἐρετριεῖς κατῴκουν· Χαρικράτους δὲ πλεύσαντος ἐκ Κορίνθου μετὰ δυνάμεως καὶ τῷ πολέμῳ κρατοῦντος, ἐμβάντες εἰς τὰς ναῦς οἱ Ἐρετριεῖς ἀπέπλευσαν οἴκαδε. προαισθόμενοι δ' οἱ πολῖται, τῆς χώρας εἶργον αὐτοὺς καὶ ἀποβαίνειν ἐκώλυον σφενδονῶντες. μὴ δυνάμενοι δὲ μήτε πεῖσαι μήτε βιάσασθαι πολλοὺς καὶ ἀπαραιτήτους ὄντας, ἐπὶ Θρᾴκης ἔπλευσαν καὶ κατασχόντες χωρίον, ἐν ᾧ πρότερον οἰκῆσαι Μέθωνα τὸν Ὀρφέως πρόγονον ἱστοροῦσι, τὴν μὲν πόλιν ὠνόμασαν Μεθώνην, ὑπὸ δὲ τῶν προσοίκων 'ἀποσφενδόνητοι' προσωνομάσθησαν; see also Chapter 2.

73 Plutarch's source for the story may have been Aristotle's now lost *Constitution of the Methonaians*, see Halliday 1928, p. 63. Hammond (1972, pp. 425–426) accepts it as the immediate source, but supposes an earlier original source, for which he later (Hammond 1998, p. 393, n. 3) suggests Hekataios' *Γῆς περίοδος* of the late 6th century B.C. Ephoros may be another candidate for Plutarch's source, as is demonstrated for a similar case in Strabo (see Wheeler 1987, pp. 175–178).

74 Hawkins 1847, p. 100: "frequent use in the [Israelite] prophecies of the expression to 'sling-out' a people, as a synonym for total extermination"; see also Plut. *Comm. Not.* 1062a: ὁ Λίχας, ὑπὸ τοῦ Ἡρακλέους ἀποσφενδονώμενος (Soph. *Trach.* 779–780: μάρψας ποδός νιν, ἄρθρον ᾗ λυγίζεται, | ῥιπτεῖ πρὸς ἀμφίκλυστον ἐκ πόντου πέτραν; Apollod. 2.7: τὸν μὲν Λίχαν τῶν ποδῶν ἀράμενος κατηκόντισεν ἀπὸ τῆς †Βοιωτίας); and cf. Ov. *Met.* 9.216–225 (text in Appendix III.3). In all the cases above, Lichas himself is slung, not shot at.

75 Diod. 16.34.5: καὶ μέχρι μέν τινος οἱ Μεθωναῖοι διεκαρτέρουν, ἔπειτα κατισχυόμενοι συνηναγκάσθησαν παραδοῦναι τὴν πόλιν τῷ βασιλεῖ ὥστε ἀπελθεῖν τοὺς πολίτας ἐκ τῆς Μεθώνης ἔχοντας ἓν ἱμάτιον ἕκαστον. Bruno Helly (2006) has suggested that the refugees from Methone passed to Thessaly and settled on the southwest coast of Mt Pelion, where they founded the Magnesian Methone; however, contemporary (but perhaps intentionally misleading) sources indicate that at least part of the population was enslaved: [Plut.] *X Orat.* 11, 850f–851a: Δημοχάρης Λάχητος Λευκονοεὺς αἰτεῖ Δημοσθένει τῷ Δημοσθένους Παιανιεῖ δωρεὰν εἰκόνα χαλκῆν ἐν ἀγορᾷ καὶ σίτησιν ἐν πρυτανείῳ καὶ προεδρίαν αὐτῷ καὶ ἐκγόνων ἀεὶ τῷ πρεσβυτάτῳ εὐεργέτῃ καὶ συμβούλῳ γεγονότι πολλῶν καὶ καλῶν τῷ δήμῳ τῷ Ἀθηναίων καὶ τήν τε οὐσίαν εἰς τὸ κοινὸν καθεικότι τὴν ἑαυτοῦ . . . [τριηραρχίες] . . . καὶ λυτρωσαμένῳ πολλοὺς τῶν ἁλόντων ἐν Πύδνῃ καὶ Μεθώνῃ καὶ Ὀλύνθῳ ὑπὸ Φιλίππου· καὶ χορηγίαν ἀνδράσιν ἐπιδόντι, ὅτε ἐκλιπόντων τῶν Πανδιονιδῶν τοῦ χορηγεῖν ἐπέδωκε καὶ καθώπλισε τοὺς πολίτας τῶν ἐλλειπόντων . . . ; cf. Dem. 18.268:

ἐν μὲν τοίνυν τοῖς πρὸς τὴν πόλιν τοιοῦτος· ἐν δὲ τοῖς ἰδίοις εἰ μὴ πάντες ἴσθ' ὅτι κοινὸς καὶ φιλάνθρωπος καὶ τοῖς δεομένοις ἐπαρκῶν, σιωπῶ καὶ οὐδὲν ἂν εἴποιμι οὐδὲ παρασχοίμην περὶ τούτων οὐδεμίαν μαρτυρίαν, οὔτ' εἴ τινας ἐκ τῶν πολεμίων ἐλυσάμην, οὔτ' εἴ τισιν θυγατέρας συνεξέδωκα, οὔτε τῶν τοιούτων οὐδέν; Dem. 8.70: ὦ ἄνδρες Ἀθηναῖοι, καὶ τριηραρχίας εἰπεῖν καὶ χορηγίας καὶ χρημάτων εἰσφορὰς καὶ λύσεις αἰχμαλώτων καὶ τοιαύτας ἄλλας φιλανθρωπίας; and also Dem. 19.40, 166, and 169–171; Aeschin. 2.100.

76 Kanatsoulis 1948, pp. 64–77; Borel 2007, pp. 105–111; Greenwalt 2015, 2017.

77 Diod. 16.31.6 and 16.34.4: Φίλιππος δ' ὁρῶν τοὺς Μεθωναίους ὁρμητήριον παρεχομένους τὴν πόλιν τοῖς πολεμίοις ἑαυτοῦ πολιορκίαν συνεστήσατο; Dem. 1.12–13: Φίλιππος τὸ πρῶτον Ἀμφίπολιν λαβών, μετὰ ταῦτα Πύδναν, πάλιν Ποτείδαιαν, Μεθώνην αὖθις, εἶτα Θετταλίας ἐπέβη; Dem. 9.26: Ὄλυνθον μὲν δὴ καὶ Μεθώνην καὶ Ἀπολλωνίαν καὶ δύο καὶ τριάκοντα πόλεις ἐπὶ Θρᾴκης ἐῶ. On Methone being an Athenian stronghold in the north Aegean, see Dem. 4.4–5: ὅτι εἴχομέν ποθ' ἡμεῖς, ὦ ἄνδρες Ἀθηναῖοι, Πύδναν καὶ Ποτείδαιαν καὶ Μεθώνην καὶ πάντα τὸν τόπον τοῦτον οἰκεῖον κύκλῳ, καὶ πολλὰ τῶν μετ' ἐκείνου νῦν ὄντων ἐθνῶν αὐτονομούμενα κἀλεύθερ' ὑπῆρχε, καὶ μᾶλλον ἡμῖν ἐβούλετ' ἔχειν οἰκείως ἢ 'κείνῳ. εἰ τοίνυν ὁ Φίλιππος τότε ταύτην ἔσχε τὴν γνώμην, ὡς χαλεπὸν πολεμεῖν ἐστιν Ἀθηναίοις ἔχουσι τοσαῦτ' ἐπιτειχίσματα τῆς αὐτοῦ χώρας ἔρημον ὄντα συμμάχων, οὐδὲν ἂν ὧν νυνὶ πεποίηκεν ἔπραξεν οὐδὲ τοσαύτην ἐκτήσατ' ἂν δύναμιν; and also Dem. 7.12: καίτοι πλείους γε ἦσαν αἱ ἐπιμειξίαι τότε πρὸς ἀλλήλους ἢ νῦν εἰσίν· ὑφ' ἡμῖν γὰρ ἦν ἡ Μακεδονία καὶ φόρους ἡμῖν ἔφερον, καὶ τοῖς ἐμπορίοις τότε μᾶλλον ἢ νῦν ἡμεῖς τε τοῖς ἐκεῖ κἀκεῖνοι τοῖς παρ' ἡμῖν ἐχρῶντο, καὶ ἐμπορικαὶ δίκαι οὐκ ἦσαν, ὥσπερ νῦν, ἀκριβεῖς, αἱ κατὰ μῆνα, ποιοῦσαι μηδὲν δεῖσθαι συμβόλων τοὺς τοσοῦτον ἀλλήλων ἀπέχοντας, in which it is unclear as to which period Demosthenes is referring: that of the Delian League or the Second Athenian Empire. The Macedonian king, more particularly, is presented as subject to the Athenians in Dem. 3.24 (the same claim repeated in Arr. *Anab.* 7.9.4: φόρους τελεῖν Ἀθηναίοις, 2nd century A.D.), but whether this is Perdikkas II, Amyntas III, or one of his sons remains unclear; on the possibility that Amyntas III was a member of the Second Athenian League, see Cargill 1981, pp. 85–87; and also Harding 2006, p. 232. On the Athenian inaction, see Diod. 16.34.5: . . . καὶ μέχρι μέν τινος οἱ Μεθωναῖοι διεκαρτέρουν; and also Dem. 1.9: καὶ πάλιν ἡνίκα Πύδνα, Ποτίδαια, Μεθώνη, Παγασαί, τἄλλα, ἵνα μὴ καθ' ἕκαστα λέγων διατρίβω, πολιορκούμεν' ἀπηγγέλλετο, εἰ τότε τούτων ἑνὶ τῷ πρώτῳ προθύμως καὶ ὡς προσῆκεν ἐβοηθήσαμεν αὐτοί, ῥᾴονι καὶ πολὺ ταπεινοτέρῳ νῦν ἂν ἐχρώμεθα τῷ Φιλίππῳ; Dem. 4.35: καίτοι τί δήποτ', ὦ ἄνδρες Ἀθηναῖοι, νομίζετε τὴν μὲν τῶν Παναθηναίων ἑορτὴν καὶ τὴν τῶν Διονυσίων ἀεὶ τοῦ καθήκοντος χρόνου γίγνεσθαι, ἄν τε δεινοὶ λάχωσιν ἄν τ' ἰδιῶται οἱ τούτων ἑκατέρων ἐπιμελούμενοι, εἰς ἃ τοσαῦτ' ἀναλίσκεται χρήματα, ὅσ' οὐδ' εἰς ἕνα τῶν ἀποστόλων, καὶ τοσοῦτον ὄχλον καὶ παρασκευὴν ὅσην οὐκ οἶδ' εἴ τι τῶν ἁπάντων ἔχει, τοὺς δ' ἀποστόλους πάντας ὑμῖν ὑστερίζειν τῶν καιρῶν, τὸν εἰς Μεθώνην, τὸν εἰς Παγασάς, τὸν εἰς Ποτίδαιαν;

78 Diod. 16.31.6: ἅμα δὲ τούτοις . . . (sc. defeat of Philomelos, leadership assumed by Onomarchos, 354 B.C.).

79 *IG* II² 130 (*SEG* 24.85, lines 8–12) = *IGLPalermo* 128, lines 8–12: . . . ἐπαινέ[σ|αι Σωχάρη]ν Χάρητος Ἀπολλωνιάτη[ν] | [. . . . 8 . . . .]ον ὅτι πρόθυμος ἦν ṭ[οῖς π|ολίταις ὑ]πηρετεῖν καὶ ἔπεμψ[εν . .]|[. . . 7 . . .]ον ἑαυτοῦ εἰς Μεθώνη[ν, . . .].

80 Buckler (1989, p. 176) discredits Diodoros' dates 353/2 (16.34.4) or 354/3 (16.31.6) B.C. for the beginning of the siege as wrong on the basis of this inscription. He infers that there was a voluntary and private venture to help Methone. On the debate over the date of the fall of Methone, see Buckler 1989, p. 177.

81 For a full chronology and the debate over the dates, see Buckler 1989, pp. 176–181.

82 See Chapter 29.

83 Lee 2001.

84 Polyainos *Strat.* 4.2.5: Φίλιππος τοῖς Μεθωναίων τείχεσι κλίμακας προσήγαγεν καὶ δι' αὐτῶν πολλοὺς Μακεδόνας ἀνεβίβασε πολιορκητάς. ἐπεὶ δὲ ἀνέβησαν ἐπὶ τὰ τείχη, ἀφεῖλε τὰς κλίμακας, ὅπως ἐλπίδα τοῦ καταβῆναι μὴ ἔχοντες προθυμότερον τῶν τειχῶν κρατήσειαν; also, *Anonyma Tactica Byzantina, Syllogae*

tacticorum 90.3: ὁ Φίλιππος πολεμῶν τὴν Μεθώνην καὶ ταύτην ἑλὼν ἤδη, ἐπεὶ τὴν πόλιν εἰσιόντες οἱ Μακεδόνες ὑπὸ τῶν ἐν τοῖς τείχεσιν ἱσταμένων πολεμίων κακῶς πάσχοντες ἐνδιδόναι ἤρξαντο, κλίμακας ἐξ ἑτέρων τῆς πόλεως ἐπιθεὶς μερῶν ἀναβαίνειν δι᾽ αὐτῶν τοῖς στρατιώταις ἐπέταξε. Πρὸς τοῦτο τῶν πολιτῶν ἀντιπερισπασθέντων καὶ πρὸς τὸν Φίλιππον συνδραμόντων εὐχερῶς Μεθώνη ἑάλω.

85 Bessios 2003; Bessios et al. 2004, pp. 367–373; Bessios, Athanassiadou, and Noulas 2008, pp. 241–245. See also Chapter 18.

86 Bessios, Athanassiadou, and Noulas 2008, p. 245; see Chapters 1 and 29; see also Appendix I.

87 Excavation Notebook 2004 (A. Athanassiadou), p. 7 (7/7/2006); Bessios, Athanassiadou, and Noulas 2008, p. 245; see also Chapter 1, Fig. 1.1, for the location of Plot 278.

88 Cf. an interior space by the walls filled with evidence for the hurried production of sling bullets during a siege in Populonia, Etruria (Coccolutto 2006).

89 Bessios, Athanassiadou, and Noulas 2008, p. 246, and 2021a, pp. 122–123.

90 We thank the excavators for notifying us of this find. For the discovery of a trench whence the Macedonian army probably collected the earth for the ramp, see Bessios et al. 2014, p. 229; Bessios, Athanassiadou, and Noulas 2021a, p. 123.

91 On ramps as a siege tactic to scale fortification walls, see Garlan 1974, pp. 142–143.

92 Bessios, Athanassiadou, and Noulas 2008, p. 246.

93 On tunneling operations by both sides, the besieged and the besiegers, as well as the use of javelins and hand-held mechanical artillery in the tunnels, see Philo *On Sieges* 99/D30–33 (Whitehead 2016).

94 Bessios et al. 2004, pp. 373–374.

95 Excavation Notebook 2004 (A. Athanassiadou), p. 48; Bessios et al. 2004, p. 374.

96 Gehrke 1985, pp. 237–245, esp. p. 241; Lee 2001, p. 19. See also Philo *On Sieges* 93/C23–27 (Whitehead 2016) on provisioning urban houses with projectile weaponry in anticipation of a siege, and especially C26 where it is provided that "at public expense a ten-mina stone-projector (λιθοβόλον δέκα μνῶν) and two three-span catapults (καταπάλτας δύο τρισπιθάμους) are to be issued to each *amphodon*" (LSJ, s.v. ἄμφοδον, block of houses).

97 Athanassiadou 2011, pp. 178–179; and Chapter 29.

98 Lee 2001; on p. 19, Lee notes that "the agora seems curiously devoid of missile finds," a fact that seems to support his reconstruction of events including guerrilla warfare in the neighborhoods of the city; the Olynthian agora, however, is not identified with certainty. The only residential area identified so far at Methone has not yet been explored, see Morris et al. 2020, pp. 671–672, fig. 13.

99 Lee 2001, p. 16.

100 Cahill 1991, pp. 164–165.

101 Wiseman 1963, p. 263. For mud-brick fortification walls in northern Greece, see Ouellet 2021.

102 Nankov 2004–2005, p. 171. The Athenian decree *IG* II^2 463, lines 52–74, of 307/6 B.C. was specifically concerned with the roofing of *parodoi* on curtain walls located in open and flat areas, such as the Kerameikos, which were more prone to damage caused by artillery attack (especially lines 52–53: καταστεγάσει δὲ κα[ὶ] τὴν πάροδον | [τοῦ κύκλ]ου τοῦ περὶ [τὸ ἄστυ ἄνευ το]ῦ διατειχί[σμ]α[τ]ος καὶ τοῦ ὑπὲρ τῶν πυλῶν, and lines 69–70: [κ]αὶ κεραμώσει Λακων[ι]κ[ῶ]ι κεράμωι τοῦ μὲν κύκλου πᾶσαν τὴν π[άρο]||[δ]ον; reconstructions in Caskey 1910; discussion in Maier 1959, pp. 48–67). On closed battlements and galleried curtains, see Lawrence 1979, pp. 367–375, especially pp. 369–370: the roof prevented missiles discharged from siege towers (rising higher than walls) and the placement of ladders or landing bridges from such towers, and was useful mostly on even terrain; and p. 375: being weak structures, they were often further protected by ditches and *diateichismata*.

103 The caliber of the sling bullets from Methone is within the standard size and weight of the period. Their weight ranges between (inscribed) 23.4–29.1 and (uninscribed) 28.7–34.5 g, their length between (inscribed) 0.026–0.0315 and (uninscribed) 0.029–0.0332 m, their width between (inscribed)

0.014–0.0167 and (uninscribed) 0.0141–0.018 (plus one deformed at 0.0204) m, their thickness between (inscribed) 0.0109–0.0153 and (uninscribed) 0.0132–0.0162 m (partially preserved bullets are not taken into account).

104 Corresponds to Type Ic according to Völling 1990, pp. 34–35; "almond" and "olive" according to Rihll 2009, p. 155.

105 Voutiropoulos 1996, pp. 65–66; Adamidou 2008, pp. 52–55.

106 Semper 1859; Kerviler 1883; Fougères 1896b, p. 1609; Paunov and Dimitrov 2000, p. 46; see also Pritchett 1991b, p. 43: "the spin imparted by the ovoid form added to the accuracy of the missile in flight"; cf. Pind. *Ol.* 13.93–95: ἐμὲ δ' εὐθὺν ἀκόντων | ἱέντα ῥόμβον παρὰ σκοπὸν οὐ χρὴ | τὰ πολλὰ βέλεα καρτύνειν χεροῖν ("But I, while casting the whirling javelins with straight aim, must not miss the mark as I speed many shafts with the strength of my hands," trans. J. Sandys, Cambridge, Mass., and London, 1937), where the poet presents himself as a javelin thrower who must be repeatedly accurate; according to Boeke (2007, pp. 154–155), the "'whirling javelin' embodies the emphasis on accuracy." The *rhombos* (Suda, s.v. ῥομβεῖν· σφενδονᾶν, καὶ ῥόμβος ἡ κίνησις) is repeatedly referred to in war contexts, especially in association with missiles whirling as they are flying toward their target, e.g., *Anth. Pal.* 6.111.4: πλήξας ῥομβωτῷ δούρατος οὐριάχῳ.

107 See, e.g., Brélaz 2007, pp. 77–81.

108 Völling 1990, pp. 34–36 (six types, Roman); Bosman 1995 (five types, Roman): amygdaloid (V), hammered all around (IV), half-hammered (III), cast in depressions made in sand with a stick (II) or a finger (I); Rihll 2009, p. 155 (12 types, Greek and Roman).

109 This typological criterion has been used to discern between production standards seeking to identify issues of different states by Tsaravopoulos (2004–2009, pp. 332–339 = 2012, p. 209).

110 Weight, although largely analogous to the dimensions, is not a safe criterion (on the futility of such attempts, see Rihll 2009, p. 159), as it may vary for several reasons, among which the existence of holes, the exact length at which the bullet was cut from the casting stem, and corrosion effects. Rihll (2009, p. 151) cautions that corrosion can result in gain (with patina) or loss of weight (when a shiny surface develops), and, therefore, a reasonable fluctuation of weight is to be expected.

111 This particular defect seems to be a commonality in the MEPNA bullets, the majority of which exhibit more or less protruding edges due to mold shift (the most significant cases are **28/9** [ΜΕΘ 2854], **28/16** [ΜΕΘ 2868], **28/22** [ΜΕΘ 2875], **28/23** [ΜΕΘ 2878], **28/28** [ΜΕΘ 2895], **28/30** [ΜΕΘ 2897] , **28/32** (ΜΕΘ 2903)), while even uninscribed bullets, which are generally cruder than inscribed ones, do not (except **28/74** [ΜΕΘ 1703]). This was the result of incorrect alignment of the two halves of the mold, and proves that the mold for MEPNA bullets had no alignment pins.

112 See **28/1** (ΜΕΘ 281), **28/2** (ΜΕΘ 285), **28/3** (ΜΕΘ 287), **28/5** (ΜΕΘ 655), **28/8** (ΜΕΘ 1709), **28/17** (ΜΕΘ 2869), **28/21** (ΜΕΘ 2873), **28/33** (ΜΕΘ 2907), and **28/36** (ΜΕΘ 2911) (all MEPNA), and three uninscribed: **28/69** (ΜΕΘ 650), **28/78** (ΜΕΘ 2849), and **28/105** (ΜΕΘ 2915). In several cases, remaining pieces of casting flash have been folded against the side of the bullet (e.g. **28/5** [ΜΕΘ 655], **28/14** [ΜΕΘ 2866], **28/32** [ΜΕΘ 2903], **28/56** [ΜΕΘ 2901], **28/60** [ΜΕΘ 2847]).

113 The Chalkidian bullets have been identified by the inscriptions Ὀλυ(νθίων) (*Olynthus* X, nos. 2220–2227) and Χαλκι(δέων) (*Olynthus* X, nos. 2260–2264).

114 Cf. similar molds of the Medieval period for round bullets: one limestone mold with six small and one large cavity for spherical bullets(?) found on the Pnyx in Athens, date uncertain (Davidson and Burr Thompson 1943, p. 102, no. 39); three bronze molds for a single spherical bullet found at Corinth, Byzantine–Late Byzantine period (*Corinth* XII, nos. 1576–1578); one bronze mold with eight cavities for spherical bullets found at Corinth, Byzantine–Late Byzantine period (*Corinth* XII, no. 1579). Cf. Suda, s.v. ἐπίσκοπα· . . . οἱ Καρδοῦχοι σφενδονῆται ἄριστοι λίθοις τε καὶ μολυβδίναις σφαίραις, ἃς ἐξακοντίζουσιν ἐπίσκοπα.

115 *Olynthus* X, p. 419.

116 Bruneau 1968, p. 650.

117 Empereur 1981, p. 555.

118 For examples of clusters of bullets (of the Roman era) from such a mold, see Vicente, Punter, and Ezquerra 1997, p. 195 with fig. 39.

119 Papakonstantinou-Diamantourou 1997, pp. 258–259, no. 1.

120 Makaronas 1960, p. 82; Papakonstantinou-Diamantourou 1997, p. 259, no. 2.

121 Flevari 2015, pp. 109–110. The Aptera find verified the arrangement of cavities that Zangemeister (1885, pp. XI–XII with fig. III) had presumed, even though he based his assumption on bullets probably made from a treelike channeling mold.

122 Zangemeister 1885, pp. XI–XII.

123 Flevari 2015, p. 109.

124 Flevari 2015, p. 109.

125 *Olynthus* X, p. 437; not illustrated.

126 Poux and Guyard 1999; no channel is visible in the photograph.

127 To take this a step further, given that the ΜΕΡΝΑ, Μικίνα, and Κλεοβούλō bullets are in fact Macedonian products, and that a finer shape performs better in flight (otherwise, why bother?), perhaps Philip II invested in numbers of slingers, rather than their expertise.

128 Colivicchi 2004, no. 204: no date given; Fiorini and Torelli 2007, pp. 88–89, and p. 91, where they note metallurgical waste pits of 4th–3rd century B.C. in the area.

129 *Olynthus* X, p. 419, n. 148; Brélaz and Ducrey 2003, pl. 23.3.

130 Weiss 1997, p. 147, no. III.1–6.

131 Karageorghis 1978, p. 163, no. 45; also Nicolaou 1977, p. 213.

132 Varoucha-Christodoulopoulou 1953–1954, p. 333.

133 Coccolutto 2006.

134 Brélaz and Ducrey 2003, pp. 99–101.

135 Manov 2016.

136 Olson 2014, p. 157.

137 This is referred to by Plato in *Rep.* 519a–b: τὸ τῆς τοιαύτης φύσεως εἰ ἐκ παιδὸς εὐθὺς κοπτόμενον περιεκόπη (pruned, trimmed) τὰς τῆς γενέσεως συγγενεῖς ὥσπερ μολυβδίδας.

138 Brélaz and Ducrey 2003, p. 102; Brélaz 2007, p. 72. Such a forcible detachment of the bullets from the stem is probably referred to in Plut. *Non posse* 1107c: κατατείναντες δὲ τὸ θεωρητικὸν εἰς τὸ σῶμα καὶ κατασπάσαντες ὥσπερ μολυβδίσι ταῖς τῆς σαρκὸς ἐπιθυμίαις.

139 Rihll (2009, pp. 151, 159–160) reinforces her argument that these holes are intentionally created after casting by pointing out that they also occur in stone *glandes*.

140 Zangemeister (1885, pp. XIII–XIV) addresses Woodhouse's argument that messages were inserted in the holes to carry information to the enemy, but, although not rejecting it, considers other possibilities, such as villagers in modern times perforating such finds to turn them into amulets. Vischer (1878b, p. 255) also considers the insertion of messages in the holes, as well as of poison, especially in the case of a bullet with a hole below the depiction of a snake, wherefore the inscription σῶσαι ("save") on the other side would have a special meaning for the army surgeon extracting the bullet; the possibility of drilling a hole as a receptable for poison is also proposed by Rihll (2009, pp. 159–160) and Tsaravopoulos (2012, p. 211, no. 7). On lead bullets penetrating the body, see Celsus, *De Medicina* 7.5.4; Paul. Aeg. 6.88.9; Onasander 19.3 (text in Appendix III.1); Livy 38.21.11. This proposition, however, raises more questions: How would they secure the poison in the hole? Would the temperature of the human body be enough to make, say, wax melt in order to release the poison? And why does only a portion of the bullets have this feature? As for the insertion of messages in holes this small, it is highly unlikely.

141 Also noted by Rihll (2009, p. 155).

142 Incised inscriptions are extremely rare. Apart from very few Latin examples of cutting a (military division?) number on the side (see, e.g., Zangemeister 1885, p. XX, no. 4, and p. 42, no. 37; Manganaro 2000, fig. 29), only two other bullets with incised inscription are reported: one from Iberia (García Garrido and Lalana 1991–1993, no. 20: inscription in Iberian script) and one from Cyprus (Nicolaou 1977, p. 215, no. 3: incised signs of the Cypriot syllabary).

143 *Olynthus* X, p. 418; Romero 2021, p. 212.

144 Similar summaries in Zangemeister 1885, pp. XV–XVI; Fougères 1896b, p. 1610; Rihll 2009, pp. 153–154.

145 Cf. the inscriptions on Macedonian shields (e.g., Adam-Veleni 1993; Pantermalis 2000; Tsouggaris 2009).

146 For attempts toward a "military prosopography" see *Olynthus* X, pp. 418–443; Empereur 1981; Tuck 1999–2001, pp. 17–22; Cambitoglou et. al. 2001; Hourlier 2006; Avram 2011a, 2014; Kelly 2012, pp. 282–285; Avram, Chiriac, and Matei 2013; Nankov 2016.

147 In the Roman era legions and auxiliary cohorts were often named after their commanders until this practice ended in A.D. 27 (Birley 1978; Speidel 1982). Isler (1994, p. 252) identified on clay bullets of the early Hellenistic period from Sicily military units of slingers divided by phratry, represented by a number, and the name and patronym of the commander (cf. *IG* XIV 2407.11: δευ(τέρα) φυλ(ά) | φα(τρία) Ἀλτρι | Φιλωνίδας | Εὐπολέμου, Sicily, 104–100 B.C.); earlier, Manni Piraino (1971, p. 175) had similarly suggested reading these inscriptions as the number of a λόχος (company) and the name of commander.

148 A "corpus" of nominatives in Ma 2010b, p. 161, n. 30.

149 Maiuri 1925, p. 250, no. V: Σωκρ|άτης | ἐπό|ησε = Segre and Pugliese Carratelli 1949–1951, p. 275, no. 192; Michailidou-Nikolaou 1969–1970, no. M. 2999/25: Σω[κρ]άτ(ης) | ἐπ[ό]ησεν; Manganaro 2000, p. 129: Σωκρά|[της] | ἐπόησε; Nicolaou 1977, pp. 211–214: three (1976/V-31/11(ii), 1976/VI-29/3(ii), 1976/XI-9/34) inscribed Ἄνδρων ἐπόησε, from Dhekeleia, Cyprus; Buonopane 2014: *T(itus) Fabricius fecit*; see further Avram, Chiriac, and Matei 2013, pp. 292–293. Flemberg (1978, p. 84) considers the possibility of the manufacturer featuring in the genitive as in some amphora stamps. Weiss and Draskowski (2010, pp. 151–152) suggest that inscriptions in the nominative record the commissioner, not the artisan ("[the one who] had the bullets made, rather than the fabricant himself").

150 This is suggested by Michailidou-Nikolaou 1969–1970, p. 368: the nominative probably the subject of an implied verb σφενδονᾶν, βάλλειν, or ποιεῖν, e.g., ὁ δεῖνα (ἐσφενδόνησεν); and Foss 1975, p. 28: maker or distinguished slinger. Perhaps the rather unusual formula *name + ethnic* could belong to this category, as it is uncustomarily explicit and the ethnics happen to coincide with regions known for their distinguished slingers (Weiss 1997, no. 2: Δ̣ρόμας | Α̣ἰνιάν; Weiss and Draskowski 2010, no. 9: Ἀντίμαχος | Αἰνιάν, no. 10: Δαμοκλῆς | Ἀχαιός, and no. 19: [Μά]νης | Α̣ἰολίδας [the editors consider the latter as a case of two personal names]; Vischer 1878b, no. 79: Σωσάνδρου | Μαλιέος); similarly, Weiss (1997, p. 151) suggested that these were the commanders of mercenary companies of slingers. It is worth noting that the most renowned slingers in Greece were the Rhodians (Thuc. 6.43.2; Xen. *Anab.* 3.3.16–17) and those from the *ethne* of central Greece, more particularly the Dolopes (Strab. 9.5.5: Πίνδαρος μνησθεὶς τοῦ Φοίνικος 'ὃς Δολόπων ἄγαγε θρασὺν ὅμιλον σφενδονᾶσαι, ἱπποδάμων Δαναῶν βέλεσι πρόσφορον'; Eust. *Il.* 2.638 (van der Valk, vol. 1, p. 483): Πίνδαρος δὲ τοὺς ὑπὸ τῷ Φοίνικι Δόλοπάς φησι «θρασὺν ὅμιλον σφενδονᾶσαι», ὡς καὶ τῶν Δολόπων δεξιῶν ὄντων σφενδονητῶν), the Malieis (Thuc. 4.100.1), the Ainianes (Appendix II.23), the Akarnanes (Thuc. 2.81.8, and 7.31.5; Pollux 1.137: . . . τόξον Κρητικόν, σφενδόνη Ἀκαρνάνων, ἀκόντιον Αἰτωλικόν . . .), the Achaeans (Livy 38.29.3–7; Suda, s.v. Ἀχαΐα καὶ ἐπὶ τῶν εὐστόχως βαλλόντων, παρ' ὅσον πάντων ἐπιτηδειότατόν ἐστι τὸ

τοιοῦτον βέλος πρὸς πολιορκίαν, τὸ τῶν ἐξ Ἀχαΐας σφενδονητῶν βέλος; Weiss and Draskowski 2010, p. 132, suggest that Achaia Phthiotis in Thessaly is meant by this ethnic); and cf. Diod. 15.85.4 (text in n. 64).

151 E.g., *IC* I.xvi.12 and I.xxviii.28: Γορ(τυνίων); *Olynthus* X, nos. 2181–2183: Ἀθηναίων, nos. 2220–2225: Ὀλυ(νθίων), nos. 2260–2264: Χαλκι(δέων); Foss 1974–1975, no. 12–13: Κνω(σίων); Kosmidou and Malamidou 2006, p. 135: Ἀμφ( ) or Ἀμ|φι(πολιτῶν). See also Guarducci 1969, p. 518.

152 A fair number of bullets have been identified as such; however, the readings are often not correct and personal names have been misread. Such cases are: κράτε, "hold it" (Hellmann 1982, no. 26), identified as an abbreviated name by Weiss and Draskowski (2010, p. 147: ΚΡΑ|ΤΕ(–); also Martínez Fernández 2007, p. 403); αἶνε, "strike" (Papadakis 1984, pp. 138–139; Martínez Fernández 2007, p. 403), identified as an abbreviated name by Kelly 2012, pp. 294–295: Αἰνε(σίδαμος); αἰσχρὸ(ν) δῶρο(ν), "foul gift" (*Olynthus* X, no. 2176), on which see the commentary on *Εὐγένεος* below; ἄ<φ>νις (αἴφνης), "suddenly" (Foss 1974–1975, no. 9), identified as a name by Tsaravopoulos (2004–2009, nos. 10–11: Αἶνις) and Avram (2011b, pp. 347–348); φαῖνε, "appear," identified as an abbreviated name by Ma (2010b, p. 169: Φαινέ(ας), with references); καλά, "a nice one," identified as an abbreviated name by Ma (2010b, pp. 169–170: Κάλα(ς), with references). To these could be added Ναμέρ(της), not ναμερτής/-ές, "unfailing" (Ma 2010b, p. 170, n. 74; see also the commentary on *Μερ|να(–)? vel Να|μερ(–)* below); Βαβύρτας, which is most probably also a personal name, not an insult as in Hsch., s.v. βαβύρτας· ὁ παράμωρος, "greatest fool" (Vischer 1878b, no. 65; Reinach 1889; Michon 1894, no. 6); and the, if accurately read, female Νεολύτη, "recently cast" according to Michailidou-Nicolaou (1969-1970, no. M. 2999/24 and p. 369), but certainly not an adjective (ὁ/ἡ νεόλυτος), which strangely reads as a woman's name. Another most likely false reading is αἰσίως, "auspiciously," according to Nicolaou 1985, nos. 16a: ΑΙΣ̣[ΙΩΣ] and 16c: [ΑΙΣ]ΙΩΣ, who restores the inscription by combining the two, regarding them as complementary to each other, but as they differ considerably in dimensions, weight, and form it is impossible that they are of the same issue and highly unlikely that they had the same inscription (letter forms not visible in the photograph). As for some inscribed loomweights that Manganaro (1965, p. 166) thinks were actually sling missiles, see the objections by Guarducci (1969, p. 523, n. 5). Apparently secure readings are: δέξαι, "take this" (Vischer 1878b, no. 17; Hellmann 1982, no. 18: δέξαι | thunderbolt; Cerchiai 1984, nos. 58 and 58a); γεῦσαι, "taste this" (Gera 1985 = 1995; *CIIP* II 2137; *CIIP* III 2276–2277; it is noteworthy that γεῦσαι, as well as τρῶγε and τρωγάλιον (see below), refers directly to the sense of taste, a war metaphor used already in the Homeric epics, see Hom. *Il.* 20.257–258: ἀλλ' ἄγε θᾶσσον | γευσόμεθ' ἀλλήλων χαλκήρεσιν ἐγχείῃσιν, *Il.* 21.60–61: ἀλλ' ἄγε δὴ καὶ δουρὸς ἀκωκῆς ἡμετέροιο | γεύσεται, *Od.* 21.98: ἦ τοι ὀϊστοῦ γε πρῶτος γεύσασθαι ἔμελλεν; see also *Anth. Pal.* 16.251, line 4: πικρῶν γευσάμενος βελέων); τρῶγε, "eat it" (Lenormant 1866a, no. 143); τρωγάλιον, "a snack" (de Minicis 1844, p. 64, no. 4: ΤΡΩΓ|Ε|ΑΛΙΟΝ, "eat this nut"; Goettling 1851, p. 18: τρῶγε Ἅλιον (the name of the slinger), but τρῶγε ἅλιον, "bite it in vain," is better (see also n. 257); *CIG* IV, no. 8530c (E. Curtius): τρωγάλιον and a numeral; McCaul 1864, p. 99: τρῶγε τρωγάλιον; *IG* IV 384 (M. Fraenkel): τρωγάλιον | Ε, initial of an ethnic; cf. Mnesim. fr. 7.1–10, where the speaker consumes Cretan arrowheads as chickpeas: ἆρ' οἶσθα, | ὁτιὴ πρὸς ἄνδρας ἐστί σοι μαχητέον, | οἳ τὰ ξίφη δειπνοῦμεν ἠκονημένα, | ὄψον δὲ δᾶδας ἡμμένας καταπίνομεν; | ἐντεῦθεν εὐθὺς ἐπιφέρει τραγήματα | ἡμῖν ὁ παῖς μετὰ δεῖπνον ἀκίδας Κρητικάς, | ὥσπερ ἐρεβίνθους, δορατίων τε λείψανα | κατεαγότ', ἀσπίδας δὲ προσκεφάλαια καὶ | θώρακας ἔχομεν, πρὸς ποδῶν δὲ σφενδόνας | καὶ τόξα, καταπέλταισι δ' ἐστεφανώμεθα); ζάθειον, "most sacred" (Michailidou-Nikolaou 1969–1970, nos. M. 2999/14–17, no. M. 265, no. 1963/IV–20/98, and p. 367, no. 5; see also Nicolaou 1979, no. 9b: [ΔΗ]ΜΟCΙΟΝ, which is more likely Ζ̣ά̣θ̣ε̣ιον); λαβέ, "take this" (Vischer 1878b, no. 18; Hellmann 1982, no. 21: Ἡρακ̣λείδα | λα̣βέ); λῆγε, "expire" (Hawkins 1847, p. 104 [no reference given]); πρόσεχε, "watch out" (Lenormant 1866a, no. 142); ὀδυνηρῶς, "painfully" (Paunov and Dimitrov 2000, pp. 54–55, no. 6c: ΟΔΥΝΗ|Π(ΩΣ?); *SEG* 52.700: ὀδυνη|ρῶς);

ὀδύνη, "pain" (Paunov and Dimitrov 2000, no. 6c; Nankov 2016, no. 3: ὀδύνη | τοῖς . . . κοις); αἷμα, "blood" (Vischer 1878b, no. 21; Lenormant 1862, no. 63: αἷμα | Ἀθε(ναίων), the two sides not to be necessarily read continuously); κύε, "get pregnant" (Michailidou-Nikolaou 1969–1970, p. 367, no. 2; this particular inscription could be read as an exhortation with sexual connotations addressed to the slinger, whose masculinity and pugnacity are praised by calling him to impregnate the target, but also as an insult to the "effeminate" enemy who will become pregnant by the slinger; on sexual connotations in war, see further Kelly 2012, pp. 293–294); ἥτις αἶσα, "what a lot" (Lenormant 1862, no. 64: "quelle qu'en soit la Fortune!," "Au hazard!"); σοῦ(?), "all yours" (Nicolaou 1977, p. 215, no. 3: *se-u*, reading unclear, see also n. 396); τύχα, "luck" (Lenormant 1866b, no. 361); Μο<ῖ>ρα, "fate" (Papadakis 1984, p. 139); πεῖρα, "pierce" (Cuming 1864, p. 75 [no reference given]); ἀγωνίς, "anguish" (Cuming 1864, p. 75 [no reference given]). Note, however, that François Lenormant is known to have been forging inscriptions (Masson 1993). Latin inscriptions of this category are more numerous and more illustrative, see, e.g., Zangemeister 1885, no. 13: *fugitivi peristis*, and no. 62: (phallus) | *sede laxe Octavi*; de Minicis 1844, pp. 23–24: *Pompeii*, pp. 30–31: *feri Pompeium*, p. 35, no. 12 (p. 43): *L. Antoni Calvii peristi* | *C. Caiisarus victoria*, p. 39: *peto culum* | *Octaviani*.

153 *Olynthus* X, no. 2180: Ἀρχίης | ὡραῖος; Cambitoglou et al. 2001, no. 18.11: Ὀρ - - δας | καλός. Weiss and Draskowski (2010, pp. 149–150) also consider the possibility of two personal names (*LGPN* 2: Κάλος, Athens, earliest attestation in the 2nd century B.C.; *LGPN* 5A: Ὡραῖος, Smyrna, 3rd century B.C.; more common is the female Ὡραῖα, earliest attestation in the 3rd century B.C., Athens, see *LGPN* 2), as in their nos. 17–20.

154 Βάσκε ἄν, "make haste" (Michailidou-Nikolaou 1969–1970, no. M. 2999/28 and p. 368), is an uncertain case, while ΕΥΣΚΑΝΟΥ, understood as εὖ σκάνου, "lodge well" (addressed to the injured victim lodging and recovering in a tent), by Vischer (1878a, no. 4 = *IG* IX.1 836), has been rejected as an exhortation and read as the genitive of the unattested personal name Εὔσκανος by Guarducci (1969, p. 520) and Martínez Fernández (2007, p. 401). Note, however, the hapax term εὐσκήνοιο in an epigram from Miletos (*Milet* VI.3 1085: 2nd century B.C.) referring to a theatrical scene, not an army tent, as well as the term σκῆνος (Dor. σκᾶνος), tent, body, corpse (LSJ, s.v.), which could render the inscription an exhortation to the bullet to lodge (the verb σκηνάω/-έω/-όω) well (εὖ) in the victim's body (also Ernst Curtius, *CIG* IV, no. 8530b/d).

155 The inscription ΠΑΠΑΙ was justifiably identified as the common exclamation of pain παπαῖ (Papadogiannaki 2007, pp. 220–221 [βαβαῖ], pp. 272–274 [παπαῖ], p. 275 [ποποῖ]), but the reading was corrected after the publication of further examples on which the inscription was clearly ΠΑΠΑC, the quite common personal name Πάπ(π)ας (Ma 2010b, p. 169; Avram 2014, pp. 134–135: Παππᾶς; Weiss and Draskowski 2010, p. 147). Only Tuck (1999–2001, no. 21) maintains that it is an exclamation of pain, although on the bullet he publishes the lunate C (sigma) at the end is clear.

156 E.g., de Minicis 1844, pp. 54–55, no. 1: ΗΑΚΕΟΣ νίκη, nos. 2–6: Ἀθηνίωνος νίκη, and pp. 59–60: Διὸς νίκη and νίκη Ματέρων; Gera 1985 = 1995: Τρύφωνος νίκη; Vischer 1878b, no. 47: Νίκα; see further Manganaro 2000, pp. 130–133.

157 McCaul (1864, p. 96) interprets phrases such as Διὸς νίκη as referring to "gods and goddesses, whose aid was specially invoked by the combatants on either side, or to whom the missiles were consecrated."

158 E.g., Papakonstantinou-Diamantourou 1997, no. 1: ΦΙ(λίππου), identified as Philip V of Macedon.

159 E.g., the ligatures X͡A or A͡X and A͡O or Λ͡O (see nn. 271–272).

160 E.g., Isler 1994: number of phratry/military division; the single letter featuring in the middle in the inscription ΤΡΩΓ|Ε|ΑΛΙΟΝ may be a number according to Ernst Curtius (*CIG* IV, no. 8530c: "a numeral denoting the number of bullets thus inscribed").

161 See an extensive collection in Rihll 2009, p. 154.

162 The phallus, in contrast to all other depictions, is contextually connected to the inscription on the single example on which it occurs (Zangemeister 1885, nos. 61–62), and, therefore, it should not be considered as a device, but rather as a pictogram.

163 Fougères 1896b, p. 1610: lethal symbolism; Kelly 2012, p. 299.

164 Rihll (2009, p. 163, no. 7) points out that several devices correspond to the names of many of the "slinging" machines we know of, as, for instance, the scorpion for the scorpion catapult, the thunderbolt (*fulmen*) for *fulminalis* (ballista), and the trident for *tragularii.*

165 Fougères 1896b, p. 1610: the crest of the city. See, e.g., Isler 1994, pp. 252–254, who notices the same stamp depicting Achelôos on bullets and other public issues, such as coins and seals; Kosmidou and Malamidou 2006, p. 135, who identify the torch depicted on bullets from Amphipolis as a "visual representation and substitute of the ethnic" (the torch serves as the city emblem on its coinage; see Gaebler 1935, pp. 30–33); Manov 2016, who identifies a bullet of Philip V of Macedon by the emblems it carries, as they also appear on his coinage.

166 A theory promoted by Ma 2010b, pp. 170–173.

167 Ma 2010b, p. 172.

168 Kelly 2012, p. 299.

169 Simon 1989, no. 339: Κεραυ(thunderbolt)νίου | Διὸς νίκ[η]; Weiss 1997, p. 149: a bullet found at Miletos carrying the star of Apollo and the inscription Θρασυβούλō.

170 McCaul 1864, p. 94: "The names of men inscribed on these objects were those of the chiefs, or commanding officers, or persons who ordered the casting of the bullets"; Zangemeister 1885, pp. XV–XVI: (1) the people or the state occupied in a war, (2) he who commissioned the bullets, (3) legion, (4) possibly slingers, (5) fabricant, (6) exclamations; Fougères 1896b, p. 1610: (1) ethnic of the issuing authority, (2) chief of army in genitive, rarely in nominative, (3) legion number, (4) exhortation to the bullet, (5) invocation to gods, (6) irony and insults to the enemy.

171 Tuck 1999–2001, p. 26.

172 Kelly 2012, pp. 297–299.

173 Kelly 2012, p. 299. On the possibility that the slingers and enemy soldiers were able to read the inscriptions, whatever they meant for them, it is noteworthy that a particular kind of literacy, "military literacy"—an addition, perhaps, to the specialists' and functional "literacies" of William Harris (1989) and Rosalind Thomas (2009)—has been acknowledged in its own right in recent decades after the discovery of the Vindolanda tablets, the wooden sheets with the bureaucratic and personal correspondence of the personnel of the Roman army stationed at Hadrian's Wall in Britain. The social and professional class of officers provided and demanded advanced skills in writing and reading, but apparently even low-ranking officers and soldiers were literate to a degree (of competence and extent). Apart from clerks in the military bureaucratic machine, regular soldiers had motives (promotion, appointment to better posts or clerical positions), as well as obligations (ability to read passwords, duties/services, orders; cf. the order of Peukestas, 331–323 B.C. [Turner 1974]), that demanded or presupposed training in writing and reading. Still, mass literacy, even among the military, was not the case (Bowman 1994), and the reality must have been rather closer to Harris' (1989) view on the rather restricted extent of literacy.

174 Ma 2010b, pp. 170–171.

175 Ma 2010b, pp. 171–173; see also Kelly 2012, p. 284: "The inscribed *onomastica* on the slingshots serve to both promote a sense of group identity, among the firing troops, and instill a corresponding fear in their targets."

176 This is specifically attested about Philip II in Diod. 16.3.1: τὰς δὲ στρατιωτικὰς τάξεις ἐπὶ τὸ κρεῖττον διορθωσάμενος καὶ τοὺς ἄνδρας τοῖς πολεμικοῖς ὅπλοις δεόντως κοσμήσας, συνεχεῖς ἐξοπλασίας καὶ γυμνασίας ἐναγωνίους ἐποιεῖτο; Treister 1996, p. 227; Themelis 2000, p. 499. See also *IG* II^2 468

(inventory of siege equipment including [μ]ολυ[βδ–], Athens, end of 4th century B.C.); *IG* II² 1488, esp. line 6: μολυβδίδω[ν –] (inventory of missiles, Athens, end of 4th century B.C.); and possibly *IG* II² 1627, lines 322–324 (330/29 B.C.), 1628, lines 505–506 (326/5 B.C.), 1629, lines 980–981 (325/4 B.C.), and 1631, lines 217–218 (323/2 B.C.): naval inventories from Piraeus including "μολυβδίδων σταθμὸν καὶ μολύβδου τῶν ἐν τῆι τάρπηι [sum of weight]."

177 See above, "On Slings, Slinging, and Slingers."

178 *CPG* 7.80 (Diogenianus): Πολλὰ κενὰ τοῦ πολέμου: ἤτοι διὰ τὸ πολλὰ καθ' ὑπόνοιαν φέρειν· ἢ ὅτι Λακεδαιμόνιοι κεναῖς σφενδόναις καὶ νευραῖς ἐψόφουν πρὸς ἔκπληξιν τῶν πολεμίων. Another feint action that slingers could have used to intimidate their enemies was swinging their slings just to produce sonic fuss. In the works of lexicographers, the terms ῥομβεῖν and ῥεμβονᾶν are synonymous to σφενδονᾶν, slinging (Photios, *Lexicon*, s.v. ῥομβεῖν; Hsch., s.v. ῥεμβονᾶν; Suda, s.v. ῥομβεῖν), which may be simply due to the whirling motion of swinging a sling, but it could, perhaps, also be with reference to the *rhombos* (ῥόμβος), the "bull-roarer," an instrument made of a wooden airfoil fastened on a cord, which, when swung, produced a low-frequency vibrato sound.

179 Hdt. 8.128.1–2: ὅκως βυβλίον γράψειε ἢ Τιμόξεινος ἐθέλων παρὰ Ἀρτάβαζον πέμψαι ἢ Ἀρτάβαζος παρὰ Τιμόξεινον, τοξεύματος παρὰ τὰς γλυφίδας περιειλίξαντες καὶ πτερώσαντες τὸ βυβλίον ἐτόξευον ἐς συγκείμενον χωρίον. ἐπάιστος δὲ ἐγένετο ὁ Τιμόξεινος προδιδοὺς τὴν Ποτίδαιαν· τοξεύων γὰρ ὁ Ἀρτάβαζος ἐς τὸ συγκείμενον, ἁμαρτὼν τοῦ χωρίου τούτου βάλλει ἀνδρὸς Ποτιδαιήτεω τὸν ὦμον, τὸν δὲ βληθέντα περιέδραμε ὅμιλος, οἷα φιλέει γίνεσθαι ἐν πολέμῳ, οἳ αὐτίκα τὸ τόξευμα λαβόντες ὡς ἔμαθον τὸ βυβλίον, ἔφερον ἐπὶ τοὺς στρατηγούς (= Aen. Tact. 31.25–27); Heliodor. *Aeth.* IX.5.2–3: ὁ δὲ ἐπείθετο μέν, δοῦλος καὶ ἄκων τῆς τύχης γινόμενος, ἀποτετειχισμένος δὲ τῷ ὕδατι καὶ ὅπως ἂν τινα διαπέμψαιτο ὡς τοὺς πολεμίους ἀδυνατῶν ἐπίνοιαν ὑπὸ τῆς ἀνάγκης ἐδιδάσκετο· γραψάμενος γὰρ ἃ ἐβούλετο καὶ λίθῳ τὴν γραφὴν ἐναψάμενος σφενδόνῃ πρὸς τοὺς ἐναντίους ἐπρεσβεύετο διαπόντιον τὴν ἱκεσίαν τοξευόμενος· ἤνυε δὲ οὐδέν, ἐλαττουμένης τοῦ μήκους τῆς βολῆς καὶ τῷ ὕδατι προεμπιπτούσης. Ὁ δὲ καὶ αὖθις τὴν αὐτὴν γραφὴν ἐκτοξεύων ἀπετύγχανε, πάντων μὲν τοξοτῶν καὶ σφενδονητῶν ἐφικέσθαι τῆς βολῆς φιλοτιμουμένων οἷα δὴ τὸν περὶ ψυχῆς σκοπὸν ἀθλούντων, ἁπάντων δὲ τὰ ὅμοια πασχόντων; Polyaen. 2.29: Κλεώνυμος, Λακεδαιμονίων βασιλεύς, Τροιζῆνα πολιορκῶν κατὰ πολλὰ μέρη τῆς πόλεως ὀξυβελεῖς περιστήσας ἐκέλευσεν ἀφιέναι τοῖς βέλεσιν ἐπιγράψας "ἥκω τὴν πόλιν ἐλευθερώσων." ἔχων δὲ καὶ Τροιζηνίους αἰχμαλώτους ἀφῆκεν ἄνευ λύτρων. οἱ μὲν αἰχμάλωτοι εἴσω παρελθόντες εὐηγγελλίζοντο; Plut. *Cim.* 12.3: ἐπιπλεύσας δὲ τῇ πόλει τῶν Φασηλιτῶν, Ἑλλήνων μὲν ὄντων, οὐ δεχομένων δὲ τὸν στόλον οὐδὲ βουλομένων ἀφίστασθαι βασιλέως, τήν τε χώραν κακῶς ἐποίει καὶ προσέβαλλε τοῖς τείχεσιν. οἱ δὲ Χῖοι συμπλέοντες αὐτῷ, πρὸς δὲ τοὺς Φασηλίτας ἐκ παλαιοῦ φιλικῶς ἔχοντες, ἅμα μὲν τὸν Κίμωνα κατεπράϋνον, ἅμα δὲ τοξεύοντες ὑπὲρ τὰ τείχη βιβλίδια προσκείμενα τοῖς οἰστοῖς ἐξήγγελλον τοῖς Φασηλίταις; Caes. *BHisp.* 13: *glans missa est inscripta, quo die ad oppidum capiendum accederent, sese scutum esse positurum*, *BHisp.* 18: *servus... clam a Caesaris praesidiis in Pompei castra discessit et indicium glande scriptum misit, per quod certior fieret Caesar, quae in oppido ad defendendum compararentur*, and *BHisp.* 19: *hoc praeterea tempore tabellae de muro sunt deiectae, in quibus scriptum est inventum: L. Munatius Caesari. Si mihi vitam tribues, quoniam ab Cn. Pompeio sum desertus, qualem me illi praestiti tali virtute et constantia futurum me in te esse praestabo* (intelligence and treachery inscribed on sling bullets sent from the besieged settlement of Attegua in Spain to Caesar's camp). Cf. a rather extraordinary case in Alkidamas fr. 2, 30–41: . . . συνιόντων δὲ ἡμῶν ὁμόσε τοῖς ἀνδράσιν, ἐκδραμὼν τοξότης ἐκ τῶν πολεμίων ἐστοχάσατο τούτου, ἁμαρτὼν δὲ αὐτοῦ βάλλει ἐγγὺς ἐμοῦ· οὗτός τε λόγχην ἀφίησιν ἐπ' αὐτόν, καὶ ἐκεῖνος ἀνελόμενος ᾤχετο εἰς τὸ στρατόπεδον. ἐγὼ δὲ ἀνελὼν τὸν οἰστὸν δίδωμι Εὐρυβάτῃ δοῦναι Τεύκρῳ, ἵνα χρῷτο. ἀνοχῆς δὲ γενομένης ἀπὸ τῆς μάχης ὀλίγον χρόνον, δείκνυσί μοι τὸν οἰστὸν ὑπὸ τοῖς πτεροῖς γράμματα ἔχοντα. ἐκπλαγεὶς δὲ ἐγὼ τῷ πράγματι, προσκαλεσάμενος Σθένελόν τε καὶ Διομήδη ἐδείκνυον αὐτοῖς τὰ ἐνόντα. ἡ δὲ γραφὴ ἐδήλου τάδε· «Ἀλέξανδρος Παλαμήδει. ὅσα συνέθου Τηλέφῳ, πάντα σοὶ ἔσται, ὅ τε πατὴρ Κασάνδραν γυναῖκα δίδωσί σοι, καθάπερ ἐπέστειλας· ἀλλὰ τὰ ἀπὸ

σοῦ πραττέσθω διὰ τάχους». ἐνεγέγραπτο μὲν ταῦτα· καί μοι προσελθόντες μαρτυρήσατε οἱ λαβόντες τὸ τόξευμα; and also fr. 2, 50–52: τεκμαίρεσθαι δὲ δεῖ ἐκ τούτων εἰκότως καὶ τὴν ἄφεσιν τῆς λόγχης. φημὶ γὰρ καὶ ἐν ἐκείνῃ γράμματα εἶναι, πηνίκα τε καὶ πότε προδώσει. Note that in most instances the message is wrapped around the shaft of the missile, rather than inscribed on it. See also Plut. *Pyrrh.* 2.6: οἱ δ' οὐ κατήκουον διὰ τραχύτητα καὶ πάταγον τοῦ ῥεύματος, ἀλλ' ἦν διατριβὴ τῶν μὲν βοώντων, τῶν δὲ μὴ συνιέντων, ἄχρι τις ἐννοήσας καὶ περιελὼν δρυὸς φλοιὸν ἐνέγραψε πόρπῃ γράμματα φράζοντα τήν τε χρείαν καὶ τὴν τύχην τοῦ παιδός, εἶτα λίθῳ τὸν φλοιὸν περιελίξας καὶ χρησάμενος οἷον ἕρματι τῆς βολῆς ἀφῆκεν εἰς τὸ πέραν· ἔνιοι δέ φασι σαυνίῳ περιπήξαντας ἀκοντίσαι τὸν φλοιόν; and Caes. *BGall.* 5.45.3–4: *hic servo spe libertatis magnisque persuadet praemiis, ut litteras ad Caesarem deferat. Has ille in iaculo illigatas effert et Gallus inter Gallos sine ulla suspicione versatus ad Caesarem pervenit.*

180 Riginos 1994, pp. 106–114 (full catalogue and commentary on the sources). The story is referred to in Them. *Soph.* 284b–c: (being attacked by adversaries) ἐπεὶ οὖν οἱ μὲν βάλλοντες εἰς τοὐμφανὲς προελθεῖν οὐκ ἐθέλουσι καὶ στῆναι ἐν μέσῳ παρ' ὑμῖν καὶ ἐν περιόπτῳ, ἀλλ' ἐν γωνίαις που καταδεδύκασιν ἢ χηραμοῖς, τοὺς δὲ ὀϊστοὺς ὁρῶ πίπτοντας οὐκ οἶδα ὅθεν καὶ ἐν ποσὶ κυλινδομένους, φέρε ἐξαριθμήσωμαί τε αὐτοὺς ἀνελόμενος ἐκ τῆς γῆς καὶ πειραθῶ διακλάσαι, ἣν δύνωμαι, καὶ ἐπιδεῖξαι τῶν ὄγκων τὴν μαλακότητα καὶ διαθρῆσαι εἰ δή τινες εἶεν φαρμάκῳ ἀληλιμμένοι. ἴσως δ' ἂν καὶ πυκνὰ ἐπαφώμενοι καὶ μεταστρέφοντες εὕροιμεν ἀγχοῦ τῶν γλυφίδων καὶ τοὔνομα τοῦ βάλλοντος ἐγκεχαραγμένον· ὅθενπερ καὶ Φιλίππῳ ἐφωράθη τῷ Μακεδόνι πολιορκοῦντι Μεθώνην ὁ βαλὼν ἐκ τοῦ τείχους τοξότης. Ἀστὴρ ὄνομα ἦν τῷ ἀνθρώπῳ, καὶ ἐγκέκαυτο ἐν τῷ βέλει. The narrative draws so heavily on the anecdote of Philip II that it makes it impossible to infer whether the author actually had any real circumstances in mind and only used the story as common knowledge or was just adapting it.

181 Plut. *Prae. ger. reip.* 825e–f: ἐν δὲ ταῖς κρίσεσι καὶ ταῖς δίκαις πρὸς τοὺς πολίτας ἄμεινόν ἐστι καθαραῖς καὶ ψιλαῖς ταῖς αἰτίαις χρώμενον ἀγωνίζεσθαι, καὶ μὴ καθάπερ βέλη τὰ πράγματα χαράσσοντα καὶ φαρμάσσοντα ταῖς βλασφημίαις καὶ ταῖς κακοηθείαις καὶ ταῖς ἀπειλαῖς ἀνήκεστα καὶ μεγάλα καὶ δημόσια ποιεῖν.

182 For a representative example from World War II, see McDermott 1942, p. 35.

183 See nn. 152 and 154–155; also, Ma 2010b, pp. 167–170; Kelly 2012, pp. 291–294.

184 *Olynthus* X; Michailidou-Nicolaou 1969–1970, p. 367, no. 6, and p. 369; Cambitoglou et al. 2001; Christov and Manov 2011; Mikulčić and Sokolovska 1991, p. 79, and Paunov and Dimitrov 2000, p. 52 (Κλεομάχου).

185 These are: Φιλίππ(ου) | spearhead (*Olynthus* X, no. 2241), found at Olynthos, and thus securely dated before 348 B.C.; Θρασυβούλō | star, Κλεάνδρō | bucranium, and Χαριξένō | thunderbolt, all dated on account of the genitive ending in –ō in the second half of the 4th century B.C. (Avram, Chiriac, and Matei 2013, s.v.), but should all be dated before ca. 325 B.C. when the grapheme –ō goes out of use (see Threatte 1980, pp. 258–259); Βαβύρτα | spearhead, Εὐβουλίδα | pitchfork, Θεάρō | pitchfork (which should be counted with the above), and Θάρυπος | pitchfork(?), which are associated with the siege of Kameiros by Demetrios Poliorcetes in 305 B.C. (Ma 2010b, pp. 164–165; Avram, Chiriac, and Matei 2013, s.v.). The dating of the bullets inscribed ΠΑΠΑϹ | thunderbolt to ca. 400 B.C. on account of the lunate sigma, also employed on the bullets of ΤΙϹϹΑΦΕΡΝ(–)—apparently taking for granted the identification with the satrap of Lydia (Avram 2011a, no. 1; Avram, Chiriac, and Matei 2013, p. 259)—is rather arbitrary: the lunate sigma is extremely uncommon before the 3rd century B.C. (see also n. 59), and the form of alpha with the broken crossbar in most bullets of Παπᾶς (see, e.g., Bates 1930, p. 44; Tuck 1999–2001, no. 21) is characteristic of the late 3rd–1st century B.C. (Chaniotis 1996, p. 452).

186 Ἀρχίης | ὡραῖος (*Olynthus* X, no. 2180) was, according to the editor, a Macedonian military officer in his prime, but, as Weiss and Draskowski (2010, p. 150) point out, the Ionic form of the name resists his identification as a Macedonian.

187 Vischer 1878b, no. 14 (bucranium) and no. 46 (star); Manov and Torbov 2016, no. 14 (star); Michailidou-Nicolaou 1969–1970, no. M. 2999/29 (anchor); Weiss and Draskowski 2010, no. 13 (shield).

188 See n. 146. The most prominent relevant example is the identification by David Robinson (*Olynthus* X, pp. 426–427) of Ἱππόνικος with a general of Philip II, but the name is fairly common throughout the Greek world (*LGPN* 1–5).

189 See, e.g., Weiss and Draskowski 2010, pp. 151–152 (referring to Ma 2010b, pp. 170–173), who see the inscriptions and devices on sling bullets as "signs directed only at the circle of those involved in a combat situation for which these very objects were destined" (p. 151); they even suggest that in the case of bullets with two personal names both named individuals were military personnel, and, although it is impossible for us to understand how that would work in hierarchy as ancient miltary organization is largely unknown, "in the situation for which the bullets were cast, everyone knew."

190 Ma 2010b, pp. 170–173; a view also adopted by Weiss and Draskowski 2010, p. 151: "They were intended for their own soldiers and apparently had the function to address by means of certain keywords the identity and group feeling and thus to strengthen motivation and fighting confidence."

191 Ma 2010b, p. 170.

192 See also Tuck 1999–2001, p. 17: "[personal names of commanders] might have been meant as statements of the attacking general's power, if those attacked had the interest and ability to read them during or after the assault."

193 See Avram, Chiriac, and Matei 2013, pp. 234–236, with the addition of Manov and Torbov 2016, nos. 1–12: Ἀλεξάνδρου | Φιλίππου, which is actually the only name that can be identified with certainty as Alexander III (see also n. 210); Philip was a common name, and identification of Tissaphernes with the satrap of Lydia is only one possibility (Foss 1975; Weiss and Draskowski 2010, nos. 1–2; see also nn. 59 and 185).

194 Avram, Chiriac, and Matei (2013, p. 280) suppose that there were two individuals by the name Μικίνας, in different periods and unrelated to each other, and so they date the bullets with the name in the genitive to the end of the 4th century B.C. (note that until the present publication, these were without known provenance and archaeological context). It is now clear that both are of the mid-4th century B.C. and in all likelihood refer to the same individual.

195 Rihll 2009, p. 154.

196 Tuck 1999–2001, p. 17; also Ma 2010b, p. 170.

197 McLean 2002, pp. 200–201 (portability); Cooley 2012, p. 185 (convenience). Margherita Guarducci (1969, pp. 444–535) rightly categorizes sling bullets among other *instrumenta publica*.

198 Harris 1993; Pucci 2001; Chaniotis 2005. Note also Daniele Manacorda's (1993, p. 37) suggested methodological approach to the study of stamped products of the Roman era, according to which the chronological, geographical, and typological barriers should be dismissed and a common thread should be sought throughout the practice of all forms of marking products.

199 Lead weights are not very dissimilar, but they are excluded as they only carry ethnics or state emblems (on which see Killen 2017) or weight symbols (Lang 1964, pp. 6–13), and only from the Hellenistic period onward were the date and the official involved also included (see, e.g., Kroll 2012; Gitler and Finkielsztejn 2015).

200 Kroll 2008b; Wartenberg 2015, p. 356.

201 Thompson 1961; Mørkholm 1991, pp. 31–35; and especially de Callataÿ 2012 for an overview of interpretations.

202 *Agora* XXXVII, p. 7.

203 *Agora* XXXVII, p. 8. See also Guarducci 1969, pp. 502–516.

204 *Agora* XXXVII, pp. 15–19.

205 Guarducci 1969, pp. 505–511.

206 See especially Felsch 1979, 1990.

207 Wace 1906, 1907 (Sparta); Paris 1892, pp. 113–117 (Elateia). See further Guarducci 1969, pp. 491–497.

208 Misailidou-Despotidou 1993. See further Guarducci 1969, pp. 497–501.

209 *Agora* XXXVII, p. 12.

210 Sling bullets with certain references to kings only occur in the period from the late 4th to the 2nd century B.C., but they are far too few. The earliest ones are those inscribed Ἀλεξάνδρου | Φιλίππου (Manov and Torbov 2016, nos. 1–12) and Βασιλέ(ως) | Ἀλεξάν(δρου) (Avram, Chiriac, and Matei 2013, pp. 230, nos. 1–2; Avram 2016; Nankov 2016, nos. 6–9; cf. Manov, Talmaţchi, and Custurea 2019, who dissociate them from the Macedonian king and date them to the 3rd century B.C.), referring to Alexander III of Macedon, while contemporary ones inscribed Στρατη(γοῦ) | Ἀλεξάνδ(ρου) (Avram, Chiriac, and Matei 2013, pp. 230, no. 3; Nankov 2016, no. 10; Manov, Talmaţchi, and Custurea 2019) probably refer to his marshal Alexander of Lyncos. Avram (2016, 490) also identifies those inscribed ΑΛΕΞΑΝ|ΔΡΟΥ and ΑΛΕΞΑΝΔΡΟΥ | eagle as probably of Alexander III, but others inscribed ΑΛΕ | blank and ΑΛΕΞΑΝΔΡΟΥ | blank as probably not, on account of their provenance or date. A later example, also from Macedonia, is a bullet carrying two devices, a club and a thunderbolt, both coinage insignia of Philip V of Macedon (Manov 2016). *CIIP* III 2274: Βα(σιλέως) Τρύ(φωνος), probably refers to the rebel king of the Seleukid Empire of the 2nd century B.C., while it is not impossible that the plain Βασιλέως (Tsaravopoulos 2004–2009, nos. 1–6) is a personal name (*LGPN* 1: Βασιλεύς, Peparethos, 3rd? century B.C.). See further Avram, Chiriac, and Matei 2013, pp. 234–236. Cf. Appendix I: Φιλίππō.

211 See a general account in Rhodes and Osborne 2003, pp. 294–296.

212 Weiss 1997, p. 151.

213 *Olynthus* X, no. 2226: ΟΛΥ(–) | ΑΝΔ(–), no. 2227: ΟΛΥ(–) | ΣΩΣΙΟ ←. Unless the abbreviation stands for the individual's ethnic, although they would hardly abbreviate a name which was to be further specified with an ethnic.

214 Most of these interpretations have been rejected as far as coinage is concerned (see de Callataÿ 2012), but they should not be completely dismissed until our understanding of this practice is clearer. Another useful comparandum may be the practice of stamping loaves of bread (e.g., *CIL* X 8058.18). Daniele Manacorda (1993, p. 45) interpreted these stamps as certifications of meeting size, weight, and content specifications, but Claire Holleran (2012, pp. 134–135) has convincingly argued that each household would bring its own homemade bread, stamped to declare ownership, to be baked in a private (or communal, one may add) bakery, as the building and maintainance, as well as the fuel demands of everyday heating, of an oven would be a considerable expense for individual households. Accordingly, one could argue that, as each military division would not have its own foundry—even nowadays, it certainly does not have its own cook-house—the quartermaster would bring the mold, presumably having been manufactured by and belonging to each unit/division, and the lead, presumably allocated in specific amounts to each unit/division by the central military authority, to the foundry of the camp and would expect to bring back a certain number of sling bullets recognized by the commander's name and/or insignia.

215 Ἀχαιός was a common personal name (*LGPN* 1–5), but Αἰνιάν and Μαλιεύς are not attested as names.

216 Thompson 1961, pp. 263–351.

217 Wace 1907, nos. 33a–b, and cf. nos. 34–35a–b, on which these names appear individually.

218 See also Spier 1990, who concludes from a wide-ranging study on emblems in the Archaic period that devices on gems, shields, coins, etc. were merely signs of personal or civic identification, and, although they may occasionally have functioned as puns or as straightforward references to state/family cults or regional traditions, it is highly doubtful that they had any deeper meanings, symbolic or allegorical.

219 See Chase 1902.

220 Tsaravopoulos 2010–2013, nos. 1–3, who identifies him with Ptolemy II Philadelphos, 285–246 B.C.; also Tsaravopoulos 2016, no. 1.

221 Tsaravopoulos 2010–2013, no. 4: Demetrios Poliorcetes or Demetrios II Aitolikos or a military officer or Δη(μόσιον).

222 Tsaravopoulos 2016, no. 2: a personal name Φρασίτων or a military unit Φρασιτῶν (Γ or Λ denoting the subunit).

223 *Olynthus* X, nos. 2217–2218.

224 Despoini 1976, p. 250. Also, Hammond (1984, p. 32) reported an unspecified number of bullets inscribed MEPNA from Pydna. Actually, a total of 112 such bullets have been found and are being studied for publication by the present authors.

225 Empereur 1981, p. 561, no. 20.

226 So, Ma 2010b, p. 170, n. 74, although the editors (see n. 227) published it as found in Osuna; cf. Rihll's (2009, p. 153) remark that "neither of the current hypotheses to explain MER|NA fits a Spanish context"; and Mainardis 2007, p. 874, who in order to explain the find in Spain suggests that Greek mercenaries were soldiering with the Carthaginians prior to 340 B.C.

227 García Garrido and Lalana 1991–1993, p. 104, n. 10, fig. 1.10 (as Latin inscription); *CIL* II^2.5 1106; Díaz Ariño 2005, p. 230, and annex. no. 89; Díaz Ariño 2008, G21: abbreviated name.

228 Radman Livaja 1999–2000, p. 110, and p. 113, n. 1.

229 Tuck 1999–2001, no. 15: ME[. . .]|NA.

230 Kousoulakou 2000a, p. 703: a few in a probably Hellenistic context, plus one in an early 5th century B.C. context; Ma (2010b, p. 170, n. 74) rightly presumes that this must be an intrusion into an earlier stratum; Kousoulakou 2000b, p. 325.

231 Cambitoglou et al. 2001, nos. 18.1 and 18.10: NA|MEP.

232 Kosmidou and Malamidou 2006, p. 136.

233 Mainardis 2007, pp. 870–872, no. 6 = *SEG* 57.2045, no. 1.

234 Angelovski 2011, p. 258. On the date, see Angelovski 2011, p. 260; Nankov 2015, p. 3: "I suggest . . . a siege operation conducted by Philip II officers, Kleoboulos and Hipponikos, perhaps in 342–339 BC."

235 Avram 2014, p. 134.

236 Avram, Chiriac, and Matei 2013, p. 281.

237 BM 1842/0728.555: NA|MEP.

238 Brixhe and Panayotou 1988, pp. 247, 251, drawing on Despoini 1976, p. 250, but see also p. 249; cf. *BÉ* 1987, no. 124 (M. Sève), where the find is reported as found in a tomb of the 2nd century B.C., but this is false. Ma 2010b, p. 170, n. 74, simply presumes it was an intrusion to an earlier stratum.

239 García Garrido and Lalana 1991–1993, no. 10, p. 104, where they speculate that the context was the conflict between Julius Ceasar and the sons of Pompey; also *CIL* II^2.5 1106.

240 Radman Livaja 1999–2000, p. 110.

241 *Olynthus* X, p. 429.

242 These are, in fact, rare in Greek inscriptions prior to the 4th century A.D. (McLean 2002, p. 151).

243 Tsaravopoulos 2004–2009, no. 12; cf. no. 13: παρὰ Φα(λασαρνίων).

244 Although there is no (known) word or proper name that starts with μερν–, there is a settlement by the name Morna (modern Photeina) in Pieria, which, if ancient, could also be Μόρνα/Μέρνα, and its ethnic Μορναίων/Μερναίων, not unlike Τορώνη/Τερώνη (Cambitoglou and Papadopoulos 2001, pp. 40–41) and Κόρκυρα/Κέρκυρα (e.g., on the latter Isocr. 15.108–109; Arist. *Av.* 1463).

245 Brixhe and Panayotou 1988, pp. 247, 251.

246 Koukouli 1967 (*BÉ* 1970, no. 382) = Collart and Ducrey 1975, no. 20 = Pilhofer 2009, no. 167: Philippi, 2nd–3rd century A.D. (*LGPN* 4, s.v.).

247 Λέρνα (Forrer 1938, pp. 195–197: Hattic term); Κέρνη ([Scylax] 112.32–34: Κατὰ δὲ ταῦτα νῆσός ἐστιν, ᾗ ὄνομα Κέρνη. Παράπλους δὲ ἀπὸ Ἡρακλείων στηλῶν ἐπὶ Ἑρμαῖαν ἄκραν ἡμερῶν δύο; Lycoph. *Alex.* 18: Τιθωνὸν ἐν κοίτῃσι τῆς Κέρνης πέλας; Strab. 1.3.2.15: Κέρνην τε νῆσον); Θέρνη (Steph. Byz. s.v. Θέρνη, πόλις Θρᾴκης. τὸ ἐθνικὸν Θερναῖος); Πέρνη (Steph. Byz. Πέρνη· πόλις Θρᾴκης ἀντικρὺ Θάσου. τὸ ἐθνικὸν Περναῖος καὶ Περναία).

248 Exceptions include *Olynthus* X, no. 2242; Brélaz and Ducrey 2003, pl. 23.3; an unpublished bullet from Pydna (Πυ 14295); possibly Nankov 2015, pp. 3–4, fig. 1d; and also Brélaz and Ducrey 2003, pp. 99–101, where the inscription runs on one side only.

249 Among the Εὐγένεος bullets, which most likely were cast in a single mold, this is the only one on which the inscription starts from and ends before the bullet point.

250 See also Díaz Ariño 2005, p. 230; Mainardis 2007, pp. 871–872, no. 6; Díaz Ariño 2008, G21: regarded as abbreviated name, but the text is given as ΜΕΡ|ΝΑ. Derivative names of the adjective ναμερτής/–ές are Ναμέρτης (*LGPN* 5A: Ephesos, ca. 405–390 B.C.; Pergamon, 1st century B.C.–1st century A.D.) or Ναμέρτας (*LGPN* 3A: Sparta, undated) or Νημέρτης (*LGPN* 5b: Iasos, 3rd–2nd century B.C. [gen. Νημέρτεως]), Ναμερτίδας (*LGPN* 3A: Corinth, 6th–5th century B.C.), and Ναμέρτιος (*LGPN* 2: Oinoe, ca. 300–275 B.C.).

251 Cambitoglou et al. 2001, p. 725. Although smaller letters are a usual solution to fit a name on a bullet, abbreviation even down to four letters is quite common; e.g., Christov and Manov 2011, nos. 7–17: Ἀνα|ξάν(δρου); Weiss and Draskowski 2010, p. 147: ΚΡΑ|ΤΕ(–), ΛΥ|ΣΑΝ(–), ΔΙΔΥ(–); Kelly 2012, p. 283: Αἰνε(σίδαμος).

252 Avram 2014, p. 134.

253 See also BM 1842/0728.553: ΝΑ | blank (reading uncertain), in the British Museum.

254 Ma 2010b, p. 170, n. 74.

255 Hom. *Il.* 13.518: ἀλλ' ὅ γε καὶ τόθ' ἅμαρτεν, ὃ δ' Ἀσκάλαφον βάλε δουρὶ, *Il.* 17.609: δίφρῳ ἐφεσταότος· τοῦ μέν ῥ' ἀπὸ τυτθὸν ἅμαρτεν, *Il.* 22.290: καὶ βάλε Πηλεΐδαο μέσον σάκος οὐδ' ἀφάμαρτε; also in a game, when Nausikaa misses her target throwing the ball (*Od.* 1.115–116: σφαῖραν ἔπειτ' ἔρριψε μετ' ἀμφίπολον βασίλεια ἀμφιπόλου μὲν ἅμαρτε, βαθείῃ δ' ἔμβαλε δίνῃ); Hdt. 8.128.2: τοξεύων γὰρ ὁ Ἀρτάβαζος ἐς τὸ συγκείμενον (sc. χωρίον), ἁμαρτὼν τοῦ χωρίου τούτου βάλλει ἀνδρὸς Ποτιδαιήτεω τὸν ὦμον (full text in n. 179); Xen. *Anab.* 3.4.15: ἐπεὶ δὲ διαταχθέντες οἱ Ῥόδιοι ἐσφενδόνησαν καὶ οἱ Σκύθαι τοξόται ἐτόξευσαν καὶ οὐδεὶς ἡμάρτανεν ἀνδρός; Alkidamas fr. 2, 30–31: ἐκδραμὼν τοξότης ἐκ τῶν πολεμίων ἐστοχάσατο τούτου, ἁμαρτὼν δὲ αὐτοῦ βάλλει ἐγγὺς ἐμοῦ; *Scholia in Lycoph.* 64 (Scheer, vol. 2, p. 42): ἀχθέντος γὰρ ἐκ Λήμνου τοῦ Φιλοκτήτου *τοξικῇ* ἐμονομάχησαν αὐτός τε καὶ Ἀλέξανδρος. καὶ πρῶτος μὲν ἀφεὶς Ἀλέξανδρος ἥμαρτε τοῦ Φιλοκτήτου, δεύτερος δὲ τοξεύσας ὁ Φιλοκτήτης βάλλει κατὰ χεῖρα λαιὰν τὸν Ἀλέξανδρον; Eust. *Il.* 8.300–302 (van der Valk, vol. 2, p. 584): ὅτι ἀποτυχίαν τοξότου φράζει ἐν τῷ "καὶ ἄλλον ὀϊστὸν ἀπὸ νευρῆφιν ἴαλλε τοῦ δεῖνος ἀντικρύ, βαλέειν δὲ ἑ ἵετο θυμός· καὶ τοῦ μὲν ἀφάμαρτε."

256 For instance, Hom. *Il.* 3.204: ἔπος νημερτές, *Od.* 1.86: νημερτέα βουλήν, *Od.* 3.19: νημερτέα εἴπῃ; Aesch. *Pers.* 246: ναμερτῆ λόγον.

257 See, for instance, Aesch. *Supp.* 243: ἀψευδεῖ λόγῳ; and Eur. *Med.* 354: μῦθος ἀψευδής, along with *Anth. Pal.* 9.265, lines 5–6: μηκέτ' ἐφ' ὑμετέροις ἀψευδέσι Κρῆτες ὀϊστοῖς αὐχεῖθ', ὑμνείσθω καὶ Διὸς εὐστοχίη; and Hom. *Il.* 18.324: ἅλιον ἔπος, *Il.* 5.715: ἅλιον τὸν μῦθον, along with *Il.* 4.498: ἅλιον βέλος.

258 There are two unlikely readings, but nevertheless worth mentioning, that do not involve an abbreviation. A particular gloss in Hesychius, s.v. μορνάμενος· μαχόμενος, for μαρνάμενος (see, e.g., Eur. *Phoen.* 1141–1143: καὶ πρῶτα μὲν τόξοισι καὶ μεσαγκύλοις ἐμαρνάμεσθα σφενδόναις θ' ἑκηβόλοις πέτρων τ' ἀραγμοῖς), could be a contextually plausible parallel form of *μέρνα = battle, but it presents linguistic problems as to the change between the phonemes /e/, /o/, and /a/ (on this see Chantraine 1980, s.v. βερνώμεθα: κληρωσώμεθα, Λάκωνες [Hsch.], which, as Chantraine notes, is probably a corrupted lemma, with doubtful links to μέρος, μείρομαι, by a stem μερ-ν- (by dissimilation); and cf. LSJ s.v.

βάρναμαι = μάρναμαι, also by dissimilation according to Chantraine (1980, s.v.), who notes that no derivative nouns of this verb are known. Another gloss in Hesychius, s.v. ἀμερνός· ἄπειρος, without the privative affix would give an unattested adjective *μερνός, –ή, –όν, "experienced," that could be read as a qualification of the bullet itself (i.e., μολυβδίς), an inscription of Type 3b.ii.

259 Mitrevski 2016, p. 48; Mitrevski 2019, p. 324: found along with arrowheads in a destruction layer dated in the early 3rd century B.C. and associated with the Gallic invasion.

260 García Garrido and Lalana 1991–1993, no. 12; *CIL* II^2.5 1106; Díaz Ariño 2005, p. 230: MIKINA *vel* MIKINΔ ← / device. See also n. 226.

261 Weiss and Draskowski 2010, no. 15: MIKINA ← | fork with four prongs.

262 Avram 2014, pp. 133–134.

263 Romero 2021, pp. 213–214: MIKINA | fork with four prongs. See also Romero 2015, pp. 32–33, nos. B-349.01–06.

264 Cf. Garcia Ramon, Helly, and Tziafalias 2007, pp. 94–95: Σμικίνας or Σμικινᾶς, from a form σμικ(κ)ός.

265 *LGPN* 1, 2, and 3b: Euboia, Attica, and central Greece.

266 *LGPN* 3a–b: central Greece and Korkyra, 3rd–2nd century B.C.; and also as Μικίννας, *LGPN* 3b: Thespiai, 3rd century B.C., *LGPN* 5a: Troas, 3rd–2nd century B.C.

267 A single bullet of the former type has been found in Pydna (Πυ 14365; unpublished). Other published examples are: one bullet of unknown provenance, undated (Vischer 1878b, p. 275, no. 75: MIK|?IN; Avram, Chiriac, and Matei 2013, p. 280 [Μικίνας (I)]: MIK|IN[ΑΣ]); one bullet found at Torone, ante 349 B.C. (Cambitoglou et al. 2001, pp. 725–726, no. 18.2); unspecified number of bullets found at Amphipolis, mid-4th century B.C. (Kosmidou and Malamidou 2006, p. 136).

268 Avram, Chiriac, and Matei 2013, p. 280 (Μικίνας I–II).

269 Ma 2010b, pp. 164–165.

270 See Avram, Chiriac, and Matei 2013, p. 273, who, based on Ma's suggestion, date the bullet to 306 B.C. (conquest of Cyprus by Demetrios Poliorcetes) or to 294 B.C. (recapture of the island by Ptolemy I).

271 Maiuri 1925, p. 251, no. IV: θεαρõ | X͡A + *penteakontion*? = Segre and Pugliese Carratelli 1949–1951, p. 275, no. 192q: Θεάρο | X͡A + five-pronged object; Hellmann 1982, no. 4: Θεαρõ | X͡A + "une fourche à cinq pointes—la pointe centrale étant plus longue—qui est peut-être aussi un monogramme"; BM 1959/0721.1, 1861/1024.32, 1861/1024.39, and 1861/1024.43: ΘΕΑΡΟ | five shorter prongs. The symbol that the curator of the British Museum identifies as the Coptic symbol Ϫ is the monogramme X͡A, as Hellmann (1982, no. 4) correctly remarks. Ma (2010b, p. 163) speculates that the monogram stands for Ἀχαιοί, Achaean, slingers. All of Thearos' bullets with known provenance come from Kameiros, Rhodes. For an overview, see Avram, Chiriac, and Matei 2013, p. 273.

272 Maiuri 1925, p. 251, no. II = Segre and Pugliese Carratelli 1949–1951, p. 275, no. 192o: Εὐβουλίδας | A; Weiss and Draskowski 2010, no. 16: Εὐβουλίδας | (pitch?)fork with four bent prongs and short handle, next to a ligature of an O inside a Λ or A, which lies in the middle; Beden and Manucci 2005, p. 110: ΕΤΒΟΓΛΙΔΑΣ (*BÉ* 2206, no. 75 [M. Sève]: Εὐβουλίδας) | "fourche à quatre pointes" (*SEG* 55.1270: hay fork) and an A; Avram 2014, p. 132; Manov and Torbov 2016, no. 18: Εὐβουλίδας | (pitch?)fork with four bent prongs and short handle, next to a ligature of an O inside a Λ or A, which lies in the middle. Most of Euboulidas' bullets with known provenance come from Kameiros, Rhodes. For an overview, see Avram, Chiriac, and Matei 2013, p. 271.

273 Moore et al. 2012, p. 5: ΘΑΡΥΓΟΣ [should be read Θάρυπος] | five-pronged fork, from Vigla, Cyprus.

274 Zangemeister 1885, p. XVIII: *agricolarum furca*.

275 Weiss and Draskowski 2010, no. 14: blank | (pitch?)fork with five straight prongs and short handle.

276 BM 1955/0920.279, a Knidian amphora with a round stamp containing an inscription and a four-pronged "trident," according to the curator of the museum.

277 Maiuri 1925, p. 251, no. IV.

278 García Garrido and Lalana 1991–1993, no. 12.

279 Hellmann 1982, no. 4.

280 Weiss and Draskowski 2010, pp. 136–143, esp. p. 143.

281 Weiss and Draskowski 2010, p. 136.

282 Weiss and Draskowski 2010, p. 139.

283 Aiolic term for an implement used in sacrifices, see Hom. *Il.* 1.463 and *Od.* 3.460; cf. Apoll. *Lex. hom.* s.v. πεμπώβολα· πέντε ὀβελίσκοι τριαινοειδεῖς ἐκ μιᾶς ἀρχῆς; Hsch., s.v. πεμπωβόλους· πέντε ὀβελίσκους ἐκ μιᾶς λαβῆς συνεχομένους τριαινοειδῶς.

284 Weiss and Draskowski 2010, p. 141.

285 Bon and Bon 1957, no. 646 (*fourche?*), no. 656 (*fourche?*), no. 762 (*fourche ou râteau*), and no. 812 (*fourche*); *Agora* XXXVII, nos. 257–258 (five-pronged pitchforks).

286 Bon and Bon 1957, no. 656 (*fourche?*) and no. 1707 (*torche*).

287 All known examples are on amphora stamps from Akanthos (Filis 2011, nos. Ακ.2-8, Ακ.2-12, Ακ.2-13, and Ακ.2-16), but there may be more.

288 Kosmidou and Malamidou 2006, pp. 135, 138, fig. 9.

289 *Olynthus* X, nos. 2202–2216: ΚΛΕΟ|ΒΟΥΛΟ.

290 Sismanidis 1994b, p. 460 = 1994a, p. 283: ca. 100 bullets of which ca. 50 inscribed with the names Φιλίππου, Πωτάλου, Κλεοβούλου; Sismanidis 1992, p. 460: ΚΛΕΟΒΟΥΛΟΥ; Sismanidis 1993, p. 435: no mention of names; Sismanidis 1995, p. 390: ΚΛΕΟΒΟΥΛΟΥ; Sismanidis 1997, p. 473: ΚΛΕΟΒΟΥΛΟΥ (the renderings of the texts are non-diplomatic; the ending could be either in –ου or –ō).

291 Adam-Veleni 2000, p. 693.

292 Cambitoglou et al. 2001, pp. 725–726, no. 18.3: ΚΛΕΟ|ΒΟΥΛΟ.

293 Kosmidou and Malamidou 2006, p. 136, fig. 11–12: ΚΛΕΟΒ|ΟΥΛΟΥ ← (the reading is confirmed from the photograph).

294 Angelovski 2011, p. 258: ΚΛΕΟ|[ΒΟΥΛΟΣ], "relatively damaged but could be identified as 'ΒΟΥΛΟS'."

295 Christov and Manov 2011, nos. 1–2, 5: ΚΛΕΟ|ΒΟΥΛΟΥ, nos. 3–4: ΚΛΕΟ|ΒΟΥΛ[ΟΥ], and no. 6: ΚΛΕΟ|ΒΟΥ[ΛΟΥ] (photographs are not clear enough to verify the readings).

296 Avram, Chiriac, and Matei 2013, p. 277.

297 Nankov 2015, pp. 3–4: ΚΛΕΟ|ΒΟΥΛ[ΟΥ].

298 *LGPN* 4.

299 *Olynthus* X, pp. 428–429.

300 See *Olynthus* X, pp. 426–427.

301 See, e.g., *Olynthus* X, nos. 2163–2201; Adam-Veleni 2000, p. 693; Angelovski 2011, p. 258.

302 Rihll 2009, p. 159.

303 For the use of both graphemes ō and ου for the phoneme [oˑ], see Threatte 1980, pp. 238–259.

304 Christov and Manov (2011, p. 27) date the siege of the Kozi Gramadi fortress to 347–342/1 B.C. on the assumption that the ΚΛΕΟΒΟΥΛΟ bullets were manufactured during the siege of Olynthos, and whatever was left over was used in subsequent military operations; thus all Κλεοβούλō bullets must postdate the siege of Olynthos. Those from Methone, as well as Amphipolis (besieged in 357 B.C.; Diod. 16.8.2), invalidate their argument, but their dating for the siege of Kozi Gramadi fortress may still be correct.

305 *LGPN* 3b.

306 *IG* II^2 10366: (gen.) Εὐγένōς, early 4th century B.C.

307 *LGPN* 4.

308 *LGPN* 1.

309 *LGPN* 5a: (gen.) Εὐγένευς, 311–306 B.C.

310 For the uncontracted genitive ending –εος, see Buck 1955, p. 90, no. 108.1.

311 See Denniston 1954, p. 128, on the sarcastic function of the exclamatory particle γε when combined with adjectives and adverbs; for instances of ironical use of the adverb εὖ γε, see LSJ, s.v.

312 Smyth 1920, p. 313, no. 1288.

313 *LGPN* 3a: Ṇέος?, Tegea, mid-4th century B.C.; *LGPN* 3b: Chorsiai, Hellenistic period; *LGPN* 5b: Miletos, 3rd century B.C.

314 *Olynthus* X, no. 2180, and Cambitoglou et al. 2001, no. 18.11, respectively. Weiss and Draskowski (2010, pp. 150–151), in line with the theory developed by Ma (2010b, pp. 170–173), see these as illustrative examples of "the expression of the *esprit de corps* and emotional attachment to the commander by the praise of his masculinity and charisma."

315 *Olynthus* X, no. 2176.

316 Pritchett 1991b, pp. 62–63.

317 *LGPN* 1–5.

318 Tod 1945, p. 84, n. 660; *BÉ* 1948, no. 7 (J. and L. Robert); Weiss and Draskowski 2010, p. 147.

319 Ma 2010b, pp. 167–171; see also nn. 152, 154–155.

320 As determined by the finds at Amphipolis (Κλεοβούλō) and Pydna (ΜΕΡΝΑ).

321 *Olynthus* X, p. 433.

322 Tsaravopoulos 2004–2009, pp. 332–339 = 2012, p. 209; but the validity of the method is uncertain, as the uninscribed bullets are not taken into account. See also Hristov 2012, p. 81, for bullets with the same inscription found both inside and outside the walls, and n. 4 on the reuse of missiles.

323 Tsaravopoulos 2004–2009, p. 340; Nankov 2015, p. 7.

324 XRF results on a sample of ten bullets (**28/1** [ΜΕΘ 281], **28/2** [ΜΕΘ 285], **28/38** [ΜΕΘ 286], **28/63** [ΜΕΘ 289], **28/58** [ΜΕΘ 292], **28/62** [ΜΕΘ 651], **28/42** [ΜΕΘ 656], **28/65** [ΜΕΘ 2891], **28/61** [ΜΕΘ 2900], **28/34** [ΜΕΘ 2909]) identified only pure lead alloy, no copper or silver (Vanessa Muros, pers. comm.). Lead isotope analysis, which was not performed, could produce provenance indicators for the lead and by extension for each of the issues of bullets. Isotopic and chemical analyses on the sling bullets from Pistiros showed that the lead used for their manufacture originated from the Chalkidike and Laurion in Attica (Kuleff et al. 2006, no. Pb 39: Chalkidike, no. Pb 40: Laurion, no. Pb 41: Chalkidike, no. Pb 48: Laurion). Determining the provenance of the lead for these "early" bullets from Methone could potentially show whether or not the lead resources of Philip II were any different before the capture of Chalkidike.

325 See also Manacorda 1993.

326 Type C according to Robinson (*Olynthus* X, p. 382); Type 3B4 according to Snodgrass (1964, p. 153); Type IIB1 according to Baitinger (2001, pp. 17–20). This type of arrowhead was probably called τριγλώχις (ὀϊστός) in antiquity (Pollux 1.137: καὶ τοῦ βέλους [μέρη] τὸ μὲν ἐπτερωμένον εἴποις ἂν κεφαλὴν βέλους, ὁ δὲ σίδηρος ἀκίς, καὶ τῆς ἀκίδος ὄγκοι μὲν αἱ πρὸς τῷ καλάμῳ, γλωχῖνες δὲ αἱ πρὸς τῇ ἀκμῇ προβολαί; Apoll. *Lex. hom.* s.v. "γλωχῖνα" τὴν γωνίαν, καὶ "τριγλώχινας ὀϊστούς" τοὺς τριγώνους τὸ σχῆμα; Hsch., s.v. γλωχῖνα· τὴν γωνίαν τοῦ βέλους Ω 274 καὶ "τριγλώχινας ὀιστούς" Ε 393. καὶ γλῶσσαν. καὶ ἄκρον. κυρίως δὲ "γλωχῖνες" αἱ τῶν ἀκίδων ἐξοχαὶ καὶ αἱ τοῦ ζυγοῦ γωνίαι Ω 274; Paul. Aeg. 6.88.1–2: διαφέρουσι τοίνυν τὰ βέλη ὕλῃ, σχήματι, μεγέθει, ἀριθμῷ, σχέσει, δυνάμει, ὕλη . . . σχήματι δέ, καθ' ὃ τὰ μέν εἰσι στρογγύλα, τὰ δὲ γωνιωτά, οἷον τρίγωνα ἢ τετράγωνα, τὰ δὲ γλωχινωτά, καὶ τούτων τὰ μὲν διγλώχινα τὰ καὶ λογχωτὰ καλούμενα, τὰ δὲ τριγλώχινα, καὶ τὰ μὲν ἀκιδωτά, τὰ δὲ χωρὶς ἀκίδων, καὶ τῶν ἀκιδωτῶν τὰ μὲν ἐπὶ τὰ ὀπίσω νευούσας τὰς ἀκίδας ἔχουσιν; Eust. *Il.* 8.297 (van der Valk, vol. 2, p. 584): τανυγλώχινες δὲ ὀϊστοί ἀντὶ τοῦ ὀξυγώνιοι, μακρογώνιοι. γλωχίν γὰρ καὶ ἀλλαχοῦ ἡ γωνία δηλοῦται, see Eust. *Il.* 5.393 (van der Valk, vol. 2, p. 106): "γλωχίν δὲ ξίφους ἡ γωνία"); see also Snodgrass 1964, p. 153.

327 *Olynthus* X, p. 383, nos. 1907–1911; no. 1912 is similar but bears no inscription.

328 Inv. no. 1960.490, Department of Asian and Mediterranean Art, Arthur M. Sackler Museum, Harvard,

bequest of D. M. Robinson.

329 Snodgrass 1967, pp. 116–117; Snodgrass 1971b, p. 108 (accepted by Hammond and Griffith 1979, p. 447).

330 Marsden 1977, pp. 213–217.

331 *Olynthus* X, p. 382.

332 See the plan in Lee 2001, p. 17.

333 See above, "Commentary on the Inscriptions."

334 *Olynthus* X, nos. 2228–2240, 2241: ΦΙΛΙΠΠ ← | spearhead.

335 Hellmann 1982, nos. 32–34.

336 Sismanidis 1992, p. 460; 1994a, p. 283; 1997, p. 473.

337 Christov and Manov 2011, p. 25.

338 Karamitrou-Mentesidi 2011c, pp. 38–39, fig. 2 (= Karamitrou-Mentesidi 2016, p. 816).

339 Romero 2021, p. 214: ΦΙΛΙΠΠΟΥ | spearhead.

340 Robinson (*Olynthus* X, p. 382) actually writes: "All of the arrowheads inscribed were found along the west side of the North Hill."

341 Borza 1990, p. 299.

342 Lee 2001, p. 15.

343 For a survey and a catalogue of slinger iconography in Italy in the Roman period, see Völling 1990, pp. 27–33, 54–55 (Liste 2), with the addition of a funerary relief stele with a frontal depiction of a slinger in Arneth 1851, p. 236, and pl. IV; Fougères 1896a, p. 1365, and fig. 3328.

344 Tsountas 1891, pp. 11–21, pl. 2.2.

345 Rizza 2011, p. 39, 43, fig. 26; Biondi 2019, fig. 4.2.

346 Zapheiropoulou 2000, fig. 7a and 10 (detail); Croissant 2008, "amphore B."

347 *Délos* X, no. 459.

348 BAPD no. 300770; Richter 1932.

349 BAPD no. 300000; Benndorf 1889, pl. IV.1b.

350 BAPD no. 301062; De Witte 1876, pl. 3.

351 BAPD no. 301063; Lasteyrie 1890, pp. 92–93.

352 BAPD no. 310312; *ABV* p. 136, no. 52; Mannack 2012, p. 120, fig. 69.

353 Dawkins 1929a, p. 92, pls. XV–XVI.

354 BAPD no. 2183; Paul 1995, p. 21, no. 11.

355 BAPD no. 340267; Vierneisel and Kaesar 1990, p. 116, fig. 14.7a–b.

356 BAPD no. 16407.

357 BAPD no. 200290; Walters 1921, pp. 118–119, no. 1.

358 BAPD no. 7590; Lissarrague 1999, p. 166.

359 BAPD no. 6956; Simon 1982, pp. 80–83, no. 34.

360 There are many versions of the scene; a comparable one is on an Attic red-figure calyx krater of ca. 430 B.C. (British Museum E 466), in which Kephalos is depicted carrying two spears and a rock in his hand, ready to throw it at Eos. Another version, this time with Kephalos fleeing, depicts him with hunting attire (a pair of spears, sword, hunting boots, cap) and two more items floating in the background between the two figures, a club and a sling, on an Attic red-figure bell krater, 450–425 B.C. (Musée du Louvre G491). For the sling used in hunting, see n. 31; see also Strab. 15.3.18: θηρεύουσι δὲ σαύνια ἀφ᾽ ἵππων βάλλοντες καὶ τοξεύματα καὶ σφενδονῶντες; and Verg. *Georg.* 1.308–309: *auritosque sequi lepores, tum figere dammas, | stuppea torquentem Balearis verbera fundae* (hunting hare, deer, etc.).

361 BAPD no. 206076; Pellegrini 1912, no. 204.

362 BAPD no. 207547; Froehner 1883, no. 379.

363 BAPD no. 206001.

364 Wide 1901, no. 4.

365 BAPD no. 215872; *ARV*[2] p. 1200, no. 38; Stähler 1992, pl. 3.6; Oakley 2010, p. 94, fig. 1.

366 Gardner 1883, pls. X.10 (431–371 B.C.), XIII.5 (335–280 B.C.).

367 Liampi 1993, p. 33.

368 BAPD no. 200583; *ARV*[2] p. 69 ("athletes, several of them characterized as acontists"); Oakley, Coulson, and Palagia 1997, p. 45, fig. 15 ("sfendonistes"); Giudice and Panvini 2007, pp. 40, 41, fig. 7.

369 Baralis, Panayotova, and Nedev 2019, no. 51 (A. Hermary).

370 Maiuri 1927, pp. 69–70.

371 The slinger on no. 2 seems dressed just like the spearmen behind him, also carrying a shield, but the depiction is too rudimentary to allow any further inferences.

372 Hom. *Il.* 2.527–530: Λοκρῶν δ' ἡγεμόνευεν Ὀϊλῆος ταχὺς Αἴας | μείων, οὔ τι τόσος γε ὅσος Τελαμώνιος Αἴας | ἀλλὰ πολὺ μείων· ὀλίγος μὲν ἔην λινοθώρηξ, | ἐγχείῃ δ' ἐκέκαστο Πανέλληνας καὶ Ἀχαιούς ("And the Locrians had as leader the swift son of Oïleus, Aias the less[er], in no ways as great as Telamonian Aias, but far less. Small of stature was he, with corselet of linen, but with the spear he far excelled the whole host of Hellenes and Achaeans," transl. A. T. Murray, Cambridge, MA, and London, 1924); cf. Eust. *Il.* 2.259 (van der Valk, vol. 1, p. 422–423): λέγει δὲ καὶ ὅτι λινοθώρηξ ἦν (sc. Αἴας). φανήσεται γὰρ ὅτι πεζῶν ἦρχεν, ὅθεν οὐδὲ αὐτὸς σιδηροῦ χιτῶνος πάνυ ἐδέετο. (p. 423) «ἐγχείῃ δέ», φησίν, «ἐκέκαστο Πανέλληνας καὶ Ἀχαιούς», ἤγουν ἐγχέσπαλος ἦν καὶ αἰχμητής, εἰ καὶ μὴ τοιούτων ἦρχεν ἀλλὰ σφενδονητῶν τε καὶ τοξοτῶν καὶ τοιούτων τινῶν; *Scholia in Hom. Il.* 2.830b: (BCE3E4) ex. <λινοθώρηξ:> σφενδονήτης ἢ τοξότης; *Scholia in Hom. Il.* (*scholia recentiora Theodori Meliteniotis*, e cod. Genevensi gr. 44), 529: λινοθώρηξ· λινοῦν θώρακα ἔχων· οἱ γὰρ τοξόται λινοῦς θώρακας φοροῦσιν; *Anonyma tactica byzantina* 30.3 (Dain 1938): Οἵ γε μὴν ψιλοὶ τῶν ἀναγεγραμμένων ὅπλων εἶχον οὐδέν, ἐκηβόλοι δ' ἐτύγχανον πάντες τοξεύοντες ἢ ἀκοντίζοντες ἢ λίθους ἀφιέντες, οὓς μὲν ἀπὸ χειρός, τοὺς δέ γε πλείστους διὰ σφενδόνης. Στολὰς δὲ παχυτάτας εἶχον ἐκ λινοῦ πεποιημένας μέχρι τῶν γονάτων κατιούσας καὶ μικρόν τι πρός.

373 On this type of armor, see especially Aldrete, Bartell, and Aldrete 2013.

374 "Even as you see all things become hot and catch fire through motion, yea, even a ball of lead too, whirling in a long course, will melt" (transl. C. Bailey, Oxford, 1910).

375 "In no other way than often a ball of lead grows hot in its course, when dropping many bodies of stiff cold it has taken in fire in the air" (transl. C. Bailey, Oxford, 1910).

376 "Mezentius his spear laid by, and whirled three times about his head the thong of his loud sling: the leaden liquefied bullet clove the youth's mid-forehead, and his towering form fell prostrate its full length along the ground" (transl. Th. C. Williams, Boston, 1910; modified by the authors).

377 "In the same way a leaden bullet is liquefied when discharged from a sling, and falls in drops by reason of atmospheric friction just as it would do through fire" (transl. J. Clarke, London, 1910).

378 "Then blazing torches flew, arrows and stones, and ponderous balls of lead molten by speed of passage through the air" (transl. E. Ridley, London, 1905).

379 "The son of Jove, astonished, while he wheeled on balanced pinions through the yielding air, burned hot; as oft from Balearic sling the leaden missile, hurled with sudden force, burns in a glowing heat beneath the clouds" (transl. B. More, Boston, 1922); cf. Maximus Planudes *Publii Ovidii Nasonis Metamorphoseon, graece versi* 2.922: ἢ ὡς ὁπότε Βαλιαρικὴ σφενδόνη μόλιβδον βάλλει, | ὃς ἵπταταί τε καὶ προϊὼν ἐκθερμαίνεται, καί, ὅπερ | οὐκ εἶχε, πῦρ ὑπὸ ταῖς νεφέλαις εὑρίσκει.

380 "His mortal flesh dissolved | into thin air, as when a ball of lead | shot up from a broad sling melts all away | and soon is lost in heaven" (transl. B. More, Boston, 1922). For a commentary and translations of the two similes in Ov. *Met.*, see also von Glinski 2012, p. 50.

381 "But the Tyrians—their only means of safety—crown the summit of the battlements, and hurl charred stakes and shining darts of steel against the foe, and stones torn from their own walls, and missiles that catch fire as they go through the void of air; a fierce deluge streams from the roof-tops, and the barred windows spew forth hissing javelins" (transl. J. H. Mozley, London and New York, 1928).

382 "The sling is the most deadly weapon that is used by the light-armed troops, because the lead slug is the same colour as the air and is invisible in its course, so that it falls unexpectedly on the unprotected bodies of the enemy, and not only is the impact itself violent but also the missile, heated by the friction of its rush through the air, penetrates the flesh very deeply, so that it even becomes invisible and the swelling quickly closes over it" (transl. Members of the Illinois Greek Club, Cambridge, MA, and London, 1948).

383 Note also the possible reading πυρί, "to the fire," of an incised inscription on a lead bullet from Cyprus (Åström and Nikolaou 1980, no. 5).

384 "On the seventh day of the attack, when a very high wind having sprung up, they began to discharge by their slings hot balls made of burned or hardened clay, and heated javelins, upon the huts, which, after the Gallic custom, were thatched with straw. These quickly took fire, and by the violence of the wind, scattered their flames in every part of the camp" (transl. W. A. McDevitte and W. S. Bohn, New York, 1869). Cf. Dion. Hal. *Ant. Rom.* 10.16.4: καὶ συνεκινδύνευον οὗτοι τῷ Οὐαλερίῳ μόνοι καὶ συνεξεῖλον τὰ φρούρια πᾶσαν εὔνοιαν καὶ προθυμίαν ἀποδειξάμενοι. ἐγένετο δ' ἡ προσβολὴ τοῖς φρουρίοις πανταχόθεν· οἱ μὲν γὰρ ἀπὸ τῶν πλησίον οἰκιῶν ἀσφάλτου καὶ πίσσης πεπυρωμένης ἀγγεῖα σφενδόναις ἐναρμόττοντες ἐπέβαλλον ὑπὲρ τὸν λόφον.

385 "Caresus strikes down Dipsas and Strymon who scatters wounds in concealment from a sling" (transl. J. H. Mozley, Cambridge, MA, 1972); see also Wijsman 2000, p. 96: "the death caused by a sling apparently comes out of the air as if from nowhere, the sling responsible is not visible."

386 "One hurled volleys of bullets with Balearic sling: standing erect, he brandished the light thong thrice round his head, and concealed his missile in the air, for the winds to carry; another poised whizzing stones with strong arm; a third threw a lance speeded by a light strap" (transl. J. D. Duff, London and Cambridge, MA, 1961; modified by the authors).

387 See also Brélaz and Ducrey 2007, pp. 340–341.

388 "So shouted forth the twain, and aroused the battle of the Achaeans. And as flakes of snow fall thick on a winter's day, when Zeus, the counsellor, bestirred him to snow, shewing forth to men these arrows of his, and he lulled the winds and shedded the flakes continually, until he had covered the peaks of the lofty mountains and the high headlands, and the grassy plains, and the rich tillage of men; aye, and over the harbours and shores of the grey sea is the snow strewn, albeit the wave as it beat against it kept it off, but all things beside are wrapped therein, when the storm of Zeus drove it on: even so from both sides their stones flew thick, some upon the Trojans, and some from the Trojans upon the Achaeans, as they cast at one another; and over all the wall the din arose" (transl. A. T. Murray, London and New York, 1928; modified by the authors).

389 "The Macedonians standing in front of the rampart at first easily held off the Romans, who were trying the approaches from every direction, with much assistance from those who from the higher ground were hurling a veritable cloud of missiles from their slings as well as darts and arrows at the same time" (transl. J. C. Yardley, Cambridge, MA, 2018).

390 ". . . and to hurl their weapons from all sides at the same time. It was as if a storm hit the horses—the wounds dealt by the missiles hurled from every quarter on the one hand, the discordant shouts on the other—and it so terrified them that they suddenly bolted in all directions indiscriminately, as though they had no reins" (transl. C. Yardley, Oxford and New York, 2000).

391 "And stones rain hissing from the slings, swift bullets, and dread arrows winged with a double death rival the lightning-stroke" (transl. J. H. Mozley, London and New York, 1928).

392 "Yet the relentless rain turns aside neither face nor breast, the warriors keep their gaze steady upon the walls, forgetful of death and seeing nought but their own weapons" (transl. J. H. Mozley, London and New York, 1928).

393 "Others were throwing stones, others were sending arrows like rain coming from the sky, others were throwing spears, and others were slinging bullets obscuring the light of day . . . and the air was dusky and bloody" (transl. by the authors).

394 "The swoop of forked lightning, the arrow sped by Skythian string, the trail of the swiftly-falling star, the leaden hurricane of bullets whirled from Balearic slings has never so rapidly split the airy paths of the sky" (transl. W. B. Anderson, Cambridge, MA, and London, 1963).

395 Καταπάλτης according to the Attic phonology, see Threatte 1980, p. 121.

396 LSJ s.v. καταπαλτός· *hurled down,* ἐξ αἰθέρος ὕδωρ A. ap. Aristid. Or. 36(48).53. Note also a bullet from Hala Sultan Tekke (Cyprus) with an incised and a dotted inscription on either side, both of them doubtful, the latter of which Nicolaou (1977, p. 215, no. 3) reads in the Cypriot syllabic script as: se-u (σεῦ = σοῦ, "yours") *vel* u-se (ὗσε, "it rained"). See further a bullet inscribed κύε, "get pregnant" (Michailidou-Nikolaou 1969–1970, p. 367, no. 2; see also n. 152) in comparison with Aesch. fr. 44.3–4: ὄμβρος δ' ἀπ' εὐνάεντος οὐρανοῦ πεσὼν ἔκυσε γαῖαν, which is reminiscent of the prayer addressed by the hierophants of Eleusis to Sky and Earth (*IG* II² 4876: ὁ Πὰν ὁ Μήν, χαίρετε νύνφαι καλαί. ὕε κύε ὑπέρχυε, Attica, Imperial period; Hippol. *Haer.* 5.7.34: ἐστὶ τὸ μέγα καὶ ἄρρητον <τῶν> Ἐλευσινίων μυστήριον «ὕε, κύε»; Proclus *Pl. Tim. comm.* (Diehl 1906, p. 176): εἰς δὲ τούτους βλέποντες καὶ ἐν τοῖς Ἐλευσινίοις ἱεροῖς εἰς μὲν τὸν οὐρανὸν ἀναβλέποντες ἐβόων 'ὕε', καταβλέψαντες δὲ εἰς τὴν γῆν τὸ 'κύε'. The entire idea of "impregnating rain" may lend some credibility to the readings ὗσε and κύε, although the former remains extremely doubtful (both as an inscription and as to its reading).

397 "For when his olives and grapes burgeon forth, they shall be cut down with the flail of the pelleted storm. And if we see one of you making bricks, we will pour down our cataracts, and with our gun-stones of ice beat flat his house tiles" (transl. W. J. M. Starkie, Amsterdam, 1966; modified by the authors).

398 "It snows spears, lead and stones it hails" (transl. E. H. Warmington, Cambridge, MA, and London, 1936).

399 "As he was speaking and trying to get hold of the hero's knees, Alcides (i.e., Herakles) seized him and, swinging him round three times and a fourth, hurled him, more powerfully than a catapult, into the Euboean waves. While hanging in the air, he got hardened by the wind, just as rain-drops are said to be frozen by the wind, thus becoming snowflakes, which as they whirl congregate into a soft mass and then, by the pressure of twisting together, into round hailstones. So, ancient tradition says, he (sc. Lichas), flung by strong arms through space, became bloodless with fright, and as all moisture in him dried up he turned into a hard flint-stone." (transl. by the authors).

400 ". . . such a volley of stones, like the densest hail, was rained upon the fleet now approaching land" (transl. F. G. Moore, Cambridge, MA, 1957).

401 See the "Commentary on the Inscriptions."

402 See, e.g., Eur. *Tr.* 78–79: καὶ Ζεὺς μὲν ὄμβρον καὶ χάλαζαν ἄσπετον πέμψει. See also Pairman Brown 2000, p. 146: "Jupiter and Zeus Pater both came into the Mediterranean bearing the name of the Indo-European god of the bright sky; but in these texts they are assimilated to an indigenous High God responsible for things that fall from the dark sky—the thunderbolt, hail and snow as well as beneficent rain. In Hebrew absolutely, and in Greek and Latin more obliquely, those falling things are identified as the God's *arrows.*"

403 See also Eust. *Il.* 12.280 (van der Valk, vol. 3, p. 390): ἀστείως δὲ τὴν ἄνωθεν ἐν χειμῶνι μάλιστα κατασκήπτουσαν νιφοβολίαν ἐπίδειξιν λέγει Διός, ὡς οἷα ἐκηβολοῦντος. δῆλον δὲ ὅτι Διός, ἤγουν ἀέρος, βέλη οὐ μόνον νιφάδες, ἀλλὰ καὶ κεραυνοὶ καὶ εἴ τι ἄλλο τοιοῦτον ἀέριον πάθος, ἐν οἷς καὶ χάλαζα. ὅθεν καὶ τὸ χαλαζοβολεῖν.

29

THE ANCIENT AGORA OF METHONE: POTTERY FROM THE DESTRUCTION LAYER

Athena Athanassiadou

In 354 B.C. Philip II besieged and razed Methone and forced the inhabitants to leave. After the abandonment of the settlement, the roofs of the buildings in the agora fell onto the floors, the walls collapsed, and as a result, a solid deposit of disintegrated bricks was created, which sealed the destruction layers from that time on. The excavation of these layers brought to light a well-dated group of pottery, the bulk of which dates to the second quarter of the 4th century B.C. It comprises black-glazed vases, a few examples with painted decoration, plain pottery, and several cooking pots. Most numerous are the amphoras, usually found in fragments that are scattered on the floors, indoors and outdoors. Finally, fragments of lamps of several types have been identified which are dated from the 6th to the mid-4th century B.C.

This particular group of pottery is very important because it enriches our knowledge of late Classical ceramic production and also because it is connected with the historical events which determined the fate of Methone, as the fragmentary pots bespeak the use of the agora buildings during Philip's siege of 354 B.C.

THE AGORA OF METHONE

The ancient agora of Methone developed in the hollow between two adjacent hills, where there is evidence of residential and fortification activity long before the arrival of settlers from Eretria in the 8th century B.C. Excavations on the East Hill—specifically in Plot 274—in the years between 2003 and 2009 revealed a series of buildings that developed around a large central square.[1] These buildings were of a public character, as indicated by their monumental size. The excavations brought to light extensive workshop and commercial activity.

The most thoroughly excavated buildings of this complex are Buildings A and B, located south and north of the large central square, Plateia A (Fig. 29.1). Their excavation has not been completed, as both continue to the north and south into adjacent plots of private land. The masonry of Building A (Fig. 29.2) revealed various building phases, the earliest of which dates back to the second quarter of the 6th century B.C., when the building first received monumental dimensions. In the last quarter of the same century, the building was curtailed toward the west, while in the 5th century B.C. a colonnaded stoa gallery or porch was added along the north side of the building facing the central square, Plateia A. The initial building phase of Building B (Fig. 29.3) dates to the end of the 6th century B.C., but various interventions and repairs were carried out throughout its history, not least an extension of it to the south, which probably dates

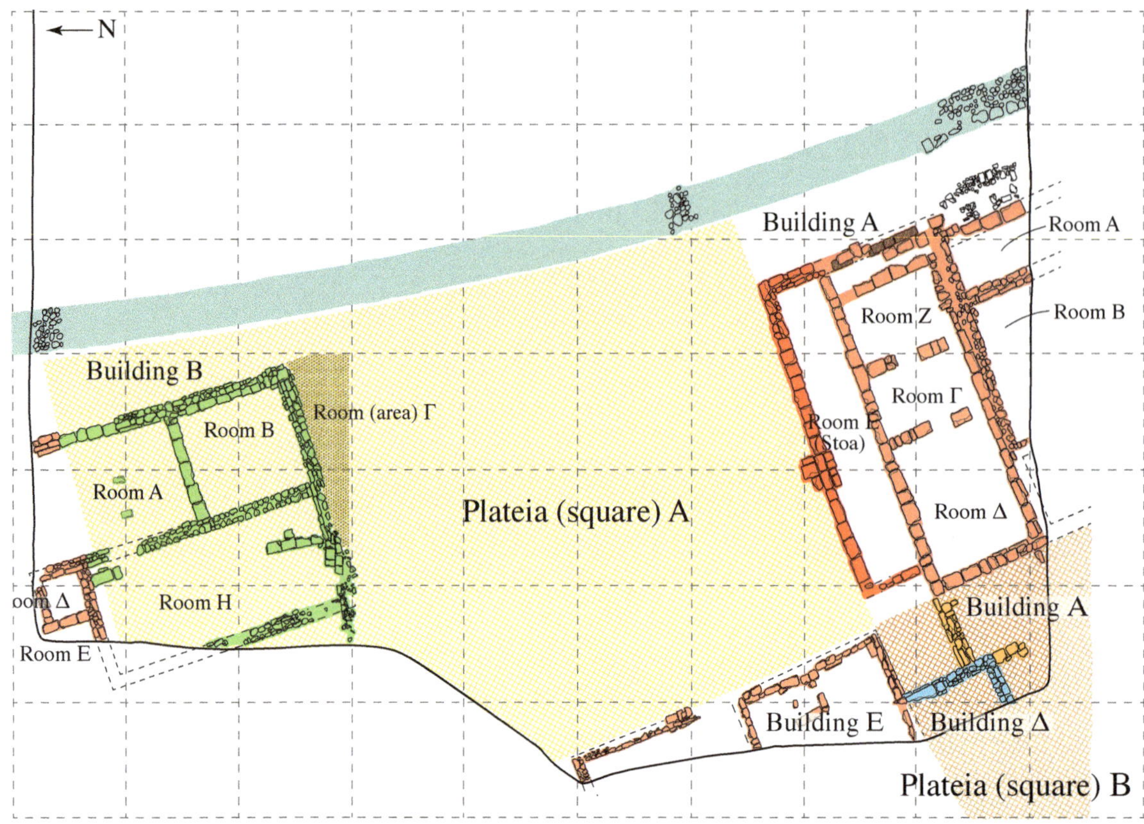

FIGURE 29.1. Plan of the ancient agora of Methone.
Drawing I. Moschou

FIGURE 29.2. Building A from west. Photo A. Athanassiadou

FIGURE 29.3. Building B from southwest.
Photo A. Athanassiadou

to the first half of the 4th century B.C. The extension of the building occupied a significant part of the square.

The excavation of the destruction layer of both buildings and their surrounding areas revealed a remarkable assemblage of ceramics, for which the historical and archaeological data provide a useful chronological fixed point. When Philip II destroyed Methone, expelled its inhabitants, and established a new settlement about 700 m northwest, a new population of Macedonians was installed. The scale of the destruction and abandonment is clearly reflected in the agora. Over time, the roofs of the buildings fell onto the floors, and the subsequent collapse of the walls resulted in the formation of a solid layer of broken and disintegrated mud bricks, which sealed the destruction horizon. A substantial dark layer, up to 2.00 m thick, formed later due to collapse and weathering, further protecting the underlying structures. Without any subsequent building interventions, the Methone agora now offers a well-dated closed set of vessels, thus enriching our knowledge of the pottery of the late Classical era.

As anticipated, most of the pottery dates to the second quarter of the 4th century B.C., although there is, of course, no shortage of earlier material.[2] Beside black-gloss tableware, there are a few vessels with painted decoration, in addition to undecorated domestic and cooking ware and kitchen utensils, as well as commercial amphoras and lamps.

FINE WARES

This category includes black-gloss, slipped, and painted pottery (red-figure, black-painted, banded vases). The order in which the material is presented is based, as far as possible, on a representative sample of each type or shape in the destruction deposit.[3]

Bowl, Small Bowl, and Footed Saltcellar (Figs. 29.4–29.16)

The most common shape found in the pottery of the destruction deposit is the small bowl or footed saltcellar with incurved rim. The examples examined vary in shape and size, but they share a number of common features, such as a ring base, echinus-shaped body, and rim turned inward to varying degrees. Seven of the catalogued pieces are imports from Attica (**29/1**, **29/2**, **29/4**, **29/5**, **29/10**, **29/11**, **29/12**), while another five are products of various local workshops (**29/3**, **29/6**, **29/7**, **29/8**, **29/9**).[4] In contrast, the small bowl with outturned rim (**29/13**) is represented by a solitary example of Attic origin.

Bowl, incurving rim

Among the larger bowls with incurving rim are the Attic examples **29/1** and **29/2**, which are distinguished by their pure orangey-red clay, glossy black glaze, and the high quality of their manufacture.[5] They are almost identical, with **29/2** enjoying a more robust base with a wider resting surface and a slightly taller body that defines a sharper curve. The resting surface is unpainted, as is the groove at the juncture of the base and body. The interior floor is decorated with alternately linked stamped palmettes surrounded by rouletting. Their form is close to examples of the second quarter of the 4th century B.C. from the Athenian Agora,[6] Olynthos,[7] Akanthos,[8] and Thasos,[9] while the distinctive decoration is typical for the time.[10]

A similar body profile, with a thickish incurved rim, is found on the local bowl **29/3**, but with the curvature of the rim less emphasized. It differs from the Attic examples in its substantial base with a wide resting surface, resulting in a proportionately smaller underside, which is covered with *miltos*, and has a small painted circle around the center (the inner edge of the foot on the underside is also painted). This bowl has no exact parallel. The general form of the body recalls the typical bowls with incurved rims,[11] such as those examined above, but the form of the base represents another version of the products of the Athenian Kerameikos, with smaller proportions, which make their appearance around 380 B.C.[12] If the treatment of the underside is a chronological criterion—and not an idiosyncratic preference of the potter—then **29/3** may be a little earlier than **29/1** and **29/2**.[13]

The remaining examples are clearly smaller in size and correspond to four different types. The earliest is represented by the Athenian bowls **29/4** and **29/5**, which belong to the "later and light" type, according to the terminology of the Athenian Agora.[14] They have a ring base with a concave molding underneath, a very shallow body with thin walls, and a gently incurved rim, with **29/4** having a more accented profile externally at the point where the rim curves in. The same piece has a reserved underside adorned with a black band around the outer edge, and two painted circles and a small dot at center; the resting surface is reserved, as is the juncture between the foot and lower body on the exterior.[15] It can be compared with an example dating to the last quarter of the 5th century B.C. from the Athenian Agora,[16] but also with a later example from Akanthos.[17] Its context, however, favors a dating in the first 20 years of the 4th century B.C.;[18] **29/5** should be more or less contemporary.

The local bowl **29/6** is coarsely made, with the glaze applied by dipping. It has a shallow, gently curved body that is slightly angular, with a thick rounded rim that is not incurved. The bowl recalls examples from Olynthos[19] and Pylos.[20] The form is a little earlier than the next group of bowls with incurved rim, which are very common in the second quarter of the 4th century B.C.; consequently, a date for **29/6** around the transition from the first to the second quarter of the 4th century B.C. is likely.

The locally made bowls of the third group are essentially the smallest versions of the bowls typified by **29/1** and **29/2**.[21] They have a ring base with a flat resting surface, a shallow, echinus-shaped body, and a thickish incurved rim. **29/7** is an elaborate piece covered entirely with glaze; **29/8** is not unlike it, but here the glaze is applied by dipping, as on **29/9**, where the loose molding and asymmetrical walls betray hasty work. **29/7** and **29/8** find comparanda from the Athenian Agora,[22] Olynthos,[23] Akanthos,[24] Mieza,[25] and Thasos.[26] **29/9**, which is formed in the simplest possible way, is also compared with examples from Olynthos[27] and from Nea Philadelphia.[28]

The three well-made Attic examples of the fourth group (**29/10–29/12**) share common morphological features with many of the above, but have thicker walls and a more sharply incurved rim. The base has a flat or grooved resting surface and the body is echinus-shaped or hemispherical. They belong to the type of saltcellars with a ring base, which is primarily produced in the 2nd and 3rd quarters of the 4th century B.C.[29] Similar examples are published from various sites, such as the Athenian Agora,[30] Olynthos,[31] Akanthos,[32] Pella,[33] and Thasos.[34]

Bowl, Outturned Rim

The form of the bowl with outturned rim is rare in the destruction level,[35] **29/13** being the solitary example, and is characteristic of Athenian manufacture.[36] This is an elegant vessel with smooth surfaces and a good metallic black glaze. It has a peculiar base which—rather than the usual ring foot—is formed of two very thin rings, one on top of the other, separated from the body by a distinct cylindrical stem. The other elements are typical, such as the groove on the resting surface and the small nipple at the center of the underside. The body is shallow, surmounted by a rounded, outturned rim. The center of the floor is embellished with the typical pattern of alternately linked stamped palmettes enclosed by rouletting.

This bowl finds no exact parallel in its overall form. The base profile, combined with the low stem, is probably taken from stemless cups of the late 5th century B.C.,[37] the production of which stretches into the second quarter of the 4th century B.C.[38] The body is similar to no. 803 from the Athenian Agora,[39] while the treatment of the underside and the stamped and rouletted decoration recalls some later examples,[40] placing the vessel in the same chronological context as the bowls with incurved rims, **29/1** and **29/2**.

Attic-type Skyphos (Type A) (Figs. 29.17–29.19)

The Attic-type skyphos is represented by five fragmentary examples, not all illustrated here, but the number of the fragments found scattered across almost the entire extent of the destruction deposit testifies to its popularity. Attic products predominate, while local imitations are not lacking. There are also a few fragments that come from red-figure examples.

The best preserved skyphoi, **29/14–29/16**, together with the more fragmentary examples from the deposit, typify the form that the shape takes in the 4th century B.C.[41] The body forms a double curve, the lower body is narrow, the upper body is broader, convex-concave in profile as the rim turns outward. The handles are attached to the upper body, directly below the rim, and, as is seen on **29/16**, are triangular in shape. The form of the base is typical, with a torus profile, a reserved resting surface, and reserved underside adorned with two or three black circles around the center. A reserved band or groove highlights the juncture of foot and body. In general, the skyphoi of the destruction deposit, which are characteristic for their time, have proportions intermediate between the bulkier examples of the early 4th century B.C. and those with the very narrow lower body that are found from the middle of the century onward.[42] They can be compared with contemporary examples from the Athenian Agora,[43] Corinth,[44] Olynthos,[45] Thasos,[46] Nea Philadelphia,[47] Edessa,[48] and Pydna.[49]

Plate (Figs. 29.20–29.24)

The group of plates includes two examples with a rolled rim (**29/17**, **29/18**), one with a rilled rim (**29/19**), and two fish plates (**29/20**, **29/21**). The latter must have been more popular at Methone, judging by the fact that they occur more often than any other type of plate among the fragmentary pottery. Of the catalogued plates, four are of Attic origin and only **29/18** is the product of a local workshop.

Plate, rolled rim

Plate **29/17**, with its sophisticated profile and elaborate interior decoration, is one of the earliest examples of the type.[50] It has a broad ring base, a flat floor, and a protruding lip that forms a groove at the inner circumference. There is a concave molding on the outside edge of the rim, resulting in a fillet of sorts. The impressed decoration on the floor interior consists of palmettes around a circle of enclosed ovules. The same pattern is repeated a second time around the center of the floor.[51] The profile is close to the earliest examples of the series from the Athenian Agora,[52] even though none of these rims extend as far as we see on the Methone plate. Quite apart from the repair of the vessel in antiquity, its early date in relation to the destruction deposit is reinforced by the fact that some of the fragments of the plate were found deeper than the floor of the final phase of Building A.[53]

The smaller local plate **29/18** is not devoid of diligent work, but its profile is more simplified,[54] as is the impressed decoration, which consists of five consecutive rows of horizontal marks.[55] The orange-yellow hue does not correspond to the fabric of other examples from Methone and may be the result of an attempt by the potter to imitate the surface of bronze vessels.

Plate, rilled rim

Plate **29/19** has a broad base, a particularly shallow body with a flat floor, and its wall rising vertically; the rim is flat on top, with one broad rill. The impressed decoration extends over most of the floor and consists of twelve stamped and alternately linked palmettes enclosing two central circles of rouletting, and enclosed by four rows of rouletted lines. This particular piece does not find an exact parallel from the Athenian potters' quarter, but the groove on the rim indicates a type of plate invented around 430 B.C.[56] The simplified profile represents the form that this shape takes in the 4th century B.C.,[57] whereas the pattern of the impressed decoration leads to a closer dating in the second quarter of the century.[58]

Fish plate

This particular shape, which appears in Attica at the end of the 5th century B.C., consists of a sturdy ring base, a broad floor that slopes down toward a central depression, and an overhanging sloping rim.[59] At Methone it appears quite often in the pottery of the destruction layer, but only two examples are well preserved, which differ from one another in size and in a number of individual features. The larger of the two, **29/20**, rests on a sturdy base with a flat and reserved resting surface and glazed underside which is curved; the floor slopes toward the central depression, with a deep overhanging rim. There is a reserved groove around the central depression, and another around the outer periphery of the floor.[60] In the case of **29/21**, the lip hangs less prominently downward, leaving more of the body visible, while the visibly lower base has a groove on the resting surface. Despite their variation, the two examples are contemporary.[61]

ONE-HANDLER (FIGS. 29.25–29.27)

Frequently present in the destruction deposit are shallow one-handlers.[62] Few examples are well preserved, but many pieces or individual sherds can safely be attributed to this shape. Demand for these small utensils is mainly met by local production, which is characterized by a wide variety of clay and morphological characteristics.[63] However, the best-preserved examples discussed here have a ring base, a shallow body, and a vertical rim with a narrow lip, which slopes inward either sharply or less so. None preserves the entire handle.

In the case of the Attic one-handler, **29/22**, the foot is relatively tall with a slightly curved profile, while the body forms an imperceptible double curve as the lip turns slightly outward. The floor is decorated with four stamped palmettes in a cruciform arrangement. The underside is reserved and adorned with a black circle around the center, whereas **29/23** has a black band and a circle on its underside. In the latter example, the body gradually opens upward in a single curve.

In contrast to the two previous examples, the local one-handler, **29/24**, is a hasty piece of work in which the shape is unsuccessfully rendered. The molding is loose, the surface rough, and the glaze of low quality, applied by dipping. The contour of the body forms a gentle angle near the midpoint and the rim terminates in a rounded lip.

On the basis of parallels from the Athenian Agora,[64] Olynthos,[65] and Pella,[66] **29/22** can be dated to the transition from the first to the second quarter of the 4th century B.C. In contrast, **29/23**, with the continuous curve of its body, stands somewhere between **29/22** and the one-handlers of the late 5th century B.C.,[67] and should probably be dated to the first quarter of the 4th century B.C. Similar examples have been found in the cemeteries of Edessa[68] and Mieza.[69] **29/24** can be compared to local one-handlers from Mieza[70] and Nea Philadelphia[71] and, on the basis of its profile, can be dated to the second quarter of the 4th century B.C.

Saltcellar, Concave Wall (Figs. 29.28–29.32)

The five Attic "saltcellars" with concave walls, **29/25–29/29**, exhibit only minor or negligible morphological variations: they have a ring base with a flat resting surface, which sometimes bears a groove, a shallow body with a concave contour, and a rounded rim.[72] Four have post-firing graffiti on their undersides. This type is particularly popular in the 2nd and 3rd quarters of the 4th century B.C. Similar examples are published from the Athenian Agora,[73] Corinth,[74] Thasos,[75] Mieza,[76] Sindos,[77] Olynthos,[78] and Vergina.[79]

Bolsal (Figs. 29.33–29.35)

The low skyphos with the conventional name "bolsal" appears in Attica in the third quarter of the 5th century B.C.[80] In its typical form it has a low base, similar to that of the Corinthian-type skyphos, a shallow body with a hollow concave lower wall and vertical upper walls, and two horizontal handles attached immediately below the rim. The shape is not common in the destruction deposit at Methone. Three examples are well preserved, of which one (**29/30**) is Attic, while the other two (**29/31**, **29/32**) come from different local workshops and imitate the Attic products fairly well, even though they lag behind in quality.[81]

The examples from Methone follow the basic features of the shape and do not show any substantial differences among them, even though the larger proportions of **29/32** dictate a somewhat different approach. The foot does not have the usual flaring profile but rises vertically, and the high and broad lower wall is not clearly separated from the upper body, which is deep; the handle does not have a circular section but is ribbon-shaped. The underside of both **29/32** and **29/30** is reserved, whereas that of **29/31** is totally glazed.

As far as dating is concerned, **29/30** with its distinctive body profile and reserved underside can be placed in the first quarter of the 4th century B.C. It can be compared with no. 556 in the Athenian Agora,[82] and with examples from Akanthos,[83] Nea Philadelphia,[84] and Mieza.[85] **29/32** must be contemporary; apart from the peculiarities imposed by its size, it also has common features with no. 556 from the Athenian Agora,[86] but also with the earliest group of bolsals from Nea

Philadelphia.[87] Analogous parallels may be cited for **29/31**,[88] but its glazed underside indicates a slightly later dating, probably at the transition from the first to the second quarter of the 4th century B.C.[89]

Askos, Shallow Type (Figs. 29.36, 29.37)

The only closed vessel form to speak of in the destruction deposit is the shallow type of askos, a shape that appears at the beginning of the 5th century B.C. but is more systematically produced in the last decades of the century, in both black-gloss[90] and red-figure versions.[91] It consists of a wide disk-shaped base, a shallow body domed at the top, an obliquely set spout, and a wide arched handle. The best preserved examples (**29/33** and **29/34**) share these characteristics. In addition to these, a few very fragmentary examples of the same type, of Attic origin, have been identified in the destruction deposit.

The askos **29/33** is one of the very few red-figure vases found in the destruction deposit. The top of the body is domed and ends in a central nipple, surrounded by two concentric plastic rings and a shallow groove.[92] It is decorated with two pairs of front-facing female busts or protomai wearing head caps, alternating with stylized vegetal ornaments. This pictorial theme is typical for the second quarter of the 4th century B.C. and is often found on the lids of red-figure lekanides.[93] An askos from Pella probably had similar decoration.[94]

The locally produced askos **29/34** is completely covered with glaze except for the underside. The carinated body is relatively tall and has a steep lower wall, while the domed top converges toward a central nipple. The handle is unusually thin. The shape, in general, follows the trends of the 4th century B.C., when askoi develop higher bodies, but its outline betrays local traditions. Several similarities are presented in two examples from Olynthos.[95]

Lekanis (Figs. 29.38–29.40)

The shape of the lekanis differs from that of the more open domestic lekane, because it is articulated to receive a lid.[96] The black-glaze version exists in several variants,[97] while the shape is not absent from the repertoire of household ceramics.[98] The destruction deposit yielded the bodies of two black-glaze or black-painted lekanides and a small black-gloss lid from a third example.

Lekanis, lidded, with ribbon handles

One of the earliest vessels of the destruction deposit is the impressively large lekanis **29/35**, which represents one of the most common variants in the Attic series. It has a ring base with a broad resting surface, a deep body with lower walls sloping outward, and an upper body that is nearly vertical, articulated to form a deep ledge to accommodate a lid and that terminates in a perpendicular lip; horizontal ribbon handles (only one is preserved), plano-concave in section, are flanked on either side by a spur.[99] The ledge is reserved and decorated with a black-painted branch-and-leaf pattern.[100]

This particular lekanis does not correspond in its overall form to any of the published examples from the Athenian Agora.[101] For its dating we should look at individual morphological features, which include the broad resting surface that appears after the middle of the 5th century B.C.,[102] although the form of the lower body, with its rising walls, corresponds to earlier examples.[103] In addition, the spurs of the handle are still made in one piece with the ribbon handle.[104] The decorative motif of the branch-and-leaf pattern, rendered in black-painted technique, is unusual for this shape,[105] but corresponds to similar decoration on other shapes,[106] and, combined with the other features, leads to a dating between the third and the fourth quarters of the 5th century B.C. In addition, extensive surface wear and the repair to the heavy handle indicate long-term use.

Lekanis, lidded, with horizontal handles

The vessel **29/36** was found very close to the previous lekanis (**29/35**), in the area of the stoa porch of Building A. This is a local product that, thanks to its good quality glaze and carefully made form, is one of the most remarkable products of the local black-glaze repertoire. It has a particularly shallow and wide body and preserves a horizontal horseshoe-shaped handle. The groove on the upper surface of the rim, which seems to have facilitated a lid, but also the form of the base with its broad resting surface, allow us to classify it among the lekanides. The unusual configuration of the rim does not correspond to any of the variants of the Attic black-glaze lekanides.[107] The general form of the shape, however, is close to the examples of the 4th century B.C. of the version discussed above.[108]

Lekanis lid

The lid **29/37** comes from a small lekanis,[109] which is also a remarkable product of, in all probability, a local workshop. It has a gently sloping body on top that nearly forms a right angle to the vertical downturned rim, without however interrupting the contour. This is surmounted by a disk-shaped knob that stands on a very low cylindrical shaft; the disk has a raised rib and a small conical depression at the center. The upper surface of the knob is reserved and adorned with two black rings, while the upper surface of the raised circumference is also reserved (the inner surface of the raised rib is also painted). Lids similar in overall form, but also with similarly shaped and decorated knobs, have been found at Olynthos[110] and Pella.[111]

LOCALLY PRODUCED SKYPHOI/BOWLS (FIGS. 29.41, 29.42)

The class of pottery with painted decoration is represented by some examples of local workshops. **29/38** and **29/39**, with their ring bases, deep conical bodies, and sharply incurving rims, could be classified as skyphoi or bowls. **29/38** does not have handles, is not well made, with rough surfaces and design weaknesses, and is simply decorated with broad red bands inside and out, and a red painted disk at the center of the floor. A better-made product, **29/39** has two horizontal handles that are pinched in at the center and were possibly surmounted by button-shaped knobs. Its surfaces are covered with a red glaze that was applied by dipping.

The shape of **29/39** is unusual, but not entirely unknown in Macedonia. A similar vessel, with an incurved rim and bifurcated handle, was found in Pit C of the Double Trapeza of Anchialos-Sindos.[112] A similar handle, very fragmentary, is known at Edessa.[113] In contrast, **29/38** does not have exact parallels, but the decorative treatment is similar to that of the "lekanis-shaped vessels" from Anchialos-Sindos.[114] A date, therefore, for both vessels in the second quarter of the 4th century B.C., based on the examples from Pit C, seems assured.

STAMNOID PYXIS (FIG. 29.43)

The locally made **29/40** is, in the context of the destruction deposit, an isolated example of a shape which is usually given the conventional name "stamnoid pyxis."[115] Very small in size, it has a ring-shaped, almost conical base, an ovoid body with the lower wall rising steeply, the shoulder curving sharply in, and a vertical rim; the horizontal, almost upright, handles are obliquely placed on the shoulder, which, if preserved, would rise well above the level of the rim. The decoration combines bands and dots that are rendered in black on a reserved surface.

This vessel seems to have certain characteristics from East Greece. Similar pots were made in Rhodes and are typical of tombs of the 4th and early 3rd centuries B.C.[116] In Macedonia, the shape is known since Archaic times,[117] and has been found in various versions in burial and, less often, residential contexts.[118] The shape also brings to mind the so-called "sipyes," the large storage vessels with painted decoration that were often used as cinerary urns for cremation tombs.[119]

The Methone pyxis represents a stage in the evolution of the shape in which the body eliminates the more spherical form of the earlier examples as it tapers toward the base. The shape of **29/40** can be compared to an example from Olynthos,[120] but is closer to pyxides from Akanthos[121] and Rhodes,[122] which strengthens a date in the second quarter of the 4th century B.C.

PLAINWARES

This category includes domestic pottery that was designed for everyday use and is completely devoid of decoration or, in a few cases, bears only rudimentary decoration (banding or burnishing/polishing). This pottery is considered to be local utilitarian pottery, which could have been made in Methone or in a ceramic workshop in the wider region. The closed vessels are discussed first, followed by the open shapes, in order of their frequency in the destruction deposit. In the absence of good parallels, the date of this pottery is often based on the stratigraphic data provided by the destruction deposit itself.

Closed Shapes

Oinochoe/jug (Figs. 29.44–29.46)

The oinochoai from the destruction deposit make up a heterogeneous group, as they exhibit much variety in form, size, and fabric. The focus here is only on those examples that have complete profiles.

29/41 is a well-crafted vessel, the surface of which has been polished. It has a ring base, a short but full body with a strongly curved profile, an almost horizontal shoulder, a very tall neck, and a thick rounded lip. There is a broad groove between the neck and the rim.[123] The handle extends from the top of the body to the height of the groove. I know of no exact parallel. The treatment of the body resembles an oinochoe from Olynthos,[124] but also some examples of Corinthian manufacture.[125]

29/42 is an example of the type with a tall neck and round mouth, which probably had a disk base. The body is relatively short, but it gains in height thanks to its tall sloping shoulder; the body and shoulder are biconical. The neck is lightly ridged, the mouth is defined by an outturned and chamfered rim, and the handle is attached from the shoulder directly to the rim. The yellowish creamy clay of the vessel is not often found among the pottery of Methone.

The small oinochoe **29/43** represents a different type. It is coarsely made with a rough outer surface, of poor-quality brown clay that was divided into strips or slices. It has a disk base, a small ovoid body, a low narrow neck, a round mouth with beveled lip, and a strap handle attached from the shoulder directly to the rim. Oinochoai with a narrow neck and globular body, in both black-glaze and unpainted versions, are produced in Corinth during the Classical and Hellenistic periods.[126] Numerous examples are also published from Olynthos,[127] and a few from the Athenian Agora.[128] Vases of this type usually functioned as containers, since the narrow neck ensured the leak-free transfer of their liquid contents. Morphologically, the Methone oinochoe is more akin to the globular version of the Deianeira lekythos type,[129] but differs in the treatment of the rim.[130] By observing the evolution of these lekythoi, we can incorporate **29/43** into the ceramic tradition of the 4th century B.C.[131]

Lekythos (Figs. 29.47, 29.48)

Belonging to the class of large, unpainted lekythoi, **29/44** and **29/45** were found as fragments scattered across the roofed courtyard of Building B. In particular, **29/45** is a capacious vessel, unusually large for the type, but the shape of both vessels is similarly rendered, with very small variations in the treatment of their individual elements. They have a low disk base, a tall ovoid body that forms a single curve with the shoulder, a narrow and low neck with a plastic ring (drip ring) at the top, an echinus-shaped rim with a beveled upper surface, and a narrow strap handle attached from shoulder to neck.

The Methone examples illustrate, on a larger scale, the form of the Athenian black-glaze Deianeira lekythoi,[132] which were reproduced by the local ceramic workshops in Macedonia in Classical and Hellenistic times.[133] A similar type is made at Corinth throughout the 5th and first half of the 4th century B.C.[134] The only unusual element of **29/44** and **29/45** is the rim with chamfered upper surface. Otherwise, **29/44** is not unlike some examples from Olynthos;[135] in contrast, **29/45** has no close parallels.

Olpe (Figs. 29.49, 29.50)

The olpe was produced in a wide variety of local ceramic workshops from Archaic to Hellenistic times.[136] It can have an oval or more cylindrical body, with or without a clearly articulated base, a round or trefoil mouth, and a narrow handle, usually rising well above the level of the rim. Only two examples of the shape were found in the destruction deposit at Methone, both in the same place.[137]

The olpe **29/46** has a flat and a relatively short and wide cylindrical body that narrows a little toward the bottom. The shoulder follows the contour of the body and converges with a low neck, round mouth, and chamfered rim. The handle, only a small portion of which is preserved, rises well above the level of the rim. The exterior surface is rough and banded,[138] highlighting the conservative tendencies of some of the local workshops.[139] The olpe **29/47**, which survives in three non-joining pieces, has a low disk base, an oval body, and a wide neck with an equally wide round mouth.[140] The upper part of the vessel, from the shoulder to the rim and inside the mouth, is covered with brown-black glaze.

Pelike (Fig. 29.51)

For **29/48** the term "pelike"[141] was preferred to "amphora," despite the fact that its body does not have a low center of gravity, and because the shape of the rim and handles resembles those of red-figured pelikai of the 4th century B.C.[142] Its clay has the same composition as that of the Methone cooking ware. The shortcomings of **29/48** are reflected in its loose molding, sharp contours, disproportionately short body, and the poor application of one of the handles. Morphologically, it has a ring-shaped base, a cylindrical body that forms an angle with the sloping shoulder, a tall neck that flares toward the top, an almost perpendicularly downturned rim, and vertical handles that are triangular in section.

The shape is rare in the unpainted version.[143] The Methone pelike finds no exact parallel, but can be compared to an example of the early 4th century B.C. from Olynthos,[144] and also with later examples from Mieza[145] and Edessa.[146] **29/48** belongs to a stage just prior to the examples from Edessa—to which it is most closely related—as the rim is still at some distance from the upper handle attachments.

Open Shapes

Lekane (Figs. 29.52, 29.53)

In the modern literature, the term "lekane" is usually given to the large open household vessel, which was not intended to receive a lid and was mainly used as a mixing bowl.[147] The shape was produced in a wide variety of forms, as can be seen from the collection in the Athenian Agora.[148] Various examples are also published from Corinth.[149] From the destruction deposit at Methone, we have two almost complete examples (**29/49**, **29/50**), a third very fragmentary one, and a few fragments among the uncatalogued pottery, which are attributed to different types of lekanai.

The lekane **29/49** has a rudimentary disk base, a hemispherical body with curved walls, a horizontal protruding lip, and two horizontal handles placed high on the body. A similar example from Olynthos dates to the late 5th century B.C.,[150] but **29/49** may be later. The vessel was repaired with a lead clamp, potentially indicating long-term use, but the thin walls made it quite sensitive, especially since it was intended for constant use. It could, therefore, be dated to the second quarter of the 4th century B.C., but perhaps not very close to the time of the destruction.

The lekane **29/50** has a disk base, a relatively deep conical body with slightly curved walls, a horizontal protruding rim with a perpendicular overhang, and handles that curve upward and are pressed against the upper face of the rim. The type of lekane with such handles (normally referred to as "handles turned up to rim")[151] appears in Attica in the middle of the 6th century B.C., but is rare in the 4th century B.C.[152] **29/50** closely follows the Attic shape, as it developed from the last quarter of the 5th century B.C. and later,[153] and which did not show any substantial changes in the 4th century B.C.[154] In addition, the body is rendered in the same way as it is in late Attic lekanai of the type with horizontal handles.[155] Finally, the profile is related to a lekane, also with horizontal handles, from Pydna, which was used as lid for a pot burial (*enchytrismos*),[156] as well as to two Corinthian examples of the 4th century B.C., which lack handles.[157]

Mortar (Figs. 29.54–29.57)

Shallow basins with thick walls and a thick rim, known as "*igdia*" (ἰγδία),[158] are one of the most enduring utensils of household equipment, essential in the preparation of food. The shape and construction made them particularly durable and suitable for laborious tasks such as grinding, rubbing, mashing grains, spices, herbs, etc.[159] The shape in clay shows several variations, depending on the workshop or the period.[160] Corinth is one of the first regions in mainland Greece where clay versions were both imported and manufactured since the middle of the 7th century B.C.,[161] while representative examples are also published from the Athenian Agora.[162]

The Methone destruction deposit brought to light three better-preserved mortaria (**29/51–29/53**), which are considered local products.[163] They are made of coarse orange clay of various shades, with plenty of inclusions and abundant mica. The interior surface is intentionally rough, while the exterior surface has received a rudimentary finish and preserves wheelmarks, without implying that all three were wheelmade.[164] The handles and spouts are handmade and subsequently attached.

29/51 has a disk base, thick curved walls, and a thick protruding rim, convex on top. It preserves two seal-impressed handles, each of which has two rectangular sealings depicting a branch with leaves and some indistinguishable letters.[165] On the missing side there would have been another handle, and only a small portion of the spout survives. **29/52** preserves about one-half of the mortar. It has a broad disk base and a wide shallow body with curved walls. The rim protrudes both outward and slightly on the interior, and it has a groove on its upper surface. The spout is fluked and the surviving handle is adorned with vertical ribs.[166] Some small roughly impressed circles on the upper rim[167] may have been decorative.[168]

The overall form of the shape of the above examples is reminiscent of the mortaria from Corinth with protruding rims,[169] but the comparison stops there. **29/52** closely resembles an example from Olynthos,[170] which is securely dated to the second quarter of the 4th century B.C., a date that is in keeping with the form of the spout.[171] **29/51** finds no close parallel. The profile of another Olynthian example of the later 5th century B.C. is not unlike,[172] but given the dearth of exact comparanda, it would be best to date **29/51** to the first half of the 4th century B.C. on the basis of its context.

29/53 represents a different type, which has a disk base and a particularly shallow body. The rim is thick and very pronounced and is separated from the body by a wide groove on its underside, while its upper surface slopes downward. The spout is similar to that of **29/52**, as are the two ribbed handles. The handle opposite the spout is more sophisticated, as it forms three shallow circular depressions defined by vertical ribs. In terms of construction, the heavy walls and the particularly shallow body indicate the use of a mold, at least for the primary construction of the basic shape.[173] At a second stage of production, perhaps with the aid of a potter's wheel, a separate layer of clay was spread over the entire surface, even on the rim, which accounts for its thickness. The handles were formed separately and were decorated after their attachment to the rim,[174] when the clay was still malleable, and the attachment of the spout appears to belong to the final stage of production.

The shape of **29/53** recalls examples, such as no. 1912 from the Athenian Agora,[175] or A145 from the Alonnisos shipwreck,[176] both dating to the late 5th century B.C., that belong to the type of "heavy-rim mortaria," according to the classification of Alexandra Villing and Elizabeth Pemberton.[177] This type, however, is quite different from **29/53**, mainly in terms of the treatment of the rim with its angular profile. The handle with the shallow decorated circular depressions of **29/53** corresponds to an example from Olynthos,[178] and resembles similar handles decorated with triple ovolo ornament.[179] The form of the spout corresponds, as we have seen in the case of **29/52**, to a date in the second quarter of the 4th century B.C.[180]

There is one final mortar, **29/54**, only a small part of which is preserved, and which is made of a completely different fabric from that of the previous examples. Its clay is yellowish orange, medium-grained, with minimal impurities, a little fine mica, and a texture reminiscent of powder. The vessel is coarse, heavy-duty, and moldmade. It has a disk base, a very shallow body, a thick rounded rim, articulated on the exterior by a notch, and a ribbed handle in one piece with the rim. It belongs to the type of "heavy-rim" mortaria,[181] and is imported to Methone, although its origin remains unknown. The type is in use mainly during the late 5th and early 4th centuries B.C. and is often considered Corinthian, though its production in Corinth remains to be documented.[182] Examples are known from Aigina,[183] the Athenian Agora,[184] the Alonnisos wreck,[185] and, in the north Aegean, from Thasos.[186] The Methone example is similar to one at Corinth[187] and another from Aigina,[188] and can be dated on the basis of its context to the first half of the 4th century B.C.

Ladle (Fig. 29.58)

Terracotta ladles are not commonly found,[189] despite the fact that the shape was useful in the kitchen, perhaps because ancient households were supplied with wooden ladles that do not survive.[190] **29/55** is the sole example from the destruction deposit, and was found in fragments scattered inside and outside the stoa of Building A (Room E). It has a hemispherical body and a long straight horizontal double handle, which is formed of one roll of clay bent back onto itself and pressed together for its entire length, except for the loop at its end designed for hanging, which is painted in red. Red dots decorate the rest of the long handle, while the edge of the rim is also painted with the same color. Similar ladles are made in Attica from the middle of the 5th century B.C.[191] Analogous examples have been found at Olynthos,[192] which reinforce the dating of the Methone ladle to the second quarter of the 4th century B.C.

COOKING WARES

The cooking wares found in the excavation of the destruction deposit form a large group that includes various shapes, such as two-handled lidded chytrai, one-handled lidless chytrai,[193] lopades, and lids. The most commonly encountered shape is the one-handled lidless chytra, with seven complete or well-preserved examples and another five that are very fragmentary, while the two-handled lidded chytra is represented by just two examples. The lopades outnumber the two-handled lidded chytrai (even taking into account the more fragmentary uncatalogued pottery), while the presence of lids is similar.

The vast majority of the cooking wares came from Building B, with the highest concentration observed in Room A. They are locally produced and made of orange or gray coarse clay containing many impurities and mica.[194] They were thrown on the potter's wheel,[195] and their walls are sufficiently thin to ensure rapid cooking. Two examples (**29/56**, **29/59**) are decorated with off-white vertical stripes, while the surface of the lid **29/69** was burnished.[196] The whole group is dated to the second quarter of the 4th century B.C. and—if we consider that such utensils were brittle and therefore unsuitable for long-term use—they were probably made not long before the destruction of Methone.

Chytra (Figs. 29.59–29.67)

The shape of the chytrai is quite varied and their distinction into individual types is mainly based on the number of handles and the form of the rim, and on whether or not it was designed to accommodate a lid.[197] Their common feature is the globular body with a plain rounded base. The collections of the Athenian Agora[198] and Corinth[199] include numerous Archaic, Classical, and Hellenistic cooking wares, including chytrai. From Macedonia, representative sets of cooking wares have been published from Souroti,[200] Olynthos,[201] Akanthos,[202] and Veroia.[203]

Two-handled chytra, lidded

The chytrai **29/56** and **29/57** show no significant differences between them, apart from the configuration of the handles. They have a globular body without a neck and a flaring lip articulated to receive a lid.[204] The body of **29/56** is very inflated, with a strongly curved outline that defines a full body at the point of maximum diameter; the rim is tall, with a straight exterior. It has two vertical strap handles, attached from just above the point of maximum diameter directly to the rim. In the case of **29/57**, the walls are slightly more flattened and the shoulder slopes inward. The rim has a slightly convex profile on the exterior, which is almost imperceptible, and the horizontal handles rise obliquely, almost vertically, on the shoulder, to well above the level of the rim. Both chytrai are fire-affected from use. **29/56** is of particular interest as its body is decorated with pairs of vertical stripes that are rendered in white or off-white.[205] Morphologically, it is close to an example from Olynthos,[206] and to an example of Group III at Akanthos.[207] The general shape of **29/57** falls between no. 1955[208] and no. 1956[209] from the Athenian Agora.

One-handled chytra, lidless

The examples of lidless one-handled chytrai from Methone can be divided into two groups based on size. The first group (**29/58–29/61**) has a height of 0.170–0.205 m and a body diameter of 0.214–0.219 m; the second (**29/62–29/64**) has a height of 0.130–0.158 m and a body diameter of 0.152–0.173 m. Regardless of their size, some are fire-affected, having been placed on a fire.[210] It is important to note that while the two-handled lidded chytrai discussed above are fire-affected over the entire perimeter of their body, the chytrai of this group are more heavily fire-affected on the side of the body opposite the handle. This different distribution of fire damage is related to how they were placed on or in the fire.[211]

The primary features of this group of chytrai are the globular body with a plain rounded base, which forms a continuous profile to the outturned rim, and a vertical strap handle. The rim has a convex, or more rarely flat, upper surface indicating that these vessels were never intended to receive a lid. The first group is characterized by a greater variety in their shape, while examples of the second group follow the same basic lines without being identical to one another.

There are no substantial differences between **29/58** and **29/59**, and their basic form is close to the lidded variety discussed above. The body—which is a little squatter in the case of **29/59**—defines an accentuated curve which includes the shoulder, while the neck has no clear articulation, even though it is more distinct on **29/59**. The latter is close to **29/56** on account of its decoration, with small vertical off-white stripes,[212] and it is even possible that these two vessels are products of the same workshop. **29/60** is a capacious vessel with a tall body, the sphericality of which is further accentuated by the absence of a distinct neck. Its vertical handle is wide but very thin and attached from the upper body directly to the rim, forming a right angle with it. The body of **29/61** is more cylindrical, with the slightly flattened lower walls converging toward the bottom. The shoulder rises upward, the neck is tall, and the handle is attached at the upper shoulder, rather than to the point of maximum diameter of the body, at the rim, forming a loop.

The examples of the second group have a spherical-cylindrical body and a clearly formed neck. **29/63** has a short body and short neck; the neck of **29/62** is taller, with a concave contour. In both, the handle is almost loop-shaped. **29/64** has a taller body with more flattened sidewalls than the previous examples. The shoulder rises sharply upward without being separated from the conical neck,[213] while the vertical strap handle forms a larger opening, attached from the upper body directly to the rim.

The one-handled lidless variety at Methone corresponds to the common type of chytra in the Athenian Agora,[214] and to the unflanged cooking pots of the Corinthian potters' quarter,[215] without, however, finding an exact parallel. Comparison with examples from other sites is usually of limited chronological value, since the shape develops slowly throughout its production.

Lopas (Figs. 29.68–29.71)

The lopas[216] is essentially a shallow version of the chytra,[217] and in its typical form it is composed of an echinus-shaped body with a plain rounded base,[218] a wide mouth suitably configured to take a lid, and two horizontal handles, circular in section, rising above the level of the rim. Representative of the shape are the many examples of the form from the Athenian Agora[219] and Corinth,[220] of Classical and Hellenistic date, while from the north Aegean there are published collections from Akanthos,[221] Olynthos,[222] and Thasos.[223] Methone now joins this group of northern sites, with lopades that can be distinguished into three subtypes largely on the basis of the rim and the body: in Types 2 and 3 the rim interior is articulated to receive a lid, while in Type 1 the lid would have rested directly on the shoulder of the vessel.[224] Of these three types, the most common appears to be Type 1.[225] Type 2 is barely represented, and there is to date just one example of Type 3.

Type 1: low vertical/slightly upturned rim and echinus-shaped body

The lopas **29/65** has an echinus-shaped body that probably ended in a conical base. Its outline defines an accentuated curve before meeting the shoulder, which is almost flat and ends at a very low vertical rim. The handle is attached almost at right angles to the juncture of the shoulder and body, and rises well above the level of the rim. In the case of **29/66**, the body is even shallower, the shoulder slopes gently toward the top, and the rim is only slightly upturned. At the beginning of the shoulder there is a small mastos-like appliqué.[226] Lopades of this type are known from various parts of Macedonia, including Akanthos,[227] Olynthos,[228] and southern Pieria,[229] with examples of late Classical and Hellenistic date. A recent excavation in the area of the west cemetery of Pydna has brought to light an analogous example in a storage pit with pottery dating to the late 5th century B.C.[230]

Type 2: banded rim and hemispherical body

The lopas **29/67** has a shallow hemispherical body with curved walls and a somewhat flattened rounded base. The lip flares upward and has straight walls on the exterior, while it is articulated at its base on the interior to receive a lid. The handle rises obliquely at the juncture of the body and rim, and extends above the level of the rim. Related lopades, but without close similarity, have been found at Corinth[231] and Thasos.[232]

Type 3: flaring flanged rim and echinus-shaped body

The lopas **29/68** has an echinus-shaped body with a strongly curved outline and a tall flaring rim, with a prominent flange on the interior to receive a lid. The profile of the rim is curved, while its upper surface is flattened and flares slightly outward. Similar examples are known from the Athenian Agora,[233] Corinth,[234] and Thasos.[235]

Lid (Figs. 29.72–29.75)

The four best-preserved lids from the destruction deposit belong to the type of domed lid which, according to Brian Sparkes and Lucy Talcott, was suitable for lopades.[236] They have either a hemispherical (**29/69**, **29/70**) or an echinus (**29/71**, **29/72**) shape. **29/69** stands apart from the rest as it is carefully made of a rather pure, fine-grained clay, with thin walls and burnished surface. It has a relatively high dome, at the top of which there is a low plastic ring which formed the handle knob. In contrast, **29/70** has thicker walls with a thickish beveled lip. The handle knob consists of a short stem with a conical finial at the top. Lids with domed shapes and a compact handle that end in a knob are known from deposits of the 5th[237] and 4th[238] centuries B.C. in the Athenian Agora, while similar examples from Corinth cover a wider chronological range.[239]

The two echinus-shaped lids have particularly low domes. The upper surface of **29/71** rises rather abruptly at the center to form the handle knob, which appears to be hollow on the underside. On **29/72** the outer edge turns downward to form an almost vertical rim.

LAMPS

The lamps from the destruction deposit belong to various types dating from the 6th to the middle of the 4th century B.C. The sample presents quite a variety, but mainly consists of a limited number of examples of each type; for this reason, their classification is based primarily on chronological criteria and, secondly, on morphology. Only one lamp survives nearly complete, twelve preserve only a small portion, while many lamp fragments, which can be securely attributed to particular types, have been identified among the uncatalogued sherds.[240]

For the typological classification of the lamps from Methone I have followed the classification of Richard Howland,[241] since most of the Methone lamps correspond to types known from the Athenian Agora. Where possible, correlation with the corresponding types of Oscar Broneer[242] and Ingeborg Scheibler[243] is made. A common reference is also the publication of Olynthos,[244] as the lamps from this site cover a wide chronological range, like that of Methone, and represent a wide variety of types.

Early Lamp Types (second half 6th–beginning of the 5th centuries B.C.) (Figs. 29.76, 29.77)

The presence of lamps of early types in the destruction deposit is quite common. The majority are fragmentary and only two examples (**29/73**, **29/74**) retain full profiles, even though they are not complete. Even in their fragmentary form, however, the examples of this group, as well as of the next group, are of particular significance, given the limited occurrence of lamps in the north Aegean during the 6th and 5th centuries B.C.[245]

The lamp **29/73** has a particularly shallow body with walls curving toward the base and a narrow flat rim, which protrudes slightly outward and slopes gently toward the filling hole. The rim top is covered with glossy black glaze, while traces of glaze are also visible on the interior bottom. The exterior is covered with clay slip. The lamp is Attic and belongs to Howland Type 16 B, which is manufactured from the last quarter of the 6th century, but does not continue beyond 480 B.C.[246] **29/73** can be compared to no. 98 in the Athenian Agora,[247] while its profile is also close to no. 107 of the following group (Howland Type 16 Variants).[248] The type also corresponds to the second variety of Broneer Type II[249] and to Scheibler DRL Group.[250]

The Attic lamp **29/74** belongs to roughly the same time. It has a very shallow body with a flat underside and convex walls that continue as a continuous profile to the rim, defining a prominent curve. The interior is covered with black glaze, and the exterior with a thin clay slip. A thin black band adorns the side of the rim around the filling hole. The profile corresponds to Howland Type 21 A, which is mainly in use in the first two decades of the 5th century B.C., but appears a little earlier.[251] It can be compared with the earliest example of the series, in which the lip is unpainted but is also very narrow,[252] as well as an example from the Sanctuary of Demeter at Dion.[253] Analogous lamps with continuous body contours, but with little similarity to the Methone example, are classified under Broneer Type IV[254] and Scheibler Group RSL 1.[255]

Among the early lamps some fragments can be identified, such as a Corinthian lamp of Howland Type 16 A[256] (= Broneer Type II);[257] four open handmade nozzles that originate from the Attic Howland Type 6 B;[258] one local example, the shape and decoration of which can be compared to Howland Type 12 B;[259] and, finally, two fragments that can be characterized as Howland Type 19 A.[260]

Lamps of the Late 5th to Early 4th Century B.C. (Figs. 29.78–29.83)

Lamps with curved walls and wide filling holes

The type of "open" lamp, with convex walls that define a continuous curve up to the rim, is represented by an example consisting of non-joining fragments (**29/75**), three additional examples that preserve only a small part of each lamp (**29/76–29/78**), and also numerous uncatalogued fragments, of which the majority are of Attic lamps.

The lamp **29/75** is Attic. It has a low but well-defined disk base, a shallow body with a curved shoulder, incurved rim, and a horizontal strap handle. The good quality black glaze covers all surfaces except the underside of the base. The body of **29/76**, which is also Attic, is similarly shaped but of lesser quality.

The lamps **29/77** and **29/78** are attributed to local workshops, and preserve the nozzle together with a small part of the body. **29/77** is covered with glaze only on the interior, while traces of glaze are also visible on the outer sides of the nozzle, which is short, with a rounded end and the wick hole occupying almost all of its surface. The body is even more shallow and open than the other examples of the type. On the black-glaze lamp **29/78** the nozzle is more elongated and the wick hole is at a distance from the rim.

This group of lamps corresponds to the Attic Howland Types 21 B[261] and 21 C,[262] as well as Broneer Type IV[263] and Scheibler Group RSL 1.[264] In Macedonia, the oldest examples of the type come from the Sanctuary of Demeter at Dion and date to the 5th century B.C.,[265] while the corresponding group of open lamps from Pella (ΠΛ 1) belongs mainly to the early 4th century B.C.[266] In the publication of Olynthos, lamps with these characteristics are designated as Group IV.[267]

The lamps **29/75** and **29/76** find parallels among examples of both Howland types,[268] which date from the last quarter of the 5th century B.C.;[269] they can also be compared to examples from the Kerameikos,[270] Corinth,[271] and Pella.[272] Their respective contexts indicate a date in the late 5th or early 4th century B.C. **29/77** seems to be earlier. The form of the nozzle connects it more closely to Howland Type 21 B, which, according to parallels, can be dated between the 3rd and the 4th quarters of the 5th century B.C.[273] In contrast, **29/78** reflects a more developed stage, called by Howland Type 21 C;[274] it should be placed in the last quarter of the 5th century B.C., without excluding a later date for this lamp, as well as for the two Attic examples of the group.

Lamp with narrow flat rim and wide filling hole

Only a small portion of the Attic black-glaze lamp **29/79** survives. It has thick walls which externally define a subtle curve that is clearly separated from the rim, which is flat and leans slightly toward the large filling hole. The nozzle would have been relatively long, with the wick hole at a distance from the edge of the rim. These characteristics correspond to Howland Type 23 A, which is in use in the late 5th and early 4th centuries B.C.[275] The very narrow rim, which leaves open the upper part of the body, indicates the first stages in the development of the type,[276] and suggests a date in the last quarter of the 5th century B.C.[277] Similar features are found in the so-called "Steilwand" lamps of Group KSL 1 from the Athenian Kerameikos,[278] while similar lamps from Corinth are classified as Broneer Type VI.[279] An example from Sindos shows the reproduction of this type by workshops in the north Aegean.[280]

Lamp with grooved rim

Only a very small part of the body and rim of the Attic black-glaze lamp **29/80** survives. Its state of preservation does not allow for a certain attribution to a particular type. The rather shallow body and the horizontal rim, with grooves around a probably large filling hole, are characteristic of Howland Type 24 A,[281] which corresponds to Scheibler Group KSL 2,[282] and the second variety of Broneer Type V.[283] Examples that correspond to these types, and which are similar to those from Methone, are known from the Pnyx in Athens,[284] Aigina,[285] and Thasos,[286] where the use of similar lamps seems to continue into the early 4th century B.C.[287] **29/80** should date, on the basis of the type in the Athenian Agora, to the last quarter of the 5th century B.C.

Lamps of the Second Quarter of the 4th Century B.C. (Figs. 29.84–29.88)

Tall-bodied lamp with vertical walls and small filling hole

Although fragmentary, the Attic black-glaze lamp **29/81** is easily recognizable. It has a tall body with vertical walls and a wide flat rim that slopes downward toward a very small filling hole. The handle would be of ribbon type and rather wide. It belongs to Howland Type 23 C[288] and Scheibler Group DSL 1,[289] which were in use at the time when Methone was destroyed.[290] Analogous lamps are classified as Broneer Type VI.[291] Similar examples have been found at the Pnyx in Athens,[292] Isthmia,[293] Olynthos,[294] Dion,[295] and Pella.[296]

Lamp with a groove on rim and small filling hole

The Attic black-glaze lamp **29/82** preserves about half of the rim together with a small part of the body, where the point of attachment of a strap handle is visible. The upper wall curves slightly in, forming an angle with the flat upper surface of the rim, which has a deep reserved groove around the lip. The filling hole is narrow. Lamps of this type are not represented in the Athenian Agora but are known from the Athenian Kerameikos and are included in Scheibler Group DSL 3, which is in use beginning in the second quarter of the 4th century B.C.[297] Similar lamps, all Attic, have been found in Olynthos and constitute the earliest examples of Group VIII at the site, which Robinson places at the end of the 5th century B.C.[298]

Lamps with spherical body, unglazed exterior

The latest lamps from the destruction deposit (**29/83–29/85**) have a spherical body and unpainted exterior, which marks the passage from the late Classical to the early Hellenistic period. They are probably of Attic origin.

The nearly complete **29/83** has a narrow disk base, a spherical body with very shallow ridges on the shoulder, and a curved rim, surrounded by a shallow groove and enclosing a narrow filling hole. The nozzle is relatively long, with a small circular wick hole at its end. Opposite there would have been a horizontal ribbon or strap handle. **29/84** and **29/85**, which preserve only a very small part of the rim and body, also had a spherical body with ridges on the shoulder, but their shoulders are more clearly articulated from the rim.

The above lamps belong to Howland Types 24 C′[299] and 25 A′/Scheibler Group RSL 5 respectively,[300] and they correspond to a later variety of Broneer Type VII.[301] Even closer parallels, however, are examples of Group IX at Olynthos,[302] which were in use in the years before the destruction of that city in 348 B.C.,[303] and which allow us to place the Methone lamps near the end of the second quarter of the 4th century B.C.

CONCLUSION

By examining the pottery from the destruction deposit in the agora of Methone as a group, we can make a few observations. First of all, almost all the various classes of pottery are represented, such as black-glaze and unpainted vessels, cooking wares, commercial amphoras, and terracotta lamps. Very few examples have painted or red-figured decoration, most notably the kylix **23/17** (ΜΕΘ 1362), the pelike **23/15** (ΜΕΘ 5161) (both illustrated in Chapter 23),[304] the askos **29/33**, the lekanis **29/35**, the stamnoid pyxis **29/40**, and also a small surviving portion of a Rhodian amphora which is adorned with painted bands and dot rosettes (Fig. 29.89).[305]

With regard to the repertoire of shapes, the black-glaze pottery largely comprises tablewares, with bowls with incurved rims and Type A skyphoi among the most popular shapes. Kantharoi are rare, represented by a very few uncatalogued fragments, while there is only one sufficiently preserved bowl with outturned rim. Corinthian-type skyphoi are also rare. The open shapes prevail, while the closed shapes include askoi, a few uncatalogued fragments only of squat lekythoi, and parts of an amphoriskos and a small hydria. Among the plain, unpainted wares, we find pots for daily use in the kitchen, related to cooking and preparation of food, transportation, storage, serving of liquids, and so on. Among the lamps, several types are found, dating from the 6th to the middle of the 4th century B.C., with the predominant type being the open lamp with curved walls.

The most common category of pottery in the destruction deposit are the amphoras, found in fragments scattered on the floors of enclosed and open spaces. Their study is still at a preliminary stage, as many are undergoing conservation.[306] Consequently, I provide only the most rudimentary summary here. There are many examples of Mendaian amphoras (e.g., ΜΕΘ 4153, ΜΕΘ 4156, ΜΕΘ 4159) (Figs. 29.90–29.92),[307] while others similarly belong to the same tradition of the northeast Aegean (e.g., ΜΕΘ 4152, ΜΕΘ 4157) (Figs. 29.93, 29.94). The Chian amphora ΜΕΘ 4158 can be distinguished (Fig. 29.95), as well as the Phoenician amphora ΜΕΘ 3878 (Fig. 29.96).[308]

Demand for black-glaze pottery products was covered by imports from Attica, but local workshops also produced black-glaze vases that are more or less faithful to Attic standards. There are quite a few good examples, next to, of course, those of inferior quality. Very often, dipping was used to apply the glaze. A few decorated vessels, such as the bowls **29/38** and **29/39**, reflect the preferences of local potters. Pottery for everyday domestic use was largely covered by the local ceramic workshops, those of Methone and of the wider region. The operation of such workshops in Methone had been established since the foundation of the colony.[309]

We may well ask: how were the vessels found in the agora, the center of the commercial activities of ancient Methone, used? Almost all are household utensils, cooking ware, and tableware. The wear and tear seen on many of them, and the repairs they sometimes received (e.g., the plate **29/17**, or the lekane **29/49**), or the traces of soot that most of the cooking ware displays from having come in contact with fire, allow us to consider that a part, at least, of the vessels of the destruction deposit were not marketable items but were in daily use at the time. The rough fireplaces found scattered in almost all areas of Building A, in some cases even leaving slight fire damage on the walls, must be associated with the installation of various groups of people during the siege of the city. The concentration of lead sling bullets in the eastern part of the stoa porch, as well as in Building Γ which was found to the south (in Plot 278),[310] leaves no doubt about the occupation of public buildings, either by the besieged Methonaians or by troops of the army of Philip II. Whoever was settled here, they had to meet their everyday needs for food. Consequently, the pottery from the destruction deposit should be interpreted in the light of historical events.

It is no coincidence, therefore, that most of the pots found in the long stoa porch of Building A (Room E) were concentrated in the eastern part, which was closed on three sides.[311] From this one area alone, more than ten vessels were collected, including the chytra **29/62**, the oinochoe **29/41**, the lekane **29/49**, the ladle **29/55**, the plate **29/18**, the local bowl/skyphos **29/38**, the bowl **29/3**, and the Attic skyphos **29/14**, as well as 25 coins, the majority being issues of Amyntas III (ca. 393–370/369 B.C.) and Perdikkas III (365–359 B.C.).[312] From the open area of the stoa porch, two amphoras were encountered, together with the black-glaze lekanides **29/35** and **29/36**.

In a similar vein, the adjacent Room Z was also used to prepare food. Of the two hearths found on its floor, one was made with rough fieldstones and in it were found animal bones. An amphora was found in this area, as was the pelike **29/48**, the lekane **29/50**, and the small bowl **29/8**, which contained red paint, as well as the lamp **29/85**.

The other areas of Building A yielded very little pottery. The excavation of the south wing of the building, with Rooms A and B, was not completed. The destruction deposit here contained few finds, among which the fragmentary Rhodian amphora with painted decoration stands out (Fig. 29.89, A 247).[313] In Room Γ, which constituted the anteroom between Rooms Δ and Z, the largest surviving portion of the plate **29/17** was found, together with the local bowl/skyphos **29/39** and the small stamnoid pyxis **29/40**. In the large Room Δ no well-preserved vessel was found, except the large Attic red-figure kylix by the Bonn Painter **23/17** (ΜΕΘ 1362),[314] found fallen in front of the entrance to the space, and which must have been hung on the wall. This kylix, which dates to the last decades of the 6th century B.C.—some 150 years before the destruction of Methone—is perhaps the only vessel that relates to the original phase of the building.

In contrast, part of the pottery found in Building B can be attributed to its original use or function. The excavation of this building showed it to have been largely used as a workshop space, which does not preclude other uses, by the besieged or the besiegers. On the north side of Room A,[315] a hearth made of clay was found, and this must have served as an outdoor oven/furnace, which would have been particularly useful during the siege. Near it were found three chytrai (**29/58–29/60**) and the Phoenician amphora ΜΕΘ 3878 (Fig. 29.96). In addition, all of the lopades and lids of the destruction deposit were found in Room A. This space seems to have been semi-open, since the fallen roof tiles found here were barely proportionate to the extent of the space, while two parallel stones embedded in the floor probably served as bases for wooden columns. In the southwest corner, a little deeper than the floor, in the so-called "Εστία," over ten vessels were found, which were probably placed on a wooden shelf. They include both Attic and local pottery, mostly tablewares (e.g., the bowls **29/1**, **29/4**, **29/6**, **29/7**, **29/10**; the "saltcellar" **29/26**; the bolsals **29/30**, **29/31**, and the like), some of which date to the first quarter of the 4th century B.C.

Room A communicated to the west with a paved roofed courtyard (Room H), which was closed to the west by a wall with an entrance that probably led to some other space.[316] Here, more than 20 vessels were found, mainly unpainted household wares (the chytrai **29/63**, **29/64**; the olpai **29/46**, **29/47**; the lekythoi **29/44**, **29/45**; the mortars **29/52** and the fragmentary **29/54**), but also a few black-glaze vessels (the small bowl **29/11**; the skyphos **29/15**; the "saltcellar" **29/29**, and a fragment of a kantharos); the red-figure askos **29/33** and the lamp **29/83** were also found here. There was, finally, a large concentration of amphoras, primarily along the western wall, which suggests that the area may have also been used for storage purposes.

The southern part of the building served as a blacksmith's shop, for the working of iron. In Room B, only a few fragmentary vessels were found (the small bowl **29/5**; the one-handler **29/23**; the lamp **29/82**), together with some sherds of cooking wares. The floor was covered with workshop waste—primarily iron slag—as well as many scattered iron nails and bronze coins. Room B did not communicate either with Room A or with the paved courtyard, and the only entrance to it was through Area Γ, which was immediately to the south and represents a later addition, since it even covered a part of Plateia A. Area Γ was open and its floor was characterized by extensive burning and a high concentration of iron slag and other iron waste products. Several vessels were found on this floor, such as the "saltcellars" **29/27** and **29/28**, the small bowl **29/12**, the oinochoe **29/42**, the chytra **29/61**, a miniature Corinthian pot of the "bowl-on-saucer" type (ΜΕΘ 2181, not illustrated),[317] and scattered fragments of at least three amphoras. The fish plate **29/21**, from which the floor had been largely detached, may have been here in secondary use.

Another issue arising from the examination of the pottery from the destruction deposit is how much time elapsed between the abandonment of the site after the expulsion of the Methonaians, and the total collapse of the buildings. The excavation of part of Plateia A and B[318] showed that outside Building A there was a large concentration of fragmentary pottery, including some complete or near-complete vessels. Scattered among the roof tiles were fragments of at least 14 amphoras, fragments or larger parts of cooking wares, among them the chytrai **29/56** and **29/57**, the mortaria **29/51** and **29/53**, and the oinochoe **29/43**. The black-glaze pottery, equally fragmented, is abundant and covers a wide range of shapes, predominantly plates, bowls, one-handlers, and Type A skyphoi. Among the most complete examples worth noting are the bowls **29/2** and **29/13**, the plate **29/19**, the fish plate **29/20**, the askos **29/34**, and the lid **29/37**. In some cases sherds that are broken into very small fragments seem to have been used to reinforce the earth floor. The general picture presented here indicates that, after the abandonment, the site must have remained exposed for a reasonable period of time and was open to all sorts of looting until the final collapse of the buildings. An indication of the wide scattering of the pottery is the fact that, in some cases, pieces or small fragments of the same vessel were found at a great distance from one another.[319]

The pottery from the destruction deposit of the agora of Methone is undoubtedly a very important assemblage, as a closed and well-dated context that yielded a complex collection of pottery.[320] This is all the more true as it relates to a period—the first half of the 4th century B.C.—for which we do not have corresponding assemblages in Macedonia, with the exception of Olynthos. On account of this, the study of this assemblage acquires special importance, magnified as it is by its association with the historical events of the time.

CATALOGUE

FINE WARES

29/1. (ΜΕΘ 1997) BG Bowl with Incurving Rim Fig. 29.4

East Hill #274/018003 [2]: Εστία(Building B: Room A).

H. 0.042; Diam. (foot) 0.091; p.Diam. (rim) 0.115.

Mended from three joining frr. Small part of foot and about two-thirds of body and rim missing.

Ring foot with grooved resting surface and nipple on underside. Groove at junction of foot and wall. Shallow bowl with strongly incurving rim.

Clay color: reddish yellow (7.5YR 7/6).

Thick, shiny black glaze. Glazed inside and out. Reserved: resting surface and groove at junction of foot and wall. Impressed decoration inside: nine alternately linked palmettes enclosing a central circle, within rouletting.

Attic.

Second quarter of 4th century B.C.

29/2. (ΜΕΘ 2629) BG Bowl with Incurving Rim Fig. 29.5

East Hill #274/059011 [2]: Δάπεδο (Plateia A).

H. 0.046; Diam. (foot) 0.088; p.Diam. (rim) 0.132.

Mended from five joining frr. About two-thirds of body and rim missing.

Ring foot with shallow and broad groove in resting surface. Nipple on underside. Groove at junction of foot and wall. Shallow bowl with strongly incurving rim.

Clay color: reddish yellow (7.5YR 7/6).

Thick, shiny black glaze, peeled on part of rim and in a few small areas on the exterior wall, fired red on the underside. Glazed inside and out. Reserved: resting surface, with traces of *miltos*(?) and groove at junction of foot and wall. Impressed decoration inside: eight alternately linked palmettes enclosing a central circle, within rouletting.

Graffito on underside, as shown.

Attic.

Second quarter of 4th century B.C.

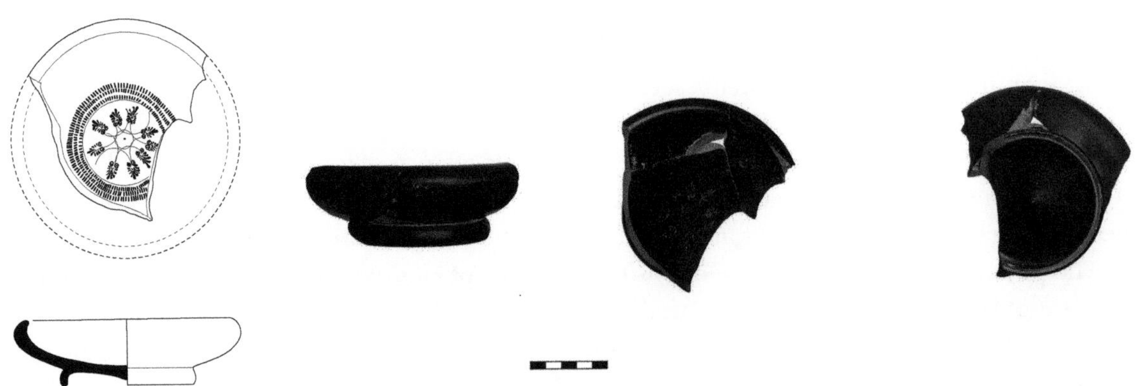

FIGURE 29.4. BG bowl with incurving rim, **29/1** (ΜΕΘ 1997).
Drawing I. Moschou, photos J. Vanderpool

FIGURE 29.5. BG bowl with incurving rim, **29/2** (ΜΕΘ 2629).
Drawing I. Moschou, photos J. Vanderpool

29/3. (ΜΕΘ 1371) BG Bowl with Incurving Rim Fig. 29.6

East Hill #274/066: Στρώμα καταστροφής (Building A: Room E).

H. 0.042; Diam. (foot) 0.074; Diam. (rim) 0.127.

Mended from 16 joining frr. Small parts of wall and rim missing.

Ring foot with broad resting surface. Shallow bowl with incurving rim.

Clay color: pale yellow (2.5Y 7/3).

Thick, dull black glaze, peeled in parts of exterior, but generally of good quality. Glazed inside and out. Reserved: resting surface, underside with glazed circle and junction of foot and wall. The underside is covered with a thick and well-preserved coat of *miltos*. Traces of *miltos* on the reserved band at junction of foot and wall.

Local.

Early(?) in second quarter of 4th century B.C.

29/4. (ΜΕΘ 2005) Small BG Bowl (Later and Light) Fig. 29.7

East Hill #274/018003 [2]: Εστία(Building B: Room A).

H. 0.025; Diam. (foot) 0.054; p.Diam. (rim) 0.065.

Mended from four joining frr. Large part of body and rim along with a small part of foot missing.

Ring foot with concave molding beneath. Very shallow bowl with plain, rounded rim, incurving.

Clay color: reddish yellow (7.5YR 7/6).

Thick black glaze, peeled in large part of the exterior wall. Glazed inside and out. Reserved: resting surface, underside with glazed band, two circles and central dot and junction of foot and wall.

Graffiti on underside, as shown.

Attic.

400–380 B.C.

FIGURE 29.6. BG bowl with incurving rim, **29/3** (ΜΕΘ 1371).
Drawing I. Moschou, photos I. Coyle

FIGURE 29.7. BG bowl with incurving rim (later and light), **29/4** (MEΘ 2005).
Drawing I. Moschou, photos I. Coyle

FIGURE 29.8. BG bowl with incurving rim (later and light), **29/5** (MEΘ 4064).
Drawing I. Moschou, photo I. Coyle

29/5. (MEΘ 4064) Small BG Bowl (Later and Light) Fig. 29.8

East Hill #274/027006 [4] (Building B: Room B).

H. 0.026; p.Diam. (foot) 0.057; p.Diam. (rim) 0.037.

Single fr preserving about one-quarter of body and rim and rather more of foot.

Ring foot with concave molding beneath. Very shallow bowl with plain, slightly incurving rim rounded on top.

Clay color: reddish yellow (5YR 6/6).

Thick, shiny black glaze. Glazed inside and out. Reserved: resting surface.

Attic.

400–380 B.C.

29/6. (MEΘ 1999) Small BG Bowl with Rounded Rim Fig. 29.9

East Hill #274/018003 [2]: Εστία(Building B: Room A).

H. 0.029; Diam. (foot) 0.047; Diam. (rim) 0.076.

Intact.

Ring foot with flat resting surface. Shallow bowl, slightly angular in profile, with plain, rounded rim.

Clay color: reddish yellow (7.5YR 6/6). Fabric contains few inclusions and mica.

Dull glaze, variously fired black and red, peeled in parts, especially in the area of the rim. The glaze is applied by dipping and covers the interior, most of the exterior of the body, and small part of the exterior of the foot.

Local.

Ca. 380 B.C.

FIGURE 29.9. BG bowl with rounded rim, **29/6** (ΜΕΘ 1999).
Drawing I. Moschou, photos I. Coyle

FIGURE 29.10. BG bowl with incurving rim, **29/7** (ΜΕΘ 1996).
Drawing I. Moschou, photo I. Coyle

FIGURE 29.11. BG bowl with incurving rim, **29/8** (ΜΕΘ 1372).
Drawing I. Moschou, photo I. Coyle

29/7. (ΜΕΘ 1996) Small BG Bowl with Incurving Rim Fig. 29.10
East Hill #274/018003 [2]: Εστία(Building B: Room A).
H. 0.030; Diam. (foot) 0.054; Diam. (rim) 0.085.
Intact.
Ring foot with narrow resting surface and slight nipple on underside. Shallow bowl with incurving rim.
Clay color: reddish yellow (7.5YR 7/6). Micaceous fabric.
The glaze is fired red for the most part and peeled in large areas. Totally glazed.
Local.
Second quarter of 4th century B.C.

29/8. (ΜΕΘ 1372) Small BG Bowl with Incurving Rim Fig. 29.11
East Hill #274/076: Στρώμα καταστροφής (Building A: Room Z).
H. 0.028; Diam. (foot) 0.049; Diam. (rim) 0.081.
Intact.
Ring foot with flat resting surface and slight nipple on underside. Shallow bowl with incurving rim.
Clay color: reddish yellow (7.5YR 7/6). Micaceous fabric.
Glaze fired black to red, peeled in parts. Glazed inside and out, applied by dipping. Reserved: resting surface and underside. Traces of red pigment on interior.
Local.
Second quarter of 4th century B.C.

29/9. (MEΘ 1379) Small BG Bowl with Incurving Rim Fig. 29.12

East Hill #274/067: Ανατολικός μάρτυρας (Plateia A).

H. 0.028; Diam. (foot) 0.050; Diam. (rim) 0.074.

Mended from nine joining frr. Parts of body and rim missing.

Ring foot with narrow resting surface. Shallow bowl with incurving rim.

Clay color: gray (5Y 6/1). Fabric contains inclusions and mica.

Poor, dull black glaze, worn and peeled in most of the exterior. Glazed inside and out, applied by dipping. Probably the resting surface and underside remained unglazed.

Local.

Second quarter of 4th century B.C.

29/10. (MEΘ 1998) Small BG Bowl with Incurving Rim (Footed Saltcellar) Fig. 29.13

East Hill #274/018003 [2]: Εστία(Building B: Room A).

H. 0.030; Diam. (foot) 0.036; Diam. (body, max, just below rim) 0.064.

Intact.

Ring foot with narrow resting surface and nipple on underside. Rather deep bowl with pronouncedly incurving rim.

Clay color: reddish yellow (7.5YR 7/6).

Thick, shiny black glaze, well preserved on the interior and on the underside, worn and peeled on rim and on the exterior wall. Glaze inside and out. Reserved: resting surface and junction of foot with wall.

Attic.

Second quarter of 4th century B.C.

FIGURE 29.12. BG bowl with incurving rim, **29/9** (MEΘ 1379).
Drawing I. Moschou, photo I. Coyle

FIGURE 29.13. BG bowl with incurving rim (footed saltcellar), **29/10** (MEΘ 1998).
Drawing I. Moschou, photo I. Coyle

29/11. (ΜΕΘ 2177) Small BG Bowl with Incurving Rim (Footed Saltcellar) Fig. 29.14

East Hill #274/029001 [1]: Δάπεδο (Building B: Room H).

P.H. 0.030; Diam. 0.069.

Mended from three frr. About one-quarter of body and rim along with foot missing.

Deep bowl with pronouncedly incurving rim.

Clay color: reddish yellow (7.5YR 7/6).

Thick, shiny black glaze, peeled in parts of body and rim, especially on exterior. Glazed inside and out. Reserved: junction of foot and wall.

Attic.

Second quarter of 4th century B.C.

29/12. (ΜΕΘ 4065) Small BG Bowl with Incurving Rim (Footed Saltcellar) Fig. 29.15

East Hill #274/027023 [3] (Building B: Room Γ).

H. 0.034; p.Diam. (foot) 0.025; p.Diam. (body, max, just below rim) 0.053.

Single fr preserving about one-quarter of body and rim and rather less of foot.

Ring foot with grooved resting surface. Shallow rounded bowl with curving sides and pronouncedly incurving rim.

Clay color: reddish yellow (5YR 6/6).

Thick, shiny black glaze, peeled in small parts and in a larger part on the exterior. Glazed inside and out. Reserved: resting surface and junction of foot and wall.

Attic.

Second quarter of 4th century B.C.

FIGURE 29.14. BG bowl with incurving rim (footed saltcellar), **29/11** (ΜΕΘ 2177). Photo I. Coyle

FIGURE 29.15. BG bowl with incurving rim (footed saltcellar), **29/12** (ΜΕΘ 4065). Drawing I. Moschou, photo I. Coyle

29/13. (ΜΕΘ 4790) BG Bowl with Outturned Rim Fig. 29.16

East Hill #274/069 (Plateia A).

H. 0.048; Diam. (foot) 0.074; p.Diam. (rim) 0.134.

Mended from several joining frr. Several parts missing, but it retains full profile.

Ring foot, formed by two fine plastic rings and a low stem above them that joins the base and the body. The inner face of the foot rises in a single curve. The resting surface is grooved and there is a central nipple on the underside. Broad shallow bowl with angled wall and slightly thickened rim projecting outward.

Clay color: reddish yellow (7.5YR 6/6).

Thick, metallic black glaze, fired black to red in a small area on the exterior wall and rim. Glazed inside and out. Reserved: groove in resting surface, with traces of *miltos.* Impressed decoration inside: alternately linked palmettes within rouletting. Five palmettes are preserved, but there must have been seven.

Attic.

Second quarter of 4th century B.C.

29/14. (ΜΕΘ 1367) BG Skyphos, Attic Type Fig. 29.17

East Hill #274/076: Βόρειος μάρτυρας/Στρώμα καταστροφής (Building A: Room E).

P.H. 0.119; Diam. (foot) 0.066; p.Diam. (body) 0.121.

Mended from many joining frr. Large part of body along with entire rim and handles missing.

Torus ring foot. Groove at junction of foot and wall. S-shaped body with outturned rim.

Clay color: reddish yellow (7.5YR 7/6).

Thick black glaze. Glazed inside and out. Reserved: underside with three glazed circles, resting surface and groove at junction of foot and wall. Traces of *miltos* on underside.

Attic.

Second quarter of 4th century B.C.

FIGURE 29.16. BG bowl with outturned rim, **29/13** (ΜΕΘ 4790). Drawing I. Moschou, photos J. Vanderpool

FIGURE 29.17. BG Attic-type skyphos, Type A, **29/14** (ΜΕΘ 1367). Drawing I. Moschou, photo I. Coyle

29/15. (ΜΕΘ 4746) BG Skyphos, Attic Type Fig. 29.18

East Hill #274/019001 [1] (Building B: Room H).

H. 0.113; p.Diam. (foot) 0.053; p.Diam. (rim) 0.047.

Mended from eight joining frr. It preserves less than one-quarter, from foot to rim, and part of a handle.

Torus ring foot. S-shaped body with outturned rim. Horizontal, slightly angled handle, round in section, attached at top of wall, below rim.

Clay color: reddish yellow (5YR 6/6).

Thick, shiny black glaze. Glazed inside and out. Reserved: underside and resting surface.

Attic.

Second quarter of 4th century B.C.

29/16. (ΜΕΘ 2000) BG Skyphos, Attic Type Fig. 29.19

East Hill #274/018003 [2]: Εστία(Building B: Room A).

P.H. 0.094; Diam. (rim) 0.105.

Mended from nine joining frr. Foot, large parts of body, about one-third of rim and one handle missing.

S-shaped body with outturned rim. Horizontal, slightly angled triangular handle, round in section, attached at top of wall, below rim.

Clay color: reddish yellow (7.5YR 7/6), colored gray in a large part because of misfiring.

Thick, shiny black glaze, peeled on most of handle, in small part of outer wall and in parts of rim area.

Attic.

Second quarter of 4th century B.C.

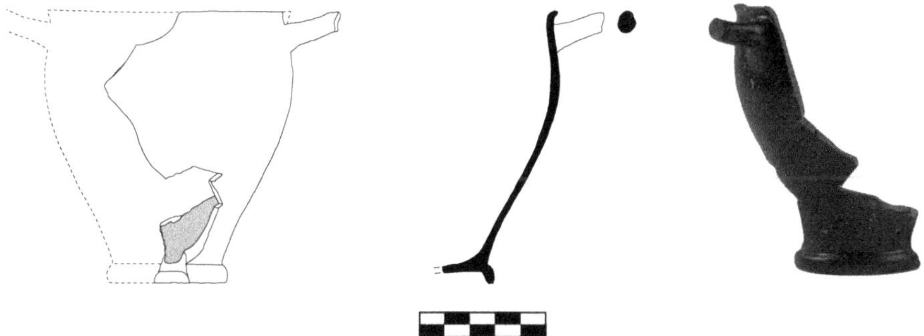

FIGURE 29.18. BG Attic-type skyphos, Type A, **29/15** (ΜΕΘ 4746). Drawing I. Moschou, photo I. Coyle

FIGURE 29.19. BG Attic-type skyphos, Type A, **29/16** (ΜΕΘ 2000). Photo I. Coyle

29/17. (ΜΕΘ 1374) BG Plate, Rolled Rim Fig. 29.20

East Hill #274/077: Ανατολικός μάρτυρας (Building A: Room Γ).

H. 0.024; p.Diam. (foot) 0.118; p.Diam. (rim) 0.164; est. Diam. (rim) 0.173.

Mended from a large piece and three small joining frr. About half of vase missing. Vessel repaired with a lead clamp in the area of the rim in antiquity.

Ring foot with inner face merging into underside in a single curve. Slight nipple at center of underside. Projecting rim, with a rill in inner circumference. Concave molding beneath rim, with a fillet.

Clay color: reddish yellow (7.5YR 6/6), colored gray over most parts because of misfiring.

Thick, shiny black glaze peeled on part of exterior wall and foot. Totally glazed. Impressed decoration on floor: palmettes around a circle of enclosed ovules. Pattern repeated.

Attic.

Beginning of 4th century B.C.

29/18. (ΜΕΘ 1364) Glazed Plate, Rolled Rim Fig. 29.21

East Hill #274/076: Βόρειος μάρτυρας/Στρώμα καταστροφής (Building A: Room E).

H. 0.022; p.Diam. (foot) 0.091; p.Diam. (rim) 0.088; est. Diam. (rim) 0.139.

Mended from nine joining frr. Several parts missing, but it retains full profile.

Ring foot with the inner face merging into the underside in a single curve. A downward-pointing nipple at center of underside. Thickened rim, flat on top, fillet beneath.

Clay color: reddish yellow (7.5YR 7/6). Micaceous fabric.

Dull orange glaze, peeled in large areas. Quite thick, but with a tendency to flake. Totally glazed, except for resting surface, which is reserved. Impressed decoration on floor: five successive rows of horizontal marks, in the style of stitched rouletting.

Local.

Second quarter of 4th century B.C.

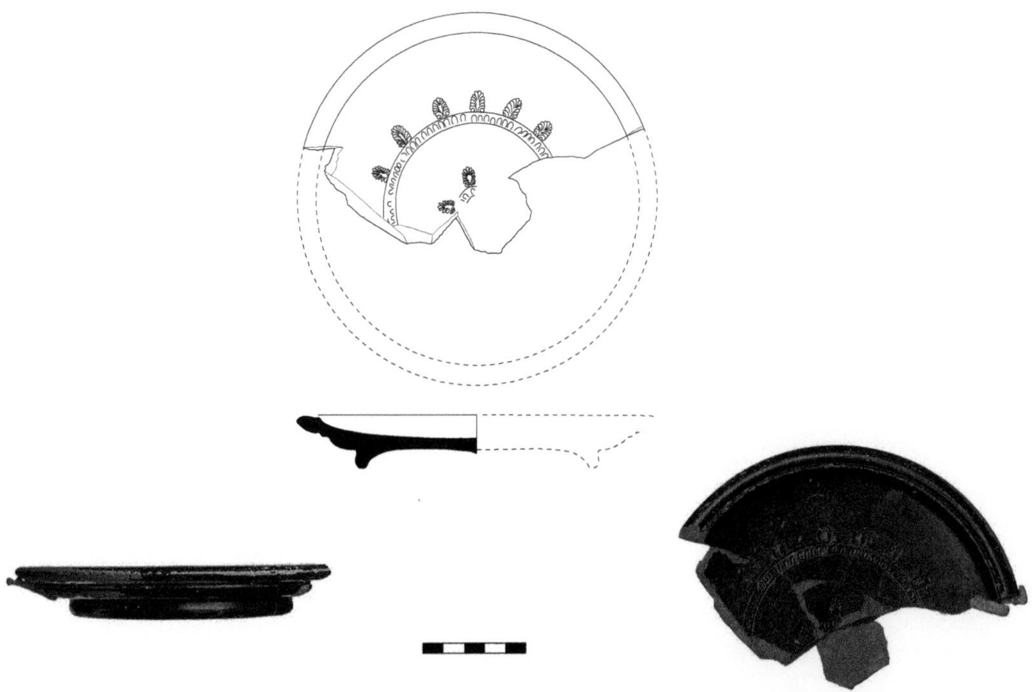

FIGURE 29.20. BG plate with rolled rim, **29/17** (ΜΕΘ 1374).
Drawing I. Moschou, photos J. Vanderpool

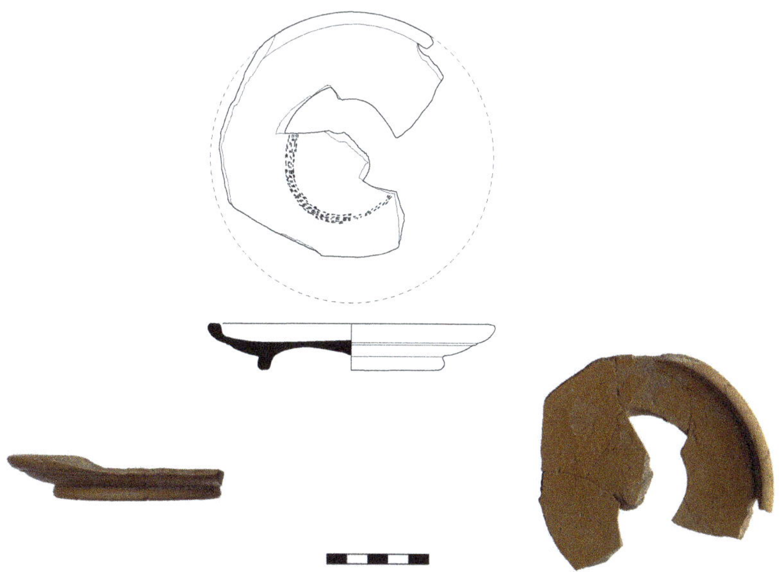

FIGURE 29.21. Glazed plate with rolled rim, **29/18** (ΜΕΘ 1364). Drawing I. Moschou, photos J. Vanderpool

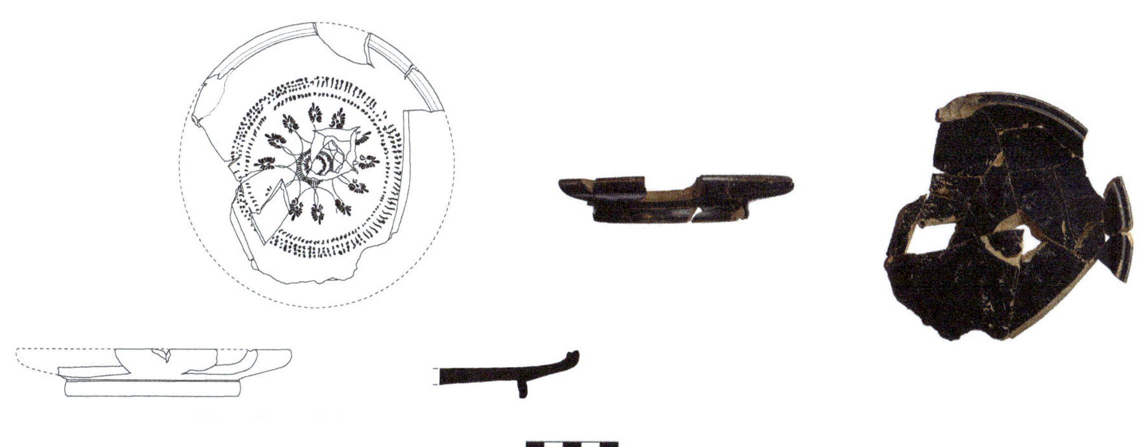

FIGURE 29.22. BG plate with rilled rim, **29/19** (ΜΕΘ 4791). Drawing I. Moschou, photos J. Vanderpool

29/19. (ΜΕΘ 4791) BG Plate, Rilled Rim Fig. 29.22

East Hill #274/079: Ανατολικό τμήμα (Plateia A–B).

H. 0.025; Diam. (foot) 0.095; p.Diam. (rim) 0.132; est. Diam. (rim) 0.151.

Mended from many joining frr. Several parts missing, but it retains full profile.

Ring foot with narrow resting surface. Underside with light incised concentric circles and a very slight nipple at center. Very shallow body, with wall rising vertically from edge of flat floor. Rim flat on top, with one broad rill.

Clay color: reddish yellow (7.5YR 6/6).

Thick, shiny black glaze, peeled in just a few small areas. Totally glazed. Impressed decoration on floor: twelve alternately linked palmettes enclosing two central circles of rouletting, within rouletting.

Attic.

Second quarter of 4th century B.C.

29/20. (ΜΕΘ 2178) BG Fish Plate Fig. 29.23

East Hill #274/059009 [2]: Δάπεδο (Plateia A).

H. 0.033; Diam. (foot) 0.114; p.Diam. (rim) 0.207; est. Diam. (rim) 0.214.

Mended from several joining pieces and smaller frr. About one-third of floor along with the rim missing.

High ring foot with flat resting surface and nipple on underside. Flat floor sloping down to a central depression. Groove around central depression and on outer edge of floor. Deep overhanging rim.

Clay color: reddish yellow (7.5YR 6/6).

Thick black glaze well preserved on underside, peeled and worn on floor and rim. Totally glazed. Reserved: resting surface, outer edge of underside, junction of wall and foot, grooves/bands around central depression and on outer edge of floor.

Attic.

Second quarter of 4th century B.C.

29/21. (ΜΕΘ 2175) BG Fish Plate Fig. 29.24

East Hill #274/028003 [1]: Δάπεδο (Building B: Room Γ).

H. 0.023; Diam. (foot) 0.092; Diam. (rim) 0.152.

Mended from three joining frr. Central part of floor along with depression missing.

Ring foot with grooved resting surface. Flat floor sloping down to center. Scraped groove on outer edge of floor. Slightly downturned rim.

Clay color: reddish yellow (7.5YR 6/6).

Thick black glaze, peeled over a large area of underside. Totally glazed. Reserved: outer edge of resting surface.

Attic.

Second quarter of 4th century B.C.

FIGURE 29.23. BG fish plate, **29/20** (ΜΕΘ 2178). Drawing I. Moschou, photos I. Coyle

FIGURE 29.24. BG fish plate, **29/21** (ΜΕΘ 2175). Drawing I. Moschou, photo I. Coyle

FIGURE 29.25. BG one-handler, **29/22** (MEΘ 2003).
Drawing I. Moschou, photos J. Vanderpool

29/22. (MEΘ 2003) BG One-handler Fig. 29.25
East Hill #274/018003 [2]: Εστία(Building B: Room A).
H. 0.038; Diam. (foot) 0.052; Diam. (rim) 0.086.
Mended from six joining frr. About one-quarter of body and rim along with handle missing.
Ring foot with flat resting surface. Fairly deep body with slightly flaring rim.
Clay color: reddish yellow (7.5YR 7/6).
Thick black glaze, peeled in area of rim and in small parts mostly on exterior wall. Glazed inside and out. Reserved: resting surface and underside with glazed circle. Traces of *miltos* on underside. Impressed decoration inside: palmette cross.
Attic.
Turn from first to second quarter of 4th century B.C.

29/23. (MEΘ 4641) BG One-handler Fig. 29.26
East Hill #274/028001 [1] (Building B: Room B).
H. 0.038; p.Diam. (foot) 0.049; p.Diam. (rim) 0.068.
Single fr preserving very little of foot to rim and a stump from handle.
Flaring ring foot with flat resting surface. Broad shallow body. Rim sloping inward. Horizontal handle, round in section, attached just below rim.
Clay color: very pale brown (10YR 7/4), with light gray core in parts because of misfiring. Although the color does not resemble normal Attic red-orange clay, the fabric is Attic. It is possible that the brownish color is the result of secondary firing.
Thick black glaze, discolored, peeled in small parts mostly on exterior wall. Glazed inside and out. Reserved: resting surface, underside with glazed band and circle and a broad band from exterior of foot to junction with wall.
Attic.
First quarter of 4th century B.C.

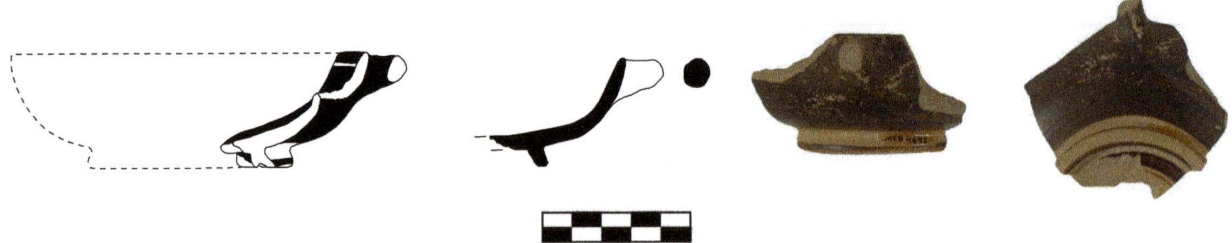

FIGURE 29.26. BG one-handler, **29/23** (MEΘ 4641).
Drawing I. Moschou, photos I. Coyle

FIGURE 29.27. Glazed one-handler, **29/24** (MEΘ 1380).
Drawing I. Moschou, photo I. Coyle

29/24. (MEΘ 1380) Glazed One-handler Fig. 29.27

East Hill #274/007030 [10] (Building B: Room A).

H. 0.038; Diam. (foot) 0.063; Diam. (rim) 0.100.

Mended from 16 joining frr. Several parts of body and rim along with handle missing.

Ring foot with narrow resting surface. Broad shallow body, slightly angular in profile. Rounded rim.

Clay color: reddish yellow (7.5YR 6/6). Fabric contains inclusions and mica.

Poor, dull red glaze, much worn on interior. Glazed inside and out, applied by dipping, leaving foot and part of lower body on exterior unglazed.

Local.

Second quarter of 4th century B.C.

29/25. (MEΘ 1994) BG Saltcellar with Concave Wall Fig. 29.28

East Hill #274/018002 [2]: Δάπεδο (Building B: Room A).

H. 0.028; Diam. (foot) 0.064; Diam. (rim) 0.066.

Intact.

Ring foot with flat resting surface and recessed underside. Shallow body with concave wall. Rim rounded on top.

Clay color: reddish yellow (7.5YR 7/6).

Shiny silver-black glaze, peeled just in small parts on rim and foot. Totally glazed.

Graffito on underside, as shown.

Attic.

Second quarter of 4th century B.C.

29/26. (MEΘ 2001) BG Saltcellar with Concave Wall Fig. 29.29

East Hill #274/018003 [2]: Εστία(Building B: Room A).

H. 0.026; Diam. (foot) 0.063; Diam. (rim) 0.065.

Intact.

Ring foot with slight groove in resting surface and recessed underside. Shallow body with concave wall. Rim rounded on top, sloping outward.

FIGURE 29.28. BG saltcellar with concave wall, **29/25** (MEΘ 1994).
Drawing I. Moschou, photos I. Coyle

FIGURE 29.29. BG saltcellar with concave wall, **29/26** (MEΘ 2001).
Drawing I. Moschou, photos I. Coyle

Clay color: reddish yellow (7.5YR 6/6).
Dull black glaze, peeled in parts. Totally glazed.
Graffito on underside: incised line, as shown.
Attic.
Second quarter of 4th century B.C.

29/27. (MEΘ 1136) BG Saltcellar with Concave Wall Fig. 29.30
East Hill #274/027017 [2] (Building B: Room Γ).
H. 0.029; Diam. (foot) 0.066; p.Diam. (rim) 0.065.
Single fr preserving most part from foot to rim.
Ring foot with slight groove in resting surface and recessed underside. Shallow body with concave wall. Rim rounded on top, sloping outward.
Clay color: reddish yellow (7.5YR 6/6).
Thick, shiny black glaze, peeled in parts. Totally glazed.
Graffito on underside, as shown.
Attic.
Second quarter of 4th century B.C.

FIGURE 29.30. BG saltcellar with concave wall, **29/27** (ΜΕΘ 1136).
Drawing I. Moschou, photos I. Coyle

FIGURE 29.31. BG saltcellar with concave wall, **29/28** (ΜΕΘ 2176).
Drawing I. Moschou, photos I. Coyle

29/28. (ΜΕΘ 2176) BG Saltcellar with Concave Wall — Fig. 29.31

East Hill #274/028003 [1] (Building B: Room Γ).

H. 0.028; Diam. (foot) 0.065; p.Diam. (rim) 0.063.

Mended from two joining frr. Full profile from foot to rim, about half missing.

Ring foot with grooved resting surface and recessed underside. Shallow body with concave wall. Rim rounded on top.

Clay color: reddish yellow (7.5YR 6/6).

Thick, shiny black glaze, peeled in parts and over large area on underside. Totally glazed.

Graffito on underside, as shown. There is also an incised line at the bottom.

Attic.

Second quarter of 4th century B.C.

29/29. (ΜΕΘ 2174) BG Saltcellar with Concave Wall — Fig. 29.32

East Hill #274/028002 [1]: Δάπεδο (Building B: Room H).

H. 0.029; p.Diam. (foot) 0.047; p.Diam. (rim) 0.063.

Mended from large piece and a small joining fr. About half part from foot to rim missing.

Ring foot with flat resting surface and recessed underside. Shallow body with concave wall. Rim rounded on top.

FIGURE 29.32. BG saltcellar with concave wall, **29/29** (ΜΕΘ 2174).
Drawing I. Moschou, photo I. Coyle

FIGURE 29.33. BG bolsal, **29/30** (ΜΕΘ 2004).
Drawing I. Moschou, photos I. Coyle

Clay color: reddish yellow (7.5YR 6/6), turned gray in most areas because of misfiring(?).

Thick, shiny black glaze, peeled in part of rim area and in small parts on body and foot. Totally glazed.

Attic.

Second quarter of 4th century B.C.

29/30. (ΜΕΘ 2004) BG Bolsal Fig. 29.33

East Hill #274/018003 [2]: Εστια (Building B: Room A).

H. 0.042; Diam. (foot) 0.063; est. Diam. (rim) 0.090.

Single fr preserving foot and about one-quarter of body and rim. Large part of body and rim, along with handles, missing.

Flaring ring foot. Concave lower part of wall, slightly curved sides on upper part. Plain rim.

Clay color: reddish yellow (7.5YR 6/6).

Thick black glaze, peeled in small parts. Glazed inside and out. Reserved: underside with glazed circle and central dot. Traces of *miltos* on underside.

Attic.

First quarter of 4th century B.C.

29/31. (ΜΕΘ 2002) BG Bolsal Fig. 29.34

East Hill #274/018003 [2]: Εστία(Building B: Room A).

H. 0.043; Diam. (foot) 0.060; Diam. (rim) 0.090.

Mended from six joining frr. Parts of body and rim and one handle missing.

Flaring ring foot. Concave lower part of wall, slightly flaring sides on upper part. Plain rim. Long horizontal horseshoe handle, round in section, attached just below rim.

Clay color: reddish yellow (7.5YR 7/6).

Fairly thick glaze, variously fired black and red, peeled in a few small areas, mostly on resting surface. Totally glazed.

Local.

Turn from first to second quarter of 4th century B.C.

FIGURE 29.34. BG bolsal, **29/31** (MEΘ 2002).
Drawing I. Moschou, photos I. Coyle

FIGURE 29.35. BG bolsal, **29/32** (MEΘ 4744).
Drawing I. Moschou, photos I. Coyle

29/32. (MEΘ 4744) BG Bolsal Fig. 29.35

East Hill #274/017005 [3] (Building B: Room A).

H. 0.061; p.Diam. (foot) 0.045; p.Diam. (rim) 0.060.

Mended from five joining frr. Most of foot, large parts of body and rim, one handle and small portion of the other missing.

Heavy ring foot. Concave lower part of wall, nearly vertical sides on upper part. Plain rim. Horizontal, slightly angled, horseshoe ring handle, attached just below rim.

Clay color: pink (7.5YR 7/4). Micaceous fabric.

Dull glaze variously fired black and brown, peeled in parts. Glazed inside and out. Reserved: underside with glazed band.

Local.

First quarter of 4th century B.C.

29/33. (MEΘ 2007) Red-figured Askos, Shallow Type Fig. 29.36

East Hill #274/018004 [2]: Δάπεδο (Building B: Room H).

P.H. 0.101; max Diam. (foot) 0.138; Diam. (body) 0.149.

Mended from many joining frr. Large parts of foot, few small parts of body, part of spout, and almost entire handle missing.

Disk foot, slightly projecting from wall. Body with tall dome-shaped top. Prominent nipple at center of top, surrounded by two plastic rings and a groove around them. Light groove at edge of shoulder on top. Flaring spout. Broad overarching handle, triangular in section.

Clay color: reddish yellow (7.5YR 7/6), more pinkish (7.5YR 7/4 "pink") in parts due to firing.

Thick, shiny black glaze. Glazed outside and on interior of spout. Reserved: underside, with traces of *miltos*, grooves around shoulder and center, upper plastic ring, top of nipple. Red-figured decoration on top: two pairs of women's heads, facing. Between them, spiral plants. The women in each pair are wearing different kinds of headgear.

Attic.

Second quarter of 4th century B.C.

FIGURE 29.36. RF askos, shallow type, **29/33** (ΜΕΘ 2007).
Drawing I. Moschou, photos I. Coyle

FIGURE 29.37. BG askos, shallow type, **29/34** (ΜΕΘ 3267).
Drawing I. Moschou, photos I. Coyle

29/34. (ΜΕΘ 3267) BG Askos, Shallow Type Fig. 29.37

East Hill #274/066: Βόρειο τμήμα/Δάπεδο (Plateia A).

P.H. 0.064; Diam. (foot) 0.084; Diam. (body) 0.108.

Mended from several joining frr. Part of foot, two small and one larger part of body, part of spout, and almost entire handle missing.

Disk foot, slightly projecting from the wall. Body with steep lower wall and tall conical top, angular in profile. Nipple at center of top. Broad, thin strap overarching handle.

Clay color: gray to greenish (between 2.5Y5/2 "grayish brown" and 5/3 "light olive brown"), because of misfiring. Fabric contains inclusions and mica.

Thick, shiny black glaze, fired black to red. Glazed outside. Bottom reserved.

Local.

Second quarter of 4th century B.C.

29/35. (ΜΕΘ 1373) Black-painted Lidded Lekanis, with Ribbon Handles Fig. 29.38

East Hill #274/077: Στρώμα καταστροφής (Building A: Room E).

H. 0.119; Diam. (foot) 0.139; Diam. (body) 0.321; Diam. (rim) 0.306.

Mended from many joining frr. Major part of body and rim and several smaller ones, along with one handle, missing. Remaining handle had been broken and rejoined to body with a lead clamp in antiquity.

Low ring foot with broad resting surface. Deep body, with lower wall rising steeply from foot. Upper part of wall is nearly vertical, forming a deep ledge on which lid rests. Thin vertical lip. Horizontal tilted ribbon handle, concave in section, attached at top of wall.

Clay color: reddish yellow (7.5YR 6/6), grayish in several areas.

Thick, shiny black glaze, discolored, worn and peeled in large areas on exterior, well preserved on interior. Glazed inside and out. Reserved: resting surface, underside with glazed band and circle around center, band above foot, handle panel, and space between handle roots. The ledge is also reserved and decorated with black-painted branch-and-leaf pattern.

Attic.

Between third and fourth quarters of 5th century B.C.

FIGURE 29.38. Black painted lidded lekanis with ribbon handles, **29/35** (ΜΕΘ 1373). Drawing I. Moschou, photos I. Coyle

FIGURE 29.39. BG lidded lekanis with horizontal handles, **29/36** (ΜΕΘ 1376). Drawing I. Moschou, photos I. Coyle

29/36. (ΜΕΘ 1376) BG Lidded Lekanis, with Horizontal Handles Fig. 29.39

East Hill #274/078: Ανατολικός μάρτυρας (Building A: Room E).

H. 0.057; Diam. (foot) 0.111; p.Diam. (rim) 0.205.

Mended from several joining pieces and small frr. Large part of body and rim along with one handle missing.

Ring foot with broad resting surface. Low broad body, with lower wall rising smoothly from foot. Upper part of wall is nearly vertical, with a slight flare at top of wall. Rim flat on top, with one broad rill. There is a slight central depression in floor. Horizontal tilted horseshoe-shaped handle, attached at top of wall.

Clay color: pink (7.5YR 7/4), brownish in parts because of misfiring.

Thick black glaze, discolored, peeled in small parts and in large area on exterior wall. Glazed inside and out. Reserved: resting surface, underside with glazed band, circle, and a central dot, junction of foot and wall.

Local.

Second quarter of 4th century B.C.

29/37. (ΜΕΘ 5354) BG Lekanis Lid Fig. 29.40

East Hill #274/059003 [2] (Plateia A).

H. 0.040; Diam. 0.121.

Mended from several joining frr. Large parts of lid and small part of knob missing.

Echinus-shaped lid with nearly flat, slightly sloping top and downturned rim. Very low stem with disk knob at the top. Knob forms raised edge and small conical depression at center.

Clay color: reddish yellow, creating two bands (5YR 7/6 and 7.5YR 7/6) because of misfiring. Fabric contains very few inclusions and mica.

Thick black glaze. Glazed inside and out. Reserved: upper surface of knob, decorated with two glazed bands around conical depression, bottom of depression, top of raised edge of knob.

Local.

Second quarter of 4th century B.C.

FIGURE 29.40. BG lekanis lid, **29/37** (ΜΕΘ 5354).
Drawing I. Moschou, photos J. Vanderpool

FIGURE 29.41. Locally produced skyphos/bowl, **29/38** (ΜΕΘ 1365).
Drawing I. Moschou, photos I. Coyle

29/38. (ΜΕΘ 1365) Handleless Skyphos/Bowl with Banded Decoration Fig. 29.41

East Hill #274/076: Βόρειος μάρτυρας/Στρώμα καταστροφής (Building A: Room E).

H. 0.083; Diam. (foot) 0.082; Diam. (rim) 0.207.

Mended from many joining frr. Several parts of wall, rim and floor missing.

Ring foot with flat resting surface. Deep broad conical body with incurving rim.

Clay color: reddish yellow (5YR 6/6). Micaceous fabric.

Decoration: band of red glaze outside, broader one at top of interior that continues to rim, red disk in floor.

Local.

Second quarter of 4th century B.C.

29/39. (ΜΕΘ 1375) Two-handled Skyphos/Bowl with Banded Decoration Fig. 29.42

East Hill #274/077: Ανατολικός μάρτυρας (Building A: Room Γ).

H. 0.066; Diam. (foot) 0.073; Diam. (rim) 0.166.

Mended from many joining frr. Large parts missing, but it retains full profile.

Ring foot with flat resting surface. Deep broad conical body with incurving rim. Horizontal band handles, squeezed at center, probably ending in knobs, attached at rim.

Clay color: reddish yellow (7.5YR 7/6). Fabric contains inclusions and mica.

Thick glaze of very good quality, fired red to brown, peeled only in small parts. Center of floor fired orange from stacking. Glazed inside and out, applied by dipping, leaving foot and lower body on exterior unglazed.

Local.

Second quarter of 4th century B.C.

FIGURE 29.42. Locally produced skyphos/bowl, **29/39** (ΜΕΘ 1375).
Drawing I. Moschou, photos I. Coyle

FIGURE 29.43. Locally made stamnoid pyxis, **29/40** (ΜΕΘ 1363).
Drawing I. Moschou, photos I. Coyle

29/40. (ΜΕΘ 1363) Stamnoid Pyxis with Painted Decoration Fig. 29.43

East Hill #274/077: Στρώμα καταστροφής (Building A: Room Γ).

H. 0.086; Diam. (foot) 0.050; max Diam. (body) 0.101; p.Diam. (rim) 0.068.

Mended from many joining frr. Large part of rim and handles, small fr of shoulder, and very few small parts of body missing.

Ring foot. Deep ovoid body with rounded sloping shoulder. High vertical flat-topped rim. Rolled handles attached diagonally on shoulder, probably rising above rim.

Clay color: reddish yellow (7.5YR 6/6). Micaceous fabric.

Decoration: glazed band at foot that continues to lowest part of body, two bands around body, dots at junction of body and shoulder, above them a glazed shapeless band that continues on outer face of handles. Top of rim is also glazed.

Local.

Second quarter of 4th century B.C.

PLAINWARES

29/41. (ΜΕΘ 1370) Tall-necked Oinochoe Fig. 29.44

East Hill #274/066 and #274/076: Both Στρώμα καταστροφής (Building A: Room E).

H. 0.240; Diam. (foot) 0.100; max Diam. (body) 0.192; Diam. (rim) 0.099.

Mended from many joining frr. Very few small parts missing.

Flaring ring foot with flat resting surface. Squat, globular body with nearly flat shoulder. Tall cylindrical neck with wide groove on top. Rounded mouth with rolled rim, which is undercut. Thick handle from just below shoulder to top of neck.

Clay color: reddish yellow (5YR 7/6). Fabric contains inclusions.

FIGURE 29.44. Plain ware oinochoe/jug, **29/41** (ΜΕΘ 1370).
Drawing I. Moschou, photo I. Coyle

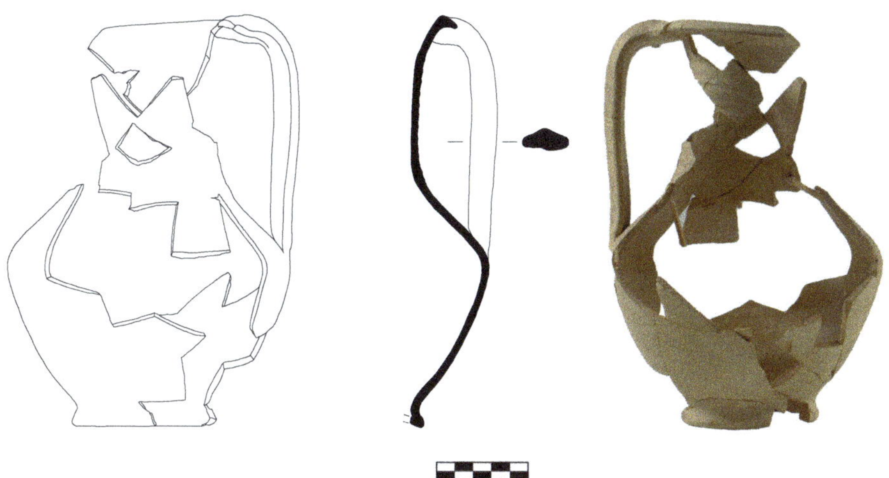

FIGURE 29.45. Plain ware oinochoe/jug, **29/42** (ΜΕΘ 4958).
Drawing I. Moschou, photo I. Coyle

Unglazed exterior with polished surface.
Local.
Second quarter of 4th century B.C.

29/42. (ΜΕΘ 4958) Tall-necked Oinochoe Fig. 29.45
East Hill #274/027013 [3] and #274/027023 [3] (Building B: Room Γ).
H. 0.216; Diam. (foot) 0.083; max Diam. (body) 0.153; p.Diam. (rim) 0.108.
Mended from many joining frr. Large parts missing, but it retains full profile.
Disk(?) foot. Low body with high sloping shoulder, biconical in profile. Tall cylindrical neck with ridges. Rounded mouth with beveled rim projecting outward. Handle triangular in section, from shoulder to rim.
Clay color: pale yellow (2.5Y 8/3), unevenly fired. Fabric quite soft and creamy.
Unglazed exterior.
Local.
Second quarter of 4th century B.C.

FIGURE 29.46. Plain ware oinochoe/jug, **29/43** (ΜΕΘ 1378).
Drawing I. Moschou, photo I. Coyle

FIGURE 29.47. Plain ware lekythos, **29/44** (ΜΕΘ 2170).
Drawing I. Moschou, photo A. Athanassiadou

29/43. (ΜΕΘ 1378) Narrow-necked Oinochoe Fig. 29.46

East Hill #274/067: Δοκιμαστική τομή/Στρώμα καταστροφής (Plateia A).

H. 0.128; Diam. (foot) 0.068; max Diam. (body) 0.126; Diam. (rim) 0.039.

Mended from several joining pieces and smaller frr. Parts of body and foot missing.

Disk foot. Squat ovoid body with broad sloping shoulder. Low narrow neck, with very low ridge at base of neck, with round mouth and beveled rim. Strap handle from shoulder to rim.

Clay color: reddish brown (5YR 5/4), with gray core. Micaceous fabric with tendency to flake.

Unglazed exterior, with rough and worn surface.

Local.

Second quarter of 4th century B.C.

29/44. (ΜΕΘ 2170) Globular Lekythos Fig. 29.47

East Hill #274/028002 [1]: Δάπεδο (and few frr above the roof tiles of the destruction layer) and #274/018007 [2]: Κάτω από το στρώμα κεραμιδιών (Building B: Room H).

H. 0.211; Diam. (foot) 0.081; max Diam. (body) 0.166; Diam. (rim) 0.063.

Mended from many joining frr. Large parts of body and smaller parts of shoulder, neck, and mouth missing.

Disk foot. Tall ovoid body with broad sloping shoulder. Low narrow neck with a drip ring at junction with mouth. Low and broad echinus-shaped mouth with beveled rim. Strap handle from shoulder to neck.

Clay color: reddish yellow (5YR 6/6), with gray core. Fabric contains inclusions and mica.

Unglazed exterior, with rough surface.

Local.

Second quarter of 4th century B.C.

FIGURE 29.48. Plain ware lekythos, **29/45** (ΜΕΘ 4853).
Drawing I. Moschou, photo I. Coyle

29/45. (ΜΕΘ 4853) Globular Lekythos Fig. 29.48

East Hill #274/018007 [2]: Κάτω από το στρώμα κεραμιδιών (and few frr above the roof tiles of the destruction layer) and #274/018004 [2]: Πάνω και κάτω από το στρώμα κεραμιδιών (Building B: Room H).

P.H. 0.245; Diam. (foot) 0.094; max Diam. (body) 0.187; Diam. (rim) 0.066.

Mended from many joining frr and non-joining mouth. Several parts missing.

Disk foot. Tall and broad ovoid body with broad sloping shoulder. Low narrow neck, possibly with drip ring at junction with mouth. Quite tall and broad echinus-shaped mouth with beveled rim. Strap handle, concave in section, from shoulder to neck.

Clay color: reddish yellow (5YR 6/6), with gray core. Fabric contains inclusions and mica.

Unglazed exterior, with rough surface.

Local.

Second quarter of 4th century B.C.

29/46. (ΜΕΘ 2171) Footless Olpe with Banded Decoration Fig. 29.49

East Hill #274/028002 [1]: Δάπεδο (Building B: Room H).

P.H. (handle) 0.136; H. (rim) 0.108; Diam. (foot) 0.062; max Diam. (body) 0.076; Diam. (rim) 0.047.

Almost intact, except for two small joining frr on the neck area. Large part of handle missing.

Flat bottom. Rather short cylindrical body slightly contracted toward base, in continuous curve with shoulder and up to mouth. Short neck with concave wall. Round mouth with beveled rim. Strap handle that rises well above rim, ending on upper body.

Clay color: light brown (7.5YR 6/4). Fabric contains inclusions and mica.

Unglazed exterior, with rough surface. Banded decoration: black band around rim and on interior of mouth, which continues to back of handle and until bottom of wall. Traces of a band around body, at level of handle root.

Local.

Second quarter of 4th century B.C.

FIGURE 29.49. Plain ware olpe, **29/46** (ΜΕΘ 2171).
Drawing I. Moschou, photos I. Coyle

FIGURE 29.50. Plain ware olpe, **29/47** (ΜΕΘ 2172).
Photo J. Vanderpool

29/47. (ΜΕΘ 2172) Footed Olpe, Partly Glazed Fig. 29.50

East Hill #274/028002 [1]: Δάπεδο (Building B: Room H).

Diam. (foot) 0.039; Diam. (rim) 0.049.

Three non-joining pieces, each one mended from several joining frr: a) part of lower body with foot, b) part of upper body with shoulder, c) part of neck and mouth.

Low disk foot, slightly projecting, slightly concave beneath. Ovoid body. Tall, broad neck with concave wall. Round mouth with thin beveled rim.

Clay color: pink (7.5YR 7/4), unevenly fired. Micaceous fabric.

Thick brown to black glaze. Unglazed exterior, except for from shoulder to rim and interior of mouth, which are covered with glaze probably by dipping.

Local.

Second quarter of 4th century B.C.

29/48. (ΜΕΘ 1559) Pelike Fig. 29.51

East Hill #274/076: Δοκιμαστική τομή/Στρώμα καταστροφής and #274/076: Ανατολικός μάρτυρας/Στρώμα κεραμιδιών (Building A: Room Z).

H. 0.254; Diam. (foot) 0.107; max Diam. (body) 0.185; Diam. (rim) 0.147.

Mended from many joining frr. Large parts missing, but it retains full profile. Part of missing body restored in plaster.

FIGURE 29.51. Plain ware pelike, **29/48** (ΜΕΘ 1559).
Drawing I. Moschou, photos I. Coyle

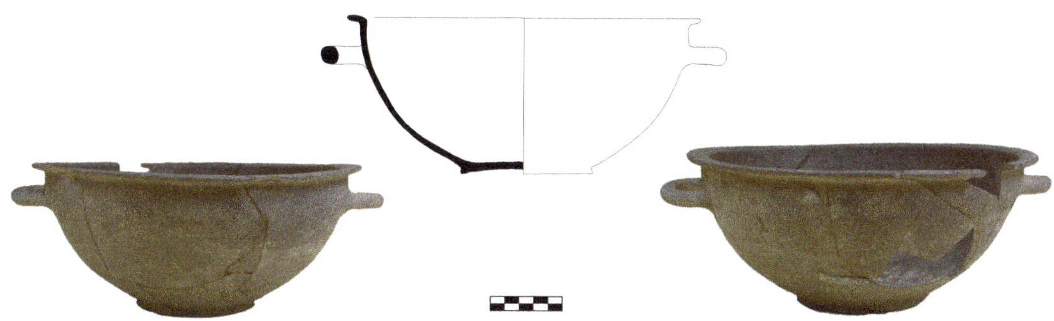

FIGURE 29.52. Plain ware lekane, **29/49** (ΜΕΘ 1369).
Drawing I. Moschou, photos I. Coyle

Ring foot. Low broad body with cylindrical wall and sloping shoulder. Junction between body and shoulder forms an angular profile. Tall neck tapering upward. Vertical overhanging rim. Handles attached from neck to junction of body and shoulder, triangular in section.

Clay color: yellowish red (5YR 5/6), with light reddish brown core (5YR 6/4). Fabric contains inclusions and mica.

Unglazed exterior, with rough and worn surface. Rim chipped.

Local.

Second quarter of 4th century B.C.

29/49. (ΜΕΘ 1369) Lekane with Horizontal Handles Fig. 29.52

East Hill #274/066: Στρώμα καταστροφής (Building A: Room E).

H. 0.127; Diam. (foot) 0.112; max Diam. (rim) 0.305.

Mended from many joining frr. Very few small parts of body and rim missing. Repaired in antiquity in side wall with three lead clamps.

Disk foot, slightly concave beneath. Broad hemispherical body with curved sides. Flat projecting rim. Horizontal rolled handles.

Clay color: gray (2.5YR 5/1), unevenly fired. Micaceous fabric.

Unglazed exterior, with rough surface.

Local.

(Early?) second quarter of 4th century B.C.

29/50. (ΜΕΘ 2164) Lekane with Handles Turned Up to Rim Fig. 29.53

East Hill #274/076: Στρώμα καταστροφής (Building A: Room Z).

H. 0.132; Diam. (foot) 0.103; Diam. (rim) 0.297.

Mended from many joining frr. Parts of foot, body, and rim missing.

Disk foot, concave beneath. Broad conical body with curved sides. Flat projecting rim, with vertical overhang at edge. Horizontal rolled handles, curving directly up to rim and attached to it.

Clay color: pink (7.5YR 7/4), with gray core, unevenly fired. Fabric contains inclusions and mica.

Unglazed exterior.

Local.

Second quarter of 4th century B.C.

29/51. (ΜΕΘ 2166) Mortar with Projecting Rim Fig. 29.54

East Hill #274/069: Δάπεδο and #274/079: ΒΔ τμήμα (Plateia A).

H. 0.096; Diam. (foot) 0.171; Diam. (rim) 0.352.

Mended from 11 joining pieces. Parts of foot, body, and rim along with one handle and spout missing.

Disk foot, concave beneath. Broad body with convex wall. Outcurved rim. Two lug handles; each one bears a pair of rectangular sealings depicting a branch with leaves and the letters "O N" (?) on the left corner below and "Σ" (?) on the left corner above. Wheelmarks on exterior. Surface of interior is rough.

Clay color: reddish yellow (7.5YR 6/6). Fabric contains inclusions and mica. On about half of vase, surface is lighter in color (2.5Y8/3 "pale yellow") on exterior, rim, and a few centimeters below rim on interior. Probably a slip covered all of exterior, rim, and upper part of interior, now worn away.

Wheelmade?

Local.

First half of 4th century B.C.

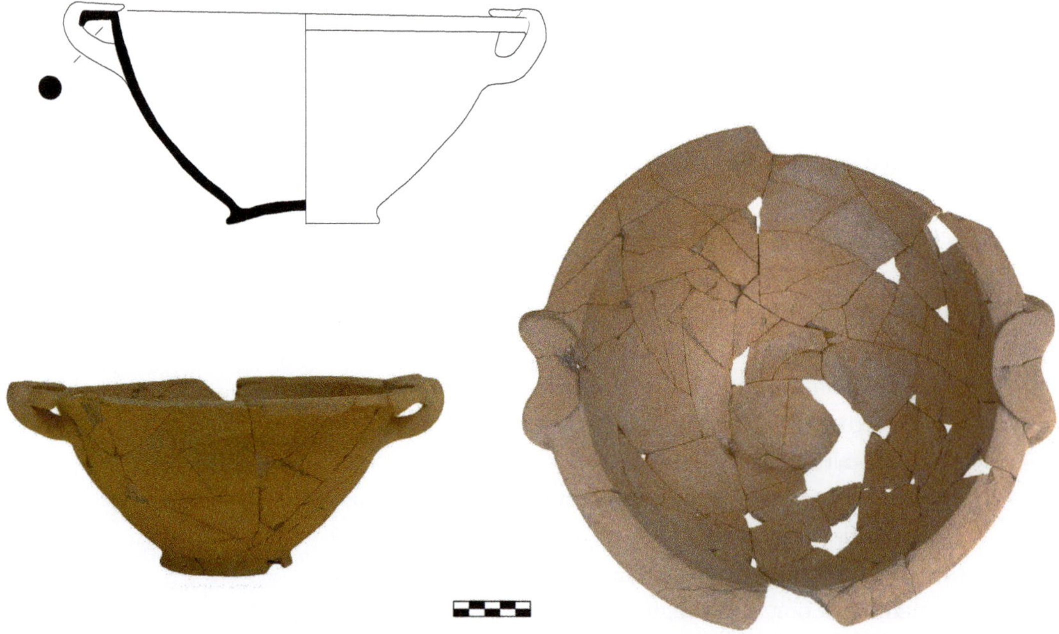

FIGURE 29.53. Plain ware lekane, **29/50** (ΜΕΘ 2164).
Drawing I. Moschou, photos I. Coyle

FIGURE 29.54. Plain ware mortar, **29/51** (ΜΕΘ 2166).
Drawing I. Moschou, photos J. Vanderpool

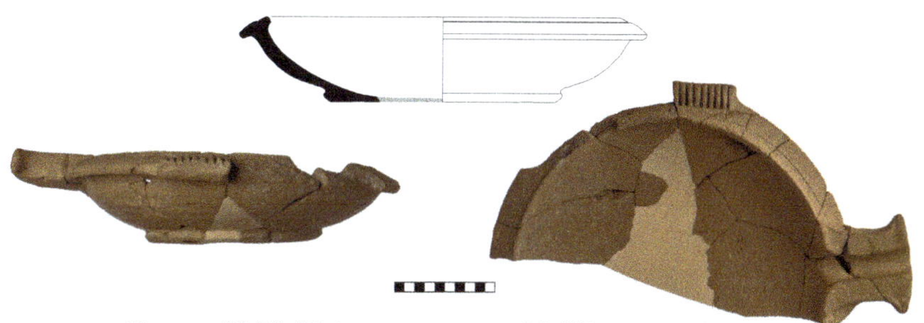

FIGURE 29.55. Plain ware mortar, **29/52** (ΜΕΘ 2168).
Drawing I. Moschou, photos J. Vanderpool

29/52. (ΜΕΘ 2168) Mortar with Projecting Rim Fig. 29.55

East Hill #274/009012 [5]: Δάπεδο (Building B: Room H).

H. 0.093; Diam. (foot) 0.195; Diam. (rim) greater than 0.350.

Mended from 16 joining pieces and smaller frr. Almost half of vase, from body to rim, along with two(?) handles and also several smaller pieces from bottom, body, rim, and part of remaining handle missing. Restored with plaster.

Broad disk foot. Broad shallow body with convex wall. Sloping rim projecting outward and inward. Narrow groove on upper surface of rim, broad shallow groove on underside. Handle with vertical ribs on upper surface. Impressed circles on top of rim, in handle area. Fluked spout. Wheelmarks on exterior. Surface on interior is rough.

Clay color: light yellowish brown (10YR 6/4), lighter in surface (10YR 7/4 "very pale brown"). Fabric contains inclusions and mica.

Wheelmade or combined technique. Handle and spout handmade, added separately.

Local.

Second quarter of 4th century B.C.

FIGURE 29.56. Plain ware mortar, **29/53** (ΜΕΘ 2667).
Drawing I. Moschou, photos I. Coyle and O. Kourakis

29/53. (ΜΕΘ 2667) Mortar with Heavy Rim Fig. 29.56

East Hill #274/079: Ανατολικό τμήμα/Δάπεδο and #274/079: Δυτικό τμήμα/Στρώμα κεραμιδιών (Plateia B).

H. 0.067; Diam. (foot) 0.178; Diam. (rim) 0.357.

Mended from six large and two smaller joining frr. One handle and small part of another missing. Part of base also missing, but has been restored with plaster. Spout is not joining.

Broad disk foot, slightly concave beneath. Shallow open body with thick convex wall. Heavy rim, angular in profile, with raised inner edge. Rim is separated on underside from body by broad shallow groove. Two handles opposite each other decorated with vertical ribs on upper surface. Handle opposite spout decorated with circular depressions defined by vertical ribs. Fluked spout. Wheelmarks on exterior. Surface on interior is rough.

Clay color: very pale brown (10YR 7/4). Fabric contains inclusions and mica.

Moldmade and probably finished on wheel. Handles and spout handmade, added separately.

Local.

Second quarter of 4th century B.C.

29/54. (ΜΕΘ 7533) Mortar with Heavy Rounded Rim Fig. 29.57

East Hill #274/018007 [2]: Κάτω από το στρώμα κεραμιδιών (Building B: Room H) and #274/027023 [3] (Building B: Rooms B and Γ).

H. 0.067; p.Diam. (foot) 0.078; p.Diam. (max) 0.088.

Mended from two joining pieces found in different rooms of Building B. It preserves tiny part from body to rim and handle.

Disk foot. Shallow open body with thick wall, straight on exterior, slightly concave on interior. Heavy rounded rim that merges with bowl, articulated on exterior by notch. Handle ribbed.

Clay color: very pale brown (between 10YR 8/3 and 8/4), fired yellow (2.5Y 8/3 "pale yellow") in parts of surface. Fabric contains few inclusions and mica and is of fine powdery quality. Surface worn on both interior and exterior.

Moldmade.

Unknown origin.

First half of 4th century B.C.

FIGURE 29.57. Plain ware mortar, **29/54** (ΜΕΘ 7533).
Drawing I. Moschou, photos J. Vanderpool

FIGURE 29.58. Plain ware ladle, **29/55** (ΜΕΘ 1366).
Drawing I. Moschou, photos J. Vanderpool

29/55. (ΜΕΘ 1366) Ladle Fig. 29.58

East Hill. Handle: #274/066: Βόρειο τμήμα/Δάπεδο and #274/067: Ανατολικός μάρτυρας (Plateia A); Bowl: #274/076: Βόρειος μάρτυρας/Στρώμα καταστροφής (Building A: Room E).

L. 0.194; H. (bowl) 0.034; Diam. (bowl) 0.079.

Mended from eight joining pieces or smaller frr. Parts of bowl missing.

Low bowl with rounded base and curved sides. Long double strap handle with loop at end.

Clay color: reddish yellow (7.5YR 6/6), with gray core in parts. Fabric contains inclusions and mica.

Unglazed exterior. Red glaze on upper surface and outer wall of loop. Crude dots of red glaze on upper surface of handle sections that are pressed together. Thin red line on rim.

Local.

Second quarter of 4th century B.C.

COOKING WARES

29/56. (ΜΕΘ 1377) Two-handled Chytra, Lidded Fig. 29.59

East Hill #274/067: Δοκιμαστική τομή/Στρώμα καταστροφής (Plateia A).

H. 0.158; Diam. (body) 0.199; Diam. (rim) 0.127.

Mended from many joining frr. Small parts of body and rim and almost entire of one handle missing.

Globular/squat body with rounded bottom, in continuous curve of profile to shoulder. High flaring rim, straight in profile, flanged inside to accommodate a lid. Vertical strap handles from upper part of body to rim.

Clay color: yellowish red (5YR 5/8). Fabric contains many inclusions and mica.

FIGURE 29.59. Cooking ware two-handled lidded chytra, **29/56** (ΜΕΘ 1377).
Drawing I. Moschou, photo I. Coyle

FIGURE 29.60. Cooking ware two-handled lidded chytra, **29/57** (ΜΕΘ 4854).
Drawing I. Moschou, photo I. Coyle

Unglazed exterior. Pairs of vertical lines of thin white paint on body. Traces of fire on bottom and lower body.

Local.

Second quarter of 4th century B.C.

29/57. (ΜΕΘ 4854) Two-handled Chytra, Lidded Fig. 29.60

East Hill #274/078: Δυτικό τμήμα (Plateia A–B).

H. (max) 0.165 (handle); H. 0.151 (rim); Diam. (body) 0.209; Diam. (rim) 0.134.

Mended from many joining frr. Large parts missing, but it retains full profile.

Globular body with rounded bottom, in continuous curve of profile with sloping shoulder. Flaring rim, slightly convex in profile, with flat upper surface projecting outward, flanged inside to accommodate a lid. Horizontal rolled handles set diagonally on shoulder, rising well above rim.

Clay color: yellowish red (5YR 5/6). Fabric contains many inclusions and mica.

Unglazed exterior. Slight ridges on shoulder. Traces of fire on bottom, body, rim, and handles.

Local.

Second quarter of 4th century B.C.

29/58. (ΜΕΘ 1560) One-handled Chytra, Lidless Fig. 29.61

East Hill #274/008008 [3] (Building B: Room A).

P.H. 0.185; Diam. (body) 0.219; p.Diam. (rim) 0.131; est. Diam. (rim) 0.150.

Mended from many joining frr, preserving part of vase, from base to rim and handle.

Globular body with rounded bottom, in continuous curve of profile with shoulder. No distinction between shoulder and neck, which is short and tapering toward top. Rim projecting outward. Vertical strap handle from upper part of body to rim.

Initial color of clay cannot be detected because vase is burnt. Fabric contains many inclusions and mica.

Unglazed exterior. Surface burned.

Local.

Second quarter of 4th century B.C.

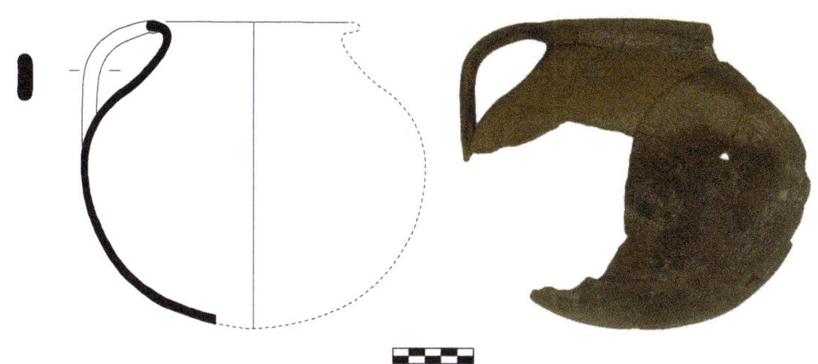

FIGURE 29.61. Cooking ware one-handled lidless chytra, **29/58** (MEΘ 1560).
Drawing I. Moschou, photo I. Coyle

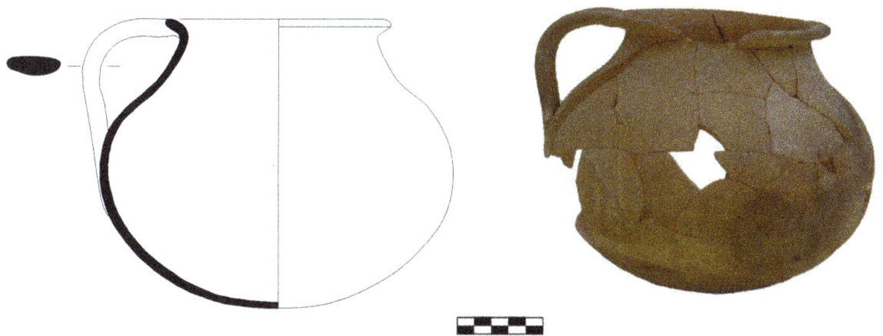

FIGURE 29.62. Cooking ware one-handled lidless chytra, **29/59** (MEΘ 1561).
Drawing I. Moschou, photo I. Coyle

29/59. (MEΘ 1561) One-handled Chytra, Lidless Fig. 29.62
East Hill #274/008014 [7] (Building B: Room A).
H. 0.170; Diam. (body) 0.215; Diam. (rim) 0.147.
Mended from many joining frr. Large parts of body and shoulder and small part of rim missing.
Globular/squat body with rounded bottom, in continuous curve of profile with shoulder. The latter is slightly distinct from neck, which is quite tall and tapering toward top. Rim projecting outward. Vertical strap handle from upper part of body to rim.
Clay color: reddish yellow (5YR 6/8). Fabric contains many inclusions and mica.
Unglazed exterior. Vertical lines of thin white paint on body. Traces of fire on base, body, and lower part of handle, more intense on side opposite handle where they reach up to shoulder.
Local.
Second quarter of 4th century B.C.

29/60. (MEΘ 1562) One-handled Chytra, Lidless Fig. 29.63
East Hill #274/008015 [7] (Building B: Room A).
H. 0.185; Diam. (body) 0.214; p.Diam. (rim) 0.129.
Mended from many joining frr. Small parts of body, bottom, and rim missing.
Deep globular body with rounded bottom, in continuous curve of profile with sloping shoulder, almost neckless. Outcurved rim. Vertical thin strap handle, concave above, from upper part of body to rim.
Clay color: yellowish red (5YR 5/8). Fabric contains many inclusions and mica.
Unglazed exterior. Traces of fire on bottom and body, on wall opposite handle.
Local.
Second quarter of 4th century B.C.

FIGURE 29.63. Cooking ware one-handled lidless chytra, **29/60** (ΜΕΘ 1562). Drawing I. Moschou, photo I. Coyle

FIGURE 29.64. Cooking ware one-handled lidless chytra, **29/61** (ΜΕΘ 2165). Drawing I. Moschou, photo I. Coyle

29/61. (ΜΕΘ 2165) One-handled Chytra, Lidless Fig. 29.64

East Hill #274/027023 [3] (Building B: Rooms B and Γ).

H. 0.205; Diam. (body) 0.215; Diam. (rim) 0.135.

Mended from many joining frr. About half of body, from bottom to neck, along with several smaller parts missing.

Broad cylindrical body with rounded bottom, in continuous curve of profile with sloping shoulder. No distinction between shoulder and neck, which is quite tall and concave in profile. Rim projecting outward. Vertical strap handle from shoulder to rim.

Clay color: red (2.5YR 5/8). Fabric contains inclusions and mica.

Unglazed exterior.

Local.

Second quarter of 4th century B.C.

29/62. (ΜΕΘ 1368) One-handled Chytra, Lidless Fig. 29.65

East Hill #274/066: Στρώμα ερυθρό με πλιθιά καταςτροφής 4 (Building A: Room E).

H. (max) 0.145 (handle); H. 0.140 (rim); Diam. (body) 0.161; p.Diam. (rim) 0.083; est. Diam. (rim) 0.110.

Mended from many joining frr. Part of neck along with rim and a few small frr of body and shoulder missing.

Low cylindrical body with rounded bottom, flattened in center, in continuous curve of profile with shoulder. No distinction between shoulder and neck, which is quite tall and concave in profile. Rim projecting outward. Vertical strap handle from shoulder to rim, rising a few centimeters above rim.

Clay color: dark gray (2.5Y 4/1), with brown core (10YR 4/3). Fabric contains inclusions and mica.

Unglazed exterior.

Local.

Second quarter of 4th century B.C.

FIGURE 29.65. Cooking ware one-handled lidless chytra, **29/62** (ΜΕΘ 1368). Drawing I. Moschou, photo I. Coyle

FIGURE 29.66. Cooking ware one-handled lidless chytra, **29/63** (ΜΕΘ 2167). Drawing I. Moschou, photo I. Coyle

29/63. (ΜΕΘ 2167) One-handled Chytra, Lidless Fig. 29.66

East Hill #274/009012 [5]: Δάπεδο (Building B: Room H).

H. 0.130; Diam. (body) 0.152; p.Diam. (rim) 0.108; est. Diam. (rim) 0.120.

Mended from many joining frr. Parts of rim and few small frr of body missing.

Low cylindrical body with rounded bottom, in a continuous curve of profile with the shoulder. Short neck, concave in profile. Rim projecting outward. Vertical strap handle from junction of body and shoulder to rim.

Clay color: reddish yellow (5YR 6/6). Fabric contains many inclusions and mica.

Unglazed exterior. Slight traces of fire on bottom, more intense on body, wall opposite handle.

Local.

Second quarter of 4th century B.C.

29/64. (ΜΕΘ 2180) One-handled Chytra, Lidless Fig. 29.67

East Hill #274/018007 [2]: Κάτω από το στρώμα κεραμιδιών (Building B: Room H).

H. (max) 0.160 (handle); H. 0.158 (rim); Diam. (body) 0.173; Diam. (rim) 0.112.

Mended from many joining frr. Large part and a few small frr of body, small fr of rim missing.

Cylindrical body with rounded bottom, slightly distinct from shoulder; latter rising steeply to neck, which is tall and tapering toward top. No distinction between shoulder and neck. Rim projecting outward. Vertical strap handle from upper part of body to rim, slightly rising above rim.

Clay color: dark gray (2.5Y4/1), with grayish brown core (2.5Y5/2). Fabric contains many inclusions and mica.

Unglazed exterior.

Local.

Second quarter of 4th century B.C.

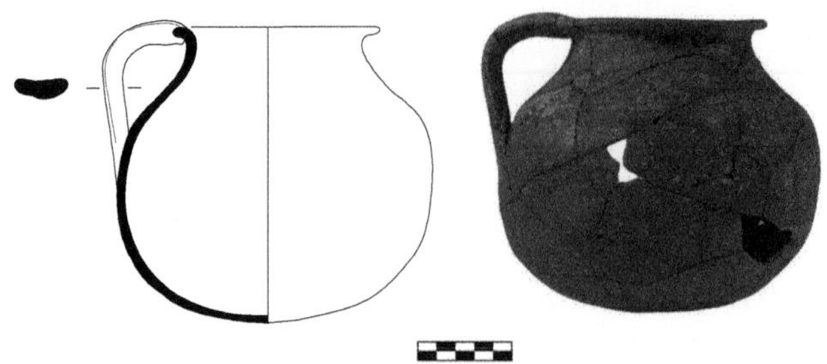

FIGURE 29.67. Cooking ware one-handled lidless chytra, **29/64** (MEΘ 2180). Drawing I. Moschou, photo I. Coyle

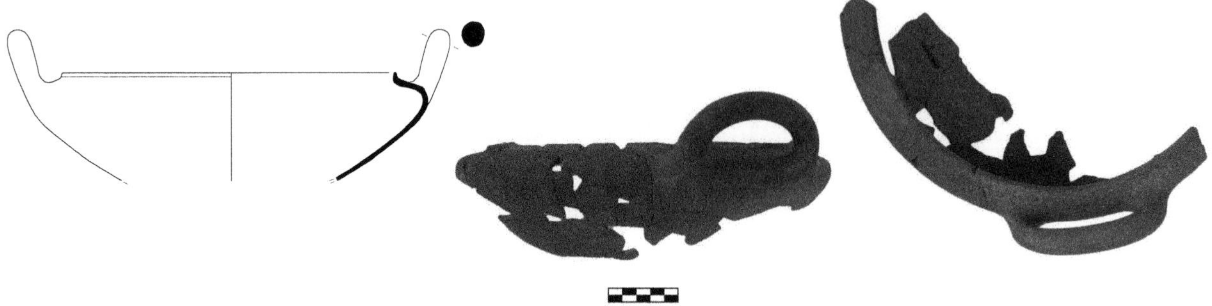

FIGURE 29.68. Cooking ware lopas, Type 1, with low vertical/slightly upturned rim and echinus-shaped body, **29/65** (MEΘ 4858). Drawing F. Skyvalida, photos I. Coyle

29/65. (MEΘ 4858) Lopas Fig. 29.68

East Hill #274/018002 [2] and #274/018003 [2] (Building B: Room A).

Fr a) P.H. (max) 0.105 (handle); p.H. 0.073 (rim); p.Diam. (rim) 0.223; est. Diam. (rim) 0.240.

It preserves two non-joining parts, each one mended from many smaller frr: a) about one-third of the vase, from nearly bottom to rim, along with a handle, b) small part from nearly the bottom to rim. It also preserves several non-joining frr. Large part from bottom to rim and one handle missing.

Echinus-shaped body with conical(?) base and pronounced curve to shoulder, which is almost flat. There is a slight ridge at junction of body and shoulder. Very low vertical rim with no reception for lid. Horizontal rolled handle set upright at junction of body and shoulder, rising well above rim.

Clay color: dark gray (5Y4/1), fired brown-orange in parts. Fabric contains many inclusions and mica.

Unglazed exterior. Traces of burning.

Local.

Second quarter of 4th century B.C.

29/66. (MEΘ 5317) Lopas Fig. 29.69

East Hill #274/018002 [2]: Δάπεδο (Building B: Room A).

P.H. 0.048; p.Diam. (body) 0.100.

It preserves small part from base to rim, mended from six frr.

Shallow echinus-shaped body with rounded(?) bottom, in single curve with gently sloping shoulder. Thick rounded rim slightly upturning from shoulder, with no reception for lid. Small knob on shoulder.

Clay color: red (2.5YR 6/8). Fabric contains many inclusions and mica.

Unglazed exterior. Traces of burning.

Local.

Second quarter of 4th century B.C.

FIGURE 29.69. Cooking ware lopas, Type 1, with low vertical/slightly upturned rim and echinus-shaped body, **29/66** (MEΘ 5317). Drawing I. Moschou

FIGURE 29.70. Cooking ware lopas, Type 2, with banded rim and hemispherical body, **29/67** (MEΘ 4859). Drawing F. Skyvalida, photos I. Coyle

29/67. (MEΘ 4859) Lopas Fig. 29.70

East Hill #274/018002 [2] and #274/018003 [2] (Building B: Room A).

Fr a) P.H. (max) 0.077 (handle); p.H. 0.053 (rim); p.Diam. (rim) 0.180; est. Diam. (rim) 0.250.

It preserves three non-joining parts, each one mended from several smaller frr: a) about one-quarter of vase, from upper part of body to rim, along with a handle, b) small part from upper part of body to rim, preserving roots of a second handle, c) small part from nearly base to rim. It also preserves several non-joining frr. Large part from bottom to rim and most part of one handle missing.

Shallow open body with curved sides and flat bottom. Flaring rim, straight in profile, flanged inside to accommodate a lid. Horizontal rolled handle set diagonally at junction of body and rim, rising above level of rim.

Clay color: yellowish red (5YR 5/6). Fabric contains many inclusions and mica.

Unglazed exterior. Traces of burning.

Local.

Second quarter of 4th century B.C.

29/68. (MEΘ 5584) Lopas Fig. 29.71

East Hill #274/018003 [2] (Building B: Room A).

Fr a) P.H. 0.048; p.Diam. (rim) 0.128; est. Diam. (rim) 0.160.

It preserves two non-joining parts, each one mended from smaller frr: a) small part from nearly base to rim, b) very small part of body and rim. Most of vase from bottom to rim, along with handles, missing.

FIGURE 29.71. Cooking ware lopas, Type 3, with flaring flanged rim and echinus-shaped body, **29/68** (ΜΕΘ 5584). Drawing I. Moschou, photo J. Vanderpool

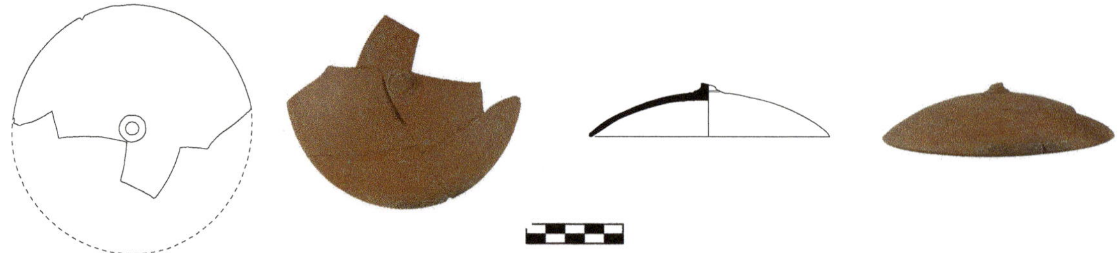

FIGURE 29.72. Cooking ware lid, **29/69** (ΜΕΘ 2006).
Drawing I. Moschou, photos I. Coyle

Echinus-shaped body in a continuous curve with the short shoulder. Tall rim with convex-concave profile, flanged inside to accommodate a lid.
Clay color: gray (10YR 5/1), fired brown-orange in parts. Fabric contains many inclusions and mica.
Unglazed exterior. Traces of burning.
Local.
Second quarter of 4th century B.C.

29/69. (ΜΕΘ 2006) Lid Fig. 29.72
East Hill #274/018003 [2]: Εστία(Building B: Room A).
P.H. 0.026; p.Diam. 0.122.
Mended from six joining frr. About half of lid along with knob missing.
Domed lid with plastic ring at center of top, on which stem of knob rests.
Clay color: reddish yellow (5YR 6/6). Fabric contains very few inclusions and some mica.
Unglazed. Burnished concentric circles on upper surface. Traces of burning in small part of outer edge.
Local.
Second quarter of 4th century B.C.

29/70. (ΜΕΘ 1985) Lid Fig. 29.73
East Hill #274/017005 [3] (Building B: Room A).
H. 0.040; p.Diam. 0.129; est. Diam. greater than 0.150.
Intact. About two-thirds of lid missing.
Domed lid with thick beveled outer edge. Small solid knob consisting of stem tapering upward and small conical finial.
Clay color: red (2.5YR 6/8), with purple-brown core in parts due to misfiring. Fabric contains many inclusions and mica.
Unglazed.
Local.
Second quarter of 4th century B.C.

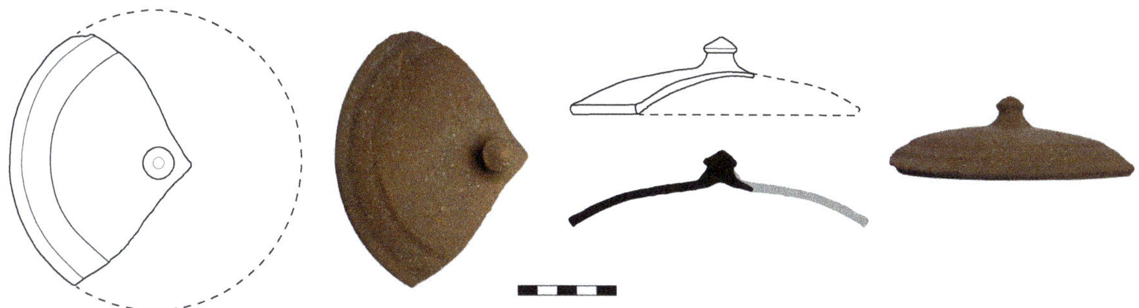

FIGURE 29.73. Cooking ware lid, **29/70** (ΜΕΘ 1985).
Drawing I. Moschou, photos J. Vanderpool

FIGURE 29.74. Cooking ware lid, **29/71** (ΜΕΘ 4856).
Drawing F. Skyvalida, photos I. Coyle

FIGURE 29.75. Cooking ware lid, **29/72** (ΜΕΘ 4857).
Drawing F. Skyvalida, photos I. Coyle

29/71. (ΜΕΘ 4856) Lid — Fig. 29.74

East Hill #274/018002 [2]: Δάπεδο (Building B: Room A).

P.H. 0.028; Diam. 0.130.

Mended from nine joining frr. About half of lid along with knob missing.

Echinus-shaped lid with probably hollow knob.

Clay color: reddish yellow (7.5YR 6/6). Fabric contains many inclusions and mica.

Unglazed.

Local.

Second quarter of 4th century B.C.

29/72. (ΜΕΘ 4857) Lid — Fig. 29.75

East Hill #274/018002 [2]: Δάπεδο (Building B: Room A).

P.H. 0.026; p.Diam. 0.155; est. Diam. 0.200.

Small part of lid preserved, mended from four joining frr.

Echinus-shaped lid with downturned edge.

Clay color: dark gray (2.5Y 4/1). Fabric contains many inclusions and mica.

Unglazed.

Local.

Second quarter of 4th century B.C.

LAMPS

29/73. (ΜΕΘ 6486) Lamp with Overhanging Rim (HT 16 B) Fig. 29.76

East Hill #274/066 (Building A: Room E).

H. 0.018; p.Diam. 0.054.

Mended from three joining frr preserving about one-quarter of lamp, from bottom to rim.

Flat base in continuous curve with low sides. Narrow overhanging rim, slightly sloping downward on interior, terminating in sharply cut lip. Rim extending slightly to exterior.

Clay color: reddish yellow (between 5YR and 7.5YR 7/6). Fabric contains small inclusions.

Quite shiny black glaze on top of rim. Dull black glaze at center of floor. Exterior of lamp covered with fine slip.

Attic.

End of 6th–early 5th century B.C.

29/74. (ΜΕΘ 6487) Lamp with Curved Rim (HT 21 A) Fig. 29.77

East Hill #274/077: Δυτικά (Building A: Room E).

H. 0.017; p.Diam. 0.066.

Single fr preserving about one-third of lamp, from bottom to rim.

Flat bottom curving into low rounded sides that form continuous curve to rim.

Clay color: reddish yellow (7.5YR 7/6). Fabric contains small inclusions.

Dull black glaze on interior. Black glaze on inner edge of rim. Entire exterior is covered with fine slip, better preserved on underside, much worn on upper walls.

Attic.

End of 6th–early 5th century B.C.

29/75. (ΜΕΘ 6305) BG Lamp with Curved Rim (HT 21 B-C) Fig. 29.78

East Hill #274/018003 [2]: Εστία(Building B: Room A).

Diam. (foot) 0.047; p.Diam. (body) 0.061.

It preserves four non-joining pieces: a) foot with beginning of body and very small portion of nozzle, b) part of body with handle attachment, mended from two frr, c) small part of body with handle attachment, d) handle.

FIGURE 29.76. Fragmentary partly glazed lamp, **29/73** (ΜΕΘ 6486). Drawing I. Moschou, photos J. Vanderpool

FIGURE 29.77. Fragmentary partly glazed lamp, **29/74** (ΜΕΘ 6487). Drawing I. Moschou, photos J. Vanderpool

FIGURE 29.78. Fragmentary BG lamp, **29/75** (MEΘ 6305). Drawing I. Moschou, photos J. Vanderpool

FIGURE 29.79. Fragmentary BG lamp, **29/76** (MEΘ 6306). Drawing I. Moschou, photos J. Vanderpool

Raised base, slightly concave underneath, rising to nipple at center of floor. Low sides curving into rim. Horizontal band handle.

Clay color: reddish yellow (5YR 7/6).

Thick, shiny black glaze, peeled in small areas and in large area on exterior of body. Glazed inside and out, reserved underside.

Attic.

Late 5th–early 4th century B.C.

29/76. (MEΘ 6306) BG Lamp with Curved Rim (HT 21 B-C) Fig. 29.79

East Hill #274/059010 [3]: Αυλάκι (Plateia A).

P.H. 0.025; p.L. 0.066.

Mended from four joining frr preserving about half of body, with beginning of nozzle and handle attachment.

Thick wall. Low sides curving into rim. Horizontal band handle, now missing, probably set at angle to wall.

Clay color: reddish yellow (5YR 6/6 and 6/8), unevenly fired.

Thick black glaze, variously fired black to brown-black on exterior, brown on interior, peeled in small parts. Glazed inside and out.

Attic.

Late 5th–early 4th century B.C.

29/77. (MEΘ 6307) Lamp with Curved Rim (HT 21 B) Fig. 29.80

East Hill #274/059011 [2] (Plateia A).

P.H. 0.020; p.Diam. 0.058.

Single fr preserving about one-quarter of body, along with nozzle.

Very low sides curving into rim. Short nozzle, flat on top, with rounded edge. Oval wick hole, filling entire nozzle.

Color of clay varies from orange to light gray, latter may be caused by use. Fabric of clay cannot be determined because edges are very worn, but certainly contains mica. Surface worn.

Dull black glaze on interior. Unglazed exterior. Traces of glaze outside nozzle. Nozzle is burnt.

Local.

Between third and fourth quarters of 5th century B.C.

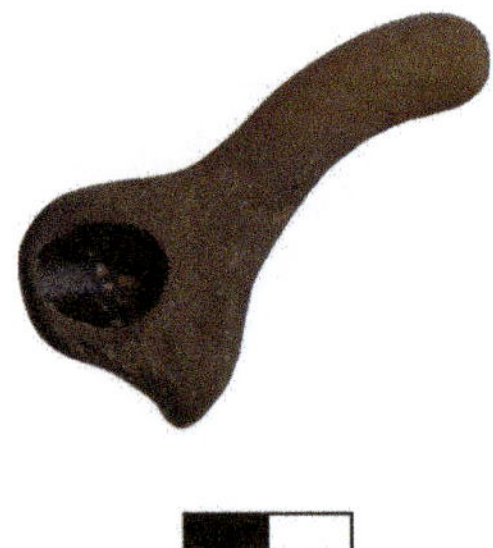

FIGURE 29.80. Fragmentary partly glazed lamp, **29/77** (ΜΕΘ 6307). Photo J. Vanderpool

FIGURE 29.81. Fragmentary BG lamp, **29/78** (ΜΕΘ 6308). Photo J. Vanderpool

FIGURE 29.82. Fragmentary BG lamp, **29/79** (ΜΕΘ 6309). Photo J. Vanderpool

29/78. (ΜΕΘ 6308) BG Lamp with Curved Rim (HT 21 C) Fig. 29.81

East Hill #274/068: Στρώμα καστανέρυθρο 3 (Plateia A).

P.H. 0.021; p.Diam. 0.044.

Single fr preserving very small portion of body and rim along with nozzle.

Incurved rim. Short nozzle, flat on top, with small wick hole, placed at a distance from rim area.

Clay color: pale yellow (2.5Y 7/3). Fabric contains fine particles of mica.

Dull black glaze, peeled in parts. Glazed inside and out.

Local.

Fourth quarter of 5th century B.C.

29/79. (ΜΕΘ 6309) BG Lamp with Broad Open Body (HT 23 A) Fig. 29.82

East Hill #274/089: Ανατολικό τμήμα (Plateia B).

P.H. 0.034; p.Diam. 0.072.

Single fr preserving very little of body and rim along with part of nozzle.

Broad body with slightly curved sides that form an angle with the flat narrow rim. Long wide nozzle, flat on top, with wick hole opened toward end.

Clay color: reddish yellow (7.5YR 6/6).

Thick, shiny black glaze, peeled in parts. Glazed inside and out.

Attic.

Fourth quarter of 5th century B.C.

29/80. (ΜΕΘ 6311) BG Lamp with Grooves on Rim (HT 24 A) Fig. 29.83

East Hill #274/066: Βόρειο τμήμα/Δάπεδο (Plateia A).

P.H. 0.021; p.Diam. 0.050.

Single fr preserving very small portion of rim and upper body.

Low(?) body with vertical upper wall, inclined toward base. Horizontal rim with two grooves on top surrounding concave lip.

Clay color: reddish yellow (5YR between 7/6 and 6/6), unevenly fired.

Quite thick black glaze, fired brown to black, peeled in parts. Glazed inside and out.

Attic.

Fourth quarter of 5th century B.C.

29/81. (ΜΕΘ 6310) BG Lamp with Tall Closed Body and Flat Rim (HT 23 C) Fig. 29.84

East Hill #274/069 and #274/079: Ανατολικό τμήμα (Plateia A).

P.H. 0.030; p.Diam. 0.056.

Mended from four joining frr preserving about half of body and rim, along with handle attachment.

Tall body with straight sides in smooth angle with rim. Wide rim sloping to small filling hole. Horizontal band handle, now missing.

Clay color: reddish yellow (7.5YR 7/6).

Thick, shiny black glaze, peeled in small parts mostly on exterior. Glazed inside and out.

Attic.

Second quarter of 4th century B.C.

29/82. (ΜΕΘ 6312) BG Lamp with Groove on rim (Scheibler DSL 3) Fig. 29.85

East Hill #274/027020 [2]: Βόρειος μάρτυρας/γκρίζο αμμώδες ςτρώμα (Building B: Room B).

P.H. (max) 0.023; p.Diam. 0.068.

Single fr preserving almost half part of rim and less of body.

Tall(?) body with slightly curved sides at top, angled at junction of rim. Flat rim with one deep groove around lip, which slopes into small filling hole. Side wall shows stub of a (band?) handle attachment.

Clay color: reddish yellow (7.5YR 7/6).

Thick, shiny glaze fired red and black, peeled from large area on interior. Glazed inside and out, except for groove on rim.

Attic.

Second quarter of 4th century B.C.

FIGURE 29.83. Fragmentary BG lamp, **29/80** (ΜΕΘ 6311). Drawing I. Moschou, photo J. Vanderpool

FIGURE 29.84. Fragmentary BG lamp, **29/81** (ΜΕΘ 6310). Drawing I. Moschou, photos J. Vanderpool

FIGURE 29.85. Fragmentary BG lamp, **29/82** (MEΘ 6312).
Drawing I. Moschou, photo J. Vanderpool

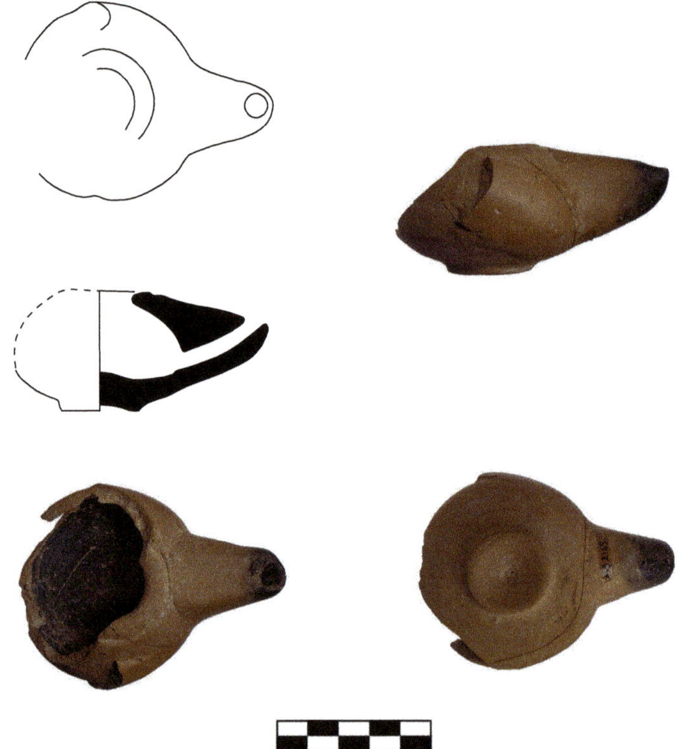

FIGURE 29.86. Lamp with curved closed body and groove on rim, **29/83** (MEΘ 2169).
Drawing I. Moschou, photos J. Vanderpool

29/83. (MEΘ 2169) Lamp with Curved Closed Body and Groove on Rim (HT 24 C′) Fig. 29.86

East Hill #274/019001 [1]: Κάτω από το στρώμα κεραμιδιών (Building B: Room H).

H. 0.037; p.L. 0.083; Diam. (foot) 0.027; Diam. (body) 0.062.

Mended from two pieces and a small fr preserving most of lamp, except for part of body and rim and nearly entire handle.

Small raised base, concave underneath, rising to low cone at center on interior. Quite tall body with curving sides, distinguished from rim by shallow groove. Slight ridges at shoulder. Rounded rim, surrounding small filling hole. Long nozzle tapering outward, flat on top, with small wick hole at end. Horizontal ribbon or strap handle probably set at an angle to wall, now missing.

Clay color: reddish yellow (7.5YR 7/6).

Dull black glaze on interior. Exterior is finished with thin slip. Trickle of black glaze on underside of nozzle. End of nozzle is burnt.

Attic.

Late(?) second quarter of 4th century B.C.

FIGURE 29.87. Fragmentary lamp with curved closed body and ridges on shoulder, **29/84** (ΜΕΘ 6313). Drawing I. Moschou, photo J. Vanderpool

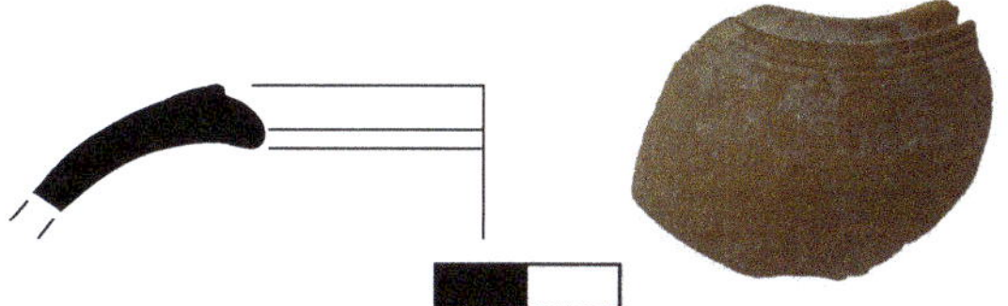

FIGURE 29.88. Fragmentary lamp with curved closed body and ridges on shoulder, **29/85** (ΜΕΘ 5018). Drawing A. Hooton, photo J. Vanderpool

29/84. (ΜΕΘ 6313) Lamp with Curved Closed Body and Ridges on Shoulder (HT 25 A′) Fig. 29.87

East Hill #274/018003 [2]: Εστία(Building B: Room A).

P.H. 0.026; p.Diam. (max) 0.037.

Mended from two joining frr preserving very small portion of rim and less of upper body.

Rounded body with curving sides. Slight ridges at shoulder, which rises above rim. Rounded rim, surrounding small filling hole.

Clay color: pink (7.5YR 7/4).

Good quality brown to black glaze on interior. Unglazed exterior, with very few traces of red slip.

Attic.

Late(?) second quarter of 4th century B.C.

29/85. (ΜΕΘ 5018) Lamp with Curved Closed Body and Ridges on Shoulder (HT 25 A′) Fig. 29.88

East Hill #274/076: Δοκιμαστική τομή/στρώμα ερυθρό με πλιθιά 4 (Building A: Room Z).

P.H. 0.024; p.Diam. 0.041.

Single fr preserving very small portion of rim and upper body.

Rounded body with curving sides. Slight ridges at shoulder, which is distinct from the rim. Rounded rim, surrounding small filling hole.

Clay color: light brown (7.5YR 6/4).

Dull and dilute black glaze on interior. Unglazed exterior.

Attic.

Late(?) second quarter of 4th century B.C.

TRANSPORT AMPHORAS

FIGURE 29.89. Fragmentary Rhodian amphora (A 247), decorated with painted bands and dot rosettes. Photos J. Vanderpool

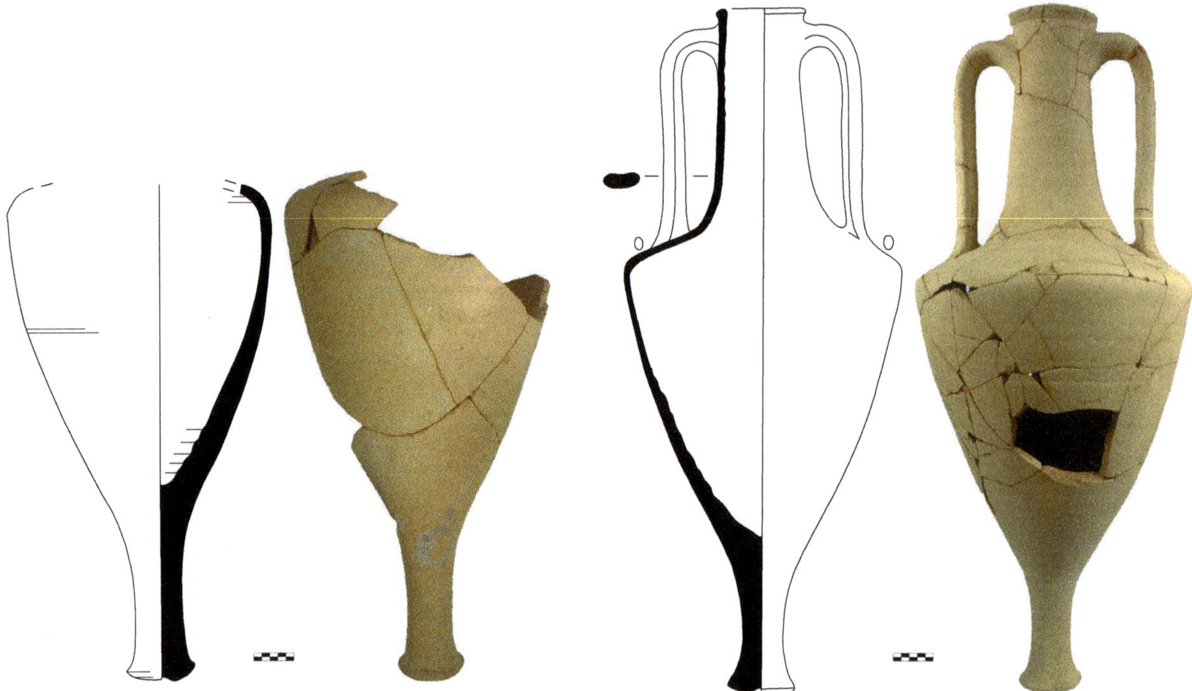

FIGURE 29.90. Mendaian amphora, ΜΕΘ 4153. Drawing F. Skyvalida, photo I. Coyle

FIGURE 29.91. Mendaian amphora, ΜΕΘ 4156. Drawing F. Skyvalida, photo I. Coyle

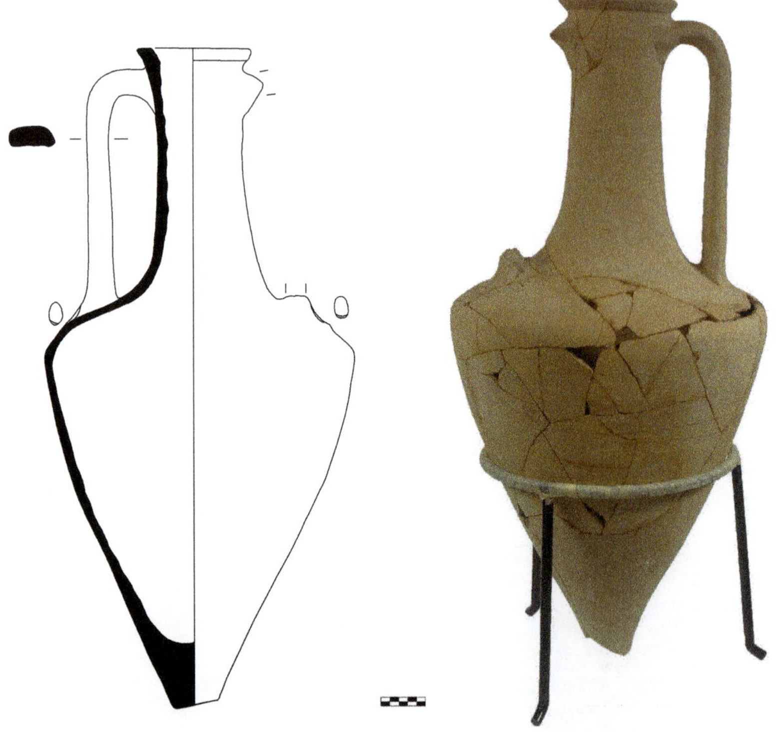

FIGURE 29.92. Mendaian amphora, ΜΕΘ 4159. Drawing F. Skyvalida, photo I. Coyle

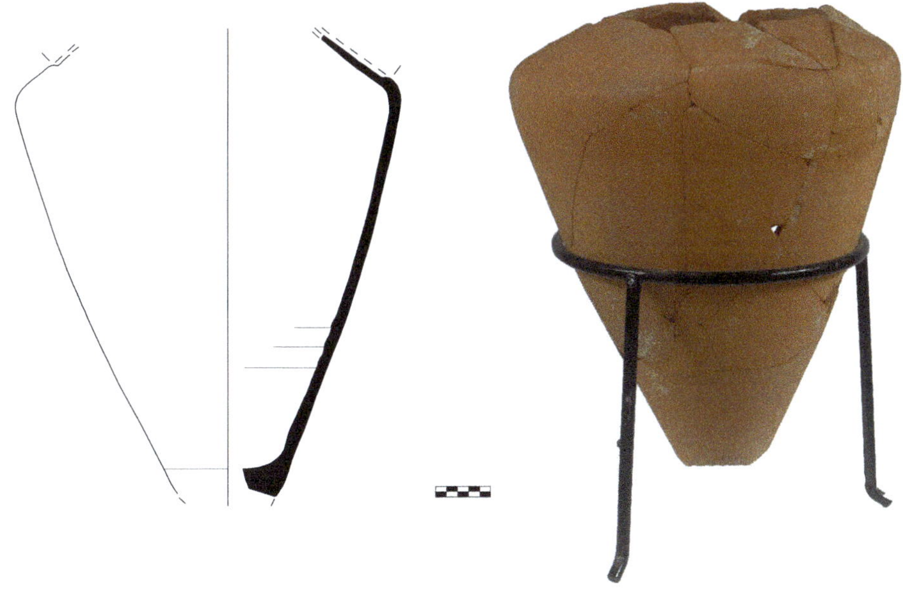

FIGURE 29.93. Northeast Aegean amphora, ΜΕΘ 4152.
Drawing F. Skyvalida, photo I. Coyle

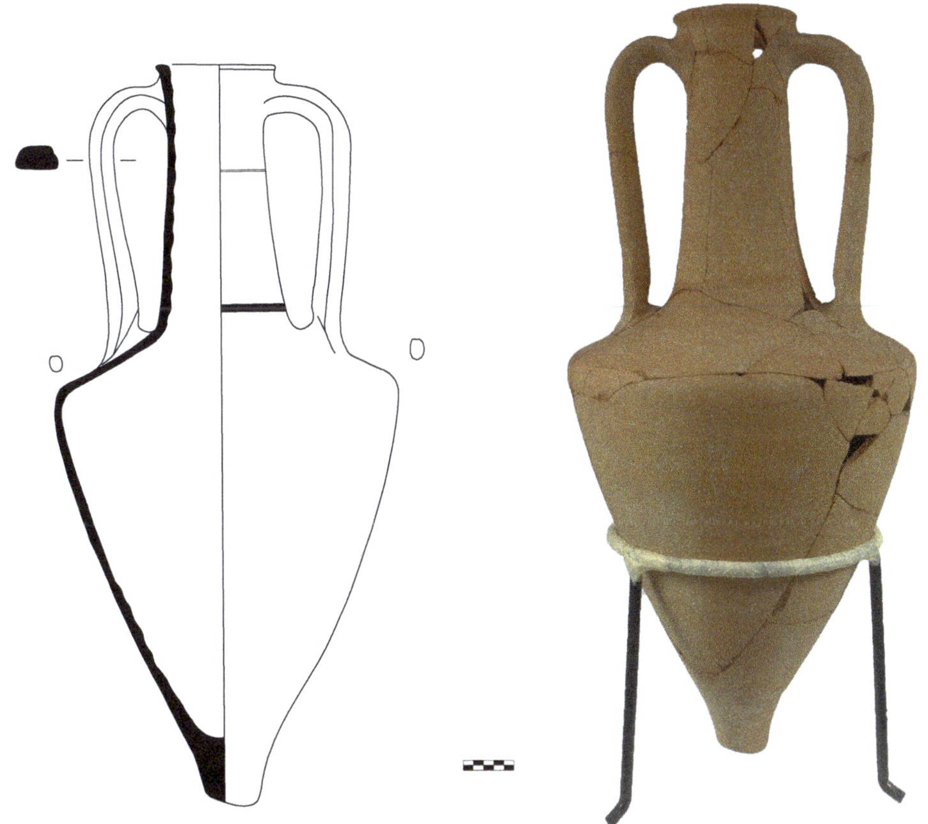

FIGURE. 29.94. Northeast Aegean amphora, ΜΕΘ 4157.
Drawing F. Skyvalida, photo I. Coyle

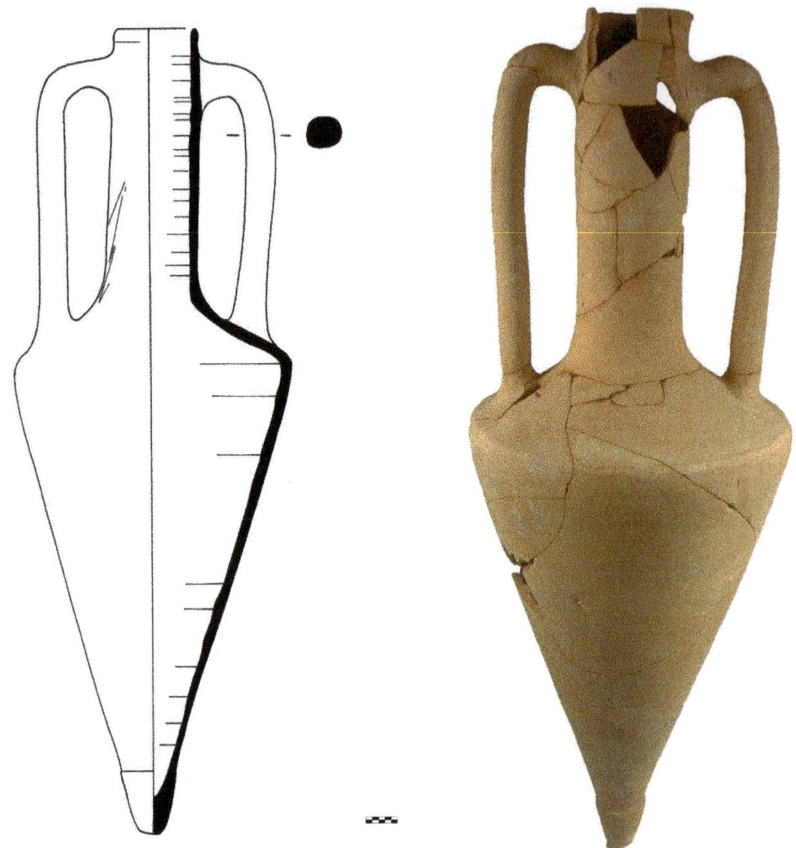

FIGURE 29.95. Chian amphora, ΜΕΘ 4158.
Drawing F. Skyvalida, photo I. Coyle

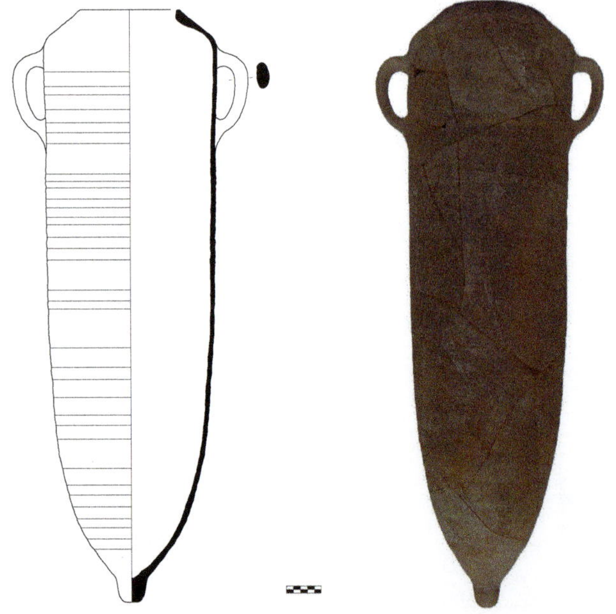

FIGURE 29.96. Phoenician amphora, ΜΕΘ 3878.
Drawing T. Ross, photo A. Athanassiadou

INDEX OF DESTRUCTION DEPOSIT CONTEXTS

Building A

Room B

A 247

Room Γ

29/17
29/39
29/40

Room Δ

23/17

Room E

29/3
29/14
29/18
29/35
29/36
29/38
29/41
29/49
29/55 (and in Plateia A)
29/62
29/73
29/74

Room Z

29/8
29/48
29/50
29/85

BUILDING B

Room A	*Room B*	*Room Γ*	*Room H*
29/1	**29/5**	**29/12**	**29/11**
29/4	**29/23**	**29/21**	**29/15**
29/6	**29/82**	**29/27**	**29/29**
29/7		**29/28**	**29/33**
29/10		**29/42**	**29/44**
29/16		**29/61** (Rooms B–Γ)	**29/45**
29/22			**29/46**
29/24			**29/47**
29/25			**29/52**
29/26			**29/54** (and in Rooms B–Γ)
29/30			**29/63**
29/31			**29/64**
29/32			**29/83**
29/58			
29/59			
29/60			
29/65			
29/66			
29/67			
29/68			
29/69			
29/70			
29/71			
29/72			
29/75			
29/84			

PLATEIA A AND B

23/15
29/2
29/9
29/13
29/19
29/20
29/34
29/37
29/43
29/51
29/53
29/56
29/57
29/76
29/77
29/78
29/79
29/80
29/81

NOTES

1 For the excavations of ancient Methone, see Bessios 2003, pp. 443–450; Bessios et al. 2004, pp. 367–376; Bessios, Athanassiadou, and Noulas 2008, pp. 241–248; Athanassiadou 2011; Chapter 1. For Building A, see Chapter 18.

I am grateful to Manthos Bessios, who encouraged me to work on this material from the destruction deposit and supported me in all aspects. I also thank Professor John Papadopoulos for the translation of the text. The translation of the catalogue was made by the author. The profile drawings are by Ioannis Moschou (Ephoreia of Antiquities of Pieria), except for **29/65**, **29/67**, **29/71**, **29/72**, and the uncatalogued commercial amphoras in Figs. 29.90–29.95, which were drawn by Fani Skyvalida, the uncatalogued commercial amphora in Fig. 29.96 by Tina Ross, and **29/85** by Anne Hooton. The plan of the ancient agora of Methone (Fig. 29.1) is also by Ioannis Moschou. Photos of Buildings A and B (Figs. 29.2, 29.3) were taken by the author. Photos of **29/1**, **29/2**, **29/13**, **29/17**, **29/18**, **29/19**, **29/22**, **29/37**, **29/47**, **29/51**, **29/52**, **29/54**, **29/55**, **29/68**, and **29/70**, as well as the lamps and the uncatalogued A 247 (Fig. 29.89), were taken by Jeff Vanderpool. The uncatalogued amphora ΜΕΘ 3878 (Fig. 29.96) and **29/44** were photographed by the author and the top view of **29/53** by Orestis Kourakis. The remainder were taken by Ian Coyle; for assistance with the editing of the photographs I would like to thank Myles Chykerda (UCLA). Finally, the conservation of the material was undertaken by Christos Avramidis, Charilaos Karanikas, and Dimitra Makantasi (Ephoreia of Antiquities of Pieria). Christos Avramidis, especially, had the patience to check with me numerous bags with ceramic sherds from the destruction layer, as well as from other related deposits, and managed to reconstruct or complete already known pieces and to discover new ones.

2 In the presentation of the pottery that follows, dates are provided for the earlier examples where possible, although the greater part dates to the second quarter of the 4th century B.C.

3 In addition to the catalogued pieces, I also consider the more fragmentary examples of each type of pottery represented in the deposit.

4 A similar typology and provenance is found among the numerous fragments that are uncatalogued.

5 For the shape, see *Agora* XII, pp. 131–132, nos. 825–842, fig. 8, pl. 33.

6 *Agora* XII, p. 295, nos. 827, 828, fig. 8, pl. 33; Shear 1984, p. 46, P 31363, pl. 11:e.

7 *Olynthus* XIII, pp. 352–354, nos. 768, 769, 771, 774, pls. 219, 220, 222.

8 *Akanthos* I, p. 33, no. 763, fig. 21 (p. 252), pl. 14:α.

9 Blondé 1985, pp. 299–301, nos. 100–106, fig. 13; Blondé 1989, p. 493, no. 26, fig. 6 (p. 492).

10 See, among others, *Agora* XII, p. 275, no. 560, pl. 53 (bolsal); p. 290, no. 759, pl. 56 (one-handler); p. 293, no. 805, pl. 58 (bowl, outturned rim); p. 309, no. 1052, pl. 59 (plate, rolled rim).

11 See *Agora* XII, p. 295, no. 827, pl. 33; *Akanthos* I, p. 33, no. 763, fig. 21 (p. 252), pl. 14:α.

12 See *Agora* XII, p. 135, nos. 882–889, fig. 9, pl. 33.

13 The early examples of the form, from the Athenian Agora (see, e.g., *Agora* XII, no. 882, p. 299 [ca. 380 B.C.]), with analogous treatment of the underside, are not unlike **29/3**. This treatment, however, is quickly abandoned and, from the second quarter of the 4th century B.C. on, the underside is covered with glaze and has a small central nipple.

14 *Agora* XII, p. 134, nos. 863–876, fig. 9, pl. 33. The type first appears around 430 B.C. and does not continue beyond the first quarter of the 4th century B.C.

15 The underside of **29/5** is not preserved.

16 *Agora* XII, p. 298, no. 871, pl. 33; for the treatment of the underside see also no. 867, which dates to the same period, as well as no. 876, which is dated ca. 380 B.C.

17 *Akanthos* I, p. 123, no. 1057, fig. 21 (p. 252), pl. 139:γ (dated around 380 B.C.).

18 It was found a little below the floor of the final phase of Building B.

19 *Olynthus* V, p. 231, no. 870, pl. 175 (early 4th century B.C.).

20 Coleman 1986, p. 108, D174, pl. 42. The pottery from the Classical phases of the settlement at Pylos dates mainly between 410 and 365 B.C.; see Coleman 1986, pp. 106–107.

21 For the type, see n. 5 above.

22 *Agora* XII, p. 295, no. 828, fig. 8, pl. 33 (375–350 B.C.); Shear 1984, p. 46, P 31363, pl. 11:e (first half of the 4th century B.C.).

23 *Olynthus* V, pl. 176; *Olynthus* XIII, pp. 352–354, nos. 768, 769, 771, 774, pls. 219, 220, 222 (early 4th century B.C.).

24 *Akanthos* I, p. 33, no. 763, fig. 21 (p. 252), pl. 14:α. (375–350 B.C.).

25 Rhomiopoulou and Touratsoglou 2002, p. 42, Π 1536 (middle of the 4th century B.C.); p. 85, Π 1642 (4th century B.C.); p. 122, Π 1749 (third quarter of the 4th century B.C.).

26 Blondé 1985, p. 300, nos. 98, 99, fig. 13; Blondé 1989, p. 493, no. 25, fig. 6 (p. 492); dating to the second quarter of the 4th century B.C.

27 *Olynthus* XIII, p. 357, nos. 785, 786, pl. 224 (5th or early 4th century B.C.).

28 Misailidou-Despotidou 1999, p. 777, inv. nos. 18327, 18376, pls. 18, 21 (second quarter of the 4th century B.C.).

29 See *Agora* XII, pp. 137–138, nos. 942–950, fig. 9, pl. 34.

30 *Agora* XII, p. 302, nos. 943, 944 (375–350 B.C.), no. 945 (ca. 350 B.C.), fig. 9, pl. 34.

31 *Olynthus* V, p. 232, no. 876, pl. 175 (4th century B.C.) and pl. 176 (first and second rows, first column).

32 *Akanthos* I, p. 29, nos. 653, 654, pl. 9:δ, ε (middle of the 4th century B.C.); p. 33, no. 762, pl. 14:β (375–350 B.C.); p. 76, no. 718, pl. 77:ζ (380–370 B.C.); see also fig. 21 (p. 252).

33 Lilibaki-Akamati 2007, p. 587, fig. 6 (first half of the 4th century B.C.).

34 Blondé 1985, p. 299, nos. 96, 97, fig. 13 (p. 300); Blondé 1989, pp. 491–493, nos. 22–24, fig. 6 (second quarter of the 4th century B.C.).

35 For the shape, see *Agora* XII, pp. 128–130, nos. 777–808, fig. 8, pl. 32.

36 The presence of this type is also rare among the fragmentary uncatalogued pottery from the destruction deposit, with only one sherd securely attributed to the shape.

37 See *Agora* XII, p. 270, nos. 493–496, fig. 5, pls. 22, 23.

38 See Corbett 1955, p. 181, no. 9, fig. 2 (p. 180); p. 184, no. 23, fig. 3.

39 *Agora* XII, p. 293, no. 803, fig. 8, pl. 32 (ca. 380 B.C.).

40 For the treatment of the underside, see *Agora* XII, p. 293, no. 804 (380–350 B.C.), no. 805 (375–350 B.C.). For the stamped decoration, see above, n. 10.

41 For the shape and its development, see *Agora* XII, pp. 84–85, nos. 334–354, fig. 4, pls. 16, 17.

42 See the series of the 4th century B.C. from the Athenian Agora, *Agora* XII, pp. 259–260, nos. 348–354.

43 *Agora* XII, p. 260, no. 350, pl. 16 (375–350 B.C.).

44 *Corinth* VII.3, p. 69, no. 323, pls. 13, 50 (375 B.C.); *Corinth* XIV, p. 132, nos. 6, 7, pl. 48.

45 *Olynthus* V, pls. 184, 185 (esp. no. 971); *Olynthus* XIII, pls. 200, 202.

46 Blondé 1985, pp. 306–307, nos. 137, 138, fig. 17; Blondé 1989, p. 502, nos. 75, 76, fig. 9 (p. 501); p. 513, no. 137, fig. 12 (p. 512).

47 Misailidou-Despotidou 1999, p. 775, inv. no. 18345, pl. 14 (second quarter of the 4th century B.C.).

48 Chrysostomou 2013, pp. 107, 431–432, no. 35, fig. 14, pl. A, A (second quarter of the 4th century B.C.).

49 Kotitsa 2012b, p. 91, fig. 16 (385–365 B.C.).

50 The shape appears in Attica at the beginning of the 4th century B.C. and continues to be produced, with increasing popularity, into Hellenistic times, see *Agora* XII, p. 147, nos. 1046–1060, fig. 10, pl. 36.

51 For the same pattern see, among others, *Olynthus* XIII, p. 352, no. 770, pl. 220 (first half of the 4th century B.C.); Shear 1970, p. 217, D 13, pl. 57 (ca. 390 B.C.); Williams 1979, p. 134, no. 49, pl. 50 (early 4th century B.C.). All three examples cited are bowls with outturned rims. In the example from Olynthos, the palmettes are free-standing and in the other two examples they are linked.

52 *Agora* XII, p. 309, nos. 1047, 1048 (400–375 B.C.) and 1049 (ca. 375 B.C.), fig. 10, pl. 36.

53 The largest part of the plate was found on the floor of Room Γ (Trench 077), but three of its fragments were found at some distance, in the fill of a cutting that passed in front of the stoa of the building (Trench 067), which predated the destruction deposit.

54 For the shape, see *Agora* XII, p. 310, nos. 1056, 1057, fig. 10, pl. 36 (ca. 350 B.C.); *Olynthus* XIII, pl. 226.

55 It recalls the less common pattern of stitched rouletting, which occurs in the early 4th century B.C., for which see *Agora* XII, pp. 30, 278–279, no. 604 (ca. 375 B.C.), no. 608 (ca. 380 B.C.), pl. 55; Talcott 1935, no. 115, fig. 8 (p. 485).

56 See *Agora* XII, pp. 146–147, nos. 1022–1045, fig. 10, pl. 36.

57 *Agora* XII, p. 308, no. 1033, fig. 10 (400–375 B.C.).

58 Cf. the bowls **29/1** and **29/2** and the parallels cited in n. 10. See also *Olynthus* V, pls. 157–159; *Olynthus* XIII, pls. 226–230.

59 For the shape and its development until the end of the 4th century B.C., see *Agora* XII, pp. 147–148, nos. 1061–1076, fig. 10, pl. 37.

60 Among the more fragmentary pottery from the destruction deposit there are examples where the underside is reserved and adorned with black bands and circles.

61 For **29/20** see *Agora* XII, pp. 310–311, no. 1067 (ca. 375 B.C.), no. 1070 (375–350 B.C.), pl. 37; *Olynthus* XIII, p. 133, no. 76, pls. 94, 232 (first half of the 4th century B.C.); pp. 377–378, no. 892, pl. 231 (second quarter of the 4th century B.C.). For **29/21** see *Agora* XII, p. 311, no. 1070 (375–350 B.C.), no. 1071 (ca. 350 B.C.), fig. 10, pl. 37.

62 For the black-glazed version with a shallow body, see *Agora* XII, pp. 126–127, nos. 744–763, fig. 8, pls. 30, 31.

63 For the various uses of the shape, see *Agora* XII, p. 124.

64 *Agora* XII, p. 290, no. 758, pl. 31 (ca. 375 B.C.).

65 *Olynthus* XIII, pl. 218, with examples primarily from the first quarter of the 4th century B.C.

66 Lilibaki-Akamati and Akamatis 2014, pp. 112, 171–172, no. 427, fig. 444, drawing 101 (beginning of the second quarter of the 4th century B.C.).

67 See *Agora* XII, p. 290, nos. 752–754, fig. 8, pl. 31 (420–400 B.C.).

68 Chrysostomou 2013, pp. 98, 433, no. 16, pl. XIII (end of the 5th–beginning of the 4th century B.C.).

69 Rhomiopoulou and Touratsoglou 2002, p. 52, Π 1563 (beginning of the 4th century B.C.).

70 Rhomiopoulou and Touratsoglou 2002, p. 59, Π 1584 (from a grave dating to the third quarter of the 4th century B.C.); p. 114, Π 1728 (from a grave dating to the first quarter of the 4th century B.C.).

71 Misailidou-Despotidou 1999, p. 776, inv. no. 18344, pl. 34.

72 For the shape and its varieties, see *Agora* XII, pp. 136–137, nos. 921–938, fig. 9, pl. 34.

73 *Agora* XII, p. 302, no. 936 (375–350 B.C.), no. 937 (350–325 B.C.), fig. 9, pl. 34; Thompson 1940, p. 133, fig. 98:d (second quarter of the 4th century B.C.).

74 *Corinth* XIV, p. 133, nos. 27, 28, pl. 48; Williams 1979, pp. 134–135, no. 52, pl. 50 (late first–early second quarter of the 4th century B.C.).

75 Blondé 1985, pp. 298–299, nos. 90–93, fig. 12; Blondé 1989, p. 491, nos. 20, 21, fig. 6 (p. 492); p. 509, no. 114, fig. 11 (p. 507).

76 Rhomiopoulou and Touratsoglou 2002, p. 116, Π 1732 (around the middle of the 4th century B.C.).

77 Saripanidi 2012, pp. 103–104, no. 205, pl. 45 (second quarter of the 4th century B.C.).

78 *Olynthus* V, pl. 189; *Olynthus* XIII, pp. 386–387, pls. 232, 238.

79 Drougou 2011, pp. 107–116.

80 For the history of the shape, see *Agora* XII, pp. 107–108, nos. 532–561, fig. 6, pl. 24; Corbett 1949, pp. 331–332 (under no. 77); Gill 1984, pp. 102–106.

81 Among the more fragmentary pottery from the destruction deposit, the few pieces assigned to this shape are primarily Attic.

82 *Agora* XII, p. 275, no. 556, pl. 24 (early 4th century B.C.).

83 *Akanthos* I, p. 43, no. 952, pl. 24:ε; p. 210, no. 1259, pl. 217:στ, dating to the first quarter of the 4th century B.C.

84 Misailidou-Despotidou 1999, p. 772, inv. no. 18352, pl. 5 (around 400 B.C.); p. 773, inv. no. 18339, pl. 6 (early 4th century B.C.).

85 Rhomiopoulou and Touratsoglou 2002, p. 114, Π 1726 (first quarter of the 4th century B.C.).

86 *Agora* XII, p. 275, no. 556, pl. 24.

87 Misailidou-Despotidou 1999, pp. 774–775 (type with elongated handles).

88 *Agora* XII, p. 275, no. 556, pl. 24; Misailidou-Despotidou 1999, p. 773, inv. no. 18339, pl. 6 (early 4th century B.C.), inv. no. 18342, pl. 8 (first quarter of the 4th century B.C.).

89 The underside does not have the molded nipple seen in examples dating to the second quarter of the 4th century B.C.; cf. no. 558 in *Agora* XII, p. 275, fig. 6 (380–350 B.C.); also *Corinth* VII.6, p. 179, VI-50, fig. 38 (late first or early second quarter of the 4th century B.C.).

90 For the type, see *Agora* XII, pp. 157–160, nos. 1173–1178, fig. 11, pl. 39.

91 For red-figure examples, see *Agora* XXX, p. 56, nos. 1149–1182, pls. 109–111.

92 For the shape, see *Agora* XII, p. 318, no. 1177 (400–375 B.C.), no. 1178 (375–350 B.C.), pl. 39. For the plastic decoration at the center of the dome, which probably imitates a lid handle, see *Olynthus* V, pl. 140; Massei 1978, pp. 36–37, no. 24, pls. VIII:2, IX:1 (around 390 B.C.); pp. 66–67, no. 45, pl. XVIII:4 (beginning of the 4th century B.C.); p. 77, no. 51, pl. XX:1, 2 (near the middle of the 4th century B.C.).

93 See *Agora* XXX, p. 286, no. 1121, pl. 107 (second quarter of the 4th century B.C.); p. 287, no. 1135, pl. 108 (middle of the 4th century B.C.).

94 Akamatis 2008, p. 21, askos no. 7 (around the middle of the 4th century B.C.).

95 *Olynthus* V, p. 257, no. 1075, pl. 192 (4th century B.C.); *Olynthus* XIII, p. 261, no. 465, pl. 176 (first half of the 4th century B.C.).

96 For the name, the distinction between the shape and that of the lekane, and its various uses, see *Agora* XII, p. 164; Amyx 1958, pp. 202–205; Kanowski 1984, pp. 91–92.

97 See *Agora* XII, pp. 164–173.

98 For the household lekanis, see *Agora* XII, p. 197, nos. 1547–1561, fig. 13, pl. 69.

99 For the shape, see *Agora* XII, pp. 165–167, nos. 1213–1223, fig. 11, pl. 40.

100 For other reserved areas and the treatment of the underside, see the description in the catalogue.

101 *Agora* XII, pp. 165–167, nos. 1213–1223, fig. 11, pl. 40.

102 *Agora* XII, pp. 321–322, no. 1220 (ca. 425 B.C.) and no. 1221 (425–400 B.C.), fig. 11, pl. 40.

103 *Agora* XII, p. 321, no. 1219, pl. 40 (ca. 450 B.C.).

104 From the end of the 5th century B.C. the spurs are placed separately; see *Agora* XII, p. 166.

105 Similar Attic examples are usually decorated with zigzags; see *Agora* XII, nos. 1217, 1221, pl. 40 and p. 166, n. 16. Similar decoration is also found on examples from Olynthos, see *Olynthus* V, p. 84, nos. 79, 81, pls. 57, 58, whereas another example from Olynthos is decorated with a wave pattern, see p. 86, no. 91, pl. 60.

106 Such as, for example, on lekythoi: see, among others, Rhomiopoulou and Touratsoglou 2002, p. 49, Π 1557, pl. 8 (second half of the 5th century B.C.); *Corinth* XIII, pp. 254–255, Grave 367-11, 12, pl. 59 (third to fourth quarters of the 5th century B.C.).

107 See *Agora* XII, pp. 164–173.

108 *Agora* XII, p. 322, no. 1222 (ca. 375 B.C.), no. 1223 (350–325 B.C.), pl. 40.

109 For lids of Attic black-glazed lekanides, see *Agora* XII, pp. 167–168.

110 See *Olynthus* V, pp. 248–250, nos. 1006, 1007, 1014, 1016, pls. 187–188 (4th century B.C.); *Olynthus* XIII, pp. 321–322, nos. 635 (lid no. 975), 636, pl. 206 (later 5th or early 4th century B.C.).

111 Lilibaki-Akamati and Akamatis 2014, pp. 86, 168, no. 287, figs. 330, 331 (beginning of the third quarter of the 4th century B.C.).

112 Kalliga 2004, p. 296, no. 5, pl. 30:α. This vase is part of the group of "lekanis-shaped vessels" of Pit C, the date of which is placed between 375 and 325 B.C., see pp. 295–297.

113 Chrysostomou 1987, fig. 2:α (second row) (p. 171).

114 Kalliga 2004, p. 296.

115 For the term see Drougou and Touratsoglou 1998, p. 159. For further discussion, see Kotitsa 2006, p. 84, where the author adopts the term "λεβητοειδής πυξίδα"; for more general discussion of the shape and its uses, see *Agora* XXXIII, pp. 92–93, 96.

116 Yiannikouri, Patsiada, and Philimonos 1990, pp. 176–178, pls. 92–95. The most common decoration of the Rhodian pyxides consists of bands across the body, whereas the shoulder is often decorated with wavy lines or tear-shaped motifs.

117 See *Olynthus* V, pp. 38–40, P 64–68, pls. 36, 37, decorated with bands and wavy lines rendered in white or dark color.

118 See, among others, an example from the 5th century B.C. in *Olynthus* XIII, p. 195, no. 219, pl. 137. For 4th century B.C. examples, see Kalliga 2004, pp. 299–300, pls. 30:e, 31:a, b (Anchialos-Sindos); Kotitsa 2006, pp. 84–85, no. 118, pl. 34 (the cemetery of Macedonian Methone); *Olynthus* V, p. 251, no. 1023, pl. 188; Panti 2008, pp. 95–96, no. 150, pl. 29:στ; pp. 122–123, no. 291, pl. 50:ζ (Akanthos); Chrysostomou and Chrysostomou 2011, p. 403, pl. 169:α (Archontiko, Pella).

119 See, among others, Saripanidi 2012, pp. 139–140, nos. 248, 249, pl. 55. For the large storage bins often referred to in the modern Greek bibliography as "sipyes"—a term that also appears in the Attic stelai as a large storage container (see Amyx 1958, esp. pp. 195–196)—see *Agora* XII, p. 195.

120 *Olynthus* V, p. 251, no. 1023, pl. 188 (4th century B.C.).

121 Panti 2008, pp. 95–96, 324, no. 150, fig. 9:ε, pl. 29:στ (middle of the 4th century B.C.).

122 Yiannikouri, Patsiada, and Philimonos 1990, p. 177, Π 1381, pl. 93:α (middle of the 4th century B.C.); Kotitsa (2006, p. 85) suggests a slightly later date.

123 This feature probably had a practical purpose. In some Attic oinochoai of the Hellenistic period, a similar groove served to secure a piece of cloth tied to the mouth. See also in this respect *Agora* XXXIII, pp. 73–74.

124 *Olynthus* V, p. 213, no. 733, pl. 166 (5th or early 4th century B.C.).

125 Pease 1937, p. 303, no. 203, fig. 32 (p. 300) (later 5th century B.C.); Merker 2006, pp. 101–104, nos. 215, 219, fig. 66 (4th century B.C.).

126 *Corinth* VII.3, pp. 113–115, nos. 633–642, pls. 24, 60; *Corinth* XIII, pp. 136–137, fig. 14 (p. 131), pl. 92 (round-mouthed oinochoai, Type B).

127 *Olynthus* V, pls. 168–169; *Olynthus* XIII, pls. 153, 156, 158, 161, 165, 166.

128 *Agora* XII, p. 352, pl. 76 (nos. 1660–1662).

129 *Agora* XII, pp. 151–152, nos. 1105–1108, fig. 11, pl. 38.

130 These lekythoi have a nicely formed rim. In the case of **29/43** the rim is not formed separately, but is essentially a continuation of the neck, and for this reason this vase was included among the oinochoai rather than the unpainted lekythoi examined on pp. 1248–1249.

131 From the later 5th century B.C. onward, the shoulder gradually becomes flatter, the lower part of the body shrinks, and the base loses its protruding profile and turns into a simple ring, see *Agora* XII, pp. 151–152, nos. 1105–1108, pl. 38.

132 For the shape, see *Agora* XII, pp. 151–152, nos. 1100–1108 (esp. nos. 1105–1108), fig. 11, pl. 38.

133 See, among others, *Akanthos* I, pp. 255–256, fig. 22, pls. 39:α–γ, 109:α; *Olynthus* V, pls. 168–169; *Olynthus* XIII, pls. 153, 156, 158, 161, 165, 166; Panti 2008, pp. 116–118, fig. 18, pls. 47, 48; Drougou 2005, pp. 128–129, fig. 146.

134 *Corinth* XIII, pp. 136–137, fig. 14 (p. 131), pl. 92 (round-mouthed oinochoai, Type B).

135 *Olynthus* V, p. 215, no. 747, pl. 168 (5th century B.C.); *Olynthus* XIII, p. 238, no. 384, pl. 165 (first half of the 4th century B.C.).

136 For Attic examples, see, among others, *Agora* XII, pp. 76–79, fig. 3, pls. 12, 13. For Corinthian versions see *Corinth* VII.3, pp. 50–51, pls. 9, 48; *Corinth* XIII, p. 133, fig. 14 (p. 131), pl. 57 (tall trefoil oinochoai). From the north Aegean plenty of examples have come to light from Olynthos, see *Olynthus* V, pls. 162–165; *Olynthus* XIII, pp. 226–228, pls. 162–166. At Akanthos, the shape has a long tradition since its production begins in the late 7th century B.C. and continues into the 4th century B.C.; see Panti 2008, pp. 31–37, figs. 4, 5, pls. 7, 8; pp. 85–86, pl. 27; pp. 105–106, fig. 12, pls. 37, 38; *Akanthos* I, p. 263, fig. 32, pls. 115:β, 221:γ.

137 The same dearth of the form from the destruction deposit is true for the more fragmentary uncatalogued pottery. In contrast, the shape is better represented in the earlier stages of habitation at Methone, judging by the number of examples found in the Hypogeion on the East Hill (late 8th to early 7th century B.C.).

138 Olpai with banded decoration are produced in East Greek (Ionian) workshops during Archaic times, and their dispersal seems to have influenced ceramic production in the north Aegean area and beyond, for which see Panti 2008, pp. 31–35, pl. 7, with references. See also the corresponding series of olpai from the Athenian Agora, *Agora* XII, p. 78, nos. 255–260 (Attic) and no. 261 (imported), pl. 12.

139 For other examples of the 4th century B.C. with banded decoration, see Panti 2008, pp. 33–35, 313, no. 40, fig. 4:η, pl. 7:γ, and no. 42, fig. 5:β, pl. 7:στ; *Olynthus* XIII, pp. 229–230, no. 335, pl. 162.

140 For the shape, see analogous examples from Olynthos in *Olynthus* XIII, pp. 226–228, pls. 162–166.

141 The term exists in antiquity, but its application to this particular shape in modern literature is arbitrary. It was adopted by early archaeologists to distinguish the shape from the amphora, and became entrenched and maintained in the literature. The ancients probably used the term "amphora" for what we call today both a pelike and an amphora. Moreover, both forms served the same function. For further discussion, see *Agora* XII, p. 49; Kanowski 1984, pp. 113–114; Tzouvara-Souli 1992, pp. 50–51.

142 See *Agora* XXX, p. 12.

143 Apart from the red-figure examples, which were very popular, the more common are the black-glaze pelikai, for which see *Agora* XII, pp. 49–50, pls. 1, 2. Unpainted and black-glaze examples are published in *Olynthus* V, pls. 160, 161, where no distinction is made for the shape and all are referred to as amphoras; see also *Olynthus* XIII, pls. 137–139.

144 *Olynthus* V, p. 201, no. 638, pl. 160. For the chronology, see also *Olynthus* XIII, p. 199.

145 Rhomiopoulou and Touratsoglou 2002, p. 68, Π 1607, which was found in a tomb that dates to the third quarter of the 4th century B.C.

146 Chrysostomou 2013, p. 113, no. 59, fig. 19 (middle of the 4th century B.C.); p. 116, no. 72, pl. 24 (third quarter of the 4th century B.C.); these examples are described as "amphoras" (see p. 448).

147 For the term and its various uses, see Amyx 1958, pp. 202–205; Kanowski 1984, pp. 91–92; Sparkes 1962, pp. 128–129.

148 *Agora* XII, pp. 211–216, fig. 15, pls. 81–87. For the typology of Attic lekanai, the study by Lüdorf (2000) is very informative.

149 See, among others, Pease 1937, fig. 24 (p. 292), nos. 144, 145, fig. 32 (p. 300), nos. 187, 188; *Corinth* VII.6, pp. 138–143, V-19–V-30, figs. 26, 27, pl. 22.

150 *Olynthus* XIII, p. 418, no. 1044, pl. 253.

151 For the type, see *Agora* XII, pp. 214–215, nos. 1821–1834, fig. 15, pl. 86.

152 The fragmentary ΜΕΘ 5366 belongs to the same type, and is adorned with a wavy band on the upper surface of the rim and a thick black central dot surrounded by a black circle at the center of the floor.

153 See *Agora* XII, pp. 364–365, nos. 1831–1833, pl. 86.

154 Cf. *Agora* XII, no. 1834, p. 365, pl. 86 (second half of the 4th century B.C.).

155 *Agora* XII, pp. 213–214, nos. 1816–1819, pl. 85 (first and second half of the 4th century B.C.).

156 Kotitsa 2012b, p. 82, fig. 5 (Πυ 5979), from an infant burial of the third quarter of the 4th century B.C., for which see p. 85.

157 *Corinth* XVIII.1, p. 153, no. 383, pl. 44; Williams and Fisher 1973, pp. 24–25, no. 25, pl. 10.

158 It is likely that the ancient name was *thyeia* or *igdis* (θυεία or ἴγδις); see esp. Sparkes 1962, p. 125; Villing and Pemberton 2010, p. 557. The corresponding Latin term *mortarium* is confirmed by inscriptions on Roman examples; see Villing and Pemberton 2010, p. 557, with n. 10.

159 *Agora* XII, p. 221, n. 2; *Agora* XXXIII, pp. 99–100. More specifically, see Villing and Pemberton 2010, pp. 602–624, with extensive reference to iconographic evidence, literary sources, and archaeological context providing information on their use.

160 Clay and stone are the main materials from which mortars were made, but the medical texts also mention metallic versions (see Villing and Pemberton 2010, p. 623), while it cannot be ruled out that there were also wooden examples (p. 606, n. 141).

161 The examples that came to light from the excavations of Corinth show remarkable variety and cover a wide chronological range; see Villing and Pemberton 2010, pp. 566–602, detailing the types represented in Corinth from the Archaic period to the destruction of the city in 146 B.C.

162 *Agora* XII, pp. 221–223, pls. 90–92; *Agora* XXXIII, pp. 99–103, pls. 24–27. Villing and Pemberton (2010, p. 556 and n. 7) note that some examples from the Athenian Agora were wrongly identified as Corinthian.

163 There were only a few pieces of mortaria among the fragmentary pottery from the destruction deposit, which do not add anything to the general picture seen in the better-preserved examples, beyond the homogeneity of their fabric.

164 The clay mortars were made either on the wheel or with a mold, or in a combination of the two techniques, see Villing and Pemberton 2010, p. 559, and p. 565, n. 50, where older views on how Corinthian mortars were made are reviewed.

165 The same sealings are found on a mortar handle (ΜΕΘ 7535) found to the east of Building A but not in the destruction deposit. Its clay is different from that of **29/51**, and closer to that of **29/52**.

166 For the construction details of the handle, see also **29/53**.

167 Two circles next to the preserved handle and one opposite the spout.

168 Cf. a mortar of the early Hellenistic period from the Athenian Agora, with impressed circles on the handles and spout; see *Agora* XXXIII, p. 264, no. 182, fig. 30, pl. 24.

169 Villing and Pemberton 2010, pp. 578–582 (projecting-rim mortaria). This is not a very popular variant, and one that seems to be limited to the 5th century B.C.

170 *Olynthus* XIII, p. 414, no. 1030, pl. 250 (first half of the 4th century B.C.). This particular example has no spout but four reel bars adorned with ribs, while ribs are also found on the rim.

171 According to Edwards, the fluked spout occurs in the 4th century B.C. (see *Corinth* VII.3, p. 109), but Villing and Pemberton (2010, p. 584, n. 92) note that this suggestion has not been confirmed. Cf., among others, Villing and Pemberton 2010, Να γίνει αντιστροφή; p. 582, no. 37, fig. 12 (early 4th century B.C.), but also *Agora* XII, p. 369, no. 1898, pl. 92 (context of the second half of the 4th century B.C.).

172 *Olynthus* XIII, p. 413, no. 1025, pl. 250; this particular example has a shallower body.

173 For the necessity of using a mold in the construction of mortaria, see *Agora* XII, p. 37; Villing and Pemberton 2010, p. 625.

174 From the point where the rib handle is broken, we can distinguish the original core of the rim, which should have dried well before the attachment of the handle.

175 *Agora* XII, p. 370, no. 1912, fig. 16, pl. 91 (context ca. 450–425 B.C.).

176 Hadjidaki 1996, p. 577, A145 (cat. no. 5), fig. 15 (ca. 425–400 B.C.).

177 Villing and Pemberton 2010, pp. 590–594. The type is widely distributed throughout the Mediterranean, but its main production center has not been confirmed. The examples from Corinth should date to the early 4th century B.C.

178 *Olynthus* II, pl. 254 (lower right), with two shallow cavities defined by individual ribs.

179 Cf. *Agora* XII, pp. 370–371, no. 1914 (context ca. 425–400 B.C.), no. 1917 (context ca. 375–340 B.C.), pl. 92; see also Shear 1975, p. 357, P 30458, pl. 81:g.

180 See above, n. 171.

181 See above, n. 177.

182 Very few examples have been found at Corinth, and of these the clay is different from that used for the Corinthian mortars; see Villing and Pemberton 2010, pp. 590–594.

183 Klebinder-Gauss 2012, p. 263, cat. no. 348 (CKOL 39), pls. 58, 99; pp. 287–288, CKOL 35, 36, 38, 40, pls. 58, 119. The examples on Aigina come from deposits of the second half of the 5th century B.C.; extensive discussion of the fabric and shape is given on pp. 90–92.

184 *Agora* XII, p. 370, no. 1912 (context ca. 450–425 B.C.), no. 1913 (context of the 5th century B.C.), fig. 16, pl. 91 (for a drawing of no. 1913, see Villing and Pemberton 2010, p. 591, fig. 18).

185 See above, n. 176.

186 Blondé 1985, pp. 342–343, no. 384, fig. 61; Blondé 1989, p. 522, no. 191, fig. 16 (p. 520).

187 Villing and Pemberton 2010, p. 593, no. 51, fig. 21 (p. 594) (first half of the 4th century B.C.).

188 Klebinder-Gauss 2012, p. 288, CKOL 38, pls. 58, 119.

189 The usual ancient name was *κύαθος*, but the term *ἀρύταινα*, which is also found in the literature, has prevailed nowadays for ladles with long straight handles. For the name see Tzouvara-Souli 1992, pp. 122–123 and n. 4; Sparkes 1962, p. 131, n. 90.

190 More often, bronze ladles are found, which were intended solely for serving wine; see above, n. 189.

191 *Agora* XII, pp. 143, 306, no. 999 (425–400 B.C.), no. 1000 (ca. 350 B.C.), pl. 35.

192 *Olynthus* XIII, pp. 418–419, nos. 1047–1049, pl. 253 (first half of the 4th century B.C.).

193 In Greek publications, one-handled lidless chytrai are frequently referred to as "αρυτήρες," a term proposed by Manolis Andronikos (1955, p. 45, n. 1) and accepted by many scholars (see, e.g., Drougou and Touratsoglou 1998, p. 120; Kotitsa 2006, p. 37, n. 80), as the main function of the shape was to draw/pour liquids. Some of the examples of this type from Methone bear traces of fire, while some do not, but to avoid confusion we keep the term "chytra" for all and for both one-handled and two-handled varieties.

194 With the exception of the lid **29/69**, made of fine-grained purer clay.

195 For the manner of production of cooking wares, see *Agora* XII, pp. 34–35; *Agora* XXXIII, pp. 57–58; *Corinth* VII.6, p. 38.

196 For similar types of decoration of cooking wares, see *Corinth* VII.6, pp. 40–41.

197 For its shape and uses as reflected in the literary testimonia, see Amyx 1958, pp. 211–212.

198 *Agora* XII, pp. 224–226, fig. 18, pls. 93, 94; *Agora* XXXIII, pp. 165–178, figs. 71–81, pls. 61–67.

199 *Corinth* VII.2, pp. 155–157, An 291, An 301, pls. 82, 111; *Corinth* VII.3, pp. 120–124, nos. 648–658, pls. 27, 28, 61; *Corinth* VII.6, pp. 77–80, 89–91, figs. 11, 16, 17, pls. 11, 14; *Corinth* XV.3, p. 354, nos. 2217–2219, pl. 77; *Corinth* XVIII.1, pp. 72–74.

200 Soueref and Chavela 2002, pp. 270–271, figs. 5, 9; Allamani-Souri 2008, pp. 356–359, fig. 10.

201 *Olynthus* V, pp. 19–23, P 4–16, P 21, pls. 19, 21 (pre-Persian); p. 227, nos. 838–841, pl. 173; *Olynthus* XIII, pp. 194–195, nos. 217, 218, pl. 137; pp. 208–212, nos. 261–278, pls. 148, 149.

202 *Akanthos* I, pp. 265, 267–268, fig. 36; Panti 2008, pp. 107–115, figs. 13–17, pls. 38–47.

203 Drougou and Touratsoglou 1998, pp. 120–122.

204 For the type, see *Agora* XII, pp. 225–226, nos. 1943–1958, pl. 94; *Corinth* VII.3, p. 121, nos. 648, 649, pls. 27, 61 (Chytra I); *Corinth* VII.6, p. 80, III-11, III-12, fig. 11. The Corinthian examples have a single handle.

205 Similar decoration is found on **29/59**, discussed on pp. 1252–1253. Painted decoration on cooking ware is unusual, but not unknown, e.g. *Agora* XXXIII, p. 309, no. 617, fig. 78, pl. 66; Miller 1974, p. 206, no. 51, pl. 33. See also *Corinth* VII.6, pp. 40–41, with extensive discussion on the manner of decorating Corinthian cooking pots.

206 *Olynthus* XIII, pp. 194–195, no. 218, pl. 137 (5th century B.C.). According to Sparkes and Talcott (*Agora* XII, p. 226, n. 13), this vessel dates to the first half of the 4th century B.C.

207 Panti 2008, pp. 109, 329, no. 213, fig. 13:στ, pl. 40:ε (around 400 B.C.), with vertical rim and one handle.

208 *Agora* XII, p. 373, no. 1955, pl. 94 (context ca. 425–400 B.C.).

209 *Agora* XII, p. 373, no. 1956, pl. 94 (context ca. 350–310 B.C.).

210 Size does not play a decisive role in their use, that is, it has not been demonstrated that the smaller versions served as water jars rather than cooking pots. For discussion of this topic, see Saripanidi 2012, p. 150.

211 Brian Sparkes argues that the chytrai with smoke marks on the side opposite the handle were placed on semi-cylindrical supports that were pushed toward the fire, with only one side coming in contact with it; see Sparkes 1962, p. 130, pl. V: 4, but also pls. V: 6, VI: 5 for different types of supports. In contrast, David Robinson thinks that they were placed at the edge of the fire, not directly on it; see *Olynthus* V, p. 21. Nikolaos Kaltsas believes that, since these vessels had traces of soot also on the lower part of the body, they must have been placed in and among the coals; see *Akanthos* I, p. 268. Methone has not produced examples of λάσανα that support chytrai directly over a fire (Morris 1985).

212 For the decoration of cooking ware, see above, n. 205.

213 The shape is close to **29/61**.

214 *Agora* XII, pp. 224–225, nos. 1922–1940, fig. 18, pl. 93.

215 *Corinth* VII.6, pp. 89–91, figs. 16, 17, pl. 14.

216 For the name, see *Agora* XII, p. 3, n. 4; Amyx 1958, p. 210, n. 76. It is often referred to in the literature as a "casserole."

217 For the uses of the form, see *Agora* XII, p. 227; *Agora* XXXIII, pp. 178–179.

218 For a likely form of support, see Sparkes 1962, p. 131, pl. VI: 5.

219 *Agora* XII, pp. 227–228, nos. 1960–1976, fig. 18, pl. 95; *Agora* XXXIII, pp. 178–186, figs. 82–85, pls. 67–69.

220 *Corinth* VII.3, pp. 124–126, nos. 659–682, pls. 29, 62; *Corinth* VII.6, pp. 80–85, figs. 12, 13, pls. 11, 12; *Corinth* XVIII.1, pp. 74–75.

221 *Akanthos* I, pp. 260–261, fig. 28; Panti 2008, pp. 118–122, figs. 19, 20, pls. 48–50.

222 *Olynthus* V, p. 247, nos. 1003, 1004, pl. 186; *Olynthus* XIII, pp. 316–318, nos. 612–619, pl. 203. Some examples from Olynthos have painted decoration.

223 Blondé 1985, pp. 335–338, nos. 329–350, figs. 53–55; Blondé 1989, pp. 532–533, nos. 232–237, figs. 21 (p. 531), 22.

224 See, for example, a lopas with its lid from Akanthos in Panti 2008, pl. 50:α.

225 The incidence of the types is based not only on the better-preserved catalogued examples, but also on the basis of the uncatalogued fragmentary pottery.

226 See *Olynthus* V, p. 247, no. 1004, pl. 186. According to Panti (2008, p. 119), the mastoid appliqués on the main side of lopades perhaps represent the remnants of the open pouring spout of cooking pots. See also an Attic example with similar protrusions on either side of the spout: *Agora* XII, p. 374, no. 1968, pl. 95.

227 *Akanthos* I, pp. 260–261, fig. 28; Panti 2008, pp. 120–121, fig. 19, pls. 48–50 (Types I, II).

228 *Olynthus* XIII, pp. 316–318, nos. 612–619, pl. 203, especially the unglazed examples nos. 618–619.

229 Bachlas and Syros 2014, p. 213, Κρ216, pls. 61:δ, 68:ε (where it is characterized as a "small lebes"); Mourati 2014, pp. 115–116, Π 81, pl. 34:2.

230 Athanassiadou and Bessios 2019, p. 272.

231 *Corinth* VII.3, p. 126, no. 679, pls. 29, 62 (second quarter of the 4th century B.C., though MacPhee and Pemberton do not exclude a later date, see *Corinth* VII.6, p. 82, n. 51); *Corinth* XVIII.1, p. 188, no. 659, pl. 59 (probably later 4th century B.C.).

232 Blondé 1985, p. 337, no. 334, fig. 53 (p. 335), no. 335, fig. 54 (p. 336).

233 *Agora* XII, p. 373, no. 1963, pl. 95 (context ca. 375–350 B.C.).

234 *Corinth* VII.6, p. 82 (n. 51), C-1947-889, fig. 53 (= *Corinth* VII.3, p. 126, no. 675), dating to the first quarter of the 4th century B.C.

235 Blondé 1985, p. 338, nos. 348, 349, fig. 55 (p. 337); for the shape of the rim, see also no. 331, fig. 53 (p. 335), no. 350, fig. 55 (p. 337).

236 Whereas the flat lids were intended for chytrai: *Agora* XII, p. 227; such a distinction is not so assured in Hellenistic times (*Agora* XXXIII, p. 195).

237 *Agora* XII, p. 374, no 1978, pl. 95 (context ca. 480–450 B.C.); Boulter 1953, p. 95, no. 114, pl. 35 (mid-5th century B.C.).

238 *Agora* XII, p. 373, no. 1962, fig. 18 (context ca. 400–380 B.C.), no. 1963, pl. 95 (context ca. 375–350 B.C.).

239 *Corinth* VII.3, pp. 129–130, nos. 688–692 (Lid I), pls. 31, 62 (6th century to 146 B.C.[?]).

240 This publication is primarily concerned with the most representative examples of lamps.

241 *Agora* IV.

242 *Corinth* IV.2.

243 *Kerameikos* XI.

244 *Olynthus* II; *Olynthus* V; *Olynthus* XIV.

245 For discussion on this topic, see Drougou 2012, pp. 86–87. If one excludes Olynthos, few of the early lamps are known from other parts of Macedonia, for example, the lamps from the Sanctuary of Demeter at Dion, Pingiatoglou 2005, p. 63. See also the lamps from Torone, *Torone* I, pp. 647–648 (John Tidmarsh). For lamps from several other contexts at Methone, see Chapter 24.

246 *Agora* IV, pp. 31–33, nos. 94–105, pls. 4, 32. Lamps of this type, which originated in the Corinthian Kerameikos, do not have an articulated base but a concave raised underside, and lack a handle. They are provided with a short, wide nozzle, which has a broad oval opening that often overlaps the rim.

247 *Agora* IV, p. 33, no. 98, pls. 4, 32 (last years of 6th century to ca. 480 B.C.). See also Rotroff and Oakley 1992, p. 122, no. 335, fig. 26, pl. 59 (late 6th to early 5th century).

248 *Agora* IV, p. 34, no. 107, pls. 4, 32 (ca. 500–480 B.C.).

249 *Corinth* IV.2, pp. 35–38, fig. 14 (p. 32), esp. profile 12, pl. I. For the type, see also *Isthmia* III, pp. 6–8, pls. 1, 14. The type dominates in the 6th century B.C. and probably continues into the first two decades of the 5th century B.C.; see also Campbell 1938, p. 610, nos. 229, 230, figs. 30 (p. 609), 31 (second half of the 6th century B.C.).

250 *Kerameikos* XI, pp. 16–17, nos. 10–14, pls. 6–7 (520–480 B.C.); see esp. nos. 12, 13.

251 *Agora* IV, pp. 44–46, nos. 156–163, pls. 6, 34 ("later years of 6th century B.C. down to ca. 480 B.C."). Lamps of this type have a flat or slightly concave underside, a triangular nozzle with a comparatively large opening that usually extends into the area of the rim, and a horizontal handle, which is sometimes omitted.

252 *Agora* IV, p. 45, no. 156, pls. 6, 34 (end of the 6th century B.C.).

253 Pingiatoglou 2005, p. 69, K 4, pl. 2 (first half of the 5th century B.C.).

254 *Isthmia* III, p. 9, nos. 36, 37, pls. 2, 15 (Type IV A).

255 *Kerameikos* XI, p. 23, nos. 51, 52, pls. 12, 13 (around 450 B.C.).

256 *Agora* IV, pp. 30–31, no. 92, pls. 4, 32 ("early 6th century B.C. and well into third quarter of the century").

257 See, among others, *Corinth* IV.2, no. 53, pl. I; *Isthmia* III, no. 13, pls. 1, 14.

258 *Agora* IV, pp. 16–17, nos. 43, 49, pl. 30 ("middle of 6th century B.C. to end of century").

259 *Agora* IV, pp. 26–27, nos. 76–78, pls. 3, 31 ("late third and fourth quarters of 6th century B.C., perhaps into early years of 5th century").

260 *Agora* IV, pp. 39–40, nos. 131–135, pls. 5, 33 ("last quarter of 6th century B.C. to ca. 480 B.C.").

261 *Agora* IV, pp. 46–47, nos. 164–170, pls. 6, 34 ("between 480 B.C. and ca. 415 B.C.").

262 *Agora* IV, pp. 48–49, nos. 171–176 ("last quarter of 5th century B.C. and well into early years of 4th century"). Essentially this type, which continues the shape chronologically down into the 4th century B.C., is slightly different from the former, and the only development is primarily in the nozzle.

263 Type IV is produced over a long period, from the 6th to the 4th century B.C., but mainly in the 5th century B.C., see *Corinth* IV.2, pp. 39–42, fig. 14 (p. 32), esp. profiles 17, 18, pl. II. For other examples of the type from Corinth see *Corinth* XIII, pp. 150–151, 166, fig. 19, pl. 100 (first and second row from the top); *Corinth* XIV, pp. 129–130, nos. 1–5, pl. 47. For the type see also *Isthmia* III, pp. 10–12, pls. 2, 15 (Type IV B).

264 *Kerameikos* XI, pp. 23–24, nos. 53–63, pls. 12–15 (5th century B.C.).

265 Pingiatoglou 2005, pp. 70–77, K 6–K 22 (Attic), K 23–K 26 (locally produced), pls. 3–11.

266 This is the earliest group of ΠΛ 1 open lamps, which includes Attic products but also local imitations or variants of Howland Type 21 and Scheibler RSL 1; see Drougou 1992, p. 29.

267 *Olynthus* XIV, pp. 343–347, pl. 144, with references to earlier publications. Robinson dates Group IV between the end of the 6th and the early 5th century B.C., but Drougou (1992, p. 24) considers a later date possible.

268 Without the nozzle, it is difficult to distinguish between the two types accurately.

269 *Agora* IV, p. 47, no. 169 (21 B), p. 48, nos. 171, 172 (21 C), pls. 6, 34; Corbett 1949, p. 338, no. 110, fig. 8, pl. 99.

270 *Kerameikos* XI, pp. 23–24, nos. 57, 58, pls. 14, 15 (third quarter of the 5th century B.C.).

271 *Corinth* IV.2, p. 135, nos. 65, 66, figs. 58, 59.

272 Drougou 1992, p. 92, Τομή Ο.Υ.Θ., cat. no. 1 (77.412), pl. 85 (5th century B.C.; for the date see p. 101).

273 *Agora* IV, p. 47, no. 168 (ca. 430–420 B.C.), no. 169 (last quarter of the 5th century B.C.), pls. 6, 34; *Corinth* XIII, p. 260, Grave 388–14, fig. 19 (p. 150), pl. 100 (late third quarter of the 5th century); see also *Kerameikos* XI, esp. the nozzles of lamps nos. 58–60, pl. 15 (third quarter of the 5th century B.C.).

274 See *Agora* IV, p. 48, nos. 171, 172, pls. 6, 34 (last quarter of the 5th century B.C.).

275 *Agora* IV, pp. 56–57, nos. 209–220, pls. 7, 36 ("late in third quarter of 5th century B.C. into first quarter of 4th century"). In addition to the above features, lamps of this type have a disk-shaped or ring base, a shallow body, and usually a ribbon handle, which is sometimes replaced by a second nozzle.

276 In their development, Howland Type 23 lamps gradually acquire a taller and narrower body and a larger rim with a smaller filling hole. Cf. *Agora* IV, p. 57, no. 213, pls. 7, 36, but also an example of the first quarter of the 4th century B.C., Shear 1970, p. 218, D 17, pl. 58. The final step is represented by Howland Type 23 C, for which further reference is made on p. 1256, in relation to lamp **29/81**.

277 See *Agora* IV, p. 57, no. 212 for the profile, and esp. no. 217, pls. 7, 36.

278 *Kerameikos* XI, pp. 19–20, esp. no. 30 (last quarter of the 5th century B.C.), no. 33, pls. 8, 9.

279 *Corinth* XIII, p. 271, Grave 419–15, 16, fig. 19 (p. 150), pls. 69, 100 (later 5th century B.C.). For the type, see below, n. 291.

280 Saripanidi 2012, pp. 172–173, no. 305, pl. 63 (last quarter of the 5th century B.C.).

281 *Agora* IV, pp. 63–64, nos. 243–249, pls. 8, 37 ("late in third quarter of 5th century B.C. and well through the last quarter of the century"), and esp. no. 249, with more convex walls (last quarter of the 5th century B.C.).

282 *Kerameikos* XI, pp. 21–22, nos. 45–49, pls. 12, 13 (450–400 B.C.).

283 *Corinth* IV.2, pp. 42–43, fig. 14 (p. 32), esp. profiles 24, 25, and p. 138, no. 95, pl. II. This variety is dated by Broneer to the first half of the 5th century B.C.

284 Kourouniotes and Thompson 1932, pp. 133–134, no. 2, fig. 20 (second half of the 5th century B.C.).

285 Klebinder-Gauss 2012, pp. 72–73, 271, no. 401, pls. 38, 102 (third and fourth quarters of the 5th century B.C.).

286 Blondé 1985, p. 310, no. 167, fig. 23 (second half of the 5th century B.C.).

287 Blondé 2007, p. 155, Type ATT. 2.1, pl. 42, fig. 6 (first half of the 4th century B.C.).

288 *Agora* IV, pp. 59–60, nos. 228–230, pls. 8, 36 ("first and especially second quarters of 4th century B.C."). The other features of the type include a disk base with reserved underside and a long and narrow nozzle with a small wick hole at its end. For other examples from the Athenian Agora, see Shear 1970, p. 218, D 18, pl. 58 (ca. 380–370 B.C.); Shear 1975, p. 361, L 5850, pl. 81:f.

289 *Kerameikos* XI, p. 36, nos. 166–171, pls. 30, 31 (first half of the 4th century B.C.), esp. no. 171 (second quarter of the 4th century B.C.).

290 The type, however, is rare in the destruction deposit since, apart from **29/81**, only one fragment of the type was found in the deposit.

291 For the type, see *Corinth* IV.2, pp. 43–45, fig. 14 (p. 32), profiles 28–30, and esp. p. 139, no. 104, fig. 62 and nos. 102, 105, pl. III. In this publication, Broneer dates the type early, namely in the 5th century B.C.

292 Davidson and Burr Thompson 1943, pp. 51–52, no. 27, fig. 19 (p. 48), no. 31, fig. 20 (p. 50).

293 *Isthmia* III, p. 14, nos. 85, 86, pls. 2, 16 (first half of the 4th century B.C.).

294 *Olynthus* II, p. 142, no. 74, fig. 305 (Series 7, 4th century B.C.); *Olynthus* XIV, p. 354, no. 27, pl. 146 (Group VI, second third of the 5th century B.C.).

295 Pingiatoglou 2005, pp. 78–79, K 30–K 31, pl. 14 (second half of the 4th century B.C.).

296 Drougou 1992, p. 92, Τομή Ο.Υ.Θ., cat. no. 3 (77.409), pl. 86 (400 B.C., for the date see p. 45), with shallower body.

297 *Kerameikos* XI, pp. 38–39, no. 186 (about 370/60 B.C.), no. 188 (350 B.C.), no. 189, pls. 32, 33.

298 *Olynthus* V, pp. 279–280, no. 106, pl. 200; *Olynthus* XIV, pp. 385–389, nos. 143, 147, pl. 163. Two more examples, found in the excavation of 1928, are classified in Series 7 of the earlier publication of the Olynthos lamps, *Olynthus* II, p. 142, nos. 77, 79, fig. 306 (4th century B.C.). The examples from Olynthos and the Kerameikos complement our knowledge of the type; they have a tall body with slightly curved walls, a robust base that rises in the center, and a long flat nozzle.

299 *Agora* IV, pp. 66–67, nos. 259–266, pls. 9, 37 ("late years of fifth century B.C. into second quarter of 4th century"); see no. 265, without handle.

300 *Agora* IV, pp. 70–71, nos. 285–300, pls. 10, 38 ("late in second quarter of 4th century B.C. into second quarter of 3rd century"); cf. the later no. 287, which is not a close parallel; *Kerameikos* XI, pp. 30–33, esp. no. 133 (third quarter of the 4th century B.C.), no. 135 (around 350–340 B.C.) and no. 136, pls. 24, 25.

301 *Corinth* IV.2, pp. 45–46, fig. 14 (p. 32), profiles 33–34. According to Broneer, Type VII begins in the 5th century B.C. and continues throughout the entire 4th century B.C.

302 See *Olynthus* V, p. 283, no. 125, pl. 201 (with glaze on the exterior) for **29/84** and **29/85**. See also *Olynthus* XIV, p. 393, nos. 155, 156, pl. 164 for **29/84** and **29/85**, and no. 157, pl. 165 for **29/83**.

303 For the general characteristics and date of Group IX, see *Olynthus* V, pp. 282–283; *Olynthus* XIV, pp. 391–392. In an earlier publication of the Olynthian lamps, analogous examples were assigned to Series 8, see *Olynthus* II, p. 143, nos. 89, 90, pl. 307 ("just before 348 B.C.").

304 ΜΕΘ 5161 (**23/15**) is discussed and illustrated in Chapter 23A, by Seth Pevnick.

305 Amphora Methone A 247. For Rhodian amphoras, see Yiannikouri, Patsiada, and Philimonos 1989, pp. 68–69 (p. 74 in the second edition); Yiannikouri, Patsiada, and Philimonos 1990, pp. 172–173, 181. This kind of decoration dates back to Archaic times and survives into the 4th century B.C.

306 I would like to thank warmly Dr. Mark Lawall, who was kind enough to view the material and provide me with useful information on their typological classification and dating.

307 For Mendaian amphoras and their various production centers, see Papadopoulos and Paspalas 1999.

308 For the Phoenician amphora, see Adam-Veleni and Stephani 2012, p. 162, no. 111 (A. Athanassiadou). For the earlier transport amphoras from Methone (Late Geometric and Archaic), including, among others, north Aegean, Chian, Lesbian, Lakonian, Phoenician, and SOS types, see Chapters 12 (Kotsonas) and 21 (Kasseri).

309 Bessios et al. 2004, p. 369, fig. 2.

310 See Bessios, Athanassiadou, and Noulas 2008, p. 245; Chapter 28.

311 The stoa opened onto the large central square (Plateia A). Along the northern side there was a wooden colonnade that stood on a stone stylobate, but its eastern part was closed from the north, east, and south. For a fuller description of the building, see Chapter 18.

312 The coins include those with the following excavation numbers: N 21–29, N 38–49, and N 50–53. Twenty-four of these are bronze and only one is silver. Many of the coins of Perdikkas III were recut coins of Amyntas III. One coin is unrecognizable and the identification of another remains unclear (Amyntas III or Pydna?). For the coins of Methone, see Gatzolis 2010, vol. 1, pp. 115–129; vol. 2, pp. 39–50.

313 See above, n. 305.

314 The kylix is fully presented above, in Chapter 23B, by Maria Tolia-Christakou.

315 Room A could not be investigated completely, as it continued north, outside the area of Plot 274.

316 The excavation did not extend in this direction.

317 For analogous examples, see *Corinth* XV.3, p. 355, nos. 2240, 2241, pl. 78; Proskynitopoulou 2011, p. 159, K 23, with further references.

318 The excavation at Plateia A was limited to the section north and northwest of Building A. Only a small part of Plateia B was located and investigated, as it continued to the west and south into adjacent privately owned plots.

319 For example, part of the surviving handle of the lekanis **29/35**, from the stoa porch of Building A, was found about 6 m from the rest of the vessel, outside the porch. The same is true in the case of plate **29/17** (see n. 53). In the case of the ladle **29/55**, the body was found in the closed part of the stoa, while the handle was found broken into two segments scattered outside the stoa.

320 For a definition of a closed assemblage, see Drougou and Touratsoglou 1994, pp. 128–129.

ΠΕΡΙΛΗΨΗ

(translation: Angelos Boufalis)

ΤΟΜΟΣ 1

Εισαγωγή: Το αρχαιολογικό ερευνητικό πρόγραμμα της αρχαίας Μεθώνης

John K. Papadopoulos και Sarah P. Morris (με τη συμβολή του Αντώνη Κ. Κοτσώνα)

Η αρχαία Μεθώνη βρίσκεται στη Βόρεια Πιερία κοντά στο σημερινό δέλτα του ποταμού Αλιάκμονα, τον μεγαλύτερο σε μήκος ποταμό της Ελλάδας (297 χλμ.), βόρεια του όρους Ολύμπου, και κατοικείτο από τη νεότερη νεολιθική εποχή (περ. 4.000 π.Χ.) μέχρι την καταστροφή της από τον Φίλιππο Β′ το 354 π.Χ. (Κεφάλαιο 1· Fig. I.1). Στις αρχαίες πηγές (Κεφάλαιο 2) εμφανίζεται ως μια από τις αρχαιότερες αποικίες στο Βόρειο Αιγαίο, ιδρυθείσα κατά την παράδοση από Ερετριείς που εκδιώχθηκαν από την Κέρκυρα το περ. 733/2 π.Χ. (Πλούτ. *Ἠθ.* 293β). Η θέση της σε ένα ακρωτήριο και στους γειτονικούς λόφους, κοντά στην εκβολή του Αλιάκμονα (Κεφάλαιο 3), την κατέστησε μια πύλη προς την πλούσια σε πρώτες ύλες ενδοχώρα (ιδίως σε ξυλεία και μέταλλα, βλ. Κεφάλαια 12–15, 20, 26), ενώ διέθετε έναν λιμένα προστατευμένο από τους νότιους ανέμους και ως εκ τούτου ασφαλές αγκυροβόλιο για πλοία από όλο το Αιγαίο. Από τον 5ο αιώνα π.Χ. η Μεθώνη αποτελούσε μέρος της αθηναϊκής συμμαχίας και προμήθευε τους Αθηναίους με ξυλεία, ιδίως ξυλεία κατάλληλη για την κατασκευή κουπιών για τις τριήρεις. Το 354 π.Χ. η Μεθώνη πολιορκήθηκε από τον Φίλιππο Β′, ο οποίος έχασε ένα μάτι στη μάχη και κατέστρεψε την πόλη (Κεφάλαιο 2). Οι επιζώντες κάτοικοι απελάθηκαν και σε μικρή απόσταση βορειοδυτικά εγκαταστάθηκαν Μακεδόνες (Fig. I.2).

Η εξέχουσα θέση της Μεθώνης κατά την εποχή του χαλκού (Κεφάλαια 4–6), την πρώιμη εποχή του σιδήρου (Κεφάλαια 7–9, 10–17) και την αρχαϊκή και κλασική περίοδο (Κεφάλαια 18–29) γίνεται καλύτερα αντιληπτή από τον χάρτη αναγλύφου με τεχνολογία δορυφορικής ραδιομέτρησης θερμικών εκπομπών και ανάκλασης (ASTER) (Fig. I.3), όπου απεικονίζεται η περιοχή του Θερμαϊκού Κόλπου κατά την αρχαιότητα, πριν από τις εκτεταμένες προσχώσεις των ποταμών Αλιάκμονα, Λουδία, Αξιού και Γαλλικού. Η θέση της Μεθώνης στη δυτική ακτή του στομίου του κόλπου εξασφάλισε την πρόσβασή της στα θαλάσσια δίκτυα επικοινωνίας του Αιγαίου, καθώς και τις οδούς προς τη μακεδονική ενδοχώρα, την Ήπειρο και τα Βαλκάνια. Από τη θέση αυτή ανάμεσα στο Αιγαίο και την αχανή μακεδονική και βαλκανική ενδοχώρα, η Μεθώνη εξυπηρετούσε τη μετακίνηση εμπορευμάτων, ανθρώπων και ιδεών. Ο Αλιάκμονας υπήρξε πλωτός ποταμός, όπως μάλιστα διαπιστώθηκε το καλοκαίρι του 2012 χάρη σε μία εξόρμηση με πλωτό μέσο έως την εκβολή του και προς το εσωτερικό του (Fig. I.4, 3.2). Δυτικότερα, μετά τη μονή του Αγίου Ιωάννη του Βαπτιστή (Fig. 3.7) και τη Βεργίνα (αρχ. Αιγαί), ο ποταμός σχηματίζει ένα εντυπωσιακό φαράγγι (Fig. I.5), και ακόμα δυτικότερα, θέσεις όπως η Αιανή παρουσιάζουν από την προϊστορική περίοδο ομοιότητες στα υλικά κατάλοιπα με την αρχαία Μεθώνη. Ονόματα «Πιέρων» σε πινακίδες Γραμμικής Β από την Πύλο και τις Μυκήνες (Κεφάλαια 2, 6) δείχνουν πιθανές επαφές με τον νότο πριν από το 1200 π.Χ., ενώ η ομηρική Μεθώνη (*Ἰλ.* 2.716–719) ίσως ήταν η πιερική. Η ανάμνηση θέσεων όπως η Μεθώνη, οχυρωμένη με διαρκώς υπό συντήρηση πλίνθινα τείχη έως και την πολιορκία του 354 π.Χ., ίσως ήταν που ενέπνευσε τη θρυλική «κατάρα του Αγαμέμνονα» (Στράβ. 8.6.15· Κεφάλαια 2, 6).

Η αρχαία πόλη της Μεθώνης εντοπίστηκε το 1970 στους λόφους αμέσως βόρεια της Νέας Αγαθούπολης, από Έλληνες αρχαιολόγους (Κεφάλαιο 1). Ανασκαφές από τον Μάνθο Μπέσιο ξεκίνησαν το 2003 και συνεχίστηκαν ετησίως έως το 2013, αλλά η θέση παρέμενε ελάχιστα γνωστή πέραν προκαταρκτικών εκθέσεων έως το 2012, όταν παρουσιάστηκαν σε μια σειρά συνεδρίων, εκθέσεων και βιβλίων πρώιμες ελληνικές επιγραφές από τη θέση αυτή (Κεφάλαιο 11). Κατόπιν συναντήσεων στον χώρο το 2012 (πάνω σε 60 εκ. χιονιού, Figs. I.6a–d) ο Μ. Μπέσιος προσκάλεσε επισήμως τους επιμελητές του ανά χείρας συλλογικού έργου σε συνεργασία με την ομάδα του για τη δημοσίευση των ευρημάτων αλλά και περαιτέρω έρευνες στη Μεθώνη. Ο παρών δίτομο έργο εκπληρώνει τον πρώτο στόχο, συγκεντρώνοντας μια ομάδα ειδικών για τη δημοσίευση του υλικού των ανασκαφών έως το 2013 σε ένα συνθετικό αλλά και επιλεκτικό τόμο. Ο δεύτερος στόχος εκπληρώθηκε μέσω μιας συνεργασίας ανάμεσα στην ΚΖ′ Εφορεία Προϊστορικών και Κλασικών Αρχαιοτήτων (νυν Εφορεία Αρχαιοτήτων Πιερίας) και του Πανεπιστημίου της Καλιφόρνια στο Λος Άντζελες (UCLA), διά της Αμερικανικής Σχολής Κλασικών Σπουδών στην Αθήνα, και ολοκληρώθηκε σε τέσσερις περιόδους εργασιών πεδίου, αλλά και γεωφυσικής διασκόπησης και γεωαρχαιολογικής έρευνας, τοπογραφικής αποτύπωσης με τη μέθοδο LiDAR, εντατικής έρευνας επιφανείας και στοχευμένης ανασκαφικής έρευνας (μια προκαταρκτική έκθεση των αποτελεσμάτων των ετών 2014–2017 δημοσιεύθηκε το 2020 στο περιοδικό *Hesperia*, τόμος 89, τεύχος 4). Συνολικά 15 έτη έρευνας έχουν αποκαλύψει ένα από τα σημαντικότερα λιμάνια και βιοτεχνικά κέντρα του Βόρειου Αιγαίου.

Μια σύνοψη των ανασκαφών της περιόδου 2003–2013 στη Μεθώνη προσφέρει το Κεφάλαιο 1, ακολουθούμενο από μια επισκόπηση της Μεθώνης στις αρχαίες πηγές (Κεφάλαιο 2) και μια λεπτομερή περιγραφή του τοπίου (Κεφάλαιο 3). Τα κυριότερα αποτελέσματα των ανασκαφικών ερευνών της περιόδου 2003–2013 περιλαμβάνουν την αποκάλυψη μιας πρώιμης αγοράς κάτω από τον Ανατολικό Λόφο με δημόσια κτήρια (Κεφάλαια 1, 18, 29)· τον εντοπισμό μιας ακρόπολης στον Δυτικό Λόφο με οικίες και εργαστήρια της αρχαϊκής και κλασικής περιόδου (Κεφάλαιο 19) πάνω από ταφές της εποχής του χαλκού (Κεφάλαιο 6) και κτίσματα της πρώιμης εποχής του σιδήρου (Κεφάλαιο 19)· και οχυρωματικά έργα, όπως σήραγγες σκαμμένες από τους Μεθωναίους και μία ράμπα από τον στρατό του Φιλίππου Β′ κατά την πολιορκία της πόλης (Κεφάλαιο 1· Fig. 1.26). Τομές σε διάφορα σημεία επιβεβαιώνουν την κατάληψη του χώρου από τη νεότερη νεολιθική έως την εποχή του χαλκού και την πρώιμη εποχή του σιδήρου, αλλά και την αρχαϊκή και κλασική περίοδο, με τον προϊστορικό οικισμό στον Ανατολικό (Κεφάλαια 4–5) και το νεκροταφείο του στον Δυτικό Λόφο (Κεφάλαιο 6), και κατοίκηση και στους δύο πριν από την έλευση των Ερετριέων (Κεφάλαια 7, 9, 12). Ιδιαιτέρως σημαντικό είναι το αδιατάρακτο στρώμα καταστροφής του 354 π.Χ. στην αγορά (Κεφάλαιο 29), το οποίο περιείχε πλήθος μολύβδινων βλημάτων σφενδόνης (Κεφάλαιο 28) και χάλκινων και σιδηρών όπλων (Κεφάλαιο 26) σχετιζόμενων με την καταστροφή της πόλης. Η πλέον εντυπωσιακή ανακάλυψη ήταν το βαθύ (πλέον των 11,5 μ. από την επιφάνεια) ορθογώνιο «Υπόγειο» στον Ανατολικό Λόφο (Figs. 1.4, 1.5), γεμάτο με θραύσματα εκατοντάδων αγγείων (συμπεριλαμβανομένων εμπορικών αμφορέων) κυρίως του ύστερου 8ου και πρώιμου 7ου αιώνα π.Χ. από κάθε γωνιά του Αιγαίου αλλά και εκτός αυτού, περιλαμβάνοντας και πέντε φοινικικούς αμφορείς (Κεφάλαια 1, 8–9, 12). Σχεδόν 200 από τους αμφορείς και τα αγγεία πόσης ήταν ενεπίγραφα με εγχάρακτα (graffiti) ή γραπτά (dipinti) γράμματα και άλλα σημεία, τουλάχιστον 25 στην ελληνική αλφαβητική γραφή, αποτελώντας το μεγαλύτερο και περισσότερο ποικίλο πρώιμο σύνολο έως τώρα (Κεφάλαιο 11).

Όπως αναφέρθηκε παραπάνω, τα Κεφάλαια 4–7 (Μέρος Ι) παρουσιάζουν την κεραμική της νεολιθικής εποχής και αυτών του χαλκού και του σιδήρου από τον Ανατολικό Λόφο, καθώς και το νεκροταφείο της υστερης εποχής του χαλκού στον Δυτικό Λόφο. Τα ευρήματα αυτά φανερώνουν έναν ευημερούντα προ- και πρωτο-ιστορικό οικισμό στη Μεθώνη, καλά δικτυωμένο με περιφερειακά δίκτυα στο Βόρειο Αιγαίο και πέραν αυτού, τουλάχιστον τρεις χιλιετίες πριν από τον αποικισμό του από τους Ερετριείς. Το ίδιο το όνομα Μεθώνη θα μπορούσε να είναι προελληνικό (με ένα επίθεμα που απαντά και σε άλλες θέσεις, όπως η Τορώνη και η Σκιώνη). Αντιθέτως, μια πρόσφατη πρόταση το συνδέει με το ελληνικό ρήμα *μεθίημι* και το ερμηνεύει ως μια τοποθεσία όπου κανείς μπορούσε να απαλλαχθεί ή ανακουφιστεί από τη ναυτική ζωή, ένα όνομα κατάλληλο για λιμένα. Σε κάθε περίπτωση, η Μεθώνη ήταν παλαιά θέση και πιθανώς φημισμένη για το αγκυροβόλιό της.

Το Μέρος II, το οποίο περιλαμβάνει τα Κεφάλαια 8–17, πραγματεύεται την ανασκαφή και το υλικό που ανασύρθηκε από το Υπόγειο, εστιάζοντας στο εμπόριο, τη βιοτεχνία και τον τρόπο ζωής στη Μεθώνη της πρώιμης εποχής του σιδήρου, ιδίως στην ύστερη γεωμετρική περίοδο και τον πρώιμο 7ο αιώνα π.Χ. Το Κεφάλαιο 8 περιγράφει την ανασκαφή του Υπογείου και το Κεφάλαιο 9 παρουσιάζει επιλεγμένη κεραμική από αυτό το αξιοπρόσεκτο εύρημα. Το Κεφάλαιο 10 παρέχει μια προκαταρκτική επισκόπηση των στοιχείων περί της χλωρίδας και πανίδας που αντλούνται από το Υπόγειο, μελετώντας μεταξύ άλλων απανθρακωμένα υλικά και όστρεα, και αποτελεί μια από τις πρώτες συνολικές μελέτες τέτοιων υλικών από στρωματογραφημένες επιχώσεις στην Ελλάδα της πρώιμης εποχής του σιδήρου. Το Κεφάλαιο 11 συνοψίζει την ενεπίγραφη κεραμική από τη Μεθώνη του περ. 700 π.Χ. (για την οποία, βλ. αναλυτικότερα το *Μεθώνη Πιερίας I)* και το Κεφάλαιο 12, μέσω της ανάλυσης των εμπορικών αμφορέων από το Υπόγειο, αναδεικνύει τη σημασία του εμπορίου για τον ερετριακό οικισμό στη Μεθώνη αλλά και ευρύτερα για τον ελληνικό αποικισμό. Τα επόμενα τρία κεφάλαια ασχολούνται με τη μεταλλουργία και τα μεταλλικά ευρήματα από το Υπόγειο. Το Κεφάλαιο 13 παρουσιάζει μια ευρεία ομάδα προϊστορικών λίθινων εργαλείων που επαναχρησιμοποιήθηκαν για μεταλλουργικές εργασίες κατά τη γεωμετρική περίοδο. Το Κεφάλαιο 14 αναδεικνύει τη σημασία της χρυσοχοΐας για τη Μεθώνη, όπου ο χρυσός κυριαρχεί μεταξύ των υπολειμμάτων στα κεραμικά μεταλλουργικά σκεύη από το Υπόγειο, όπως και στη μητρόπολη της Μεθώνης, την Ερέτρια. Το Κεφάλαιο 15 παρουσιάζει μια σύνοψη των κύριων κατηγοριών αντικειμένων από ευτελή μέταλλα (χαλκός, σίδηρος, μόλυβδος) από το Υπόγειο. Το Κεφάλαιο 16 παρουσιάζει μια επιλογή πήλινων συνέργων από το Υπόγειο, ιδίως σφονδυλιών, αγνύθων, και άλλων σχετικών με την υφαντική. Και τέλος, το Κεφάλαιο 17 παρουσιάζει όστρακα επεξεργασμένα δισκοειδώς.

Στο Μέρος III παρουσιάζεται η Μεθώνη της αρχαϊκής και κλασικής περιόδου, ξεκινώντας με το Κτήριο Α στην αγορά (Κεφάλαιο 18). Ακολουθεί μια παρουσίαση των κεραμικών εργαστηρίων στον Δυτικό Λόφο και μια επισκόπηση της αρχαϊκής τους κεραμικής (Κεφάλαιο 19). Το Κεφάλαιο 20 προσφέρει μια επισκόπηση της φυσικής ιστορίας και των λογοτεχνικών πηγών της μακεδονικής ξυλείας, πρώτης ύλης κρίσιμης σημασίας για την οικονομία της Μεθώνης, καθώς και της Μακεδονίας και των Αθηνών. Τα υπόλοιπα τέσσερα κεφάλαια αφορούν την κεραμική. Το Κεφάλαιο 21 συνοψίζει ορισμένους από τους αντιπροσωπευτικούς τύπους εμπορικών αμφορέων της αρχαϊκής περιόδου από τον Δυτικό Λόφο. Το Κεφάλαιο 22 παρουσιάζει τις κυριότερες κατηγορίες εισηγμένης από την Ανατολική Ελλάδα κεραμικής στη Μεθώνη. Το Κεφάλαιο 23 παρουσιάζει μια μικρή επιλογή αττικής μελανόμορφης και ερυθρόμορφης κεραμικής, και το Κεφάλαιο 24 μια σύνθεση των εισηγμένων (αττικών και κορινθιακών) και τοπικών κεραμικών λύχνων (επιπλέον των λύχνων του Κεφαλαίου 29).

Μια άλλη σημαντική κατηγορία βιοτεχνικών προϊόντων που παράγονταν στη Μεθώνη αποτελούν τα πρώιμα υάλινα αντικείμενα (Κεφάλαιο 25), συμπεριλαμβανομένων υάλινων ράβδων και απορριμμάτων κατεργασίας, σημάδια ενός πρωτοπόρου παραγωγικού κέντρου του Βόρειου Αιγαίου. Το Κεφάλαιο 26 δημοσιεύει τα μεταλλικά αντικείμενα από την αρχαϊκή και κλασική Μεθώνη. Το Κεφάλαιο 28 παρουσιάζει έναν μεγάλο αριθμό ενεπίγραφων και ανεπίγραφων μολύβδινων βλημάτων σφενδόνης, μεταξύ των τελευταίων αποθέσεων στη θέση αυτή και μαρτύρων της πολιορκίας της πόλης από τον Φίλιππο Β′ και της άμυνας που προέβαλε. Ο δεύτερος τόμος ολοκληρώνεται με το αξιοπρόσεκτο στρώμα καταστροφής στην αγορά της Μεθώνης (Κεφάλαιο 29), ένα εξαιρετικής σημασίας κλειστό σύνολο του 354 π.Χ.

Αν και ο στόχος ήταν η περιεκτική σύνθεση των ανασκαφικών αποτελεσμάτων της περιόδου 2003–2013, δεν κατέστη δυνατόν να συμπεριληφθεί κάθε κατηγορία ευρημάτων. Ο Χρήστος Γκατζόλης και η Σελήνη Ψωμά πρόκειται να δημοσιεύσουν ένα σημαντικό θησαυρό νομισμάτων από την αγορά τη Μεθώνης (για μια πρώτη παρουσίαση, βλ. https://www.youtube.com/watch?v=3z_YYI1ZIec). Μια εκτενέστερη αναφορά της εισηγμένης αρχαϊκής κορινθιακής κεραμικής (Figs. 1.35, 19.6–9) έχει αναλάβει ο Κωνσταντίνος Νούλας, ενώ η παλαιότερη κεραμική παρουσιάζεται από τον Μάνθο Μπέσιο (Κεφάλαιο 9). Μια από τις σημαντικότερες κατηγορίες υλικού, τα «εργαστηριακά», ιδίως από το Υπόγειο, βρίσκονται υπό μελέτη από τον Μάνθο Μπέσιο και περιλαμβάνουν εργαλεία και απορρίμματα μετάλλου, υαλιού, ελεφαντόδοντου και οστού, κεράτου, και άλλων φυσικών και μη υλικών (ορισμένα ήδη στα Κεφάλαια 13–14, 25). Οι πάμπολλες λίθινες και πήλινες μήτρες μεταλλοτεχνίας παρουσιάζονται επιλεκτικά (Figs. 1.15–16, 1.36, 14.3–4) και σε μια αναλυτική μελέτη τριών μητρών στο Μουσείο Θεσσαλονίκης (Κεφάλαιο 27), παράλληλα με παραδείγματα υποπροϊόντων κατεργασίας ελεφαντόδοντου και μια σφραγίδα από ελεφαντόδοντο (Figs. 1.14, 1.37). Στο μέλλον προβλέπεται και η ανάλυση των όστρεων, των απανθρωκωμένων ξύλων, και των λοιπών καταλοίπων χλωρίδας και πανίδας, συμπεριλαμβανομένων εκείνων του Υπογείου που παρουσιάζονται στο Κεφάλαιο 10.

Τα 29 κεφάλαια σε αυτό το δίτομο έργο έχουν συνταχθεί από περισσότερους από 30 συνεργάτες και παρουσιάζουν περισσότερα από 1.200 αντικείμενα. Η συγκέντρωση, μετάφραση και επιμέλεια αυτών πήρε πολύ περισσότερο χρόνο από όσο αναμενόταν το 2012 και καθυστέρησε επιπλέον λόγω της συνέχειας των ανασκαφών από το 2014. Αν και ογκώδε, το παρόν έργο δεν είναι παρά συνθετικό, καθώς η ποσότητα και η ποιότητα του υλικού της Μεθώνης απαιτεί πολλά έτη συντήρησης, μελέτης και καταγραφής, πόσω μάλλον μετά τον εμπλουτισμό του από τις ανασκαφές της περιόδου 2014–2017.

Η ιστορική σημασία της Μεθώνης έγκειται στην καταστροφή της από τον Φίλιππο Β′ το 354 π.Χ., και η κοινότητα της σύγχρονης Μεθώνης και Νέας Αγαθούπολης ανήγειρε έναν αδριάντα του το 2010 (Fig. I.7). Το ερευνητικό μας πρόγραμμα επεδίωξε να τιμήσει νεότερα κεφάλαια της ελληνικής ιστορίας, συγκεκριμένα της Νέας Αγαθούπολης, του οικισμού που διαδέχθηκε στη θέση αυτή την αρχαία Μεθώνη. Πρόκειται για έναν από τους οικισμούς προσφύγων από την ανατολική Θράκη στη Βόρεια Ελλάδα, άλλοτε συνδεδεμένος με βορρά και νότο μέσω σιδηροδρόμου, ώσπου έχασε τον ζωτικό αυτόν σύνδεσμο μετά τη μετατόπιση της σιδηροδρομικής γραμμής δυτικά πριν από κάποιες δεκαετίες. Ο εγκαταλειμμένος σταθμός στάθηκε ως ευκαιρία για την εμπλοκή της τοπικής κοινότητας και το πολυχωρικό κτήριο αποκαταστάθηκε το 2015. Εγκαινιάστηκε επισήμως το 2016 ως πολιτιστικό κέντρο, ανοίγοντας τις θύρες του στο κοινό με μια έκθεση φωτογραφιών, και πλέον διευθύνεται από τον τοπικό πολιτιστικό σύλλογο γυναικών «Αγάθωνες», χρησιμοποιούμενος για περιστασιακές συγκεντρώσεις και εορτασμούς. Περαιτέρω πληροφορίες για το ερευνητικό μας πρόγραμμα και τον σιδηροδρομικό σταθμό μπορεί κανείς να δει στο διαδίκτυο μέσω του συνδέσμου https://www.ascsa.edu.gr/news/newsDetails/webinar-the-ancient-methone-archaeological-project-the-movie.

Ολοκληρώνουμε με μια έκκληση για τη διατήρηση της αρχαίας Μεθώνης. Εκτός ενός μικρού τμήματος δημόσιας γαίας (στον Δυτικό Λόφο), το μεγαλύτερο τμήμα του αρχαιολογικού χώρου βρίσκεται σε ιδιωτικούς αγρούς και η ανασκαφή είναι δυνατή μόνο με την άδεια του ιδιοκτήτη. Ωστόσο, ο εκτεταμένος υδροβιότοπος των δέλτα των ποταμών βόρεια και βορειοανατολικά της θέσης (Fig. I.8a), στις παρυφές του οποίου στέκει παρατηρήριο πτηνών (Fig. I.8b), προστατεύεται από το πρόγραμμα Natura 2000, ένα δίκτυο περιοχών αναπαραγωγής και ανάπαυσης για σπάνια και απειλούμενα είδη και περιοχών αξιόλογου φυσικού περιβάλλοντος. Διαρκές όνειρο όλων των αρχαιολόγων που εμπλέκονται στην έρευνα της αρχαίας Μεθώνης είναι να προστατευθεί το σύνολο αυτό με τον καθορισμό μιας αρχαιολογικής ζώνης, η οποία θα ενοποιήσει τον υδροβιότοπο και τον αρχαιολογικό χώρο της Μεθώνης.

Κεφάλαιο 1. Ανασκαφές στη Μεθώνη (2003–2013)

Ματθαίος Μπέσιος, Αθηνά Αθανασιάδου και Κωνσταντίνος Νούλας

Οι ανασκαφές στην αρχαία Μεθώνη από το 2003 έχουν αποδώσει πλούσιο υλικό. Το παρόν κεφάλαιο παρουσιάζει τις αρχικές σωστικές ανασκαφές από την ΙΣΤ΄ και αργότερα ΚΖ΄ Εφορεία Προϊστορικών και Κλασικών Αρχαιοτήτων, όχι μόνο εντός του τειχισμένου οικισμού (αγροτεμάχια 229, 245, 274 και 278· Fig.1.1), αλλά και στον περιβάλλοντα χώρο.

Ο οικισμός αναπτύχθηκε σε δύο γειτονικούς λόφους και στον επίπεδο χώρο βόρεια αυτών. Ο Ανατολικός Λόφος είναι χαμηλότερος και με μικρότερες κλίσεις, ο Δυτικός ψηλότερος με πιο απότομες πλαγιές, σε φυσικά οχυρή θέση και ως εκ τούτου θεωρείται ως η ακρόπολη του οικισμού. Η κατοίκηση στον Ανατολικό Λόφο ήταν συνεχής από τη νεότερη νεολιθική εποχή (Κεφάλαιο 4) έως το 354 π.Χ. (Κεφάλαιο 29), αλλά η δράση των θαλάσσιων κυμάτων από ανατολάς είχε ως αποτέλεσμα να απομείνει μόνο το δυτικότερο τμήμα των φάσεων της νεότερης νεολιθικής και της πρώιμης εποχής του χαλκού (Fig. 1.2). Περιορισμένης έκτασης ανασκαφικές έρευνες στο αγροτεμάχιο 278, στην ανατολική πλαγιά, εντόπισαν οικιστικά κατάλοιπα και στη θέση αυτή, ίσως λόγω ενός δευτερεύοντος αγκυροβολίου, απροστάτευτου από τους νότιους ανέμους που πλήττουν την περιοχή, σε αντίθεση με τον κύριο βόρειο λιμένα, ο οποίος ήταν από τους ασφαλέστερους στον Θερμαϊκό Κόλπο. Σε συνδυασμό με την άμεση γειτνίασή της με τον παράκτιο οδικό άξονα βορρά νότου, η θέση αυτή προσέδωσε στη Μεθώνη στρατηγική σημασία και την ενέταξε στο χερσαίο δίκτυο της Κεντρικής και Δυτικής Μακεδονίας και, πέραν αυτής, των Βαλκανίων.

Οι ανασκαφικές έρευνες εστίασαν στο αγροτεμάχιο 274 και ιδίως σε ένα βαθύ όρυγμα της ύστερης γεωμετρικής περιόδου (Fig. 1.2). Το «Υπόγειο» της Μεθώνης (Figs. 1.3–5), διαστάσεων 4,20 x 3,60 μ. και βάθους άνω των 11,50 μ., απέδωσε ένα τεράστιο πλήθος αρχαιολογικού υλικού, στην πλειονότητά του χρονολογούμενο στην πρώτη φάση του αποικισμού της Μεθώνης από τους Ερετριείς στον ύστερο 8ο και πρώιμο 7ο αιώνα π.Χ. (Μέρος II). Η κεραμική από αυτό αποτελεί το μεγαλύτερο σύνολο της περιόδου αυτής από τη Μακεδονία και το Βόρειο Αιγαίο και περιλαμβάνει τόσο τοπική όσο και εισηγμένη κεραμική από την Ερέτρια και την Εύβοια (Figs. 1.6–7), το Ανατολικό (Fig. 1.8) και Βόρειο Αιγαίο, την Κόρινθο (Fig. 1.9) και την Αθήνα (Fig. 1.10), και ακόμα την Ανατολική Μεσόγειο (συγκεκριμένα, φοινικικούς αμφορείς· Figs. 1.11–12). Ο μεγάλος αριθμός ενεπίγραφων αγγείων, τα οποία φέρουν μικρά κείμενα, μεμονωμένα γράμματα, εμπορικά σημεία και άλλα σύμβολα (Figs. 1.13–14), αποτελεί το μεγαλύτερο σύνολο πρώιμης ελληνικής αλφαβητικής γραφής στο Αιγαίο. Η πληθώρα εργαστηριακών απορριμμάτων (Figs. 1.15–20) υποδεικνύει ότι η Μεθώνη, εκτός από εμπορικό, ήταν και σημαντικό βιοτεχνικό κέντρο. Δείχνει ακόμα πως μια τολμηρή ομάδα Ερετριέων εγκαθίδρυσε ένα *ἐμπόριον* στον Θερμαϊκό Κόλπο, εφάρμοσε νέες τεχνολογίες και επιδόθηκε στο εμπόριο, και, εν τέλει, μετέτρεψε τον οικισμό των αυτοχθόνων σε αποικία.

Η δυτική πλαγιά του Ανατολικού Λόφου είχε διαμορφωθεί με εκτενή αναλήμματα, με στόχο τη συγκράτηση και σταθεροποίηση του ανώτερου επιπέδου του λόφου, στην πρωτογεωμετρική, ύστερη γεωμετρική και πρώιμη αρχαϊκή περίοδο. Αμέσως δυτικά, αποκαλύφθηκε μέρος της αγοράς της Μεθώνης (Figs. 1.21–22) με καλοδιατηρημένα μνημειακά κτήρια, τα πρώτα γνωστά στην Κάτω Μακεδονία, τα οποία μπορούν να χαρακτηριστούν ως δημόσια (Κεφάλαιο 18). Οι καλοχτισμένοι πολυγωνικοί τοίχοι στα Κτήρια Α, Β και Δ χρονολογούνται στο τέλος του 7ου και την αρχή του 6ου αιώνα π.Χ. (Fig. 1.23). Μια μείζονος κλίμακας μνημειακή φάση των κτηρίων κατά το ισόδομο σύστημα στο Κτήριο Α χρονολογείται στο πρώτο μισό του 6ου αιώνα π.Χ. και ένα εκτενέστερο οικοδομικό πρόγραμμα (στο οποίο ανήκουν οι λίθινοι τοιχοβάτες και πλίνθινες ανωδομές) στον ύστερο 6ο αιώνα π.Χ. (Fig. 1.24). Τον 5ο αιώνα π.Χ. χρονολογείται η προσθήκη μιας στοάς κατά μήκος της βόρειας όψης του Κτηρίου Α, προς την Πλατεία Α. Τα κτήρια αυτά και οι πλατείες φιλοξένησαν βιοτεχνικές δραστηριότητες εμπορικής φύσης, σε μια από τις καλύτερα σωζόμενες αγορές της αρχαϊκής περιόδου στον ελληνικό κόσμο. Κεραμική από το στρώμα καταστροφής (Fig. 1.25· Κεφάλαιο 29), καθώς και μολύβδινα βλήματα σφενδόνης (Κεφάλαιο 28) και αιχμές βελών (Figs. 26.51–52), δίνουν μια εικόνα των τελευταίων ημερών του οικισμού της Μεθώνης.

Οι ανασκαφές στον Δυτικό Λόφο, ο οποίος ταυτίζεται με την ακρόπολη της Μεθώνης, ανίχνευσαν τη θέση του νότιου τείχους, που έχει λιθολογηθεί ολοκληρωτικά, και αποκάλυψαν υπόγειες σήραγγες που σχετίζονται με αμυντικά έργα (Fig. 1.26). Στον αυχένα του υψώματος αμέσως νότια του τείχους εντοπίστηκε μεγάλος όγκος χώματος (μετά το 2013 εντοπίστηκε και ο λάκκος από όπου προήλθε το χώμα), κατά τη γνωστή πολιορκητική πρακτική της δημιουργίας μιας ράμπας ώστε οι επιτιθέμενοι να υπερσκελίσουν τα τείχη (Πολύαινος *Στρατηγήματα* 4.2.15), αναμφίβολα σχετιζόμενος με την πολιορκία από τον Φίλιππο Β′ το 354 π.Χ. Νοτιότερα, οχυρωματικές τάφροι περιέβαλαν μάλλον το μακεδονικό στρατόπεδο σε απόσταση ικανή να επιτρέψει σε μια βολή να τραυματίσει το δεξιό μάτι του Φιλίππου (Σχόλια στο Δημ. *Ὀλυνθιακός* III.43α).

Την αραιή κατοίκηση και τις λιγοστές λακκοειδείς ταφές στην κορυφή του Δυτικού Λόφου κατά την πρώιμη εποχή του χαλκού διαδέχεται σημαντικά μεγαλύτερος αριθμός τάφων της ύστερης εποχής του χαλκού (Κεφάλαιο 6), παραδίδοντας ενδιαφέροντα κτερίσματα (Fig. 1.27a–b), όπως τροχήλατη και γραπτή κεραμική (Fig. 1.28a–d), τοπική χειροποίητη κεραμική (Fig. 1.28e–f) και διάφορα κοσμήματα (Fig. 1.29). Οι ταφές είναι σχεδόν αποκλειστικά ενταφιασμοί σε ξύλινες σαρκοφάγους ή σε λάκκους με ξύλινη κάλυψη, εκτός από μία καύση, με τα καμμένα οστά τοποθετημένα μέσα σε πήλινο χειροποίητο αγγείο (Fig. 1.30). Κατά τη διάρκεια της πρώιμης εποχής του σιδήρου (πρωτογεωμετρική και υπο-πρωτογεωμετρική), αυξάνεται σαφώς η έκταση του οχυρωμένου οικισμού επί του Δυτικού Λόφου, όπου μια οχυρωματική τάφρος στην ανώτερη ανατολική πλαγιά, διορυχθείσα στην πρώιμη εποχή του σιδήρου, επέκτεινε τον οικισμό προς νότο (Fig. 1.31). Στην κορυφή του λόφου, αψιδωτά κτήρια της πρώιμης εποχής του σιδήρου, όπως υποδεικνύουν πασσαλότρυπες (Fig. 1.32), εντοπίστηκαν στα κατώτερα στρώματα των επιχώσεων. Αποθέσεις της αρχαϊκής περιόδου σχετίζονται με τουλάχιστον τρία κτήρια (Fig. 1.33) του δεύτερου μισού του 7ου και πρώτου μισού του 6ου αιώνα π.Χ., καλυμμένα από ένα εκτεταμένο στρώμα καταστροφής, την οποία προκάλεσε πυρκαγιά στο πρώτο μισό του 6ου αιώνα π.Χ., με πλούσια κεραμικά ευρήματα (Figs. 1.34–35· Κεφάλαια 19, 21). Η ανασκαμμένη περιοχή παρουσιάζει σαφείς ενδείξεις βιοτεχνικής δραστηριότητας, συμπεριλαμβανομένων δύο κλιβάνων κεραμικής (Figs. 1.33, 6.3a, 19.1c), λίθινων μητρών μεταλλουργίας (Fig. 1.36a–f) και θραυσμάτων υποπροϊόντων κατεργασίας ελεφαντόδοντου, εύρημα σπάνιο στην αρχαϊκή Ελλάδα (Fig. 1.37). Στον μεγάλο βαθμό διάβρωσης οφείλεται η συνολική απώλεια των στρωμάτων της κλασικής περιόδου, με τα περισσότερα ευρήματα της τελευταίας φάσης της Μεθώνης να συλλέγονται από υπόγειες σήραγγες, εγκαταλειμμένες μετά το 354 π.Χ. Ο οχυρωμένος οικισμός εκτιμάται ότι καταλάμβανε έκταση 100 στρεμμάτων, αλλά από το 2013 ανασκαφικές έρευνες για την εγκατάσταση αποχετευτικού δικτύου στις παρυφές του οικισμού παρέχουν πρόσθετα στοιχεία που υποδεικνύουν διαχρονική χρήση της ευρύτερης περιοχής.

Ανακεφαλαιώνοντας, ο οικισμός φθάνει σε ακμή κατά την πρώιμη εποχή του αποικισμού του, δηλαδή κατά την ύστερη γεωμετρική και την αρχαϊκή περίοδο. Μετά τους Περσικούς Πολέμους, η Μεθώνη εισέρχεται στην αθηναϊκή σφαίρα επιρροής ως μέλος της Δηλιακής Συμμαχίας, μια διαρκής στρατιωτική και οικονομική απειλή για το μακεδονικό βασίλειο, ενώ νότια, η Πύδνα λειτουργεί ως ο κύριος λιμένας για τους Μακεδόνες. Στον 5ο αιώνα π.Χ., η Μεθώνη υποστηρίζεται από τους Αθηναίους, οι οποίοι και ψήφισαν την ειδική προνομιακή μεταχείριση της πόλης (Fig. 1.38). Οι πολιτικές και στρατιωτικές εξελίξεις κατά τον 4ο αιώνα π.Χ. προδιέγραψαν το τέλος της Μεθώνης. Το 354 π.Χ., ο Φίλιππος Β′ πολιόρκησε και κατέλαβε την πόλη, απέλασε του Μεθωναίους και μοίρασε τη γη τους σε Μακεδόνες, και εγκατέστησε ένα μακεδονικό οικισμό σε μικρή απόσταση βορειοδυτικά της αρχαίας Μεθώνης, σε μια ακόμα παραθαλάσσια εκείνη την εποχή θέση (Fig. 1.39). Η θέση του νέου μακεδονικού οικισμού απέδωσε επιφανειακά ευρήματα, όπως θραύσματα αρχιτεκτονικών μελών (παραστάδων) και βοτσαλωτά δάπεδα καταστραμμένα από την άροση των αγρών. Τμήμα ενός μαρμάρινου ανδρικού αγάλματος από την περιοχή και ένα θραύσμα στήλης παραπέμπουν σε κάποιο κοντινό ιερό, ενώ επιφανειακά ευρήματα δείχνουν ότι ο οικισμός αυτός κατοικείτο έως και τα πρώιμα χριστιανικά χρόνια. Ένας άλλος μακεδονικός οικισμός στη θέση «Παλαιοκαταχάς» (Fig. 1.39) διήρκησε ακόμα περισσότερο, από τον 4ο αιώνα π.Χ. έως και τον 19ο αιώνα μ.Χ. Και στους δύο ερευνήθηκαν νεκροταφεία, τα οποία απέδωσαν πλούσια ευρήματα. Στο νεκροταφείο της παράλιας θέσης, το οποίο εντοπίστηκε στη θέση «Μελίσσια» Αιγινίου, εντοπίστηκαν λίγοι τάφοι χρονολογούμενοι στην πρώιμη περίοδο του αποικισμού της Μεθώνης, μεταξύ των οποίων ένας κιβωτιόσχημος τάφος πολεμιστή της πρώιμης εποχής του σιδήρου με όπλα και μια ύστερη πρωτογεωμετρική ευβοϊκή οινοχόη (Figs. 1.40–41), στοιχείο προ-αποικιακών επαφών μεταξύ Ευβοίας και Μεθώνης. Ένα όστρακο σώματος αττικού αμφορέα της μέσης γεωμετρικής περιόδου από το Υπόγειο (Fig. 1.42) με ίχνη φθοράς από νερό στο εσωτερικό, ίσως φερμένο από έναν έμπορο από την Ερέτρια στον λιμένα της πόλης, αντικατοπτρίζει τους τρεις παράγοντες που καθόρισαν τη μοίρα της Μεθώνης: Ερέτρια, Αθήνα και θάλασσα.

Κεφάλαιο 2. Η Μεθώνη στις αρχαίες πηγές
Γιάννης Ζ. Τζιφόπουλος

Το παρόν κεφάλαιο εξετάζει το όνομα και τις παραδόσεις σχετικά με την πόλη της Μεθώνης (μία εκ των τεσσάρων ή πέντε οικισμών με το όνομα αυτό), και τη θέση της στην αρχαία ιστορία και λογοτεχνία. Ενώ θρύλοι αποδίδουν το όνομα της πόλης σε μυθικούς οικιστές, όπως ο πρόγονος του Ορφέα *Μέθων* (Πλούτ. *Αἴτ. Ἑλλ.* 293α–β), ή το θεωρούν παράγωγο της μέθης, λόγω του τοπικού οίνου (Στέφ. Βυζ. *Ἐθν.* 440–441), η ρίζα του ίσως σχετίζεται με το ρήμα *μεθίημι* και η σημασία του με έναν τόπο "απελευθέρωσης" από τη ναυτική ζωή (όπως υποστήριξε πρόσφατα ο Blanc). Ένα απόσπασμα από τον Θεόπομπο (Στράβ. 8.6.15) αναφέρεται στη Μεθώνη ως *ὑλήεσσα*, δηλαδή δασωμένη, στο πλαίσιο αιτήματος των *ναυστολόγων* του Αγαμέμνονα για την επισκευή των πλοίων της Τρωικής εκστρατείας, αίτημα το οποίο οι κάτοικοι της Μεθώνης αρνήθηκαν και οι ναυστολόγοι τους καταράστηκαν. Η θέση της πόλης εντός του ομηρικού βασιλείου του Φιλοκτήτη (*Ἰλ.* 2.716–719), το όνομά της, και οι παλαιοί θρύλοι μαρτυρούν την ύπαρξη του οικισμού ήδη στην εποχή του χαλκού, άποψη που υποστηρίζεται από τα αρχαιολογικά ευρήματα (Κεφάλαια 4–6). Ομοίως, αναφορές σε Πίερες, είτε ως ανθρωπωνύμιο είτε ως εθνικό, σε πινακίδες Γραμμικής Β ίσως συνδέουν την περιοχή αυτή της Βόρειας Ελλάδας με τον μυκηναϊκό κόσμο της ύστερης εποχής του χαλκού. Στους πρώιμους ελληνικούς μύθους, η Πιερία ήταν η κατοικία των Ολύμπιων θεών (*Ἰλ.* 14.193) και ο τόπος γέννησης των Μουσών (Ησ. *Θεογ.* 53).

Οι Πίερες "Θράκες" εκτοπίστηκαν από τους Μακεδόνες και μετοίκησαν στον Πιερικό Κόλπο, πέραν του Στρυμόνα (Θουκ. 2.99.3). Οι Πίερες αυτοί κάτοικοι του Φάγρη συμμετείχαν στους Περσικούς Πολέμους στο περσικό στρατόπεδο (Ηρόδ. 7.112, 185), όταν ο Ξέρξης προέλαυνε στη Βόρεια Ελλάδα και μέσω της παράλιας Πιερίας στη Θεσσαλία (Ηρόδ. 7.131). Η Μεθώνη εμφανίζεται για πρώτη φορά στην ελληνική ιστορία ως αποικία της ευβοϊκής Ερέτριας, ιδρυθείσα το περ. το 733 π.Χ. από Ερετριείς πρότερα εγκατεστημένους στην Κέρκυρα, εκδιωγμένους από τους Κορινθίους και έπειτα και από την πατρίδα τους, όπου τους απώθησαν με σφενδόνες, και για τον λόγο αυτό απέκτησαν το παρωνύμιο «ἀποσφενδόνητοι» (Πλούτ. *Αἴτ. Ἑλλ.* 293α–β).

Μετά τους Περσικούς Πολέμους, η τύχη της Μεθώνης ήταν στενά συνδεδεμένη με το γειτονικό και αντίπαλο λιμάνι της Πύδνας και με τον επεκτατισμό των Αθηνών και του μακεδονικού βασιλείου. Οι τοπικές πρώτες ύλες, όπως ξυλεία και πίσσα (Κεφάλαιο 20), αλλά και τα ορυκτά γύρω από τον Θερμαϊκό Κόλπο, στη Χαλκιδική και στη Θράκη, καθιστούσαν τη Μεθώνη σημαντικό σύμμαχο για τους Αθηναίους παρά την εξέγερση των Ευβοέων (η οποία κατεστάλη το 446/5 π.Χ., Θουκ. 1.114), και ιδίως μετά την εξέγερση της Ποτείδαιας (432/1–429 π.Χ.), και τελικά εμφανίζεται τη δεκαετία του 420 π.Χ. ως μέλος της αθηναϊκής αυτοκρατορίας (Fig. 2.1). Τέσσερα ψηφίσματα της δεκαετίας αυτής (*IG* I^3 61) υπογραμμίζουν τη δύσκολη θέση της Μεθώνης, παγιδευμένης ανάμεσα σε Μακεδονία και Αθήνα, και ορίζουν ειδικές οικονομικές διευκολύνσεις ώστε η πόλη να παραμείνει πιστή στους Αθηναίους. Τα προνόμια αυτά εξακολουθούσαν να ισχύουν την επόμενη δεκαετία, όταν οι Αθηναίοι χρησιμοποίησαν τη Μεθώνη ως βάση από όπου το ιππικό τους λεηλατούσε τη Μακεδονία (Θουκ. 6.7.3). Η Μεθώνη έπειτα εξαφανίζεται από το προσκήνιο μέχρι την επόμενη σύρραξη μεταξύ Αθηνών και μακεδονικού βασιλείου, όταν το 362/1 π.Χ. ο Αθηναίος στρατηγός Τιμόθεος "απελευθέρωσε" τη Μεθώνη, την Πύδνα και την Ποτείδαια (Δίν. *κατὰ Δημοσθένους* 14). Ο Φίλιππος Β′ ανήλθε στον θρόνο της Μακεδονίας το 359 π.Χ. και πέρασε στην αντεπίθεση. Αφού κατέλαβε την Πύδνα το 357 π.Χ., η Μεθώνη ήταν πλέον το μόνο λιμάνι κοντά στις Αιγές και την Πέλλα που δεν βρισκόταν υπό τον έλεγχό του. Τρία έτη αργότερα, ο Φίλιππος, μετά από μια συντριπτική ήττα εις βάρος του διεκδικητή του βασιλείου Αργαίου, ο οποίος υποστηριζόταν από 3.000 Αθηναίους οπλίτες που είχαν αποσταλεί στη Μεθώνη, πολιόρκησε την πόλη ώστε να κρατήσει τον αθηναϊκό στόλο έξω από τον Θερμαϊκό Κόλπο και απέλασε τους κατοίκους, αφήνοντας μια μακεδονική φρουρά σταθμευμένη βόρεια της πόλης (Διόδ. Σικ. 16.31.6, 34.4–5· Δημ. 9.26).

Κεφάλαιο 3. Στην ακροθαλασσιά
Samantha L. Martin

Το παρόν κεφάλαιο εξετάζει τη θέση της αρχαίας Μεθώνης από θαλάσσια σκοπιά ή, με άλλα λόγια, προσφέρει μια άποψη του θαλάσσιου και ηπειρωτικού τοπίου μιας πόλης φημισμένης ως λιμένα από τη σκοπιά της θάλασσας. Η άποψη αυτή βασίζεται σε αναλυτική μελέτη του αρχαίου τοπίου τόσο της θέσης όσο και του περιβάλλοντος χώρου μέσω εκτεταμένης επιφανειακής έρευνας, κατά τους μήνες Αύγουστο και Σεπτέμβριο του 2012 (Fig. 3.1). Ένας κατάλογος φωτογραφιών και περιγραφών αποτελεί τη βάση για την κατανόηση της αρχαίας Μεθώνης εντός του αρχαίου και του σημερινού περιβάλλοντός της, ως μέρος ενός ζωντανού τοπίου και οικοσυστήματος της ανθρώπινης δραστηριότητας.

Η διερεύνηση αυτή οργανώνεται γύρω από τρεις θεματικές με δυνατότητες περαιτέρω έρευνας. Ως προς την πρώτη θεματική, *συνέχεια και μεταβολή*, μια εξόρμηση με σκάφος έως το δέλτα του Αλιάκμονα (Fig. 3.2) επέτρεψε μια άποψη της Μεθώνης από θαλάσσης και εντός του περιβάλλοντος τοπίου (Figs. 3.3), με τα όρη ως διαρκές φόντο, ενώ η πορεία και το μήκος του ποταμού έχουν αλλάξει δραματικά. Τοπόσημα, όπως τα Πιέρια όρη (Fig. 3.5), το Πάικο (Fig. 3.8), ο Χορτιάτης (Fig. 3.9), και ο Όλυμπος (Fig. 3.10), δεσπόζουν στον ορίζοντα, ενώ το δέλτα του Αλιάκμονα και η ακτογραμμή πλησίον της Μεθώνης (Fig. 3.11) προχωρούν αντιληπτά στο πέρασμα του χρόνου, και αλλαγές των ανέμων στην περιοχή ορίζουν την περίοδο πλεύσης κάθε χρόνο (Fig. 3.12). Η δεύτερη θεματική, *κίνηση και επικοινωνία*, εστιάζει στην αγορά της αρχαίας Μεθώνης ως πολιτικό κέντρο και εμπορικό κόμβο. Συγκεκριμένα, το Κτήριο Α και η στοά του αντικρύζουν μια πλατεία αλλά κοιτούν και βορειοδυτικά προς τον λιμένα, όπου έφταναν και αναχωρούσαν πολύτιμα εμπορεύματα, όπως μαρτυρούν τα πλούσια αρχαιολογικά ευρήματα (Fig. 3.13). Τέλος, όσον αφορά τη θέση της πόλης εκεί όπου ο Θερμαϊκός Κόλπος σμίγει με το δέλτα του Αλιάκμονα και τη χώρα της Πιερίας (Fig. 3.14), πρόκειται για μια θέση οριακή αλλά και κομβική για ένα ευρύ δίκτυο διασύνδεσης (connectivity), το υπομόχλιο του εμπορίου στο Αιγαίο. Κατά τα ομηρικά *ὑγρὰ κέλευθα*, η θάλασσα αποτελούσε οδό επικοινωνίας, και η Μεθώνη εξυπηρετούσε την περαιτέρω διασύνδεση με τις χερσαίες και ποτάμιες οδούς. Για την τρίτη αυτή θεματική, *παρυφή και σύγκλιση*, παρατίθενται ως παράδειγμα οι σύγχρονοι "αγρότες της θάλασσας" και τα πρόχειρα καταλύματά τους στο δέλτα του Αλιάκμονα (Fig. 3.15).

ΜΕΡΟΣ Ι. Η Μεθώνη πριν από την Ερέτρια: Ο οικισμός από τη νεότερη νεολιθική έως την πρώιμη εποχή του σιδήρου

Κεφάλαιο 4. Ο οικισμός και η κεραμική της νεολιθικής και της πρώιμης εποχής του χαλκού
Μαριάννα Νικολαΐδου

Η προϊστορική κεραμική που παρουσιάζεται στο παρόν κεφάλαιο ανήκει στην αρχαιότερη περίοδο κατοίκησης επί του Ανατολικού Λόφου της Μεθώνης και χρονολογείται στη νεότερη και τελική νεολιθική και την πρώιμη εποχή του χαλκού (πρώιμη 5η έως ύστερη 3η – πρώιμη 2η χιλιετία π.Χ.). Ένα μικρό αλλά σημαντικό μέρος του πρώιμου υλικού συλλέχθηκε μέσα και γύρω από τα αποσπασματικά κατάλοιπα τριών τάφρων και τεσσάρων λάκκων, οι οποίοι εντοπίστηκαν στην κορυφή του λόφου (Figs. 4.1–3). Ο υπόλοιπος προϊστορικός οικισμός έχει οριστικά χαθεί εξαιτίας της διάβρωσης από τη δράση των κυμάτων και χιλιετίες συνεχούς κατάληψης του λόφου, με αποτέλεσμα τη διασπορά της κεραμικής και τη δευτερογενή απόθεσή της ανάμεσα στα κτίσματα της ύστερης εποχής του χαλκού και της πρώιμης εποχής του σιδήρου, καθώς και κάτω από κτήρια της αρχαϊκής και κλασικής περιόδου. Η εκτεταμένη διασπορά των οστράκων της νεολιθικής και πρώιμης εποχής του χαλκού ίσως υποδεικνύει ότι οι πρώιμοι οικισμοί ήταν εκτενέστεροι του περιορισμένου χώρου της κορυφής του ακρωτηρίου.

Η κεραμική είναι στο σύνολό της χειροποίητη και αντιπροσωπεύεται από ποικιλία σχημάτων και κεραμικών υλών, ενώ συνεχίζει κεραμικές παραδόσεις και διαπεριφερειακές πρακτικές, όπως και άλλες προϊστορικές κοινότητες στην ακτή της Βόρειας Πιερίας και γύρω από τον Θερμαϊκό Κόλπο, όπου η κατοίκηση είναι επαρκώς τεκμηριωμένη ήδη από την 7η χιλιετία π.Χ. Σε όλη την έκταση της Πιερίας, η μακράς διάρκειας νεολιθική εποχή αντιπροσωπεύεται από παράλιους, πεδινούς και ημιορεινούς οικισμούς, αλλά και κάποιους σε μεγαλύτερα υψόμετρα. Ο οικισμός στον Ανατολικό Λόφο της Μεθώνης ανήκει στον επίπεδο εκτεταμένο τύπο, χαρακτηριστικό της Πιερίας και του Θερμαϊκού Κόλπου, σε αντίθεση με τις τούμπες που συναντώνται αλλού, και είναι συγκρίσιμος με τους γειτονικούς του οικισμούς.

Ένα μικρό τμήμα μιας τάφρου και μια πασσαλότρυπα εντός αυτής, η οποία αποκαλύφθηκε στη βορειοανατολική γωνία του ανασκαφικού κάνναβου (Fig. 4.3, Τάφρος 1), αποτελεί το μοναδικό αρχιτεκτονικό κατάλοιπο της παλαιότερης οικιστικής περιόδου. Σε μορφή και μέγεθος ομοιάζει με τάφρους των Φάσεων Ι και ΙΙ του οικισμού στο «Αγίασμα» Μακρυγιάλου και ίσως χρονολογείται στη νεότερη νεολιθική Ι, όπως υποδεικνύει ένα μελανόχρωμο στιλβωμένο αμφικωνικό αγγείο με ψηλό λαιμό (Fig. 4.10). Η τάφρος ομοιάζει γενικότερα με περιβόλους και εσωτερικά χωρίσματα (μονές ή πολλαπλές τάφροι, τείχη πασσάλων ή λίθινα), τυπικά στοιχεία των οικισμών του Βόρειου Αιγαίου και των Βαλκανίων κατά τη νεολιθική εποχή.

Η διαγνωστική κεραμική που σχετίζεται με δύο παράλληλες τάφρους και τους τέσσερις λάκκους (Fig. 4.3, Τάφροι 2 και 3), όσο και όστρακα σε δευτερογενείς αποθέσεις, παρέχουν στοιχεία κατάληψης του χώρου κατά τα μέσα της 4ης χιλιετίας π.Χ., στο μεταβατικό στάδιο από τη τελική νεολιθική ΙΙ στη πρώιμη εποχή του χαλκού. Υποδεικνύει έτσι μια μακρά διάρκεια του οικισμού της τελικής νεολιθικής, ίσως συνεχούς με τη νεότερη νεολιθική, με επαναλαμβανόμενη κατασκευή και αναδιάταξη των αμυντικών τάφρων στην κορυφή του λόφου (όπως στη νεολιθική). Μικτή κεραμική της νεολιθικής και πρώιμης εποχής του χαλκού χαρακτηρίζει την επίχωση των λάκκων και των τάφρων, με πολύ λίγα όστρακα να έπονται της πρώιμης εποχής του χαλκού. Το σημαντικότερο τεμάχιο (Fig. 4.23) είναι ένα βαθύ κύπελλο με εσωστρεφές χείλος και κεραμική ύλη πλούσια σε προσμείξεις από όστρεα, με στιλβωμένη και διάστικτη όψη, το οποίο βρέθηκε στον πυθμένα της Τάφρου 2. Το σχήμα, το υλικό και το φινίρισμα της εξωτερικής επιφάνειας θυμίζουν έντονα κεραμικά της τελικής νεολιθικής και πρώιμης εποχής του χαλκού Ι από θέσεις στην ευρύτερη περιοχή, συγκεκριμένα από την «Αποχέτευση Μεθώνης» (αγροτεμάχιο 617) και τη θέση «Χασάν Βρύση» Κίτρους. Αυτές οι τρεις θέσεις στη Βόρεια Πιερία βρίσκονται σε κομβικές τοποθεσίες ανάμεσα στις εύφορες πεδιάδες της Δυτικής και Κεντρικής Μακεδονίας και τις ακτές και πεδιάδες της Θεσσαλίας. Τα κοινά στοιχεία στον υλικό πολιτισμό και τις κοινωνικές και συμβολικές πτυχές του μαρτυρούν ένα εξωστρεφές τολμηρό πνεύμα κατά την τελική νεολιθική, όταν ιδέες, αγαθά και άνθρωποι μετακινούνταν εντός και διαμέσου περιοχών σε θαλάσσιους και χερσαίους δρόμους.

Η διαγνωστική κεραμική υποδεικνύει κατάληψη της θέσης καθ' όλη τη διάρκεια της πρώιμης εποχής του χαλκού, από την ύστερη 4η χιλιετία π.Χ. (ΠΕΧ Ι) έως τη μετάβαση από την πρώιμη στη μέση εποχή του χαλκού κατά την 2η χιλιετία π.Χ. Το υλικό της πρώιμης εποχής του χαλκού μέσα και γύρω από τις τρεις προϊστορικές τάφρους τεκμηριώνει ότι ο οικισμός καταλάμβανε την κορυφή και εξακολουθούσε να χρησιμοποιεί τις τάφρους αυτές. Μεγάλες ποσότητες κεραμικής της πρώιμης εποχής του χαλκού συγκεντρώθηκαν στις επιχώσεις κάτω από τη βορειοδυτική πλαγιά και αποτέθηκαν δευτερογενώς στα στρώματα της αγοράς, συγκεκριμένα στο στρώμα δαπέδου ενός κτηρίου της πρώιμης εποχής του σιδήρου κάτω από το επίπεδο του Κτηρίου Α. Τα ευρήματα αυτά σχετίζονται στενά με τους λιγοστούς τάφους της ΠΕΧ στον Δυτικό Λόφο και όστρακα από την επιφανειακή έρευνα του 2014 βόρεια της πόλης. Φαίνεται λοιπόν ότι ο οικισμός κατά την ΠΕΧ επεκτάθηκε σημαντικά σε σχέση με τις προηγούμενες περιόδους, κάτι που αρμόζει στο αυξημένο ενδιαφέρον για παράλια κατοίκηση κατά την εποχή αυτή. Η εγκαθίδρυση ενός ξεχωριστού νεκροταφείου στον Δυτικό Λόφο είναι άλλη μια κρίσιμη εξέλιξη, σύμφωνη με ευρύτερες εξελίξεις σε Μακεδονία και Βόρεια

Πιερία. Η Μεθώνη συγκαταλέγεται σε ένα πλήθος οικισμών της ΠΕΧ με συνεχή κατοίκηση χιλιετιών από τη νεολιθική εποχή, της οποίας η χωροταξική οργάνωση συνεχίστηκε κατά παράδοση. Γεωαρχαιολογικά και αρχαιολογικά στοιχεία φέρνουν στο προσκήνιο τη μακρά προϊστορία των δύο σημαντικότερων αστικών κέντρων της κλασικής περιόδου στην Πιερία: τα λιμάνια της Μεθώνης και της Πύδνας.

Κεφάλαιο 5. Η κεραμική της μέσης και ύστερης εποχής του χαλκού
Trevor Van Damme

Οι ανασκαφές έχουν αποδείξει κατοίκηση κατά τη μέση και ύστερη εποχή του χαλκού επί του Ανατολικού Λόφου της Μεθώνης, άλλοτε ενός ακρωτηρίου που προέβαλε στον Θερμαϊκό Κόλπο, με φυσικά αγκυροβόλια βόρεια και νότια (Κεφάλαια 1, 3). Αν και μεγάλο μέρος του οικισμού έχει χαθεί εξαιτίας της διάβρωσης από τη δράση των κυμάτων και ύστερων οικοδομικών δραστηριοτήτων, ένα μικρό αλλά σημαντικό σύνολο κεραμικής της μέσης και ύστερης εποχής του χαλκού σε δευτερογενείς αποθέσεις μαρτυρά τη συνέχεια της κατοίκησης. Το παρόν κεφάλαιο παρουσιάζει μια αντιπροσωπευτική επιλογή σχημάτων και κεραμικών υλών της μέσης και ύστερης εποχής του χαλκού από τις ανασκαφές της περιόδου 2003–2013, εντός ενός διερευνητικού ερμηνευτικού πλαισίου.

Η παρούσα μελέτη διακρίνει το υλικό της μέσης και της αρχικής περιόδου της υστερης εποχής του χαλκού σε τέσσερις κατηγορίες: τροχήλατη μινυακή κεραμική και χειροποίητες απομιμήσεις· άλλη τοπική χειροποίητη κεραμική· τροχήλατη κεραμική μυκηναϊκής τεχνοτροπίας· και αμαυρόχρωμη και δίχρωμη χειροποίητη κεραμική. Το σύνολο της μινυακής αποτελείται κυρίως από αγγεία πόσης και μετάγγισης, ένα μοτίβο που επαναλαμβάνεται στην ύστερη εποχή του χαλκού, ίσως επειδή μια μικρή ελίτ επεδίωκε να αναδειχθεί κοινωνικά μέσω της χρήσης επιτραπέζιων αγγείων νέας τεχνοτροπίας και της υιοθέτησης νέων καταναλωτικών συνηθειών. Για τα περισσότερα αγγεία τα κοντινότερα παράλληλα εντοπίζονται στην ώριμη και ύστερη περίοδο της νότιας μινυακής κεραμικής, με ανοιχτά σχήματα, όπως το κύπελλο με πόδι (Figs. 5.7–9), ο κάνθαρος (Fig. 5.6, 5.10), και το κύπελλο (Fig. 5.5), να κυριαρχούν παράλληλα με μικρά κλειστά σχήματα όπως πιθοειδή αγγεία (Fig. 5.3) και αμφορίσκοι (Fig. 5.2). Χειροποίητες απομιμήσεις τροχήλατης μινυακής κεραμικής εμφανίζονται επίσης συχνά (Figs. 5.9–10). Τοπικά χειροποίητα αγγεία έχουν μακρόβια βόρεια παράλληλα, ιδίως το κύπελλο με λαβή τύπου wishbone (Figs. 5.14–16).

Ο οικισμός της ύστερης εποχής του χαλκού βρισκόταν επίσης επί του Ανατολικού Λόφου, συνδεδεμένος με ένα σημαντικού μεγέθους νεκροταφείο στον Δυτικό Λόφο, δεν ήταν όμως ιδιαίτερα μεγάλος σύμφωνα με τα κεραμικά ευρήματα. Παρά τις πρώιμες επαφές με τη Νότια Ελλάδα, συμπεριλαμβανομένης μιας αιγινήτικης εισαγωγής (Fig. 5.21), πρώιμη μυκηναϊκή διακοσμημένη κεραμική δεν έχει ακόμα βρεθεί στη Μεθώνη. Τα σποραδικά στοιχεία εισηγμένης κεραμικής ή συνδέσεων με τον νότο διαρκούν ως την κατάρρευση των ανακτόρων στο Νότιο Αιγαίο (ΥΕ ΙΙΙΒ2), όταν η τοπική παραγωγή μυκηναϊκής κεραμικής και η επίγνωση περί των κεραμικών εξελίξεων στη Νότια Ελλάδα απογειώνονται. Μυκηναϊκά σχήματα εμφανίζονται αρχικά (ίσως στην ΥΕ ΙΙΙΑ· Κεφάλαιο 6) σχεδόν αποκλειστικά με τοπικό ή περιφερειακό χαρακτήρα, χαρακτηριστικό των μικρών μεσόγειων οικισμών στη Βόρεια Ελλάδα. Μια πιθανή πηγή έμπνευσης ήταν η νότια Πιερία, με την ισχυρή τοπική μυκηναϊκή παράδοση, ή η Θεσσαλία, παρά η απευθείας σύνδεση με τη Νότια Ελλάδα. Αρκετά χειροποίητα ήταν προσεκτικά φινιρισμένα ώστε να δίνουν την εντύπωση τροχήλατης κατασκευής, ως εάν οι τεχνικές της μυκηναϊκής παραγωγής να είχαν αποκτηθεί από δεύτερο χέρι.

Μεταξύ των ευρημάτων της ύστερης εποχής του χαλκού από το Υπόγειο, δύο πόδια κυλίκων μυκηναϊκής τεχνοτροπίας στη πρώτη φάση της επίχωσης (Figs. 5.18–19) ίσως είχαν χρησιμοποιηθεί ως πώματα. Ένας χειροποίητος αμαυρόχρωμος κάνθαρος (Fig. 5.26) στην πρώτη φάση της επίχωσης χρονολογείται μάλλον στην πρώιμη εποχή του σιδήρου, κρίνοντας από το προφίλ του, την εισηγμένη(;) κεραμική ύλη και το αρχαιολογικό του πλαίσιο, αφού η αμαυρόχρωμη τεχνοτροπία παρέμεινε δημοφιλής στη Βόρεια Ελλάδα πολύ μετά την ύστερη εποχή του χαλκού. Σε γενικές γραμμές, η αμαυρόχρωμη κεραμική είναι παρούσα στη Μεθώνη σε ποσότητες μικρότερες της τοπικής μυκηναϊκής και ίσως ανήκει σε μια προηγούμενη ή μετέπειτα περίοδο. Τα περισσότερο δημοφιλή αμαυρόχρωμα αγγεία είναι ανοιχτά σχήματα, ιδίως ο κάνθαρος και το κύπελλο (Figs. 5.26–27), υποστηρίζοντας την άποψη ότι αντικατέστησαν, ή αντικαταστάθηκαν από, τροχήλατα μυκηναϊκά σχήματα. Τέλος, η ποσότητα της χειροποίητης κεραμικής που μπορεί να χρονολογηθεί στη μέση και ύστερη εποχή του χαλκού είναι δύσκολο να εκτιμηθεί από τα όστρακα από δευτερογενείς αποθέσεις, και συνεπώς το δείγμα που παρουσιάζεται στο παρόν κεφάλαιο αποτελεί μικρό μόνο μέρος του συνόλου της χειροποίητης κεραμικής της 2ης χιλιετίας π.Χ.

Συνολικά, η κεραμική της μέσης και ύστερης εποχής του χαλκού στη Μεθώνη δεν διαφέρει από άλλες σύγχρονες θέσεις της Μακεδονίας, ιδίως γύρω από τον Θερμαϊκό Κόλπο, στην κοιλάδα του Αλιάκμονα και στη Χαλκιδική. Η κυριαρχία ανοιχτών σχημάτων δείχνει υιοθέτηση και παραγωγή μινυακής, αμαυρόχρωμης και μυκηναϊκής κεραμικής επικεντρωμένης σε 'συμποσιακές' πρακτικές, υποδηλώνοντας διάθεση κοινωνικής διάκρισης και προσφέροντας δυνατότητες περαιτέρω μελέτης του υλικού αυτού.

Κεφάλαιο 6. Το νεκροταφείο της ύστερης εποχής του χαλκού

Sarah P. Morris, Σέβη Τριανταφύλλου και Βάσω Παπαθανασίου
(με τη συμβολή των John K. Papadopoulos, Vanessa Muros, Brian Damiata και John Southon)

Οι ανασκαφές στον Δυτικό Λόφο της Μεθώνης αποκάλυψαν 28 λακκοειδείς τάφους της ύστερης εποχής του χαλκού ανοιγμένους στο φυσικό έδαφος, μοιρασμένους σε δύο αγροτεμάχια, οι οποίοι ανήκαν μάλλον στο ίδιο νεκροταφείο (Fig. 6.1). Η εκσκαφή τουλάχιστον 80 αποθηκευτικών και απορριμματικών λάκκων κατά την περίοδο κατοίκησης της πρώιμης εποχής του σιδήρου και σηράγγων κατά την πολιορκία της πόλης (357–354 π.Χ.) είχαν ως αποτέλεσμα τη διατάραξη πολλών ταφών, μεταξύ των οποίων ίσως και νεογνών. Ωστόσο, τα σκελετικά και υλικά κατάλοιπα προσφέρουν πολύτιμες πληροφορίες σχετικά με τον πληθυσμό της Μεθώνης στο τέλος της 2ης χιλιετίας π.Χ. Παλαιότερες ταφές νότια του Δυτικού Λόφου δείχνουν ότι η τοποθεσία αυτή χρησιμοποιείτο ως νεκροταφείο από την πρώιμη εποχή του χαλκού (περ. 3.000 π.Χ.). Οι ταφές που παρουσιάζονται στο παρόν κεφάλαιο εμπλουτίζουν την εικόνα των νεκροταφείων της εποχής του χαλκού στην Πιερία, τα οποία εντοπίζονται στην παράκτια χώρα και γύρω από τον Όλυμπο, υποδηλώνοντας σημαντική αύξηση του πληθυσμού, ιδιαίτερα κατά την περίοδο 1.800–1.200 π.Χ.

Οι ταφές της εποχής του χαλκού στη Μεθώνη ακολουθούν πρακτικές κοινές σε όλη την Πιερία. Πρόκειται για ορθογώνιους λάκκους σκαμμένους στο μαλακό πέτρωμα της περιοχής, οι οποίοι περιείχαν ενταφιασμούς σε εκτεταμένη ή σε συνεσταλμένη στάση. Ορισμένοι διαθέτουν περιμετρικά αναβαθμό, είτε για τον σχηματισμό γείσου όπου θα πατούσε ξύλινη κάλυψη είτε επειδή ήθελαν να τοποθετήσουν το λείψανο βαθύτερα στη γη και σχημάτιζαν μια βαθύτερη κοιλότητα στο μέσον του σκάμματος. Δεν υπάρχουν ενδείξεις κάλυψης με λίθινες πλάκες ή σήματα όπως στη Νότια Πιερία. Μόλις έξι τάφοι περιείχαν περισσότερους του ενός ενταφιασμούς, συνήθως ως σκόρπια οστά (συχνά νεογνών) στην επίχωση του τάφου. Οι περισσότεροι σκελετοί βρίσκονταν σε ύπτια θέση με τα χέρια σταυρωμένα στο στήθος ή την κοιλιακή χώρα, και ορισμένοι με τα πόδια ελαφρώς λυγισμένα προς τη μια πλευρά. Τα κτερίσματα ήταν είτε κοσμήματα (χάλκινες περόνες, χρυσά ενώτια και χάντρες, και περιδέραια και ψέλια με λίθινες, χάλκινες, υάλινες, οστέινες, πήλινες και κεχριμπαρένιες χάντρες) είτε προσφορές (πήλινα αγγεία και χάλκινα μαχαίρια) τοποθετημένες κοντά στην κεφαλή και τα άνω και κάτω άκρα. Μια μόνο χειροποίητη τεφροδόχος αβέβαιης χρονολόγησης περιείχε τα λείψανα ενός ενήλικου ατόμου μαζί με ένα σφονδύλι (Fig. 6.35).

Μεταξύ των κεραμικών κτερισμάτων, όλων τοπικής παραγωγής, το συχνότερο είδος είναι μια εκδοχή του μυκηναϊκού αλάβαστρου, ένα σχήμα που επιβιώνει στην περιοχή κατά τη μετα-ανακτορική μυκηναϊκή περίοδο (όπως και ο αμφορίσκος). Συχνότατα ευρισκόμενα σε ταφικά σύνολα της ύστερης εποχής του χαλκού ανά την Ελλάδα, συχνά με οστέινες περόνες στο εσωτερικό τους (Figs. 6.8, 6.18, 6.36d), τα αγγεία αυτά ίσως περιείχαν αρωματικά έλαια για τη χρίση του νεκρού κατά την προετοιμασία του λειψάνου για ενταφιασμό ή πριν από τη σφράγιση του τάφου. Ορισμένες ταφές περιείχαν επίσης τοπικές όψιμες παραλλαγές του μικρού άωτου πιθοειδούς αγγείου με ταινιωτή και κατά το ήμισυ ή ολόβαφη διακόσμηση

(Fig. 6.37). Τοπικά χειροποίητα αγγεία συνοδεύουν απομιμήσεις νοτιοελλαδικών αλάβαστρων σε σχήματα εξίσου κοινά σε άλλες θέσεις της Πιερίας και συχνά ανώτερης ποιότητας κατασκευής και διακόσμησης από τροχήλατους τύπους (Fig. 6.39). Ένα μοναδικό αμαυρόχρωμο αμφικωνικό πιθοειδές αγγείο σε έναν από τους παλαιότερους τάφους (Fig. 6.6), μαζί με λίγα αμαυρόχρωμα όστρακα στην επίχωση του Τάφου 229/10, αντιπροσωπεύει μια τοπική κεραμική παράδοση που φθίνει στη Βόρεια Ελλάδα καθώς έρχεται στη μόδα το μυκηναϊκό στυλ (Κεφάλαιο 5). Κάποιες ταφές (συγκεκριμένα νέων γυναικών, Figs. 6.12–13) ήταν πλουσιοπάροχα κτερισμένες με χάλκινα, υάλινα, πήλινα, λίθινα, κεχριμπαρένια και χρυσά κοσμήματα (Fig. 6.39), ενώ τα χάλκινα μαχαίρια λογίζονται ως εργαλεία παρά ως όπλα. Πολλές ταφές πραγματοποιήθηκαν στη μετα-ανακτορική περίοδο (ΥΕ ΙΙΙΓ), ορισμένες αρκετά μετά το 1.200 π.Χ. (Fig. 6.45). Τα σκελετικά κατάλοιπα είναι ανεπαρκώς διατηρημένα, πολλά καταστραμμένα από τη διάνοιξη λάκκων σε ύστερες περιόδους, αλλά στον βαθμό που σώζονται μαρτυρούν την ηλικία, το φύλο και δίνουν πληροφορίες για τη σωματική υγεία. Από τα σκελετικά κατάλοιπα ελήφθησαν δείγματα για χρονολόγηση με τη μέθοδο της φασματομετρίας με επιταχυντή μάζας ραδιενεργού άνθρακα (^{14}C) και τη μέθοδο της ανάλυσης σταθερών ισοτόπων (Appendix).

Κεφάλαιο 7. Ο οικισμός και η κεραμική της πρώιμης εποχής του σιδήρου: Γενική επισκόπηση
John K. Papadopoulos

Η κεραμική η οποία δημοσιεύεται στο παρόν κεφάλαιο προέρχεται από τις επιχώσεις της πρώιμης εποχής του σιδήρου οι οποίες κάλυπταν τα κτήρια και την πλατεία της αγοράς της αρχαϊκής και κλασικής περιόδου και περιείχαν υλικό προερχόμενο από προγενέστερα στρώματα επί του Ανατολικού Λόφου, τα οποία διαβρώθηκαν και κατέληξαν να καλύψουν τα μεταγενέστερα που βρίσκονταν σε χαμηλότερο υψόμετρο. Παρουσιάζεται ένα αντιπροσωπευτικό δείγμα διαφόρων ειδών κεραμικής, από τροχήλατη και γραπτή έως χειροποίητη, συμπεριλαμβανομένων χονδροειδών αγγείων και μαγειρικών σκευών, όλων σε αποσπασματική κατάσταση.

Το πλέον διαγνωστικό στοιχείο του υλικού αυτού, το οποίο εν πολλοίς προηγείται του ευβοϊκού αποικισμού, είναι ο διάκοσμός του (ομόκεντροι κύκλοι και ημικύκλια), αλλά η χαρακτηριστική του δεύτερου μισού του 8ου και των αρχών του 7ου αιώνα π.Χ. διακόσμηση στα αγγεία του Υπογείου απουσιάζει. Το αρχαιότερο υλικό, προερχόμενο από μια βαθειά επιμήκη ανασκαφική τομή κατά μήκος της βόρειας πλευράς του αγροτεμαχίου 274, χρονολογείται στην πρωτογεωμετρική περίοδο, ενώ η ανασκαφή δεν προχώρησε βαθύτερα για λόγους ασφαλείας. Η χειροποίητη κεραμική αποτελεί σημαντικό ποσοστό του υλικού αυτού, ενώ αντιπροσωπεύεται κατά μικρό μόνο ποσοστό εντός του Υπογείου.

Μεταξύ των τροχήλατων κλειστών αγγείων, ο αμφορέας του Βόρειου Αιγαίου αναγνωρίζεται με ευκολία (Figs. 7.1–6) και ακολουθεί το πλέον διαγνωστικό ανοιχτό σχήμα, ο σκύφος με κρεμάμενα ημικύκλια, αντιπροσωπευόμενος από εισηγμένα ευβοϊκά αλλά και τοπικά παραδείγματα (Fig. 7.7), όλα χρονολογούμενα στην ύστερη πρωτογεωμετρική και υπο-πρωτογεωμετρική περίοδο, δηλαδή αρκετές γενεές πριν από την άφιξη των Ερετριέων αποίκων τον ύστερο 8ο αιώνα π.Χ. Τα μεγαλύτερου μεγέθους ανοιχτά σχήματα περιλαμβάνουν τον κρατήρα και τη λεκανίδα, σχήματα γνωστά από την Τορώνη και το Λευκαντί (Fig. 7.9). Η χειροποίητη κεραμική της πρώιμης εποχής του σιδήρου από τη Μεθώνη είναι ίσως η πιο χαρακτηριστική και περιλαμβάνει ορισμένα από τα καλύτερα προϊόντα της τοπικής παράδοσης. Η ευδιάκριτη στίλβωση, ιδιαιτέρως στα ανοιχτά σχήματα, και η σπανιότητα της χειροποίητης οπισθότμητης πρόχου με εγχάρακτη, ραβδωτή, αυλακωτή και πλαστική διακόσμηση, καθιστούν τη Μεθώνη ξεχωριστή περίπτωση σε σχέση με άλλες θέσεις στον βορρά. Το συχνότερο και χαρακτηριστικότερο σχήμα είναι ο μακρόβιος και δημοφιλής κάνθαρος με κομβιόσχημες λαβές (Figs. 7.13–16), ακολουθούμενος από κύπελλα (Figs. 7.17–20). Τα μαγειρικά σκεύη, συμπεριλαμβανομένου του τριποδικού λέβητα (Figs. 7.25–26), ολοκληρώνουν το υλικό από τον οικισμό της πρώιμης εποχής του σιδήρου στον Ανατολικό Λόφο.

ΜΕΡΟΣ ΙΙ. Εμπόριο, βιομηχανία και βίος στη Μεθώνη της πρώιμης εποχής του σιδήρου: το Υπόγειο

Κεφάλαιο 8. Η ανασκαφή του Υπογείου

Ματθαίος Μπέσιος

Ο οικισμός της αρχαίας Μεθώνης και η θέση του στη δυτική ακτή του Θερμαϊκού Κόλπου σημειώνεται στο Κεφάλαιο 1, και επιπλέον στοιχεία παρέχονται στο Κεφάλαιο 3. Σήμερα η θέση απέχει περίπου 500 μέτρα από την ακτή, όμως στην αρχαιότητα η θάλασσα έγλυφε την ανατολική πλευρά του οικισμού και εισχωρούσε στη βόρεια πλευρά, η οποία ήταν προστατευμένη από τους νοτιοανατολικούς ανέμους και συνεπώς από τα ασφαλέστερα αγκυροβόλια στον Θερμαϊκό Κόλπο (Figs. 8.1–2). Ανασκαφές στην αρχαία Μεθώνη από το 2003 έχουν δείξει τη συνεχή κατοίκηση της θέσης από τη νεότερη νεολιθική εποχή έως το 354 π.Χ. και ότι ο λιμένας της υπήρξε εμπορικός κόμβος από τις πρώιμες φάσεις της εποχής του χαλκού (Μέρος Ι). Η ανασκαφή έχει επίσης εντοπίσει την αγορά της αρχαϊκής και κλασικής περιόδου στο διάσελο μεταξύ Δυτικού και Ανατολικού Λόφου (Figs. 1.21–22). Στην κορυφή του Ανατολικού Λόφου αποκαλύφθηκε ένα ιδιαιτέρως σημαντικό εύρημα για την πρώιμη εποχή του σιδήρου και ειδικότερα για τον αποικισμό, το οποίο ονομάστηκε συμβατικά «Υπόγειο» (Fig. 8.3). Η εκσκαφή του μπορεί να χρονολογηθεί στο τέλος της γεωμετρικής περιόδου και μετά την ίδρυση της Μεθώνης ως ερετριακής αποικίας στη θέση ενός προϋπάρχοντος οικισμού. Η αφθονία ευρημάτων από το Υπόγειο επιβεβαιώνει τις εκτεταμένες επαφές μεταξύ Μεθώνης και μεγάλου πλήθους εμπορικών κέντρων στο Αιγαίο και την Ανατολική Μεσόγειο, καθώς και τη λειτουργία εργαστηρίων για την παραγωγή προϊόντων από διάφορα υλικά ήδη από την ίδρυση της αποικίας.

Είναι σαφές ότι ο Ανατολικός Λόφος κατοικείτο από τη νεότερη νεολιθική εποχή, όμως μεγάλο μέρος από τα στρώματα της προϊστορικής εποχής, και επιπλέον 1 μ. φυσικού εδάφους, έχει διαβρωθεί και κυλήσει σε χαμηλότερο υψόμετρο. Εξαιτίας της συνθήκης αυτής, το Υπόγειο απέμεινε ως το μόνο αξιόλογο κατασκευαστικό στοιχείο επί του Ανατολικού Λόφου (Fig. 8.3). Κανένα υπέργειο κτίσμα δεν εντοπίζεται επί της κορυφής του λόφου, αλλά το όρυγμα θα είχε ασφαλώς κάποιου είδους ανωδομή, πλέον παντελώς αφανισμένη, καθιστώντας την ταύτιση της χρήσης του χώρου ιδιαιτέρως δύσκολη.

Το Υπόγειο είναι ένα πολύ βαθύ, ευρύ, σχεδόν ορθογώνιο λαξευτό όρυγμα, πλάτους πλευρών 3,6 x 4,2 μ. στον πυθμένα και σωζόμενου βάθους τουλάχιστον 11,5 μ. Κατά την ανασκαφή του Υπογείου, η οποία ξεκίνησε το 2003 και συνεχίστηκε το 2004 (Figs. 8.4a–b), υποτέθηκε αρχικά ότι επρόκειτο για υπόγειο αποθηκευτικό χώρο. Η υπόθεση αυτή διαψεύστηκε κατά τη συνέχεια της ανασκαφής κατά τα έτη 2006–2007, όταν διαπιστώθηκε ότι η εκσκαφή του Υπογείου δεν ολοκληρώθηκε ποτέ. Εγκαταλείφθηκε τον ύστερο 8ο αιώνα π.Χ. λόγω της αστάθειας του γεωλογικού υποβάθρου, αποτελούμενου από αλλεπάλληλα στρώματα πηλού και μαργαϊκού ασβεστόλιθου με κάποια ενδιάμεσα λεπτά στρώματα άμμου ή ψαμμίτη. Η επίχωση του ορύγματος ξεκίνησε βιαστικά και ολοκληρώθηκε σε σύντομο χρονικό διάστημα. Το κατώτατο 1 μέτρο της επίχωσης αποτελείται από ωμό πρασινωπό πηλό, ωμές πλίνθους, λίθους, ξυλεία, κεραμικά και οστά ζώων, σε ένα ομοιογενές στρώμα, το οποίο ονομάστηκε Φάση Ι (Figs. 8.5–10a–b). Η επίχωση αυτή δείχνει ότι το Υπόγειο ουδέποτε λειτούργησε ως υπόγειο οποιοσδήποτε και αν ήταν ο σκοπός του. Το επόμενο στρώμα, της Φάσης ΙΙ, βάθους άνω των 2 μ., ολοκληρώθηκε επίσης γρήγορα, αλλά διαφαίνεται ένας κάποιος σχεδιασμός, αφού βρέθηκε ξυλεία (Fig. 8.12), τόσο στρογγυλή όσο και τετράγωνη, προσεκτικά τοποθετημένη παράλληλα προς τις πλευρές του ορύγματος σε αλλεπάλληλα στρώματα. Ένα στρώμα πηλού στο ανώτερο επίπεδο της Φάσης ΙΙ ανήκει μάλλον στη Φάση ΙΙΙ, η οποία χαρακτηρίζεται από στρώσεις πηλού, τυπικό στοιχείο απορριμματικών λάκκων στην περιοχή του Θερμαϊκού Κόλπου. Ανάμεσα στις στρώσεις πηλού βρίσκονταν αλλεπάλληλα στρώματα που περιείχαν κάθε λογής υλικά (κεραμική, πήλινες λεκάνες, μεταλλικά αντικείμενα, οστά ζώων, όστρεα, εργαλεία, διαφόρων ειδών εργαστηριακά απορρίμματα, τέφρα και απανθρακωμένα ξύλα), με σκοπό να εξασφαλίσουν, κατά το δυνατόν, τη σταθερότητα του εδάφους γύρω από το Υπόγειο.

Ένας αρκετά παχύς τοίχος (Τ14) θεμελιώθηκε στα ανώτερα στρώματα της επίχωσης της Φάσης ΙΙΙ, δεν ανήκει όμως σε αυτή (Figs. 8.15–17) και ίσως πρόκειται για μέρος αναλήμματος που κατασκευάστηκε μετά την πλήρωση του Υπογείου για να φιλοξενήσει νέες υπέργειες δραστηριότητες. Η αρχική επιφάνεια των επιχώσεων του Υπογείου (Φάσεις I–III) βρισκόταν τουλάχιστον 8,5 μ. από τον πυθμένα του ορύγματος. Η σταδιακή καθίζηση και η βύθιση των στρωμάτων προκάλεσε την υποχώρηση του τοίχου εντός της επίχωσης. Η καθίζηση και συρρίκνωση της συνολικής επίχωσης επέβαλε την κατασκευή ενός άλλου τοίχου (Τ5, Figs. 8.18–19), ο οποίος ίσως αντικατέστησε τον Τ14, μάλλον στον 7ο αιώνα π.Χ. Όλα τα στρώματα άνωθεν της «φάσης α» («επίχωση Α») βρίσκονταν κάποτε επιφανειακά όμως βυθίστηκαν εντός του ορύγματος καθώς η αρχική επίχωση συμπιέστηκε, και χρήζουν περαιτέρω μελέτης, ιδίως η επίχωση πάνω από τη Φάση ΙΙΙ, μια διακριτή φάση πλούσια σε διαγνωστική κεραμική και πηλό από διαλυμένες πλίνθους, με κορινθιακές και ιωνικές εισαγωγές από το τελευταίο τέταρτο του 7ου έως τα μέσα του 6ου αιώνα π.Χ. (Figs. 9.42–43), αλλά και ένα αττικό ερυθρόμορφο όστρακο από το τέλος του 6ου αιώνα π.Χ.

Είναι σαφές ότι το Υπόγειο επιχώθηκε σε σύντομο χρονικό διάστημα με δομικά υλικά και εργαστηριακά και οικιακά απορρίμματα προερχόμενα όλα από μια συγκεκριμένη βιοτεχνική συνοικία, τα οποία μεταφέρθηκαν και αποτέθηκαν συγχρόνως. Η κεραμική των Φάσεων I–III, η οποία αποτελεί τη μεγαλύτερη και διαγνωστικότερη κατηγορία ευρημάτων, χρονολογείται από το τέλος της εποχής του λίθου έως την ύστερη πρώιμη εποχή του σιδήρου, με τη συντριπτική πλειονότητα της τοπικής και εισηγμένης, ιδίως των πολλών ολόκληρων αγγείων, να συμφωνούν με μια χρονολόγηση στην ύστερη γεωμετρική ΙΙβ περίοδο (720–690 π.Χ.). Η χρονολόγηση αυτή βασίζεται στην εισηγμένη λεπτή κεραμική από καλά μελετημένες και χρονολογημένες ακολουθίες ιδίως σε Εύβοια, Αττική και Κόρινθο (Κεφάλαιο 9), με το πλέον συγκρίσιμο παράδειγμα στον Λάκκο 53 της Δυτικής Συνοικίας της μητρόπολης της Μεθώνης, της Ερέτριας, όπως επιβεβαιώνεται από την κορινθιακή κεραμική και αττικές εισαγωγές. Το Υπόγειο παραμένει μοναδική κατασκευή με εξαιρετικά πλούσιο επιγραφικό (Κεφάλαιο 11) και κεραμικό υλικό (Κεφάλαια 9, 12), αλλά και άλλα ευρήματα, όπως εργαστηριακά απορρίμματα (Κεφάλαια 13–14), μέταλλα (Κεφάλαιο 15), κατεργασμένο ελεφαντόδοντο, κέρατο ελάφου και οστό, και πολλά ακόμα αντικείμενα (Κεφάλαια 16–17). Ως σύνολο έχει ήδη προσελκύσει αρκετό ενδιαφέρον από την επιστημονική κοινότητα. Στον παρόντα τόμο παρουσιάζεται ένα δείγμα μόνο του υλικού, το οποίο απαιτεί συντήρηση, μελέτη και παρουσίαση ως σύνολο που έχει ακόμα πολλά να προσφέρει.

Κεφάλαιο 9. Κατάλογος επιλεγμένης κεραμικής από το Υπόγειο
Ματθαίος Μπέσιος

Το παρόν κεφάλαιο αποτελεί μεταφρασμένη και διευρυμένη εκδοχή του *Μεθώνη Πιερίας* Ι, σελ. 65–111, και παρουσιάζει 98 αντιπροσωπευτικά παραδείγματα τοπικής, αττικής, ευβοϊκής, ιωνικής, και πρωτοκορινθιακής/-ίζουσας κεραμικής της πρώιμης εποχής του σιδήρου (ύστερη/υπο-γεωμετρική περίοδος) από το Υπόγειο, χρονολογούμενης στο διάστημα 720–690 π.Χ. Η κεραμική παρουσιάζεται σε μορφή καταλόγου μαζί με πίνακες όπου δίδεται το ακριβές αρχαιολογικό τους πλαίσιο και η φάση στην οποία ανήκουν.

Κεφάλαιο 10. Βίος και διατροφή στη Μεθώνη της εποχής του σιδήρου: Προσέγγιση μέσω του φθαρτού υλικού πολιτισμού
Αλεξάνδρα Λιβάρδα, Ρένα Βεροπουλίδου, Αναστασία Βασιλειάδου και Llorenç Picornell-Gelabert

Ένα από τα μεγαλύτερα και περισσότερο εντυπωσιακά σύνολα βιοαρχαιολογικού υλικού στο Αιγαίο της πρώιμης εποχής του σιδήρου συλλέχθηκε κατά την ανασκαφή του Υπογείου της Μεθώνης. Το παρόν κεφάλαιο αποτελεί μια συστηματική και ολοκληρωμένη αποτίμηση του συνόλου των οικοδεδομένων της πρώτης φάσης της επίχωσης, ώστε να διαφωτιστούν οι βιοτικές και διατροφικές συνήθειες των κατοίκων της πόλης κατά την πρώιμη περίοδο της αποικίας. Όλες οι συνισταμένες της βιοαρχαιολογικής έρευνας συμβάλλουν στην ανασύσταση του φυσικού περιβάλλοντος και την κατανόηση του διατροφικού και γαστρονομικού πολιτισμού του οικισμού, των αλληλεπιδράσεων μεταξύ ανθρώπων και περιβάλλοντος, και της εδραίωσης νεωτερισμών και της ενσωμάτωσής τους στην κοινωνική ζωή. Τα φθαρτά πολιτισμικά υλικά από το Υπόγειο προσφέρουν ένα εναλλακτικό μέσο και μια σπάνια ευκαιρία να διαφωτιστεί η ιστορία της πρώιμης αποικίας. Πιο συγκεκριμένα, το σύνολο των όστρεων (περ. 330 κιλά) είναι ένα από τα μεγαλύτερα που έχουν βρεθεί έως τώρα στο Αιγαίο οποιασδήποτε χρονικής περιόδου. Υποβοηθούμενη από ξηρό κόσκινο, συλλογή και επίπλευση των 92 δειγμάτων χώματος με ορατά απανθρακωμένα υλικά και ταύτιση και ποσολόγηση των οικοδεδομένων σύμφωνα με κατάλληλα πρωτόκολλα, η καλή διατήρηση του βιοαρχαιολογικού υλικού επέτρεψε λεπτομερή παρατήρηση και αυξημένη δυνατότητα ταύτισης των διαφόρων ειδών και της χρήσης τους.

Η μελέτη ξεκινά με μια περιγραφή του φυσικού περιβάλλοντος γύρω από τη Μεθώνη της εποχής του σιδήρου, στις νοτιοδυτικές ακτές του Θερμαϊκού Κόλπου, με εκτεταμένες λιμνοθάλασσες και εκβολές ποταμών προς βορρά και τα όρη Πιέρια και Όλυμπος προς δυσμάς και νότο. Παλυνολογικά στοιχεία από την Πιερία, τη Βόρεια Ελλάδα και τα Βαλκάνια μαρτυρούν δάση κωνοφόρων και βελανιδιάς σε μεγαλύτερα υψόμετρα κατά την εποχή του σιδήρου και μάλλον την επικράτηση ενός εκτεταμένου δάσους φυλλοβόλων στα χαμηλά υψόμετρα (Κεφάλαιο 20, Appendix I). Η μελέτη των απανθρακωμένων υλικών από το Υπόγειο ταύτισε τόσο δασικά όσο και χαμηλών υψομέτρων είδη, καθώς και άλλα είδη από διάφορα οικοσυστήματα, με κυρίαρχη τη φυλλοβόλο βελανιδιά (*Quercus*). Παλυνολογικά στοιχεία υποδηλώνουν σοβαρή διατάραξη των δασών κωνοφόρων και βελανιδιάς από την πρώιμη εποχή του σιδήρου και εξής. Τα αρχαιοβοτανολογικά και ζωοαρχαιολογικά στοιχεία από το Υπόγειο δείχνουν επίσης συστηματική εκμετάλλευση του περιβάλλοντος τοπίου, υποδηλώνοντας μια πιθανώς εντατική μικτή αγροκτηνοτροφική οικονομία συμβατή με τα αποτελέσματα της γεωαρχαιολογικής έρευνας στην περιοχή.

Τα παράκτια τοπία που ανασυστάθηκαν βάσει της γεωαρχαιολογικής και παλαιοπεριβαλλοντικής έρευνας στην περιοχή δείχνουν ότι περ. το 10.000 π.Χ. το τοπίο του Πλειστόκαινου κατακλύστηκε εξαιτίας της ταχείας ανόδου της στάθμης της θάλασσας και σχηματίστηκε μια εκτεταμένη ρηχή θαλάσσια περιοχή στην πεδιάδα της Θεσσαλονίκης. Η στενή παράκτια πεδιάδα ανατολικά των Πιερίων κατέληγε σε μια ακτή με ρηχά νερά διακοπτόμενη από εκβολές μικρών ποταμών και ήταν μεταβλητή ως προς τις υδρόβιες συνθήκες, εξ αιτίας των τακτικών εισροών γλυκού νερού. Το υπόστρωμα αυτών ήταν αμμώδες με κυμαινόμενη αλμυρότητα, φιλοξενώντας τυπική μαλακιοπανίδα όπως μαρτυρείται από τα πάμπολλα όστρεα στη Μεθώνη. Η παρουσία ομοιογενούς ευρυαλοειδούς μαλακιοπανίδας στο Υπόγειο δείχνει επιπλέον ότι οι αρχαίοι κάτοικοι επισκέπτονταν συχνά και εκμεταλλεύονταν τα αμμώδη-λασπώδη υποστρώματα των εκβολών των ποταμών και των παράκτιων λιμνοθαλασσών στην περιοχή. Τυπική θαλάσσια πανίδα ήταν επίσης παρούσα, σημάδι της αλληλεπίδρασης και εκμετάλλευσης του συνόλου του ενάλιου περιβάλλοντος. Λεπτομερέστερη εξέταση των καταλοίπων μαλακίων δείχνει ότι οι κάτοικοι του οικισμού εστίασαν κυρίως στην εκμετάλλευση των οικοσυστημάτων των εκβολών των ποταμών με στόχο τη μαζική προμήθεια ευρέως διαθέσιμων ειδών υφάλμυρων νερών, κυρίως ενήλικων ατόμων τα οποία συλλέγονταν με απλό εξοπλισμό που δεν έβλαπτε τον πυθμένα και επομένως τον γόνο. Η ποσότητα και συχνότητα των καταλοίπων κυδωνιού, πλέον του 97% του συνόλου (Fig. 10.2), συμφωνεί με την προτίμηση του είδους αυτού καθ' όλες τις περιόδους και σε όλες τις θέσεις της Κεντρικής Μακεδονίας.

Η επίχωση του Υπογείου περιείχε πλήθος βιοαρχαιολογικών καταλοίπων μιας πλούσιας διατροφικής βάσης. Ένας συνδυασμός εξημερωμένων ζώων, δημητριακών, οσπρίων και μαλακίων υφάλμυρων νερών κυριαρχεί στο υλικό. Μεταξύ των ζώων, τα αιγοπρόβατα είναι το κοινότερο είδος, ακολουθούμενο από τους χοίρους και έπειτα τα βοοειδή. Η θνητότητα των αιγοπροβάτων και των χοίρων υποδηλώνει κτηνοτροφία με στόχο πρωτίστως την παραγωγή κρέατος. Η κατάτμηση των πολλών οστών βοοειδών και αιγοπροβάτων υποδηλώνει συχνή εξαγωγή του μυελού, ενώ τα σχετικά ίχνη σε οστά χοίρων είναι λιγότερα, ίσως επειδή ήταν προτιμότερη η όπτηση ολόκληρου του χοίρου ή ολόκληρων μερών του ζώου. Ίχνη φιλεταρίσματος (Fig. 10.1) σε οστά όλων των ειδών με παρόμοια συχνότητα δείχνουν ότι η κατανάλωση του κρέατος γινόταν απευθείας από το οστό. Μεταξύ των βασικών διατροφικών φυτικών ειδών, το μονόκοκκο και δίκοκκο σιτάρι, το αποφλοιωμένο κριθάρι και το κεχρί είναι τα δημητριακά που βρέθηκαν στη Μεθώνη με τη μεγαλύτερη συχνότητα, ενδεικτικά καλλιέργειας και επεξεργασίας καθ' όλη τη διάρκεια του έτους για την κατά το δυνατόν μεγαλύτερη επισιτιστική ασφάλεια. Η ποικιλία δημητριακών στη Μεθώνη, παράλληλα με τα όσπρια τα οποία βελτιώνουν το χώμα, υποδεικνύει ποικιλία γεύσεων, χρωμάτων και 'πιάτων'. Η σχετικά μικρή παρουσία αχύρων και σταχύων στο Υπόγειο δείχνει αποθήκευση αναποφλοίωτου σίτου και καθαρισμό του κάθε φορά πριν από την παρασκευή του φαγητού.

Άλλες δραστηριότητες, όπως το κυνήγι και η συγκομιδή άγριων ειδών, συνέβαλαν όχι μόνο στον εμπλουτισμό των διατροφικών συνηθειών αλλά και στη σφυρηλάτηση κοινωνικών δεσμών και ταυτοτήτων μεταξύ των κατοίκων. Στη Μεθώνη, το κυνήγι ήταν σχετικά σπάνιο, αφού τα ποσοστά των άγριων ζώων (έλαφος, πλατώνι, ζαρκάδι, αγριόχοιρος, αλεπού και λαγός), με συχνότερο τον έλαφο, ήταν μικρά συγκριτικά με των οικόσιτων. Άγριοι καρποί και άλλα βρώσιμα φυτά συλλέγονταν, όμως και αυτά σε ποσοστά παρόμοια των άγριων ζώων· ωστόσο, είναι δύσκολο να ανιχνευτούν και να ποσοτικοποιηθούν χωρίς απανθρακωμένα δείγματα.

Κοσμήματα και τέχνεργα από όστρεα αφθονούν στο προϊστορικό Αιγαίο και πιο συγκεκριμένα στον βορρά, όμως δεν απαντούν παρά μόνο σποραδικά κατά την πρώιμη εποχή του σιδήρου εκτός ταφών. Στην αρχαία Μεθώνη υπάρχουν μόνο λιγοστά διάτρητα όστρεα διαφόρων ειδών, μεταξύ των οποίων συχνότερο το κυδώνι (Fig. 10.3), συμπεριλαμβανομένων φθαρμένων από την έκθεσή τους στη δράση των κυμάτων και φυσικώς διάτρητων δειγμάτων. Σε αντίθεση με άλλες θέσεις της πρώιμης εποχής του σιδήρου στην περιοχή (π.χ. Τούμπα Θεσσαλονίκης), ενδείξεις βαφής υφασμάτων (π.χ. πορφύρας) δεν έχουν βρεθεί έως τώρα στη Μεθώνη.

Η μελέτη ορισμένων από τα πιο σημαντικά βιοαρχαιολογικά ευρήματα από το Υπόγειο της Μεθώνης αναδεικνύει πώς η συστηματική και ολοκληρωμένη μελέτη αυτού του είδους υλικού μπορεί να συμβάλει σε μια λιγότερο αποσπασματική αξιολόγηση των τρόπων ζωής κατά την πρώιμη εποχή του σιδήρου. Ένα μικτό αγροτικό σύστημα με ποικιλία φυτικών και ζωικών ειδών συμπληρωνόταν από τη συστηματική εκμετάλλευση των υδρόβιων οικοσυστημάτων στις εκβολές των ποταμών κοντά στον οικισμό. Η εκμετάλλευση της δασικής και χαμηλής βλάστησης συνέβαλε στη μεταβολή και διαμόρφωση του φυσικού περιβάλλοντος του οικισμού, ενώ άλλες δραστηριότητες, όπως η συλλογή μαλακίων και το κυνήγι, επιδεικνύουν πιθανώς μέριμνα για τη μακροπρόθεσμη βιωσιμότητα και συντήρηση των διατροφικών πηγών. Η εξέταση όλων των κατηγοριών βιοαρχαιολογικών ευρημάτων προσφέρει τη δυνατότητα να ανιχνεύσουμε πτυχές της ζωής που αποτελούν μέρος των κεντρικών κοινωνικών και πολιτισμικών ταυτοτήτων ενός πληθυσμού και υπαγορεύουν τη θέση του στον σύγχρονο κόσμο.

Κεφάλαιο 11. Επιγραφές, graffiti/dipinti και (εμπορικά) σύμβολα στη Μεθώνη (περ. 700 π.Χ.)

Γιάννης Ζ. Τζιφόπουλος

Το επιγραφικό σύνταγμα της Μεθώνης περιλαμβάνει ενεπίγραφα όστρακα κεραμικής από το Υπόγειο και ένα σύνολο ενεπίγραφων βλημάτων σφενδόνης, καθώς και μία ενεπίγραφη αιχμή βέλους, από την πολιορκία της πόλης από τον Φίλιππο Β′ (Κεφάλαιο 28). Μεταξύ της ενεπίγραφης κεραμικής, 191 αγγεία και όστρακα με επιγραφές, graffiti, και (εμπορικά) σύμβολα από το Υπόγειο δημοσιεύθηκαν το 2012. Η πλειονότητα αυτών, 166 αγγεία και όστρακα, φέρουν μη αλφαβητικά σύμβολα, σημεία, graffiti, και ελάχιστα dipinti, πιθανότατα σημεία ιδιοκτησίας ή/και σχετιζόμενα με το εμπόριο. Μεταξύ των υπόλοιπων 25 αμφορέων και αγγείων πόσης, 18 φέρουν αλφαβητικά σύμβολα, σημεία και graffiti που δηλώνουν ιδιοκτησία ή/και σχετίζονται με το εμπόριο. Το παρόν κεφάλαιο παρουσιάζει τα υπόλοιπα επτά, κυρίως αγγεία πόσης με πλήρεις ή αποσπασματικές επιγραφές, όλες δηλώσεις ιδιοκτησίας, σε χρονολογική σειρά βάσει των σχημάτων των γραμμάτων. Τόσο η θέση εύρεσης όσο και η χρονολόγηση είναι αξιοσημείωτη, αφού ανασκαφές στο Βόρειο Αιγαίο έχουν αποδώσει λιγοστά μόνο ενεπίγραφα ευρήματα τόσο πρώιμης χρονολόγησης (Τορώνη, Ποσείδι, Καραμπουρνάκι, Κρανιά Πλαταμώνα). Πέντε από τις επτά επιγραφές της Μεθώνης είναι γραμμένες επί τα λαιά και δύο ες ευθύ, δείχνοντας ότι κάποιες περιοχές του ελληνικού κόσμου χρησιμοποιούσαν και τις δύο κατευθύνσεις στα πρώιμα στάδια της γραφής. Αν και η Μεθώνη ήταν ερετριακή αποικία, η ποικιλία των σχημάτων των γραμμάτων στα κείμενα αυτά (Fig. 11.6) μαρτυρά ότι δεν χρησιμοποιούσαν όλοι οι εγγράμματοι έμποροι και κάτοικοι της πόλης το ερετριακό αλφάβητο. Ως ιδιωτικά κείμενα δηλωτικά ιδιοκτησίας, αυτά τα επτά, συμπεριλαμβανομένου του παλαιότερου επιγράμματος σε ιαμβικό μέτρο (Fig. 11.4), υποδηλώνουν επιπλέον δημόσια έκθεση με φιλοπαίγμονα διάθεση σε συμπόσια, προοίμιο της επέκτασης του αλφαβητισμού και της ανάπτυξης ποιητικών ειδών της λυρική ποίηση.

Κεφάλαιο 12. Γιατί ο αποικισμός της Μεθώνης; Εμπορικοί αμφορείς και η οικονομία του ελληνικού αποικισμού μεταξύ ιστορίας και αρχαιολογίας

Αντώνης Κοτσώνας

Ένα νέο ρεύμα στη σύγχρονη ιστορική έρευνα περί του ελληνικού αποικισμού της Μεσογείου εισηγείται την κατάργηση και αντικατάσταση του όρου «αποικισμός». Ο David Ridgway αμφισβήτησε την αντίληψη ότι ο ελληνικός αποικισμός χαρακτηριζόταν από την επικράτηση πολιτισμικώς και οικονομικώς προηγμένων λαών επί υποδεέστερων εντόπιων πληθυσμών, οι οποίοι είχαν απλώς παθητικό ρόλο σε οποιαδήποτε αλληλεπίδραση, συμπεριλαμβανομένου του εμπορίου. Το παρόν κεφάλαιο ακολουθεί την προσέγγιση αυτή και εξετάζει τους οικονομικούς ωθητικούς και ελκυστικούς παράγοντες στους οποίους οφείλεται η μετακίνηση ελληνικών πληθυσμών σε ξένες χώρες, δίνοντας ιδιαίτερη έμφαση στη Μεθώνη στον Θερμαϊκό Κόλπο, κατά την παράδοση την παλαιότερη (ύστερος 8ος αιώνας π.Χ.) ελληνική αποικία στο Βόρειο Αιγαίο. Το παράδειγμα της Μεθώνης είναι ενδεικτικό της δυνατότητας να αμφισβητηθούν παραδοχές περί των αιτιών του αποικισμού ενώπιον νέων ευρημάτων, με επίκεντρο τους εμπορικούς αμφορείς και το περιεχόμενό τους.

Οι ιστορικοί της ελληνικής αρχαιότητας διαφωνούν ως προς τη σημασία του εμπορίου ως κινήτρου του ελληνικού αποικισμού. Ορισμένοι εμμένουν στην άποψη ότι ήταν δευτερεύουσας σημασίας, άλλοι όμως υποστηρίζουν μια "εκ των κάτωθεν" υπόθεση, κατά την οποία Έλληνες έμποροι εγκαθιστούσαν πρώτα ένα *ἐμπόριον*, το οποίο στη συνέχεια προσέλκυε Έλληνες αποίκους, οι οποίοι με επικεφαλής έναν οικιστή ίδρυαν την αποικία. Ακολουθώντας την προσέγγιση αυτή με σχετική συζήτηση σε συγκεκριμένες θέσεις, το παρόν κεφάλαιο εξετάζει τη σχέση ανάμεσα σε εμπόριο και αποικισμό βάσει ιστορικών μαρτυριών και αρχαιολογικών στοιχείων, μεταξύ των οποίων οι πρώιμοι εμπορικοί αμφορείς από τη Μεθώνη.

Κατά γενική παραδοχή ο ρόλος του εμπορίου στην ίδρυση της ευβοϊκής αποικίας στη Μεθώνη ήταν μηδαμινός, ενώ τα αρχαιολογικά στοιχεία επιβεβαιώνουν τη στενή σχέση ελληνικού αποικισμού και εμπορίου κατά τον ύστερο 8ο αιώνα π.Χ. Οι ιστορικοί έχουν εν πολλοίς βασιστεί στην ιστορία που παραδίδει ο Πλούταρχος, η ιστορικότητα της οποίας καθώς και η χρονολόγηση των σχετικών γεγονότων του 733/732 π.Χ. έχουν γίνει αποδεκτά από τους περισσότερους μελετητές. Ωστόσο, ο παράλιος οικισμός της Μεθώνης, μάλιστα πλάι σε ένα εξαιρετικό αγκυροβόλιο, προϋπήρχε, όπως σημειώνουν ο Πλούταρχος αλλά και δύο μυθολογικές παραδόσεις, και όπως πλέον επιβεβαιώνεται από αρχαιολογικά τεκμήρια (Μέρος I). Η ομοφωνία μεταξύ των ιστορικών σχετικά με τον μικρό ρόλο του εμπορίου στην ίδρυση της Μεθώνης είναι επηρεασμένη από παραδοσιακές αντιλήψεις περί συντηρητικού κοινωνικοπολιτικού συστήματος και αποκλειστικά αγροτικής οικονομίας κατά την πρώιμη αρχαϊκή περίοδο. Το στερεότυπο ενός απομονωμένου και εσωστρεφούς βορειοδυτικού Αιγαίου, με αγροτική οικονομία και υπανάπτυκτη συγκριτικά με νοτιότερες περιοχές οικονομία, έχει αντληθεί από ιστορικές πηγές. Η καθυστερημένη εντατική αρχαιολογική έρευνα πεδίου στο Βόρειο Αιγαίο και η σπανιότητα ολοκληρωμένων δημοσιεύσεων της τοπικής κεραμικής της πρώιμης εποχής του σιδήρου έχουν επίσης συντελέσει σε αυτή την άποψη, αν και πρόσφατα ορισμένοι μελετητές έχουν αναδείξει τον ρόλο του εμπορίου με ιδιαίτερη αναφορά στη Μεθώνη.

Ανασκαφές στη Μεθώνη έχουν αποδώσει πληθώρα στοιχείων ενδεικτικών των εισαγωγών πολλών διαφορετικών προϊόντων και μεταλλουργικών δραστηριοτήτων (Κεφάλαιο 14) κατά τον ύστερο 8ο αιώνα π.Χ. (περίοδο ίδρυσης της αποικίας), και βιοτεχνικών εγκαταστάσεων του 6ου αιώνα π.Χ. (Κεφάλαιο 19), καθώς και λεπτής κεραμικής χρονολογούμενης πριν από την ίδρυση της αποικίας (Κεφάλαια 7, 9). Όμως ο πλέον αξιόπιστος δείκτης εμπορικών ανταλλαγών είναι οι εμπορικοί αμφορείς. Πρόσφατες έρευνες παρουσιάζουν ένα προσεγγιστικό πλαίσιο του μεγάλου συνόλου εμπορικών αμφορέων από το Υπόγειο στη Μεθώνη, μέσω στρωματογραφίας, τυπολογίας, μορφολογίας, πετρογραφίας, και ανάλυσης οργανικών και ανόργανων υπολειμμάτων. Οι αμφορείς από τη Μεθώνη υποστηρίζουν την άποψη ότι το χονδρικό εμπόριο τροφίμων ξεκίνησε τον 8ο αιώνα π.Χ. και προτρέπουν να αναθεωρήσουμε παλαιότερες απόψεις σχετικά με το εμπόριο στη Μεσόγειο κατά την πρώιμη εποχή του σιδήρου. Οι ενεπίγραφοι εμπορικοί αμφορείς από το Υπόγειο, δημοσιευμένοι το 2012, είναι πολλών διαφορετικών τύπων. Η κατά πολύ μεγαλύτερη ομάδα των ανεπίγραφων αποκαλύπτει πολλά ακόμα παραδείγματα των ίδιων τύπων, αλλά και φοινικικών αμφορέων, και πολλών άλλων άγνωστης προέλευσης.

Ο συχνότερα αντιπροσωπευόμενος τύπος στο Υπόγειο της Μεθώνης είναι ο αμφορέας του Θερμαϊκού Κόλπου (1/5 του συνόλου) (Figs. 12.2a–b), επίσης γνωστός ως αμφορέας του Βόρειου Αιγαίου. Ο τύπος αυτός ξεκίνησε να παράγεται τον πρώιμο 8ο αιώνα π.Χ. και συνεπώς προηγείται χρονολογικά του αποικισμού του Βόρειου Αιγαίου, και μάλιστα της παραγωγής αμφορέων στα περισσότερα μέρη του Αιγαίου. Η πρώιμη χρονολόγησή τους, η αποκεντρωμένη παραγωγή τους, και η εκτεταμένη διασπορά τους αμφισβητούν ανοιχτά εικασίες μιας υπανάπτυκτης αγροτικής οικονομίας γύρω από τον Θερμαϊκό Κόλπο. Το Υπόγειο απέδωσε οκτώ παραδείγματα ενός όμοιου τύπου, όμως παλαιότερου και με πηλό λεπτότερης σύστασης. Οι αμφορείς αυτοί, τύπου Catling I και I/II (μεταβατικός τύπος), παράγονταν σε διαφορετικά μέρη του Κεντρικού και Βόρειου Αιγαίου από τον 11ο έως και τον 9ο αιώνα π.Χ.

Πολύ συχνό εύρημα από το Υπόγειο είναι και οι αμφορείς της Ανατολικής Ελλάδας, μεταξύ των οποίων οι σαμιακοί (Fig. 12.5a–b) αποτελούν τον συνηθέστερο ενεπίγραφο εισηγμένο τύπο, ακολουθούμενο από τους λέσβιους. Οι χιακοί αμφορείς είναι λιγότεροι από αυτούς της αρχαϊκής περιόδου (Κεφάλαιο 21), και 20 πρώιμοι μιλησιακοί είναι ασυνήθιστοι για το Βόρειο Αιγαίο. Το Υπόγειο περιείχε ακόμα 15 αττικούς και ευβοϊκούς αμφορείς τύπου SOS, και μόλις τρεις κορινθιακούς. Τέλος, πέντε φοινικικοί αμφορείς από το Υπόγειο συνιστούν το μεγαλύτερο σύνολο στο Αιγαίο της πρώιμης εποχής του σιδήρου μετά από αυτό του Κομμού. Πολλοί αμφορείς άγνωστου τύπου υποδεικνύουν πολλά ακόμα κέντρα παραγωγής στην πρώιμη Ελλάδα σε σχέση με τα έως τώρα γνωστά, στοιχείο με αντίκτυπο στην επικρατούσα εικόνα για την πρώιμη ελληνική οικονομία. Ανάλυση υπολειμμάτων δείχνει λιπαρά οξέα (έλαια;) σε κάποιους αμφορείς (συμπεριλαμβανομένων χιακών), ενώ ρητίνη στο εσωτερικό λέσβιων αμφορέων και κερί σε αμφορείς τύπου SOS και Θερμαϊκού Κόλπου ίσως ήταν στεγανωτικά υλικά.

Η πρώιμη χρονολόγηση, η μεγάλη ποσότητα και ποικιλία τύπων, και τα πολυάριθμα εμπορικά σημεία στους εμπορικούς αμφορείς από το Υπόγειο της Μεθώνης υποδηλώνουν μια σύνθετη οικονομική δραστηριότητα κατά τις πρώτες δεκαετίες της αποικίας. Άλλωστε η Μεθώνη και η περιοχή της προσέφεραν οικονομικά κίνητρα σχετικά με φυσικούς πόρους (ξυλεία) και μεταλλουργία. Ήδη από τον 8ο αιώνα π.Χ. η οικονομία της περιοχής αυτής ήταν μικτή και το εμπόριο αναπτυγμένο σε κλίμακα που δεν έχει ακόμα εκτιμηθεί ορθώς, ενώ σημαντικές οικονομικές πρωτοβουλίες λαμβάνονταν από τους εντόπιους πληθυσμούς. Συνεπώς δεν επιτρέπεται πλέον ιστορικά αφηγήματα και γνωστικοί χάρτες να αντιμετωπίζουν την περιοχή του Θερμαϊκού Κόλπου ως μια παθητική οικονομικώς και πολιτισμικώς περιοχή της περιφέρειας.

Κεφάλαιο 13. Μεταλλουργική δραστηριότητα στη Μεθώνη: Η μαρτυρία των λίθινων τέχνεργων από το Υπόγειο

Ιωάννης Μάνος και Ιωάννης Βλασταρίδης

Η παρούσα μελέτη κατέγραψε 86 λίθινα μακροτέχνεργα από το Υπόγειο της Μεθώνης, των οποίων καταλογογραφούνται 18. Αν και φέρουν ίχνη κατεργασίας, δεν πρόκειται για προϊόντα πελεκητής λιθοτεχνίας, ενώ ορισμένα χρησιμοποιήθηκαν στη φυσική τους μορφή. Το σύνολο αυτό ήταν κατανεμημένο σε επιχώσεις συνολικού βάθους έως και 11,70 μ. εντός ενός ορύγματος (Fig. 13.1a–b), το οποίο παρουσιάζει διαφορετικές φάσεις πλήρωσης, επιβεβαιώνοντας τις παρατηρήσεις του ανασκαφέα. Πέντε αντικείμενα βρέθηκαν στην κατώτερη επίχωση, εκείνη της Φάσης I, ένα ομοιόμορφο στρώμα που αποτέθηκε σε πολύ σύντομο χρονικό διάστημα. Δύο ακόμα αντικείμενα βρέθηκαν στην επίχωση της Φάσης II. Μεταξύ αυτής και της Φάσης I μεσολαβεί επίχωση πάχους περ. 2 μ. χωρίς λίθινα μακροτέχνεργα. Έξι αντικείμενα, τα οποία βρέθηκαν σε συνάρτηση με το στρώμα πηλού που σφραγίζει την επίχωση της Φάσης II, ανήκουν στη Φάση III. Το πολυπληθέστερο σύνολο λίθινων τεχνέργων στην επίχωση του Υπογείου, ανερχόμενο σε 43 αντικείμενα, ανήκει στη Φάση III, πάχους περ. 4 μ., και παρουσιάζει ομοιόμορφη κατανομή στον κατακόρυφο άξονα. Η συχνότητα λίθινων τέχνεργων πάνω από τις επιχώσεις των Φάσεων I–III είναι σαφώς μειωμένη, ενώ απουσιάζουν τέχνεργα από πυριγενή πετρώματα.

Στο σύνολο των αντικειμένων, δέκα παρουσιάζουν εμφανή ίχνη θερμικής αλλοίωσης, συμπεριλαμβανομένων εργαλείων της εποχής του λίθου τα οποία επαναχρησιμοποιήθηκαν ως δομικό υλικό σε πυροτεχνικές εγκαταστάσεις (Fig. 13.2). Η πρώτη ύλη περιλαμβάνει πυριγενή πετρώματα, ιζηματογενή με λεπτόκοκκη και χονδρόκοκκη διαβάθμιση, μεταμορφωμένα (π.χ. μάρμαρο, σερπεντινίτης, αμφιβολίτης), ορυκτά (π.χ. χαλαζίας) και άλλα αδιάγνωστα. Είκοσι αντικείμενα χρησιμοποιήθηκαν στη φυσική τους μορφή. Πρόκειται για κροκάλες, οι μισές από τις οποίες ανήκουν στη Φάση III, ενώ έξι κυριαρχούν μορφολογικά στα ανώτερα στρώματα. Αντιθέτως, 27 πλακοειδή αντικείμενα ήταν κατανεμημένα σε όλο το βάθος της επίχωσης του Υπογείου.

Η μεταλλουργία διακρίνεται σε δύο στάδια: (α) την παραγωγή του μετάλλου, και (β) τη μεταλλοτεχνία. Η επεξεργασία κατά το πρώτο στάδιο περιλαμβάνει θραύση και τήξη του μεταλλεύματος, συχνά κοντά στο μεταλλείο (Fig. 13.3). Η επεξεργασία κατά το δεύτερο στάδιο περιλαμβάνει, μετά τη χύτευση, σφυρηλάτηση, ανόπτηση, τριβή, λείανση, διακόσμηση και αφύγρανση (Fig. 13.4). Η υλικοτεχνική υποδομή για τη σφυρηλάτηση αποτελείται από παθητικά εργαλεία με επιφάνειες κρούσης άλλοτε κυρτές (Fig. 13.5) και άλλοτε κοίλες, επίπεδες, κυλινδρικές (Fig. 13.6) ή κωνικές (Fig. 13), και από ενεργητικά εργαλεία με επιφάνειες σφαιρικές (Fig. 13.8), κυρτές (Fig. 13.9) ή επίπεδες (Fig. 13.10). Η μορφοποίηση του μετάλλου μπορεί επίσης να επιτευχθεί με εφαρμογή έμμεσης πίεσης χρησιμοποιώντας κατάλληλα εργαλεία, ενώ η επιφάνεια του μετάλλου ενδέχεται να υποστεί τριβή και λείανση με λίθινα εργαλεία, αρχικά από χονδρόκοκκο πέτρωμα (Fig. 13.11) και από λεπτόκοκκο στα τελικά στάδια της κατεργασίας (Fig. 13.12). Η διακόσμηση πραγματοποιείται με έμμεση ή άμεση κρούση (Fig. 13.14–13.17).

Ο συνδυασμός ανάλυσης των τεχνο-λειτουργικών παραμέτρων, μακροσκοπικής παρατήρησης και κατηγοριοποίησης των ιχνών χρήσης επιτρέπει την αναγνώριση του συνόλου ως εργαλειακής υποδομής ενός εργαστηρίου μεταλλουργίας και μεταλλοτεχνίας, το οποίο ανανέωνε και ανακύκλωνε τα λίθινα εργαλεία του. Το λιθοτεχνικό σύνολο από το Υπόγειο ερμηνεύεται ως εργαλειακός εξοπλισμός, ο οποίος χρησιμοποιείτο για κρούση και τριβή και μαρτυρά εντονότερη εργαστηριακή δραστηριότητα κατά τη Φάση III (ύστερη γεωμετρική περίοδος έως περ. 690 π.Χ.).

Κεφάλαιο 14. Πήλινα σκεύη μεταλλουργίας από το Υπόγειο

Samuel Verdan

Το Υπόγειο στη Μεθώνη απέδωσε διάφορα κατάλοιπα μεταλλουργικών δραστηριοτήτων: απορρίμματα, σκωρίες εκκαμίνευσης, και θραύσματα πυρίμαχων πήλινων σκευών. Πολυπληθές και υψηλής ποιότητας, το σύνολο αυτό είναι μοναδικό για τον ύστερο 8ο – πρώιμο 7ο αιώνα π.Χ. στην Ελλάδα, προσφέρει πληροφορίες σχετικά με τις τέχνες και βιοτεχνικές δραστηριότητες που εξασκούνταν συμπληρωματικά προς την εμπορική δραστηριότητα, και διαφωτίζει σχετικά με τις μεταλλουργικές τεχνικές της πρώιμης αρχαϊκής περιόδου, ιδίως αυτές της χρυσοχοΐας. Μία προκαταρκτική οπτική εξέταση των πήλινων σκευών μεταλλουργίας, περίπου 1.000 πήλινων τέχνεργων, αναγνώρισε ενδείξεις επεξεργασίας σιδήρου, χαλκού και χρυσού. Τα ευρήματα του Υπογείου υποδηλώνουν ότι η επεξεργασία σιδήρου στη Μεθώνη περιοριζόταν στη σιδηρουργία, ίσως για να εξυπηρετήσει την επεξεργασία άλλων μετάλλων. Η επεξεργασία χαλκού μαρτυρείται σε 44 θραύσματα χοάνης (χωνευτηριού) ή καμίνου (Fig. 14.1), λιγοστά ακροφύσια (Fig. 14.2) και πήλινες μήτρες για την παραγωγή χυτών κοσμημάτων (Figs. 14.3–4). Υπολείμματα τήξης χρυσού σώζονται σε μορφή σφαιριδίων ή σβώλων και αποτυπωμάτων αυτών σε χονδροειδή δοχεία τήξης (Figs. 14.5–8), μάλλον για την παραγωγή ράβδων (Figs. 14.9–10) από τοπικές προσχωματικές αποθέσεις χρυσού. Τα ευρήματα της Μεθώνης αποτελούν ισχυρές ενδείξεις ότι ο μακεδονικός χρυσός ήταν αντικείμενο εντατικής εκμετάλλευσης στον ύστερο 8ο – πρώιμο 7ο αιώνα π.Χ. από τους Ερετριείς, και ανακαλούν την αναφορά του Στράβωνα (5.4.9) περί ευβοϊκών χρυσείων στις Πιθηκούσες.

Κεφάλαιο 15. Μεταλλικά ευρήματα από το Υπόγειο
John K. Papadopoulos

Μεταλλικά αντικείμενα βρέθηκαν σε όλες τις φάσεις του Υπογείου (Table 15.1). Το παρόν κεφάλαιο παρουσιάζει ένα αντιπροσωπευτικό δείγμα χαλκών, σιδηρών και μολύβδινων αντικειμένων, κυρίως του ύστερου 8ου – πρώιμου 7ου αιώνα π.Χ., παράλληλα με τα μεταλλικά αντικείμενα από τον Ανατολικό και Δυτικό Λόφο (Κεφάλαιο 26). Βρέθηκε επίσης πλήθος σκωριών εκκαμίνευσης, θραύσματα ελασμάτων (απορρίμματα μεταλλουργίας, σπασμένα αντικείμενα και αποκόμματα ή ανακυκλωμένα μέταλλα). Τα χαλκά αντικείμενα περιλαμβάνουν κοσμήματα (περίαπτα, πόρπες και περόνες διαφόρων τύπων, χάντρες και δακτυλίους, αμφίκυρτα κωνικά κομβία «tutuli»), καθώς και εργαλεία, όπως βελόνες, μαχαίρια, σφιγκτήρες, άγκιστρα, μεταξύ των οποίων και ψαρέματος, και καρφιά. Τα σιδηρά αντικείμενα περιλαμβάνουν όπλα (αιχμές δοράτων και βελών, λεπίδες μαχαιριών) και διάφορα εργαλεία, όπως πελέκεις, σκεπάρνια, σφύρες, σμίλες και οπείς. Ιδιαίτερο ενδιαφέρον παρουσιάζουν θραύσματα λαβίδων ή σκάλευθρων μεταλλουργών (Figs. 15.50–15.51), γνωστών από παραστάσεις αττικών μελανόμορφων αγγείων της αρχαϊκής εποχής (Fig. 15.52). Τον κατάλογο των 107 αντικειμένων ολοκληρώνουν μολύβδινα σταθμία και σύνδεσμοι.

Κεφάλαιο 16. Πήλινα σύνεργα υφαντουργίας από τη Μεθώνη: σφονδύλια και υφαντικά βάρη από το Υπόγειο
Sarah P. Morris

Μια επιλογή υφαντουργικών αντικειμένων σχετικών με το γνέσιμο και την ύφανση, ενταγμένων σε πέντε κατηγορίες κατά μέγεθος και σχήμα, αντιπροσωπεύει οικιακά σύνεργα απορριμμένα σε όλες τις φάσεις του Υπογείου (Fig. 16.1). Τα 128 καταγεγραμμένα σφονδύλια ανήκουν σε κωνικούς, αμφικωνικούς και δισκοειδείς τύπους με βάρος έως 100 γρ. (Figs. 16.2–3). Τα υφαντικά βάρη ανήκουν σε πυραμιδοειδείς (περ. 50 δείγματα) και δισκοειδείς τύπους (Fig. 16.4). Τουλάχιστον 15 πηνία (Fig. 16.5) και ημισφαιρικά βάρη (Fig. 16.6) αντιπροσωπεύουν λιγότερο κοινούς τύπους, γνωστούς ομώς στη Μακεδονία, οι οποίοι σύμφωνα με τα ευρήματα του Υπογείου είχαν μακρά διάρκεια χρήσης.

Κεφάλαιο 17. Δισκοειδή όστρακα από το Υπόγειο
John K. Papadopoulos

Μια επιλογή 41 κυκλικού σχήματος οστράκων, αποκομμένων από τοιχώματα αγγείων, χωρίς διανοιγμένη οπή έχουν καταγραφεί (44 επιπλέον παραδείγματα από το Υπόγειο), διαστάσεων 0,09–0,21 μ. και βάρους 1,5–125 γρ., αντιπροσωπεύει μια κατηγορία αντικειμένων που εμφανίζεται συχνά στην Ελλάδα κατά την 1η χιλιετία π.Χ., της οποίας όμως η λειτουργία παραμένει αμφίβολη. Είτε πρόκειται για πούλια παιχνιδιού, είτε για πώματα, είτε εξυπηρετούσαν την προσωπική υγιεινή, τα περισσότερα από τα καταλογογραφημένα παραδείγματα απορρίφθηκαν στις πρώιμες φάσεις του Υπογείου, και επομένως φαίνεται ότι ήταν αντικείμενα κοινής χρήσης.

ΤΟΜΟΣ 2

ΜΕΡΟΣ III. Η Μεθώνη στην αρχαϊκή και κλασική περίοδο

Κεφάλαιο 18. Το Κτήριο Α στον Ανατολικό Λόφο της αρχαίας Μεθώνης

Samantha L. Martin

Ο Ανατολικός Λόφος αποτελούσε άλλοτε μέρος ενός ακρωτηρίου που πρόβαλε βορειοανατολικά στον Θερμαϊκό Κόλπο, αλλά σήμερα σώζεται μόνο το δυτικό τμήμα του, όπου βρίσκεται η αρχαία αγορά της Μεθώνης (Fig. 18.1). Το Κτήριο Α, ένα από τα πρώτα κτήρια που κατασκευάστηκαν γύρω από την αγορά (Fig. 18.2), είναι κρίσιμης σημασίας για την κατανόηση της τοπογραφίας της αρχαίας πόλης και για τη χρονολόγηση των δημοσίων κτηρίων στην Ελλάδα του 6ου αιώνα π.Χ. και εξής. Μαζί με τα Κτήρια Β–Ε και την τετράγωνη πλατεία στο μέσον (Figs. 17.2–3), αποτελεί το αρχαιότερο έως τώρα γνωστό δείγμα δημόσιας μνημειακής αρχιτεκτονικής σε αστικό οικισμό στη Μακεδονία.

Τρεις κύριες οικοδομικές φάσεις ορίζουν μια επιμήκη αίθουσα, χωρισμένη σε τρία διαμερίσματα, με δύο ακανόνιστου σχήματος προσκτίσματα στη νότια πλευρά και προσθήκη μιας στοάς στην κλασική περίοδο (Fig. 18.3). Οι πρώτες δύο φάσεις, χρονολογούμενες στον πρώιμο και ύστερο 6ο αιώνα π.Χ., χαρακτηρίζονται από ισόδομη δόμηση με δόμους από τοπικό ασβεστόλιθο και πλίνθινη ανωδομή επίσης κατά το ισόδομο σύστημα (Fig. 18.13), αλλά και τμήματα παλαιότερων τοίχων αργολιθοδομής και πολυγωνικής δόμησης (Figs. 18.19, 18.26). Στην τελική φάση του 5ου αιώνα π.Χ. προστέθηκε μια στοά, πλάτους περ. 2,5 μ., κατά μήκος της βόρειας πλευράς, με μάλλον ξύλινους κίονες επί του λίθινου στυλοβάτη (Fig. 18.29). Σύμφωνα με τα ευρήματα, το Κτήριο Α κατασκευάστηκε για να φιλοξενήσει εμπορικές και βιοτεχνικές δραστηριότητες, οι οποίες χαρακτηρίζουν αυτό το τμήμα της αγοράς, έως την πολιορκία του 354 π.Χ., όταν κατά τα φαινόμενα είχε καταληφθεί από μαχητές μέχρι την καταστροφή του (Κεφάλαιο 29).

Κεφάλαιο 19.
(a) Κεραμικά εργαστήρια της αρχαίας Μεθώνης

Ματθαίος Μπέσιος

Όπως σημειώθηκε στο Κεφάλαιο 1, η αρχαία Μεθώνη καταλαμβάνει μια ευνοϊκή παράλια θέση, η οποία βρίσκεται επιπλέον σε άμεση γειτνίαση με τον κύριο οδικό άξονα βορρά-νότου κατά την αρχαιότητα, θέση στην οποία οφείλεται η ακμή του οικισμού ιδίως κατά την ύστερη γεωμετρική και την αρχαϊκή περίοδο. Επιπρόσθετη σπουδαιότητα προσέδωσε η αποκάλυψη, για πρώτη φορά στη Βόρεια Πιερία, καλά διατηρημένων αρχιτεκτονικών καταλοίπων, μεταξύ των οποίων και το διοικητικό και εμπορικό κέντρο της πόλης, η αγορά. Τα ευρήματα υποδεικνύουν έντονη βιοτεχνική δραστηριότητα στην αγορά κατά την αρχαϊκή και κλασική περίοδο, και περιλαμβάνουν δύο μερικώς εντοπισμένους κλιβάνους στα Κτήρια Α και Β, οι οποίοι πρόκειται να ερευνηθούν περαιτέρω στο μέλλον.

Οι ανασκαφές στην κορυφή του Δυτικού Λόφου αποκάλυψαν κατάλοιπα μιας σαφώς βιοτεχνικής περιοχής. Πρόκειται πιο συγκεκριμένα για τουλάχιστον τρία μερικώς ανασκαμμένα κτήρια (Fig. 19.1), τα οποία βρίσκονταν σε χρήση από το δεύτερο ήμισυ του 7ου αιώνα π.Χ. έως τα μέσα του 6ου αιώνα π.Χ. Τα κτήρια αυτά ήταν απλής κατασκευής και περιείχαν ελάχιστα θραύσματα κεράμων, επομένως ήταν μάλλον στεγασμένα με φθαρτά υλικά. Στα στοιχεία της βιοτεχνικής δραστηριότητας περιλαμβάνονται μικρού μεγέθους λάκκοι για την τήξη χαλκού στο δάπεδο του Χώρου 2 του Κτηρίου Α και ίχνη φωτιάς και τεμάχια τηγμένου χαλκού στον Χώρο 3, καθώς και θραύσματα λίθινων μητρών, πήλινων χωνευτηριών κ.ά. στον Χώρο 3 και τους γειτονικούς σε αυτόν χώρους. Επιπλέον, οι περισσότεροι χώροι στην περιοχή αυτή απέδωσαν άφθονα απορρίμματα διαφόρων σταδίων της κατεργασίας ελεφαντόδοντου (Fig. 1.37). Οι ανασκαφές αποκάλυψαν ακόμα δύο κεραμεικούς κλιβάνους στον Χώρο 4 του Κτηρίου Α, έναν μεγάλο μάλλον υπαίθριο ή ίσως μερικώς στεγασμένο χώρο, όπως συχνά διαθέτουν τα κεραμικά εργαστήρια. (Figs. 19.2–3). Αμέσως δυτικά των δύο αυτών κλιβάνων, ένα παχύ γκρίζου χρώματος στρώμα ενδεχομένως σχετίζεται με κάποιο εργαστήριο, αφού περιείχε μεγάλη ποσότητα κεραμικής από την Κόρινθο, την Αττική, το ανατολικό Αιγαίο, και άλλες περιοχές, καθώς και πλήθος τεφρόχρωμης κεραμικής, όχι όμως και απορρίμματα ή αποτυχημένα κατά την όπτηση αγγεία, ώστε να συνδεθούν ασφαλώς με το εργαστήριο αυτό. Η κύρια συμβολή της ανασκαφικής έρευνας στη Μεθώνη είναι ότι πλέον διαθέτουμε έναν βιοτεχνικό οικισμό, όπου παράγονταν όλων των ειδών προϊόντα από διάφορα υλικά, είτε για να καλύψουν την τοπική ζήτηση είτε για να πάρουν τον δρόμο του περιφερειακού και υπερπόντιου εμπορίου.

(b) Αρχαϊκή κεραμική από την ακρόπολη (Δυτικός Λόφος) της αρχαίας Μεθώνης
Ματθαίος Μπέσιος και Κωνσταντίνος Νούλας

Όπως σημειώθηκε ανωτέρω, η συμβολή της ανασκαφικής έρευνας στη Μεθώνη από το 2003 έγκειται στο ότι τεκμηριώθηκε ένα σημαντικό βιοτεχνικό κέντρο, το οποίο παρήγαγε αντικείμενα από χρυσό, άργυρο, χαλκό, σίδηρο, ελεφαντόδοντο, οστό, κέρατο ελάφου και υαλί. Επιπλέον αυτών των πολυτελών υλικών, των οποίων η κατεργασία απαιτούσε εξειδίκευση, κεραμικά εργαστήρια κάλυπταν τις καθημερινές ανάγκες με απλά τεχνικά μέσα. Από την ύστερη γεωμετρική περίοδο, τα κεραμικά εργαστήρια της πόλης παρήγαγαν μεγάλη ποικιλία κεραμικών ειδών με σαφείς επιδράσεις από την Εύβοια, την τοπική μακεδονική παράδοση, την Κόρινθο, και πολύ πιθανόν επίσης από το Ανατολικό Αιγαίο. Στο κεφάλαιο αυτό παρουσιάζεται η κεραμική της αρχαϊκής περιόδου από τον Δυτικό Λόφο της Μεθώνης, ξεκινώντας από τμήματα πίθων της πρώιμης εποχής του σιδήρου και κυκλικούς αποθηκευτικούς λάκκους, οι οποίοι αργότερα χρησίμευσαν ως απορριμματικοί (Figs. 1.31–32). Οι περισσότεροι φαίνεται ότι επιχώθηκαν στο δεύτερο τέταρτο του 7ου αιώνα π.Χ. με κορινθιακή κεραμική και αγγεία του Ανατολικού Αιγαίου, μεταξύ των οποίων χιακοί αμφορείς και ιωνικές κύλικες, καθώς και τοπική και εισηγμένη τεφρόχρωμη κεραμική. Στα τοπικά εργαστήρια θα πρέπει να αποδοθούν γραπτά ανοιχτά αγγεία, ο διάκοσμος των οποίων διατηρεί γεωμετρικά στοιχεία (π.χ. Fig. 19.4). Το σημαντικότερο σύνολο αρχαϊκής κεραμικής ανασκάφηκε στην κεντρική περιοχή του πλατώματος της ακρόπολης, όπου αποκαλύφθηκαν τρία κτήρια σαφώς εργαστηριακού χαρακτήρα. Η πλουσιότερη σε ευρήματα φάση τους χρονολογείται στο τέλος του πρώτου μισού του 6ου αιώνα π.Χ. και παρουσιάζει εμφανή ίχνη πυρκαγιάς, ίσως συνέπεια της ευρείας χρήσης της φωτιάς στις δραστηριότητες που λάμβαναν χώρα στα κτήρια αυτά σε συνδυασμό με τα φθαρτά υλικά στην κατασκευή τους. Το αδιατάρακτο στρώμα καταστροφής απέδωσε πλήθος κινητών ευρημάτων, ιδιαιτέρως κεραμικών (Fig. 19.5).

Πρόκειται για έναν ακμάζοντα οικισμό σε επικοινωνία με πολλά διαφορετικά εμπορικά κέντρα του αρχαίου κόσμου. Αυτό προκύπτει από την ποικιλία των εμπορικών αμφορέων με παραδείγματα από την Αττική, τη Χίο, τη Σάμο, τη Λέσβο, τη Μίλητο και την Κόρινθο, καθώς και έναν λακωνικό (Κεφάλαιο 21). Έχουν ακόμα συλλεχθεί τύποι αμφορέων άγνωστης προέλευσης, μεταξύ των οποίων θα πρέπει να αναγνωριστεί η τοπική παραγωγή της Μεθώνης αλλά και της ευρύτερης περιοχής του Θερμαϊκού Κόλπου, πολλοί εκ των οποίων φέρουν εγχάρακτα σημεία και γράμματα (Fig. 21.10). Όσον αφορά τη λεπτή κεραμική, η συντριπτική πλειονότητα των αγγείων πόσης είναι κορινθιακά (Figs. 19.6–9) με αμέσως μικρότερη ομάδα εκείνη των εργαστηρίων του Ανατολικού Αιγαίου, ενώ η Αττική παραγωγή αντιπροσωπεύεται από θραύσματα κρατήρων, κυλίκων (Fig. 19.10=23.2) και πινακίων. Τα περισσότερα από τα επιτραπέζια αγγεία ανήκουν στην τοπική παραγωγή του ευρύτερου Θερμαϊκού Κόλπου, και ένας γραπτός αμφορέας ανήκει σε εκείνη της Χαλκιδικής (Fig. 19.11). Ένα σταθερό ποσοστό επί του συνόλου καταλαμβάνει η τεφρόχρωμη κεραμική, η οποία παρουσιάζει ευδιάκριτες διαφορές ως προς την ποιότητά της.

Κεφάλαιο 20. Ο ρόλος της Μεθώνης στο μακεδονικό εμπόριο ξυλείας

Άγγελος Μπούφαλης

Η παρούσα μελέτη προτείνει την Πιερία ως την πηγή της μακεδονικής ξυλείας και τη Μεθώνη ως τον κύριο λιμένα για την εξαγωγή της, βάσει γεωγραφικών, παλαιοπεριβαλλοντικών και βοτανολογικών δεδομένων, σε συνδυασμό με ιστορικά και αρχαιολογικά τεκμήρια. Η μακεδονική ξυλεία, γνωστή από τα έργα του Θεόφραστου και του Πλίνιου του πρεσβύτερου, θεωρείτο η καλύτερη σε Αιγαίο και Μαύρη Θάλασσα, ενώ ιστορικές πηγές μαρτυρούν τις προμήθειες των Αθηναίων σε ναυπηγήσιμη ξυλεία, κουπιά και πίσσα κατά τον 5ο και 4ο αιώνα π.Χ., όχι όμως και το πώς ακριβώς λειτουργούσε το εμπόριο αυτό.

Κατά τους Περσικούς Πολέμους ενδέχεται οι Μακεδόνες να προμήθευαν τους Αθηναίους με ξυλεία για τον πρώτο τους στόλο. Δασικά είδη της Πιερίας, ιδίως κωνοφόρα και πιο συγκεκριμένα η πεύκη (*Pinus nigra* και *sylvestris*) και η ελάτη (*Abies borisii regis*), ήταν τα πλέον κατάλληλα για σκάφη και κουπιά, ενώ διαθέτουν ρητίνη, από την οποία παράγεται η πίσσα. Στα Πιέρια όρη συναντάται η υποαλπική ζώνη κωνοφόρων, όπου φύεται το μοναδικό δάσος του είδους *P. sylvestris* στη Μακεδονία (Figs. 20.2–3) άνωθεν ενός εκτεταμένου δάσους οξιάς-ελάτης και *P. nigra*. Ορισμένες ασυνέπειες στην πραγματεία του Θεόφραστου υποδηλώνουν ότι οι πληροφορίες του μάλλον συνέχεαν ορισμένα είδη εξαιτίας τοπικών διαφορών στην ονομασία των δένδρων. Επομένως, ενδέχεται με τον όρο *ελάτη* ο Θεόφραστος (ή ο πληροφοριοδότης του) να εννοούσε ένα είδος πεύκης, συγκεκριμένα το *P. sylvestris*. Η παρουσία αυτού του είδους σε συνδυασμό με τη μεγάλη ποικιλία δασικών ειδών (Appendix 2) καθιστούσε το δάσος των Πιερίων μια πρώτης τάξης πηγή ναυπηγικής και ναυπηγήσιμης ξυλείας. Τα παλαιότερα δείγματα γύρης από την Πιερία χρονολογούνται μόλις στην ελληνιστική περίοδο και τότε τα στοιχεία δείχνουν επιλεκτική υλοτόμηση ελάτης και σημύδας. Ωστόσο, στα απανθρακωμένα ξύλα από το Υπόγειο (περ. 700 π.Χ.) περιλαμβάνονται δείγματα ορεινών πεύκων (Chapter 10).

Οι πλησιέστεροι στα Πιέρια όρη λιμένες ελέγχονταν από τις πόλεις Μεθώνη και Πύδνα (Fig. 20.1). Μια σειρά αθηναϊκών ψηφισμάτων (Fig. 2.1) παρέχουν οικονομικές διευκολύνσεις στους Μεθωναίους, ώστε να εξακολουθήσουν να εξυπηρετούν τους Αθηναίους, μάλλον σχετικά με την προμήθεια ξυλείας, ένα μέλημα έκδηλο στη συνθήκη του 423 π.Χ. με τον Περδίκκα, η οποία απαγορεύει την εξαγωγή κουπιών, εκτός αν αυτά προορίζονταν για την Αθήνα (*IG* I[3] 89). Η πρόσβαση σε πρώτης τάξης ξυλεία, η εγγύτητα στη Μακεδονία, και η καταλληλότητα του λιμένα έθεσαν τη Μεθώνη στο προσκήνιο των πολιτικών και στρατιωτικών εξελίξεων της κλασικής περιόδου και του ανταγωνισμού ανάμεσα σε δύο μεγάλες δυνάμεις, έως ότου το 354 π.Χ. καταστράφηκε ολοκληρωτικά από τον Φίλιππο Β΄.

Κεφάλαιο 21. Εμπόριο στο αρχαϊκό Βόρειο Αιγαίο: Εμπορικοί αμφορείς από τον Δυτικό Λόφο της Μεθώνης

Αλεξάνδρα Κασσέρη

Τρία κτήρια της αρχαϊκής περιόδου με βιοτεχνικά κατάλοιπα στον Δυτικό Λόφο της Μεθώνης (Figs. 1.33, 19.1) βρέθηκαν καλυμμένα από ένα στρώμα καταστροφής του περ. 550 π.Χ., με άφθονη κεραμική, οπού κυριαρχούν τα αγγεία μεταφοράς (αμφορείς), τα οποία αποτελούν το αντικείμενο της συμβολής αυτής. Το πλέον χαρακτηριστικό στοιχείο του συνόλου αυτού είναι η ποικιλία των τύπων, τόσο εισηγμένων από διάφορα κέντρα παραγωγής σε Νότια και Ανατολική Ελλάδα όσο και τοπικής παραγωγής από το Βόρειο Αιγαίο.

Μεταξύ των αμφορέων της αρχαϊκής περιόδου από τον Δυτικό Λόφο η πολυπληθέστερη ομάδα προέρχεται από τη Χίο (τουλάχιστον 15 αγγεία), και σε συνδυασμό με παλαιότερα παραδείγματα από το Υπόγειο (Κεφάλαιο 12) μαρτυρά τις εισαγωγές από την Ανατολική Ελλάδα από τον 8ο έως και τα μέσα του 6ου αιώνα π.Χ. Τουλάχιστον 13 αμφορείς από τη Σάμο, από έξι διαφορετικούς πηλούς, και δέκα μιλησιακοί αμφορείς, αυξάνουν τις εισαγωγές από την Ανατολική Ελλάδα. Αμφότεροι οι τύποι αυτοί παρουσιάζουν περιορισμένη διασπορά σε άλλες θέσεις του Βόρειου Αιγαίου, σε αντίθεση με τους Λέσβιους αμφορείς (εννέα δείγματα, ορισμένα πιθανώς τοπικής παραγωγής). Μια άλλη συχνά εμφανιζόμενη ομάδα προέρχεται από την Αττική και την Εύβοια και περιλαμβάνει 19 δείγματα αμφορέων τύπου SOS. Από τον Δυτικό Λόφο προέρχονται ακόμα τουλάχιστον πέντε κορινθιακά αγγεία, και ένα μοναδικό λακωνικό παράδειγμα. Εκτός 20 θραυσμάτων αμφορέων του Θερμαϊκού Κόλπου (δεν παρουσιάζονται στο παρόν κεφάλαιο), ο Δυτικός Λόφος απέδωσε επτά διαφορετικούς τύπους τοπικών αμφορέων, όλοι ενεπίγραφοι (ορισμένοι πριν από την όπτηση), μαρτυρώντας τη συνέχεια της τοπικής παραγωγής και το περιφερειακό, καθώς και υπερπόντιο, εμπόριο στην αρχαϊκή Μεθώνη. Συμπερασματικά, υπερπόντιο εμπόριο λάμβανε ασφαλώς χώρα κατά τη διάρκεια του 6ου αιώνα π.Χ. και, παράλληλα με συναλλαγές σε περιφερειακό επίπεδο, επιτρέπει την αναγνώριση της αρχαϊκής Μεθώνης ως ένα μείζον διαμετακομιστικό λιμάνι της Κεντρικής Μακεδονίας.

Κεφάλαιο 22. Η λεπτή κεραμική της Ανατολικής Ελλάδας
John K. Papadopoulos

Μια επιλογή της κεραμικής της Ανατολικής Ελλάδας που βρέθηκε στη Μεθώνη μεταξύ 2003 και 2013, με σειρά παρουσίασης από τη βορειοδυτική Μικρά Ασία προς νότο, ακολουθεί τη νέα ταξινόμηση των Michael Kerschner και Udo Schlotzhauer. Το σύστημά τους αντικαθιστά τον συλλογικό όρο «Ανατολική Ελλάδα», ο οποίος αναφέρεται σε μία ευρύτατη περιοχή, συμπεριλαμβανομένων των γειτονικών νήσων, με αναφορά σε συγκεκριμένες θέσεις και παραγωγικά κέντρα, ένα σύστημα το οποίο μάλιστα επιδέχεται προσθηκών και διεύρυνσης. Η τοπική παραγωγή του Βόρειου Αιγαίου συζητείται στις σχετικές ενότητες, και το παρόν κεφάλαιο θα πρέπει να διαβαστεί συνδυαστικά με τα Κεφάλαια 12 και 21 περί των αμφορέων της Ανατολικής Ελλάδας από το Υπόγειο και τον Δυτικό Λόφο.

Η «αιολική» τεφρόχρωμη κεραμική αποτελεί σημαντικό ποσοστό των περισσότερων συνόλων της αρχαϊκής περιόδου στη Μεθώνη, ιδίως στον Δυτικό Λόφο. Το σύνολο της τεφρόχρωμης κεραμικής που παρουσιάζεται στο παρόν κεφάλαιο προέρχεται από επιχώσεις του Δυτικού Λόφου χρονολογούμενες στον 7ο και στο πρώτο μισό του 6ου αιώνα π.Χ. Σε αντίθεση με τη σχετική σπανιότητα σε άλλες θέσεις του Βόρειου Αιγαίου, το πλήθος της στη Μεθώνη υποδεικνύει περιορισμένη εισαγωγή και μάλλον τοπική παραγωγή σημαντικής ποσότητας αυτής της ιδιαίτερης κεραμικής. Τα πλησιέστερα παράλληλα προς την τεφρόχρωμη κεραμική της Μεθώνης εντοπίζονται σε διάφορες θέσεις της Λέσβου, στην Κύμη, στην Άσσο, στη Λάρισα και στην Πέργαμο της προκλασικής περιόδου, αλλά πολλά από τα σχήματα αγγείων της Μεθώνης δεν απαντούν με ιδιαίτερη συχνότητα αλλού και ίσως ανήκουν σε τοπική παραγωγή. Επιπλέον των λεπτών τεφρόχρωμων αγγείων και οστράκων του καταλόγου, υπάρχει πλήθος παραδειγμάτων της πλούσιας σε μαρμαρυγία τεφρόχρωμης κεραμικής του Βόρειου Αιγαίου. Ακολουθεί η περιοχή της βόρειας Ιωνίας, πατρίδα των (άλλοτε «ροδιακών») κοτυλών με πουλιά. Το πλήθος αυτών στο Υπόγειο (Table 22.1) ενισχύει σημαντικά τον συνολικό αριθμό τους στο Βόρειο Αιγαίο, μαρτυρώντας στενές σχέσεις μεταξύ Μεθώνης και βόρειας Ιωνίας (ειδικά της Τέω) κατά τον αποικισμό της πόλης από τους Ερετριείς, πριν από τον αποτυχημένο αποικισμό των Αβδήρων από τους Κλαζομένιους το 654 π.Χ. Ο αριθμός των ύστερων υπογεωμετρικών και αρχαϊκών κοτυλών με πουλιά στη Μεθώνη είναι μικρότερος και προέρχεται κυρίως από τον Δυτικό Λόφο. Η καλής ποιότητας χιακή και μιλησιακή κεραμική είναι σπάνια στη Μεθώνη, σε αντίθεση με τους αμφορείς από τις ίδιες αυτές πόλεις (Κεφάλαιο 12), ενώ οι Knickrandschalen της νότιας Ιωνίας είναι άφθονοι (όπως άλλωστε και στο Βόρειο Αιγαίο) και περιλαμβάνουν ένα από τα μεγαλύτερα σε μέγεθος γνωστά παραδείγματα από τον ελληνικό κόσμο (Fig. 22.27). Ο κατάλογος ολοκληρώνεται με ένα καλής διατήρησης παράδειγμα «σαμιακής» ληκύθου (Fig. 22.30), ένα σχήμα με σαφώς φοινικικές ρίζες.

Κεφάλαιο 23. (a) Επιλεγμένη αττική μελανόμορφη και ερυθρόμορφη κεραμική από τη Μεθώνη
Seth Pevnick
Κεφάλαιο 23. (b) Μια αττική ερυθρόμορφη κύλικα του ζωγράφου της Βόννης από τη Μεθώνη
Μαρία Τόλια-Χριστάκου

Οι ανασκαφές της περιόδου 2003–2013 στη Μεθώνη απέδωσαν άφθονα θραύσματα αττικής κεραμικής με εικονιστικές παραστάσεις, από πρώιμα μελανόμορφα έως και ύστερα ερυθρόμορφα, δείγματα μακράς και διαρκούς επικοινωνίας μεταξύ των Αθηνών και της Μεθώνης. Στην πλειονότητά τους τα θραύσματα αυτά βρέθηκαν στον Ανατολικό Λόφο, και μόλις τρία στον Δυτικό, όπου τα ευρήματα μετά την καταστροφή του 550 π.Χ. ήταν λίγα. Ο Seth Pevnick (Κεφάλαιο 23a) παρουσιάζει 16 παραδείγματα μελανόμορφων κυλίκων (Figs. 23.1–7) και ερυθρόμορφου κρατήρα, λεκανίδας, πελίκης και ληκύθου (Figs. 23.8–14). Μια ερυθρόμορφη κύλικα από το Κτήριο Α (Figs. 23.15–16) εξετάζεται περισσότερο επισταμένως και αποδίδεται στον ζωγράφο της Βόννης από τη Μαρία Τόλια-Χριστάκου (Κεφάλαιο 23b).

Κεφάλαιο 24. Πήλινοι λύχνοι
John K. Papadopoulos

Ένα δείγμα 16 ελληνικών πήλινων λύχνων από τον Ανατολικό Λόφο (εκτός του στρώματος καταστροφής του Κτηρίου Α· Κεφάλαιο 29) και το αγροτεμάχιο 278 στο νοτιοανατολικό τμήμα του οικισμού (Fig. 1.1), χρονολογούμενων από την αρχαϊκή έως και την ύστερη κλασική περίοδο, επιλέχθηκε λόγω της κατάστασης διατήρησης και ως αντιπροσωπευτικό της τυπολογίας και των πηλών. Δέκα είναι αττικής παραγωγής ή μελαμβαφείς της τοπικής παραγωγής, δύο πρώιμοι κορινθιακοί και τέσσερις ανήκουν σε γραπτούς ή ακόσμητους τύπους της τοπικής παραγωγής.

Κεφάλαιο 25. Πρώιμο υαλί στη Μεθώνη
Δέσποινα Ιγνατιάδου
(με τη συμβολή των Ελισσάβετ Ντότσικα, Πέτρου Κάραλη και Antonio Longinelli)

Ανασκαφές στη Μεθώνη έχουν αποκαλύψει 130 υάλινα ευρήματα σε όλη την έκταση της θέσης, σε αγορά, Υπόγειο και ακρόπολη (Table 25.1). Οφθαλμωτές και ακόσμητες χάντρες και αγγεία κατασκευασμένα με την τεχνική του πυρήνα χρησιμοποιούνταν από την εποχή του αποικισμού τον ύστερο 8ο αιώνα π.Χ., σύμφωνα με ευρήματα από το Υπόγειο. Τον 6ο αιώνα π.Χ., ραβδωτές χάντρες που βρέθηκαν εντός και εκτός των Κτηρίων Α και Β στον Ανατολικό Λόφο, πολλές σπασμένες και απορριμμένες, ήταν κατασκευασμένες από υάλινες ράβδους που επίσης βρέθηκαν στην αγορά. Υάλινα αντικείμενα της αρχαϊκής περιόδου στον Δυτικό Λόφο συλλέχθηκαν κυρίως από το Κτήριο Β (πέντε ακόσμητες χάντρες), εκτός μιας ραβδωτής χάντρας από το Κτήριο Α. Αν και αποσπασματικά, τα ευρήματα από τη Μεθώνη μαρτυρούν τη χρήση υαλιού καθ' όλη την ιστορία της αποικίας. Κατά την αρχαϊκή περίοδο η πόλη διέθετε τοπική παραγωγή γαλάζιων ραβδωτών χαντρών από προκατασκευασμένες υάλινες ράβδους. Χημική και ισοτοπική ανάλυση οκτώ δειγμάτων από το Υπόγειο και την αγορά επιβεβαίωσε την αρκετά ομοιογενή ανθρακική-ασβεστιτική-χαλαζιακή σύσταση ορισμένων αντικειμένων, ομοία με τη ανάλυση υαλινών αντικειμένων από την Πύδνα. Δύο οφθαλμωτές χάντρες από το Υπόγειο έδωσαν πολύ διαφορετικές τιμές ισοτόπων οξυγόνου και επομένως προέρχονται από διαφορετικές παραγωγικές διαδικασίες. Η χημική σύσταση μιας ράβδου υαλιού και δύο ραβδωτών χαντρών δείχνει ότι κατασκευάστηκαν με άμμο θαλάσσης από την Ανατολή, ενώ οι πρώτες ύλες ενός αγγείου κατασκευασμένου με την τεχνική του πυρήνα από την αγορά προήλθαν πιθανώς από την Αίγυπτο. Επομένως, η χημική και ισοτοπική ανάλυση δείχνει ότι τα ελληνικά δείγματα υαλιού κατασκευάζονταν με πρώτες ύλες από τη συρο-παλαιστινιακή ακτή, και αποτελούν στοιχεία της εμπορικής δραστηριότητας μεταξύ Ελλάδας και Εγγύς Ανατολής.

Κεφάλαιο 26. Μεταλλικά αντικείμενα στην αρχαϊκή και κλασική Μεθώνη: ακρόπολη και η ανατολική της πλαγιά, η αγορά και η περιοχή του νότιου λιμένα
John K. Papadopoulos

Το παρόν κεφάλαιο στοχεύει να προσφέρει μια περιληπτική επισκόπηση των μεταλλικών αντικειμένων από την αρχαϊκή και κλασική Μεθώνη, από τις τέσσερις περιοχές του οικισμού που αναφέρονται στον τίτλο (τα μεταλλικά ευρήματα του Υπογείου παρουσιάζονται στο Κεφάλαιο 15). Το υλικό από τον Δυτικό Λόφο (Table 26.1) προέρχεται κυρίως από στρώματα της αρχαϊκής περιόδου, όταν μεγάλο μέρος του καταλήφθηκε από βιοτεχνικές εγκαταστάσεις, περιλαμβάνει όμως και ορισμένα ύστερα κλασικά ή επιφανειακά ευρήματα. Το υλικό από την αγορά και την περιοχή του νότιου λιμένα προέρχεται κυρίως από το στρώμα καταστροφής του 354 π.Χ. Πρόκειται για αντικείμενα αποκλειστικώς χάλκινα, σιδηρά και μολύβδινα, και παρουσιάζονται με αυτή τη σειρά. Ο κατάλογος ξεκινά με κοσμήματα (περίαπτα, πόρπες, περόνες, χάντρες, δακτύλιοι) και ακολουθούν όπλα και εργαλεία. Ιδιαίτερο ενδιαφέρον παρουσιάζει ένα μεγάλο σιδερένιο ξέστρο, το οποίο ενδέχεται να χρησιμοποιείτο στην επεξεργασία του ξύλου (Fig. 26.56).

Κεφάλαιο 27. Μήτρες κοσμημάτων από τη Μεθώνη στο Αρχαιολογικό Μουσείο Θεσσαλονίκης (Συλλογή Σταμάτιου Τσάκου)
Στυλιάνα Γκαλινίκη

Τρεις λίθινες μήτρες από τη Συλλογή Σταμάτιου Τσάκου στο Αρχαιολογικό Μουσείο Θεσσαλονίκης, οι οποίες εκτίθενται στη μόνιμη συλλογή, αποτελούν κατ' ισχυρισμό τυχαία εκ περισυλλογής ευρήματα από τη Μεθώνη. Και οι τρεις φέρουν εγχάρακτα μοτίβα για την παραγωγή κοσμημάτων. Οι μήτρες εξετάστηκαν οπτικά και αναλύθηκαν με μη επεμβατικές μεθόδους (ακτίνες Χ, φασματοσκοπία φθορισμού ακτίνων Χ [XRF], αξονική τομογραφία) ώστε να εξακριβωθεί ο τρόπος χρήσης τους και οι δυνατότητες εφαρμογής διαφορετικών τεχνολογιών. Μια δίλοβη μήτρα από απολιθωματοφόρο ασβεστόλιθο για χύτευση οκτώσχημης πόρπης αποτελείται από δύο τμήματα (Figs. 27.1–4), τα οποία είναι ακόμα ενωμένα, και φέρει γόμφους από κασσίτερο, χοάνες, οπές και εγχαράξεις αβέβαιης λειτουργίας. Η δεύτερη μήτρα από υπόλευκο ασβεστόλιθο (Figs. 27.25–27, 30–33) είναι πυραμιδοειδούς σχήματος με επτά όψεις, πέντε με εγχάρακτα σχέδια και δύο με χοάνες, επιτρέποντας την αναπαραγωγή διαφόρων τύπων κοσμημάτων, μάλλον από μόλυβδο (Figs. 27.27–29). Η τρίτη μήτρα (Figs. 27.34–37) ήταν σχεδιασμένη για παραγωγή χάλκινων περονών. Και οι τρεις βρίσκουν πλησιέστερα παράλληλα στη νότια Ελλάδα και ίσως ήταν εισηγμένες.

Κεφάλαιο 28. Τα μολύβδινα βλήματα σφενδόνης από τη Μεθώνη
Άγγελος Μπούφαλης, Νίκη Οικονομάκη και Γιάννης Ζ. Τζιφόπουλος

Η παρούσα μελέτη παρουσιάζει ένα σύνολο 108 μολύβδινων βλημάτων σφενδόνης (68 ενεπίγραφων και 40 ανεπίγραφων), προερχόμενων από την αγορά της Μεθώνης και την περιοχή των τειχών επί του Δυτικού Λόφου, τα οποία συνδέονται με την πολιορκία της πόλης από τον Φίλιππο Β′ το 354 π.Χ. και σχετίζονται με όμοια βλήματα που έχουν βρεθεί σε διάφορες θέσεις της Μακεδονίας, της Χαλκιδικής και της Θράκης. Πολύ πριν από την πολιορκία της πόλης τους, οι Μεθωναίοι είχαν ιδιαίτερη σχέση με τις σφενδόνες, αφού κατά την παράδοση οι πρώτοι Ερετριείς άποικοι έφεραν το παρωνύμιο *ἀποσφενδόνητοι* (Chapter 2). Ένας πλήρης αρχαιολογικός, ιστορικός και επιγραφικός σχολιασμός συζητά τη σημασία, τη λειτουργία και τον σκοπό των επιγραφών και των εμβλημάτων πάνω στα βλήματα (αφορούν μάλλον την παραγωγή παρά τη χρήση τους), καθώς και θεωρίες σχετικά με τον πόλεμο και τον αλφαβητισμό στην αρχαιότητα. Μετά από ένα σύντομο ιστορικό της χρήσης των βλημάτων σφενδόνης στην αρχαιότητα (με αρχή τη νεολιθική εποχή) ακολουθεί ο κατάλογος, ο οποίος συνοδεύεται από ένα σύντομο σημείωμα σχετικά με την τυπολογία και τις κατασκευαστικές μεθόδους. Η διασπορά των βλημάτων, τα οποία βρέθηκαν σε στρώματα εντός των κτηρίων της αγοράς σχετιζόμενα με το στρώμα καταστροφής (Κεφάλαιο 29) και κατά μήκος των τειχών στον Δυτικό Λόφο, δείχνουν ότι κατά τη διάρκεια της πολιορκίας μάχες έλαβαν χώρα και εντός της πόλης, πιθανότατα αφού οι πολιορκητές είχαν περάσει τα τείχη.

Κεφάλαιο 29. Η αρχαία αγορά της Μεθώνης:
Κεραμική από το στρώμα καταστροφής
Αθηνά Αθανασιάδου

Μετά την πολιορκία και καταστροφή της Μεθώνης από τον Φίλιππο Β′ και την απέλαση των κατοίκων της, οι στέγες και οι τοίχοι των κτηρίων της αγοράς κατέρρευσαν και ένα συμπαγές στρώμα διαλυμένων πλίνθων σφράγισε τις υποκείμενες επιχώσεις. Η ανασκαφή αυτών έφερε στο φως ένα καλά χρονολογημένο σύνολο κεραμικής, κυρίως του δεύτερου τετάρτου του 4ου αιώνα π.Χ., αποτελούμενο από μελαμβαφή αγγεία, λίγα γραπτά, ακόσμητη κεραμική και μαγειρικά σκεύη. Πολυπληθέστεροι είναι οι αμφορείς, οι οποίοι βρέθηκαν σε θραύσματα στο επίπεδο των δαπέδων, ενώ η ομάδα των λύχνων αντιπροσωπεύεται από τύπους μιας ευρύτερης χρονικής περιόδου, από τον 6ο έως τα μέσα του 4ου αιώνα π.Χ. Το σύνολο αυτό συμβάλλει σημαντικά στη γνώση μας για την κεραμική παραγωγή της ύστερης κλασικής περιόδου και παρουσιάζει ειδικότερο ενδιαφέρον, αφού μαρτυρά τη χρήση των κτηρίων της αγοράς κατά τη διάρκεια της πολιορκίας του 354 π.Χ.

Η αγορά της αρχαίας Μεθώνης αναπτύχθηκε στον χώρο μεταξύ δύο γειτονικών λόφων, όπου γύρω από μια κεντρική πλατεία ανεγέρθηκαν μνημειακού χαρακτήρα κτήρια (Fig. 29.1). Τα δημόσια αυτά κτήρια εξυπηρετούσαν βιοτεχνικές και εμπορικές δραστηριότητες. Η πλειονότητα της κεραμικής χρονολογείται στο δεύτερο τέταρτο του 4ου αιώνα π.Χ., ενώ δεν είναι λίγη η παλαιότερη κεραμική. Η λεπτή κεραμική περιλαμβάνει μελαμβαφή, ολόβαφα και γραπτά αγγεία (ερυθρόμορφα, μελανόγραφα, ταινιωτά), τόσο εισηγμένα όσο και τοπικής παραγωγής, τα οποία βρίσκουν παράλληλα σε Αθήνα, Όλυνθο και άλλες ελληνικές πόλεις. Τα τοπικά εργαστήρια, της Μεθώνης ή/και της ευρύτερης περιοχής, παρήγαγαν γραπτούς σκύφους ή κύπελλα (Figs. 29.41–42), ακόσμητα οικιακά σκεύη καθημερινής χρήσης, ιγδία και μαγειρικά σκεύη. Οι λύχνοι ανήκουν σε τύπους της ύστερης κλασικής περιόδου, αλλά εμφανίζονται και άλλοι του 6ου αιώνα π.Χ. Τη συχνότερη κατηγορία κεραμικής αποτελούν οι αμφορείς, με διασπορά θραυσμάτων σε όλους τους χώρους, περιλαμβάνοντας μενδαίους τύπους ή άλλους που ανήκουν στην παράδοση του βορειοανατολικού Αιγαίου, ενώ ξεχωρίζουν ένας χιακός και ένας φοινικικός αμφορέας.

Πώς όμως χρησίμευαν τα αγγεία αυτά στο εμπορικό κέντρο της Μεθώνης; Στην πλειονότητά τους αποτελούν οικιακό εξοπλισμό και παρουσιάζουν ορατά σημάδια φθοράς, επισκευής και αιθάλης από την εναπόθεση σε πυρά, υποδηλώνοντας ότι δεν πρόκειται για εμπορεύσιμα αλλά για χρηστικά σκεύη, τα οποία βρίσκονταν σε καθημερινή χρήση κατά τη διάρκεια της πολιορκίας. Πρόχειρες εστίες που βρέθηκαν σε όλους τους χώρους του Κτηρίου Α, ορισμένες με οστά ζώων, προφανώς σχετίζονται με την κατάληψη των κτηρίων της αγοράς από διάφορες ομάδες ανθρώπων κατά τη διάρκεια της πολιορκίας. Η συγκέντρωση μολύβδινων βλημάτων σφενδόνης δεν αφήνει αμφιβολία για τη στρατιωτική ιδιότητα των καταληψιών, είτε επρόκειτο για τους πολιορκημένους Μεθωναίους είτε για τον στρατό του Φιλίππου Β′. Η διασπορά της κεραμικής σε διαφορετικά κτήρια και δωμάτια δείχνει ότι ακόμα και εργαστηριακοί χώροι χρησιμοποιούνταν για παρασκευή και κατανάλωση φαγητού.

Συνεπώς, η κεραμική του στρώματος καταστροφής θα πρέπει να ερμηνευθεί υπό το φως των ιστορικών γεγονότων, ενώ παρέχει στοιχεία και για το χρονικό διάστημα που μεσολάβησε μεταξύ της εγκατάλειψης της πόλης και της πλήρους κατάρρευσης των κτισμάτων. Η γενική εικόνα δείχνει ότι μεσολάβησε μια περίοδος λεηλασίας, όπως υποδεικνύουν συνανήκοντα όστρακα που βρέθηκαν σε μεγάλη απόσταση το ένα από το άλλο, ως να είχαν διασπαρεί από εκτεταμένη διατάραξη. Επομένως, το σύνολο κεραμικής από το στρώμα καταστροφής της αγοράς της Μεθώνης δεν είναι απλώς ένα κλειστό και καλά χρονολογημένο σύνολο από μια περίοδο (πρώτο μισό του 4ου αιώνα π.Χ.) με λιγοστά, πέραν της Ολύνθου, δημοσιευμένα συγκρίσιμα σύνολα στην ευρύτερη περιοχή της Μακεδονίας, αλλά και ιδιαίτερης σημασίας λόγω της σύνδεσής του με τα ιστορικά γεγονότα της περιόδου.

BIBLIOGRAPHY AND ABBREVIATIONS

ABBREVIATIONS

In addition to the abbreviations listed in the *American Journal of Archaeology*, the following abbreviations are used:

ABFV = Boardman, J. 1985. *Athenian Black Figure Vases: A Handbook*, London.

ABV = Beazley, J. D. 1956. *Attic Black-Figure Vase-Painters*, Oxford.

AEMTh = Το Αρχαιολογικό Έργο στη Μακεδονία και Θράκη, Thessaloniki.

ARV = Beazley, J. D. 1942. *Attic Red-Figure Vase-Painters*, 1st ed., Oxford.

ARV[2] = Beazley, J. D. 1963. *Attic Red-Figure Vase-Painters*, 2nd ed., Oxford.

ATL 3 = Meritt, B. D., H. Th. Wade-Gery, and M. Fr. McGregor. 1950. *The Athenian Tribute Lists* 3. Princeton.

BAMK = *Beiträge zur ur- und frühgeschichtlichen Archäologie des Mittelmeer-Kulturraumes*.

BAPD = *Beazley Archive Pottery Database*. https://www.beazley.ox.ac.uk/pottery/default.htm

BÉ = *Bulletin Épigraphique* in *Revue des Études Grecques*, Paris 1888–.

CID 2 = Bousquet, J. 1989. *Corpus des inscriptions de Delphes* 2 : *Les Comptes du quatrième et du troisième siècle*, Paris.

CIG = Boeckh, A., et al., *Corpus Inscriptionum Graecarum* (Berlin 1828–1877).

CIIP II = Ameling, W., H. M. Cotton, W. Eck, B. Isaac, A. Kushnir-Stein, H. Misgav, J. Price, and A. Yardeni, eds. 2011. *Corpus Inscriptionum Iudaeae/Palestinae* 2: *Caesarea and the Middle Coast: Nos. 1121–2160*, Berlin and Boston.

CIIP III = Ameling, W., H. M. Cotton, W. Eck, B. Isaac, A. Kushnir-Stein, H. Misgav, J. Price, and A. Yardeni, eds. 2014. *Corpus Inscriptionum Iudaeae/Palaestinae* 3: *South Coast*, Berlin and Boston.

CIL = *Corpus Inscriptionum Latinarum* (Königliche Preussische Akademie der Wissenschaften zu Berlin), Berlin 1893–.

CPG I–II = Leutsch, E. L. von, and F. G. Schneidewin, eds. 1839–1851. *Corpus Paroemiographorum Graecorum* 1–2, Göttingen.

CVA = *Corpus Vasorum Antiquorum*.

CVA Athens 1 = Rhomaios, K., and S. Papaspyridi. 1930. *CVA Grèce 1, Athènes, Musée National 1*, Athens.

CVA Basel 2 = Slehoverova, V. 1984. *CVA Schweiz 6, Basel, Antikenmuseum und Sammlung Ludvig 2*, Bern.

CVA Bologna = Laurinsich, L. 1929. *CVA Italia 5, Bologna, Museo Civico 1*, Rome.

CVA Boston = Hoffmann, H., ed. 1973. *CVA U.S.A. 14, Boston, Museum of Fine Arts 1*, Boston.

CVA Mainz = Hampe, R., and E. Simon. 1959. *CVA Deutschland Bd. 15. Mainz: Universität, Bd. 1*, Munich.

CVA Netherlands 11 = Borgers, O. E., and H. A. G. Brijder. 2007. *CVA Netherlands* 11, *Amsterdam, Allard Pierson Museum* 5, Amsterdam.

CVA Oxford = Beazley, J. D. 1927. *CVA Great Britain* 3, *Oxford, Ashmolean Museum* 1, Oxford.

CVA The Hague 2 = Scheurleer, C., and W. Lusingh. 1931. *CVA The Hague 2, Musée Scheurleer 2*, Paris.

EAA = *Enciclopedia dell'arte antica, classica e orientale*, Rome 1958–1984.

FM = Furumark Motif; *FS* = Furumark Shape. Furumark, A. 1941. *The Mycenaean Pottery, Analysis and Classification*, Stockholm.

GHI = Tod, M. N. 1946. *A Selection of Greek Historical Inscriptions* 1: *To the End of the Fifth Century B.C.*, 2nd ed.; 2: *From 403 to 323 B.C.*, Oxford 1946 and 1948.

IG = *Inscriptiones Graecae*, Berlin 1895–.

IGLPalermo = Manni Piraino, M. T. 1973. *Iscrizioni greche lapidarie del Museo di Palermo* (ΣΙΚΕΛΙΚΑ, serie storica 6), Palermo.

LGPN = *A Lexicon of Greek Personal Names*, ed. P. M. Fraser and E. Matthews. Vol. I: *The Aegean Islands, Cyprus, Cyrenaica*, ed. M. J. Osborne and S. G. Byrne, Oxford 1987; Vol. II: *Attica*, ed. P. M. Fraser and E. Matthews, Oxford 1994; Vol. IIIA: *The Peloponnese, Western Greece, Sicily and Magna Graecia*, ed. P. M. Fraser and E. Matthews, Oxford 1997; Vol. IIIB: *Central Greece: From the Megarid to Thessaly*, ed. P. M. Fraser and E. Matthews, ass. ed. R. W. V. Catling, Oxford 2000; Vol. IV: *Macedonia, Thrace, Northern Regions of the Black Sea*, Oxford 2005. (*http://clas-lgpn5.classics.ox.ac.uk:8080/exist/apps/lgpn1-search/index.html.*)

LIMC = *Lexicon Iconographicum Mythologiae Classicae*, Zurich 1981–2009.

LSJ[9] = H. G. Liddell, R. Scott, and H. S. Jones, *A Greek-English Lexicon*, 9th ed., Oxford 1940.

Paralipomena = Beazley, J. D. 1971. *Paralipomena*, Oxford.

PAS = Prähistorische Archäologie in Südosteuropa

PBF = *Prähistorische Bronzefunde*, Munich and Stuttgart.

RE = Pauly, A., and G. Wissowa, *Real-Encyclopädie der Classischen Altertumswissenschaft* (1893–1978).

SEG = *Supplementum Epigraphicum Graecum*, Leiden 1923– (see https://brill.com/view/db/sego).

WORKS CITED

Abbott, T. R. 1989. *Compendium of Landshells*, Burlington.

Abdelhamid, S. 2013. "Against the 'Throw-away-Mentality': The Reuse of Amphoras in Ancient Maritime Transport," in *Mobility, Meaning and the Transformations of Things*, ed. H. P. Hahn and H. Weiss, Oxford, pp. 91–106.

Åberg, N. 1932. *Bronzezeitliche und früheisenzeitliche Chronologie* 3: *Kupfer- und Frühbronzezeit*, Stockholm.

Acheilara, L. 2012. "Τα γκριζόχρωμα αγγεία από το αρχαϊκό νεκροταφείο της Μυτιλήνης: η περίπτωση του οικοπέδου Χ. Κρικλένη—Δ. Κουτσοβίλη," in Tiverios et al. 2012, pp. 55–68.

Adam, S. 1967. *The Technique of Greek Sculpture in the Archaic and Classical Periods* (*BSA* Suppl. 3), London.

Adamesteanu, D. 1965–1966. "Candelabro di bronzo di Melfi," *AttiMMGraecia* 6–7, pp. 199–208.

Adamesteanu, D., and H. Dilthey. 1992. *Macchia dj Rossano. Il santuario della Mefitis, rapporto preliminare*, Galatina.

Adamidou, A. 2008. "Με αφορμή τα βλήματα σφεντόνας από το Νεολιθικό Δισπηλιό," *Ανάσκαμμα* 1, pp. 49–65.

Adam-Veleni, P., ed. 1985. *Θεσσαλονίκην Φιλίππου Βασίλισσαν. Μελέτες για την Αρχαία Θεσσαλονίκη*, Thessaloniki.

———. 1993. "Χάλκινη ασπίδα από τη Βεγόρα της Φλώρινας," in *Ancient Macedonia* 5.1 (Institute for Balkan Studies 240), ed. D. Pantermalis, Thessaloniki, pp. 17–28.

———. 2000. "Νομός Θεσσαλονίκης, Νέα Απολλωνία, Θέση Μπουντρούμια," *ArchDelt* 55, B2, pp. 692–694.

Adam-Veleni, P., E. Kefalidou, and D. Tsiafaki, eds. 2013. *Κεραμικά Εργαστήρια στο Βορειοανατολικό Αιγαίο (8ος–αρχές 5ου αι. π. Χ.). Ημερίδα ΑΜΘ 2010. Pottery Workshops in Northeastern Aegean (8th–early 5th Century BC). Scientific Meeting AMTh 2010*, Thessaloniki.

Adam-Veleni, P., E. Poulaki, and K. Tzanavari. 2003. *Ancient Country Houses on Modern Roads: Central Macedonia*, Athens.

Adam-Veleni, P., and E. Stefani, eds. 2012. *Greeks and Phoenicians at the Mediterranean Crossroads*, Thessaloniki.

Adam-Veleni, P., and K. Tzanavari, eds. 2009. *Το Αρχαιολογικό Έργο στη Μακεδονία και Θράκη (AEMTh), 20 χρόνια. Επετειακός Τόμος*, Thessaloniki.

Adam-Veleni, P., M. Violatzis, P. Karatasios, and A. Stangos. 2002. "Προϊστορικές θέσεις στην ενδοχώρα του Στρυμονικού κόλπου: νεολιθική θέση στην Ασπροβάλτα," *AEMTh* 16 [2004], pp. 171–190.

Adrimi-Sismani, V. 2007. "La site Chalcolithique de Microthèbes au carrefour du monde Égéen et des Balkans du Nord," in Galanaki et al. 2007, pp. 73–79.

———. 2010. "Το Διμήνι στη Μέση Εποχή Χαλκού," in *Mesohelladika: The Greek Mainland in the Middle Bronze Age*, ed. A. Philippa-Touchais, G. Touchais, S. Voutsaki, and J. Wright, Athens, pp. 301–313.

———. 2012. "Ο ρόλος του μυκηναϊκού οικισμού Διμηνίου στην περιοχή γύρω από τον μυχό του Παγασητικού κόλπου," in *Αρχαιολογικό Έργο Θεσσαλίας και Στερεάς Ελλάδας 3. Παν/μιο Θεσσαλίας (Τμήμα ΙΑΚΑ) και Εφορείες Αρχαιοτήτων ΥΠΠΟΤ, Βόλος, 17–19 Μαρτίου 2009*, ed. A. Mazarakis Ainian, Volos, pp. 159–176.

———. 2013. *Ο μυκηναϊκός οικισμός Διμηνίου: 1977–1997. 20 χρόνια ανασκαφών*, Volos.

———. 2014. *Ιωλκός: Η εϋκτιμένη πόλη του Ομήρου. Ένα αστικό κέντρο στον μυχό του Παγασητικού Κόλπου. Το διοικητικό κέντρο, οι οικίες και το νεκροταφείο*, Volos.

Adrimi-Sismani, V., and L. Godart. 2005. "Les inscriptions en Linéaire B de Dimini/Iolkos et leur contexte archéologique," *ASAtene* 83, series 3.5, vol. 1, pp. 47–70.

Agora = *The Athenian Agora: Results of Excavations Conducted by the American School of Classical Studies at Athens*, Princeton

IV = R. H. Howland, *Greek Lamps and Their Survivals*, 1958.

VIII = E. T. H. Brann, *Late Geometric and Protoattic Pottery: Mid 8th to Late 7th Century B.C.*, 1962.

X = M. Lang and M. Crosby, *Weights, Measures, and Tokens*, 1964.

XII = B. A. Sparkes and L. Talcott, *Black and Plain Pottery of the 6th, 5th and 4th Centuries B.C.*, 1970.

XIII = S. A. Immerwahr, *The Neolithic and Bronze Ages*, 1971.

XVI = A. G. Woodhead, *Inscriptions: The Decrees*, 1997.

XXVIII = A. L. Boegehold (with contributions by J. McK. Camp II, M. Crosby, M. Lang, D. R. Jordan, and R. F. Townsend), *The Lawcourts at Athens: Sites, Buildings, Equipment, Procedure, and Testimonia*, 1995.

XXX = M. B. Moore, *Attic Red-Figured and White-Ground Pottery*, 1997.

XXXIII = S. I. Rotroff, *Hellenistic Pottery: The Plain Wares*, 2006.

XXXVI = J. K. Papadopoulos and E. L. Smithson, *The Early Iron Age: The Cemeteries*, 2017.

XXXVII = Ch. Tzochev, *Amphora Stamps from Thasos*, 2016.

Akamatis, I. 2011. "Pella from the Third Millennium to the Third Quarter of the Fourth Century BC: The Bronze Age Cemetery," in *The Archaeological Museum of Pella*, M. Lilimbaki-Akamati, I. Akamatis, A. Chrysostomou, and P. Chrysostomou, Athens, pp. 35–39.

Akamatis, N. 2008. "Ερυθρόμορφη κεραμική από την Πέλλα," *ArchEph* 2008, pp. 1–78.

Akanthos I = N. E. Kaltsas, *Άκανθος* 1: *Η ανασκαφή στο νεκροταφείο κατά το 1979*, Athens 1998.

Aktseli, D. 1996. *Altäre in der archaischen und klassischen Kunst. Untersuchungen zu Typologie und Ikonographie* (Internationale Archäologie 28), Espelkamp.

Akurgal, E. 1950. *Bayraklı Kazısı, ön rapor*, Ankara.

———. 1983. *Alt-Smyrna* 1: *Wohnschichten und Athenatempel*, Ankara.

Alberti, I. B. 1992. *Thucydidis Historiae* 2, *libri* 3–5, Rome.

Albizzati, C. 1924–1938. *Vasi antichi dipinti del Vaticano*, Rome.

Aldrete, G. S., S. Bartell, and A. Aldrete. 2013. *Reconstructing Ancient Linen Body Armor: Unraveling the Linothorax Mystery*, Baltimore.

Alexander, J. 1962. "Greeks, Italians and the Earliest Balkan Iron Age," *Antiquity* 36, pp. 123–130.

———. 1964. "The Pins of the Jugoslav Early Iron Age," *PPS* 30, pp. 159–185.

———. 1965. "The Spectacle Fibulae of Southern Europe," *AJA* 69, pp. 7–23.

———. 1973a. "The History of the Fibula," in *Archaeological Theory and Practice*, ed. D. E. Strong, London, pp. 217–230.

———. 1973b. "The Study of Fibulae (Safety-pins)," in *The Explanation of Culture Change: Models in Prehistory*, ed. C. Renfrew, London, pp. 185–194.

Alexander, J., and S. Hopkins. 1982. "The Origins and Early Development of European Fibulae," *PPS* 48, pp. 401–416.

Alexandrescu, P., and S. Dimitriu. 1968. *CVA Roumanie* 2: *Bucarest* 2, Bucharest.

Alexandri, O. 1973. "Κράνος 'βοιωτουργές' ἐξ Ἀθηνῶν," *ArchEph* 1973, pp. 93–105.

———. 1977. "Ἀθήνα: Ὁδὸς Δράκου 19," *ArchDelt* 32, B′1, pp. 18–20.

Alexandridou, A. 2020. "One More Node to the Thessalo-Euboean Small World: The Evidence from the Site of Kephala on the Island of Skiathos," in *Euboica II. Pithekoussai and Euboea between East and West* (*AION, Annali di Archeologia e Storia Antica, Università degli Studi di Napoli L'Orientale*, n.s. 26, 2019), vol. 1, ed. T. E. Cinquantaquattro and M. D'Acunto, Naples, pp. 263–275.

Alexandrov, S. 2009. "Golden Jewelry from a 2nd Millennium BC Tumulus at Ovchartzi, Radnevo District," in *Aegean and Balkan Prehistory*, ed. B. Horejs and P. Pavúk, http://www.aegeobalkanprehistory.net/index.php?p=article&id_art=15

———. 2017. "Der Grabhügel-Komplex (Grabstätte Nr. 7) von Ovčarci," in *Das erste Gold. Ada Tepe: Das älteste Goldbergwerk Europas*, ed. S. Haag, C. Popov, B. Horejs, S. Alexandrov, and G. Plattner, Vienna, pp. 130–132.

Alexiou, E. B. 2015. *Ρητορική και ιδεολογία: Ο Φίλιππος Β΄ της Μακεδονίας στον Ισοκράτη*, Thessaloniki, http://ancdialects.greek-language.gr/sites/default/files/studies/ritoriki_kai_ideologia_0.pdf.

Allamani, V. 2013. "Νεκροταφείο Θέρμης νομού Θεσσαλονίκης: επιλεγμένα κτερίσματα τοπικής κεραμικής," in Adam-Veleni, Kefalidou, and Tsiafaki 2013, pp. 183–191.

Allamani-Souri, V. 2008. "Σουρωτή: η εξέλιξη του ανασκαφικού έργου στο αρχαίο νεκροταφείο," *AEMTh* 22 [2011], pp. 351–360.

———. 2012. "Κλειστά σύνολα αρχαϊκής κεραμικής από το νεκροταφείο της Σουρωτής στον Νομό Θεσσαλονίκης και δείγματα αγγείων από τον οικισμό της Τούμπας Θεσσαλονίκη," in Tiverios et al. 2012, pp. 283–296.

Allen, S. H. 1990. "Northwest Anatolian Grey Wares in the Late Bronze Age: Analysis and Distribution in the Eastern Mediterranean" (diss. Brown Univ.).

Alram-Stern, E. 2014. "Times of Change: Greece and the Aegean during the 4th Millennium BC," in *Western Anatolia before Troy: Proto-Urbanisation in the 4th Millennium BC? Proceedings of the International Symposium Held at the Kunsthistorisches Museum Wien, Vienna, Austria, 21–24 November 2012* (*OREA* 1, Austrian Academy of Sciences), ed. B. Horejs and M. Mehofer, Vienna, pp. 305–327.

Amandry, P. 1953. *Collection Hélène Stathatos* 1: *Les bijoux antiques*, Strasbourg.

Ambrose, S. H. 1990. "Preparation and Characterization of Bone and Tooth Collagen for Isotopic Analysis," *JAS* 17, pp. 431–451.

Ambrose, S. H., and L. Norr. 1992. "On Stable Isotope Data and Prehistoric Subsistence in the Soconusco Region," *Current Anthropology* 33, pp. 401–404.

Amyx, D. A. 1958. "The Attic Stelai: Part III. Vases and Other Containers," *Hesperia* 27, pp. 163–254.

———. 1988. *Corinthian Vase-Painting of the Archaic Period* 1–3, Berkeley, Los Angeles, and London.

Anagnostopoulou-Chatzipolychroni, E., and S. Gimatzidis. 2009. "Αρχαία Μένδη: Κεραμική από τις πρώϊμες φάσεις της πόλης," *AEMTh* 23 [2013], pp. 369–376.

Anagnostou, I., D. Kyriakou, E. Kyriatzi, and A. Vargas. 1990. "Ανασκαφή στην Τούμπα Θεσσαλονίκης," *AEMTh* 4 [1993], pp. 277–287.

Andersson Strand, E., and M.-L. Nosch, eds. 2015. *Tools, Textiles and Contexts: Investigating Textile Production in the Aegean and Eastern Mediterranean Bronze Age* (Ancient Textiles Series 21), Oxford and Philadelphia.

André, J. 1964. "La résine et la poix dans l'antiquité. Technique et terminologie," *AntCl* 33, pp. 86–97.

Andreiomenou, A. K. 1975. "Γεωμετρικὴ καὶ Ὑπογεωμετρικὴ κεραμεικὴ ἐξ Ἐρετρίας," *ArchEph* 1975, pp. 206–229.

———. 1977. "Γεωμετρικὴ καὶ Ὑπογεωμετρικὴ κεραμεικὴ ἐξ Ἐρετρίας II," *ArchEph* 1977, pp. 128–163.

———. 1980. "Πρωτογεωμετρικὸς ἀμφορεὺς ἐκ Τάχι Θηβῶν," in *Στήλη: Τόμος εἰς μνήμην Νικολάου Κοντολέοντος*, Athens, pp. 55–58.

———. 1981. "Ἀνασκαφὲς στὴ Βοιωτία," *ASAtene* 59, n.s. 43, pp. 251–261.

———. 1982. "Γεωμετρικὴ καὶ Ὑπογεωμετρικὴ κεραμεικὴ ἐξ Ἐρετρίας IV (κάνθαροι, κοτύλαι, κύπελλα, κρατῆρες-δίνοι)," *ArchEph* 1982, pp. 161–186.

———. 1983. "Γεωμετρικὴ καὶ Ὑπογεωμετρικὴ κεραμεικὴ ἐξ Ἐρετρίας (τελευταῖον). Κλειστὰ ἀγγεῖα, λαβαί, ὑπογεωμετρικὴ καὶ χειροποίητος κεραμεική," *ArchEph* 1983, pp. 161–192.

Andreou, I. 1977. "Νομός Ιωαννίνων: Ανασκαφή Πανεπιστημιούπολης," *ArchDelt* 32, Chron., pp. 149–152.

———. 2000. "Το αρχαίο νεκροταφείο στη Δουρούτη Ιωαννίνων," in *ΜΥΡΤΟΣ: Μνήμη Ιουλίας Βοκοτοπούλου*, ed. P. Adam-Veleni, Thessaloniki, pp. 23–38.

Andreou, S. 1997. "Σίνδος: αποθέτης κεραμικής της πρώιμης εποχής του χαλκού," *ArchDelt* Α΄ (*Μελέτες*) 31–32 [2000], pp. 51–84.

———. 2001. "Exploring the Patterns of Power in the Bronze Age Settlements of Northern Greece," in *Urbanism in the Aegean Bronze Age*, ed. K. Branigan, Sheffield, pp. 160–173.

———. 2003. "Η μυκηναϊκή κεραμική και οι κοινωνίες της κεντρικής Μακεδονίας κατά την Ύστερη εποχή του Χαλκού," in *2nd International Interdisciplinary Colloquium, the Periphery of the Mycenaean World, 26–30 September, Lamia 1999*, ed. N. Kyparissi-Apostolika and M. Papakonstantinou, Athens, pp. 191–210.

———. 2009. "Stratified Wheel Made Pottery Deposits and Absolute Chronology of the LBA to the EIA Transition at Thessaloniki Toumba," in *LH IIIC Chronology and Synchronisms III: LH IIIC Late and the Transition to the Early Iron Age. Proceedings of the International Workshop Held at the Austrian Academy of Science at Vienna, February 23rd and 24th, 2007*, ed. S. Deger-Jalkotzy and A. E. Bächle, Vienna, pp. 15–40.

———. 2014. "Εκατό χρόνια έρευνας στην Εποχή του Χαλκού της Μακεδονίας. Τι άλλαξε;" in Stefani, Merousis, and Dimoula 2014, pp. 141–152.

———. 2020. "The Thermaic Gulf," in *A Companion to the Archaeology of Early Greece and the Mediterranean*, ed. I. S. Lemos and A. Kotsonas, Hoboken, N.J., pp. 913–938.

Andreou, S., and K. Eukleidou. 2008. "Η πανεπιστημιακή ανασκαφή στην Τούμπα Θεσσαλονίκης, 2008," *AEMTh* 22 [2011], pp. 323–328.

Andreou, S., K. Eukleidou, and S. Triantaphyllou. 2010. "Η πανεπιστημιακή ανασκαφή στην Τούμπα Θεσσαλονίκης," *AEMTh* 24 [2014], pp. 359–364.

Andreou, S., M. Fotiadis, and K. Kotsakis. 2001. "Review of Aegean Prehistory V: The Neolithic and Bronze Age of Northern Greece," in *Aegean Prehistory: A Review*, ed. T. Cullen, Boston, pp. 259–327.

Andreou, S., C. Heron, G. Jones, V. Kiriatzi, K. Psaraki, M. Roumpou, and M. Valamoti. 2013. "Smelly Barbarians or Perfumed Natives? An Investigation of Oil and Ointment Use in Late Bronze Age Northern Greece," in *Diet, Economy and Society in the Ancient Greek World: Towards a Better Integration of Archaeology and Science. Proceedings of the International Conference Held at the Netherlands Institute at Athens on 22–24 March 2010*, ed. S. Voutsaki and S. M. Valamoti, Leuven, pp. 173–185.

Andreou, S., and K. Kotsakis. 1996. "Η προϊστορική Τούμπα της Θεσσαλονίκης. Παλιά και νέα ερωτήματα," *AEMTh* 10A [1997], pp. 369–387.

Andreou, S., and K. Psaraki. 2007. "Tradition and Innovation in the Bronze Age Pottery of the Thessaloniki Toumba," in *The Struma/Strymon Valley in Prehistory: In the Steps of James Harvey Gaul* 2, ed. H. Todorova, M. Stefanovich, and G. Ivanov, Sofia, pp. 397–420.

Andrews, J. H. 1997. *Shapes of Ireland: Maps and Their Makers 1564-1839*, Dublin.

Andronikos, M. 1954. "Η δωρική εισβολή και τα αρχαιολογικά ευρήματα," *Ελληνικά* 13, pp. 221–240.

———. 1955. "Ελληνιστικός τάφος Βεροίας," *ArchEph* 1955, pp. 22–50.

———. 1984. *Vergina: The Royal Tombs and the Ancient City*, Athens.

Angelovski, B. 2011. "Survey for the Studying of the Lead Projectiles and Findings from the Carevi Kuli-Strumica," in *Stephanos Archaeologicos in Honorem Professoris Ivani Mikulčić* (Folia archaeologica Balkanica 2), Skopje, pp. 255–261.

Aperghis, G. 2013. "Athenian Mines, Coins and Triremes," *Historia* 62, pp. 1–24.

Apostolou, M. 1988. "Ανασκαφή στην Κυψέλη Ημαθίας," *AEMTh* 2 [1991], pp. 307–315.

———. 1991. "Ανασκαφή στην Κυψέλη Ημαθίας," *AEMTh* 5 [1994], pp. 31–37.

Aquilué Abadias, X., P. Castanyer i Masoliver, M. Santos Retolaza, and J. Tremoleda i Trilla. 2000. "Les ceràmiques gregues arcaiques de la *Palaià Polis* d'Empòrion," in *Ceràmiques jònies d'època arcaica: centres de producció i comercialització al Mediterrani Occidental: Actes de la Taula Rodona celebrada a Empúries els dies 26 al 28 de maig de 1999*, ed. P. Cabrera Bonet and M. Santos Retolaza, Barcelona, pp. 285–346.

Arachoviti, P. 1994. "Θολωτός πρωτογεωμετρικός τάφος στην περιοχή των Φερών," in *La Thessalie: Quinze années de recherches archeologiques, 1975–1990. Bilans et perspectives. Actes du Colloque international, Lyon, 17–22 avril 1990*, 2, ed. E. Kypraiou and D. Zapheiropoulou, Athens, pp. 125–138.

Aravantinos, V. 2010. *Το Αρχαιολογικό Μουσείο των Θηβών*, Athens.

Archibald, Z. H. 1998. *The Odrysian Kingdom of Thrace: Orpheus Unmasked*, Oxford.

———. 2010. "Macedonia and Thrace," in *A Companion to Ancient Macedonia*, ed. J. *Roisman and I. Worthington*, Oxford, *pp.* 326–341.

———. 2011–2012. "Archaeology in Greece 2011–2012: Macedonia and Thrace (Prehistoric to Hellenistic)," *AR* 58, pp. 96–106.

———. 2013. *Ancient Economies of the Northern Aegean: Fifth to First Centuries B.C.*, Oxford.

Ardovino, A. M. 1980. "Nuovi oggetti sacri con iscrizioni in alfabeto archeo," *ArchCl* 32, pp. 50–66.

Argissa-Magoula = *Die deutschen Ausgrabungen auf dem Argissa-Magoula in Thessalien. BAMK.*

III = E. Hanschmann and V. Milojčić, *Die frühe und beginnende Mittlere Bronzezeit, Bände* I–II (*BAMK* 23–24), Bonn 1976.

IV = E. Hanschmann, *Die mittlere Bronzezeit*, Bonn 1981.

Arianoutsou, M., and G. Ne'eman. 2000. "Post-fire Regeneration of Natural *Pinus halepensis* Forests in the East Mediterranean Basin," in *Ecology, Biogeography and Management of* Pinus halepensis *and* P. brutia *Forest Ecosystems in the Mediterranean Basin*, ed. G. Ne'eman and L. Trabaud, Leiden, pp. 269–289.

Arletti, R., A. Ciarallo, S. Quartieri, G. Sabatino, and G. Vezzalini. 2006a. "Archaeometric Analyses of Game Counters from Pompeii," *Geological Society, London, Special Publications* 257 (1), pp. 175–186.

———. 2006b. "Roman Coloured and Opaque Glass: A Chemical and Spectroscopic Study," *Applied Physics* 83 (2), pp. 239–245.

Arletti, R., D. Ferrari, and G. Vezzalini. 2012. "Pre-Roman Glass from Mozia (Sicily-Italy): The First Archaeometrical Data," *JAS* 39 (11), pp. 3396–3401.

Arletti, R., C. Maiorano, D. Ferrari, G. Vezzalini, and S. Quartieri. 2010. "The First Archaeometric Data on Polychrome Iron Age Glass from Sites Located in Northern Italy," *JAS* 37 (4), pp. 703–712.

Arletti, R., L. Rivi, D. Ferrari, and G. Vezzalini. 2011. "The Mediterranean Group II: Analyses of Vessels from Etruscan Contexts in Northern Italy," *JAS* 38 (9), pp. 2094–2100.

Arneth, M. 1851. "Archäologische Analekten," *SBWien* 7, pp. 235–238.

Αρχαία Ζώνη = *Αρχαία Ζώνη. Εφορεία Αρχαιοτήτων Έβρου, Περιφέρεια Ανατολικής Μακεδονίας-Θράκης*

I = P. Tsatsopoulou-Kaloudi, C. Brixhe, Ch. Pardalidou, S. Iliopoulou, K. Kaloudis, M. Galani-Krikou, A. Zournatzi, P. Tselekas, R. Veropoulidou, and D. Nikolaïdou, *Το ιερό του Απόλλωνα*, Komotini 2015.

Asheri, D. 1980. "La colonizzazione grece," in *La Sicilia antica I,1: Indigeni, Fenici-Punici e Greci*, ed. E. Gabba and G. Vallet, Palermo, pp. 89–142.

Asirvatham, R. S. 2008. "The Roots of Macedonian Ambiguity in Classical Athenian Literature," in *Macedonian Legacies: Studies in Ancient Macedonian History and Culture in Honor of Eugene N. Borza*, ed. T. Howe and J. Reames, Claremont, Calif., pp. 235–255.

Aslan, C. C. 2009. "Gray Ware at Troy in the Protogeometric through Archaic Periods," in *Pontic Grey Wares: International Conference, Bucharest-Constantza, September 30–October 3, 2008* (Pontica 42), Constanta, pp. 267–283.

———. 2011. "A Place of Burning: Hero or Ancestor Cult at Troy," *Hesperia* 80, pp. 381–429.

———. 2019. "The West Sanctuary at Troy in the Protogeometric, Geometric, and Archaic Periods," in *Troy Excavation Project Final Reports. The West Sanctuary at Troy: Iron Age Through Classical* (Studia Troica Monograph 10), ed. C. Aslan, M. Lawall, and K. Lynch, Bonn, pp. 28–418.

Aslan, C. C., L. Kealhofer, and P. Grave. 2014. "The Early Iron Age at Troy Reconsidered," *OJA* 33 (3), pp. 275–312.

Aslan, C. C., and E. Pernicka. 2013. "Wild Goat Style Ceramics at Troy and the Impact of Archaic Period Colonisation on the Troad," *Anatolian Studies* 63, pp. 35–53.

Aslanis, I. 1985. *Kastanas. Ausgrabungen in einem Siedlungshügel der Bronze- und Eisenzeit Makedoniens 1975–1979. Die Frühbronzezeitlichen Funde und Befunde* (*PAS* 4), Berlin.

———. 1990. "Οι οχυρώσεις στους οικισμούς του Βορειοελλαδικού χώρου και η περίπτωση του Διμηνίου," *Μελετήματα* 10, pp. 19–53.

———. 1993. "Η Χαλκολιθική περίοδος στο βορειοελλαδικό χώρο. Προβλήματα αναγνώρισης και διάρκειας," in *Ancient Macedonia 5.1* (Institute for Balkan Studies 240), ed. D. Pantermalis, Thessaloniki, pp. 134-145.

———. 2009. "Άγιος Μάμας Νέας Ολύνθου (Προϊστορική Όλυνθος). Ένας περιφερειακός οικισμός του μεσοελλαδικού κόσμου—Τα δεδομένα της μινυακής κεραμικής," in Adam-Veleni and Tzanavari 2009, pp. 31–40.

———. 2010. "Η κατοίκηση στην Ελλάδα κατά την 5η και 4η χιλιετία π.Χ.," in Papadimitriou and Tsirtsoni 2010, pp. 39–53.

———. 2017. *Das prähistorische Olynth: Ausgrabungen in der Toumba Ayios Mamas 1994–1996. Die mittelbronzezeitliche Keramik der Schichten 18 bis 12* (*PAS* 29), Rahden/Westfalen.

Aslanis, I., and B. Hänsel. 1999. "Ανασκαφές για τη Μεσοελλαδική της Μακεδονίας στον Άγιο Μάμα," in *Ancient Macedonia 6* (Institute for Balkan Studies 272), ed. D. Pantermalis, Thessaloniki, pp. 99–108.

Asouchidou, S. 2009. "Κριαρίτσι Συκιάς νομού Χαλκιδικής 1996–2000. Συνολική παρουσίαση των αρχαιολογικών ερευνών και των αποτελεσμάτων τους," in Adam-Veleni and Tzanavari 2009, pp. 41–50.

Åström, P., and I. Nikolaou. 1980. "Lead Sling-bullets from Hala Sultan Tekke," *OpAth* 13, pp. 29–33.

Athanasiadis, N. H. 1975. "Zur postglacialen Vegetationsentwicklung von Litochoro Katerinis und Pertouli Trikalon (Griechenland)," *Flora* 164, pp. 99–132.

———. 1988. "Η ανάλυση της γύρης και η σημασία της από ιστορικο-αρχαιολογική άποψη με βάση τα δεδομένα διαγράμματος από το Βαρικό Λιτοχώρου," *Scientific Annals of the Department of Forestry and Natural Environment* 31, pp. 143–152.

Athanasiadis, N. H., and A. M. Gerasimidis. 1986. "Μεταπαγετώδης εξέλιξη της βλάστησης στο Βόρα Αλμωπίας," *Scientific Annals of the Department of Forestry and Natural Environment* 29, pp. 211–249.

———. 1987. "Μεταπαγετώδης εξέλιξη της βλάστησης στο όρος Πάικον," *Scientific Annals of the Department of Forestry and Natural Environment* 30, pp. 403–445.

Athanassiadou, A. 2011. "Αρχαία αγορά Μεθώνης: κεραμική από το στρώμα καταστροφής," *AEMTh* 25 [2015], pp. 173–180.

———. 2012. "Phoenician Amphoras," in *Greeks and Phoenicians at the Mediterranean Crossroads*, ed. P. Adam-Veleni and E. Stefani, Thessaloniki, pp. 161–162.

Athanassiadou, A., and M. Bessios. 2019. "Κεραμική του 5ου αι. π.Χ. από αγροικίες της Πύδνας," in *Η κεραμική της κλασικής εποχής στο Βόρειο Αιγαίο και την περιφέρειά του (480–323/300 π.Χ.), Πρακτικά του διεθνούς αρχαιολογικού συνεδρίου, Θεσσαλονίκη, 17–20 Μαΐου 2017*, Thessaloniki, pp. 265–275.

Aubet, M. E. 1994. *The Phoenicians and the West: Politics, Colonies and Trade*, Cambridge.

Aupert, P. 1980. "Édifice avec bain (Philippes)," *BCH* 104, pp. 699–712.

Averdung, D., and R. K. Pedersen. 2012. "The Marsala Punic Warships: Reconsidering Their Nature and the Function of the Ram," *Skyllis* 12, pp. 125–131.

Avila, R. A. J. 1983. *Bronzene Lanzen- und Pfeilspitzen der griechischen Spätbronzezeit* (*PBF* V.1), Munich.

Avram, A. 2011a. "Marginalien zu griechisch beschrifteten Schleudergeschossen (I)," in *Scripta Classica: Radu Ardevan sexagenario dedicata*, ed. I. Piso, V. Rusu-Bolindeţ, R. Varga, S. Mustaţă, E. Beu-Dachin, and L. Ruscu, Cluj-Napoca, pp. 195–199.

———. 2011b. "Marginalien zu griechisch beschrifteten Schleudergeschossen (II)," in *Archaeology: Making of and Practice. Studies in Honor of Mircea Babeş at His 70th Anniversary*, ed. D. Măgureanu, Dr. Măndescu, and S. Matei, Piteşti, pp. 345–350.

———. 2014. "Marginalien zu griechisch beschrifteten Schleudergeschossen (IV)," *Ephemeris Napocensis* 24, pp. 131–138.

———. 2016. "Marginalien zu griechisch beschrifteten Schleudergeschossen (III)," in *Moesiaca et Christiana: Studies in Honour of Professor Alexandru Barnea*, ed. A. Panaite, R. Cîrjan, and C. Căpiţă, Brăila, pp. 489–493.

Avram, A., C. Chiriac, and I. Matei. 2013. "Balles de fronde grecques en pays gète et ailleurs. Sur les traces de Zopyrion dans le bas Danube," *RA* 2, pp. 227–448.

Aydıngün, H. 2015. "Archaeological Findings of Thracian/Phrygian Tribes' Crossing of Bosporus: (ITA) İstanbul Prehistoric Research Project," in *SOMA 2013. Proceedings of the 17th Symposium on Mediterranean Archaeology, Moscow, 25–27 April 2013*, ed. S. Fazlullin and M. M. Antika, Oxford, pp. 24–33.

Aytaçlar, N. 2004. "The Early Iron Age at Klazomenai," in *Klazomenai, Teos and Abdera: Metropoleis and Colony. Proceedings of the International Symposium Held at the Archaeological Museum of Abdera, Abdera, 20–21 October 2001*, ed. A. Moustaka, E. Skarlatidou, M.-C. Tzannes, and Y. E. Ersoy, Thessaloniki, pp. 17–41.

Baatz, D. 1990. "Schleudergeschosse aus Blei—eine waffentechnische Untersuchung," *SaalbJb* 45, pp. 59–67.

Babbitt, F. C. 1936a. *Plutarch Moralia* 4 (Loeb Classical Library 305), Cambridge, Mass. and London.

———. 1936b. *Plutarch Moralia* 5 (Loeb Classical Library 306), Cambridge, Mass. and London.

Babelon, E., and J. A. Blanchet. 1895. *Catalogue des bronzes de la Bibliothèque Nationale*, Paris.

Bachlas, V. 2018. "Ενσφράγιστοι εμπορικοί αμφορείς του Πιερικού Ηρακλείου και της χώρας Λειβήθρων," in *Proceedings of 9th Scientific Meeting on Hellenistic Pottery, Thessaloniki, 5–9 December 2012*, 2, ed. S. Drougou, Athens, pp. 857–880.

Bachlas, V., and A. Syros. 2014. "Ελληνιστική κεραμική από δύο πηγάδια-αποθέτες του Πιερικού Ηρακλείου," in *Η΄ Επιστημονική Συνάντηση για την Ελληνιστική Κεραμική, Ιωάννινα, 5–9 Μαΐου 2009*, Athens, pp. 205–233.

———. 2018. "Εργαστηριακές εγκαταστάσεις κλασικής εποχής στο Πιερικό Ηράκλειον," in *Η κεραμική της κλασικής εποχής στο Βόρειο Αιγαίο και την περιφέρειά του (480–323/300 π.Χ). Classical Pottery of the Northern Aegean and its Periphery (480–323/300 BC)*, ed. E. Manakidou and A. Avramidou, Thessaloniki, pp. 277–294.

———. Forthcoming. "Πιερικό Ηράκλειον: Εργαστηριακές εγκαταστάσεις κλασικής εποχής," *AEMTh* 30 [2016].

Bachmann, H.-G. 1982. *The Identification of Slags from Archaeological Sites*. London.

Bader, T. 1983. *Die Fibeln in Rumänien* (*PBF* XIV.6), Munich.

Badian, E. 1994. "Herodotus on Alexander I of Macedon: A Study in Some Subtle Silences," in *Greek Historiography*, ed. S. Hornblower, Oxford, pp. 107–130.

Bailey, D. M. 1975. *A Catalogue of Lamps in the British Museum* 1: *Greek, Hellenistic, and Early Roman Pottery Lamps*, Oxford.

Bailey, G. N. 1981. "Concepts of Resource Exploitation: Continuity and Discontinuity in Palaeoeconomy," *WorldArch* 13, pp. 1–15.

Baitinger, H. 2001. *Die Angriffswaffen aus Olympia* (*OlForsch* 29), Berlin and New York.

Bakalakis, G. 1938a. "Ἐκ τοῦ ἱεροῦ τῆς Παρθένου ἐν Νεαπόλει (Καβάλᾳ)," *ArchEph* 1938, pp. 106–154.

———. 1938b. "Ἀνασκαφαὶ ἐν Καβάλᾳ καὶ τοῖς πέριξ," *Prakt* 1938, pp. 75–102.

Bakalakis, G., and A. Sakellariou. 1981. *Paradimi* (Heidelberger Akademie der Wissenschaften, Internationale Interakademische Kommission für die Erforschung der Vorgeschichte des Balkans, Monographien 2), Mainz.

Bakhuizen, S. C. 1976. *Chalcis-in-Euboea, Iron and Chalcidians Abroad*. Leiden.

Bakır, T. 1974. *Der Kolonettenkrater in Korinth und Attica zwischen 625 und 550 v. Chr.*, Würzburg.

Baldacci, G. 2008. "La doppia ascia decorate con farfalle da Festos," *ASAtene* 86, pp. 71–86.

Ballard, R. D., L. E. Stager, D. Master, D. Yoerger, D. Mindell, L. L. Whitcomb, H. Singh, and D. Piechota. 2002. "Iron Age Shipwrecks in Deep Water off Ashkelon, Israel," *AJA* 106 (2), pp. 151–168.

Balmuth, M. S., ed. 2001. *Hacksilber to Coinage: New Insights into the Monetary History of the Near East and Greece* (Numismatic Studies 24), New York.

Bammer, A. 1990. "Bronzen aus dem Artemision von Ephesos," in *Echo: Beiträge zur Archäologie des Mediterranen und Alpinen Raumes. Johannes B. Trentini zum 80. Geburtstag* (Innsbrucker Beiträge zur Kulturwissenschaft 27), ed. B. Otto and F. Ehrl, Innsbruck, pp. 21–35.

Bankel, H.-G. 1984. "Griechische Bleistifte," *AA* 99, pp. 409–411.

Bankoff, H. A., N. Meyer, and M. Stefanovich. 1996. "Handmade Burnished Ware and the Late Bronze Age of the Balkans," *JMA* 9, pp. 193–209.

Baralis, A., K. Panayotova, and D. Nedev, eds. 2019. *Apollonia du Pont: Sur les pas des archéologues. Collections du Louvre et des musées de Bulgarie*, Sofia.

Barry, J. 1999. *Environment and Social Theory*, London.

Bartoloni, G., A. M. Bietti Sestieri, M. A. Fugazzola Delpino, C. Morigi Govi, and E. Parise Badoni, eds. 1980. *Dizionari terminologici: Materiali dell'età del Bronzo finale e della prima età del Ferro*, Florence.

Bartoněk, A., and Buchner, G. 1995. "Die ältesten griechischen Inschriften von Pithekoussai (2. Hälfte des VIII. bis 1. Hälfte des VI. Jh.)," *Die Sprache* 37, pp. 129–231.

Bass, G. F. 1967. *Cape Gelidonya: A Bronze Age Shipwreck* (*TAPS* n.s. 57, part 8), Philadelphia.

———. 1986. "A Bronze Age Shipwreck at Ulu Burun (Kaş): 1984 Campaign," *AJA* 90, pp. 269–296.

Bass, G. F., C. Pulak, D. Collon, and J. Weinstein. 1989. "The Bronze Age Shipwreck at Ulu Burun: 1986 Campaign," *AJA* 93, pp. 1–29.

Bates, W. N. 1930. "Two Inscribed Slingers' Bullets from Galatista," *AJA* 34, pp. 44–46.

Bather, A. G. 1892–1893. "The Bronze Fragments of the Acropolis," *JHS* 13, pp. 124–130.

Bats, M., and B. d'Agostino, eds. 1998. *Euboica: L'Eubea e la presenza euboica in Calcidica e in Occidente. Atti del Convegno Internazionale di Napoli, 13–16 novembre 1996*, Naples.

Batziou-Eustathiou, A. 1984. "Πρωτογεωμετρικὰ ἀπὸ τὴ δυτικὴ Θεσσαλία," *AAA* 17, pp. 74–87.

———. 2015. "The Mycenaean Settlement at Pefkakia: The Harbour of Iolkos?" in *Tradition and Innovation in the Mycenaean Palatial Polities*, ed. J. Weilhartner and F. Ruppenstein, Vienna, pp. 51–86.

Bayne, N. 2000. *The Grey Wares of North-west Anatolia in the Middle and Late Bronze Age and the Early Iron Age and Their Relation to the Early Greek Settlements* (Asia Minor Studien 37), Bonn.

Béal, J.-C. 1983. *Catalogue des objets de tabletteries du Musée de la civilization gallo-romaine de Lyon*, Lyon.

Beazley, J. D. 1927. *CVA Great Britain* 3, *Oxford, Ashmolean Museum* 1, Oxford.

———. 1932. "Little-Master Cups," *JHS* 52, pp. 167–204.

———. 1941. "Some Inscriptions on Vases IV," *AJA* 45, pp. 593–602.

Becher, W. 1932. "Methon," *RE* 15 (2), p. 1381.

Bechtel, F. 1917. *Die historischen Personennamen des Griechischen bis zur Kaiserzeit*, Halle.

Beck, A. 1980. *Beiträge zur frühen und älteren Urnenfelderkultur im nordwestlichen Alpenvorland* (*PBF* XX.2), Munich.

Beck, C. W., and C. Borromeo. 1990. "Ancient Pine Pitch: Technological Perspectives from a Hellenistic Shipwreck," in *Organic Contents of Ancient Vessels: Materials Analysis and Archaeological Investigation* (MASCA Research Papers in Science and Archaeology 7), ed. A. R. Biers and P. E. McGovern, Philadelphia, pp. 51–58.

Beck, H. C. 1928. "Classification and Nomenclature of Beads and Pendants," *Archaeologia* 77, pp. 1–171.

———. 1973 [1926]. *Classification and Nomenclature of Beads and Pendants*, 2nd ed., York, Pa.

Becker, C. 1986. *Kastanas: Ausgrabungen in einem Siedlungshügel der Bronze- und Eisenzeit Makedoniens 1975–1979. Die Tierknochenfunde* (*PAS* 5), Berlin.

Becker, C., and H. Kroll. 2008. *Das prähistorische Olynth. Ausgrabungen in der Toumba Agios Mamas 1994–1996. Ernährung und Rohstoffnutzung im Wandel* (*PAS* 22), Rahden/Westfalen.

Becks, R., and D. Thumm. 2001. "Untergang der Stadt in der Frühen Eisenzeit," in *Troia: Traum und Wirklichkeit. Begleitband zur Ausstellung "Troia—Traum und Wirklichkeit," 17. März bis 17. Juni 2001, Stuttgart*, Stuttgart, pp. 419–424.

Bedello, M., and E. Fabricotti. 1975. "Veio (Isola Farnese): Continuazione degli scavi nella necropolis villanoviana in località 'Quattro Fantanili,'" *NSc* 1975, pp. 63–184.

Beden, H., and Fr. Manucci. 2005. "Une ville inconnue en Ionie," *NumAntCl* 34, pp. 107–117.

Beekes, R. 2010. *Etymological Dictionary of Greek* (Leiden Indo-European Etymological Dictionary Series 10), Leiden and Boston.

Behrends, R.-H. 1982. "Studien der Funktion und Typenkombination der Lausitzer Grabkeramik," *JRGZM* 29, pp. 156–248.

Bell, S., R. D. de Puma, L. C. Pieraccini, and S. Steingräber. 2012. "David Ridgway: 1938–2012," *Etruscan Studies* 15 (2), pp. 238–242.

Bellas, I. N. 2018. "Τόξα, βέλη, και φαρέτρες στον αρχαίο ελληνικό κόσμο" (diss. Aristotle Univ. Thessaloniki).

Belon, P. 2001. *Voyage au Levant. Les Observations de Pierre Belon du Mans. De plusieurs singularités et choses mémorables, trouvées en Grèce, Turquie, Judée, Égypte, Arabie et autres pays étranges,* trans. A. Merle, Paris.

Benac, A., and B. Čović. 1956. *Glasinac* 1: *Bronzezeit*, Sarajevo.

———. 1957. *Glasinac* 2: *Eisenzeit*, Sarajevo.

Benndorf, O. 1889. *Wiener Vorlegeblätter für archäologische Übungen (1888)*, Vienna.

Ben-Shlomo, D., E. Nodarou, and J. B. Rutter. 2011. "Transport Stirrup Jars from the Southern Levant: New Light on Commodity Exchange in the Eastern Mediterranean," *AJA* 115 (3), pp. 329–353.

Benton, S. 1934–1935. "The Evolution of the Tripod-Lebes," *BSA* 35, pp. 74–130.

———. 1939–1940. "Bronzes from Palaikastro and Praisos," *BSA* 40, pp. 51–59.

———. 1950. "The Dating of Horses on Stands and Spectacle Fibulae in Greece," *JHS* 70, pp. 16–22.

———. 1952. "Note on Spectacle Fibulae and Horses," *JHS* 72, p. 119.

———. 1953. "Further Excavations at Aetos," *BSA* 48, pp. 255–360.

Bentz, M., W. Geominy, and J. M. Müller, ed. 2010. *Ton Art: Virtuosität antiker Töpfertechnik*, Petersberg.

Benzi, M. 1975. *Ceramica micenea in Attica*, Milan.

Béquignon, Y. 1932. "Études théssaliennes," *BCH* 56, pp. 89–191.

———. 1937. *Recherches archéologiques à Phères de Thessalie*, Paris.

Beresford, J. 2013. *The Ancient Sailing Season* (*Mnemosyne* Suppl. 351), Leiden and Boston.

Berger, E., and R. Lullies, eds. 1979. *Antike Kunstwerke aus der Sammlung Ludwig I. Frühe Tonsarkophage und Vasen. Katalog und Einzeldarstellungen*, Basel.

Bernabò-Brea, L. 1964. *Poliochni* 1: *Citta preistorica nell'isola di Lemnos*, Rome.

———. 1976. *Poliochni* 2: *Citta preistorica nell'isola di Lemnos*, Rome.

Bernard, P. 1964. "Céramique de la première moitié du VIIe siècle à Thasos," *BCH* 88, pp. 77–146.

Bernstein, F. 2004. *Konflikt und Migration: Studien zu griechischen Fluchtbewegungen im Zeitalter der sogenannten Grossen Kolonisation*, St. Katharinen.

Bertini, M., A. Shortland, K. Milek, and E. M. Krupp. 2011. "Investigation of Iron Age North-eastern Scottish Glass Beads Using Element Analysis with LA-ICP-MS," *JAS* 38 (10), pp. 2750–2766.

Beschi, L. 2001. "Frammenti di *auloi* dal Cabirio di Lemno," in *Ιθάκη: Festschrift für Jörg Schäfer zum 75. Geburtstag am 25. April 2001*, ed. S. Böhm and K.-V. von Eickstedt, Würzburg, pp. 175–180.

———. 2005. "Culto e riserva delle acque nel santuario arcaico di Efestia," *ASAtene* 81, pp. 95–220.

Bessios, M. 1990. "Ανασκαφή κλασσικών τάφων στη Μεθώνη, 1986," in *Οι αρχαιολόγοι μιλούν για την Πιερία (Καλοκαίρι 1986)*, ed. D. Tsirou, Thessaloniki, pp. 68–83.

———. 1993. "Μαρτυρίες Πύδνας. Το ψήφισμα του Απόλλωνος Δεκαδρύου," in *Ancient Macedonia* 5.2 (Institute for Balkan Studies 240), ed. D. Pantermalis, Thessaloniki, pp. 1111–1121.

———. 2003. "Ανασκαφή Μεθώνης 2003," *AEMTh* 17 [2005], pp. 443–450.

———. 2010. *Πιερίδων Στέφανος: Πύδνα, Μεθώνη και οι Αρχαιότητες της Βόρειας Πιερίας*, ed. Y. Z. Tzifopoulos, Katerini.

———. 2012a. "Κεφάλαιο 2. Η ανασκαφή του 'Υπογείου,'" in Bessios, Tzifopoulos, and Kotsonas 2012, pp. 41–112.

———. 2012b. "Ανασκαφές στη βόρεια Πιερία," *Οι Αρχαιολόγοι Μιλούν για την Πιερία*, pp. 14–20.

———. 2013. "Κεραμικά εργαστήρια Μεθώνης," in Adam-Veleni, Kefalidou, and Tsiafaki 2013, pp. 89–92.

———. 2017. "Μεθώνη," in *Αρχαιολογία. Μακεδονία και Θράκη*, ed. A. Vlachopoulos and D. Tsiafaki, Athens, pp. 162–165.

Bessios, M., and F. Adaktylou. 2008. "Τάφρος της τελικής Νεολιθικής στον Κάτω Αγιάννη Πιερίας," *AEMTh* 22 [2011], pp. 235–240.

Bessios, M., F. Adaktylou, A. Athanassiadou, E. Gerophoka, K. Gkagkali, and M. Christakou-Tolia. 2003. "Ανασκαφές Βόρειας Πιερίας," *AEMTh* 17 [2005], pp. 435–441.

Bessios, M., A. Athanassiadou, M. Deoudi, K. Papazoglou, G. Savvaki, N. Sachini, and P. Tsilogianni. 2014. "Σωστικές ανασκαφές στα αποχετευτικά δίκτυα δήμου Πύδνας-Κολινδρού," *AEMTh* 28 [2019], pp. 229–234.

Bessios, M., A. Athanassiadou, E. Gerofoka, and M. Christakou-Tolia. 2004. "Μεθώνη 2004," *AEMTh* 18 [2006], pp. 367–376.

Bessios, M., A. Athanassiadou, and K. Noulas. 2008. "Ανασκαφή Μεθώνης," *AEMTh* 22 [2011], pp. 241–248.

———. 2021a. "Ancient Methone (354 B.C.): Destruction and Abandonment," in *The Destruction of Cities in the Ancient Greek World: Integrating the Archaeological and Literary Evidence*, ed. S. Fachard and E. Harris, Cambridge, pp. 108–128.

———. 2021b. "Από τον αποικισμό του Θερμαϊκού: ανασκαφές Μεθώνης," in *Argilos, 25 années de recherches. Organisation de la ville et de la campagne dans les colonies du Nord de l'Égée, VIIIe–IIIe siècles av. n.è. Actes du colloque de Thessalonique, 25–27 mai 2017* (Publications of the Canadian Institute in Greece 13), ed. Z. Bonias and J.-Y. Perreault, Athens, pp. 407–422.

———. Forthcoming. "Ανασκαφές στη Μεθώνη και τη 'χώρα' της," *AEMTh* 30 [2017].

Bessios, M., A. Athanassiadou, K. Noulas, and M. Christakou-Tolia. 2003. "Ανασκαφές στον Αγωγό Ύδρευσης Βόρειας Πιερίας," *AEMTh* 17 [2005], pp. 451–458.

Bessios, M., and A. Krahtopoulou. 2001. "Η εξέλιξη του τοπίου στη Βόρεια Πιερία," *AEMTh* 15 [2003], pp. 385–400.

Bessios, M., and K. Noulas. 2012. "Αρχαϊκή κεραμική από την ακρόπολη της αρχαίας Μεθώνης," in Tiverios et al. 2012, pp. 399–407.

Bessios, M., and M. Pappa. 1995. *Πύδνα*, Katerini.

Bessios, M., and E.-B. Tsigarida. 2000. "Χρυσά κοσμήματα από το νεκροταφείο του Αιγινίου κοντά στην αρχαία Πύδνα," in *ΜΥΡΤΟΣ: Μελέτες στη μνήμη της Ιουλίας Βοκοτοπούλου*, ed. P. Adam-Veleni, Thessaloniki, 179–197.

Bessios, M., Y. Z. Tzifopoulos, and A. Kotsonas [ed. Y. Z. Tzifopoulos]. 2012. *Μεθώνη Πιερίας 1: Επιγραφές, χαράγματα και εμπορικά σύμβολα στη γεωμετρική και αρχαϊκή κεραμική από το "Υπόγειο" της Μεθώνης Πιερίας στη Μακεδονία*, Thessaloniki.

Best, J. G. P. 1969. *Thracian Peltasts and Their Influence on Greek Warfare*, Groningen.

Betancourt, P. P. 1985. *A History of Minoan Pottery*, Princeton.

Betcher, D. 2012. "Independent Colonies Emerge into Flourishing Independent City-States," *Constructing the Past* 13 (1), Article 5, http://digitalcommons.iwu.edu/constructing/vol13/iss1/5.

Bettles, E. A. 2003. *Phoenician Amphora Production and Distribution in the Southern Levant: A Multi-disciplinary Investigation into Carinated-shoulder Amphorae of the Persian Period (539–332 BC)* (*BAR-IS* 1183), Oxford.

Betzler, P. 1974. *Die Fibeln in Süddeutschland, Österreich und der Schweiz* 1 (*Urnenfeldzeitliche Typen*) (*PBF* XIV.3), Munich.

Bevan, A. 2014. "Mediterranean Containerization," *Current Anthropology* 55, pp. 387–418.

Bianco, S., and M. Tagliente, eds. 1985. *Il Museo Nazionale della Siritide di Policoro*, Bari.

Bianco Peroni, V. 1976. *Die Messer in Italien: I coltelli nell'Italia continentale* (*PBF* VII.2), Munich.

Bielefeld, E. 1968. *Schmuck* (*Archaeologia Homerica* 1.C), Göttingen.

Bikai, P. M. 2000. "Phoenician Ceramics from the Greek Sanctuary," in *Kommos 4: The Greek Sanctuary*, ed. J. W. Shaw and M. C. Shaw, Princeton, pp. 302–312.

Billows, R. A. 1995. *Kings and Colonists: Aspects of Macedonian Imperialism* (Columbia Studies in the Classical Tradition 22), Leiden.

Bilouka, A., and E. Euthymoglou. 2011. "Νέα Καλλικράτεια Χαλκιδικής 2011: ταφές αρχαϊκών χρόνων," *AEMTh* 25 [2015], pp. 411–416.

Biondi, G. 2019. "La ceramica protogeometrica della necropoli di Siderospilia. Osservazioni preliminari," in *Proceedings of the 12th International Congress of Cretan Studies, Herakleion, 21–25.9.2016*, https://12iccs.proceedings.gr.

Birley, E. 1978. "*Alae* Named after Their Commanders," *Ancient Society* 9, pp. 257–273.

Bîrzescu, I. 2005. "Die Handelsamphoren der 'Lesbos rot'-serie in Istros," *AM* 120, pp. 45–69.

———. 2009. "Funde aus Milet XXI: Drei Typen archaischer Reifenamphoren aus Milet," *AA* 2009/1, pp. 121–134.

Bischop, D. 1996. "Fibeln der archaischen bis römischen Zeit in Assos," in *Ausgrabungen in Assos 1992* (Asia Minor Studien 21), ed. Ü. Serdaroğlu and R. Stupperich, Bonn, pp. 139–165.

Biskowski, M. 2003. "Appendix 5.1. Supplementary Report on the Sitagroi Groundstone Tools," in *Sitagroi* 2, pp. 196–203.

Bissa, E. M. A. 2009. *Governmental Intervention in Foreign Trade in Archaic and Classical Greece* (*Mnemosyne* Suppl. 312), Leiden and Boston.

Blackwell, N. 2011. "Middle and Late Bronze Age Metal Tools from the Aegean, Eastern Mediterranean, and Anatolia: Implications for Cultural/Regional Interaction and Craftsmanship" (diss. Bryn Mawr College).

———. 2018. "Contextualizing Mycenaean Hoards: Metal Control on the Greek Mainland at the End of the Bronze Age," *AJA* 122, pp. 509–539.

———. 2020. "Tools," in *A Companion to the Archaeology of Early Greece and the Mediterranean*, ed. I. S. Lemos and A. Kotsonas, Hoboken, N.J., pp. 523–537.

Blakeway, A. 1932–1933. "Prolegomena to the Study of Greek Commerce with Italy, Sicily and France in the Eighth and Seventh Centuries B.C.," *BSA* 33, pp. 170–208.

Blanc, A. 2018. "Le toponyme grec Méthônê/Mêthônê: localisations, étymologie, métrique," in *Vina diem celebrent: Studies in Linguistics and Philology in Honor of Brent Vine*, ed. D. Gunkel, S. W. Jamison, A. O. Mercado, and K. Yoshida, Ann Arbor, pp. 1–11.

Blatter, R. 1964. "Rüstungsszene auf einer attischen Schale," *AntK* 7, pp. 48–50.

Blegen, C. W. 1928. "The Coming of the Greeks II: The Geographical Distribution of Prehistoric Remains in Greece," *AJA* 32 (2), pp. 146–154.

———. 1937. *Prosymna: The Helladic Settlement Preceding the Argive Heraion*, Cambridge.

———. 1952. "Two Athenian Grave Groups of about 900 B.C.," *Hesperia* 21, pp. 279–294.

Blegen, C. W., and M. Rawson. 1966. *The Palace of Nestor at Pylos in Western Messenia* 1: *The Buildings and Their Contents*, Princeton.

Blinkenberg, C. 1926. *Fibules grecques et orientales* (Lindiaka V), Copenhagen.

———. 1931. *Lindos: Fouilles et recherches, 1902–1914,* 1: *Les petits objets*, Berlin.

Blinkenberg, C. S., and K. Friis Johansen. 1932. *CVA Denmark*, Fasc. 2, *Copenhagen National Museum*, Fasc. 2, Copenhagen.

Bliquez, J. L. 1994. *Roman Surgical Instruments and Other Minor Objects in the National Archaeological Museum of Naples*, Mainz.

Bloesch, H. 1940. *Formen attischer Schalen von Exekias bis zum Ende des strengen Stils*, Bern.

Blomme, A., P. Degryse, E. Dotsika, D. Ignatiadou, A. Longinelli, and A. Silvestri. 2017. "Provenance of Polychrome and Colourless 8th–4th Century B.C. Glass from Pieria, Greece: A Chemical and Isotopic Approach," *JAS* 78, pp. 134–146.

Blondé, F. 1985. "Un remblai thasien du IVe siècle avant notre ère," *BCH* 109, pp. 281–344.

———. 1989. "Les abords N.-E. de l'agora de Thasos. 3. La céramique," *BCH* 113, pp. 481–545.

———. 2007. *Les céramiques d'usage quotidien à Thasos au IVe siècle avant J.-C.* (Études Thasiennes 20), Athens.

Boardman, J. 1952. "Pottery from Eretria," *BSA* 47, pp. 1–48.

———. 1957. "Early Euboean Pottery and History," *BSA* 52, pp. 1–29.

———. 1960. "Protogeometric Graves at Ayios Ioannis near Knossos. Knossos Survey 3," *BSA* 55, pp. 128–148.

———. 1961. *The Cretan Collection in Oxford: The Dictaean Cave and Iron Age Crete*, Oxford.

———. 1967. *Excavations in Chios, 1952–1955: Greek Emporio* (*BSA* Suppl. 6), Oxford.

———. 1970. *Greek Gems and Finger Rings: Early Bronze Age to Late Classical*, London and New York.

———. 1971. "Ship Firedogs and Other Metalwork from Kavousi," *Κρητικά Χρονικά* 23, pp. 5–8.

———. 1978. "The Problems of Analysis of Clay and Some General Observations on Possible Results," in *Les céramiques de la Grèce de l'Est et leur diffusion en Occident* (Colloques Internationaux du Centre National de la Recherche Scientifique 569), Paris and Naples, pp. 287–289.

———. 1985. *Athenian Black Figure Vases: A Handbook*, London.

———. 1989. "The Finds," in *Excavations in Chios, 1952–1955: Byzantine Emporio*, ed. M. Balance, Oxford, pp. 86–142.

———. 1994. "Settlement for Trade and Land in North Africa: Problems of Identity," in *The Archaeology of Greek Colonisation: Essays Dedicated to Sir John Boardman* (Oxford Committee for Archaeology Monograph 40), ed. G. R. Tsetskhladze and F. De Angelis, Oxford, pp. 137–149.

———. 1998. *Early Greek Vase Painting, 11th–6th B.C.: A Handbook*, London.

———. 1999. *The Greeks Overseas: Their Early Colonies and Trade*, 4th ed., London.

———. 2007. "Athenian Theseus and Some Ancient Greek Punishments and Executions," in *Ἀμύμονα ἔργα: Τιμητικός τόμος για τον καθηγητή Βασίλη Κ. Λαμπρινουδάκη*, ed. E. Simantoni-Bournia, A. Lemou, L. G. Mendoni, and N. Kourou, Athens, pp. 257–264.

Boardman, J., and J. W. Hayes. 1966. *Excavations at Tocra 1963–1965: The Archaic Deposits I* (*BSA* Suppl. 4), Oxford.

———. 1973. *Excavations at Tocra 1963–1965: The Archaic Deposits II and Later Deposits* (*BSA* Suppl. 10), Oxford.

Bodley, N. B. 1946. "The Auloi of Meroë: A Study of the Greek-Egyptian Auloi Found at Meroë, Egypt," *AJA* 50, pp. 217–240.

Boehlau, J. 1898. *Aus ionischen und italischen Nekropolen: Ausgrabungen und Untersuchungen zur Geschichte der nachmykenischen griechischen Kunst*, Leipzig.

Boehlau, J., and E. Habich (with J. Fabricius, P. Gercke, H. J. Kienast, W. Löwer, and K. Tsakos). 1996. *Samos: Die Kasseler Grabung 1894 in der Nekropole der archaischen Stadt*, Kassel.

Boehlau, J., and K. Schefold. 1942. *Larisa am Hermos. Die Ergebnisse der Ausgrabungen 1902–1934* 3: *Die Kleinfunde*, Berlin.

Boehm, R. A. 2011. "Synoikism, Urbanization, and Empire in the Early Hellenistic Period" (diss. Univ. of California, Berkeley).

Boehmer, R. M. 1972. *Boğazkoy-Hattuša: Ergebnisse der Ausgrabungen des Deutschen Archäologischen Instituts und der Deutschen Orient-Gesellschaft* 7: *Die Kleinfunde von Boğazköy: Aus den Grabungskampagnen 1931–1939 und 1952–1969*, Berlin.

Boeke, H. 2007. *The Value of Victory in Pindar's Odes: Gnomai, Cosmology and the Role of the Poet* (*Mnemosyne* Suppl. 285), Leiden and Boston.

Boessneck, J. 1969. "Osteological Differences between Sheep (*Ovis aries* Linne) and Goat (*Capra hircus* Linne)," in *Science in Archaeology: A Survey of Progress and Research*, ed. D. Brothwell and E. S. Higgs, London, pp. 331–358.

Bogucki, P. I. 1984. "Ceramic Sieves of the Linear Pottery Culture and Their Economic Implications," *OJA* 3, pp. 15–30.

Bohen, B. 2017. *Kratos & Krater: Reconstructing an Athenian Protohistory*, Oxford.

Boitani, F. 1990. "Le ceramiche laconiche a Gravisca," *Lakonikà* 2, pp. 19–67.

Bökönyi, S. 2005. "The Animal Remains Found in Tombs," in Papadopoulos 2005, pp. 317–320.

Boldrini, S. 2000. "Coppe ioniche e altro: una produzione occidentale a Gravisca," in *Ceràmiques jònies d'època arcaica: centres de producció i comercialització al Mediterrani Occidental: Actes de la Taula Rodona celebrada a Empúries els dies 26 al 28 de maig de 1999*, ed. P. Cabrera Bonet and M. Santos Retolaza, Barcelona, pp. 101–110.

Bon, A.-M., and A. Bon. 1957. *Les timbres amphoriques de Thasos* (Études thasiennes 4), Paris.

Bonanno-Aravantinou, M. 1999. "Μεταφορά τοπωνυμίων και μύθων από τη Μακεδονία στη Βοιωτία," in *Ancient Macedonia* 6 (Institute for Balkan Studies 272), ed. D. Pantermalis, Thessaloniki, pp. 167–180.

Bonfante, L. 1989. "Nudity as a Costume in Classical Art," *AJA* 93, pp. 543–570.

Bonias, Z., and J.-Y. Perreault. 1996. "Άργιλος. Πέντε χρόνια ανασκαφής," *AEMTh* 10B [1997], pp. 663–680.

———. 1997. "Άργιλος, ανασκαφή 1997," *AEMTh* 11 [1999], pp. 539–548.

Borel, A. N. 2007. "L'armée macédonienne avant Philippe II," in *Ancient Macedonia* 7: *Macedonia from the Iron Age to the Death of Philip II* (Institute for Balkan Studies 280), E. Voutiras, Thessaloniki, pp. 97–111.

Borrini, M., St. Marchiaro, and P. Mannucci. 2012. "La lesività delle armi antiche: la frombola a mano," *Archivio per l'antropologia e la etnologia* 142, pp. 27–42.

Borza, E. N. 1982. "Athenians, Macedonians, and the Origins of the Macedonian Royal House," in *Studies in Attic Epigraphy, History and Topography Presented to Eugene Vanderpool* (*Hesperia* Suppl. 19), Princeton, pp. 7–13.

———. 1987. "Timber and Politics in the Ancient World: Macedon and the Greeks," *ProcPhilAs* 131, pp. 32–52.

———. 1990. *In the Shadow of Olympus: The Emergence of Macedon*, Princeton.

———. 1995. *Makedonika*, Claremont.

Bosman, A. V. A. J. 1995. "Pouring Lead in the Pouring Rain: Making Lead Slingshot under Battle Conditions," *Journal of Roman Military Equipment Studies* 6: *Roman Military Equipment: Experiment and Reality. Proceedings of the Ninth International Roman Military Equipment Conference, Leiden, 1994*, ed. C. van Driel-Murray, pp. 99–103.

Bottema, S. 1994. "The Prehistoric Environment of Greece: A Review of the Palynological Record," in *Beyond the Site: Regional Studies in the Aegean Area*, ed. N. P. Kardulias, Boston, pp. 45–68.

Boufalis, A. 2020. "Οι επιγραφές της αρχαϊκής και κλασικής εποχής στη Μακεδονία" (diss. Aristotle Univ. Thessaloniki).

Boufalis, A., N. Oikonomaki, and Y. Z. Tzifopoulos. 2021. "Ενεπίγραφη κεραμική από την Άργιλο," in *Argilos, 25 années de recherches. Organisation de la ville et de la campagne dans les colonies du Nord de l'Égée, VIIIe–IIIe siècles av. n.è. Actes du colloque de Thessalonique, 25–27 mai 2017* (Publications of the Canadian Institute in Greece 13), ed. Z. Bonias and J.-Y. Perreault, Athens, pp. 77–94.

Boulter, C. 1953. "Pottery of the Mid-fifth Century from a Well in the Athenian Agora," *Hesperia* 22, pp. 59–115.

Bound, M. 1991a. "A Wreck of Likely Etruscan Origin off the Mediterranean Island of Giglio (c. 600 B.C.)," in *Recent Advances in Marine Archaeology. Proceedings of the Second Indian Conference on Marine Archaeology of Indian Ocean Countries, January, 1990*, ed. S. R. Rao, Goa, pp. 43–50.

———. 1991b. *The Giglio Wreck: A Wreck of the Archaic Period (c. 600 BC) off the Tuscan Island of Giglio. An Account of Its Discovery and Excavation; a Review of the Main Finds* (*ENAΛIA* Supplement 1), Athens.

Bourogiannis, G. 2018. "The Transmission of the Alphabet to the Aegean," in *Change, Continuity, and Connectivity: North-eastern Mediterranean at the Turn of the Bronze Age and in the Early Iron Age*, ed. L. Niesiołowski-Spanò and M. Węcowski (Philippika: Marburger altertumskundliche Abhandlungen 118), Wiesbaden, pp. 235–257.

———. 2019. "Between Scripts and Languages: Inscribed Intricacies from Geometric and Archaic Greek Contexts," in *Understanding Relations Between Scripts II: Early Alphabets*, ed. Ph. J. Boyes and Ph. M. Steele, Oxford and Philadephia, pp. 151–180.

Boussios, S. A. 2008. "Δασοκομική έρευνα σε συστάδες μαύρης πεύκης στο δημόσιο δάσος Καταφυγίου-Αγίας Κυριακής, νομού Κοζάνης" (diss. Aristotle Univ. Thessaloniki).

Bouzek, J. 1969. "The Beginnings of the Protogeometric Pottery and the 'Dorian Ware,'" *OpAth* 9, pp. 41–57.

———. 1974a. "The Attic Dark Age Incised Ware," *Sbornik*, Ser. A, *Historia* 28:1, pp. 1–55.

———. 1974b. *Graeco-Macedonian Bronzes: Analysis and Classification*, Prague.

———. 1983. "Der Vardar- und Morava-Bereich in seinem Verhältnis zu Griechenland zwischen 1200 und 900 v.u.Z.," in *Griechenland, die Ägäis und die Levante während der 'Dark Ages' vom 12. bis zum 9. Jh. v.Chr.*, ed. S. Deger-Jalkotzy, Vienna, pp. 271–284.

———. 1985. *The Aegean, Anatolia and Europe: Cultural Interrelations to the Second Millennium B.C.* (SIMA 29), Göteborg.

———. 1987. "Macedonian and Thessalian Bronzes: Macedonian Beads," *Acta Universitatis Carolinae, Philologica 1, Graecolatina Pragensia* 11, pp. 77–101.

———. 1997. *Greece, Anatolia, and Europe: Cultural Interrelations During the Early Iron Age* (SIMA 122), Jonsered.

Bovon, A. 1966. *Lampes d'Argos* (Études péloponnésiennes 5), Paris.

Bowman, A. K. 1994. "The Roman Imperial Army: Letters and Literacy on the Roman Frontier," in *Literacy and Power in the Ancient World*, ed. A. K. Bowman and G. Woolf, Cambridge, pp. 109–125.

Boyd, M. 2014. "The Materiality of Performance in Mycenaean Funerary Practices," in *World Archaeology* 46 (2), *The Archaeology of Performance*, pp. 192–205.

Boyle, R. W. 1979. *The Geochemistry of Gold and Its Deposits* (Geological Survey of Canada Bulletin 280), Ottawa.

Bozkova, A., and P. Delev. 2012. "Archaic Pottery with Painted Geometric Design from South-western Bulgaria," in Tiverios et al. 2012, pp. 69–77.

Brachionidou, S. 2019. "Εμπορικοί αμφορείς της κλασσικής περιόδου από την βόρεια Πιερία," in *Η Κεραμική της Κλασσικής Εποχής στο Βόρειο Αιγαίο και την Περιφέρειά του (480–323/300 π. Χ.). Classical Pottery of the Northern Aegean and Its Periphery (480–323/300 BC)*, ed. E. Manakidou and A. Avramidou, Thessaloniki, pp. 225–241.

Bradley, R. 2000. *An Archaeology of Natural Places*, London.

Branigan, K. 1974. *Aegean Metalwork of the Early and Middle Bronze Age*, Oxford.

———. 1992. "Metalwork and Metallurgical Debris," in *Knossos from Greek City to Roman Colony: Excavations at the Unexplored Mansion* II, ed. L. H. Sackett (*BSA* Suppl. 21), Oxford, pp. 363–378.

Brann, E. T. H. 1956. "A Well of the 'Corinthian' Period Found in Corinth," *Hesperia* 25, pp. 350–374.

———. 1961. "Protoattic Well Groups from the Athenian Agora," *Hesperia* 30, pp. 305–379.

Braudel, F. 1992. *The Mediterranean and the Mediterranean World in the Age of Philip II*, trans. S. Reynolds, New York.

Bräuning, A., and I. Kilian-Dirlmeier. 2013. *Die eisenzeitlichen Grabhügel von Vergina. Die Ausgrabungen von Photis Petsas 1960–1961*, Mainz.

Bravo, B. 1983. "Le commerce des céréales chez les grecs de l'époque archaïque," in *Trade and Famine in Classical Antiquity*, ed. P. Garnsey and C. R. Whittaker, Cambridge, pp. 17–29.

Brélaz, C. 2007. "Des balles de fronde à Daskyleion: armes de guerre ou armes de chasse?" *Anatolia Antiqua* 15, pp. 71–82.

Brélaz, C., and P. Ducrey. 2003. "Une grappe de balles de fronde en plomb à Érétrie: la technique de fabrication des projectiles et l'usage de la fronde en Grèce ancienne," *AntK* 46, pp. 99–115.

———. 2007. "Réalités et images de la fronde en Grèce ancienne," in *Les armes dans l'antiquité, de la technique à l'imaginaire. Actes du colloque international du SEMA, Montpellier, 20 et 22 mars 2003*, ed. P. Sauzeau and Th. van Compernolle, Montpellier, pp. 325–351.

Bresson, A. 2016. *The Making of the Ancient Greek Economy*, Princeton and Oxford.

Brijder, H. A. G. 1983. *Siana Cups I and Komast Cups* (Allard Pierson Series 4), Amsterdam.

———. 1993. "Simply Decorated, Black Siana Cups by the Taras Painter and Cassel Cups," *BABesch* 68, pp. 129–145.

Brill, R., R. Clayton, T. Mayeda, and C. Stapleton. 1999. "Oxygen Isotope Analyses of Early Glasses," *Chemical Analyses of Early Glasses* 2, pp. 303–322.

Brixhe, C., and A. Panayotou. 1988. "L'atticisation de la Macédoine: l'une des sources de la koiné," *Verbum* 11, pp. 245–260.

Brixhe, C., and G. D. Summers. 2007. "Les inscriptions phrygiennes de Kerkenes Dağ (Anatolie centrale)," *Kadmos* 45, pp. 93–135.

Brize, P. H. 1989–1990. "Archaische Bronzevotive aus dem Heraion von Samos," *Scienze dell'antichità* 3–4, pp. 317–326.

Brock, J. K. 1957. *Fortetsa: Early Greek Tombs near Knossos* (*BSA* Suppl. 2), Cambridge.

Brock, J. K., and G. Mackworth Young. 1949. "Excavations at Siphnos," *BSA* 44, pp. 1–92.

Brokalakis, G. 2013. "Γυάλινα και μετάλλινα τέχνεργα," in *Κύθηρα. Το μινωϊκό ιερό κορυφής στον Άγιο Γεώργιο στο Βουνό 3: Τα ευρήματα*, ed. I. Sakellarakis, Athens, pp. 329–418.

Brokaw, C. 1963. "Concurrent Styles in Late Geometric and Early Protoattic Vase Painting," *AM* 78, pp. 63–73.

Broneer, O. 1933. "Excavations on the North Slope of the Acropolis at Athens, 1931–1932," *Hesperia* 2, pp. 329–417.

———. 1939. "A Mycenaean Fountain on the Athenian Acropolis," *Hesperia* 8, pp. 317–433.

———. 1958. "Excavations at Isthmia: Third Campaign, 1955–1956," *Hesperia* 27, pp. 1–37.

Bronk Ramsey, C. 2001. "Development of the Radiocarbon Calibration Program OxCal," *Radiocarbon* 43, pp. 355–363.

———. 2009. "Bayesian Analysis of Radiocarbon Dates," *Radiocarbon* 51, pp. 337–360.

Bronk Ramsey, C., and S. Lee. 2013. "Recent and Planned Developments of the Program OxCal," *Radiocarbon* 55 (2–3), pp. 720–730.

Broodbank, C. 2013. *The Making of the Middle Sea: A History of the Mediterranean from the Beginning to the Emergence of the Classical World*, London.

Brouskari, M. 1980. "A Dark Age Cemetery in Erechtheion Street, Athens," *BSA* 75, pp. 13–31.

Brown, T. A., D. E. Nelson, J. S. Vogel, and J. R. Southon. 1988. "Improved Collagen Extraction by Modified Longin Method," *Radiocarbon* 34, pp. 279–291.

Brown Vega, M., and N. Craig. 2009. "New Experimental Data on the Distance of Sling Projectiles," *JAS* 36, pp. 1264–1268.

Brück, J. 1999. "Ritual and Rationality: Some Problems of Interpretation in European Archaeology," *Journal of European Archaeology* 2 (3), pp. 313–344.

Brun, J.-P. 2003. *Le vin et l'huile dans la Méditerranée antique: Viticulture, oléiculture et procédés de transformation*, Paris.

Bruneau, Ph. 1968. "Contribution à l'histoire urbaine de Délos," *BCH* 92, pp. 633–709.

Buchholz, H.-G. 1962. "Der Pfeilglätter aus dem VI. Schachtgrab von Mykene und die helladischen Pfeilspitzen," *JdI* 77, pp. 1–58.

———. 1975. *Methymna: Archäologische Beiträge zur Topographie und Geschichte von Nordlesbos*, Mainz.

Buchholz, H.-G., S. Foltiny, and O. Höckmann. 1980. *Kriegswesen*, Teil 2: *Angriffswaffen: Schwert, Dolch, Lanze, Speer, Keule* (*ArchHom* I E 2), Göttingen.

Buchholz, H-G., G. Jöhrens, and I. Maull. 1973. *Jagd und Fischfang* (*ArchHom* 2 J), Göttingen.

Buchner, G. 1979. "Early Orientalizing: Aspects of the Euboean Connection," in *Italy Before the Romans: The Iron Age, Orientalizing and Etruscan Periods*, ed. D. Ridgway and F. R. Ridgway, London, pp. 129–144.

Buck, C. D. 1955. *The Greek Dialects*, Chicago and London.

Buckler, J. 1989. *Philip II and the Sacred War* (*Mnemosyne* Suppl. 109), Leiden.

———. 2003. *Aegean Greece in the Fourth Century B.C.*, Leiden.

Buonopane, A. 2014. "Due ghiande missili col nome del fabbricante nel Museo Archeologico al Teatro Romano di Verona," in *Hoc quoque laboris praemium. Scritti in onore di Gino Bandelli*, ed. M. Chiabà, Trieste, pp. 19–32.

Burr, D. 1933. "A Geometric House and a Proto-Attic Votive Deposit," *Hesperia* 2, pp. 542–640.

Burrows, R. M., and P. N. Ure. 1907–1908. "Excavations at Rhitsóna in Boeotia," *BSA* 14, pp. 226–318.

Butler, H. C. 1914. "Fifth Preliminary Report on the American Excavations at Sardes in Asia Minor," *AJA* 18, pp. 425–437.

Buxeda I Garrigós, J., R. E. Jones, V. Kilikoglou, S. T. Levi, Y. Maniatis, J. Mitchell, L. Vagnetti, K. A. Wardle, and S. Andreou. 2003. "Technology Transfer at the Periphery of the Mycenaean World: The Cases of Mycenaean Pottery Found in Central Macedonia (Greece) and the Plain of Sybaris (Italy)," *Archaeometry* 45, pp. 263–284.

Buxó, R. 2009. "Botanical and Archaeological Dimensions of the Colonial Encounter," in *Colonial Encounters in Ancient Iberia: Phoenician, Greek, and Indigenous Relations*, ed. M. Dietler and C. López-Ruiz, Chicago, pp. 155–168.

Caddy, J., and D. Defeo. 2003. *Enhancing or Restoring the Productivity of Natural Populations of Shellfish and Other Marine Invertebrate Resources* (Fisheries Technical Paper 448), Food and Agriculture Organization of the United Nations.

Cahill, N. D. 1991. "Olynthus: Social and Spatial Planning in a Greek City" (diss. Univ. of California, Berkeley).

Cahn, H. C. 1973. "Dokimasia," *RA* 1973, pp. 3–22.

Callaghan, P. J., and A. W. Johnston. 2000. "The Pottery from the Greek Temples at Kommos," in *Kommos IV: The Greek Sanctuary*, ed. J. W. Shaw and M. C. Shaw, Princeton, pp. 210–301.

Calvet, Y., and M. Yon. 1977. "Céramique trouvée à Salamine (Fouilles de la ville)," in *Greek Geometric and Archaic Pottery Found in Cyprus*, ed. E. Gjerstad, Stockholm, 9–22.

———. 1978. "Salamine de Chypre et le commerce ionien," in *Les céramiques de la Grèce de l'est et leur diffusion en occident. Centre Jean Bérard, Institut Français de Naples, 6–9 juillet 1976*, Paris, pp. 43–51.

Cambitoglou, A., and J. K. Papadopoulos. 1988. "Excavations at Torone, 1986: A Preliminary Report," *MeditArch* 1, pp. 180–217.

———. 1989. "Οι ανασκαφές στην Τορώνη το 1989," *AEMTh* 3 [1992], pp. 439–449.

———. 1991. "Excavations at Torone, 1989," *MeditArch* 4, pp. 147–171.

———. 1993. "The Earliest Mycenaeans in Macedonia," in *Wace and Blegen: Pottery as Evidence for Trade in the Aegean Bronze Age 1939–1989*, ed. C. Zerner, P. Zerner, and J. Winder, Amsterdam, pp. 299–302.
———. 1994. "Excavations at Torone, 1990," *MeditArch* 7, pp. 141–163.
———. 2001. "Historical and Topographical Introduction," in *Torone* I, pp. 37–88.
Cambitoglou, A., S. Pierce, O. Segal, and J. K. Papadopoulos. 1981. *Archaeological Museum of Andros: Guide to the Finds from the Excavations of the Geometric Town at Zagora*, Athens.
Cambitoglou, A., O. Tudor Jones, Gr. Joyner, and B. McLoughlin. 2001. "The Metal Objects," in *Torone* I, pp. 721–763.
Camp, J. M. 1979. "A Drought in the Late Eighth Century B.C.," *Hesperia* 48, pp. 397–411.
Campbell, D. B. 2011. "Ancient Catapults: Some Hypotheses Reexamined," *Hesperia* 80, pp. 677–700.
Campbell, M. T. 1938. "A Well of the Black-Figured Period at Corinth," *Hesperia* 7, pp. 557–611.
Caner, E. 1983. *Fibeln in Anatolien* 1 (*PBF* XIV.8), Munich.
Cappers, R. T. J., R. M. Bekker, and J. E. A. Jans. 2006. *Digital Seed Atlas of the Netherlands* (Groningen Archaeological Studies 4), Eelde.
Cappers, R. T. J., R. Neef, and R. M. Bekker. 2009. *Digital Atlas of Economic Plants 1, 2a and 2b*, Groningen.
Carancini, G. L. 1975. *Die Nadeln in Italien* (*PBF* XIII.2), Munich.
Carapanos, C. 1878. *Dodone et ses ruines*, Paris.
Cargill, J. 1981. *The Second Athenian League: Empire or Free Alliance?*, Los Angeles and London.
Carington Smith, J. 1975. "Spinning, Weaving and Textile Manufacture in Prehistoric Greece" (diss. Univ. of Tasmania, Hobart).
———. 1991. "Τρεις κάνθαροι και ένας κρατήρας από τη θέση Κούκος Συκιάς," *AEMTh* 5 [1994], pp. 335–348.
———. 2000. "The Cooking Vessels of Koukos, Sykia," in *ΜΥΡΤΟΣ. Μέλετες στη Μνήμη της Ιουλίας Βοκοτοπούλου*, ed. P. Adam-Veleni, Thessaloniki, pp. 219–228.
Carington Smith, J., and I. Vokotopoulou. 1988. "Ανασκαφή στον Κούκο Συκιάς, Ν. Χαλκιδικής," *AEMTh* 2 [1991], pp. 357–370.
———. 1989. "Ανασκαφή στον Κούκο Χαλκιδικής," *AEMTh* 3 [1993], pp. 425–438.
———. 1990. "Η ανασκαφή στον Κούκο Συκιάς, 1990," *AEMTh* 4 [1993], pp. 439–454.
———. 1992. "Excavation at Koukos, Sykia," *AEMTh* 6 [1995], pp. 495–502.
Carl, P. 2011. "Type, Field, Culture, Praxis," *Architectural Design* 81, pp. 38–45.
Carlson, D. N. 2003. "The Classical Greek Shipwreck at Tektaş Burnu, Turkey," *AJA* 107, pp. 581–600.
Carpenter, T. H. 1989. *Beazley Addenda: Additional References to* ABV, ARV^2, *and* Paralipomena, Oxford.
Carter, J. C., and J. Hall. 1998. "Burial Descriptions," in *The Chora of Metaponto: The Necropoleis* 1, ed. J. C. Carter, Austin, pp. 237–447.
Cartledge, P. 1983. "'Trade and Politics' Revisited: Archaic Greece," in *Trade in the Ancient Economy*, ed. P. Garnsey, K. Hopkins, and C. R. Whittaker, Berkeley and Los Angeles, pp. 1–15.
Caskey, J. D. 1910. "The Roofed Gallery on the Walls of Athens," *AJA* 14, pp. 298–309.
Caskey, J. L. 1960. "Objects from a Well at Isthmia," *Hesperia* 29, pp. 168–176.
Caskey, J. L., and P. Amandry. 1952. "Investigations in the Heraion of Argos, 1949," *Hesperia* 21, pp. 165–221.
Caskey, J. L., and E. G. Caskey. 1960. "The Earliest Settlements at Eutresis," *Hesperia* 29, pp. 126–167.
Caskey, L. D. 1936. "Recent Acquisitions of the Museum of Fine Arts, Boston," *AJA* 40, pp. 306–313.
Cassimatis, H. 1988. "À propos de l'utilisation du motif iconographique: autel-trône? Une bizarrerie de l'imagerie," in *Proceedings of the 3rd Symposium of Ancient Greek and Related Pottery, Copenhagen, August 31 to September 4 1987*, ed. J. Christiansen and T. Melander, Copenhagen, pp. 117–129.
Casson, L. 1991. "The Ram and Naval Tactics," in *The Athlit Ram* (The Nautical Archaeology Series 3), ed. L. Casson and J. R. Steffy, College Station, Tex., pp. 76–82.
Casson, S. 1919–1921. "Excavations in Macedonia," *BSA* 24, pp. 1–33.
———. 1921. "The Dorian Invasion Reviewed in the Light of Some New Evidence," *AntJ* 1, pp. 199–221.
———. 1923–1925. "Excavations in Macedonia, 2," *BSA* 26, pp. 1–29.
———. 1926. *Macedonia, Thrace and Illyria: Their Relations to Greece from the Earliest Times down to the Time of Philip, Son of Amyntas*, Oxford.
———. 1933. *The Technique of Early Greek Sculpture*, Oxford.
Catling, H. W. 1964. *Cypriot Bronzework in the Mycenaean World*, Oxford.
Catling, H. W., and E. A. Catling. 1981. "'Barbarian' Pottery from the Mycenaean Settlement at the Menelaion, Sparta," *BSA* 76, pp. 71–82.
Catling, R. W. V. 1996. "A Tenth-century Trademark from Lefkandi," in *Minotaur and Centaur: Studies in the Archaeology of Crete and Euboea Presented to Mervyn Popham*, ed. D. Evely, I. S. Lemos, and S. Sherratt, Oxford, pp. 126–132.
———. 1998. "The Typology of the Protogeometric and Subprotogeometric Pottery from Troia and its Aegean Context," *Studia Troica* 8, pp. 151–187.
Cavalier, M. 1985. *Les amphores du VIe au IVe siècle dans les fouilles de Lipari*, Naples.
Cavanagh, W. G. 1998. "Innovation, Conservatism, and Variation in Mycenaean Funerary Ritual," in *Cemetery and Society in the Aegean Bronze Age*, ed. K. Branigan, Sheffield, pp. 103–114.
Cavanagh, W. G., and R. R. Laxton. 1984. "Lead Figurines from the Menelaion and Seriation," *BSA* 79, pp. 23–36.
Cawkwell, G. L. 1992. "Early Colonisation," *CQ* 42, pp. 289–303.
Cerchiai, C. 1984. "Les glandes plumbeae della Collezione Gorga," *BullCom* 88 (1982–1983), pp. 191–211.
Chambers, J. T. 1986. "Perdiccas, Thucydides, and the Greek City-States," in *Ancient Macedonia* 4 (Institute for Balkan Studies 204), ed. A. Vakalopoulos, Thessaloniki, pp. 138–145.
Chamoux, F. 1983. "Diodore et la Macédoine," in *Ancient Macedonia* 3 (Institute for Balkan Studies 193), ed. C. Svolopoulos, Thessaloniki, pp. 57–66.
Chaniotis, A. 1996. *Die Verträge zwischen kretischen Poleis in der hellenistischen Zeit* (Heidelberger althistorische Beiträge und epigraphische Studien 24), Stuttgart.
———. 2005. "Inscribed instrumenta domestica and the Economy of Hellenistic and Roman Crete," in *Making, Moving, and Managing: The New World of Ancient Economies*, ed. Z. H. Archibald, J. K. Davies, and V. Gabrielsen, Oxford, pp. 92–116.
Chantraine, P. 1980. *Dictionnaire étymologique de la langue grecque: Histoire des mots*, Paris.
Chapman, J. 2000. *Fragmentation in Archaeology: People, Places, and Broken Objects in the Prehistory of South-eastern Europe*, London.

Chapman, R., B. Leake, and M. Styles. 2002. "Microchemical Characterization of Alluvial Gold Grains as an Exploration Tool," *Gold Bulletin* 35 (2), pp. 53–65.

Charalambidou, X. 2017. "Viewing Euboea in Relation to Its Colonies and Relevant Sites in Northern Greece and Italy," in *Regional Stories Towards a New Perception of the Early Greek World*, ed. A. Mazarakis Ainian, A. Alexandridou, and X. Charalambidou, Volos, pp. 85–126.

———. 2020. "Chalcidian Deposits and Their Role in Reconstructing Production and Consumption Practices and the Function of Space in Early Iron Age and Archaic Chalcis: Some First Thoughts," in *Euboica II. Pithekoussai and Euboea between East and West* (*AION, Annali di Archeologia e Storia Antica, Università degli Studi di Napoli L'Orientale*, n.s. 26, 2019), vol. 1, ed. T. E. Cinquantaquattro and M. D'Acunto, Naples, pp. 55–71.

Charitonidis, S. 1955. "A Geometric Grave at Clenia in Corinthia," *AJA* 59, pp. 125–128.

Chase, G. H. 1902. "The Shield Devices of the Greeks," *HSCP* 13, pp. 61–127.

Chatziangelakis, L. 1984. "Ο προϊστορικός οικισμός της Πετρομαγούλας," *Ανθρωπολογικά* 5, pp. 75–85.

Chatzidimitriou, A. 2004–2009. "Ενεπίγραφα όστρακα από τους Ζάρακες Καρυστίας," *HOROS* 17–21, pp. 521–540.

Chatzis, N. S. 2010. "Κεραμική Γεωμετρικών χρόνων από τον αρχαίο οικισμό στο Καραβουρνάκι. Μια μελέτη των κατώτερων στρωμάτων της τομής 23–13α," *Εγνατία* 14, pp. 155–192.

Chatzitoulousis, S., T. Sianos, G. Stavridopoulos, and K. Touloumis. 2014. "Περίκλειστος κόσμος. Μια συζήτηση για τους περιβόλους στην προϊστορική Μακεδονία με αφορμή το Δισπηλιό Καστοριάς," in Stefani, Merousis, and Dimoula 2014, pp. 373–380.

Chavela, K. E. 2006. "Η χωροχρονική διάσταση του αρχαίου πολίσματος στην Τούμπα Θεσσαλονίκης: Η κεραμική ως πιλότος ερμηνείας" (diss. Aristotle Univ. Thessaloniki).

———. 2013. Rev. of Bessios, Tzifopoulos, and Kotsonas 2012, in *AJA* 117 (3), https://www.ajaonline.org/book-review/1619

———. 2018. "Transformations and Formations around the Thermaic Gulf in the Late Bronze and Early Iron Age: The Evidence of Burial Practices," in *Archaeology Across Frontiers and Borderlands: Fragmentation and Connectivity in the North Aegean and the Central Balkans from the Bronze Age to the Iron Age*, ed. S. Gimatzidis, M. Pieniążek, and S. Mangaloğlu-Votruba, Vienna, pp. 159–186.

Cheddadi, R., H. J. B. Birks, P. Tarroso, S. Liepelt, D. Gömöry, S. Dullinger, E. S. Meier, K. Hülber, L. Maiorano, and H. Laborde. 2014. "Revisiting Tree-migration Rates: *Abies alba* (Mill.). A Case Study," *Vegetation History and Archaeobotany* 23, pp. 113–122.

Chemsseddoha, A.-Z. 2019. *Les pratiques funéraires de l'Âge du Fer en Grèce du Nord: étude d'histoires regionales* (Scripta Antiqua 121), Bordeaux.

Cherry, J. F., and J. L. Davis. 2007. "The Other Finds," in *Excavations at Phylakopi in Melos 1974–1977* (*BSA* Suppl. 42), ed. C. Renfrew, N. Brodie, C. Morris, and C. Scarre, London, pp. 401–464.

Childe, V. G. 1929. *The Danube in Prehistory*, Oxford.

Chochliouros, S. P. 2005. "Χλωριδική και φυτοκοινωνιολογική έρευνα του όρους Βερμίου—Οικολογική προσέγγιση" (diss. University of Patras).

Chondroyianni-Metoki, A. 1997. "Αλιάκμων 1997. Στοιχεία από την επιφανειακή έρευνα και την ανασκαφή δυο νεκροταφείων, της ΥΕΧ και ΠΕΣ," *AEMTh 11* [1999], pp. 31–42.

———. 2009. "Μη οικιστικές χρήσεις χώρου στους νεολιθικούς οικισμούς. Το παράδειγμα της Τούμπας Κρεμαστής Κοιλάδας" (diss. Aristotle Univ. Thessaloniki).

———. 2010. "Η καύση των νεκρών στο νεολιθικό οικισμό της Τούμπας Κρεμαστής Κοιλάδας στην Κίτρινη Λίμνη Κοζάνης," in *ΙΡΙΣ. Μελέτες στη μνήμη της καθηγήτριας Αγγελικής Πιλάλη-Παπαστερίου από τους μαθητές της στο Πανεπιστήμιο Θεσσαλονίκης*, ed. N. Merousis, E. Stefani, and M. Nikolaidou, Thessaloniki, pp. 213–234.

Choremis, A. 1973. "Μυκηναϊκοὶ καὶ Πρωτογεωμετρικοὶ τάφοι εἰς Καρποφόρον Μεσσηνίας," *ArchEph* 1973, pp. 25–74.

Christov, I., and M. Manov. 2011. "Ancient Macedonian Sling Bullets from the Area of a Thracian Rulers' Residence near the Peak of Kozi Gramadi," *Archaeologia Bulgarica* 15, pp. 21–33.

Chrysostomou, A. 1987. "Το τείχος της Έδεσσας," *AEMTh* 1, pp. 161–172.

———. 1994. *Ancient Almopia*. Thessaloniki.

———. 1995. "Το νεκροταφείο των τύμβων Εποχής Σιδήρου στην Κωνσταντία Αλμωπίας," *AEMTh* 1 [1988], pp. 155–166.

———, ed. 2008. *Αρχαία Έδεσσα*, Edessa.

———. 2013. *Αρχαία Έδεσσα, Τα Νεκροταφεία*, Volos.

———. 2016. "Η ανασκαφή και τα ευρήματα από το νεκροταφείο Εποχής Σιδήρου στη θέση 'Ναυτικός Όμιλος' Άρνισσας," in *Φίλιππος· τριμηνιαία έκθεση της Ιστορικής και Λαογραφικής Εταιρείας Γιαννιτσών "Ο Φίλιππος,"* ed. A. Chrysostomou, Giannitsa, pp. 7–36.

Chrysostomou, A., and P. Chrysostomou. 1995. "Ανασκαφή στην τράπεζα του Αρχοντικού Γιαννιτσών κατά το 1994," *AEMTh* 9 [1998], pp. 73–82.

———. 2011. "Κεραμική ύστερων κλασικών–πρώιμων ελληνιστικών χρόνων από το δυτικό νεκροταφείο του αρχαίου οικισμού στο Αρχοντικό Πέλλας," in *Ζ' Επιστημονική Συνάντηση για την Ελληνιστική Κεραμική, Αίγιο, 4–9 Απριλίου 2005*, Athens, pp. 393–406.

———. 2012. "Ιωνικά bucchero από τα νεκροταφεία του Αρχοντικού Πέλλας," in Tiverios et al. 2012, pp. 239–251.

Chrysostomou, P. 2011. "Ο αρχαίος οικισμός του Αρχοντικού," in *Το Αρχαιολογικό Μουσείο Πέλλας*, ed. E. Louvrou, Athens, pp. 299–389.

Chrysostomou, P., and Pan. Chrysostomou. 1990. "Νεολιθικές έρευνες στα Γιαννιτσά και στην περιοχή τους," *AEMTh* 4 [1993], pp. 169–177.

Chrysostomou, Pan. 1996. "Η νεολιθική κατοίκηση στη βόρεια παράκτια ζώνη του άλλοτε Θερμαϊκού κόλπου (Επαρχία Γιαννιτσών)," *AEMTh* 10A [1997], pp. 159–172.

———. 2001. "Νέα στοιχεία από την προϊστορική έρευνα στην επαρχία Γιαννιτσών: μια άγνωστη μορφή προϊστορικής γραφής," *AEMTh* 15 [2005], pp. 489–498.

Chykerda, M.C., and M. A. Kontonicolas. Forthcoming. "The Ancient Methone Archaeological Survey: A Balanced Approach to an Intraurban Landscape in Pieria, Greece."

Claassen, C. 1991. "Gender, Shellfishing, and the Shell Mound Archaic," in *Engendering Archaeology: Women and Prehistory*, ed. J. M. Gero and M. W. Conkey, Oxford, pp. 276–300.

Claveau, Y., C. Messier, P. G. Comeau, and K. D. Coates. 2002. "Growth and Crown Morphological Responses of Boreal Conifer Seedlings and Saplings with Contrasting Shade Tolerance to a Gradient of Light and Height," *Canadian Journal of Forest Research* 32, pp. 458–468.

Cleal, R. 1988. "The Occurrence of Drilled Holes in Later Neolithic Pottery," *OJA* 7, pp. 139–145.

Clinkenbeard, B. G. 1982. "Lesbian Wine and Storage Amphoras: A Progress Report on Identification," *Hesperia* 51, pp. 248–268.

———. 1986. "Lesbian and Thasian Wine Amphoras: Questions Concerning Collaboration," in *Recherches sur les amphores grecques*, ed. J.-Y. Empereur and Y. Garlan (*BCH* Suppl. 13), Paris, pp. 353–362.

Coates, J. 1997. "Some Comments on the Article on Shipworm in (and Beaching of) Ancient Mediterranean Warships in *IJNA*, 25.2: 104–121," *IJNA* 26, pp. 82–83.

———. 1999. "Long Ships, Slipways and Beaches," in *Tropis V. Proceedings of the 5th International Symposium on Ship Construction in Antiquity, Nauplia, 26–28 August 1993*, ed. H. Tzalas, Athens, pp. 103–118.

Coccolutto, M. 2006. "Un gruppo di ghiande missili dal saggio III," in *Materiali per Populonia* 5, ed. M. Aprosio and C. Mascione, Pisa, pp. 187–195.

Cohen, B., ed. 2006. *The Colors of Clay: Special Techniques in Athenian Vases* (Exhibition catalogue, The J. Paul Getty Museum 2006), Los Angeles.

Cohen, G. M. 2013. *The Hellenistic Settlements in the East from Armenia and Mesopotamia to Bactria and India* (Hellenistic Culture and Society 54), Berkeley, Los Angeles, and London.

———. 2015. "Polis Hellenis," in *East and West in the World Empire of Alexander: Essays in Honour of Brian Bosworth*, ed. P. Wheatley and E. Baynham, Oxford, pp. 259–276.

Coldstream, J. N. 1960. "A Geometric Well at Knossos," *BSA* 55, pp. 159–171.

———. 1968. *Greek Geometric Pottery: A Survey of Ten Local Styles and Their Chronology,* London.

———. 1973. *Knossos: The Sanctuary of Demeter* (*BSA* Suppl. 8), Oxford.

———. 1977. *Geometric Greece*, London.

———. 1981. "The Greek Geometric and Plain Archaic Imports," in *Excavations at Kition* 4: *The Non-Cypriote Pottery*, ed. V. Karageorghis, J. N. Coldstream, P. M. Bikai, A. W. Johnston, M. Robertson, and L. Jehasse, Nicosia, pp. 17–22.

———. 1995. "Euboean Geometric Imports from the Acropolis of Pithekoussai," *BSA* 90, pp. 251–267.

———. 2003. "The BSA's Geometric Collection: Kynosarges et alia," *BSA* 98, pp. 331–346.

———. 2008. *Greek Geometric Pottery: A Survey of Ten Local Styles and Their Chronology*, 2nd ed., Bristol.

Coldstream, J. N., and H. W. Catling. 1996. *Knossos North Cemetery: Early Greek Tombs* (*BSA* Suppl. 28), London.

Cole, J. W. 1974. "Perdiccas and Athens," *Phoenix* 28 (1), *Studies Presented to Mary E. White on the Occasion of Her Sixty-fifth Birthday*, pp. 55–72.

Coleman, J. E. 1977. *Kephala: A Late Neolithic Settlement and Cemetery* (*Keos* 1), Princeton.

———. 1986. *Excavations at Pylos in Elis* (*Hesperia* Suppl. 21), Princeton.

———2000. "An Archaeological Scenario for the 'Coming of the Greeks' ca. 3200 B.C.," *Journal of Indo-European Studies* 28, pp. 101–153.

———. 2011. "The Petromagoula-Doliana Group and the Beginning of the Aegean Early Bronze Age," *HELIKE* 4, pp. 13–41.

Colivicchi, F. 2004. *Gravisca. Scavi nel santuario greco* 16: *I materiali minori (con contributi di G. Gorini—le monete, e C. Sorrentino—i reperti osteologici)*, Bari.

Collart, P., and P. Ducrey. 1975. *Philippes 1: Les reliefs rupestres* (*BCH* Suppl. 2), Athens.

Connan, J., and A. Nissenbaum. 2003. "Conifer Tar on the Keel and Hull Planking of the Ma'agan Mikhael Ship (Israel, 5th century B.C.): Identification and Comparison with Natural Products and Artefacts Employed in Boat Construction," *JAS* 30, pp. 709–719.

Consolo Langher, S. N. 2007. "La Macedonia da Aminta III a Filippo II (la formazione del grando stato territoriale Macedone)," in *Ancient Macedonia* 7: *Macedonia from the Iron Age to the Death of Philip II* (Institute for Balkan Studies 280), ed. E. Voutiras, Thessaloniki, pp. 229–238.

Constantakopoulou, C. 2007. *The Dance of the Islands: Insularity, Networks, the Athenian Empire, and the Aegean World*, Oxford.

Conte, S., R. Arletti, J. Henderson, P. Degryse, and A. Blomme. 2016a. "Different Glassmaking Technologies in the Production of Iron Age Black Glass from Italy and Slovakia," *Archaeological and Anthropological Sciences* 3 (10), pp. 503–521.

Conte, S., R. Arletti, F. Mermati, and B. Gratuze. 2016b. "Unravelling the Iron Age Glass Trade in Southern Italy: The First Trace-element Analyses," *European Journal of Mineralogy* 28 (2), pp. 409–433.

Cook, E. F. 2000. Rev. of I. Malkin, *The Returns of Odysseus: Colonization and Ethnicity*, *BMCR* 2000.03.22.

Cook, J. M. 1947. "Athenian Workshops Around 700," *BSA* 42, pp. 139–155.

———. 1958–1959. "Old Smyrna, 1948–1951," *BSA* 53–54, pp. 1–34.

———. 1965. "Old Smyrna: Ionic Black Figure and Other Sixth-Century Figured Wares," *BSA* 60, pp. 114–142.

———. 1973. *The Troad: An Archaeological and Topographical Study*, Oxford.

———. 1975. "Greek Settlement in the Eastern Aegean and Asia Minor," in *CAH* II.2: *History of the Middle East and the Aegean Region c. 1380–1000 BC*, 3rd ed., ed. I. E. S. Edwards, C. J. Gadd, N. G. L. Hammond, and E. Sollberger, Cambridge, pp. 773–804.

———. 1982. "The Eastern Greeks," in *CAH* III.3: *The Expansion of the Greek World, Eighth to Sixth Centuries BC*, 2nd ed., ed. J. Boardman and N. G. L. Hammond, Cambridge, pp. 196–221.

Cook, R. M. 1946. "Ionia and Greece in the Eighth and Seventh Centuries B.C.," *JHS* 66, pp. 67–98.

———. 1972. *Greek Painted Pottery*, 2nd ed., London.

Cook, R. M., and P. Dupont. 1998. *East Greek Pottery*, London and New York.

Cooley, A. E. 2012. *The Cambridge Manual of Latin Epigraphy*, Cambridge.

Cooney, G. 2003. "Introduction: Seeing the Land from the Sea," *World Archaeology* 35, *Seascapes*, pp. 323–328.

Corbett, P. E. 1949. "Attic Pottery of the Later Fifth Century from the Athenian Agora," *Hesperia* 18, pp. 298–351.

———. 1955. "Palmette Stamps from an Attic Black-Glaze Workshop," *Hesperia* 24, pp. 172–186.

Corinth = *Corinth. Results of Excavations Conducted by the American School of Classical Studies at Athens*, Princeton

IV.2 = O. Broneer, *Terracotta Lamps*, Cambridge, Mass., 1930.

VII.1 = S. S. Weinberg, *The Geometric and Orientalizing Pottery*, Cambridge, Mass., 1943.

VII.2 = D. A. Amyx and P. Lawrence, *Archaic Corinthian Pottery and the Anaploga Well*, 1975.

VII.3 = G. R. Edwards, *Corinthian Hellenistic Pottery*, 1975.

VII.6 = I. McPhee and E. G. Pemberton, *Late Classical Pottery from Ancient Corinth: Drain 1971-1 in the Forum Southwest*, 2012.

XII = G. R. Davidson, *The Minor Objects*, 1952.

XIII = C. W. Blegen, H. Palmer, and R. S. Young, *The North Cemetery*, 1964.

XIV = C. Roebuck, *The Asklepieion and Lerna*, 1951.

XV.1 = A. N. Stillwell, *The Potters' Quarter*, 1948.

XV.3 = A. N. Stillwell and J. L. Benson, *The Potters' Quarter: The Pottery*, 1984.

XVIII.1 = E. G. Pemberton, *The Sanctuary of Demeter and Kore: The Greek Pottery*, 1989.

Coudin, F. 2009. *Les Laconiens et la Méditerranée à l'époque archaïque*, Naples.

Coulié, A. 1996. "Το θασιακό εργαστήριο μελανόμορφων αγγείων· γιατί θασιακό;" *AEMTh* 10B [1997], pp. 825–834.

Coulson, W. D. E. 1985. "The Dark Age Pottery of Sparta," *BSA* 80, pp. 29–84.

Courbin, P. 1954. "Travaux de l'École française: Argos. 4: Nécropoles et céramiques," *BCH* 78, pp. 175–183.

———. 1957. "Une tombe géomètrique d'Argos," *BCH* 81, pp. 322–386.

———. 1966. *La céramique géométrique de l'Argolide*, Paris.

———. 1974. *Tombes géométriques d'Argos* I *(1952–1958)* (Etudes péloponnésiennes 7), Paris.

———. 1978. "La céramique de la Grèce de l'est à Ras el Bassit," in *Les céramiques de la Grèce de l'est et leur diffusion en occident. Centre Jean Bérard, Institut Français de Naples, 6–9 juillet 1976*, Paris, pp. 41–42.

Courtois, J.-C. 1984. *Alasia* 3: *Les objets des niveaux stratifiés d'Enkomi (Fouilles C. F.-A. Schaeffer, 1947–1970)*, Paris.

Courtois, L. 2004. "Les techniques de la céramique," in *Dikili Tash, village préhistorique de Macédoine Orientale* 1: *Fouilles de Jean Deshayes 1961–1975* 2 (*BCH* Suppl. 37), ed. R. Treuil, Paris, pp. 1–25.

Craddock, P. T. 1995. *Early Metal Mining and Production*. Edinburgh.

Craddock, P. T., M. R. Cowell, and M. F. Guerra. 2005. "Controlling the Composition of Gold and the Invention of Gold Refining in Lydian Anatolia," in *Anatolian Metal* 3 (*Der Anschnitt*, Beiheft 18), ed. Ü. Yalcun, Bochum, pp. 67–77.

Craddock, P. T., I. C. Freestone, and C. D. Dawe. 1997. "Casting Metals in Limestone Moulds," *Historical Metallurgy* 31 (1), pp. 1–7.

Craig, H. 1957. "Isotopic Standards for Carbon and Oxygen and Correction Factors for Mass-spectrometric Analysis of Carbon Dioxide," *Geochimica et Cosmochimica Acta* 12, pp. 133–149.

Crandell, O., C. Ionescu, and P. Mirea. 2016. "Neolithic and Chalcolithic Stone Tools Used in Ceramics Production: Examples from the South of Romania," *Journal of Lithic Studies* 3 (1), pp. 1–18, doi:10.2218/jls.v3i1.1134.

Crielaard, J. P. 2012. "*Hygra Keleutha*: Maritime Matters and the Ideology of Seafaring in the Greek Epic Tradition," in *Alle origini della Magna Grecia. Mobilità, migrazioni, fondazioni. Atti del Cinquantesimo Convegno di Studi sulla Magna Grecia*, Taranto, pp. 135–157.

Cristofani, M. M. 1978. "La ceramica greco-orientale in Etruria," in *Les céramiques de la Grèce de l'est et leur diffusion en occident. Centre Jean Bérard, Institut Français de Naples, 6–9 juillet 1976*, Paris, pp. 150–212.

Critchfield, W. B., and E. L. Little. 1966. *Geographic Distribution of the Pines of the World*, Washington, D.C.

Croissant, F. 2008. "Batailles géométriques pariennes," in *Alba della città, l'alba delle immagine?* (Tripodes 7), ed. B. d'Agostino, Athens, pp. 31–62.

Csapo, E., A. W. Johnston, and D. Geagan. 2000. "The Iron Age Inscriptions," in *Kommos* 4: *The Greek Sanctuary*, Part 1, ed. J. W. Shaw and M. Shaw, Princeton and Oxford, pp. 101–134.

Cucuzza, N. 1998. "Geometric Phaistos: A Survey," in *Post-Minoan Crete. Proceedings of the First Colloquium on Post-Minoan Crete Held by the British School at Athens and the Institute of Archaeology, University College London, 10–11 November 1995*, ed. W. G. Cavanagh, M. Curtis, J. N. Coldstream, and A. W. Johnston (*BSA* Studies 2), London, pp. 62–68.

Culican, W. 1975. "Sidonian Bottles," *Levant* 7, pp. 145–150.

Cullen, T., L. E. Talalay, D. R. Keller, L. Karimali, and W. R. Farrand. 2013. *The Prehistory of the Paximadi Peninsula, Euboea* (Prehistory Monographs 40), Philadelphia.

Cuming, H. S. 1864. "On the History of Slings," *The Journal of the British Archaeological Association* 1864, pp. 73–81.

Cuomo di Caprio, N. 2007. *La Ceramica in Archeologia* 2. *Antiche tecniche di lavorazione e moderni metodi di indagine*, Rome.

Dafis, S. 1972. *Δασική Φυτοκοινωνιολογία*, Thessaloniki.

———. 2010. *Τα δάση της Ελλάδας*, Thessaloniki.

Dain, A. 1938. *Sylloge tacticorum quae olim "Inedita Leonis Tactica" dicebatur*, Paris.

Dakaris, S. I. 1974. "Δωδώνη," *Ergon* 1974, pp. 44–50.

———. 1998. *Δωδώνη. Αρχαιολογικός οδηγός*, Ioannina.

Dakoronia, Ph. 1987. "Αταλάντη: Οδός Δημοτική (οικόπεδο Αχ. Γκούρα)," *ArchDelt* 42.B'1, pp. 226–228.

———. 1989. "Κρίκοι: Προνομισματικὲς μορφὲς γεωμετρικῆς ἐποχῆς," *ArchEph* 128, pp. 115–120.

———. 2003. "The Transition from Late Helladic III C to the Early Iron Age at Kynos," in *LH III C Chronology and Synchronisms. Proceedings of the International Workshop Held at the Austrian Academy of Sciences at Vienna, May 7th and 8th, 2001*, ed. S. Deger-Jalkotzy and M. Zavadil, Vienna, pp. 37–51.

Dakoronia, Ph., and P. Kounouklas. 2009. "Kynos' Pace to the Early Iron Age," in *LH III C Chronology and Synchronisms* 3: *LH III C Late and the Transition to the Early Iron Age. Proceedings of the International Workshop Held at the Austrian Academy of Sciences at Vienna, February 23rd and 24th, 2007*, ed. S. Deger-Jalkotzy and A. E. Bächle, Vienna, pp. 61–76.

D'Andrea, A. C., and H. Mitiku. 2002. "Traditional Emmer Processing in Highland Ethiopia," *Journal of Ethnobiology* 22, pp. 179–217.

Danile, L. 2009. "Lemnian Grey Ware," in *Pontic Grey Wares. International Conference, Bucharest-Constantza, September 30–October 3, 2008* (Pontica 42), Constanta, pp. 305–326.

———. 2011. *Lemno* 2: *Scavi ad Efestia* 1: *La ceramic grigia di Efestia dagli inizi dell'età del ferro all'età alto-arcaica*, Athens.

———. 2012. "Local Productions and Imports at Hephaestia (Lemnos): From the Early Iron Age to the Archaic Period," in Tiverios et al. 2012, pp. 79–90.

Daragan, M. 2009. "Grey Pottery from Monuments of the Early Scythian Period in the Middle Dnestr Region (Western Podolian Group of Monuments)," in *Pontic Grey Wares. International Conference, Bucharest-Constantza, September 30–October 3, 2008* (Pontica 42), Constanta, pp. 119–147.

Darcque, P., H. Koukouli-Chrysanthaki, D. Malamidou, R. Treuil, and Z. Tsirtsoni. 2007. "Recent Researches at the Neolithic Settlement of Dikili Tash, Eastern Macedonia, Greece: An Overview," in *The Struma/Strymon Valley in Prehistory: In the Steps of James Harvey Gaul* 2, ed. H. Todorova, M. Stefanovich, and G. Ivanov, Sofia, pp. 247–256.

Daux, G. 1957. "Chronique des fouilles et découvertes archéologique en Grèce en 1956," *BCH* 81, pp. 496–713.

Davaras, K. 1992. "Bronze Double Axes," in *Minoan and Greek Civilization from the Mitsotakis Collection*, ed. L. Marangou, Athens, pp. 262–267.

Davey, C. J., and I. Edwards. 2008. "Crucibles from the Bronze Age of Egypt and Mesopotamia," in *Proceedings of the Royal Society of Victoria* 120 (1), pp. 146–154.

David, W. 2002. *Studien zu Ornamentik und Datierung der bronzezeitlichen Depotfundgruppe Hajdúsamson-Apa-Ighel-Zajta* 1–2, Karlsberg.

Davidson, G. R., and D. Burr Thompson. 1943. *Small Objects from the Pnyx* 1 (*Hesperia* Suppl. 7), Amsterdam.

Davies, J. K. 2001. "Hellenistic Economies in the Post-Finley Era," in *Hellenistic Economies*, ed. Z. H. Archibald, J. Davies, V. Gabrielsen, and G. J. Oliver, London, pp. 11–62.

———. 2013. "Corridors, Cleruchies, Commodities, and Coins: The Pre-history of the Athenian Empire," in *Trade and Finance in the 5th c. BC Aegean World* (BYZAS 18), ed. A. Slawisch, Istanbul, pp. 43–66.

Davison, J. M. 1961. *Attic Geometric Workshops* (*YCS* 16), New Haven.

Dawkins, R. M. 1909–1910. "Laconia. I: Excavations at Sparta, 1910. 2: The Mycenaean City near the Menelaion," *BSA* 16, pp. 4–11.

———, ed. 1929a. *The Sanctuary of Artemis Orthia at Sparta, Excavated and Described by Members of the British School at Athens, 1906–1910* (The Society for the Promotion of Hellenic Studies, Suppl. 5), London.

———. 1929b. "Objects in Carved Ivory and Bone," in Dawkins 1929a, pp. 203–248.

Dawkins, R. M., A. J. B. Wace, J. P. Droop, G. Dickens, M. N. Tod, H. J. W. Tillyard, and A. M. Woodward. 1906–1907. "Laconia, I: Excavations at Sparta, 1907," *BSA* 13, pp. 1–218.

Day, J. W. 2010. *Archaic Epigram and Dedication: Representation and Reperformance*, Cambridge.

———. 2019."The Origins of Greek Epigram: The Unity of Inscription and Object," in *A Companion to Ancient Epigram*, ed. C. Henriksén, Hoboken, N.J., pp. 231–247.

Day, L. P. 2011. "Appropriating the Past: Early Iron Age Mortuary Practices at Kavousi, Crete," in *The "Dark Ages" Revisited. Acts of an International Symposium in Memory of William D. E. Coulson, University of Thessaly, Volos, 14–17 June 2007*, ed. A. Mazarakis Ainian, Volos, pp. 745–757.

Day, L. P., W. D. E. Coulson, and G. C. Gesell. 1986. "Kavousi, 1983–1984: The Settlement at Vronda," *Hesperia* 55, pp. 355–387.

Day, P. M., P. S. Quinn, J. B. Rutter, and V. Kilikoglou. 2011. "A World of Goods: Transport Jars and Commodity Exchange at the Late Bronze Age Harbor of Kommos, Crete," *Hesperia* 80, pp. 511–558.

De Angelis, F. 1994. "The Foundation of Selinous: Overpopulation and Opportunities," in *The Archaeology of Greek Colonisation: Essays Dedicated to Sir John Boardman* (Oxford Committee for Archaeology Monograph 40), ed. G. R. Tsetskhladze and F. De Angelis, Oxford, pp. 87–110.

———. 1998. "Ancient Past, Imperial Present: The British Empire in T. J. Dunbabin's *The Western Greeks*," *Antiquity* 72, pp. 539–549.

———. 2002. "Trade and Agriculture at Megara Hyblaia," *OJA* 21, pp. 299–310.

———. 2010. "Ancient Greek Colonization in the 21st Century: Some Suggested Directions," *Bollettino di Archeologia On Line* (volume speciale), pp. 18–30.

———. 2016. *Archaic and Classical Greek Sicily: A Social and Economic History*, Oxford.

De Angelis, S., and M. Gori. 2017. "The Wheel and the Sun: 'Glocal' Symbologies of Wheel-pendants across Europe," in *New Perspectives on the Bronze Age. Proceedings of the 13th Nordic Bronze Age Symposium Held in Gothenburg 9th to 13th June 2015*, ed. S. Bergerbrant and A. Wessman, Oxford, pp. 355–366.

de Callataÿ, Fr. 2012. "Control Marks on Hellenistic Royal Coinages: Use, and Evolution Toward Simplification?" *RBN* 158, pp. 39–62.

Decavallas, O. 2007. "Beeswax in Neolithic Perforated Sherds from the Northern Aegean: New Economic and Social Implications," in *Cooking Up the Past: Food and Culinary Practices in the Neolithic and Bronze Age Aegean*, ed. C. Mee and J. Renard, Oxford, pp. 148–157.

DeCou, H. F. 1905. "The Bronzes of the Argive Heraeum," in *The Argive Heraeum* 2: *Terra-cotta Figurines, Terra-cotta Reliefs, Vases and Vase Fragments, Bronzes, Engraved Stones, Gems, and Ivories, Coins, Egyptian, or Graeco-Egyptian Objects*, ed. C. Waldstein, Boston, pp. 191–399.

de Domingo, C., and A. Johnston. 2003. "A Petrographic and Chemical Study of East Greek and Other Archaic Transport Amphorae," *Eulimene* 4, pp. 27–60.

Deger-Jalkotzy, S. 1977. *Fremde Zuwanderer im spätmykenischen Griechenland*, Vienna.

———. 1983. "Das Problem der 'Handmade Burnished Ware' von Myk. IIIC," in *Griechenland, die Ägäis und die Levante während der 'Dark Ages' vom 12. bis zum 9. Jh. v.Chr.*, ed. S. Deger-Jalkotzy, Vienna, pp. 161–168.

———. 2009. "From LH III C Late to the Early Iron Age: The Submycenaean Period at Elateia," in *LH III C Chronology and Synchronisms* 3: *LH III C Late and the Transition to the Early Iron Age. Proceedings of the International Workshop Held at the Austrian Academy of Sciences at Vienna, February 23rd and 24th, 2007*, ed. S. Deger-Jalkotzy and A. E. Bächle, Vienna, pp. 77–116.

Deith, M. R., and J. C. Shackleton. 1988. "The Contribution of Shells to Site Interpretation: Approaches to Shell Material from Franchthi Cave," in *Conceptual Issues in Environmental Archaeology*, ed. J. Bintliff, D. Davidson, and E. Grant, Edinburgh, pp. 49–58.

de Juliis, E. M., A. Alessio, and M. di Puolo. 1989. *Gli ori di Taranto in età ellenistica*, Milan.

Dekoulakou, I. N. 1973. "Γεωμετρικοὶ ταφικοὶ πίθοι ἐξ Ἀχαΐας," *ArchEph* 1973, pp. 15–29.

de la Genière, J. 1968. *Recherches sur l'âge du fer en Italie méridionale, Sala Consilina*, Naples.

———. 1971. "Amendolara (Cosenza): Campagne del 1967 e 1968 (relazione preliminare)," *NSc* 1971, pp. 439–475.

———. 1979. "The Iron Age in Southern Italy," in *Italy Before the Romans: The Iron Age, Orientalizing, and Etruscan Periods*, ed. D. Ridgway and F. R. Ridgway, London, pp. 59–93.

———. 1984. "'Perfumés comme Crésus': De l'origine du lécythe attique," *BCH* 108, pp. 91–98.

Delamotte, M., and E. Vardala-Theodorou. 1994. *Shells from the Greek Seas*, Athens.

Deliopoulos, G. 2010. "Η εγχάρακτη κεραμική της Ύστερης Εποχής του Χαλκού στον προϊστορικό οικισμό του Αρχοντικού Γιαννιτσών," in *ΙΡΙΣ: μελέτες στη μνήμη της καθηγήτριας Αγγελικής Πιλάλη-Παπαστερίου από τους μαθητές της στο Αριστοτέλειο Πανεπιστήμιο Θεσσαλονίκης*, ed. N. Merousis, E. Stefani, and M. Nikolaidou, Thessaloniki, pp. 75–92.

Deliopoulos, G., I. Papadias, and A. Papefthymiou-Papantimou. 2014. "Η κεραμική των προχωρημένων φάσεων της Πρώιμης Εποχής του Χαλκού στη Μακεδονία," in Stefani, Merousis, and Dimoula 2014, pp. 561–576.

Dell, H. J. 1970. "The Western Frontier of the Macedonian Monarchy," in *Ancient Macedonia* 1 (Institute for Balkan Studies 122), ed. B. Laourdas and Ch. Makaronas, Thessaloniki, pp. 115–126.

Dell'Oro, F. 2017. "Alphabets and Dialects in the Euboean Colonies of Sicily and Magna Graecia, or What Could Have Happened in Methone," in Strauss Clay, Malkin, and Tzifopoulos 2017b, pp. 165–181.

Délos = *Exploration Archéologique de Délos, faite par l'École française d'Athènes*, Paris

VIII = J. Chamonard, *Le quartier du théatre: Études sur l'habitation à l'époque hellénistique* 3: *Construction et technique*, 1924.

X = C. Dugas, *Les vases d'Héraion*, 1928.

XV = C. Dugas and C. Rhomaios, *Les vases préhelléniques et géométriques*, 1934.

XVIII = W. Deonna, *Le Mobilier Délien*, 1938.
Demesticha, S., and A. B. Knapp. 2016a. *Maritime Transport Containers in the Bronze Age–Iron Age Aegean and Eastern Mediterranean*, Uppsala.
———. 2016b. "Introduction: Maritime Transport Containers in the Bronze and Iron Age Aegean and East Mediterranean," in *Maritime Transport Containers in the Bronze Age–Iron Age Aegean and Eastern Mediterranean*, ed. S. Demesticha and A. B. Knapp, Uppsala, pp. 1–16.
Demetriou, D. 2011. "What Is an Emporion? A Reassessment," *Historia* 60, pp. 255–272.
De Minicis, G. 1844. "Sulle antiche ghiande missili e sulle loro iscrizioni" (diss. Pontificia Accademia Romana di Archeologia).
Demoule, J.-P. 2004. "Les récipients en céramique du Néolithique Récent (Chalcolithique): description, évolution et contexte régional," in *Dikili Tash, village préhistorique de Macédoine Orientale* 1: *Fouilles de Jean Deshayes 1961–1975* 2 (*BCH* Suppl. 37), ed. R. Treuil, Paris, pp. 63–270.
DeNiro, M. J. 1985. "Postmortem Preservation and Alteration of *in-vivo* Bone Collagen Isotope Ratios in Relation to Paleodietary Reconstruction," *Nature* 317, pp. 806–809.
Denker, A., and H. Oniz. 2015. "3D Modeling of the Archaic Amphoras of Ionia," in *The International Archives of the Photogrammetry, Remote Sensing and Spatial Information Sciences, vol. XL-5/W5, 2015 Underwater 3D Recording and Modeling, 16–17 April 2015*, Piano di Sorrento, pp. 84–92, https://www.int-arch-photogramm-remote-sens-spatial-inf-sci.net/XL-5-W5/85/2015/isprsarchives-XL-5-W5-85-2015.pdf
Denniston, J. D. 1954. *The Greek Particles*, 2nd ed., Oxford.
Deonna, W. 1959. "Haches, broches et chenets dans une tombe géométrique d'Argos," *BCH* 83, pp. 247–253.
Deppert-Lippitz, B. 1985. *Griechischer Goldschmuck*, Mainz.
de Ridder, A. 1895. "Fouilles d'Orchomène," *BCH* 19, pp. 137–224.
———. 1896. *Catalogue des bronzes trouvés sur l'acropole d'Athènes*, Paris.
Desborough, V. R. d'A. 1948. "What Is Protogeometric?" *BSA* 43, pp. 260–272.
———. 1952. *Protogeometric Pottery*, Oxford.
———. 1954. "Mycenae 1939–1953. Part 5: Four Tombs," *BSA* 49, pp. 258–266.
———. 1955. "Mycenae 1939–1954. Part 6: Three Geometric Graves," *BSA* 50, pp. 239–247.
———. 1956. "Mycenae 1939–1955. Part 3: Two Tombs," *BSA* 51, pp. 128–130.
———. 1960. Rev. of Verdelis 1958, in *JHS* 80, pp. 234–235.
———. 1963. "Appendix II: The Low-footed Skyphoi with Pendent Semicircles," in "A 'Royal' Tomb at Salamis, Cyprus," ed. P. Dikaios, *AA* 78, pp. 204–206.
———. 1964. *The Last Mycenaeans and Their Successors: An Archaeological Survey c. 1200–c. 1000 B.C.*, Oxford.
———. 1965. "The Greek Mainland, c. 1150–c. 1000 B.C.," *PPS* 31, pp. 213–228.
———. 1972. *The Greek Dark Ages*, London.
———. 1973. "Late Burials from Mycenae," *BSA* 68, pp. 87–101.
———. 1976. "The Background to Euboean Participation in Early Greek Maritime Enterprise," in *Tribute to an Antiquary: Essays Presented to Marc Fitch by Some of His Friends*, ed. F. Emmison and R. Stephens, London, pp. 27–40.
———. 1979. "A Postscript to an Appendix," in *Studies Presented in Memory of Porphyrios Dikaios*, ed. V. Karageorghis et al., Nicosia, pp. 119–122.
Descamps-Lequime, S., ed. 2011. *Au royaume d'Alexandre le Grand: la Macédoine antique*, Paris.
Descoeudres, J.-P. 1976. "Die vorklassische Keramik aus dem Gebiet des Westtors," in *Eretria* V, pp. 13–58.
———. 1978. "Euboeans in Australia: Some Observations on the Imitations of Corinthian Kotylai Made in Eretria and Found in Al Mina," in *Eretria* IV, pp. 7–19.
———. 2008. "Central Greece on the Eve of the Colonisation Movement," in *Greek Colonisation: An Account of Greek Colonies and Other Settlements Overseas* 2, ed. G. Tsetskhladze, Leiden, pp. 289–382.
Descoeudres, J.-P., and R. A. Kearsley. 1983. "Greek Pottery at Veii: Another Look," *BSA* 78, pp. 9–53.
Deshayes, J. 1960. *Les outils de bronze, de l'Indus au Danube (IVe au IIe millénaire)*, Paris.
———. 1966. *Argos, les fouilles de la Deiras* (Études péloponnésiennes 4), Paris.
Despoini, A. 1976. "Νομός Πιερίας," *ArchDelt* 31, Β΄2, pp. 247–251.
———. 1996. *Αρχαία χρυσά κοσμήματα*, Athens.
Despinis, G. 1979. "Ανασκαφή Τήνου," *Prakt* 1979, pp. 228–235.
De Witte, J. 1876. "Hercule et les oiseaux de Stymphale," *GazArch* 1876, pp. 8–10.
Díaz Ariño, B. 2005. "Glandes inscriptae de la península ibérica," *ZPE* 153, pp. 219–236.
———. 2008. *Epigrafía latina republicana de Hispania* (Colecció instrumenta 26), Barcelona.
DiBattista, A. 2021. "Transformations of Animal Materials in Early Greece" (diss. University of California, Los Angeles).
Dickinson, O. T. P. K. 1977. *The Origins of Mycenaean Civilisation*, Göteborg.
———. 2006. *The Aegean from Bronze Age to Iron Age*, Oxford and New York.
Diehl, E. 1906. *Procli Diadochi in Platonis Timaeum commentaria* 3, Leipzig.
Diessl, W. G. 1979. "La balística de la honda," *Relaciones de la sociedad argentina de antropologia* 13, pp. 7–20.
Dietler, M. 2010. *Archaeologies of Colonialism: Consumption, Entanglement, and Violence in Ancient Mediterranean France*, Berkeley and Los Angeles.
Di Fraia, T. 2017. "Tablet Weaving in Prehistory and Proto-history: The Contribution of the Italian Record," in *Material Chains in Late Prehistoric Europe and the Mediterranean: Time, Space and Technologies of Production* (Ausonius Mémoires 48), ed. A. Gorgues, K. Rebay-Salisbury, and R. B. Salisbury, Bordeaux, pp. 139–155.
Dikaios, P. 1969. *Enkomi: Excavations 1948–1958*, 1: *The Architectural Remains, the Tombs*, Mainz on Rhein.
Dimakopoulou, K. 1974. "Μυκηναϊκόν Ἀνακτορικὸν Ἐργαστήριον εἰς Θήβας," *AAA* 8, pp. 162–171.
———. 1988. *Ο Μυκηναϊκός κόσμος. Πέντε αιώνες πρώιμου ελληνικού πολιτισμού, 1600–1100 π.Χ.*, Athens.
———, ed. 1990. *Troy, Mycenae, Tiryns, Orchomenos. Heinrich Schliemann: The 100th Anniversary of His Death* (Exhibition catalogue, Athens, National Archaeological Museum 1990/Berlin, Altes Museum 1990–1991), Athens.
Dimitrakoudi, E. A. 2009. "Προσδιορισμός χημικής σύστασης οργανικών κατάλοιπων σε αρχαία κεραμικά σκεύη" (diss. Aristotle Univ. Thessaloniki).
Dimitrakoudi, E. A., S. A. Mitkidou, D. Urem-Kotsou, K. Kotsakis, J. Stephanidou-Stefanatou, and J. A. Stratis. 2011. "Characterization by Gas Chromatography-Mass Spectrometry of Diterpenoid Resinous Materials in Roman-Age Amphorae from Northern Greece," *European Journal of Mass Spectrometry* 17, pp. 581–591.
Dimitsas, M. G. [1988] 1874. *Αρχαία γεωγραφία της Μακεδονίας* 1–2, repr. Thessaloniki.
———. [2006] 1896. *Η Μακεδονία εν λίθοις φθεγγομένοις και μνημείοις σωζομένοις* 1–2, repr. Katerini.

Dimoula, A. 2014. *Πρώιμη κεραμική τεχνολογία και παραγωγή. Το παράδειγμα της Θεσσαλίας*, Thessaloniki.

Dindorf, W. ed. 1863. *Scholia graeca in Euripidis tragoedias ex codicibus aucta et emendata*, Oxford.

Di Sandro, N. 1986. *Le anfore arcaiche dallo scarico Gosetti, Pithecusa*, Naples.

Di Stefano, G., and C. Giardino. 1990–1991. "Scicli (Ragusa): Il ripostiglio di bronzi in contrada Castelluccio sull'Irminio," *NSc* 1990–1991, pp. 489–546.

Dittenberger, W. 1907. "Methana und Hypata," *Hermes* 42, pp. 542–547.

Dobres, M. A., and J. E. Robb. 2005. "'Doing' Agency: Introductory Remarks on Methodology," *Journal of Archaeological Method and Theory* 12, pp. 159–166.

Docter, R. F. 1997. "Archaische Amphoren aus Karthago und Toscanos: Fundspektrum und Formentwicklung. Ein Beitrag zur phönizischen Wirtschaftsgeschichte" (diss. Univ. of Amsterdam).

———. 2000. "East Greek Fine Wares and Transport Amphorae of the 8th–5th Century BC from Carthage and Toscanos," in *Ceràmiques jònies d'època arcaica: Centres de producció i comercialització al Mediterrani occidental. Actes de la Taula Rodona celebrada a Empúries, 26–28 maig 1999*, ed. P. Cabrera Bonet and M. Santos Retolaza, Barcelona, pp. 63–88.

Dohrenwend, R. E. 2002. "The Sling: Forgotten Firepower of Antiquity," *Journal of Asian Martial Arts* 11 (2), pp. 28–49.

Donlan, W. 1970. "Strabo and the Lelantine War," *TAPA* 101, pp. 131–142.

Donnart, K. 2007. *Première approche diachronique du macro-outillage dans le massif armoricain (France): du Néolithique moyen au début de l'âge du Bronze*, https://www.academia.edu/1107537/Premi%C3%A8re_approche_diachronique_du_macro_outillage_dans_le_Massif_armoricain_France_du_N%C3%A9olithique_moyen_au_d%C3%A9but_de_l_%C3%A2ge_du_Bronze

Donnellan, L. 2016. "'Greek Colonisation' and Mediterranean Networks: Patterns of Mobility and Interaction at Pithekoussai," *Journal of Greek Archaeology* 1, pp. 109–148.

———. 2020. "Pithekoussan Amphorae and the Development of a Mediterranean Market Economy," *Journal of Greek Archaeology* 5, pp. 263–297.

D'Onofrio, A. M. 2011. "Athenian Burials with Weapons: The Athenian Warrior Graves Revisited," in *The "Dark Ages" Revisited. Acts of an International Symposium in Memory of William D. E. Coulson, University of Thessaly, Volos, 14–17 June 2007*, ed. A. Mazarakis Ainian, Volos, pp. 645–673.

D'Onofrio, A. M., ed. 2007. *Tallies, Tokens and Counters from the Mediterranean to India. Proceedings of the Meeting Held at the Università degli Studi di Napoli "L'Orientale," Naples, 31st May 2004*, Naples.

Doonan, R., and A. Mazarakis Ainian. 2007. "Forging Identity in Early Iron Age Greece: Implications of the Metalworking Evidence from Oropos," in *Oropos and Euboea in the Early Iron Age. Acts of an International Round Table, University of Thessaly (June 18–20, 2004)*, ed. A. Mazarakis Ainian, Volos, pp. 361–379.

Dotsika, E., D. Poutoukis, I. Tzavidopoulos, Y. Maniatis, D. Ignatiadou, and B. Raco. 2009. "A Natron Source at Pikrolimni Lake in Greece? Geochemical Evidence," *Journal of Geochemical Exploration* 103 (2–3), pp. 133–143.

Dotsika, E., I. Tzavidopoulos, D. Poutoukis, B. Raco, Y. Maniatis, and D. Ignatiadou. 2012. "Isotope Contents, Cl/Br Ratio and Origin of Water at Pikrolimni Lake: A Natron Source in Greece, as Archive of Past Environmental Conditions," *Quaternary International* 266, pp. 74–80.

Dougherty, C. 1993. *The Poetics of Colonization: From City to Text in Archaic Greece*, New York and Oxford.

Doumas, Ch. 1975. "Αρχαιότητες και μνημεία Δωδεκανήσων," *ArchDelt* 30, Chr. B΄1, pp. 361–372.

Douzougli, A. 1996. "Pottery: Epirus—The Ionian Islands," in Papathanassopoulos 1996, pp. 117–119.

Douzougli, A., and J. K. Papadopoulos. 2010. "Liatovouni: A Molossian Cemetery and Settlement in Epirus," *JdI* 125, pp. 1–87.

Douzougli, A., and K. Zachos. 2002. "L'archéologie des zones montagneuses: modèles et interconnexions dans le néolithique de l'Épire et de l'Albanie méridionale," in *Albanie dans l'Europe préhistorique: Actes du colloque de L'orient, organisé par l'École Française d'Athènes et l'Université de Bretagne-Sud, Lorient, 8–10 June 2000* (*BCH* Suppl. 42), ed. G. Touchais and J. Renard, Paris, pp. 111–143.

Dow, S. 1963. "Dikasts' Bronze Pinakia," *BCH* 87, pp. 653–687.

Drescher, H. 1989. "Römisches Schreibgerät aus dem Hafen von Ostia Antica," *AntW* 20 (1), pp. 59–60.

Droop, J. P. 1905–1906. "Dipylon Vases from the Kynosarges Site," *BSA* 12, pp. 80–92.

———. 1906–1907. "Laconia," *BSA* 13, pp. 109–136.

———. 1926. "Bronzes," in Dawkins 1929a, pp. 196–202.

Drougou, S. 1992. *Ανασκαφή Πέλλας, 1957–1964. Οι πήλινοι λύχνοι*, Athens.

———. 2005. *Βεργίνα. Τα πήλινα αγγεία της Μεγάλης Τούμπας*, Athens.

———. 2011. "Μελαμβαφείς 'αλατιέρες' από ταφικά σύνολα της νεκρόπολης των Αιγών," in *ΕΠΑΙΝΟΣ Luigi Beschi* (Μουσείο Μπενάκη, 7ο Παράρτημα), ed. A. Delivorrias, G. Despinis, and A. Zarkadas, Athens, pp. 107–116.

———. 2012. "Πήλινοι λύχνοι στην αρχαία Μακεδονία," in *Θέματα της Ελληνιστικής Κεραμικής στην αρχαία Μακεδονία*, ed. St. Drougou and I. Touratsoglou, Athens, pp. 86–106.

Drougou, S., and I. Touratsoglou. 1994. "Τα χρονολογημένα σύνολα Ελληνιστικής Κεραμικής από τη Μακεδονία," in *Γ' Επιστημονική Συνάντηση για την Ελληνιστική Κεραμική, Θεσσαλονίκη, 24–27 Σεπτεμβρίου 1991*, Athens, pp. 128–137.

———. 1998. *Ελληνιστικοί λαξευτοί τάφοι Βεροίας*, Athens.

Dugas, C. 1921. "Le sanctuaire d'Aléa Athéna à Tégée avant le IVe siècle," *BCH* 45 (1), pp. 335–435.

Dumitrescu, V., A. Bolomey, and F. Mogoşanu. 1982. "The Prehistory of Romania: From the Earliest Times to 1000 B.C.," in *CAH* III.1: *The Prehistory of the Balkans, the Middle East and the Aegean World, Tenth to Eighth Centuries BC*, ed. J. Boardman, I.E.S. Edwards, N. G. L. Hammond, and E. Sollberger, Cambridge, pp. 1–74.

Dunbabin, T. J. 1940. "Objects in Other Metals," in *Perachora* I, pp. 184–189.

. 1948. *The Western Greeks: The History of Sicily and South Italy from the Foundation of the Greek Colonies to 480 B.C.*, Oxford.

———. 1962. "Lamps," in *Perachora* II, pp. 389–392.

Dunst, G. 1972. "Archaische Inschriften und Dokumente der Pentekontaetia aus Samos," *AM* 87, pp. 99–163.

Dupont, P. 1982. "Amphores commerciales archaïques de la Grèce de l'Est," *PP* 37, pp. 193–209.

———. 1983. "Classification et détermination de provenance des céramiques grecques orientales archaïques d'Istros: Rapport préliminaire," *Dacia* 27, series 2, pp. 19–43.

———. 1998. "Chapter 23: Archaic East Greek Trade Amphoras," in *East Greek Pottery*, ed. R. M. Cook and P. Dupont, London, pp. 142–191.

———. 1999. "Marques signalétiques avant-cuisson sur les amphores ioniques archaïques: cercles et croix," *Pontica* 32, pp. 9–18.

———. 2000. "Amphores 'samiennes' archaïques: sources de confusion et questionnements," in *Ceràmiques jonies di època arcaica: Centres de producció i comercialització al Mediterrani occidental*, ed. P. Cabrera Bonet and M. Santos Retolaza, Barcelona, pp. 57–62.

———. 2001. "Le commerce amphorique dans le Pont archaïque," *Dossiers d'Archéologie* 266, pp. 82–86.

———. 2007a. "Diffusion des amphores commerciales de type milesien dans le Pont archaïque," in *Frühes Ionien: Eine Bestandsaufnahme. Panionion-Symposion Güzelçamlı, 26. September–1. Oktober 1999*, ed. J. Cobet, V. von Graeve, W.-D. Niemeier, and K. Zimmermann, Mainz on Rhein, pp. 621–630.

———. 2007b. "Amphores 'samiennes' archaïques de mer Noire (approche archéométrique)," in *Greeks and Natives in the Cimmerian Bosporus 7th–1st Centuries B.C. Proceedings of the International Conference, October 2000, Taman, Russia*, ed. S. D. Solovov, Oxford, pp. 41–50.

———. 2009. "Données archéométriques préliminaires sur les amphores du type de Lesbos," in *Synergia Pontica and Aegeo-Anatolica*, ed. P. Dupont and V. Lungu, Galati, pp. 37–72.

———. 2018. "The Lessons of Archaeometric Data on East Greek Pottery Finds from Bayraklı," in *Archaic and Classical Western Anatolia: New Perspectives in Ceramic Studies. In Memoriam Prof. Crawford H. Greenewalt, Jr.*, ed. R. G. Gürtekin Demir, H. Cevizoğlu, Y. Polat, and G. Polat, Leuven, pp. 43–56.

Dupont, P., M. Angelscu, C, Dubosse, L. Noca, and P. Séjalon. 1999. "Les enceintes grecques d'Histria: vers une nouvelle approche?" in *Religions du Pont-Euxin, Actes du VIIIe Symposium de Vani*, ed. O. Lordkipanidze, P. Lévêque, A. Fraysse, and É. Geny, Besançon, pp. 37–52.

Dupont, P., and E. Skarlatidou. 2012. "Archaic Transport Amphoras from the First Necropolis of Clazomenian Abdera," in Tiverios et al. 2012, pp. 253–264.

Dupont, P., and A. Thomas. 2006. "Naukratis: Les importations grecques orientales archaïques: Classification et détermination d'origine en laboratoire," in *Naukratis: Greek Diversity in Egypt: Studies on East Greek Pottery and Exchange in the Eastern Mediterranean*, ed. A. Villing and U. Schlotzhauer, London, pp. 77–84.

Durand, J. N. L. 1802–1805. *Précis des leçons d'architecture données à l'École polytechnique*, Paris.

Duru, R. 2008. *From 8000 B.C. to 2000 B.C.: Six Thousand Years of the Burbur-Antalya Region*, Antalya.

Echols, E. C. 1950. "The Ancient Slinger," *The Classical Weekly* 43, pp. 227–230.

Eder, B. 1998. *Argolis, Lakonien, Messenien: Vom Ende der mykenischen Palastzeit bis zur Einwanderung der Dorier*, Vienna.

———. 2001. *Die submykenischen und protogeometrischen Gräber von Elis*, Athens.

———. 2007. "Im Spiegel der Siegel: Die nördlichen und westlichen Regionen Griechenlands im Spannungsfeld der mykenischen Paläste," in *Keimelion. Elitenbildung und elitarer Konsum von der mykenischen Palastzeit bis zur homerischen Epoche, Akten des internationalen Kongresses vom 3. bis 5. Februar 2005 in Salzburg*, ed. E. Alram-Stern and G. Nightingale (Veröffentlichungen der Mykenischen Kommission 27), Vienna, pp. 81–124.

———. 2008. "The Northern Frontier of the Mycenaean World," in *Aegean and Balkan Prehistory*, ed. B. Horejs and P. Pavúk, April 3, http://www.aegeobalkanprehistory.net/index.php?p=article&id_art=11.

———. 2009. "The Northern Frontier of the Mycenaean World," in *Αρχαιολογικό Έργο Θεσσαλίας και Στερεάς Ελλάδας 2 (2006). Πρακτικά Επιστημονικής Συνάντησης, Βόλος 16.3–19.3.2006* 1: Θεσσαλία, Βόλος, ed. A. Mazarakis Ainian, Volos, pp. 113–131.

Edmonds, J. M. 1957. *The Fragments of Attic Comedy after Meineke, Bergk, and Kock*, Leiden.

Edson, C. F. 1947. "Notes on the Thracian Phoros," *CP* 42, pp. 88–105.

———. 1970. "Early Macedonia," in *Ancient Macedonia* 1 (Institute for Balkan Studies 122), ed. V. Laourdas and Ch. Makaronas, Thessaloniki, pp. 17–44.

Ekroth, G. 2001. "Altars on Attic Vases: The Identification of *Bomos* and *Eschara*," in *Ceramics in Context. Proceedings of the International Colloquium in Ancient Pottery, Stockholm 13–15 June 1997*, Stockholm, pp. 115–126.

Elezi, G. 2014. "Κεραμική από το Νεολιθικό οικισμό Θέρμης Θεσσαλονίκης. Χωρική κατανομή και προσδιορισμός λειτουργίας των χώρων" (MA thesis Aristotle Univ. Thessaloniki).

Ellis, J. R. 1970. "The Security of the Macedonian Throne under Philip II," in *Ancient Macedonia* 1 (Institute for Balkan Studies 122), ed. V. Laourdas and Ch. Makaronas, Thessaloniki, pp. 68–75.

Elster, E. S. 1986. "Tripods, Plastic Vessels, and Stands: A Fragmentary Collection of Social Ceramics," in *Sitagroi* 1, pp. 303–332.

———. 1997. "Construction and Use of the Early Bronze Age Burnt House at Sitagroi: Craft and Technology," in *TEXNH: Craftsmen, Craftswomen and Craftsmanship in the Aegaean Bronze Age. Proceedings of the 6th International Aegean Conference/6e Rencontre égéenne internationale, Philadelphia, Temple University, 18–21 April 1996* (*Aegaeum* 16), ed. R. Laffineur and P. P. Betancourt, Liège, pp. 19–36.

———. 2003a. "Chapter 5. Grindstones, Polished-stone Tools, and Other Stone Artifacts," in *Sitagroi* 2, pp. 175–203.

———. 2003b. "Tools of the Spinner, Weaver, and Matmaker," in *Sitagroi* 2, pp. 229–251.

———. 2003c. "*Paralipomena* and Other Plastic Forms," in *Sitagroi* 2, pp. 421–430.

Empereur, J.-Y. 1981. "Collection Paul Canellopoulos (XVII): Petits objets inscrits," *BCH* 105, pp. 537–568.

Empereur, J.-Y., and A. Simosi. 1989. "Θάσος," *ArchDelt* 44, pp. 379–380.

Emre, K. 1978. *Yanarlar: Afyon yöresinde bir hitit mezarliği (Yanarlar: A Hittite Cemetery near Afyon)*, Ankara.

Engels, J. 2010. "Macedonians and Greeks," in *A Companion to Ancient Macedonia*, ed. J. Roisman and I. Worthington, Oxford, pp. 81–98.

Eretria = *Eretria: Fouilles et recherches/Ausgrabungen und Forschungen*, Swiss School of Archaeology in Greece

III = C. Bérard, *L'Hérôon à la porte de l'ouest*, Berne 1970.

IV = J.-P. Descoeudres, "Euboeans in Australia"; C. Dunant, "Stèles funéraires"; Ingrid R. Metzger, "Gefässe mit Palmetten-Lotus Dekor"; I. R. Metzger, "Die Funde aus den Pyrai"; C. Bérard, "Topographie et urbanisme de l'Erétrie archaïque: l'Hérôon," Berne 1978.

V = A. Hurst, "Ombres de l'Eubée?"; J.-P. Descoeudres, "Die vorklassische Keramik aus dem Gebiet des Westtors"; P. Auberson, "Le temple de Dionysos," 1976.

XIV = S. Huber, *L'aire sacrificielle au nord du sanctuaire d'Apollon Daphnéphoros*, Gollion 2003.

XVII = B. Blandin, *Les pratiques funéraires d'époque géométrique à Érétrie: Espace des vivants, demeures des morts*, Gollion 2007.

XX = S. Verdan, A. Kenzelmann Pfyffer, and C. Léderrey, *Céramique géométrique d'Érétrie*, Gollion 2008.

XXII = S. Verdan, *Le sanctuaire d'Apollon Daphnéphoros à l'époque géométrique*, Gollion 2013.

Errington, R. M. 1990. *A History of Macedonia*, trans. C. Errington, Berkeley, Los Angeles, and Oxford.

———. 2007. "The Importance of the Capture of Amphipolis for the Development of the Macedonian City," in *Ancient Macedonia* 7: *Macedonia from the Iron Age to the Death of Philip II* (Institute for Balkan Studies 280), ed. E. Voutiras, Thessaloniki, pp. 275–282.

Ersoy, Y. E. 1993. "Clazomenae: The Archaic Settlement" (diss. Bryn Mawr College).

———. 2000. "East Greek Pottery Groups of the 7th and 6th Centuries BC from Clazomenae," in *Die Ägäis und das westliche Mittelmeer: Beziehungen und Wechselwirkungen 8. bis 5. v. Chr., Wien, 24. bis 27. März 1999*, ed. F. Krinzinger, Vienna, pp. 399–406.

———. 2003. "Pottery Production and Mechanism of Workshops in Archaic Clazomenae," in *Griechische Keramik im kulturellen Kontext: Akten des Internationalen Vasen-Symposiums in Kiel vom 24.–28.9.2001 veranstaltet durch das Archäologische Institut der Christian-Albrechts-Universität zu Kiel*, ed. B. Schmaltze and M. Söldner, Münster, pp. 254–257.

———. 2004. "Klazomenai: 900–500 BC. History and Settlement Evidence," in *Klazomenai, Teos and Abdera: Metropoleis and Colony. Proceedings of the International Symposium Held at the Archaeological Museum of Abdera, Abdera, 20–21 October 2001*, ed. A. Moustaka, E. Skarlatidou, M.-C. Tzannes, and Y. E. Ersoy, Thessaloniki, 43–76.

———. 2007. "Notes on the History and Archaeology of Early Clazomenae," in *Frühes Ionien: Eine Bestandsaufnahme. Panionion-Symposion Güzelçamlı 26. September–1. Oktober 1999* (Milesische Forschungen 5), ed. J. Cobet, V. von Graeve, W.-D. Niemeier, and K. Zimmermann, Mainz on Rhein, pp. 149–178.

———. 2018. "Painting with Fire and Smoke: Standardisation and Variation of Pottery from Clazomenae during the Archaic Period (7th–Early 5th Century BC)," in *Archaic and Classical Western Anatolia: New Perspectives in Ceramic Studies. In Memoriam Prof. Crawford H. Greenewalt, Jr.*, ed. R. G. Gürtekin Demir, H. Cevizoğlu, Y. Polat, and G. Polat, Leuven, pp. 57–85.

Ertuğ, F. 2000. "An Ethnobotanical Study in Central Anatolia (Turkey)," *Economic Botany* 54, pp. 155–182.

Evangelidis, D. E. 1912. "Ἐκ τῆς Μυκηνῶν γεωμετρικῆς νεκροπόλεως," *ArchEph* 1912, pp. 127–141.

———. 1952. "Ἡ ἀνασκαφὴ τῆς Δωδώνης," *Prakt* 1952, pp. 279–306.

———. 1955. "Ἀνασκαφὴ ἐν Δωδώνῃ," *Prakt* 1955, pp. 169–173.

———. 1956. "Ἀνασκαφὴ ἐν Δωδώνῃ," *Prakt* 1956, pp. 154–157.

. 1957. "Ἀνασκαφὴ ἐν Δωδώνῃ," *Prakt* 1957, pp. 76 78.

Evans, A. J. 1928. *The Palace of Minos: A Comparative Account of the Successive Stages of the Early Cretan Civilization as Illustrated by the Discoveries at Knossos* 2, Part 1: *Fresh Lights on Origins and External Relations: The Restoration in Town and Palace After Seismic Catastrophe Towards Close of M. M. III, and the Beginnings of the New Era*, London.

Evans, H. C., and W. D. Wixom, eds. 1997. *The Glory of Byzantium: Art and Culture of the Middle Byzantine Era, A.D. 843–1261* (Exhibition catalogue, Metropolitan Museum of Art 1997), New York.

Evans, J. D. 1964. "Excavations in the Neolithic Settlement at Knossos, 1957–60. Part I," *BSA* 59, pp. 132–240.

Evans, J. G. 2003. *Environmental Archaeology and the Social Order*, London.

Evans, R. K. 1986. "The Pottery of Phase III," in *Sitagroi* 1, pp. 393–428.

Evely, D. 2006. "The Small Finds," in *Lefkandi* IV, pp. 265–302.

Evely, D., A. Hein, and E. Nodarou. 2012. "Crucibles from Palaikastro, East Crete: Insights into Metallurgical Technology in the Aegean Late Bronze Age," *JAS* 39, pp. 1821–1836.

Faklaris, P. V., and V. G. Stamatopoulou. 2021. "Η ελιά και το λάδι στην αρχαία Μακεδονία. Επισκόπηση των στοιχείων για την ελαιοκαλλιέργεια και την ελαιοποίηση στον μακεδονικό χώρο," in *Άργιλος, 25 Χρόνια Έρευνας. Οργάνωση Πόλης και Χώρας στις Αποικίες του Βορείου Αιγαίου, 8ος–3ος αι. π.Χ.*, ed. Z. Bonias and J.-Y. Perreault, Athens, pp. 609–623.

Fantalkin, A. 2001. "Low Chronology and Greek Protogeometric and Geometric Pottery in the Southern Levant," *Levant* 33, pp. 117–125.

———. 2006. "Identity in the Making: Greeks in the Eastern Mediterranean during the Iron Age," in *Naukratis: Greek Diversity in Egypt. Studies on East Greek Pottery and Exchange in the Eastern Mediterranean*, ed. A. Villing and U. Schlotzhauer, London, pp. 199–208.

Fantalkin, A., I. Finkelstein, and E. Piasetzky. 2015. "Late Helladic to Middle Geometric Aegean and Contemporary Cypriot Chronologies: A Radiocarbon View from the Levant," *BASOR* 373, pp. 25–48.

Fantalkin, A., and O. Tal. 2010. "Reassessing the Date of the Beginning of the Gray Series of Transport Amphorae from Lesbos," *BABesch* 85, pp. 1–12.

Faraguna, M. 1998. "Aspetti administrativi e finanziari della monarchia macedone tra IV e III secolo A.C.," *Athenaeum* 86, pp. 349–395.

Faraone, C. A. 1996. "Taking the 'Nestor's Cup Inscription' Seriously: Erotic Magic and Conditional Curses in the Earliest Inscribed Hexameters," *ClAnt* 15, pp. 77–112.

Farooq Swati, M., and M. Khan. 2001. "A Note on Jewellery Moulds from Miadam, Swat," *South Asian Studies* 17 (1), pp. 189–198.

Faucher, T., F. Téreygeol, L. Brousseau, and A. Arles. 2009. "À la recherche des ateliers monétaires grecs: l'apport de l'expérimentation," *RN* 165, pp. 43–80.

FdD = *Fouilles de Delphes, École française d'Athènes*, Paris

V.1 = P. Perdrizet, *Monuments figurés: Petits bronzes, terre-cuites, antiquités diverses*, 1908.

V.3 = C. Rolley, *Monuments figurés. Les trépieds à cuve clouée*, 1977.

V.5 = H. Aurigny, *Bronzes du haut-archaïsme à Delphes: Trépieds, chaudrons, et vaisselle de bronze (fin VIIIe–VIIe siècle)*, 2019.

Feinman, G. M. 2016. "Reframing Ancient Economies: New Models, New Questions," in *Eurasia at the Dawn of History: Urbanization and Social Change*, ed. M. Fernández-Götz and D. Krausse, New York, pp. 139–149.

Felsch, R. C. S. 1979. "Boiotische Ziegelwerkstätten archaischer Zeit," *AM* 94, pp. 1 40.

———. 1990. "Further Stamped Roof Tiles from Central Greece, Attica, and the Peloponnese," *Hesperia* 59, pp. 301–323.

———. 2007. "Die Bronzefunde," in *Kalapodi* II, pp. 28–388.

Felten, F., C. Reinholdt, E. Pollhammer, W. Gauss, and R. Smetana. 2008. "Ägina-Kolonna 2007: Vorbericht über die Grabungen des Fachbereichs Altertumswissenschaften/Klassische und Frühägäische Archäologie der Universitat Salzburg," *ÖJh* 77, pp. 47–76.

Fentress, E., and J. Fentress. 2001. "The Hole in the Doughnut," *Past and Present* 173, pp. 203–219.

Ferrara, S. 2012. *Cypro-Minoan Inscriptions* 1: *Analysis*, Oxford and New York.

Figueira, T. J. 2015. "Modes of Colonization and Elite Integration in Archaic Greece," in *"Aristocracy" in Antiquity: Redefining Greek and Roman Elites*, ed. N. Fisher and H. van Wees, Swansea, pp. 313–347.

Filipovic, D. Z., E. Allué, and D. R. Boric. 2010. "Integrated Carpological and Anthracological Analysis of Plant Record from the Mesolithic Site of Vlasac, Serbia," *Journal of the Serbian Archaeological Society* 26, pp. 145–161.

Filis, K. 2011. "Εμπορικοί αμφορείς από την αρχαία Άκανθο και το τοπικό εργαστήριο" (diss. Aristotle Univ. Thessaloniki).

———. 2012a. "Ιωνικοί εμπορικοί αμφορείς στο Βόρειο Αιγαίο," in Tiverios et al. 2012, pp. 265–280.

———. 2012b. "Εμπορικοί αμφορείς από το Καραμπουρνάκι," in *Κεραμέως παῖδες: Αντίδωρο στον Καθηγητή Μιχάλη Τιβέριο από τους μαθητές του*, ed. E. Kefalidou and D. Tsiafaki, Thessaloniki, pp. 309–320.

———. 2013. "Transport Amphorae from Akanthus," in *PATABS III, Production and Trade of Amphorae in the Black Sea. Production et commerce amphoriques en mer noir. Actes de la Table Ronde internationale de Constanta, 6–10 octobre 2009*, ed. L. Buzoianu, P. Dupont, and V. Lungu, Constanza, pp. 67–88.

———. 2014. "Karabournaki: The Transport Amphorae from a Semi-Subterranean Structure in Trench 27/89D," *Eirene. Studia Graeca et Latina* 50, pp. 233–265.

———. 2019. "Τα τοπικά εργαστήρια και οι εισαγωγές εμπορικών αμφορέων στο Βόρειο Αιγαίο στους κλασσικούς χρόνους. Εμπορικά δίκτυα και αγορές καταναλωτικών αγαθών," in *Η Κεραμική της Κλασσικής Εποχής στο Βόρειο Αιγαίο και την Περιφέρεια του (480–323/300 π. Χ.)*, ed. E. Manakidou and A. Avramidou, Thessaloniki, pp. 243–261.

Filow, B. D. 1927. *Die archaische Nekropole von Trebenischte am Ochrida-See*, Berlin and Leipzig.

———. 1934. *Die Grabhügelnekropole bei Duvanlij in Südbulgarien*, Sofia.

Finkelstein, I., and E. Piasetzky. 2009. "Radiocarbon-dated Destruction Layers: A Skeleton for Iron Age Chronology in the Levant," *OJA* 28, pp. 255–274.

Finley, M. I. 1976. "Colonies: An Attempt at a Typology," *Transactions of the Royal Historical Society* 26, pp. 167–188.

Fiorini, L., and M. Torelli. 2007. "La fusione, Afrodite e l'emporion," *Facta* 1, pp. 75–106.

Flemberg, J. 1978. "Two Lead Sling Bullets," in *From the Gustavianum Collections in Uppsala* 2: *The Collection of Classical Antiquities. History and Studies of Selected Objects* (Acta Univ. Upsaliensis. *Boreas*: Uppsala Studies in Ancient Mediterranean and Near Eastern Civilizations 9), Stockholm, pp. 81–85.

Flensted-Jensen, P. 2004. "Thrace from Axios to Strymon," in Hansen and Nielsen 2004, pp. 810–853.

Flensted-Jensen, P., and M. H. Hansen. 1996. "Pseudo-Skylax' Use of the Term Polis," in *More Studies in the Ancient Greek Polis* (*Historia*: Einzelschriften 108), ed. M. H. Hansen and K. Raaflaub, Stuttgart, pp. 137–167.

Fletcher, R. 2008. "Fragments of Levantine Iron Age Pottery in Chalkidike," *MeditArch* 21, pp. 3–7.

———. 2011. "Greek–Levantine Cultural Exchange in Orientalizing and Archaic Pottery Shapes," *Ancient West and East* 10, pp. 11–42.

Flevari, L. 2015. "Μήτρες μολυβδίδων και μολυβδίδες από την κύρια είσοδο της Απτέρας," in *Αρχαιολογικό Έργο Κρήτης, Πρακτικά της 3ης Συνάντησης, Ρέθυμνο, 5–8 Δεκεμβρίου 2013* 2, ed. P. Karanastasi, A. Tzigkounaki, and Chr. Tsigonaki, Rethymno, pp. 109–114.

Fluzin, P., A. Ploquin, and V. Serneels. 2000. "Archéométrie des déchets de production sidérurgique. Moyens et méthodes d'identification des différents éléments de la chaîne opératoire directe," *Gallia* 57, pp. 101–121.

Fluzin, P., V. Serneels, E. Huysecom, P. Benoit, and H. T. Kienon. 2001. "Reconstitution of the Operating Chain in Paleo-iron and Steel Metallurgy from the Archaeological Remains: Comparative Studies with the African Ethno-archaeology," in *Ethno-archaeology and Its Transfers. Papers from a Session Held at the European Association of Archaeologists Fifth Annual Meeting in Bournemouth 1999*, ed. S. Beyries and P. Pétrequin (*BAR-IS* 983), Oxford, pp. 113–122.

Foley, B. P., M. C. Hansson, D. P. Kourkoumelis, and T. A. Theodoulou. 2012. "Aspects of Ancient Greek Trade Re-evaluated with Amphora DNA Evidence," *JAS* 39, pp. 389–398.

Foltiny, S. 1961. "Athens and the East Halstatt Region: Cultural Interrelations at the Dawn of the Iron Age," *AJA* 65, pp. 283–297.

Forrer, E. 1938. "Quelle und Brunnen in Alt-Vorderasien," *Glotta* 26, pp. 178–202.

Forrest, W. G. G. 1982. "Euboea and the Islands," in *CAH* III.3: *The Expansion of the Greek World, Eighth to Sixth Centuries BC*, 2nd ed., ed. J. Boardman and N. G. L. Hammond, Cambridge, pp. 249–260.

Forsdyke, E. J. 1925. *Catalogue of the Greek and Etruscan Vases in the British Museum* 1.1: *Prehistoric Aegean Pottery*, London.

———. 1931. "Geometric Bronzes from Potidaea," *British Museum Quarterly* 6 (3), pp. 82–83.

Foss, C. 1974–1975. "Greek Sling Bullets in Oxford," *AR* 21, pp. 40–44.

———. 1975. "A Bullet of Tissaphernes," *JHS* 95, pp. 25–30.

Foster, P. 1978. *Greek Arms and Armour*, Newcastle-upon-Tyne.

Fotheringham, I. K. 1923. *Eusebii Pamphili Chronici Canones, latine vertit, audaxit, ad sua tempora produxit S. Eusebius Hieronymus*, London.

Fotiadis, M. 2001. "Imagining Macedonia in Prehistory, ca. 1900–1930," *JMA* 14 (2), pp. 115–135.

Fotiadis, M., and A. Chondroyianni-Metoki. 1993. "Κίτρινη Λίμνη: διαχρονική σύνοψη, ραδιοχρονολογήσεις και η ανασκαφή του 1993," *AEMTh* 7 [1997], pp. 19–32.

Fouache, E., M. Ghilardi, K. Vouvalidis, G. Syrides, M. Styllas, S. Kunesch, and S. Stiros. 2008. "Contribution on the Holocene Reconstruction of Thessaloniki Coastal Plain, Greece," *Journal of Coastal Research* 24, pp. 1161–1173.

Fougères, G. 1896a. "Funda," *DarSag* 2 (2), Paris, pp. 1363–1366.

———. 1896b. "Glans," *DarSag* 2 (2), Paris, pp. 1608–1611.

Foxhall, L. 1998. "Cargoes of the Heart's Desire: The Character of Trade in the Archaic Mediterranean World," in *Archaic Greece: New Approaches and New Evidence*, ed. N. Fisher and H. van Wees, London and Oakville, pp. 295–309.

Franchthi = *Excavations at Franchthi Cave, Greece*, Bloomington

I.1–2 = K. Vitelli, *Franchthi Neolithic Pottery* 1: *Classification and Ceramic Phases 1 and 2*, 1993.

I.3–5 = K. Vitelli, *Franchthi Neolithic Pottery* 2: *The Later Neolithic Ceramic Phases 3 to 5*, 1999.

II = T. Van Andel and S. B. Sutton, *Landscape and People of the Franchthi Region*, with contributions by J. M. Hansen and C. J. Vitaliano, 1987.

Frasca, M. 1993. "Osservazioni preliminari sulla ceramica protoarcaica ed arcaica di Kyme eolica," *Cronache di Archeologia* 32 (ed. G. Rizza, *Studi su Kyme eolica. Attic della giornata di studio della scuola di specializzazione in archeologia dell'università di Catania, Catania, 16 maggio 1990*), pp. 51–70.

———. 1998. "Ceramiche greche d'importazione a Kyme eolica nell'VIII secolo a.C.," in Bats and d'Agostino 1998, pp. 273–279.

———. 2000. "Ceramiche tardo geometrico a Kyme eolica," in *Die Ägäis und das westliche Mittelmeer: Beziehungen und Wechselwirkungen 8. bis 5. v. Chr., Wien, 24. bis 27. März 1999*, ed. F. Krinzinger, Vienna, pp. 393–398.

Freedman, P. 2007. "Introduction," in *Food: The History of Taste*, ed. P. Freedman, London, pp. 7–33.

Freestone, I. C., M. Ponting, and M. J. Hughes. 2002. "The Origins of Byzantine Glass from Maroni Petrera, Cyprus," *Archaeometry* 44 (2), pp. 257–272.

Friedländer, P., and H. B. Hoffleit. 1948 [1987]. *Epigrammata: Greek Inscriptions in Verse from the Beginnings to the Persian Wars*. Berkeley and London, repr. Chicago.

French, D. H. 1971. "An Experiment in Water-sieving," *AnatSt* 21, pp. 59–64.

French, E., and J. B. Rutter. 1977. "The Hand-made Burnished Ware of the Late Helladic IIIC Period: Its Modern Historical Context," *AJA* 81, pp. 111–112.

Friis Johansen, K. 1958. *Exochi: Ein frührhodisches Gräberfeld* (*ActaArch* 28), Copenhagen.

Frizell, B. S. 1986. *Asine* II.3: *Results of the Excavations East of the Acropolis, 1970–1974: The Late and Final Mycenaean Periods*, Stockholm.

Frödin, O., and A. W. Persson. 1938. *Asine: Results of the Swedish Excavations, 1922–1930*, Stockholm.

Froehner, W. 1883. *Terres cuites de Tanagra et d'Asie Mineure. Collection Camille Lecuyer*, Paris.

Frontisi-Ducroux, F. 1998. "Kalé. Le féminin facultatif," *Métis* 13, pp. 175–181.

Frost, H. 1973. "First Season of Excavation on the Punic Wreck in Sicily," *IJNA* 2, pp. 33–49.

———. 1974. "The Punic Wreck in Sicily: Second Season of Excavation," *IJNA* 3, pp. 35–54.

———. 1975. "The Ram from Marsala," *IJNA* 4, pp. 219–228.

Funke, P. 2018. "A Politician in Exile: The Activities of the Athenian Kallistratos of Aphidnai in Macedonia," in *Βορειοελλαδικά: Tales from the Lands of the Ethne: Essays in Honour of Miltiades B. Hatzopoulos* (Μελετήματα 78), ed. M. Kalaïtzi, P. Paschidis, C. Antonetti, and A.-M. Guimier-Sorbets, Athens, pp. 159–166.

Furmánek, V., L. Veliačik, and J. Vladár. 1999. *Die Bronzezeit im slowakischen Raum* (*PBF* XV), Rahden.

Furtwängler, A. 1906. *Aegina. Das Heiligtum der Aphaia*, Munich.

Furtwängler, A. E. 1981. "Heraion von Samos: Grabungen im Südtemenos 1977, II. Kleinfunde," *AM* 96, pp. 73–138.

———. 1986. "Neue Beobachtungen zur frühesten Münzprägung," *SNR* 65, pp. 153–165.

Furumark, A. 1972. *Mycenaean Pottery* 1: *Analysis and Classification*, Stockholm and Lund.

Gàbrici, E. 1927. "Il santuario della Malophoros a Selinunte," *MontAnt* 32, cols. 1–414.

Gadolou, A. 2008. *Η Αχαΐα στους πρώιμους ιστορικούς χρόνους. Κεραμική παραγωγή και έθιμα ταφής*, Athens.

Gaebler, H. 1935. *Die antiken Münzen Nord-Griechenlands* 3: *Makedonia und Paionia*, Berlin.

Gagarin, M., and D. M. MacDowell. 1998. *Antiphon and Andocides* (The Oratory of Classical Greece Series 1), Austin, Tex.

Gailledrat, E. 2000. "Les céramiques grecques archaïques en Languedoc occidental," in *Ceràmiques jònies d'època arcaica: centres de producció i comercialització al Mediterrani Occidental: Actes de la Taula Rodona celebrada a Empúries els dies 26 al 28 de maig de 1999*, ed. P. Cabrera Bonet and M. Santos Retolaza, Barcelona, pp. 147–164.

Galanaki, I., H. Tomas, Y. Galanakis, and R. Laffineur, eds. 2007. *Between the Aegean and Baltic Seas: Prehistory Across Borders. Proceedings of the International Conference Bronze and Early Iron Age Interconnections and Contemporary Developments between the Aegean and the Regions of the Balkan Peninsula, Central and Northern Europe, University of Zagreb, 11–14 April 2005* (*Aegaeum* 27). Liège.

Galiniki, S. 2006. "Μήτρες κοσμημάτων από τη συλλογή Στ. Τσάκου," in *Αρχαία Ελληνική Τεχνολογία, Πρακτικά 2ου Διεθνούς Συνεδρίου*, ed. G. Kazazi, Athens, pp. 347–354.

Gallis, K. 1982. *Καύσεις νεκρών από τη Νεολιθική εποχή στη Θεσσαλία*. Athens.

———. 1987. "Die stratigraphische Einordnung der Larisa-Kultur: Eine Richtigstellung," *PZ* 62, pp. 14–163.

Galpin, T. J. 1984. "The Democratic Roots of Athenian Imperialism in the Fifth Century B.C.," *CJ* 79, pp. 100–109.

Gam, T. 1993. "Experiments in Glass, Present and Future," *Annales du 12e Congrès de l'Association Internationale pour l'Histoire du Verre, Vienna, August 1991*, Amsterdam, pp. 261–270.

Gantès, L.-F. 2000. "Un atelier de Grèce d'occident à l'époque archaïque: l'exemple de Marseille," in *Ceràmiques jònies d'època arcaica: centres de producció i comercialització al Mediterrani Occidental: Actes de la Taula Rodona celebrada a Empúries els dies 26 al 28 de maig de 1999*, ed. P. Cabrera Bonet and M. Santos Retolaza, Barcelona, pp. 111–123.

Garašanin, M. 1982a. "The Bronze Age in the Central Balkan Area," in *CAH* III.1: *The Prehistory of the Balkans, the Middle East and the Aegean World, Tenth to Eighth Centuries BC*, ed. J. Boardman, I. E. S. Edwards, N. G. L. Hammond, and E. Sollberger, Cambridge, pp. 163–186.

———. 1982b. "The Early Iron Age in the Central Balkan Area, c. 1000–750 B.C.," in *CAH* III.1: *The Prehistory of the Balkans, the Middle East and the Aegean World, Tenth to Eighth Centuries BC*, 2nd ed., ed. J. Boardman, I. E. S. Edwards, N. G. L. Hammond, and E. Sollberger, Cambridge, pp. 582–618.

———. 1982c. "The Stone Age in the Central Balkan Area," in *CAH* III.1: *The Prehistory of the Balkans, the Middle East and the Aegean World, Tenth to Eighth Centuries BC*, 2nd ed., ed. J. Boardman, I. E. S. Edwards, N. G. L. Hammond, and E. Sollberger, Cambridge, pp. 75–135.

———. 1982d. "The Eneolithic Period in the Central Balkan Area," in *CAH* III.1: *The Prehistory of the Balkans, the Middle East and the Aegean World, Tenth to Eighth Centuries BC*, 2nd ed., ed. J. Boardman, I. E. S. Edwards, N. G. L. Hammond, and E. Sollberger, Cambridge, pp. 136–162.

García Garrido, M., and L. Lalana. 1991–1993. "Algunos glandes de plomo con inscripciones latinas y púnicas hallados en Hispania," *Homenatge al Dr. Leandre Villaronga* (*ActaNum* 21–23), ed. M. Crusafont i Sabater, A. M. Balaguer, and P. P. Ripollès Alegre, pp. 101–107.

Garcia Ramon, J. L., Br. Helly, and A. Tziafalias. 2007. "Inscriptions inédites de Mopsion: décrets et dédicaces en dialecte thessalien," in *Φωνῆς χαρακτὴρ ἐθνικός. Actes du Ve congrès international de dialectologie grecque, Athènes 28–30 septembre 2006* (Μελετήματα 52), ed. M. B. Hatzopoulos and V. Psilakakou, Athens, pp. 63–103.

Gardner, E. A., and S. Casson. 1918–1919. "Macedonia II: Antiquities Found in the British Zone, 1915–1919," *BSA* 23, pp. 10–43.

Gardner, P. 1883. *The Types of Greek Coins: An Archaeological Essay*, Cambridge.

Garlan, Y. 1970. "Études d'histoire militaire et diplomatique," *BCH* 94, pp. 625–635.

———. 1974. *Recherches de poliorcétique grecque* (Bibliothèque des Écoles Françaises d'Athènes et Rome 223), Paris.

Gartziou-Tatti, A. 1999. "Θάνατος και ταφή του Ορφέα στη Μακεδονία και τη Θράκη," in *Ancient Macedonia* 6 (Institute for Balkan Studies 272), ed. D. Pantermalis, Thessaloniki, pp. 439–451.

Gassner, V. 2011. "Fabrics from Chios," *FACEM*, June 6, http://www.facem.at/project-papers.php

Gatzolis, Ch. 2010. "Η κυκλοφορία του χάλκινου νομίσματος στη Μακεδονία (5ος–1ος αι π.Χ.)," 2 vols. (diss. Aristotle Univ. Thessaloniki).

Gatzolis, Ch., and S. Psoma. 2017. "Θησαυροί αργυρών νομισμάτων από την Μεθώνη: Ένας ή δύο [;] θησαυροί από την Μεθώνη της Πιερίας," Rencontres Numismatiques, École Française d'Athènes, May 8, 2017. https://www.youtube.com/watch?v=3z_YYI1ZIec.

Gaudio, N., P. Balandier, S. Perret, and C. Ginisty. 2011. "Growth of Understorey Scots Pine (*Pinus sylvestris L.*) Saplings in Response to Light in Mixed Temperate Forest," *Forestry* 84, pp. 187–195.

Gauß, W., M. Lindblom, R. A. K. Smith, and J. C. Wright, eds. 2011. *Our Cups Are Full: Pottery and Society in the Aegean Bronze Age*, Oxford.

Gauss, W., and R. Smetana. 2007. "Aegina Kolonna, the Ceramic Sequence of the SCIEM 2000 Project," in *Middle Helladic Pottery and Synchronisms. Proceedings of the International Workshop Held at Salzburg, October 31st–November 2nd, 2004*, ed. F. Felton, W. Gauss, and R. Smetana, Vienna, pp. 57–80.

Gazis, M. 2017. "Τείχος Δυμαίων: 5.500 χρόνια ιστορίας," in *Αρχαιολογικοί χώροι και μνημεία του Δήμου Δυτικής Αχαΐας. Πρακτικά ημερίδας, 19 Σεπτεμβρίου 2016*, ed. V. Argyropoulos, E. Simoni, and K. Papagiannopoulos, Kato Achaia, pp. 15–24.

Gebauer, J. 1992. "Die archaische geglättete graue Keramik," in *Ausgrabungen in Assos 1990* (Asia Minor Studien 5), ed. Ü. Serdaroğlu and R. Stupperich, Bonn, pp. 65–101.

———. 1993. "Verschiedene graue Waren," in *Ausgrabungen in Assos 1991* (Asia Minor Studien 10), ed. Ü. Serdaroğlu and R. Stupperich, Bonn, pp. 73–100.

Geddes, A. G. 1987. "Rags and Riches: The Costume of Athenian Men in the Fifth Century," *CQ* 37, pp. 307–331.

Gedl, M. 2004. *Die Fibeln in Polen* (*PBF* XIV.10), Munich.

Gehrig, U. L. 1964. *Die geometrischen Bronzen aus dem Heraion von Samos*, Hamburg.

Gehrke, H.-J. 1985. *Stasis. Untersuchungen zu den inneren Kriegen in den griechischen Staaten des 5. und 4. Jahrhunderts v. Chr.* (Vestigia 35), Munich.

Genz, H. 1997. "Northern Slaves and the Origin of Handmade Burnished Pottery," *JMA* 10, pp. 109–111.

Georgiadou, A., and A. Lagoudi. 2014. "Η κεραμική από τον οικισμό της ύστερης εποχής χαλκού στην Άψαλο Αλμωπίας," *AEMTh* 28 [2019], pp. 279–286.

Gera, D. 1985. "Typhon's Sling Bullet from Dor," *IEJ* 35, pp. 153–163.

———. 1995. "Typhon's Sling Bullet from Dor," in *Qedem Reports* 2: *Excavations at Dor, Final Report* 1B: *Areas A and C: The Finds*, ed. E. Stern, Jerusalem, pp. 491–496.

Gerasimidis, A. M. 1985. "Σταθμολογικές συνθήκες και Μεσοπαγετώδης εξέλιξη της βλάστησης στα δάση Λαϊλιά Σερρών και Καταφυγίου Πιερίας" (*Scientific Annals of the Department of Forestry and Natural Environment* 26, Suppl. 7) (diss. Aristotle Univ. Thessaloniki).

———. 1995. "Ανθρωπογενείς επιδράσεις στην εξέλιξη της δασικής βλάστησης στην Ελλάδα: Στοιχεία από διαγράμματα γύρης," *Scientific Annals of the Department of Forestry and Natural Environment* 38, pp. 169–203.

———. 2000. "Palynological Evidence for Human Influence on the Vegetation of Mountain Regions in Northern Greece: The Case of Lailias, Serres," in *Landscape and Land Use in Postglacial Greece*, ed. P. Halstead and C. D. Frederick, Sheffield, pp. 28–37.

Gerasimidis, A., and N. Athanasiadis. 1995. "Woodland History of Northern Greece from the mid Holocene to Recent Time Based on Evidence from Peat Pollen Profiles," *Vegetation History and Archaeobotany* 4, pp. 109–116.

Gerasimidis, A., N. Athanasiadis, and S. Panajiotidis. 2009. "Mount Voras (North-West Greece)," *Grana* 48, pp. 316–318.

Gerasimidis, A., and S. Panajiotidis. 2010. "Flambouro, Pieria Mountains (Northern Greece)," *Grana* 49, pp. 76–78.

Gerasimidis, A., S. Panajiotidis, and N. Athanasiadis. 2008. "Five Decades of Rapid Forest Spread in the Pieria Mountains (N. Greece) Reconstructed by Means of High-resolution Pollen Analysis and Aerial Photographs," *Vegetation History and Archaeobotany* 17, pp. 639–652.

Gerasimidis, A., S. Panajiotidis, S. Hicks, and N. Athanasiadis. 2006. "An Eight-year Record of Pollen Deposition in the Pieria Mountains (N. Greece) and Its Significance for Interpreting Fossil Pollen Assemblages," *Review of Palaeobotany and Palynology* 141, pp. 231–243.

Gergova, D. 1987. *Früh- und ältereisenzeitliche Fibeln in Bulgarien* (*PBF* XIV.7), Munich.

Gesell, G. C., W. D. E. Coulson, and L. P. Day. 1991. "Excavations at Kavousi, Crete, 1988," *Hesperia* 60, pp. 145–177.

Gesell, G. C., L. P. Day, and W. D. E. Coulson. 1988. "Excavations at Kavousi, Crete, 1987," *Hesperia* 57, pp. 279–301.

Ghali-Kahil, L. 1960. *La céramique grecque (Fouilles 1911–1956)* (Études Thasiennes 7), Paris.

Ghilardi, M. 2006. *Apport et intérêt de la Modélisation Numérique de Terrain en géomorphologie: étude du site de Méthoni (Piérie–Grèce)* (Mémoire du laboratoire de géomorphologie et d'environnement littoral de l'École Pratique des Hautes Études 45), Dinard.

———. 2007. "Dynamiques spatiales et reconstitutions paléogéographiques de la plaine de Thessalonique (Grèce) à l'Holocène récent" (diss. Univ. Paris XII Val-de-Marne).

Ghilardi, M., E. Fouache, F. Queyrel, G. Syrides, K. Vouvalidis, S. Kunesch, M. Styllas, and S. Stiros. 2008a. "Human Occupation and Geomorphological Evolution of the Thessaloniki Plain (Greece) since mid Holocene," *JAS* 35, pp. 111–125.

Ghilardi, M., S. Kunesh, M. Styllas, and E. Fouache. 2008b. "Reconstruction of Mid-Holocene Sedimentary Environments in the Central Part of the Thessaloniki Plain (Greece), Based on Microfaunal Identification, Magnetic Susceptibility and Grain-size Analyses," *Geomorphology* 97, pp. 617–630.

Ghilardi, M., J. Le Rhun, M. F. Courel, P. Chamard, F. Queyrel, M. Styllas, and T. Paraschou. 2007. "Apport et intérêt de la Modélisation Numérique de Terrain (MNT) en géomorphologie: étude du site antique de Methoni (Piérie, Grèce)," *AEMTh* 19 [2005], pp. 317–321.

Giardino, C. 2006. "Il ripostiglio di Monte Rovello: Una nota archeometallurgica," in *Studi di protostoria in onore di Renato Peroni*, Florence, pp. 62–65.

Giberson, D. F., Jr. 1996. "Ancient Glassmaking: Its Efficiency and Economy," *Ornament* 19 (4), pp. 76–79.

Gilboa, A., P. Waiman-Barak, and R. Jones. 2015. "On the Origin of Iron Age Phoenician Ceramics at Kommos, Crete: Regional and Diachronic Perspectives across the Bronze Age to Iron Age Transition," *BASOR* 374, pp. 75–102.

Gill, D. W. J. 1984. "The Workshops of the Attic Bolsal," in *Ancient Greek and Related Pottery. Proceedings of the International Vase Symposium in Amsterdam 12–15 April 1984*, ed. H. A. G. Brijder, Amsterdam, pp. 102–106.

Gill, M. V. 1986. "The Small Finds," in *Excavations at Saraçhane in Istanbul* 1: *The Excavations, Structures, Architectural Decoration, Small Finds, Coins, Bones, and Molluscs*, ed. R. M. Harrison, Princeton, pp. 226–277.

Gimatzidis, S. 2006. Die Stadt Sindos. Eine Siedlung von der späten Bronze- bis zur klassischen Zeit am Thermaischen Golf in Makedonien (diss. Freie Univ. Berlin).

———. 2010. *Die Stadt Sindos: eine Siedlung von der späten Bronze- bis zur klassischen Zeit am thermaischen Golf in Makedonien* (*PAS* 26), Rahden/Westfalen.

———. 2011. "The Northwest Aegean in the Early Iron Age," in *The "Dark Ages" Revisited: International Conference in Memory of William D. E. Coulson, University of Thessaly, Volos, 14–17 June 2007*, ed. A. Mazarakis Ainian, Volos, pp. 957–970.

———. 2013. Rev. of Bessios, Tzifopoulos, and Kotsonas 2012, in *BMCR* 2013.1.53, https://bmcr.brynmawr.edu/2013/2013.01.53/

———. 2017. "Πρώϊμοι Ελληνικοί εμπορικοί αμφορείς και οικονομία στο βόρειο Αιγαίο," in *Thasos. Métropole et colonies. Symposium International à la mémoire de Marina Sgourou, 21–22 septembre 2006*, ed. Z. Bonias and E. Lafli, Paris, pp. 259–293.

———. 2020. "The Economy of Early Greek Colonisation in the Northern Aegean," *Journal of Greek Archaeology* 5, pp. 243–262.

Gimatzidis, S., and R. Jung. 2008. "Νέα στοιχεία για την εποχή χαλκού και σιδήρου από την Πιερία: Κάστρο Νεοκαισάρειας και Μοσχοχώρι," *AEMTh* 22 [2011], pp. 211–218.

Gimbutas, M. 1965. *Bronze Age Cultures in Central and Eastern Europe*, The Hague.

Giouri, E. 1971. "Τὸ ἱερὸν τοῦ Ἄμμωνος Διὸς παρὰ τὴν Ἄφυτιν," *AAA* 4, pp. 356–367.

Giouri, E., and Ch. Koukouli. 1987. "Ανασκαφή στην αρχαία Οισύμη," *AEMTh* 1, pp. 363–387.

Girtzy, M. 2001. *Historical Topography of Ancient Macedonia: Cities and Other Settlement-Sites in the Late Classical and Hellenistic Period*, Thessaloniki.

Gitler, H., and G. Finkielsztejn. 2015. "An Official Hellenistic Inscribed Disk from Ascalon," *Israel Numismatic Research* 10, pp. 37–54.

Giudice, F., and R. Panvini, eds. 2007. *Il greco, il barbaro e la ceramica attica: Immaginario del diverso, processi di scambio e autorappresentazione degli indegni* 4, Rome.

Gjerstad, E. 1977. "Pottery from Various Parts of Cyprus," in *Greek Geometric and Archaic Pottery Found in Cyprus*, ed. E. Gjerstad, Stockholm, pp. 23–59.

———. 1979. "A Cypro-Greek Royal Marriage in the 8th Century B.C.," in *Studies Presented in Memory of Porphyrios Dikaios*, ed. V. Karageorghis et al., Nicosia, pp. 89–93.

Gjerstad, E., with Y. Calvet, M. Yon, V. Karageorghis, and J. P. Thalmann. 1977. *Greek Geometric and Archaic Pottery Found in Cyprus*, Stockholm.

Gkaniatsas, K. 1938. "Ἔρευναι επί της χλωρίδας του όρους Χορτιάτου," *Επιστημονική επετηρίς της Σχολής Φυσικών και Μαθηματικών Επιστημών του Πανεπιστημίου Θεσσαλονίκης* 5, pp. 5–32.

Glogović, D. 2003. *Fibeln im kroatischen Küstengebiet (Istrien, Dalmatien)* (*PBF* XIV.13), Munich.

Goettling, C. W. 1851. *Gesammelte Abhandlungen aus dem klassischen Altertum* 1, Halle.

Golani, A. 2019. "Technological Observations on Two-Part Stone Jewelry-Casting Molds of the Late Bronze Age in the Near East," *Journal of Eastern Mediterranean Archaeology and Heritage Studies* 7 (1), pp. 44–62.

Goldman, H. 1931. *Excavations at Eutresis in Boeotia*, Cambridge, Mass.

———. 1940. "The Acropolis of Halae," *Hesperia* 9, pp. 381–514.

Gómez Bellard, C. 1995. "The First Colonization of Ibiza and Formentera (Balearic Islands, Spain): Some More Islands out of the Stream?" *WorldArch* 26 (3): *Colonization of Islands*, ed. J. F. Cherry, pp. 442–455.

Gomme, A. W. 1945. *A Historical Commentary on Thucydides* 1, Oxford.

———. 1956. *A Historical Commentary on Thucydides* 2–3, Oxford.

Gomme, A. W., A. Andrewes, and K. J. Dover. 1970. *A Historical Commentary on Thucydides* 4, Oxford.

———. 1981. *A Historical Commentary on Thucydides* 5, Oxford.

Gorissen, P. 1978. "Litterae Lunatae," *Ancient Society* 9, pp. 149–163.

Gotsinas, A. 2016. "Παράρτημα 5. Τα ζωοαρχαιολογικά κατάλοιπα από τον Αποθέτη 39," in Pantelidou-Gofa 2016, Athens, pp. 361–375.

Gracia Alonso, Fr. 2000. "Análisis táctico de las fortificaciones ibéricas," *Gladius* 20, pp. 131–170.

Graham, A. J. 1971. "Patterns in Early Greek Colonization," *JHS* 91, pp. 35–47.

———. 1982. "The Colonial Expansion of Greece: The Western Greeks," in *CAH* III.3: *The Expansion of the Greek World, Eighth to Sixth Centuries BC*, 2nd ed., ed. J. Boardman and N. G. L. Hammond, Cambridge, pp. 83–162.

———. 2001. *Collected Papers on Greek Colonization* (*Mnemosyne* Suppl. 214), Leiden.

Graham, J. W. 1933. "Lamps from Olynthus, 1931," in *Olynthus* V, pp. 265–284.

Graikos, I. 2006. "Μια νέα θέση της νεότερης νεολιθικής στον Τρίλοφο Ημαθίας," *AEMTh* 20 [2008], pp. 795–804.

Grammenos, D. V. 1975. "Από τους προϊστορικούς οικισμούς της ανατολικής Μακεδονίας," *ArchDelt* 30A΄, pp. 193–234.

———. 1979. "Τύμβοι της ύστερης εποχής του Χαλκού και άλλες αρχαιότητες στην περιοχή του Νευροκοπίου Δράμας," *ArchEph* 1979, *Chronika*, pp. 26–71.

———. 1981. "Ανασκαφή σε οικισμό της Εποχής του Χαλκού στην Πεντάπολη του νομού Σερρών," *ArchEph* 120, pp. 91–153.

———. 1997a. "Μέρος Ι, Δήμητρα. Προϊστορικός οικισμός κοντά στις Σέρρες," in *Νεολιθική Μακεδονία*, ed. D. V. Grammenos, Athens, pp. 27–57.

———. 1997b. "Μέρος ΙΙ, Κεφάλαιο Γ. Οι οικισμοί και η δημογραφία," in *Νεολιθική Μακεδονία*, ed. D. V. Grammenos, Athens, pp. 276–290.

Grammenos, D. V., and M. Fotiadis. 1980. "Από τους προϊστορικούς οικισμούς της ανατολικής Μακεδονίας," *Ανθρωπολογικά* 1, pp. 15–53.

Grammenos, D. V., and S. Kotsos. 1996. "Ανασκαφή στον προϊστορικό οικισμό Μεσημεριανή Τούμπα Τριλόφου. Περίοδοι 1992, 1994–1996," *AEMTh* 10 (A) [1997], pp. 356–368.

Grammenos, D. V., S. Kotsos, and A. Chatzoudi. 1997. "Σωστικές ανασκαφές στο νεολιθικό οικισμό της Σταυρούπολης," *AEMTh* 11 [1999], pp. 305–315.

Grammenos, D. V., and K. Skourtopoulou. 1992. "Μεσημεριανή Τούμπα Τριλόφου Νομού Θεσσαλονίκης. Ανασκαφική περίοδος 1992," *AEMTh* 6 [1995], pp. 339 348.

Grandjean, Y. 1992. "Contribution à l'établissement d'une typologie des amphores thasiennes, le matériel amphorique du quartier de la porte du Silene," *BCH* 116, pp. 541–584.

Graninger, D. 2010. "Macedonia and Thessaly," in *A Companion to Ancient Macedonia*, ed. J. Roisman and I. Worthington, Oxford, pp. 306–325.

Gras, M. 1985. *Trafics tyrrhéniens archaïques*, Rome.

———. 1999. "Georges Vallet et le commerce," in *La colonisation grecque en Méditerranée occidentale. Actes de la rencontre scientifique en hommage à George Vallet, Rome–Naples 15–18 novembre 1995*, Rome, pp. 7–22.

———. 2010. "Plus de vin, moins d'huile? Retour sur les amphores corinthiennes dans la Méditerranée du VIIe s.," in *La Méditerranée au VIIe siècle av. J.-C. (essais d'analyses archéologiques)* (Travaux de la Maison René Ginouvès 7), ed. R. Étienne, Paris, pp. 110–116.

Grassi, G., and R. Giannini. 2005. "Influence of Light and Competition on Crown and Shoot Morphological Parameters of Norway Spruce and Silver Fir Saplings," *Annals of Forest Science* 62, pp. 269–274.

Greco, E. 1994. "Pithekoussai: Empòrion o apoikìa?" *Annali di Archeologia e Storia Antica* n.s. 1 (*ΑΠΟΙΚΙΑ: I più antichi insediamenti Greci in Occidente. Scritti in onore di Giorgio Buchner*), ed. B. d'Agostino and D. Ridgway, Naples, pp. 11–18.

Greenfield, H., K. D. Fowler, M. Fotiadis, and E. Arnold. 2005. *The Secondary Products Revolution in Macedonia: The Zooarchaeological Remains from Megalo Nisi Galanis, a Late Neolithic–Early Bronze Age Site in Greek Macedonia* (*BAR-IS* 1414), Oxford.

Greenwalt, W. S. 1999. "Why Pella?" *Historia* 48, pp. 158–183.

———. 2010. "Macedonia, Illyria and Epirus," in *A Companion to Ancient Macedonia*, ed. J. Roisman and I. Worthington, Oxford, pp. 279–305.

———. 2015. "Infantry and the Evolution of Argead Macedonia," in *Greece, Macedon and Persia: Studies in Social, Political and Military History in Honour of Waldemar Heckel*, ed. T. Howe, E. E. Garvin, and G. Wrightson, Oxford and Philadelphia, pp. 41–46.

———. 2017. "Alexander II of Macedon," in *Ancient Historiography on War and Empire*, ed. T. Howe, S. Müller, and R. Stoneman, Oxford and Philadelphia, pp. 80–91.

Groot, M. 2005. "Palaeopathological Evidence for Draught Cattle on a Roman Site in the Netherlands," in *Diet and Health in Past Animal Populations: Current Research and Future Directions*, ed. J. Davies, M. Fabis, I. Mainland, M. Richards, and R. Thomas, Oxford, pp. 52–57.

Grose, D. F. 1989. *The Toledo Museum of Art. Early Ancient Glass: Core-formed, Rod-formed, and Cast Vessels and Objects from the Late Bronze Age to the Early Roman Empire, 1600 B.C. to A.D. 50*, New York.

Gschnitzer, F., and E. Schwertheim. 1996. "Aioleis," in *Der Neue Pauly: Enzyklopädie der Antike* 1, Stuttgart, cols. 336–341.

Guarducci, M. 1969. *Epigrafia Greca* 2: *Epigrafi di carattere pubblico*, Rome.

Guglielmino, R., and C. Pagliara. 2006. "Rocavecchia (LE): Testimonianze di rapporti con Creta nell'eta del Bronzo," in *Studi di protoistoria in onore di Renato Peroni*, Florence, pp. 117–124.

Gumbricht, T., J. McCarthy, and C. Mahlander. 1996. "Digital Interpretation and Management of Land Cover: A Case Study of Cyprus," *Ecological Engineering* 6, pp. 273–279.

Güthenke, C. 2006. "Watching the Great Sea of Beauty: Thinking the Ancient Greek Mediterranean," paper, Princeton/Stanford 2006, version 1.1, https://www.princeton.edu/~pswpc/papers/authorAL/guthenke/guthenke.html

Guzzo, P. G. 1978. "Importazione fittili greco-orientali sulla costa Jonica d'Italia," in *Les céramiques de la Grèce de l'est et leur diffusion en occident. Centre Jean Bérard, Institut Français de Naples, 6–9 juillet 1976*, Paris, pp. 107–130.

Gwynn, A. 1918. "The Character of Greek Colonisation," *JHS* 38, pp. 88–123.

Gyulai, F., and K. Kelertas. 2005. "Appendix D: The Plant Remains from Tombs," in Papadopoulos 2005, pp. 339–342.

Haag, S., C. Popov, B. Horejs, S. Alexandrov, and G. Plattner. 2017. *Das erste Gold. Ada Tepe: Das älteste Goldbergwerk Europas*, Vienna.

Haarer, P. 2000. " Ὀβελοί and Iron in Archaic Cyprus" (diss. Oxford Univ.).

Haas, C. J. 1985. "Athenian Naval Power Before Themistocles," *Historia* 34, pp. 29–46.

Habicht, C. 1970. *Gottmenschentum und griechische Städte* (Zetemata 14), Munich.

Hadjichambis, A. C. H., D. Paraskeva-Hadjichambi, A. Della, M. E. Guisti, K. de Pasquale, C. Lenzarini, E. Censorii, M. R. Gonzales-Tejero, C. Sanchez-Rojas, J. Ramiro-Gutierrez, M. Skoula, Ch. Johnson, A. Sarpaki, M. Hmamoushi, S. Jorhi, M. El-Demerdash, M. El-Zayat, and A. Pieroni. 2007. "Wild and Semi-domesticated Food Plant Consumption in Seven Circum-Mediterranean Areas," *International Journal of Food Sciences and Nutrition* 1, pp. 1–32.

Hadjidaki, E. 1996. "Underwater Excavations of a Late Fifth Century Merchant Ship at Alonnesos, Greece: the 1991–1993 Seasons," *BCH* 120, pp. 561–593.

Hagerman, C. 2014. "Weapons: Catapults, Arrowheads, Javelin and Spear Heads, and Sling Bullets," in Schaus 2014a, pp. 79–102.

Hägg, I. 1967–1968. "Some Notes on the Origin of the Peplos-type Dress in Scandinavia," *Tor* 12, pp. 81–127.

Hägg, I., and R. Hägg. 1978. *Excavations in the Barbouna Area at Asine*, Fasc. 2: *Finds from the Levendis Sector, 1970–1972*, Uppsala.

Hägg, R. 1971. "Protogeometrische und geometrische Keramik in Nauplion," *OpAth* 10, pp. 41–52.

———. 1974. *Die Gräber der Argolis in submykenischer, protogeometrischer und geometrischer Zeit* 1: *Lage und Form der Gräber*, Uppsala.

Hale, C. 2016. "The Middle Helladic Fine Gray Burnished (Gray Minyan) Sequence at Mitrou, East Lokris," *Hesperia* 85, pp. 243–295.

Haley, J. B. 1928. "The Coming of the Greeks I: The Geographical Distribution of Pre-Greek Place-Names," *AJA* 32 (2), pp. 141–145.

Hall, E. H. 1914. *Excavations in Eastern Crete: Vrokastro*, Philadelphia.

Hall, J. M. 2001. "Contested Ethnicities: Perceptions of Macedonia Within Evolving Definitions of Greek Ethnicity," in *Ancient Perceptions of Greek Ethnicity* (Center for Hellenic Studies Colloquia 5), ed. I. Malkin, Cambridge, Mass., pp. 159–186.

———. 2008. "Foundation Stories," in *Greek Colonisation: An Account of Greek Colonies and Other Settlement Overseas* 2, ed. G. R. Tsetskhladze, Boston and Leiden, pp. 383–426.

Hallett, C. 2005. *The Roman Nude: Heroic Portrait Statuary 200 B.C.–A.D. 300*, Oxford.

Halliday, W. R. 1928. *The Greek Questions of Plutarch*, Oxford.

Halstead, P. 1985. "A Study of Mandibular Teeth from Romano-British Contexts at Maxey," in *Archaeology and Environment in the Lower Welland Valley* (East Anglian Archaeology Report 27), ed. F. M. M. Pryor and C. A. I. French, Cambridge, pp. 219–224.

———. 2011. "Faunal Remains," in *Nemea Valley Archaeological Project: Early Bronze Age Village on Tsoungiza Hill*, ed. D. J. Pullen, Princeton, pp. 741–803.

Halstead, P., and P. Collins. 1995. *The Taxonomic Identification of Limb Bones of European Farmyard Animals and Deer*, A Multimedia Tutorial, Glasgow.

Halstead, P., P. Collins, and V. Isaakidou. 2002. "Sorting the Sheep from the Goats: Morphological Distinctions Between the Mandibles and Mandibular Teeth of Adult Ovis and Capra," *JAS* 29, pp. 545–553.

Halstead, P., and V. Isaakidou. 2011. "A Pig Fed by Hand is Worth Two in the Bush: Ethnoarchaeology of Pig Husbandry in Greece and Its Archaeological Implications," in *Ethnozooarchaeology: The Present Past of Human:Animal Relationships*, ed. U. Albarella, Oxford, pp. 160–174.

Halstead, P., and G. Jones. 1980. "Early Neolithic Economy in Thessaly: Some Evidence from Excavations at Prodromos," *Anthropologica* 1, pp. 93–108.

Hamilakis, Y. 2003. "The Sacred Geography of Hunting: Wild Animals, Social Power and Gender in Early Farming Societies," in *Zooarchaeology in Greece*, ed. E. Kotjabopoulou, Y. Hamilakis, P. Halstead, C. Gamble, and P. Elefanti, Athens, pp. 239–247.

Hamilton, R. W. 1935. "Excavations at Tell Abu Hawam," *QDAP* 4, pp. 1–69.

Hammond, N. G. L. 1967. *Epirus: The Geography, the Ancient Remains, the History and Topography of Epirus and Adjacent Areas*, Oxford.

———. 1972. *A History of Macedonia* 1: *Historical Geography and Prehistory*, Oxford.

———. 1982. "Illyris, Epirus and Macedonia," in *CAH* III.3: *The Expansion of the Greek World, Eighth to Sixth Centuries BC*, 2nd ed., ed. J. Boardman and N. G. L. Hammond, Cambridge, pp. 261–285.

———. 1984. "The Battle of Pydna," *JHS* 104, pp. 31–47.

———. 1989. *The Macedonian State: Origins, Institutions, and History*, Oxford.

———. 1995a. "Connotations of 'Macedonia' and of 'Macedones' until 323 B.C.," *CQ* 45.1, pp. 120–128.

———. 1995b. "The Location of the Trout-River Astraeus," *GRBS* 36, pp. 173–176.

———. 1998. "Eretria's Colonies in the Area of the Thermaic Gulf," *BSA* 93, pp. 393–399.

Hammond, N. G. L., and G. T. Griffith. 1979. *A History of Macedonia* 2: *550–336 B.C.*, Oxford.

Hampe, R. 1936. *Frühe griechische Sagenbilder in Böotien*, Athens.

Handberg, S. 2010. "East Greek Pottery," in *Excavation on the Timpone della Motta, Francavilla Marittima (1992–2004)* 1: *The Greek Pottery*, ed. J. K. Jacobsen and S. Handberg, Bari, pp. 289–332.

Hanfmann, G. M. A. 1956. "On Some Eastern Greek Wares Found at Tarsus," in *The Aegean and the Near East: Studies Presented to Hetty Goldman on the Occasion of Her Seventy-fifth Birthday*, ed. S. S. Weinberg, Locust Valley, N.Y., pp. 165–184.

Hänsel, B. 1973. "Policoro (Matera): Scavi eseguiti nell'area dell'acropoli di Eraclea negli anni 1965–1967," *NSc* 28, pp. 400–492.

———. 1976. *Beiträge zur regionalen und chronologischen Gliederung der älteren Hallstattzeit an der unteren Donau*, Bonn.

———. 1979. "Ergebnisse der Grabungen bei Kastanas in Zentralmakedonien 1975–1978," *JRGZM* 26, pp. 167–202.

———. 1989. *Kastanas. Ausgrabungen in einem Siedlunghügel der Bronze- und Eisenzeit Makedoniens, 1975–1979. Die Grabung und der Baubefund* (*PAS* 7), Berlin.

Hänsel, B., and I. Aslanis. 2010. *Das prähistorische Olynth: Ausgrabungen in der Toumba Ayios Mamas 1994–1996. Die Grabung und der Baubefund* (*PAS* 23), Rahden/Westfalen.

Hansen, H. D. 1933. *Early Civilization in Thessaly*, Baltimore.

———. 1937. "The Prehistoric Pottery on the North Slope of the Acropolis, 1937," *Hesperia* 6, pp. 539–570.

Hansen, M. H. 1997. "Emporion: A Study of the Use and Meaning of the Term in the Archaic and Classical Periods," in *Yet More Studies in the Ancient Greek Polis* (*Historia* Einzelschriften 117), ed. T. H. Nielsen, Stuttgart, pp. 83–105.

———. 2004. "Colonies and Indigenous Hellenised Communities," in Hansen and Nielsen 2004, pp. 150–153.

———. 2006a. "Emporion: A Study of the Use and Meaning of the Term in the Archaic and Classical Periods," in *Greek Colonisation: An Account of Greek Colonies and Other Settlements Overseas* 1, ed. G. R. Tsetskhladze, Leiden and Boston, pp. 1–39.

———. 2006b. *Polis: An Introduction to the Ancient Greek City-State*, Oxford.

Hansen, M. H., and T. H. Nielsen. 2004. *An Inventory of Archaic and Classical* Poleis: *An Investigation Conducted by the Copenhagen Polis Centre for the Danish National Research Foundation*, Oxford.

Hansson, M. C., and B. P. Foley. 2008. "Ancient DNA Fragments Inside Classical Greek Amphoras Reveal Cargo of 2400 Year Old Shipwreck," *JAS* 35, pp. 1169–1176.

Harding, A. 1975. "Mycenaean Greece and Europe: The Evidence of Bronze Tools and Implements," *PPS* 41, pp. 183–202.

Harding, P. 2006. *Didymos: On Demosthenes*, Oxford.

Harris, E. M. 2018. "The Stereotype of Tyranny and the Tyranny of Stereotypes: Demosthenes on Philip II of Macedon," in *Βορειοελλαδικά. Tales from the Lands of the Ethne: Essays in Honour of Miltiades B. Hatzopoulos* (Μελετήματα 78), ed. M. Kalaïtzi, P. Paschidis, C. Antonetti, and A.-M. Guimier-Sorbets, Athens, pp. 167–178.

Harris, P. 1960. "Production of Pine Resin and Its Effect on Survival of *Rhyacionia buoliana* (Schiff.) (Lepidoptera: Olethreutidae)," *Canadian Journal of Zoology* 38, pp. 121–130.

Harris, W. H. 2013. "Defining and Detecting Mediterranean Deforestation, 800 BCE to 700 CE," in *The Ancient Mediterranean Environment Between Science and History*, ed. W. H. Harris, Leiden and Boston, pp. 173–194.

Harris, W. V. 1989. *Ancient Literacy*, Cambridge, Mass., and London.

———, ed. 1993. *The Inscribed Economy: Production and Distribution in the Roman Empire in the Light of instrumentum domesticum* (*JRA* Suppl. 6), Ann Arbor.

Harrison, C. M. 1999. "Triremes at Rest: On the Beach or in the Water?" *JHS* 119, pp. 168–171.

———. 2003. "A Note on the Care and Handling of Triremes," *IJNA* 32, pp. 78–84.

Hasebroek, J. 1928. *Staat und Handel im alten Griechenland. Untersuchungen zur antiken Wirtschaftsgeschichte*, Tübingen.

Haskell, H. W., R. E. Jones, P. E. Day, and J. T. Killen. 2011. *Transport Stirrup Jars of the Bronze Age Aegean and East Mediterranean*, Philadelphia.

Haspels, C. H. E. 1936. *Attic Black-Figured Lekythoi*, Paris.

Hatzopoulos, M. B. 1985. "La Béotie et la Macédoine à l'époque de l'hégémonie thébaine: le point de vue macédonien," in *La Béotie antique. Colloques internationaux du Centre National de la Recherche Scientifique, Lyon, Saint-Etienne, 16–20 Mai 1983*, ed. P. Roesch and G. Argoud, Paris, pp. 217–248.

———. 1987. "Strepsa: A Reconsideration, or New Evidence on the Road System of Lower Macedonia," in Hatzopoulos and Loukopoulou 1987, pp. 17–60.

———. 1995. "Τα όρια της Μακεδονίας," *Πρακτικά της Ακαδημίας Αθηνών*, April 6, 1995, pp. 164–177.

———. 1996. *Macedonian Institutions under the Kings* 1: *A Historical and Epigraphic Study*; 2: *Epigraphic Appendix* (Μελετήματα 22), Athens.

———. 2011a. "Macedonia and Macedonians," in *Brill's Companion to Ancient Macedon: Studies in the Archaeology and History of Macedon, 650 BC–300 AD*, ed. R. J. Lane Fox, Leiden, pp. 43–49.

———. 2011b. "Macedonians and Other Greeks," in *Brill's Companion to Ancient Macedon: Studies in the Archaeology and History of Macedon, 650 BC–300 AD*, ed. R. J. Lane Fox, Leiden, pp. 51–78.

———. 2021. "Thucydides, Historical Geography and the 'Lost Years' of Perdikkas II," in *Sidelights on Greek Antiquity: Archaeological and Epigraphical Essays in Honour of Vasileios Petrakos*, ed. K. Kalogeropoulos, D. Vassilikou, and M. Tiverios, Berlin/Boston 2021, pp. 3–16.

Hatzopoulos, M. B., D. Knoepfler, and V. Marigo-Papadopoulos. 1990. "Deux sites pour Méthone de Macédoine," *BCH* 114, pp. 639–668.

Hatzopoulos, M. B., and L. D. Loukopoulou. 1987. *Two Studies in Ancient Macedonian Topography* (Μελετήματα 3), Athens.

———. 1992. *Recherches sur les marches orientales des Téménides (Anthémonte–Kalindoia): Ière partie* (Μελετήματα 11), Athens.

Hatzopoulos, M. B., and P. Paschidis. 2004. "Makedonia," in Hansen and Nielsen 2004, pp. 794–809.

Hauben, H. 1978. "The Ships of the Pydnaeans: Remarks on Kassandros' Naval Situation in 314/313 B.C.," *Ancient Society* 9, pp. 47–54.

Hawkins, W. 1847. "Observations on the Use of the Sling, as a Warlike Weapon, Among the Ancients," *Archaeologia* 32, pp. 96–107.

Hayden, B. D. 1995. "The Emergence of Prestige Technologies and Pottery," in *The Emergence of Pottery: Technology and Innovation in Ancient Societies*, ed. W. K. Barnett and J. W. Hoopes, Washington, pp. 257–265.

Hayes, J. W. 1980. *A Supplement to Late Roman Pottery*, London.

Hedges, R. E. M. 2000. "Appraisal of Radiocarbon Dating of Kiore Bones (Pacific rat *Rattus exulans*)," *Journal of the Royal Society of New Zealand* 30, pp. 385–398.

Hedreen, G. M. 2001. *Capturing Troy: The Narrative Functions of Landscape in Archaic and Early Classical Greek Art*, Ann Arbor.

———. 2007. "Involved Spectatorship in Archaic Greek Art," *Art History* 30 (2), pp. 217–246.

———. 2016. "So-and-so καλή: A Reexamination," in *Epigraphy of Art. Ancient Greek Vase-Inscriptions and Vase-Paintings*, ed. D. Yatromanolakis, Oxford, pp. 53–72.

Heesen, P. 2011. *Athenian Little-Master Cups*, 2 vols., Amsterdam.

Heiden, B. 2008. "Common People and Leaders in *Iliad* Book 2: The Invocation of the Muses and the Catalogue of Ships," *TAPA* 138, pp. 127–154.

Heilmeyer, W.-D. 1981. "Wagenvotive," in *X. Bericht über die Ausgrabungen in Olympia*, ed. A. Mallwitz, Berlin, pp. 59–71.

———. 1982. *Frühgriechische Kunst: Kunst und Siedlung im geometrischen Griechenland*, Berlin.

———. 1994. "Frühe olympische Bronzefiguren: Die Wagenvotive," in *IX. Bericht über die Ausgrabungen in Olympia*, ed. E. Kunze, Berlin, pp. 172–208.

Hein, A., I. Karatasios, N. S. Müller, and V. Kilikoglou. 2013. "Heat Transfer Properties of Pyrotechnical Ceramics Used in Ancient Metallurgy," *Thermochimica Acta* 573, pp. 87–94.

Hein, A., V. Kilikoglou, and V. Kassianidou. 2007. "Chemical and Mineralogical Examination of Metallurgical Ceramics from a Late Bronze Age Copper Smelting Site in Cyprus," *JAS* 34, pp. 141–154.

Heinrichs, J. 2017. "Coins and Constructions: The Origins of Argead Coinage under Alexander I," in *The History of the Argeads: New Perspectives*, ed. S. Müller, T. Howe, H. Bowden, and R. Rollinger, with the collaboration of S. Pal (Classica et Orientalia 19), Wiesbaden, pp. 79–98.

Hellmann, M.-Chr. 1982. "Collection Froehner: balles de fronde grecques," *BCH* 106, pp. 75–87.

Helly, B. 2006. "Démétrias, Méthoné de Piérie, Méthoné de Magnésie et la malédiction d'Agamemnon contre les Méthonéens," in *Maiandros: Festschrift für Volkmar von Graeve*, ed. R. Biering, V. Brinkmann, U. Schlotzhauer, and B. F. Weber, Munich, pp. 115–130.

———. 2007. "Le dialecte thessalien, un autre modèle de développement," in *Die altgriechischen Dialekte: Wesen und Werden, Akten des Kolloquiums Freie Universität Berlin 19.–22. September 2001* (Innsbrucker Beiträge zur Sprachwissenschaft 126), ed. I. Hajnal, Innsbruck, pp. 177–222.

———. 2018. "La Thessalie au 4e s. av. J.-C.: entre autonomie et sujétion," in *Βορειοελλαδικά. Tales from the Lands of the Ethne: Essays in Honour of Miltiades B. Hatzopoulos* (Μελετήματα 78), ed. M. Kalaïtzi, P. Paschidis, C. Antonetti, and A.-M. Guimier-Sorbets, Athens, pp. 123–158.

Hemingway, S. 1996. "Minoan Metalworking in the Postpalatial Period," *BSA* 91, pp. 213–252.

Henry, A. 1991. "A Lead Letter from Torone," *ArchEph* 130, pp. 65–70.

———. 2001. "A Lead Letter," in *Torone* I, Part 2, pp. 765–771.

Herda, A. 2006. "Panionion-Melia, Mykalessos-Mykale, Perseus und Medusa: Überlegungen zur Siedlungsgeschichte der Mykale in der frühen Eisenzeit," *IstMitt* 56, pp. 43–102.

Herrero de Jauregui, M. 2008. "The Protrepticus of Clement of Alexandria: A Commentary" (diss. Alma Mater Studiorum–Università di Bologna).

Hertel, D. 2007. "Der aiolische Siedlungsraum (Aiolis) am Übergang von der Bronze- zur Eisenzeit," in *Frühes Ionien: Eine Bestandsaufnahme. Panionion-Symposion Güzelçamlı 26. September–1. Oktober 1999* (Milesische Forschungen 5), ed. J. Cobet, V. von Graeve, W.-D. Niemeier, and K. Zimmermann, Mainz on Rhein, pp. 97–122.

———. 2008a. "Die frühe griechische Keramik in der Berliner Sammlung (1020–650/25 bzw. 600/550 v. Chr.)," in *Heinrich Schliemanns Sammlung trojanischer Altertümer—Neuvorlage* 1: *Forschungsgeschichte, keramische Funde der Schichten VII bis IX, Nadeln, Gewichte und durchlochte Tongeräte*, ed. M. Wemhoff, D. Hertel, and Al. Hänsel, Berlin, pp. 93–173.

———. 2008b. *Das frühe Ilion: Die Besiedlung Troias durch die Griechen (1020–650/25 v. Chr.)*, Munich.

———. 2011. "Das vorklassische Pergamon und sein Siedlingsprofil," *IstMitt* 61, pp. 21–84.

Herzog-Hauser, G. 1956a. "Pieria 1–6," *RE* Suppl. 8, pp. 494–495.

———. 1956b. "Pieros 1–2," *RE* Suppl. 8, pp. 498–499.

Heskel, J. 1997. *The North Aegean Wars, 371–360 B.C.* (*Historia*: Einzelschriften 102), Stuttgart.

Heurtley, W. A. 1925. "Report on an Excavation at the Toumbas of Vardino, Macedonia," *Liverpool Annals of Archaeology and Anthropology* 12, pp. 15–36.

———. 1939. *Prehistoric Macedonia: An Archaeological Reconnaissance of Greek Macedonia (West of the Struma) in the Neolithic, Bronze, and Early Iron Ages*, Cambridge.

Heurtley, W. A., and H. Lorimer. 1932–1933. "Excavations at Ithaca, Vol. 1," *BSA* 33, pp. 22–65.

Heurtley, W. A., and T. C. Skeat. 1930–1931. "The Tholos Tombs of Marmariane," *BSA* 31, pp. 1–55.

Heuzey, H. 1927. "Notes sur quelques manteaux Grecs: l'éphaptide et la zeira," *REG* 40, pp. 5–16.

Heymans, E. 2018a. "Heads or Tails: Metal Hoards from the Iron Age Southern Levant," in *Gifts, Goods and Money: Comparing Currency and Circulation Systems in Past Societies*, ed. D. Brandherm, E. Heymans, and D. Hofmann, Oxford, pp. 85–104.

———. 2018b. "Argonauts of the Eastern Mediterranean: The Early History of Money in the Eastern Mediterranean Iron Age" (diss. Tel Aviv University).

———. 2021. *The Origins of Money in the Iron Age Mediterranean World*, Cambridge.

Higgins, R. A. 1980. *Greek and Roman Jewellery*, 2nd ed., London.

Himmelmann, N. 1990. *Ideale Nacktheit* (*JdI* Ergänzungsheft 26), Berlin and New York.

Histria XV = I. Bîrzescu, *Die archaischen und frühklassischen Transportamphoren* (Histria 15), Bucharest 2012.

Hitsiou, E. 2003. "Production and Circulation of the Late Neolithic Pottery from Makrygialos (Phase II), Macedonia, Northern Greece" (diss. University of Sheffield).

Hochstetter, A. 1984. *Kastanas. Ausgrabungen in einem Siedlungshügel der Bronze- und Eisenzeit Makedoniens 1975–1979. Die handgemachte Keramik. Schichten 19 bis 1* (*PAS* 6), Berlin.

———. 1987. *Kastanas. Ausgrabungen in einem Siedlungshügel der Bronze- und Eisenzeit Makedoniens 1975–1979. Die Kleinfunde* (*PAS* 6), Berlin.

Hodges, H. 1964. *Artifacts: An Introduction to Early Materials and Technology*, New York.

Hodos, T. 2006. *Local Responses to Colonization in the Iron Age Mediterranean*, London.

———. 2020. *The Archaeology of the Mediterranean Iron Age: A Globalising World c.1100–600 BCE*, Cambridge.

Hogarth, D. G. 1899–1900. "The Dictaean Cave," *BSA* 6, pp. 94–116.

———. 1908. *Excavations at Ephesus: The Archaic Artemisia*, London.

Holleran, Cl. 2012. *Shopping in Ancient Rome: The Retail Trade in the Late Republic and the Principate*, Oxford.

Holloway, R. R. 1981. *Italy and the Aegean 3000–700 B.C.* (Archaeologia Transatlantica 1), Louvain-La-Neuve.

Holste, F. 1953. *Die Bronzezeit in Süd- und Westdeutschland* (Handbuch der Urgeschichte Deutschlands 1), Berlin.

Hood, M. S. F. 1982. *Excavations in Chios 1938–1955: Prehistoric Emporio and Ayio Gala*, 2 vols. (*BSA* Suppl. 15), London.

Hood, M. S. F., and J. N. Coldstream. 1968. "A Late Minoan Tomb at Ayios Ioannis near Knossos," *BSA* 63, pp. 205–218.

Hood, M. S. F., G. Huxley, and N. Sandars. 1958–1959. "A Minoan Cemetery at Upper Gypsades (Knossos Survey 156), *BSA* 53–54, pp. 194–262.

Horden, P., and N. Purcell. 2000. *The Corrupting Sea: A Study of Mediterranean History*, Oxford.

Horejs, B. 2005. "Kochen am Schnittpunkt der Kulturen—zwischen Karpathenbecken und Ägäis," in *Interpretationsraum Bronzezeit: Bernhard Hänsel von seinen Schülern gewidmet* (Universitätsforschungen zur prähistorischen Archäologie 121), ed. B. Horejs, R. Jung, E. Kaiser, and B. Terzan, Bonn, pp. 71–94.

———. 2007a. *Das prähistorische Olynth: Ausgrabungen in der Toumba Ayios Mamas 1994–1996. Die Spätbronzezeitliche handgemachte Keramik der Schichten 13 bis 1* (*PAS* 21), Rahden/Westfalen.

———. 2007b. "Transition from Middle to Late Bronze Age in Central Macedonia and Its Synchronism with the 'Helladic World,'" in *Middle Helladic Pottery and Synchronisms. Proceedings of the International Workshop Held at Salzburg, October 31st–November 2nd, 2004*, ed. F. Felton, W. Gauss, and R. Smetana, Vienna, pp. 183–200.

———. 2017. "The Çukuriçi Höyük Research Project," in *Çukuriçi Höyük* 1: *Anatolia and the Aegean from the 7th to the 3rd Millennium BC*, (*OREA* 5, Austrian Academy of Sciences), ed. B. Horejs, Vienna, pp. 11–26.

Hornblower, S. 1991, 1996, 2008. *A Commentary on Thucydides* 1: *Books 1–3*; 2: *Books 4–5.24*; 3: *Books 5.25–8.109*, Oxford.

———. 1997. "Thucydides and 'Chalkidic' Torone (IV.110.1)," *OJA* 16, pp. 177–186.

Hourlier, M. 2006. "Une balle de fronde au nom d'Onomarchos et sa monnaie," *RN* 162, pp. 51–55.

How, W. W., and J. Wells. 1928. *A Commentary on Herodotus* 1–2, Oxford.

Howe, T. 2017. "Plain Tales from the Hills: Illyrian Influences on Argead Military Development," in *The History of the Argeads: New Perspectives*, ed. S. Müller, T. Howe, H. Bowden, and R. Rollinger, with the collaboration of S. Pal (Classica et Orientalia 19), Wiesbaden, pp. 99–111.

Howes Smith, P. H. G. 1981. "Two Oriental Bronze Bowls in Utrecht," *BABesch* 56, pp. 3–36.

———. 1984. "Bronze Ribbed Bowls from Central Italy and Etruria: Import and Imitation," *BABesch* 59, pp. 73–112.

Hristov, I. 2012. "Military Operations Before the Walls of the Residence in 341 BC in Accordance with the Evidence of the Lead Sling-Balls from the Site," in *Kozi Gramadi: Studies of an Odrysian Ruler's Residence and Sanctuaries in Sredna Gora Mt., 8th–1st Cent. BC* 2, ed. I. Hristov, Sofia, pp. 79–89.

Hughes-Brock, H. 2005. "Amber and Some Other Travelers in the Bronze Age Aegean and Europe," in *Autochthon: Papers Presented to O. T. P. K. Dickinson on the Occasion of His Retirement*, ed. A. Dakouri-Hild and S. Sherratt, Oxford, pp. 301–316.

Humphreys, S. L. 1965. "Il commercio in quanto motivo della colonizzazione greca dell'Italia e della Sicilia," *Rivista Storica Italiana* 77, pp. 421–433.

Hunter, J. R. 1994. "Maritime Culture: Notes from the Land," *IJNA* 23, pp. 261–264.

Hürmüzlü, B. 2004. "Burial Grounds at Klazomenai: Geometric Through Hellenistic Periods," in *Klazomenai, Teos and Abdera: Metropoleis and Colony. Proceedings of the International Symposium Held at the Archaeological Museum of Abdera, Abdera, 20–21 October 2001*, ed. A. Moustaka, E. Skarlatidou, M.-C. Tzannes, and Y. E. Ersoy, Thessaloniki, 77–95.

Hurwit, J. M. 2007. "The Problem with Dexileos: Heroic and Other Nudities in Greek Art," *AJA* 111, pp. 35–60.

Hüttel, H.-G. 1980. "Ein mitteleuropäischer Fremdling in Tiryns?" *JRGZM* 27, pp. 159–165.

Huxley, G. L. 1966. *The Early Ionians*, London.

Iakovidis, S. 1969–1970. *Περατή. Τὸ Νεκροταφεῖον*, 3 vols., Athens.

———. 1977. "On the Use of Mycenaean 'Buttons'," *BSA* 72, pp. 113–119.

———. 1989. *Γλᾶς 1: Ἡ ἀνασκαφὴ 1955–1961*, Athens.

Ignatiadou, D. 1993. "Γυάλινα κτερίσματα από το νεκροταφείο της Πύδνας," *AEMTh* 7, pp. 207–214.

———. 2002. "Royal Identities and Political Symbolism in the Vergina Lion-hunt Painting," *ArchDelt* 57, A, pp. 119–154.

———. 2004. "Glass Vessels," in *The Maussolleion at Halikarnassos. Reports of the Danish Archaeological Expedition to Bodrum. Subterranean and Pre-Maussolan Structures on the Site of the Maussolleion, the Finds from the Tomb Chamber of Maussollos*, ed. J. Zahle and K. Kjeldsen, Aarhus, pp. 181 201.

———. 2006. "Psychoactive and Poisonous Plants on Achaemenid-style Vases," in *Ancient Greece and Ancient Iran: Cross-cultural Encounters*, ed. S. M. R. Darbandi and A. Zournatzi, Athens, pp. 327–337.

———, ed. 2010. *Glass Cosmos* (Exhibition catalogue, Archaeological Museum of Thessaloniki 2009), Thessaloniki.

Ignatiadou, D. 2012a. "Sacerdotal Vessels and Jewellery," in *Δινήεσσα. Τιμητικός τόμος για την Κατερίνα Ρωμιοπούλου. Festschrift for Katerina Rhomiopoulou*, ed. P. Adam-Veleni and K. Tzanavari, Thessaloniki, pp. 621–628.

———. 2012b. "Το διακοσμητικό θέμα των μακρών πετάλων," in *VII Conference on Hellenistic Pottery (Aigion 2005)*, Athens, pp. 645–650.

Ignatiadou, D., and A. Antonaras. 2008. *Glassworking, Ancient and Medieval: Terminology, Technology and Typology, A Greek–English, English–Greek Dictionary*, Thessaloniki.

Ignatiadou, D., and A. Athanassiadou. 2012."Υαλουργία Μεθώνης," *AEMTh* 26 [2017], pp. 199–204.

Ignatiadou, D., and K. Chatzinikolaou. 2002. "Γυάλινες χάντρες από το αρχαίο νεκροταφείο της Θέρμης (Σέδες) Θεσσαλονίκης," in *Το γυαλί από την Αρχαιότητα έως Σήμερα, Β Συνέδριο Μαργαριτών Μυλοποτάμου Κρήτης 1997*, ed. P. G. Themelis, Athens, pp. 57–72.

Ignatiadou, D., and A. Chatzipanagiotou. 2018. "Χρήσεις και συμβολισμοί των κοσμημάτων. Από τη Γεωμετρική έως και τη Ρωμαϊκή εποχή," in *Οι αμέτρητες όψεις του ωραίου στην αρχαία τέχνη*, ed. M. Lagogianni-Georgakarakou, Athens, pp. 265–281.

Immerwahr, H. R. 1990. *Attic Script: A Survey*. Oxford.

Ingold, T. 2000. *The Perception of the Environment: Essays in Livelihood, Dwelling and Skill*, London.

Ingram, R. S. 2005. "Faience and Glass Beads from the Late Bronze Age Shipwreck at Uluburun" (MA thesis, Texas A&M University, College Station).

Intze, Z. 2011. "Ο Νεολιθικός οικισμός της Ρητίνης Πιερίας: η κεραμική από το μεγάλο λάκκο" (MA thesis, Aristotle Univ. Thessaloniki).

İren, K. 1993. "Archaische ostgriechische Keramik 1991," in *Ausgrabungen in Assos 1991* (Asia Minor Studien 10), ed. Ü. Serdaroğlu and R. Stupperich, Bonn, pp. 37–52.

———. 2002. "Die Werkstatt des Londoner Dinos: Eine phokäische Werkstatt?" *IstMitt* 52, pp. 165–207.

———. 2003. *Aiolische orientalisierende Keramik*, Istanbul.

———. 2008. "The Necropolis of Kyme Unveiled: Some Observations on the New Finds," in *Euergetes: Festschrift für Prof. Dr. Haluk Abbasoğlu zum 65. Geburtstag*, ed. İ. Delemen, S. Çokay-Kepçe, A Özdizbay, and Ö. Turak, Antalya, pp. 613–637.

Isaakidou, V. 2006. "Ploughing with Cows: Knossos and the 'Secondary Products Revolution,'" in *Animals in the Neolithic of Britain and Europe*, ed. D. Serjeantson and D. Fields, Oxford, pp. 95–112.

Isler, H. P. 1994. "Glandes: Schleudergeschosse aus den Grabungen auf den Monte Iato," *AA* 1994, pp. 239–254.

Isthmia = *Isthmia. Excavations by the University of Chicago Under the Auspices of the American School of Classical Studies at Athens*, Princeton

III = O. Broneer, *Terracotta Lamps*, 1977.

VII = I. K. Raubitschek, *The Metal Objects (1952–1989)*, 1998.

VIII = C. Morgan, *The Late Bronze Age Settlement and Early Iron Age Sanctuary*, 1999.

X = Lindros Wohl, B. *Terracotta Lamps*, II: *1967-2004*, 2017.

Jacob-Felsch, M. 1988. "Compass-Drawn Concentric Circles in Vase Painting: A Problem of Relative Chronology at the End of the Bronze Age," in *Problems in Greek Prehistory. Papers Presented at the Centenary Conference of the British School of Archaeology at Athens, Manchester, April 1986*, ed. E. B. French and K. A. Wardle, Bedminster, pp. 193–199.

———. 1996. "Die spätmykenische bis frühprotogeometrische Keramik," in *Kalapodi* I, pp. 1–213.

Jacobsthal, P. 1932. "Λέαινα ἐπὶ τυροκνήστιδος," *AM* 57, pp. 1–7.

———. 1956. *Greek Pins and Their Connexions with Europe and Asia*, Oxford.

Jacomet, S. 2006. *Identification of Cereal Remains from Archaeological Sites*, 2nd ed., Basel.

Jacopi, G. 1929. *Scavi nella necropolis di Jaliso 1924–1928* (*ClRh* 3), Bergamo.

———. 1931. *Esplorazione archeologica di Camiro I: Scavi nelle necropoli camiresi 1929–1930* (*ClRh* IV), Bergamo.

———. 1932–1933. *Esplorazione archeologica di Camiro* 2 (*ClRh* 6–7), Bergamo.

Janko, R. 1994. *The Iliad: A Commentary* 4: *Books 13-16*, Cambridge.

———. 2015. "From Gabii and Gordion to Eretria and Methone: The Rise of the Greek Alphabet," *BICS* 58, pp. 1–32.

———. 2017. "From Gabii and Gordion to Eretria and Methone: The Rise of the Greek Alphabet," in Strauss Clay, Malkin, and Tzifopoulos 2017b, pp. 135–164.

Jantzen, U. 1953. "Geometrische Kannenverschlüsse," *AA* 1953, pp. 56–67.

———. 1955. *Griechische Greifenkessel*, Berlin.

Jeffery, L. H. 1980. "Commentary on the Graffiti, with a Note on the Greek Use of the Long Sigma," in *Lefkandi* I, pp. 89–93.

———. 1982. "Greek Alphabetic Writing," in *The Cambridge Ancient History*, vol. 3.1: *The Prehistory of the Balkans, the Middle East, and the Aegean World, Tenth to Eighth Centuries B.C.*, ed. J. Boardman, I. E. S. Edwards, N. G. L. Hammond, and E. Sollberger, Cambridge, pp. 819–833.

Jeffery, L. H., and A. W. Johnston. 1990. *The Local Scripts of Archaic Greece: A Study of the Origin of the Greek Alphabet and Its Development from the Eighth to the Fifth Centuries B.C.*, rev. ed., Oxford.

Johannowsky, W. 1978. "Importazioni greco-orientali in Campania," in *Les céramiques de la Grèce de l'est et leur diffusion en occident. Centre Jean Bérard, Institut Français de Naples, 6–9 juillet 1976*, Paris, pp. 137–139.

Johnston, A. W. 1990. "Aegina, Aphaia-Tempel XIII: The Storage Amphorae," *AA* 1990, pp. 37–64.

———. 1993. "Pottery from Archaic Building Q at Kommos," *Hesperia* 62, pp. 339–382.

———. 2004. "Amphorae and Text," in *Anfore e testo in età greca arcaica: Atti del seminario dell'Università degli studi di Milano* (26 marzo 2001) (*MÉFRA* 116), ed. F. Cordano, pp. 735–760.

———. 2005. "Kommos: Further Iron Age Pottery," *Hesperia* 74, pp. 309–393.

———. 2010. "Curiouser and Curiouser, from Histria?" *Il Mar Nero* 8, pp. 181–186.

———. 2016. "Trademarks, West . . . and East," in *A Diachronic Approach. Potters—Painters—Scribes. Inscriptions on Attic Vases. Proceedings of the Colloquium Held at the Universities of Lausanne and Basel from 20th to 23rd September 2012*, ed. R. Wachter, Zurich, 43–54.

———. 2017. "Texts and Amphoras in the Methone 'Ypogeio,'" in Strauss Clay, Malkin, and Tzifopoulos 2017b, pp. 123–132.

Johnston, A. W., and A. K. Andreiomenou. 1989. "A Geometric Graffito from Eretria," *BSA* 84, pp. 217–220.

Johnston, A. W., and R. E. Jones. 1978. "The 'SOS' Amphora," *BSA* 73, pp. 103–141.

Jones, G., K. Wardle, P. Halstead, and D. Wardle. 1986. "Crop Storage at Assiros," *Scientific American* 254, pp. 96–103.

Jones, R. E. 1986. *Greek and Cypriot Pottery: A Review of Scientific Studies* (Fitch Laboratory Occasional Paper 1), Athens.

Jung, R. 2002. *Kastanas. Ausgrabungen in einem Siedlungshügel der Bronze- und Eisenzeit Makedoniens 1975–1979. Die Drehschreibenkeramik der Schichten 19 bis 11* (*PAS* 18), Kiel.

Jung, R., S. Andreou, and B. Weninger. 2009. "Synchronisation of Kastanás and Thessaloníki Toumba at the End of the Bronze Age and the Beginning of the Iron Age," in *LH III C Chronology and Synchronisms* 3: *LH III C Late and the Transition to the Early Iron Age. Proceedings of the International Workshop Held at the Austrian Academy of Sciences at Vienna, February 23rd and 24th, 2007*, ed. S. Deger-Jalkotzy and A. E. Bächle, Vienna, pp. 183–202.

Jung, R., and S. Gimatzidis. 2008. "Ο αρχαίος οικισμός στη θέση Κάστρο της Νεοκαισάρειας Πιερίας," *Εστιακά Σύμμεικτα* 1, pp. 133–150.

Kadıoğlu, M., C. Ozbil, M. Kerschner, and H. Mommsen. 2015. "Teos im Licht der neuen Forschungen," in *Anatolien—Brücke der Kulturen: Aktuelle Forschungen und Perspektiven in den deutsch-türkischen Altertumswissenschaften* (Der Anschnitt: *Zeitschrift für Kunst und Kultur in Bergbau* 27), ed. Ü. Yalçın and H.-D. Bienert, pp. 345–366.

Kahane, P. 1940. "Die Entwicklungsphasen der attisch-geometrischen Keramik," *AJA* 44, pp. 464–482.

Kahrstedt, U. 1953. "Städte in Makedonien," *Hermes* 81, pp. 85–111.

Kakavoyiannis, E. 1984. "Production of Lead from Litharge in Hellenistic Rhodes," *AAA* 17, pp. 124–140.

Kalaitzoglou, G. 2008. *Assesos: Ein geschlossener Befund südionischer Keramik aus dem Heiligtum der Athena Assesia* (Milesische Forschungen 6), Mainz.

Kalapodi = *Kalapodi. Ergebnisse der Ausgrabungen im Heiligtum der Artemis und des Apollon von Hyampolis in der antiken Phokis*, Mainz

I = M. Jacob-Felsch, "Die spätmykenische bis frühprotogeometrische Keramik," pp. 1–213; K. Braun, "Die korinthische Keramik," pp. 215–269; A. Palme-Koufa, "Die Graffiti auf der Keramik," pp. 271–331; P. Armstrong, "The Byzantine and Later Pottery," pp. 333–363.

II = R. C. S. Felsch, "Zur Stratigraphie des Heiligtums" (mit einem Beitrag von J. Riederer); "Die Bronzefunde," pp. 28–338; H.-O. Schmidt, "Die Angriffswaffen," pp. 423–551, 2007.

Kalléris, J. N. 1954. *Les anciens Macédoniens: étude linguistique et historique 1* (Collection de l'Institut français d'Athènes 81), Athens.

———. 1976. *Les anciens Macédoniens: étude linguistique et historique* 2 (Collection de l'Institut français d'Athènes 81), Athens.

Kalliga, K. 2004. "Anchialos-Sindos Double Trapeza. Pit C: Observations on the Painted and Black-glazed Pottery of Local Fourth-century B.C. Workshops," *BSA* 99, pp. 291–313.

Kallipolitis, V. G. 1961. "Ἀνασκαφὴ Παλαιοπόλεως Κερκύρας," *Prakt* 1961, pp. 120–128.

Kalogiropoulou, E. 2014. "Αναζητώντας κοινωνικές ταυτότητες: η συμβολή των θερμικών κατασκευών στην οργάνωση του χώρου στη Νεολιθική Μακεδονία," in Stefani, Merousis, and Dimoula 2014, pp. 359–372.

Kalogirou, A. 1994. "Production and Consumption of Pottery in Kitrini Limni, West Macedonia, Greece, 4500 BC–3500 BC" (diss. Indiana Univ. Bloomington).

———. 1997. "Pottery Production and Craft Specialization in Neolithic Greece," in *TEXNH: Craftsmen, Craftswomen and Craftsmanship in the Aegaean Bronze Age. Proceedings of the 6th International Aegean Conference/6e Rencontre égéenne internationale, Philadelphia, Temple University, 18–21 April 1996* (*Aegaeum* 16), ed. R. Laffineur and P. P. Betancourt, Liège, pp. 11–18.

Kaltsas, N., S. Fachard, A. Psalti, and M. Yiannopoulou. 2010. *Ερέτρια. Ματιές σε μια αρχαία πόλη*, Athens.

Kanatsoulis, D. K. 1948. *Ὁ Ἀρχέλαος καὶ αἱ μεταρρυθμίσεις του ἐν Μακεδονίᾳ*, Thessaloniki.

Kaniuth, K. 2006. *Metallobjekte der Bronzezeit aus Nordbaktrien* (Archäologie in Iran und Turan 16), Mainz.

Kanowski, M. G. 1984. *Containers of Classical Greece. A Handbook of Shapes,* St. Lucia Qld/Lawrence, Mass.

Kanta-Kitsou, A., O. Palli, and I. Anagnostou. 2008. *Αρχαιολογικό Μουσείο Ηγουμενίτσας*, Igoumenitsa.

Karadima, H., and M. Koutsoumanis. 1992. "Σαμοθράκη," *ArchDelt* 47, Chr. B΄2, pp. 496–497.

Karadima, X. 2009. "Ο οίνος της Θράκης στην αρχαιότητα. Φιλολογικές μαρτυρίες και αρχαιολογική έρευνα," in *Οίνον ιστορώ 8: Πότνια οίνου. Διεθνές επιστημονικό συμπόσιο προς τιμήν της Σταυρούλας Κουράκου-Δραγώνα*, ed. G. A. Pikoulas, Volos, pp. 146–167.

Karageorghis, V. 1963. *CVA Cyprus* 1, *Cyprus Museum*, Fasc. 1, Nicosia.

———. 1973. *Salamis 5: Excavations in the Necropolis of Salamis* III, Nicosia.

———. 1974. "Pikes or Obeloi from Cyprus and Crete," in *Antichità Cretesi: Studi in onore de Doro Levi* (*CronCatania* 13), ed. G. Pugliese Carratelli and G. Rizza, Catania, pp. 168–172.

———. 1977. "Pottery from Kition," in *Greek Geometric and Archaic Pottery Found in Cyprus*, ed. E. Gjerstad, Stockholm, pp. 61–63.

———. 1978. "A 'Favissa' at Kazaphani," *RDAC* 1978, pp. 156–193.

———. 1983. *Palaepaphos-Skales: An Iron Age Cemetery in Cyprus* (*Ausgrabungen in Alt-Paphos auf Zypern* 3), Konstanz.

Karali, L. 1999. *Shells in Aegean Prehistory* (*BAR-IS* 761), Oxford.

Karamitrou-Mentesidi, G. 1990. "Ρύμνιο," *ArchDelt* 45, p. 355.

———. 2003. "Μυκηναϊκά Αιανής—Ελιμιώτιδας και Άνω Μακεδονίας," in *2nd International Interdisciplinary Colloquium, the Periphery of the Mycenaean World, 26–30 September, Lamia 1999*, ed. N. Kyparissi-Apostolika and M. Papakonstantinou, Athens, pp. 167–190.

———. 2008. *Aiani: A Guide to the Archaeological Site and Museum*, Athens.

———. 2011a. "Aiani," in *Au Royaume d'Alexandre le Grand: La Macédoine Antique*, ed. S. Descamps-Lequime, Paris, pp. 158–163.

———. 2011b. *Το Αρχαιολογικό Έργο στην Άνω Μακεδονία* 1. Aiani.

———. 2011c. "Από το ανασκαφικό έργο της Λ΄ Εφορείας Προϊστορικών και Κλασικών Αρχαιοτήτων κατά το 2011," *AEMTh* 25 [2015], pp. 37–60.

———. 2013. "Αιανή, Βασιλική Νεκρόπολη: Η έρευνα σε 'μυκηναϊκές,' αρχαϊκές, κλασικές, ελληνιστικές ταφές," in *Το Αρχαιολογικό Έργο στην Άνω Μακεδονία ΙΙ*, Aiani, pp. 84–153.

———. 2016. "Νομός Κοζάνης: Αιανή," *ArchDelt* 66 [2011], B2, pp. 814–819.

Karanika, M. 2014. "Κάτω Άγιος Ιωάννης Πιερίας. Κεραμική από το λάκκο 1 και 2 του αγροτεμαχίου 174" (MA thesis, Aristotle Univ. Thessaloniki).

Karathanasis, K. 2019. "A Game of Timber Monopoly: Atheno-Macedonian Relations on the Eve of the Peloponnesian War," *Hesperia* 88, pp. 707–726.

Kardamaki, E., P. M. Day, M. Tenconi, J. Maran, and A. Papadimitriou. 2016. "Transport Stirrup Jars in Late Mycenaean Tiryns: Maritime Transport Containers and Commodity Movement in Political Context," in Demesticha and Knapp 2016, pp. 145–167.

Kardara, Ch. P. 1963. *Ροδιακή Αγγειογραφία*, Athens.

———. 1988. *Ἀφροδίτη Ἐρυκίνη. Ἱερὸν καὶ μαντεῖον εἰς τὴν Β. Δ. Ἀρκαδίαν*, Athens.

Karetsou, A. 1981. "The Peak Sanctuary of Mt. Juktas," in *Sanctuaries and Cults in the Aegean Bronze Age. Proceedings of the First International Symposium at the Swedish Institute in Athens, 12–13 May, 1980*, ed. R. Hägg and N. Marinatos, Stockholm, pp. 137–153.

Karliampas, G., M. Bessios, and S. Triantaphyllou. 2004. "Νεκροταφεία της Πρώιμης Εποχής του Σιδήρου στη βόρεια Πιερία," in *Το Αιγαίο στην Πρώιμη Εποχή του Σιδήρου*, ed. N. Ch. Stampolidis and A. Yiannikouri, Athens, pp. 341–352.

Karo, G. 1930–1933. *Die Schachtgräber von Mykenai*, Munich.

Kasseri, A. 2012. "Φοινικικοί εμπορικοί αμφορείς από τη Μεθώνη Πιερίας," in *Κεραμέως παῖδες: Αντίδωρο στον Καθηγητή Μιχάλη Τιβέριο από τους μαθητές του*, ed. E. Kefalidou and D. Tsiafaki, Thessaloniki, pp. 299–318.

———. 2015. "Archaic Trade in the Northern Aegean: The Case of Methone in Pieria, Greece" (diss. Oxford Univ.), https://ora.ox.ac.uk/objects/uuid:48f2cf91-f266-4d32-9521-680da39f0acd

Katsarou, S. 2013. "Λατρεία Πανός και Νυμφών σε σπήλαιο της αρχαίας Φωκίδας στον Παρνασσό," *Grammateion* 2, pp. 33–40.

Katsikaridis, N. 2021. "Νεολιθική κεραμική από τον οικισμό Αυγής Καστοριάς: τεχνολογία, χρήση και κατανομή στο χώρο" (diss. Aristotle University Thessaloniki).

Käufler, S. 2004. "Die archaischen Kannen von Milet" (diss. Ruhr-Universität Bochum).

Kearsley, R. A. 1989. *The Pendent Semi-circle Skyphos: A Study of its Development and Chronology and an Examination of it as Evidence for Euboean Activity at Al Mina* (BICS Suppl. 44), London.

———. 1995. "The Greek Geometric Wares from Al Mina Levels 10–8 and Associated Pottery," *MeditArch* 8, pp. 7–81.

Kedrou, G., and S. Andreou. 2012. "Τούμπα Θεσσαλονίκης: τροχήλατη κεραμική της ΥΕΧ και ΠΕΣ από το κτήριο Β," *AEMTh* 26 [2017], pp. 429–438.

Kefalidou, G. 2012. "Κεραμική από τη Νέα Καλλικράτεια στο Αρχαιολογικό Μουσείο Θεσσαλονίκης," in Tiverios et al. 2012, pp. 91–104.

Kelly, A. 2012. "The Cretan Slinger at War—A Weighty Exchange," *BSA* 107, pp. 273–311.

Kennedy, B. V. E. 1988. "Variation in δ^{13}C Values of Postmedieval Europeans" (diss. Univ. of Calgary, Alberta).

Kenzelmann Pfyffer, A., Th. Theurillat, and S. Verdan. 2005. "Graffiti d'époque géométrique provenant du sanctuaire d'Apollon Daphnéphoros à Erétrie," *ZPE* 151, pp. 51–83.

Kerameikos = *Kerameikos. Ergebnisse der Ausgrabungen*, Berlin

I = W. Kraiker and K. Kübler, *Die Nekropolen des 12. bis 10. Jahrhunderts*, 1939.

IV = K. Kübler, *Neufunde aus der Nekropole des 11. und 10. Jahrhunderts*, 1943.

V.1 = K. Kübler, *Die Nekropole des 10. bis 8. Jahrhunderts*, 1954.

IX = U. Knigge, *Der Südhügel*, 1976.

XI = I. Scheibler, *Griechische Lampen*, 1976.

XIII = B. Bohen, *Die geometrischen Pyxiden*, 1988.

XVIII = F. Ruppenstein, *Die submykenische Nekropole: Neufunde und Neubewertung*, Munich 2007.

Keramopoullos, A. D. 1917. "Θηβαϊκά," *ArchDelt* 3, pp. 1–503.

———. 1932. "Ἀνασκαφαὶ καὶ ἔρευναι ἐν τῇ ἄνω Μακεδονίᾳ," *ArchEph* 1932, cols. 48–133.

Keramopoullos, A. D., and E. Pelekidis. 1915. "Περὶ τῶν ἐργασιῶν ἐν τοῖς μουσείοις τῆς Ἀκροπόλεως," *ArchDelt* 1, Parartema, pp. 19–41.

Kerschner, M. 1997. "Ein stratifizierter Opferkomplex des 7. Jhs. v. Chr. aus dem Artemision von Ephesos," *ÖJh* 66, Beiblatt, pp. 84–226.

———. 2000a. "Zur Keramik der geometrischen und archaischen Epoche," in M. Kerschner, M. Lawall, P. Scherrer, and E. Trinkl, "Ephesos in archaischer und klassischer Zeit. Die Ausgrabungen in der Siedlung Smyrna," in *Die Ägäis und das westliche Mittelmeer: Beziehungen und Wechselwirkungen 8. bis 5. v. Chr., Wien, 24. bis 27. März 1999*, ed. F. Krinzinger, Vienna, pp. 45–54.

———. 2000b. "Die bemalte ostgriechische Keramik auf Sizilien und ihr Zeugniswert für den archaischen Handel," in *Die Ägäis und das westliche Mittelmeer: Beziehungen und Wechselwirkungen 8. bis 5. v. Chr., Wien, 24. bis 27. März 1999*, ed. F. Krinzinger, Vienna, pp. 487–491.

———. 2001. "Perspektiven der Keramikforschung in Naukratis 75 Jahre nach Elinor Price," in *Naukratis: Die Beziehungen zu Ostgriechenland, Ägypten und Zypern in archaischer Zeit. Akten der Table Ronde in Mainz, 25.–27. November 1999*, ed. U. Höckmann and D. Kreikenbom, Möhnesee, pp. 69–94.

———. 2002a. "Archäologische Fragestellung und Interpretation der Analysedaten. 3.1.2. Die bemalte spätgeometrische und archaische ostgriechische Keramik," in *Töpferzentren der Ostägäis: Archäometrie und archäologische Untersuchungen zur mykenischen, geometrischen und archaischen Keramik aus Fundorten in Westkleinasien*, ed. M. Akurgal, M. Kerschner, H. Mommsen, and W.-D. Niemeier, Vienna, pp. 28–50.

———. 2002b. "Archäologische Fragestellung und Interpretation der Analysedaten. 3.5. Ostgriechischen Kalottenschalen (Vogelkotylen, Vogel-, Rosetten-, Mäander- und Reifenschalen) und Vogelkannen," and "3.6. Die nichtlokalisierten chemischen Gruppen B/C, E, F, G und ihr Aussagewert für die spätgeometrische und archaische Keramik des nördliche Ioniens und der Äolis," in *Töpferzentren der Ostägäis: Archäometrie und archäologische Untersuchungen zur mykenischen, geometrischen und archaischen Keramik aus Fundorten in Westkleinasien*, ed. M. Akurgal, M. Kerschner, H. Mommsen, and W.-D. Niemeier, Vienna, pp. 63–92.

———. 2006a. "On the Provenance of Aiolian Pottery," in *Naukratis: Greek Diversity in Egypt. Studies on East Greek Pottery and Exchange in the Eastern Mediterranean*, ed. A. Villing and U. Schlotzhauer, London, pp. 109–126.

———. 2006b. "Zur Herkunftsbestimmung archaisch-ostgriechischer Keramik: Die Funde aus Berezan im Akademischen Kunstmuseum der Universität Bonn und im Robertinum der Universität Halle-Wittenberg," *IstMitt* 56, pp. 129–156.

———. 2007. "Das Keramikbild von Ephesos im 7. und 6. Jh. v. Chr.," in *Frühes Ionien: Eine Bestandsaufnahme. Panionion-Symposion Güzelçamlı 26. September–1. Oktober 1999* (Milesische Forschungen 5), ed. J. Cobet, V. von Graeve, W.-D. Niemeier, and K. Zimmermann, Mainz on Rhein, pp. 221–245.

Kerschner, M., and H. Mommsen. 1997. "Neutronenaktivierungs-Analysen zur Herkunft der ostgriechischen Vogelschalen," in *Archäometrie und Denkmalpflege, Kurzberichte des Jahrestagung in Wien*, ed. G. Schulze and K. Slusallek, Vienna, pp. 138–140.

———. 2005. "Transportamphoren milesischen Typs in Ephesos: Archäometrische und archäologische Untersuchungen zum Handel im archaischen Ionien," in *Synergia: Festschrift für Friedrich Krinzinger*, ed. B. Brandt, V. Gassner, and S. Ladstätter, Vienna, pp. 119–130.

———. 2009. "Imports of East Greek Pottery to Sicily and Sicilian Productions of East Greek Type: Archaeometric Analyses of Finds from the Votive Deposit in Katane," in *Stipe votive del Santuario di Demetra a Catania: La ceramica greco-orientale*, ed. A. Pautasso, Catania, pp. 125–150.

Kerschner, M., H. Mommsen, T. Beier, D. Heimermann, and A. Hein. 1993. "Neutron Activation Analysis of Bird Bowls and Related Archaic Ceramics From Miletus," *Archaeometry* 35, pp. 197–210.

Kerschner, M., and U. Schlotzhauer. 2005. "A New Classification System for East Greek Pottery," *Ancient West and East* 4, pp. 1–56.

———. 2007. "Ein neues Klassifikationssystem der ostgriechischen Keramik," in *Frühes Ionien: Eine Bestandsaufnahme. Panionion-Symposion Güzelçamlı 26. September–1. Oktober 1999* (Milesische Forschungen 5), ed. J. Cobet, V. von Graeve, W.-D. Niemeier, and K. Zimmermann, Mainz on Rhein, pp. 295–317.

Kerviler, R. 1883. "Des projectiles cylindro-conique ou en olive depuis l'antiquité à nos jours," *RA* 2, 3rd series, pp. 281–287.

Kessisoglou, M. D., E. A. Mirtsou, and I. A. Stratis. 1985. "Συμβολή στην έρευνα της τεχνολογίας της μακεδονικής κεραμεικής. Πρώιμη Εποχή Χαλκού, " *Ανθρωπολογικά* 7, pp. 7–16.

Keyser, P. T., and D. D. Clark. 2001. "Analyzing and Interpreting the Metallurgy of Early Electrum Coins," in Balmuth 2001, pp. 105–126.

Kidd, S. E. 2019. *Play and Aesthetics in Ancient Greece*, Cambridge.

Kilian, K. 1970. *Früheisenzeitliche Funde aus der Südostnekropole von Sala Consilina (Provinz Salerno)* (Archäologische Forschung in Lukanien 3), Heidelberg.

———. 1973. "Zum italischen und griechischen Fibelhandwerk des 8. und 7. Jahrhunderts," *Hamburger Beiträge zur Archäologie* 3 (1), pp. 1–39.

———. 1975a. *Fibeln in Thessalien von der mykenischen bis zur archaischen Zeit* (*PBF* XIV.2), Munich.

———. 1975b. "Trachtzubehör der Eisenzeit zwischen Ägäis und Adria," *PZ* 50, pp. 9–140.

———. 1981. "Ausgrabungen in Tiryns 1978, 1979," *AA* 1981, pp. 149–194.

———. 1983. "Weihungen aus Eisen und Eisenverarbeitung im Heiligtum zu Philia (Thessalien)," in *The Greek Renaissance of the Eighth Century B.C.: Tradition and Innovation. Proceedings of the Second International Symposium at the Swedish Institute in Athens, 1–5 June, 1981*, ed. R. Hägg, Stockholm, pp. 131–147.

Kilian-Dirlmeier, I. 1979. *Anhänger in Griechenland von der mykenischen bis zur spätgeometrischen Zeit (Griechisches Festland, Ionische Inseln, dazu Albanien und Jugoslawisch Mazedonien)* (*PBF* XI.2), Munich.

———. 1980. "Bemerkungen zu den Fingerringen mit Spiralenden," *JRGZM* 27, pp. 249–269.

———. 1981. "Bronzeanhänger der geometrischen und archaischen Zeit," in *OlForsch* XIII, pp. 345–377.

———. 1984a. *Nadeln der frühhelladischen bis archaischen Zeit von der Peloponnes* (*PBF* XIII.8), Munich.

———. 1984b. "Gjilpërat e kohës së hekurit në Shqipëri (Die Nadeln der Eisenzeit in Albanien)," *Iliria* 14 (1), pp. 69–109.

———. 1984c. "Der dorische Peplos: Ein archäologisches Zeugnis der Dorischen Wanderung?" *Archäologisches Korrespondenzblatt* 14, pp. 281–291.

———. 1993. *Die Schwerter in Griechenland (ausserhalb der Peloponnes), Bulgarien, und Albanien* (*PBF* IV.12), Stuttgart.

———. 2002. *Kleinfunde aus dem Athena Itonia-Heiligtum bei Philia (Thessalien)* (Römisch-Germanisches Zentralmuseum, Monographien 48), Mainz.

Kilikoglou, V., G. Vekinis, and Y. Maniatis. 1995. "Toughening of Ceramic Earthenwares by Quartz Inclusions: An Ancient Art Revisited," *Acta metallurgica et materialia* 43 (8), pp. 2959–2965.

Kilikoglou, V., G. Vekinis, Y. Maniatis, and P. M. Day. 1998. "Mechanical Performance of Quartz-tempered Ceramics: Part I, Strength and Toughness," *Archaeometry* 40 (2), pp. 261–279.

Killen, S. 2017. *Parasema: offizielle Symbole griechischer Poleis und Bundesstaaten* (Archäologische Forschungen 36), Wiesbaden.

Kinch, K. F. 1914. *Fouilles de Vroulia (Rhodes)*, Berlin.

King, C. J. 2018. *Ancient Macedonia*, London and New York.

Kiriatzi, E. 2000. "Κεραμική τεχνολογία και παραγωγή: η κεραμική της Ύστερης Εποχής Χαλκού από την Τούμπα Θεσσαλονίκης" (diss. Aristotle Univ. Thessaloniki).

Kiriatzi, E., S. Andreou, S. Dimitriadis, and K. Kotsakis. 1997. "Co-existing Traditions: Handmade and Wheelmade Pottery in Late Bronze Age Central Macedonia," in *ΤΕΧΝΗ: Craftsmen, Craftswomen and Craftsmanship in the Aegean Bronze Age. Proceedings of the 6th International Aegean Conference/6e Rencontre égéenne internationale, Philadelphia, Temple University, 18–21 April 1996* (*Aegaeum* 16), ed. R. Laffineur and P. P. Betancourt, Liège, pp. 361–367.

Kiriatzi, E., X. Charalambidou, A. Kotsonas, M. Roumbou, M. Bessios, and Y. Tzifopoulos. 2013. "Παραγωγή και διακίνηση κεραμικής στο Θερμαϊκό κόλπο κατά τον ύστερο 8ο–πρώιμο 7ο αι. π. Χ. Πρώτα αποτελέσματα της διεπιστημονικής μελέτης κεραμικής από το 'Υπόγεο της Μεθώνης Πιερίας" (paper, *AEMTh* 27, 2013).

Kiriatzi, E., X. Charalambidou, M. Roumpou, M. Bessios, and A. Kotsonas. 2012. "Inscribed Transport Amphorae at Methone: Provenance and Content" (paper, "Panhellenes at Methone: graphê in Late Geometric and Protoarchaic Methone, Macedonia (ca 700 BCE)," Thessaloniki, 8–10 June 2012).

Kiriatzi, E., A. Kotsonas, X. Charalambidou, N. Müller, M. Roumpou, and M. Bessios. 2015. "Transport Amphorae from Methone, Northern Greece: An Interdisciplinary Study of Production and Trade c. 700 BC" (paper, "Pots on the Water: Maritime Transport Containers in the Mediterranean Bronze and Iron Ages," 21st Annual Meeting of the European Association of Archaeologists, Glasgow, 2–5 September 2015).

Kiriatzi, E., N. Merousis, and E. Stefani. 2014. "Κεραμική της Ύστερης Εποχής του Χαλκού από το Αγγελοχώρι Ημαθίας: Προκαταρκτικές παρατηρήσεις από τη μελέτη του υλικού" (paper, *AEMTh* 28, 2014).

Kirk, G. S. 1985. *The Iliad: A Commentary* 1: *Books 1–4*, Cambridge.

Kish, G., ed. 1978. *A Source Book in Geography*, Cambridge.

Klapanes, P., and Th. Abatzes. 2011. "Διαχειριστική μελέτη του δημόσιου δασικού συμπλέγματος Ρητίνης-Βρύας. Διαχειριστική περίοδος 2011–2020" (unpublished report, Forestry Service of Pieria Prefecture).

Klebinder-Gauss, G. 2003. "Zwei bronzene Doppeläxte aus dem Artemision von Ephesos," *ÖJh* 72, pp. 133–140.

———. 2007. *Bronzefunde aus dem Artemision von Ephesos* (Forschungen in Ephesos 12.3), Vienna.

———. 2012. *Keramik aus klassischen Kontexten im Apollon-Heiligtum von Ägina-Kolonna. Lokale Produktion und Importe,* (Ägina-Kolonna, Forschungen und Ergebnisse 6), Vienna.

Kletter, R. 2003. "Iron Age Hoards of Precious Metals in Palestine—an 'Underground Economy'?" *Levant* 35, pp. 139–152.

Klingborg, P. 2017. *Greek Cisterns: Water and Risk in Ancient Greece, 600–50 B.C.*, Uppsala.

Klug, R. D. 2013. *Griechische Transportamphoren im regionalen und überregionalen Handel: Untersuchungen in griechischen und nicht-griechischen Kontexten in Unteritalien und Sizilien vom 8. bis zum 5. Jh. v. Chr.*, Rahden/Westfalen.

Knapp, A. B., and S. Demesticha, eds., with contributions by Robert Martin and Catherine E. Pratt. 2017. *Mediterranean Connections: Maritime Connections and Seaborne Trade in the Bronze and Early Iron Ages*, New York.

Knappett, C. 2011. *An Archaeology of Interaction: Network Perspectives on Material Culture and Society*, Oxford.

Knigge, U., and F. Willemsen. 1964. "Die Ausgrabungen im Kerameikos 1963, 2: Die Höhe östlich des Querweges," *ArchDelt* 19, B´1, pp. 42–46.

Knox, R., Jr., R. Maddin, P. Meyers, J. D. Muhly, G. Rapp, Jr., and L. P. Stodulski. 1983. "Chemical and Metallurgical Analyses of Metal Objects from Sardis," in *Sardis* 8, pp. 154–191.

Koçak Yaldır, A. 2011. "Imported Trade Amphoras in Daskyleion from the Seventh and Sixth Centuries B.C. and the Hellespontine–Phrygian Route," *World Archaeology* 43, pp. 364–379.

Koehler, C. G. 1992. "A Brief Typology and Chronology of Corinthian Transport Amphoras," in *Greek Amphoras*, ed. V. I. Kats and S. Monachov, Saratov, pp. 265–279.

Kokkinidou, D., and M. Nikolaidou. 1999. "Neolithic Enclosures in Greek Macedonia: Violent and Nonviolent Aspects of Territorial Demarcation," in *Ancient Warfare: Archaeological Perspectives*, ed. J. Carman and A. Harding, Stroud, U.K., pp. 88–99.

Kokkorou-Alevra, G., E. Poupaki, A. Eustathopoulos, and A. Chatzikonstantinou. 2014. *Corpus Αρχαίων Λατομείων. Λατομεία του ελλαδικού χώρου από τους προϊστορικούς έως τους μεσαιωνικούς χρόνους* (Τομέας Αρχαιολογίας και Ιστορίας της Τέχνης Πανεπιστημίου Αθηνών), Athens.

Kokkou-Vyridi, K. 1977. "Τέσσερεις πρωτογεωμετρικοὶ τάφοι στὸ Ἄργος," *ArchEph* 116, pp. 171–194.

———. 1999. *Ελευσίς: πρώϊμες πυρές θυσιών στο Τελεστήριο της Ελευσίνος*, Athens.

Konsolaki, E. 2001. "New Evidence for the Practice of Libations in the Aegean Bronze Age," in *Potnia: Deities and Religion in the Aegean Bronze Age. Proceedings of the 8th International Aegean Conference/8e Rencontre égéenne internationale. Göteborg, Göteborg University, 12–15 April 2000* (*Aegaeum* 22), ed. R. Laffineur and R. Hägg, Liège, pp. 213–220.

Konstantinidi, E. 2001. *Jewelry Revealed in the Burial Contexts of the Greek Bronze Age* (*BAR-IS* 912), Oxford.

Konstantinidi-Syvridi, E., and M. Kontaki. 2009. "Casting Finger Rings in Mycenaean Times: Two Unpublished Moulds at the National Archaeological Museum, Athens," *BSA* 104, pp. 311–319.

Konstantinidis, K. A. 1989. *Land Reclamation Project of the Plain of Thessaloniki*, Thessaloniki.

Konstantinidis, P. 1995. "Το πρόβλημα της καταγωγής της κουκουναριάς (*Pinus pinea* L.)," *Γεωτεχνικά Επιστημονικά Θέματα* 6 (3), pp. 27–31.

Kontaxi, Ch., V. Giannopoulos, and A. Kaznesi. 2004. "Το σπήλαιο του 'Ορφέα' Αλιστράτης Σερρών και η ευρύτερη περιοχή: πρώτες σπηλαιολογικές και αρχαιολογικές έρευνες," *AEMTh* 18 [2006], pp. 57–61.

Kontis, I. D. 1949–1951. "Δύο αρχαϊκαί ἐπιγραφαὶ ἐκ Καμίρου," *ASAtene* 27–29, n.s. 11–13, pp. 347–349.

Kontoleon, N. M. 1963. "Οἱ ἀειναῦται τῆς Ἐρετρίας," *ArchEph* 1963, pp. 1–45.

Kontonicolas, M. 2018. "Cremation, Society and Landscape in the North Aegean, 6000–700 B.C.E." (diss. Univ. of California, Los Angeles).

Kopcke, G. 2002. "1000 B.C.E.? 900 B.C.E.? A Greek Vase from Lake Galilee," in *Leaving No Stones Unturned: Essays on the Ancient Near East and Egypt in Honor of Donald P. Hansen*, ed. E. Ehrenberg, Winona Lake, Ind., pp. 109–117.

Kopytoff, I. 1986. "The Cultural Biography of Things: Commoditization as Process," in *The Social Life of Things: Commodities in Cultural Perspective,* ed. A. Appadurai, Cambridge, pp. 64–91.

Korfmann, M. 1973. "The Sling as a Weapon," *Scientific American* 229, pp. 34–42.

Korkuti, M. 1995. *Neolithikum und Chalkolithikum in Albanien*, Mainz.

Kosmidou, E., and D. Malamidou. 2006. "Arms and Armour from Amphipolis, Northern Greece: Plotting the Military Life of an Ancient City," in *Anodos: Studies of the Ancient World* 4. *Proceedings of the International Symposium Arms and Armour through the Ages (from the Bronze Age to the Late Antiquity), Modra-Harmónia, 19th–22nd November 2005*, ed. M. Novotná and W. Jobst, Trnava, pp. 133–147.

Kossatz-Deissmann, A. 1981. "Achilleus," *LIMC* 1, Zürich, pp. 87–90.

Kotitsa, Z. 2006. *Αιγίνιο Πιερίας. Κεραμική από το νεκροταφείο στη θέση "Μελίσσια,"* Thessaloniki.

———. 2012a. "Metal-coated Pottery from Macedonia in the Late Classical and Hellenistic Period," in *Θέματα της ελληνιστικής κεραμικής στην Αρχαία Μακεδονία. Topics on Hellenistic Pottery in Ancient Macedonia*, ed. S. Drougou and I. Touratsoglou, Athens, pp. 108–125.

———. 2012b. "Tombes d'enfants du IVe s. av. J.-C. à Pydna," in *L'enfant et la mort dans l'antiquité* 3: *Le matériel associé aux tombes d'enfants. Actes de la table ronde internationale organisée à la Maison Méditerranéenne des Sciences de l'Homme (MMSH) d'Aix-en-Provence, 20–22 janvier 2011*, ed. A. Hermary and C. Dubois, Arles, pp. 77–96.

Kotsakis, K. 2010. "Η κεραμική της Νεότερης Νεολιθικής στη Βόρεια Ελλάδα," in Papadimitriou and Tsirtsoni 2010, pp. 67–75.

———. 2014. "Εκατό χρόνια νεολιθικής έρευνας στη Μακεδονία: τάσεις και κατευθύνσεις," in Stefani, Merousis, and Dimoula 2014, pp. 133–140.

Kotsakis, K., and P. Halstead. 2002. "Ανασκαφή στα Νεολιθικά Παλιάμπελα Κολινδρού," *AEMTh* 16 [2004], pp. 407–415.

Kotsakis, K., A. Papanthimou-Papaefthymiou, A. Pilali-Papasteriou, T. Savvopoulou, Y. Maniatis, and B. Kromer. 1989. "Carbon 14 Dates from Mandalo, W. Macedonia," in *Archaeometry. Proceedings of the 25th International Symposium*, ed. Y. Maniatis, Amsterdam, pp. 679–685.

Kotsonas, A. 2012. "Η ενεπίγραφη κεραμική του 'Υπογείου': προέλευση, τυπολογία, χρονολόγηση και ερμηνεία," in Bessios, Tzifopoulos, and Kotsonas 2012, pp. 113–304.

———. 2013. Rev. of S. Gimatzidis, *Die Stadt Sindos: Eine Siedlung von der späten Bronze- bis zur klassischen Zeit am Thermaïschen Golf in Makedonien* (Prähistorische Archäologie in Südosteuropa Band 26), in *AJA* 117 (3), https://www.ajaonline.org/book-review/1618.

———. 2015. "What Makes an Euboean Colony or Trading Station? Zagora in the Cyclades, Methone in the Thermaic Gulf and Aegean Networks in the 8th Century BC," in *Zagora in Context: Settlements and Intercommunal Links in the Geometric Period (900–700 BC). Proceedings of the Conference Held by the Australian Archaeological Institute at Athens and the Archaeological Society at Athens, Athens, 20–22 May, 2012* (*MeditArch* 25), pp. 243–257.

———. 2020. "Euboeans & Co. in the North Aegean: Ancient Tradition and Modern Historiography of Greek Colonization," in *Euboica* II: *Pithekoussai and Euboea between East and West* (*AION, Annali di Archeologia e Storia Antica, Università degli Studi di Napoli L'Orientale*, n.s. 26), vol. 1, ed. T. E. Cinquantaquattro and M. D'Acunto, Naples, pp. 301–324.

Kotsonas, A., E. Kiriatzi, X. Charalambidou, M. Roumbou, N. S. Miller, and M. Bessios. 2017. "Transport Amphorae from Methone: An Interdisciplinary Study of Production and Trade ca. 700 BCE," in Strauss Clay, Malkin, and Tzifopoulos 2017b, pp. 9–19.

Kotsonas, A., and J. Mokrisova. 2020. "Mobility, Migration, Colonization," in *A Companion to the Archaeology of Early Greece and the Mediterranean*, ed. I. S. Lemos and A. Kotsonas, Hoboken, N.J., pp. 217–246.

Kotsos, S. 2014. "Settlement and Housing During the 6th Millennium BC in Western Thessaloniki and the Adjacent Langadas Province," in Stefani, Merousis, and Dimoula 2014, pp. 315–322.

Kottaridi, A. 2000. "Από τη νεκρόπολη των Αιγών στο νεολιθικό οικισμό των Πιερίων," *AEMTh* 14 [2002], pp. 526–535.

Koufovasilis, D. 2016. "Παράρτημα 2. Αποτυπώματα πλέγματος στην κεραμική του Αποθέτη 39," in Pantelidou-Gofa 2016, pp. 297–328.

Kouka, O. 2015. "Prehistoric Heraion Reconsidered: Glimpses on the Excavations 2009–2013 North of the Sacred Road," in *Ein Minoer im Exil: Festschrift für Wolf-Dietrich Niemeier* (Universitätsforschungen zur prähistorischen Archäologie 270), ed. D. Panagiotopoulos, I. Kaiser, and O. Kouka, Bonn, pp. 223–242.

Koukouli, Ch. 1967. "Φίλιπποι," *ArchDelt* 22, B΄2, p. 422.

Koukouli-Chrysanthaki, Ch. 1970. "Travaux de l'École française: Nécropole et céramique," *BCH* 78, pp. 175–183.

———. 1971. "Προϊστορικὴ Θάσος," *ArchEph* 1971, *Chronika*, pp. 16–22.

———. 1973–1974. "Αρχαιότητες και μνημεία ανατολικής Μακεδονίας," *ArchDelt* 29, B΄2, pp. 777–787.

———. 1980. "Οικισμός της ύστερης εποχής Χαλκού στον Σταθμό Αγγίστας Σερρών," *Anthropologika* 1, pp. 54–85.

———. 1987. "Οικισμός Πρώιμης Εποχής Χαλκού στη Σκάλα Σωτήρος Θάσου," *AEMTh* 1 [1988], pp. 389–406.

———. 1988. "Οικισμός Πρώιμης Εποχής Χαλκού στη Σκάλα Σωτήρος Θάσου (II)," *AEMTh* 2 [1991], pp. 423–431.

———. 1992. *Πρωτοϊστορικὴ Θάσος. Τὰ νεκροταφεῖα τοῦ οἰκισμοῦ Καστρί* (Publications of *ArchDelt* 45), Athens.

———. 1996. "Pottery: Macedonia—Thrace," in Papathanassopoulos 1996, pp. 112–116.

———. 2011. "Amphipolis," in *Brill's Companion to Ancient Macedon: Studies in the Archaeology and History of Macedon, 650 BC–300 AD*, ed. R. J. Lane Fox, Leiden and Boston, pp. 409–436.

Koukouli-Chrysanthaki, Ch., I. Aslanis, I. Vaisov, and M. Valla. 2003. "Προμαχώνας-Topolniča 2002–2003," *AEMTh* 17 [2005], pp. 91–110.

Koukouli-Chrysanthaki, Ch., and A. Marangou-Lerat. 2012. "Αρχαϊκή κεραμική απο την αρχαϊκή αποικία στην Οισύμη," in Tiverios et al. 2012, pp. 321–338.

Koukouli-Chrysanthaki, Ch., H. Todorova, I. Aslanis, I. Vaisov, and M. Valla. 2014. "Γεωφυσική έρευνα και αρχαιολογική πραγματικότητα στο νεολιθικό οικισμό Προμαχών-Topolniča," in Stefani, Merousis, and Dimoula 2014, pp. 251–260.

Koukouli-Chrysanthaki, Ch., R. Treuil, L. Lespez, and D. Malamidou. 2008. *Dikili Tash, village préhistorique de Macédoine orientale: Recherches franco-helléniques dirigées par la Société Archéologique d'Athènes et l'École française d'Athènes (1986–2001)*, Athens.

Koukouli-Chrysanthaki, Ch., R. Treuil, and D. Malamidou. 1996. "Προϊστορικός οικισμός Φιλίππων 'Ντικιλί Τας': δέκα χρόνια ανασκαφικής έρευνας," *AEMTh* 10B [1997], pp. 681–704.

Koukoulidou, C. 2017. "Silver Jewelry," in *Les sanctuaires archaïques des Cyclades, Recherches récentes,* ed. A. Mazarakis Ainian, Rennes, pp. 200–205.

Koukouvou, A. 2012. *ΛΙΘΩΝ ΛΑΤΟΜΕΙΝ. Από τα λατομεία των Ασωμάτων Βέροιας στα οικοδομήματα των Μακεδόνων Βασιλείων. Μελέτη για την εξόρυξη πωρόλιθου στην αρχαιότητα*, Thessaloniki.

Koulidou, S. 2007. "'Μυκηναϊκή' παρουσία στη νότια Πιερία. Η περίπτωση της Πηγής Αρτέμιδος," *AEMTh* 24 [2010], pp. 143–152.

———. 2015. "'Πηγή Αρτέμιδος' Πιερίας: ορθογώνιες κατασκευές σε ταφικές και οικιστικές συνάφειες κατά την Ύστερη Εποχή Χαλκού," *Archaiologiko Ergo Thessalias kai Stereas Helladas* 1 (2012), pp. 105–112.

———. 2021. "Mycenaean-type Ceramic Evidence from the Lower Slopes of Macedonian Olympos: The Cases of the LBA Cemeteries at 'Trimpina/Platamon Stop' and 'Rema Xydias'," in *Third International Interdisciplinary Colloquium, The Periphery of the Mycenaean World: Recent Discoveries and Research Results, 18–21 May 2018, Cultural Center of the Municipality of Lamia*, ed. E. Karantzali, Athens, pp. 417–432.

Koulidou, S., Z. Andrias, E. Mastora, K. Panteliadou, M. Papavasileiou, and D. Patis. 2014. "'Πέρασμα' στον χρόνο. Ζωή και θάνατος στον Κάτω Όλυμπο κατά την Ύστερη Εποχή Χαλκού: η περίπτωση της θέσης 'Ρέμα Ξυδιάς', Πλαταμώνας Πιερίας," *AEMTh* 28 [2019], pp. 163–178.

Koulidou, S., E. Zagkou, E. Batzikosta, K. Pentelaidou, A. Tsianaka. 2012. "Πλαταμών Στοπ! 'Μυκηναϊκό' νεκροταφείο και οικισμός της Ύστερης Εποχής Χαλκού στη θέση 'Τριμπίνα 2/Πλαταμών Στοπ', στον Πλαταμώνα Πιερίας," *AEMTh* 26 [2017], pp. 213–224.

Kountouri, E. 2011. "The Mycenaean Presence in Macedonia: New Evidence from the Region of Emathia," in *Heracles to Alexander the Great: Treasures from the Royal Capital of Macedon, a Hellenic Kingdom in the Age of Democracy* (Exhibition Catalogue, Ashmolean Museum and Hellenic Ministry of Culture and Tourism, 17th Ephorate of Prehistoric and Classical Antiquities), Oxford, pp. 59–66.

Kourakou-Dragona, S. 2009. "Ο Κανείς τύφλωσε τον Κύκλωπα, αλλά κανείς δεν τον μέθυσε . . . ," in *Οίνον ιστορώ* 8: *Πότνια οίνου. Διεθνές Επιστημονικό Συμπόσιο προς τιμήν της Σταυρούλας Κουράκου-Δραγώνα,* Βόλος, 27–28 Σεπτεμβρίου 2008, ed. G. A. Pikoulas, Volos, pp. 19–39.

Kourayos, Y., and B. Burns. 2004. "Exploration of the Archaic Sanctuary at Mandra on Despotiko," *BCH* 128 (1), pp. 133–174.

Kourou, N. 2017. "The Archaeological Background of the Earliest Graffiti and Finds from Methone," in Strauss Clay, Malkin, and Tzifopoulos 2017b, pp. 20–35.

Kourouniotes, K., and H. A. Thompson. 1932. "The Pnyx in Athens," *Hesperia* 1, pp. 90–217.

Kourouniotis, K. 1910. "Τὸ ἐν Βάσσαις ἀρχαιότερον ἱερὸν τοῦ Ἀπόλλωνος," *ArchEph* 49, cols. 273–332.

———. 1916. "Ἀνασκαφαὶ καὶ ἔρευναι ἐν Χίῳ," *ArchDelt* 2, pp. 190–215.

Kousoulakou, K. 2000a. "Νομός Χαλκιδικής, Ποτείδαια, Περιοχή Διώρυγας," *ArchDelt* 55, B2, pp. 702–704.

———. 2000b. "Ποτίδαια 2000: Κτηριακό συγκρότημα δημόσιου χαρακτήρα," *AEMTh* 14 [2002], pp. 321–329.

Krahtopoulou, A. 2010. *The Geoarchaeology of Northern Pieria, Macedonia, Greece*, Katerini.

Krahtopoulou, A., J. Turner, R. Veropoulidou, L. Picornell-Gelebert, A. Livarda, and B. Damiata. 2020. "Geoarchaeology," in Morris et al. 2020, pp. 667–669.

Krahtopoulou, A., and R. Veropoulidou. 2014. "Linking Inland and Coastal Records: Landscape and Human Histories in Pieria, Macedonia, Greece," in *PHYSIS: Environnement naturel et la relation homme-milieu dans le monde Égéen protohistorique* (*Aegaeum* 37), ed. G. Touchais, R. Laffineur, and F. Rougemont, Louvain, pp. 153–160.

———. 2017. "Late Pleistocene-Holocene Shoreline Reconstruction and Human Exploitation of Molluscan Resources in Northern Pieria, Macedonia, Greece," *JAS* 15, pp. 423–436.

Kranz, P., and R. Lullies. 1975. *CVA Deutschland* 38; *Kassel, Antikenabteilung der staatlichen Kunstsammlungen* 2, Munich.

Krebber, B. 1972. "Ναυστολόγοι bei Strabon: ein neues Papyrusfragment," *ZPE* 9, pp. 204–221.

Kritikos, P., and S. Papadaki. 1963. "Μήκωνος καί ὀπίου ἱστορία καί ἐξάπλωσις ἐν τῇ περιοχῇ τῆς Ἀνατολικῆς Μεσογείου κατὰ τὴν ἀρχαιότητα," *ArchEph* 1963, pp. 80–150.

Kritzas, C. B. 1972. "Ἀρχαιότητες καὶ μνημεῖα Ἀργολιδοκορινθίας: Ἄργος," *ArchDelt* 27, B′1, pp. 192–219.

Kroll, H. 1983. *Kastanas. Ausgrabungen in einem Siedlungshügel der Bronze- und Eisenzeit Makedoniens 1975–1979. Die Pflanzenfunde* (*PAS* 2), Berlin.

Kroll, J. H. 1967. "Dikasts' Pinakia from the Fauvel Collection," *BCH* 91, pp. 379–396.

———. 1972. *Athenian Bronze Allotment Plates*, Cambridge, Mass.

———. 2001. "Observations on Monetary Instruments in Precoinage Greece," in Balmuth 2001, pp. 77–91.

———. 2008a. "Early Iron Age Balance Weights at Lefkandi, Euboea," *OJA* 27 (1), pp. 37–48.

———. 2008b. "The Monetary Use of Weighed Bullion in Archaic Greece," in *The Monetary Systems of the Greeks and Romans*, ed. W. V. Harris, Oxford, pp. 12–37.

———. 2012. "Three Inscribed Corinthian Bronze Weights," in *Stephaneforos. De l'économie antique à l'Asie Mineure. Hommage à Raymond Descat* (Mémoires 28), ed. K. Konuk, Bordeaux, pp. 111–116.

Kron, U. 1998. "Sickles in Greek Sanctuaries: Votives and Cultic Instruments," in *Ancient Greek Cult Practice from the Archaeological Evidence. Proceedings of the Fourth International Seminar on Ancient Greek Cult, Organised by the Swedish Institute at Athens, 22–24 October 1993*, ed. R. Hägg, Stockholm, pp. 187–215.

Kuleff, I., I. Iliev, E. Pernicka, and D. Gergova. 2006. "Chemical and Lead Isotope Compositions of Lead Artefacts from Ancient Thracia (Bulgaria)," *Journal of Cultural Heritage* 7, pp. 244–256.

Kunter, K. 1995. *Schichtaugenperlen, Glasperlen der vorrömischen Eisenzeit* 4 (Marburger Studien zur Vor- und Frühgeschichte 18), Marburg.

Kurke, L. 1999a. "Ancient Greek Board Games and How to Play Them," *CP* 94, pp. 247–267.

———. 1999b. *Coins, Bodies, Games and Gold: The Politics of Meaning in Archaic Greece*, Princeton.

Kurtz, D. C. 1983. *The Berlin Painter*, with drawings by Sir John Beazley, Oxford.

Lacy, A. D. 1967. *Greek Pottery in the Bronze Age*, London.

Lagona, S., and M. Frasca. 2009. "La ceramica griglia a Kyme e in eolide," in *Pontic Grey Wares. International Conference, Bucharest-Constantza, September 30–October 3, 2008* (Pontica 42), Constanta, pp. 285–304.

Lalonde, G. V. 1968. "A Fifth Century Hieron Southwest of the Athenian Agora," *Hesperia* 37, pp. 123–133.

Lamb, W. 1926–1927. "Excavations at Sparta, 1906–1910: Notes on Some Bronzes from the Orthia Site," *BSA* 28, pp. 96–106.

———. 1930–1931. "Antissa," *BSA* 31, pp. 166–178.

———. 1931–1932. "Antissa," *BSA* 32, pp. 41–67.

———. 1932. "Grey Wares from Lesbos," *JHS* 52, pp. 1–12.

———. 1934–1935. "Excavations at Kato Phana in Chios," *BSA* 35, pp. 138–164.

———. 1936. *Excavations at Thermi in Lesbos*, Cambridge.

Lambrino, M. 1938. *Les vases archaïques d'Histria*, Bucarest.

Lambrinoudakis, B. K. 1981. "Remains of the Mycenaean Period in the Sanctuary of Apollon Maleatas," in *Sanctuaries and Cults in the Aegean Bronze Age. Proceedings of the First International Symposium at the Swedish Institute in Athens, 12–13 May, 1980*, ed. R. Hägg and N. Marinatos, Stockholm, pp. 59–65.

———. 1982. "Τὸ ἱερὸ τοῦ Ἀπόλλωνα Μαλεάτα στὴν Ἐπίδαυρο καὶ ἡ χρονολογία τῶν κορινθιακῶν αγγείων," *ASAtene* 60, n.s. 44, pp. 49–56.

Landau, O. 1958. *Mykenisch-Griechische Personennamen*. Göteborg.

Lane Fox, R. J. 2008. *Travelling Heroes: Greeks and Their Myths in the Epic Age of Homer*, London.

———. 2011a. "399–369 BC," in *Brill's Companion to Ancient Macedon: Studies in the Archaeology and History of Macedon, 650 BC–300 AD*, ed. R. J. Lane Fox, Leiden and Boston, pp. 209–234.

———. 2011b. "The 360s," in *Brill's Companion to Ancient Macedon: Studies in the Archaeology and History of Macedon, 650 BC–300 AD*, ed. R. J. Lane Fox, Leiden and Boston, pp. 257–269.

———. 2011c. "Philip of Macedon: Accession, Ambitions, and Self-Presentation," in *Brill's Companion to Ancient Macedon: Studies in the Archaeology and History of Macedon, 650 BC–300 AD*, ed. R. J. Lane Fox, Leiden and Boston, pp. 335–366.

Lang, M. 1964. "Weights and Measures," in *Agora* X, pp. 1–68.

Langdon, M. K. 1976. *A Sanctuary of Zeus on Mount Hymettos* (*Hesperia* Suppl. 16), Princeton.

———. 2015. "Herder's Graffiti," in *ΑΞΩΝ: Studies in Honor of Ronald S. Stroud*, ed. A. P. Matthaiou and N. Papazarkadas, Athens, pp. 49–58.

———. 2016. "Additions to the Corpus of Greek Erotic Inscriptions," *Grammateion* 5, pp. 83–104.

Langlotz, E. 1975. *Studien zur nordostgriechischen Kunst*, Mainz.

Lapatin, K. 2006. "Kerch-style Vases: The Finale," in Cohen 2006, pp. 318–326.

Larisa am Hermos = *Larisa am Hermos: Die Ergebnisse der Ausgrabungen 1902–1934*, Berlin

III = J. Boehlau and K. Schefold, eds., *Die Kleinfunde*, 1942.

Lasteyrie, R. de. 1890. *Album archéologique des musées de province*, Paris.

Laughy, M. 2018. "Figurines in the Road: A Protoattic Votive Deposit from the Athenian Agora Reexamined," *Hesperia* 87, pp. 633–679.

Laum, B. 1924. *Heiliges Geld. Eine historische Untersuchung über den sakralen Ursprung des Geldes*, Tübingen.

Laurenzi, L. 1936. "Necropoli Ialisie (Scavi dell'anno 1934)," *ClRh* 8, pp. 7–207.

Laux, F. 1973. *Die Fibeln in Niedersachsen* (*PBF* XIV.1), Munich.

Lawall, M. L. 1995. "Transport Amphoras and Trademarks: Imports to Athens and Economic Diversity in the Fifth Century BC" (diss. Univ. of Michigan, Ann Arbor).

———. 1998. "Ceramics and Positivism Revisited: Greek Transport Amphorae and History," in *Trade, Traders and the Ancient City*, ed. H. Parkins and C. Smith, London and New York, pp. 75–101.

———. 2002. "Ilion Before Alexander: Amphoras and Economic Archaeology," *Studia Troica* 12, pp. 197–243.

———. 2010. "Imitative Amphoras in the Greek World," *Marburger Beiträge zur Antiken Handels-, Wirtschafts- und Socialgeschichte* 28, pp. 45–88.

———. 2011a. "Socio-economic Conditions and the Contents of Amphorae," in *PATABS* 2: *Production and Trade of Amphorae in the Black Sea. Proceedings of the International Round Table, Kiten, Nessebar and Sredetz, 26–30 September 2007*, ed. C. Tzochev, T. Stoyanov, and A. Bozkova, Sofia, pp. 23–33.

———. 2011b. "Greek Amphorae in the Archaeological Record," in *Pottery in the Archaeological Record: Greece and Beyond* (Gönsta Enbom Monographs 1), ed. M. L. Lawall and J. Lund, Aarhus, pp. 38–50.

———. 2016a. "Maritime Transport Containers of the Bronze and Early Iron Age as Viewed from Later Periods," in Demesticha and Knapp 2016, pp. 215–231.

———. 2016b. "Transport Amphoras, Markets and Changing Practices in the Economies of Greece, Sixth to First Centuries BCE," in *The Ancient Greek Economy: Markets, Households, and City-states*, ed. E. M. Harris, D. M. Lewis, and M. Woolmer, Cambridge, pp. 254–273.

———. 2021. "The Transport Amphoras at Argilos: A Preliminary Report," in *Άργιλος, 25 Χρόνια Έρευνας. Οργάνωση Πόλης και Χώρας στις Αποικίες του Βορείου Αιγαίου, 8ος–3ος αι. π.Χ.*, ed. Z. Bonias and J.-Y. Perreault, Athens, pp. 189–202.

Lawall, M. L., N. A. Lejpunskaja, P. D. Diatroptov, and T. L. Samojlova. 2010. "Transport Amphoras," in *The Lower City of Olbia (Sector NGS) in the 6th Century BC to the 4th Century AD*, ed. A. Lejpunskaja, P. Guldager Bilde, J. Munk Højte, V. V. Krapivina, and S. D. Kryžickij, Aarhus, pp. 355–405.

Lawall, M. L., and C. Tzochev. 2019–2020. "New Research on Aegean and Pontic Transport Amphorae of the Ninth to First Century B.C., 2010–2020," *AR* 66, pp. 117–144.

Lawrence, A. W. 1979. *Greek Aims in Fortification*, Oxford.

Lawton, C. L. 1995. *Attic Document Reliefs: Art and Politics in Ancient Athens*, Oxford.

Lazaridis, D. I. 1964. "Ἀνασκαφαὶ καὶ ἔρευναι εἰς Ἀμφίπολιν," *Prakt* 1964, pp. 35–40.

———. 1965. "Ἀνασκαφαὶ καὶ ἔρευναι εἰς Ἀμφίπολιν," *Prakt* 1965, pp. 47–52.

Lazaridou, K. D. 2015. "Εφηβαρχικός νόμος από την Αμφίπολη," *ArchEph* 154, pp. 1–48.

Leake, W. M. 1835. *Travels in Northern Greece*, London.

Lee, J. W. I. 2001. "Urban Conflict at Olynthus, 348 BC," in *Fields of Conflict: Progress and Prospect in Battlefield Archaeology* (*BAR-IS* 958), ed. P. W. M. Freeman and A. Pollard, Oxford, pp. 11–22.

Lefkandi = *British School of Archaeology at Athens, BSA Supplementary Volumes*

I = M. R. Popham, L. H. Sackett, and P. G. Themelis, eds., *Lefkandi* 1: *The Iron Age* (*BSA* Suppl. 11), Oxford 1979–1980.

II.1 = R. W. V. Catling and I. S. Lemos, *Lefkandi* 2.1: *The Protogeometric Building at Toumba: The Pottery* (*BSA* Suppl. 22), Oxford 1990.

II.2 = M. R. Popham, P. G. Calligas, and L. H. Sackett, eds., with J. J. Coulton and H. W. Catling, *Lefkandi* 2.2: *The Protogeometric Building at Toumba: The Excavation, Architecture and Finds* (*BSA* Suppl. 23), Oxford 1993.

III = M. R. Popham, with I. S. Lemos, *Lefkandi* 3: *The Early Iron Age Cemetery at Toumba: The Excavations of 1981 to 1994, Plates* (*BSA* Suppl. 29), Oxford 1996.

IV = D. Evely, ed., *The Late Helladic IIIC Settlement at Xeropolis* (*BSA* Suppl. 39), London 2006.

Lehmann, K. 1953. "Samothrace: Sixth Preliminary Report," *Hesperia* 22, pp. 1–24.

Leinas, C. 1973. "Inter duas januas à la maison du Lac," in *Etudes Déliennes, publiées à l'occasion du centième anniversaire du debut des fouilles de l'École française d'Athènes à Délos* (*BCH* Supplement 1), Paris, pp. 291–328.

Lembesi, A. 1970. "Ἀνασκαφικαὶ ἔρευναι εἰς ἀνατολικὴν Κρήτην," *Prakt* 1970, pp. 256–297.

Lemos, A. A. 1986. "Archaic Chian Pottery on Chios," in *Chios: A Conference at the Homereion in Chios*, ed. J. Boardman and C. E. Vaphopoulou-Richardson, Oxford, pp. 233–249.

———. 1991. *Archaic Pottery of Chios: The Decorated Styles*, Oxford.

———. 1992. "Un atelier archaïque de Chios en Macédoine orientale," in *Les ateliers de potiers dans le monde grec aux époques géométrique, archaïque et classique* (*BCH* Supplément 23), Paris, pp. 157–173.

———. 2000. "Aspects of East Greek Pottery and Vase Painting," in *Die Ägäis und das westliche Mittelmeer: Beziehungen und Wechselwirkungen 8. bis 5. v. Chr., Wien, 24. bis 27. März 1999*, ed. F. Krinzinger, Vienna, pp. 377–391.

Lemos, I. S. 1986. "Protogeometric Skyros and Euboea," *OJA* 5, pp. 323–337.

———. 1998. "Euboea and Its Aegean Koine," in Bats and d'Agostino 1998, Naples, pp. 45–58.

———. 2002. *The Protogeometric Aegean: The Archaeology of the Late Eleventh and Tenth Centuries B.C.*, Oxford.

———. 2012. "A Northern Aegean Amphora from Xeropolis, Lefkandi," in *Δινήεσσα: Τιμητικός τόμος για την Κατερίνα Ρωμιοπούλου. Festschrift for Katerina Rhomiopoulou*, ed. P. Adam-Veleni and K. Tzanavari, Thessaloniki, pp. 177–182.

Lenk, B. 1932. "Methone 7," *RE* 15 (2), pp. 1385–1387.

Lenormant, F. 1862. *Recherches archéologiques à Éleusis. Recueil des inscriptions*, Paris.

———. 1866a. "Inscriptionum Graecarum ineditarum centuria secunda et tertia," *RhM* 21, pp. 362–404.

———. 1866b. "Inscriptionum Graecarum ineditarum centuria quarta," *RhM* 21, pp. 510–533.

Lentacker, A., A. Ervynck, and W. Van Neer. 2004. "Gastronomy or Religion? The Animal Remains from the Mithraeum at Tienen (Belgium)," in *Behaviour Behind Bones: The Zooarchaeology of Ritual, Religion, Status and Identity*, ed. S. O'Day, W. Van Neer, and A. Ervycnk, Oxford, pp. 77–94.

Lenz, D., F. Ruppenstein, M. Baumann, and R. Catling. 1998. "Protogeometric Pottery at Troia," *Studia Troica* 8, pp. 189–211.

Lepore, E. 1969. "Osservazioni sul rapporto tra fatti economici e fatti di colonizzazione in Occidente," *DialArch* 3, pp. 175–212.

Le Rider, G. 2001. *La naissance de la monnaie. Pratiques monétaires de l'Orient ancient*, Paris.

Le Rider, G., and S. Verdan. 2002. "La trouvaille d'Erétrie: réserve d'un orfèvre ou dépôt monétaire?" *AntK* 45, pp. 133–152.

Leroi-Gourhan, A. 1971. *L'homme et la matière*, Paris.

Leukart, A. 1994. *Die frühgriechischen Nomina auf -tas und -as: Untersuchungen zu ihrer Herkunft und Ausbreitung (unter Vergleich mit den Nomina auf -eús)*, Vienna.

Liampi, K. 1993. "Παρουσίαση και εικονογραφία των νομισματικών εκδόσεων των Αινιάνων," *Hypate* 1993, pp. 17–34.

Lierke, R. 1992. "Early History of Lampwork: Some Facts, Findings and Theories, Part 2. Fire or Flame? Lampworking Techniques in Antiquity," *Glastechnische Berichte* 65, pp. 341–348.

Lightfoot, J. L. 2009. *Hellenistic Collection: Philitas, Alexander of Aetolia, Hermesianax, Euphrion, Parthenius* (Loeb Classical Library 508), Cambridge, Mass. and London.

Lilibaki-Akamati, M. 2007. "Στοιχεία για την Πέλλα του πρώτου μισού του 4ου αι π.Χ.," in *Ancient Macedonia 7: Macedonia from the Iron Age to the Death of Philip II*, ed. E. Voutiras, Thessaloniki, pp. 585–604.

Lilibaki-Akamati, M., and I. Akamatis. 2012. "Pella from the Bronze to the Hellenistic Age," in *Θρεπτήρια. Μελέτες για την Αρχαία Μακεδονία*, ed. M. Tiverios, P. Nigdelis, and P. Adam-Veleni, Thessaloniki, pp. 8–25.

Lilibaki-Akamati, M., and N. Akamatis. 2014. *Ανατολικό νεκροταφείο Πέλλας. Ανασκαφικές περίοδοι 1991–2007*, Thessaloniki.

Lindblom, M. 2001. *Marks and Makers: Appearance, Distribution and Function of Middle and Late Helladic Manufacturers' Marks on Aeginetan Pottery* (*SIMA* 128), Jonsered.

———. 2007. "Early Mycenaean Mortuary Meals at Lerna IV with Special Emphasis on Their Aeginetan Components," in *Middle Helladic Pottery and Synchronisms. Proceedings of the International Workshop Held at Salzburg, October 31st–November 2nd, 2004*, ed. F. Felton, W. Gauss, and R. Smetana, Vienna, pp. 115–136.

Lindenlauf, A. 2004. "The Sea as a Place of No Return in Ancient Greece," *World Archaeology: Seascapes* 35 (3), pp. 416–433.

Lioutas, A., and E. Gkioura. 1997. "Τοπογραφικές αναζητήσεις ΒΔ της αρχαίας Θεσσαλονίκης με αφορμή τις ανασκαφές σε νεκροπόλεις στους δήμους Σταυρούπολης και Πολίχνης," *AEMTh* 11 [1999], pp. 317–326.

Lis, B. 2017. "Foodways in Early Mycenaean Greece: Innovative Cooking Sets and Social Hierarchy at Mitrou and Other Settlements on the Greek Mainland," *AJA* 121 (2), pp. 183–217.

Lissarrague, F. 1990. *L'autre guerrier: archers, peltastes, cavaliers dans l'imagerie attique*, Paris.

———. 1999. *Vases grecs: les Athéniens et leurs images*, Paris.

Lister, A. M. 1996. "The Morphological Distinction Between Bones and Teeth of Fallow Deer (*Dama dama*) and Red Deer (*Cervus elaphus*)," *International Journal of Osteoarchaeology* 6, pp. 119–143.

Livarda, A. 2008. "Introduction and Dispersal of Exotic Food Plants into Europe during the Roman and Medieval Periods" (diss. Univ. of Leicester).

———. 2011. "Spicing up Life in Northwestern Europe: Exotic Food Plant Imports in the Roman and Medieval World," *Vegetation History and Archaeobotany* 20, pp. 143–164.

———. 2012. "The Archaeobotanical Evidence of the Late Bronze Age and Protogeometric Occupation under the Roman Villa Dionysus, Knossos, Crete, and an Overview of the Protogeometric Data of Greece," *BSA* 107, pp. 189–209.

Livarda, A., and G. Kotzamani. 2014. "The Archaeobotany of Neolithic and Bronze Age Crete: Synthesis and Prospects," *BSA* 108, pp. 1–29.

Livarda, A., H. A. Orengo, N. Cañellas-Boltà, S. Riera-Mora, L. Picornell-Gelabert, V. Tzevelekidi, R. Veropoulidou, R. Marlasca Martín, and A. Krahtopoulou. 2021. "Mediterranean Polyculture Revisited: Olive, Grape and Subsistence Strategies at Palaikastro, East Crete, Between the Late Neolithic and Late Bronze Age," *JAnthArch* 61, 101271 (https://doi.org/10.1016/j.jaa.2021.101271).

Longin, R. 1971. "New Method for Collagen Extraction for Radiocarbon Dating," *Nature* 230, pp. 241–242.

Lo Porto, F. G. 1970–1971. "Tomba messapica di Ugento," *AttiMGraecia* 11–12, pp. 99–152.

———. 1978. "Le importazioni della grecia dell'est in Puglia," in *Les céramiques de la Grèce de l'est et leur diffusion en occident. Centre Jean Bérard, Institut Français de Naples, 6–9 juillet 1976*, Paris, pp. 131–136.

Lorimer, H. L. 1950. *Homer and the Monuments*, London.

Lo Schiavo, F. 1970. *Il gruppo Liburnico-Japodico per una definizione nell'ambito della protostoria balcanica*, Rome.

———. 1983–1984a. "Le fibule di bronzo: Catalogo degli esemplari dale Tombe T.57-93," *AttiMGraecia* 24–25, pp. 111–126.

———. 1983–1984b. "Fibule dell'acropoli sulla Motta," *AttiMGraecia* 24–25, pp. 127–134.

Lüdorf, G. 2000. *Die Lekane: Typologie und Chronologie einer Leitform der attischen Gebrauchskeramik des 6.–1. Jahrhunderts v. Chr.*, Rahden/Westfalen.

Lullies, R. 1968. *"Griechische Kunstwerke, Sammlung Ludwig, Aachen. Eine Auswahl" (Exhibition Catalogue, Ausstellung im Hessischen Landesmuseum Kassel vom 25 Mai bis 6 Oktober 1968),* (Aachener Kunstblätter 37), Düsseldorf.

Lungu, V. 2009. "Projet d'atlas de référence des céramiques grises monochromes du Pont-Euxin à l'époque grecque," in *Pontic Grey Wares. International Conference, Bucharest-Constantza, September 3–October 3, 2008* (Pontica 42), Constanta, pp. 13–40.

———. 2010. "Lesbiaca II: Données typologiques préliminaires sur les amphores à pâte grise de Mytilène," in *Synergia Pontica et Aegeo-Anatolica*, ed. P. Dupont and V. Lungu, Galaţi, pp. 48–68.

Luppe, W. 1994. "Die Verfluchung der Methonaier (zum Strabon-Papyrus P. Köln I 8)," *Archiv für Papyrusforschung und verwandte Gebiete* 40 (2), pp. 115–118.

Luraghi, N. 2010. "The Local Scripts from Nature to Culture," *ClAnt* 29, pp. 68–91.

Lyons, C. L. 1996. *Morgantina Studies* V: *The Archaic Cemeteries*, Princeton.

Lyons, C. L., and J. K. Papadopoulos, eds. 2002. *The Archaeology of Colonialism*, Los Angeles.

Ma, J. 2010a. "A Note on Lead Projectiles (*glandes, molybdides*) in Support of Sling Bullets: A Reply to T. Rihll," *JRA* 23, pp. 427–428.

———. 2010b. "Autour des balles de fronde 'camiréennes,'" *Chiron* 40, pp. 155–173.

———. 2018. "The *Polis* in a Cold Climate: Propositions, Consequences, Questions," in *Βορειοελλαδικά. Tales from the Lands of the Ethne: Essays in Honour of Miltiades B. Hatzopoulos* (Μελετήματα 78), ed. M. Kalaïtzi, P. Paschidis, C. Antonetti, and A.-M. Guimier-Sorbets, Athens, pp. 309–327.

Maass, M. 1977. "Kretische Votivdreifüsse," *AM* 92, pp. 33–59.

———. 1981. "Die geometrischen Dreifüsse von Olympia," *AntK* 24, pp. 6–20.

Maass, M., and I. Kilian-Dirlmeier. 1998. "Aegina—Aphaiatempel. Bronzefunde ausser Waffen," *AA* 1998, pp. 57–104.

Mack, E. 1964. "Die Goldvorkommen in Griechisch-Makedonien," *Erzmetall* 17, pp. 9–18.

Macnamara, E. 2006. "Pithecusan Gleaning II: Other Bronze Objects," in *Across Frontiers: Etruscans, Greeks, Phoenicians, and Cypriots. Studies in Honour of David Ridgway and Francesca Romana Ridgway*, ed. E. Herring, I. Lemos, F. Lo Schiavo, L. Vagnetti, R. Whitehouse, and J. Wilkes, London, pp. 267–279.

Mac Sweeney, N. 2017. "Separating Fact from Fiction in the Ionian Migration," *Hesperia* 86, pp. 379–421.

Maddin, R., T. S. Wheeler, and J. D. Muhly. 1977. "Tin in the Ancient Near East: Old Questions and New Finds," *Expedition* 19 (2), pp. 35–47.

Madrigali, E., and A. Zara. 2018. "Anfore fenicie e puniche con contenuti alimentari dai rinvenimenti di Michel Cassien a Nora," *Folia Phoenicia* 2, pp. 54–58.

Maier, F. 1956. "Zu einigen bosnisch-herzegowinischen Bronzen in Griechenland," *Germania* 34, pp. 63–75.

Maier, F. G. 1959. *Griechische Mauerbauinschriften*, Part 1, *Texte und Kommentare*, Heidelberg.

Mainardis, F. 2007. "Tra storia, collezionismo e falsificazione: le ghiande missili dei Civici Musei di Trieste," in *XII Congressus Internationalis Epigraphiae Graecae et Latinae, Provinciae Imperii Romani Inscriptionibus Descriptae, Barcelona, 3–8 Septembris 2002*, 2 (Monografies de la secció historico-arqueologica 10), ed. M. Mayer i Olivé, G. Baratta, and A. Guzmán Almagro, Barcelona, pp. 869–876.

Maiuri, A. 1925. *Nuova silloge epigrafica di Rodi e Cos*, Firenze.

———. 1927. "Relazione sui lavori di scavo dal marzo 1924 al marzo 1926," *NSc*, series 6 (3), pp. 3–83.

Makaronas, Ch. 1960. "Ἀνασκαφαὶ Πέλλης 1957–1960," *ArchDelt* 16, pp. 74–83.

Makridis, Th. 1937. "Χαλκᾶ μακεδονικὰ τοῦ Μουσείου Μπενάκη," *ArchEph* 1937, cols. 512–521.

Malamidou, D. 2007. "Kryoneri: A Neolithic and Early Bronze Age Settlement in the Lower Strymon Valley," in *The Struma/Strymon River Valley in Prehistory: In the Steps of James Harvey Gaul* 2, ed. H. Todorova, M. Stefanovich, and G. Ivanov, Sofia, pp. 297–308.

Malamidou, D., and S. Papadopoulos. 1993. "Ανασκαφική έρευνα στον προϊστορικό οικισμό Λιμεναρίων Θάσου," *AEMTh* 7 [1997], pp. 559–572.

———. 1997. "Προϊστορικός οικισμός Λιμεναρίων: Η πρώιμη εποχή του χαλκού," *AEMTh* 11 [1999], pp. 585–596.

Malamidou, D., Z. Tsirtsoni, P. Yiouni, L. Lespez, V. Kilikoglou, and A. Tsolakidou. 2006. "Les poteries néolithiques à décor peint 'noir sur rouge' en Grèce du Nord: matières premières et production," *BCH* 130 (2), pp. 571–611.

Malkin, I. 1987. *Religion and Colonisation in Ancient Greece* (Studies in Greek and Roman Religion 3), Leiden.

———. 1998. *The Returns of Odysseus. Colonization and Ethnicity*, Berkeley.

———, ed. 2001. *Ancient Perceptions of Greek Ethnicity* (Center for Hellenic Studies Colloquia 5), Cambridge, Mass.

———. 2009. "Foundations," in *A Companion to Archaic Greece*, ed. K. A. Raaflaub and H. van Wees, Chichester, pp. 373–394.

———. 2011. *A Small Greek World: Networks in the Ancient Mediterranean*, Oxford.

———. 2016. "Greek Colonisation: The Right to Return," in *Conceptualising Early Colonisation*, ed. L. Donnellan, V. Nizzo, and G.-J. Burgers, Brussels, pp. 27–50.

Malkin, I., C. Constantakopoulou, and K. Panagopoulou, eds. 2009. *Greek and Roman Networks in the Mediterranean*, London and New York.

Mallios, G. 2011. "Μύθος και ιστορία: Η περίπτωση της αρχαίας Μακεδονίας" (diss. Aristotle Univ. Thessaloniki).

Manacorda, D. 1993. "Appunti sulla bollatura in età romana," in *The Inscribed Economy: Production and Distribution in the Roman Empire in the Light of instrumentum domesticum* (*JRA* Suppl. 6), ed. W. V. Harris, Ann Arbor, pp. 37–54.

Manakidou, E. 2010. "Céramiques 'indigènes' de l'époque géométrique et archaïque du site de Karabournaki en Macédoine et leur relation avec les céramiques importées," in *Grecs et indigènes de la Catalogne à la Mer Noire. Actes des rencontres du programme européen Ramses, 2006–2008*, ed. H. Tréziny, Paris and Aix-en-Provence, pp. 463–470.

———. 2017. "Η αρχαία Χαλάστρα και η περιοχή της," in *Χαλάστρα και η ευρύτερη περιοχή: Ιστορικό, πολιτιστικό και οικιστικό απόθεμα*, ed. E. G. Gavra, Thessaloniki, pp. 3–36.

———. 2018. "Protocorinthian and Corinthian Ceramic Imports in Macedonia: Different People, Different Tastes?" in *Archaeology Across Frontiers and Borderlands: Fragmentation and Connectivity in the North Aegean and the Central Balkans from the Bronze Age to the Iron Age*, ed. S. Gimatzidis, M. Pieniążek, and S. Mangaloğlu-Votruba, Vienna, pp. 187–202.

Manganaro, G. 1965. "Per la storia dei culti in Sicilia," *PP* 20, pp. 163–178.

———. 2000. "Onomastica greca su anelli, pesi da telaio e glandes in Sicilia," *ZPE* 133, pp. 123–134.

Mangold, M. 2000. *Kassandra in Athen. Die Eroberung Trojas auf attischen Vasenbildern*, Berlin.

Mannack, Th. 2012. *Griechische Vasenmalerei: eine Einführung*, 2nd ed., Darmstadt.

Manning, W. H. 1980. "Blacksmiths' Tools from Waltham Abbey, Essex," in *Aspects of Early Metallurgy*, ed. W. A. Oddy, London, pp. 87–96.

Manni Piraino, M. T. 1971. "Revisioni epigrafiche siceliote," *Kokalos* 17, pp. 170–183.

Manoledakis, M. 2016. "From Macedonia to Anatolia: Phrygians and Their Migration," in *Ηχάδιν* II. *Τιμητικός τόμος για τη Στέλλα Δρούγου*, ed. M. Giannopoulou and Ch. Kallini, Athens, pp. 48–72.

Manov, M. 2016. "A Lead Sling Bullet of the Macedonian King Philip V (221–179 B.C.)," *Bulgarian e-Journal of Archaeology* 6, pp. 191–201.

Manov, M., G. Talmaţchi, and G. Custurea. 2019. "New Lead Sling Bullets with Inscriptions ΣΤΡΑΤΗ | ΑΛΕΞΑΝ and ΒΑΣΙΛΕ | ΑΛΕΞΑΝ Found in Dobrudja (in Romania and Bulgaria)," *Numismatics, Sigillography and Epigraphy* 15, pp. 133–155.

Manov, M., and N. Torbov. 2016. "Inscribed Lead Sling Bullets with the Names of Alexander the Great and with Other Names and Symbols Found in Thrace," *Archaeologia Bulgarica* 20, pp. 29–43.

Maran, J. 1998. *Kulturwandel auf dem griechischen Festland und den Kykladen im späten 3. Jahrtausend v. Chr.*, Teile 1–2, Bonn.

———. 2007. "Emulation of Aeginetan Pottery in the Middle Bronze Age of Coastal Thessaly: Regional Context and Social Meaning," in *Middle Helladic Pottery and Synchronisms. Proceedings of the International Workshop Held at Salzburg, October 31st–November 2nd, 2004*, ed. F. Felton, W. Gauss, and R. Smetana, Vienna, pp. 167–182.

———. 2013. "Bright as the Sun: The Appropriation of Amber Objects in Mycenaean Greece," in *Mobility, Meaning and the Transformations of Things*, ed. H. P. Hahn and H. Weiss, Oxford, pp. 147–169.

Marangou, Ch. 1992. *Eidolia: Figurines et miniatures du néolithique récent et du bronze ancien en Grèce* (*BAR-IS* 576), Oxford.

———. 1996. "Figurines and Models," in Papathanassopoulos 1996, pp. 161–162.

———. 2004. "Les récipients zoomorphes et anthropomorphes du Néolithique Moyen et du Néolithique Récent (Chalcolithique)," in *Dikili Tash, village préhistorique de Macédoine Orientale* 1: *Fouilles de Jean Deshayes 1961–1975*, 2 (*BCH* Suppl. 37), ed. R. Treuil, Paris, pp. 270–312.

Marangou, L. 2002. *Ἀμοργὸς* 1: *Ἡ Μινώα: Ἡ πόλις, ὁ λιμὴν καὶ ἡ μείζων περιφέρεια*, Athens.

Marazov, I., A. Fol, M. Tacheva-Khitova, and I. Venedikov, eds. 1997. *Ancient Gold: The Wealth of the Thracians. Treasures from the Republic of Bulgaria*, New York.

Margomenou, D., S. Andreou, and K. Kotsakis. 2005. "Τούμπα Θεσσαλονίκης· προσεγγίσεις στη μελέτη των πίθων και στο θέμα της αποθήκευσης κατά την Ύστερη Εποχή του Χαλκού," *AEMTh* 19 [2007], pp. 157–171.

Margomenou, D., and M. Roumpou. 2011. "Storage Technologies as Embedded Social Practices: Studying Pithos Storage in Prehistoric Northern Greece," in *Tracing Prehistoric Social Networks Through Technology: A Diachronic Perspective on the Aegean*, ed. A. Brysbaert, New York, pp. 126–142.

Mari, M. 2002. *Al di la dell'Olimpo: Macedoni e grandi santuari della Grecia dall'eta arcaica al primo ellenismo* (Μελετήματα 34), Athens.

———. 2007. "Macedonian Poleis and Ethnē in the Greek Sanctuaries Before the Age of Philip II," in *Ancient Macedonia* 7: *Macedonia from the Iron Age to the Death of Philip II* (Institute for Balkan Studies 280), ed. E. Voutiras, Thessaloniki, pp. 31–49.

. 2011. "Archaic and Early Classical Macedonia," in *Brill's Companion to Ancient Macedon: Studies in the Archaeology and History of Macedon, 650 BC–300 AD*, ed. R. J. Lane Fox, Leiden and Boston, pp. 79–92.

Mariaud, O. 2011. "The Geometric Graves of Colophon after the Exccavations of H. Goldman, 1922: Reflexions on the Burial Customs of Early Iron Age Ionia," in *The Dark Ages Revisited: From the Dark Ages to the Rise of the Polis. Proceedings of the International Symposium in Memory of William D. E. Coulson, Volos, June 2007*, ed. A. Mazarakis Ainian, Volos, pp. 687–703.

———. 2019. "Nouvelle datation des tumuli de la necropole nord-est de Colophon: l'apport du mobilier métallique," in *"Colofoni, città della Ionia." Nuovi ricerche e studi. Atti del Convegno Internazionale di Studi di Salerno, 20 aprile 2017*, ed. L. Vecchio, Salerno, pp. 225–242.

Marinatos, S. N. 1932. "Αἱ ἀνασκαφαὶ Goekoop ἐν Κεφαλληνίᾳ," *ArchEph* 71, pp. 1–47.

Marinova, E. M., D. Z. Filipovic, D. Obradovic, and E. Allué. 2013. "Wild Plant Resources and Land Use in Mesolithic and Early Neolithic South-East Europe: Archaeobotanical Evidence from the Danube Catchment of Bulgaria and Serbia," *Offa* 69–70, pp. 467–478.

Mariotti, A. 1983. "Atmospheric Nitrogen is a Reliable Standard for Natural ^{15}N Abundance Measurements," *Nature* 303, pp. 685–687.

Marriott Keighley, J. 1986. "The Pottery of Phases I and II," in *Sitagroi* 1, pp. 345–390.

Marsden, E. W. 1977. "Macedonian Military Machinery and Its Designers under Philip and Alexander," in *Ancient Macedonia* 2 (Institute for Balkan Studies 155), ed. K. Mitsakis, Thessaloniki, pp. 211–223.

Mårtensson, L., E. Andersson, M.-L. Nosch, and A. Batzer. 2007. "Technical Report: Experimental Archaeology, Part 4 Spools, 2007," Center for Textile Research, Copenhagen, https://ctr.hum.ku.dk/research-programmes-and-projects/previous-programmes-and-projects/tools/technical_report_4__experimental_arcaheology.pdf

Martha, J. 1889. *L'art étrusque*, Paris.

Martin, R. 2016. "The Development of Canaanite and Phoenician Style Maritime Transport Containers and Their Role in Reconstructing Maritime Exchange Networks," in Demesticha and Knapp 2016, pp. 111–128.

Martínez Fernández, A. 2007. "Glandes con inscripciones atestiguados en la antigua Grecia," *Revista de Filología* 25, pp. 399–405.

Maryon, H. 1938. "Some Prehistoric Metalworkers' Tools," *AntJ* 18, pp. 243–250.

Marzoli, D. 1989. *Bronzefeldflaschen in Italien* (*PBF* II.4), Munich.

Mason, P. 1996. *The Early Iron Age of Slovenia* (*BAR-IS* 643), Oxford.

Massei, L. 1978. *Gli askoi a figure rosse nei corredi funerari delle necropoli di Spina*, Milan.

Masson, O. 1993. "François Lenormant (1837–1883), un érudit déconcertant," *MusHelv* 50, pp. 44–60.

Mastrokostas, E. 1966. "Τεῖχος Δυμαίων," *Ergon* 1966, pp. 156–165.

Matthaiou, A. P. 2004–2009. "Θραύσμα ενεπίγραφου πίθου από τους Ζάρακες Καρυστίας," *HOROS* 17–21, pp. 541–544.

Matthäus, H. 1980. *Die Bronzegefässe der kretisch-mykenischen Kultur* (*PBF* II.1), Munich.

———. 1985. *Metallgefässe und Gefässuntersätze der Bronzezeit, der geometrischen und archaischen Periode auf Zypern* (*PBF* II.8), Munich.

Mattingly, H. B. 1961. "The Methone Decrees," *CQ* 11, pp. 154–165.

———. 1996a. "Periclean Imperialism," in *The Athenian Empire Restored: Epigraphic and Historical Studies*, Ann Arbor, pp. 147–179.

———. 1996b. "Athens, Methone, and Aphytis, *IG* I^{3} 61 and 62," in *The Athenian Empire Restored: Epigraphic and Historical Studies*, Ann Arbor, pp. 525–527.

Mauel, S. 2009. "Die Spinnwirtel und Webgewichte der bronze- und eisenzeitlichen Siedlung von Kastanas. Zur Textilproduktion Nordgriechenlands im 2. vorchristlichen Jahrtausend" (MA thesis, University of Copenhagen).

———. 2012. "Summarizing Results of a New Analysis of the Textile Tools from the Bronze Age Settlement of Kastanas, Central Macedonia," in *KOSMOS: Jewellery, Adornment and Textiles in the Aegean Bronze Age. Proceedings of the 13th International Aegean Conference/Rencontre égéenne internationale, University of Copenhagen, Danish National Research Foundation's Centre for Textile Research, 21–26 April 2010* (*Aegaeum* 33), ed. M.-L. Nosch and R. Laffineur, Leuven/Liège, pp. 139–146.

Mauri, A., D. de Rigo, and G. Caudullo. 2016. "*Abies alba* in Europe: Distribution, Habitat, Usage and Threats," in *European Atlas of Forest Tree Species*, ed. J. San-Miguel-Ayanz, D. de Rigo, G. Caudullo, T. Houston Durrant, and A. Mauri, Luxembourg, pp. 48–49.

Mavroeidi, I. 2012. "Ο οικισμός του Αγίου Αθανασίου, νομού Θεσσαλονίκης: οι ενδοκοινοτικές σχέσεις σε μία κοινότητα της Πρώιμης Εποχής του Χαλκού μέσα από τη μελέτη της κεραμικής και της αρχιτεκτονικής οργάνωσης" (diss. Aristotle Univ. Thessaloniki).

———. 2014. "Η Πρώιμη Εποχή του Χαλκού στη Μακεδονία. Μία συνθετική επαναπροσέγγιση των αρχαιολογικών δεδομένων," in Stefani, Merousis, and Dimoula 2014, pp. 261–270.

Mavroeidi, I., S. Andreou, and M. Pappa. 2006. "Οικισμός της πρώιμης εποχής του χαλκού στον Άγιο Αθανάσιο Θεσσαλονίκης," *AEMTh* 20 [2008], pp. 479–490.

Maxwell-Hyslop, R. 1953. "Bronze Lugged Axe or Adze Blades from Asia," *Iraq* 15, pp. 69–87.

Mazar, A., and C. Bronk Ramsey. 2008. "14C Dates and the Iron Age Chronology of Israel: A Response," *Radiocarbon* 50, pp. 159–180.

Mazarakis Ainian, A. 1996. "Ανασκαφή Σκάλας Ωρωπού," *Prakt* 1996, pp. 21–124.

———. 1998. "Oropos in the Early Iron Age," in Bats and d'Agostino 1998, pp. 179–215.

———. 2017. "Η Σκιάθος της Πρώιμης Εποχής του Σιδήρου," in *Το αρχαιολογικό έργο στα νησιά του Αιγαίου. Διεθνές επιστημονικό συνέδριο, Ρόδος 27 Νοεμβρίου–1 Δεκεμβρίου 2013*, ed. P. Triantafyllidis, Mytilene, pp. 131–140.

———. 2010. "Ein antikes Heiligtum auf Kythnos," in *Neue Forschungen zu griechischen Städten und Heiligtümern. Festschrift für Burkhardt Wesenberg zum 65. Geburtstag*, ed. H. Frielinghaus and J. Stroszeck, Möhnesee, pp. 21–53.

———. 2019. *The Sanctuaries of Ancient Kythnos*, Rennes.

Mazarakis Ainian, A., and A. Alexandridou. 2015. "Νέα δεδομένα για τις Σποράδες κατά τους πρώιμους ιστορικούς χρόνους: Ο οικισμός της Κεφάλας Σκιάθου," *Archaiologiko Ergo Thessalias kai Stereas Helladas* 5 (2020), pp. 421–430.

Mazarakis Ainian, A., and A. P. Matthaiou. 1999. "Ενεπίγραφο αλιευτικό βάρος των γεωμετρικών χρόνων," *ArchEph* 1999, pp. 143–153.

Mazza, F., ed. 1992. *Crotone: Storia, Cultura, Economia*, Crotone.

Mazzoli, M. 2018. "Metal Finds," in *The Chora of Metaponto* 7: *The Greek Sanctuary at Pantanello* 2, ed. J. C. Carter and K. Swift, Austin, Tex., pp. 919–933.

McCaul, J. 1864. "On Inscribed Sling-Bullets," *The Canadian Journal of Industry, Science, and Art*, n.s. 9, no. 50, March, pp. 92–102.

McClellan, J. A. 1975. "The Iron Objects from Gordion: A Typological and Functional Analysis" (diss. Univ. of Pennsylvania).

McClellan, M. C. 1992. "The Core-formed Vessels," in Weinberg 1992, pp. 19–20.

McDermott, W. C. 1942. "Glandes Plumbeae," *CJ* 38, pp. 35–37.

McInerney, J. 2018. *Greece in the Ancient World*, London.

McLean, B. H. 2002. *An Introduction to Greek Epigraphy of the Hellenistic and Roman Periods from Alexander the Great down to the Reign of Constantine (323 B.C.–A.D. 337)*, Ann Arbor.

Meehan, B. 1982. *Shell Bed to Shell Midden*, Canberra.

Meeks, N. D., and P. T. Craddock. 2013. "Scientific Examination of Two Sherds with Gold Particles," in *Eretria* XXII, pp. 271–273.

Megaloudi, F. 2006. *Plants and Diet in Greece from Neolithic to Classic Periods: The Archaeobotanical Remains* (*BAR-IS* 1516), Oxford.

Meiggs, R. 1982. *Trees and Timber in the Ancient Mediterranean World*, Oxford.

Meiggs, R., and D. M. Lewis. 1969. *A Selection of Greek Historical Inscriptions* 1: *To the End of the Fifth Century B.C.*, Oxford.

———. 1988. *A Selection of Greek Historical Inscriptions to the End of the Fifth Century B.C.*, rev. ed., Oxford.

Mellaart, J. 1955. "Iron Age Pottery from Southern Anatolia," *Belleten* 19, pp. 115–136.

Méndez Dosuna, J. V. 2017. "Methone of Pieria: A Reassessment of Epigraphical Evidence (with Special Attention to Pleonastic Sigma)," in Strauss Clay, Malkin, and Tzifopoulos 2017b, pp. 242–258.

Meritt, B. D. 1936. "Archelaos and the Decelean War," in *Classical Studies Presented to Edward Capps on His Seventieth Birthday*, Princeton, pp. 246–252.

———. 1944. "The American Excavations in the Athenian Agora, Twenty-Fifth Report: Greek Inscriptions," *Hesperia* 13, pp. 210–265.

———. 1980. "The Athenian Colony at Poteidaia," in *Στήλη. Τόμος εις μνήμην Νικολάου Κοντολέοντος*, Athens, pp. 21–25.

Merkelbach, R. 1973. "Methone—Methana," *ZPE* 10, pp. 194–196.

Merker, G. 2006. *The Greek Tile Works at Corinth: The Site and the Finds* (*Hesperia* Suppl. 35), Princeton.

Merousis, N. 2002. "Η διακοσμημένη κεραμική από το νεολιθικό Πολυπλάτανο: προκαταρκτικές παρατηρήσεις," *AEMTh* 16 [2004], pp. 519–530.

———. 2004. "Early Bronze Age in the Pella-Imathia Plain, W. Macedonia," in *Die Ägäische Frühzeit, 2. Serie: Forschungsbericht 1975–2002. 2. Band*, Teile 1-2: *Die Frühbronzezeit in Griechenland mit Ausnahme von Kreta*, ed. E. Alram-Stern, Wien, pp. 1285–1295.

Merousis, N., and M. Nikolaidou. 1997. "Η κεραμική της Νεολιθικής και της Πρώιμης Εποχής του Χαλκού από τον προϊστορικό οικισμό του Μάνδαλου Πέλλας: η τεχνολογική διαφοροποίηση," *AEMTh* 11 [1999], pp. 155–163.

Merrillees, R. S. 1962. "Opium Trade in the Bronze Age Levant," *Antiquity* 36, 287–292.

Messier, C., R. Doucet, J.-C. Ruel, Y. Claveau, C. Kelly, and M. J. Lechowicz. 1999. "Functional Ecology of Advance Regeneration in Relation to Light in Boreal Forests," *Canadian Journal of Forest Research* 29, pp. 812–823.

Metallinou, G., ed. 2008. *Atlas Historiko-arkeologjik i Zones Kufitare Greko-Shqiptare*, Athens.

Metaponto I = D. Adamesteanu, D. Mertens, and F. D'Andria, *Metaponto* 1, *NSc* Supplemento 29: 1975, Rome 1980.

Meyer, E. 1932. "Methone 5," *RE* 15 (2), p. 1384.

Michailidou, A., and I. Tzachili. 1986. "Λίθινη μήτρα για κοσμήματα από τη Βεργίνα. Ένα αινιγματικό τυχαίο εύρημα," *Ancient Macedonia* 4 (Institute for Balkan Studies 204), ed. A. Vakalopoulos, pp. 365–376.

Michailidou-Nikolaou, I. 1969–1970. "Ghiande Missili di Cipro," *ASAtene* 47–48, pp. 359–369.

Michon, E. 1894. Untitled, *BAntFr* 1894, pp. 268–271.

Mihovilić, K. 2007. "Istrian Contacts with the Aegean Throughout the Early Iron Age," in Galanaki et al. 2007, pp. 343–346.

Mikrogiannakis, E. 2007. "Αρχέλαος," in *Ancient Macedonia* 7: *Macedonia from the Iron Age to the Death of Philip II* (Institute for Balkan Studies 280), ed. E. Voutiras, Thessaloniki, pp. 221–227.

Mikulčić, I., and V. Sokolovska. 1991. "Grobnica vo Brasda kaj Skopje (Eine Herrschersgruft in Brasda bei Skopje)," *Macedoniae Acta Archaeologica* 11, pp. 79–92.

Milet VI.3 = P. Herrmann, W. Günther, and N. Ehrhardt, eds., *Inschriften von Milet* (*Milet* 6.3), Berlin and New York.

Militello, P. 2001. "Amministrazione e contabilità a Festos. I: Gettoni di età prepalaziale," *Creta Antica* 2, pp. 29–40.

Miller, M. A. 1997. "Jewels of Shell and Stone, Clay and Bone: The Production, Function and Distribution of Aegean Stone Age Ornaments" (diss. Boston Univ.).

Miller, S. G. 1974. "Menon's Cistern," *Hesperia* 43, pp. 194–245.

———. 1976. "Excavations at Nemea, 1975," *Hesperia* 45, pp. 174–202.

———. 1978. "Excavations at Nemea, 1977," *Hesperia* 47, pp. 58–88.

———. 1979. "Excavations at Nemea, 1978," *Hesperia* 48, pp. 73–103.

———. 1983. "Excavations at Nemea, 1982," *Hesperia* 52, pp. 70–95.

———. 1984. "Excavations at Nemea, 1983," *Hesperia* 53, pp. 171–192.

Millett, P. 2010. "The Political Economy of Macedonia," in *A Companion to Ancient Macedonia*, ed. J. Roisman and I. Worthington, Oxford, pp. 472–504.

Milne, J. S. 1907. *Surgical Instruments in Greek and Roman Times*, Oxford.

Milojčić, V. 1948–1949. "Die dorische Wanderung im Lichte der vorgeschichtlichen Funde," *AA* 1948–1949, pp. 12–36.

———. 1961. *Samos* 1: *Die prähistorische Siedlung unter dem Heraion, Grabung 1953 und 1955*, Bonn.

Miron, E. 1992. *Axes and Adzes from Canaan* (*PBF* IX.19), Stuttgart.

Misailidou-Despotidou, V. 1993. "Ενσφράγιστες κεραμίδες από το ανάκτορο της Πέλλας," in *Ancient Macedonia* 5.2 (Institute for Balkan Studies 240), ed. D. Pantermalis, Thessaloniki, pp. 975–997.

———. 1998. "Νέα Φιλαδέλφεια. Ανασκαφική έρευνα στην 'Τράπεζα' και στο νεκροταφείο της Εποχής Σιδήρου," *AEMTh* 12 [2000], pp. 259–268.

———. 1999. "Χρονολογικά στοιχεία από ταφικά σύνολα του 4ου αι π.Χ. από τη Ν. Φιλαδέλφεια," in *Ancient Macedonia 6.2* (Institute for Balkan Studies 272), ed. D. Pantermalis, pp. 771–785.

———. 2008. "Νέα Φιλαδέλφεια: Οικιστικές εγκαταστάσεις και νεκροταφεία στην ενδοχώρα της Θεσσαλονίκης," in *Αρχαιολογικές Τροχιοδρομήσεις: Από τη Θεσσαλονίκη στον Πλαταμώνα*, ed. K. Tsouni, Athens, pp. 24–69.

———. 2009. "Άφυτις 1997–2006," in Adam-Veleni and Tzanavari 2009, pp. 221–237.

———. 2011. *Χάλκινα κοσμήματα αρχαϊκών χρόνων από τη Μακεδονία*, Thessaloniki.

———. 2012a. "Η αρχαϊκή κεραμική από το νεκροταφείο της αρχαίας Άφυτης," in Tiverios et al. 2012, pp. 371–384.

———. 2012b. "Ο διπλός πέλεκυς στο νεκροταφείο της Νέας Φιλαδέλφειας," in *Δινήεσσα. Τιμητικός τόμος για την Κατερίνα Ρωμιοπούλου. Festschrift for Katerina Rhomiopoulou*, ed. P. Adam-Veleni and K. Tzanavari, Thessaloniki, pp. 471 480.

———. 2013. "Τοπική κεραμεική από τη Νέα Φιλαδέλφεια Θεσσαλονίκης," in Adam-Veleni, Kefalidou, and Tsiafaki 2013, pp. 225–233.

Mitkidou, S., E. Dimitrakoudi, D. Urem-Kotsou, D. Papadopoulou, K. Kotsakis, J. A. Stratis, and I. Stephanidou-Stephanatou. 2008. "Organic Residue Analysis of Neolithic Pottery from North Greece," *Microchimica Acta* 160, pp. 493–498.

Mitrevski, D. 2016. *Ancient Bylazora, the Capital of Independent Paeonians*, trans. A. Atanasov, Sveti Nikole.

———. 2019. "Classical Pottery from the Royal Palace in Bylazora—Capital of the Independent Paeonians," in *H κεραμική της κλασικής εποχής στο Βόρειο Αιγαίο και την περιφέρειά του (480–323/300 π.Χ.)*, ed. E. Manakidou and A. Avramidou, Thessaloniki, pp. 323–338.

Mitsopoulou-Leon, V. 2001. "Zum Halsschmuck oder Drogen für die Götter?" *AM* 116, pp. 51–65.

———. 2012. *Das Heiligtum der Artemis Hemera in Lousoi: Kleinfunde aus den Grabungen 1986–2000*, Vienna.

Mommsen, H., D. Hertel, and P. A. Mountjoy. 2001. "Neutron Activation Analysis of the Pottery from Troy in the Berlin Schliemann Collection," *AA*, pp. 169–211.

Mommsen, H., and M. Kerschner. 2006. "Chemical Provenance Determination of Pottery: The Examples of the Aiolian Group G," in *Naukratis: Greek Diversity in Egypt. Studies on East Greek Pottery and Exchange in the Eastern Mediterranean*, ed. A. Villing and U. Schlotzhauer, London, pp. 105–108.

Mommsen, H., with U. Schlotzhauer, A. Villing, and S. Weber. 2012. "Teil 3: Herkunftsbestimmung von archaischen Scherben aus Naukratis und Tell Defenneh in Ägypten durch Neutronenaktivierungsanalyse," in *Griechische Keramik des 7. und 6. Jhs. v. Chr. aus Naukratis und anderen Orten in Ägypten* (Archäologische Studien aus Naukratis 3), ed. U. Höckmann, Worms, pp. 433–477.

Mommsen, H., M. von Haugwitz, and G. Johrens. 2010. "Herkunftsbestimmung von Amphoren mit gestempelten Henkeln aus den Grabungen von Milet durch Neutronenaktivierungsanalyse," *AA* 2012, pp. 47–58.

Monachov, S. J. 1999. *Grecheskie Amfory v Prichernomore: Kompleksy Keramicheskoi Tary VII–II Vekov do. n. e.*, Moscow.

———. 2000. "Quelques séries d'amphores grecques des VIIe–Ve S. av. n. è. au Nord de la Mer Noire," in *Production et commerce des amphores anciennes en Mer Noire*, ed. Y. Garlan, Aix-en-Provence, pp. 163–193.

———. 2003a. *Grecheskie Amfory v Prichernomore: Tipologiia Amfor Vedushchikh tsentrov-eksportero Tovarov V Keramicheskoi Tare Katalog-Opredelitel*, Moscow.

———. 2003b. "Amphorae from Unidentified Centres in the North Aegean," in *The Cauldron of Ariantas. Studies Presented to A. N. Ščeglov on the Occasion of His 70th Birthday*, ed. P. Guldager Bilde, J. M. Højte, and V. F. Stolba, Aarhus, pp. 247–261.

Montanari, F. 2013. *Vocabulario della lingua greca*, 3rd ed., Torino.

Montelius, O. 1895. *La civilisation primitive en Italie* 1, Stockholm and Berlin.

———. 1904. *La civilisation primitive en Italie* 2, *Planche 2¹ et 2²*, Stockholm and Berlin.

Moog, F. P. 2002. "Zur Traumatologie der antiken Schleuderbleie," *Medizinhistorisches Journal* 37, pp. 123–137.

Moore, A. D., and W. D. Taylour. 1999. "The Temple Complex," in *Well Built Mycenae: The Helleno-British Excavations Within the Citadel at Mycenae, 1959–1969*, Fasc. 10, ed. W. D. Taylour, E. B. French, and K. A. Wardle, Exeter.

Moore, R. S., W. R. Caraher, Br. R. Olson, and D. K. Pettegrew. 2012. "Pyla-Vigla: Life and Times on a Ptolemaic Garrison Camp in Southern Cyprus" (paper, Annual Meeting of the American Schools of Oriental Research, November 2012).

Morakis, A. 2011. "Thucydides and the Character of Greek Colonization in Sicily," *CQ* 61 (2), pp. 460–492.

Morel, J.-P. 1984. "Greek Colonization in Italy and in the West: Problems of Evidence and Interpretation," in *Crossroads of the Mediterranean: Papers Delivered at the International Conference on the Archaeology of Early Italy, Haffenreffer Museum, Brown University, 8–10 May 1981*, ed. T. Hackens, N. D. Holloway, and R. R. Holloway, Louvain and Providence, pp. 123–161.

Morgan, C. 1998. "Euboians and Corinthians in the Area of the Corinthian Gulf?" in Bats and d'Agostino 1998, pp. 281–302.

———. 2013–2014. "The Work of the British School at Athens, 2013–2014," *AR* 60, pp. 25–37.

Morgan, C., R. K. Pitt, D. Mulliez, and D. Evely. 2010. "Archaeology in Greece. 2009–2010," *AR* 56, pp. 1–201.

Mørkholm, O. [ed. Ph. Grierson and U. Westermark]. 1991. *Early Hellenistic Coinage from the Accession of Alexander to the Peace of Apamea (336–186 B.C.)*, Cambridge.

Morley, I., and C. Renfrew, eds. 2010. *The Archaeology of Measurement: Comprehending Heaven, Earth and Time in Ancient Society*, Cambridge.

Morricone, L. 1978. "Sepolture della prima Eta del Ferro a Coo," *ASAtene* 56, n.s. 40, pp. 9–427.

Morris, I. 2003. "Mediterraneanization," *Mediterranean Historical Review*, 18 (2), pp. 30–55.

Morris, S. P. 1985. "ΛΑΣΑΝΑ: A Contribution to the Ancient Greek Kitchen," *Hesperia* 54, pp. 393–400.

———. 2008. "Προϊστορική Τορώνη (1986–1990): προκαταρκτικά αποτελέσματα των ανασκαφών στη θέση 'Λήκυθος,'" *AEMTh* 22 [2011], pp. 435–442.

———. 2009–2010. "Prehistoric Torone: A Bronze Age Emporion in the Northern Aegean. Preliminary Report on the Lekythos Excavations 1986 and 1988–1990," *MeditArch* 22–23 [2011], pp. 1–69.

———. 2014. "Dairy Queen: Churns and Milk Products in the Aegean Bronze Age," *OpAth* 7, pp. 205–222.

———. 2015. "*Pieria Capta*: Methone, Pella, and the Urbanization of Macedonia" (paper, Archaeological Institute of America, January 2015).

———. Forthcoming. "The Kingdom of Philoktetes and the Curse of Agamemnon: Pieria in the Bronze Age," in *Stellar Ventures*, ed. S. Triantaphyllou, K. Eukleidou, and L. Vokotopoulos, Philadelphia.

Morris, S. P., and J. K. Papadopoulos. 1998. "Phoenicians and the Corinthian Pottery Industry," in *Archäologische Studien in Kontaktzonen der antiken Welt* (Veröffentlichungen der Joachim Jungius-Gesellschaft der Wissenschaften e.V. Hamburg, Band 87), ed. R. Rolle, K. Schmidt, and R. Docter, Hamburg, pp. 251–263.

Morris, S. P., J. K. Papadopoulos, M. Bessios, A. Athanassiadou, and K. Noulas. 2020. "The Ancient Methone Archaeological Project (AMAP): A Preliminary Report on Fieldwork, 2014–2017," *Hesperia* 89, pp. 659–723.

Morrison, J. S., J. F. Coates, and N. B. Rankov. 2000. *The Athenian Trireme: The History and Reconstruction of an Ancient Greek Warship*, 2nd ed., Cambridge.

Moschonissioti, S. 2010. "Child Burials at the Seaside Cemetery of Ancient Mende," in *L'enfant et la mort dans l'Antiquité* 1: *Nouvelles recherches dans les nécropoles grecques. Le signalement des tombes d'enfants (Actes d'une table ronde, Athènes, École française d'Athènes, 29–30 May 2008)*, ed. A. De Boccard, M. Guimier-Sorbets, and Y. Morizot, Paris, pp. 207–225.

———. 2012. "Αρχαϊκή κεραμική από το ιερό του Ποσειδώνα στο Ποσείδι της Χαλκιδικής," in Tiverios et al. 2012, pp. 385–398.

Moschonissioti, S., A. Pentedeka, E. Kiriatzi, and M. Mexi. 2005. "Πετρογραφικές αναλύσεις Γεωμετρικής και Πρώιμης Αρχαϊκής κεραμικής από το νεκροταφείο της αρχαίας Μένδης. Μερικές σκέψεις για την παραγωγή και διακίνηση κεραμικής στην κεντρική Μακεδονία," *AEMTh* 19 [2007], pp. 249–267.

Motsianos, I., and E. Bintsi, eds. 2011. *Light on Light: An Illuminating Catalogue* (Exhibition catalogue, Folklife and Ethnological Museum of Macedonia-Thrace, 31 October 2011–11 June 2012), Thessaloniki.

Mountjoy, P. A. 1981. *Four Early Mycenaean Wells from the South Slope of the Acropolis at Athens*, Gent.

———. 1986. *Mycenaean Decorated Pottery: A Guide to Identification*, Göteborg.

———. 1993. *Mycenaean Pottery: An Introduction*, Oxford.

———. 1999. *Regional Mycenaean Decorated Pottery*, Rahden/Westfalen.

Mourati, A. 2014. "Σκεύη και εργαλεία από το 'Κομπολόι.' Συμβολή στη μελέτη μιας αγροικίας ελληνιστικών χρόνων από τη Πιερία" (MA thesis, Aristotle Univ. Thessaloniki).

Muller, A. 2012. "The Other Greece: The Archaeology of Macedonia," in *Ancient Macedonia: Language, History, Culture*, ed. G. K. Giannakis, Thessaloniki, pp. 101–119.

Müller, S. 2010. "Philip II," in *A Companion to Ancient Macedonia*, ed. J. Roisman and I. Worthington, Oxford, pp. 166–185.

Müller-Karpe, H. 1959. *Beiträge zur Chronologie der Urnenfelderzeit Nördlich und Südlich der Alpen*, Berlin.

———. 1962. "Die Metallbeigaben der früheisenzeitlichen Kerameikos-Gräber," *JdI* 77, pp. 59–129.

Mulliez, D. 1982. "Notes sur le transport du bois," *BCH* 106, pp. 107–118.

Munaretto, M., and G. P. Schaus. 2014. "Constructing the Sanctuary: Iron Nails for Building and Binding," in Schaus 2014a, pp. 184–192.

Mureddu, P. 1972. "Χρυσεῖα a Pithecussai," *PP* 27, pp. 407–409.

Muros, V., and D. A. Scott. 2014. "Analytical Studies of the Metal Objects from Lofkënd," *The Excavation of the Prehistoric Burial Tumulus at Lofkënd, Albania*, ed. Papadopoulos et al., Los Angeles, pp. 389–410.

Murray, O. 1980. *Early Greece*, Brighton.

———. 2016. "The Symposion between East and West," in *The Cup of Song: Studies on Poetry and the Symposion*, ed. V. Cazzato, D. Obbink, and E. E. Prodi, Oxford, pp. 17–27.

Muscarella, O. W. 1967. *Phrygian Fibulae from Gordion*, London.

Mylona, D. 2014. "Aquatic Animal Resources in Prehistoric Aegean, Greece," *Journal of Biological Research—Thessaloniki* 21(2), http://www.jbiolres.com/content/21/1/2.

Mylonas, G. E. 1973. *Ὁ ταφικὸς κύκλος Β τῶν Μυκηνῶν*, Athens.

———. 1975. *Τὸ δυτικὸν νεκροταφεῖον τῆς Ἐλευσῖνος*, Athens.

Myres, J. L. 1930. *Who Were the Greeks?* Berkeley.

Nakassis, D. 2013. *Individuals and Society in Mycenaean Pylos* (*Mnemosyne* Suppl. 357), Leiden.

Nankov, E. 2004–2005. "Preliminary Observations on the Use of Artillery on the Early Hellenistic Fortifications at Halai in Opountian Lokris: New Evidence," in *Anodos: Studies of the Ancient World* 4–5: *Proceedings of the International Symposium Arms and Armour through the Ages (from the Bronze Age to the Late Antiquity), Modra-Harmónia, 19th–22nd November 2005*, pp. 165–174.

———. 2015. "The Mobility of Macedonian Army in Thrace during the Reign of Philip II and the Inscribed Lead Sling Bullets from Kozi Gramadi," *Bulgarian e-Journal of Archaeology* 5, pp. 1–13.

———. 2016. "Inscribed Lead Sling Bullets from the Regional Museum of History in Shumen: New Data on the Macedonian Campaigns in the Lands of the Getae in the Time of Philip II and Alexander III," in *Тракия и Околният Свят. Сборник с доклади от Национална научна конференция, 27–29 октомври 2016,* ed. I. Marazov, Shumen, pp. 282–293.

Nantet, E. 2010. "Les épaves du VIIe siècle: Un témoignage sur les échanges maritimes à l'époque archaïque," in *La Méditerranée au VIIe siècle av. J.-C. (essais d'analyses archéologiques)* (Travaux de la Maison René Ginouvès 7), ed. R. Étienne, Paris, pp. 96–109.

Naso, A. 2005. "Funde aus Milet XIX: Anfore commerciali arcaiche a Mileto: rapporto preliminare," *AA* 2005, pp. 75–84.

Naveh, J. 1982. *Early History of the Alphabet: An Introduction to West Semitic Epigraphy and Palaeography*, Jerusalem.

Nease, A. S. 1949. "Garrisons in the Athenian Empire," *Phoenix* 3, pp. 102–111.

Nedev, D., and M. Gyuzelev. 2011. "The 6th Century BC Chian White-slipped Amphorae from Apollonia (Results of the Most Recent Archaeological Investigations)," in *PATABS* 2: *Production and Trade of Amphorae in the Black Sea. Acts of the International Round Table Held in Kiten, Nessebar and Sredetz, September 26–30, 2007*, ed. C. Tzochev, T. Stoyanov, and. A. Bozkova, Sofia, pp. 63–71.

Neeft, C. W. 1975. "Corinthian Fragments from Argos at Utrecht and the Corinthian Late Geometric Kotyle," *BABesch* 50, pp. 97–134.

Neils, J. 1994. "Priamos," *LIMC* 7, Zürich, pp. 516–520.

Newton, M., K. A. Wardle, and P. I. Kuniholm. 2003. "Dendrochronology and Radiocarbon Determinations of the Greek Iron Age," *AEMTh* 17 [2005], pp. 173–190.

Nichoria III = W. A. McDonald, W. D. E. Coulson, and J. Rosser, eds., *Excavations at Nichoria in Southwest Greece* III: *Dark Age and Byzantine Occupation*, Minneapolis 1983.

Nicolaou, I. 1977. "Inscriptiones cypriae alphabeticae XVI, 1976," *RDAC* 1977, pp. 209–221.

———. 1979. "Inscriptiones cypriae alphabeticae XVIII, 1978," *RDAC* 1979, pp. 344–351.

———. 1985. "Inscriptiones cypriae alphabeticae XXIV, 1984," *RDAC* 1985, pp. 325–334.

Niemeyer, H. G. 2006. "The Phoenicians in the Mediterranean: Between Expansion and Colonization. A Non-Greek Model of Overseas Settlement and Presence," in *Greek Colonisation: An Account of Greek Colonies and Other Settlement Overseas* 1, ed. G. R. Tsetskhladze, Boston and Leiden, pp. 143–168.

Nieto, X. 2008. "L'arquitectura del vaixell," in *El vaixell grec arcaic de Cala Sant Vicenç* (Monografies del CASC 7), ed. X. Nieto and M. Santos, Girona, pp. 23–64.

Nikolaïdou, D. 2010. "Ανάλυση και μελέτη ζωοαρχαιολογικού υλικού από την Τούμπα Θεσσαλονίκης (Τομή 761, Κτήριο Ζ, Δρόμος Χ1)" (diss. Aristotle Univ. Thessaloniki).

Nikolaïdou, M. 2003a. "Items of Adornment," in *Sitagroi* 2, pp. 331–360.

———. 2003b. "Miniatures and Models," in *Sitagroi* 2, pp. 431–442.

Nikolaïdou, M., E. S. Elster, and J. M. Renfrew. 2013. "Sitagroi in 2013: A Fresh Evaluation of Wild Resource Exploitation during the Neolithic and Early Bronze Age," *Backdirt: Annual Review of the Cotsen Institute of Archaeology at UCLA* 2013, pp. 54–69.

Nikolaïdou, M., N. Merousis, A. Papanthimou, and A. Papasteriou. 2003. "From *Metron* to Context in Neolithic/Early Bronze Age Mandalon, Northwestern Greece: The Example of Ceramics," in *METRON: Measuring the Aegaean Bronze Age. Proceedings of the 9th International Aegean Conference/9e Rencontre égéenne internationale, Yale University, 18 21 April 2002* (*Aegaeum* 24), ed. K. P. Foster and R. Laffineur, Liège, pp. 317–326.

Nikolaïdou-Patera, M. 2007. "Συμποτικά αγγεία από τον Φάγρητα," in *Οἶνον ἱστορῶ* 7: *Στα οινόπεδα του Παγγαίου*, ed. G. A. Pikoulas, Athens, pp. 87–96.

Noble, J. V. 1988. *The Techniques of Painted Attic Pottery*, London.

Nordquist, G. C. 1987. *A Middle Helladic Village: Asine in the Argolid*, Uppsala and Stockholm.

Novotná, M. 2001. *Die Fibeln in der Slowakei* (*PBF* XIV.11), Munich.

Ntinou, M. 2002. *La Paleovegetación en el Norte de Grecia Desde el Tardiglaciar Hasta el Atlántico: Formaciones Vegetales, Recursos y Usos* (*BAR-IS* 1038), Oxford.

Oakley, J. H. 2004. *Picturing Death in Classical Athens: The Evidence of the White Lekythoi*, Cambridge.

———. 2010. "Barbarians on Attic White Lekythoi," in *Il greco, il barbaro e la ceramica attica: Immaginario del diverso, processi di scambio e autorappresentazione degli indigeni* 1, ed. F. Giudice and R. Panvini, Rome, pp. 93–100.

Oakley, J. H., W. D. E. Coulson, and O. Palagia, eds. 1997. *Athenian Potters and Painters: The Conference Proceedings*, Oxford.

Oettli, M. 1994. "Importierte Handelsamphoren archaischer und klassischer Zeit von der 'Doppelten Trapeza' von Anchialos (in der Nähe des heutigen Sindos)" (diss. Univ. of Basel).

O'Halloran, B. 2019. *The Political Economy of Classical Athens: A Naval Perspective*, Leiden.

Oikonomaki, A. 2010. "Τα τοπικά αλφάβητα της Κρήτης στην αρχαϊκή και κλασική περίοδο" (diss. Aristotle Univ. Thessaloniki).

———. 2017. "Local 'Literacies' in the Making: Early Alphabetic Writing and Modern Literacy Theories," in Strauss Clay, Malkin, and Tzifopoulos 2017b, pp. 261–284.

OlForsch = *Olympische Forschungen. Deutsches Archäologisches Institut*, Berlin

I = E. Kunze and H. Schlief, eds., *Olympische Forschungen* 1, 1944.

III = F. Willemsen, *Dreifusskessel von Olympia. Alte und neue Funde*, 1957.

IX = P. C. Bol, *Grossplastik aus Bronze in Olympia*, 1978.

X = M. Maas, *Die geometrischen Dreifüsse von Olympia*, 1978.

XII = W.-D. Heilmeyer, *Frühe olympische Bronzefiguren: Die Tiervotive*, 1979.

XIII = H. Philipp, *Bronzeschmuck aus Olympia*, 1981.

XVIII = W. Schiering, *Die Werkstatt des Pheidias in Olympia* 2, 1991.

XX = W. Gauer, *Die Bronzegefässe von Olympia* 1. *Kessel und Becken mit Untersätzen, Teller, Kratere, Hydrien, Eimer, Situlen und Cisten, Schöpfhumpen und verschiedenes Gerät*, 1991.

XXV = K. Hitzl, *Die Gewichte griechischer Zeit aus Olympia*, 1996.

XXXII = H. Baitinger and T. Völling, *Werkzeug und Gerät aus Olympia*, 2007.

Olofsson, L., E. Andersson Strand, and M.-L. Nosch. 2015. "Experimental Testing of Bronze Age Textile Tools," in *Tools, Textiles and Contexts: Investigating Textile Production in the Aegean and Eastern Mediterranean Bronze Age* (Ancient Textile Series 21), ed. E. Andersson Strand and M.-L. Nosch, Oxford and Philadelphia, pp. 75–100.

Olson, B. R. 2014. "A Contextual and Epigraphic Analysis of the Inscribed Glandes (Sling Bullets) from Vigla," in *Pyla-Koutsopetria* 1: *Archaeological Survey of an Ancient Coastal Town* (American Schools of Oriental Research, Archeological Reports 21), ed. W. Caraher, R. Scott Moore, and D. K. Pettegrew, Boston, pp. 155–164.

Olympia IV = A. Furtwängler, *Die Bronzen und die übrigen kleineren Funde*, Berlin 1890.

Olynthus = *Excavations at Olynthus Conducted by The Johns Hopkins University Expedition under the Auspices of the American School of Classical Studies at Athens, Greece*, Baltimore

I = G. E. Mylonas, *The Neolithic Settlement*, 1929.

II = D. M. Robinson, *Architecture and Sculpture: Houses and Other Buildings*, 1930.

V = D. M. Robinson, *Mosaics, Vases, and Lamps of Olynthus Found in 1928 and 1931*, 1933.

VIII = D. M. Robinson and J. W. Graham, *The Hellenic House: A Study of the Houses Found at Olynthus with a Detailed Account of Those Excavated in 1931 and 1934*, 1938.

X = D. M. Robinson, *Metal and Minor Miscellaneous Finds*, 1941.

XIII = D. M. Robinson, *Vases Found in 1934 and 1938*, 1950.

XIV = D. M. Robinson, *Terracottas, Lamps and Coins Found in 1934 and 1938*, 1952.

Onassoglou, A. 1981. "Οι γεωμετρικοί τάφοι της Τραγάνας στην ανατολική Λοκρίδα," *ArchDelt* 36Α′ (Mel.), pp. 1–57.

———. 1995. *Ἡ Οικία του Τάφου τῶν Τριπόδων στὶς Μυκῆνες*, Athens.

O'Neil, E. N. 2004. *Plutarch: Moralia. Index* (Loeb Classical Library 499), Cambridge, Mass. and London.

Orchomenos = Bayerische Akademie der Wissenschaften (BAW), Munich

IV = K. Sarri, *Orchomenos in der mittleren Bronzezeit* (BAW 135), 2010.

V = P. A. Mountjoy, *Mycenaean Pottery from Orchomenos, Eutresis and Other Boeotian Sites* (BAW 89), 1983.

Orlandini, P. 1978. "Ceramiche della grecia dell'est a Gela," in *Les céramiques de la Grèce de l'est et leur diffusion en occident. Centre Jean Bérard, Institut Français de Naples, 6–9 juillet 1976*, Paris, pp. 93–98.

Orlandos, A. K., ed. 1960. *Τὸ Ἔργον τῆς Ἀρχαιολογικῆς Ἑταιρείας κατὰ τὸ 1960*, Athens.

———, ed. 1961. *Τὸ Ἔργον τῆς Ἀρχαιολογικῆς Ἑταιρείας κατὰ τὸ 1961*, Athens.

———. 1966. *Les matériaux de construction et la technique architecturale des anciens Grecs*, Part 1, Paris.

———. 1967–1968. *Ἡ Αρκαδική, Ἀλίφειρα καὶ τα μνημεία της*, Athens.

———. 1968. *Les matériaux de construction et la technique architecturale des anciens Grecs*, Part 2, Paris.

Orsi, P. 1911. "Rapporto preliminare sulla quinta campagna di scavi nelle Calabrie durante l'anno 1910," *NSc* 1911, supplemento.

———. 1913. "Scavi di Calabria nel 1913 (relazione preliminare)," *NSc* 1913, supplemento, pp. 3–145.

———. 1914. "Caulonia. Campagne archeologische del 1912, 1913 e 1915," *MontAnt* 23, cols. 685–948.

———. 1917. "Campagne di scavo degli anni 1914 e 1915 nella necropolis di Locri Epizefiri," *NSc* 1917, pp. 101–167.

———. 1926. "Le necropolis preelleniche calabresi di Torre Galli e di Canale Janchina, Patarita," *MontAnt* 31, cols. 1–376.

———. 1933. *Templum Apollinis Alaei ad Crimisa Promontorium*, Rome.

Osborne, R. 1996. "Pots, Trade and the Archaic Greek Economy," *Antiquity* 70, pp. 31–44.

———. 1998. "Early Greek Colonization? The Nature of Greek Settlement in the West," in *Archaic Greece: New Approaches and New Evidence*, ed. N. Fisher and H. van Wees, London, pp. 251–269.

———. 2008. "Colonial Cancer," *JMA* 21, pp. 281–284.

———. 2016. "Greek 'Colonisation': What Was, and What Is, at Stake?" in *Conceptualising Early Colonisation*, ed. L. Donnellan, V. Nizzo, and G.-J. Burgers, Brussels, pp. 21–26.

Ouellet, K. 2021. "Argilos et les défenses en briques crues: étude comparative des fortifications en adobe dans le nord de la Grèce," in *Argilos 3: Argilos, 25 années des recherches. Organisation de la ville et de la campagne dans le Nord de l'Égée, VIIIe–IIIe siècles av. n.è., Actes du colloque de Thessalonique, 25–27 mai 2017* (Publications de l'Institut canadien en Grèce, No. 13), ed. Z. Bonias and J.-Y. Perreault, Athens, pp. 279–313.

Özer, B. 2004. "Clazomenian and Related Black-Figured Pottery from Klazomenai: Preliminary Observations," in *Klazomenai, Teos and Abdera: Metropoleis and Colony. Proceedings of the International Symposium Held at the Archaeological Museum of Abdera, Abdera, 20–21 October 2001*, ed. A. Moustaka, E. Skarlatidou, M.-C. Tzannes, and Y. E. Ersoy, Thessaloniki, 199–219.

Özgünel, C. 2003. "Geometrische Keramik von Alt-Smyrna aus der Akurgal-Grabung," in *Probleme der Keramikchronologie des südlichen und westlichen Kleinasiens in geometrischer und archaischer Zeit. Internationales Kolloquium, Tübingen 24.3.–26.3.1998*, ed. B. Rückert and F. Kolb, Bonn, pp. 69–89.

Pacala, S. W., C. D. Canham, J. A. Silander, and R. K. Kobe. 1994. "Sapling Growth as a Function of Resources in a North Temperate Forest," *Canadian Journal of Forest Research* 24, pp. 2172–2183.

Pache, C. O. 2001. "Barbarian Bond: Thracian Bendis Among the Athenians," in *Between Magic and Religion: Interdisciplinary Studies in Ancient Mediterranean Religion and Society*, ed. S. R. Asirvatham, C. O. Pache, and J. Watrous, Lanham, pp. 3–12.

Pairman Brown, J. 2000. *Israel and Hellas* 2: *Sacred Institutions with Roman Counterparts* (Beihefte zur Zeitschrift für die alttestamentliche Wissenschaft 276), Berlin and New York.

Palagia, O. 2008. "Marble Carving Techniques," in *Greek Sculpture: Function, Materials, and Techniques in the Archaic and Classical Period*, ed. O. Palagia, Cambridge, pp. 243–279.

Palaiokrassa, L. 1991. *Τὸ ἱερὸ τῆς Ἀρτέμιδος Μουνιχίας*, Athens.

Palma, P., and L. N. Santhakumaran. 2014. *Shipwrecks and Global "Worming,"* Oxford.

Panagou, T. M. 2010. "Η σφράγιση των αρχαίων ελληνικών εμπορικών αμφορέων: Κέντρα παραγωγής και συνθετική αξιολόγηση" (diss. Univ. of Athens).

Panajiotidis, S., A. Gerasimidis, and G. Fotiadis. 2009. "Variation in Quantitative Pollen Parameters of *Pinus nigra* and *P. sylvestris* (*Pinaceae*) Populations of Mts Pieria (N Greece)," in *Plant, Fungal and Habitat Diversity Investigation and Conservation. Proceedings of IV Balkan Botanical Congress, Sofia, 20–26 June 2006*, ed. D. Ivanova, Sofia, pp. 23–25.

Panayotou-Triantaphyllopoulou, A. 2017. "The Impact of Late Geometric Greek Inscriptions from Methone on Understanding the Development of Early Euboean Alphabet," in Strauss Clay, Malkin, and Tzifopoulos 2017b, pp. 232–241.

Panighello, S., E. F. Orsega, J. T. van Elteren, and V. S. Šelih. 2012. "Analysis of Polychrome Iron Age Glass Vessels from Mediterranean I, II and III Groups by LA-ICP-MS," *JAS* 39, pp. 2945–2955.

Pantelidou-Gofa, M. 2016. *Τσέπι Μαραθώνος. Ο Αποθέτης 39 του προϊστορικού νεκροταφείου* (Βιβλιοθήκη της εν Αθήναις Αρχαιολογικής Εταιρείας 310), Athens.

Pantermali, E., and E. Trakosopoulou. 1995. "Καραμπουρνάκι 1995. Η ανασκαφή της ΙΣΤ΄ ΕΠΚΑ," *AEMTh* 9 [1998], pp. 283–292.

Pantermalis, D. 2000. "ΒΑΣΙΛΕ[ΩΣ ΔΗΜΗΤΡ]ΙΟΥ," in *ΜΥΡΤΟΣ. Μελέτες στην μνήμη Ιουλίας Βοτοκοπούλου*, ed. P. Adam-Veleni, Thessaloniki, pp. xviii–xxii.

Panti, A. 2008. "Τοπική κεραμική από τη Χαλκιδική και το μυχό του Θερμαϊκού Κόλπου (Άκανθος, Καραμπουρνάκι, Σίνδος)" (diss. Aristotle Univ. Thessaloniki).

———. 2013. "Τεφρή κεραμική από το νεκροταφείο της Θέρμης νομού Θεσσαλονίκης," in Adam-Veleni, Kefalidou, and Tsiafaki 2013, pp. 193–200.

Papadakis, M. 1994. *Ilias- und Iliupersisdarstellungen auf frühen rotfigurigen Vasen*, Frankfurt am Main.

Papadakis, N. P. 1984. "Παραδόσεις αρχαίων αντικειμένων από ιδιώτες στη Σητεία (Γ΄)," *Αμάλθεια* 15, pp. 133–142.

Papadimitriou, G. D. 2008. "Η παραγωγή μολύβδου στο αρχαίο Λαύριο στη διάρκεια των κλασικών και των ρωμαϊκών χρόνων," in *Πρακτικά Θ΄ Επιστημονικής Συνάντησης ΝΑ. Αττικής, Λαύριο Αττικής, 13–16 Απριλίου 2000*, Kalyvia Thorikou, pp. 111–127.

Papadimitriou, N., and Z. Tsirtsoni, eds. 2010. *Η Ελλάδα στο ευρύτερο πολιτισμικό πλαίσιο των Βαλκανίων κατά την 5η και 4η χιλιετία π.Χ. Έκδοση με την ευκαιρία της έκθεσης "Το ξεχασμένο παρελθόν της Ευρώπης. Η κοιλάδα του Δούναβη, 5000–3500 π.Χ. και οι σχέσεις της Ελλάδας με τα Βαλκάνια στη Νεολιθική Εποχή,"* Athens.

Papadogiannaki, E. 2007. "Τα επιφωνήματα στην ποίηση από την αρχαϊκή ως την κλασική εποχή: η σημασία και η λειτουργία τους" (diss. Univ. of Crete).

Papadopoulos, J. K. 1989. "An Early Iron Age Potter's Kiln at Torone," *MeditArch* 2, pp. 9–44.

———. 1994. "Early Iron Age Potters' Marks in the Aegean," *Hesperia* 63, pp. 437–507.

———. 1996. "Euboians in Macedonia? A Closer Look," *OJA* 15, pp. 151–181.

———. 1997. "Phantom Euboians," *JMA* 10, pp. 191–219.

———. 1998. "From Macedonia to Sardinia: Problems of Iron Age Chronology and Assumptions of Greek Maritime Primacy," in *Sardinia and Aegean Chronology: Toward the Resolution of Relative and Absolute Dating in the Mediterranean*, ed. M. S. Balmuth and R. H. Tykot, Oxford, pp. 363–369.

———. 2001. "The Bronze Age Pottery," in *Torone* 1, pp. 273–291.

———. 2002a. "Minting Identity: Coinage, Ideology and the Economics of Colonization in Akhaian Magna Graecia," *CAJ* 12 (1), pp. 21–55.

———. 2002b. "Παίζω ἢ χέζω?: A Contextual Approach to *Pessoi* (Gaming Pieces, Counters, or Convenient Wipes?" *Hesperia* 71, pp. 423–427.

———. 2003a. *La dea di Sibari e il santuario ritrovato: Studi sui rinvenimenti dal Timpone Motta di Francavilla Marittima* 2.1: *The Archaic Votive Metal Objects* (*Bollettino d'Arte*, special volume), Rome.

———. 2003b. *Ceramicus Redivivus: The Early Iron Age Potters' Field in the Area of Classical Athenian Agora* (*Hesperia* Suppl. 31), Princeton.

———. 2005. *The Early Iron Age Cemetery at Torone* (Monumenta Archaeologica 24), Los Angeles.

———. 2011. "'Phantom Euboians'—A Decade On," in *Euboea and Athens. Proceedings of a Colloquium in Memory of Malcolm B. Wallace, Athens 26–27 June 2009*, ed. D. W. Rupp and J. E. Tomlinson, Athens, pp. 113–133.

———. 2012. "Money, Art, and the Construction of Value in the Ancient Mediterranean," in *The Construction of Value in the Ancient World*, ed. J. K. Papadopoulos and G. Urton, Los Angeles, pp. 261–287.

———. 2015. "The Charitonidis Class: A Group of Large Athenian Late Protogeometric Skyphoi," *OpAthRom* 8, pp. 7–26.

———. 2016. "The Early History of the Greek Alphabet: The New Evidence from Eretria and Methone," *Antiquity* 90 (353), pp. 1238–1254.

———. 2017a. "To Write and to Paint: More Early Iron Age Potters' Marks in the Aegean," in Strauss Clay, Malkin, and Tzifopoulos, pp. 36–104.

———. 2017b. "An Epirote Pastoral: Wind Instruments in Tombs in Epirus," in *Σπείρα. Επιστημονική συνάντηση προς τιμήν της Αγγέλικας Ντούζουγλη και του Κωνσταντίνου Ζάχου. Πρακτικά*, ed. E. Merminka, Athens, pp. 265–278.

———. 2021a. "The Painter of Athens 897: An Athenian Late Geometric Vase-Painter at Home and Abroad," in *Ἔξοχος ἄλλων. Τιμητικός τόμος για την Ε. Σημαντώνη-Μπουρνιά*, ed. V. Lambrinoudakis, L. Mendoni, M. Koutsoumbou, T.-M. Panagou, A. Sfyroera, and X. Charalambidou, Athens, pp. 591–608.

———. 2021b. "Torone and Its Colonial Experiences: Thoughts on the Early History of the North Aegean," in *Άργιλος, 25 Χρόνια Έρευνας. Οργάνωση Πόλης και Χώρας στις Αποικίες του Βορείου Αιγαίου, 8ος–3ος αι. π.Χ.*, ed. Z. Bonias and J.-Y. Perreault, Athens, pp. 423–449.

———. 2022. "Greeks, Phoenicians, Phrygians, Trojans, and Other Creatures in the Aegean: Connections, Interactions, Misconceptions," in *The Connected Iron Age: Interregional Networks in the Eastern Mediterranean, 900–600 BCE*, ed. J. Osborne and J. R. Hall, Chicago, pp. 142-168.

Papadopoulos, J. K., G. M. Cross, R. E. Jones, and L. Sharpe. 1999. "The Prehistoric Fortifications of Torone," in *POLEMOS: Le contexte Guerrier en Égée à l'Âge du Bronze. Actes de la 7e Rencontre égéenne internationale Université de Liège, 14–17 avril 1998 (Aegaeum 19)*, ed. R. Laffineur, Liege, pp. 163–170.

Papadopoulos, J. K., B. N. Damiata, and J. M. Marston. 2011. "Once More with Feeling: Jeremy Rutter's Plea for the Abandonment of the Term 'Submycenaean' Revisited," in *Our Cups are Full: Pottery and Society in the Aegean Bronze Age*, ed. W. Gauss, M. Lindblom, A. Smith, and J. Wright, Oxford, pp. 187–202.

Papadopoulos, J. K., and R. Kurti. 2014. "Objects of Terracotta, Metal (Gold/Electrum, Bronze, Iron, and Bimetallic), Semiprecious Stone, Faience, Glass, and Worked Bone," in Papadopoulos et. al., *The Excavation of the Prehistoric Burial Tumulus at Lofkënd, Albania*, Los Angeles, pp. 325–388.

Papadopoulos, J., S. P. Morris, L. Bejko, and L. A. Schepartz. 2014. *The Excavation of the Prehistoric Burial Tumulus at Lofkënd, Albania*, Los Angeles.

Papadopoulos, J. K., and S. A. Paspalas. 1999. "Mendaian as Chalkidian Wine," *Hesperia* 68, pp. 161–188.

Papadopoulos, J. K., J. F. Vedder, and T. Schreiber. 1998. "Drawing Circles: Experimental Archaeology and the Pivoted Multiple Brush," *AJA* 102, pp. 507–529.

Papadopoulos, S. 2002. *Η μετάβαση από τη Νεολιθική στην Εποχή του Χαλκού στην ανατολική Μακεδονία* (Δημοσιεύματα του Αρχαιολογικού Δελτίου 82), Athens.

———. 2007. "Decline of the Painted Pottery in Eastern Macedonia and North Aegean at the End of the Final Neolithic/Chalcolithic Period," in *The Struma/Strymon River Valley in Prehistory: In the Steps of James Harvey Gaul* 2, ed. H. Todorova, M. Stefanovich, and G. Ivanov, Sofia, pp. 317–328.

Papadopoulos, S., G. Aristodimou, D. Kouyioumtzoglou, and F. Megaloudi. 2001. "Η Τελική Νεολιθική και η Πρώιμη Εποχή του Χαλκού στη Θάσο: η ανασκαφική έρευνα στις θέσεις Άγιος Ιωάννης και Σκάλα Σωτήρος," *AEMTh* 15 [2005], pp. 55–65.

Papadopoulos, S., and A. Bechtsi. 2003. "Ανασκαφικές και επιφανειακές έρευνες σε προϊστορικές θέσεις της Θάσου," *AEMTh* 17 [2005], pp. 61–68.

Papadopoulos, S., and D. Malamidou. 2000. "Οι πρώιμες φάσεις κατοίκησης του νεολιθικού οικισμού των Λιμεναρίων," *AEMTh* 14 [2002], pp. 25–32.

Papadopoulos, S., O. Palli, S. Vakirtzi, and E. Psathi. 2018. "Ayios Ioannis, Thasos: The Economy of a Small Coastal Site Dated to the Second Half of the 4th Millennium BC," in *Communities in Transition: The Circum-Aegean Area During the 5th and 4th Millennia BC*, ed. S. Dietz, F. Mavridis, Z. Tankosič, and. T. Takaoglu, Oxford, pp. 357–366.

Papadopoulos, S., V. Papalazarou, and S. Tsoutsoumpei-Lioliou. 2007. "Νέα δεδομένα από τον οικισμό της Σκάλας Σωτήρος Θάσου," *AEMTh* 21 [2010], pp. 427–433.

Papadopoulou, D., A. Sakalis, N. Tsirlinganis, and N. Merousis. 2006. "Μελέτη διακοσμημένης νεολιθικής κεραμικής από την τούμπα στον Πολυπλάτανο Ημαθίας με τη μέθοδο της μικρο-φθορισμομετρίας ακτίνων X," *AEMTh* 20 [2008], pp. 780–794.

Papaefthymiou-Papanthimou, A. 1973. "Μινωική μήτρα από τον Πόρο Ηρακλείου," *Κρητικά Χρονικά* 25, pp. 375–396.

———. 1979. *Σκεύη και σύνεργα του καλλωπισμού στον κρητομυκηναϊκό χώρο*, Thessaloniki.

Papaefthymiou-Papanthimou, A., and E. Papadopoulou. 2014. "Αρχοντικό Γιαννιτσών, ένας οικισμός της Πρώιμης Εποχής του Χαλκού στη Μακεδονία," in Stefani, Merousis, and Dimoula 2014, pp. 271–280.

Papaefthymiou-Papanthimou, A., and A. Pilali-Papasteriou. 1988. "Ανασκαφή στο Μάνδαλο (1988)," *AEMTh* 2 [1991], pp. 127–135.

———. 1997. *Οδοιπορικό στην προϊστορική Μακεδονία/Prehistoric Macedonia: An Itinerary*, Thessaloniki.

Papakonstantinou-Diamantourou, D. 1997. "Μετάλλινα αντικείμενα από την Πέλλα Β΄: μολυβδίδες," in *Μνήμη Μανόλη Ανδρόνικου* (Παράρτημα Μακεδονικών 6), Thessaloniki, pp. 253–261.

Papakostas, Th. 2013. "Τοπική κεραμεική από το νεκροταφείο της Αγίας Παρασκευής Θεσσαλονίκης," in *Κεραμικά Εργαστήρια στο Βορειοανατολικό Αιγαίο (8ος-αρχές 5ου αι. π. Χ.)*, pp. 167–172.

Papathanasiou, V. 2020. "Σκελετικά κατάλοιπα και ταφικές πρακτικές στη Μακεδονία στην Ύστερη Εποχή του Χαλκού: Η περίπτωση της Μεθώνης Πιερίας" (MA thesis, Aristotle Univ. Thessaloniki).

Papathanassopoulos, G. A., ed. 1996. *Neolithic Culture in Greece*, Athens.

Papazoglou, F. 1988. *Les villes de Macédoine à l'époque romaine* (*BCH* Suppl. 16), Paris.

Pappa, E. 2013. *Early Iron Age Exchange in the West: Phoenicians in the Mediterranean and the Atlantic* (*Ancient Near Eastern Studies* Supplement 43), Leuven, Paris, and Walpole.

Pappa, M. 1990. "Εγκατάσταση Εποχής Χαλκού στο Πολύχρονο Χαλκιδικής," *AEMTh* 4 [1993], pp. 385–398.

———. 1992. "Τούμπα Αγίου Μάμαντος Χαλκιδικής: ανασκαφή νεκροταφείων," *AEMTh* 6 [1995], pp. 475–484.

———. 2007. "Neolithic Societies: Recent Evidence from Northern Greece," in *The Struma/Strymon River Valley in Prehistory: In the Steps of James Harvey Gaul* 2, ed. H. Todorova, M. Stefanovich, and G. Ivanov, Sofia, pp. 257–269.

———. 2010. "Το νεκροταφείο της Πρώιμης Εποχής του Χαλκού στην τούμπα του Αγίου Μάμαντος," in Hänsel and Aslanis 2010, pp. 382–440.

———. 2017. "Νομός Πιερίας," in *Αρχαιολογία—Μακεδονίας και Θράκης*, ed. A. Vlachopoulos and D. Tsiafaki, Athens, pp. 146–149.

Pappa, M., and M. Bessios. 1999. "The Neolithic Settlement at Makrygialos, Pieria, Greece," *JFA* 26 (2), pp. 177–195.

Pappa, M., P. Halstead, K. Kotsakis, A. Bogaard, R. Fraser, V. Isaakidou, I. Mainland, D. Mylona, K. Skourtopoulou, S. Triantafyllou, C. Tsoraki, D. Urem-Kotsou, S. M. Valamoti, and R. Veropoulidou. 2013. "The Neolithic Site of Makrygialos, Northern Greece: A Reconstruction of the Social and Economic Structure of the Settlement Through a Comparative Study of the Finds," in *Diet, Economy and Society in the Ancient Greek World: Towards a Better Integration of Archaeology and Science. Proceedings of the International Conference Held at the Netherlands Institute at Athens on 22–24 March 2010* (*Pharos* Suppl. 1), ed. S. Voutsaki and S. M. Valamoti, Leuven, pp. 77–88.

Pappa, M., P. Halstead, K. Kotsakis, and D. Urem-Kotsou. 2004. "Evidence for Large-scale Feasting at Late Neolithic Makrygialos, N. Greece," in *Food, Cuisine and Society in Prehistoric Greece*, ed. P. Halstead and J. C. Barrett (Sheffield Studies in Aegean Archaeology 5), Oxford, pp. 16–44.

Pappa, M., S. Nanoglou, and M. Efthymiadou. 2016. "Appendix 1. Vasilika, Kyparissi: A Preliminary Report on the 2013–2015 Rescue Excavation Project," in *The Anthemous Valley Archaeological Project: A Preliminary Report*, ed. S. Andreou, J, Czebreszuk, and M. Pappa, Poznan, pp. 261–278.

Pappa, M., and R. Veropoulidou. 2011. "The Neolithic Settlement at Makrygialos, Northern Greece: Evidence from the *Spondylus Gaederopus* Artifacts," in *Spondylus in Prehistory: New Data and Approaches. Contributions to the Archaeology of Shell Technologies* (*BAR-IS* 2216), ed. F. Ifantidis and M. Nikolaïdou, Oxford, pp. 105–121.

Pappas, A. 2017. "Form Follows Function? Toward an Aesthetics of Early Greek Inscriptions at Methone," in Strauss Clay, Malkin, and Tzifopoulos, pp. 285–308.

Pardalidou, Ch. 2012. "Κεραμική αρχαϊκών χρόνων από το ιερό του Απόλλωνα στην αρχαία Ζώνη νομού Έβρου," in Tiverios et al. 2012, pp. 425–435.

Paris, P. 1892. *Élatée. La ville, le temple d'Athéna Cranaia*, Paris.

Parker, A. J. 2001. "Maritime Landscapes," *Landscapes* 2:1, pp. 22–41.

Parker, H. N. 2008. "The Linguistic Case for the Aiolian Migration Reconsidered," *Hesperia* 77, pp. 431–464.

Parlama, L., and N. C. Stampolides, eds. 2000. *The City Beneath the City: Antiquities from the Metropolitan Railway Excavations*, Athens.

Parlama, L. M., S. Theochari, S. Bonatos, Ch. Romaiou, and Y. Manos. 2010. "Παλαμάρι Σκύρου· η πόλη της Μέσης Χαλκοκρατίας," in *Mesohelladika: La Grèce continental au Bronze Moyen*, ed. A. Philippa-Touchais, G. Touchais, S. Voutsaki, and J. Wright, Paris, pp. 281–289.

Pasayiannis, G. 2000. "Μελέτη της γενετικής ποικιλότητας δώδεκα φυσικών πληθυσμών της δασικής πεύκης (*Pinus sylvestris L.*) στον ελλαδικό χώρο με βιοχημικά γνωρίσματα" (diss. Aristotle Univ. Thessaloniki).

Paspalas, S. A. 1995. "The Late Archaic and Early Classical Pottery of the Chalkidike in Its Wider Aegean Context" (diss. Univ. of Oxford).

———. 2001. "The Late Geometric and Archaic Pottery," in *Torone* I, pp. 309–329.

———. 2006. "The Non-figured Wares from the Anglo-Turkish Excavations at Old Smyrna," in *Naukratis: Greek Diversity in Egypt. Studies on East Greek Pottery and Exchange in the Eastern Mediterranean*, ed. A. Villing and U. Schlotzhauer, London, pp. 93–104.

Paul, E. 1995. *Schwarzfigurige Vasen* (Kleine Reihe des Antiken-Museums der Universität Leipzig 1), Leipzig.

Paunov, E., and D. Y. Dimitrov. 2000. "New Data on the Use of War Sling in Thrace (4th–1st Century B.C.)," *Archaeologia Bulgarica* IV: 3, pp. 44–57.

Pautasso, A. 2009. *Stipe votive del Santuario di Demetra a Catania: La ceramica greco-orientale* (Stipe votive del Santuario di Demetra a Catania 2), Catania.

Pavese, C. O. 1996. "La iscrizione sulla kotyle di Nestor da Pithekoussai," *ZPE* 114, pp. 1–23.

Pavúk, P. 2012. "Of Spools and Discoid Loomweights: Aegean-type Weaving at Troy Re-considered," in *KOSMOS: Jewellery, Adornment and Textiles in the Aegean Bronze Age. Proceedings of the 13th International Aegean Conference/ Rencontre égéenne internationale, University of Copenhagen, Danish National Research Foundation's Centre for Textile Research, 21–26 April 2010* (*Aegaeum* 33), ed. M.-L. Nosch and R. Laffineur, Leuven/Liège, pp. 121–130.

———. 2014. *Troia VI Früh und Mitte: Keramik, Stratigraphie, Chronologie* (*Studia Troica* Monographien 3), Bonn.

Payne, H. 1931. *Necrocorinthia: A Study of Corinthian Art in the Archaic Period*, Oxford.

Payne, S. 1973. "Kill-off Patterns in Sheep and Goats: The Mandibles from Asvan Kale," *AnatSt* 23, pp. 281–303.

———. 1985. "Morphological Distinctions Between the Mandibular Teeth of Young Sheep, Ovis, and Goats, Capra," *JAS* 12, pp. 139–147.

Peacock, D. P. S., and D. F. Williams. 1986. *Amphorae and the Roman Economy: An Introductory Guide*, London and New York.

Pearson, L., and S. Stephens. 1983. *Didymi in Demosthenem commenta*, Stuttgart.

Pease, M. Z. 1937. "A Well of the Late Fifth Century at Corinth," *Hesperia* 6, pp. 257–316.

Peek, W. 1969. *Inschriften aus dem Asklepieion von Epidauros* (Abhandlungen der sachsischen Akademie der Wissenschaften zu Leipzig, philologisch–historische Klasse 60.2), Berlin.

Pelagatti, P. 1990. "Ceramica laconica in Sicilia e a Lipari. Materiali per una carta di distribuzione," *Bolletino d'arte* 75, 64s, pp. 123–192.

———. 1992. *Lakonikà: ricerche e nuovi materiali di ceramica laconica*, Rome.

———. 2006. "Camarina: Studi e ricerche recenti 2: Camarina: Città e necropolis," in *Camarina: 2600 anni dopo la fondazione. Nuovi studi sulla città e sul territorio. Proceedings of a National Conference, Ragusa 7 Dec 2002, 7–9 April 2003*, ed. P. Pelagatti, G. Di Stefano, and L. de Lachenal, Ragusa, pp. 45–76.

Pellegrini, G. 1912. *Catalogo dei vasi greci dipinti della necropoli felsinee*, Bologna.

Peña, J. T. 2007. *Roman Pottery in the Archaeological Record*, Cambridge.

Pendlebury, H. W., J. D. S. Pendlebury, and M. B. Money-Coutts. 1937–1938. "Excavations in the Plain of Lasithi. III. Karphi: A City of Refuge of the Early Iron Age in Crete," *BSA* 38, pp. 57–145.

Perachora = *Perachora: The Sanctuaries of Hera Akraia and Limenia: Excavations of the British School at Athens, 1930–1933*

I = H. Payne, *Architecture, Bronzes, Terracottas*, Oxford 1940.

II = T. J. Dunbabin, ed., *Pottery, Ivories, Scarabs, and Other Objects from the Votive Deposit of Hera Limenia*, Oxford 1962.

Perlès, C., and K. D. Vitelli. 1999. "Craft Specialization in the Neolithic of Greece," in *Neolithic Society in Greece* (Sheffield Studies in Aegean Archaeology 2), ed. P. Halstead, Sheffield, pp. 96–107.

Perlman, P. 2000. *City and Sanctuary in Ancient Greece: The* Theorodokia *in the Peloponnese* (Hypomnemata 121), Göttingen.

Pernicka, E. 1987. "Erzlagerstätten in der Ägäis und ihre Ausbeutung im Altertum: geochemische Untersuchungen zur Herkunftsbestimmung archäologischer Metallobjekte," *JRGZM* 34 (2), pp. 607–714.

Pernot, M. 1998. "Archéométallurgie de la transformation des alliages à base de cuivre," in *L'innovation technique au Moyen Âge. Actes du VIe Congrès international d'Archéologie Médiévale (1–5 Octobre 1996, Dijon–Mont Beuvray–Chenôve–Le Creusot–Montbard)* (Actes des congrès de la Société d'archéologie médiévale 6), ed. P. Beck, Paris pp. 123–133.

Perreault, J.-Y., and Z. Bonias. 2017. "*Άργιλος*," in *Αρχαιολογία. Μακεδονία και Θράκη*, ed. A. G. Vlachopoulos and D. Tsiafaki, Athens, pp. 428–429.

Perron, M. 2015. Rev. of M. Bessios, I. Z. Tzifopoulos, and A. Kotsonas, *Μεθώνη Πιερίας 1: Επιγραφές, χαράγματα και εμπορικά σύμβολα στη γεωμετρική και αρχαϊκή κεραμική από το "Υπόγειο" της Μεθώνης Πιερίας στη Μακεδονία*, in *Topoi: Orient-Occident* 20, pp. 683–696.

Petrakos, B. Ch. 1968. *Ὁ Ὠρωπὸς καὶ τὸ ἱερὸ τοῦ Ἀμφιαράου*, Athens.

———. 1987. "Οἱ ἀνασκαφὲς τοῦ Ραμνοῦντος," *ArchEph* 1987, pp. 265–298.

———. 1997. *Οι επιγραφές του Ωρωπού* (Βιβλιοθήκη τῆς ἐν Ἀθήναις Ἀρχαιολογικῆς Ἑταιρείας 170), Athens.

Petrie, W. M. F. 1917. *Tools and Weapons: Illustrated by the Egyptian Collection in University College, London, and 2,000 Outlines from Other Sources* (British School of Archaeology in Egypt and Egyptian Research Account 30), London.

Petropoulos, E. K. 2005. *Hellenic Colonization in Euxeinos Pontos: Penetration, Early Establishment, and the Problem of the "Emporion" Revisited* (*BAR-IS* 1394), Oxford.

Petsas, Ph. 1961–1962. "Ἀνασκαφὴ ἀρχαίου νεκροταφείου Βεργίνης," *ArchDelt* 17, A, pp. 218–288.

———. 1964. "The Multiple Brush on a Local Early Iron Age Pithos from Pieria," in *Essays in Memory of Karl Lehmann*, ed. L. F. Sandler, New York, pp. 255–258.

Pevkakia = *Die Deutschen Ausgrabungen auf der Pevkakia-Magula in Thessalien*, ed. H. Hauptmann, Bonn

I = H.-J. Weisshaar, *Das Späte Neolithikum und das Chalkolithikum* (*BAMK* 28), 1989.

III = J. Maran, *Die Mittlere Bronzezeit*, Parts 1–2 (*BAMK* 30–31), 1992.

Pfaff, C. 1988. "A Geometric Well at Corinth: Well 1981-1," *Hesperia* 57, pp. 21–80.

Pfleger, V. 1999. *Molluscs*, Leicester.

Pfuhl, E. 1903. "Der archaische Friedhof am Stadtberge von Thera," *AM* 28, pp. 1–290.

Phaklaris, P. B. 1990. *Αρχαία Κυνουρία. Ανθρώπινη δραστηριότητα και περιβάλλον*, Athens.

Philippa-Touchais, A., and G. Touchais. 2011. "Fragments of the Pottery Equipment of an Early Middle Helladic Household from Aspis, Argos," in *Our Cups Are Full: Pottery and Society in the Aegean Bronze Age. Papers Presented to Jeremy B. Rutter on the Occasion of His 65th Birthday* (*BAR-IS* 2227), ed. W. Gauss, M. Lindblom, R. A. K. Smith, and J. C. Wright, Oxford, pp. 203–216.

Pieniążek, M. 2016. "Amber and Carnelian: Two Different Careers in the Aegean Bronze Age," *Fontes Archeologici Posnanienses* 52, pp. 51–66.

Pieridou, A. G. 1973. *Ὁ πρωτογεωμετρικὸς ρυθμὸς ἐν Κύπρῳ*, Athens.

Pierro, E. 1978. "Ceramiche greco-orientali di Tarquinia," in *Les céramiques de la Grèce de l'est et leur diffusion en occident. Centre Jean Bérard, Institut Français de Naples, 6–9 juillet 1976*, Paris, pp. 231–238.

Pikoulas, Y. A. 2001. *Η χώρα των Πιέρων: Συμβολή στην τοπογραφία της*, Athens.

———. 2010. "Διασχίζοντας τον Όλυμπο: οδικό δίκτυο και άμυνα στην Περραιβία. Η έρευνα του 2010," *AEMTh* 24 [2014], pp. 121–125.

———. 2022. "Το αμαξιτό οδικό δίκτυο της αρχαίας Θεσσαλίας," *Θεσσαλικό Ημερολόγιο* 81, pp. 3-18.

Pilali-Papasteriou, A., and A. Papaefthymiou-Papanthimou. 2002. "Die Ausgrabungen auf der Toumba von Archontiko," *Prähistorische Zeitschrift* 77 (2), pp. 137–147.

Pilali-Papasteriou, A., A. Papaefthymiou-Papanthimou, K. Kotsakis, and T. Savvopoulou. 1986. "Νέος προϊστορικός οικισμός στο Μάνδαλο Δυτικής Μακεδονίας," in *Ancient Macedonia* 4 (Institute for Balkan Studies 204), ed. A. Vakalopoulos, Thessaloniki, pp. 451–465.

Pilhofer, P. 2009. *Philippi 2: Katalog der Inschriften von Philippi*, Tübingen.

Pingiatoglou, S. 2005. *Δίον. Το Ιερό της Δήμητρος. Οι λύχνοι*, Thessaloniki.

Pipili, M. 2000. "Wearing an Other Hat: Workmen in Town and Country," in *Not the Classical Ideal: Athens and the Construction of the Other in Greek Art*, ed. B. Cohen, Leiden and Boston, pp. 153–179.

———. 2012. "Λακωνική Κεραμική στο Βόρειο Αιγαίο," in Tiverios et al. 2012, pp. 197–208.

Pithekoussai I = Buchner, G., and D. Ridgway, eds. 1993. *Pithekoussai* I: *La Necropoli. Tombe 1–723 scavate del 1952 al 1961* (Monumenti Antichi, Serie Monografica 4), Rome.

Pittakis, K. S. 1838. "Σημειώσεις ἐπὶ τῶν λιθογραφημάτων," *ArchEph* 1838, pp. 92–98.

Ploug, G. 1973. *Sukas 2: The Aegean, Corinthian and Eastern Greek Pottery and Terracottas*, Copenhagen.

Podzuweit, C. 1979. "Spätmykenische Keramik von Kastanas," *JRGZM* 26, pp. 203–223.

Polat, Y., O. Zunal, and S. Üney. 2018. "Pottery from an Archaic House in Antandrus," in *Archaic and Classical Western Anatolia: New Perspectives in Ceramic Studies. In Memoriam Prof. Crawford H. Greenwalt, Jr. Proceedings of the Second KERAMOS International Conference at Ege University, Izmir, 3–5 June, 2015*, ed. R. G. Gürtekin Demir, H. Cevizoğlu, Y. Polat, with G. R. Tsetsekhladze, Leuven, Paris, and Bristol, pp. 201–230.

Pollard, A. J. 1994. "A Study of Marine Exploitation in Prehistoric Scotland with Special Reference to Marine Shells and Their Archaeological Contexts" (diss. Univ. of Glasgow).

Polzer, M. E. 2009. "Hull Remains from the Pabuç Burnu Shipwreck and Early Transition in Archaic Greek Shipbuilding" (MA thesis, Texas A&M University, College Station).

Pomadère, M. 2006. "Des enfants nourris au biberon à l'Âge du Bronze," in *Cooking Up the Past: Food and Culinary Practices in the Neolithic and Bronze Age Aegean*, ed. C. Mee and J. Renard, Oxford, pp. 270–289.

Pomey, P. 1998. "Les épaves grecques du VIe siècle av. J.-C. de la place Jules-Verne à Marseille," in *Archaeonautica* 14: *Construction navale maritime et fluviale: approches archéologiques, historiques et ethnologiques. Actes du 7e colloque international d'archéologie navale, île Tatihou, 1994*, ed. P. Pomey and E. Rieth, pp. 147–154.

Popham, M. R. 1994. "Precolonization: Early Euboean Contact with the East," in *The Archaeology of Greek Colonisation: Essays Dedicated to Sir John Boardman* (Oxford Committee for Archaeology Monograph 40), ed. G. R. Tsetskhladze and F. De Angelis, Oxford, pp. 11–34.

Popham, M., P. G. Calligas, and L. H. Sackett. 1988–1989. "Further Excavation of the Toumba Cemetery at Lefkandi, 1984 and 1986: A Preliminary Report," *AR* 1988–1989, pp. 117–129.

Popham, M., and Lemos, I. 1995. "A Euboean Warrior Trader," *OJA* 14, pp. 151–157.

Popham, M., and E. Milburn. 1971. "The Late Helladic IIIC Pottery of Xeropolis (Lefkandi), a Summary," *BSA* 66, pp. 333–352.

Popham, M., and L. H. Sackett. 1980. "Objects of Clay," in *Lefkandi* I, pp. 82–84.

———. 1984. *The Minoan Unexplored Mansion at Knossos* (*BSA* Suppl. 17), Oxford.

Popham, M., E. Schofield, and S. Sherratt. 2006. "Chapter 2. The Pottery," in *Lefkandi* IV, pp. 137–232.

Popham, M. R., E. Touloupa, and L. H. Sackett. 1982a. "Further Excavation of the Toumba Cemetery at Lefkandi, 1982," *BSA* 77, pp. 213–248.

———. 1982b. "The Hero of Lefkandi," *Antiquity* 56, pp. 169–174.

Poppe, G. T., and Y. Goto. 1991. *European Seashells* 1, Wiesbaden.

———. 1993. *European Seashells* 2, Hackenheim.

Posamentir, R. 2006. "The Greeks in Berezan and Naukratis: A Similar Story?" in *Naukratis: Greek Diversity in Egypt. Studies on East Greek Pottery and Exchange in the Eastern Mediterranean*, ed. A. Villing and U. Schlotzhauer, London, pp. 159–167.

Posamentir, R., and S. Solovyov. 2006. "Zur Herkunftsbestimmung archaisch-ostgriechischer Keramik: Die Funde aus Berezan in der Ermitage von St. Petersburg," *IstMitt* 56, pp. 103–128.

———. 2007. "Zur Herkunftsbestimmung archaisch-ionischer Keramik: Die Funde aus Berezan in der Ermitage von St. Petersburg II," *IstMitt* 57, pp. 179–207.

Poulaki, E. Ph. 2001. *Χῖα καὶ Ἀνθεμοῦσια (ιστορία αρχαιολογία)*, Katerini.

Poulaki, E. 2012. "Το Ηράκλειον," in *Μελέτες για την Αρχαία Μακεδονία: Προς τη γένεση των πόλεων*, ed. D. V. Grammenos, http://www.greek-language.gr/digitalResources/ancient_greek/macedonia/cities/page_067.html.

Poulaki-Pantermali, E. 1987. "Όλυμπος 2. Μακεδονικόν όρος, μετεωρότατον," in *ΑΜΗΤΟΣ. Τιμητικός τόμος για τον καθηγητή Μανόλη Ανδρόνικο*, Thessaloniki, pp. 697–718.

———. 1993. "Macedonian Olympus and Its Early Cemeteries," in *Greek Civilization: Macedonia* [Montreal exhibit, 1993], ed. I. Vokotopoulou, Athens, pp. 122–127.

———. 2003. "1997–2001: Έργα εθνικά και άλλα στην περιοχή του Μακεδονικού Ολύμπου," *AEMTh* 15 [2001], pp. 331–346.

———. 2007. "Πλαταμών Ολύμπου (Ηρακλείου) και η Εποχή του Σιδήρου," in *Ancient Macedonia* 7: *Macedonia from the Iron Age to the Death of Philip II*, ed. E. Voutiras, Thessaloniki, pp. 625–643.

———. 2008a. "Κρανιά-Ηράκλειο," in *Αρχαιολογικές τροχιοδρομήσεις από τη Θεσσαλονίκη στον Πλαταμώνα*, ed. G. Aikaterinidis, Athens, pp. 117–157.

———. 2008b. *Λείβηθρα*, Katerini.

———. 2013a. *Μακεδονικός Όλυμπος. Μύθος—Ιστορία—Αρχαιολογία*, Thessaloniki.

———. 2013b. "Μυκηναϊκή Εποχή," in Poulaki-Pantermali 2013a, pp. 45–63.

Poulaki-Pantermali, E., M. Vaxevanopoulos, S. Koulidou, and A. Syros. 2004. "Καταρράκτες (Φράγμα) Σιδηροκάστρου 2004," *AEMTh* 18 [2006], pp. 63–72.

Poulos, S. E., G. Th. Chronis, M. B. Collins, and V. Lykousis. 2000. "Thermaikos Gulf Coastal System, NW Aegean Sea: An Overview of Water-Sediment Fluxes in Relation to Air-Land-Ocean Interactions and Human Activities," *Journal of Marine Systems* 25, pp. 47–76.

Poux, M., and L. Guyard. 1999. "Un moule à balles de fronde inscrit d'époque tardo-républicaine à Paris (rue Saint-Martin)," *Instrumentum* 9, pp. 29–30.

Powell, B. B. 1991. *Homer and the Origin of the Greek Alphabet*, Cambridge.

Powell, J. 1992. "Archaeological and Pictorial Evidence for Fishing in the Bronze Age: Issues of Identification and Interpretation," in *EIKON. Aegean Bronze Age Iconography: Shaping a Methodology. Proceedings of the 4th International Conference, University of Tasmania, Hobart, Australia, 6–9 April 1992*, ed. R. Laffineur and J. L. Crowley, Liège, pp. 307–316.

———. 1996. *Fishing in the Prehistoric Aegean* (SIMA-PB 137), Jonsered.

———. 2003. "Fishing in the Mesolithic and Neolithic: The Cave of Cyclops, Youra," in *The Greek Mesolithic: Problems and Perspectives* (*BSA* Studies 9), ed. N. Galanidou and C. Perlès, London, pp. 75–84.

Pratt, C. E. 2015. "The 'SOS' Amphora: An Update," *BSA* 110, pp. 213–245.

———. 2016a. "The Rise and Fall of the Transport Stirrup Jar in the Late Bronze Age Aegean," *AJA* 120, pp. 27–66.

———. 2016b. "Greek Commodities Moving West: Comparing Corinthian and Athenian Amphorae in Early Archaic Sicily," in Demesticha and Knapp 2016, pp. 195–213.

———. 2021. *Oil, Wine, and the Cultural Economy of Ancient Greece: From the Bronze Age to the Archaic Era*, Cambridge.

Prendi, F. 1982. "The Prehistory of Albania," in *CAH* 3.1: *The Prehistory of the Balkans, the Middle East and the Aegean World, Tenth to Eighth Centuries BC*, ed. J. Boardman, I. E. S. Edwards, N. G. L. Hammond, and E. Sollberger, Cambridge, pp. 187–237.

Price, E. R. 1924. "Pottery of Naucratis," *JHS* 44, pp. 180–222.

Pritchard, D. M. 2018. "The Standing of Sailors in Democratic Athens," *Dialogues d'histoire ancienne* 44, pp. 231–253.

Pritchett, W. K. 1961. "Xerxes' Route over Mount Olympos," *AJA* 65, pp. 369–375.

———. 1980. *Studies in Ancient Greek Topography* 3: *Roads* (University of California Publications, Classical Studies 22), Berkeley.

———. 1991a. *Studies in Ancient Greek Topography* 7, Amsterdam.

———. 1991b. *The Greek State at War*, Part 5, Berkeley, Los Angeles, and Oxford.

———. 1993. *The Liar School of Herodotos*, Amsterdam.

Prohászka, M. 1998. "Metal Objects and Coins," in *The Chora of Metaponto: The Necropoleis* 2, ed. J. C. Carter, Austin, Tex., pp. 786–834.

Proskynitopoulou, R. 2011. *Αρχαία Επίδαυρος. Εικόνες μιας αργολικής πόλης από την προϊστορική εποχή έως την ύστερη αρχαιότητα. Αρχαιολογικά ευρήματα και ιστορικές μαρτυρίες*, Athens.

Prummel, W., and H. J. Frisch. 1986. "A Guide for the Distinction of Species, Sex and Body Size in Bones of Sheep and Goat," *JAS* 13, pp. 567–577.

Psaraki, K., and I. Mavroeidi. 2013. "Η κεραμική της Εποχής του Χαλκού στη Μακεδονία," *Περιοδικό "Προϊστορήματα" (ISSN 2241–2921). Παράρτημα* 1·*Μελέτες για την Προϊστορική Μακεδονία*, ed. D. Grammenos, https://proistoria.wordpress.com/παράρτημα, #20.

Psoma, S. E. 2002. "Μεθώνη Πιερίας: ένας νέος νομισματικός τύπος," *NomChron* 21, pp. 73–81.

———. 2011. "The Kingdom of Macedonia and the Chalcidic League," in *Brill's Companion to Ancient Macedon: Studies in the Archaeology and History of Macedon, 650 BC–300 AD*, ed. R. J. Lane Fox, Leiden, pp. 113–135.

———. 2012. "Innovation or Tradition? Succession to the Kingship in Temenid Macedonia," *Tekmeria* 11, pp. 73–87.

———. 2014. "Athens and the Macedonian Kingdom from Perdikkas II to Philip II," *RÉA* 116, pp. 133–144.

———. 2015. "Athenian Owls and the Royal Macedonian Monopoly on Timber," *Mediterranean Historical Review* 30, pp. 1–18.

Pucci, G. 2001. "Inscribed *instrumentum* and the Ancient Economy," in *Epigraphic Evidence: Ancient History from Inscriptions*, ed. J. Bodel, London and New York, pp. 137–152.

Pulak, C. 1988. "The Bronze Age Shipwreck at Ulu Burun, Turkey: 1985 Campaign," *AJA* 92, pp. 1–37.

Purcell, N. 2003. "The Boundless Sea of Unlikeness? On Defining the Mediterranean," *Mediterranean Historical Review* 18.2, pp. 9–29.

Purves, A. 2006. "Unmarked Space: Odysseus and the Inland Journey," *Arethusa* 39.1, pp. 1–20.

Quatremère de Quincy, A.-C. 1825. "Type," in *Encyclopédie Méthodique* 3, Paris.

Radman Livaja, I. 1999–2000. "Olovna tanad iz arheološkog muzeja u Zagrebu/Lead Sling-shots in the Zagreb Archaeological Museum," *Vjesnik arheološkog muzeja u Zagrebu* 32–33, pp. 107–118.

Radt, S. 2007. *Strabons Geographika* 6, Göttingen.

Radt, W. 1974. "Die früheisenzeitliche Hügelnekropole bei Vergina in Makedonien," in *Beiträge zu italienischen und griechischen Bronzefunde*, ed. H. Müller-Karpe (*PBF* 20.1), Munich, pp. 98–147.

Rahmstorf, L. 2003. "Clay Spools from Tiryns and Other Contemporary Sites: An Indication of Foreign Influence in LH IIIC?" in *2nd International Interdisciplinary Colloquium, the Periphery of the Mycenaean World, 26–30 September, Lamia 1999,* ed. N. Kyparissi-Apostolika and M. Papakonstantinou, Athens, pp. 397–415.

———. 2005. "Ethnicity and Changes in Weaving Technology in Cyprus and the Eastern Mediterranean in the 12th Century BC," in *Cyprus: Religion and Society from the Late Bronze Age to the End of the Archaic Period*, ed. V. Karageorghis, H. Matthäus, and S. Rogge, Bibliopolis, pp. 143–169.

Rahmstorf, L., M. Siennicka, E. Andersson Strand, M.-L. Nosch, and J. Cutler. 2015. "Textile Tools from Tiryns, Mainland Greece," in Andersson Strand and Nosch 2015, pp. 267–278.

Randall-MacIver, D. 1927. *The Iron Age in Italy: A Study of Those Aspects of the Early Civilization Which Are Neither Villanovan nor Etruscan*, Oxford.

Raubitschek, I. K. 1999. "The Metal Objects," in *Isthmia* VIII, pp. 157–160.

Raynor, B. 2016. "*Theorodokoi*, *Asylia*, and the Macedonian Cities," *GRBS* 56, pp. 225–262.

Reber, K. 1991. *Untersuchungen zur handgemachten Keramik Griechenlands in der submykenischen, protogeometrischen und der geometrischen Zeit* (SIMA-PB 105), Jonsered.

Reed, C. M. 2004. "Afterword to 'How Far Was Trade a Cause of Early Greek Colonisation?'" in *G. E. M. de Ste. Croix, Athenian Democratic Origins and Other Essays*, ed. D. Harvey and R. Parker, Oxford, pp. 367–370.

Reese, D. S. 2000. "Appendix 6.1: Iron Age Shell Purple-dye Production in the Aegean," in *The Greek Sanctuary. Kommos: An Excavation on the South Coast of Crete* 4, ed. J. Shaw and M. Shaw, Princeton, pp. 643–646.

Rehder, J. E. 1994. "Blowpipes Versus Bellows in Ancient Metallurgy," *JFA* 21 (3), pp. 345–350.

Rehren, T., and E. Pernicka. 2008. "Coins, Artefacts and Isotopes—Archaeometallurgy and Archaeometry," *Archaeometry* 50 (2), pp. 232–248.

Reichel, W., and A. Wilhelm. 1901. "Das Heiligtum der Artemis zu Lusoi," *ÖJh* 4, pp. 1–89.

Reimer, P. J., E. Bard, A. Bayliss, J. W. Beck, P. G. Blackwell, C. Bronk Ramsey, P. M. Grootes, T. P. Guilderson, H. Haflidason, I. Hajdas, C. Hatte, T. J. Heaton, D. L. Hoffmann, A. G. Hogg, K. A. Hughen, K. F. Kaiser, B. Kromer, S. W. Manning, M. Niu, R. W. Reimer, D. A. Richards, E. M. Scott, J. R. Southon, R. A. Staff, C. S. M. Turney, and J. van der Plicht. 2013. "IntCal13 and Marine13 Radiocarbon Age Calibration Curves 0–50,000 Years cal BP," *Radiocarbon* 55 (4), pp. 1869–1887.

Reinach, Th. 1889. "Noms méconnus (suite) (1)," *RÉG* 2, pp. 384–392.

Reinholdt, C. 1992. "Arbeitszeugnisse geometrischer und archaischer Schmuckwerkstätten," *AA* 1992, pp. 216–231.

———. 2008. *Der frühbronzezeitliche Schmuckhortfund von Kap Kolonna: Ägina und die Ägäis im Goldzeitalter des 3. Jahrtausends v. Chr.* (Ägina-Kolonna Forschungen und Ergebnisse 2), Vienna.

Renfrew, C. 1986. "The Excavated Areas," in *Sitagroi* 1, pp. 175–222.

Renfrew, J. M. 2003. "Grains, Seeds and Fruits from Prehistoric Sitagroi," in *Sitagroi* 2, pp. 1–28.

Rethemiotakis, G., and M. Englezou. 2010. *Το γεωμετρικό νεκροταφείο της Έλτυνας*, Herakleion.

Rhodes, P. J. 2010. "The Literary and Epigraphic Evidence to the Roman Conquest," in *A Companion to Ancient Macedonia*, ed. J. Roisman and I. Worthington, Oxford, pp. 23–40.

Rhodes, P. J., and R. Osborne. 2003. *Greek Historical Inscriptions, 404–323 B.C.*, Oxford.

Rhomiopoulou, K. 1971. "Ταφοὶ πρώιμης ἐποχῆς τοῦ Σιδήρου εἰς ἀνατολικὴν Πίνδον," *AAA* 4, pp. 37–42.

Rhomiopoulou, K., and I. Kilian-Dirlmeier. 1989. "Neue Funde aus der eisenzeitlichen Hügelnekropole von Vergina, Griechisch Makedonien," *PZ* 64, pp. 86–145.

Rhomiopoulou, K., and I. Touratsoglou. 2002. *Μίεζα. Νεκροταφείο υστεροαρχαϊκών-πρώιμων ελληνιστικών χρόνων*, Athens.

Richardson, T. 1998a. "The Ballistics of the Sling," *Royal Armouries Yearbook* 3, pp. 44–49.

———. 1998b. "Ballistic Testing of Historical Weapons," *Royal Armouries Yearbook* 3, pp. 50–52.

Richter, G. M. A. 1923. *The Craft of Athenian Pottery: An Investigation of the Technique of Black-Figured and Red-Figured Athenian Vases*, New Haven.

———. 1932. "An Aryballos by Nearchos," *AJA* 36, pp. 272–275.

Ridgway, D. 1992. *The First Western Greeks*, Cambridge.

———. 1997. "Nestor's Cup and the Etruscans," *OJA* 16 (3), pp. 325–344.

Ridgway, D., and O. T. P. K. Dickinson. 1973. "Pendent Semicircles at Veii: A Glimpse," *BSA* 68, pp. 191–192.

Ridley, C., and K. A. Wardle. 1979. "Rescue Excavations at Servia 1971–73: A Preliminary Report," *BSA* 74, pp. 185–230.

Ridley, C., K. A. Wardle, and C. A. Mould. 2000. *Servia* I*: Anglo-Hellenic Rescue Excavations 1971–73, directed by Katerina Rhomiopoulou and Cressida Ridley* (*BSA* Suppl. 32), London.

Riederer, J. 2007. "Die metallurgische Zusammensetzung der Kupfer- und Bronzefunde aus Kalapodi," in *Kalapodi* II, pp. 389–422.

Riginos, A. S. 1994. "The Wounding of Philip II of Macedon: Fact and Fabrication," *JHS* 114, pp. 103–119.

Riha, E. 1986. *Römisches Toilettgerät und medizinische Instrumente aus Augst und Kaiseraugst*, Augst.

Rihll, Tr. 2009. "Lead 'Slingshot' (*glandes*)," *JRA* 22, pp. 146–169.

Říhovský, J. 1993. *Die Fibeln in Mähren* (*PBF* XIV.9), Munich.

Riis, P. J. 1970. *Sukas* 1: *The North-east Sanctuary and the First Settling of Greeks in Syria and Palestine*, Copenhagen.

Rizza, G., ed. 1993. *Studi su Kyme eolica. Atti della giornata di studio della scuola di specializzazione in archeologia dell'università di Catania, Catania, 16 maggio 1990* (Cronache di Archeologia 32), Rome.

———. 2011. "Identità culturale, etnicità, processi di trasformazione a Prinias," in *Identità culturale, etnicità, processi di trasformazione a Creta fra Dark Age e arcaismo. Per i cento anni dello scavo di Priniàs, 1906–2006, Convegno di Studi, Atene 9–12 novembre 2006* (Studi e Materiali di Archeologia Greca 10), ed. G. Rizza, Catania, pp. 21–56.

Robakowski, P., T. Wyka, S. Samardakiewicz, and D. Kierzkowski. 2004. "Growth, Photosynthesis, and Needle Structure of Silver Fir (*Abies alba* Mill.) Seedlings Under Different Canopies," *Forest Ecology and Management* 201, pp. 211–227.

Robertson, C. M. 1940. "The Excavations at Al Mina, Sueidia, IV: The Early Greek Vases," *JHS* 60, pp. 1–21.

———. 1948. "Excavations at Ithaca, V: The Geometric and Later Finds from Aetos," *BSA* 43, pp. 1–124.

———. 1992. *The Art of Vase-Painting in Classical Athens*, Cambridge.

Robinson, D. M. 1930. "The Lamps," in *Olynthus* II, pp. 129–145

Robinson, J. 1969. *The Economics of Imperfect Competition*, 2nd ed., London.

Rocchetti, L. 1967–1968. "Il deposito protogeometrico di Petrokephali presso Festòs," *ASAtene* 45–46, n.s. 29–30, pp. 181–209.

———. 1974–1975. "La ceramica dell'abitato geometrico di Festòs a occidente del palazzo minoico," *ASAtene* 52–53, n.s. 36–37, pp. 169–300.

Rodden, R., and K. A. Wardle, eds. 1996. *Nea Nikomedeia: The Excavation of an Early Neolithic Village in Northern Greece 1961–1964,* 1: *The Excavation and the Ceramic Assemblage* (*BSA* Suppl. 25), London.

Roebuck, C. A. 1959. *Ionian Trade and Colonization*, New York.

Roesch, P. 1984. "Un décret inédit de la ligue thébaine et la flotte d'Épaminondas," *RÉG* 97, pp. 45–60.

Roisman, J. 2010. "Classical Macedonia to Perdiccas III," in *A Companion to Ancient Macedonia*, ed. J. Roisman and I. Worthington, Oxford, pp. 145–165.

Rolley, C. 1982. *Les vases de bronze de l'archaïsme récent en Grande-Grèce*, Naples.

———. 1984. "Objets divers de metal," in *L'antre corycien* 2 (*BCH* Suppl. 9), Paris, pp. 261–280.

Rollinger, R. 2006. "*Yaunā takabarā* und *maginnatā* tragende 'Ionier.' Zum Problem der 'griechischen' Thronträgerfiguren in Naqsch-i Rustam und Persepolis," in *Altertum und Mittelmeerraum: die antike Welt diesseits und jenseits der Levante* (Oriens et Occidens: Studien zu antiken Kulturkontakten und ihrem Nachleben 12), ed. R. Rollinger and Br. Truschnegg, Stuttgart, pp. 365–400.

Romano, D., and M. Voyatzis. 2014. "Mt. Lykaion Excavation and Survey Project, Part 1: The Upper Sanctuary," *Hesperia* 83, pp. 569–652.

Romero, F. G. 2011. "Ἀμουσότερος Λειβηθρίων (OF 1069)," in *Tracing Orpheus: Studies of Orphic Fragments in Honour of Alberto Bernabé* (Sozomena 10), ed. M. Herrero de Jáuregui, A. I. Jiménez San Cristóbal, E. R Luján Martínez, R. M. Hernández, M. A. Santamaría Álvarez, and S. Torallas Tovar, Berlin and Boston, pp. 339–343.

Romero, M. 2015. "Les armes de jet d'Argilos: catalogue typologique" (MA thesis, University of Montreal).

———. 2021. "Les armes de jet d'Argilos: pointes de flèches et balles de plomb," in *Argilos 3: Argilos, 25 années des recherches. Organisation de la ville et de la campagne dans le Nord de l'Égée, VIIIe–IIIe siècles av. n.è., Actes du colloque de Thessalonique, 25–27 mai 2017* (Publications de l'Institut canadien en Grèce, No. 13), ed. Z. Bonias and J.-Y. Perreault, Athens, pp. 203–223.

Romm, J. S. 1992. *The Edges of the Earth in Ancient Thought*, Princeton.

Rose, C. B. 2008. "Separating Fact from Fiction in the Aiolian Migration," *Hesperia* 77, pp. 399–430.

Rostoker, W., and E. R. Gebhard. 1980. "The Sanctuary of Poseidon at Isthmia: Techniques of Metal Manufacture," *Hesperia* 49, pp. 347–363.

Rotroff, S. I., and J. H. Oakley. 1992. *Debris from a Public Dining Place in the Athenian Agora* (*Hesperia* Suppl. 25), Princeton.

Rouillard, P. 1978. "Les dernières leçons de la Corse," in *Les céramiques de la Grèce de l'est et leur diffusion en occident. Centre Jean Bérard, Institut Français de Naples, 6–9 juillet 1976*, Paris, pp. 272–286.

Rubensohn, O. 1962. *Das Delion von Paros*, Weisbaden.

Ruffing, K. 2017. "The Macedonian Economy under the Argeads," in *The History of the Argeads: New Perspectives*, ed. S. Müller, T. Howe, H. Bowden, and R. Rollinger, with the collaboration of S. Pal (Classica et Orientalia 19), Wiesbaden, pp. 125–135.

Ruscillo, D. 2005. "Appendix C: Marine Remains and Land Mollusks from Terrace V," in Papadopoulos 2005, pp. 321–342.

Russell, J. B. 1982. "Byzantine Instrumenta Domestica from Anemurium: The Significance of Context," in *City, Town and Countryside in the Early Byzantine Era*, ed. R. L. Hohlfelder, New York, pp. 133–163.

Rutherford, I. 2001. "The New Simonides: Towards a Commentary," in *The New Simonides: Contexts of Praise and Desire*, ed. D. Boedeker and D. Sider, Oxford, pp. 33–54.

Rutter, J. B. 1975. "Ceramic Evidence for Northern Intruders in Southern Greece at the Beginning of the Late Helladic IIIC Period," *AJA* 79, pp. 17–32.

———. 1979. "The Last Mycenaeans at Corinth," *Hesperia* 48, pp. 348–392.

———. 1983. "Fine Gray-burnished Pottery of the Early Helladic III Period: The Ancestry of Gray Minyan," *Hesperia* 52, pp. 327–355.

———. 1990. "Some Comments on Interpreting the Dark-surfaced Handmade Burnished Pottery of the 13th and 12th Century B.C. Aegean," *JMA* 3, pp. 29–49.

Saatsoglou-Paliadeli, Ch. 2007. "Arts and Politics in the Macedonian Court before Alexander," in *Ancient Macedonia* 7: *Macedonia from the Iron Age to the Death of Philip II* (Institute for Balkan Studies 280), ed. E. Voutiras, Thessaloniki, pp. 345–356.

Sabatini, S. 2016. "Textile Tools from the East Gate at Mycenaean Midea, Argolis, Greece," *Opuscula* 9, pp. 217–247.

Sakellariou, A. 1965. "Νέα Ἀγχίαλος," *ArchDelt* 20, Β΄2, p. 421.

Sakellariou, M. B. 1979. "Quelques questions relatives à la colonization eubéenne en Occident," in *Gli Eubei in Occidente: Atti del diciottesimo convegno di studi sulla Magna Grecia, Taranto, 8–12 ottobre 1978*, Taranto, pp. 9–36.

———. 2009. *Ethné grecs à l'âge du Bronze* 1–2 (Μελετήματα 47), Athens.

Salazar, C. 1998. "Getting the Point: Paul of Aegina on Arrow Wounds," *Sudhoffs Archiv* 82, pp. 170–187.

Salviat, F. 1978. "La céramique de style Chiote à Thasos," in *Les céramiques de la Grèce de l'est et leur diffusion en occident, Centre Jean Bérard, Institut Français de Naples, 6–9 juillet 1976,* Paris, pp. 87–92.

Samos = *Deutsches Archäologisches Institut, Athens*

I = V. Milojčić, *Die prähistorische Siedlung unter dem Heraion, Grabung 1953 und 1955*, Bonn 1961.

VI = E. Walter-Karydi, *Samische Gefässe des 6. Jahrhunderts v. Chr.*, Bonn 1973.

Samothrace = *Samothrace: Excavations Conducted by the Institute of Fine Arts of New York University*, New York

4:1 = K. Lehmann, *The Hall of Votive Gifts*, 1962.

Sandars, N. K. 1955. "The Antiquity of the One-edged Bronze Knife in the Aegean," *PPS* 21, pp. 174–197.

Sapouna-Sakellarakis, E. 1978. *Die Fibeln der griechischen Inseln* (*PBF* XIV.4), Munich.

———. 1998. "Geometric Kyme: The Excavation at Viglatouri, Kyme, on Euboea," in Bats and d'Agostino 1998, pp. 59–104.

Sardis = *Archaeological Exploration of Sardis* (Monograph Series). Cambridge and London

8 = J. C. Waldbaum, *Metalwork from Sardis: The Finds Through 1974*, 1983.

11 = A. Ramage and P. Craddock, with contributions by M. R. Cowell, A. E. Geçkinli, D. R. Hook, M. S. Humphrey, K. Hyne, N. D. Meeks, A. P. Middleton, and H. Özbal, *King Croesus' Gold: Excavations at Sardis and the History of Gold Refining*, 2000.

Saripanidi, V. 2012. "Εισαγμένη και εγχώρια κεραμική στο βορειοελλαδικό χώρο. Η περίπτωση της Σίνδου" (diss. Aristotle Univ. Thessaloniki).

———. 2013. "Η εγχώρια κεραμική από το αρχαϊκό-κλασικό νεκροταφείο της Σίνδου," in Adam-Veleni, Kefalidou, and Tsiafaki 2013, pp. 217–223.

———. 2017. "Constructing Continuities with a 'Heroic' Past: Death, Feasting and Political Ideology in the Archaic Macedonian Kingdom," in *Constructing Social Identities in Early Iron Age and Archaic Greece* (Études d'archéologie 12), ed. A. Tsingarida and I. S. Lemos, Brussels, pp. 73–170.

Sarpaki, A. A. 1995. "Toumba Balomenou, Chaeronia: Plant Remains from the Early and Middle Neolithic Levels," in *Res Archaeobotanicae, International Workgroup for Palaeoethnobotany. Proceedings of the Ninth Symposium, Kiel, 1992*, ed. H. Kroll and R. Pasternak, Kiel, pp. 281–300.

———. 2012. "The Taming of an Island Environment: Crete from Dawn to Noon (Neolithic to the End of the Bronze Age)," in *Parallel Lives: Ancient Island Societies in Crete and Cyprus*, ed. G. Cadogan, M. Iacovou, K. Kopaka, and J. Whitley, London, pp. 35–45.

Šašel Kos, M. 2015. "Corcyra in Strabo's Geography," in *Prospettive corciresi*, ed. C. Antonetti and E. Cavalli, Pisa, pp. 1–31.

Savvopoulou, Th. 1987. "Ένα νεκροταφείο πρώιμης εποχής Σιδήρου στο Παλιό Γυναικόκαστρο του Κιλκίς," *AEMTh* 1 [1988], pp. 305–312.

———. 1988. "Νέα στοιχεία από το Π. Γυναικόκαστρο," *AEMTh* 2 [1991], pp. 219–229.

———. 2001. "Παλιό Γυναικόκαστρο. Το νεκροταφείο των περιβόλων,'" in *Καύσεις στην Εποχή του Χαλκού και την Πρώιμη Εποχή του Σιδήρου,* ed. N. Stambolides, Athens, pp. 169–185.

———. 2004. "Η Περιοχή του Αξιού στήν Πρώιμη Εποχή του Σιδήρου," in *Το Αιγαίο στην Πρώιμη Εποχή Σιδήρου. Πρακτικά του Διεθνούς Συμποσίου, Ρόδος, 1–4 Νοεμβρίου 2002*, ed. N. Stampolides and A. Giannikouri, Athens, pp. 307–316.

Sayre, E. V., and R. W. Smith. 1961. "Compositional Categories of Ancient Glass," *Science* 133 (3467), pp. 1824–1826.

———. 1967. "Some Materials of Glass Manufacturing in Antiquity," in *Archaeological Chemistry: A Symposium*, ed. M. Levey, Philadelphia, pp. 279–311.

Schachermeyr, F. 1980. *Die ägäische Frühzeit: Die Ausgrabungen und ihre Ergebnisse für unser Geschichtsbild 4: Griechenland im Zeitalter der Wanderungen vom Ende der mykenischen* Ära *bis auf die Dorier*, Vienna.

Schalk, E. 2008. "Die Bronzenadeln in der Berliner Sammlung," in *Heinrich Schliemanns Sammlung trojanischer Altertümer—Neuvorlage* 1: *Forschungsgeschichte, keramische Funde der Schichten VII bis IX, Nadeln, Gewichte und durchlochte Tongeräte*, ed. M. Wemhoff, D. Hertel, and Al. Hänsel, Berlin, pp. 183–226.

Schauenburg, K. 1976. "Askoi mit plastischem Löwenkopf," *RM* 83, pp. 261–271.

Schaus, G. P. 1985. *The Extramural Sanctuary of Demeter and Persephone at Cyrene, Libya, Final Reports* 2: *The East Greek, Island, and Laconian Pottery*, Philadelphia.

———. 1992. "Archaic Imported Fine Wares from the Acropolis, Mytilene," *Hesperia* 61, pp. 355–374.

———, ed. 2014a. *Stymphalos: The Acropolis Sanctuary* 1, Toronto.

———. 2014b. "Miscellaneous Small Finds," in Schaus 2014a, pp. 148–183.

Scheel, B. 1989. *Egyptian Metalworking and Tools*, Aylesbury.

Scheffer, C. 1981. *Aquarossa* 2.1: *Cooking and Cooking-stands in Italy 1400–400 B.C.*, Stockholm.

Scheibler, I. 1973. *Die archaischen Nekropole*, Athens.

Schibille, N. 2011. "Supply Routes and the Consumption of Glass in First Millennium CE Butrint (Albania)," *JAS* 38 (11), pp. 2939–2948.

Schiering, W. 1957. *Werkstätten Orientalisierender Keramik auf Rhodos*, Berlin.

Schilder, G., and M. van Egmond. 2007. "Maritime Cartography in the Low Countries during the Renaissance," in *Cartography in the European Renaissance* (The History of Cartography vol 3, part 2), ed. D. Woodward, Chicago, 1384-1432.

Schliemann, H. 1878. *Mycenae: A Narrative of Researches and Discoveries at Mycenae and Tiryns*, London.

Schlotzhauer, U. 2000. "Die südionischen Knickrandschalen: Formen und Entwicklung der sog. Ionische Schalen in archaischer Zeit," in *Die Ägäis und das westliche Mittelmeer: Beziehungen und Wechselwirkungen 8. bis 5. v. Chr., Wien, 24. bis 27. März 1999*, ed. F. Krinzinger, Vienna, pp. 407–416.

———. 2006. "Some Observations on Milesian Pottery," in *Naukratis: Greek Diversity in Egypt: Studies on East Greek Pottery and Exchange in the Eastern Mediterranean*, ed. A. Villing and U. Schlotzhauer, London, pp. 133–144.

———. 2012. "Teil 1: Untersuchungen zur archaischen griechischen Keramik aus Naukratis," in *Griechische Keramik des 7. und 6. Jhs. v. Chr. aus Naukratis und anderen Orten in Ägypten* (Archäologische Studien aus Naukratis 3), ed. U. Höckmann, Worms, pp. 21–194.

———. 2014. "Die südionischen Knickrandschalen: Eine chronologische Untersuchung zu den sog. Ionischen Schalen in Milet" (diss. Ruhr-Univ. Bochum).

Schlotzhauer, U., and A. Villing. 2006. "East Greek Pottery from Naukratis: The Current State of Research," in *Naukratis: Greek Diversity in Egypt. Studies on East Greek Pottery and Exchange in the Eastern Mediterranean*, ed. A. Villing and U. Schlotzhauer, London, pp. 53–68.

Schmid, E. 1972. *Atlas of Animal Bones*, Amsterdam.

Schmitt, A., K. Badreshany, E. Tachatou, and H. Sader. 2018. "Insights into the Economic Organization of the Phoenician Homeland: A Multidisciplinary Investigation of the Later Iron Age II and Persian Period Phoenician Amphorae from Tell El-Burak," *Levant* 50 (1), pp. 52–90.

Schmitt, H.-O. 2007. "Die Angriffswaffen," in *Kalapodi* II, pp. 423–551.

Schreiber, T. 1999. *Athenian Vase Construction: A Potter's Analysis*, Malibu.

Schweingruber, F. H. 1990. *Anatomie Europäischer Hölzer: ein Atlas zur Bestimmung Europäischer Baum-, Strauch- und Zwergstrauchhölzer*, Stuttgart.

Schweitzer, B. 1971. *Greek Geometric Art*, trans. P. Usborne and C. Usborne, London (originally published as *Die geometrische Kunst Griechenlands*, Cologne 1969).

Scott, D. A., R. Finnerty, Y. Taniguchi, E. Koseto, R. Schmidtling, and Z. S. Stos. 2003. "Analytical Studies of the Francavilla Metal Objects," in *La dea di Sibari e il santuario ritrovato: Studi sui rinvenimenti dal Timpone Motta di Francavilla Marittima*, 2.1: *The Archaic Votive Metal Objects* (*Bollettino d'Arte*, volume special), ed. J. K. Papadopoulos, Rome, pp. 167–243.

Scullion, S. 2003. "Euripides and Macedon, or the Silence of the *Frogs*," *CQ* 53, pp. 389–400.

Seel, O. 1935. *M. Iuniani Lustini Epitoma Historiarum Philippicarum Pompei Trogi*, Leipzig.

Séferiadès, M. 1983. "Dikili Tash: introduction à la préhistoire de la Macédoine orientale," *BCH* 107 (2), pp. 635–677.

Segre, M., and G. Pugliese Carratelli. 1949–1951. "Tituli Camirenses," *ASAtene* 27–29, pp. 141–318.

Seifert, M. 1996. "Überlegungen zur Anwendung naturwissenschaftlicher Methoden bei der Herkunftsbestimmung von Keramik," *Hephaistos* 14, pp. 29–43.

———. 2004. *Herkunftsbestimmung archaischer Keramik am Beispiel von Amphoren aus Milet*, Oxford.

Seifert, M., and Ü. Yalçin. 1995. "Milet'te arkeometrik araştirmalar," *Arkeometri Sonuçlari Toplantisi* 10, pp. 15–38.

Seiradaki, M. 1960. "Pottery from Karphi," *BSA* 55, pp. 1–37.

Selinus = *Selinus. Deutsches Archäologisches Institut*, Rome

V = H. Baitinger, *Die Metallfunde aus Selinunt. Der Fundstoff aus den Grabungen des Deutschen Archäologischen Instituts auf der Agora*, Wiesbaden 2016.

Semper, G. 1859. *Ueber die bleiernen Schleudergeschosse der Alten und über zweckmässige Gestaltung der Wurfkörper im Allgemeinen: ein Versuch die dynamische Entstehung gewisser Formen in der Natur und in der Kunst nachzuweisen*, Frankfurt.

Serneels, V. 1993. *Archéométrie des scories de fer: recherches sur la sidérurgie ancienne en Suisse occidentale*. Cahiers d'archéologie romande 61. Lausanne.

Serpico, M., J. Bourriau, L. Smith, Y. Goren, B. Stern, and C. Heron. 2003. "Commodities and Containers: A Project to Study Canaanite Amphorae Imported into Egypt During the New Kingdom," in *The Synchronisation of Civilisations in the Eastern Mediterranean in the Second Millennium B.C.* 3. *Proceedings of the SCIEM 2000 EuroConference, Haindorf, 2–7 May 2001*, ed. M. Bietak, Vienna, pp. 365–375.

Sezgin, Y. 2004. "Clazomenian Transport Amphorae of the Seventh and Sixth Centuries," in *Klazomenai, Teos and Abdera: Metropoleis and Colony. Proceedings of the International Symposium Held at the Archaeological Museum of Abdera, Abdera 20–21 October 2001, Thessaloniki: 19th Ephorate of Prehistoric and Classical Antiquities*, ed. A. Moustaka, E. Skarlatidou, M.-C. Tzannes, and Y. Ersoy, Thessaloniki, pp. 169–183.

———. 2012. *Arkaik Dönem İonia Üretimi Ticari Amphoralar*, Istanbul.

Shapiro, H. A. 1982. "Kallias Kratiou Alopekethen," *Hesperia* 51, pp. 69–73.

Shapiro, H. A., C. A. Picón, and G. D. Scott, eds. 1995. *Greek Vases in the San Antonio Museum of Art*, San Antonio.

Shaw, J. W., and M. C. Shaw, eds. 2000. *Kommos: An Excavation on the South Coast of Crete* 4: *The Greek Sanctuary*, Princeton.

Shear, T. L. 1930. "Excavations in the North Cemetery at Corinth in 1930," *AJA* 34, pp. 403–431.

Shear, T. L., Jr. 1970. "The Monument of the Eponymous Heroes in the Athenian Agora," *Hesperia* 39, pp. 145–222.

———. 1973. "The Athenian Agora: Excavations of 1971," *Hesperia* 42, pp. 121–179.

———. 1975. "The Athenian Agora: Excavations of 1973–1974," *Hesperia* 44, pp. 331–374.

———. 1984. "The Athenian Agora: Excavations of 1980–1982," *Hesperia* 53, pp. 1–57.

Shefton, B. B. 1962. "Other Non-Corinthian Vases," in *Perachora. The Sanctuaries of Hera Akraia and Limenia. Excavations of the British School of Archaeology at Athens, 1930–1933.* II: *Pottery, Ivories, Scarabs, and Other Objects from the Votive Deposit of Hera Limenia Excavated by Humfry Payne*, ed. T. J. Dunbabin, Oxford, pp. 368–388.

———. 1982. "Greeks and Greek Imports in the South of the Iberian Peninsula: The Archaeological Evidence," in *Phönizier im Westen: Die Beiträge des Internationalen Symposiums über "Die phönizische Expansion im westlichen Mittelmeerraum" in Köln vom 24. bis 27. April 1979*, ed. H. G. Niemeyer, Mainz, pp. 337–370.

Sheppard, A. O. 1965. *Ceramics for the Archaeologist*, 5th ed. (Publication 609, Carnegie Institution of Washington), Washington, D.C.

Sherratt, A. 1986. "Chapter 13. The Pottery of Phases IV and V: The Early Bronze Age," in *Sitagroi* 1, pp. 429–476.

Sherratt, S. 2011a. "The Aegean and the Wider World: Some Thoughts on a World-system Perspective," in *Archaic State Interaction: The Eastern Mediterranean in the Bronze Age*, ed. M. L. Galaty and W. A. Parkinson, Santa Fe, pp. 81–106.

_______. 2011b. "Between Theory, Texts and Archaeology: Working with the Shadows," in *Intercultural Contacts in the Ancient Mediterranean,* ed. K. Duistermaat and I. Regulski, Leuven, Paris, and Walpole, MA, pp. 3–29.

Sherratt, S., and A. Sherratt. 1992–1993. "The Growth of the Mediterranean Economy in the Early First Millennium B.C.," *WorldArch* 24, pp. 361–378.

Shipley, G., ed. 2011. *Pseudo-Skylax's Periplous: The Circumnavigation of the Inhabited World. Text, Translation and Commentary*, Exeter.

Shortland, A. J. 2002. "The Use and Origin of Antimonate Colorants in Early Egyptian Glass," *Archaeometry* 44 (4), pp. 517–530.

Shortland, A., and H. Schroeder. 2009. "Analysis of First Millennium B.C. Glass Vessels and Beads from the Pichvnari Necropolis, Georgia," *Archaeometry* 51 (6), pp. 947–965.

Sider, D. 2001. "Fragments 1-22 W[2]: Text, Apparatus Criticus, and Translation," in *The New Simonides. Contexts of Praise and Desire*, ed. D. Boedeker and D. Sider, Oxford, pp. 13-29.

Siennicka, M., and A. Ulinowska. 2016. "So Simple Yet Universal: Contextual and Experimental Approach to Clay 'Spools' from Bronze Age Greece," in *Textiles, Basketry and Dyes in the Ancient Mediterranean World* (Purpureae Vestes 5: Textiles and Dyes in Antiquity), ed. J. Ortiz, C. Alfaro, L. Turell, M. Martinez, and J. Martinez, Valencia, pp. 25–35.

Sillar, B. 1997. "Reputable Pots and Disreputable Potters: Individual and Community Choice in Present-day Pottery Production and Exchange in the Andes," in *Not So Much a Pot, More a Way of Life: Current Approaches to Artefact Analysis in Archaeology*, ed. C. Cumberpatch and P. Blinkhorn, Oxford, pp. 1–20.

Silvestri, A., A. Longinelli, and G. Molin. 2010. "δ^{18}O measurements of archaeological glass (Roman to Modern age) and raw materials: possible interpretation," *JAS* 37, pp. 549-560.

Silvestri, A., E. Dotsika, A. Longinelli, E. Selmo, and S. Doukata-Demertzi. 2017. "Chemical and Oxygen Isotopic Composition of Roman and Late Antique Glass from Northern Greece," *Journal of Chemistry* 2017, doi:10.1155/2017/2956075.

Simon, E. 1982. *The Kurashiki Ninagawa Museum: Greek, Etruscan and Roman Antiquities*, Mainz on Rhine.

———. 1989. *Die Sammlung Kiseleff im Martin-von-Wagner-Museum der Universität Würzburg* 2: *Minoische und griechische Antiken*, Mainz on Rhein.

Sindos = *Σίνδος. Το νεκροταφείο. Ανασκαφικές έρευνες 1980–1982*, Athens 2016

I = A. Despoini, *Η ανασκαφή των τάφων, τάφοι και ταφικά έθιμα, το σκελετικό υλικό.*

II = A. Despoini, K. Liambi, V. Misaelidou-Despotidou, V. Saripanidi, and M. Tiverios, *Πήλινα, γυάλινα και φαγεντιανά αγγεία, πήλινοι λύχνοι, μεταλλικά αγγεία, πήλινα ειδώλια και πλαστικά αγγεία, νομίσματα.*

III = A. Despoini, *Μάσκες και χρυσά ελάσματα, κοσμήματα, μικροαντικείμενα και στλεγγίδες, είδη οπλισμού.*

Sipsie-Eschbach, M. 1991. *Protogeometrische Keramik aus Iolkos in Thessalien*, Berlin.

Sismanidis, K. 1992. "Ανασκαφή Αρχαίων Σταγείρων 1992," *AEMTh* 6 [1995], pp. 451–465.

———. 1993. "Αρχαία Στάγειρα 1993," *AEMTh* 7 [1997], pp. 429–443.

———. 1994a. "Αρχαία Στάγειρα 1994," *AEMTh* 8 [1998], pp. 275–287.

———. 1994b. "Αρχαία Στάγειρα," *ArchDelt* 49, B2, pp. 459–460.

———. 1995. "Η συνέχεια της έρευνας στα αρχαία Στάγειρα κατά το 1995," *AEMTh* 9 [1998], pp. 383–393.

———. 1996. "Αρχαία Στάγειρα 1990–1996," *AEMTh* 10A [1997], pp. 279–295.

———. 1997. "Ανασκαφικά και αναστηλωτικά αρχαίων Σταγείρων 1997," *AEMTh* 11 [1999], pp. 469–479.

Sitagroi = *Prehistoric Sitagroi: Excavations in Northeast Greece, 1968–1970*

1 = C. Renfrew, M. Gimbutas, and E. S. Elster, *Excavations at Sitagroi: A Prehistoric Village in Northeast Greece* 1 (Monumenta Archaeologica 13), Los Angeles 1986.

2 = E. Elster and C. Renfrew, *Prehistoric Sitagroi: Excavations in Northeast Greece, 1968–1970* 2: *The Final Report* (Monumenta Archaeologica 20), Los Angeles 2003.

Skafida, E., A. Karnava, and J.-P. Olivier. 2012. "Two New Linear B Tablets from the Site of Kastro-Palaia in Volos," in *Études mycéniennes 2010: Actes du XIIIe colloque international sur les textes égéens. Sèvre, Paris, Nanterre, 20–23 September 2010*, ed. P. Carlier, C. de Lamberterie, M. Egetmeyer, N. Guilleux, F. Rougemont, and J. Zurbach, Pisa and Rome, pp. 55–73.

Skarlatidou, E. 2000. "Από το Αρχαϊκό Νεκροταφείο των Αβδήρων" (diss. Aristotle Univ. Thessaloniki).

———. 2004. "The Archaic Cemetery of the Clazomenian Colony at Abdera," in *Klazomenai, Teos and Abdera: Metropoleis and Colony. Proceedings of the International Symposium Held at the Archaeological Museum of Abdera, Abdera, 20–21 October 2001*, ed. A. Moustaka, E. Skarlatidou, M.-C. Tzannes, and Y. E. Ersoy, Thessaloniki, pp. 249–259.

———. 2007. *Θέρμη. Το αρχαίο νεκροταφείο κάτω από τη σύγχρονη πόλη*, Athens.

———. 2010. *Το αρχαϊκό νεκροταφείο των Αβδήρων: Συμβολή στην έρευνα της αποικίας των Κλαζομενίων στα Άβδηρα* (Αρχαιολογικό Ινστιτούτο Μακεδονικών και Θρακικών Σπουδών, Δημοσιεύματα 9), Thessaloniki.

———. 2012. "Κλειστά σύνολα με κορινθιακή και ιωνική κεραμική από το πρώιμο αρχαϊκό νεκροταφείο των Αβδήρων," in Tiverios et al. 2012, pp. 453–460.

Skarlatidou, E., Ph. Georgiadis, A. Panti, and K. Chatzinikolaou. 2012. "Επείσακτη και εγχώρια αρχαϊκή κεραμική από το αρχαίο νεκροταφείο στη Θέρμη (Σέδες) Θεσσαλονίκης," in Tiverios et al. 2012, pp. 461–474.

Skeat, T. C. 1934. *The Dorians in Archaeology*, London.

Skelton, C. 2017. "Thoughts on the Initial Aspiration of HAKESANDRO," in Strauss Clay, Malkin, and Tzifopoulos 2017b, pp. 219–231.

Skobelev, D. A. 2009. "Техника стрельбы из пращи и способы ее держания," *Para Bellum* 9, pp. 49–62.

Skoula, M., A. Sarpaki, C. Dal Cin D'Agata, P. Georgiakakis, and P. Lumperakis. 2010. "Αυλη Πολιτιστική Κληρονομιά και Βιοποικιλότητα: Εθνοβιολογική Μελέτη στην Περιοχή του Κίσσαμου στην Κρήτη," Chania, https://docplayer.gr/274482-Ayli-politistiki-klironomia-kai-viopoikilotita-ethnoviologiki-meleti-stin-periohi-toy-kissamoy-stin-kriti.html.

Skov, E. 2011. "Sling Technology: Towards an Understanding of Capabilities," *Nebraska Anthropologist* 26, pp. 112–126.

Slaska, M. 1986. "Anfore arcaiche greco-orientali e loro diffusione nel Mediterraneo. Confronto con la situazione nell' area pontica," in *Thracia Pontica III (Sozopole, 6–12 October 1985)*, ed. A. Fol, Sofia, pp. 54–67.

Sloan, K. et al. 2007. *A New World: England's First View of America*, Chapel Hill.

Small, D. B. 1990. "Handmade Burnished Ware and Prehistoric Aegean Economics: An Argument for Indigenous Appearance," *JMA* 3, pp. 1–25.

———. 1997. "Can We Move Forward? Comments on the Current Debate over Handmade Burnished Ware," *JMA* 10, pp. 223–228.

Smith, L. M. V., J. D. Bourriau, Y. Goren, M. J. Hughes, and M. Serpico. 2004. "The Provenance of Canaanite Amphorae Found at Memphis and Amarna in the New Kingdom: Results 2000–2002," in *Invention and Innovation: The Social Context of Technological Change* 2: *Egypt, the Aegean, and the Near East, 1650–1150 B.C.*, ed. J. Bourriau and J. Phillips, Oxford, pp. 55–77.

Smithson, E. L. 1961. "The Protogeometric Cemetery at Nea Ionia, 1949," *Hesperia* 30, pp. 147–178.

———. 1968. "The Tomb of a Rich Athenian Lady, ca. 850 B.C.," *Hesperia* 37, pp. 77–116.

———. 1974. "A Geometric Cemetery on the Areopagus: 1897, 1932, 1947, with Appendices on the Geometric Graves Found in the Dörpfeld Excavations on the Acropolis West Slope in 1895 and on Hadrian Street ('Phinopoulos' Lot') in 1898," *Hesperia* 43, pp. 325–390.

———. 1982. "The Prehistoric Klepsydra: Some Notes," in *Studies in Athenian Architecture, Sculpture, and Topography Presented to Homer A. Thompson* (*Hesperia* Suppl. 20), Princeton, pp. 141–154.

Smyth, H. W. 1920. *Greek Grammar for Colleges*, New York.

Snodgrass, A. M. 1962. "Greece and Central Europe," *AJA* 66, pp. 408–410.

———. 1964. *Early Greek Armour and Weapons from the End of the Bronze Age to 600 B.C.*, Edinburgh.

———. 1965. "Barbarian Europe and Early Iron Age Greece," *PPS* 31, pp. 229–240.

———. 1967. *Arms and Armour of the Greeks*, London.

———. 1971a. *The Dark Age of Greece: An Archaeological Survey of the Eleventh to the Eighth Centuries B.C.*, Edinburgh.

———. 1971b. "Ancient Artillery" (Review of E. W. Marsden, *Greek and Roman Artillery: Historical Development*), *CR* 21, pp. 106–108.

———. 1980. *Archaic Greece: The Age of Experiment*, Berkeley and Los Angeles.

———. 1983. "Heavy Freight in Archaic Greece," in *Trade in the Ancient Economy*, ed. P. Garnsey, K. Hopkins, and C. R. Whittaker, Berkeley and Los Angeles, pp. 16–26.

———. 1994. "The Nature and Standing of the Early Western Colonies," in *The Archaeology of Greek Colonisation: Essays Dedicated to Sir John Boardman* (Oxford Committee for Archaeology Monograph 40), ed. G. R. Tsetskhladze and F. De Angelis, Oxford, pp. 1–10.

———. 1996. "Iron," in *Knossos North Cemetery: Early Greek Tombs* (*BSA* Suppl. 28), ed. J. N. Coldstream and H. W. Catling, London, pp. 575–597.

Sofronidou, M., and Z. Tsirtsoni. 2007. "What Are the Legs For? Vessels with Legs in the Neolithic and Early Bronze Age Aegean," in *Cooking Up the Past: Food and Culinary Practices in the Neolithic and Bronze Age Aegean*, ed. C. Mee and J. Renard, Oxford, pp. 247–269.

Soueref, K. 1990. "Τούμπα Θεσσαλονίκης. Ανασκαφές στην Οδό Καλαβρύτων," *AEMTh* 4 [1993], pp. 299–313.

———. 1992. "Θεσσαλονίκη: Τούμπα," *ArchDelt* 47, Chr. B´2, pp. 367–373.

———. 2007. "Μία πιθανή εισαγωγή στην αρχαϊκή Μακεδονία: ενότητες χώρου στην ανατολική παραθερμαϊκή ζώνη," in *Ancient Macedonia* 7: *Macedonia from the Iron Age to the Death of Philip II* (Institute for Balkan Studies 280), ed. E. Voutiras, Thessaloniki, pp. 651–674.

———. 2011. *Τοπογραφικά και αρχαιολογικά κεντρικής Μακεδονίας*, Thessaloniki.

Soueref, K. (ed.) 2016. *Αρχαιολογία του λεκανοπέδιου Ιωαννίνων. Από τις άπαρχες ως την ύστερη αρχαιότητα*, Ioannina.

Soueref, K., and K. Chavela. 2002. "Σουρωτή 2002," *AEMTh* 16 [2004], pp. 267–276.

Sourisseau, J.-C. 1997. "Recherches sur les amphores de Provence et de la basse vallée du Rhône aux époques archaïque et classique (fin VIIe–début IVe s. av. J.-C.)" (diss. Univ. of Aix-en-Provence).

Spadea, R. 1994. "Il tesoro di Hera," *BdA* 88, pp. 1–34.

———. 1996. *Il tesoro di Hera: Scoperte nel santuario di Hera Lacinia a Capo Colonna di Crotone*, Milan.

Spaer, M. 2001. *Ancient Glass in the Israel Museum: Beads and Other Small Objects*, Jerusalem._

Sparkes, B. A. 1962. "The Greek Kitchen," *JHS* 82, pp. 121–137.

Speidel, M. P. 1982. "Auxiliary Units Named after Their Commanders: Four New Cases from Egypt," *Aegyptus* 62, pp. 165–172.

Spencer, N. 1995a. "Early Lesbos Between East and West: A 'Grey Area' of Aegean Archaeology," *BSA* 90, pp. 269–306.

———. 1995b. "Multi-dimensional Group Definition in the Landscape of Rural Greece," in *Time, Tradition and Society in Greek Archaeology: Bridging the "Great Divide,"* ed. N. Spencer, London and New York, pp. 28–42.

Spier, J. 1990. "Emblems in Archaic Greece," *BICS* 37, pp. 107–129.

Sprawski, S. 2010. "The Early Temenid Kings to Alexander I," in *A Companion to Ancient Macedonia*, ed. J. Roisman and I. Worthington, Oxford, pp. 127–144.

Stacey, R., C. Cartwright, S. Tanimoto, and A. Villing. 2010. "Coatings and Contents: Investigations of Residues on Four Fragmentary Sixth-century B.C. Vessels from Naukratis (Egypt)," *The British Museum Technical Research Bulletin* 4, pp. 19–26.

Stähler K. 1992. *Griechische Geschichtsbilder klassischer Zeit* (EIKON 1), Münster.

Stählin, F. 1932. "Methone 6," *RE* 15 (2), pp. 1385–1386.

Stais, V. 1917. "Σουνίου ἀνασκαφαί," *ArchEph* 1917, pp. 168–213.

Stampolidis, N. Ch. 1996. *ΑΝΤΙΠΟΙΝΑ: "Reprisals." Contribution to the Study of Customs of the Geometric-Archaic Period*, Rethymnon.

———, ed. 2003. *Πλόες. Από τη Σιδώνα στη Χουέλβα. Σχέσεις λαών της Μεσογείου, 16ος–6ος αι. π.Χ.*, Athens.

Stampolidis, N., Ch. E. Papadopoulou, I. G. Lourentzatou, and I. D. Fappas, eds. 2018. *Κρήτη. Αναδυόμενες Πόλεις: Άπτερα—Ελεύθερνα—Κνωσός*, Athens.

———, eds. 2019. *Crete, Emerging Cities: Aptera, Eleutherna, Knossos*, Athens.

Starr, R. F. S. 1937. *Nuzi: Report on the Excavations at Yorgan Tepa near Kirkuk, Iraq, Conducted by Harvard University in Conjunction with the American Schools of Oriental Research and the University Museum of Pennsylvania, 1927–1931* 1, Cambridge.

Starr, S. G. 1961. *The Origins of Greek Civilization 1100–650 B.C.*, New York.

Stavridopoulos, G., and T. Sianos 2009. "Ο λίθινος περίβολος του Δισπηλιού," *Ανάσκαμμα* 5, pp. 53–66.

Stavropoullos, Ph. D. 1938. "Ἱερατικὴ οἰκία ἐν Ζωστῆρι Ἀττικῆς," *ArchEph* 1938, pp. 1–31.

Ste. Croix, G. E. M. de. 2004. "How Far Was Trade a Cause of Early Greek Colonisation?" in *G. E. M. de Ste. Croix, Athenian Democratic Origins and Other Essays*, ed. D. Harvey and R. Parker, Oxford, pp. 349–367.

Stefani, E. 2011. "L'habitat à l'âge du Bronze Récent," in *Au Royaume d'Alexandre le Grand: La Macédoine Antique*, ed. S. Descamps-Lequime, Paris, pp. 153–158.

———. 2012. "'. . . ὄρος Βέρμιον ἄβατον ὑπὸ χειμῶνος': Landscape and Habitation in Semi-mountainous Imathia," in *Θρεπτήρια: Studies on Ancient Macedonia*, ed. M. Tiverios, P. Nigdelis, and P. Adam-Veleni, Thessaloniki, pp. 26–63.

———. 2013. "Εργαστήρια κεραμικής στη Λευκόπετρα Βερμίου," in Adam-Veleni, Kefalidou, and Tsiafaki 2013, pp. 93–118.

Stefani, E., and A. Koukouvou. 2019. *Copying (in) the Past: Imitation and Inspiration Stories*, Thessaloniki.

Stefani, E., and N. Merousis. 2003. "Τοπίο στην ομίχλη. Η 2η χιλιετία στην κεντρική Μακεδονία," in *2nd International Interdisciplinary Colloquium, the Periphery of the Mycenaean World, 26–30 September, Lamia 1999*, ed. N. Kyparissi-Apostolika and M. Papakonstantinou, Athens, pp. 228–242.

Stefani, E., N. Merousis, and A. Dimoula, eds. 2014. *Εκατό χρόνια έρευνας στην προϊστορική Μακεδονία 1912–2012: Πρακτικά Διεθνούς Συνεδρίου, Αρχαιολογικό Μουσείο Θεσσαλονίκης, 22–24* Νοεμβρίου *2012/A Century of Research in Prehistoric Macedonia 1912–2012: International Conference Proceedings, Archaeological Museum of Thessaloniki, 22–24 November 2012*, Thessaloniki.

Stefani, E., E. Tsagkaraki, and A. Arvanitaki. 2019. *Από τον νότο στον βορρά. Αποικίες των Κυκλάδων στο βόρειο Αιγαίο*, Thessaloniki.

Stefani, L. 2000. "Ανασκαφή στον άξονα της Εγνατίας: δύο προϊστορικές εγκαταστάσεις στην περιοχή της Λευκόπετρας Ημαθίας," *AEMTh* 14 [2002], pp. 537–553.

Steffy, J. R. 1985. "The Kyrenia Ship: An Interim Report on Its Hull Construction," *AJA* 89, pp. 71–101.

———. 1991. "The Ram and Bow Timbers: A Structural Interpretation," in *The Athlit Ram* (The Nautical Archaeology Series 3), ed. L. Casson and J. R. Steffy, College Station, Tex., pp. 6–39.

———. 1994. *Wooden Ship Building and the Interpretation of Shipwrecks*, College Station, Texas.

Stein, G. J. 2002. "From Passive Periphery to Active Agents: Emerging Perspectives in the Archaeology of Interregional Interaction," *American Anthropology* 104, pp. 903–916.

———, ed. 2005a. *The Archaeology of Colonial Encounters: Comparative Perspectives*, Santa Fe.

———. 2005b. "Introduction: The Comparative Archaeology of Colonial Encounters," in *The Archaeology of Colonial Encounters: Comparative Perspectives*, ed. G. J. Stein, Santa Fe, pp. 3–31.

Steinmann, B. 2012. *Die Waffengräber der ägäischen Bronzezeit: Waffenbeigaben, soziale Selbstdarstellung und Adelsethos in der minoisch-mykenischen Kultur* (*Philippika* 52), Wiesbaden.

Steinmayer, A. G., and J. MacIntosh Turfa. 1996. "Effects of Shipworm on the Performance of Ancient Mediterranean Warships," *IJNA* 25, pp. 104–121.

———. 1997. "Shipworms and Ancient Mediterranean Warships—A Response," *IJNA* 26, pp. 345–346.

Stephanou, A. G. 1974. "Η λατρεία των δέντρων παρά τοις αρχαίοις: τα δέντρα και η μυθολογία," in *Το δάσος που λαχτάριζες . . . εξήντα χρόνων αγώνας (1913–1973), να σωθούν τα δάση μας, τα θηράματα και το περιβάλλον*, Athens, pp. 17–23.

Stern, B., S. J. Clelland, C. C. Nordby, and D. Urem-Kotsou. 2006. "Bulk Stable Light Isotopic Ratios in Archaeological Birch Bark Tars," *Applied Geochemistry* 21, pp. 1668–1673.

Stibbe, C. M. 2000. *Laconian Oil Flasks and Other Closed Shapes* (Laconian Black-glazed Pottery, Part 3, Allard Pierson Series Scripta Minora 5), Amsterdam.

———. 2003. *Trebenishte: The Fortunes of an Unusual Excavation*, Rome.

Stoop, M. W. 1970–1971. "Francavilla Marittima B). Santuario di Athena sul Timpone della Motta," *AttiMGraecia* 11–12, pp. 37–66.

———. 1980. "Note sugli scavi nel santuario di Atenas sul Timpone della Motta (Francavilla Marittima—Calabria), 3," *BABesch* 55:2, pp. 163–189.

———. 1987. "Note sugli scavi nel santuario di Atena sul Timpone della Motta (Francavilla Marittima—Calabria), 7: Oggetti di bronzo vari (animali, ornamenti personali, armi, varia," *BABesch* 62, pp. 21–31.
Strack, S. 2007. "Regional Dynamics and Social Change in the Late Bronze and Early Iron Age: A Study of Handmade Pottery from Southern and Central Greece" (diss. Univ. of Edinburgh).
Stratouli, G. 2005. "Μεταξύ πηλών, πλίνθων και πασάλων, μαγνητικών σημάτων και αρχαιολογικών ερωτημάτων: τάφροι οριοθέτησης και θεμελίωσης στο νεολιθικό οικισμό Αυγής Καστοριάς," *AEMTh* 19 [2007], pp. 595–606.
Stratouli, G., N. Katsikaridis, T. Bekiaris, and V. Tzevelekidi. 2014. "Ενσωματώνοντας το παρελθόν, προσδιορίζοντας το παρόν, νοηματοδοτώντας το μέλλον: αναγνώριση και ερμηνεία πρακτικών δομημένης (εν)απόθεσης στο νεολιθικό οικισμό Αυγής Καστοριάς στη Βόρεια Ελλάδα," in Stefani, Merousis, and Dimoula 2014, pp. 349–358.
Stratouli, G., S. Triantafyllou, N. Katsikaridis, and T. Bekiaris. 2009. "Η διαχείριση του θανάτου: χώρος ταφικής πρακτικής στο νεολιθικό οικισμό Αυγής Καστοριάς", *AEMTh* 23 [2013], pp. 9–18.
Strauss, B. S. 2000. "Democracy, Kimon, and the Evolution of Athenian Naval Tactics in the Fifth Century BC," in *Polis and Politics: Studies in Ancient Greek History Presented to Mogens Herman Hansen on His 60th Birthday*, ed. T. H. Nielsen, L. Rubinstein, and P. Flensted-Jensen, Copenhagen, pp. 315–326.
Strauss Clay, J., I. Malkin, and Y. Z. Tzifopoulos. 2017a. "Introduction," in Strauss Clay, Malkin, and Tzifopoulos 2017b, pp. 1–5.
———, eds. 2017b. *Panhellenes at Methone:* Graphê *in Late Geometric and Protoarchaic Methone, Macedonia (ca. 700 B.C.E.)* (*Trends in Classics* Suppl. 44), Berlin and Boston.
Strøm, I. 1995. "The Early Sanctuary of the Argive Heraion and its External Relations (8th–Early 6th Cent. BC): The Greek Geometric Bronzes," in *Proceedings of the Danish Institute at Athens* 1, ed. S. Dietz, Athens, pp. 37–127.
Stubbings, F. H. 1947. "The Mycenaean Pottery of Attica," *BSA* 42, pp. 1–75.
———. 1954. "Mycenae 1939–1953, Part VIII: A Winged-axe Mould," *BSA* 49, pp. 297–298.
Stuiver, M., and H. A. Polach. 1977. "Discussion: Reporting of ^{14}C Data," *Radiocarbon* 19, pp. 355–363.
Styrenius, C.-G. 1967. *Submycenaean Studies: Examination of Finds from Mainland Greece with a Chapter on Attic Protogeometric Graves*, Lund.
Sundwall, J. 1943. *Die älteren italischen Fibeln*, Berlin.
SwCyprusExp = *The Swedish Cyprus Expedition*
II = E. Gjerstad, J. Lindros, E. Söjqvist, and A. Westholm, *Finds and Results of the Excavations in Cyprus 1927–1931*, Stockholm 1935.
Tagliente, M. 1983. "Un'oinochoe in bucchero campano dalla necropolis di Chiaromonte (PZ)," in *Studi in onore di Dinu Adamesteanu*, Galatina, pp. 17–29.
Talcott, L. 1935. "Attic Black-glazed Stamped Ware and Other Pottery from a Fifth Century Well," *Hesperia* 4, pp. 476–523.
Tarditi, C. 1996. *Vasi di bronzo in area apula: Produzioni greche ed italiche di età arcaica e classica*, Lecce.
Tarsus = *Excavations at Gözlü Kule, Tarsus*, Princeton
I = H. Goldman, *The Hellenistic and Roman Periods*, 1950.
III = H. Goldman, *The Iron Age*, 1963.
Taylour, W. D., and R. Janko. 2008. *Ayios Stephanos: Excavations at a Bronze Age and Medieval Settlement in Southern Lakonia* (*BSA* Suppl. 44), London.
Terzopoulou, D. 1995. "Αρχαία Στρύμη," *ArchDelt* 50, B΄2, pp. 657–659.
Thalmann, J. P. 1977. "Céramique trouvée à Amathonte," in *Greek Geometric and Archaic Pottery Found in Cyprus*, ed. E. Gjerstad, Stockholm, pp. 65–86.
Themelis, P. G. 1981. "Εργαστήριο χρυσοχοΐας του 8ου π.Χ. αι. στην Ερέτρια," *AAA* 14, pp. 185–208.
———. 1983. "An 8th Century Goldsmith's Workshop at Eretria," in *The Greek Renaissance of the Eighth Century B.C.: Tradition and Innovation. Proceedings of the First International Symposium at the Swedish Institute in Athens (1981)*, ed. R. Hägg, Stockholm, pp. 157–165.
———. 2000. "Μεταλλοτεχνία Μακεδονική," in *ΜΥΡΤΟΣ: Μέλετες στη Μνήμη της Ιουλίας Βοκοτοπούλου*, ed. P. Adam-Veleni, Thessaloniki, pp. 495–517.
Themelis, P., and G. Touratsoglou. 1997. *Οι τάφοι του Δερβενίου*, Athens.
Theochari, M. 1960. "Μυκηναϊκὰ ἐκ Λαρίσης," *Thessalika* 2, pp. 47–56.
———. 1962. "Δοκιμαστικὴ ἀνασκαφὴ εἰς Χασάμπαλι," *Thessalika* 4, pp. 35–50.
———. 1966. "Πρωτογεωμετρικὰ Θεσσαλίας," *Thessalika* 5, pp. 37–53.
Theocharis, D. R. 1960. "Ἀνασκαφαὶ ἐν Ἰωλκῷ," *Prakt* 1960, pp. 49–59.
———. 1961–1962. "Αρχαιότητες και Μνημεία Θεσσαλίας," *ArchDelt* 17, B΄1, pp. 175–178.
———. 1971. *Prehistory of Eastern Macedonia and Thrace* (Ancient Greek Cities 9), Athens.
Theodoropoulou, T. 2007a. "La mer dans l'assiette: l'exploitation alimentaire des faunes aquatiques en Egée pré- et protohistorique," in *Cooking Up the Past: Food and Culinary Practices in the Neolithic and Bronze Age Aegean*, ed. C. Mee and J. Renard, Oxford, pp. 72–88.
———. 2007b. "Gifts from the Gulf: The Exploitation of Molluscs in the Geometric Artisan Site of Skala Oropou, Greece," in *Oropos and Euboea in the Early Iron Age. Proceedings of the International Round Table, University of Thessaly, 18–20 June 2004*, ed. A. Mazarakis Ainian, Volos, pp. 285–301.
———. 2011. "Fishing (in) Aegean Seascapes: Early Aegean Fishermen and Their World," in *The Seascape in Aegean Prehistory*, ed. G. Vavouranakis, Athens, pp. 51–69.
———. 2014. "Οι αλιευτικές δραστηριότητες στην προϊστορία της Βόρειας Ελλάδας: ένα πανόραμα των αρχαιοζωολογικών δεδομένων," in Stefani, Merousis, and Dimoula 2014, pp. 453–464.
———. 2017. "A Sea of Luxury: Luxury Items and Dyes of Marine Origin in the Aegean during the Seventh Century B.C.," in *Interpreting the Seventh Century B.C.: Tradition and Innovation*, ed. X. Charalambidou and C. Morgan, Oxford, pp. 80–92.
Theodoropoulou, T., and G. Stratouli. 2009. "Fishbones vs. Fishhooks: A Comparative Study from the Neolithic Lakeside Settlement of Dispilio, Greece," *Environment and Culture* 7, pp. 126–130.
Thomas, C. G. 2008. "Centering the Periphery," in *Macedonian Legacies: Studies in Ancient Macedonian History and Culture in Honor of Eugene N. Borza*, ed. T. Howe and J. Reames, Claremont, Calif., pp. 1–16.
———. 2011. "The Physical Kingdom," in *Companion to Ancient Macedonia*, ed. J. Roisman and I. Worthington, Malden, pp. 65–81.
Thomas, P. 1992. "LH IIIB:1 Pottery from Tsoungiza and Zygouries" (diss. Univ. of North Carolina, Chapel Hill).
Thomas, R. 2009. "Writing, Reading, Public and Private 'Literacies': Functional Literacy and Democratic Literacy in Greece," in *Ancient Literacies: The Culture of Reading in Greece and Rome*, ed. W. A. Johnson and H. N. Parker, New York, pp. 13–45.

Thompson, C. M. 2003. "Sealed Silver in Iron Age Cisjordan and the 'Invention' of Coinage," *OJA* 22 (1), pp. 67–107.

Thompson, H. A. 1940. *The Tholos of Athens and Its Predecessors* (*Hesperia* Suppl. 4), Baltimore.

———. 1956. "Activities in the Athenian Agora: 1955," *Hesperia* 25, pp. 46–68.

Thompson, M. E. 1961. *New Style Silver Coinage of Athens* (Numismatic Studies 10), New York, http://numismatics.org/digitallibrary/ark:/53695/nnan131509.

Threatte, L. 1980. *The Grammar of Attic Inscriptions* 1: *Phonology*, Berlin and New York.

———. 1996. *The Grammar of Attic Inscriptions* 2: *Morphology*, Berlin and New York.

Threpsiadis, I. 1972. "Ἀνασκαφὴ Γαλαξιδίου," *ArchEph* 111, pp. 184–207.

Tidmarsh, J. 2001. "The Greek and Roman Lamps," in *Torone* I, pp. 647–667.

Tiryns XVI = L. Rahmstorf, *Kleinfunde. Terrakotta, Stein, Bein, und Glas/Fayence vornehmlich aus der Spätbronzezeit*, Wiesbaden 2008.

Tiverios, M. A. 1993. "Σίνδος—Αίγυπτος," in *Ancient Macedonia* 5.3 (Institute for Balkan Studies 240), ed. D. Pantermalis, Thessaloniki, pp. 1487–1493.

———. 1996. "Επτά χρόνια (1990–1996) αρχαιολογικών ερευνών στη διπλή τράπεζα Αγχιάλου–Σίνδου. Ο αρχαίος οικισμός," *AEMTh* 10A [1997], pp. 407–425.

———. 1998. "The Ancient Settlements in the Anchialos-Sindos Double Trapeza: Seven Years (1990–1996) of Archaeological Research," in Bats and d'Agostino 1998, pp. 243–253.

———. 2000. "Αθηναϊκό λάδι στον μυχό του Θερμαϊκού κόλπου κατά τον 6ο αι. π.Χ.," in *ΜΥΡΤΟΣ: Μέλετες στη Μνήμη της Ιουλίας Βοκοτοπούλου*, ed. P. Adam-Veleni, Thessaloniki, pp. 519–527.

———. 2006. "Πάρος—Θάσος—Εύβοια," in *Γενέθλιον: Αναμνηστικός τόμος για την συμπλήρωση είκοσι χρόνων λειτουργίας του Μουσείου Κυκλαδικής Τέχνης*, ed. N. Ch. Stampolidis, Athens, pp. 73–85.

———. 2008. "Greek Colonisation of the Northern Aegean," in *Greek Colonisation: An Account of Greek Colonies and Other Settlements Overseas* 2, ed. G. Tsetskhladze, Leiden, pp. 1–154.

———. 2009a. "Η διπλή τράπεζα Αγχιάλου," in Adam-Veleni and Tzanavari 2009, pp. 397–407.

———. 2009b. "Η πανεπιστημιακή ανασκαφή στο Καραμπουρνάκι Θεσσαλονίκης," in Adam-Veleni and Tzanavari 2009, pp. 385–396.

———. 2012a. "The Phoenician Presence in the Northern Aegean," in *Greeks and Phoenicians at the Mediterranean Crossroads*, ed. P. Adam-Veleni and E. Stefani, Thessaloniki, pp. 69–72.

———. 2012b. "Classification of Local Pottery in Macedonia (Primarily from Coastal Sites) in the Late Geometric and Archaic Periods," in *Θρεπτήρια: Μελέτες για την αρχαία Μακεδονία*, ed. M. Tiverios, P. Nigdelis, and P. Adam Veleni, Thessaloniki, pp. 172–198.

———. 2013a. "The Presence of Euboeans in the North Helladic Region and the Myths of Heracles," in *Studies in Ancient Art and Civilization* 17, ed. J. Bodzek, Krakow, pp. 97–110.

———. 2013b. "Ταξινόμηση ντόπιας κεραμικής στον μακεδονικό χώρο κατά την Εποχή του Σιδήρου—ορισμένες δεύτερες σκέψεις," in Adam-Veleni, Kefalidou, and Tsiafaki 2013, pp. 15–24.

———. 2019a. "Κάρανος, ο γενάρχης της μακεδονικής βασιλικής δυναστείας. Η νομισματική μαρτυρία," *ArchEph* 158, pp. 195–212.

———. 2019b. "Οι αποικίες των Παρίων και Ανδρίων στο βόρειο Αιγαίο," in *Από τον Νότο στον Βορρά: Αποικίες των Κυκλάδων στο βόρειο Αιγαίο* (Αρχαιολογικό Μουσείο Θεσσαλονίκης 43), ed. Stephani,Tsagkaraki, and Arvanitaki 2019, pp. 39–51.

Tiverios, M., and S. Gimatzidis. 2000. "Αρχαιολογικές έρευνες στη διπλή τράπεζα της Αγχιάλου κατά το 2000," *AEMTh* 14 [2002], pp. 193–203.

Tiverios, M., E. Manakidou, and D. Tsiafaki. 1997. "Ανασκαφικές έρευνες στο Καραμπουρνάκι κατά το 1997: ο αρχαίος οικισμός," *AEMTh* 11 [1999], pp. 327–335.

Tiverios, M., E. Manakidou, D. Tsiafaki, S. M. Valamoti, T. Theodoropoulou, and E. Gatzogia. 2013. "Cooking in an Iron Age Pit at Karabournaki: An Interdisciplinary Approach," in *Diet, Economy and Society in the Ancient Greek World: Towards a Better Integration of Archaeology and Science*, ed. S. Voutsaki and S. M. Valamoti, Leuven, Paris, and Walpole, pp. 205–214.

Tiverios, M., V. Misailidou-Despotidou, E. Manakidou, and A. Arvanitaki, eds. 2012. *Η κεραμική της αρχαϊκής εποχής στο Βόρειο Αιγαίο και την περιφέρειά του (700–480 π.Χ.). Πρακτικά Αρχαιολογικής Συνάντησης, 19–22 Μαΐου 2011. Archaic Pottery of the Northern Aegean and Its Periphery (700–480 B.C.). Proceedings of the Archaeological Meeting, Thessaloniki 19–22 May 2011*, Thessaloniki.

Tod, M. N. 1945. "The Progress of Greek Epigraphy, 1941–1945," *JHS* 65, pp. 58–99.

Toffolo, M. B., A. Fantalkin, I. S. Lemos, R. C. S. Felsch, W.-D. Niemeyer, G. D. R. Sanders, I. Finkelstein, and E. Boaretto. 2013. "Towards an Absolute Chronology for the Aegean Iron Age: New Radiocarbon Dates from Lefkandi, Kalapodi, and Corinth," *PLoS ONE* 8(12): e83117, doi:10.1371/journal.pone.0083117.

Tolia-Christakou, M. 2019. "Ἐρυθρόμορφη κύλικα τοῦ Ζωγράφου τῆς Βόννης ἀπὸ τὴ Μεθώνη Πιερίας," *ArchEph* 158, pp. 97–129.

Tomkins, P. 2007. "Communality and Competition: The Social Life of Food and Containers at Aceramic and Early Neolithic Knossos," in *Cooking Up the Past: Food and Culinary Practices in the Neolithic and Bronze Age*, ed. C. Mee and J. Renard, Oxford, pp. 174–199.

Torone I = A. Cambitoglou, J. K. Papadopoulos, and O. Tudor Jones, eds. *Torone* I: *The Excavations of 1975, 1976, and 1978* (Athens Archaeological Society 206, 207, 208), Athens 2001.

Torr, C. [ed. A. J. Podlecki]. 1964. *Ancient Ships*, Chicago.

Toufexis, G., S. Karapanou, and M. Mangafa. 2000. "Ανασκαφική έρευνα στη Μαγούλα Ραχμάνι. Πρώτα συμπεράσματα," in *Το έργο των Εφορειών Αρχαιοτήτων και Νεωτέρων Μνημείων του ΥΠΠΟ στη Θεσσαλία και την ευρύτερη περιοχή της (1990–1998), 1η Επιστημονική Συνάντηση*, Volos, pp. 105–115.

Touloumis, K. 1994. "Το πλεόνασμα στην προϊστορία και η αρχαιολογία της αποθήκευσης" (diss. Aristotle Univ. Thessaloniki).

Touloumtzidou, A. 2011. "Μετάλλινα αγγεία του 4ου–2ου αι. π.Χ. από τον ελλαδικό χώρο," (diss. Aristotle Univ. Thessaloniki).

———. 2017. "Small Finds from the Sanctuary of Kythnos: The Bronze Finds—Part I," in *Les Sanctuaires Archaïques des Cyclades. Recherches récentes*, ed. A. Mazarakis Ainian, Rennes, pp. 200–216, 247–252.

Touloupa, E. 1972. "Bronzebleche von der Akropolis in Athen: Gehämmerte geometrische Dreifüsse," *AM* 87, pp. 57–76.

Touratsoglou, I. 2010. *Συμβολή στην οικονομική ιστορία του βασιλείου της αρχαίας Μακεδονίας (6ος–3ος αι. π.Χ.)*, ed. K. Liampi (ΚΕΡΜΑ 2), Athens.

Tournavitou, I. 1992. "Practical Use and Social Functon: A Neglected Aspect of Mycenaean Pottery," *BSA* 87, pp. 281–210.

Trakosopoulou, E. 2002. "Glass Grave Goods from Acanthus," in *Hyalos-Vitrum-Glass, 1st International Conference,* ed. G. Kordas, Rhodes and Athens, pp. 79–89.

Trakosopoulou-Salakidou, E. 1986. *Θεσσαλονίκη 2300 χρόνια. Θεσσαλονίκη από τα προϊστορικά μέχρι τα χριστιανικά χρόνια,* Athens.

———. 1988. "Ανασκαφή στον Αη-Γιάννη Νικήτης," *AEMTh* 2 [1991], pp. 347–355.

———. 1996. "Αρχαία Άκανθος: 1986–1996," *AEMTh* 10A [1997], pp. 297–312.

Treister, M. Y. 1996. *The Role of Metals in Ancient Greek History* (*Mnemosyne* Suppl. 156), Leiden, New York, and Cologne.

———. 2007. "Archaic Pantikapaion," in *Frühes Ionien: Eine Bestandsaufnahme. Panionion-Symposion Güzelçamlı, 26. September–1. Oktober 1999* (Milesische Forschungen 5), ed. J. Cobet, V. von Graeve, W.-D. Niemeyer, and K. Zimmermann, Mainz, pp. 567–580.

Treister, M., and I. Zolotarev. 1993. "Moulds for Casting of Matrices for Roman Relief Mirrors from Chersonessus," in *Bronces y religion romana. Actas del XI Convegno internacional de bronce. Santiguos, Madrid, Mayo–Junio 1990*, ed. J. Arce and F. Burkhalter, pp. 429–448.

Treuil, R., ed. 1992. *Dikili Tash, village préhistorique de Macédoine Orientale* 1: *Fouilles de Jean Deshayes 1961–1975* 1 (*BCH* Suppl. 24), Paris.

Triantaphyllos, D., and M. Tasaklaki. 2012. "Pottery from Two Archaic Cemeteries in Aegean Thrace," in Tiverios et al. 2012, pp. 475–488.

Triantaphyllou, S. 1998. "Prehistoric Populations from Northern Greece: A Breath of Life for the Skeletal Remains," in *Cemetery and Society in the Aegean Bronze Age*, ed. K. Branigan, Sheffield, pp. 150–164.

———. 1999a. "A Bioarchaeological Approach to Prehistoric Cemetery Populations from Central and Western Greek Macedonia" (diss. Univ. of Sheffield).

———. 1999b. "Prehistoric Makrygialos: A Story from the Fragments," in *Neolithic Society in Greece* (Sheffield Studies in Aegean Archaeology 2), ed. P. Halstead, Sheffield, pp. 128–135.

———. 2001. *A Bioarchaeological Approach to Prehistoric Cemetery Populations from Central and Western Greek Macedonia*, Oxford.

———. 2003. "A Bioarchaeological Approach to Bronze Age Cemetery Populations from Western and Central Greek Macedonia," in *METRON. Measuring the Aegean Bronze Age* (*Aegaeum* 24), ed. K. P. Foster and R. Laffineur, Liège and Austin, pp. 217–224.

Triantaphyllou, S., and St. Andreou. 2020. "Claiming Social Identities in the Mortuary Landscape of the Late Bronze Age Communities in Northern Greece," in *Death in Late Bronze Age Greece: Variations on a Theme*, ed. J. M. A. Murphy, Oxford, pp. 171–197.

Triantaphyllou, S., and M. Bessios. 2005. "A Mass Burial at Fourth Century B.C. Pydna, Macedonia, Greece: Evidence for Slavery?" *Antiquity* 79 (305). http://antiquity.ac.uk/projgall/triantaphyllou305/.

Tringham, R. 2003. "Chapter 3. Flaked Stone," in *Sitagroi* 2, pp. 81–126.

Tringham, R., and M. Stevanovic. 1990. "The Nonceramic Uses of Clay," in *Selevac: A Neolithic Village in Yugoslavia* (Monumenta Archaeologica 15), ed. R. Tringham and D. Krstic, Los Angeles, pp. 323–396.

Tripodi, B. 2007. "Aminta I, Alessandro I e gli *hyparchoi* in Erodoto," in *Ancient Macedonia* 7: *Macedonia from the Iron Age to the Death of Philip II* (Institute for Balkan Studies 280), ed. E. Voutiras, Thessaloniki, pp. 67–85.

Tritsaroli, P. 2017. "The Pigi Athenas Tumuli Cemetery of Macedonian Olympus: Burial Customs and the Bioarchaeology of Social Structure at the Dawn of the Late Bronze Age, Central Macedonia, Greece," in *Bones of Contention: Bioarchaeological Case Studies of Social Organization and Skeletal Biology*, ed. H. D. Klaus, A. R. Harvey, and M. N. Cohen, Gainesville, pp. 224–261.

Troy = *Excavations Conducted by the University of Cincinnati, 1932–1938.* Princeton.

III = C. W. Blegen, J. L. Caskey, and M. W. Rawson, *The Sixth Settlement*, 1953.

IV = C. W. Blegen, C. G. Boulter, J. L. Caskey, and M. Rawson, *Troy Settlements VIIa, VIIb and VIII*, 1958.

Truhelka, Ć. 1904. "Der vorgeschichtliche Pfahlbau im Savebette bei Donja Dolina (Bezirk Bosnisch-Gradiška): Bericht über die Ausgrabungen bis 1904," *Wissenschaftliche Mitteilungen aus Bosnien und der Herzegowina* 9, pp. 3–170.

Trump, D. H. 1980. *The Prehistory of the Mediterranean*, London.

Tsakos, K. 2016. "Λίθινες μήτρες για μεταλλικά κοσμήματα από την αρχαία Σάμο," in *Ἠχάδιν. Τιμητικός τόμος για τη Στέλλα Δρούγου* 2, ed. M. Giannopoulou and Ch. Kallini, Athens, pp. 696–710.

Tsalkou, E. 2020. "Τμήμα υπομυκηναϊκού νεκροταφείου στα νότια της Ακρόπολης (Κουκάκι). Μια προκαταρκτική παρουσίαση," in *Athens and Attica in Prehistory. Proceedings of the International Conference, Athens, 27–31 May 2015*, ed. N. Papadimitriou, J. C. Wright, S. Fachard, N. Polychronakou-Sgouritsa, and E. Andrikou, Oxford, pp. 575–587.

Tsantsanoglou, K. 2000. "Ο Αρχίλοχος και ο λαός του. Αποσπάσματα 115, 93a, 94 (W.)," in *Κτερίσματα. Φιλολογικά μελετήματα αφιερωμένα στον Ιω. Σ. Καμπίτση (1938–1990)*, ed. G. M. Sifakis, Herakleio, pp. 369–393.

———. 2003. "Archilochus Fighting in Thasos: Frr. 93a+94 from the Sosthenes Inscription," *Ελληνικά* 53, pp. 235–255.

Tsaravopoulos, A. 2004–2009. "Η επιγραφή IG V 1, 948 και οι ενεπίγραφες μολυβδίδες του Κάστρου των Αντικυθήρων," *HOROS* 17–21, pp. 327–348.

———. 2010–2013. "Ενεπίγραφα καρφιά ή η λογιστική του στρατού στα ελληνιστικά χρόνια (οι «αόρατες» επιγραφές)," *HOROS* 23–25, pp. 187–198.

———. 2012. "Inscribed Sling Bullets from 'Kastro' in Antikythera (Greece)," *Gdańskie studia archeologiczne* 2, pp. 207–220.

———. 2016. "Two More Inscribed Nails from Korone, Porto Rafti (Did Persian Soldiers Really Come to Attica in 267–262 B.C.?)," *Γραμματείον* 5, pp. 43–48.

Tselekas, P. 1996. "The Coinage of Pydna," *NC* 156, pp. 11–32.

Tsetskhladze, G. R. 1994. "Greek Penetration of the Black Sea," in *The Archaeology of Greek Colonisation: Essays Dedicated to Sir John Boardman* (Oxford Committee for Archaeology Monograph 40), ed. G. R. Tsetskhladze and F. De Angelis, Oxford, pp. 111–135.

———. 1998. "Trade on the Black Sea in the Archaic and Classical Periods: Some Observations," in *Trade, Traders and the Ancient City*, ed. H. Parkins and C. Smith, London and New York, pp. 52–74.

———. 2006. "Revisiting Ancient Greek Colonization," in *Greek Colonisation: An Account of Greek Colonies and Other Settlement Overseas* 1, ed. G. Tsetskhladze, Leiden, pp. xxv–xxviii.

Tsiafaki, D. 1998. *Η Θράκη στην αττική εικονογραφία του 5ου αιώνα π.Χ.* (Παράρτημα Θρακικής Επετηρίδας 4), Komotini.

———. 2000. "On Some East Greek Pottery Found at Karabournaki in the Thermaic Gulf," in *Die Ägäis und das westliche Mittelmeer: Beziehungen und Wechselwirkungen 8. bis 5. v. Chr., Wien, 24. bis 27. März 1999*, ed. F. Krinzinger, Vienna, pp. 417–423.

———. 2008. "The East Greek and East Greek-style Pottery," in *La Dea di Sibari e il santuario ritrovato. Studi sui rinvenimenti dal Timpone Motta di Francavilla Marittima*, 1.2: *Ceramiche di importazione, di produzione coloniale e indigena* 2 (*Bollettino d'Arte*, volume speciale), ed. F. van der Wielen-van Ommeren and L. de Lachenal, Rome, pp. 7–56.

———. 2012. "Κεραμική Ανατολικής Ελλάδας στο Καραμπουρνάκι," in Tiverios et al. 2012, pp. 215–238.

———. 2020. "The Northern Aegean," in *A Companion to Greeks across the Ancient World*, ed. F. De Angelis, Hoboken, pp. 409–430.

Tsiaousi, V. 1996. *Ειδικό διαχειριστικό σχέδιο για την περιοχή Κάτω Όλυμπος*, Thessaloniki.

Tsiloyianni, P. 2014. "Οικισμός της Χαλκολιθικής περιόδου στη Μεθώνη Πιερίας," *AEMTh* 28 [2019], pp. 223–228.

Tsimpidou-Avloniti, M., A. Kagiouli, A. Kaiafa, I. Lykidou, M. Mandaki, and S. Protopsalti. 2006. "Καλαμαριά 2005–2006. Μια 'άγνωστη' ρωμαϊκή εγκατάσταση στην ακτογραμμή του Θερμαϊκού και άλλα ευρήματα," *AEMTh* 20 [2008], pp. 271–283.

Tsingarida, A. 2014. "The Attic Phiale in Context: The Late Archaic Red-Figure and Coral-red Workshops," in *Athenian Potters and Painters* 3, ed. J. H. Oakley, Oxford and Philadelphia, pp. 263–272.

Tsirtsoni, Z. 2000a. "Les poteries du début du Néolithique Récent en Macédoine: 1. Les types de récipients," *BCH* 124, pp. 1–55.

———. 2000b. "Η κεραμική της Νεότερης Νεολιθικής περιόδου από τον Γαλλικό τομέα των πρόσφατων ανασκαφών (1986–1996) στο Ντικιλί Τας (Φίλιπποι, Ν. Καβάλας)," *AEMTh* 14 [2002], pp. 45–54.

———. 2001. "Les poteries du début du Néolithique Récent en Macédoine: 2. Les fonctions des récipients," *BCH* 125, pp. 1–39.

———. 2010. "Το τέλος της Νεολιθικής εποχής στην Ελλάδα και τα Βαλκάνια," in Papadimitriou and Tsirtsoni 2010, Athens, pp. 93–103.

Tsirtsoni, Z., and F. Bourguignon. 2016. "Late Neolithic Ceramic Lamps: New Evidence from Northern Greece," in *Southeast Europe and Anatolia in Prehistory: Essays in Honor of Vasil Nikolov on his 65th Anniversary* (Universitätsforschungen zur prähistorischen Archäologie 293), ed. K. Bacvarov and R. Gleser, Bonn, pp. 209–219.

Tsouggaris, Ch. 2009. "Παιονική ασπίδα στην Ορεστίδα της Άνω Μακεδονίας," in *Κέρματα Φιλίας: Τιμητικός τόμος για τον Ιωάννη Τουράτσογλου 2*, ed. St. Drougou, D. Eugenidou, Ch. Kritzas, N. Kaltsas, B. Penna, E. Tsourti, M. Galani-Krikou, and E. Ralli, Athens, pp. 579–589.

Tsountas, Ch. D. 1891. "Ἐκ Μυκηνῶν," *ArchEph* 1891, cols. 1–43.

———. 1897. "Μῆτραι και ξίφη εκ Μυκηνῶν," *ArchEph* 1897, cols. 96–127.

———. 1899a. "Κυκλαδικά II," *ArchEph* 1899, cols. 73–134.

———. 1899b. "Ἀνασκαφὴ ἐν Θεσσαλίᾳ," *Prakt* 1899, pp. 101–102.

———. 1908. *Αἱ προϊστορικαὶ ἀκροπόλεις Διμηνίου καὶ Σέσκλου*, Athens.

Tuck, S. L. 1999–2001. "Ouch! Inscribed Greek Sling Bullets in Missouri," *Muse* 33–35, pp. 14–32.

Turner, E. 1974. "A Commander-in-Chief's Order from Saqqâra," *JEA* 60, pp. 239–242.

Turner, R. D. 1966. *A Survey and Illustrated Catalogue of the Teredinidae*, Cambridge, Mass.

Turner, V. 1969. *The Ritual Process: Structure and Anti-structure*, London.

Twede, D. 2002. "Transport Amphoras: The Earliest Consumer Packages?" *Journal of Macromarketing* 22, pp. 98–108.

Tylecote, R. F. 1973. "Casting Copper and Bronze into Stone Molds," *Bulletin of the Historical Metallurgy Group*, 7 (1), pp. 1–5.

———. 1982. "The Late Bronze Age and Bronze Metallurgy at Enkomi and Kition." In *Early Metallurgy in Cyprus, 4000–500 B.C.*, ed. J. D. Muhly, R. Maddin, and V. Karageorghis, Nicosia, pp. 81–100.

———. 1987. *The Early History of Metallurgy in Europe*, London.

———. 1992. *A History of Metallurgy*, 2nd ed., London.

Tzannes, M.-C. 2004. "The Excavations of G. Oikonomos at the Archaic Cemetery of Monastirakia in Klazomenai, 1921–22," in *Klazomenai, Teos and Abdera: Metropoleis and Colony. Proceedings of the International Symposium Held at the Archaeological Museum of Abdera, Abdera, 20–21 October 2001*, ed. A. Moustaka, E. Skarlatidou, M.-C. Tzannes, and Y. E. Ersoy, Thessaloniki, 97–120.

Tzedakis, I., and H. Martlew. 1999. *Minoans and Mycenaeans: Flavours of Their Time*, Athens.

Tzedakis, I., H. Martlew, and M. Jones, eds. 2008. *Archaeology Meets Science: Biomolecular Investigations in Bronze Age Greece. The Primary Scientific Evidence*, Oxford.

Tziaphalias, A. 1983. "Κραννών," *ArchDelt* 38, B'1, pp. 204–208.

Tzifopoulos, Y. Z. 2012a. "Ιστορικό διάγραμμα Μεθώνης," in Bessios, Tzifopoulos, and Kotsonas 2012, pp. 13–40.

———. 2012b. "Η ενεπίγραφη κεραμική του 'Υπογείου': Πανέλληνες στη Μεθώνη," in Bessios, Tzifopoulos, and Kotsonas 2012, pp. 307–319.

———. 2013. *Γράμματα από το "Υπόγειο." Γραφή στη Μεθώνη Πιερίας ύστερος 8ος πρώιμος 7ος αιώνας π.Χ. Letters from the Underground: Writing in Methone, Pieria Late 8th–Early 7th Century B.C.*, Thessaloniki.

Tzouvara-Souli, Ch. 1992. *Τεχνική και σχήματα αττικών αγγείων 6ου–4ου π.Χ. αι.*, Ioannina.

Undset, I. 1889. "Zu den ältesten Fibeltypen," *Zeitschrift für Ethnologie* 21, pp. 205–234.

Unruh, J. 2007. "Ancient Textile Evidence in Soil Structures at the Agora Excavations in Athens, Greece," in *Ancient Textiles: Production, Craft, and Society*, ed. C. Gillis and M.-L. B. Nosch, Oxford, pp. 167–172.

Untracht, O. 1986. *Τεχνικές επεξεργασίας μετάλλων για τους τεχνίτες. Ένα βασικό εγχειρίδιο για χρήση των τεχνιτών σχετικό με τις μεθόδους μορφοποίησης και διακόσμησης των μετάλλων*, Athens.

Urem-Kotsou, D. 2006. "Νεολιθική κεραμική του Μακρυγιάλου. Διατροφικές συνήθειες και οι κοινωνικές διαστάσεις της κεραμικής" (diss. Aristotle Univ. Thessaloniki).

Urem-Kotsou, D., and N. Efstratiou. 1993. "Η συμβολή της κεραμικής τυπολογίας της Μάκρης στη μελέτη της προϊστορικής εξέλιξης στη Θράκη," *AEMTh* 7 [1997], pp. 618–625.

Urem-Kotsou, D., and K. Kotsakis. 2007. "Pottery, Cuisine and Community in the Neolithic of North Greece," in *Cooking Up the Past: Food and Culinary Practices in the Neolithic and Bronze Age Aegean*, ed. C. Mee and J. Renard, Oxford, pp. 225–246.

Urem-Kotsou, D., B. Stern, C. Heron, and K. Kotsakis. 2002. "Birch-Bark Tar at Neolithic Makriyalos, Greece," *Antiquity* 76, pp. 962–967.

Utili, F. 1992. "Früh- und hocharchaische bemalte Schalen," in *Ausgrabungen in Assos 1990* (Asia Minor Studien 5), ed. Ü. Serdaroğlu and R. Stupperich, Bonn, pp. 33–63.

———. 1996a. "Archaische ostgriechische Lekanai," in *Ausgrabungen in Assos 1992* (Asia Minor Studien 21), ed. Ü. Serdaroğlu and R. Stupperich, Bonn, pp. 59–70.

———. 1996b. "Die archaischen Gräber aus E' IV'," in *Ausgrabungen in Assos 1992* (Asia Minor Studien 21), ed. Ü. Serdaroğlu and R. Stupperich, Bonn, pp. 43–57.

———. 1999. *Die archaische Nekropole von Assos* (Asia Minor Studien 31), Bonn.

Uzel, I. 1999. "Les instruments médicaux et chirurgicaux conservés au musée d'Ephèse," in *100 Jahre österreichische Forschungen in Ephesos. Akten des Symposions Wien 1995*, ed. H. Friesinger and F. Krinzinger, Vienna, pp. 211–214.

Uzun, K. 2018. "Clazomenian Wave-line Pottery," in *Archaic and Classical Western Anatolia: New Perspectives in Ceramic Studies. In Memoriam Prof. Crawford H. Greenewalt, Jr.*, ed. R. G. Gürtekin Demir, H. Cevizoğlu, Y. Polat, and G. Polat, Leuven, pp. 315–344.

Vajsov, I. 2007. "Promachon-Topolniča: A Typology of Painted Decorations and Its Use as a Chronological Marker," in *The Struma/Strymon River Valley in Prehistory: In the Steps of James Harvey Gaul* 2, ed. H. Todorova, M. Stefanovich, and G. Ivanov, Sofia, pp. 91–132.

Vakirtzi, S. 2018. "The Thread of Life Broken: Spindles as Funerary Offerings in the Prehistoric Cyclades," *Arachne* 5, pp. 100–110.

Vakirtzi, S., H. Koukouli-Chrysanthaki, and S. Papadopoulos. 2014. "Spindle Whorls from Two Prehistoric Sites on Thassos," in *Prehistoric, Ancient Near Eastern and Aegean Textiles and Dress*, ed. M. Harlow, C. Michel, and M.-L. Nosch, Oxford, pp. 43–57.

Valamoti, S.-M. 2003. "Αρχαιοβοτανικά δεδομένα από το Καραμπουρνάκι: μια προκαταρκτική έκθεση των ευρημάτων," *AEMTh* 17 [2005], pp. 201–204.

———. 2004. *Plants and People in Late Neolithic and Early Bronze Age Northern Greece: An Archaeobotanical Investigation* (*BAR-IS* 1258), Oxford.

———. 2007a. "Food Across Borders: A Consideration of the Neolithic and Bronze Age Archaeobotanical Evidence from Northern Greece," in Galanaki et al. 2007, pp. 281–292.

———. 2007b. "Traditional Foods and Culinary Novelties in Neolithic and Bronze Age Northern Greece: An Overview of the Archaeobotanical Evidence," in *Cooking Up the Past: Food and Culinary Practices in the Neolithic and Bronze Age Aegean*, ed. C. Mee and J. Renard, Oxford, pp. 89–108.

———. 2009. *Η αρχαιοβοτανική έρευνα της διατροφής στην προϊστορική Ελλάδα*, Thessaloniki.

———. 2013. "Towards a Distinction between Digested and Undigested Glume Bases in the Archaeobotanical Record from Neolithic Northern Greece: A Preliminary Experimental Investigation," *Environmental Archaeology* 18, pp. 31–42.

———. 2016. "Millet, the Late Comer: On the Tracks of *Panicum miliaceum* in Prehistoric Greece," *Archaeological and Anthropological Sciences* 8 (1), pp. 51–63.

Valamoti, S.-M., and M. Charles. 2005. "Distinguishing Food from Fodder through the Study of Charred Plant Remains: An Experimental Approach to Dung-derived Chaff," *Vegetation History and Archaeobotany* 14, pp. 528–533.

Valamoti, S. M., and E. Gkatzogia. 2010. "Plant Remains from an Iron Age Cooking Installation at Karabournaki, Northern Greece" (poster presentation, International Work Group for Palaeoethnobotany 2010).

Valamoti, S.-M., E. Gkatzogia, I. Hristova, and E. Marinova. 2018. "Iron Age Cultural Interactions, Plant Subsistence and Land Use in Southeastern Europe Inferred from Archaeobotanical Evidence of Greece and Bulgaria," in *Archaeology Across Frontiers and Borderlands: Fragmentation and Connectivity in the North Aegean and the Central Balkans from the Bronze Age to the Iron Age,* ed. S. Gimatzidis, M. Pieniążek, and S. Mangaloğlu-Votruba, Vienna, pp. 269–290.

Valamoti, S. M., E. Gkatzogia, and M. Ntinou. 2018. "Did Greek Colonisation Bring Olive Growing to the North? An Integrated Archaeobotanical Investigation of the Spread of Olea Europaea in Greece from the 7th to the 1st millennium BC," *Vegetation History and Archaeobotany* 27, pp. 177–195.

Valamoti, S.-M., and G. Jones. 2010. "Bronze and Oil: A Possible Link Between the Introduction of Tin and 'Lallemantia' to Northern Greece," *BSA* 105, pp. 83–96.

Valamoti, S.-M., A. Papanthimou, and A. Pilali. 2003. "Προϊστορικά μαγειρέματα στην Τούμπα του Αρχοντικού Γιαννιτσών: τα αρχαιοβοτανικά δεδομένα," *AEMTh* 17 [2005], pp. 497–503.

Valla, M. 2007. "A Late Bronze Age Cemetery in Faia Petra, East of the Middle Strymon Valley," in *The Struma/Strymon River Valley in Prehistory*, ed. H. Todorov, M. Stefanovich, and G. Ivanov, Sofia, pp. 359–372.

Vallet, G., and F. Villard. 1964. *Mégara Hyblaea* 2: *La céramique archaïque*, Paris.

Valmin, M. N. 1938. *The Swedish Messenia Expedition*, Lund.

Van Compernolle, T. 2000. "Les céramiques ioniennes en Méditerranée centrale," in *Ceràmiques jònies d'època arcaica: centres de producció i comercialització al Mediterrani Occidental: Actes de la Taula Rodona celebrada a Empúries els dies 26 al 28 de maig de 1999*, ed. P. Cabrera Bonet and M. Santos Retolaza, Barcelona, pp. 89–100.

Van Damme, T. 2019. "Stoppers, Transport Stirrup Jars and Wine Transport, 1450–1150 BC," *BSA* 114, pp. 93-117.

———. 2020. "The Many Lives of Attic Figured Vases from Ancient Methone," in Archaeological Institute of America, 120th Annual Meeting Abstracts, pp. 208–209.

Van der Kolf, M. C. 1932. "Methone 1–3," *RE* 15 (2), p. 1381.

Vanderpool, E. 1946. "The Rectangular Rock-cut Shaft," *Hesperia* 15, pp. 265–336.

van der Wielen-van Ommeren, F., and M. Kleibrink. 2008. "Colonial Pottery," in *La Dea di Sibari e il santuario ritrovato. Studi sui rinvenimenti dal Timpone Motta di Francavilla Marittima* 1.2: *Ceramiche di importazione, di produzione coloniale e indigena* 2 (*Bollettino d'Arte*, volume speciale), ed. F. van der Wielen-van Ommeren and L. de Lachenal, Rome, pp. 57–169.

Vandiver, P. 1983. "Glass Technology at the Mid-Second-Millennium B.C. Hurrian Site of Nuzi," *Journal of Glass Studies* 25, pp. 239–247.

van Dommelen, P. 2005. "Colonial Interactions and Hybrid Practices: Phoenician and Carthaginian Settlement in the Ancient Mediterranean," in *The Archaeology of Colonial Encounters: Comparative Perspectives*, ed. G. J. Stein, Santa Fe and Oxford, pp. 109–141.

———. 2012. "Colonialism and Migration in the Ancient Mediterranean," *Annual Review of Anthropology* 41, pp. 393–409.

Van Duivenvoorde, W. 2014. "The 5th-Century BC Shipwreck at Tektaş Burnu,Turkey: Evidence for the Ship's Hull from Nail Concretions," *Nautical Archaeology* 43, pp. 10–26.

Van Gennep, A. 1961. *The Rites of Passage*, Chicago.

Van Gijn, A., and Y. Lammers-Keijsers. 2010. "Toolkits for Ceramic Production: Informal Tools and the Importance of High Power Use-wear Analysis," *Bulletin de la Société préhistorique française* 107 (4), pp. 755–762.

Van Straten, F. T. 1995. *Hiera Kala: Images of Animal Sacrifice in Archaic and Classical Greece*, Leiden.

Van Wees, H. 1995. "Politics and the Battlefield: Ideology in Greek Warfare," in *The Greek World*, ed. A. Powell, London and New York, pp. 153–178.

———. 2010. "'Those Who Sail Are to Receive a Wage': Naval Warfare and Finance in Archaic Eretria," in *New Perspectives on Ancient Warfare*, ed. G. G. Fagan and M. Trundle, Leiden and Boston, pp. 206–226.

Vargyas, P. 2002. "The Alleged Eretria Goldsmith in Near Eastern Perspective," *Specimina Nova* 16, pp. 13–18.

Varoucha-Christodoulopoulou, I. 1953–1954. "Συμβολὴ εἰς τὸν Χρεμωνίδειον Πόλεμον, 266/5–263/2 π.Χ.," *ArchEph* Part 3, pp. 321–349.

Varvarinou, D. 2017. "Small Finds from the Sanctuary of Kythnos: The Bone and Ivory Jewelry, Part I," in *Les sanctuaires archaïques des Cyclades*, ed. A. Mazarakis Ainian, Rennes, pp. 167–173.

Vasić, R. 1977. *The Chronology of the Early Iron Age in the Socialist Republic of Serbia* (BAR, Supplementary Series 3.I), Oxford.

———. 1982. "Ein Beitrag zu den Doppelnadeln im Balkanraum," *PZ* 57, pp. 220–257.

———. 1999. *Die Fibeln im Zentralbalkan (Vojvodina, Serbien, Kosovo und Makedonien)* (*PBF* XIV.12), Stuttgart.

———. 2003. *Die Nadeln im Zentralbalkan (Vojvodina, Serbien, Kosovo und Makedonien)* (*PBF* XIII.11), Stuttgart.

Vasileiadou, A. 2009. "Ανάλυση και ερμηνεία του ζωοαρχαιολογικού υλικού από το Κτήριο Α της Τούμπας Θεσσαλονίκης της υστερης Εποχής του Χαλκού" (MA thesis, Aristotle Univ. Thessaloniki).

Vasilev, M. I. 2015. *The Policy of Darius and Xerxes Towards Thrace and Macedonia* (*Mnemosyne* Suppl. 379), Leiden and Boston.

Vassallo, S. 2004. "The Stone Casting Moulds from Colle Madore: Evidence of Metallurgy in Sikanie," in *Ancient West and East* 3.1, ed. G. Tsetskhladze, Leiden and Boston, pp. 20–37.

Vassileiadou, I. 2011. *Η αγροτική ζωή στην αρχαία Πιερία: αρχαιολογικά τεκμήρια*, Thessaloniki.

———. 2019. "Πίσσα πιερική—πίσσα μακεδονική," in *Η πανεπιστημιακή ανασκαφή του Δίου: Νεότερες μελέτες*, ed. S. Pingiatoglou, Thessaloniki, pp. 111–118.

Vassileva, M. 2007. "King Midas and the Early History of Macedonia," in *Ancient Macedonia* 7: *Macedonia from the Iron Age to the Death of Philip II* (Institute for Balkan Studies 280), E. Voutiras, Thessaloniki, pp. 773–779.

———. 2018. "Of Fibulae, of Course!" in *The Adventure of an Illustrious Scholar: Papers Presented to Oscar White Muscarella*, ed. E. Simpson, Leiden, 188–212.

Vassilogamvrou, A. 2008. "The Early Helladic Cemetery at Kalamaki, Northwest Peloponnese (ca. 3000–2700 B.C.)," in Tzedakis, Martlew, and Jones 2008, pp. 249–251.

Vassilopoulou, V. 2000. "Από το άντρο των Λειβηθρίδων στον Ελικώνα," in *Επετηρίς Εταιρείας Βοιωτικών Μελετών 3: Πρακτικά Γ΄ Διεθνούς Συνεδρίου Βοιωτικών Μελετών, Θήβα 4–8 Σεπτεμβρίου 1996*, 1, ed. V. Aravantinos, Athens, pp. 404–431.

Vassilopoulou, V., and A. Matthaiou. 2013a. "Ἐπιγραφικὰ χαράγματα ἀπὸ τὸ ἄντρον τῶν Λειβηθρίδων," *Grammateion* 2, pp. 85–90.

———. 2013b. "Ἐπιγραφικὰ χαράγματα ἀπὸ τὸ ἄντρον τῶν Λειβηθρίδων. ΠΡΟΣΘΗΚΗ," *Grammateion* 2, pp. 91–92.

Vavelidis, M. 2004. "Κοιτάσματα χρυσού και αρχαία μεταλλευτική δραστηριότητα στη Μακεδονία και Θράκη," *Thessalonikeon Polis* 14, pp. 74–93.

Vavelidis, M., and S. Andreou. 2008. "Gold and Gold Working in Late Bronze Age Northern Greece," *Naturwissenschaften* 95, pp. 361–366.

Ventris, M., and J. Chadwick. 1973. *Documents in Mycenaean Greek*, 2nd ed., Cambridge.

Verdan, S. 2006. "Un nouveau navire géométrique à Érétrie," *Antike Kunst* 49, pp. 97–107.

———. 2007. "Eretria: Metalworking in the Sanctuary of Apollo Daphnephoros During the Geometric Period (with an appendix by W. Fasnacht)," in *Oropos and Euboea in the Early Iron Age. Acts of an International Round Table, University of Thessaly (June 18–20, 2004)*, ed. A. Mazarakis Ainian, Volos, pp. 345–359.

———. 2017. "Counting on Pots? Reflections on Numerical Notations in Early Iron Age Greece," in Strauss Clay, Malkin, and Y. Z. Tzifopoulos 2017b, pp. 105–122.

Verdan, S., and E. Heymans. 2020. "Men and Metals on the Move: The Case of Euboean Gold," in *Euboica* II. *Pithekoussai and Euboea between East and West: Proceedings of the Conference, Lacco Ammeno (Ischia, Naples), 14–17 May 2018* (*AION, Annali di Archeologia e Storia Antica, Università degli Studi di Napoli L'Orientale*, n.s. 26, 2019), vol. 1, ed. T. E. Cinquantaquattro and M. D'Acunto, Naples, vol. 1, pp. 279–299.

Verdelis, N. M. 1958. *Ὁ πρωτογεωμετρικὸς ῥυθμὸς τῆς Θεσσαλίας*, Athens.

———. 1963. "Neue geometrische Gräber in Tiryns," *AM* 78, pp. 1–62.

Vergina I = M. Andronikos, *Βεργίνα* I: *Τὸ νεκροταφεῖον τῶν τύμβων*, Athens 1969.

Veropoulidou, R. 2011a. "Όστρεα από τους οικισμούς του Θερμαϊκού Κόλπου. Ανασυνθέτοντας την κατανάλωση των μαλακίων στη Νεολιθική και την Εποχή Χαλκού" (diss. Aristotle Univ. Thessaloniki).

———. 2011b. "*Spondylus gaederopus* Tools and Meals in Central Greece from the 3rd to the Early 1st Millennium BCE," in *Spondylus in Prehistory: New Data and Approaches. Contributions to the Archaeology of Shell Technologies* (*BAR-IS* 2216), ed. F. Ifantidis and M. Nikolaidou, Oxford, pp. 191–208.

———. 2012. "The Tyrian Purple, a 'Royal Dye,'" in *Greeks and Phoenicians at the Mediterranean Crossroads*, ed. P. Adam-Veleni and E. Stefani, Thessaloniki, pp. 103–105.

———. 2014. "Όψεις της διατροφής και του υλικού πολιτισμού της Νεολιθικής και της Εποχής Χαλκού στην κεντρική Μακεδονία. Μια οστρεοαρχαιολογική προσέγγιση" ["Aspects of Neolithic and Bronze Age Diet and Material Culture in Central Macedonia: The Evidence from Shell Analyses"], in Stefani, Merousis, and Dimoula 2014, pp. 465–475.

———. 2022. "'Warming the Cockles of Their Hearts': Perforated Shells in Central Macedonia, Northern Aegean, during the Neolithic, Bronze Age and Early Iron Age," in *ΜΥΡΡΙΝΗ. Μελέτες αιγαιακής προϊστορίας. Τιμητικός τόμος για την Αικατερίνη Παπαευθυμίου-Παπανθίμου*, ed. N. Merousis, M. Nikolaidou and L. Stefani, Thessaloniki (e-book).

Veropoulidou, R., G. Kazantzis, N. Orova, S. Papadopoulou, and P. Tsiloyianni. Forthcoming. "Νέα δεδομένα από τον οικισμό της Τελικής Νεολιθικής περιόδου στη Μεθώνη Πιερίας," *AEMTh* 31 [2018].

Versakis, Ph. 1916. "Τὸ ἱερὸ τοῦ Κορύνθου Ἀπόλλωνος," *ArchDelt* 2, pp. 65–118.

Vicente, J. D., M. P. Punter, and B. Ezquerra. 1997. "La catapulta tardo-republicana y otro equipamiento militar de 'La Caridad' (Camineal, Teruel)," *Journal of Roman Military Equipment Studies* 8, pp. 167–199.

Vickers, M. 1977. "Some Early Iron Age Bronzes from Macedonia," in *Ancient Macedonia 2* (Institute of Balkan Studies 155), ed. K. Mitsakis, Thessaloniki, pp. 17–31.

Vierneisel, K., and B. Kaesar, eds. 1990. *Kunst der Schale, Kultur des Trinkens*, Munich.

Villard, F. 1970. "Céramique ionienne et céramique phocéenne en Occident," *PP* 25, pp. 108–129.

Villing, A., and E. G. Pemberton. 2010. "Mortaria from Ancient Corinth: Form and Function," *Hesperia* 79, pp. 555–638.

Vischer, W. 1878a. "Epigraphische und archäologische Beiträge aus Griechenland," in *Kleine Schriften* 2, ed. A. Burckhardt, Leipzig, pp. 1–103.

———. 1878b. "Antike Schleudergeschosse," in *Kleine Schriften* 2, ed. A. Burckhardt, Leipzig, pp. 240–284.

Vitale, S. 2011. "The Late Helladic IIIA2 Pottery from Mitrou and Its Implications for the Chronology of the Mycenaean Mainland," in Gauß et al. 2011, pp. 331–344.

Vitale, S., T. Marketou, C. McNamee, E. Ballan, N. G. Blackwell, I. Iliopoulos, C. Mantello, J. E. Morrison, K. Moulo, I. Moutafi, K.-S. Passa, and E. Vika. 2016. "The Serraglio, Eleona, and Langada Archaeological Project (SELAP): Report on the Results of the 2011–2015 Study Seasons," *ASAtene* 94, series 3 (16), pp. 225–285.

Vitelli, K. D. 1989. "Were Pots First Made for Foods? Doubts from Franchthi," *World Archaeology* 21 (1), pp. 17–29.

Vlachogianni, E. 2000. "Ελλοπία: Κανάλι Μόρνου," *ArchDelt* 55, B′1, pp. 396–398.

Vlachou, V. 2007. "Oropos: The Infant and Child Inhumations from the Settlement (Late 8th–Early 7th Centuries BC)," in *Oropos and Euboea in the Early Iron Age. Acts of an International Round Table*, ed. A. Mazarakis Ainian, Volos, pp. 213–224.

Voigtländer, W. 1984. "Zur archaischen Keramik in Milet," in *Milet 1899–1980. Ergebnisse, Probleme, und Perspektiven einer Ausgrabung. Kolloquium Frankfurt am Main 1980* (*IstMitt* Beiheft 31), ed. W. Müller-Wiener, 35–56.

Vokotopoulou, I. 1969. "Πρωτογεωμετρικὰ ἀγγεῖα ἐκ τῆς περιοχῆς τοῦ Ἀγρινίου," *ArchDelt* 24, A′, pp. 74–94.

———. 1973. *Οδηγός Μουσείου Ιωαννίνων*, Athens.

———. 1984. "ΙΣΤ Εφορεία Προϊστορικών και Κλασικών Αρχαιοτήτων," *ArchDelt* 39 B′, pp. 214–227.

———. 1986. *Βίτσα: τα νεκροταφεία μιας μολοσσικής κώμης*, Athens.

———. 1988. "Macedonia: Geographical and Historical Outline," in *Ancient Macedonia* (Exhibition catalogue, Museum of Victoria, Melbourne; Queensland Museum, Brisbane; Australian Museum, Sydney), Athens, pp. 68–70.

———. 1990. *Οι ταφικοί τύμβοι της Αίνειας*, Athens.

———. 1993. "Αρχαϊκό ιερό στη Σάνη Χαλκιδικής," in *Ancient Macedonia* 5.1 (Institute for Balkan Studies 240), ed. D. Pantermalis, Thessaloniki, pp. 179–236.

Vokotopoulou, I., M. Bessios, and E. Trakosopoulou. 1990. "Παρθενώνας Χαλκιδικής· Ιερό σε κορυφή του Ιτάμου," *AEMTh* 4 [1991], pp. 427–438.

Vokotopoulou, I., and A.-P. Christidis. 1995. "A Cypriot Graffito on an SOS Amphora from Mende, Chalcidice," *Kadmos* 34, pp. 5–12.

Vokotopoulou, I., A. Despoini, V. Misailidou, and M. Tiverios. 1985. *Σίνδος. Κατάλογος τῆς ἔκθεσης*, Athens.

Voliotis, D. T. 1967. "Ἔρευναι ἐπὶ τῆς βλαστήσεως καὶ χλωρίδος τοῦ Χολομώντος καὶ ἰδίᾳ τῆς ἀρωματικῆς, φαρμακευτικς καὶ μελισσοτροφικῆς τοιαύτης" (diss. Aristotle Univ. Thessaloniki).

Völling, T. 1990. "Funditores im römischen Heer," *SaalbJb* 45, pp. 24–58.

Von den Driesch, A. 1976. *A Guide to the Measurement of Animal Bones from Archaeological Sites, as Developed by the Institut für Palaeoanatomie, Domestikationsforschung und Geschichte der Tiermedizin of the University of Munich*, Cambridge, Mass.

von Eles Masi, P. 1986. *Le fibule dell'Italia settentrionale* (*PBF* XIV.5), Munich.

Von Glinski, M. L. 2012. *Simile and Identity in Ovid's* Metamorphoses, Cambridge and New York.

Von Graeve, V. 1973–1974. "Milet. Bericht über die Arbeiten im Südschnitt an der hellenistischen Stadtmauer 1963," *IstMitt* 23–24, pp. 63–115.

Von Miller, A. C. J. 2015. "Archaic Pottery from Panayırdağ, Ephesos: New Evidence and First Results," in *Keramos. Ceramics: A Cultural Approach. Proceedings of the First International Conference at Ege University, May 9–13, 2011, İzmir*, ed. R. G. Gürtekin-Demir, H. Cevizoğlu, Y. Polat, and G. Polat, Ankara, pp. 184–196.

———. 2018. "Pottery Remains from the Archaic Settlement Underneath the Tetragonos Agora, Ephesos: A Chronological Case Study of Ionian Settlement Pottery," in *Archaic and Classical Western Anatolia: New Perspectives in Ceramic Studies. In Memoriam Prof. Crawford H. Greenewalt, Jr.*, ed. R. G. Gürtekin Demir, H. Cevizoğlu, Y. Polat, and G. Polat, Leuven, pp. 175–199.

Von Miller, A. C. J., with contributions by Michael Kerschner and Lisa Betina. 2019. *Archaische Siedlungsbefunde in Ephesos. Stratigraphie, Bauphasen, Keramik und Kleinfunde aus den Grabungen unter der Tetragonos Agora. Archaische Keramik aus dem Theater und von den Nordwestlichen Ausläufern des Panayırdağ* (Forschungen in Ephesos XIII.3), Vienna.

Von Sacken, F. 1868. *Das Grabfeld von Halstatt in Oberösterreich und dessen Alterthümer*, Vienna.

Vortuba, G. F. 2017. "Did Vessels Beach in the Ancient Mediterranean? An Assessment of the Textual and Visual Evidence," *The Mariner's Mirror* 103, pp. 7–29.

Voulgari, E. 2011. "Κοινωνική σημασία της ατομικής έκφρασης και των διακοσμητικών θεμάτων στη μελέτη της νεολιθικής κεραμικής" (diss. Aristotle Univ. Thessaloniki).

Voutiropoulos, N. 1996. "Το όπλο του Δαβίδ," *Αρχαιολογία και Τέχνες* 59, pp. 64–68.

Voyatzis, M. E. 1990. *The Early Sanctuary of Athena Alea at Tegea and Other Archaic Sanctuaries in Arcadia*, Göteborg.

———. 2014. "Objects from the Northern Sector," in *Tegea* 2: *Investigations in the Sanctuary of Athena Alea 1990–94 and 2004*, ed E. Østby, Athens, pp. 163–262.

Vukovič, J. B. 2013. "Baking Vessels in Late Neolithic: Baking-pans from Vinča," *Archéologie* 21 (1), pp. 129–144.

Waal, W. 2018. "On the 'Phoenician Letters': The Case for an Early Transmission of the Greek Alphabet from an Archaeological, Epigraphic and Linguistic Perspective," *Aegean Studies* 1, pp. 83–125.

Wace, A. J. B. 1906. "Laconia II. Excavations at Sparta, 1906: The Stamped Tiles," *BSA* 12, pp. 344–350.

———. 1907. "Laconia I. Excavations at Sparta, 1907: The Stamped Tiles," *BSA* 13, pp. 17–43.

———. 1921–1923. "Excavations at Mycenae," *BSA* 25, pp. 1–434.

———. 1929. "Lead Figurines," in Dawkins 1929a, pp. 249–284.

———. 1932. *Chamber Tombs at Mycenae* (*Archaeologia* 82), Oxford.

———. 1953. "Mycenae, 1939–1952," *BSA* 48, pp. 3–18.

Wace, A. J. B., and J. P. Droop. 1906–1907. "Excavations at Theotokou, Thessaly," *BSA* 13, pp. 309–327.

Wace, A. J. B., and M. S. Thompson. 1912. *Prehistoric Thessaly: Being Some Account of Recent Excavations and Explorations in North-Eastern Greece from Lake Kopais to the Borders of Macedonia*, Cambridge.

Wachter, R. 2001. *Non-Attic Greek Vase Inscriptions*. Oxford.

———. 2010. "Inscriptions," in *A Companion to the Ancient Greek Language*, ed. E. J. Bakker, Oxford, pp. 47–61.

Waiman-Barak, P., and A. Gilboa. 2016. "Maritime Transport Containers: The View from Phoenician Tell Keisan (Israel) in the Early Iron Age," in Demesticha and Knapp 2016, pp. 169–193.

Walbank, M. B. 1978. *Athenian Proxenies of the Fifth Century B.C.*, Toronto and Sarasota.

Walberg, G. 1976. "Northern Intruders in Mycenaean IIIC?" *AJA* 80, pp. 186–187.

Waldhauer, O. 1914. *Kaiserliche Ermitage. Die antiken Tonlampen*, St. Petersburg.

Waldstein, C. 1905. *Argive Heraeum* 2: *Terra-cotta Figurines, Terra-cotta Relief, Vase Fragments, Bronzes, Engraved Stones, Gems, and Ivories, Coins, Egyptian, or Graeco-Egyptian Objects*, Boston and New York.

Wallace, M., and M. Charles. 2013. "What Goes In Does Not Always Come Out: The Impact of the Ruminant Digestive System of Sheep on Plant Material, and Its Importance in the Interpretation of Dung-derived Archaeobotantical Assemblages," *Environmental Archaeology* 18, pp. 18–30.

Wallace, M. B. 1970. "Early Greek 'proxenoi,'" *Phoenix* 24, pp. 189–208.

Walter, H. 1968. *Frühe samische Gefässe: Chronologie und Landschaftsstile ostgriechischer Gefässe*, Bonn.

Walter, H., and F. Felten. 1981. *Alt-Ägina* 3.1: *Die vorgeschichtliche Stadt. Befestigungen, Häuser, Funde*, 2 vols., Mainz/Rhein.

Walter-Karydi, E. 1973. *Samos* VI: *Samische Gefässe des 6. Jahrhunderts v. Chr.*, Bonn.

Walters, H. B. 1921. "Red-Figured Vases Recently Acquired by the British Museum," *JHS* 41, pp. 117–150.

Wardle, K. A. 1973. "A Group of Late Helladic IIIB2 Pottery from within the Citadel at Mycenae," *BSA* 68, pp. 297–348.

———. 1980. "Excavations at Assiros, 1975–9: A Settlement Site in Central Macedonia and Its Significance for the Prehistory of South-east Europe," *BSA* 75, pp. 229–267.

———. 1983. "Assiros: A Macedonian Settlement of the Late Bronze and Early Iron Age," in *Ancient Macedonia* 3 (Institute for Balkan Studies 193), ed. C. Svolopoulos, pp. 291–305.

———. 1993. "Mycenaean Trade and Influence in Northern Greece," in *Wace and Blegen: Pottery as Evidence for Trade in the Aegean Bronze Age 1939–1989. Proceedings of the International Conference Held at the American School of Classical Studies at Athens. Athens, December 2–3, 1989*, ed. C. Zerner with P. Zerner and J. Winder, Amsterdam, pp. 117–141.

———. 2011. "Assiros and Aegean Chronology: An Update," *AEMTh* 25 [2015], pp. 415–421.

Wardle, K. A., T. Higham, and B. Kromer. 2014. "Dating the End of the Greek Bronze Age: A Robust Radiocarbon-based Chronology from Assiros Toumba," *PLoS ONE* 9(9): e106672, doi: 10.1371/journal.pone.0106672.

Wardle, K. A., and D. Wardle. 1999. "Metal Working in Late Bronze Age Central Macedonia," *AEMTh* 13 [2001], pp. 29–48.

———. 2000. "Assiros Toumba: Remains of the Later Iron Age," in *ΜΥΡΤΟΣ: Μελέτες στη Μνήμη της Ιουλίας Βοτοκοπούλου*, ed. P. Adam-Veleni, Thessaloniki, pp. 653–673.

Wartenberg, U. 2015. "Thraco-Macedonian Coinage in the Fifth Century B.C.: The Case of Ichnai," in *ΚΑΙΡΟΣ: Contributions to Numismatics in Honor of Basil Demetriadi*, ed. U. Wartenberg and M. Amandry, New York, pp. 347–364.

Waters, D. W. 1967. *The Rutters of the Sea: The Sailing Directions of Pierre Garcie. A Study of the First English and French Printed Sailing Directions*, New Haven.

Waurick, G. 1988. "Helme der hellenistischen Zeit und ihre Vorläufer," in *Antike Helme. Sammlung Lipperheide und andere Bestände des Antikenmuseums Berlin* (Monographien des Römisch-Germanisches Zentralmuseum, Forschungsinstitut für Vor- und Frühgeschichte, 14), Mainz on Rhein, pp. 151–180.

Weber, H. 1944. "Angriffswaffen," in *OlForsch* I, pp. 146–165.

Weber, S. 2012. "Teil 2: Untersuchungen zur archaischen griechischen Keramik aus anderen ägyptischen Fundorten," in *Griechische Keramik des 7. und 6. Jhs. v. Chr. aus Naukratis und anderen Orten in Ägypten* (Archäologische Studien aus Naukratis 3), ed. U. Höckmann, Worms, pp. 195–432.

Węcowski, M. 2017. "Wine and the Early History of the Greek Alphabet: Early Greek Vase-Inscriptions and the *Symposion*," in Strauss Clay, Malkin, and Tzifopoulos 2017b, pp. 309–328.

Weinberg, G. D. 1960. "Excavations at Tarrha, 1959," *Hesperia* 29, pp. 90–108.

———. 1992. *Glass Vessels in Ancient Greece: Their History Illustrated from the Collection of the National Archaeological Museum, Athens*, Athens.

Weiss, P. 1997. "Milet 1994-1995: Schleuderbleie und Marktgewichte," *AA* 1997 (2), pp. 143–156.

Weiss, P., and N. Draskowski. 2010. "Neue griechische Schleuderbleie: Tissaphernes und weitere Kommandeure," *Chiron* 40, pp. 123–153.

Weisshaar, H.-J. 1980. "Ägäische Tonanker," *AM* 95, pp. 33–49.

Wells, B. 1983a. *Asine* 2: *Results of the Excavations East of the Acropolis, 1970–1974*, Fasc. 4.2: *The Protogeometric Period: An Analysis of the Settlement* (*ActaAth* 4, 24.2), Stockholm.

———. 1983b. *Results of the Excavations East of the Acropolis 1970–1974*, Fasc. 4.3: *The Protogeometric Period*, Part 3: *Catalogue of Pottery and Other Artefacts*, Stockholm.

Weninger, B., and R. Jung. 2009. "Absolute Chronology of the End of the Aegean Bronze Age," in *LH III C Chronology and Synchronisms* 3: *LH III C Late and the Transition to the Early Iron Age. Proceedings of the International Workshop Held at the Austrian Academy of Sciences at Vienna, February 23rd and 24th, 2007*, ed. S. Deger-Jalkotzy and A. E. Bachle, Vienna, pp. 373–416.

West, A. B. 1914. "The Formation of the Chalcidic League," *CP* 9, pp. 24–34.

———. 1925. "Methone and the Assessment of 430," *AJA* 29, pp. 440–444.

West, M. L. 1992. *Ancient Greek Music*, Oxford.

West, M. L., and R. Merkelbach. 1967. *Fragmenta Hesiodea*. Oxford.

Westerdahl, C. 1992. "The Maritime Cultural Landscape," *IJNA* 21.1, pp. 5–14.

———. 1994. "Maritime Cultures and Ship Types: Brief Comments on the Significance of Maritime Archaeology," *IJNA* 23, pp. 265–270.

Wheeler, E. L. 1987. "Ephorus and the Prohibition of Missiles," *TAPA* 117, pp. 157–182.

Whitbread, I. K. 1995. *Greek Transport Amphorae: A Petrological and Archaeological Study* (The British School at Athens Fitch Laboratory Occasional Paper 4), Exeter.

Whitehead, D. 2016. *Philo Mechanicus: On Sieges. Translated with Introduction and Commentary* (*Historia*: Einzelschriften 243), Stuttgart.

Whitley, J. 2002. "Objects with Attitude: Biographical Facts and Fallacies in the Study of Late Bronze Age and Early Iron Age Warrior Graves," *CAJ* 12, pp. 217–232.

Wide, S. 1901. "Eine lokale Gattung boiotischer Gefässe," *AM* 26, pp. 143–156.

———. 1910. "Gräberfunde aus Salamis," *AM* 35, pp. 17–36.

Wiencke, M. I. 1954. "An Epic Theme in Greek Art," *AJA* 58, pp. 285–306.

———. 1998. "Mycenaean Lerna," *Hesperia* 67, pp. 125–214.

Wiethold, J. 2003. "How to Trace the 'Romanisation' of Central Gaul by Archaeobotanical Analysis? Some Considerations on New Archaeobotanical Results from France Centre-Est," in *Actualité de la Recherche en Histoire et Archéologie agraires. Actes du colloque international AGER V, septembre 2000* (Annales Littéraires, 764. Série Environnement, sociétés et archéologie 5), ed. F. Favory and A. Vignot, Besançon, pp. 269–282.

Wijsman, H. J. W. 2000. *Valerius Flaccus, Argonautica, Book VI: A Commentary* (*Mnemosyne* Suppl. 204), Leiden, Boston, and Cologne.

Willerding, U. 1971. "Methodische Probleme bei der Untersuchung und Auswertung von Pflanzenfunden in vor- und frühgeschichtlichen Siedlungen," *Nachrichten aus Niedersachsens Urgeschichte* 40, pp. 180–198.

———. 1991. "Präsenz, Erhaltung und Repräsentanz von Pflanzenresten in archäologischem Fundgut (Presence, Preservation and Representation of Archaeological Plant Remains)," in *Progress in Old World Palaeoethnobotany: A Retrospective View on the Occasion of 20 Years of the International Work Group for Palaeoethnobotany*, ed. W. van Zeist, K. Wasylikowa, and K.-E. Behre, Rotterdam, pp. 25–51.

Williams, C., and H. Williams. 1991. "Excavations at Mytilene, 1990," *Echos du Monde Classique* 35, pp. 175–191.

Williams, C. K., II. 1979. "Corinth, 1978: Forum Southwest," *Hesperia* 48, pp. 105–144.

Williams, C. K., II, and J. E. Fisher. 1973. "Corinth, 1972: The Forum Area," *Hesperia* 42, pp. 1–44.

Williams, J., ed. 1997. *Money: A History*, London.

Willis, K. 1994. "The Vegetation History of the Balkans," *Quaternary Science Reviews* 13, pp. 769–788.

Wilson, J.-P. 1997–1998. "The 'Illiterate Trader'?" *BICS* 42, pp. 29–56.

———. 2005. "The Nature of Greek Overseas Settlements in the Archaic Period: Emporion or Apoikia?" in *The Development of the Polis in Archaic Greece*, ed. L. G. Mitchell and P. J. Rhodes, 2nd ed., London and New York, pp. 110–114.

———. 2006. "Ideologies of Greek Colonization," in *Greek and Roman Colonization: Origins, Ideologies and Interactions*, ed. G. Bradley and J. P. Wilson, Swansea, pp. 25–57.

Wiseman, J. R. 1963. "A Trans-Isthmian Fortification Wall," *Hesperia* 32, pp. 248–275.

———. 1967. "Excavations at Corinth, the Gymnasium Area, 1966," *Hesperia* 36, pp. 402–428.

Wolters, P. 1892. "Βοιωτικαὶ ἀρχαιότητες," *ArchEph* 31, cols. 213–240.

Woodard, R. D. 2017. "Alphabet and Phonology at Methone: Beginning a Typology of Methone Alphabetic Symbols and an Alternative Hypothesis for Reading Ηακεσάνδρο," in Strauss Clay, Malkin, and Tzifopoulos 2017b, pp. 182–218.

Worthington, I. 2008. *Philip II of Macedonia*, New Haven.

Worthington, I., C. Cooper, and E. M. Harris. 2001. *Dinarchus, Hyperides, and Lycurgus* (The Oratory of Classical Greece Series 5), Austin, Tex.

Woytowitsch, E. 1978. *Die Wagen der Bronze- und frühen Eisenzeit in Italien* (*PBF* XVII.1), Munich.

Wright, H. E. 1972. "Vegetation History," in *The Minnesota Messenia Expedition: Reconstructing a Bronze Age Regional Environment*, ed. W. A. McDonald and G. R. Rapp, Minneapolis, pp. 188–199.

Xydopoulos, I. K. 2006. *Κοινωνικές και πολιτιστικές σχέσεις των Μακεδόνων και των άλλων Ελλήνων: Συμβολή στην έρευνα της γραμματειακής και επιγραφικής παραδόσεως για την αρχαία Μακεδονία* (Μακεδονική Βιβλιοθήκη της Εταιρείας Μακεδονικών Σπουδών 96), Thessaloniki.

———. 2007. "Η Μακεδονία και οι Μακεδόνες στη γραμματειακή παράδοση του 5ου αιώνα: όψεις του 'άλλου'; Η περίπτωση του Ηροδότου," in *Ancient Macedonia* 7: *Macedonia from the Iron Age to the Death of Philip II* (Institute for Balkan Studies 280), ed. E. Voutiras, Thessaloniki, pp. 23–30.

———. 2012. "Άνω Μακεδονία," in *Θρεπτήρια: Μελέτες για την αρχαία Μακεδονία*, ed. M. A. Tiverios, P. Nigdelis, and P. Adam-Veleni, Thessaloniki, pp. 525–542.

———. 2016. "Τα ανατολικά σύνορα της Μακεδονίας επί Αλεξάνδρου Α´," in *Ἠχάδιν* 2*: Τιμητικός τόμος για τη Στέλλα Δρούγου*, ed. M. Giannopoulou and Chr. Kallini, Athens, pp. 246–264.

Yfantidis, K. 1990. *Staatliche Kunstsammlungen Kassel. Antike Gefässe: Eine Auswahl*, Kassel.

Yiannikouri, A., V. Patsiada, and M. Philimonos. 1989. "Ταφικά σύνολα από τις νεκροπόλεις της αρχαίας Ρόδου," in *Α´ Επιστημονική Συνάντηση για την Ελληνιστική Κεραμική, Ιωάννινα, Δεκέμβριος 1986,* Ioannina, pp. 56–94.

———. 1990. "Χρονολογικά προβλήματα γραπτής κεραμεικής από τη Ρόδο," in *Β´ Επιστημονική Συνάντηση για την Ελληνιστική Κεραμική, Ρόδος, 22–25 Μαρτίου 1989,* Athens, pp. 172–184.

———. 2000. "Ταφικά σύνολα από τις νεκροπόλεις της αρχαίας Ρόδου," in *Α Επιστημονική Συνάντηση για την Ελληνιστική Κεραμική, Ιωάννινα, Δεκέμβριος 1986,* 2nd ed., Rhodes, pp. 63–84.

Yntema, D. 2000. "Mental Landscapes of Colonization: The Ancient Written Sources and the Archaeology of Early Colonial-Greek Southeastern Italy," *BaBesch* 75, 1–49.

Yon, M. 1971. *Salamine de Chypre* 2: *La Tombe T.I. du XIe s. av. J.-C.*, Paris.

Young, A. 2014. "Jewellery," in Schaus 2014a, pp. 103–147.

Young, R. S. 1939. *Late Geometric Graves and a Seventh Century Well in the Agora* (*Hesperia* Suppl. 2), Athens.

———. 1969. "Old Phrygian Inscriptions from Gordion: Toward a History of the Phrygian Alphabet," *Hesperia* 38, pp. 252–296.

Zacharias, N., and M. Kaparou. 2011. "Appendix. Archaeological Pottery from Lemnos: A Technological Study," in Danile 2011, pp. 157–164.

Zachos, G. 2012. "Αρχαϊκή κεραμική από την Ερεσό της Λέσβου," in Tiverios et al. 2012, pp. 305–319.

Zachos, K. 2010. "Η μεταλλουργία στην Ελλάδα και στη ΝΑ Ευρώπη κατά την 5η και 4η χιλιετία π.Χ.," in Papadimitriou and Tsirtsoni 2010, pp. 77–91.

Zachos, K., and A. Douzougli. 1999. "Aegean Metallurgy: How Early and How Independent?" in *MELETEMATA: Studies Presented to Malcolm H. Wiener as He Enters His 65th Year* (*Aegaeum* 20), ed. P. B. Betancourt, V. Karageorghis, R. Laffineur, and W.-D. Niemeier, Liège, pp. 959–968.

Zachou, M. 2007. "Analysis of Metal Objects from Two Late Bronze to Classical Period Cemeteries in Molossia (Epirus, Greece)" (MA thesis, Institute of Archaeology, University College London).

Zagora 1 = A. Cambitoglou, *Zagora 1: Excavation Season 1967; Study Season 1968–69* (Australian Academy of the Humanities, Sydney), Sydney 1971.

Zagora 2 = A. Cambitoglou, A. Birchall, J. J. Coulton, and J. R. Green, eds. *Zagora* 2: *Excavation of a Geometric Town on the Island of Andros. Excavation Season 1969; Study Season 1969–1970*, Athens 1988.

Zahrnt, M. 2007. "Amyntas III und die griechischen Mächte," in *Ancient Macedonia* 7: *Macedonia from the Iron Age to the Death of Philip II* (Institute for Balkan Studies 280), ed. E. Voutiras, Thessaloniki, pp. 239–251.

———. 2011. "Η Μακεδονία και η Θράκη στον Θουκυδίδη," in *Τριάντα δύο μελέτες για τον Θουκυδίδη*, ed. A. Rengakos and Ch. Tsangalis, Thessaloniki, pp. 613–638.

———. 2012. "The History of Macedonia in the Pre-Hellenistic Period," in *Ancient Macedonia: Language, History, Culture*, ed. G. K. Giannakis, Thessaloniki, pp. 83–99.

Zampas, K., E. Doudoumi, G. Thomas, and E. Pavlidis. 2021. "Η θεωρητική αποκατάσταση και η πρόταση μερικής αναστήλωσης του Αρχοντικού της Αργίλου," in *Argilos, 25 années de recherches. Organisation de la ville et de la campagne dans les colonies du Nord de l'Égée, VIIIe–IIIe siècles av. n.è. Actes du colloque de Thessalonique, 25–27 mai 2017* (Publications of the Canadian Institute in Greece 13), ed. Z. Bonias and J.-Y. Perreault, Athens, pp. 341–367.

Zampiti, A. 2012. "Λειβήθριο άντρο Ελικώνα Βοιωτίας: από την κεραμική των αρχαϊκών και κλασικών χρόνων" (diss. Univ. of Ioannina).

Zampiti, A., and V. Vassilopoulou. 2008. "Κεραμική αρχαϊκής και κλασικής περιόδου από το Λειβήθριο Άντρο του Ελικώνα," in *Επετηρίς της Εταιρείας Βοιωτικών Μελετών 4: Δ΄ (Δ΄) Διεθνές Συνέδριο Βοιωτικών Μελετών, Λιβαδειά, 9–12 Σεπτεμβρίου 2000,* 1, ed. V. Aravantinos, pp. 445–472.

Zancani Montuoro, P. 1965–1966. "L'edificio quadrato nello Heraion alla Foce del Sele," *AttiMGraecia* 6–7, pp. 23–195.

———. 1972. "Lekythoi 'samie' e bucchero 'eolico,'" *ArchCl* 24, pp. 372–377.

———. 1974–1976. "Francavilla Marittima: A) Necropoli, I. Tre notabili enotrii dell'VIII sec. a.C.," *AttiMGraecia* 15–17, pp. 9–82.

———. 1977–1979. "Francavilla Marittima: Necropoli di Macchiabate: Saggi e scoperte in zone varie," *AttiMGraecia* 18–20, pp. 7–91.

———. 1980–1982. "Francavilla Marittima A): Necropoli e ceramic a Macchiabate zona T. (Temporella)," *AttiMGraecia* 21–23, pp. 7–129.

———. 1983–1984. "Francavilla Marittima: Necropoli di Macchiabate zona T. (Temporella, continuazione)," *AttiMGraecia* 24–25, pp. 7–109.

Zangemeister, K. 1885. *Glandes plumbeae latine inscriptae* (*EphEp*: Corporis Inscriptionum Latinarum Suppl. 6), Rome and Berlin.

Zapheiropoulos, N. S. 1960. "Ἀνασκαφαὶ Νάξου," *Prakt* 115, pp. 329–340.

Zapheiropoulou, Ph. 1969. "Κυκλάδες: Δονοῦσα," *ArchDelt* 24, B'2, pp. 390–393.

———. 2000. "Το αρχαίο νεκροταφείο της Πάρου στη γεωμετρική και αρχαϊκή εποχή," *ArchEph* 2000, pp. 283–293.

Zeest, I. B. 1960. *Keramičeskaja tara Bospora*, Moscow.

Ziehen, L. 1949. "Παράσιτοι 1," *RE* 36, pp. 1377–1381.

Zimmer, G. 1990. *Griechische Bronzegusswerkstätten. Zur Technologieentwicklung eines antiken Kunsthandwerkes*, Mainz.

Ziota, Ch. 2007. "Ταφικές πρακτικές και κοινωνίες της Εποχής του Χαλκού στη Δυτική Μακεδονία. Τα νεκροταφεία στην Κοιλάδα και στις Γούλες Κοζάνης" (diss. Aristotle Univ. Thessaloniki).

———. 2010. "Ταφές σε αγγεία της Πρώιμης και Μέσης Εποχής του Χαλκού στην ευρύτερη περιοχή της Κοζάνης," in *ΙΡΙΣ. Μελέτες στη μνήμη της καθηγήτριας Αγγελικής Πιλάλη-Παπαστερίου από τους μαθητές της στο Πανεπιστήμιο Θεσσαλονίκης*, ed. N. Merousis, E. Stefani, and M. Nikolaidou, Thessaloniki, pp. 93–115.

———. 2014. "Ο οικισμός του Κλείτου Κοζάνης στο ευρύτερο φυσικό και ανθρωπογενές περιβάλλον της Νεότερης και Τελικής Νεολιθικής περιόδου," in Stefani, Merousis, and Dimoula 2014, pp. 323–336.

Zohary, D., and M. Hopf. 2000. *Domestication of Plants in the Old World*, 3rd ed., Oxford.

Zunal, O. 2015. "East Greek Pottery from Klaros," in *Keramos. Ceramics: A Cultural Approach. Proceedings of the First International Conference at Ege University, May 9–13, 2011, İzmir*, ed. R. G. Gürtekin-Demir, H. Cevizoğlu, Y. Polat, and G. Polat, Ankara, pp. 243–254.

Zurbach, J. 2008. "Question foncière et départs coloniaux. À propos des *apoikiai* archaïques," *ASAtene* 86, pp. 87–103.

Zvelebil, M. 1992. "Hunting in Farming Societies: The Prehistoric Perspective," *Anthropozoologica* 16, pp. 7–18.

CONCORDANCES OF INVENTORY (ΜΕΘ OR ΜΕ) NUMBERS AND CATALOGUE OR FIGURE NUMBERS

ΜΕΘ numbers = Μεθώνη inventory numbers

ΜΕΘ no.	Cat. no.
ΜΕΘ 40	**16/35**
ΜΕΘ 44	**16/36**
ΜΕΘ 92	**16/20**
ΜΕΘ 96	**16/27**
ΜΕΘ 105	**17/10**
ΜΕΘ 106	**17/18**
ΜΕΘ 112	**17/19**
ΜΕΘ 114	**17/4**
ΜΕΘ 125	**16/29**
ΜΕΘ 145	**16/30**
ΜΕΘ 146	**16/32**
ΜΕΘ 158	**16/34**
ΜΕΘ 160	**16/31**
ΜΕΘ 170	**25/54**
ΜΕΘ 171	**25/55**
ΜΕΘ 172	**25/56**
ΜΕΘ 173	**25/57**
ΜΕΘ 174	**25/58**
ΜΕΘ 175	**25/102**
ΜΕΘ 176	**25/59**
ΜΕΘ 177	**25/103**
ΜΕΘ 178	**25/60**
ΜΕΘ 179	**25/3**
ΜΕΘ 180	**25/96**
ΜΕΘ 182	**25/1**
ΜΕΘ 183	**25/14**
ΜΕΘ 184	**25/15**
ΜΕΘ 185	**25/16**
ΜΕΘ 186	**25/2**
ΜΕΘ 187	**25/129**
ΜΕΘ 188	**25/52**
ΜΕΘ 190A	**25/48**
ΜΕΘ 190B	**25/49**
ΜΕΘ 191	**25/17**
ΜΕΘ 194	**13/12**
ΜΕΘ 210	**13/14**
ΜΕΘ 242	**13/1**
ΜΕΘ 257	**13/2**
ΜΕΘ 269	**13/11**
ΜΕΘ 280	**28/67**
ΜΕΘ 281	**28/1**
ΜΕΘ 282	**28/66**
ΜΕΘ 283	**28/37**
ΜΕΘ 284	**28/68**
ΜΕΘ 285	**28/2**
ΜΕΘ 286	**28/38**
ΜΕΘ 287	**28/3**
ΜΕΘ 288	**28/39**
ΜΕΘ 289	**28/63**
ΜΕΘ 290	**28/64**
ΜΕΘ 291	**28/4**
ΜΕΘ 292	**28/58**
ΜΕΘ 293	**28/106**
ΜΕΘ 294	**26/176**
ΜΕΘ 295	**26/123**
ΜΕΘ 296	**26/124**
ΜΕΘ 299	**26/125**
ΜΕΘ 302	**13/14**
ΜΕΘ 332	**25/61**
ΜΕΘ 333	**25/62**
ΜΕΘ 334	**25/63**
ΜΕΘ 335	**25/104**

MEΘ 336	**25/50**
MEΘ 337	**25/51**
MEΘ 338	**25/18**
MEΘ 339	**25/64**
MEΘ 340	**25/9**
MEΘ 341	**25/4**
MEΘ 342	**25/10**
MEΘ 346	**17/1**
MEΘ 348	**17/2**
MEΘ 350	**17/34**
MEΘ 352	**17/7**
MEΘ 354	**17/3**
MEΘ 355	**17/30**
MEΘ 358	**17/8**
MEΘ 359	**17/40**
MEΘ 360	**17/6**
MEΘ 361	**17/17**
MEΘ 362	**17/5**
MEΘ 363	**17/35**
MEΘ 366	**17/16**
MEΘ 367	**17/15**
MEΘ 368	**17/38**
MEΘ 369	**17/36**
MEΘ 371	**17/22**
MEΘ 372	**17/14**
MEΘ 375	**17/23**
MEΘ 377	**17/21**
MEΘ 385	**17/11**
MEΘ 386	**17/20**
MEΘ 432	**17/28**
MEΘ 433	**17/27**
MEΘ 435	**16/2**
MEΘ 437	**16/16**
MEΘ 438	**16/4**
MEΘ 442	**16/12**
MEΘ 443	**16/7**
MEΘ 446	**16/14**
MEΘ 447	**16/10**
MEΘ 454	**16/17**
MEΘ 456	**16/15**
MEΘ 457	**16/13**
MEΘ 459	**16/6**
MEΘ 460	**16/5**
MEΘ 462	**16/18**
MEΘ 468	**16/9**
MEΘ 469	**16/1**
MEΘ 471	**16/19**
MEΘ 472	**16/3**
MEΘ 478	**16/25**
MEΘ 479	**16/24**
MEΘ 482	**16/26**
MEΘ 488	**16/21**
MEΘ 495	**16/22**
MEΘ 497	**16/46**
MEΘ 498	**16/47**
MEΘ 499	**16/48**
MEΘ 504	Fig. 1.16
MEΘ 506	Fig. 1.16
MEΘ 507	Fig. 1.14
MEΘ 513	Fig. 14.4
MEΘ 515	Fig. 1.19, 14.11
MEΘ 529	**13/18**
MEΘ 532	**13/17**
MEΘ 543	**13/15**
MEΘ 563	**13/9**
MEΘ 565	**13/4**
MEΘ 567	**13/5**
MEΘ 589	**13/6**
MEΘ 590	**13/7**
MEΘ 606	**13/3**
MEΘ 649	**28/40**
MEΘ 650	**28/69**
MEΘ 651	**28/62**
MEΘ 652	**28/70**
MEΘ 653	**28/41**
MEΘ 654	**28/71**
MEΘ 655	**28/5**
MEΘ 656	**28/42**
MEΘ 661	**16/39**
MEΘ 667	**16/23**
MEΘ 799	**25/19**
MEΘ 800	**25/20**
MEΘ 801	**25/21**
MEΘ 802	**25/22**
MEΘ 803	**25/23**
MEΘ 804	**25/24**
MEΘ 805	**25/25**
MEΘ 806	**25/26**
MEΘ 807A	**25/27**
MEΘ 807B	**25/28**
MEΘ 808	**25/65**
MEΘ 809	**25/97**
MEΘ 810	**25/98**
MEΘ 811	**25/99**
MEΘ 812	**25/66**
MEΘ 813	**25/53**

ΜΕΘ 814	**25/100**
ΜΕΘ 815	**25/67**
ΜΕΘ 816	**25/68**
ΜΕΘ 817	**25/69**
ΜΕΘ 818	**25/70**
ΜΕΘ 819	**25/105**
ΜΕΘ 820	**25/71**
ΜΕΘ 821	**25/72**
ΜΕΘ 822	**25/106**
ΜΕΘ 823	**25/115**
ΜΕΘ 824	**25/112**
ΜΕΘ 825	**25/113**
ΜΕΘ 854	**25/29**
ΜΕΘ 860	**6/1**, Fig. 1.28d
ΜΕΘ 861	**6/2**, Fig. 1.28b
ΜΕΘ 862	**6/3**, Fig. 1.28e
ΜΕΘ 863	**6/9**
ΜΕΘ 864	**6/12**, Fig. 1.28c
ΜΕΘ 865	**6/13**, Fig. 1.28a
ΜΕΘ 866	**6/15**, Fig. 1.28f
ΜΕΘ 867	**6/14**
ΜΕΘ 868	**6/27**
ΜΕΘ 869	**6/28**
ΜΕΘ 870	**6/29**
ΜΕΘ 871	**6/30**
ΜΕΘ 872	**6/35**
ΜΕΘ 873	**6/36**
ΜΕΘ 874	**6/37**
ΜΕΘ 875	**6/40**
ΜΕΘ 876	**6/41**
ΜΕΘ 877	**6/8**
ΜΕΘ 878	**6/5**
ΜΕΘ 879α	**6/16**
ΜΕΘ 879β	**6/17**
ΜΕΘ 880 + 881	**6/42**
ΜΕΘ 881 + 880	**6/42**
ΜΕΘ 882α,β	**6/18α**,β
ΜΕΘ 883α,β	**6/25α**,β
ΜΕΘ 884α,β,γ,δ	**6/6α**,β,γ,δ
ΜΕΘ 885α,β,γ	**6/38α**,β,γ
ΜΕΘ 886	**6/7**
ΜΕΘ 887	**6/39**
ΜΕΘ 888α,β	**6/20α**,β
ΜΕΘ 889 + 4164	**6/21**
ΜΕΘ 890	**6/22**
ΜΕΘ 891α,β,γ	**6/19α**,β,γ
ΜΕΘ 892α,β,γ	**6/43α**,β,γ
ΜΕΘ 893	**6/44**
ΜΕΘ 894α,β,γ	**6/10α**,β,γ
ΜΕΘ 895	**6/26**
ΜΕΘ 896	**6/31**
ΜΕΘ 897	**6/4**
ΜΕΘ 898	**6/24**
ΜΕΘ 906	**25/30**
ΜΕΘ 1064	**25/107**
ΜΕΘ 1065	**25/73**
ΜΕΘ 1066	**25/74**
ΜΕΘ 1067	**25/75**
ΜΕΘ 1068	**25/76**
ΜΕΘ 1069	**25/77**
ΜΕΘ 1070	**25/78**
ΜΕΘ 1071	**25/79**
ΜΕΘ 1072	**25/101**
ΜΕΘ 1073	**25/80**
ΜΕΘ 1074	**25/31**
ΜΕΘ 1075	**25/32**
ΜΕΘ 1076	**25/33**
ΜΕΘ 1077	**25/34**
ΜΕΘ 1078	**25/131**
ΜΕΘ 1080	**13/16**
ΜΕΘ 1110	**13/8**
ΜΕΘ 1117	**13/13**
ΜΕΘ 1136	**29/27**
ΜΕΘ 1140	**24/1**
ΜΕΘ 1216	**17/37**
ΜΕΘ 1217	**17/24**
ΜΕΘ 1218	**17/12**
ΜΕΘ 1221	**17/26**
ΜΕΘ 1224	**17/9**
ΜΕΘ 1229	**17/29**
ΜΕΘ 1230	**17/13**
ΜΕΘ 1236	**16/37**
ΜΕΘ 1237	**16/38**
ΜΕΘ 1238	**16/40**
ΜΕΘ 1241	**17/33**
ΜΕΘ 1242	**16/42**
ΜΕΘ 1243	**16/41**
ΜΕΘ 1244	**16/43**
ΜΕΘ 1249	**16/11**
ΜΕΘ 1296	**25/5**
ΜΕΘ 1297	**25/6**
ΜΕΘ 1298	**25/7**
ΜΕΘ 1307	**9/69**
ΜΕΘ 1308	**9/27**
ΜΕΘ 1309	**9/26**
ΜΕΘ 1314	**9/46**

ΜΕΘ 1318	**22/22**	ΜΕΘ 1409	**15/47**
ΜΕΘ 1319	**9/20**, Fig. 1.9	ΜΕΘ 1410	**15/24**
ΜΕΘ 1321	**9/88**, Fig. 1.7	ΜΕΘ 1417	**15/26**
ΜΕΘ 1326	**9/48**	ΜΕΘ 1418	**15/18**
ΜΕΘ 1327	**9/92**	ΜΕΘ 1434	**15/20**
ΜΕΘ 1330	**9/71**	ΜΕΘ 1459	**15/22**
ΜΕΘ 1334	**9/65**	ΜΕΘ 1467	**15/45**
ΜΕΘ 1335	**9/70**	ΜΕΘ 1468	**15/46**
ΜΕΘ 1337	**9/64**	ΜΕΘ 1472	**15/29**
ΜΕΘ 1343	**9/83**, Fig. 1.6	ΜΕΘ 1473	**15/1**
ΜΕΘ 1344	**9/61**	ΜΕΘ 1474	**15/28**
ΜΕΘ 1351	**9/85**	ΜΕΘ 1475	**15/32**
ΜΕΘ 1352	**9/49**	ΜΕΘ 1476	**15/50**
ΜΕΘ 1354	**9/77**	ΜΕΘ 1478	**15/5**
ΜΕΘ 1355	**9/55**	ΜΕΘ 1479	**15/4**
ΜΕΘ 1360	**9/89**	ΜΕΘ 1480	**15/3**
ΜΕΘ 1362	**23/17**	ΜΕΘ 1483	**15/39**
ΜΕΘ 1363	**29/40**	ΜΕΘ 1484	**15/38**
ΜΕΘ 1364	**29/18**	ΜΕΘ 1486	**15/57**
ΜΕΘ 1365	**29/38**	ΜΕΘ 1487	**15/37**
ΜΕΘ 1366	**29/55**	ΜΕΘ 1489	**15/43**
ΜΕΘ 1367	**29/14**	ΜΕΘ 1490	**15/65**
ΜΕΘ 1368	**29/62**	ΜΕΘ 1491	**15/23**
ΜΕΘ 1369	**29/49**	ΜΕΘ 1493	**15/36**
ΜΕΘ 1370	**29/41**	ΜΕΘ 1494	**15/40**
ΜΕΘ 1371	**29/3**	ΜΕΘ 1496	**15/33**
ΜΕΘ 1372	**29/8**	ΜΕΘ 1497	**15/51**
ΜΕΘ 1373	**29/35**	ΜΕΘ 1498	**15/34**
ΜΕΘ 1374	**29/17**	ΜΕΘ 1499	**15/13**
ΜΕΘ 1375	**29/39**	ΜΕΘ 1500	**15/60**
ΜΕΘ 1376	**29/36**	ΜΕΘ 1501	**15/44**
ΜΕΘ 1377	**29/56**	ΜΕΘ 1502	**15/53**
ΜΕΘ 1378	**29/43**	ΜΕΘ 1503	**15/74**
ΜΕΘ 1379	**29/9**	ΜΕΘ 1504	**15/55**
ΜΕΘ 1380	**29/24**	ΜΕΘ 1505	**15/54**
ΜΕΘ 1382	**15/15**	ΜΕΘ 1508	**15/52**
ΜΕΘ 1384	**15/12**	ΜΕΘ 1510	**15/16**
ΜΕΘ 1385	**15/11**	ΜΕΘ 1512	**15/27**
ΜΕΘ 1386	**15/35**	ΜΕΘ 1516	**15/63**
ΜΕΘ 1387	**15/7**	ΜΕΘ 1517	**15/68**
ΜΕΘ 1388	**15/10**	ΜΕΘ 1519	**15/17**
ΜΕΘ 1390	**15/6**	ΜΕΘ 1520	**15/66**
ΜΕΘ 1391	**15/2**	ΜΕΘ 1521	**15/49**
ΜΕΘ 1392	**15/14**	ΜΕΘ 1522	**15/56**
ΜΕΘ 1393	**15/8**	ΜΕΘ 1523	**15/42**
ΜΕΘ 1394	**15/9**	ΜΕΘ 1524	**15/30**
ΜΕΘ 1395	**15/21**	ΜΕΘ 1525	**15/105**
ΜΕΘ 1403	**15/19**	ΜΕΘ 1526	**26/214**

ΜΕΘ 1527	**15/104**
ΜΕΘ 1528	**15/106**
ΜΕΘ 1529	**15/108**
ΜΕΘ 1530	**15/95**
ΜΕΘ 1531	**15/94**
ΜΕΘ 1532	**15/76**
ΜΕΘ 1533	**15/75**
ΜΕΘ 1534	**15/84**
ΜΕΘ 1537	**15/81**
ΜΕΘ 1538	**15/79**
ΜΕΘ 1539	**15/82**
ΜΕΘ 1540	**15/83**
ΜΕΘ 1544	**15/98**
ΜΕΘ 1545	**15/86**
ΜΕΘ 1546	**15/88**
ΜΕΘ 1548	**15/99**
ΜΕΘ 1550	**15/97**
ΜΕΘ 1551	**15/91**
ΜΕΘ 1552	**15/103**
ΜΕΘ 1553	**15/92**
ΜΕΘ 1554	**15/93**
ΜΕΘ 1555	**15/96**
ΜΕΘ 1556	**15/89**
ΜΕΘ 1558	**15/101**
ΜΕΘ 1559	**29/48**
ΜΕΘ 1560	**29/58**
ΜΕΘ 1561	**29/59**
ΜΕΘ 1562	**29/60**
ΜΕΘ 1563	**15/87**
ΜΕΘ 1564	**15/80**
ΜΕΘ 1565	**15/90**
ΜΕΘ 1566	**15/78**
ΜΕΘ 1574	**9/67**
ΜΕΘ 1575	**9/84**
ΜΕΘ 1577	**9/66**
ΜΕΘ 1582	**4/43**
ΜΕΘ 1586	**9/79**
ΜΕΘ 1589	**9/80**
ΜΕΘ 1591	**22/23**, Fig. 1.8
ΜΕΘ 1592	**22/26**
ΜΕΘ 1599	**9/60**
ΜΕΘ 1603	**26/72**
ΜΕΘ 1604	**26/76**
ΜΕΘ 1605	**26/56**
ΜΕΘ 1608	**26/70**
ΜΕΘ 1609	**26/69**
ΜΕΘ 1610	**26/73**
ΜΕΘ 1611	**26/77**
ΜΕΘ 1613	**26/78**
ΜΕΘ 1614	**26/74**
ΜΕΘ 1621	**26/68**
ΜΕΘ 1622	**26/79**
ΜΕΘ 1627	**26/60**
ΜΕΘ 1628	**26/64**
ΜΕΘ 1629	**26/58**
ΜΕΘ 1630	**26/63**
ΜΕΘ 1631	**26/61**
ΜΕΘ 1632	**26/65**
ΜΕΘ 1633	**26/149**
ΜΕΘ 1634	**26/59**
ΜΕΘ 1635	**26/66**
ΜΕΘ 1636	**26/57**
ΜΕΘ 1637	**26/62**
ΜΕΘ 1639	**26/90**
ΜΕΘ 1640	**26/89**
ΜΕΘ 1641	**26/92**
ΜΕΘ 1642	**26/91**
ΜΕΘ 1645	**26/100**
ΜΕΘ 1646	**26/102**
ΜΕΘ 1647	**26/101**
ΜΕΘ 1648	**26/167**
ΜΕΘ 1649	**26/86**
ΜΕΘ 1650α,β,γ	**26/87**
ΜΕΘ 1651	**26/85**
ΜΕΘ 1653	**26/84**
ΜΕΘ 1654	**26/80**
ΜΕΘ 1655	**26/83**
ΜΕΘ 1658	**26/117**
ΜΕΘ 1659	**26/118**
ΜΕΘ 1665	**26/88**
ΜΕΘ 1669	**26/99**
ΜΕΘ 1670	**26/114**
ΜΕΘ 1671	**26/113**
ΜΕΘ 1672	**26/115**
ΜΕΘ 1673	**26/106**
ΜΕΘ 1674	**26/182**
ΜΕΘ 1675	**26/175**
ΜΕΘ 1676	**26/179**
ΜΕΘ 1677	**26/181**
ΜΕΘ 1678	**26/180**
ΜΕΘ 1679	**26/178**
ΜΕΘ 1681	**26/127**
ΜΕΘ 1683	**26/128**
ΜΕΘ 1685	**26/130**
ΜΕΘ 1686	**26/129**
ΜΕΘ 1688	**26/131**

ΜΕΘ 1690	**26/104**
ΜΕΘ 1691	**26/105**
ΜΕΘ 1692	**26/146**
ΜΕΘ 1693	**26/145**
ΜΕΘ 1695	**26/141**
ΜΕΘ 1698	**28/72**
ΜΕΘ 1699	**28/73**
ΜΕΘ 1700	**28/43**
ΜΕΘ 1701	**28/44**
ΜΕΘ 1702	**28/45**
ΜΕΘ 1703	**28/74**
ΜΕΘ 1704	**28/75**
ΜΕΘ 1705	**28/6**
ΜΕΘ 1706	**28/46**
ΜΕΘ 1707	**28/7**
ΜΕΘ 1708	**28/59**
ΜΕΘ 1709	**28/8**
ΜΕΘ 1710	**26/213**
ΜΕΘ 1711	**26/228**
ΜΕΘ 1712	**26/209**
ΜΕΘ 1713	**26/216**
ΜΕΘ 1723	**26/186**
ΜΕΘ 1728	**26/187**
ΜΕΘ 1730	**26/183**
ΜΕΘ 1731	**26/184**
ΜΕΘ 1734	**26/185**
ΜΕΘ 1737	**26/194**
ΜΕΘ 1746	**26/188**
ΜΕΘ 1747	**26/191**
ΜΕΘ 1751	**26/193**
ΜΕΘ 1752	**26/189**
ΜΕΘ 1753	**26/192**
ΜΕΘ 1754	**26/198**
ΜΕΘ 1755	**26/195**
ΜΕΘ 1766	**26/190**
ΜΕΘ 1769	**26/203**
ΜΕΘ 1771	**26/204**
ΜΕΘ 1774	**26/196**
ΜΕΘ 1775α	**26/157**
ΜΕΘ 1775β	**26/158**
ΜΕΘ 1776	**26/161**
ΜΕΘ 1777	**26/160**
ΜΕΘ 1778	**26/150**
ΜΕΘ 1779	**26/151**
ΜΕΘ 1780	**26/109**
ΜΕΘ 1781	**26/121**
ΜΕΘ 1784	**26/122**
ΜΕΘ 1787	**26/75**
ΜΕΘ 1791	**26/177**
ΜΕΘ 1794	**26/96**
ΜΕΘ 1795	**26/108**
ΜΕΘ 1796	**26/95**
ΜΕΘ 1797	**26/93**
ΜΕΘ 1798	**26/94**
ΜΕΘ 1898	**25/81**
ΜΕΘ 1899	**25/82**
ΜΕΘ 1900	**25/108**
ΜΕΘ 1901	**25/83**
ΜΕΘ 1902	**25/84**
ΜΕΘ 1903	**25/85**
ΜΕΘ 1904	**25/86**
ΜΕΘ 1905Α	**25/87**
ΜΕΘ 1905Β	**25/35**
ΜΕΘ 1906	**25/88**
ΜΕΘ 1907	**25/89**
ΜΕΘ 1908	**25/90**
ΜΕΘ 1909	**25/114**
ΜΕΘ 1910	**25/36**
ΜΕΘ 1911	**25/37**
ΜΕΘ 1912	**25/38**
ΜΕΘ 1913	**25/39**
ΜΕΘ 1914	**25/40**
ΜΕΘ 1915	**25/109**
ΜΕΘ 1953	**9/95**
ΜΕΘ 1956	**17/31**
ΜΕΘ 1959	**17/39**
ΜΕΘ 1960	**16/45**
ΜΕΘ 1961	**16/33**
ΜΕΘ 1981	**24/6**
ΜΕΘ 1984	**23/16**
ΜΕΘ 1985	**29/70**
ΜΕΘ 1986	**24/8**
ΜΕΘ 1988	**23/7**
ΜΕΘ 1994	**29/25**
ΜΕΘ 1996	**29/7**
ΜΕΘ 1997	**29/1**
ΜΕΘ 1998	**29/10**
ΜΕΘ 1999	**29/6**
ΜΕΘ 2000	**29/16**
ΜΕΘ 2001	**29/26**
ΜΕΘ 2002	**29/31**
ΜΕΘ 2003	**29/22**
ΜΕΘ 2004	**29/30**
ΜΕΘ 2005	**29/4**
ΜΕΘ 2006	**29/69**
ΜΕΘ 2007	**29/33**

MEΘ 2008	**4/55**
MEΘ 2009	**4/1**
MEΘ 2010	**4/14**
MEΘ 2011	**6/69**
MEΘ 2019	**9/90**
MEΘ 2021	**9/41**
MEΘ 2022	**9/97**
MEΘ 2028	Fig. 12.5
MEΘ 2031	**9/39**
MEΘ 2032	**9/37**
MEΘ 2033	Fig. 1.11a–b
MEΘ 2034	Fig. 1.11c–d
MEΘ 2039	**9/68**
MEΘ 2059	**24/14**
MEΘ 2128	**25/41**
MEΘ 2129	**26/147**
MEΘ 2130	**26/67**
MEΘ 2132	**26/81**, Fig. 1.10
MEΘ 2133α	**26/71**
MEΘ 2133β	**26/119**
MEΘ 2134	**26/116**
MEΘ 2135	**26/97**
MEΘ 2136	**26/98**
MEΘ 2138	**26/126**
MEΘ 2140	**26/172**
MEΘ 2141	**26/142**
MEΘ 2142	**26/143**
MEΘ 2143	**26/82**
MEΘ 2144	**28/47**
MEΘ 2145	**28/48**
MEΘ 2146	**26/208**
MEΘ 2147	**26/222**
MEΘ 2148	**26/224**
MEΘ 2149	**26/215**
MEΘ 2164	**29/50**
MEΘ 2165	**29/61**
MEΘ 2166	**29/51**
MEΘ 2167	**29/63**
MEΘ 2168	**29/52**
MEΘ 2169	**29/83**
MEΘ 2170	**29/44**
MEΘ 2171	**29/46**
MEΘ 2172	**29/47**
MEΘ 2174	**29/29**
MEΘ 2175	**29/21**
MEΘ 2176	**29/28**
MEΘ 2177	**29/11**
MEΘ 2178	**29/20**
MEΘ 2179	**24/12**
MEΘ 2180	**29/64**
MEΘ 2182	**26/212**
MEΘ 2184	Fig. 12.2
MEΘ 2186	Fig. 12.2
MEΘ 2206	Fig. 12.8
MEΘ 2207	Fig. 12.9
MEΘ 2237	**11/2**, Fig. 1.13
MEΘ 2238	**11/1**
MEΘ 2240	Fig. 12.7
MEΘ 2247	**11/3**
MEΘ 2248	**9/6**, **11/6**
MEΘ 2249	**11/7**, Fig. 1.12
MEΘ 2253	**11/4**
MEΘ 2255	**11/5**
MEΘ 2308 + 3241	**22/37**
MEΘ 2424	Fig. 12.12
MEΘ 2425	Fig. 12.5
MEΘ 2433	Fig. 12.12
MEΘ 2462	**21/7**
MEΘ 2464	**21/13**
MEΘ 2465	**21/1**
MEΘ 2629	**29/2**
MEΘ 2667	**29/53**
MEΘ 2675	**21/4**
MEΘ 2684	**21/11**, Fig. 1.34a
MEΘ 2693	Fig. 19.6
MEΘ 2695	Figs. 1.35, 19.7
MEΘ 2701	**22/53**
MEΘ 2704	**22/40**
MEΘ 2707	Fig. 19.11
MEΘ 2771	**26/231**
MEΘ 2773	**26/232**
MEΘ 2778	**16/8**
MEΘ 2783	**16/44**
MEΘ 2794	**16/28**
MEΘ 2797	**17/32**
MEΘ 2798	**17/25**
MEΘ 2814	**13/10**
MEΘ 2835	**25/11**
MEΘ 2836	**25/8**
MEΘ 2846	**28/76**
MEΘ 2847	**28/60**
MEΘ 2848	**28/77**
MEΘ 2849	**28/78**
MEΘ 2850	**28/79**
MEΘ 2851	**28/80**
MEΘ 2852	**28/81**

ΜΕΘ 2853	**28/49**
ΜΕΘ 2854	**28/9**
ΜΕΘ 2855	**28/82**
ΜΕΘ 2856	**28/50**
ΜΕΘ 2857	**28/51**
ΜΕΘ 2858	**28/52**
ΜΕΘ 2859	**28/53**
ΜΕΘ 2860	**28/54**
ΜΕΘ 2861	**28/55**
ΜΕΘ 2862	**28/10**
ΜΕΘ 2863	**28/11**
ΜΕΘ 2864	**28/12**
ΜΕΘ 2865	**28/13**
ΜΕΘ 2866	**28/14**
ΜΕΘ 2867	**28/15**
ΜΕΘ 2868	**28/16**
ΜΕΘ 2869	**28/17**
ΜΕΘ 2870	**28/18**
ΜΕΘ 2871	**28/19**
ΜΕΘ 2872	**28/20**
ΜΕΘ 2873	**28/21**
ΜΕΘ 2874	**28/83**
ΜΕΘ 2875	**28/22**
ΜΕΘ 2876	**28/84**
ΜΕΘ 2877	**28/85**
ΜΕΘ 2878	**28/23**
ΜΕΘ 2879	**28/24**
ΜΕΘ 2880	**28/86**
ΜΕΘ 2881	**28/87**
ΜΕΘ 2882	**28/88**
ΜΕΘ 2883	**28/89**
ΜΕΘ 2884	**28/90**
ΜΕΘ 2885	**28/91**
ΜΕΘ 2886	**28/92**
ΜΕΘ 2887	**28/93**
ΜΕΘ 2888	**28/94**
ΜΕΘ 2889	**28/95**
ΜΕΘ 2890	**28/96**
ΜΕΘ 2891	**28/65**
ΜΕΘ 2892	**28/25**
ΜΕΘ 2893	**28/26**
ΜΕΘ 2894	**28/27**
ΜΕΘ 2895	**28/28**
ΜΕΘ 2896	**28/29**
ΜΕΘ 2897	**28/30**
ΜΕΘ 2898	**28/31**
ΜΕΘ 2899	**28/97**
ΜΕΘ 2900	**28/61**
ΜΕΘ 2901	**28/56**
ΜΕΘ 2902	**28/98**
ΜΕΘ 2903	**28/32**
ΜΕΘ 2904	**28/99**
ΜΕΘ 2905	**28/100**
ΜΕΘ 2906	**28/101**
ΜΕΘ 2907	**28/33**
ΜΕΘ 2908	**28/102**
ΜΕΘ 2909	**28/34**
ΜΕΘ 2910	**28/35**
ΜΕΘ 2911	**28/36**
ΜΕΘ 2912	**28/57**
ΜΕΘ 2913	**28/103**
ΜΕΘ 2914	**28/104**
ΜΕΘ 2915	**28/105**
ΜΕΘ 2917	**22/32**
ΜΕΘ 2976	Fig. 1.36d–f
ΜΕΘ 2977	Fig. 1.36a–c
ΜΕΘ 2986	**25/120**
ΜΕΘ 3042	**6/45**
ΜΕΘ 3043	**6/46**
ΜΕΘ 3044	**25/123**
ΜΕΘ 3046	**25/122**
ΜΕΘ 3095	**26/103**
ΜΕΘ 3097	**26/133**
ΜΕΘ 3100	**26/230**
ΜΕΘ 3191	**25/110**
ΜΕΘ 3192	**25/91**
ΜΕΘ 3198	**22/28**
ΜΕΘ 3202	**21/9**, Fig. 1.34b
ΜΕΘ 3235	**24/13**
ΜΕΘ 3239	**22/24**
ΜΕΘ 3241 + 2308	**22/37**
ΜΕΘ 3263	**22/41**
ΜΕΘ 3264	**22/43**
ΜΕΘ 3265	**22/44**
ΜΕΘ 3267	**29/34**
ΜΕΘ 3300	**22/34**
ΜΕΘ 3302	**22/25**
ΜΕΘ 3303	**22/30**
ΜΕΘ 3305	**22/29**
ΜΕΘ 3306	**22/33**
ΜΕΘ 3318	**9/44**
ΜΕΘ 3343	**9/51**
ΜΕΘ 3344	**9/52**
ΜΕΘ 3368	**9/59**
ΜΕΘ 3371	**9/57**
ΜΕΘ 3373	**22/31**

ΜΕΘ 3374	**22/27**
ΜΕΘ 3384	**9/58**
ΜΕΘ 3397	**9/56**
ΜΕΘ 3406	**9/29**
ΜΕΘ 3407	**9/25**
ΜΕΘ 3408	**9/30**
ΜΕΘ 3409	**9/11**
ΜΕΘ 3410	**9/21**
ΜΕΘ 3411	**9/13**
ΜΕΘ 3412	**9/28**
ΜΕΘ 3413	**9/10**
ΜΕΘ 3415α,β,γ	**9/12**
ΜΕΘ 3420	**9/74**
ΜΕΘ 3425	**9/81**
ΜΕΘ 3442	**9/91**
ΜΕΘ 3532	**9/93**, Fig. 22.10b
ΜΕΘ 3542	**21/5**
ΜΕΘ 3543	**21/6**
ΜΕΘ 3544	**21/10**
ΜΕΘ 3545	**21/12**
ΜΕΘ 3552	**22/1**
ΜΕΘ 3554	**22/14**
ΜΕΘ 3556	Fig. 19.9
ΜΕΘ 3559	Fig. 19.4
ΜΕΘ 3567	**9/87**
ΜΕΘ 3569	**9/72**
ΜΕΘ 3578	**9/78**
ΜΕΘ 3579	**9/75**
ΜΕΘ 3581	**9/76**
ΜΕΘ 3582	**9/47**
ΜΕΘ 3588	**9/82**
ΜΕΘ 3604	**9/86**
ΜΕΘ 3606	**9/5**
ΜΕΘ 3646	**9/73**
ΜΕΘ 3807	**9/1**, Fig. 1.42
ΜΕΘ 3808	**9/18**
ΜΕΘ 3809	**9/63**
ΜΕΘ 3810	**9/23**
ΜΕΘ 3811	**9/4**
ΜΕΘ 3812	**9/54**
ΜΕΘ 3814α,β + 4061	**9/50**
ΜΕΘ 3815	**9/53**
ΜΕΘ 3816	**9/45**
ΜΕΘ 3818	**9/2**
ΜΕΘ 3819	**9/3**
ΜΕΘ 3821	**9/96**
ΜΕΘ 3822	**9/98**
ΜΕΘ 3823	**9/62**
ΜΕΘ 3878	Fig. 29.96
ΜΕΘ 3960α,β	**6/68α**,β
ΜΕΘ 3961α–θ	**6/67α**–θ
ΜΕΘ 4033α,β	**9/14**
ΜΕΘ 4034	**9/43**
ΜΕΘ 4035	**9/16**
ΜΕΘ 4035α,β,γ	**9/15**
ΜΕΘ 4037	**9/24**
ΜΕΘ 4038α,β	**9/33**
ΜΕΘ 4039	**9/36**
ΜΕΘ 4040	**9/35**
ΜΕΘ 4041	**9/34**
ΜΕΘ 4042	**9/9**
ΜΕΘ 4043α,β	**9/31**
ΜΕΘ 4044	**9/19**
ΜΕΘ 4045α,β,γ	**9/22**
ΜΕΘ 4046	**9/94**, Fig. 22.10b
ΜΕΘ 4051	**9/8**
ΜΕΘ 4052	**9/42**
ΜΕΘ 4053α,β,γ	**9/17**
ΜΕΘ 4054	**9/7**
ΜΕΘ 4058	**9/40**
ΜΕΘ 4059	**9/38**
ΜΕΘ 4060α,β	**9/32**
ΜΕΘ 4061 + 3814 α,β	**9/50**
ΜΕΘ 4064	**29/5**
ΜΕΘ 4065	**29/12**
ΜΕΘ 4067	**25/92**
ΜΕΘ 4068	**6/49**, Fig. 1.30
ΜΕΘ 4069	**6/56**
ΜΕΘ 4070	**6/51**
ΜΕΘ 4071	**6/52**
ΜΕΘ 4072	**6/55**
ΜΕΘ 4073	**6/53**
ΜΕΘ 4093	**6/54**
ΜΕΘ 4094	**6/57**
ΜΕΘ 4095	**6/58**
ΜΕΘ 4096	**6/59**
ΜΕΘ 4097	**6/61**
ΜΕΘ 4098	**6/63**
ΜΕΘ 4099	**6/60**
ΜΕΘ 4100	**6/64**
ΜΕΘ 4101	**6/62**
ΜΕΘ 4102	**6/66**
ΜΕΘ 4103	**6/65**
ΜΕΘ 4106	**15/72**
ΜΕΘ 4110	**15/70**
ΜΕΘ 4113	**15/73**

ΜΕΘ 4115	**15/71**
ΜΕΘ 4117	**15/41**
ΜΕΘ 4118	**15/58**
ΜΕΘ 4120	**15/67**
ΜΕΘ 4121	**15/64**
ΜΕΘ 4124	**15/48**
ΜΕΘ 4130	**15/31**
ΜΕΘ 4135	**15/61**
ΜΕΘ 4136	**15/62**
ΜΕΘ 4137	**15/25**
ΜΕΘ 4140	**15/59**
ΜΕΘ 4141	Fig. 1.16
ΜΕΘ 4142	**26/110**
ΜΕΘ 4143	**26/107**
ΜΕΘ 4145	**26/140**
ΜΕΘ 4146	**26/152**
ΜΕΘ 4149	**6/47**
ΜΕΘ 4152	Fig. 29.93
ΜΕΘ 4153	Fig. 29.90
ΜΕΘ 4156	Fig. 29.91
ΜΕΘ 4157	Fig. 29.94
ΜΕΘ 4158	Fig. 29.95
ΜΕΘ 4159	Fig. 29.92
ΜΕΘ 4160	**6/33**
ΜΕΘ 4161	**6/34**
ΜΕΘ 4163	**6/32**
ΜΕΘ 4164 + 889	**6/21**
ΜΕΘ 4175	**6/50**
ΜΕΘ 4182	**4/56**
ΜΕΘ 4183	**4/48**
ΜΕΘ 4187	**26/111**
ΜΕΘ 4188	**26/112**
ΜΕΘ 4190	**26/148**
ΜΕΘ 4191	**26/173**
ΜΕΘ 4192	**26/137**
ΜΕΘ 4193	**26/136**
ΜΕΘ 4194	**26/134**
ΜΕΘ 4195	**26/135**
ΜΕΘ 4196	**26/55**
ΜΕΘ 4197	**26/120**
ΜΕΘ 4199	**7/9**
ΜΕΘ 4201	**7/29**
ΜΕΘ 4202	**7/32**
ΜΕΘ 4203	**7/31**
ΜΕΘ 4204	**7/34**
ΜΕΘ 4205	**7/33**
ΜΕΘ 4207	**7/22**
ΜΕΘ 4208	**7/27**
ΜΕΘ 4209	**7/28**
ΜΕΘ 4210	**7/4**
ΜΕΘ 4211	**7/7**
ΜΕΘ 4212	**7/12**
ΜΕΘ 4213	**7/15**
ΜΕΘ 4214	**7/38**
ΜΕΘ 4220	**4/13**
ΜΕΘ 4221	**4/11**
ΜΕΘ 4222	**4/15**
ΜΕΘ 4227	**26/156**
ΜΕΘ 4228	**26/164**
ΜΕΘ 4229	**26/166**
ΜΕΘ 4230	**26/168**
ΜΕΘ 4231	**26/159**
ΜΕΘ 4232	**26/170**
ΜΕΘ 4233	**26/162**
ΜΕΘ 4234	**26/171**
ΜΕΘ 4235	**26/163**
ΜΕΘ 4237	**7/42**
ΜΕΘ 4251	**4/44**
ΜΕΘ 4253	**4/3**
ΜΕΘ 4254	**4/16**
ΜΕΘ 4256	**4/57**
ΜΕΘ 4257	**4/4**
ΜΕΘ 4258	**4/17**
ΜΕΘ 4260	**26/199**
ΜΕΘ 4264	**4/58**
ΜΕΘ 4265	**25/124**
ΜΕΘ 4266	**25/125**
ΜΕΘ 4267	**25/126**
ΜΕΘ 4268	**25/121**
ΜΕΘ 4269	**7/39**
ΜΕΘ 4270	**7/58**
ΜΕΘ 4271	**7/24**
ΜΕΘ 4272	**4/49**
ΜΕΘ 4273	**7/55**
ΜΕΘ 4274	**7/59**
ΜΕΘ 4275	**7/43**
ΜΕΘ 4276	**7/44**
ΜΕΘ 4277	**7/1**
ΜΕΘ 4278	**7/56**
ΜΕΘ 4279	**7/23**
ΜΕΘ 4280	**7/25**
ΜΕΘ 4284	**7/36**
ΜΕΘ 4286	**7/3**
ΜΕΘ 4287	**4/45**
ΜΕΘ 4288	**5/40**
ΜΕΘ 4290	**4/29**

MEΘ 4291	**26/154**
MEΘ 4292	**26/139**
MEΘ 4293	**26/138**
MEΘ 4300	**4/18**
MEΘ 4301	**4/5**
MEΘ 4304	**26/153**
MEΘ 4305	**26/144**
MEΘ 4308	**26/165**
MEΘ 4309	**26/169**
MEΘ 4310	**26/132**
MEΘ 4311	**26/155**
MEΘ 4313	**7/10**
MEΘ 4315	**7/48**
MEΘ 4316	**4/12**
MEΘ 4317	**7/8**
MEΘ 4318	**7/11**
MEΘ 4322	**7/45**
MEΘ 4323	**7/53**
MEΘ 4324	**4/19**
MEΘ 4325	**7/2**
MEΘ 4326	**4/36**
MEΘ 4328	**4/6**
MEΘ 4329	**7/26**
MEΘ 4330	**7/40**
MEΘ 4331	**7/19**
MEΘ 4332	**4/35**
MEΘ 4333	**7/60**
MEΘ 4334	**4/20**
MEΘ 4345	**26/202**
MEΘ 4363	**26/225**
MEΘ 4364	**26/223**
MEΘ 4365	**26/218**
MEΘ 4366	**26/211**
MEΘ 4367	**26/206**
MEΘ 4368	**26/205**
MEΘ 4369	**15/107**
MEΘ 4370	**26/229**
MEΘ 4371	**26/210**
MEΘ 4372	**26/207**
MEΘ 4373	**26/226**
MEΘ 4374	**26/219**
MEΘ 4375	**26/220**
MEΘ 4376	**26/221**
MEΘ 4377	**26/227**
MEΘ 4378	**26/217**
MEΘ 4407	**22/42**
MEΘ 4409	**22/45**
MEΘ 4430	**24/2**
MEΘ 4431	**24/4**
MEΘ 4432	**24/11**
MEΘ 4433	**24/9**
MEΘ 4434	**24/10**
MEΘ 4641	**29/23**
MEΘ 4644 + 5139	**23/2**
MEΘ 4648	**21/2**
MEΘ 4650	**21/3**
MEΘ 4744	**29/32**
MEΘ 4746	**29/15**
MEΘ 4790	**29/13**
MEΘ 4791	**29/19**
MEΘ 4820	**21/8**
MEΘ 4853	**29/45**
MEΘ 4854	**29/57**
MEΘ 4856	**29/71**
MEΘ 4857	**29/72**
MEΘ 4858	**29/65**
MEΘ 4859	**29/67**
MEΘ 4868	**7/16**
MEΘ 4869	**4/59**
MEΘ 4870	**5/51**
MEΘ 4871	**7/49**
MEΘ 4872	**4/50**
MEΘ 4873	**7/54**
MEΘ 4874	**7/20**
MEΘ 4875	**5/19**
MEΘ 4877	**7/13**
MEΘ 4878	**7/51**
MEΘ 4879	**5/1**
MEΘ 4880	**4/7**
MEΘ 4881	**5/20**
MEΘ 4882	**7/50**
MEΘ 4883	**7/57**
MEΘ 4884	**7/35**
MEΘ 4885	**7/52**
MEΘ 4886	**4/37**
MEΘ 4887	**4/38**
MEΘ 4889	**7/14**
MEΘ 4891	**5/8**
MEΘ 4914	**23/11**
MEΘ 4915	**23/10**
MEΘ 4919	**7/5**
MEΘ 4920	**7/6**
MEΘ 4921	**7/17**
MEΘ 4935	**23/12**
MEΘ 4938	**23/8**
MEΘ 4944	**23/14**

ΜΕΘ 4946	**23/9**
ΜΕΘ 4950	**5/46**
ΜΕΘ 4951	**5/52**
ΜΕΘ 4952	**5/53**
ΜΕΘ 4953	**5/39**
ΜΕΘ 4954	**4/8**
ΜΕΘ 4955	**4/26**
ΜΕΘ 4956	**4/9**
ΜΕΘ 4957	**4/27**
ΜΕΘ 4958	**29/42**
ΜΕΘ 4959	**4/10**
ΜΕΘ 4960	**26/37**
ΜΕΘ 4961	**26/36**
ΜΕΘ 4963	**26/34**
ΜΕΘ 4964	**26/40**
ΜΕΘ 4965	**26/38**
ΜΕΘ 4966	**26/35**
ΜΕΘ 4967	**4/30**
ΜΕΘ 4968	**26/29**
ΜΕΘ 4969	**26/30**
ΜΕΘ 4970	**26/28**
ΜΕΘ 4971	**26/31**
ΜΕΘ 4972	**26/32**
ΜΕΘ 4973	**26/27**
ΜΕΘ 4975	**26/33**
ΜΕΘ 4978	**25/130**
ΜΕΘ 4982	**5/30**
ΜΕΘ 4986	**5/33**
ΜΕΘ 4988	**7/37**
ΜΕΘ 4989	**5/41**
ΜΕΘ 4990	**5/42**
ΜΕΘ 4991	**4/39**
ΜΕΘ 4992	**5/34**
ΜΕΘ 4993	**5/35**
ΜΕΘ 4996	**4/21**
ΜΕΘ 4997	**24/16**
ΜΕΘ 4998	**24/15**
ΜΕΘ 5005	**22/10**
ΜΕΘ 5007	**22/11**
ΜΕΘ 5008	**22/12**
ΜΕΘ 5009	**22/6**
ΜΕΘ 5010	**22/5**
ΜΕΘ 5011	**22/4**
ΜΕΘ 5012	**22/9**
ΜΕΘ 5013	**22/8**
ΜΕΘ 5014	**22/7**
ΜΕΘ 5015	**22/13**
ΜΕΘ 5016	**22/3**
ΜΕΘ 5017	**26/233**
ΜΕΘ 5018	**29/85**
ΜΕΘ 5019	**7/18**
ΜΕΘ 5020	**7/47**
ΜΕΘ 5021	**4/34**
ΜΕΘ 5022	**4/22**
ΜΕΘ 5023	**4/51**
ΜΕΘ 5024	**5/43**
ΜΕΘ 5031	**26/45**
ΜΕΘ 5032	**26/47**
ΜΕΘ 5033	**26/49**
ΜΕΘ 5034	**26/43**
ΜΕΘ 5035	**26/48**
ΜΕΘ 5036	**26/46**
ΜΕΘ 5037	**26/50**
ΜΕΘ 5038	**26/41**
ΜΕΘ 5039	**26/44**
ΜΕΘ 5040	**26/42**
ΜΕΘ 5043	**26/51**
ΜΕΘ 5044	**26/52**
ΜΕΘ 5045	**26/54**
ΜΕΘ 5046	**26/53**
ΜΕΘ 5047	**4/40**
ΜΕΘ 5051	**23/6**
ΜΕΘ 5061	**4/28**
ΜΕΘ 5062	**5/2**
ΜΕΘ 5073	**5/54**
ΜΕΘ 5074	**5/9**
ΜΕΘ 5075	**5/10**
ΜΕΘ 5081	**23/5**
ΜΕΘ 5083	**4/52**
ΜΕΘ 5085	**7/30**
ΜΕΘ 5088	**5/11**
ΜΕΘ 5089	**4/41**
ΜΕΘ 5090	**4/42**
ΜΕΘ 5091	**4/31**
ΜΕΘ 5092	**5/12**
ΜΕΘ 5094	**5/13**
ΜΕΘ 5096	**5/24**
ΜΕΘ 5097	**5/3**
ΜΕΘ 5103	**5/14**
ΜΕΘ 5108	**7/21**
ΜΕΘ 5109	**22/19**
ΜΕΘ 5110	**22/17**
ΜΕΘ 5111	**22/18**
ΜΕΘ 5112	**22/15**
ΜΕΘ 5113	**5/55**
ΜΕΘ 5115	**5/21**

ΜΕΘ 5117	**5/4**
ΜΕΘ 5118	**22/38**
ΜΕΘ 5119	**22/39**
ΜΕΘ 5120	**22/36**
ΜΕΘ 5121	**22/16**
ΜΕΘ 5122	**22/20**
ΜΕΘ 5123	**22/21**
ΜΕΘ 5139 + 4644	**23/2**, Fig. 19.10
ΜΕΘ 5154	**23/13**
ΜΕΘ 5155	**5/15**
ΜΕΘ 5158	**23/4**
ΜΕΘ 5159	**23/1**
ΜΕΘ 5160	**23/3**
ΜΕΘ 5161	**23/15**
ΜΕΘ 5185	Fig. 12.10
ΜΕΘ 5186	Fig. 12.10
ΜΕΘ 5187	Fig. 12.10
ΜΕΘ 5191	Fig. 12.7
ΜΕΘ 5205	Fig. 12.11
ΜΕΘ 5206	Fig. 12.11
ΜΕΘ 5207	Fig. 12.11
ΜΕΘ 5208	Fig. 12.11
ΜΕΘ 5211	Fig. 12.4
ΜΕΘ 5212	Fig. 12.4
ΜΕΘ 5213	Fig. 12.4
ΜΕΘ 5219	Fig. 12.4
ΜΕΘ 5238	**5/5**
ΜΕΘ 5240	**22/2**
ΜΕΘ 5256	Fig. 12.6
ΜΕΘ 5272	**26/1**
ΜΕΘ 5273	**26/22**
ΜΕΘ 5274	**26/24**
ΜΕΘ 5275	**26/25**
ΜΕΘ 5276	**26/23**
ΜΕΘ 5277	**26/6**
ΜΕΘ 5278	**26/5**
ΜΕΘ 5279	**26/13**
ΜΕΘ 5280	**26/8**
ΜΕΘ 5281	**26/3**
ΜΕΘ 5282	**26/7**
ΜΕΘ 5283	**26/2**
ΜΕΘ 5284	**26/26**
ΜΕΘ 5285	**26/4**
ΜΕΘ 5286	**26/15**
ΜΕΘ 5287	**26/20**
ΜΕΘ 5288	**26/14**
ΜΕΘ 5291	**26/197**
ΜΕΘ 5292	**26/39**
ΜΕΘ 5294	**26/18**
ΜΕΘ 5295	**26/12**
ΜΕΘ 5296	**26/9**
ΜΕΘ 5297	**26/19**
ΜΕΘ 5298	**26/10**
ΜΕΘ 5299	**26/16**
ΜΕΘ 5300	**26/17**
ΜΕΘ 5302	**26/11**
ΜΕΘ 5303	**26/174**
ΜΕΘ 5304	**15/69**
ΜΕΘ 5305	**26/21**
ΜΕΘ 5308	Fig. 12.6
ΜΕΘ 5317	**29/66**
ΜΕΘ 5318	**6/11**
ΜΕΘ 5319	**15/100**
ΜΕΘ 5321	**15/85**
ΜΕΘ 5323	**15/102**
ΜΕΘ 5327	**15/77**
ΜΕΘ 5328	**17/41**
ΜΕΘ 5329	Figs. 1.20, 14.2
ΜΕΘ 5330	Figs. 1.20, 14.2
ΜΕΘ 5331	Figs. 1.18, 14.5
ΜΕΘ 5332	Fig. 14.6
ΜΕΘ 5333	**26/200**
ΜΕΘ 5335	Figs. 1.15, 14.3
ΜΕΘ 5337	Figs. 1.15, 14.3
ΜΕΘ 5339	Fig. 14.8
ΜΕΘ 5340	Fig. 14.7
ΜΕΘ 5344	Figs. 1.17, 14.1
ΜΕΘ 5345	**26/201**
ΜΕΘ 5347	**6/48**
ΜΕΘ 5348	**24/5**
ΜΕΘ 5349	**24/3**
ΜΕΘ 5350	**24/7**
ΜΕΘ 5354	**29/37**
ΜΕΘ 5563	**25/42**
ΜΕΘ 5564	**25/43**
ΜΕΘ 5565	**25/45**
ΜΕΘ 5566	**25/46**
ΜΕΘ 5567	**25/44**
ΜΕΘ 5568	**25/47**
ΜΕΘ 5570	**25/116**
ΜΕΘ 5571	**25/117**
ΜΕΘ 5572	**25/118**
ΜΕΘ 5573	**25/111**
ΜΕΘ 5574	**25/93**
ΜΕΘ 5575	**25/119**
ΜΕΘ 5576	**25/94**

ΜΕΘ 5577	**25/95**
ΜΕΘ 5584	**29/68**
ΜΕΘ 5600	**5/16**
ΜΕΘ 5601	**5/25**
ΜΕΘ 5602	**5/47**
ΜΕΘ 5603	**5/48**
ΜΕΘ 5604	**5/49**
ΜΕΘ 5605	**5/56**
ΜΕΘ 5606	**5/26**
ΜΕΘ 5607	**5/32**
ΜΕΘ 5608	**5/27**
ΜΕΘ 5610	**5/6**
ΜΕΘ 5612	**4/46**
ΜΕΘ 5613	**4/53**
ΜΕΘ 5614	**5/50**
ΜΕΘ 5615 + 5619	**5/36**
ΜΕΘ 5616	**5/22**
ΜΕΘ 5617	**5/17**
ΜΕΘ 5618	**4/32**
ΜΕΘ 5619 + 5615	**5/36**
ΜΕΘ 5620	**5/37**
ΜΕΘ 5621	**5/38**
ΜΕΘ 5622	**4/47**
ΜΕΘ 5623	**4/54**
ΜΕΘ 5624	**5/31**
ΜΕΘ 5625	**5/44**
ΜΕΘ 5626	**4/2**
ΜΕΘ 5627	**5/28**
ΜΕΘ 5628	**4/33**
ΜΕΘ 5629	**5/45**
ΜΕΘ 5630	**5/29**
ΜΕΘ 5631	**5/23**
ΜΕΘ 5632	**5/7**
ΜΕΘ 5633	**7/41**
ΜΕΘ 5634	**6/70**
ΜΕΘ 5637	**7/46**
ΜΕΘ 5638	**4/23**
ΜΕΘ 5639	**4/24**
ΜΕΘ 5641	**4/25**
ΜΕΘ 5642	**5/18**
ΜΕΘ 5652	**4/60**
ΜΕΘ 5682	**22/35**
ΜΕΘ 5683	**22/48**
ΜΕΘ 5684	**22/49**
ΜΕΘ 5689	**22/52**
ΜΕΘ 5691	**22/47**
ΜΕΘ 5698	**22/46**
ΜΕΘ 5700	**22/51**
ΜΕΘ 5701	**22/50**
ΜΕΘ 6305	**29/75**
ΜΕΘ 6306	**29/76**
ΜΕΘ 6307	**29/77**
ΜΕΘ 6308	**29/78**
ΜΕΘ 6309	**29/79**
ΜΕΘ 6310	**29/81**
ΜΕΘ 6311	**29/80**
ΜΕΘ 6312	**29/82**
ΜΕΘ 6313	**29/84**
ΜΕΘ 6486	**29/73**
ΜΕΘ 6487	**29/74**
ΜΕΘ 7528	Fig. 22.10c
ΜΕΘ 7529	Fig. 22.20
ΜΕΘ 7533	**29/54**
ΜΕΘ 8361	Fig. 19.8
ΜΕΘ 8393	**25/12**
ΜΕΘ 8394	**25/13**
ΜΕΘ 8395	**25/127**
ΜΕΘ 8396	**25/128**

A numbers = Αγγείο numbers (Pot numbers)

A 247	Fig. 29.89

ME numbers = Μικρό Εύρημα numbers (Small Find numbers)

ME 1345	Fig. 14.9
ME 1346	Fig. 14.9

Πυ numbers = Πύδνα numbers

Πυ 1516	Figs. 1.40, 1.41

Concordance of Inventory nos. and Figure nos. Acropolis Museum, Athens

EM 6596	Figs. 1.38, 2.1

Concordance of Inventory nos. and Figure nos. Archaeological Museum of Thessaloniki

ΤΣ 1080	Figs. 27.1–27.24
ΤΣ 1081	Figs. 27.25–27.33
ΤΣ 1082	Figs. 27.34–27.38

INDEX

Note: Page numbers in ***bold italics*** indicate illustrations or tables.

UCLA COTSEN INSTITUTE OF ARCHAEOLOGY PRESS

MONUMENTA ARCHAEOLOGICA

Volume 49	*Ancient Methone, 2003–2013: Excavations by Matthaios Bessios, Athena Athanassiadou, and Konstantinos Noulas,* edited by Sarah P. Morris and John K. Papadopoulos
Volume 48	*Divine Consumption: Sacrifice, Alliance Building, and Making Ancestors in West Africa,* by Stephen A. Dueppen
Volume 47	*Talepakemalai: Lapita and Its Transformations in the Mussau Islands of Near Oceania,* edited by Patrick Vinton Kirch
Volume 46	*Bikeri: Two Copper Age Villages on the Great Hungarian Plain,* edited by William A. Parkinson, Attila Gyucha, and Richard W. Yerkes
Volume 45	*Paso de la Amada: An Early Mesoamerican Ceremonial Center,* edited by Richard G. Lesure
Volume 44	*The Wari Enclave of Espíritu Pampa,* by Javier Fonseca Santa Cruz and Brian S. Bauer
Volume 43	*Landscape History of Hadramawt: The Roots of Agriculture in Southern Arabia (RASA) Project 1998–2008,* edited by Joy McCorriston and Michael J. Harrower
Volume 42	*Early Athens: Settlements and Cemeteries in the Submycenaean, Geometric, and Archaic Periods,* by Eirini Dimitriadou
Volume 41	*The History and Archaeology of Jaffa 2,* edited by Aaron A. Burke, Katherine Strange Burke, and Martin Peilstöcker
Volume 40	*Tangatatau Rockshelter: The Evolution of an Eastern Polynesian Socio-Ecosystem,* edited by Patrick Vinton Kirch
Volume 39	*The Desert Fayum Reinvestigated: The Early to Mid-Holocene Landscape Archaeology of the Fayum North Shore, Egypt,* edited by Simon J. Holdaway and Willeke Wendrich
Volume 38	*The Archaeology of Grotta Scaloria: Ritual in Neolithic Southeast Italy,* edited by Ernestine S. Elster, Eugenia Isetti, John Robb, and Antonella Traverso
Volume 37	*A Bronze Age Landscape in the Russian Steppes: The Samara Valley Project,* edited by David W. Anthony, Dorcas R. Brown, Aleksandr A. Khokhlov, Pavel F. Kuznetsov, and Oleg D. Mochalov
Volume 36	*Rural Archaeology in Early Urban Northern Mesopotamia: Excavations at Tell al-Raqa'i,* edited by Glenn M. Schwartz
Volume 35	*New Insights into the Iron Age Archaeology of Edom, Southern Jordan,* by Thomas E. Levy, Mohammad Najjar, and Erez Ben-Yosef
Volume 34	*The Excavation of the Prehistoric Burial Tumulus at Lofkënd, Albania,* by John K. Papadopoulos, Sarah P. Morris, Lorenc Bejko, and Lynne A. Schepartz
Volume 33	*Formative Lifeways in Central Tlaxcala: Volume 1: Excavations, Ceramics, and Chronology,* edited by Richard G. Lesure
Volume 32	*Integrating Çatalhöyük: The 2000-2008 Seasons (Çatal Research Project Volume 10),* edited by Ian Hodder

Volume 31 — *Substantive Technologies at Çatalhöyük: Reports from the 2000-2008 Seasons (Çatal Research Project Volume 9),* edited by Ian Hodder

Volume 30 — *Humans and Landscapes of Çatalhöyük (Çatal Research Project Volume 8),* edited by Ian Hodder

Volume 29 — *Çatalhöyük Excavations: The 2000-2008 Seasons (Çatal Research Project Volume 7),* edited by Ian Hodder

Volume 28 — *Light and Shadow: Isolation and Interaction in the Shala Valley of Northern Albania,* edited by Michael L. Galaty, Ols Lafe, Wayne E. Lee, and Zamir Tafilica

Volume 27 — *Last House on the Hill: BACH Area Reports from Çatalhöyük, Turkey,* edited by Ruth Tringham and Mirjana Stevanović

Volume 26 — *The History and Archaeology of Jaffa 1,* edited by Martin Peilstöcker and Aaron A. Burke

Volume 25 — *The Lloyd Cotsen Study Collection of Chinese Bronze Mirrors,* edited by Lothar von Falkenhausen

Volume 24 — *The Early Iron Age Cemetery at Torone,* by John K. Papadopoulos

Volume 23 — *The Plain of Phaistos: Cycles of Social Complexity in the Mesara Region of Crete,* by L. Vance Watrous, Despoina Hadzi-Vallianou, and Harriet Blitzer

Volume 22 — *K'axob: Ritual, Work, and Family in an Ancient Maya Village,* edited by Patricia A. McAnany

Volume 21 — *The Sydney Cyprus Survey Project: Social Approaches to Regional Archaeological Survey,* by Michael Given and A. Bernard Knapp

Volume 20 — *Prehistoric Sitagroi: Excavations in Northeast Greece 1968–1970.* Volume 2. *Final Report,* edited by Ernestine S. Elster and Colin Renfrew

Volume 19 — *Archaeology of Solvieux, An Upper Paleolithic Open Air Site in France,* by James Sackett

Volume 18 — *Down by the Station: Los Angeles Chinatown, 1880–1933,* by Roberta S. Greenwood

Volume 17 — *Rock Art of Easter Island: Symbols of Power, Prayers to the Gods,* by Georgia Lee

Volume 16 — *Landscape Archaeology as Long-Term History: Northern Keos in the Cycladic Islands,* by J. E. Cherry, J. L. Davis, and E. Mantzourani

Volume 15 — *Selevac: A Neolithic Village in Yugoslavia,* edited by Ruth Tringham and Dusan Krstic

Volume 14 — *Achilleion: A Neolithic Settlement in Thessaly, Greece, 6400–5600 B.C.,* by Marija Gimbutas, Shan Winn, and Daniel Shimabuku

Volume 13 — *Excavations at Sitagroi: A Prehistoric Village in Northeast Greece.* Volume 1. By Colin Renfrew, Marija Gimbutas, and Ernestine S. Elster

Volume 12 — *Petroglyphs in the Guianas and Adjacent Areas of Brazil and Venezuela: An Inventory with a Comprehensive Bibliography of South American and Antillean Petroglyphs,* by C. N. Dubelaar

Volume 11 — *Chinese Archaeological Abstracts 4,* edited by Albert E. Dien, Jeffrey K. Riegel, and Nancy T. Price

Volume 10 — *Chinese Archaeological Abstracts 3,* edited by Albert E. Dien, Jeffrey K. Riegel, and Nancy T. Price

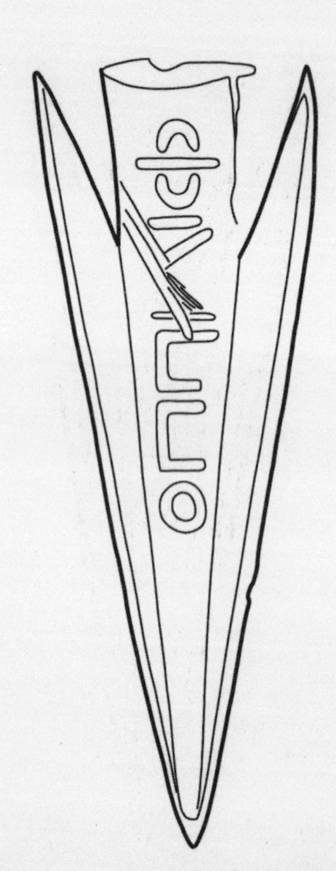